A HISTORY OF LITERARY CRITICISM
IN THE ITALIAN RENAISSANCE

A HISTORY
of
LITERARY
CRITICISM
IN THE
ITALIAN
RENAISSANCE

VOLUME I

By Bernard Weinberg

THE UNIVERSITY OF CHICAGO PRESS

Library of Congress Catalog Card Number: 60-5470
The University of Chicago Press, Chicago & London
The University of Toronto Press, Toronto 5, Canada
Published 1961
ALL RIGHTS RESERVED
Second Impression 1963
Printed by The University of Chicago Press
Chicago, Illinois, U.S.A.

Midway Reprint   1974

To

RONALD CRANE

RICHARD McKEON

ELDER OLSON

PREFACE

THE HISTORY OF LITERARY CRITICISM in the Italian Renaissance has been written several times. It is the subject of a volume by Ciro Trabalza entitled *La Critica letteraria (Dai primordi dell'Umanesimo all'Età nostra)* and published in Milan (1915) in the series "Storia dei generi letterari italiani." Inside and outside Italy the most widely read and influential treatment of the subject is to be found in Joel Elias Spingarn's *History of Literary Criticism in the Renaissance* (New York: Macmillan, 1899), published in Italian in a somewhat expanded form in 1904. The various works of Marvin T. Herrick have provided much useful information on the development of the theory of the genres during the Renaissance.

The present attempt to rewrite that history has two justifications. The first of these lies in the limited bibliography upon which the earlier histories were based. Spingarn discussed, in the briefest fashion, only some thirty documents in the original edition, a few more in the Italian translation. Trabalza and Herrick dealt with a considerably larger number of documents, but they fell far short of an adequate representation of the numerous texts that actually constitute the vast bibliography of literary criticism in the Italian Renaissance. This bibliography comprises, besides the major printed works, a great quantity of manuscript materials preserved in the libraries of Italy; these were left untouched by the earlier historians. It also includes many texts that are "minor" only in the sense that they are short or relatively unknown; they are frequently "major" because of their ideas or because of the contribution they have made to the development of literary criticism.

The second, and more important, justification derives from the way in which Spingarn and Trabalza used their materials. Their methods were those of the literary historians of an earlier generation. They tended rather to summarize texts than to analyze them, rather to disrupt texts (by isolating terms and passages) than to discover their structures, rather to construct chronologies than to write histories. What one learns from them, essentially, is the order and the content of a certain number of works; but even here one cannot be sure, since the content as they state it is often philosophically unconvincing. One cannot be sure, from the evidence they present, that their reading is a proper one. Such cautions, of course, attach to any reading of any text; the only recourse for the reader is his own reading of the text, and the only hope for the historian is that his reading, through its consistency and through the citations that support it, will convince others that it is a tenable hypothesis about the particular text.

In a sense, what I have attempted is an experiment in the writing of intellectual history. What is experimental is not the extension of the bibliography through the addition of hundreds of items not hitherto considered: this is merely the normal effect of the growth of bibliographical knowledge and the continued pursuit of the subject. It is rather the organization of the materials and the elaboration of the historical statement. I have not sought to follow any author through his career or any term or concept through the century. Instead, I have tried to distinguish the main intellectual traditions of the century as they relate to literary criticism and to trace them, year by year and text by text, up through the sixteenth century to the final, arbitrary date of 1600. These traditions were of two kinds: they were ways of regarding the art of poetry (a theoretical approach) and ways of judging poetic works (a practical approach). This distinction accounts for the two major divisions of my book.

With respect to the theoretical traditions, it has seemed to me useful to distinguish and identify them as developments and continuations of three great critical positions of the classical past: those of Plato, Aristotle, and Horace. These were the positions that provided Italians of the Renaissance with the greater part of their ideas on the art of poetry. It is rare, of course, that any one of them appears, purely and simply, in any single text; the Renaissance was not a period of intellectual purity and orderliness. But any individual text, taken in its entirety, should be classifiable under one or another of the major traditions; or at least its major tendencies may be expected to bear some resemblance to one of the major tendencies of the century—unless it is a completely eclectic work. It is only through the reading of the texts, indeed, that we discover the existence of those tendencies.

A consideration of each of the texts in its entirety should constitute another of the experimental aspects of my approach. It is, at least, one of the first principles of that approach. I have attempted, in the reading of each work, to discover its essential position; to discern what, basically and peculiarly, it was saying about the art of poetry or about a particular poem; to determine the methodological and the logical bases for its statements; to define its terms in relation to the whole complex of terms and concepts present in the work. I should point out that what I have said about any individual text is not intended to represent the totality of its contents; I have no more tried to report every idea than I have tried to account for every failure or inconsistency. My aim has been rather to state, with the greatest possible economy, its central position, to give an epitome of its premises and its conclusions, and to discover the method by which it passed from premises to conclusions. I have not undertaken to provide a substitute for the reading of any text but, instead, a guide to that reading.

Given the nature of the texts themselves, I have frequently found it necessary to discuss certain of them at two or three or four points in my study. A commentary on Aristotle's *Poetics*, for example, might also make a significant contribution to the study of Horace's *Ars poetica*, another to the development of Platonic ideas, still another to the criticism of a contemporary author. For the most part, though, each work is given major consideration only once. In a few cases I have had to deal with texts whose main subjects were not directly pertinent to my inquiry—broad philosophical treatises, works on other arts—but which did contain useful materials. Here I have been obliged, contrary to my general practice, to isolate passages or sections rather than to study entire texts.

I have limited my inquiry to literary criticism in the Italian Renaissance. The temptation was present, constantly, to associate with literary criticism such related fields as rhetorical theory and the criticism of the other arts, for the problems are the same or nearly so, and the documents themselves readily lead from one discipline to another. But I have had to resist this temptation sternly. The materials on literary criticism are themselves so abundant that to add others to them would have made the subject completely unmanageable. Moreover, the virtues of limitation to a single line of inquiry seemed to me obvious. Hence, the reader will find here no history of the important rhetorical documents of the century, even though there is much discussion of rhetorical ideas which appear in the treatises on poetry. Nor will he find any discussion of the quarrel over the Italian language, of the theory of painting or sculpture or architecture, in spite of the many resemblances of this theory to literary theory.

I have taken "Italian" in a fairly broad sense, including the works not only of Italians publishing in Italy but of foreigners publishing there and of Italians publishing abroad; the criterion for inclusion is the direct relationship of any given document to the Italian tradition. On the other hand, I have given to the term "Renaissance" a highly restricted meaning: I have limited it to the sixteenth century, except for those few cases in which I have found it necessary to trace a movement back into the Quattrocento. Here again, the decision was determined by the nature of the materials. The Cinquecento was the century of major development and full realization, both in poetic theory and in practical criticism; the Quattrocento, for all its overwhelming importance in other phases of the Renaissance, provided only a minor impetus in the domain of literary criticism, and the Seicento did little more than repeat and reorder the ideas of the preceding century. By 1600, the renaissance in criticism had run its full course, and at that date I have ended my investigation.

A word about the translations included in my text. In order to provide as nearly as possible a continuous text in one language, I have translated all quoted passages from Latin or Italian into English. The effort to make the translations both accurate and literate has been a task full of difficulties. Because in sixteenth-century usage many terms had multiple meanings and because syntax and construction, in both the Italian and the Latin texts, are frequently loose and inaccurate, it has been necessary at every point to decide upon the particular meaning intended. I present these translations with the usual reservations of the translator, urging the reader—if he thinks that I may have gone astray or if he wishes to follow the terminology in the original languages—to check them against the original texts, given in the footnotes. Among other technical matters, I have sometimes provided subheadings within the chapters for authors or subjects; but this is not done consistently for every text—merely from time to time in order to help with the chronology and to call attention to the most important documents. I have regularly reproduced original texts exactly, in spite of obvious errors; only rarely have I thought it necessary to make emendations.

As far as the source materials are concerned, I have attempted in all cases to consult the best manuscripts and the earliest printed editions. All documents are listed in a single Bibliography, arranged alphabetically by author; where more than one edition of a given work is described, I have indicated the edition used for study and citation. There is virtually no secondary bibliography. Except for light on bibliography itself and on the dating of works, I have chosen to discuss works themselves rather than the interpretations of those works by others. I was convinced that the only possibility of a fresh history of the subject lay in the rereading of all the pertinent materials (or at least of as many as I could find), by a single reader, and according to a constant method of analysis. My history, therefore, excludes some of the approaches common in the writing of intellectual and literary history. It is not concerned with sources and influences in the usual sense, with the discovery of where and how a given writer obtained his ideas. Rather, it tries to show how those ideas are related to the developing currents of Renaissance thought. I have consulted freely such bibliographical instruments as the lists of R. C. Williams and W. L. Bullock, the Cooper-Gudeman bibliography of Aristotle's *Poetics*, the bibliographies found in earlier histories of the subject; and I have also made use of various biographies and separate studies concerning the authors themselves.

I have many debts to discharge, both to those institutions which have subsidized and furthered my work over a period of some twenty-five years and to those individuals who have counseled and helped me. I can discharge them only through the simplest kind of thanks: to Washington University, to Northwestern University, and to the University of Chicago for grants in aid of my research; to the John Simon Guggenheim Memorial Foundation and the administrators of the Fulbright Program for generous fellowships; to the Institute for Advanced Study at Princeton for its hospitality. Many friends have been unsparing of time, wisdom, and material assistance; I would thank especially Donald Bryant, Ronald Crane, Phillip DeLacy, Edward Kaufmann, Paul Kristeller, and Peter Riesenberg for their reading of parts or all of the manuscript and for useful suggestions; Mrs. Anne McDonnell Heisler, for help in the preparation of the manuscript; and colleagues at the University of Chicago, too numerous to name, for the generous giving of their erudition and advice. I should wish also to thank many librarians for their kind co-operation, above all those at The University of Chicago Libraries, the Newberry Library, the Harvard University Library, the British Museum, the Bibliothèque Nationale in Paris; all the Biblioteche Nazionali in Italy, but mostly that in Florence; the other great Florentine libraries and the Vatican; and provincial libraries all over Italy.

CONTENTS

PART ONE
POETIC THEORY

CHAPTER ONE. THE CLASSIFICATION OF POETICS AMONG THE SCIENCES

A RENAISSANCE PROFESSOR, beginning a series of lessons on a topic or a text, almost invariably devoted the first lecture—the prolusio —to explaining his subject's place in the whole scheme of arts and sciences. This was not merely an academic gesture. It fulfilled an intellectual expectation of his auditors which had been passed on to them by their medieval and humanist forebears. For some centuries, it had been customary to regard each art or science as a part of the great complex of Philosophy. The individual science was defined or delimited by distinguishing it from its neighboring sciences; its ends and its means and its possibilities were discovered by determining to what faculty of the mind it belonged, what human need it served, under which of the major branches of human activity it was to be subsumed. All subsequent thinking about the science flowed from these initial and fundamental presuppositions.

To be sure, by the time of the Cinquecento the logical tightness of these systematic attitudes had been considerably weakened. The stern syllogistic discipline of the Schools had in some cases been openly attacked, in others it had been allowed to degenerate—almost imperceptibly—into the rhetorical loquacity of the universities. The academies, attracting as they did great numbers of aristocrats and bourgeois and providing them with an essentially lay instruction, frequently replaced the old severity of method by fostering enthusiasm for new fields of study and by a questioning, even a disparaging, approach to the traditional modes of thought. Nevertheless, the old framework continued to supply the usual points of reference, and the old habits of thinking continued to inform the major part of philosophical discussion. Perhaps it would be correct to say that the habit of a systematic approach to the sciences was still cultivated at a time when the instruments of analysis were no longer adequate to the task of pursuing classification to its last consequences and distinction to its final implications.

For the science of poetics, one of the old sciences made new by a fresh interest, a practical need, and the rediscovery of ancient texts, this was as true as for other sciences. Perhaps it was especially true. For poetics, formerly considered an auxiliary of grammar and rhetoric—an auxiliary whose particular concern was with versification and figures of speech—but now given new dignity as a guide to the greatest of the arts, had special need of justification. Witness the "defenses of poesy" which, from the fourteenth century on, were a standard form of literary expression. One of the most effective means of supplying that justification was to place the science in a position of dignity, honor, and utility among all the others. But even where justification was not the motive, the theorists followed the traditional pattern of exposition and somewhere—in the prolusio or later

—provided for poetics its proper place among the other sciences. The family to which poetics was assigned might be large or small, incomplete or complete, depending upon the cast of mind of the theorist or the necessities of his argument. But always it was of sufficient magnitude to throw upon the "science" or the "art" the kind of light which, for a man of the Cinquecento, could come only from classification and distinction.

Much of what a theorist was later to say about poetics would of necessity derive from his original classification of it. Hence the great importance of this initial step in the critical process. If, for example, he were to classify it with rhetoric as one of the instrumental disciplines, then his tendency would be to consider poems in terms of their probable specific effects upon specific audiences. He would, if he were an Aristotelian rhetorician, think of poems in terms of poet–poem–audience relationships; if he were a Ciceronian, in terms of invention, disposition, and elocution, and of what the poet must do to gain the acclaim of his listeners. On the other hand, should he begin by defining poetry as a branch or an instrument of moral philosophy, then his whole theory must be oriented toward the ability of the poet to produce or of the critic to judge the desired ethical effect. Any change in classification brings with it a consequent shift in the whole conception of the poetic art. The relationship of the parts within the poem, the criteria for its beauty or goodness or success, the hierarchy of the various poetic genres—all these varied with the place assigned to poetics in the total family of sciences.

THE ARTS OF DISCOURSE

The Cinquecento inherited from the immediate past a method of classifying poetry which we may characterize as the traditional system. Poetics took its place, according to this method, among the arts of discourse. Since poetry used words as its medium, it belonged with all the logical disciplines—with logic, dialectic, rhetoric, and sophistic—and with such arts as grammar and history, all of which also used words. This meant that poetry was joined on the one hand to the trivium (or to Aristotle's group of instrumental sciences), on the other hand to history. Renaissance theorists in a sense never abandoned this classification, although the sciences associated with poetry appear in different groupings and combinations. Throughout the sixteenth century we find systems modeled on this essentially medieval pattern.

For some Renaissance theorists (such as Bartolomeo Lombardi), the source and authority for so classifying poetry was Averroës. In Averroës they found poetry grouped with demonstrative logic, dialectic, rhetoric, and sophistic, and arranged with them in a hierarchy on the basis of their relationship to the truth.[1] This placed it definitely among the discursive

---

[1] I have found no single passage in Averroës making this complete association and hierarchy of the various arts mentioned. But in various scattered places individual arts are so combined; cf. the "Prooemium in libros posteriorum," in the Venice edition of Aristotle, trans. Mantinus (Iuntas, 1574), I, Pt. IIA, 9–9v: "Ad reliquas vero quinque artes se habet verè, veluti dominus

sciences. Such early humanists as Coluccio Salutati had also, in passing, placed it among these sciences; in his *De laboribus Herculis*, begun between 1383 and 1391 and left unfinished at his death in 1406, Salutati characterized poetics as a "sermocinalis philosophie pars," a part of the branch of philosophy concerned with words.[2] By the time we come to the later humanists, this particular branch has been fitted into more comprehensive views of the whole of philosophy. Thus Angelo Poliziano in the *Panepistemon*, printed in the *Opera* of 1498, sets out to find a general scheme for the sciences treated in Aristotle's works. He divides all doctrine into three kinds, the inspired (theology), the invented (philosophy), and the mixed (divination). Philosophy is then subdivided in the following way:

Spectativa	*Actualis*	*Rationalis*
De Anima	Mores	Grammatica
Mathematicae	Ethica	Historia
Arithmetica	Economica	Dialectica
Musica	Politica	Rhetorica
Geometria	Agricultura	Poetica
Sphaerica	Pastio	
Calculatoria	Venatio	
Geodesia	Architectura	
Canonice	Grafice	
Astrologia	Coquinaria	
Optica	Teatricae	
Mecanica	Etc.	

In this system, the contemplative ("spectativa") science is one which considers a given "res" or "materia," the practical ("actualis") is one which leads to useful activity, and the rational ("rationalis") is one which "iudicat, narrat, demonstrat, suadet, oblectat." Apparently one is to take the "oblectat" as referring specifically to "Poetica." Insofar as poetics is concerned, two things need to be noted: first, it is dissociated from other "creative" arts such as music (which comes under mathematics) and architecture and "graphics" (which belong to the practical sciences); and,

---

ad suos subiectos & proportio illius, cui subministratur ad ipsum seruum, adinuentae enim sunt illae artes vt inseruiant scientiae demonstratiuae, quam hęc pars nobis tradit: nempe, quod per persuasionem dialecticam, vel rhetoricam persuadetur, aut per fictionem poeticam fingitur." Also the commentary on Bk. I in the same edition, p. 13: "Potest tamen haec enuntiatio complecti quinque artes logicas, ac genera definitionum, & partes definitionum": and the *In libros rhetoricorum Aristotelis paraphrases*, trans. Balmes, same edition, II, 73*v*; "manifestum est quòd in vnoquoque istorum generum orationis sit species rhetorica, species topica, & species demonstratiua, & species sophistica: qui sicut reperiuntur in his artibus inductio & syllogismus, sic in rhetorica reperiuntur exemplum & enthymema." A 1522 volume of Averroës' paraphrases of logical works by Aristotle, containing also Abram de Balmes' translation of the Averroës paraphrase of the *Poetics* (Venice: De Sabio), is followed by a separate section (dated 1523) devoted to the *Epithoma Auerroys omnium librorum logice*. After treating other logical works, the *Epithoma* passes to a section entitled "De orationibus poeticis" (p. 26).

2 *De laboribus Herculis*, ed. B. Ullman, I, 17; also Introduction, pp. vii–viii.

second, it is associated with the three members of the medieval trivium—logic, grammar, and rhetoric—and with history. In a later passage, Poliziano places the poet close to the orator: "For the poet is very close to the orator (as Cicero says); just as he is more restricted in rhythms, so is he freer in the choice of words."[3]

At a somewhat later date another formal philosopher, Agostino Nifo (*De iis qui apte possunt in solitudine vivere*, 1531), proposed a similar classification. He divided the "contemplative intellect" into two sections, thus:

Partes principes	Partes subministrae, aut organicae
Physica	Grammatica
Mathematica	Analytica
Astrologia	Topica
Perspectiva	Sophistica
Musica	[Rhetorica]
Theologia	[Poetica]

Of the "auxiliary and instrumental parts," analytics (or logic) is the instrument of natural philosophy and rhetoric the instrument of moral philosophy. In the text, however, the connection between rhetoric and poetics is not completely clear, and the place of the latter is left ambiguous: "Though rhetoric is the instrument of moral philosophy as analytics of natural philosophy, nevertheless it is useful in all forms of discourse in which we are accustomed to express ourselves before listeners. Moreover, poetry was invented (as Aristotle suggested in the book which he wrote on poetics) for purposes both of pleasure and utility."[4] Here again, as with Poliziano, music and poetry retain their essentially medieval positions. The implication is that poetry is merely one of those "forms of discourse in which we are accustomed to express ourselves before listeners," distinguished from the others by the combined ends of utility and pleasure which it pursues.

The documents cited so far have not been specifically concerned with the art of poetry. But we find the same basis of classification in a lecture which must have been one of the first public expositions of Aristotle's *Poetics*. Around 1541, according to the testimony of Vincenzo Maggi, Bartolomeo Lombardi addressed to the Accademia degl'Infiammati at Padua the exordium of a series of lectures on the *Poetics*; Lombardi died soon thereafter, and the series was given by Maggi; but the first lecture was printed by Maggi as a preface to his and Lombardi's *In Aristotelis librum de poetica communes explanationes* (1550; p. *ij). Lombardi took Averroës as

---

[3] In *Opera* (1498), fols. Yix–Yixv and Zvi: "Quippe finitimus oratori poeta est (ut Cicero inquit). Sicut numeris astrictior. ita uerbis licentior" (quoted from Cicero, *De Oratore*, I, xvi).

[4] (1535 ed.), p. 89: "Rhetorica licet moralis philosophię sit instrumentum, ut Analytica naturalis philosophię: tamen utilis est in omnibus dicendi generibus: in quibus dicere solemus coram auditoribus. Poetica autem inuenta est (ut Aristoteles auctor est in eo Libro, quem de poetica scripsit) & ad delectandum, & ad conferendum."

his authority for placing poetry among the logical and rational sciences; it shares with demonstrative logic, dialectic, sophistic, and rhetoric certain common qualities:

... neither do they have a specific thing as their subject matter, but only words and discourse, nor do they consist in one specific genus but introduce themselves into all. These are their common characteristics. As for the particular and distinct ones, demonstration and its two companions, dialectic and sophistic, are called logical faculties, since their major and more common use is in arguments and they effect what they set out to do by means of certain concise points and in a brief and strict fashion, and if I may say so, they exist exclusively as syllogistic forms. ... Rhetoric and poetic, on the other hand, are not called logical faculties in a true and proper sense, and hardly ever use the syllogism, but they use rather the example and the enthymeme, which are, so to speak, popular devices. Their products, insofar as they are of this kind, are orations and poems, and for the most part they are concerned with political subject matters.[5]

The use of words and discourse and the cultivation of a universal rather than a particular subject matter are thus the bases for classifying poetics along with these other sciences.

In a much less systematic document, Sperone Speroni (*Dialogo della rhetorica*, 1542) again conjoins poetry and rhetoric, but for entirely different reasons. Speroni is not concerned with the whole system of the sciences, but only with the arts, which he classifies as useful (or mechanical) and pleasurable; the latter are subdivided into the arts which delight the body and those which delight the spirit:

Body	*Spirit*
Painting (eyes)	Rhetoric
Music (ears)	Poetry
Perfumery (nose)	
Cooking (taste)	
Heating (touch?)	

Poetry and rhetoric are arts of words, which are the instruments of the mind. They are distinguished by their ends: poetry aims only to please, rhetoric wishes both to please and to persuade. As a result, the orator's art is more difficult, since he must produce a much tighter rhythmic structure (pp. 138, 154–54v).

5 *Explanationes* (1550), p. 8: "quòd neque materiae loco res habeant: uerba tantum & orationem. neque in certo uno genere uersentur: sed in omnia insinuant sese. haec communia. illa propria atque distincta; quòd Demonstratiua, & eius duae comites Dialectica & Sophistica logicae ipsae appellantur: quòd harum maior quidam usus & communior in dissertationibus & quibusdam quasi punctis concisa breuiter admodum atque strictim quod proposuerunt, efficiunt, & ut ita loquar, syllogisticae prorsus existunt. . . . Rhetorica, Poeticáque contra: quòd non adeò uerè ac propriè Logicae appellantur, neque syllogismo ferè, sed exemplo atque enthymemate, rationibus quasi popularibus utuntur: atque harum quà huiusmodi sunt, extant opera, orationes atque poemata, plurimúmque in politicis occupantur argumentis."

With Francesco Robortello's *In librum Aristotelis de arte poetica explicationes* (1548) we return to the position of Lombardi (whose preface was published two years later); the classification is the same, although some of the reasons are different. Robortello's point of view is stated in his own preface, before the commentary on Aristotle actually begins:

> Discourse is placed under the poetic faculty as its material, as it is placed under all the others which concern themselves with discourse. These are five in number, demonstrative (for so it is proper to call apodeictic discourse), dialectic, rhetoric, sophistic, poetic. . . . All these have discourse as their matter; indeed, since discourse assumes a different force and form, both from the kind of things which it treats and from the person who uses it to set forth or prove something, for that reason it is necessary that every discourse be different in some way. The most proper and genuine function of discourse is to express what is true. . . . Insofar as discourse of any kind departs from truth, to that same degree it moves nearer to what is false. Between truth and falseness in a kind of interval between the two, are placed τὸ ἔνδοξον, τὸ πιθανὸν, τὸ φαινόμενον which may be expressed in Latin as the *probabile* [the probable], the *suasorium* [the persuasive], and the *apparens verum*; *seu probabile quod videtur* [the apparently true, or that which seems probable]. From among these each separate faculty seizes upon one kind: demonstration, upon the true; dialectic, upon the probable; rhetoric, upon the persuasive; sophistic, upon that which has the appearance of probability, but in the sense of verisimilitude; poetics, upon the false or the fabulous.[6]

The traditional classification, on the basis of the use of words as a medium, still prevails here.

A different kind of approach seems to be present in the thinking of Benedetto Varchi. But if to an original statement by Varchi, which antedates Robortello, is added a later one, his ultimate position turns out to be essentially the same as Robortello's. The first document is a "Lezzione della maggioranza dell'arti," delivered before the Florentine Academy in the spring of 1546. Varchi here addressed himself not so much to the problem of the place of poetics among the sciences as to the more general problem of the place of all the arts among human activities. He admittedly took as his point of departure the *Nicomachean Ethics*, especially Book VI. His division of the soul gives the following schema:

---

[6] *Explicationes* (1548), p. 1: "Subiicitur tanquàm materies poëticę facultati oratio, sicuti et aliis omnibus, quae circa orationem uersantur. Eae autem sunt quinque numero, Demonstratoria (sic enim ἀποδεικτικὴν licet appellare) dialecticε. rhetoricε. sophisticε. poëticε. . . . Omnes hae subiectam sibi habent orationem; Verùm, quoniam oratio diuersam accipit uim, & formam, tùm ex genere rerum, quas tractat; tùm ab eo, qui ipsa vtitur ad aliquid edisserendum, & probandum; ideò diuersam quoque omnium oportet esse orationem; Orationis maximè proprium, & genuinum munus est, proferre id, quod verum est. . . . Quantum autem orationis quodque genus 'à vero recedit, tantò propius accedit ad id, quod est falsum. Inter verum sanè, & falsum medio quodam interuallo posita sunt, τὸ ἔνδοξον, τὸ πιθανὸν, τὸ φαινόμενον; quę sic libet Latinè proferre; probabile, suasorium; & apparens verum; seu probabile quod videtur. Ex his quaelibet facultas vnum arripit genus, Demonstratoria verum. Dialectice probabile. Rhetorice suasorium. Sophistice id, quod probabilis, sed verisimilis habet speciem. Poëtice falsum, seu fabulos[u]m."

[6]

Anima

Ragione particolare
intenzioni individuali
cose particolari, gene-
rabili, & corruttibili
= cogitativa

Ragione universale
intenzioni uniuersali
cose private d'ogni materia,
spogliate da tutte le passioni, & accidenti ma-
teriali
cose ingenerate, et incorru-
tibili

Ragione superiore
intelletto specolativo,
contemplativo
= conoscere, intendere

Habiti contemplativi
intelletto
sapienza
scienza

Ragione inferiore
intelletto pratico,
attivo
= fare, operare

Habiti pratichi
agibile
fattibile

All the arts fall under the second of the "practical habits."[7] Varchi gives examples of the kinds of arts included under each category: horsemanship, dancing, singing, playing musical instruments under the "attiva;" architecture, painting, and sculpture (and "infinite others") under the "fattiva." Presumably, poetry is one of the "infinite others"; although poetry is not specifically mentioned here, the last section of the lecture is devoted to a detailed comparison of poetry and painting (pp. 68, 72). The major purpose of the lecture is to establish a hierarchy among the arts according to their nobility; and since the dignity of the end is set up as the criterion, and since warfare, medicine, and architecture occupy the highest positions in the hierarchy, the place assigned to poetry will be relatively humble.

These views of Varchi's are to be supplemented and perhaps corrected by those expressed, in a fuller and more careful way, in another lecture delivered to the Florentine Academy, in October, 1553. This time—referring again to the Aristotelian system but including the *Poetics*, which had been absent from the earlier materials—Varchi does offer a complete system of the sciences. He begins by dividing philosophy into "real" philosophy and "rational" philosophy:

Reale
(*cose*)

Contemplativa
Specolativa
  Metafisica
  Fisica
  Matematiche

Pratica
Attiva

Agibile
Etica

Rationale
(*parole*)

Loica giudiziale
Dialettica
Topica
Sofistica
Tentativa

7 In *Due lezzioni* (1549), pp. 58–59.

[7]

Reale (cose)		Rationale (parole)
Aritmetica	Economica	Rettorica
Musica	Politica	Poetica
Geometria	Fattibile	Storica
Astrologia	Arti meccaniche	Gramatica

In the commentary on this scheme, Varchi specifically states that poetry, coming as it does in the group of disciplines dealing with words, cannot be considered either an art or a science but merely a faculty. If it is sometimes called an art, this is only because it has been reduced to precepts and rules.[8] Moreover, its position in fourth place among the instrumental sciences shows its rank according to nobility; it is inferior not only to all the sciences but also to the disciplines above it in the same group. In a sense, it is indistinguishable from those disciplines: "It is indeed true that dialectic, logic, and poetics are almost the same thing, not being different substantially but only in accidents, and thus the dialectician, the rhetorician, and the poet may be placed at the same level of nobility and of honor."[9]

How poetics is related to the other rational faculties is indicated in another classification of these faculties in which Varchi assigns to each a subject matter and a corresponding instrument among the instruments of discourse:

Rational Faculty	Subject	Part of Discourse
loica, dimostrativa	vero	[demonstrative syllogism]
dialetica, topica	probabile	[topical syllogism]
sofistica	pare probabile, ma non è	[sophistical syllogism]
retorica	persuasivo	[enthymeme]
poetica	finto, favoloso	[example]

Once again, poetics, whose instrument is the "least worthy of all the others," is placed in a very inferior position.[10]

But this is not Varchi's final word. One must, he says later, take into consideration two things with respect to poetry: first, the host of wonderful things which become the objects of its imitation; second, the magnificent end which it serves, that of making men good, virtuous, and happy, that of perfecting the human soul. When these qualities are taken into account, poetry emerges as the greatest of all human activities:

Since poetics, then, treats of all things divine as well as human, of so sublime, desirable, and worthy an end, and in the most beautiful, useful, and delightful way, because it is language it comes to contain in itself necessarily all the sciences,

8 In *Lezzioni* (1590), pp. 571–72.
9 *Ibid.*, p. 572: "Ben'è vero, che la dialettica, la loica, e la poetica sono quasi vna medesima cosa, non essendo differenti sostanzialmente, ma per accidente, e così il dialettico, il retore, e il poeta si posson mettere in vn medesimo grado di nobiltà, e d'honore."
10 *Ibid.*, p. 573.

all the arts, and all the faculties at once, whence it is more noble, more delightful, and more perfect than each one of them in itself; thus it is deserving without any doubt of greater marvel as a faculty, and greater praise as an art, and greater honor as a science, than all the other faculties, arts, and sciences.[11]

One senses, in this last phase of the argument, a desire to break out of the restrictions imposed by the system, to elevate poetry above its systematic rank as one of the lowest of the rational faculties.

In the dedication to his *Dialogi della inventione poetica* (1554) Alessandro Lionardi allies poetics once more with rhetoric and history, although there are no traces of a more complete philosophical system. He begins by stating that the two most necessary and useful human activities are speaking and doing:

... neither the one nor the other of these actions can be completely and properly done without a knowledge of history, of orations, and of poems, as those things which teach us to do, to say, and to deliberate what is required in this life in every manner of state, of age, and of condition, showing us in actions and in discourse what is to be imitated and what avoided. ...

Poetry contains the other two within itself, and hence is the most worthy of study. It will be noted that here, again, there is an effort to ennoble the art of poetry, and that part of the process consists in assigning to poetry an important function in teaching men how to live.[12]

For Giovanni Battista Pigna (*I romanzi*, 1554), the reason for classifying poetry with rhetoric and dialectic under logic is to permit the explanation of its universality of subject matter; like the other instrumental sciences, it has no fixed subject: " ... just as rhetoric and dialectic, since they are under logic, have had no definite subject matter on which to fix themselves, so poetry, which falls under the same, will not be restricted to any specific branch of human activity. Whence it is common to say that the poet participates in every science."[13]

A division of the sciences which again presents itself as traditional, but which proceeds on a somewhat different basis, is offered by Antonio Sebastiano Minturno in his *De poeta* (1559). He groups all sciences under

11 *Ibid.*, p. 592: "Trattando dunque la poetica di tutte le cose così diuine, come humane tanto sublime desiderato, e degno fine e nel piu bello vtile, e diletteuole modo per esser prosa viene à contenere in se necessariamente tutte le scienze tutte l'arti, e tutte le facultà insieme, donde è più nobile piu piaceuole, e piu perfetta di ciascuna di loro di perse; dunque merita senza alcun dubbio maggior merauiglia, come facultà, e maggior lode, come arte e maggiore honore come scienza, di tutte quante l'altre facultà arti, e scienze."

12 *Dialogi* (1554), p.3: "nè l'una nè l'altra di queste due attioni potersi compiutamente, & conueneuolmente fare senza la cognitione dell'istoria, dell'orationi, & de' poemi, come quelli, che ci insegnano à fare, à dire, & à deliberare cioche à questa uita in ogni maniera di stato, di età, & di conditione si richiede, mostrandoci nelle operationi, & ne' parlamenti quel che si ha da imitare, & da fuggire."

13 *I romanzi* (1554), p. 19: "come la Rhetorica & la Dialettica, perche sono sotto la Logica, alcun certo soggetto su che si fermino, hauuto non hanno; cosi la Poesia, che cade sotto la medesima, ad alcuna certa professione non sarà astretta. La onde dir si suole che il poeta è d'ogni scienza partecipe."

four major headings: (1) those which are concerned with "knowing the nature and the causes of things" and with a "contemplation of divine things"; (2) those concerned with "instructions for good living"; (3) those belonging to the "faculty of discussing and speaking"; (4) mathematics.[14] Poetics, of course, belongs in the third category, along with grammar, rhetoric, logic, and history. Minturno introduces this distinction at a point where he is estimating the contribution of each of the other sciences to poetry; but the fact that it is fundamental in his thinking about poetry emerges from an analysis of his work as a whole.[15]

Alessandro Piccolomini, who wrote commentaries both on the *Rhetoric* and the *Poetics* of Aristotle, considered himself an Aristotelian and found justification for his views on the philosophical position of poetics in the works of Aristotle themselves. Thus he defends the affiliation between rhetoric and poetics as follows; he is explaining why he expects to work on the *Poetics* after he finishes his labors on the *Rhetoric* (*Piena parafrase nel terzo libro della Retorica d'Aristotele*, 1572):

... for the reason that these two faculties, rhetoric and poetics, are so closely linked together in kinship that a great many of the subjects they treat can and should be equally useful in the one and the other faculty. Thus it is that Aristotle, knowing this, in order not to repeat the same things in both [treatises] when he was writing about the one and the other, made a choice of the aforementioned common materials in such wise as to put in one faculty those considerations which were closest to it and most conjoined with it; then, writing about the other, he referred to the first when necessary.[16]

In the subsequent work on the other "faculty," *Annotationi nel libro della Poetica d'Aristotile* (1575), Piccolomini indicates his basic position by referring directly to the *Ethics*. All arts, he says, aim at "some honest utility and convenience for human life"; hence poetry will also seek as its end some such usefulness, "since poetry also is a habit of the practical intellect relevant to things which can be made, and since it may consequently be called an art, and since it is most honored among all the other habits of this kind and in nobility very close to civil prudence, which is that art to which all others are subordinated." The notion that civil prudence (a paraphrase for politics) is the "architectonic" science will gain

14 *De poeta* (1559), p. 87: "partem in cognoscendo rerum naturam, causasque posuerunt, atque cum ea rerum diuinarum perspicientiam coniunxerunt; partem in bene uiuendi institutione uersari, partem in disserendi ac loquendi ratione, partem in Mathematicis uoluerunt."

15 *Ibid.*, p. 92; cf. my article, "The Poetic Theories of Minturno," in *Studies in Honor of Frederick W. Shipley* ("Washington University Studies" [St. Louis, Mo., 1942]), pp. 101–29.

16 *Parafrase* (1572), p. *2v: "Percioche essendo queste due facultà, la Retorica, & la Poetica tanto congiunte di parentela insieme, che moltissime lor considerationi possono, & debbon communemente seruir' all'una, & all'altra: di qui è che, sì come Aristotele conoscendo questo, per non replicar' in scriuer dell'una, & dell'altra, le stesse cose in amendue; fece delle dette communi considerationi vna scelta in modo, che quelle, ch'alquanto fusser più vicine, & congiunte all'una, ch'all'altra di dette facultà, in quella poneua, & a quella scriuendo dell'altra, si rimetteua."

currency later in the century, and poetry will with increasing frequency be subsumed under it.[17]

Piccolomini's approach presupposes a purview of the Aristotelian system which extends beyond poetics and rhetoric and includes at least one other science in a different category, politics. A system which extends still farther beyond, and which really returns to the universal classifications of the first part of the century, is proposed by Federico Ceruti in a work which he presents as anonymous but which is probably his own, the *De re poetica libellus incerti auctoris* of 1588. Indeed, Ceruti outlines two possible complete schemata of the sciences. The first would be divided as follows:

Theoretice	*Practice*	*Logice*	*Mecanice*
theologia	ethice	rhetorice	lanificium
mathematica	oiconomice	grammatice	res militares
arithmetice	politice	historia	navigatio
musice		poetice	agricultura
geometria			venatio
astronomia			medicina
physice			pictura
			tectonica
			architectonica
			fabrilis

A second and somewhat different division would proceed as follows:

Theoretice	*Practice*	*Poietice*	*Instrumentales*
mathematice	de moribus	ars militaris	logice
metaphysice	de ciuili	nautica	grammatice
phisice	gubernatione	pictura	rhetorice
etc.	de legibus	musica	poetice
	etc.	etc.	historia

Whichever of these systems one adopts, says Ceruti, the place of poetics is clear. In both, in fact, it is linked with the same cognate disciplines, although in the first it is subsumed under grammar, which in turn is subsumed under logic, whereas in the second all five instrumental sciences are on the same plane. What is not clear is why a group of "poetical" arts, which for the most part make things by hand ("quae manibus vt plurimum fiunt"), should not include "poetics" itself. Apparently for Ceruti the traditional place of poetry is so firmly established that even the close etymological proximity of the terms does not raise any questions for him.[18]

Two years later—and very close to the end of the century—Gabriele Zinano (or Ginani) presents another such system of the sciences in his *Il*

17 *Annotationi* (1575), p. ††6v: "qualche honesto giouamento, & commodo dell'humana vita. . . . essendo la poesia anch'ella vn'habito dell'intelletto prattico intorno à cose fattibili; & per conseguente potendosi chiamar' arte; & essendo trà tutti gli altri così fatti habiti honoratissima, & in nobiltà alla ciuil prudentia, architectonica di tutte l'arti, vicinissima."
18 *De re poetica* (1588), chap. ix, pp. 10–11.

sogno, overo della poesia (1590). Zinano claims that the one he offers is Aristotelian:

SCIENCES

Speculative	Practical	
Metaphysics	Internal	External
Physics	Operations	Operations
Mathematics	(mind)	(words, deeds)
Geometry		
Arithmetic	will: moral philosophy	
Astrology	ethics	grammar	military art
Music	economics	rhetoric	agriculture
	politics	poetry	navigation
	intellect: dialectic	history	wool-making
	memory:		etc.
	art of remembering		

Grammar, among the practical sciences dealing with words, is concerned with "il ben dire"; rhetoric, with "l'ornato dire." As for poetry, it soon breaks out of its assigned compartment and becomes a universal science encompassing all the others; this is so because all the others furnish it with subject matter, because it teaches the lessons of all the others, and because through its allegory—moral or natural or divine— it contains the essential doctrines of all the others.[19]

The last important document, among those examined, to insist on the grouping of poetics with logic, grammar, and rhetoric is Giuseppe Malatesta's *Della poesia romanzesca* (1596). This is a sequel to an earlier dialogue of 1589, *Della nuova poesia*, in which Malatesta had not raised the question of the classification of poetry. In the present one, he does hazard a general system. He divides all the sciences into five groups: the natural sciences, the metaphysical sciences, the rational faculties, the liberal arts, and the mechanical arts. The rational faculties are arts of discourse which have no specific subject matter; they include logic and grammar. They might also include poetics:

In this group and of this kind is also poetry, to which by its nature no specific subject matter was given, but which rather remained free to treat of as many

[19] *Il sogno* (1590), pp. 19–21: "Le scienze, & l'arti in prattica, & in speculativa si diuidono, come vuole Aristotile nel primo della Metafisica, & questa divisione è presa dal fine, perciò che la speculatiua consiste in contemplatione, la prattica in operatione: l'vna contempla tutte le cose dell'vniuerso, l'altra quelle, che sono soggette all' arti, l'vna considera il vero, l'altra il buono, & di qui hanno origine l'intelletto speculatiuo, & prattico, ò più tosto le sopradette cose da lui origine hanno. Non si contenta il Peripatetico d'hauer cosi nel primo le scienze, & l'arti diuise, che ancora considerando le scienze esser varie secondo la qualità de gli enti, le subdiuide nel sesto [of the *Metaphysics*]. La speculatiua in Metafisica, in Fisica, & in Matematica subdiuide. . . . La prattica, versando circa l'operationi, secondo l'operationi si diuide. Del'operationi altre sono esterne, & altre interne. L'operationi interne prouengono dalla mente, & sono di tre sorti, di uolontà, d'intelletto, & di memoria. Nella volontà consiste la filosofia morale, che si diuide in Etica, in Economia, & in Politica." Cf. also pp. 21–31.

things as it might wish and to enter everywhere. . . . And therefore it would have been very proper for Aristotle, when he compared rhetoric to dialectic, to have added as a third, poetics, which no less than the other two occupies itself with things which can in a certain sense be understood by anyone, which does not recognize any definite or limited subject matter, and in which every subject finds itself in some way a participant by the goodness of Nature.

In this analysis, the basis of classification is uniquely the subject matter, since the initial assumption is that sciences are differentiated one from another solely on the basis of differences in subject matter.[20]

Beginning with the humanistic period—which had inherited it from the Middle Ages—and extending throughout the sixteenth century, there is thus a strong tradition that associates poetry with logic, grammar, rhetoric, and history as one of the discursive or instrumental sciences. Poetry belongs with the others as a discursive science because it uses words (or "discourse") as its means. One consequence of this association is that the resultant theories will tend to emphasize problems of language, the special kind of diction which differentiates poetry from the other discursive sciences, the matter of rhythm and rhyme, the figures and tropes which are regarded as peculiar to poetic expression. Another consequence is that, since words are symbols for things and represent meanings to the person for whom signification is intended, theories of this kind will hesitate or oscillate between emphasis on the things themselves and attention to the kinds of meanings associated with the words by the readers. Poetry is regarded as an instrumental science because it is thought to have no fixed subject matter and hence to resemble logic, grammar, and rhetoric. Resulting theories will stress on the one hand the universality of its subject and will compile long lists of the kinds of things it treats; on the other hand, they will consider its quality *qua* instrument and the ends which it achieves. This latter activity will bring such theories into close contact with another set of theories based specifically on conceptions of the end of poetry, especially those which consider it as an instrument of moral and civil philosophy, i.e., of ethics and politics.

HISTORY

A special place must be made for those classifications which include history among the discursive or instrumental sciences related to poetry. History, too, uses words, and it may be thought of as serving ethical or political ends. But it also presents other possibilities of comparison with

20 *Poesia romanzesca* (1596), pp. 27–28: "In questo numero, & di questa conditione, è ancora la Poesia, a cui non fù dalla natura sua prescritto niun soggetto particolare, anzi venne libera di poter trattare di quante cose volesse, & di ingerirsi per tutto. . . . Et per tanto non saria stato se non molto conueniente che quando Aristotele proportionò la Rethorica, alla Dialettica, hauesse aggiunta per terza la Poesia, la quale non meno che l'altre due si essercita sopra cose che ponno in certo modo capirsi da ciascuno, non riconosce materia definita, ò limitata, & ognuna se ne troua in qualche modo partecipe dal benefitio della Natura."

poetry; these may be boiled down to the essential fact that history, like so many forms of poetry, presents a "narration." One may thus apply to it (albeit equivocally) such common terms of the critical vocabulary as action, character, thought, episode, and so forth; one may discover in it such common features as descriptions of places and persons, speeches, great deeds of kings and heroes. These further possibilities of comparison led another group of theorists to set up a separate classification of poetry as a kind of history; they constitute in a sense a cognate strain of classification, beginning again with the humanists and continuing—although much less frequently—throughout the sixteenth century. It is appropriate at this point, in order to fill out the picture of this kind of classification, to examine the position of a group of theorists representing this cognate strain.

Giovanni (or Gioviano) Pontano, in a dialogue entitled *Actius de numeris poeticis et lege historiae* and written toward the end of the fifteenth century, attempted to relate poetry to such divers activities as prophecy, history, oratory, and painting; but the comparison developed most extensively is the one with history. The following bases of similarity are discovered: both relate ancient and remote deeds; both describe places, peoples, nations; both condemn vices and praise virtues; both partake of the demonstrative and deliberative types of oratory, as shown by the orations which they introduce; both treat the unexpected and accidental events which happen so frequently in life. The comparison continues in these terms, then is supplemented by a series of contrasts demonstrating in what ways the two arts differ. Finally, sets of criteria for both arts are derived from their common characteristics.[21]

The same tendency to pair poetry with history is developed at some length in an anonymous *Dialogue on History* found in MS Vat. Lat. 6528, whose date is probably around 1560–65. In this dialogue the main expositor, Hieronimo Zabbarella, claims to be presenting and defending the theory of Pomponazzi on history. He starts with the assertion of the existence of a four-way "chiasmus," a division of narration into four subordinate parts:

Poema: narration of a single action of a single man
Historia: narration of a single action of many persons
Vita: narration of many sayings and actions of a single man
Sermone: narration of many and various actions of many men

Poetry differs from history, first, in the character of the action narrated and, second, in the use of verse and a special kind of language. Both "poetry" and "history" are used in very broad senses, and the whole discussion has an essentially analogical quality (fols. 142v, 151).

Julius Caesar Scaliger's point of view, in the *Poetices libri septem* of

---

[21] In *I Dialoghi*, ed. Previtera, pp. 193–227.

1561, puts him into both categories of critics, those who classified poetry as a part of "oratio" and those who considered it a form of narration. He begins with a general division of "oratio" according to its ends, as follows:

End	Type of Expression	Audience
veritas	necessitas	philosophi
prudentia	vtilitas	cives
voluptas	delectatio	theatra

The third type of expression, "delectatio," uses the common form of narration, accompanied by ornate language. It is subdivided into history and poetry: history which "by a sure belief professes and produces truth, spinning its discourse in a simpler thread," poetry which "either adds fiction to truth, or imitates true things by means of false, but in any case with greater splendor." As is the case for history, the final end of poetry is also to teach: "This end [of imitation] is intermediate to another which is final, and which is to teach with pleasure."[22]

In a work which is essentially a treatise on history, the *De ratione scribendae historiae* of 1574, Uberto Foglietta spends a certain amount of time in drawing a comparison between history and epic poetry. Both are narrations (the essential basis for the comparison), both treat events which have actually happened. But history is different insofar as it depends upon truth and cannot exist without it, and insofar as it may dispense with the various ornaments and decorations which are required in poetry. In his discussion of the component graces of history, Foglietta indicates that these are the ones commonly cultivated by the poet. Indeed, such a document as this is more interesting for its assumption that the internal procedures of the two arts of history and poetry are the same than for its theoretical statements about them.[23]

For Lionardo Salviati, the last of this group of theorists, the two arts are related not so much because they are forms of narration as because they serve a common end, instruction by means of pleasure. His dialogue, *Il Lasca* (1584), raises the whole issue of the relationship of poetry to history. Unlike earlier theorists, he admits the possibility of history which tells not the truth but what is commonly believed, and which may even tell lies when these would be useful. Its usefulness is to "render prudent those who read it or hear it, so that . . . they may know how to govern the community well, if it is a public history, and themselves and their houses if it is a private history";[24] this end is achieved through the means of the pleasure inherent

22 *Poetice* (1581 ed.), p. 2: "Differunt autem, quòd alterius fides certa verum & profitetur & prodit, simpliciore filo texens orationem: altera aut addit ficta veris, aut fictis vera imitatur, maiore sanè apparatu. . . . Hic enim finis est medius ad illum vltimum, qui est docendi cum delectatione."

23 *De ratione*, ed. with Bodin (1576), pp. 947–48, 963.

24 *Il Lasca* (1584), p. 8: "Ch'ella sia vtile, cioè faccia prudente quei, che la leggono, o che l'ascoltano, si che, e in pace, e in guerra sappiano ben gouernare il comune, s'ella sia storia pubblica: se priuata lor medesimi, e le lor case."

[15]

in the reading. Such views, of course, bring history very close to the common conception of poetry, and Salviati sees between them the following differences (pp. 11–13):

Poetry	History
forma: imitazione	forma: narrazione
soggetto: verisimile	soggetto: quel che si crede
fine: purgar gli animi	fine: prudenza
renderci ben costumati	
stromento: verso, melodia, ballo	stromento: favellare sciolto

"For which reasons," he goes on to say, "poetry may in a way be made subordinate to the philosophy of conduct, and history to that of government; nevertheless, as far as the end is concerned there might be occasion to argue to the contrary, that is, that it is the same both in history and in poetry."[25] As the dialogue continues, however, Salviati argues that poetry achieves these ends less well than history, since it is not believed and has as a result no lasting moral effect, and hence is to be considered an inferior art.

Most of these texts, classifying poetry with all the rest of the discursive or instrumental sciences or with history singled out from among them, fall within the first sixty years of the century. The few which come later do little more than continue a tradition dating back to the humanist period. Not all of them, indeed, give so restricted a role to poetry as the mere process of classification might indicate. At times, out of the conviction that poetry is really something more than an instrument, that it serves higher purposes in a more particular way, there is an effort, not to assign it to another position, but to find some supplementary way of regarding it which will make it transcend its companion arts. This effort, as with Varchi, results in the affirmation that poetry is a universal science, a recipient of all the riches of philosophy, whose function is to contribute to the highest welfare of mankind. During the rest of the century, while the old classification continues to appear from time to time, the essential position of poetics will be one rather more in keeping with its exalted functions, that is, as a part or as an instrument of moral philosophy.

MORAL PHILOSOPHY

This position is first assigned to poetics, among the documents studied, by Scipione Ammirato in *Il Dedalione overo del poeta dialogo*, dated 1560. The work is essentially a rebuttal of Plato's banishment of the poets. Ammirato divides philosophy into two main branches, the contemplative and the active:

[25] *Ibid.*, p. 11: "Per laqual cosa la Poesia in qualche modo sotto la filosofia de' costumi: La Storia ridur potrassi sotto quella della città, tuttauia quanto è il fine, ci sarebbe forse da disputare in contrario, cioè, che fosse, e nella storia, e nella poesia il medesimo."

Contemplative	Active
Natural	"morale costumatezza" (= Ethics)
Supernatural	"domestica, familiare" (= Economics)
Mathematics	"civile" (= Politics)

Poetics is subsumed under civil philosophy: "If civil philosophy concerns the good of our minds and of our bodies, it will really concern both these arts, that is, poetics and medicine; but let us take the matter in a larger sense and say that it concerns equivocally both the one and the other medicine, that of the soul and that of the body."[26] The poet bears the same relationship to the physician as the legislator does to the surgeon, and the "end of poetry is to induce virtue into the soul by driving vice out of it."[27]

This is essentially the point of view of Antonio Posio, whose aim in the pertinent section of his *Thesaurus* (1562) is to summarize the order and the contents of Aristotle's works. The *Poetics* would fall into the sequence "Dialectica–Rhetorica–Poetica–Ethica" for the reasons given below:

Rhetoric in fact is the instrument of the moral philosopher, an instrument with which good laws are proposed and which is used in the senate for the best deliberations about the observance of the laws, of divine worship, of peace, of charity, of justice, and of all the other things that are necessary to a state. To it indeed is added poetics, which must not be rejected from a perfect state, whatever Plato seems to want to do with it in the eighth book of the *Republic*. In fact, the poet, using a certain sweetness of language, purges the soul of evil passions and brings great utility through the action and great pleasure through the imitation. Those have not been lacking, even, who have maintained that it is part of rhetoric. I leave to others to decide whether this be true. Moreover, the same poetics serves the state as an art of discourse, since the poet must arouse anger, fear, hope, and the other passions. These books having been placed as first handmaidens to moral and civil philosophy, to them were added immediately the books on ethics dedicated to Nicomachus.

Poetics remains, here, an associate of dialectic and rhetoric, maintaining its function as a discursive science; but the whole group to which it belongs becomes "ancillary" to moral and civil philosophy, and poetry itself is distinguished by the pleasure and the utility which it affords.[28]

26 In *Opuscoli* (1642), p. 386: "Se la ciuile riguarda il bene degli animi nostri & de corpi, veramente ella riguarderà amendue questi, cioè la poetica & la medicina; ma prendiamo la cosa più larga & diciamo ch'ella riguarda equiuocamente l'vna & l'altra medicina dell'anima & del corpo."

27 *Ibid.*, "il fine della poetica è indur nell'anima la virtù discacciandone il vizio."

28 *Thesaurus* (1562), fol. *5v: "Rhetorica enim est instrumentum moralis philosophi, quo bonae proponuntur leges, optimaeque fiunt in senatu deliberationes ad obseruandas leges, cultum diuinum, Pacem, pietatem, Iustitiam, & caetera quae Reipub. sunt necessaria. Accedit vero Poetica, quae ab optima Repub. non est abiicienda. Quicquid videatur velle Plato in octauo de Repub. Poeta enim cum quadam sermonis suauitate, animum malis affectibus purgat, magnamque actione vtilitatem, & imitatione delectationem affert. Non defuerunt autem, qui partem Rhetorices eam esse putauerint. An id verum sit, aliorum nunc sit iudicium seruit autem ipsa Poetica Reipublicae tanquam sermocinalis facultas, cum debeat poeta commouere iram, timorem, spem, caeterosque affectus. His praepositis ciuili, ac morali philosophiae ancillis, libri ad Nicomachum de moribus statim adiecti sunt."

The next statement is neither so systematic nor so explicit, since it relates poetry to moral philosophy without specifying the nature of the relationship. It is found in Jacopo Mazzoni's *Discorso in difesa della Comedia del divino poeta Dante* (1572, under the pseudonym of Donato Rofia), which devoted its first chapter to the proposition "that it is not improper for philosophers to discuss poets." Mazzoni here makes only the bald statement: "... elsewhere we have sufficiently clearly proved that poetry is a part of moral philosophy" (p. 3). The assertion is neither developed nor supported later in the text, nor are we told how poetry serves the end of moral philosophy. I have found no earlier text by Mazzoni to which he might be referring.

Concern with the "dignity" of the art is really the primary characteristic of a work which made public its conclusions four years later, in 1576. Just as Varchi in 1546 had been concerned with the "maggioranza dell'arti," so Lorenzo Giacomini in 1576 proposed the topic *Della nobiltà delle lettere e delle armi* for three lectures to be read in the Florentine Academy. Under letters he included moral philosophy, the art of logic, rhetoric, poetics, history, medicine, and architecture. In his final arrangement, Giacomini seems to divide letters into two subgroups: the first, the "scienzie contemplative," is superior to arms; the second, made up of moral philosophy and other forms of knowledge, is inferior to arms, since it merely supplies the doctrine which leads to action. Action itself is more noble than doctrine. Although it is not so stated, poetry presumably falls into the last category; instruction in the literary arts will include "rhetoric and poetics, which furnish us with the means to explain moral subjects for our own benefit and that of others, and music also, which like poetry used to be used for four ends, for formation of character, for the purgation of the passions, for rest from our affairs, and for recreation in our studies."[29]

By this date, 1576, the position of poetics as related to moral philosophy is firmly established; there will be very few dissenters later on. But a new question now arises: is it a part or an instrument of moral philosophy? The distinction is sometimes not clear, but much debate centers upon it, especially in a large group of documents relating to the quarrel over Dante. It will be remembered that, five years earlier, Jacopo Mazzoni had initiated the discussion in his defense of Dante with the statement that "poetry is a part of moral philosophy." Sometime between 1573 and 1576–77 Bellisario Bulgarini of Siena wrote his *Alcune considerazioni sopra'l discorso di M. Giacopo Mazzoni, fatto in difesa della Comedia di Dante*, published only in 1583. Since Bulgarini set out to counter Mazzoni on every possible point, he did not fail to take issue with him on this statement. Poetry, he insisted,

29 MS B.N. Paris, Fonds italien 982, fols. 62*v*–63: "impareremo . . . la Rettorica, et la Poetica le quali ci danno il modo di spiegare i suggetti morali in benefizio nostro et d'altrui. et la Musica ancora, la quale si come la Poesia per quattro fini soleua vsarsi, per il costume, per purgazione degli affetti, per riposo da i negozij, et per diporto negli studij."

could not be considered a part of moral philosophy because it was an art; Aristotle and Horace should be taken as authorities for this. Moreover, if it were a part of philosophy it would belong to the rational and discursive branches, not to the practical group in which moral philosophy falls.

Nor do I see, at best, how one can say anything else about it except that it might be an instrument of moral philosophy, in the way in which (by those who know best) logic is held to be an instrument of philosophy in general: and this also according to the opinion of those who claim that the principal end of this same poetics is not to delight—as is maintained by many and not without reason —but to profit.[30]

In a sense, Bulgarini's thesis is an attempt to liberate poetry from the domination of moral philosophy; to do so, he returns it to its place as an instrumental science; but he implies meanwhile that it really should be considered an independent art whose end is only to give pleasure.

The passage cited from Bulgarini was answered directly by Orazio Capponi in his manuscript *Risposte alle prime cinque particelle delle considerazioni di Bellisario Bulgarini* (1577). In reality, there are no adequate reasons given for the opposition; the following text largely illustrates a wish to retain poetry in its currently established place:

... it would not at all be an improper thing to say that poetry, insofar as it is useful to human life, as we see clearly considering it in its parts, some of which purge us of the excess of those passions which are found in us, and it teaches us good modes of conduct distinguishing them from the bad and many other such things useful for arriving at human happiness—insofar, then, as poetry can bring about this effect [it is not improper to say] that it is a part of moral philosophy whose only purpose is to direct us along the road which may lead us to happiness.[31]

Capponi does go on to say that, even according to Aristotle, there is no objection to calling an art a part of philosophy.

Bulgarini's reply came two years later in his *Repliche alle Risposte del sig. Orazio Capponi*, published in 1585 (but the work is dated at the end "Di Siena, il di 20. di Maggio 1579"). In it, he asserted the same position but at somewhat greater length: poetry is not a part of moral philosophy but an instrument of it, bearing to it the same relationship that logic bears to

---

30 *Alcune considerazioni* (1583), pp. 14–15: "Nè so veder, che di lei, al più, altro si possa dire, se non ch'ella sia istromento della moral filosofia; nella maniera, che da' più intendenti, è tenuta la Logica, per istromento, della filosofia in vniuersale: e questo anco per l'opinion di quelli, che voglion ch'il fin principale di essa Poetica sia non il dilettare, come da molti, non senza ragion si tiene; ma il giouare."

31 MS Bibl. Com. Siena G.IX.54, fol. 14v: "non sarebbe cosa del tutto sconcia il dire, che la Poesia in quanto è utile alla vita humana, come si uede manifesto risguardando nelle sue parti, alcuna delle quali ci purga dal souerchio di quelli affetti, che si trouano in noi, e ci fà conoscere i buoni costumi distinguendoli da rei, e molte delle si fatte cose utili a peruenire alla felicità humana, Inquanto dunque, che la poesia può questo effetto cagionare, sia parte della filosofia morale, laquale altro non fa, che indrizzarci per la strada, che possa condurci alla felicità."

philosophy in general. He would suggest, with respect to logic and poetics, that

the one and the other of them should perhaps be placed among the arts, or we might say sciences (taking science in a broad sense) which are called rational or discursive; and that just as logic, agreeing in this with rhetoric, has no fixed subject matter about which it operates, almost the same thing happens with respect to poetics, and particularly with relationship to the human actions that it undertakes to imitate; so that, not being confined to speaking or treating exclusively of such or such human actions, it may have free choice with respect to any and all, with one or another kind of poem. Add to this the fact that just as logic was invented primarily to serve philosophy in general as its particular instrument, so poetry perchance [was invented] to serve the moral philosophies, occupying itself with the subject matters of these latter; whence it will come to be also in a certain way their instrument, since they use it to bring profit and to form better (by means of the pleasure which it always carries with it) the moral characters of men, directing them toward practical happiness, which is the most immediate end of the moral philosopher.[32]

It would be improper, however, to consider poetry an instrument of natural science, since verse compositions treating the latter are not really poems. Bulgarini repeats, finally, his notion that, if all arts are divided into the speculative, the practical, and the instrumental, logic and rhetoric and poetics belong to the last of these; poetics cannot thus possibly be considered a part of such a practical science as moral philosophy.

Bulgarini's manuscript of this last work came to the attention of Lelio Marretti, who wrote an answer in the form of *Avvertimenti,* presumably around 1579–80; the manuscript is to be found with most of the others in this interchange in the Biblioteca Comunale at Siena. Marretti's notes are confused and show a misunderstanding of some of Bulgarini's ideas. He begins with the thesis that poetry is subordinate to politics insofar as the politician must judge of the possible moral effects of a poem. Still, it would not be proper to call it an instrument of moral philosophy, since it does not teach the principles of that science; it teaches only "how to live well, to ignorant men."[33] It is an instrument only in a special sense: "It seems to me that one might say that poetry was an instrument of the moral

[32] *Repliche* (1585), pp. 27–28: "l'vna, e l'altra di loro sia forse da riporsi infra l'arti, ò vogliam dire scienze (pigliando la Scienza in largo modo) che razionali, ò sermocinali si chiamano; e che, si come la Logica, conforme in ciò alla Retorica, non ha alcuna determinata materia, intorno alla quale s'esserciti; quasi, che questo medesimo interuiene alla Poetica, e particolarmente intorno alle azzioni vmane, ch'ella si prende ad imitare: conciosiacosa che, non essendo ristretta à dire, ò à trattar di queste, ò di quelle vmane azzioni solamente, habbia l'elezzion libera intorno à tutte quante, con' vna, ò con' vn' altra sorte di Poemi. Aggiungasi à questo, che si come la Logica è stata principalmente trouata, per seruire alla Filosofia in vniuersale, come suo proprio stromento; così la Poesia, per auentura, per seruir' alle Morali, venendo ad essercitarsi intorno alle materie di esse. laonde verrà ad esser' anco in vn certo modo loro stromento; seruendosi quelle di lei, per giouare, e formar meglio, per mezzo della dilettazione, che ella porta tuttauia seco, i costumi de gli huomini, indirizzandoli alla felicità pratica; la qual' è il fin più propinquo del moral Filosofo."

[33] *Avvertimenti,* fol. 438: "ma sol il ben viuere à gl'huomini rozzi."

philosopher, since he uses it to give proper moral character to men, rather than an instrument of moral philosophy, since the latter teaches us man's end in life and how to achieve it, for which teaching neither poetics nor poetry is useful to us. I suspect that there is considerable equivocation about this word 'instrument.'"[34] This stand rather leads Marretti to take sides with Capponi: "The opinion of Capponi seems to me quite probable, that poetry is rather a part than an instrument of moral science, since it does exactly what that science does, bringing in its own way happiness to the ordinary man."[35] As for Bulgarini's classification of poetry among the rational disciplines, Marretti will have none of it: "If poetry could be called a part of philosophy, without doubt it could not be placed anywhere else than under the branch of moral philosophy, both because it deals with the very same matter and because it concerns the very same end."[36]

During the years 1573–80, then, the Bulgarini-Capponi-Marretti controversy revolved about the designation of poetry as a part or as an instrument of moral philosophy. Some of the difficulty of decision arose from the inability of the theorists to decide to which of the Aristotelian branches of science the art of poetry belonged. They hesitated between the practical and the instrumental. About the same period, a formal philosopher, Francesco Patrizi, was concerning himself with the same question. In Book VIII of Volume I of his *Discussiones peripateticae* (1571), devoted to a division of Aristotle's works ("Aristotelicorum librorum extantium per genera distributio"), he first distinguishes eight groups of works: "Logicum, De Ente, De Sapientia, Mathematicum, Naturale, Medicum, Morale, Artificiale." Each is then subdivided, and under the group "Morale" come these treatises: *Ethics, Politics, Economics, Poetics, Rhetoric,* and sections 18, 27, 28, and 29 of the *Problemata.* The assignment of the *Poetics* to the group of moral sciences is justified by reference to Book VIII of the *Politics* and by the argument that, along with music, poetics is useful for the instruction of the young. The authority of Plato is cited in support. In Book IX of the same volume ("Aristotelicorum librorum in singulis generibus distributio"), Patrizi insists that the *Poetics* was really meant to be the last book of the *Politics.*[37]

For Jacopo Zabarella, as for several previous theorists, poetry is at one

34 *Ibid.,* fol. 438v: "Più tosto par à me si potrebbe dire, che la Poetica fusse istromento del filosofo morale, seruendosi d'essa per render costumati gli huomini, che istrumento della filosofia morale insegnandoci questa il fine dell'huomo, et il modo d'acquistarlo, al che non ci serue, ne la poetica, ne la poesia. Dubbito, che non s'equiuochi assai intorno à questa parola istromento."

35 *Ibid.,* fol. 438v: "Parmi assai probabile l'oppinion del Capponi, che la poesia sia piu tosto parte, che istromento del morale, facendo il medesimo appunto, che fa la scientia inducendo con il suo modo felicità nell'huomo ordinario."

36 *Ibid.,* fols. 439–439v: "Se la poetica se potesse chiamar parte di filosofia senza dubbio non potrebbe porsi, se non sotto il membro della morale e perche la si raggira intorno alla medesima materia, e perche la riguarda 'l medesimo fine."

37 *Discussionum peripateticarum tomi primi* (1571 ed.), pp. 66–66v, 82.

and the same time related to the rational sciences and to moral philosophy. It should be noted that the work in which he discusses the problem is a work on logic, his *De natura logicae libri duo* of 1578; the specific chapters devoted to the discussion are in Book II, chapter 13, "De Rhetorica, & Poetica quòd philosophiae contemplatiuae instrumenta non sint"; chapter 14, "Quòd Rhetorica, & Poetica neque artium, neque moralis philosophiae instrumenta sint"; and chapter 15, "Quòd Rhetorica, & Poetica solius ciuilis disciplinae instrumenta sint, & quomodo." The relationship to logic, the association with rhetoric, are thus initial assumptions. The point at issue is specifically what branch of philosophy is served by poetry as an instrument. Zabarella argues first that poetry and rhetoric do not serve contemplative (or speculative) philosophy, since the latter is concerned only with knowledge whereas the two sister faculties are concerned with action: "... their usefulness is related to action rather than to contemplation; they deal with things in action."[38] Next, he argues that they are not instrumental to moral philosophy, which has as its function to teach each man how to improve himself, but rather to the "civil discipline," by which each man attempts to improve others. Both are thus the tools of the politician. The distinction is made clear in the following passage:

> The moral man is he who does right; the citizen, however, causes others to do right; for the moral man wants to make himself good, whereas the citizen wants to make others good. ... Rhetoric and poetics are thus instrumental faculties which the citizen employs for action, namely, to make his fellow citizens good; with this distinction, however, that he uses rhetoric through his own means, but poetics by means of other persons.[39]

In later chapters Zabarella contends that they are a part of particular rather than of universal logic, and that poetics is a part of logic insofar as it uses one of the means of logic, the example. Example is taken in the broad sense of actions, characters, and passions presented to the audience for imitation or rejection.

Some expansion and clarification of the point of view of Lionardo Salviati, who has already appeared as one of those classifying poetry with history, may be seen in his *Commentary on Aristotle's Poetics*, written in 1585–86. Salviati considers the opinions of such other commentators as Maggi, Piccolomini, and Castelvetro. He decides that "with respect to the end of the poem, which is relative to moral character, the operation of the poet will have its place within moral philosophy." As for history, he rejects Castelvetro's theory that a treatise on poetry presupposes a treatise

---

[38] *De natura logicae* (1578), pp. 53–57, esp. p. 53: "ad actionem potius, quàm ad contemplationem vtilitas ipsarum pertinet."

[39] *Ibid.*, p. 55: "moralis ipse est, qui bene agit, ciuilis verò facit vt alii bene agant; moralis enim uult seipsum bonum reddere, ciuilis autem alios. ... Sunt igitur Rhetorica, atque Poetica facultates instrumentales, quibus homo ciuilis ad agendum vtitur, idest ad ciues bonos efficiendos, cum hoc tamen discrimine, quòd arte Rhetorica per semetipsum vtitur, Poetica uerò per alios."

on history. Even though the poet must know something about truth, "to the knowledge of truth, in what pertains to things that have happened, not a treatise on the writing of history but history itself is required. . . . And without reading histories the truth about things which happen may rather be derived from experience."[40] Salviati's approach is not basically systematic, and these statements show rather a preoccupation with current problems than an orderly attempt at solving them.

A much more orderly treatment is seen in Bernardino Baldino's *Discorso breve intorno all'utilità delle scienze et arti* (1586); but the order here is derived less from philosophical principle than from moral conviction. That conviction is briefly put at the outset: ". . . poetry by its essence can and must blame misdeeds, no less than certain other disciplines and arts."[41] As a result, all branches of philosophy are transformed into types of moral philosophy. All sciences are divided into speculative and practical. The speculative exist in order "to heal the soul"; theology, which presumably belongs in this group, "provides medicine against our sins." So for the practical: the moral disciplines "heal the mind of its vices," and medicine contributes to "the health of human bodies." If everything thus is analogized in medical terms, the medical science involved is specifically curative rather than preventive. Poetry, along with rhetoric, falls within the class of liberal arts, those which pertain to the soul.[42] Its curative functions are stated thus:

. . . it also, like the other noble arts, came into being to enrich our spirit with salutary and honorable precepts. But it is different from the other disciplines in this, that the others come unveiled and bear openly their bitterness and their whip, with which they freely touch and beat the hearts of the harmful and the vicious; whereas poetry with masks, and with sharp words but covered with honey, proposes as do the other doctrines to attack the guilty and scold faults and errors, and bring health to sick minds corrupted by spots and rottenness, just as the clever doctor sweetens bitter medicines. . . . And this they do to attract young people to study its works, which are full of teachings and remedies against misdeeds and crimes.[43]

40 MS BNF II, II, 11, fols. 13–13v: "risguardando al fine del poema, il quale è intorno a' costumi, l'esercizio del poeta tra la moral filosofia harà luogo . . ."; "alla cognizion del uero, in cio che all' auuenute cose appartiene, non il trattato dello scriuer la storia, ma essa storia è richiesta. . . . E senza legger le storie il uero dell'accadenti cose dall'esperienzia eziandio puo ritrarsi."
41 *Discorso* (1586), p. A2v: "la poesia di sua ragione può & deue biasimare i misfatti; non meno ch'alcune altre discipline, & arti."
42 *Ibid.*, pp. B4–B4v.
43 *Ibid.*, p. B3: "anch'essa come l'altre nobili arti, e venuta in luce, per arricchire l'animo nostro de precetti salutari, & horreuoli. In ciò questa e differente dall'altre discipline, che l'altre vengono scoperte, & portano palese l'amarezza & la sferza; conche liberamente toccano, & flagellano i cuori de i nocenti, e vitiosi; doue la poesia con maschere, & con parole pungenti, ma coperte di mele dissegna come le altre dottrine mordere i diffettosi, & riprendere le diffalte, & errori, & sanare gl'animi amalati, & corrotti dalle macchie, e magagne. come il medico auueduto ch'adolcisce le medecine amare. . . . E ciò fanno per allettare i gioueni a studiare l'opere sue piene de documenti, e remedij contra i misfatti, e delitti."

[23]

Balcino's little treatise, with its extreme moralizing tendency, is representative of a certain kind of thinking found with some frequency in the latter decades of the century.

The last of the documents in the Dante quarrel to concern itself specifically with the classification of poetry is Jacopo Mazzoni's *Della difesa della Comedia di Dante*, a voluminous work in two parts completed about 1585. Part I was published in 1587, Part II not until 1688. The argument by which Mazzoni arrives at his conclusion is very complex. He begins with the statement that the arts and sciences are distinguished from one another by the differences in the objects of which they treat. As for the meaning of "objects," he interprets it according to the opinion of the Peripatetics: "... sciences and arts derive their true and real distinction from their objects, not insofar as these are things, but insofar as they are knowable things and, if one might say so, things makable by art."[44] In the Aristotelian system, the considerations of rhetoric are all directed to the "persuasible," of poetics to the "imitable," of moral philosophy to—the phrase is untranslatable—the "beatificabile humano." For clarification of the idea of imitation he turns to Plato, *Republic*, Book X, to the three-way distinction of objects as Ideas (which are contemplated), Works (which are made), and Images (which are made by imitation). Poetics falls among the arts which deal with the last of these; all kinds and forms of poetry form images or Idols (secs. 9–10). The genus being thus established, Mazzoni differentiates the species by a determination of the means, which are harmony, rhythm, and meter; and of the subject matter, which is the credible (rather than the false or the possible). At this point, finally, comes the classification: since it deals with the credible, poetry "must properly be placed under that rational faculty which was called sophistic by the ancients."[45] But this is an incomplete classification; the complete one is given shortly afterward:

... the poetic art may be considered in two ways, that is either as it considers the rightness of the poetic Image, or as it makes and forms the latter. In the first way, I say that it should be called poetics, and in the second, poetry. In the first it is an art which controls and uses the Image, and is a part of the civil faculty. . . . In the second way it is an art which forms and makes the Image, and is a species under the rational faculty.[46]

Since he had previously stated that the means were exclusively productive of pleasure, Mazzoni can now summarize thus his reasons for placing

---

[44] *Della Difesa*, Pt. I (1587), "Proemio," Sec. 7: "le scienze, e l'arti prendano la sua vera, e reale distintione da gli oggetti, non inquanto, che sono cose: ma inquanto, che sono. . . . Scibili, e se cosi si potesse dire, artificiabili."

[45] *Ibid.*, Sec. 53: "si deue drittamente collocare sotto quella facoltà rationale, che fù da gli antichi Sophistica nominata."

[46] *Ibid.*, Sec. 54: "l'arte poetica si può prendere in due modi, cioè, o secondo, ch'ella considera la drittura dell'Idolo poetico, o secondo, che lo fabbrica, e lo forma. Nel primo modo, dico, ch'ella si deue nomare Poetica, e nel secondo Poesia. Nel primo è arte imperante, & vsante l'Idolo, & è parte della facoltà Ciuile. . . . Nel secondo modo è arte formante, e fabbricante l'Idolo, & è specie della facoltà rationale."

poetry under the rational faculty: "Poetry is a sophistic art because of imitation, which is its proper genus, and of the credible, which is its subject, and of pleasure, which is its end; since by being under that genus, by concerning itself with that subject, and by seeking that end, it is frequently constrained to admit the false."[47] The role of the civil faculty is explained as a kind of higher justification of the art: poetry is a game, a cessation or privation of serious activity, the most noble of them all. Thus it may be said that "the civil faculty should be divided into two highly important parts, one of which considers the proper form of activity, and was called by the general name of politics, or the civil faculty. The other considers the proper form of the cessation of activity or the proper form of the activity of games, and was called poetics."[48] Therefore, the *Poetics* should properly be considered as the ninth book of the *Politics*. This argument, for all its diffuseness, is remarkable for two points: first, Mazzoni insists that the end of poetry is pleasure exclusively; second, even when he places poetry under politics he does not do so because he wishes to assign to it a pedagogic end or an ethical purpose.

In Part II, the first book of which is devoted to "character" in poems, Mazzoni reopens the discussion of the relationship of poetry to politics. He emphasizes the difference between the positions of Aristotle and Plato; Aristotle, who considers poems as poems, admits both "good" and "bad" characters in poetry, whereas Plato, whose approach is ethical, admits only the "good":

> Reason is on the side of Plato; for if poetry is a part of philosophy, as has been shown above, it follows that poetic pleasure must be regulated and so to speak qualified by moral philosophy; and therefore good character will necessarily be conjoined with poetics and in such a way that bad character will not be admitted in it, since it would destroy moral goodness. But the practice of the poets is on the side of Aristotle.[49]

The divergence between the two philosophers is explained by the types of governments in terms of which they spoke: Plato of the ideal republic in which only a special kind of poetry would be useful, Aristotle of a practical government in conformity with the habits of mankind in which poetry is

---

[47] *Ibid.*, Sec. 60: "la Poesia è arte Sophistica, e per l'imitatione, che è il suo genere proprio, e per lo credibile, che è il suo soggetto, e per lo diletto, che è il suo fine, poiche per esser sotto quel genere, per esser intorno a quel soggetto, e per rimirare quel fine, viene astretta molte volte a dar luogo al falso."

[48] *Ibid.*, Secs. 66–67: "la facoltà ciuile si deua diuidere in due principalissime parti, l'vna delle quali considera la rettitudine dell' operationi, e fù nomata col nome generale Politica, cioè Ciuile. L'altra considera la rettitudine della cessatione o la rettitudine delle operationi de' giochi, e fù nomata Poetica."

[49] *Difesa*, Pt. II (1688), p. 2: "a Platone è fauoreuole la ragione; percioche se la Poetica è parte della Philosophia, come si è di sopra dimostrato, segue, che il diletto Poetico debba esser regolato, e per cosi dire qualificato dalla morale Philosophia. . . . Ma ad Aristotele è fauoreuole l'vso de Poeti."

admissible as a form of entertainment. When the two theories are so seen, the contradiction between them disappears (pp. 3–4). Similarly, the difficulty over the classification of the art is solved if one realizes, again, that there are two ways of looking at it:

> Poetry may be considered in two ways, that is, in itself insofar as it is an art having the pleasure of man as its aim, in such wise that by means of pleasure it restores the energies grown weary in serious occupations; and when so considered it has no other function but to imitate human actions in a way to delight those who listen to them or who read them. . . . One may, in the other way, consider poetry insofar as it is regulated and ordered by the civil faculty in operation. . . .[50]

Mazzoni, for the most part, considers poetry in the first way and addresses himself to problems of structure and artistry; but he never completely loses sight of the second, and there are constantly evidences of a preoccupation with moral problems and values.

The remaining documents in this group belong to another of the great literary polemics of the century, that waged over Battista Guarini's *Pastor Fido*. The central issue, whether the pastoral and the tragicomedy were legitimate forms of the literary art, led to many auxiliary questions, and one of these was the end of poetry and its classification as an art. The first document is a treatise by Giason Denores (1586) whose title itself is highly significant: *Discorso intorno à que' principii, cause, et accrescimenti, che la comedia, la tragedia, et il poema heroico ricevono dalla philosophia morale, & civile, & da' governatori delle republiche*. In accordance with this announced intention, Denores throughout seeks the contribution of philosophers and rulers to the invention and development of the various kinds of poems. Poetry sprang from natural causes; but it was soon directed by wise men to serve the purposes of the state, "to generate good principles of conduct in their republics and to direct them towards happiness . . . since poetry, as is also rhetoric, is subordinate to moral and civil philosophy, and owes to it every one of its most regulated productions."[51] The end of delight is intermediate to the more important end of utility; it should never be pursued for its own sake. Denores concludes where he had begun:

> . . . let us conclude that it does not belong to any other part of philosophy except politics. . . . everything that we have dealt with in relation to such compositions remains within the province of the moral and civil philosopher, whose duty it is

[50] *Ibid.*, p. 6: "la Poetica si può in due modi considerare, cioè in se stessa inquanto ch'ella è vn'arte, che rimira il diletto humano, accioche per mezo di quello ella ristori le forze affaticate nelle graui occupationi, & in questo modo ella non hà altro officio, che di assomigliare le attioni humane in modo ch'elle dilettino quelli che le ascoltano, e che le leggono. . . . Si può nell'altro modo considerare la Poetica in quanto ch'ella è retta, & ordinata dalla facolta ciuile operante."

[51] *Discorso* (1586), p. 2: "per generar buoni costumi nelle loro republiche & per inuiarle alla felicità. . . . essendo la poetica, come è ancho la rhetorica, soggetta alla philosophia morale, & ciuile; & da essa riceuendo ogni sua piu regolata produttione."

to direct all arts and all doctrines to their true and proper end, that is public utility and benefit.[52]

Two years later, in 1588, Denores returned to a discussion of the same genres in his *Poetica nella qual si tratta secondo l'opinion d'Arist. della tragedia, del poema heroico, & della comedia.* The second work adds little to the theories of the first, except for certain emphases not formerly present. One of these is the claim of the superiority of poetry to politics; poetry

in part is equal to moral and civil philosophy, in part is superior to it. It is equal insofar as both attend with every care to the two most noble actions already mentioned [the purgation of the passions, the inculcation of virtue]. It is superior insofar as the other proceeds by means of laws, penalties, and punishments, while this produces the same result with the greatest enjoyment and recreation of the spirit.[53]

Another such is the insistence that Aristotle in the *Poetics* treated only three genres—tragedy, comedy, and epic—because these were the three commonly recited in public gatherings and hence the only ones capable of exerting a moral influence in the state. "With the greatest perspicacity, as a moral and civil philosopher, he refused to accept as parts of the poetic art all such compositions in verse as did not receive their rules and their principles from Moral and Civil Philosophy, from the rulers and legislators of states ordered to the common weal."[54] To each of these genres Denores assigns a special ethical function, for a specific audience in specific circumstances. Finally, he insists that the poet must not only be fully instructed in ethics and politics but must be himself the kind of man he undertakes to praise in his works. This is a far cry from the early notions of the poet as a rhetorician; it is even farther from the more recent conception of him as a sophist. Poetry has become one with moral philosophy, and the poet is identified both with Cicero's ideal orator and with the Philosopher, or the Good Man.

In neither of these works would there seem to be any controversial materials, especially for the last decades of the century. But Battista Guarini saw in the first of them an attack upon his manuscript *Pastor Fido*, and in reply to this attack he wrote *Il Verrato, ovvero difesa di quanto ha scritto M. Giason Denores contra le tragicomedie, et le pastorali, in un suo*

---

[52] *Ibid.*, pp. 43–43*v*: "concluderemo, che non aspetti ad altra parte della philosophia, che alla politica. . . . tutto quel, che habbiamo trattato di tai componimenti, non è fuor della profession del philosopho morale, & ciuile, a cui aspetta dirizzar tutte le arti, & tutte le dottrine al loro uero, & proprio fine, cioe alla utilità, & al beneficio publico."

[53] *Poetica* (1588), p. ✚2*v*: "è parte vguale, parte è superiore alla philosophia Morale, & Ciuile. E vguale, inquanto che ambedue con ogni studio attendono alle predette due nobilissime attioni. E superiore, in quanto che quella procede con leggi, con pene, con castigamenti, & questa opera il medesimo con sommo godimento, & ricreation d'animo."

[54] *Ibid.*, p. ††: "egli, come Philosopho Morale, & Ciuile con sommo auedimento non si curò di ridur tutti i componimenti, fatti in verso, come parti dell'arte Poetica, che non riconosceuano le loro regole, & i loro principii dalla Philosophia Morale, & Ciuile, da' gouernatori, & da' legislatori delle Republiche a beneficio commune. . . ." See also p. 67.

discorso di poesia (1588). Guarini's stand on the classification of poetry is directly opposed to Denores':

How can you hold that poetics, which is an art and therefore a habit of the speculative intellect, can take its principles from ethics, which is a habit of the active intellect? You will tell me that from ethics it derives notions of character; and I say to you that it gets them rather from rhetoric, which is much different from ethics in the definition of the virtues. But even granted that it does get them from ethics, I insist that it does so not to teach them but solely to imitate them. . . . You will add further that it serves politics insofar as the legislator does or does not permit the people to have a given poem, depending upon whether it demonstrates good or bad mores. That is true; but it does not follow from that that it takes its principles from politics. . . . depending upon the form of the re- public, poetry has more or less freedom. . . . And in this only is it placed under the politician; but as for its intrinsic and formal principles, it has nothing to do with politics, but is a member of sophistic and rhetoric.[55]

From this general position, Guarini passes to a point-by-point denial of Denores' argument: Aristotle's intention in the *Poetics*, the status of the minor poetic genres, the nature of the poet. But he does not completely rule out a relationship between poetry and politics or ethics, as the above quotation shows. Instead, he distinguishes for each of the dramatic genres two separate ends, an instrumental end (which for all dramatic genres is the imitation of an action) and an architectonic end (which for each genre is a special kind of purgation: for comedy, the purgation of sadness through laughter; for tragedy, the purgation of pity and fear, which are moderated in a way to induce virtue; for tragicomedy, the purgation of melancholy). This theory of Guarini's will be developed and reinforced as the polemic with Denores continues.

Denores replied in 1590, in an *Apologia contra l'auttor del Verato*. Much of the essay is devoted to specific problems of the tragicomedy and the pastoral. On the matter of the classification of poetry Denores does little more than reaffirm his earlier convictions. The nature of the repetitions will be indicated by this passage on Aristotle's intention in the *Poetics*:

. . . as a moral and civil philosopher, he was not concerned with speaking of any such form of poetry as did not receive its rules and its principles from moral and civil philosophy and from the rulers and legislators of republics designed for the common good, but only of those forms which, receiving them [from these sources]

---

[55] *Il Verrato* (1588), pp. 39v–40: "Come volete, che la Poetica la quale è arte, & però habito dello 'ntelletto speculatiuo prenda i suoi principi dalla morale, ch'è habito dell'attiuo. Voi mi direte, che dal morale prende i costumi. & io vi dico, che anzi dal ritorico, il quale è molto diferente dal morale nelle difinizioni delle virtù. ma posto, che pur gli prenda dal morale. vi dico, che ciò non fà per insegnargli, ma solo per imitargli. . . soggiugnerete ancora, che serue al politico in quanto il legislatore la concede al popolo & nò, secondo ch'ella è di buoni, e di cattiui costumi. Egli è vero. ma non per tanto non seguita, che dal Politico prenda i principi . . . della poetica, la quale secondo le forme delle Republiche ha più & meno licenza. . . . E'n questo solo è sottoposta al politico, ma quanto ai suoi principi intrin- sechi, & formali non ha che fare con esso lui, ma è membro della sofistica, e della ritorica." See also pp. 20–27.

could generate good principles of conduct or not so receiving them could generate bad principles of conduct in the minds of the citizens in general.[56]

The general contention is, again, that tragedy, comedy, and the epic have as their function to exert a moral influence on the masses assembled to hear them, and that any kind of poem which does not fulfil this function is not worthy of consideration as poetry.

Although Guarini finished his answer in the following year, 1591, it was not published until 1592 (according to the colophon) or 1593 (according to the title page). He entitled it *Il Verato secondo ovvero replica dell'Attizzato accademico ferrarese in difesa del Pastor Fido*. In it, Guarini first reconsidered the whole question of the subordination of poetry to politics. Certain new principles appear at the outset; first, the achievement of the end of poetry is not necessary to the achievement of the end of politics:

If then the end of moral and civil philosophy is none other than public or individual happiness, what need does it have, in order to make man happy, of fables? Man acquires his happiness through the exercise of the virtues, which are rational and true operations; fictional works for the most part, since they are false and lying, will rather harm than aid the achievement of this end.

But what about purgation as a means to moral betterment?

I answer that, in order to subordinate poetry to morality, it is not sufficient that it should be useful for the purgation of the passions, but it would have to be necessary to the acquisition of virtue; for the superior art cannot obtain its end without the operation of the inferior art. ... man can purge the passions of terror and pity through other and better means than that of tragedy. And moral and civil philosophy has its own laws and private and public expedients for the achievement of this end.[57]

In sum, whatever moral profit may attach to poetry is merely an auxiliary accompaniment to the contemplation of pleasurable objects. What is more, there is no foundation anywhere in Aristotle for the subordination of poetry to politics. The end of the poet is not a utilitarian one but an aesthetic one: "His end is then not to imitate the good, but to imitate well, whether he imitate good or bad moral character; and if he imitates what is

---

56 *Apologia* (1590), p. 2*v*: "egli, come philosopho morale, & ciuile, non si curo di fauellar di ogni forma di poesia, che non riceuea le sue regole, & i suoi principii dalla philosophia morale, & ciuile, & da' gouernatori, & legislatori delle Republiche ad utilità commune, ma solamente di quelle, che, riceuendogli, poteuano generar buoni costumi, ò non riceuendogli poteuano generar cattiui costumi ne gli animi de' Cittadini in uniuersale."

57 *Il Verato secondo* (1593), p. 63: "Se dunque il fine della morale, e ciuile Filosofia non è altro, che la felicità o publica, ò priuata, che bisogno ha ella, per far felice l'huomo, di fauole? il qual' huomo acquista la sua felicità con l'esercizio della vertù, che son opere ragioneuoli, e vere, al qual suo fine possono, per lo più, l'opere fauolose, come false, e mentite, anzi nuocere, che giouare. ... Rispondo, che per esser subalternata alla morale, non basta che sia gioueuole alla purgazion degli affetti, ma bisogna che sia necessaria all'acquisto della vertù, perciochè l'arte superiore non può, se non con l'opera della 'nferiore, ottenere il suo fine. ... può ben l'huomo, per altra, e molto miglior maniera, purgar gli affetti del terrore, e della compassione, che per quella della Tragedia. E la Filosofia morale, e ciuile ha di ciò le sue leggi, ed ha per questo fine le sue priuate, e pubbliche cure."

good poorly, he will not be a good poet, but he may be called a good poet if he imitates well what is bad."[58] Indeed, all the important questions to be asked about a poem lie exclusively in the realm of poetics itself:

Furthermore, what does the poet have to do with the laws of the city? To whom must he give an accounting as to whether his plots are pathetic, or ethical, or sententious, or ridiculous, or complex, or simple, or single, or double, or with happy ending, or with turbulent ending, which are the essential parts of poetry; with respect to which, from whom does he get the rules, from legislators or from poets?[59]

Guarini also now develops two points made earlier, that touching the relation of poetry to rhetoric and that on the existence of the instrumental and architectonic ends. The poet derives from rhetoric, rather than from ethics, the notions of moral character which he uses. Like the rhetorician, he must consider the nature of his audience if he would achieve his architectonic end, since it is a form of persuasion; different audiences in different times require more or less violent tragic effects, purgation of a more or less vigorous kind. But in any event, this rhetorical end is a secondary one; the primary one still remains the artistic end proper to the art:

... the poet is not concerned with purging more or less, but with imitating well that subject—even though it may be little useful for purgation—which he undertakes; so that, if in a subject with a happy ending he will do his job well with a good imitation, with the required unity, with artful recognition, with judicious sententiae, with appropriate character, and (what is more proper to him than all the rest) with splendor of diction, he will without doubt avoid being charged with that mediocrity which Horace blames.[60]

This is as close as Guarini comes—or as any of his contemporaries come—to developing a theory of poetry as an independent art, subordinated neither to the rational disciplines nor to the ethical sciences and achieving its own special ends by following principles which are specifically its own.

There is a definite philosophical relationship between the large group of texts which classified poetry as an instrument or a part of moral philosophy and that earlier group which placed it among the rational or discursive or

[58] *Ibid.*, p. 66: "Non è dunque suo fine d'imitare il buono, ma di bene imitare, o buono o cattiuo che sia il costume: e'l buono, male imitando, non sarà buon poeta, ma imitando [bene] il cattiuo buon poeta potrà chiamarsi" (the original text reads "imitando male il cattiuo," but this must be an error).

[59] *Ibid.*, p. 90: "Del resto, che ha da fare il poeta con le leggi della città? A cui ha egli da render conto, se le sue fauole son patetiche, o morate, o sentenziose, o ridicole, o rannodate, o piane, o semplici, o doppie, o con fin lieto, o con fin turbulento, che sono le parti essenziali di poesia, delle quali, da chi prende le regole, da' legislatori, o pur da' poeti?"

[60] *Ibid.*, p. 118: "il . . . poeta non ha riguardo di purgar più, e meno, ma di bene imitar quel soggetto, quantunque poco purgante, che si propone, per modo, che se in soggetto di lieto fine farà bene la parte sua con la buona imitazione, con la debita vnità, con l'artifizioso riconoscimento, con la prudente sentenza, col conueneuol costume, e quello ch'è più suo proprio di tutto 'l resto, con lo splendor della locuzione, fuggirà, senza fallo, la nota di quella mediocrità, che biasima Orazio."

instrumental sciences. If the earlier group insisted upon the character of poetry as useful for serving some final purpose through its means as variously considered—words, which have powers of signification; arguments, which have powers of persuasion or conviction—the later group insisted upon the kinds of usefulness provided. If poetry was discursive, its discourse concerned itself with moral activity, ethical or civil or political. If poetry was instrumental, it served as an instrument for the achievement of moral ends—for supplying examples of good and bad conduct, for administering praise and blame, for persuading to activity or inactivity. The second group thus comes to constitute a kind of specification of the first, a pushing of assumptions to further conclusions; the earlier critics are concerned with the problem of instrumentality, the later ones with the ends for which the instrument is used. The change in concern accounts for the change in classification of the art.

ECLECTIC CLASSIFICATIONS

It should not be surprising that, among all these attempts to decide in favor of moral philosophy or history or logic or rhetoric as the closest relative of poetry among the sciences, there should be at least a few works in which all seem to occupy an equal position. Such is the case with Agnolo Segni, for whom the frames of reference are both philosophy and history. The following passage from his *Ragionamento sopra le cose pertinenti alla Poetica* (written in 1576 as a revision of lectures given in 1573; published in 1581) states the essence of his position, which is basically Platonic in its assumptions:

. . . we may consider the difference manifest among these three faculties of history, philosophy, and poetry and among their forms of discourse. For since there are two extreme species of objects, one, the things in our world with their imperfections, the other, their perfect forms which we call Ideas, the latter make up philosophy and the former history, each of the two being separate from the other; but the one and the other conjoined generate poetry. History, residing in things past and present, expounds and narrates them as different from their Ideas, just as they are or were in themselves. Philosophy rises to the Ideas of things different from the things themselves, and these she contemplates as they are in their perfect nature. Poetry joins the one part and the other, recounting things past or present, not as they are or were, but similar to their Ideas, and showing the Ideas not in themselves, but in things which have been and things which are. Whence history and philosophy, which are at the pure extremes, are each completely true; poetry, which tries to combine them, since they remain uncombined is in part true and in part false: true for the Ideas which she expresses, and false for the things in which she puts these Ideas, and because she makes things similar to these Ideas whereas they are really different. And therefore poetry is intermediate between philosophy and history because it participates in these two extremes; and insofar as it participates in philosophy and in her objects, it is better than history; but because of its participation in history and in the particular sensible things which are the objects of history, to this extent it is below philosophy, and the poet is of lesser dignity than the philosopher.[61]

Another eclectic document, and perhaps a more extreme one, is Torquato Tasso's *Discorsi del poema heroico* [1594]. Poetry, for Tasso, serves the traditional ends of pleasure and utility; but utility is foremost, pleasure auxiliary. Hence the role of the moral philosopher:

Therefore it is the task of the political philosopher to consider what poetry is to be prohibited and what pleasure, so that the pleasure . . . should not produce the effect of an infectious poison, or should not keep the mind occupied in idle reading. . . . poetry is a first philosophy which from our earliest years teaches us principles of conduct and the ways of life.[62]

But insofar as poetry achieves political ends it is subordinate to a higher art and is considered in terms of that art; considered in itself, it seeks only pleasure as its end:

If the poet as a poet pursues this end, he will not err far from that goal to which he must direct all his attention . . .; but as a political person and part of the city, or at least insofar as his art is subordinated to that art which is queen of all the others, he seeks some profit, and rather that which is honest than useful. Thus of the two ends which the poet envisages, one is proper to his own art, the other to the superior art.[63]

When one comes to consider the subject matter of poetry, the classification again changes abruptly; the poet, treating the probable and the verisimilar, is a kind of dialectician, as is the rhetorician. "Without doubt

---

61 *Ragionamento* (1581), pp. 65–66: "si può contemplare da noi la differenza tra queste tre facultà manifesta, historia, filosofia, & poesia, & tra le loro orazioni. che essendo due spezie estreme, vna le cose tra noi co' loro difetti, l'altra le loro perfezzioni, che noi chiamiamo Idee, queste fanno la filosofia, & quelle l'historia, ciascuna delle due parti da se: ma l'vna parte & l'altra congiunte insieme generano la poesia. L'historia stando nelle cose, nelle passate, & nelle presente, l'espone & le narra dalle loro Idee diuerse, così com'elle sono ò furono in se stesse. La filosofia s'alza all'Idee delle cose diuerse dalle cose, & quelle contempla com'elle sono nella natura loro perfette. La poesia congiugne l'vna parte & l'altra, narrando cose state ò presenti, non come sono ò furono, ma simili all'Idee, & mostrando l'Idee non in se, ma nelle cose state & nelle presenti. Onde l'historia & la filosofia, che stanno nelle pure estremità, è tutta vera l'vna & l'altra: la poesia, che congiugner le vuole, non essendo congiunte, è parte vera, & parte falsa: vera per l'Idee, le quali ella esprime: & falsa per le cose, doue ella le pone, et le cose fa simili à loro, essendo diuerse. Et però è mezzana tra la filosofia & l'historia la poesia, perche participa di que' due estremi: & in quanto participa della filosofia, & de suoi oggetti, è migliore dell' historia: ma per la participazione dell'historia, & de' particolari sensibili dell'historia oggetto, per questo è sotto la filosofia, & di minor degnità del filosofo il poeta."

62 *Poema heroico* [1594], p. 7: "Però al Politico s'appartiene di considerare, quale poesia debba esser prohibita, e qual diletto; accioche il piacere . . . non facesse effetto di pestifero veleno, ò non tenesse occupati gli animi in vana lettione. . . . la poesia . . . è vna prima Filosofia, la qual sin dalla tenera età, ci ammaestra ne costumi, e nelle ragioni della vita."

63 *Ibid.*, p. 8: "Se'l Poeta dunque in quanto Poeta hà questo fine, non errerà lontano da quel segno, alquale egli deue dirizzare tutti i suoi pensieri . . .; ma in quanto è huomo ciuile, e parte della Città, ò almeno in quanto la sua Arte è sottordinata à quella, ch'è Regina delle altre, si propone il giouamento, il quale è honesto più tosto, che vtile. de due fini dunque, i quali si prepone il Poeta, l'vno è proprio dell'arte sua, l'altro dell'arte superiore."

poetry is placed in order under dialectic, along with rhetoric. ... the probable insofar as it is verisimilar belongs to the poet, for the poet uses proofs less effectively than does the dialectician."[64] Or the poet may be regarded as a kind of logician, if one attends now to the kinds of proofs he uses. If there are three kinds of logic, so there are three kinds of poetry (or parts of poetry), each of which employs different proofs (p. 28):

Logic	Poetry
Demonstrative	"dimostrando co' Filosofi, e usando il Filosofema"
Probable	"seguendo il verisimile, & seruendosi dell'essempio, e dell'enthimema"
Sophistic (or apparent probable)	"equiuoco, fallaci argomenti"

Poetry is then a part of moral philosophy if one looks at its external or "superior" end, a part of dialectic according to its subject matter, a part of logic on the basis of the arguments it uses; it is also a part of logic, but related to grammar and rhetoric, as a result of its use of "poetic diction":

... poetry is an art subordinated to logic, or really a part of it, not only because it is an art of discourse which seeks to produce pleasure, just as grammar produces regulated speech and rhetoric persuasion, but because in poetic diction, which is not without imitation, there is a kind of tacit proof which is frequently most effective; for one cannot imitate without the simile and the example, but in the example and in everything which appears verisimilar there is a kind of proof.[65]

These shifts in Tasso's position are interesting not only as they represent in one work a kind of epitome of all the theories of the century but as they demonstrate some of the characteristics and the deficiencies of the methods of thinking used by the critics. I shall have occasion to speak of them again in the following chapter.

ARISTOTELIAN CLASSIFICATIONS

From the thinking of Tasso as from that of most theorists of the century one type of classification is strikingly absent, the one we might call Aristotelian in the strict or proper sense. Of this type there were, among the documents examined, really only two examples: that of Lionardo Salviati, a very slight one, and that of Francesco Buonamici, a much more considerable one. For Lionardo Salviati, in his *Trattato della poetica*,

64 *Ibid.*, p. 27: "senza dubio la poesia è collocata in ordine sotto la dialettica insieme con la rhetorica . . . il probabile inquanto egli [è] verisimile appertiene al Poeta: percioche il Poeta vsa le proue men efficacemente che non fà il dialettico."

65 *Ibid.*, p. 129: "la poesia, è vn'arte subordinata alla logica, ò veramente vna sua parte, non solamente perch'ella è arte dell'oratione, laqual cerca il diletto, non altrimente che la Grammatica il regolato parlare, e la Rhetorica, la persuasione. ma perche nel parlar poetico, il quale non è senza imitatione, è vna tacita proua: e molte volte efficacissima: perche non si può imitare senza similitudine, e senza essempio, ma nell'essempio, & in ogni cosa, che paia verisimile è la proua."

Lezzion prima (1564), the problem is less to relate poetry to other arts than to establish the fact that it is an intellectual habit and hence susceptible of cultivation. He is replying to Plato, to the assertion that poetry is merely a furor. The skeleton plan which he suggests is essentially Aristotelian: all habits are either moral or intellectual; the intellectual are either active (inducing perfection in the operator) or factitive (inducing perfection in some external matter); poetry belongs in the latter group.[66] Salviati, it is clear, is not establishing an Aristotelian system of the sciences but is merely inquiring into the kind of activity involved in the production of poetry.

This is not the case with Francesco Buonamici, who wrote a treatise in which he set out to restore to Aristotle's *Poetics* whatever glory and authority may have been removed from it by such critics as Castelvetro. He called it *Discorsi poetici nella Accademia fiorentina in difesa d'Aristotile* (1597). He thought that he could solve some of the difficulties of the text by presenting an elaborate system of the sciences in which the place of poetics would explain some of the operations of the "art." But the system so presented is itself confused, difficult to follow, and lacking in examples; I offer the following schematic reduction only with reservations. The first step is clear enough: all knowledge is divided into two kinds, one of which seeks truth and contemplates the nature of things (the speculative sciences), the other of which seeks truth for purposes of applying it later to some activity (the practical sciences). Poetics is among the latter, which perhaps may be represented as follows:

Practical Sciences

(with specific subject matters)		*(with no specific subject matters)*
Doing	Making	Instrumental
(activities)	*(works)*	Sciences
(πράττειν)	(ποιεῖν)	
Politics	Poetics	Logic
Medicine		Dialectic
		Rhetoric

Each of the subgroups under the practical sciences has itself a theoretical and a practical phase: there is a theory of medicine which affords precepts and a practice which applies them, a theory of poetry (the *Poetics*) and an application of this theory in the writing of poems, a theory of logic and its use in every other science. Moreover, in each of the main divisions there is one master science, from which all the others derive. In the contemplative or speculative sciences, this is metaphysics; in the practical sciences, it is politics (pp. 10–12).

It is perhaps worthy of note that a century which considered itself Aristotelian in poetic matters should have waited until its very last years to produce a text, such as Buonamici's, showing some comprehension of

[66] MS BNF, Magl. VII, 307, fol. 29.

Aristotle's general system of the sciences and of the place of poetry among them. Buonamici lists poetry neither among the instrumental sciences nor among the parts or instruments of moral philosophy. He sees it as specifically a "poetic" science whose function is to make poems. Along with the rest of his contemporaries, however, he continues to regard it, in a broader view, as auxiliary to politics; its artistic end is intermediate to a larger "architectonic" end, that of contributing to man's happiness. It would be possible, of course, so to regard poetry without ceasing to be a good Aristotelian; everything would depend upon how, in general, one interprets the text of the *Poetics* in relation to the other sciences. I reserve that analysis and that judgment for a later chapter.

CONCLUSIONS

Although there may seem to be a certain amount of similarity among the various theories proposed during the century—one might even say monotony—a close questioning of the reasons for the predominant classifications leads rather to an impression of diversity. Let us take, for example, the earliest and most persistent classification, where poetry is assigned to the group constituted by logic, grammar, rhetoric (with the occasional addition of dialectic, sophistic, and history). This assignment may be made, first, because all the arts in the group use language as their medium or material; they are all "discursive" sciences. Second, it may be made because poetry is regarded, along with the others, as neither an "art" nor a "science" but a "faculty" of the mind; hence it will belong with the others in the family of rational faculties. Or it may, third, result from a consideration of the subject matter of poetics, which deals not with the truth (as do certain other sciences) but with one of the variations of the probable or the false or the verisimilar; this will relate it to sophistic on the one hand and to rhetoric on the other. Or, fourth, the whole group may be composed of those disciplines which could be classified as "instrumental sciences," since in themselves they produce no knowledge or activity but are useful only as means of investigating, expounding, or presenting for persuasion the materials of some other science.

It is easy to see how the reason for the assignment of position will in each case predetermine the emphasis which the critic will give to his theory of the poetic art (unless, contrariwise, the classification proceeds from the emphasis). If poetry is a discursive science, then the important thing to investigate is its qualities as language, how these differ from the language of the other discursive sciences, how its language may be made to conform to the special norms established. If it is a rational faculty, one will wish to know about the peculiarities of its operation as a faculty, about what special characteristics of the mind are manifested in its products. If it is an art determined by its subject matter—the false, the probable, or the verisimilar—whether or not it is acceptable will depend upon the total philosophical outlook of the theorist; moreover, the plots to be used, the traits to be attributed to the characters, the handling of situation and story, will all depend upon this conception of subject matter. If it is an instrumental science, finally, its uses will vary with the sciences which it is made to serve and the ends which it is made to seek; it will be caught inextricably between the principles of the architectonic science and the devices required for achieving the purposes of that science. Thus although the classification "logic, rhetoric, poetic" may seem to be simple enough and traditional enough, it is susceptible of a broad range of interpretations and may produce a whole gamut of diverging theories of the poetic art.

The same is true of the classification of poetry as a part or an instrument of moral philosophy. This may result, for example, from the observation that poetry deals with the moral characters of persons, with their conduct, just as does the science of ethics; both would then have the same subject matter. The principles of behavior established in the theorist's ethics would have to be reflected in poems produced according to his poetics. Or it may result from a conviction with respect to the ends of the sciences: if ethics has as its end to produce happiness in the individual and politics to produce happiness in the state, then poetics belongs to both, since it offers examples of how happiness is achieved or lost by various kinds of persons in various situations. It must therefore offer these examples in such a way that the right moral lessons will be taught and the proper effect produced. But even within these limits there is a fair breadth of possibilities. The poet may be regarded as completely subservient to the moral philosopher or the politician, using his art to achieve the ends of the other. Or he may be on a par with the other, achieving ethical or political ends (determined by himself) by using the resources of his own art. Or he may be completely independent of the other, functioning as an artist who merely happens to cross the path of the moral philosopher when he touches upon character and conduct. According as this theory varies, politics or ethics will be considered as being the "architectonic" science for poetry, or as belonging to the same family, or as having merely a slight and accidental resemblance.

Several explanations might be offered for this great divergency of opinion over the classification of poetics. The most obvious one, of course, would be the nature of the antecedent philosophical tradition and the character of the texts which were being explained or paraphrased or commented upon. Of this, much will be said in subsequent chapters. Another one, and more germane to the present discussion, would be the method of classification itself. Any art may, in the abstract, be considered from a multiplicity of points of view; one may look at it from innumerable external positions, consider it in a large variety of contexts. But these possibilities of discussion need not affect its essence as an art or its place in a total system of philosophy; these may remain firm and fixed if the system itself provides constant principles of classification. For the critics and philosophers of the Cinquecento, two things happened, one dependent upon the other. First, they used each of the many points of view as a basis for classification: if poetry may be considered in the light of the principles of ethics, it is an ethical science; if it uses words as its means, it is a discursive science; and so on. Second, the philosophical systems into which they fitted poetics were incompletely or improperly understood. Various systems which claimed to be Aristotelian resulted in widely different conceptions of the poetic art and of its relationship to the rest of the parts of philosophy. So for those which were admittedly Platonic. The critic might begin with principles which he thought satisfactory for the classification of the sciences; but he might pursue them imperfectly, or he might abandon them without realizing it and pass into an entirely different context of analysis. Such insufficiencies will be found frequently in the documents to be studied. Perhaps this is because the large majority of the men writing on literary matters were not philosophers but critics, not specialists in the formal disciplines of analysis but critics and poets curious about the literary art. This was not always true, however, and in no event should be taken as an explanation or an exculpation.

One may ask, also, whether any change or progress or evolution in the theories of classification is perceptible through the century. This question is difficult to answer. It should be clear that the major theories exist simultaneously throughout the century. Perhaps in the early years the tendency to occupy oneself with complete philosophical systems is more prevalent than in the later. Perhaps also the classification as a discursive science or rational faculty is more prominent in the first part of the century, whereas the classification as a relative of moral philosophy is more frequent in the second part; the "rhetorical" approach gradually gives way to the "ethical." It may also be that only in the last decades of the century do we find any insistence that poetry has the right to be considered an art in itself, that it might be approached from an "artistic" or "aesthetic" point of view. But this is at best a very mild insistence and might almost pass unperceived among the dominant tendencies of the century.

CHAPTER TWO. THE METHODOLOGY OF THE THEORISTS

THE PROBLEM of literary criticism in the Cinquecento was largely a problem in aesthetics. This would, of course, be true of criticism in any place and in any period. But it is true in sixteenth-century Italy in a very special way and for two special reasons. Perhaps more than in any other time and place, the problem of criticism was essentially a theoretical problem. The major effort of the critics was to develop a theory of the literary art; even when they were engaged in practical criticism, their preoccupation was primarily with theory and with the possibilities of applying theory to the judgment of specific works. At all times, they were aware of theoretical cruxes, theoretical difficulties, theoretical modes of approach. Perhaps nowhere else in the intellectual history of the West can one find so continual, so abundant, and so diverse a centering of attention upon problems of literary theory. Moreover, and this is the second reason, the literary aesthetics of the Cinquecento did not develop independently as a free and indigenous flowering. Instead, it was transplanted from Greece and Rome and the European soils of the Middle Ages. It must therefore manifest at all times two concerns, concern with fidelity to the borrowed tradition which it pretended to continue and concern with the usefulness of this tradition for a new age and a new literature.

For the theorist, the task was thus extremely complex. He must discover, first, the meaning of the ancient text or texts which he had set out to interpret—and this at a time when the texts themselves were imperfectly established. The texts, moreover, were difficult ones, which are still subject to much uncertainty and diversity of interpretation. Next, he must decide whether it was possible to reach a satisfactory reading of the text by remaining within the *données* and the arguments of the text itself, or whether he must seek assistance by reference to another of the available ancient texts. Then, when he proceeded to develop his own theory, he must choose between the alternative possibilities of basing it upon a single ancient author or upon a conflation of several ancient authors. Finally, he must see to it that his theory not only fitted the text out of which it grew but that it accounted for and explained and permitted him to judge more recent works by his countrymen and his contemporaries. We should not assume that these problems were posed and solved in a deliberate and conscious fashion by all theorists; they are merely the problems which, somewhere or other in the process of developing a theory, must be considered and resolved.

For the practical critic, the procedure was only slightly less complicated. He, too, had to find a theoretical basis for his criticism, whether he developed his own theory or borrowed one from a contemporary or an ancient philosopher. He had to be versed in the literature of a long and diversified critical tradition. Most important of all, he had to convert the theoretical statements from which he started into guides for the reading of poems, into criteria for the judging of poems, into norms for the admission or exclusion of new literary types, into weapons for current controversy. Perhaps he had also to reconcile the findings of his intellectual explorations with the promptings of his sensitivity, his enthusiasms with contrary theoretical conclusions, his dislikes with the acceptances of a long tradition.

Both the theorist and the practical critic stood at a crucial point in the history of Western criticism, that point at which the doctrines of classical antiquity were transformed into something new and different, which in its turn became the basis of modern literary criticism. From their point of view, the critical process looked essentially backward: it attempted to extract from classical and medieval traditions the lessons needed for the solution of contemporary critical problems. From our point of view, the whole process had consequences for the future of even greater significance; at four centuries' remove, the specific nature of the transformation, the exact character of the new orientations become matters of considerable importance in intellectual history.

It is in the light of these last considerations that the matter of method or methodology becomes vital in the history of Renaissance criticism. Given a limited number of ancient texts; given a medieval tradition in which these texts, when not forgotten, had already suffered a certain transmutation; given a desire to find in these ancient and medieval materials a new critical apparatus: what results from this desire operating on these materials will depend in large part upon the way in which theorists and critics go about the solution of their problems. If the individual theorist comes to his problem with one set of intellectual habits, with one discipline for the reading and interpretation of texts, with one attitude toward the procedures of his predecessors, the theory that he himself propounds will be of one kind. Another habit, another discipline, another attitude might produce an entirely different kind of theory.

In such a situation there are really no constants. The basic texts themselves change from reader to reader; the mode of procedure of each critic will differ in some way from those of all the others; no two of the resulting theories will be exactly identical. Hence the tremendous variety and complexity of critical thought in the Cinquecento. In a sense, the only valid statements one can make are statements about individual authors and individual texts. Nevertheless, there was such a thing as a general current of intellectual discipline through the century. There was a fairly constant formation of habits of mind in the schools, a fairly definite tradition about how certain subjects were to be treated, a relatively widespread assumption with respect to the conduct of an argument. This general tendency—always with variations—formed the basis of the method employed by the individual writer in his theorizing or in his criticism. It is this general method which I wish to describe in the present chapter, as a means to aiding the reader in his understanding of subsequent textual analyses.

CLASSIFICATION AMONG THE SCIENCES

The first characteristic of this method has already been described: the tendency to preface discussion of the poetic art by indicating its position with reference to the other arts and sciences. This effort at classification might take one of several forms: that of situating poetics in the whole family of the components of philosophy; that of relating it to a smaller group of cognate arts such as logic and rhetoric, or to a single sister art such as history; that of transforming it, by a kind of analogy, into a universal art encompassing all other branches of philosophy. The first of these forms has already been studied as symptomatic of a general philosophical approach which in its essence was systematic; the same approach, but reduced in the scope of its intention, is apparent in the second. Of the third and fourth, something further needs to be said.

Let us take, to illustrate how poetics was assimilated to another art, several examples of the relating of poetics to history throughout the century. The problem here, as distinguished from that of the preceding chapter, is not so much to discover the fact or the basis of classification as to determine what methodological approaches are involved in the coupling of the two arts. An early case, from the fifteenth century, is Rodolphus Agricola's *De inventione dialectica*. Here, the two arts are compared, since both of them use words to narrate an order of events which have happened. But whereas history, bent upon representing the truth, gives events in the "natural" order in which they actually occurred, poetry may permit itself an "artificial" order. The typical case is that of the beginning "in medias res" with a later summation of antecedent happenings. As far as method is concerned, Agricola's consists in seeking a factor common to the two arts and in using this factor as a means to comparison and differentiation. Any other features of the arts are left out of consideration.[1]

The procedure of Dionigi Atanagi in his *Ragionamento de la eccellentia et perfettione de la historia* (1559) is much more complex. Atanagi wishes essentially to characterize the art of history; he adopts as the best expedient a lengthy set of likenesses and differences between history and poetry, which incidentally provides a complete theory of poetry. The important

---

[1] *De inventione dialectica* (Louvain: Martin, 1515), Liber Tertius, fol. b vi*v*: "Est tamen differentia poetice dispositionis ab historia vel maxima: quod poeta solum quantum ad ipsius: hoc est ad narrantis personam pertinet: in speciem tantum. sequitur temporum ordinem. quantum autem est ex rerum gestarum natura: plerunque perturbat eas atque a mediis orditur rebus: deinde quae primae fuerant earum: posterius personae colore alicuius aut alio quouis commento infert mentionem. [Example of *Aeneid*.] Sin vero res ipsas respicimus non personas quibus dat orationem poeta: iam videmus contrarium naturali: id est artificialem ordinem esse. . . . Historie cuius prima laus est veritas: naturalis tamen ordo conuenit. . . ."

difference is not between the use of prose and the use of verse (since some poems are also found in prose), but between the use, or not, of imitation. The differences may be summarized thus:

History	Poetry
1. No imitation	Imitation
2. Many actions of many men	Single action of one man
3. Treats the particular, things as they are	Treats the universal, the pure Idea of things
4. Narrates things done as they were done	Narrates things as they should be done, according to necessity, verisimilitude, and probability
5. Presents characters as they were, varied, unstable, etc.	Maintains constancy of character
6. Uncertain and confused order, following events themselves	Certain order, subordinating all events to central plot
7. Natural order, as events happened	Artificial order; beginning "in medias res"
8. Limited by the materials, the truth of the facts	Not limited by facts; extensive additions to produce the marvelous, the stupendous, the delightful
9. Invents speeches attributed to men; real art consists in writing dialogues, orations	Also makes men speak as they should speak
10. Rarely introduces gods or uses personifications	Introduces gods, uses personification, at will
11. Restricted in use of words, sententiae	Freer in use of words, sententiae
12. Literal meanings only for words	Allegorical meanings hidden under literal meanings

The points of likeness or similarity may also be summarized briefly:

1. Both use "proposition" and "narration," but only poetry uses "invocation"
2. Both use the "demonstrative" and the "deliberative" types of rhetoric
3. Both use the "judicial" type, which is, however, more proper to history
4. Both observe prudence and decorum
5. Both seek to teach, to delight, to move, and to bring profit; history especially seeks utility
6. Both use ancient and distant subjects, describe places, peoples, laws, customs, etc.
7. Both use sudden and unexpected accidents, changes of fortune, leading to a wide variety of emotions
8. Both use digressions, amplifications, variety

9. Both use numbers, figures of speech, although different ones
10. Both must represent things in so graphic a way as to make them visible to the eye

What was for Agricola the whole basis of comparison becomes for Atanagi only one of many points of contact between the two arts. His method is to multiply such points of juxtaposition as far as his ingenuity will permit. Each additional point further circumscribes the material or the operation of the art. One ends up with a conception of what poetry is not—as compared to history—and of what it is. What it is is not determined by discovery of a definition (inductively) and by derivation of the consequences of that definition; rather, it comes from an accumulation of isolated descriptive statements, generated dialectically by considering how it resembles and differs from something else. Moreover, the topics which give rise to these statements are themselves significant of a method of thinking about poetry. Roughly, the topics are these: the genus, kind of action, relation to truth and probability, character, order, factualness, dialogue, use of the supernatural, diction, literalness, type of rhetoric, decorum, ends, ornaments, nature of plot, figures, numbers, visual qualities. Presumably, a poem which satisfied all the conditions established by consideration of these topics would be a good poem, whether or not it conformed to such other artistic demands as might be required by a more systematic approach.[2]

A similar approach, but again fairly restricted, is that of the anonymous *Dialogue on History* in MS Vat. Lat. 6528, which I have dated roughly around 1565. As, however, the principal protagonist claims to be maintaining the point of view of Pomponazzi, the ideas would belong to the early part of the century. Here, as we have seen in the preceding chapter, both history and poetry are species of the genus narration, differentiated by the fact that poetry narrates a single action of one man whereas history narrates a single action of many men. The various poetic genres spring from a single source, historical annals: these give rise to the epic through the selection of one exceptionally great man and one of his exceptionally great actions; from the epic springs tragedy; and so on for the rest. Once the poet has dedicated himself to treating the exceptional, he must find a decorum and a style and a diction appropriate to it; thence come into being the various "modes" of poems, the use of verse and of poetic diction, allegory, and prosopopoeia. The procedure is once more to select a single common factor—the narration of an action—to seek a basis of differentiation, and from the single elementary difference so discovered to construct a whole theory of the poetic art.[3]

Giovanni Antonio Viperano, in the first of two treatises on history, the *De scribenda historia* of 1569, also uses as his starting point the genus

2 *Ragionamento* (1559), pp. 3v–6.
3 MS Vat. Lat. 6528, fols. 142v, 150v–151.

narration. Within this genus he finds three species, history, poetry, and oratory. (Oratory is included because, according to currently accepted rhetorical doctrines, "narration" was one of the component parts of any speech: "Habet quoque Orator narrationes suas.") Further distinctions sometimes include oratory, sometimes do not. History and poetry differ in the kinds of actions they represent, history using only "res gestas" and poetry "res fictas." Each of the three species has a separate end; indeed, each seems to have several ends, one serving the other. History tries immediately to "narrate well," ultimately to teach proper modes of action and to form character; it is also useful to the other arts, by supplying examples and materials, and should be accompanied by pleasure. Poetry tries immediately to "invent what is proper to each character," finally to bring pleasure through its narration. For oratory, the immediate end is to praise and to blame, but it too seeks to please through narration. Finally, while history guides the mind, poetry arouses and calms the passions. What is interesting in this method is the kind of equivocation by which oratory falls into the same genus as history and poetry and the multiple distinctions applied to these arts.[4]

Viperano's second work, *De scribendis virorum illustrium vitis* (1570), applies the general ideas of the first to the more specific field of biography. The general ideas are not repeated. Instead, biography is discussed in such a way as to indicate that the trilogy history–poetry–oratory is still present in the author's mind. For example, the main task of biography is to present the character of the hero; this will be done properly if all the topics of decorum—age, sex, condition, nation, and so forth—are treated in the way prescribed by the best rhetorical tradition and practised by the best poets.[5]

One final example: A position similar to that of the anonymous *Dialogue on History* is found in Sperone Speroni's *Dialogo dell'historia*, to which I have not been able to assign a date (published 1596). For Speroni also, history and poetry are kinds of narration; poetry narrates one action of one man, history one action of many men. But he goes beyond the *Dialogue* when he introduces the question of truthfulness of subject matter; contrary to what is commonly believed, he says, both poetry and history treat the truth. If one takes three such forms as the annal, history, and poetry, the following distinctions apply: "the annal is true, history is true and worthy, poetry is true and worthy and marvelous." The truth of poetry is changed into something higher and more wonderful through the process of treating it "as it should be" according to necessity and probability; it is this that makes of poetry an imitation. Thus, although poetry is like history in treating the truth, it is unlike it, since it transforms the particular of history into the universal; hence it is a higher and more noble art.[6]

[4] *De scribenda historia* (1576 ed.), esp. pp. 845–48.
[5] *De scribendis vitis* (1570), esp. pp. B4–B4v, Cv.
[6] In *Dialoghi* (1596 ed.), esp. pp. 376, 394–403, 411–412.

What is involved, essentially, in these multiple comparisons of the art of history to the art of poetry is not classification but delimitation. The critic is faced with the problem of explaining the nature of one art. He finds that it is like another art in some salient respect—the use of language, the narration of an action, the treatment of the truth—and he proceeds to search for other points of agreement or disagreement. The more such points he can find, the more complete will be his comparison of the two arts, and hence the more satisfactory will be his description of either one. For poetry, the comparison may be with history or with rhetoric or with painting or with logic; the resulting delineation of the poetic art will be more or less adequate as the other art is ill or well chosen or as the initial point of comparison is appropriate or inappropriate. The potential danger in the method is that the original basis of equivalence may be some aspect of the poetic art which is not really of the essence of the art, and that the whole resulting discussion may therefore deal with auxiliary or incidental or accidental features of the art. Its distinguishing characters as an art may thus never be apprehended. Such a method may also result merely in a collection of traditional statements about the art, of commonplace pros and cons relative to the central topics, with no attempt to examine the art in itself in a systematic way.

The method by which poetry becomes a universal science, containing and transcending all others, is not too different. Once again the critic selects for consideration a single aspect of the poetic art; this is always the same one, the subject matter—or rather the subject matters—of poetry. Subject matters are here taken in the broadest sense: not "human action" or "character" or "the verisimilar," but all the infinite variety of things about which a poet may speak in a poem. If he speaks of the stars, he encompasses astronomy; if he describes a battle, he applies his knowledge of the military art; the wanderings of Odysseus display Homer's expertness in geography; and so forth without end. This is the kind of thinking about poetry which, in the late Greek world, gave rise to such a document as the pseudo-Plutarchian *De Homeri poesi,* which made of Homer the "ocean" of all knowledge. In the Quattrocento, the *De Homeri poesi* was copied in large part by Angelo Poliziano in his *Oratio in expositione Homeri.*[7] In the Cinquecento the same ideas were expressed in such texts as Varchi's *Lezzioni della poetica* (already referred to), Giacopo Grifoli's *Oratio de laudibus poetarum* (1557),[8] Bernardino Parthenio's *Della imitatione poetica* (1560),[9] and numerous others. If, by using this method, it is possible to make of poetry a universal science, it is because that aspect of poetry singled out for attention, its "subject matters," is in no way a distinguishing feature of the art. How the method came to have a degree of authority in

---

[7] See ed. Lyon, Gryphius (1527–28), *Alter Tomus Operum Angeli Politiani,* pp. 339–75.

[8] In *Orationes* (1557); see p. 48.

[9] See pp. 3–5.

the Renaissance is easily understood. For the systematic philosopher, every science had its specific subject matter, which separated it from all others; but poetry rather than having a single subject matter included all the materials of all the other sciences; hence it must be a universal science and preferable to all the others. The ambiguities involved here in the use of the term "subject matter," the misconceptions with respect to the definition of sciences by their subject matters, the imperfections of the systems which could permit such a logical impossibility, will be immediately apparent.

GLOSSES AND COMMENTARIES

All the procedures involved in classification and in assimilation of poetry to another art were procedures which came to the Renaissance as a part of the antecedent intellectual tradition. The principal method of treating a text, that of the gloss or the extended commentary, was another such heritage from the recent past; as applied to the chief critical texts of antiquity, it constituted one of the standard ways of approaching problems of criticism during the Cinquecento. The method was fairly constant, although as the century progressed some variants were introduced and some refinements added. One took a small section of the text—a short paragraph if it was in prose, or a small number of verses—and printed after it a section of commentary, long or short. Sometimes a marginal notation summarized the content of the commentary. Then the same was done for the next section of the text, and so on to the end. Sometimes at the end, by way of conclusion, a digest or a summary of the comments was given. If the text was in Greek, usually a Latin translation followed it, and after this the commentary; later in the century, the same procedure was followed for vernacular translations and commentaries. Certain authors chose to provide further enlightenment by inserting a paraphrase between translation and commentary, so that the order would be text–translation–paraphrase–commentary. Thus, as time went on, the whole apparatus became more complicated and the commentary much longer. What is important for the student of criticism, of course, is what was said in the commentaries and how they were conceived. A few examples should suffice to illustrate this method.

Pomponio Gaurico's *Super Arte poetica Horatii* was the earliest of the Cinquecento commentaries on the *Ars poetica*; it was written shortly before 1510. Gaurico himself claims in his dedicatory epistle to Francesco Pucci that it is a new kind of commentary, not written "grammaticorum more" as were the earlier ones. Instead of writing a grammatical gloss on the separate words of the text, Gaurico does a continuous prosification of the epistle, in which he attempts to distinguish and clarify Horace's meaning. At intervals corresponding to sections of the text, he reduces that meaning to concise precepts and these precepts (some forty in all) are collected together in a brief final section of the commentary. There is little in the way of explanation, although occasionally examples from ancient art or literature are added. A commentary of this type does little more than extract the barest meaning from the *Ars poetica* and isolate a given number of critical ideas. It makes no attempt to discover the philosophical structure of the work, the reasons for the order of presentation of ideas, the conception of the poetic art contained within it. The later edition of Gaurico, published in 1541, intercalates the commentary among passages of the text, divided into thirty-seven sections; in this form, both text and commentary are fragmented, and any semblance of synthesis is destroyed. Indeed, such fragmentation may prevent the reader from seeing the work as a whole; and if it is badly done, if the points of separation are badly chosen, a totally false conception of the meaning of the text may result.

A much more highly developed form of the same method is found in Giovanni Battista Pigna's *Poetica Horatiana* of 1561. Once the text has been divided into sections—there are eighty in Pigna's division—and the "precept" stated for each fragment, the commentator proceeds to an elaborate exposition of the ideas of the text. He cites supporting or illustrative passages from innumerable other theorists—Cicero, Quintilian, Aristotle, Plutarch, Donatus, Plato—from miscellaneous philosophical texts on other sciences, finally from many poets who demonstrate Horace's principles. He goes into lengthy discussions of individual words and phrases, citing the authority of previous expositors of the text and seeking clarification from other texts. Sometimes this leads to the most astonishing results: the first four lines of the *Ars poetica* are made to refer, for example, to the four genres distinguished by Aristotle, with the "caput humanum" standing for the epic, the "ceruicem equinam" for tragedy, the "collatas plumas" for the dithyramb and the lyric, and the "atrum piscem" for comedy. Moreover, certain distinctions from other sciences are made to bear upon the text; in an introduction, Pigna insists that the work must be studied in the light of "res" and "verba" (an essentially grammatical distinction) and these in turn in their relationship to "invention, disposition, and elocution" (an essentially rhetorical distinction). Thus, in spite of his contention that all of Horace's precepts are linked in a tight chain, the work becomes more confused as he expounds it, and all sense of an orderly development is lost.[10]

Some of the same characteristics—not to say vices—of procedure are apparent in Pietro Vettori's extensive commentary on the *Poetics*, his *Commentarii in primum librum Aristotelis de arte poetarum* (1560). Here the approach is much more carefully philological; the Greek text is closely studied, useful emendations are suggested, better translations are proposed. But there is still no comprehensive interpretation of the text as a whole. At best, there are certain general notions which determine the interpretation of specific passages: the idea that all poetry must be in verse, the idea that

10 *Poetica Horatiana* (1561); see p. 3.

the treatment of the poem must be such as to assure the persuasion and the pleasure of the audience. Unfortunately, these ideas are such as to lead to a warping rather than to a clarification of Aristotle's meaning, and they are not capable of binding into an organized whole the multiple passages into which the text has been broken.

Even so few examples as these—and many others will be examined in detail in later chapters—are sufficient to illustrate the disruptive effect of the consistent use of the textual gloss. Such a gloss was frequently helpful from the linguistic or philological standpoint, and the Cinquecento contributed considerably to the accuracy and the intelligibility of the critical texts involved. From the philosophical standpoint, it was almost always disadvantageous. It inculcated and promoted the habit of regarding texts as collections of fragments and hence as collections of isolated precepts; contrariwise, it prevented any effort to see over and beyond the single line or paragraph to the total philosophical form of the work. It encouraged a miscellaneous citing of parallel or similar passages from other works and a kind of frantic search for outside "authorities" of no matter how different a general philosophical tendency. As a result, Horace ceased to be Horace and Aristotle never became Aristotle; each grew, instead, into a vast monument containing all the multiform remains of the literary past.

SCHOLASTIC APPROACHES

I have characterized this use of the textual commentary as a method which came to the Cinquecento from the antecedent literary tradition; I might have called it frankly a "scholastic" method. Certain other approaches could also be described, somewhat loosely, as remains of the scholastic tradition. One such approach would be the use of a fairly standard formula for the introduction of any subject. After the prolusio, in which the author indicated the place of his particular subject among the other sciences, he might well indicate how he meant to go about treating it. For many authors, the pattern would be the same. In the prefatory materials to his great commentary on Aristotle (1548), for example, Francesco Robortello says that he means to discuss "what the poetic faculty is, and what effect it has; what end it proposes for itself; what is the subject matter out of which it makes its product."[11] Similarly, the "Prolegomena" to Vincenzo Maggi's *In Aristotelis librum de poetica communes explanationes* (1550) contains a program for Maggi's own treatment of the Aristotelian text. He will discuss, in order, the "subject, its usefulness, the title, in what order the author should be read, the divisions of the text, the method of instruction, and under what faculty the latter falls."[12] In the field of practical

11 *In librum Aristotelis de arte poetica explicationes* (1548), p. 1: "Qualis sit poëtica facultas, & quam habeat uim; Quem finem propositum; Quam materiem subiectam, ex qua opus suum conficiat."

12 *Explanationes* (1550 ed.), p. 13: "scriptionis Propositum, Vtilitas, Inscriptio, Quo ordine auctor legi debeat, Diuisio, Doctrinae uia, Quamque haec sub facultatem cadat."

criticism, Marcantonio Maioragio applies to the analysis of Book IV of the *Aeneid* a set of eight topics which he admittedly borrows from Averroës; the text is Preface VIII of the *Orationes et praefationes*, written around 1550, published in 1582; the topics are, respectively, "the purpose, the utility, the order, the division, the proportion, the method of instruction, the name of the book, the name of the author."[13] Such programs as these made for a semblance of order in the handling of a subject, providing as they did a kind of advance outline for the consecutive discussion of a number of important points relevant to the materials. They came into being, indeed, as a means of assuring the consideration of these points somewhere in the course of the discussion. But as is the case with many rules of thumb, they tended to replace active thinking about poetics by routine answering of a set of questions. The various parts of the outline were considered as isolated topics, without the necessary illumination of any one of the topics by the answers found for the others.

For the same advantages of order and completeness, theorists and critics used another such fixed system for organizing their ideas on the poetic art. It was one which had very ancient and very firm philosophical bases and which had contributed to the later Middle Ages and to the humanistic period a mold for their intellectual procedures: namely, the method of the "four causes." In the Cinquecento, the mold was sometimes used in a much reduced form, sometimes fully developed and realized. An example of the former type might be found in Maggi's *Explanationes* (1550), where he points out first that the end of poetry is, "by imitating human actions through pleasant language, to ennoble the mind," and later that its material is the "human mind, which it proposes to refine with the best principles of conduct";[14] another would be Alessandro Lionardi's *Dialogi della inventione poetica* (1554), where—almost in passing—the author remarks that "every oration and speech consists in the form, which is eloquence, in the matter, which is the thing proposed, and in the end, which is the listener."[15] Here there is obviously only a vague reflection of the method and little comprehension of it. As employed by Filippo Sassetti in his marginalia to Piccolomini's *Annotationi* (1575), the form is still abbreviated; he merely says that "one might say that the efficient cause of poetry was the poet himself, the formal cause the imitation, the material cause the verse, and the final cause pleasure."[16] In spite of its brevity, this statement is revela-

---

13 *Orationes et praefationes* (1582), p. 178: "intentionem, utilitatem, ordinem, diuisionem, proportionem, uiam doctrinae, nomen Libri, nomen authoris."

14 *Explanationes* (1550 ed.), p. 13: "actiones humanas imitando, suaui sermone animum excultum reddere"; and "animus scilicet humanas: quem . . . optimis moribus sibi expoliendum proponit."

15 *Dialogi* (1554), p. 15: "nella forma che è l'eloquenza, nella materia, che è la cosa proposta, et nel fine, che è l'uditore, consiste ogni oratione & parlamento."

16 BNF Postillati 15, p. 65: "si potrebbe dire, che la causa efficiente della Poesia fusse lo stesso Poeta la formale l'imitatione la materiale il uerso, e la finale il diletto."

tory of the whole theory of poetics held by Sassetti; it indicates the usefulness of the method for concentrating the attention on certain central
problems of the art and for eliciting definite pronouncements about those
problems.

All four of the causes are present in Julius Caesar Scaliger's *Poetices libri*
(*septem* 1561), but in a strange way; they are introduced at a point where
Scaliger is making the traditional distinction among the terms poesis,
poema, and poeta. "Poema," he says, "is the work itself, the matter . . .
which is made. But poesis is the reason and the form of the poem"; poeta
is of course the poet. Then he concludes his argument: "Thus you have
three causes, the material, the formal, and the efficient; and in the preceding
commentary the final, that is, imitation, or the ultimate end, instruction."
What is strange is the assigning of the meanings of poema and poesis to
the first two causes (to say nothing of the interpretations given the other
two) and the attempt to combine this analysis with the traditional definitions.[17]

Lionardo Salviati, in his *Commentary on Aristotle's Poetics*, 1585–86,
exploits the method to a much fuller extent, actually basing upon it a good
deal of his preliminary discussion of the *Poetics*. In a section entitled
"Agente, materia, forma, fine, e difinizione del poema," he interprets the
causes thus: "The cause of the poem, that cause I say which is called acting
or efficient, is the soul of the poet operating through habit or disposition
or moved by the divine spirit as the case may be. . . . The matter of the
same poem is indeed the verisimilar expressed through ornamented
speech. . . . The form is the flawless disposition." The final cause, "which
concerns moral character," is treated only much later, when Salviati finally
decides that the special and ultimate final cause of poetry is "to profit and
delight by imitating with verse." Since the major part of the work is,
however, a running commentary on Aristotle, the method is soon abandoned and does not in any sense inform the rest of the treatment.[18]

In various other texts—for example, Niccolò Rossi's *Discorsi intorno
alla tragedia* (1590, p. 21v) and Jacopo Mazzoni's *Della difesa della
Comedia di Dante* (1587; pp. 63 ff.)—all or several of the causes appear
incidentally in the course of the development. Indeed, it is because, essentially, the method is employed as incidental to some other frame of discussion, because it is never fully exploited in its own right as capable of
producing a total and exhaustive analysis, that it fails to contribute as

17 *Poetice* (1581 ed.), p. 13: "Poema est opus ipsum: materia . . . quae fit. Poesis autem,
ratio ac forma Poematis . . ." and "Ita habes causas tres, Materiam, Formam, Efficientem:
& in superiori commentario Finem, id est, Imitationem, siue vlteriorem finem, doctionem . . ."
18 MS BNF II, II, 11, fols. 9–9v: "La cagione del poema, la cagione dico, la quale agente,
o uero efficiente è chiamata, è l'anima del poeta, o habituata, o disposta, o mossa da diuino
spirito, ch'ella si sia. . . . La materia del medesimo poema si è il uerisimile espresso col
fauellar condito. . . . La forma è la disposizione senza fallo"; fol. 13, "il quale è intorno a'
costumi"; fol. 151v: "Giouare e dilettare imitando col uerso."

completely as it might to a clarification of critical ideas. The eclectic tendency, the wish to amalgamate all possible methods of approach within a single treatise, easily led to the nullification of the best characteristics of the best methods. Moreover, knowing of the existence of a method and something about its general nature did not assure that it would be properly applied; the few examples cited here, with the variety of solutions proposed, should suffice to suggest that there was, in this century, no sure grasp on the logical instruments that would have been needed to make of the device of the four causes a valid basis for discussion of the poetic art.

In the field of practical criticism, one of the favorite devices was the full-scale "Sposizione" of a text. Since it wished to be full-scale, it operated most readily on shorter texts such as the sonnet. There are, throughout the Cinquecento, as there had been in the Quattrocento, innumerable lectures, discourses, epistles which take the form of the "Exposition"; mostly, they concern themselves with sonnets of Petrarch. The intention in this form is usually to develop and expound the ideas contained in the poem. After a paraphrase of the sonnet and a restatement of its principal idea, the author usually proceeds to a discussion of the idea itself, its philosophical backgrounds and implications, its validity and usefulness for human conduct. The poem, in a sense, provides the text for a sermon or a philosophical disquisition that soon leaves the poem entirely out of consideration. Rarely do these expositions make any reference to the artistic structure and qualities of the poem or attempt to evaluate it as a work of art. Such documents belong rather to the history of some other branch of philosophy than aesthetics in the Cinquecento, and I have hence omitted them almost entirely from the materials to be considered in the present work.

FOUR CHARACTERISTIC METHODS

All that the Italian sixteenth century did in the way of method was not, however, a piecemeal and imperfect combination of approaches inherited from its recent past. Writers of the century developed, as the years went by, a set of characteristic methods that were their own—which had, to be sure, many ties with the past, which had been practiced before and which have been practiced since, but which nevertheless may be studied as representing the predominant modes of development and presentation of ideas. As the first among these, we may examine the method of imitation of a single ancient text. Theorists who wished to develop a theory of a literary genre which had not been satisfactorily treated in antiquity— comedy, say, or the romance of chivalry—would take as their model some ancient theoretical text. The rules for the new genre would merely be the old rules transposed to fit the special circumstances of subject matter or end or manner of the genre in question. The ancient text most frequently used as the model was, of course, Aristotle's *Poetics*; hence the production of a large number of "Aristotelian" theories of the minor or the recent literary genres—or, in fact, of any genre which Aristotle himself had not completely explored.

We may take, as an example of this methodological phenomenon, Giovanni Battista Pigna's *I romanzi* (1554), which is a lengthy study of the "romance" form as practiced by Italian poets. Pigna himself, at the end of Book I, which is devoted to the general theory of the romance, confesses his indebtedness to Aristotle:

> This is what I have thought proper to say about the romance considering it in general. Although I have never mentioned Aristotle while speaking about it, that does not mean that I have not used the whole of his *Poetics*, making use of every part of its. And just as this same Aristotle gave us light on the subject of the duel, which he had never seen, so here he has been our guide on the subject of romances, even though he had never spoken of them.

The way in which Aristotle is "used" is of the highest interest. The skeleton outline of Book I, called "Argomento del primo libro," shows in brief how the framework of the *Poetics* is transferred in part to the discussion of the new form:

> First words and subject matters are treated generally. And then the epic is taken up, which is considered with respect to the plot; and thence springs the conclusion that imitation and narration are practically opposites; and then the role of truth and of verisimilitude, and how the action may be made illustrious and how it may be made one. Similarly we derive the plot of one and of two kinds, and the simple, complex, passionate, and ethical types of plot. Under the complex type come the six kinds of recognition, and reversal; which last contains the question as to whether good poets should be banned from the republic. Under the ethical type the four requirements for character are expounded. And all of this discussion concerns the qualitative parts. With respect to the quantitative parts there is the matter of composition, and the introduction of beginnings without going back to the first origins of the story; and in giving the reason for this we then discuss why tragedy is greater than epic. And then there is the resolution, which brings with it the treatment of the "deus ex machina" and of the Fates. Next come the episodes both good and bad, which are divided into "epangelia" [those narrated] and "amaprattomena" [those actually acted], under which fall the cantos and the knights errant and the paladins, all of which are explained. . . .

This outline is followed fairly closely in Book I, although many other ideas intervene and there are lengthy digressions; moreover, at many points not referred to in the outline, Aristotle is called upon for distinctions and clarification. Thus the initial distinction between poetry and history (p. 2) is from *Poetics* 1451b5; the definition of plot as imitation (p. 15) from 1450a4; the differentiation of imitations according to object, manner, and means (p. 15) from 1447a15; and so on down the line. All this does not mean, however, that Pigna agrees with Aristotle on all points or even that he accepts the general body of Aristotelian doctrine. It merely means that he borrows from the *Poetics* a relatively complete schematism for the handling of the genre.[19]

Francesco Robortello appended to his commentary on Aristotle's *Poetics* (1548), a short treatise on comedy, in which the method is again the imitation of the procedures of the basic text. The treatise is very short (less than ten folio pages); hence it presents a kind of epitome of all that Aristotle said about tragedy translated into terms of comedy. All of Aristotle's direct statements about comedy are of course included, and to them are added whatever materials Robortello could find in such supplementary sources as Donatus, Vitruvius, and Cicero. A brief outline of the contents will show how the method works. Robortello begins with a statement of the end of poetry. He then differentiates imitations according to means, object, and manner, indicating in each case which are used by comedy. There follows (as in Aristotle) a brief history of the origins of the genre; then the causes for its invention—man's instinct to imitate, and so forth; then the growth and development of the form, and the time of its invention as compared with that of tragedy. For a long section on the types of comedy, he draws heavily on Donatus; but his imitation of Aristotle on tragedy is apparent. In the discussion of the qualitative parts, he paraphrases or transposes Aristotle, making almost identical statements about plot, the kinds of recognition, knot, and solution; about the four requirements for character (with some parallels taken from Horace); about sententiae and diction. For what he has to say about apparatus or spectacle, however, he rests upon Vitruvius, and for the quantitative parts he refers directly to Donatus. The final statements about the limitation to five acts and the number of interlocutors are ascribed to Horace and Donatus. In spite of these supplementary borrowings, however, the core of the work still follows the outline of the *Poetics*.[20]

A clear statement of the intention to imitate a single text is found in the prefatory section of Antonio Riccoboni's *De re comica*, which is itself an

19 *I romanzi* (1554), p. 65: "Questo è quello che intorno al Romancio m'è paruto di dire, generalmente considerandolo. del quale mentre ho fauellato, quantunque d'Aristotile mai mentione fatto non habbia; non è stato però che di tutta la sua Poetica seruito non mi sia, tutta maneggiandola. Et come in tutto il Duello non mai da lui veduto, lume ne diede esso Aristotile; cosi quiui ne Romanzi è stato la nostra guida: benche egli mai non ne parlasse"; p. a2: "Prima delle parole, & delle materie generalmente si tratta. Et pigliasi l'Epopeia: la quale è considerata in quanto alla fauola. & cosi ne nasce, come l'imitare & il narrare sieno quasi contrarij: & la parte del uero & del uerisimile. & come l'attione sia illustre: & come una. ne nasce parimente la fauola d'un genere & di due: & il genere semplice, il composto, il perturbato & il costumato. sotto il composto sono sei agnitioni, & la peripetia: che contiene la quistione, che è, se i poeti da una buona republica si scaccino. sotto il costumato i quattro decori si espongono. & tutto cio intorno alla qualità. Nella quantità euui il comporre: & l'introducimento de principij senza la prima origine. & nel render la cagione di cio, segue perche da piu sia la Tragedia che la Epopeia: & ui è lo sciorre: che con seco porta il trattare della machina, & delle Fate. Vengono gli Episodij & i uitiosi & i buoni, che diuisi sono in epangelia & in amaprattomena. sotto i quali cadono i canti & i cauaglieri erranti & i paladini: che tutti si dichiarano. . . ."

20 Part II of the *In librum Aristotelis de arte poetica explicationes* (1548), pp. 41–50.

appendix to his translation of the *Poetics* (1579). The full title is "De re comica ex Aristotelis doctrina," and the purpose is summarized thus:

... with respect to comedy, on the one hand to collect together everything that is found in that most authoritative philosopher, on the other hand also, in imitation of those things which have been written down about tragedy and the epic, to devise some precepts which will in no way disagree with the Aristotelian theory, and by means of which comedy may be created in a laudable fashion. We shall do this in such a way as to investigate first the origin of comedy; then what comedy is; in the third place what qualitative parts it has; in the fourth place, what quantitative parts; finally, what kinds of ridiculous things they are that serve the purposes of comedy.

The program here outlined is virtually a complete listing of the later chapter headings, except for such additions as the chapters for the various "parts."[21]

Such imitative treatises, long or short, constituted a large part of the theoretical effort of the century. They will be examined, along with the theories they produced, in later chapters.

The second of the characteristic methods of the Cinquecento was the systematic comparison or combination of two different texts of classical antiquity. The method was most constantly applied to Horace's *Ars poetica*, which presented to the commentators grave problems of understanding and interpretation; therefore, they sought clarification in a point-by-point paralleling of the text with Aristotle's *Poetics*. The initial assumption was that the two works said essentially the same things about the poetic art and that if one sought carefully one could find identical statements in both. Moreover, since the order of the *Poetics* was clearer, it was even thought that the same order was followed by Horace. If, then, order and ideas were generally the same, Horace could be easily understood as a kind of Latinization of the Greek *Poetics*. Such indeed is the point of view of Vincenzo Maggi in his *In Q. Horatii Flacci de arte poetica librum ad Pisones, Interpretatio*, appended to his 1550 commentary on the *Poetics*. His statement could not be more specific:

Since indeed those two parts of this little book which we have declared the fundamental ones were written almost entirely in imitation of Aristotle's *Poetics*, I believed that it would be useful if, after having explained all matters pertinent to the *Poetics* of Aristotle, . . . I were able to demonstrate that those things which

21 In *Aristotelis ars poetica* (1579 ed.), pp. 433–34: "tum de Comoedia ea colligere omnia, quaecunque apud grauissimum philosophum reperiuntur: tum uero ad imitationem eorum, quę de Tragoedia, & de Epopoeia tradita sunt, praecepta quaedam conformare, ab Aristotelica doctrina non abhorrentia, quibus confici Comoedia laudabiliter possit. Quod ita faciemus, vt primum originem Comędiae inuestigemus: deinde quid sit Comoedia: tertio loco quas partes habeat qualitatis: quarto quas quantitatis: postremo cuiusmodi sint ridicula illa, quae rei comicae seruiunt." The 1587 ed., p. 140, substitutes the following sentence: "ut naturam eius inuestigemus ex genere, & differentijs Poesis: ex ipsius origine: ex similitudine, & dissimilitudine, quam habet cum alijs Poesibus, & imitationibus: ex definitione: ex partibus qualitatis: ex partibus quantitatis: ex pulcherrima constitutione."

are found in Horace are already found in Aristotle, as in a spring from which he made this book flow like a small river.

In the treatise that follows, Maggi's only interest is to demonstrate the conformity between the two texts. The first thirteen lines of Horace, for example, are equivalent to what Aristotle has to say about plot; no less than five passages in Aristotle—referred to by the numbers earlier assigned by Maggi in his commentary on the *Poetics*—are adduced as parallels. Lines 14–23 refer to episodes; compare passages from Aristotle on episodes. The same procedure continues for the whole of the Horatian text. Wherever Maggi is unsuccessful in finding a comparable text in Aristotle, he declares that the passage in the *Ars poetica* is a digression; for example, most of the final section on the poet, lines 412 ff. to the end, is so labeled. Besides the indication of the parallels, there is little of interest for the theory of poetry in the Maggi text.[22]

Sometimes the search for parallels is less dogged and unimaginative. At the very end of the century, for example, in 1599, Antonio Riccoboni published his *De Poetica Aristoteles cum Horatio collatus*. In the course of the work he cited all the *Ars poetica*, broken up into small sections and rearranged according to the needs of his outline. That outline itself was very simple, containing the following general headings: On the nature of poetry; On the causes of poetry; On the kinds of imitations and poems; On the qualitative parts; On the quantitative parts; On faults and their excuse. Under each of these headings he placed a prose passage meant to summarize the doctrine of Aristotle relevant to that heading; then followed the passages from Horace which he thought pertinent. Riccoboni's approach differs from Maggi's insofar as he seeks correspondence only between the doctrine of Aristotle and the passages from Horace, not between passage and passage.

A variant on this technique, which really constitutes a third method characteristic of the century, is the conflation of one text with several others. Rather than limiting himself to a Horace-Aristotle comparison, the theorist introduces a triple or a quadruple analogy, thereby enriching his commentary and making his interpretation more complex. This is the procedure of Giacopo Grifoli in the *In Artem poeticam Horatii interpretatio* (1550). An initial statement in the introduction makes the point that, whereas Horace treats the same materials as Aristotle, he does so in a different order:

Seeing then that in Aristotle's opinion tragedy is composed of plot, character, thought, diction, spectacle, and melody, he decided to discuss the constitution of

---

22 *Interpretatio* (1550), esp. p. 328: "Quoniam uero partes illae duae libelli huius, quas praecipuas esse diximus, totae ferè ad Poetices Aristotelis imitationem conscriptae sunt: non inutile futurum existimaui, si postquam ea, quae ad Aristotelis Poeticam attinebant, explicauimus; cuius ratione omnis mihi fuerat susceptus labor; quae hic ab Horatio habentur, in Aristotele, uelut in fonte demonstrarem, à quo uelut riuulum, librum hunc deduxit."

the plot first since it contains the basis for the imitation of the whole object; then, since character and thought are expressed through words, he began to elaborate on style immediately after plot. In this he did not follow either the order or the plan of Aristotle; for the latter treated character after plot, then thought, then diction, and he handled all of these in detail. But Horace, seeing that, although it is said that a play is "acted", there is no place in thought or character (that is, περὶ διανοίας, ἢ περὶ μύθου) which is not treated by means of speech, believed that by discussing speech, even changing the order of Aristotle and omitting all those points over which there is no controversy, he could most conveniently progress in both to those places to which he might wish to come. And so in the second place he spoke of diction. . . .[23]

This analysis of Horace's attitude toward the text of Aristotle prepares the way for the second of the fundamental analogies in Grifoli's text. This is an implicit one. The order suggested in the passage above—plot, then diction —brings to mind the traditional divisions of Ciceronian or pseudo-Ciceronian rhetoric, i.e., invention, disposition, and elocution. It is not long before Grifoli specifically sees these divisions as supplying the ordering principle of at least certain parts of Horace's text. Thus the passage in the commentary on verses 32–45:

And at the same time he touches upon the three points which belong to the orator's faculty, invention, elocution, and disposition. And because he had used a turned-about order, placing elocution before disposition (a thing which he did for a reason, since he here is treating of language proper to the matter and this is the right place for language), and then speaking lightly and in passing about disposition, nevertheless returning to his order, after having said a little about disposition he now comes back to elocution . . . .[24]

To the first assumption that Horace is following Aristotle's division into six qualitative parts is added, then, a second assumption that he is following the commonplace three-way rhetorical distinction. Grifoli's commentary will, therefore, shift back and forth between these two analyses, although the comparison with Aristotle remains the dominant one.

The situation is in a sense reversed in the commentary of Giason

[23] *Interpretatio* (1550), esp. pp. 11–12: "Videns igitur Aristotelis iudicio Tragoediam constare fabula, moribus, sententia, dictione, apparatu, & melodia; primum de constitutione fabulae disserendum esse statuit, nam rei totius imitandae rationem ea continet: deinde, cum mores, & sententiae verbis explicentur, orationem statim post fabulam coepit expolire; in quo non est secutus nec ordinem, nec rationem Aristotelis, nam hic post fabulam mores, tum sententiam, post dictionem explicauit, atque de his omnibus omnia diligenter executus est. Videns autem Horatius, quamuis agi fabula dicatur, tamen nullum esse locum aut de sententia, aut de more idest περὶ διανοίας, ἢ περὶ μύθου qui non tractetur oratione, existimauit de ea disserendo, etiam mutata Aristotelis dispositione, ac omissis ijs omnibus de quibus nulla est controuersia, se posse quàm commodissimè ad quos vellet vtriusque locos peruenire. Itaque secundo loco de oratione dixit. . . ."

[24] *Ibid.*, pp. 24–25: "Atque simul tres partes attigit quae sunt in oratoris vi sitae. Inuentionem, elocutionem & dispositionem. Et quia praepostero vsus erat ordine, praeponens elocutionem dispositioni, quod tamen cum causa fecit, cum de oratione hic apta rei tractet, & proprius orationis sit hic locus. Et de dispositione casu, & obiter loquatur, tamen in ordinem hęc suum redigens, vbi pauca de Dispositione dixit, ad Elocutionem redijt. . . ."

Denores, *In epistolam Q. Horatij Flacci de arte poetica* (1553). Here the major point of reference is the invention—disposition—elocution schema, as Denores indicates at the beginning: ". . . in this same epistle to the Pisos are collected together by Horace, who chose them from various works by many authors, the points which seemed to him to be essential for the judging of the writings of poets or for the formation of our taste with respect to every rule of invention, disposition, and elocution in every type of poetry."[25] Denores follows this schematism faithfully throughout. The first lines of the *Ars poetica*, he says, concern invention; lines 24–31 make distinctions relative to elocution; lines 32–41 are on disposition, as are lines 42–45; lines 46–72 treat certain problems of elocution; and so forth. However, from the very beginning the parallels with Aristotle are presented either implicitly or explicitly. So Denores' first remark about invention is that it is the "anima" of poetry: the term comes directly from Aristotle's characterization of plot. Figurative language (*in re* lines 46–72) is pleasurable because of the imitation involved, and imitation itself is enjoyable because it is a source of knowledge; compare Aristotle. In a similar way, Denores constantly brings in from the *Poetics* statements or comparisons which illuminate his essentially rhetorical interpretation.

Such a method is among the most dangerous of those used by theorists of the Cinquecento: dangerous in the sense that it must inevitably result in hopeless deformation of the texts involved. The mere fact that it should have been practiced so widely is symptomatic of the philosophical naïveté of its users. They discovered certain obvious parallels or similarities between texts; this led them to seek other less obvious agreements, to the point where the texts became totally equivalent. What they did not realize was that two texts having occasional similarities may, in their essence, present completely different theories of the poetic art. Aristotle and Horace do touch upon a certain number of common topics; but the one is essentially concerned with the internal structures of poems as these become beautiful objects of contemplation, the other with the making of poems which will have a specific effect upon a given audience at a particular time. To generalize from the accidental similarities to an identity of doctrine in the *Poetics* and the *Ars poetica* is to indicate complete failure to understand either text. To read Horace as if he were Aristotle or Aristotle as if he were Horace is to eliminate all possibility of ever arriving at a proper interpretation of either. This error on the part of the Cinquecento was of course correlative to other errors already noted, especially the tendency to reduce texts to series of isolated fragments, thereby destroying their basic philosophical integrity.

---

[25] *In epistolam* (1553), p. 5*v*: "in hac ipsa ad Pisones uel de poetarum scriptis diiudicandis, uel communiter de nostris ingenijs ad omnem inuentionis, dispositionisque, ac elocutionis rationem in quocunque poematum genere formandis, quae praecipua uidebantur, ex uarijs multorum libris excerpta diligentissime ab Horatio colliguntur."

A fourth characteristic approach of critics in this century was the constant attempt to reconcile divergent positions. When "authorities" were recognized as equally valid, differences of opinion between them must be explained away and ultimate agreement must be discovered. Perhaps the central figure in such discussions was Plato, whose attacks upon poetry in the *Republic* needed to be reconciled on the one hand with his own defences of it in other dialogues and on the other hand with the numerous "apologies" by other "authorities" and with such a position as Aristotle's. The passages in the *Republic* on the banishment of the poets were at the center of attention and controversy all through the humanistic period and the Cinquecento. One of the favorite arguments in the attempt to reconcile Plato with himself was to insist that he banished, after all, only those poets whose writings contained undesirable moral teachings. That is the point of view of such a writer as Lodovico Ricchieri (Caelius Rhodiginus) in his *Lectionum antiquarum libri XXX* (1516):

> But with respect to these [fables for the young] we must note carefully that the poets are not condemned outright by Plato; since to the degree in which he holds that they should be rejected when they disturb the state and invent shameful things, to that same degree he embraces them and kisses them tenderly when they exhort to moral improvement, celebrating elegantly and eloquently in their praises of heroes or their hymns to the gods.[26]

After this statement, Ricchieri goes on to cite others of the *Dialogues* in which Plato praises poets and poetry. Giacopo Grifoli's opinion, in the *Oratio de laudibus poetarum* (1557), is similar: despite all that might be said in favor of poets, Plato banished them because of their wicked doctrines:

> In truth we must believe that that famous philosopher condemned the teachings of poets, even though he himself had called them the fathers of all wisdom; or that he banished them because they were harmful, even though he himself had declared that they were the go-betweens of the gods; and although he held that their poems are not human inventions but gifts of the gods, he ordered that they should be driven from the territory of his state because they were wicked.[27]

This type of analysis of the various Platonic texts does one of two things: it concludes that good poets remain acceptable in the state while bad ones are excluded, or it decides that only poems with undesirable moral tendencies are the objects of Plato's attack. What it does not do is discover that different conclusions about poetry are reached in different texts because of the fact that the problems posed and the contexts established are themselves

---

[26] *Lectionum* (1516), p. 158: "Sed in iis illud impense animaduertendum, non damnari prorsum à Platone Poetas, Siquidem quantum, ubi perturbant, aut turpia fingunt, reiiciendos putat, tantundem amplexatur, exosculaturǫue, si ad bonam frugem hortentur, laudibus heroum aut Deorum hymnis eleganter, facundeǫue concelebratis."

[27] In *Orationes* (1557), p. 59: "est vero credendum illum philosophum doctrinam damnasse poetarum, qui eosdem ipse sapientiae patres appellarit, aut tanquam perniciosos exclusisse, quos idem interpretes deorum testetur esse, & quorum poemata non hominum inuenta, sed munera coelestia esse ducat, hos tanquàm impios arcendos à finibus ciuitatis suae statuisse."

different. Plato is seeking answers to widely divergent questions in the *Symposium* and the *Republic* and the *Laws*; hence, what he has to say about poetry will in each case be influenced by the special context in which he is considering it. That this was not realized, or was realized rarely, by the critics of the Renaissance is again explained by their general method: fragmentation and the concentration on the isolated passage did not lead to an awareness of the total philosophical meaning of texts and of the relationship of any individual passage to that meaning. At times, of course, this kind of awareness was present. We may take as an example Marcantonio Maioragio's statement in the "Oratio XXIV: De arte poetica" of the *Orationes et praefationes* (*ca.* 1550):

> The fact that Plato led the poets out of his state is no argument against them, especially since in many other places Plato himself praises them to the skies with almost divine commendations and admires them to a most extraordinary degree. Indeed, just as in that state, where nobody is sick at all but all are healthy and sound of body, there is no need for doctors, so Plato, since he was inventing a state most blessed and most wise in all things, removed the poets from it, because for that state, which had already achieved the highest end, there seemed to be no further need for any teachers of living, for any instructions, for any precepts of conduct, for in itself it was ready for good and blessed living.[28]

Here Maioragio realizes that, within the assumption of the *Republic* that all things are considered with reference to the achievement of justice within the state, poetry is unnecessary or undesirable as a means to that justice. But such a realization, along with the making of distinctions that it involves, is relatively rare in the Cinquecento.

It was this wish to explain away Plato's banishment of the poets which led, to a large degree, to the most common construction put upon the "purgation" clause in Aristotle's *Poetics.* Here we are confronted not so much with an attempt to reconcile two contradictory texts as with the interpretation of one text in the light of the other, on the grounds that both are talking about the same thing. Plato had banished the poets because of their undesirable moral effects; Aristotle, who wished in all things to contradict Plato, said that their moral effect was desirable; it consisted precisely in the "purgation" of pity and fear. So runs the argument. One variation of it is found in Lodovico Castelvetro's *Chiose intorno al libro del comune di Platone* (*ca.* 1570); Castelvetro argues that whereas Plato assumes that the examples found in poems must be followed by their readers, Aristotle answers that they may be either followed or rejected:

28 *Orationes et praefationes* (1582), p. 147v: "quod autem è ciuitate sua Plato poetas eduxerit, id quidem nullum est contra illos argumentum. cum praesertim alijs in locis plurimis idem Plato propè diuinis in cęlum laudibus eosdem efferat, & mirandum in modum admiretur. Verum quemadmodum in ea ciuitate, ubi nullus omnino sit aegrotus, sed omnes bene ualentes, & corpore bene constituto, nihil medicis opus est, ita Plato cum omnium beatissimam & sapientissimam fingeret ciuitatem, ex ea poetas eduxit, quoniam ei ciuitati, quae iam optimum finem esset consecuta, nullis uitae magistris, nullis institutionibus, nullis morum praeceptis amplius opus esse uidebatur, cum per se contenta esset ad benè beatéque uiuendum."

In this passage [*Rep.* III, 395] Plato supposes that poetry was invented for no other reason than to teach by means of examples and that whatever is found in poetry, be it good or bad, can and must of necessity be followed by others. This is false; for what is contained in poetry is proposed, before we wish that it should teach, as a matter for careful consideration, and so that we may have examples of all kinds—to frighten the wicked, and to console the good, and to learn about the nature of men and women. And therefore Aristotle said that tragedy, through fears and injustices, drove out fears and injustices from the heart of the men who listened to it, contradicting what Plato says in this passage.[29]

Another variation is presented by Girolamo Frachetta's *Dialogo del furore poetico* (1581). Frachetta's general thesis is that Aristotle assigns to poetry only the single end of pleasure, never that of instruction. Why then should he include purgation, with its pedagogical intent, in the definition of tragedy?

He does this because he was always eager to contradict Plato, so much so that we might almost say that at times he went about begging and borrowing the occasions to do so. Wherefore seeing that he [Plato] forbids in his Republic the horrible and pitiable subjects of the poets, which in his opinion make us fearful and full of pity, and consequently of low and poor heart; and wishing to correct him on this matter, he [Aristotle] said in defining tragedy that by means of pity and of fear it frees our minds of such passions.[30]

Lorenzo Giacomini's opinion on the matter is stated in his academic discourse *Sopra la purgazione della tragedia*, delivered to the Accademia degli Alterati in 1586; his general position is, again, that Aristotle develops his theory of purgation as an answer to Plato's banishment of poets and poetry. He ascribes it to tragedy specifically because of the nature of the audience, the circumstances of performance, and the special kind of utility which the genre is meant to have.[31]

In all these variations of the same argument, what is never questioned is the assumption that catharsis, in the *Poetics*, is a pedagogical device or an instrument to moral improvement. That assumption itself is in part the

---

[29] In *Opere varie critiche* (1727), pp. 215–16: "561. *Nihil aliud agere, vel imitari oportet.* In questo luogo presuppone Platone, che la Poesia non sia trovata per altro, se non per insegnare per Esempio, e ciò, che si truova in Poesia, o bene o male che sia, altri lo possa, o debba seguire. Il che è falso; perciocchè è proposta, prima che vogliamo che insegna, per materia da farvi pensamenti sopra, & acciocchè abbiamo esempj d'ogni maniera e da spaventare i rei, e da consolare i buoni, e da conoscere la natura de gli uomini, e delle donne. E perciò diceva Aristotele, che la Tragedia con le paure, e con le ingiustizie scacciava le paure, e le ingiustizie dal cuore de gli uomini ascoltanti, riprovando quello, che dice Platone in questo luogo."

[30] *Dialogo* (1581), p. 92: "ciò fà perche egli fu sempre uago di contradire a Platone, intantoche si può dir per poco, ch'egli sia andato alle uolte limosinando, & accattando le occasioni. La onde ueggendo ch'egli diuieta nella sua Republica le cose de poeti horribili, & compassioneuoli, perciò, che a suo parere ci fanno paurosi, & pieni di misericordia, & conseguentemente di stremo, & pouero cuore. & uolendol di cio ripigliare; disse in definendo la tragedia, che ella per la compassione, & per lo spauento ci libera l'animo da cotai passioni."

[31] In *Orationi e discorsi* (1597), pp. 29–52.

result of reading Platonic intentions into Aristotle. For Plato, in the *Republic*, the "effect" of poetry is a pedagogical or a moral one; therefore, in Aristotle, the "effect" of tragedy must also be pedagogical or moral. The two texts are more than reconciled; the second is read as if its premises, its procedures, and its conclusions were the same as those of the first.

These, then, would seem to be the four characteristic methods or approaches of Cinquecento critics: (1) the imitation of a single text for the development of new theories; (2) the conflation of one text with another; (3) the conflation of several texts; (4) the reconciliation of divergent positions. If we would explain certain of the difficulties of Renaissance criticism, two auxiliary problems must be considered: the problem of terminology and the meanings of words and the problem of the procedure of argumentation.

TERMINOLOGY AND MEANINGS

The matter of terminology and meanings is in a sense related to the subject just discussed, the attempt to reconcile differing texts. For if one tried to reconcile the major ideas one also had to try to reconcile the terms of the discussions; the latter attempt was a concomitant of the former. Perhaps the best example of the multitude of meanings—and hence the confusion of meaning—associated with a single term is the case of "imitation." One sense of the word not subject to confusion was the "Ciceronian" meaning of the imitation of earlier poets—the use of a model for matters of language, expression, style. This meaning, as it is found in Giovambattista Giraldi Cintio's *Super imitatione epistola ad Coelium Calcagninum* (dated 1532), or in Celio Calcagnini's *Super imitatione commentatio* (1532), or in Bernardino Parthenio's *Della imitatione poetica* (1560), is clear and remains distinct from the others. Indeed, Parthenio states the difference between two major kinds of imitation:

... it seems to me reasonable and necessary to recall that there are two kinds of poetic imitation. One, which consists in expressing in an excellent fashion the nature and characters of those persons whom we undertake to imitate. And this is the end of poetry. ... But leaving this type of imitation to Aristotle, we shall treat only the other one, which consists in words and in figures of speech.[32]

It is the second of these, which might be called "rhetorical" imitation— the type that the "Ciceronians" were talking about and that interested such a theorist as Du Bellay in the *Deffence et illustration de la langue française*— that was free of confusion and ambiguity. The difficulty arises when we wish

---

[32] *Della imitatione poetica* (1560), pp. 92–94: "mi pare ragioneuole, et douuto ricordar, due esser le sorti della Imitatione poetica. Vna, laquale consiste nell'esprimere eccellentemente le nature et i costumi di quelle persone, che ci proponiamo d'imitare. Et questo è il fine della poesia. ... Ma di queste sorti di imitationi lasciando la cura ad Aristotele, solamente tratteremo dell'altra, laquale consiste nelle parole, et ne modi di dire."

to consider the meaning of "poetic" imitation. And the difficulty springs from two causes: first, the variety of meanings assigned to the term in the various dialogues of Plato; and, second, the superimposition of several or all of these meanings upon the term as it is used in the *Poetics*.

Perhaps the single passage in Plato which led to the greatest uncertainty was the discussion in Book III of the *Republic* (Steph. 392–93) where Socrates distinguishes three "styles" of poetry: the narrative, in which the poet speaks in his own person; the imitative, in which the poet takes the person of another, whom he thus "imitates"; and the mixed, in which the two other styles are combined. Now critics of the Renaissance saw in this passage an exact parallel to *Poetics* 1448a19, on the manners of imitation. They thus saw also an equivalence between Plato's διά μιμήσεως (for the second style) and Aristotle's πράττοντας καὶ ἐνεργοῦντας (for the second or "dramatic" manner). The next step in reasoning was the basis of the later confusion: if Aristotle here uses "dramatic" as equivalent to Plato's "imitative," then when he himself uses "imitative" or "imitation" he means "dramatic." This assumption led to interminable discussion of the meaning of "imitation" in Aristotle and of related problems: Is the lyric an imitation, and does it come within the categories of poetry considered by Aristotle? Or are tragedy and comedy the only true imitations? To what extent is the epic an imitation? If a narrative poem is not an imitation, does it need to have unity? And so on, into manifold ramifications.

Echoes of these doubts and uncertainties and misunderstandings are to be found in such texts as Pigna's *I romanzi* (1554). The following passage may be taken as an example:

... there are three ways of imitating: the first is the imitation of one single thing through different kinds of imitation, as would be the case if a horse were represented by art, by means of lines and colors by the painter, by descriptions in words by the poet. The second is the imitation of things which differ from one another, through one kind of imitation, as if I were to represent beautiful things in verse alone and ugly things in verse alone. The last is the imitation of one single thing through one kind of imitation, but in a different manner, as is the case with the epic and the tragic poet, who treat of heroes in poetry; but the latter introduces persons in action on the stage, the former narrates how they accomplish their actions. And this epic procedure is also appropriate to our own [writers of romance], since these relate how matters stand, and when the opportunity presents itself to them, they quote the conversations that have taken place between one person and another, which, the more frequently it is done, the more the poet imitates, since introducing the actors themselves so that they may speak together is a way of making the action come more directly before our eyes. And therefore tragic and comic plots are called dramatic, because of the events which are seen and not merely heard. And it is said that these compositions come closest to being true imitations, in the same way as paintings are truly praised when they really come close to life itself. Therefore since the word "poet" means nothing else but "imitator," the more we introduce people in conversation the more will we be worthy of that name. Nevertheless it would seem to be better to avoid this kind of imitation and to use narration more continuously.[33]

I quote the text at such length because it is important to see how the shift in terminology takes place. Pigna begins with a distinction of the three kinds of imitation (which he calls "modi"), paraphrasing *Poetics* 1447a16. The third distinction, that of manner, leads him to use "imitation" as equivalent to "dramatic" and as opposed to "narrative." Follow all the consequences of the use of the term in this Platonic sense.

Another document which involves such a progression of meanings, not only of "imitation" but also of "fable," is a fragment in MS Laurenziana Ashb. 531. The fragment is anonymous, but I attribute it to Lorenzo Giacomini, whose translation of the *Poetics* it follows in the manuscript. Giacomini is attempting to arrive at a definition of poetry; once more, the passage is such as to merit lengthy quotation:

In the Third book of the *Republic*, Plato says that to imitate is to make one thing resemble another, and that poetic imitation exists when the poet speaks in the person of another. In the Tenth, differentiating imitation as a whole, he says that it is a fabrication, that is a making of idols, that is of images, and that the imitator is a fabricator and maker of idols, that is of images ... whence he is led to say also that poetic imitation is a fabrication of idols. But surely it is not necessary to fabricate idols only by speaking in the person of another, but this can be done in another way. But since the proper instrument of the poet with which he imitates is speech, it follows that poetic imitation is a fabrication of idols with speech. But that form of speech which fabricates idols and images of things is none other than fable and mythology. Aristotle, therefore, when he says that all poetry is imitation means not that first imitation of the Third book of Plato, but this second one of the Tenth, that is, mythology and fable. And this is clear, furthermore, because Aristotle himself applies to imitation the same division with which Plato in the Third book divides mythology; for Plato assigns three kinds to mythology, and Aristotle three kinds to imitation, and the same ones. But when Aristotle says that poetry is an imitation, meaning by imitation mythology, he agrees with Plato, who in the Third book conjoins poetry with mythology and

[33] *I romanzi* (1554), pp. 15–16: "tre sono i modi dell'imitare. L'uno in vna istessa cosa di genere diuersa; come nell'esprimere con l'arte vn cauallo: il quale mostrato sarà dal dipintore con lineamenti & con colori, & dal poeta con descrittion di parole. l'altro in cose tra se diuerse d'un genere istesso: come s'io in versi solo le belle cose rappresentar voglia: & in versi solo le sozze. L'ultimo in vna cosa medesima d'un medesimo genere, ma di diuerso modo: come l'Epico & il Tragico, che poeticamente de gli heroi trattano. ma questi in su la scena le persone induce à negociare: & quegli narra come i fatti loro trattino. Et tale tutta uia con i nostri si confà: conciosia cosa ch'essi dicono come le cose stiano: & quando l'opportunità loro s'offre, riferiscono i parlamenti corsi tra l'una parte & l'altra. il che quanto piu si frequenta di fare, tanto maggiormente s'imita: essendo che l'introducere i proprij negociatori insieme à fauellare, è far che piu la cosa dinanzi à gli occhi ci venga. & perciò Dramatiche si chiamano le Tragiche & le Comiche fauole da gli affari che non vditi, ma veduti sono. Et dicesi che cotesti componimenti piu alla imitatione s'accostano: nel modo che le dipinture, le quali veramente lodate sono, quando al viuo veramente s'appressano. Adunque perche la voce di poeta altro non suona che imitatore, di tal nome degni tanto piu saremo, quanto piu i parlamenti induceremo. Con tutto ciò pare che meglio sia fuggir questa sorte d'imitatione, & essere nel narrar piu continouo."

the poet with the mythologist, that is, the teller of fables. If then poetry is an imitation, and the poet an imitator, and to imitate is to feign and compose fables, it follows that the poet can imitate even if he speaks in his own person. . . . There being then two kinds of imitation, these two authors mean now the one, now the other; but in the definition of poetry Aristotle means that broader one, that is, mythology, that is, fable-telling speech.

Besides, it seems that fable has two meanings according to the aforementioned two authors, because Plato in the Second book of the *Republic* says that fable generally is a lie; later he takes it for discourse which is lying and tells fables. But Aristotle in the poetic art, taking the "fable" as a part of tragedy or of the epic, means by fable the actions themselves, feigned and false; whence fable has a double meaning, that is, false discourse and false action. When therefore we say that poetry is mythology, we mean the first kind of fable, that is, lying dicourse. . . . Poetry is thus a feigned and mendacious form of speech, which by means of narrated discourses not true in themselves, and with a certain lying and falseness, imitates true actions and real things.[34]

This is not an extreme case of the errors produced by careless or unintelligent handling of terms; such procedures are common in much of the critical writing of the Cinquecento.

PROCEDURES OF ARGUMENTATION

To this matter of terminology is also related the even more important question of argumentation. For if the theorist's use of terms is shifting and

[34] MS Laur. Ashb. 531, fols. 39–39v: "Nel terzo libro de la Rep^a Platone dice lo imitare essere assimigliare una cosa ad unaltra, et la imitazion poetica essere quando il poeta parla in persona d'altri. Nel X ponendo la differenza di tutta l'imitazione dice lei essere fabricamento, cio è facimento di idoli cio è di imagini et lo imitatore essere fabricatore et facitore di idoli cio è di imagini . . . onde viene a dire ancora che l'imitazione poetica sia fabricamento di idoli. ma certo è che non è necessario fabricare idoli parlando in persona d'altri, ma che questo si puo fare ancora in altro modo. ma essendo il proprio instrumento del poeta col quale egli imita l'orazione seguita la poetica imitazione essere fabricamento di idoli con orazione. ma l'orazione la quale fabrica gli idoli et le imagini di le cose altro non è che la favola et la mythologia. Aristotile adunque quando dice ogni poesia essere imitazione intende non quella prima del terzo libro di Platone, ma questa seconda del X, ciò è mythologia et favola. et questo è manifesto ancora, perche esso Aristotile divide l'imitazione con la divisione medesima con la quale Platone nel 3 divide la mythologia, perche tre modi à la mytologia assegna Platone, et tre Aristotile al imitazione, et i medesimi. Ma dicendo Aristotele la poesia essere imitazione, et per imitazione intendendo mytheologia convien con Platone, il quale nel terzo con la poesia congiunge la mithologia, et col poeta il mythologo, cio è il favoleggiatore. Se adunque la poesia è imitazione, et il poeta imitatore, et l'imitare è fingere et comporre favole seguita che il poeta puo imitare parlando ancora in propria persona. . . . essendo adunque due l'imitazioni, ora questa, et ora quella intendono questi due autori, ma ne la diffinitione de la poesia Aristotile intende quella piu larga, cio è la mythologia, cio è l'orazione fauolosa.

"Ancora pare che la fauola sia doppia secondo i due autori predetti, perche Platone nel secondo de la Republica dice la favola generalmente essere mendacio dipoi la piglia per orazione mendace et favolosa. Ma Aristotile nel arte poetica pigliando la favola per una parte de la tragedia et del epopeia intende la favola essere l'azzioni stesse finte et false, per la qual cosa la favola è doppia, cio è l'orazion falsa, et l'azzione falsa. quando adunque diciamo la poesia essere mythologia intendiamo il primo genere de la favola, cio è l'orazion mendace. . . . E adunque la poesia orazione finta et mendace, la quale con l'orazioni non vere da se narrate, et con qualunque mendacio et falsità imita le vere azzioni et le cose veraci."

uncertain, he can with difficulty pursue an orderly argument or achieve a convincing demonstration. Among critics of the Cinquecento the two deficiencies, of terminology and of argumentation, were sometimes concomitant, sometimes separate. That weakness in logical method should appear is not surprising, given the wilful rejection of the Aristotelian logic of the schools, the failure to discover the essence of Plato's method of dialectic, and the unawareness of the art of considering and analyzing texts as complete and consistent philosophical documents.

The best way to illustrate these deficiencies or peculiarities of argumentation is, of course, to analyze some work or works in entirety. Since I shall be doing that frequently and repeatedly in the later chapters, perhaps it will be sufficient at this point—in order to avoid repetition—to study a section of a work which presents a typical example. Let us take the sections of Francesco Patrizi's *Della poetica: La deca disputata* (1586) in which he attacks Aristotle's proposition that poetry is an imitation. Patrizi is a reputable philosopher; much of his philosophy was based upon a wish to controvert the theories of Aristotle; his method in controverting them must have been the best he could find and the object of careful attention and consideration. This particular attack begins with Book III. Starting with the objection that Aristotle had nowhere defined the term imitation, Patrizi collects six passages from Aristotle in which the term μίμησις has six different meanings, two from the *Rhetoric* and four from the *Poetics*. For several of these passages the meaning is found by consulting texts of Plato. Patrizi concludes that these are six separate meanings, with distinct definitions. Asking, then, whether individually these meanings supply a proper definition for poetry, he concludes that they do not: (1) If poetry is an imitation because words are imitations (*Rhet.* III, I, 8; cf. *Cratylus*, 423), then all forms of discourse would be poetry. (2) If imitation means "enargia" or vivid description (*Rhet.* III, XI, 2; cf. Hermogenes, καὶ τὸ μέγιστον ποιήσεως, μίμησιν ἐναργῆ), then only some parts of poetry would contain imitation, which would also be found in rhetoric and history. (3) If imitation means "favola" (plot, or fable, or mythology; *Poetics* 1450a3), then two propositions must necessarily follow: every poem will be a "favola," and every "favola" will be a poem. Leaving the first of these propositions for discussion in Book IV, Patrizi demonstrates that the second is false, for the ancients wrote many "favole" (here, fables) which were not poems because they were in prose, and many ancient authorities made a careful distinction between poetry and mythology. Moreover, he says, if we reduce Aristotle's argument to the following syllogism:

> Every poem is an imitation
> Every "favola" is an imitation
> Therefore every "favola" is a poem,

we obtain a conclusion which is in accord neither with the first premise nor with the facts. (4) If by imitation is meant a dramatic representation, as in comedy and tragedy (*Poetics* 1449*b*24; cf. *Rep*. III, 394), then it would admit neither epic nor dithyrambic poetry, but it would include both comedy and dialogues in prose. (5) If imitation does include the epic and the dithyramb (*Poetics* 1447*a*13), then Aristotle contradicts himself when he later says (1460*a*5) that many epic poets "imitate" very little because they speak constantly in their own persons; and imitation consists in speaking in the person of another. (6) If imitation is constituted by auletic, citharistic, syringic, and orchestic poetry, which would be equivalent to encomia, hymns, blames, and gnomes (*Poetics* 1447*a*15, 25, –48*a*9), then it is not poetry at all, for these are not forms of poetry; if these are taken, metaphorically, as forms of poetry, then they will be imitations only when they are represented on the stage. Patrizi summarizes thus:

> All six "imitations," therefore, have different meanings; of which some are not appropriate to poetry, others are common to other writings also and not proper to poetry, others make the compositions of writers both poetry and non-poetry, and others make all of them non-poetry. And none of them is sufficient to provide the genus for all poems.[35]

The weaknesses of this argument are immediately apparent. Not only are all the terms from the *Poetics*—"poetry, imitation, plot"—given meanings which are not justified by the context in Aristotle or which are directly excluded by that context, but these terms and others shift their meaning as Patrizi passes from stage to stage in the argument. Moreover, there is a kind of pseudological analysis of the propositions being attacked, which is itself very unsure; e.g., his treatment of the proposition (itself incorrectly derived) that "every 'favola' is a poem." The careful reader, working his way through such a series of arguments, feels himself driven to a point of complete confusion where words no longer have fixed meanings and demonstration has no validity. Perhaps Patrizi felt that he was following the example of the Platonic dialectic; instead, he was violating the very principles of that dialectic, in which change of meaning is accompanied by redefinition, justified by context, and submitted always to searching analysis and careful distinction.

These remarks on the methodology of the critics have been, I fear, fairly damaging. They would seem to point to a degree of philosophical incompetence, both in the reading and interpretation of earlier texts and in the development of new theories. I have ventured to make them for two reasons: first and primarily, so that they might serve as a partial explanation of how the ancient theories came to be interpreted as they were and

---

35 *Della poetica* (1586), pp. 59–74; v. p. 74: "Tutte adunque le sei imitazioni, hanno tra loro significati differenti. De quali altri a poesia non conuengono. Altre sono communi ad ad [*sic*] altri scrittori, e non proprie de poeti. Altre che fanno le composizioni altrui, e poesie, e non poesie. e altre del tutto non poesie. E niuna bastante ad essere genere alle poesie tutte."

how the new theories came to assume the form that they did; second, so that the reader might be more acutely aware, as he reads the subsequent chapters, of what is taking place in the individual texts analyzed. He should not, however, conclude from these remarks either that method was universally bad or that the theorists never succeeded in making consistent sense in their treatises. There were examples of good method; there were cases of solid contribution to theory; there were completely consistent and well developed documents.

Perhaps we may thus analyze the situation with respect to the procedure of the best of the theorists. A given critic has developed, let us say, a clearly thought out and perfectly self-contained poetics. He may undertake, then, to write a commentary on Aristotle's *Poetics*. The peculiarities or the deficiencies of his general philosophical method permit him to read his own theory into the text of Aristotle, even though the two may be worlds apart. Or he may set out to write an art of poetry which will expound his own theory. The peculiarities or the deficiencies of his general philosophical method permit him to cite in support of his doctrine a whole set of miscellaneous texts which might, taken separately, be entirely irreconcilable with it. In either situation, it is essentially the interpretation of the ancient text or texts which suffers; his own theory remains undamaged except insofar as the proofs offered may appear at places to be inadequate or inappropriate. By way of illustration of such procedures, I wish to summarize briefly my findings (published previously) on four of the most prominent of Cinquecento critics, Robortello, Scaliger, Minturno, and Castelvetro.

Francesco Robortello published in 1548 the first extensive commentary on Aristotle's *Poetics* in his *In librum Aristotelis de arte poetica explicationes*.[36] But far from approaching his basic text without prior suppositions about the poetic art and with the intention of interpreting the text only in and for itself, he brought to the text a completely worked out theory of poetics. He had derived this theory from his reading of Horace's *Ars poetica* and the Greek and Roman rhetoricians; hence it was essentially rhetorical in character. Robortello conceived of poetry as written for the purpose of producing certain effects of pleasure and of utility on a given audience. The audience was composed of an elite of wise men of good moral character, who would be persuaded only if certain kinds of actions and characters were presented to them; persuasion was a necessary antecedent of both utility and pleasure. The work itself would produce a variety of utilities and pleasures, not as a whole, but through different parts and elements. For example, certain lessons about human destiny would be learned from watching the action of a tragedy develop on the stage, certain lessons about character from the observation of characters in poems; certain truths would be demonstrated by the sententiae, and on the

36 "Robortello on the *Poetics*," in R. S. Crane *et al.*, *Critics and Criticism: Ancient and Modern* (Chicago: University of Chicago Press, 1952), pp. 319–48.

basis of these the audience would be moved to undertake action or to refrain from it. With respect to pleasure, again it would be produced by separate parts of the poem: that related to imitation would come from the plot itself, that associated with the *difficulté vaincue* from successful treatment of unpleasant subjects, that ascribable to admiration from certain kinds of episodes, from diction, from various ornaments.

Now this is a completely conceived system of poetics, which Robortello could defend upon philosophical or pragmatic grounds. But when he proceeds to read Aristotle as if this were Aristotle's theory, too, he completely deforms the meaning of his basic text. What happens to Aristotle may be summarized thus:

... what emerges is a poetic method essentially different from Aristotle's. The fundamental alteration comes in the passage from a poetic to a rhetorical position, from a position in which the essential consideration is the achievement of the internal and structural relationship which will make the poem beautiful to one in which the main problem is the discovery of those devices which will produce a desired effect upon a specified audience. I do not mean that in Aristotle no consideration is given to the effect of the poem upon the audience; indeed, at every crucial point in the *Poetics* the relationship of object of contemplation to contemplator is maintained constant. Such concepts as the pleasure derived from imitation, the "effect" proper to a given species, the pity and fear of tragedy and their "purgation," the "likeness" of hero to audience among the requisites of character are integral to the argument; they are fundamental if the work of art is to fulfil its function of giving a certain kind of artistic pleasure to the men who see it or hear it. But herein lies the basic departure of Robortello: the effect produced is no longer one of artistic pleasure resulting from the formal qualities of the work, but one of moral persuasion to action or inaction, in which the pleasure involved is merely an accompaniment or an instrument; and the audience is composed of men capable of yielding to this persuasion rather than of men capable of enjoying this pleasure.

This means that the problem for the poet is no longer to compound out of the constitutive parts an artistic whole which, as a whole, will produce the desired aesthetic effect, but rather to insert into the work such parts as will, by themselves, produce multiple utilities and pleasures, each part producing a separate utility or a separate pleasure. The bases for the inclusion of any given part is its capacity, by itself, to awaken in a highly specified audience a given reaction of persuasion or of pleasure. This means, in turn, that the artistic unity and integrity of the work disappear as part of the problem: "plot" may be removed from among the poetic elements of a work and may be transferred to its specifically histrionic functions. Only the vaguest notions of a unifying and ordering structure for the work need be retained; these are not vital. On the other hand, such elements as diction and the means by which diction is made ornate assume great importance.

Moreover, since the sense of the total poetic structure is lost, there is no longer any possibility of deriving from such a structure the criteria for the appropriateness, for the goodness or badness, of individual parts. Instead, criteria for each separate part will be separately derived by a reference to the character of the audience as it specifically affects that part and in the light of the utility or the pleasure which that part should produce. At each step, there will be reference outside the poem. The poem becomes, as a result, a collection rather than a unit. From it the audience derives utility of a moral character and pleasure of a non-aesthetic kind, since it is not related to the structure or the form of the work as a whole.[37]

Julius Caesar Scaliger, who died in 1558, left behind him the completed manuscript of his *Poetices libri septem*, which was published in 1561.[38] Unlike Robortello's work, this is an original art of poetry; it presents in an orderly and highly systematic fashion Scaliger's theory of the art. Indeed, so orderly and systematic is the presentation that this work might well be taken as an example of a "good" method employed by a Renaissance theorist. The theory as a whole might be described as a grammatical one, in the sense that Scaliger is essentially preoccupied with poetry as an art of discourse. Poetry is conceived primarily as language. As language, it must enter into two distinct relationships: (1) the relationship with the things which are signified by the words employed and (2) the relationship with the audience for whom the signification is intended. Scaliger will thus concern himself with things as they are in nature—or in Vergil's *Aeneid*, which represents perfectly the norm of nature—and with the effects of pleasure and utility produced in the audience. Both nature and the needs of the audience impose conditions upon poetry, which has no conditions or principles of its own except those that are purely prosodic. Such a system is, of course, diametrically opposed to that of Aristotle; and Scaliger recognizes this fact when he takes direct issue with Aristotle on such points as the definition of tragedy, its constituent parts, the end of poetry, and the internal economy of the poem. This does not prevent him, however, from using the *Poetics* constantly as a source of definitions, distinctions, and arguments.

The *De poeta* of Antonio Sebastiano Minturno (1559), almost exactly contemporary with Scaliger's work, is much less successful in achieving order and system.[39] It draws heavily upon a wide variety of works—Plato's *Republic, Laws, Ion*, etc., Aristotle's *Poetics* and *Rhetoric*, Horace's *Ars poetica*, Quintilian, Cicero's *Orator, De oratore, De optimo genere oratorum, Topica*. Such works as the *Poetics* and the *Ars poetica* are almost completely incorporated into Minturno's treatise; others contribute more or less extensive developments. But from these disparate elements no single, central approach emerges. Not only does Minturno fail to apply certain of his distinctions consistently, but there are whole groups of concepts—the rules

---

[37] *Ibid.*, pp. 346–47.

[38] "Scaliger versus Aristotle on Poetics," *Modern Philology*, XXXIX (1942), 337–60.

[39] "The Poetic Theories of Minturno," in *Studies in Honor of Frederick W. Shipley* ("Washington University Studies," [St. Louis, Mo., 1942]), pp. 101–29.

and precepts for the specific genres, for example—which do not in any way derive from the more general concepts of the work. Even among these more general ideas, a complete ordering to a central problem is lacking. Some of them relate to the poet himself, to his faculties and his character as a good man; some of them to the audience with its desire for pleasure and its need for moral improvement; some of them to the poem as an imitation composed of qualitative and quantitative parts. But no one of these analyses is complete; each is presented in a fragmentary form and Minturno passes rapidly from one context to another. Insofar as there is an ordering of ideas, it is an ordering to rhetorical principles. For the various chains of relationships established within the work there is, at one end of each chain, an effect upon the audience; at the other end, some faculty of the poet capable of producing that effect; in the middle, the poem serving as a means or instrument. This arrangement is essentially rhetorical and is vaguely reminiscent of Aristotle's system in the *Rhetoric*, in which the nature of the audience, the character of the orator, and the proofs presented in the speech itself must all be taken into consideration. In the detail of the treatment, however, Minturno's system is really Ciceronian, and most of the discussion in specific passages comes from one or another of Cicero's rhetorical works. Here again, the lack of order, the lack of discipline, the failure to arrive at a synthesis or to impose a central organization upon a mass of irreconcilable materials are evident.

Lodovico Castelvetro's *Poetica d'Aristotele vulgarizzata et sposta* (1570) is, like Robortello's work, a commentary on the *Poetics*.[40] Unlike Robortello, however, Castelvetro sets out to refute Aristotle and to suggest his own theories instead. He begins with the basic assumption that poems are written for a specific audience, the ignorant multitude, which has no knowledge, no imagination, no memory, and which demands that its comfort be respected. In order to please this audience—and pleasure is the only end—the poet must above all seek credibility or verisimilitude in combination with the marvelous: credibility so that the unimaginative audience will believe, the marvelous so that it will find pleasure in the uncommon and the extraordinary. These two factors determine the nature of plots, episodes, character, the choice of materials; they make of poetry a kind of history which differs from history only in the use of verse. The audience's demand for comfort introduces the requirement of a "unity" of time, its lack of imagination adds the "unity" of place; the unity of action (which Castelvetro does not really consider essential, even though it is the only one of the three required by Aristotle) comes as an adjunct to the unities of time and place; it serves as an additional ornament and shows the excellence of the poet. Moreover, the audience will impose upon the work a whole set of special conditions which will be codified in the rules and precepts which the poet must follow. Such a system as this, in which every-

40 "Castelvetro's Theory of Poetics," in R. S. Crane *et al.*, *op. cit.*, pp. 349–71.

thing results from the necessity of pleasing a specific audience, is rhetorical in a sense; besides, it is historical to the degree that it concerns itself with credibility. It is, of course, clearly distinct from Aristotle's conception of poetics; and what is amazing from the point of view of methodology is that the vehicle for its presentation should be a commentary on the *Poetics*. Little light will be thrown on the *Poetics* in the course of the commentary, but much illumination of Castelvetro's own doctrine will result.

These four documents are representative, in their general outlines, of the results produced by application of the methods that I have described in this chapter. An examination of the details of discussion would show other procedures at work. We should not, of course, expect to find all the methods exemplified in any single work, all the faults and failings epitomized by any one theorist, who would thus become the arch-sinner of Renaissance critical theory. Rather, we should expect that the various habits of intellectual approach, the major difficulties, the characteristic ways of solving those difficulties, would manifest themselves variously and in varying combinations in the numerous documents which constitute the body of critical materials of the Cinquecento. If we are concerned not only with what the theoretical and the practical critics said in their writings, but with why they said what they did, we should anticipate that a constant awareness of methodological factors will enable us both to understand and to judge their writings. The problem of reading Renaissance critical texts is complex, not only because of the complexities of the critical situation itself but because of our distance from it in time and in intellectual habits. By constantly asking what virtues or vices of method are present in a given document, we shall without doubt be able to discover some simplicity in complexity and some clarity in confusion.

CHAPTER THREE. THE TRADITION OF HORACE'S *ARS POETICA*: I. THE EARLIEST COMMENTARIES

THIS CHAPTER and the three succeeding ones will be concerned with tracing through the course of the sixteenth century in Italy the intellectual fortunes of Horace's *Ars poetica*. Of all theoretical documents relative to the art of poetry in classical antiquity, this was the only one which had some currency during the Middle Ages and which came to the humanistic period and the Renaissance as a part of their more immediate intellectual heritage.[1] Throughout both periods, it continued to be a dominant text in the molding of critical opinion and in the formation of new doctrines. Horace's work represented, in addition to the specific recommendations of the text itself, a general way of thinking about poetry which was highly acceptable to the Renaissance mind and which continued to dominate critical thinking in spite of the emergence of such new points of view as that contained in Aristotle's *Poetics*.

Essentially, the *Ars poetica* regards poems in the context of the society for which they are written. It considers above all the dramatic forms, in relation both to nature and to their capacity to please and to instruct an audience of a given kind that would see them in a given age under given circumstances. What goes into the making of any poem will be determined in large part by the expectations, the requirements, the taste of this particular audience. Translated into terms of the poem, these requirements become certain precepts for its ordering and unification (the audience dislikes disorder and laughs at disunity), certain conventions for its superficial forms (the audience expects that plays will have five acts and a limited number of interlocutors), certain recommendations for the decorum of its characters (the audience has fixed notions both about types and about traditional heroes), and certain generalizations about diction (the audience associates specific kinds of diction and styles of writing with each of the literary genres). Moreover, since the various age groups and the divers social sectors in the audience make different demands upon the poem, it will have to provide a proper combination of pleasurable and profitable elements.

The fact that, in Horace's theory, the internal characteristics of the poem are determined largely, if not exclusively, by the external demands of the audience brings his theory very close to specifically rhetorical approaches. In theories of this kind, the determining factor in the production of the work is not an internal principle of structural perfection, but rather an acceptance of the assumption that all those elements are included in the work that will be susceptible of producing the desired effect upon the

---

[1] For the scattered appearances of Aristotle's *Poetics* during the medieval period, see below, chap. ix, p. 352.

audience envisaged, arranged in an order calculated to achieve the maximum degree of that effect. However, in proper and complete rhetorical approaches, one essential element—absent from Horace—enters at all times into consideration: the character of the orator (or poet) as it really is (Quintilian) or as it is made to appear to be (Aristotle's *Rhetoric*). If Horace's thesis is a rhetorical one, it is incomplete rhetoric because it omits this essential aspect.

For theorists and critics of the Renaissance, the rhetorical tendency of Horace's *Ars poetica* was perhaps its most appealing characteristic. Indeed, as we have already seen in Chapter I, their own thinking about poetry inclined most frequently toward considering it as a kinsman of rhetoric or as an instrumental science serving the ends of moral philosophy. Whatever doubts they may have had about how specific passages in Horace's text were to be interpreted, they seem to have sensed immediately to what extent the whole corresponded to their favorite ways of looking at the art of poetry. Perhaps they merely continued in the paths of their medieval ancestors, for many of whom poetry was an adjunct to rhetoric and for whom the *Ars poetica* provided occasional ideas for the arts of poetry (which were otherwise largely arts of rhyming) and for passing allusions to the broader aspects of poetry.

Horace's verse epistle may thus be taken—and in fact was so taken by Renaissance critics—as the epitome of an essentially rhetorical approach to the art of poetry. Indeed, this is true to such an extent that it is frequently difficult to distinguish a predominantly "Horatian" text of the Cinquecento from one which sprang primarily from Cicero or Quintilian transmuted into an authority on the art of poetry. The details of the treatment, the specific ideas, might be different; but the basic assumptions, the fundamental ways of considering the poetic art, would be the same. For this reason, I shall include in the present chapter and the following ones not only those works which are commentaries upon Horace but all such works as are related to it in a secondary way, insofar as they represent the kind of approach indicated. As I stated in the Preface, I do not mean to trace through the Cinquecento the history of the rhetorical documents themselves, since that in itself would be a vast and complex undertaking. But a treatment of poetic theory in the period would be incomplete if cognizance were not taken of the impact of rhetorical theory upon poetics; and since this rhetorical theory is most closely associated, in the Renaissance, with the interpretation of Horace's *Ars poetica*, the present series of chapters seems to be the logical place for its treatment.

THE LATE-CLASSICAL COMMENTATORS: ACRON AND PORPHYRION

The *Ars poetica* did not come to the Renaissance as a naked text for which the simplest and most elementary interpretations had to be provided. The earliest printed editions were accompanied by two commentaries of the late Roman period, that attributed to Helenius Acron (second century A.D.) and that of Porphyrion (third century A.D.).[2] Moreover, these printed editions continued an ancient manuscript tradition (extant manuscripts date back to the ninth and tenth centuries) in which the same commentaries accompanied the Horatian text.[3] To these were added, before 1500, the commentary of Cristoforo Landino, and, around 1500, the commentary of Iodocus Badius Ascensius; and although Badius' annotations were for a number of years printed only in Paris editions, they ultimately were added to the earlier commentaries in Italian editions.[4] By the time, then, that the major Cinquecento studies of the text were made, all four glosses were a standard part of the available editions, and critics and theorists took them as a point of departure for their own interpretations.

Much of what Acron has to say in his commentary is essentially grammatical or explanatory in character. He explains the meanings of words, word order, matters of syntax; sometimes, when the sense is particularly obscure, he gives a paraphrase. He provides classifications for the various figures of speech used by Horace, cites parallels from other poets, explains legends and allusions, brings to the text a kind of grammatical and historical *explication*. However, for numerous passages he makes remarks—in a sentence or sometimes in a single word—which suggest an interpretation of the basic work, and these remarks taken together constitute a fairly complete theory of poetry as Acron discovers it in Horace. One thing that he does (and I presume that he was the first to do it for this particular text) is to distinguish a series of precepts, definitely labeled as such, in the *Ars poetica*. He prefaces these indications with a statement at the very beginning of his commentary: "De inaequalitate operis loquitur, et dat praecepta scribendi poema. Et primum praeceptum est de dispositione et conuenientia carminis."[5] Subsequently, some dozen or more precepts of this kind are pointed out. At a few other places, although he does not specifically call his remark a "praeceptum," he uses some such word as "docet" to show that he is thinking in essentially the same terms. This procedure is not without importance for the subsequent history of Horace's text. It establishes a precedent for reducing the text to a set of fixed rules for the writing of poetry, a precedent which Renaissance commentators were to follow constantly.

More important still, however, was the general orientation which Acron

[2] E.g., the *editio princeps*, the so-called "editio Romana," printed by Bartholomew Guldin-beck around 1475; the edition of Milan, 1474; of Venice, 1481; and so forth.

[3] For a list of the manuscripts, see the edition by Ferdinand Hauthal, *Acronis et Porphyrionis commentarii in Q. Horatium Flaccum* (Berlin, 1864), I, iii; also II, 574, 648, 649, and 665.

[4] See the Index, s.v. Badius Ascensius, of *Quintus Horatius Flaccus: Editions in the United States and Canada* (Mills College, California, 1938); the earliest Italian edition listed here as containing the Badius commentary is Item 85, Milan, 1518.

[5] Ed. Hauthal, cited in note 3 above, II, 575. All subsequent references to Acron will be to this volume; comments not specifically located by page will be found under the line number indicated.

gave to the *Ars poetica* in his reading of it. This was an essentially rhetorical orientation which, if it did not introduce any new ideas, emphasized and exaggerated tendencies latent in the Horatian text. One such tendency is to consider poetry in terms of the conventional rhetorical distinction of invention, disposition, and elocution. The passage previously cited ("primum praeceptum est de dispositione") already shows this intention. The other two terms of the trilogy appear in the commentary on line 40: "if one selects a subject matter which he is capable of fulfilling, neither inventions nor eloquence can be lacking to him."[6] The term "dispositio" appears in close conjunction in the gloss on the following line. But the three-way distinction is little more than suggested and does not constitute the major effort of the commentary.

If one were to attempt to find a guiding principle for Acron's whole reading of the text, it would probably be a principle of appropriateness. Everywhere, the attempt is made to reduce all matters to questions of "propriety," of "fittingness" of this to that. This attempt is apparent, again, in the first precept already cited, "et primum praeceptum est de dispositione et *conuenientia* carminis." From then on, one hardly ever loses sight of the central principle. The second precept restates it: "Praecipit, poetam *conuenientiam* seruare debere"; here, it is Acron's summation of the meaning of the first three lines of the text (p. 576). So does the third: "Docet, *non inportune* inducendam esse parabolam aut descriptionem" (p. 577). The same organizing concept is invoked in the commentaries on line 20 ("Ita ergo qui scribit, nisi *opportune* scribat . . ."), line 31 ("Docet hic, non esse indulgendum eloquentiae, *quae careat arte et ratione*, ne quis incidat in opinionem *inepti et superflui*"), lines 35–37 (". . . ita enitor omni parte poeta uideri, *nulla in parte ab alia discrepans*"), lines 47–48 ("si tota uerba *opportune* et *proprie* ponantur"); and so on through innumerable passages. The principle is in itself vague, since no criterion for appropriateness is presented. When one has said that the style must fit the subject, the diction must fit the characters, the conception of characters must fit the notion of decorum, the end must fit the beginning, one has made a rule whose application depends almost exclusively upon the sensitivity of the poet, upon his sense of what is right in a given relationship. But the principle is no more vague than it was in the Horatian text itself; the only difference is that Acron sees it as operating in many places where the original text of Horace seems not to imply it at all. For example, lines 125–27 of the *Ars poetica*—

> Siquid inexpertum scaenae committis et audes
> personam formare novam, servetur ad imum,
> qualis ab incepto processerit, et sibi constet

—undoubtedly contain a recommendation that character be kept constant

6 *Ibid.*, p. 581: "qui eligit materiam, quam possit inplere, huic nec inuentiones, nec eloquentia deesse possunt."

or consistent throughout a work; but Acron's gloss on "sibi constet" is as follows: "Let the material finish within itself, nor should it pass on to something else. Do not pass to anything else before you have finished it."[7] The idea is generalized and is made into another expression of the central notion of "fittingness" or "belongingness."

That central notion itself provides in effect a rhetorical rather than a poetic basis of organizing and constructing a work. I do not mean that a norm of "appropriateness" does not or could not apply to poetic works. But in such a document as Aristotle's *Poetics,* the relationship between one part and another of the poem is stated in other terms: in terms of the hierarchical interdependence of such component parts as plot, character, thought, and diction, or in terms of the specifically poetic devices which link the parts together, necessity and probability. That is, a given element (a word or an action or a passion) is "appropriate" to the whole work in a special way determined by the total unity and the total order of the given work itself. But for Acron (following and simplifying Horace), the principle of appropriateness is general rather than specific; it applies in the same way to all works, regardless of their particular natures; it involves such diverse kinds of appropriateness as that of meters to subject matters and of traits of character to historical personages. If it is thus unspecified, it is because, in the last analysis, appropriateness is not determined from within the work, but is at all times judged from without by the particular audience. In this resides its peculiarly rhetorical quality.

As Acron interprets Horace, the constant search for the appropriateness of all elements within a poem is a part of the constant search to please the audience. This is, of course, a Horatian principle; but Acron extends it and states it much more explicitly. For example, the "commendare" of line 225 clearly means "to render acceptable to the public"; Acron expands the statement, applied originally to satiric drama, into a general statement about all poetry: ". . . nam omnia, quae dicimus, placere desideramus, ac per hoc uidentur conmendare, quae dicimus, auribus auditorum. Omnia enim, quae dicuntur a poetis, ita debent dici, ut conmendari uideantur, id est, ut libenter adspiciantur." In a similar way, Horace's emphasis on the audience is everywhere pointed up by Acron. The "semper ad euentum festinat" of line 148 is the occasion for the gloss: "Considering the possible distaste of the reader, he hastens to the end of the work."[8] In explaining the "in medias res" beginning (line 148) he goes on to say: ". . . the good poet leads his listener immediately to known things"; and then, for the next line, ". . . the good poet excludes those things which cannot please, that is, he passes over those things which are not agreeable in the treatment."[9]

7 *Ibid.,* p. 598: "In se finiatur materia, nec ad aliud transeat. Ne transeas ad aliam, ante-quam illam finias."
8 *Ibid.,* p. 601: "Cogitans fastidium lectoris ad exitum operis properat."
9 *Ibid.,* p. 602: "adducit bonus poeta auditorem [suum] quasi ad nota" and "bonus poeta relinquit ea, quae placere non possunt, hoc est, praeterit ea, quae in tractatu ingrata sunt."

Line 153 is elucidated thus: "... what I and the people might desire, that is, what all would willingly listen to. ..."[10] For "omne tulit punctum" in line 343 he provides this explanation: "He alone obtains the votes and the [favorable] judgment of the people who writes a poem in a useful and pleasant fashion and who can both profit and delight."[11]

The general thesis is stated in connection with the phrase "Ut pictura poesis" in line 361: "indeed, an excellent poem pleases even when frequently repeated."[12] Within this audience, various segments must be pleased in special ways: Acron again emphasizes Horace's ideas. Part of the audience is low, ignorant, and wicked, and it must be pleased by special kinds of poetic fare; so the commentary on lines 213-14: "He indicates the cause for the increase of licence: because of the ignorance of the people and because there was no difference between the good and the bad," and "because the people was uneducated."[13] Another segment consists of grave persons, officials and noblemen, who will be offended by anything dishonorable; the commentary on line 248 reads: "The meaning is this: The Roman knights and senate fathers, who have great wealth and hence are noble and enjoy honorable reputation, are offended if anything shameful is expressed before them."[14] Some of the audience are young and will find delight in light things, some are old and want serious materials (commentary on line 342): "The meaning is this: Old men are pleased by the gravity of the verse and the weight of the diction, young men do not like austere and grave things."[15] The introduction to the same gloss shows that the pleasure of poetry is intended for the young, its profit for the old: "The poem must be properly tempered, so that through its pleasure it will serve the younger men and through its severity it will satisfy the older."[16] Apparently, the insistence upon moral precepts, philosophical arguments, and the arousing of the passions—because these are "grave" matters—is intended especially for the older men. The effort to find everywhere both pleasure and utility may account for the somewhat startling construction put on line 99—

Non satis est pulchra esse poemata: dulcia sunto

—when, after the gloss "Therefore, let those poems which are morally

---

10 *Ibid.*, p. 602: "quid ego et populus desideret, id est, quid libenter audiant omnes. ..."

11 *Ibid.*, p. 632: "Solus suffragia et iudicium populi tulit, qui utile et dulce poema scripsit et qui prodest et delectare potest."

12 *Ibid.*, p. 634: "probum uero poema placet etiam saepe repetitum."

13 *Ibid.*, p. 611: "Dicit autem causam, per quam creuit licentia; propter inperitiam populi, et quia nulla erat differentia inter bonos et malos" and "quia indoctus erat populus."

14 *Ibid.*, p. 619: "Sensus est: Equites Romani et patres senatores, quibus sunt substantiae magnae, ac per hoc nobiles et honestate gaudentes, offenduntur, si aliquid coram eis inhonestum fuerit prolatum."

15 *Ibid.*, p. 631: "Sensus est: Senes grauitate carminis et dictionis pondere delectantur, iuuenes austera et grauia non amant."

16 *Ibid.*, p. 631: "Poema debet temperari, et ut uoluptati seruiat iuniorum, et seueritati satisfaciat seniorum."

recommendable have beauty as well and carry the mind of the auditor wherever they will, either to pity or to indignation," the phrase "dulcia sunto" is translated by the formula "Ethica sint," which I take to mean "having moral implications."[17] In any case, the pleasure-profit distinction comes to be crossed with another grammatical and rhetorical one, the "res-verba" juxtaposition; cf. the gloss on line 320:

> He shows only to what extent is important the consideration of customs, saying that sometimes a story through the suitableness of the persons introduced and the expression of the mores, even though it may be without art, without beauty, without gravity of sententiae, pleases more than high-sounding verses which are lacking in the observation of the mores. Things without ornament can please more than poems adorned with words without substance.[18]

One special aspect of Acron's conception of the role of the audience is his interpretation of "nature" as it figures in Horace's work. Clearly, if for many things in a poem the precise way of judging "appropriateness" is not made apparent, for some at least the judgment is possible through a reference to nature. The audience is the custodian of a certain conception of nature, and it uses this conception as its criterion; what nature *is* does not count, but what the audience thinks it to be does. This is of course true in Horace, and the laughter of the spectator in the first lines indicates that the monster he sees does not conform to his notion of nature. Acron merely states the idea more explicitly. Thus for line 23—

Denique sit quod vis, simplex dumtaxat et unum

—he adds a highly significant phrase: "Quiduis scribe, simplex ut sit *et ueri simile.*" Similarly, the "specie recte" of line 25 is interpreted as "imagine boni, dum praeferimus imaginem ueritatis." The whole series of comments on lines 108 ff. is interesting in the same connection. The "intus" of line 108 is glossed as follows: "We have all passions within our souls by nature, and they are moved singly whenever they see their own images in others."[19] For the "iuvat aut impellit ad iram" of line 109 he says this: "Nature delights us when we see it charmingly presented. For through nature we become angry, we feel pleasure, we have pity."[20] The "angit" of line 110 is explained as meaning that "Nature herself [troubles] the spec-

[17] *Ibid.,* p. 593: "Habeant ergo haec, quae sunt probata, etiam uenustatem, et, quocumque uoluerint, animum auditoris trahant, siue ad misericordiam, siue ad indignationem."

[18] *Ibid.,* p. 629: "Ostendit modo, quantum prodest consideratio consuetudinis, dicens, quod interdum fabula opportunitate personarum inductarum et expressione morum, quamuis sit sine arte, sine uenustate, sine grauitate sententiarum, plus placet quam uersus bene quidem sonantes, sed morum obseruatione carentes. Magis possunt delectare res sine ornatu, quam ornata poemata uerbis sine rebus."

[19] *Ibid.,* p. 594: "adfectus omnes habemus in animis nostris ex natura, et singuli mouentur, cum imagines suas uiderint in aliis."

[20] *Ibid.,* p. 594: "Delectat nos natura, cum delicata uidemus. Nam natura irascimur, delectamur, miseremur."

tator."[21] The commentary on line 111 is essentially the same in intent.[22] Finally, the distinction between historical and newly invented subjects is transformed by Acron into a distinction between the true and the verisimilar; for line 119 he says: "Si ergo certam scribis, famam sequere, aut si *fingis*, habeat artem et uerisimilitudinem figmentum tuum. Aliud praeceptum: aut notam historiam scribe, aut uerisimilia finge." In all these passages, the introduction of the term "verisimilitude," the insistence upon nature, the indication of the interaction between nature and the spectator, are signs of an approach to poetry in which the role of the audience is even more emphatically stressed than in Horace himself.

In such an approach, the goal pursued by the poet must also be related to the audience. Acron begins with the "applause" or the "laughter" of the audience and extends it to mean "fame, glory," something very close to the Ciceronian "victory." "Whoever writes, unless he write appropriately, will not obtain glory for himself" (on line 20).[23] The single word "finis" in line 406 (which Acron apparently mistakes as referring to the "end" of poetry) is translated by "laudatio," and several comments on line 412—

Qui studet optatam cursu contingere metam

—insist that the goal is glory: "Qui studet ad gloriam uenire ...";
"*Optatam* ergo *metam* dicit gloriam, quia finis istiusmodi uitae parit gloriam sempiternam"; "Id est, propositi finem, gloriam."

If I have insisted at such length on so ancient a commentator as Acron, it is because his remarks, for readers of the Cinquecento, are in a sense contemporary both with the text of Horace and with themselves. They accompany that text in all scholarly and critical editions, are read along with it almost as if they had been written by Horace himself. Moreover, Renaissance students of the text have these remarks constantly in mind, cite them when they need support or authority for their own ideas. Finally, the salient tendencies of Acron's commentary—the reduction to precepts, the emphasis upon rhetorical elements, the attention to the role of the audience—enter bodily into the thinking of later critics about the Horatian text and in large measure determine their orientation.

As compared with the commentary of Acron, that of Porphyrion is brief, pedestrian, and relatively unimportant. It repeats a certain amount of material from Acron; but this is usually material of the grammatical or explanatory type, which constitutes the bulk of Porphyrion's contribution. The major emphases of Acron are lacking, save perhaps that upon the reduction of the work to a series of precepts. Only a few points are worthy of special mention here. As with Acron, the basis for judging appropriate-

21 *Ibid.*, p. 594: "Ipsa natura spectatorem."
22 *Ibid.*, pp. 594–95: "Id est: natura, quae me deiecit rerum miseratione, extollit prosperitate, et modo deducit ad humanitatem, modo ad iracundiam."
23 *Ibid.*, p. 578: "qui scribit, nisi opportune scribat, non sibi conparat gloriam."

ness—and hence for assuring the audience's approval—is by reference to nature. The reason that the audience laughs, says Porphyrion, is "quod contra naturam omnia faciat."[24] Poets should choose subjects equal to their strength not (as we presume Horace to have meant) so that they can complete all parts of the work properly, but so that they may please the audience: "ut eam materiam eligant, qua possint placere" (p. 651). In the gloss on line 119—

Aut famam sequere aut sibi conuenientia finge

—Porphyrion states a precept different from that of Acron: "For the poet who is going to write must either describe something according to the common opinion of men, or if he does not wish to handle a dry history, as it were, he must introduce known things in a proper way."[25] The distinction here is not between history and what is invented in a verisimilar way, but between a known history and some other known fact. The "res-verba" distinction again appears in connection with lines 319–20 in terms very similar to those of Acron. These few ideas, insofar as they corroborate or insist upon those of Acron, made of the commentary of Porphyrion an addendum to that of Acron which was not without its influence upon critics of the Cinquecento.

CRISTOFORO LANDINO (1482)

Acron, second century, Porphyrion, third century: between them and the critics of the Cinquecento there is a long gap. This gap is filled in part by the late-classical grammarians, Donatus and Diomedes, in part by the humanists of the fifteenth century. Both groups enter the Horatian tradition through the intermediary of two commentators who stand at the threshold of the sixteenth century, Cristoforo Landino and Badius Ascensius.

Landino's commentary on the *Ars poetica* appeared first, as far as I know, in the edition of Horace's *Opera* which he published in Florence in 1482. By way of incorporating into his remarks typical medieval thinking about poetic matters, he introduced lengthy quotations from Diomedes; by way of taking cognizance of the humanist contribution, he quoted Plato, cited Aristotle, called frequently upon Cicero, and in a long prefatory section presented a defence of poesy in the fashion of Boccaccio. Moreover, he referred to his own dialogue on poetry in his edition of Vergil. Landino's defence comprises the arguments which were already traditional: the poet is a creator inspired by the divine furor; no other writer equals him in wisdom and eloquence; he exerts a civilizing influence, is an instrument of religion, has always been held in high esteem by kings

---

24 In the comment on the first line, p. 649 of the Hauthal edition, which is cited throughout for Porphyrion as for Acron.

25 *Ibid.*, p. 655: "Nam poeta scripturus aut secundum hominum consensum debet aliquid describere, aut si historiam tamquam tritam non uult adtingere, debet conuenienter notam inducere."

and rulers. Great philosophers have always praised him, especially Plato in the *Ion* and Aristotle—"et ipse de facultate poetica duos: de poetis autem tres libros elegantissime scripserit." One passage in this preface indicates clearly how Landino conceives of the art of poetry and of its allegorical uses:

Indeed its matter [is] much more divine than that of other writings; for embracing all of them, and bound together by varied rhythms, and circumscribed by separated measures, and adorned in short by various ornaments and various flowers, it embellishes with admirable fictions whatever men have heretofore done, whatever they have accomplished, whatever they have known and contemplated with a divine genius; and for fear that they cannot be understood except through allegories perceived by us, it transposes completely into things of different kinds. For when it most appears to be narrating something most humble and ignoble or to be singing a little fable to delight idle ears, at that very time it is writing in a rather secret way the most excellent things of all, and which are drawn forth from the fountain of the gods.[26]

In the commentary itself, Landino goes far beyond Acron by way of interpreting Horace in terms of invention, disposition, and elocution. His gloss on the first words of the text reads as follows: "Because in the writing of a poem the first thing to be investigated is invention, disposition, and elocution, at the very beginning he explains immediately those things which relate to invention and disposition." In this regard Landino points out how close poetry is to rhetoric; the precepts for elocution are common to both (cf. Cicero), whereas the differences occur in the other two parts. He then proceeds to subdivide the text according to these distinctions: after the lines in which the relationship of the subject matter to nature and to decorum is treated, Horace passes on to disposition (beginning with line 41, "lucidus ordo"), then to elocution (beginning with line 46, "In verbis").[27] A cognate rhetorical distinction, that of the "three styles," is introduced in an interesting fashion. If subject matters (which are invented) divide themselves into three groups, the "high," the "middle," and the "low," then the types of poems used to develop them and the kinds of diction used to express them must also fall into the same three groups. Vergil's three major poems, the *Aeneid*, the *Georgics*, and the *Bucolics*, may serve as examples of proper adaptation.

26 *Opera* (1482 ed.), pp. clviv–clvii: "Verum rem esse multo illis diuiniorem quę illas omnes amplectens uariisque numeris colligata: distinctisque pedibus circumscripta: ac uarias denique luminibus uariisque floribus illustrata quęcunque hactenus homines fecerint; quęcunque egerint: quęcunque cognouerint: ac ingenii diuinitate contemplati fuerint admirandis figmentis exornat: et ne nisi allegoriis a nobis perceptis intelligi possint in diuersas omnino species traducit. Nam cum ostendat se aliud quippiam longe humilius ignobiliusque narrare aut fabellam ad ociosas aures oblectandas canere tunc res omnino egregias et a diuinitatis fonte exhaustas occultius scribit."

27 *Ibid.*, p. clvii: "Quoniam in poemate scribendo inuentio dispositioque atque elocutio in primis inuestiganda est: statim a principio quę ad inuentionem dispositionemque spectant exequitur"; also pp. clviii–clviiii.

As far as Horace is concerned, the principle is intimated in lines 86 ff., "Descriptas servare vices, etc." Elocution thus fits invention, always within the framework of one of the three "figures," and a mixing of styles becomes as impossible as a mixing of matters: "neither may we write a tragedy about comic matters nor a comedy about tragic ones."[28] This fittingness of style to genre to subject matter is expressed in the general term decorum, which for Landino is one of the concerns most "proper" to poets. As for invention itself, subjects must be natural, verisimilar, but "feigned" or created; this is because the end of poetry is to please or delight—"Nos enim delectare uult"—and there is no delight without belief. The false, the ridiculous, the monstrous will cause laughter or disdain because they are not representations of nature, and one of the fundamental notions about poetics is that every art imitates nature—"omnis ars naturam imitetur."[29] The same end of delight necessitates the cultivation of variety: "The major virtue is to distinguish the poem by much variety; for by variety we delight the soul of the listener, and render him attentive, and remove him from all boredom." It will be noted to what extent these remarks depend upon a rhetorical conception of the audience, which is either to be given pleasure or to be moved—"ut auditores in quemcunque affectum mouere possit"; and although Landino makes the appropriate comments on Horace's demands for moral utility, he emphasizes much more in his commentary elements of pleasure and feeling. The audience itself, however, is superior to that for rhetoric, being more erudite and having more time to engage in reading and rereading of the work. Hence, in disposition, for example, the poet may use an artificial order, whereas the orator is restricted to a natural one.[30] In Landino, all circles close in this same consistent fashion, and whether we start with the audience, or the elements of invention, disposition, and elocution, or the three styles, we end with some other of these factors or with all of them. A totally self-consistent rhetorical system is imposed bodily upon the Horatian poetic, and made to coincide with it at every point.

BADIUS ASCENSIUS (1500)

With the publication of the commentary of Iodocus Badius Ascensius in 1500, the interpretation of the *Ars poetica* takes another step forward. Not only is Badius' discussion much longer and more complete than any of the earlier ones, but it is enriched by a vast quantity of materials brought in from new sources. Acron, Porphyrion, and Landino are of course quoted. To them are added the grammarians who figured so importantly in the

[28] *Ibid.*, pp. clxv and clxi: "ne de re comica tragediam: aut de tragica comediam scribamus."

[29] *Ibid.*, p. clviiv; see also p. clxiiv.

[30] *Ibid.*, p. clviiiv: "Virtus maxima est poema multa uarietate distinguere. Animum enim auditoris ex uarietate delectamus: et attentum reddimus: et ab omni fastidio remouemus"; p. clxii and p. clviiii.

medieval conceptions of poetry, Diomedes, Donatus, and Priscian. There are also references to Plato.[31] But most significant of all, Badius calls constantly upon the *Institutes* of Quintilian and upon the various rhetorical works of Cicero for explanations, clarifications, and examples of Horace's ideas. In a sense, then, the commentary of Badius at once bridges the gap between the late-classical period and the Renaissance by incorporating the principal "medieval" sources, and it relates Horace specifically to the chief Latin rhetoricians.

Badius is a lover of divisions and a maker of distinctions almost in the scholastic fashion. Hence in a prologue to his commentary he indicates that the *Ars poetica* is divided into five sections: "Item quarum prima inquiunt poeta vitia extirpat. In secunda verbi decorum instituit. In tertia rerum qualitatum & personarum decora & discrimina. Item poematos genera & inuentores demonstrat. In quarta actores: formam agendi & quomodo consummata fuit docet. Et in quinta ad diligentem castigationem cohortatur" (fol. II*v*). In the ideas of the work, Badius sees almost everywhere three-way distinctions: "Pro descriptione poetice subnotandum est triplicem esse materiam scribentium, triplicem stylum, triplex potissimum decorum, triplicem qualitatem, triplicem finem & his similia" (*ibid.*). The three "matters" so distinguished are the true (which supplies the facts for history), the verisimilar (which supplies the arguments for comedy), and the fictional, which is neither true nor verisimilar (and which supplies the fables for poetry). It should be noted that the distinction is made as a gloss upon the "materiam" of line 38 and that it is derived from the *Rhetorica ad Herennium*, at that time ascribed to Cicero. But Badius goes on to say that there is another three-way division of matters, into the "sublime" or elevated, which involves gods, heroes, and kings; the "mediocre" or middling, which consists of the scientific information exploited in didactic poetry; and the "humble" or low, containing pastoral and trivial subjects. To each of these is adapted a style and a form of verse: result, a three-way distinction of styles (also called "characteres, figurae, genera dicendi") and of meters. This is of course the commonplace rhetorical division of the Middle Ages, epitomized in the "wheel of Vergil."[32] The three "decorums" are of things, of words, and of persons; the three "qualities" of verse correspond to the three styles, the elevated, the middle, and the low; the three kinds of poems are the narrative, the dramatic, and the mixed; the three ends of the poet are to bring profit, to please, or to do both at the same time (fol. VIII*v*).

It is significant that the first statement of this set of trilogies should come in the author's preface to his commentary and that the second, expanded

---

31 I quote Badius passages from the edition of Paris, Gerlier, 1500, the earliest edition that I know; all references are to this edition.

32 *Ibid.*, fols. VIII–VIII*v* (on the "wheel of Vergil," cf. E. Faral, *Les Arts poétiques du XII* et du XIII* siècle* [Paris: Champion, 1923], p. 87).

statement should appear very early in his remarks on the text. For the schematism is in every sense prior to his interpretation of Horace. His standard procedure will be to wait for some point in the text where a key word (such as the "materiam" of line 38) gives him the opportunity to exploit one of his distinctions and then to develop it fully in connection with that word. Thus the "In *verbis* etiam *tenuis*" of line 46 becomes the occasion for expatiating on the "low" style and for citing what Cicero has to say about it: "De hac re ita dicit Cicero in de oratore" (fol. X). And the passage beginning with line 112—

Si dicentis erunt *fortunis* absona dicta

—leads to a long development on the decorum of persons, prefaced by the remark "Quia decorum personarum imprimis obseruandum est ostendit quo pacto id seruabitur," and continuing to the discussion of the fortune or condition of life of various kinds of characters, their age, and their country (fol. XIX*v*).

This matter of decorum is indeed central to the whole conception of the work, even more so than it is in Horace. For if Badius separates his ideas on poetry into small groups of three, he must find some device for collecting them together again into larger units, and that device is precisely the principle of decorum. Decorum accepted in this broader sense is really little more than a principle of appropriateness, similar to that which we have seen in Acron. Once again, Badius' ideas fall into a major group of three, as he sees all things dividing themselves according to the major distinction of the "elevated," the "middle," and the "low." One may represent these relationships in a rough tabular form as follows:

	Elevated	Middle	Low
Matters:	gods, heroes, kings	information	shepherds
Styles:	*sublime*	*mediocre*	*humile*
	altisonum		*tenue*
Meters:	hexameter	pentameter	iambic
Genres:	epic, tragedy	didactic	comedy, pastoral

The table is inexact and incomplete, since certain subsequent refinements of the ideas necessitate a crossing over from column to column. But it does represent the fundamental concept in Badius' thinking: a "high" genre such as the epic or tragedy will present persons of a certain kind, each of whom has the proper traits of character (hence the decorum of persons), speaking or spoken of in a style fitted to them (hence the decorum of words), in verse suited to them both in its general rhythmic patterns and in the structure of its sounds. Moreover, these persons will engage in actions appropriate to their characters and stations (hence the decorum of things). All but two of the smaller trilogies (manner of representation and end of the poet) are combined in this set of major relationships.

The *Ars poetica* is thus read as if it were part of the classical-medieval rhetorical tradition, which culminated in the rigorous hierarchy of the literary types as it is symbolized in the "wheel of Vergil." What is more, Badius introduces other essentially rhetorical distinctions which complete the transformation of the Horatian text. As the above table shows, the "res-verba" division is made to apply in a very real way, "matters" being the "res" and "styles" the "verba." Such a statement as the following, offered as explanation of lines 310–11—

> Rem tibi Socraticae poterunt ostendere chartae:
> Verbaque provisam rem non invita sequentur

—may be cited in corroboration: "Poema enim constat ex re & oratione. Res autem ex philosophia originem trahit vt praecepta contineat. Oratio in grammatica & rhetorica dicitur" (fol. XXXVI*v*). There is, thus, no separate art of poetry, merely a combination of philosophy, grammar, and rhetoric. The rhetorical categories of invention, disposition, and elocution are introduced at the very outset, in the conclusion to the first set of remarks: "Three things are therefore necessary at first: The careful consideration and invention of the whole matter; an economy or disposition fitted with deliberation, for the events to be narrated will be placed otherwise in a poem than in a history; and their embellishment ("exornatio") in accordance with their arrangement."[33] As for the rhetorical ideas of Cicero and Quintilian, they are introduced whenever Badius can find a plausible reason for bringing them in. For example, the requirement of unity stated in line 23 elicits the following remark: "Apta autem digressio tribus modis fieri ex quarto Quintiliani colligitur"; and Quintilian's enumeration follows (fol. V). Where Horace speaks of the danger of falling into obscurity when brevity is sought (lines 25–26), Badius finds the antidote in Cicero: "De apta tamen breuitate non nihil dicemus de qua Cicero in rhetorice veteri de enarratione loquens ita inquit . . ."; and the quotation follows (fol. VII).

As for the medieval ideas incorporated into the commentary, those of Diomedes and Donatus (which I call "medieval" since they were the standard sources of ideas about poetry throughout the Middle Ages), they frequently come into the discussion even when there is no justification in the Horatian text itself. Badius opens his prologue with a number of general matters, among them the title, "Quinti Horatii Flacci ad Pisones de arte poetica institutio"; "to understand this," he goes on to say, "let us listen to Diomedes. Poetics, he says, is a metrical structure of narration of true and false things, composed in proper rhythm or meter, suitable for pleasure

---

[33] *Ibid.*, fol. IIII*v*: "Tria ergo primum sunt necessaria. Materiae totius excogitatio atque inuentio. Excogitate apta oeconomia seu dispositio. aliter enim in poemate: aliter in historia locabuntur res narrande & disposite exornatio: in qua elegantie & decori habenda est ratio."

or utility."[34] Much later, after he has finished his gloss on lines 189–201, he adds: "Since we have promised to speak of the decorum of comedies and tragedies a little later, let us now set forth a few things about their description and parts, taken from Diomedes"; and he writes over three full pages, collecting together all of Diomedes' dicta about the dramatic forms, which, essentially, have nothing to do with Horace.[35] Similarly, after his remarks on lines 275 ff., treating the history of tragedy and comedy, he adds what Donatus has to say on the same subject: "With respect to the invention of satires, tragedies, and comedies, let us recite a few things found in the grammarian Donatus. . . ."[36] Obviously, the intention is no longer merely to provide elucidation for Horace's text, but to use the commentary as a repository for everything that Badius knew or could find about the art of poetry, to transform it into a vade mecum of the kind which the Renaissance found so useful.

One final remark: The tendency found in Acron and Porphyrion to reduce Horace to a set of precepts is here carried to its inevitable conclusion. For whereas the earlier commentators had only occasionally labeled their remarks as "precepts," Badius constantly and invariably supplies a "regula" at the end of each section of the commentary. There are twenty-five such rules corresponding to the first twenty-five of the twenty-six portions of the text. Were one to assemble them in the order in which they are given, one would have a complete epitome of Badius' interpretations of the *Ars poetica*.

The net result of the addition of these four pre-Cinquecento commentaries to the text of Horace was to make of that text something very special for Cinquecento readers. The latent rhetorical characteristics of the *Ars poetica* had been made explicit and stated overtly by the two earlier commentators. The two later ones had produced as further evidence of its rhetorical character a number of parallel quotations from classical rhetoricians and had completed the rhetorical distinctions. Moreover, they had made of their commentaries compendiums of all knowledge about the poetic art, so that Horace's work was no longer a theory of poetry, but the theory of poetry, the summum of all useful ideas about the art. Text and commentaries, taken together as they always were, provided for the Cinquecento reader an initiation to poetics—which was, let it not be forgotten, an initiation of a very special kind.

---

[34] *Ibid.*, fol. IIv: "Pro quo intelligendo audiamus Diomedem. Poetica inquit est ficte vereque narrationis congruenti rythmo vel pede composita: metrica structura ad vtilitatem voluptatemque accommodata."

[35] *Ibid.*, fol. XXVv: "Quia de comoediarum & tragoediarum decoro paulo post loqui polliciti sumus. Nunc de ipsarum descriptione & partibus pauca praemittemus ex Dyomede. . . ."

[36] *Ibid.*, fol. XXXIIIv: "Circa inuentionem satyrarum tragoediarum & comoediarum pauca ex Donato grammatico recitabimus. . . ."

QUATTROCENTO THEORISTS

During the Quattrocento, evidences that this Horatian-rhetorical mode of thinking about poetry was common are found in various documents. I shall cite here only a few cases, which are not in themselves directly related to the Horatian text but which show the continuation, into the humanistic period, of the standard medieval distinctions about the art of poetry. A brief example is found in the *In errores Antonii Raudensis adnotationes* of Lorenzo Valla (d. 1457). Antonio had provided the following definition: "Clamare, deinde mouere tragoedias, est mouere exclamationes & exclamare." To which Lorenzo objects thus:

> And he cites the example of Quintilian; but neither in Quintilian nor in Cicero is it found in this sense. Rather, [it means] to make things more terrible and shameful by the use of the right words, which is the function of the writers of tragedy, who always speak of sad and terrible things; just as, on the contrary, to make comedies or *comoediari* is used by Aristophanes and certain other Greeks to mean "to speak ridiculously or bitingly."

To Antonio's remarks on comedy he offers these corrections:

> The author seems not to know that the "toga" is the dress of the Romans just as the "pallium" is the dress of the Greeks; and that the "togatae" were comedies which were not translated from the Greek but composed by Romans and Latins. . . . Indeed, all or nearly all the works of the best comic writers, Caecilius, Plautus, and Terence, were translated from the Greek; and therefore Antonio should not have have said that Plautus was the greatest "inventor" of comedies, . . . for certainly Afranius and others like him are much more properly called "inventors" than Caecilius, Plautus, and Terence, since they themselves invented and did not translate.

What is significant here is the reference to Quintilian and Cicero, the simple distinction between tragedy and comedy, and the meaning attached to the rhetorical term "invention."[37]

In the *De regno et regis institutione, libri IX* of Francesco Patrizi, Bishop of Gaeta (d. 1494), Horatian notions of the pleasure and utility of poetry are crossed with Platonic ideas of moral criteria. The utility of comedy is also made to comprise its usefulness for teaching of the language, another medieval conception. The pertinent passage occurs in Book II, chapter IX,

---

[37] In *Opera* (1543 ed.), p. 399: "Affertque exemplum Quintiliani, sed neque apud Quintilianum, neque apud Ciceronem in hanc significatiorem inuenitur. Imò rem uerbis atrocem magis, & indignam efficere, quale est opus tragicorum de rebus atrocibus semper, moestisque loquentium: sicut e contrario, comoedias agere, siue comoediari, pro ridicule, ac dicaciter loqui apud Aristophanem, & alios nonnullos Graecorum"; and p. 400: "Autor uidetur nescire togam esse uestem Romanorum, ut pallium, uestem Graecorum. Et togatas esse comoedias, non è Graeco traductas, sed à Romanis, Latinisque compositas. . . . Etenim omnes, aut ferè omnes summorum comicorum libri è Graeco traducti sunt, Caecilij, Plauti, Terentij: eoque non fuit Raudensi dicendum, fuisse Plautum maximum fabularum inuentorem, nam . . . certe Afranius, & alij similes magis inuentores, quàm Caecilius, Plautus, Terentius dicendi sunt, qui ipsi inuenerunt non transtulerunt."

"A Futuro Rege Qui Scriptores Legendi Discendique sint, quíue negligendi":

It is not without utility that one may also read tragedies, if morality is respected in them; for they carry weight, and have elegance of expression and gravity of thought, especially Euripides. . . . In the same way the writers of comedy are also to be read. For they nourish everyday conversation, and by the propriety and the elegance of their words they make the art of speaking more polished and richer. But to conclude briefly, individual poets, even if they are read with a certain pleasure, have certain virtues of their own, and a certain wonderful grace which is not at all unsuitable to the dignity of a king.

Obscene poets must be absolutely rejected, because they corrupt good mores and imbue the soul with wickedness. . . . But let us listen to Plato, who orders the poets to write those things which will make men good and will teach them that the good are happy and the bad are unhappy even if they are rich and lucky.[38]

A much more complete representation of this Horatian-rhetorical point of view is contained in Giovanni Pontano's dialogue, *Actius,* already mentioned as one of those documents which classified poetry with history. On the one hand, the dialogue is full of rhetorical distinctions applied to poetry: both history and poetry fall within the deliberative and demonstrative categories of oratory; each proposes as its ends "ut doceat, delectet, moveat"; the functions of both are divided into invention, disposition, and elocution; the personal goal of "victory" for the orator is very similar to that of "fame" or "glory" for the poet. On the other hand, differences between poetry and either history or rhetoric are usually explained in terms of distinctions found in Horace or in his commentators: poetry is more studied and elegant in its vocabulary and rhythms, especially in the use of new words; history is restricted to the truth, whereas poetry treats as well "probabilia, ficta," and sometimes things which are in no wise "veri similia"; history follows a natural order of narration, while poetry cultivates the "in medias res" beginning. The language of the orator is fitted to the forum and the senate; that of the poet must display a special kind of magnificence, elevation, and excellence:

The end of both orater and poet is to move and carry away the listener. Indeed to what end, I ask, to what end is directed this capacity to move and to carry away and the extraordinary attention that both men give to it? The orator

[38] *De regno* (1567 ed.), pp. 56*v*–57: "Non sine vtilitate etiam leguntur Tragoedi, si mores in tuto fuerint, habent enim pondus, ac nitorem verborum, & sententiarum grauitatem, pręcipuè Euripides. . . . Eodem etiam modo Comici legendi sunt. Alunt siquidem quotidianum sermonem, & proprietate elegantiáque verborum eloquentiam nitidiorem uberiorémque reddunt. Sed vt breuiter concludam, singuli poëtae, si cùm delectu quodam leguntur, proprias quasdam virtutes habent, & mirificam quandam gratiam, quae à regia dignitate nequaquam aliena est. . . . Obscoeni poëtae omnino negligendi sunt, bonos enim mores corrumpunt, & animum nequitiis imbuunt. . . . Nos autem Platonem audiamus, qui ea poëtas scribere iubet, quae viros bonos efficiant, doceantǫue bonos beatos esse, malos verò miseros, etiam si fortunati ac diuites essent."

clearly wishes to persuade the judge, the poet wishes to obtain the admiration of the listener and the reader, since the first strives for victory, the second for fame and glory. . . . The poet will be completely cheated of his end unless he has aroused and impressed admiration in the soul of the listener or the reader, by means of which he will acquire fame and reverence.

Such a passage as this is almost completely Ciceronian in tone; taken together with the other ideas of the text, it demonstrates to what extent rhetoric and poetics were combined under the aegis of Horace.[39]

What Pietro Ricci (Petrus Crinitus) had to offer in the way of theoretical statements in his *Libri de poetis Latinis* (1505) was very slight. His work is a series of notices on the Latin poets, containing brief remarks on the poets' place and time of birth, family, studies, protectors and friends, the genres which they practiced, their characters, lists of their works, some ancient opinions about them. If it has any interest at all for us, it is because for each poet passing estimates of his work are offered, usually in the form of epithets or concise critical formulas. In these occasional attempts at practical criticism, the standards of judgment remain essentially the same as those of the Middle Ages, reflecting the tradition which I am here discussing. Plautus excelled, he says, "scribendi elegantia & salibus"; Pacuvius cultivated the "amplum ac sonorum dicendi genus"; Terence was perfect "sermonis elegantia & proprietate," and moreover, according to the opinion of Donatus, "he controlled the emotions in such a way that he neither swells to the magnitude of tragedy nor descends to the level of simple history." Sextus Turpilius is praised for his "senarii de officio & ratione uiuendi," Publius Syrius for his "sententiarum grauitatem atque singularem elegantiam" (a standard formula used also for other writers), Horace because "plenus est iucunditatis & gratiae." The Horatian ends appear in such a phrase as this, applied to Manilius: "ut magis instruere: ac docere uideatur: quam delectare."[40] Brief though they may be, statements of this kind are indicative of the current ways of thinking about poetic works and of the persistence, into the sixteenth century, of older orientations toward the art.

POMPONIO GAURICO (1510)

The earliest formal commentary on the *Ars poetica* in the Cinquecento, as far as I have been able to discover, was that of Pomponio Gaurico

---

[39] In *I Dialoghi*, ed. Previtera (1943), pp. 193–94, 202, 232; and p. 233: "Utriusque etiam, oratoris ac poetae officium est movere et flectere auditorem; verum quonam, quo, inquam, haec et commotio et flexio et maximum utriusque in hoc ipso studium? Oratoris scilicet ut persuadeat iudici, poetae ut admirationem sibi ex audiente ac legente comparet, cum ille pro victoria nitatur, hic pro fama et gloria. . . . poeta fine omnino defraudabitur suo nisi in audientis ac legentis animo pepererit infixeritque admirationem, per quam sit famam venerationemque assecuturus."

[40] *De poetis Latinis* (1505), pp. Aiii, Aiv, Av, Avv: "ita temperauit affectus ut neque ad tragicam magnitudinem intumescat: neque abiciatur ad historicam," Avi, Bv, D2.

(*ca.* 1482–1530). Published with the text of Horace in 1541 under the title *Pomponius Gauricus super Arte poetica Horatii*, the commentary alone had been previously printed as the *De Arte poetica* in an undated edition which must go back to about 1510.[41] Gaurico declares in his dedication to Francesco Pucci that he does not wish to give a word-for-word gloss on the text in the fashion of the grammarians, but to "collect together the precepts themselves and to tell what he himself [Horace] had warned against."[42] Nevertheless, he does not reduce the text to a set of precepts as certain of his predecessors had done. Instead, what he gives is little more than a running paraphrase or prosification of the original text. In that paraphrase, little is added to the ideas of the text, little that might be said to be the contribution of Gaurico. What he does contribute follows the lines previously indicated in this chapter. He emphasizes what he thinks to be the most important ideas by putting brief formulas in the margin, such as "De speciebus concipiendis," "De totius operis aequabilitate," "De proposito," "De stilo." These provide a kind of outline for his reading of Horace. For lines 38 ff., the marginalia read "De Inuentione," "De Dispositione," "De Elocutione," indicating that Gaurico is once again effecting the conflation between Horace and the standard rhetorical approach. Other significant remarks are found in such formulas as "Numeros ad materiam accomodandos," "De Comoediae Tragoediaeque decoro," "De optima Ratione compositionis," and "Quid in Comoedia Tragoediaque necessarium." In the text itself, Gaurico tends to reduce all Horace's suggestions to a universal principle of appropriateness. Frequently, this "appropriateness" is to a norm of nature; thus the comment on the first lines: "as for what is said about poets and painters, that they may do what they please, this is valid to the extent that they do not depart from nature."[43] Or the remarks on style relevant to lines 24 ff.: "That style turns out to be the best which will imitate the nature of the thing treated."[44] A somewhat longer passage, on the "Sumite materiam uestris" of line 38, further circumscribes this "nature" and indicates the essential orientations of the commentary:

You will have to find a subject matter of this kind: not absurd, not difficult, not far removed from daily usage, but appropriate, susceptible of ornament, and such that you will know it thoroughly and be capable of sustaining it to the very end. If it is such, you will understand better in what manner the disposition is to

41 The *De Arte poetica*, the first edition, prints on page Bivv a "Sanctio" given by Pope Julius II; since Julius was Pope between 1503 and 1513, this would presumably be the ten-year period during which the edition was printed.

42 *De Arte poetica* (*ca.* 1510 ed.), p. A: "sed tantummodo praecepta ipsa colligerem: & quid ille commonuerit: enarrarem."

43 *Ibid.,* p. Av: "Nam quod aiunt Pictoribus ac Poetis licere quod uelint: eatenus licet: quatenus a natura non recedant."

44 *Ibid.,* pp. Av–Aii: "optimum illum uideri stilum: qui eius rei de qua agitur naturam imitabitur."

be treated and you will be able to express the matter in words much more appropriately.[45]

At other times, "appropriateness" merely means following the norms of decorum; for example, the use of comic verse for a tragic subject would be like an impropriety of dress (p. Aiiv). A few isolated passages are worthy of attention: (1) the "prodesse" of line 333 is explained as meaning "ad institutiones uitaeque praecepta referamus," thus putting the emphasis upon moral teaching (p. Bv); (2) the pendant "delectare" is made to depend upon verisimilitude, "if we invent things which make for pleasure, the things invented must appear as similar to the truth as possible; lest by chance you may suppose that you must invent things which cannot be in any way believed to have happened";[46] (3) the end of the lyric is also made one of utility, in the following terms: "ut hominibus uiam ad uirtutem significaremus: Regum gratiam aucuparemur" (p. Biii). The main directions of Gaurico's development of the Horatian text would thus seem to be toward a pointing up of the rhetorical tendencies of the *Ars poetica* and their association with Ciceronian rhetorical principles, toward an extension or even exaggeration of the idea of appropriateness, and toward an insistence upon the conception of nature held by the audience addressed.

During the same years, Vittore Fausto published his brief *De comoedia libellus* (1511). He declares that it will be an expansion upon Donatus and Diomedes, and it soon becomes clear that this expansion will take the form of a few references to Aristotle and some crossing with the rhetorical mode. The *Ars poetica* does not enter directly into cause, but some of the positions of the earlier commentators are approximated. For example, the "res-verba" distinction is present in the following statement, in which Fausto is telling how the goals of comedy may be achieved: "Since poets used to try to bring this about with things and with words, they will have two ways of doing so. . . ." The two ways refer to types of plot. For the rest, Fausto's treatise is concerned with the seven kinds of words which cause laughter, with the importance of stage action and apparatus, with the appropriateness of intonation to action, and with historical matters.[47]

Le selvette of Niccolò Liburnio (1513) is a collection of short dialogues on sundry matters. In the first one, the art of poetry is discussed in what is essentially another defence of poesy. The poet is said to require great

[45] *Ibid.*, p. Aii: "Inuenienda uero uobis scribendi materia erit: non absurda: non aspera: non longius a cotidiana consuetudine remota: sed que conueniat: que ornamenta suscipiat: quam et uos pulcherrime cognitam habeatis et constanter substinere ualeatis. Sic enim quemadmodum dispositio tractanda sit melius intelligetis: et rem ipsam multo conuenientius eloqui poteritis."

[46] *Ibid.*, p. Bii: "si que ad uoluptatem faciunt confingemus: hec que confingentur ueri simillima uideri debebunt: ne forte putetis fingenda uobis: ea que facta fuisse: nullo modo credi possunt."

[47] *De comoedia libellus* (1511), p. AA3: "Quandoquidem illud in primis poetae rebus, & uerbis efficere conabantur, ipsa quidem re bifariam. . . ."

erudition, especially in Greek literature; he must be adept in language (acquired through art) and in subject matters (acquired through extensive reading). To achieve perfection in a work he must combine art, nature, and diligence. Horace's precepts for the comportment of the poet are cited, and various models for the writer are proposed, including Dante, Petrarch, Antonio Tibaldeo, Sannazaro, and Bembo. Follows at last a long series of the conventional arguments in defence of the art. The "Selvetta terza" urges the poet to imitate earlier models, as Dante imitated Vergil and Vergil imitated Homer. Both "materia" and "stile" may benefit from such imitation. The ends of all poetic writing, as in Horace, are to profit and to please: "for the first of these it is necessary to read ... a great mass of ancient authors; for the second, in whatever you write, it is necessary to weave so lovely and elegant a garland of varied flowers that whoever is tricked into assaying it with the eyes of the mind may derive from it pleasure and utility, in a way which will teach good and happy living."[48]

As a matter of record, it should be pointed out that Matteo Bonfini's *In Horatianis operibus centum et quindecim annotationes* appeared at about this time, although the exact date is unknown. Bonfini's annotations on the *Ars poetica* are, however, disappointing, since they are exclusively grammatical and lexicographical in character and throw no light upon the interpretation of the text as a theoretical document.

In the 1517 Aldine edition of Terence there appeared for the first time a prefatory letter entitled "In Terentium epistola," which has since been attributed to Andrea Navagero.[49] It is an interesting letter because it judges Terence in terms of the criteria supplied by Horace and is thus a kind of essay in practical Horatian criticism. The author proceeds on the basis of a comparison between Terence and Plautus, indicating throughout the reasons for Terence's superiority. In language, first Terence excels in "elegantia," is "cultior," "limatior." These are the standard terms of rhetorical criticism. In the general construction of his comedies, Terence satisfies all the requirements of Horace:

> The comedies of Plautus often gape at the seams and do not have sufficient cohesion. Those of Terence are all so well woven within themselves, make so complete a unity out of all the elements, that nothing could be more completely realized than those compositions, nothing more perfect. And this is precisely the thing in which all poets and writers must principally excel, and which demands the greatest art—if indeed there be any others. For that decorum which is to be so carefully observed in all things, if it be not observed in dramatic compositions,

---

[48] *Le selvette* (1513), pp. 9–14v and pp. 33v–34: "alla prima fa di mestieri leggere . . . selue d'authori antichi; alla seconda, in cio tu iscriui, bisogna de fiori uarii tessere si uaga & pulita ghirlanda; che chiunque s'inueschi d'assagiarla co gli occhi dello'ntelletto, posse dillettatione & utilita sciugharne, con modo maestreuole al buono & beato viuere."

[49] For the basis of the attribution, see Navagero, *Opera omnia* (Padua: Volpi-Camino, 1718), p. 427. On the 1517 ed., see A. Firmin-Didot, *Alde Manuce et l'Hellénisme à Venise* (Paris: Firmin-Didot, 1875), pp. 465–66.

where everything must be contrived appropriately to each personage, then nothing at all is accomplished.[50]

Furthermore, of the two possible types of humor, that of actions and that of words, Terence cultivates the former and hence appeals to a superior audience.

GIOVANNI BRITANNICO DA BRESCIA (1518)

To approximately the same period belongs another extensive commentary on the *Ars poetica*, that of Giovanni Britannico da Brescia (Ioannes Britannicus Brixianus). Britannico flourished toward the end of the fifteenth century and produced commentaries on various Latin authors; the standard biographical dictionaries give the date of his death as 1510, but Tiraboschi (Venice, 1796 ed., VI[3], 992) cites a document by him dated November 26, 1518. I do not know when the commentary on Horace was written or first appeared; but since the first edition that I have been able to discover is that of Milan, Scinzenzeler, 1518 (*Q. Horatij Flacci poemata*), I am discussing the commentary at this chronological position. It is a conventional commentary in every respect, frequently calling, as did others of the time, upon Acron, Porphyrion, Diomedes, and Donatus. It makes no mention of Badius and may possibly be earlier than his exegesis. It goes beyond most other early glosses, however, in the extent of its references to a multitude of classical writers; Plato, Cicero, Quintilian, Pliny, Valerius Flaccus, Vitruvius, Vergil, and Homer are called upon frequently for examples and explanations. One realizes that the whole richness of humanistic erudition is being brought to bear upon the explanation of the *Ars poetica*. What emerges is in a sense disappointing, since few new critical orientations are discovered. Britannico continues to make a systematic reduction of the Horatian text to a series of precepts, and most of these precepts repeat the traditional rhetorical admonitions. The undercurrent of thinking in terms of invention, disposition, and elocution rises to the surface at the proper places: when, for example, he wishes to provide remarks on the "Rem" of line 310—

Rem tibi Socraticae poterunt ostendere chartae

—he says: "Thus he indicates that the invention of the materials is necessary above all else in the poet." Or with respect to the "ordinis" of line 42 he defines: "for order is the disposition and distribution of the materials which shows what is to be put in each place." The "verba" of line 311 (following the "rem" of line 310) provides the occasion for a definition of elocution: "for elocution (as Cicero teaches in the *Rhetorica*) is the fitting

---

50 (1517 ed.), p. a2: "Hyant nonnunquam, neque satis cohaerent Plauti Comoediae. ita omnia Terentij inter se nexa: ita ex omnibus unum quoddam conficitur: ut nihil aptius illius fabulis, nihil magis fieri ad unguem possit. atqui hoc id est, quod praecipue praestari & ab poetis, & ab scriptoribus omnibus debeat: ac maximam, si aliud quippiam, artem exigat. iam decorum illud, quod in omnibus tantopere custudiendum rebus est: in fabulis uero, ubi congrua unicuique personae effingenda sunt omnia: nisi seruetur, nihil prorsus fiat."

of proper words and of sententiae to the invention."[51] What Britannico says in the sentences immediately following shows that he is also making the usual association of these elements with the "res-verba" distinction: "For every poem," he says, "consists of words and things. The things are these same moral precepts, and the words are the diction itself."[52]

What is perhaps a more distinctive contribution on Britannico's part is his development of a dichotomy between the parts of poems providing pleasure and utility to the audience. Pleasure is a product of both "verba" and "res": of "verba," insofar as pleasantness and elegance of language are delightful in themselves (of the "dulci" in line 343 he says: "iucunditatem, elegantiamque sermonis intelligit: quae multum delectat," after which he states that it is another expression of the "delectare" in line 333); of "res," insofar as a "natural" and "verisimilar" representation of objects is pleasurable. The conditions here imposed are important; for if Horace's monster is ridiculous rather than pleasurable, it is because it is "contra naturam," and however fictional and imaginary the ornaments of a poem may be, they must nevertheless be like the truth. Another principle is really involved here: that part of "res" which is imitated from nature—e.g., the characters assigned to people according to decorum—must actually be faithfully copied from nature in a consistent and appropriate way; whereas that part which is "feigned" or created by the poet must be "like" nature. Both the real and the fictional must impress the audience as being true if they are to give it pleasure. Utility, however, is a product of "res" only. It consists in the lessons to be learned by the audience from the moral precepts and the moral examples presented by the poet. Hence, it is not sufficient for the poet to imitate the mores of men; he must limit himself to the imitation of "good" mores. Britannico interprets "morataque recte" of line 319 not as meaning "having correct mores" but as meaning "quae bonis moribus sit instructa: quae a turpitudine sit aliena."[53]

Into this central scheme Britannico has no difficulty in fitting the standard elements of Horatian theory and of the traditional interpretations. Simplicity or unity of plot is merely a reflection of the natural oneness of the materials imitated (v. pp. CXIIIv–CXIV). In the same way, the universal principle of appropriateness is merely a transposition into literary terms of the notion that things of the same kind are assorted by nature and that such things as would not be put together by nature must not be

[51] *Poemata* (Milan, 1518 ed.), p. CXXXVI: "sicque ostendit in poeta necessariam imprimis esse rei inuentionem"; p. CXVIv: "Est autem ordo dispositio & distributio rerum: qui demonstrat: quid quibusque locis sit collocandum," and cf. p. CXXXIv: "Per seriem igitur intellige ordinem & rerum dispositionem, quae distribuit quid quibusque locis sit collocandum"; and p. CXXXVI: "est enim elocutio: ut docet Cicero in rhetoricis idoneorum uerborum & sententiarum ad inuentionem accommodatio."

[52] *Ibid.*, p. CXXXVI: "omne enim poema rebus & uerbis constat: res enim sunt ipsa praecepta: uerba uero ipsa oratio."

[53] *Ibid.*, p. CXXXVIIv; pp. CXIV–CXVv, especially the last page: "debet enim fictio artificiosa naturam imitari"; p. CXXXVI.

combined by art. Therefore the three styles, each of which assembles coherent and consonant elements, and the interdiction against crossing or mixing them: literary "species" are as distinct and discrete as natural species. The theory of the literary genres is rounded out by prescription of the subject matters and of the meters for each. Thus, as compared with earlier or with contemporary commentators, Britannico would seem to place greater emphasis on the relationships between poetry and nature, although he by no means decreases the time and attention devoted to rhetorical matters.

The *Epistola* of Andrea Navagero, cited a few pages back, had been dedicated to Pietro Bembo. In 1525, Bembo himself published his *Prose della volgar lingua*. This is essentially a linguistic document, as its title indicates; but it belongs to the present inquiry in two ways: first, because it was the earliest important document in the quarrel over Dante which raged later in the century, and second, because when he speaks of the relationship between language and poetry, Bembo does so in terms of the current Horatian tradition. In Book II, for example, Bembo discusses the choice and disposition of words to be used for any given subject matter by referring to the three styles:

> If one is speaking of a high subject matter, the words to be chosen should be grave, elevated, sonorous, clear, luminous; if of a low and vulgar subject matter, they should be light, plain, humble, popular, quiet; if of a subject midway between these two, one should speak with middling and temperate words and ones which tend to move as little as possible in the direction of the one or the other extreme. It is necessary, nevertheless, to use discretion in the observance of these rules, and above all to avoid satiety by varying occasionally both grave words with temperate ones and temperate words with light ones. ... Nevertheless, a most general and universal rule is that, in each one of these manners and styles, we must choose the purest, the cleanest, the clearest, the most beautiful and agreeable words possible and bring them to our compositions.[54]

In Bembo's linguistic theory, styles and words exist in self-determined categories, with the only reference to an external context being to the general types of subject matters which they express. As for his dicta on Dante, they will be treated in the appropriate chapter.

Like Navagero's *Epistola*, Mario Equicola's *Libro de natura de amore* of 1525 may serve as an example of an application in practical criticism of the

<hr />

[54] *Prose* (1525 ed.), p. xxiiiv: "Da scieglere adunque sono li uoci; se di materia grande si ragiona; graui, alte, sonanti, apparenti, luminose: se di bassa et uolgare; lieui, piane, dimesse, popolari, chete: se di mezzana tra queste due: medesimamente con uoci mezzane et temperate, et lequali meno all'uno et all'altro pieghino di questi due termini che si puo. È di mestiero nondimeno in queste medesime regole seruar modo, et schifare sopra tutto la satieta uariando alle uolte et le uoci graui con alcuna temperata, et le temperate con alcuna leggiera. . . . Tuttafiata generalissima et uniuersale regola è in ciascuna di queste maniere et stili le piu pure, le piu monde, le piu chiare sempre, le piu belle et piu grate uoci scieglere et arrecare alle nostre compositioni, che si possa."

Horatian and rhetorical principles which are here occupying us. The occasion for such an application comes in the first book, where Equicola is discussing the poets who have treated of love. In his remarks on Guittone d'Arezzo he speaks of the pleasure afforded by poets through the use of music and rhythms, and Guido Cavalcanti is praised for the everyday flavor of his diction. Petrarch seems to occupy his high position in Italian poetry largely because he added to Tuscan many words from other regions of Italy, and Boccaccio because (like Lucian and Apuleius) he wrote poetically in prose and "embraced delightful poetry and beautiful materials." Most of Equicola's critical remarks, though, concern the work of Jacopo Calandra of Mantua, in connection with whom he states a number of critical principles. He speaks of the difficult task of the poet who must "delight and move with ornamented language" and of the remarkable talent required to "discover, and to take care to dispose and order well, whatever he invents." Even if invention and disposition are provided by nature, the poet will fail to delight and move unless he be a master of diction; and this requires erudition, study, labor, art. "The invention may be as beautiful as you please; without ornament it is a mass of gold that does not shine." To achieve ornament, the poet must know many things, cultivate exquisite sententiae, tend to the propriety of words; above all, he must choose words in common usage and those which will please the ear. All these qualities are found in Calandra. In his *Aura* he observes the decorum of persons throughout; above all, his style displays great virtues: words purely and properly derived from Latin, well-chosen diction, a great impression of naturalness and perfect rhythms.[55] In the last analysis, all of Equicola's criteria reduce to matters of language, and he is almost as exclusively concerned with the "volgar lingua" as was Bembo.

Another work essentially linguistic in character is Niccolò Liburnio's *Le tre fontane* of the following year, 1526. Liburnio studies the language of Dante, Petrarch, and Boccaccio, after having made a preliminary statement to the effect that for the poet as for the orator language is fitted to materials on the basis of the three styles. He debates at length—as the commentators on Horace had so frequently done—the question of art versus nature in the work of the poet, citing Plato's *Ion* and Cicero's *Pro Archia* on the side of nature. Of the five parts of oratory which he distinguishes—invention, disposition, elocution, memory, and pronunciation—he accords most time to elocution. The reasons are clear, for this is the part which is most admirable, which is involved in the three styles, and which demands the greatest application. Of the three styles, Vergil is cited as the consummate master; the opinion of the Middle Ages endures. The advice to young writers is to learn thoroughly all Tuscan words and to cultivate all the best authors of the past, who will provide them with invention as well as with

---

55 *Libro de natura de amore* (1525), pp. 3v–5v, 39: "la inuentione quanto uoi bella, senza ornamento e una massa d'oro che non risplende."

elocution. Cicero and Quintilian and Horace are cited as authorities for this opinion.[56]

In the light of these last documents, it is perhaps not fortuitous that Giovan Giorgio Trissino should have published his Italian translation of Dante's *De vulgari eloquentia* in 1529. Clearly, we are in a period of intense interest in problems of language and especially the problem of the Italian language. Dante's *De la volgare eloquenzia* comes appropriately just a few years after Bembo's *Prose della volgar lingua*. Moreover, for readers of the time, it was a contemporary document. Many of them believed that Trissino himself had written it—no version of Dante's text had previously been printed—and was merely trying to gain authority for his ideas by assigning them to Dante. What Dante had to say, besides, sounded so much like what writers in these years were saying that it did not fall at all strangely upon the ears of contemporaries. The basis of Dante's treatment of poetry is a division of language into three levels, the "illustre," the "mediocre," and the "humile," which conform to three kinds of subject matter, the tragic, the comic, and the elegiac. It should be noted that these are kinds of materials, not literary genres, and that the meanings attached to the terms are different from the conventional ones. The tragic style, for example, is adapted to poems about war, about love, and about virtue:

> It appears certain that we use the tragic style when the gravity of the sententiae and the loftiness of the verse and the elevation of the constructions and the excellence of the words all are assorted to one another; but because . . . it has already been proved that the highest things are worthy of the highest, and this style, which we call the tragic, seems to be the highest of the styles, therefore those things which we have already distinguished as demanding to be sung in the highest manner must be sung in this style only: that is, safety, love, and virtue.[57]

Poetry itself is defined as "a rhetorical fiction [or invention] set to music"; it may be written in any language, but that composed in the "regulated" classical languages is the best, and that composed in the vulgar tongues will achieve excellence to the degree to which it imitates the other. This way of thinking in terms of the three styles and of the subject matters to which they belong, this tendency to regard poetry as a kind of rhetoric whose problems are essentially linguistic, would of course sound very familiar to the reader of the 1520's.

AULO GIANO PARRASIO (1531)

To the same decade of the twenties should probably be attributed Aulo Giano Parrasio's *In Q. Horatii Flacci Artem poeticam commentaria*, pub-

---

[56] *Le tre fontane* (1526), pp. *iiv, 46, 64v.

[57] *De la volgare eloquenzia*, trans. Trissino (1529), pp. b viii–c and cv: "Appare certamente, che noi usiamo il stilo tragico, quando e la gravità de le sentenzie, e la superbia de i versi, e la elevazione de le construzioni, e la excellenzia de i vocabuli si concordano insieme; ma perche . . . gia è provato, che le cose somme sono degne de le somme, e questo stilo, che kiamiamo tragico, pare essere il sommo de i stili, però quelle cose, che havemo gia distinte doversi sommamente cantare, sono da essere in questo solo stilo cantate; cioè la salute, lo amore, e la virtù" (spelling modified; I have replaced Trissino's omegas by conventional o's).

lished posthumously by Bernardino Martirano in 1531. This is another full-scale commentary that was to be incorporated frequently into later editions of the Horatian text.[58] Parrasio's position is essentially the same as that of his predecessors, but there are certain notable departures that show some forward movement in the thinking about Horace's epistle. Before beginning his study of the text, Parrasio writes a lengthy introduction, which is in itself a kind of miniature *ars poetica*. He develops, on the basis of Plato, the theory of the divine origin of poetry, of the divine furor, of the poet as prophet. He may be alluding indirectly to Averroës' paraphrase of the *Poetics* when he insists that harmony and rhythm are natural or instinctive in man, that poetry was used originally for purposes of praising virtue and attacking vice, that the poet must form in advance a complete conception of the poem before beginning to write it.[59] From Quintilian he derives not only the idea that the poet must be a good man, but also that he must be "peritus" in an infinity of subjects. Both of these ideas are developed in passages which are interesting because they are so frequently re-echoed in later critical writing of the century. On the "goodness" of the poet: "First of all it is essential that the poet himself be a wise man, that he understand what things are proper to a good man. This he will not be able to do unless he be a good man himself, unless he himself abound in all the virtues, unless he have absorbed the whole of poetry, that is of wisdom, unless he lack all vices."[60] And on his infinite "knowledge":

It is necessary then that every poet be an expert on all matters, so that he may be able to speak copiously about everything. He must know well the customs of the various peoples, the usages, the laws, the details about maritime and inland cities, the descriptions of places, agriculture, the military art, the sayings and the acts of illustrious men; let him be expert with the stylus, erudite in geometry, learned in architecture and music, experienced as well in natural and moral science as in the art of writing, not ignorant of medicine. He must remember the opinions of lawyers, have certain knowledge of astrology and astronomy. But above all a knowledge of histories and of myths is necessary, and of everything that is related to grammar.[61]

[58] For references to some of these editions, see the Index to the Mills College check-list (note 4 above), s.v. Parrhasius, Aulus Janus. The date of Parrasio's death is commonly given as 1534 in the standard biographical dictionaries; but note that the dedication to the 1531 edition, by Martirano, refers to him as already dead.

[59] *Commentaria* (1531), pp. 1, 2, 6*v*; cf. Averroës (1481 ed.), p. f2*v*, p. f ("Omne itaque poema & omnis oratio poetica aut est uituperatio aut est laudatio"), p. g*v*.

[60] *Ibid.*, pp. 3–3*v*: "Ante omnia oportet ipsum poetam esse sapientem, quae boni uiri sint intelligat. quod non faciet, nisi ipse sit bonus, nisi omnibus abundet uirtutibus, nisi poeticam omnem, id est sapientiam imbiberit, careat uitijs"; cf. Quintilian, Bk. XII, ch. I.

[61] *Ibid.*, pp. 2*v*–3: "Quemcunque autem poetam rerum omnium peritum esse oportet, ut de una quaque re possit copiose dicere. Mores populorum, consuetudines, iura, terrestrium, maritimarumque cognitiones urbium, locorumque descriptiones, agriculturam, rem militarem, clarorum uirorum dicta factaque pernoscat, graphidos peritus sit, geometriae eruditus, architecturam edoctus, musicam sciat, scientiam cum naturae & morum, tum disserendi calleat, medicinae non ignaris, iurisconsultorum responsa teneat, astrologiam, coelique rationes compertas habeat. Nam historiarum, fabularumque cognitio, quaeque grammaticae copulantur, in primis sunt necessaria"; cf. Quintilian, Bk. I, ch. X.

Parrasio's introduction contains, moreover, other elements that reveal his attitudes toward poetry. He conceives of the end of poetry as being both rhetorical and moral: rhetorical insofar as it must "inflame the souls of men, extinguish wrath, arouse hate and sorrow, or lead them away from these same passions to gentleness and pity"; moral insofar as it must "invite men to good living by means of examples and reasoning, teach character and the passions, prescribe in a pleasant way what things are to be done."[62] The insistence, in the above paragraph concerning knowledge, on a mastery of grammar and, in this last citation, on the "pleasant way" is explained by Parrasio's stand on diction. For whereas most of his remarks so far have pertained to the poet and the effect of the poem upon the audience, when he actually does speak about the poem itself, he speaks of it largely in terms of diction. "Nothing," he says, "is as poetic as the diction." This emphasis will be apparent in the commentary itself; it is also prominent in the concluding section of the introduction, where he outlines Horace's general procedure. This procedure consists in dividing the work into two parts, the function of the first being to show what things are to be avoided ("uitanda ostendere") and of the second to prescribe what things are to be done ("sequenda praecipere"). Five precepts contain the essence of the first: (1) admit nothing inappropriate, lest there be discrepancies in the invention and a lack of total harmony; (2) avoid placing things where they do not belong, or introducing digressions or superfluous ornaments; (3) do not pursue the various kinds of style ("dicendi figuras") to the point of falling into the opposite vices; (4) in the search for variety, so important to the poet, refrain from the excessive cultivation of mythology, the excessive desire for eloquence, for superfluous and inappropriate ornament; (5) never depart from the most important matters. For the second, there seem to be seven brief precepts: (1) know how to provide a fitting order for the whole work; (2) narrate elegantly; (3) write beautifully; (4) cultivate variety constantly; (5) attend to the perfection of the whole; (6) start from an advance idea of the structure of the total poem; (7) achieve a tight correspondence of beginning, middle, and end. It is in the set of negative precepts especially that the emphasis on style is found.[63]

In the commentary itself, Parrasio develops and expands the notions epitomized in his precepts. As he does so, certain of the distinctions now so familiar—invention, disposition, and elocution, "res" and "verba," the three styles, nature, art, and practice in the poet—come to light and are exploited. These cross one another in interesting ways: "res" becomes equivalent to invention, "verba" to elocution; the three styles all belong to elocution, which is more important than invention ("poetis maiori obser-

---

62 *Ibid.*, p. 3: "inflammare animos hominum, & extinguere iram, odium, dolorem incendere, aut ab his ijsdem ad lenitatem & misericordiam reuocare"; and p. 4v: "ad bene uiuendum rationibus exemplisque inuitare, mores, affectionesque docere, res gerendas cum iocunditate praecipere."
63 *Ibid.*, p. 3: "Nihil tam est poeticum, quam eloquutio"; pp. 6–6v.

uanda diligentia," p. 12) since it depends more completely upon genius (or nature) than upon art, which is sufficient for invention and disposition. The further distinction of pleasure and utility is also related, because in a general way utility comes from the "res" and pleasure from the "verba." One might reduce his argument in connection with Horace's line 333 as follows:

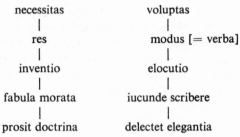

necessitas   voluptas

res   modus [= verba]

inventio   elocutio

fabula morata   iucunde scribere

prosit doctrina   delectet elegantia

Furthermore, a kind of distinction among genres seems to be made on the same basis: tragedy aims primarily at utility, comedy at pleasure.[64] The principle of decorum applies to both "res" and "verba." With respect to "res," it involves a correspondence between the things imitated in the work of art and things in nature; this is the most important thing for the poet to observe. "Not only in our lives but also in speech nothing is more difficult than to perceive what is proper, what the Greeks call πρέπον and we call *decorum.* . . . We must pay due attention to appropriateness, so that we imitate what really happens in nature and do not disturb its order."[65] With respect to "verba," the principle of decorum involves an appropriateness of words to things; all words must be chosen and placed "in a way fitting and proper to the dignity of the things."[66] Considerations of "nature" enter prominently in the commentary, not only in connection with decorum but as related to the origins of poetry (there are again strong echoes of Averroës in the statement that imitation is instinctive in man[67]), to the definition of poetry as an "imitatio naturae" (p. 78), to the genius of the poet. In a general way, all matters of "res" are referred to criteria of nature insofar as they involve verisimilitude and decorum, and to the audience insofar as they must persuade and move through credibility. On

[64] *Ibid.,* pp. 69*v*, 72: "habent inter se nonnullam similitudinem uescentes & scribentes, ut quibusdam utantur ad uoluptatem, quibusdam ad necessitatem. Docendi necessitas, in rebus est constituta, delectatio uero, in modo, quo docemus. Prosumus autem, cum morata recte est fabula. delectamus cum iucunde scribimus. . . . Laus poetae est ut prosit doctrina, delectet elegantia"; and p. 38.

[65] *Ibid.,* p. 7: "non solum in omni uita, sed etiam in oratione nihil est difficilius quam uidere quid deceat, πρέπον Graeci uocant, nostri decorum. . . . Est & suus conuenientiae labor adhibendus, ut quae in naturam cadunt fingantur, illius ordo non perturbetur."

[66] *Ibid.,* p. 12*v*: "ad rerumque dignitatem apte & decore."

[67] *Ibid.,* p. 68*v*: "Nihil enim aliud est poesis nisi imitatio uitae & morum, quae hominis propria est, facitque ut uel hac una differat a caeteris animalibus"; with which cf. Averroës (1481 ed.), p. f2*v*: "Prima quidem quum in homine existit naturaliter a prima sua natiuitate assimilatio rei ad rem: . . . & istud proprium est homini respectu ceterorum animalium."

the other hand, all matters of "verba" are referred to art, which consists essentially in the proper exploitation of the three styles according to the usual rhetorical precepts.

These interrelationships of distinctions perhaps indicate in Parrasio a more tightly knit conception of the art of poetry than was present in earlier commentators. He provides just as many disconnected remarks on isolated passages as did his predecessors, refers to as many different authorities. But over and above these, one senses some fairly definite orientations in his thinking: toward seeing a system in what had hitherto been independent sets of distinctions; toward emphasizing diction as the really poetic element and as the product of a special talent furthered by a special art; toward analyzing more searchingly the relationships of the poem to nature, to the poet, and to the audience.

In connection with line 128 of the *Ars poetica*, "Difficile est proprie communia dicere . . . ," Parrasio had developed his ideas on another kind of "imitation," that of other writers whom the poet might take as his models; he had previously recommended Vergil as the model to be followed unfailingly for all three styles (pp. 43–43*v*, 20). These were not, of course, new ideas, and they had before this appeared in conjunction with the Horatian text. But their timeliness here is indicated by the fact that they appear almost contemporaneously with the writing of two letters on the subject of imitation by Giovambattista Giraldi Cintio and by Celio Calcagnini. Giraldi's letter to Calcagnini, dated 1532, is concerned exclusively with the art of oratory and with what it may gain from proper imitation; but so completely, by this time, has the Horatian tradition assimilated the standard language of the rhetoricians that Giraldi's statements bear close resemblance to the commentaries on the *Ars poetica*. I cite the following passage, in which Giraldi is praising Cicero, in the original so that it may be compared with similar ones in the commentators:

. . . quis ad animos uel ad iram, uel ad odium, uel dolorem incitandos uegetior? quis ab ijsdem permotionibus ad amorem, ad lenitatem, ad misericordiam reuocandos aptior? quis uerborum copia locupletior? quis sententiarum pondere grauior? quis figuris iucundior? quis trallationibus magnificentior? quis totius orationis serie magis elaboratus? quis in dicendo candidior.[68]

Giraldi's letter is occupied with the debate between those who insist that many different authors should be imitated and those who maintain that the best results are obtained by imitating a single model. The subject of this "imitation" is exclusively diction: choice of words, figures of speech, rhythms and harmonies. Giraldi decides in favor of the single model, who for Latin must be Cicero, and he speaks of the components of imitation in terms long familiar in the Horatian-rhetorical tradition.

[68] In *Poematia* (1540 ed.), pp. 202–3.

Celio Calcagnini, to whom the letter had been addressed, answered in the same year in another letter entitled *Super imitatione commentatio.* In it, he defended the necessity of practicing imitation, especially for modern Italians who wished to rise out of barbarism. Then, basing his discussion on the three elements of invention, disposition, and elocution, he pointed out that the first of these is inherent in the material itself, the second is within the power of the writer, the third comes entirely from without. That is, the ability to handle language in an excellent manner is learned from the teacher or the models; it is here that imitation plays its part. The greatest lesson taught by proper imitation is the proper fitting of words to things ("uerba inuenire rei propositae accommodata"), a phrase which is almost the battle cry of the Horatians (p. 217).

Two other favorite ideas of the Horatians, the interpretation of poetry as an allegory concealing moral lessons and the insistence upon the necessity of verse, are the main points of emphasis in a short critical document of the following year, 1533. This is Alessandro Vellutello's letter to the readers printed as a preface to Agostino Ricchi's *I tre tiranni.* With respect to the first, Vellutello argues that the principal requirement of comedy is, "under the veil of joyous and pleasant discourse, to hide always some useful and appropriate morality." He then interprets the allegory or "senso mistico" of Ricchi's play. He defends Ricchi's use of verse on the basis of the whole history of comedy, the usage of the Greeks and the Romans, the authority of Aristotle in the *Poetics.* Poetry is verse, and as such is opposed to prose: "... everything that is true history or a rhetorical oration, or any part of them, belongs to prose; but the fictional fables of the poets never do. Since we do not believe that to the same things one can equally well adapt verse or write them in prose, we think that when this happens it must rather be attributed to lack of judgment than to an oversight." He admits blank verse as closer to everyday speech than rhymed verse—which would be "contra al naturale, et al uero"—and goes as far as to accept the use of prose in comedies with a modern subject, alive in themselves and necessitating no "imitation."[69]

In 1535, Lodovico Dolce published his translation of the *Ars poetica* into Italian verse; it was accompanied by a dedication to Pietro Aretino in which Dolce raises the practical question of the usefulness of Horace's precepts in the present day. His first argument is itself Horatian. Starting from the premiss that the poet depends both upon nature and upon art for the excellence of his work, he suggests that the mediocrity against which Horace had warned may be avoided only by the practice of art; and the

---

[69] In Ricchi, *I tre tiranni* (1533), p. Aijv: "sotto uelo di lieto, et piaceuole discorso sempre nascondere utile et accomodata moralità"; p. Aiij; p. Aiijv: "tutto quello che è fidele Historia, o uero Oration rethorica, o parte di loro, appartiene a la prosa, ma le finte fauole de i Poeti non mai. A le quali cose non considerando, potendosi nel medesimo modo adattare al uerso, et scriuere in Prosa, pensiamo che sempre questo ci saria piu tosto attribuito a mancamento di giuditio, che a trascuraggine."

Ars poetica is the best source of wisdom on all phases of the art. "He composed a book in which he collected together, wonderfully in a small space, everything that a good poet needs."[70] Dolce feels that such a work is especially needed today, when poets are ignorant of the basic elements of their art:

And this comes to pass because, writing today for the most part in the vulgar tongue (since we are born and grow up in it), we think that, having studied Petrarch, we can with little effort write some verse or sonnet that will give off a perfect odor of poetry. And we do not understand that this same Petrarch, and in our own century Sannazaro, Bembo, and also Ariosto, from all of whom not a little splendor has come to our language, all spent all their time, not without labor, in studies.[71]

Dolce does not fail to include Aretino himself among the distinguished writers of the century, praising him for the purity and appropriateness of his diction, for the felicity of his invention, for the art of his disposition, for his judgment in observing decorum, for the pleasantness and gravity of his thoughts—all of them Horatian qualities. Nor does he fail, in passing, to make a brief defence of poetry.

Like Giraldi and Calcagnini, Bartolomeo Ricci is concerned with the imitation of models, but in a more complete and in a more philosophical way than they had been. His *De imitatione libri tres* (1541) is a Horatian document in several respects. It justifies "imitation" as the ingredient of art that must be added to nature; it maintains that a writer imitates the invention, disposition, and elocution of his model; it selects and classifies models according to the genres that they represent; and it provides a certain number of precepts for each of the more important genres. Ricci recognizes the existence of two theories of imitation (and of a current debate over their respective merits). The first proposes that any writer imitate only his own nature, with no help at all from outside; the second proposes that he devote himself exclusively to the imitation of another. Both positions, thinks Ricci, are extreme, for the first neglects the contribution that art can make to nature, while the second unnecessarily restricts the writer to a single model. The best solution consists in supplementing nature with art, in correcting one's genius by adding to it the experience of a variety of other authors. "I therefore believe this: that in imitation as in other matters artifice is of great benefit to nature as nature is to artifice, and that each one needs

[70] *Poetica d'Horatio* (1535), pp. A2v–A3: "vn Libro compose; in cui tutto quello, che a buon Poeta è necessario, in breue campo mirabilmente racolse."

[71] *Ibid.*, p. A3: "E questo auiene; che scriuendosi hoggidi per la maggior parte nella lingua volgare; per esser noi nati e cresciuti in essa; ci pare, che hauendo il Petrarcha studiato; con poca fatica si possa dettare alcun verso o Sonetto, che renda perfetto odore di Poesia: e non comprendemo; che esso Petrarcha, e nel secol nostro il Sannazaro, il Bembo, e l'Ariosto anchora; da i quali n'è vscito non poco splendore alla lingua; hanno tutto il lor tempo, non senza fatica, consumato ne gli studi."

entirely the help of the other."[72] By this process, the deficiencies of the individual's talent will be compensated by the experience of his predecessors.

Such a procedure, says Ricci, merely follows the normal patterns of nature. All the arts derive ultimately from nature; one may take rhetoric as an example: "Indeed, in the universal art of speaking, what else do the rhetoricians propose than to adapt all their precepts to Nature herself?"[73] Just as any art is a reduction of nature to precepts, so the activity of any artist should consist in reducing his own nature to the satisfactory modes of artistry, and for this purpose the best device is imitation. "Thus will my imitator do: he will preserve carefully the many natural gifts with which he may be endowed; but if any then are lacking . . . , he will have to obtain them from elsewhere by his study, through the imitation of the good writers."[74] The problem then becomes one of selecting the best models, those which will best complement one's native genius. Late in Book I, Ricci indicates that his criteria for the choice of models are essentially their invention and elocution; but some of his discussions of the narrative and dramatic genres reveal that he also accords some importance to disposition.

Since his greatest concern is with Latin eloquence, Ricci surveys the whole field of Latin poetry and selects those poets who may best serve as models in each of the genres. This involves, of necessity, criteria for the genre and for poetry in general. For comedy, only Plautus and Terence are acceptable; Plautus is better for continuous comedy and laughter (but one must beware of triviality), Terence for seriousness and decorum. Seneca is the only model for tragedy. He satisfies the requirements of excellence in the arousing of suspense, in the conduct of the action, and in its denouement; with respect to the latter, he makes his endings sufficiently sad, whether they be related in words or enacted on the stage (following Horace's distinction). His whole conduct of the tragedy, in the serious action, in the royal personages, in the grave words is such as to achieve the desired goal of applause for the poet: "The more a tragic writer arouses pity in the spectator, the more he makes the subject cruel and terrible, the more will he elicit a greater applause for himself from the spectator, the more will he obtain for himself a merited esteem."[75] In this discussion of

---

[72] *De imitatione* (1545 ed.), pp. 12v–13: "Ego igitur sic sentio, & naturae artificium, & artificio naturam, ut in caeteris rebus, sic in imitatione plurimum prodesse, atque alterum alterius auxilio omnino indigere."

[73] *Ibid.*, p. 4v: "In uniuersa uero dicendi arte quid aliud Rhetores attendunt, quàm ut eius praecepta omnia ad naturam ipsam accommodentur?"

[74] *Ibid.*, p. 14: "ita meus faciat imitator, cui naturae bonum plurimum affuerit, id diligenter conseruabit, si quae uero desiderabuntur . . ., ea suo studio aliunde bonorum imitatione comparare debebit."

[75] *Ibid.*, p. 22v: "Quanto tragoediae scriptor magis misericordiam auditori commouebit, quanto rem crudeliorem, ac magis atrocem faciet, tanto ab hoc maiorem sibi plausum excitabit, tanto eius gratiam inibit aequiorem."

tragedy, Ricci's sources and orientations become apparent. Horace is accompanied by some allusions to Aristotle; Cicero provides the general rhetorical goal; moreover, the old medieval conception of the genre still serves as a basis. Similar recommendations are made for the other forms: Tibullus is first among the elegiac poets, Horace for the lyric and hexameter, Martial for the epigram, Vergil for the epic.

Books II and III of the *De imitatione* treat the practical rules for imitation. Once again, Ricci declares that one may imitate the invention and disposition of a work as well as elocution. He authorizes the copying or translation of whole passages and points to the great achievements of modern imitators. Yet there are important theoretical statements. In his insistence that the moderns can equal the ancients, that Nature has been as generous to us as to men of the classical past, he presents an idea that was soon to be exploited by Sperone Speroni and then by Du Bellay. He distinguishes natural from artificial order in the development of a plot, discerns a rhetorical order of parts (demonstration, narration, and so forth) in the poems and cantos of Vergil. On the purely practical side, all Book III is devoted to a consideration of language. Ricci's treatise, as a whole, represents a bridge between works of rhetorical theory and works of poetic theory, at a time when the latter were just beginning to come into prominence.

Imitation in the Giraldi-Calcagnini sense is again the subject of two treatises by Giulio Camillo Delminio, although only one of them is formally called a treatise on imitation. The work is his *Due trattati: l'uno delle materie, che possono uenir sotto lo stile dell'eloquente: l'altro della imitatione*, published in 1544. The first of these, on eloquence, is strictly rhetorical in character and derives its materials and its basic theses rather from Cicero than from Horace. The second is more remote from Horace than the letters on imitation already studied, largely because its approach is almost exclusively linguistic and it evinces no higher rationale in terms of the effects of language upon a potential audience. Camillo distinguishes language as literal, or as figurative, or as "topically figurative," and concludes that one author may borrow the first two types from another without engaging either in imitation or in plagiarism. The third provides the occasion for true imitation, and hence is the special prerogative of the poet, although the orator may also use it at times. Cicero is, as usual, held up as the sole model for imitation in Latin, and the ways in which proper imitation may be achieved are outlined.

In 1545, Lilio Gregorio Giraldi published his long *Historiae poetarum dialogi*, which belongs to the Horatian tradition by virtue not only of its numerous borrowings from the *Ars poetica* itself but also of its reflection of many of the ideas added by the expositors. In the course of the ten dialogues, certain of which are devoted to a mere biographical account of poets practicing the separate genres, Giraldi finds occasion to discuss a number of theoretical matters. The first dialogue, especially, is a full-scale defence of the art and a statement of its principles. In it, he finds it useful to call not only upon the witness of the standard commentators but also upon such ancient authorities as Plato, Strabo, Maximus of Tyre, and Theophrastus. Moreover, he patterns certain sections closely after Aristotle's *Poetics*, as I shall indicate in a subsequent chapter. In connection with his defence of poetry, he cites the recent apologies of Petrarch, Boccaccio, Budé, and Pontano. The defence itself follows the traditional lines: the early esteem in which poetry was held as a kind of first theology and first philosophy; its civilizing function; its uses in sacred writings. In connection with these, Giraldi insists upon the hidden meanings of all poetry, upon the mysteries concealed beneath its literal statements, upon its essentially allegorical nature: "it seems that generally in the art of poetry one thing is said whereas another is meant, and that the meaning is hidden, so to speak, under a veil."[76] The defence also requires an answer to Plato's ban and a demonstration of the usefulness of the art—topics long familiar to the Horatians. For the first, Giraldi declares that Plato had exiled only poets who lied about the gods; he quotes Petrarch to the effect that only scenic poets had been excluded from the Republic. For the second, he discusses the arguments of Eratosthenes (that poetry need only delight), of Strabo (that it need only instruct), and of Horace (that it must both "prodesse" and "delectare"). His own conclusion would seem to be that instruction is necessary and that it takes several forms. For one thing, as Cicero pointed out, poetry offers us in fictional guise an image of our daily lives: "Indeed these things have been feigned by the poets in such wise that we see our own characters represented in other persons, and we see expressed in them our image of daily life."[77] For another, specific moral lessons are contained in such genres as tragedy and comedy; in tragedy:

... this is the opinion of the comic poet Timocles, who says that in tragedy are found the models and the teachings for all of life and for every human condition. ... thus from some writers you will learn to bear with equanimity certain things, and from other writers how to bear other things; indeed, the sum of all misfortunes is greater than those which any one person suffers, and the man who has observed that they have befallen others, has become accustomed to bear his own more easily and more imperturbably.[78]

Giraldi's general notions of tragedy and comedy are derived from the

[76] *Historiae poetarum* (1545), p. 9: "in poëtica enim unum plerunque dici uidetur, aliud uerò significatur, & sensus quodam, ut ita dicam, uelamine occultatur."

[77] *Ibid.*, pp. 81, 72, 10: "Haec enim ... conficta sunt à Poëtis, ut effictos nostros mores in alienis personis, expressamque imaginem nostram uitae quotidianae uideamus."

[78] *Ibid.*, p. 676: "idque ex Timocle Comico, qui ait, apud Tragoediam totius uitae & conditionis esse exempla, atque documenta. ... & sic ab alijs alia aequo animo ferre disces: omnia enim maiora quàm quiuis patitur infortunia, qui alijs accidisse contemplatus, suas ipsius calamitates aequius faciliusque ferre consueuit."

medieval-Horatian school, and this in spite of the fact that he cites definitions and discussions from Aristotle. Dialogue VI is devoted to tragedy. He defines the genre thus: "Tragoedia est heroicae fortunae in aduersis comprehensio, ut nostri definiunt" ("*nostri*" being critics writing in Latin, such as Diomedes); then, after citing Theophrastus' definition in Greek, he paraphrases it in Latin: "Tragoedia est fortunę heroicae calamitas, seu infortunium. tragoediae enim propria est tristia, & luctus." Aristotle is cited on the antiquity of tragedy, and then Giraldi remarks that "in prouerbium Tragoedia exiuit, de re turbulenta, & molestiae plena." I cite these passages as samples of the continued use by Giraldi of traditional ideas and formulas.[79] When he comes to compare tragedy and comedy, he again does so in terms familiar to readers of Donatus and Diomedes:

> In comedy indeed the ordinary fortunes of men, the minor shocks and perils, are represented, and the ends of the actions are happy. In tragedy everything is the opposite: imposing personages, great fears, calamitous outcomes. In the former, unsettled events at the beginning, calm ones at the end; whereas in tragedy things transpire in the opposite order. Then in tragedy life is represented in such a way as to make us wish to flee it, in comedy so as to make us desire it. Finally, every comedy is derived from subjects invented by the poet, but tragedy frequently springs from historical truth.[80]

Similarly, his definition of the poet himself is a composite of elements derived from various accepted sources: "Perhaps one would not be wrong if he were to define the poet as a man who, moved by the divine afflatus, speaks nobly and appropriately of great things in such a way as to arouse admiration. If to this definition verse is added as an equal element, everything will seem to be plainly included in it."[81] In his treatment of the details of poetic composition—the handling of the three styles, the five acts in comedy and its various kinds, the histories of the genres, the definitions of the minor types—Giraldi refers directly and specifically to Horace and to the various expositors who, by the Renaissance commentators, were integrated into the corpus of "Horatian" ideas.

CONCLUSIONS

The gradual emergence of references to Aristotle's *Poetics* and the appearance in Lilio Gregorio Giraldi of formal definitions and discussions

---

[79] *Ibid.*, pp. 671–74; for the formulas, cf. Isidore, *Etymologiae*, VIII, vii; Evanthius, ed. Wessner, IV. 2; Diomedes, ed. Keil, I, 487; Donatus, ed. Wessner, V. 1.

[80] *Ibid.*, p. 681: "In Comoedia quidem mediocres fortunae hominum, parui impetus, periculaque, laetique sunt exitus actionum: at in Tragoedia omnia contraria, ingentes personae, magni timores, exitus funesti habentur, & illic turbulenta prima, tranquilla ultima, in Tragoedia contrario ordine res aguntur. tum in Tragoedia fugienda uita, in Comoedia capessenda exprimitur, postremò omnis Comoedia de fictis argumentis, Tragoedia saepe de historica fide petitur."

[81] *Ibid.*, p. 86: "non malè fortasse is dixerit, qui poëtam ita definierit, hominem esse, qui spiritu afflatus magna egregiè appositéque cum admiratione loquatur. . . . cui definitioni si par carmen addatur, omnia planè comprehensa uidebuntur."

derived from Aristotle indicate the arrival at a turning point in the Horatian tradition. The next text to be studied will be the first in a long series of texts which effect an intermingling of Horace's theories with those of Aristotle, and which produce in the end a complete confusion of Horace with Aristotle. Before proceeding to that study, however, it will be well to estimate the effects of the growth of the Horatian tradition in Italy up to about the year 1545.

In the first place, there is what we might call the material growth of the tradition. By that I mean the gradual accretion to the text of Horace of a host of other texts, which first become attached to it and then become inseparably identified with it. The earliest of these would be the ancient commentators, who persist with the text throughout the Middle Ages and bring to it an initial interpretation. Next would come the commentators of the end of the fifteenth century, who add not only their own glosses and their own ideas but who incorporate as well relevant materials from the late-classical grammarians and from the Latin rhetoricians. To some degree, also, these writers bring into the tradition the growing humanist knowledge of ancient texts, including both theoretical documents and various kinds of poems. Finally, the commentators of the first half of the sixteenth century expand the number of Greek and Latin theorists who are considered to have said things relevant to the interpretation of the *Ars poetica.* Plato, Aristotle, and Averroës are called upon increasingly, as well as many minor writers on poetic and rhetorical theory. There is another sense in which we may perceive a material growth of the tradition: to formal commentaries on the Horatian text are added, first, independent theoretical statements in other contexts or in separate works, and, second, essays in practical criticism in which principles belonging to the tradition are applied to poems of one kind or another. Not only are more things added to the text of the *Ars poetica,* but it is constantly applied to more things.

In the second place, we discern what might be called a methodological growth of the tradition. The earliest form of commentary is essentially a grammatical commentary, in which the exegesis of the text as a linguistic document is the primary problem. To be sure, philosophical interpretation is already present, but it is present in a secondary way. This type of grammatical commentary will continue throughout the later phases, but will gradually be subordinated to other types. To it is added, in the fifteenth century, more and more interpretation of a philosophical and literary character. At the outset, this kind of interpretation is applied to separate lines or passages in the text, for which analogues or explanations are found in other texts and for which illustrations are found in the poets. But already, because of the character of the documents which are cited as analogues, a totality of interpretation (which, as we have seen, is a rhetorical one) is present. In the sixteenth-century commentaries, the large body of disparate distinctions brought into the tradition in connection with one passage or another is organized into a set of related distinctions, and systematic interpretations of Horace appear with some frequency. None of the earlier forms of gloss is abandoned, and the increasing length and complexity of the commentaries is a reflection of the greater number of things done with the text and their greater diversity.

In the third place, and by far the most important, the tradition presents evidences of considerable doctrinal growth. Two words of caution are necessary about the meaning given to "growth" at this point. For one, it should not be thought that during the period under consideration there was any notable change in the over-all understanding of the Horatian epistle, any appreciable shift from one way of regarding the text to another. Throughout these years, the *Ars poetica* was read as a kind of rhetoric that indicated how certain effects of utility or pleasure could be brought about in a specific audience by treating nature in certain ways and by making certain kinds of adaptations of words to subject matter. For another, "growth" should not be understood as meaning necessarily that the later documents were more sophisticated or more complicated philosophically, or that they contained a larger and richer body of ideas. What doctrinal growth there was must be sought in the tradition as a whole, in the sum of doctrine during the later years as compared with the sum during the middle years as compared with the sum during the early years. Here there is substantial progress. If we see the general process of development as consisting of a more and more complete identification of Horace with the rhetorical tradition, then the first stages would be present in the simplest assimilation of the invention-disposition-elocution analysis to Horace's statements. This assimilation will grow as the division is made to correspond more and more completely with parts of the *Ars poetica*. At the same time appears another way of looking at the text, its main point being the emphasis upon the necessity of appropriateness in all poetic matters—of character traits to character or to type or to historical conceptions, of diction to subject matter, of style to genre, of social station to genre, of verse to material or genre, and so forth. The canon of appropriateness will likewise be enlarged and expanded as the tradition grows. Consonant with the increasing complexity of the rhetorical associations of the text, critics will tend to orient their thinking more definitely toward the audience and its requirements and to develop theories fitting to such an orientation. The end of poetry with respect to the audience, that of pleasing or instructing or both, is clarified by explanations and examples. At times one of these ends is emphasized as the only one (as pleasure with Landino); at times all are said to be achieved through separate parts of the work; at times each one is sought for some special segment of the audience. The constantly greater attention to moral considerations is a part of this manner of considering the ends.

For certain other relevant distinctions, one needs to go back again to the earliest commentators and from them trace a widening and diversified set of ramifications. This would be the case for the insistence, with respect to Horace, upon the "res-verba" dichotomy, an essentially grammatical distinction which comes to belong to all the arts of discourse. It would be the case, again, for the three styles; especially in the postmedieval years, these styles are called upon to provide a basis of organization for nearly all of the ideas connected with the text. To them is also related the matter of diction, and in an interesting way. For if all poetic concerns may be reduced to the three styles, then they may also be reduced to questions of diction; one of the ways of considering poetry, which will never lose its popularity during the Renaissance, will be to consider it exclusively in terms of words or expression or style. If there are thus several separate approaches of a verbal character, there are also several which spring from preoccupations with "res." The most prominent of these is the reading of Horace essentially as a document centered about a principle of decorum, a reading which reaches complete expression in Badius. Such an interpretation is of course related to those which were insistent upon appropriateness, but in a specialized way. Similarly, the persistent return to considerations of nature and verisimilitude is a facet of the theorists' attention to "res." One special phase of this is the insistence, in certain writers, that when the poet deals with historical matters he must be true, whereas when his subjects are feigned or invented it is sufficient for him to be verisimilar.

Still another direction of doctrinal growth is discerned in what we may characterize as the transforming of the *Ars poetica* into a "total poetics." Horace himself had treated a large number of matters pertinent to the art of poetry: the internal order of poems, the appropriateness of diction, the history and the materials of certain genres, the behavior of the poet, the function of the critic, and so forth. All these matters are developed in great detail by the commentators, either through the addition of examples or through the expansion of the ideas. Moreover, other developments occur. The transformation of the text into a set of rules or precepts would probably be one of these. Horace's fairly fluid organization of materials is made more solid and substantial by the declaration that every statement constitutes a "praeceptum" (as for Acron) or a "regula" (as for Badius). At times, this effort results in the discovery of dogmas for which there is actually no basis in the Horatian text itself. The aggregation of the defence of poetry to the Horatian tradition expands and enriches it to a notable degree, since it soon involves the crossing with other traditions and the appeal to other authorities. A part of this defence consists in the allegorical interpretation of poetry, where again both a renewed Platonism and a continued medievalism enter into the sum of "Horatian" ideas. Finally, the commentators introduce a large number of concepts relevant to the character of the poet: his inspiration through divine furor, his essential goodness, the universality of his knowledge, his capacities as a seer and a prophet. Through such accretions as these, the *Ars poetica*—with its attendant glosses—becomes a repository for everything that was being thought about poetry in the humanistic period and during the Renaissance up to about 1545.

In the following years, another impulsion to material and methodological and doctrinal growth is given to the Horatian tradition, and in such a way as to merit separate and detailed study. This impulsion comes from the text and the interpretation of Aristotle's *Poetics*.

CHAPTER FOUR. THE TRADITION OF HORACE'S *ARS POETICA*: II. THE CONFUSION WITH ARISTOTLE

IT WOULD BE ERRONEOUS to believe that in the years before 1545 work on Horace's *Ars poetica* had been done exclusively by persons who did not know Aristotle's *Poetics*. The passing allusions and references to the *Poetics* mentioned in the preceding chapter would disprove such a belief. A more correct statement would be that although these scholars knew Aristotle's treatise or knew of it, such knowledge did not fundamentally affect their general reading and interpretation of the Horatian text. They read it in the same way as did their colleagues who lacked this knowledge; and allusion and reference were incidental to an interpretation which had nothing to do with the *Poetics*. In the years that we shall now be studying, however, a number of theorists brought Horace's work into clear juxtaposition to and explicit comparison with Aristotle's, and in some cases at least, a new analysis of Horace resulted. What happened to Aristotle will be treated in a later section.[1]

Nor should it be thought that the comparison with Aristotle produced a revolution in the interpretation of Horace. We shall increasingly discover commentators and theorists who make the assimilation of the Greek to the Roman; but we shall also continue to meet—and perhaps more frequently—writers who persist in the earlier tradition. Both in theory and in practical criticism, it may be that the "un-Aristotelians" or the "non-Aristotelians" constitute the dominant element in the Horatian tradition of the later years as they did in the earlier. To determine the proportion, to weigh the importance of the two trends, will be one of the problems of this and the succeeding chapters.

FRANCESCO FILIPPI PEDEMONTE (1546)

The first of the Cinquecento commentaries on the *Ars poetica* to make extensive use of Aristotle was Francesco Filippi Pedemonte's *Ecphrasis in Horatii Flacci Artem poeticam*, published by his pupil Puresius in 1546. In some respects this is a conventional commentary, but in others it presents notable innovations. For example, Pedemonte follows the usual routine of dividing Horace's text into small sections, with a commentary for each section; but he varies the technique by giving a heading to each section. Thus lines 1–13 are preceded by "De Idea Concipienda," lines 14–23 by "Non esse à materia discedendum," and so on. These headings themselves indicate the direction of the interpretation. But the great innovation con-

---

[1] The same subject with respect to Horace is treated by Marvin T. Herrick in *The Fusion of Horatian and Aristotelian Literary Criticism, 1531–1555* (Urbana: University of Illinois Press, 1946); but since Herrick proceeds by a fragmentation of texts and an arrangement according to critical ideas, he does not achieve the kind of historical statement of the development which I am here seeking.

sists in the use made of Aristotle. Let us see how this is done in several typical passages. In the first passage, lines 1–13, Pedemonte sees an expression of Plato's theory that Ideas precede forms; from this theory he derives Horace's contention that "it is necessary that the artist have a preconceived notion of the things which are made by him before putting his hand to them, and that he see in advance in his mind's eye the Form according to the model of which he may give form to every work." This is the procedure, he goes on to say, in all the arts, and "especially in the arts of painting, molding, and sculpturing, which indeed seem to Aristotle to proceed in the same way of imitation as does poetry." Thus Aristotle's theory of imitation is made equivalent to Plato's theory of the imitation of Forms and to Horace's initial statements in the *Ars poetica*. Later in the same passage, when he is speaking of the impossibility of unity when disparate elements are combined, Pedemonte again quotes Aristotle: "the first parts of the poem will not fit with the last, and the poem as a whole, which (as Aristotle says) consists of a beginning, a middle, and an end, will in no way be complete." Here, Aristotle's principle of unity is identified with Horace's principle of appropriateness. Finally, Horace's recommendations that nature must be followed are said to be corroborated by Aristotle's insistence that Homer be taken as the best model, since he best taught how a "lie" (which would be something out of nature) should be told. In each of these cases, a new light is shed upon the Horatian passage by the reference to Aristotle.[2]

Pedemonte's procedure is similar in his commentary on lines 92–107, headed "De decoro, atque affectibus exprimendis. quae res ad actionem pertinere uidetur." After an initial sentence about the importance of observing decorum, he quotes Aristotle (I have been unable to locate the passage), thus making Horace's "quid deceat" equivalent to Aristotle's τò πρέπον. As the Horatian passage goes on to the effects produced by the poem—

> Non satis est pulchra esse poemata: dulcia sunto,
> et quocumque volent animum auditoris agunto

—Pedemonte first cites Cicero on the closeness of the poet to the orator and the necessity for both to sway their audiences, then both Cicero and Aristotle on the need for the poet to feel the passions that he is portraying; the reference to Aristotle is to *Poetics* 1455a31. At the end of the com-

---

2 *Ecphrasis* (1546), p. 3v: "necesse enim est artificem earum rerum, quae à se fiunt, priusquam manum admoueat, pręcognitam habere notitiam; animoque praeuidere formam, cuius exemplo opus quodque informet. sic itaque in omni arte, pingendi maxime, fingendi, atque sculpendi; quae quidem eodem imitationis tramite cum poesi Aristoteli incedere uidentur"; p. 4: "poematis primę partes cum postremis non conuenient; miniméue totum ipsum, quod (ut inquit Aristoteles) ex principio, medio ac fine constat, absoluetur"; also pp. 4v, 16. I use the name "Pedemonte" rather than "Filippi" since he was called Pedemonte by his own pupil, Puresius, and by the whole tradition of scholars up to and including Tiraboschi (Venice, 1796 ed., VII¹, 235).

mentary—and for reasons difficult to discern—he quotes Aristotle on the beautiful animal and on the proper magnitude of a poem (1450*b*35).

These passages in the *Ecphrasis* are typical. For an indication of the extent to which Pedemonte seeks parallels in Aristotle, a simple list of the texts involved will suffice:

Ars poetica	Poetics
1–13	1447*a*18, 1450*b*27, 1460*a*18
42–45	1459*b*31
46–72	1458*b*31
73–88	1459*b*31, 1448*b*32, 1459*a*11
89–91	1449*b*9, 1448*a*16
92–107	1455*a*31, 1450*b*35
128–34	1448*b*35, 1460*b*16
149–52	1451*a*32
179–88	1448*a*36, 1449*b*21, 1448*a*30, 1449*b*4, 1449*a*31, 1451*a*16, 1453*b*3, 1453*b*19
189–92	1451*a*9
193–95	1456*a*25
202–19	1455*b*32
220–24	1449*a*21
234–39	1458*b*31, 1456*a*20
275–80	1449*a*9
281–84	1449*a*36
338–40	1451*a*36
457–69	1447*b*19

As compared with earlier commentators, the extent of these references is considerable; but the study of later commentators will show that we have here only the beginning of an important tendency.

What is important, however, is not the fact of reference, but the degree to which such reference causes a change in the interpretation of the text of Horace. A careful reading of Pedemonte's commentary shows that while several new ideas are added to the Horatian tradition as the result of the parallel with Aristotle, none of the old ideas is in any way modified; the process is one of accretion rather than change. I have already referred to several of these new ideas: Aristotle's theories of imitation and of the magnitude of beautiful poems compared to that of beautiful animals. Other added elements are the notion of necessary order, in which no part of a poem may be moved or removed without destroying the total structure; the definition of tragedy and the explanation of the various components of that definition; the insistence that unity of plot is not provided by unity of hero; the declaration that tragedy should attain its effect even in the reading, through the constitution of the plot rather than through stage spectacle; the distinction of four kinds of plot; and the statement that the domain of poetry is the presentation of things as they should be, according to necessity and probability. In connection with this last, it should be noted that both the idea of the "verisimile" and the idea of "things as they should be" had appeared in earlier commentators (cf. Acron on the first and Parrasio on the second); Pedemonte's contribution consists in grouping them together and in adding to them the notion of necessity, which he does not explain.

The addition of these Aristotelian concepts does not mean, however, that any of the old components of the Horatian theory are lost or diminished. The work is still read in the light of Cicero, Quintilian, Acron, and Donatus, and the essentially rhetorical interpretation still obtains. Thus, lines 38–72 of the *Ars poetica* are divided into three sections, entitled respectively "De Inventione," "De Dispositione," and "De Vocabulorum compositione"; and as he passes on to the next section Pedemonte remarks: "So far we have abundantly discoursed about poetic invention, disposition, and the artistry of elocution."[3] Similarly, when he speaks of comedy, Pedemonte insists: "It is not sufficient to have invention, but it is also necessary to understand disposition and elocution and to fashion the poem itself according to the rules."[4] The related "res-verba" distinction appears in a somewhat special form, since the "verba" are replaced by "rhythmi" and these in turn are called "colores" (contrary to the usual practice, which reserved the term "colores" for figures of speech). The distinction is formulated thus: "So in poetry two principal things are considered, namely the material of the things which are taken by the poet for treatment, and the numbers from which this material receives its form and is made distinct by its own colors."[5]

With respect to the ends of poetry, Pedemonte seems to remain undecided between the two rival positions most commonly held by his predecessors, that which maintained that the end was pleasure and that which declared that pleasure must be mingled with utility. Commenting on the "variare" of line 29 of the *Ars poetica*, he insists on the necessity of variety in the poetic work, "for otherwise it will by no means produce admiration and pleasure, which are the poets' aim."[6] Much later, however, when he discusses line 333 ("Aut prodesse volunt, aut delectare poetae"), he is obliged by the text itself to consider the dual end, and he does so in these terms:

Yet since poetry seems to have been invented in part to give pleasure and in part also to be of utility, lest someone might think that it was entirely alien to

---

3 *Ibid.*, p. 12v: "Hactenus de inuentione poetica, dispositione, elocutionisque artificio abunde disseruimus."

4 *Ibid.*, p. 40v: "Non enim satis est inuentionem habere, uerum etiam dispositionem, ac elocutionem callere oportet; ipsumque poema rite intexere."

5 *Ibid.*, p. 14v: "Ita in poesi duo praecipua considerantur; rerum uidelicet, quae tractandę à poeta sumuntur, materia; ac numeri, à quibus informatur, efficiturque suis coloribus distincta."

6 *Ibid.*, p. 6: "cum alioquin admirationem, oblectationemque, qui poetarum est scopus, nequaquam praebeat."

pleasure he [Horace] felt it necessary to remove such a concern from men's minds by making a universal distinction among all poets. [The three kinds of poets distinguished.] Those provide utility, I say, who communicate in verse the precepts of the disciplines and of the arts, especially the precepts which are called moral, and who teach the norm of proper living. . . . These poets [Empedocles, Lucretius, Aratus, etc.] seem to have created many things in their poems for purposes of pleasure, in addition to moral portraits and a sculptured image of life which they include under the appearance of fiction. In fact, those very ancient poets who first invented poetic lies seem to have set for themselves that same purpose: to envelop, in the wrappings of fables, doctrinal mysteries and moral instructions and a way of life.[7]

By such a statement as the last one, Pedemonte allies himself with those theorists who had seen the chief utility of poetry as residing in an allegorical function. Moreover, he indicates in the passage that his whole conception of the ends of poetry is unaffected by his study and his citation of Aristotle.

As for the actual production of utility, it seems to be brought about almost entirely by the introduction of proverbs or *sententiae*. In connection with lines 202–19, Pedemonte insists that ethical philosophy "filled tragedy and comedy with most weighty *sententiae*, apposite to the teaching of right living."[8] There appears to be, in the same passage, some connection between poems offering such *sententiae* and the "moral" type of plot distinguished by Aristotle (*Poetics* 1456a1). The same position with respect to *sententiae* is present in the commentary on lines 309–22 where, among other related things, Pedemonte says this: "Indeed, unless all comedies and tragedies derived their seriousness from precepts and *sententiae* pertaining to everyday life, what would we say they were other than a dry discourse and a sterile matter?"[9] At the end of the same commentary, Pedemonte gives priority to this kind of utility over pleasure itself: "A poem faithfully reflecting mores, adorned with philosophical passages, or containing useful matter, even if it is without the seduction of beauty, or grandeur of words, or cleverness of construction, will better delight and hold the public than a poem with the most highly embellished verses if no wisdom or knowledge

---

[7] *Ibid.*, pp. 51–51*v*: "cum tamen poesis ad oblectandum partim, partim uero ad iuuandum inuenta uideatur, ne aliquis existimaret omnino à uoluptate eam esse alienam, uatum omnium uniuersali distinctione eiusmodi scrupulum euellere ex animis necessarium duxit. . . . Prosunt inquam qui disciplinarum praecepta, artiumúe, tum praesertim quę moralia uocantur, carminibus tradunt, rectéque uiuendi normam edocent. . . . multa enim ab illis oblectationis causa efficta uidentur, alioquin expressos mores, insculptamque uitae imaginem sub falsitatis umbra continent. Nam & uetustissimi illi, qui ab initio poetica mendacia excogitarunt, illud sibi scopum proposuisse uidentur; ut sub fabularum inuolucris doctrinarum mysteria, mores, uiuendíque modum inuoluerent."

[8] *Ibid.*, p. 36: "quae tragoedias comoediasque grauissimis sententijs, & ad recte uiuendum appositis repleuit."

[9] *Ibid.*, p. 49*v*: "comoedias omnes, tragoediasque, ni pondus à praeceptis, ac sententijs ad quottidianam uitam spectantibus accepissent, quid aliud esse, quàm ieiunum sermonum, sterilemque materiam diceremus?"

supports it." The position is of course that of Acron and later commentators;[10] it would not be that of Aristotle at any point in the *Poetics*. A little later, Horace's dictum on brevity (1. 335) is expanded to refer specifically to these moral precepts: "He advises us to make every possible effort toward brevity, which indeed is held to be particularly suitable for teaching the mind, and to stray as little as possible from the line of profiting and teaching; so that the learners may more easily grasp the precepts and may keep them as long as possible locked within the storehouse of the memory."[11]

We have already examined the tenor of Pedemonte's discussion of decorum in connection with *Ars poetica* 92–107; as in the Horatian text, decorum will be throughout one of the commentator's primary concerns. It should be pointed out further, relative to the above passage, that Pedemonte tends to make a proper observance of decorum one of the conditions both of sound teaching and of audience attention. Two sentences show this: "All of those who have undertaken the task of writing poetry, let them pay attention especially, according to their powers of judgment, to what is decorous, so that the proper qualities be attributed to each person; and let them observe decorum itself, through ignorance of which offense results, not only in life but most frequently in poetry and in speeches"; and "Furthermore, the writer who fails to give to each personage speech that is in keeping with character will by no means obtain the attentive minds or the open ears of his listeners."[12] Decorum also provides one of the bases for distinguishing poetry from history; for whereas the historian treats what is true, the poet pays attention "only to those things which can be treated with decorum, or which seem likely to confer splendor upon the work."[13] The treatment of the decorum of ages follows Horace with no significant additions.

Aside from these major emphases, what Pedemonte adds to the text of Horace had already been added by his predecessors. The basic principle of unity is stated in the conventional terms: "unum," "simplex," "congruens"

10 *Ibid.*, p. 50: "poema bene moratum, locisque philosophicis ornatum, utilemúe continens materiam, sine tamen uenustatis lenocinio, aut uerborum maiestate, aut constructionis artificio, melius spectantem populum oblectat, detinetque, quàm exornatissimis uersibus, nulla subiecta sententia, neque scientia"; cf. Acron, ed. Hauthal, II, 629: "dicens, quod interdum fabula opportunitate personarum inductarum et expressione morum, quamuis sit sine arte, sine uenustate, sine grauitate sententiarum, plus placet quam uersus bene quidem sonantes, sed morum obseruatione carentes."

11 *Ecphrasis*, pp. 51v–52: "quae quidem ad docendos animos admodum idonea habetur, maxime studendum esse monet; minimeque à iuuandi ac praecipiendi linea errandum; ut discentes praecepta facilius comprehendant, memoriaeque thesauro recondita quamdiutissime seruent."

12 *Ibid.*, p. 15v: "Omnes qui poeticam prouinciam susceperint, pro suo iudicio maxime quid deceat animaduertant, ut unicuique personę suę partes tribuantur; ipsumque decorum obseruent; cuius ignoratione non modo in uita, sed sępissime in poemate, & in oratione peccatur"; and p. 16: "Praeterea qui personae cuique congruentem orationem nequaquam tribuet, nullo pacto attentos animos, patentesúe aures habebit."

13 *Ibid.*, p. 24v: "sic Poeta non omnia, sed ea tantummodo attendere debet, quae tractari cum decoro possint, quaeúe splendorem operi allatura uideantur."

(p. 5). For each of the "simple" styles, Vergil may be taken as the model
(p. 5v). But lest simplicity cloy, one introduces variety into the poem—
always keeping appropriateness in mind—and in so doing one follows the
example of nature; "for poetry and numerous noble arts follow nature as
their guide, and nature, indeed, rejoices to an astonishing degree in
variety."[14] The "following of nature" is one of the kinds of imitation; but
in addition to the Platonic and Aristotelian meanings assigned to the term,
the text also uses it to mean the adaptation of old plots and the following
of models. Hence the section of the commentary on lines 128 ff. ("Difficile
est proprie communia dicere") is entitled "De imitatione atque conver-
tendis fabulis," and the general thesis is stated in this way: "Finally, the
poem which we undertake to imitate must be as a model and a sort of
image, in whose likeness everyone should execute his own work; he should,
I say, make the sum total and not merely separate parts conform to this
image."[15] Finally, the poet who executes such works, if he is to excel and
exert a proper moral influence, must himself be a good man: "castum decet
esse pium poetam" (p. 56v).

In its main lines, then, Pedemonte's *Ecphrasis* of 1546 adds to the tradition of commentary on Horace a sizable amount of reference to the *Poetics*.
This reference adds some new ideas to the corpus of interpretation, and at
times it results in changes in that interpretation. But for the most part the
construction put upon the *Ars poetica* remains unaltered, and Pedemonte
merely adds another document to the series which by this time had established a standard reading for the text.

A similar alliance of Aristotelian and rhetorical elements is found in a
letter by Claudio Tolomei to Marcantonio Cinuzzi, dated July 1, 1543, but
published in 1547. Once more, the rhetorical elements are predominant.
Tolomei is discussing Cinuzzi's translation of Claudian's *Rape of Proser-
pine*; he praises the three books of the work because they are "ingenious
in invention, clear in disposition, elevated in their great sentiments, terse in
selected words, lovely through their varied ornamentation"; he finds that
the translation is distinguished by its clarity, the kind of clarity which
derives both from the words and from their ordering.[16] This insistence on
clarity may in itself be a reference to Aristotle (*Poetics* 1458a18), although
not necessarily so; what is directly from Aristotle is the discussion of the
hexameter: "I remember what Aristotle says in the *Poetics* [1459b31], who
praises greatly the hexameter verse appropriate to the heroic style, since

---

14 *Ibid.*, p. 6: "Nam poetica & artes quamplurimae nobiles naturam tanquam ducem
sequuntur; quae quidem mirum in modum uarietate gaudet."
15 *Ibid.*, p. 21: "Poema denique, quod imitandum suscipimus, debet esse exemplar &
imago quasi quaedam; ad cuius similitudinem opus suum quisque effingat; totum inquam
corpus, & non partes singulas conformet."
16 *Delle lettere* (1547), p. 8: "son ingegnosi per inuenzione, chiari per disposizione, alti
per gran sentimenti, tersi per iscelte parole, uaghi per uario ornamento"; also p. 9.

that kind of verse does not as easily happen in the speech of men at all times as do six-syllable verses and other similar forms."[17] Here again, critical elements of all kinds are slight and commonplace; they are assembled from various sources with no systematic readjustments.

ROBORTELLO (1548) AND MAGGI (1550)

Continuing the lead of Pedemonte, although to a lesser degree, Francesco Robortello seeks to establish parallels between Horace and Aristotle in his *Paraphrasis in librum Horatii, qui vulgo de arte poetica ad Pisones inscribitur* (1548); this is one of the appendices to Robortello's commentary on the *Poetics*. As his title promises, he limits himself almost exclusively to paraphrasing Horace's epistle, and there is little if any doctrinal value in Robortello's statements. If a paraphrase is necessary at all, it is because—so he says—the order of Horace's treatise is obscure and many points need expansion and clarification. Indeed, Horace's work is not an "art" of poetry at all, but merely a "sermo" touching upon all current errors in the writing of poetry. The expositor's function will therefore be to distinguish what order is perceptible and to expand and clarify the text. In the course of his paraphrase, Robortello finds occasion to cite a number of passages from the *Poetics* which (he claims) say the same things as Horace does and thus corroborate his opinions. These are the parallels established:

Horace	Aristotle
42–45	1460a5 (Homer's narration)
73–74	1459b31 (hexameter for epic)
79	1449a23 (iambic)
82	(no definite passage; necessity of meter)
101–13	1454a16 (mores)
125–27	1453a17, 1451b11 (few families)
	1454a25 (ὁμαλίαν)
151–52	1460a18 (παραλογισμός)
191–92	1454a37 (deus ex machina)
193–201	1456a25 (chorus)
220 ff.	1449a19 (tragedy from satire)
281–88	1449a2 (old comedy)
317–20	1456a1 (ethical plot)

A mere listing of the comparisons shows, first, the kinds of subject matters for which Robortello was interested in juxtaposing the two texts (metrics, ethics and decorum, certain rules for the handling of narration, and historical considerations) and, second, the miscellaneous character of these problems. Robortello goes to Aristotle for scattered details which resemble

---

17 *Ibid.*, p. 8v: "mi souuiene di qvel che dice Aristotile ne la poetica, ilqval loda molto il uerso Hesametro atto a lo stile Heroico: percio che qvella sorte di uerso, non cade cosi ageuolmente nel parlar che l'hvom fa a tvtte l'hore, come i uersi senarii, e alcvne altre simili forme."

isolated remarks in Horace, not for any consistent or particularized theory of poetry.

In this series of the early "comparers" of Horace to Aristotle, the first to read Horace in the light of the Aristotelian text was Vincenzo Maggi, who appended to his commentary on the *Poetics* an *In Q. Horatii Flacci de arte poetica librum ad Pisones, Interpretatio* (1550). I have already referred to this text in Chapter II and quoted Maggi's assumption that the important sections of Horace's work "were written almost entirely in imitation of Aristotle's *Poetics*" and his intention "to demonstrate that those things which are found in Horace are already found in Aristotle."[18] But the text merits more complete and more intensive study. Maggi discovers three separate purposes in Horace: (1) to teach the laws for the proper making of poems; (2) to treat of poetry itself; (3) to criticize, satirize, and render ridiculous.[19] Only the first two are essential to the work, and all materials belonging to them derive from Aristotle; anything concerning the third is labeled a digression and promptly dismissed. Since lla fundamental parts of the work have their source in Aristotle, their meaning can be clarified by a citation of the parallel Aristotelian text, and Maggi is for the most part satisfied with the discovery and adducing of parallels. This is clearly stated in the introduction, where Maggi declares that he will not repeat the explanations of others but merely treat of those things "quae huic nostro cum Aristotele communia sunt." The procedure is not novel, of course; but what is new is Maggi's *parti pris* to begin with Aristotle and work forward to Horace rather than following the usual, inverse process.

An example of this method of reading is found in the commentary on the very first section of the Horatian text, lines 1–13. Maggi quotes five separate texts from the *Poetics*, all relating to the distinction between plot and episode and to the importance of plot itself. Then he goes on to say:

Therefore, since from all these texts it may be clearly concluded that Aristotle himself divided Homer's poetry into two parts, that is, plot and episodes, and that plot is so to speak the soul of poetry, that is, the thing which is most important of all, it seems to me reasonable that Horace should have given at the beginning of this work the precepts for the proper making of the plot, so that he evidently treats at once and on the very threshold of his work what is first and foremost in poetry; especially since there is no other place in Horace's *Ars poetica*, except this one, which explicitly deals with the plot, that is to say, the composition of events.[20]

18 See above, p. 53.

19 *In Aristotelis librum de poetica communes explanationes* (1550), p. 328: "partim leges rectè Poesim conficiendi docere, partim de Poesi ipsa tractare, partim criminari, ac perinde ut satyricum mordere, irrideréque.

20 *Ibid.,* pp. 329–30: "Quare cùm ex omnibus his locis plane colligi possit, Aristotelem ipsum Homeri Poesim in duas diuisisse partes, fabulam inquam, & episodia; & fabulam esse ueluti Poeseos animam, hoc est, quiddam omnium maximum: rationi consentaneum esse mihi uidetur, Horatium praecepta, quibus recte fabula confici posset, in operis huius initio tradidisse, ut quod in Poesi primum & potissimum est, in ipso statim libri limine tractare uideretur: cùm praesertim nullus in tota Horatii arte Poetica locus sit, hoc excepto, qui de fabula, id est rerum constitutione ex instituto pertractet."

He then asks whether the precepts for plot suggested by the two theorists are the same and concludes that they are, with Aristotle's requirements of necessity and probability corresponding to Horace's insistence upon the properly constituted animal. Plainly, the argument runs this way: Horace is imitating Aristotle; he finds in Aristotle precepts for the proper constitution of the plot, the most important part of any poem; he introduces at the beginning of his treatise an equivalent set of precepts. As far as the interpretation of Horace is concerned, this means that lines 1–13 will be read as a section on the proper organization of poetic plot.

In general, Maggi's procedure is to seek for each passage in Horace as many equivalents in Aristotle as he can possibly discover. We may take as an example his treatment of lines 312 ff., on the general subject of decorum; Maggi's references to the "particulae" of the *Poetics* are to his own divisions of the text in the commentary preceding. He has this to say:

... mihi uidetur Horatius intelligere, poetam oportere rectè actiones exprimere personis congruas. quae pars desumpta esse uidetur ex .II.VIII. et .IX. particulis [= 1447a13, 1447b13–24]: in quibus dicitur Poesim necessario imitari. Illud autem: Respicere exemplar uitae, ex .LXXX. particula [= 1454b8] Aristotelis sumptum uidetur: siquidem ibi ait: [translation of Aristotle quoted]. Pars uero illa:
Interdum speciosa iocis: moratáque rectè,
ubi Horatius uerba cum rebus confert, docetque multo maiorem in rebus ipsis, quàm in uerbis curam esse adhibendam: particulae Poetices Aristotelis .XLI. [= 1450a29] proportione respondere uidetur. fabulam enim eo loco cum moribus, dictionibus, et sententiis conferens, principatum ac praecipuum locum in Poesi obtinere docuit. ita Horatius illum imitatus, res uerbis comparans, ipsas primas sibi uendicare asserit. Verba autem Aristotelis sunt haec. [translation of Aristotle quoted] (p. 360).

It can readily be seen how such a determination will lead, at times, to the discovery of parallels that are very farfetched indeed. A case in point is the remark on lines 38–41, where Horace advises the poet to select a subject matter suited to his own genius in order to achieve "facundia" and "ordo"; for Maggi, this "seems to correspond" to *Poetics* 1450a35, in which Aristotle insists upon the greater difficulty of treating plot than character or diction (p. 334). But Maggi is unaware of any such discrepancies. Indeed, he finds it possible to justify, as clever imitations, all of Horace's departures from the order or the doctrine of the Aristotelian text. Horace follows his own precept "Nec uerbum uerbo curabis reddere fidus/Interpres" (l. 133); "In fact, he made the *Poetics* his own, which had already been made generally known and public by Aristotle, handing it down in a different order and not translating it word for word."[21] Thus Horace "dissimulated" his borrowings by treating epic first instead of

---

21 *Ibid.*, p. 345: "nam uulgatam iam, communemque factam ab Aristotele, propriam Poeticam effecit, alio eam ordine tradens, nec uerbum uerbo reddens."

tragedy, as Aristotle had done (p. 335), and by introducing his counsels on new words in connection with the epic rather than with tragedy, since the epic demands high-sounding speech (p. 336).

This generous conception of parallelism leads Maggi to find equivalent passages in Aristotle for almost all sections of the *Ars poetica* except those which he characterizes as satirical digressions. A complete listing follows:

Horace	Aristotle
1–13 (plot)	1455b12, 1450a3, 1450a15, 1450a38, 1451b27, 1451a23, 1451a36
14–23 (episodes)	1451b33, 1456a25, (last two above)
24–31 (diction)	1458a18
32–37	(digression)
38–41 (genius: subject)	1450a33
42–45 (epic)	1460a1, 1459a29
46–59 (new words)	1458b31–1459a16
60–72	(digression)
73–85 (meters)	1460a1, 1448b28, 1449a21
86–88	(digression)
89–95 (tragic, comic verse)	1448a14
96–103 (passions, pity)	1455a31, 1456a33
104–11 (diction)	1456b8
112–18 (decorum)	1454a15, 1461b9
119–27 (old, new characters)	1453b21, 1454a15
128–35 (imitation of poets)	1456a7, 1448b34
136–45 (epic beginning)	(no equivalent; but cf. 1462b3)
146–50 (epic plot)	1459a29
151–52 (true and false)	1460a18–33
153–78 (decorum of age)	1454a33; also *Rhetoric*
179–88 (incredible)	1460a11, 1453b1, 1461b26
189–92 (plot)	1452b14
192 (3 interlocutors)	1449a14
193–201 (chorus)	1456a25
201–19	(digression; but cf. 1458b31)
220–33 (satire and tragedy)	1449a19, 1451a6
234–43 (satire)	(no equivalent)
244–50 (rustic audience)	(„ „)
251–59 (iamb)	1449a21, 1459b31
260–74	(digression)
275–84 (tragedy, old comedy)	1448a29, 1449a14
285–94	(digression)
295–308	(„)
309–16 (wisdom)	(no equivalent)
317–22 (imitation)	1447a13, 1447b13–24, 1454b8, 1450a29
323–32	(digression)
333–46 (utility, pleasure)	1449b21, 1453a1, 1453b11 (also *Rhetoric* on brevity)
347–60 (defences)	1460b6 ff.

Horace	Aristotle
361–65 (poetry and painting)	1454b8
366–78	(digression)
379–90	(„)
391–407 (natural origins)	1448b4
408–11 (nature vs. art)	1461b26
412–18	(digression)
419–44	(„)
445–52 (meter and poetry)	1456b24
453–76	(digression)

Maggi's initial thesis that Horace was versifying Aristotle and his demonstration of the parallelism of the two texts did not fail to produce changes in the interpretation of the *Ars poetica*. Not only are all traces of the late-classical and the humanistic commentators removed (this had already been accomplished in Robortello's *Paraphrasis*), but certain new orientations in the reading of the text are introduced. And these concern really important poetic matters. Horace's somewhat vague distinction between "res" and "verba" becomes the much more specific division of plot and diction. The general admonition to make all parts of the poem cohere is read as equivalent to the organizing principles of necessity and probability. Horace's digressions are identified with Aristotle's episodes. The vices of diction pointed out by the Roman are found to be the opposites of the virtues of diction extolled by the Greek. The "dulcia sunto" of Horace (l. 99), long since identified by the commentators with the arousing of the audience's passions, is now related to Aristotle's pity; similarly, "prodesse" is taken as an exemplification of the arousal of pity, fear, and τὸ φιλάνθρωπον, while "delectare" becomes synonymous with the pleasure produced by imitation. Horace's mixture of truth with falsehood is traced back to Aristotle's παραλογισμός and the impossible probable. Notions of imitation, which had already been related by earlier commentators to a copying of nature, are, by Maggi, more definitely connected with Aristotles' conception of action. Finally, Maggi follows his predecessors in associating Horace's precepts on decorum with Aristotle's recommendations for character. All in all, this is not an inconsiderable reorientation of the reading of Horace, and Maggi becomes a kind of pioneer in this respect.

GRIFOLI (1550)

Some of the same credit for pioneering may also be accorded to Giacopo Grifoli, who in the same year of 1550 published his *In Artem poeticam Horatii interpretatio*.[22] For Grifoli also rereads the *Ars poetica* in the light of the *Poetics*. Two factors, however, decrease his originality: first, he

[22] There is no indication in the Grifoli volume as to whether it was published early or late in the year; the same is true for the Maggi volume. But since the dedication of the latter is dated September, 1549, I am assuming that it was published fairly early in 1550 and hence antedated Grifoli.

[122]

came after Maggi and probably knew his *Interpretatio*; second, in certain senses, his "rereading" reverts to a much earlier tradition. Grifoli's commentary is long and complete; it follows the usual pattern of citing a passage of the text, giving a general interpretation of the passage, and then providing a line-for-line or word-for-word gloss. Its total position is a very curious one. The basic assumption is that Horace in the *Epistle* is imitating Aristotle and adopting, paraphrasing, and reorganizing Aristotle's central ideas. This is clear from such statements as the one found in the dedication to Fabio Mignanelli, Bishop of Lucera: "This certainly I do not hesitate to affirm, that I have expounded the passages in Horace and that this work was culled almost entirely from Aristotle's *Art of Poetry*," and others in the body of the text proper: "Seeing then that in Aristotle's opinion tragedy consists of plot, characters, thought, diction, spectacle, and melody, he decided that the first thing to discuss was the construction of the plot"; "nor does he follow any the less here than elsewhere the teaching of Aristotle."[23] Starting from this assumption, he seeks a way of explaining Horace's organization in terms of the *Poetics*. He finds, first, that Horace is concerned essentially with tragedy, just as Aristotle was, and that he treats the epic only insofar as it has characteristics in common with tragedy (p. 11). Second, he believes that Horace has ordered his work around the six qualitative parts of tragedy, altering, however, the sequence of treatment. Thus lines 1–23 are devoted to plot, lines 114–18 and 319–22 to character, lines 93–113, 114–18, and 319–22 to thought, lines 24–31, 32–45, 114–18, and 319–22 to diction, and lines 179–83 and 275–80 to spectacle and melody. But there is much uncertainty, as the overlappings and repetitions indicate; this is a result of the corruption of the original assumption by other positions derived from other systems.

I have already pointed out in Chapter II how Grifoli adds to the system just outlined the set of rhetorical distinctions of invention, disposition, and elocution, thereby introducing a third layer of meanings. What Horace says is read not only under the influence of preconceptions about the *Poetics* but also as a representation of well-known rhetorical topics. This makes it possible to attach to given passages a variety of associated meanings. In lines 32–45, for example, Horace is speaking of the necessity of choosing a subject fitted to one's genius; if this is done, eloquent words and a proper order will ensue. Grifoli sees in the lines "things more abstruse than most people suspect." First, he paraphrases and quotes Aristotle on the two types of errors in poems, those ascribable to the poetic art and those ascribable to some other art (*Poetics* 1460b15); a craftsman like the one Horace mentions sins in the poetic art when he

---

23 *Interpretatio* (1550), p. 7: "Illud certe affirmare non dubito, ostendisse me locos Horatianos, ac totum ferè hoc opus ex Aristotelis Arte poetica decerptum"; p. 11: "Videns igitur Aristotelis iudicio Tragoediam constare fabula, moribus, sententia, dictione, apparatu, & melodia; primum de constitutione fabulae disserendum esse statuit"; p. 39: "neque nunc minus, quàm vnquam alias praeceptionem Aristotelis secutum."

undertakes a task superior to his capacities. Next (for ll. 38–41), Grifoli states that Horace is here beginning a new section of the work: after having expounded the proper composition of the plot, he now indicates how beauty may be achieved through diction. We shall see that this division between plot and diction is fundamental in the commentary. Finally, Horace's statement about "facundia" and "ordo" leads Grifoli to draw a parallel between the poet and the orator: the proper choice of subject matter is equivalent to invention, "ordo" to disposition, and "facundia" to elocution (see the passage quoted above in Chapter II). The general rhetorical preoccupations of the work are confirmed by Grifoli's frequent references to Cicero, Quintilian, and other masters of the art.

A further distinction is necessary, however, in order to understand completely what is going on in Grifoli's commentary. In his introduction, Grifoli twice insists that, in speaking about tragedy (and incidentally the epic), Horace was concerned essentially with the matter of appropriateness: "quaecunque ad rerum *congruentiam, & decorum* attinent, ea diligenter est persecutus" (p. 11) and "Constat igitur hic libellus ex ijs praecipuè rebus, in quibus maxime *quid deceat* apparet" (p. 12). In his effort to reconcile this emphasis with the Aristotelian system that he sees in the work, Grifoli arrives at this solution: The major form of appropriateness in a poetic work is of words to things. Of Aristotle's six qualitative parts, therefore, the two most important are μῦθος or "fabula" and λέξις or "oratio," and the *Ars poetica* thus divides its time between these two parts. Thus lines 1–23 concern "fabula," but the section of commentary on lines 24–31 begins with "Transit ad alteram partem, quae λέξις nominatur" (p. 17), and the commentary on line 280 starts thus: "ad λέξιν redit. supra quoque: & tulit eloquium insolitum" (p. 82). But what of the other four parts? The answer is fairly simple: spectacle and melody are dismissed as belonging to the instruments of poetry, and character and thought are in a sense collapsed with diction. Already in the introduction, Grifoli has declared that there is no point concerning sententiae or mores that is not treated by means of diction; moreover, "since speech is the translator of the mind and this is the indicator of character, in speaking of its decorum one has also spoken of the decorum of the rest."[24] Without consideration of language it would hardly be possible to know if the "officium, proprietas, similitudo, constantia" of character are properly observed or not (under these four terms are hidden Aristotle's requisities for character). The same idea is made even more explicit later:

Although the subject discussed is περὶ τῆς λέξεως, nevertheless nature and character are here treated, from which diction normally derives. Otherwise it will not be appropriate, and from the beginning we have warned that whenever the poet spoke about diction, he would be speaking in the proper places about

[24] *Ibid.*, p. 12: "quoniam oratio est interpres mentis, & haec est morum index, de illius decoro dicendo de reliquorum quoque decoro dixit."

sententia and character, as he does here [*A.p.*, ll. 119–135] and in what follows.[25]

For these reasons, when Grifoli comes to assign the six qualitative parts to object, manner, and means (p. 97), the three belonging to object of imitation are identified as diction, thought, and character, the two belonging to means as spectacle and melody, and the one belonging to manner as plot. From his explanation of this last assignment, it is apparent that he gives to "imitation" the meaning of "representation": "Since plot is the composite of the events in a tragedy, let it be imitated both in that way and in that sequence in which the plot itself has been composed."[26]

Horace, thus, in the last analysis, reduces Aristotle to the old "res-verba" dichotomy—and then in turn reduces it to "verba" alone. For if the object of imitation is character, thought, and diction, and if diction contains the essence of the other two, then one treats all of the essential problems of poetry when one speaks about language. Grifoli's analysis is, in fact, largely a reduction of Horace's poetics to linguistic problems. In the list of parallel passages following, I shall indicate for the most significant passages how this is true:

Horace	*Aristotle*	
1–23	1451a16	Horace's "natural" corresponds to Aristotle's "necessary and probable." Unity of action, which does not even result from having a single hero, cannot possibly come from mixed subjects. Unity and simplicity are required, mixture of styles and genres is condemned.
24–31	(none)	λέξις; in passing, spectacle and melody. In language, as in character, vices exist which imitate virtues. Of the three styles, Horace here is treating the middle. Cross references to rhetorical works. Excess of ornament in *diction* creates a monster comparable to the monster in *plot* of ll. 1–23.
32–45	1460b16	First, proper choice of subject to avoid artistic error. Then, return to λέξις; beauty of diction after beauty of plot. Invention, disposition, and elocution.
73–85	1459b32	Epic verse.
	1449a23	Iamb and daily speech; in tragedy, produces admiration.
86–92	(none)	Diction adapted to "quod decet"; the "color" of the iamb adapted to the quality of persons in tragedy or comedy.
93–113	1449b27	Language adapted to characters, situation, etc.
	1455a31	Arousal of passions in the audience; cf. the orator. In comedy, pleasure; in tragedy, "metus, misericordia, horror."

25 *Ibid.*, p. 41: "Quamuis enim περὶ τῆς λέξεως disputetur, tamen natura, & mores exprimuntur, & ab his ea emanare solet. alioqui decorum suum non habebit, & nos à principio monuimus, cum de Oratione dissereret poëta, de Sententia, & Moribus suis locis eum dicturum, vt hic, & in sequentibus cum dicit."

26 *Ibid.*, p. 97: "cum fabula sit compositio rerum omnium in tragoedia, & eo modo, & ordine imitandum sit, quo composita sit ipsa fabula."

Horace	Aristotle	
114–18	1454a16	Language appropriate to persons: Aristotle's τὸ ὅμοιον.
	1454a33	Horace's equivalents for Aristotle's four requisites of character: line 312 for τὰ χρηστά; line 156 for τὰ ἁρμόττοντα; line 114 for τὸ ὅμοιον; line 119 for τὸ ὁμαλόν. Differences in λέξις from differences in character.
119–35		In new characters, τὸ ὁμαλόν.
136–52	1448a25 [1460a20]	Epic characters insofar as they resemble tragic; mixture of the true and the false.
153–78		Decorum of age; τὰ ἁρμόττοντα.
179–83	1452b19 1455b24 1453b1 1449b27	Parts of tragedy; on- and off-stage action.
189–201	1454a37	Deus ex machina.
202–19	1447a22	Spectacle and melody. Horace's primitive audience.
220–43	1456b2	The diction of satire. Cicero against the mixing of genres. Sententiae and "verba" as appropriate to "res"; reference to the rhetoricians.
275–80	1450a13	ὄψις. Spectacle and melody as instruments of imitation; cf. action and memory in rhetoric. λέξις again.
295–308	(none)	Art vs. nature. Horace's double intention: (1) precepts for poem, (2) precepts for the end of poetry, i.e., for "delectatio" and "utilitas."
309–18	1454b8	Imitation of Platonic Ideas and Forms.
319–22	1450a7 1454a16 1450a25 1451b27 1453b11	Six parts of tragedy (distributed as indicated in discussion above). Diction from character and thought. Diction as deriving its meaning from character, and meaningless without it. Pleasure from the "fabula morata," from pity and fear in tragedy. For affecting the audience, necessity of properly constituted plot and decorum.
323–32	(none)	Both diction and materials must be great. Nature and art.
333–60	(none)	Utility and pleasure; need of "brevitas" for the first and "natura, verosimilia" for the second. Utility: "quae doceant, corrigant, moueant." Appeal to the young through pleasure, to the old through utility.
366–78	1448b4	Two natural causes of poetry. Imitation as a source of pleasure, which in turn leads to utility.
391–407	(none)	Pleasure as leading to utility.

As far as Grifoli's general interpretation of Horace is concerned, then, it is a strange combination of an attempt to read Horace as an imitator of Aristotle and a reversion to the rhetorical approaches of earlier years. Aristotle is soon made subject to the rhetoricians, and rhetoric itself is reduced to its minimal term, the study of language and all its problems.

That these were the ideas about poetry still most current is indicated by such a work as Lodovico Dolce's *Osservationi nella volgar lingua* (1550), whose first three books are exclusively linguistic and grammatical but whose fourth book deals with poetry. Here again, a few ideas are borrowed from Aristotle: poetry is an imitation; not all writers of verse are poets. But the main body of doctrine is in the old Horatian-rhetorical tradition. Immediately after the statement that poetry is an imitation, Dolce says: "for the function of the poet is to imitate the actions of men, and his end, under lovely veils of useful and moral inventions, to delight the soul of him who reads."[27] The poet must possess not only wisdom, but also invention, order, artifice, and words; of these, the most important are the last two. The real poetic gift is that of expressing the invented materials by means of "beauties and ornaments," in order to delight the reader, to arouse his passions. The whole position of Dolce, which is not too distant from that of Grifoli, is contained in the following passage:

> Nevertheless, since verses and words are the brush and the paints of the poet with which he shades and colors the canvas of his invention to make so marvelous a portrait of nature that the minds of men are ravished by it, he must devote his greatest attention and industry to composing them in this way, and with words so beautiful and so appropriate to the matter of which he treats that that end, sought and desired by him who reads, will be achieved; without which all his labors are exerted and consumed in vain.[28]

Lilio Gregorio Giraldi's *Dialogi duo de poëtis nostrorum temporum* (1551) is even more backward looking in its few passages relevant to poetics. Essentially the work is a catalogue of recent and contemporary poets of various European countries. The listing is summary, providing merely names, an occasional fact, and, for each poet, a conventional bouquet. The complimentary phrases that Giraldi accords the poets he admires sound for all the world like those used by Pietro Ricci at the beginning of the century; the epithets applied in 1505 to Latin poets are now applied to modern poets writing in Latin or in the vulgar tongues. So Pico della Mirandola is praised for his "ingenium, doctrina," for his "facilitas, affectus"; Pontano is "doctus, elegans, absolutus, enucleatus, exquisitus"; Sadoleto has as his qualities "grauitas, modestia," Bembo's poems are "dulcia, mollia, delicata"; Sannazaro has created "ingenij exquisita monumenta," and Calcagnini is noteworthy for "eruditio, doctrina."[29]

---

27 *Osservationi* (1550), p. 87v: "percioche l'ufficio del Poeta è di imitare le attioni de gli huomini: e il fine sotto leggiadri ueli di morali & utili inuentioni dilettar l'animo di chi legge."

28 *Ibid.*, p. 88v: "Non di meno, perche i uersi e le parole sono il pennello, & i colori del Poeta, con che egli ua adombrando e dipingendo la tauola della sua inuentione per fare un ritratto cotanto marauiglioso della natura, che ne stupiscano gli intelletti de glihuomini; dee porre ogni suo principale studio e diligenza in comporgli tali, e con uoci cosi belle & appartinenti alla materia, di che egli tratta, che ne riesca quel fine ricercato e desiderato da chi legge; e senza ilquale ogni sua fatica è posta e consumata in darno."

29 *Dialogi duo* (1551), pp. 16–20, 40.

These epithets indicate no more than certain kinds of knowledge on the part of the poet and certain qualities of style in his writing; they do not presuppose any poetic theory beyond the simplest rhetorical preconceptions.

DENORES (1553)

After Grifoli's fairly complex and experimental commentary, that of Giason Denores in his *In epistolam Q. Horatij Flacci de arte poetica Interpretatio* (1553) seems like a return to the patterns and the procedures of an earlier generation. Indeed, Denores takes frequent issue with the interpretations of both Maggi and Grifoli, claiming that he is reflecting instead the lectures of Trifon Gabriele on Horace, as he had heard them and as he had summarized them even before Gabriele's death in 1549. Gabriele's ideas, if they are accurately represented here, are very close to those of Giovanni Britannico and Parrasio. For Denores organizes the whole of the Horatian text around the invention–disposition–elocution distinction, and in a way even more systematic than that of his predecessors. Almost all the precepts he states—and he returns also to the preceptive form—are concerned with one of the three terms. The initial statement that he intends to follow this pattern is found in connection with the first lines of the *Ars poetica*, when he affirms that one of Horace's aims is "the formation of our taste with respect to every rule of invention, disposition, and elocution in every type of poetry."[30] Lines 1–23, he says, are concerned with invention, which is the "soul" of poetry. To explain the subsequent passages, he calls upon the rhetorical division into three parts of elocution itself: "genus" or "ratio dicendi" or "character" (the particular kind or quality of style), "verba," and "numeri" (meters or verses). Lines 24–31 treat the first of these, "character." General notions of disposition appear in lines 32–41, and the more particular problem of natural versus artificial order in lines 42–45. The second part of elocution, "verba," figures in lines 46–72, and the third part, "numeri," in lines 73–88. Lines 89–98 make special applications of the rules for "character" and "verba" to tragedy and comedy. Then, after long sections on other matters, Horace returns to the distinction in lines 220–50, pointing out that it is disposition and elocution, rather than invention, that give quality to commonplace materials. Lines 251–74, on the verse of tragedy and comedy, treat its "numeri" (rounding out the materials of lines 89–98). Finally, when Horace speaks of "sapere" and Socratic philosophy in lines 309–32, he is returning to the problem of invention. In all, somewhat over a third of the text is made to fit into this general scheme. As for the rest of it, Denores sees the long central section as devoted primarily to problems of arousing the audience's emotions, of decorum, and of conventions for the stage; but even here the major dis-

---

30 *In epistolam* (1553), p. 5v; see above, chap. II, p. 56 and n. 25 for the full text.

tinction is sometimes applicable. For example, if the poet wishes to arouse the passions, he must attend to "ornaments" and "figures" (ll. 99–113); if he uses old, traditional characters, he exercises no invention, but he makes these characters his own through proper disposition and elocution (ll. 119–30). The last part of the text (aside from the recommendations for the behavior of the poet) seems to be of interest to Denores mostly for the discussion of utility and pleasure as the ends of poetry.

Throughout the *Ars poetica*, although in comparatively small number, Denores finds analogies to the Aristotelian poetics. Sometimes these are merely implied, with no direct reference to Aristotle—as, for example, the characterization of invention as the "anima" of poetry (ll. 1–23), or the suggestion that the five-act magnitude of dramas is related to the proper size of animals (ll. 189–90), or the inclusion of "timor" and "misericordia" among the passions to be aroused by the poet (ll. 99–113). Elsewhere, the references are explicit and the text is cited: Aristotle on the pleasure derived from imitation, in connection with Horace's remarks on the choice of words and figures (ll. 46–72); on the difference between poetry and history, relevant to Horace's "res gestae" (ll. 73–88); on history and verisimilitude, apropos of Horace's three types of narrative (ll. 131–52); on the necessity of producing pity and fear by plot rather than by spectacle, in connection with Horace's precept on off-stage action (ll. 179–88); on purgation, as a means of producing Horace's "prodesse" (ll. 333–46); and on artistic and nonartistic errors (ll. 347–60). The list of parallels is not long, and it will be readily seen that they merely indicate an association of Aristotle's text with Horace's, without any important influence upon the interpretation of the latter.

For Denores' reading of Horace remains essentially rhetorical. This is true not only because of his persistence in applying the invention–disposition–elocution terminology to so large a portion of the text, but also because other rhetorical tendencies are evident. The whole conception of the relationship of audience to work and to poet is in the Ciceronian tradition: the poet, like the orator, seeks to induce the audience to admiration (in part for his own genius) and to awaken in it a wide variety of passions (ll. 46–113). To do so, he must pay particularly close attention to the decorum of persons, just as the orator does and just as Aristotle recommends in the *Rhetoric* (ll. 114–18, 153–78). Such arousing of the passions is itself merely a means to a further end, that of correcting and directing its lives by providing moral precepts and examples. It is interesting in this connection to note that Denores insists that "delectare" does not mean "oblectare" but rather "movere" and that pleasure itself is thus a form of utility; pleasure operates on the will of the audience as utility concerns its mind, and the two together produce the desired moral effects (ll. 333–46). Many details of the construction of poems are determined by this desire to produce stated effects on audiences by means of rhetorical devices.

[129]

LOVISINI (1554)

As compared with Denores, the Aristotelian flavor of Francesco Lovisini's *In librum Q. Horatii Flacci de arte poetica commentarius* (1554) is much more considerable. This results in part from the generous citation of the *Poetics* to explain passages in the *Ars poetica*, in part from the numerous references to various other works of Aristotle, especially the *Nicomachean Ethics* and the *Rhetoric*. Indeed, the whole impression of erudition is much greater; Lovisini brings into his commentary on Horace every possible quotation from Greek and Latin literature that seems to him to have some relevance to the words or the lines in question. Much of this erudition, however, turns out to be historical in content—very like that of the expositors at the beginning of the century—and adds little to the meaning of the text as an art of poetry. For Lovisini's interpretation of Horace, the most significant references are those to rhetorical treatises, primarily Aristotle's *Rhetoric*, but also Cicero, Quintilian, Demetrius, Hermogenes, and others. These sources, plus all the others he invokes, enable him to contest and correct the older commentators such as Acron and Porphyrion and the more recent ones such as Maggi, Grifoli, and Denores; but these corrections concern points of detail rather than any general reading of the text. This is also true of the majority of the texts cited from the *Poetics* as parallels to Horace, a list of which follows:

Horace	*Aristotle*
1–13 (congruous subject)	1447*b*13 (poet from imitation)
	1450*a*38 (plot as soul)
	1448*a*4 (poetry and painting)
14–23 (simplicity, unity)	1451*b*33 (episodic plot)
	1451*a*19 (unity not from hero)
24–31 (vices in style)	(none)
32–37 (total excellence)	(none)
38–41 (choice of subject)	(none)
42–45 (order of epic)	(none)
46–51 (elocution)	1456*b*20 (diction)
52–59 (new words)	(none)
60–72 (usage)	(none)
73–85 (meters for genres)	1460*a*1 (mixture of meters)
	1447*a*15 (poetic genres)
	1459*b*34 (epic meter)
	1448*b*31 (iamb)
	1449*a*21 (iamb in tragedy)
	1449*a*26 (iamb in daily speech)
86–88 (poetic styles)	(none)

Horace		Aristotle	
89–92	(trag. and comedy)	1448a16	(trag. and comedy)
		1453a18	(Thyestes)
93–95	(style of tr., com.)	1453b1	(pity and fear)
96–103	(speech of tragedy)	1453a21	(tragic families)
		1453b1	(pity and fear)
	(audience emotion)	1455a30	(emotion of poet)
		1452a4	(sources of emotion)
104–13	(action and speech)	(none)	
114–18	(decorum of speech	(none)	
119–27	(old, new heroes)	1460a35	(improbabilities in *Odyssey*)
		1453b22	(traditional plots)
		1454a20	(τὰ ἁρμόττοντα)
		1454a22	(τὸ ὅμοιον)
		1454a25	(τὸ ὁμαλόν)
128–35	(old subjects)	1448b38	(Homeric subjects)
136–39	(epic beginning)	(none)	
140–45	(„ „)	(none)	
146–52	("in medias res")	1451a36	(necessary, probable)
	(true, false)		
153–57	(decorum of age)	(none)	
158–60	(child)	(none)	
161–65	(youth)	(none)	
166–68	(adult)	(none)	
169–74	(old man)	(none)	
175–78	(traits for each)	(none)	
179–88	(on-, off-stage)	1453b1	(emotions from spectacle)
189–90	(five acts)	1450b35	(magnitude)
		1449b12	(time of tragedy, epic)
191–92	("deus ex machina")	1454b2	("deus ex machina")
193–201	(chorus)	1452a15	(parts of tragedy)
		1456a29	(choral songs)
202–7	(melody, music)	1450a7	(qualitative parts)
		1450b18	(melody)
		1447a23	(harmony, rhythm)
208–19	(licence, vulgarity)	1447a26	(„ „)
220–24	(satyrs in tragedy	1449b27	(pity and fear)
		1449a19	(satyric tragedy)
		1451b37	(dramatic contests)
		1462b11	(tr. superior to epic)
225–33	(decorum of satyrs)	(none)	
234–39	(satyric diction)	(none)	
240–43	(satyric invention)	(none)	

Horace		*Aristotle*	
244–50	(speech of satyrs)	1449a35 (αἰσχρόν, φθαρτικόν)	
251–59	(iamb and spondee)	(none)	
260–69	(Gk. *vs.* Lat. poets)	1454a28 (Euripides' errors)	
270–74	(Plautus censured)	(none)	
275–80	(history of tragedy)	1448a29 (origins of tragedy)	
		1449a15 (Aeschylus' additions)	
281–84	(old comedy)	1449a31 (definition of comedy)	
		1449a37 (chorus in comedy)	
285–94	(Latin poets)	(none)	
295–301	(art and nature)	1455a33 (talent, poetic furor)	
301–8	(poetic problems)	1447a13 (imitation as "officium")	
309–16	(knowledge)	(none)	
317–22	(life as model)	1447a15 (poetry as imitation)	
		1449b7 (qualitative parts)	
323–32	(Roman avarice)	(none)	
333–46	(ends of poetry)	1451a36 (necessary, probable)	
347–60	(errors of poet)	1460b15 (two kinds of errors)	
		1454a29 (errors of Homer)	
361–65	(poetry, painting)	1454b9 (poetry, painting)	
		1450a38 („ „)	
366–73	(no mediocrity)	(none)	
374–78	(poetry for delight)	(none)	
379–85	(ignorant poets)	(none)	
386–90	(correction)	(none)	
391–99	(civilizing role)	(none)	
400–7	(praise of poetry)	1447a24 (music and poetry)	
408–11	(nature, art)	(none)	
412–18	(advice to poet)	(none)	
419–25	(flatterers)	(none)	
426–33	(friends)	(none)	
434–37	(„)	(none)	
438–44	(true critic)	(none)	
445–52	(role of critic)	(none)	
453–63	(mad poet)	(none)	
463–69	(„ „)	(none)	
470–76	(„ „)	(none)	

I have given this list in such detail, respecting all of Lovisini's divisions of the Horatian text, for several reasons. First, it is interesting to see to what an extent the text is now subdivided—Lovisini's divisions number sixty-eight—and what topics are indicated as the subject-matter of each division. Second, the list shows how many passages from the *Poetics* are brought into association with the text, and to what ideas in Horace they are said to be parallel. It is easy to see how commentators and critics, finding so many recurrences of ideas in the two documents, might be strengthened in their conviction that Horace was merely imitating or paraphrasing Aristotle and that the two theorists were saying essentially the same things. But a close study of the parallels in the above list shows that the resemblances are largely topical; in some cases they concern purely historical matters, such as the identity of Thyestes or Aeschylus' additions to the tragic form; in others they show that the two theorists were writing about the same topics, but do not indicate conclusions by any means similar. For example, to take a case of "multiple reference," three passages from Aristotle are cited as parallel to lines 1–13 of the *Ars poetica.* In the first of these Aristotle states that the poet is a poet by reason of his imitation, and not because he writes in verse; in the second, that plot is the soul of tragedy; in the third, that poets represent characters as better or worse than we, or as like us, just as painters do. Now the first is cited in support of the general idea, attributed to these lines in Horace, that the poet follows fantasy rather than opinion; the second, to show that it is proper for Horace to treat, at the very beginning, the "constitution of the argument and the plot"; the third, because Horace had drawn the comparison "pictoribus atque poetis. . . ." This juxtaposition of passages neither indicates a clear conception of Aristotle's theory of imitation or of his definition of plot, nor, for that matter, does it throw any additional light on the comprehension of Horace's lines. Or for another such example: five passages from Aristotle are fitted to lines 119–27, in which Horace says that when traditional characters are introduced they must be handled in keeping with the tradition and that when new ones are used, they must be made to be self-consistent. Aristotle is first quoted to show that traditional materials must be followed exactly, no matter how improbable they may be; second, that traditional plots must not be modified; third, that τὰ ἁρμόττοντα is equivalent to "sibi conuenientia"; fourth, that τὸ ὅμοιον means similarity to historical or traditional character, such as the "honoratum . . . Achillem"; fifth, that τὸ ὁμαλόν states a principle of consistency identical with that of Horace. These parallels, interesting as they may be for Lovisini's interpretation of Aristotle, add little to the interpretation of Horace—unless it be a certain number of irrelevant and inappropriate considerations.

Finally, I have produced the complete list above to demonstrate what passages in Horace, at this stage of scholarship, were still regarded as independent of Aristotle. These, it will be seen, largely concern Latin poetry and certain practical counsels to poets which Aristotle's theoretical position did not admit.

Out of all this elaborate commentary and this extensive juxtaposition of texts, there emerges very little that might be called Lovisini's interpretation of Horace. Erudition and the conventional explanations have taken the place of independent reading. Lovisini assigns the usual passages to invention, disposition, and elocution, makes the usual comparisons between poetry and rhetoric, insists as did his predecessors on the decisive role of the audience in determining the nature of poems. A few points that he makes are, however, original enough to deserve special mention. For one, he seems to be more of a Platonist than many of his forerunners; in the first section of commentary, he quotes the *Symposium* to the effect that all artisans and artificers are poets in a sense, and the *Apology* on the divine furor; he identifies Horace's "exemplar vitae" (l. 317) with the "Idea which, as Plato says in the *Parmenides*, contains all particular things and is separate from them."[31] Moreover, many passages are quoted from Plato in connection with incidental matters. For another, Lovisini emphasizes certain ideas about the relationship between poetry and nature. From his comments on lines 14–23 it is clear that he thinks of probability as natural probability, for he defends the Dido episode in the *Aeneid* in this way: "that episode is not completely inconsistent with the matter at hand, but rather produces pleasure through the variety of materials; frequently, in fact, voyagers driven by storms have arrived at the outermost lands."[32] The fact that a thing may happen in nature is taken as justification for a particular happening in a specific poem. Lastly, Lovisini expands Horace's notions about utility and pleasure as the ends of poetry. He quotes Theon on the ends proposed by Homer: in the *Iliad*, that he might inspire men to justice, in the *Odyssey*, to exhort us to bear adverse fortune with equanimity.[33] He sees the "prodesse" as resulting from allegory in plots, "which teach us wisely and thoroughly what is best in life," and from the representation of character, which teaches us our duty.[34] Utility and pleasure are expanded into the triple "ut doceret, ut delectaret, ut moueret" of Cicero, with the third member of the trilogy making the other two effective (p. 24v).

Lovisini's commentary of 1554 was the last of a series of five formal expositions of the *Ars poetica* which appeared in the short space of six years: Robortello's in 1548, Maggi's and Grifoli's in 1550, Denores' in 1553, Lovisini's in 1554. The next such formal discussion will not be published for seven years, in 1561, when Pigna produces his *Poetica Horatiana*. But in the intervening years, many documents in the "Horatian mode" were written and published, and the tradition was by no means interrupted.

---

[31] *Commentarius* (1554), p. 63v: "Idaea, quae, ut ait Plato in Parmenide, singularia omnia continet, & ab ijs seiuncta est."

[32] *Ibid.*, p. 7v: "res illa à re proposita non penitus abhorret, quin potius rerum uarietate delectationem affert: nauigantes enim saepe in ultimas terras tempestate appulsi peruenerunt."

[33] *Ibid.*, p. 4v: "ut homines ad iustitiam inflammet, in Odyssaea ad ferendam aequo animo aduersam fortunam nos cohortatur."

[34] *Ibid.*, p. 66: "fabularum allegoria, quibus, quid optimum in uita sit, prudenter edocent" and "moribus etiam nos ad officium poetae boni inflammant."

In fact, during the last two of these six years, while the formal commentaries were being published, Benedetto Varchi was delivering a series of lectures to the Accademia Fiorentina which reflected, in part at least, the same Horatian ideas. The lectures, dated 1553 and 1554, were not published until 1590. As we shall see later, Varchi's point of departure was specifically the text of the *Poetics*; but most of the *Lezzioni della poetica* move rapidly away from Aristotle in the direction of Horace. In a sense, he ascribes the same movement to Horace himself, since he speaks of the *Poetics* as the text "from which Horace drew his own art" ("dal quale cauò Horazio la sua," p. 677). With Horace, also, Varchi insists that the knowledge of the art, derived from arts of poetry ancient or modern, is insufficient without the poet's natural gifts; to both art and nature must be added a firm knowledge of several languages and of the poets who have written in them. This emphasis upon knowledge of various kinds finds authority in Cicero, whom Varchi cites, and brings Varchi's position into close contact with that of the rhetoricians.

Cicero is the authority, as well, for Varchi's declaration that the qualities requisite for the poet are three in number: eloquence, goodness, and knowledge. All three are required if the ends of poetry are to be achieved. As Varchi explains the relationship between qualities and ends, he produces an extremely interesting statement, one in which, to a degree, certain distinctions are lost. The ends, as Horace would wish them, are utility and pleasure. We discover, in the following sentence, an initial dependence of ends from qualities, in which utility springs from goodness and knowledge, and pleasure from eloquence: "It is therefore necessary . . . that good and perfect poets should be eloquent, virtuous, and erudite; otherwise we could never derive and learn from them either delightfulness of words, or goodness of behavior, or knowledge of things."[35] But pleasure, we are soon told, is not only of the sensual kind which comes from the harmonies of poetry, but also of the intellectual kind and of a kind combining the two others. For this reason, utility itself will be a source of pleasure for the soul:

. . . because pleasure is of three sorts, of the mind (which we shall call intellectual pleasure), of the body (which we shall call sensual pleasure), and of the soul and the body together (which we shall call mixed or common pleasure), we must know that in the poets alone, or surely more so in the poets than in all other writers, all these three kinds of pleasures are found together. For the harmony of the words which are heard . . . delights properly the body; and the utility of the things which are understood delights properly the mind; but because words cannot be separated from things . . . and things cannot be expressed without words, it

---

35 *Lezzioni* (1590 ed.), p. 630: "Bisogna dunque . . . che i poeti buoni, e perfetti siano eloquenti, virtuosi, e dottrinati, altramente mai da loro trarre, o imparare non si potrebbe ne leggiadria di parole, ne bontà di costumi, ne scienza di cose."

comes to pass that the soul as well as the body, at the very same time, are delighted by words through things and by things through words.[36]

In these passages, an additional distinction has been introduced. It is the distinction between "res" and "verba," taken both as components of the poem and as causes of its effects. All in all, some such schematism as the following results:

Qualities of the poet	Parts of the poem	Ends or effects
goodness	things	utility, pleasure
knowledge	things	utility, pleasure
eloquence	words	pleasure

Much of what Varchi has to say, in this Horatian context, relates to the end of utility, which he sees as essentially a form of teaching. What is taught is primarily lessons for ethics, secondarily information pertaining to all branches of knowledge: the rewards of virtue, the punishments for vice, the elements of the sciences (p. 576). On the basis of their success or failure in this kind of teaching, one will classify poets as good or bad: "Those alone merit all praise who remove men from the vices and inspire them to the virtues; then the others, as they do this more or less, are to be more or less praised and held in esteem."[37] Those who do the opposite should be punished. Among them, Varchi distinguishes four separate classes: (1) The plebeian poets, "all those who without art, or judgment, or knowledge write only to please the common people and to make the crowd laugh." Examples are the authors of the *Morgante* and the *Girone Cortese*. (2) The ridiculous poets, "all those poets who write for the sake of nonsense and of plays on words." Examples: Burchiello, Antonio Alamanni, Berni. (3) The obscene poets, such as Ovid and Catullus; these especially should be punished. (4) The satirical poets, who "through their wicked nature, or through hatred, or because they have been besought or paid, or merely for the joy of it, speak ill of others." These, in keeping with Plato's recommendation, should be banished.[38]

[36] *Ibid.*, pp. 631–32: "perchè il diletto è di tre ragioni, d'animo, il quale chiameremo intellettuale; di corpo, il quale chiameremo sensuale; e d'anima, e di corpo insieme, il quale chiameremo misto, ouero comune, deuemo sapere, che ne' poeti soli, o certamente piu ne i poeti, che in tutti gli altri scrittori, si ritrouano tutte e tre queste maniere di diletti insiememente, percioche l'armonia delle parole, che s'odono, . . . diletta propriamente il corpo, e l'vtilità delle cose, che s'intendono diletta propiamente l'animo; ma perche le parole non possono separarsi dalle cose . . . e le cose non possono senza le parole sprimersi, quinci è, che l'vne per l'altre, e l'altre per l'vne dilettano à vn medesimo tempo, cosi l'animo, come il corpo."

[37] *Ibid.*, p. 585: "quegli soli meritano tutte le lodi, i quali rimuouono gli huomini da' vizij, o gl'accendono alle virtù, gli altri poi, secondo, che piu, o meno cio fanno, deono essere piu, o meno lodati, e tenuti in pregio."

[38] *Ibid.*, pp. 585–87: "tutti quegli, che senza arte, o giudizio, o dottrina scriuono solo per piacere alla Plebe, e far ridere il Volgo"; "tutti quei poeti, che scriuono per ciancia, e da motteggio"; "o per loro cattiua Natura, o per odio, o per preghi, o per danari, o per sollazzo scriuono male d'Altrui."

There are, in Varchi's lengthy *Lezzioni*, a number of miscellaneous borrowings from the *Ars poetica*. The recommendations for the proper use of decorum (p. 583) are derived specifically from Horace, as is the demand for the hexameter as the correct epic verse (p. 616). But these, by 1553, are completely commonplace and make very little contribution to the development of the Horatian mode.

The "Horatian mode" is clearly present in Alessandro Lionardi's *Dialogi della inventione poetica* of 1554. The set of two dialogues represents a kind of converse of the commentaries of the preceding years, for instead of introducing rhetorical distinctions into a basically Horatian exposition, it introduces Horatian elements into a basically rhetorical treatise. The treatise is rhetorical in spite of the fact that its title refers to "poetical invention." Lionardi begins with a consideration of three associated arts—rhetoric, history, and poetry—which belong together not only because they are arts of discourse but also because they serve the same practical ends of teaching men how to speak and to act. Of these arts, poetry is the most excellent because it embraces the other two, which serve it as auxiliaries and instruments. All three make use of invention, disposition, and elocution, of which invention is the most important for various reasons: it requires the greatest and most special talent; it is most directly responsible for the teaching of speaking and action; it is the equivalent of imitation in poetry (to which Aristotle had given primacy over other elements). If these things be true about poetry and invention, then the poet must be above all else a man possessed of various kinds of knowledge. He must be a natural and moral philosopher in order to describe nature and contrive plots, an orator in order to write speeches and deliberations for his personages and to move the passions of his audience, a historian so that he may know the virtuous and vicious actions of great men and the pertinent facts about countries and peoples. Moreover, he must be erudite in astrology (presumably because of the relationships between the constellations and the myths about the gods) and in numerous other arts not needed by the historian or the orator.

His art, as well as his information, includes the arts of the historian and the orator and goes beyond them. It is here that invention is predominant. For the poet takes the true materials provided by the historian, imposes upon them an artificial order, expresses them in a special kind of language, and treats them in verse. His inventive powers are manifested, besides, in the transformation of truth into verisimilitude. From the rhetorician he obtains his knowledge of the passions, of actions and their causes, of necessity and probability, of how to argue in various circumstances; these are all matters which pertain to invention. From the rhetorician, also, he learns such aspects of disposition and elocution as the proper ordering of various kinds of speeches and the many figures of speech by which language is made more ornate. From both of these he obtains the means for achieving his ends of teaching men how to live and speak properly; he will argue with the reasons they provide him, persuade with the truth, move with the passions, and delight with the eloquent diction.

Into this context, many Horatian ideas are readily incorporated. This is done not so much by way of the citation of corroborating arguments as by the casual use of formulas borrowed directly from the *Ars poetica*. Thus at the very beginning of Dialogue I, Lionardi says that one of the main tasks of the poetic art is so to operate "that common materials become one's own" (p. 7); later in the same dialogue he treats decorum and natural versus artificial order in terms which suggest Horace's (pp. 16–18); at the end of it, the phrase "it is proper to the poet to delight and profit" reflects line 333 of the *Ars poetica*. In Dialogue II, the passing discussion of the "in medias res" beginning is again reminiscent of Horace (p. 67). In spite of such allusions, however, Lionardi's work belongs in the present series rather because of its associations with the rhetorical tradition now currently attached to the Horatian text than because of the direct textual reference. It is also significant of current trends that there is perhaps an even larger number of citations of the *Poetics* and of other Aristotelian works. Lionardi cites the *Poetics* on the distinction between poetry and history (p. 14), on poetry as deriving its essence not from verse but from imitation (p. 14), on the necessary and the probable (p. 15), on Nature as the source of imitation, rhythm, and harmony (p. 51), on the possibility of plot without character (p. 58), on the impossible probable (p. 67), and on other subjects. He also calls upon various Platonic texts for support of his ideas: on the *Republic* and the *Phaedo* for the requisites of the poet (p. 62), on the *Republic* for the condemnation of the arousing of certain passions (p. 76) and for the distinction between narration and "imitation," as also for the division between the passions banned and those permitted (p. 80)—all this in connection with a defence of the utility of poetry. I cite these various borrowings not for their own sake but as an indication of the extent to which the divers intellectual traditions are by this time mixed and confused. For Lionardi, the essential approach is a rhetorical one; but poetic elements of a formal character from Aristotle and moral elements from Plato are intermingled to serve the purposes of the discussion.

A similar mixture of other elements into a basically rhetorical analysis is found in Book II of Matteo San Martino's *Osservationi grammaticali e poetiche della lingua italiana* (1555), for it is Book II that contains the poetical observations. It begins with a defence of poesy in the standard fashion; nothing of interest is present here. Then comes an expanded definition of poetry, which merits quotation:

> Poetry is nothing else but an imitation of human actions accompanied by wonder on the part of the listener. . . . perhaps I might be so bold as to say that poetics is a lovely fiction which, restricted within harmonized rhythms, imitating human actions, brings profit along with delight to him who listens; so that

imitation is its secondary, not its principal part. . . . it is certain that an imitation cannot be made unless the invention with which one imitates is prepared first. And as for the function of the poet and the end toward which he should tend, I say that in the poems he must investigate things which can profit and delight, and in such wise that they really do profit and delight (else he is not worthy of the name of poet), constantly filling the reader with joy and with wonder, ever feigning new things, so that with such novelty he may delight, mixing true things with false, that is not as they were, but as they should be; in such a way that neither the beginning will be in discord with the middle nor the middle with the end.[39]

One begins, in such a definition, with Aristotle, continues with Cicero, passes on to Horace, encounters nameless rhetoricians, and concludes with a final statement in which all are lumped together in the most helter-skelter fashion. The same kind of confusion prevails in other parts of the work. There are, for example, five statements on the role, or the function, or the main concern of the poet; all are different. In the passage just quoted, the function and end are to "giovar e dilettare"; a few pages later, the principal part of poetry is said to be the "fittione" or "inventione" (p. 133); farther on, "the final intention of the poets is in the imitation"— almost in direct contradiction to the passage above (p. 135); still later, a longer text of considerable interest in which the poet is said to need "persuasion, in which consists the principal strength of the intent of the poet, which is to acquire belief for his incitements; for which purpose, in order to profit through delight, he strives to move or to placate others under the veil of his fictions" (p. 178); finally, his activities are directed toward "teaching, delighting, and profiting readers at the same time" (p. 180). There is, through all these texts, a certain concentration upon the end of poetry as instructing and giving pleasure; but there is at the same time an unwillingness to make a clear subordination of any one source document to another.

As he operates in the making of poems, the poet for San Martino is essentially a rhetorician; he must be provided with precepts for invention, disposition, and elocution. But really there are no precepts for the first, since the number of subjects is infinite and the poet has free choice among them (p. 133). However, San Martino provides the usual suggestions for

---

39 *Osservationi* (1555), pp. 129–31: "la Poesia altro non è che imitatione delle humane attioni con merauiglia di chi l'ascolta. . . . temerario forse mi mouero a dire, che la Poetica sia una uaga fittione che fra harmonizzati numeri ristretta, imitando l'humane attioni, con diletto gioui a chi l'ascolta; Si che la imitatione è sua parte secondaria, e non principale. . . . certo è non potersi far imitatione, che prima non si prepari la inuentione con cui si imitti. Et quanto a lo officio del Poeta, & al fine oue tender debbia, dico che nei Poemi de inuestigar cose che giouar possano e dilettare, e si che in effecto giouino e dilettino, o che degno non è di tal nome, di continuo riempiendo il lettor di giocondita e merauiglia, nuoue cose sempre fingendo, si che con simil nouita diletti, le cose uere con le false mescolando, cioè non quali furono, ma quali esser deueano; per maniera che ne'l principio dal mezzo ne questo dal fine si discordino."

what he calls "the six parts of invention," i.e., exordium, narration, division, confirmation, confutation, and conclusion; the poet's invention is thus the same as the orator's (p. 159). Disposition, or the "ordinatione" of the materials, largely concerns words; Horace is called upon for many of the precepts here. As for elocution, the largest part of San Martino's treatment is devoted to it; for words constitute the "materia" of poetry (p. 159) and if they are properly chosen and arranged, "from them will result in the minds of the readers a most sweet harmony adorned with inconceivable loveliness" (p. 179). For all these elements, the counsels are those which might be found in any of the standard rhetorics. To them are added generous materials from the *Ars poetica*—incorporated in the way exemplified in the long quoted passage—and occasional borrowings from Aristotle and Plato. These remain, however, auxiliary and subsidiary, and they are introduced only as they furnish additional authority for points in the rhetorical system, which is unchanged by their accretion.

Giovambattista Giraldi Cintio's *Letter to Bernardo Tasso*, dated October 10, 1557, is more limited in scope than the preceding document in two ways: first it deals only with epic poetry, since Giraldi is defending his practice in his *Ercole*; and second, it is Horatian almost solely in the conception of the ends of poetry. Giraldi takes as his point of departure the thesis—by no means original—that poetry is a kind of "first philosophy"; hence, of the two ends of pleasure and utility proposed for it, utility is indisputably the more important. The theory is expounded in the following passage:

I strove, insofar as wit was granted to me to do so, to see to it that the whole work was composed in the light of the useful and the honest, since it seemed to me that this must be the end of the poet, and not pleasure alone. For, if we believe what the ancient writers have to say about it, poetry is nothing else but a first philosophy which, like a schoolmistress of life working secretly, proposes to us under poetic covering the image of a civilized and praiseworthy life drawn from the fountain of that philosophy; to which life, as to an assigned goal, we must direct our actions—as Horace showed us when he said:

Rem tibi Socraticae poterunt ostendere chartae.[40]

The utility proposed is thus exclusively moral. The poet must seek to represent behavior which is appropriate to "honest and honorable living, to praiseworthy actions, and to the whole scale of social procedures."[41]

---

[40] In *Lettere di XIII. huomini illustri* (1565 ed.), p. 871: "usai, quanto meglio mi fu concesso l'ingegno, perche l'opera tutta fusse composta all'utile, & all'honesto, parendomi che questo debba essere il fine del Poeta, & non il diletto solo. Però che, per quanto ne dicono gli auttori antichi; La Poesia non è altro, che una prima filosofia, la quale, quasi occulta maestra della uita, sotto uelame poetico, ci propone la imagine di una ciuile, & lodeuole uita tratta dal fonte di essa filosofia, alla qual uita, quasi a proposto segno, habbiamo a drizzare le nostre attioni, il che ci mostrò Horatio, quando disse.

Rem tibi Socraticae poterunt ostendere chartae."

[41] *Ibid.*, p. 872: "che si conuiene alla uita honesta, et honorata, alle lodeuoli attioni, & alla uarietà delle cose ciuili."

Applying this theory in his own poem, Giraldi has depicted the life of a man who was an example of praiseworthy and honorable actions (p. 868); he has universalized the illustrious actions, making sure that honesty was everywhere respected (p. 874); he has tried to arouse compassion and move his audience (*ibid.*); above all, he has attended to morality, "by praising the virtues, condemning the vices, and giving wherever necessary the rewards to the former and the punishments to the latter, in order to instruct persons of various ranks, according to their station, in the praiseworthy life."[42]

Pleasure is a means to the achievement of this utility. "I saw that, in order to make this utility enter into the mind of the reader with greater efficacy, a very wide pathway could be made by pleasure, whence I sought to make of it a companion to the profit, and I did not wish to take it as my primary object."[43] Pleasure is produced by writing the work "poeticamente," that is, by stopping at given places to intercalate ornaments and by devising entertaining digressions (p. 873). These add beauty to the composition and make the reader follow it with greater attention. Even the ugly may be rendered beautiful (as Aristotle and Horace have pointed out) if it is treated with the proper decorum, and it then becomes an additional source of pleasure. Similarly the use of the pagan gods, acceptable in an ancient subject such as the *Ercole*, may increase the marvelous of the poem and hence its possibilities for delight (p. 882). Finally, verse itself is an additional ornament which, when it is allied with appropriate diction, serves the purposes of both utility and pleasure (p. 888).

Giraldi's conception of the poem, made to conform to these requirements, clearly involves no notion of the unity of artistic structure. Indeed, he specifically rejects the need for unity of action and replaces it by unity of hero (p. 868). The life of Hercules is the only unifying element—unless one take into consideration the general moralizing intent or the prevailing concern with decorum. Around this life, Giraldi has gathered many "actions," some of them taken from ancient poets, some of them invented by himself. Since the subject is ancient, he has treated it in the manner of the ancients, except for the addition of such modern devices as transitions from one canto to another in order to hold the interest of his readers (pp. 879–80). Everything that he does, he insists, is calculated to please and instruct the specific audience that he has in mind. This is not an audience of the "vulgo"—no poet worthy of praise ever wrote in order to give pleasure to this vulgar crowd, or made of it his judges—but of the "best

---

[42] *Ibid.*, p. 881: "con lodare le uirtù, biasimare i uitij, & dare, oue è stato bisogno, a quelle il premio, a queste la pena, per formare persone di uarie qualità, secondo la loro conditione alla lodeuole uita."

[43] *Ibid.*, p. 872: "uidi ch'a fare, che con maggiore efficacia questo utile entrasse nell'animo a chi leggeua, ui poteua fare assai ampia strada il diletto, onde cercai ch'egli al giouamento fussi compagno, & no'l uolli prendere per primo oggetto."

judges," those who know why the poem pleases them and are capable of evaluating its artistic excellences (pp. 876–78).

In these ways, the Horatian conception of the ends of poetry comes to inform Giraldi's whole theory of the poetic art. Almost everything in it is subordinated to the wish to instruct, and even the devices for pleasure are ancillary to this. In its general supposition of the work and of a certain effect upon that audience as the goal proposed, it again falls into broadly rhetorical patterns. But much of the detailed treatment of diction, the figures, and the styles present in the more ambitious treatises is absent here, as are the numerous cross references to ancient theorists.

Similar ideas about the poetic art are at work, in an even briefer compass, in Girolamo Ruscelli's dedication to his *Fiori delle rime de' poeti illustri* of 1558—similar, that is, in the general application of rhetorical criteria to poetry. Ruscelli starts out with a defence, not of poetry in general, but of Italian poetry, declaring that in spite of the prejudice in favor of Greek and Latin literature, there is a possibility that Italian will soon come to equal them "both in delight and in profit." Ariosto has already proved this in the epic and Petrarch in the lyric, others in elegiac verse. One may judge for oneself: "This may easily be discovered by those who, having the art and the judgment to be able to know entirely the degrees and the places of perfection in invention, in disposition, in style and in all the other parts of elocution, will consider those compositions of Bembo, of Guidiccioni, of Sannazaro, of Molza, of La Pescara."[44] The proof, in a word, will be found in Ruscelli's anthology of poetry, "in which one may see the true portrait of all the beauties of poetry, where one finds the examples of every splendor and of every ornament that a language is capable of receiving, and where there are subjects and cases of history, of philosophy, of spiritual things, and almost of as many other subjects as all of the sciences are able to furnish to poetry."[45]

Although the passages in Cristoforo Rufo's *Antexegemata* (1559) which are of interest for poetic theory largely concern the *Poetics*, there are several commentaries on lines of Horace and a few places where a rhetorical interpretation is applied to Aristotle. This is not true everywhere, however; in connection with *Poetics* 1452b11, for example, he takes issue with Robortello's interpretation of πάθος as referring to the audience and insists that it refers rather to the plot (p. 13). The work is a collection of isolated

---

44 *Fiori delle rime* (1558), p. *iijv: "Ilche . . . possono ageuolmente conoscer coloro, che hauendo arte & giudicio da poter conoscere interamente i gradi e i luoghi di perfettione, nella inuentione, nella dispositione, nello stile, & in tutte l'altre parti della elocutione, haueranno considerati quei componimenti del Bembo, del Guidiccioni, del Sannazaro, del Molza, della Pescara." "La Pescara" is Vittoria Colonna.

45 *Ibid.*, p. *vij: "oue si vede il vero ritratto di tutte le bellezze della Poesia, oue sono gli essempi d'ogni candidezza & d'ogni ornamento, che vna lingua possa riceuere, & oue si hanno soggetti & occasioni d'istorie, di filosofia, di cose spirituali, & quasi di tanti altri soggetti, quanti alla Poesia ne possono somministrar tutte le scienze."

remarks on passages selected by Rufo because he disagrees with previous commentators. On *Poetics* 1456b8, disagreeing with Maggi's reading, he maintains that the writer of tragedy may derive arguments from the same topics as does the rhetorician, since both seek to arouse the emotions; but the poet must do so in a hidden way, whereas the orator's devices are apparent. On 1456b3, adding to "pity and fear" the additional effects of "amplification, proof, and persuasion," he again points out that these must be sought in the appropriate topics. For the *Ars poetica*, he provides commentary on two lines, on line 1 (where he disagrees with Maggi's gloss) to insist that the initial passage does not refer to plot alone but to the combination of plot and episodes, and on line 132 (rejecting Maggi again) to clarify the proper manner of adapting borrowed materials.[46] On the whole, however, the document is more interesting as it relates to the history of the *Poetics*, and I shall discuss it again later in that context.

In the same year, 1559, Lodovico Dolce appended to his translation of the satires, epistles, and *Ars poetica* of Horace a set of three short discourses, one for each of the works. In the first, *Origine della satira*, he traced also the origins of tragedy and of comedy, emphasizing above all the moral purposes for which they were invented: tragedy to demonstrate "how much the condition of human frailty is different from that of divine felicity and beatitude," comedy "to scold men for their vices."[47] In the second, *Discorso sopra le epistole*, he said that the satires and the epistles had complementary functions: "In the satires it was his intention to remove the vices from the breast of men, and in these [the epistles] to plant there the virtues."[48] The third, the *Discorso sopra la poetica*, is by far the most important; since it gives a brief *summa* of what Dolce considered to be the salient points of Horace's text, I translate it below almost in its entirety:

> This little book composed by Horace on the art of poetry may be divided into five parts. For he demonstrates first the vices that the poet must flee; then he speaks of the appropriateness that must be observed in words; in the third place he touches on the quality of materials and persons, and on the differences that are present in them. In the fourth he treats of actions, and in the fifth he counsels poets to correct diligently their compositions, submitting them to the judgment of those who know. The reader will thus learn from the notes that Horace gives us in this brief but most useful work of his, to consider first very carefully all the material that these poets have proposed to write about; then to dispose it, that is to order it and to give it such form that there will not be in it anything discordant or contrary, but that everything will be in conformity and appropriate. From this it results that when poets have begun or promised to write serious things, they should not descend to low ones, or to describe others that are lovely

---

[46] *Antexegemata* (1559), pp. G6, G5–G5v, H, and H8 respectively.

[47] In *I dilettevoli sermoni* (1559), p. 313: "quanto la conditione della fragilità humana fosse differente dalla felicità e beatitudine Diuina" and "per riprendere i uitij de gli huomini."

[48] *Ibid.*, p. 316: "Nelle Satire fu la sua intentione di leuare i uitij dal petto de gli huomini, & in queste di piantarui le uirtù."

and delightful but not pertinent, to show that they are clever. And in this, as in every other aspect, Ariosto merits infinite praise. Also, when we need to pass from one subject to another, we should do it in such a way that the composition will not resemble a monster. Nor, fleeing one vice, should we fall into another; but taking upon ourselves a burden equal to our strength, we should see to it that the end corresponds to the beginning and the middle; and although we may treat divers things, and although the parts be varied, it should be a single body which is not discordant in any of its parts. And as for the order, they should begin from the middle or after the middle of the subject, as Homer, Vergil, and our Ariosto did.[49]

Such a summary as this indicates what points in the *Ars poetica* seemed, to a vulgarizer like Dolce, to be worthy of emphasis. It will be noted that invention and disposition are clearly intimated and that the dominant principle of appropriateness appears again as it had in the earliest Horatian exegesis.

Girolamo Ruscelli, who only the year before had published his *Fiori delle rime*, published in 1559 a work called *Del modo di comporre in versi nella lingua italiana*; this was really a combination of two works: a treatise on verse, comprising also a fairly complete poetics; and a very lengthy rhyming dictionary. In the section on poetics, Ruscelli is most concerned with two problems, the superiority of poetry over other forms of expression and the superiority of verse over prose. He regards all forms of speech as having the function of persuading, delighting, and moving. But whereas other forms are written to appeal only to contemporaries, poetry has added beauties which give it eternal life and bring glory to its author. Hence its excellence. These beauties—if one is to respect the basic dichotomy of his analysis—are both of material and of words. For the subject matter of poetry must itself be of a special kind. It may well be false, "invented" by the poet; if so, it must be handled in such a way as to produce belief on the part of the reader. If it is true (as a historical subject is), it is rendered more

---

49 *Ibid.*, pp. 317–18: "Si puo diuidere questo libricciolo composto da Horatio sopra l'arte della Poetica in cinque parti. Percioche egli prima dimostra i uitij, che dee fuggire il Poeta: dipoi fauella della conueneuolezza, che si conuien serbare nelle parole: nel terzo luogo tocca la qualità delle materie, e delle persone, e le differenze, che ui entrano. Nel quarto tratta dell'attioni; e nel quinto conforta i Poeti a corregger diligentemente le lor compositioni, rimettendole al giudicio di coloro, che sanno. Il lettore adunque apparerà da i ricordi, che ci da Horatio in questa sua brieue, ma utilissima fatica, di considerar primieramente molto bene tutta la materia, che essi hanno proposto di scriuere: poi disponerla, cioè ordinarla, e darle una cotal forma, che non u'habbia in lei cosa discordante, e contraria, ma tutto sia conforme e corrispondente. Onde hauendo i Poeti cominciato, o promesso di scriuer cose graui, non discendano alle basse, ouero a discriuere alcune uaghe e diletteuoli, ma impertinenti, per dimostrarsi ingeniosi. Et in questa, come in ogni altra parte, merita infinita lode l'Ariosto. Douendo anco passar d'uno in altro soggetto, ci facciano in guisa, che'l componimento non sia simile a un Mostro. Ne schifando un uitio, incorriamo in un'altro: ma prendendo peso eguale alle nostre forze, procuriamo, che'l fine corrisponda al principio & al mezo: e se ben trattiamo diuerse cose, quantunque le membra siano diuerse, sia un solo corpo, ilquale punto nelle sue parti non discordi. E, quanto all'ordine, debbono cominciar dal mezo, o dopo il mezo della materia; come fece Homero, Virgilio, e'l nostro Ariosto."

perfect by the kind of selection and rearrangement which are the prerogative of the poet, and all the imperfections of reality are removed. In either case, it must be something that is "pleasing, lovely, gay, grave, or pleasant, and that in the end will delight or profit, or better still, that will profit and delight at the same time."[50] The words are the "beautiful dress" in which the subject is clothed. Great attention must be paid to the purity of language, the placing or organizing of the words, the qualities of style—all things which constitute the virtues of elocution. Disposition, it is clear, is an element to be watched closely by the poet in connection with both words and things.

Even if all these precepts be followed, however, the ultimate in perfection will not be achieved unless verse is added. For verse adds harmony, and harmony is an additional source of persuasion and of arousal of the passions. The sequence of events in the soul of the reader is as follows: the beauty of verse, added to all the other beauties of poetry, gives increased delight; this delight leads the reader to have a higher estimate of the poet's genius; the work thereby becomes more credible and more capable of producing its utilitarian effects; the profit that results is hence greater. As in so many of these texts, the end term in the argument as developed is that of utility. Indeed, the same is true for the argument about subject matter: "much greater utility, to say nothing of the pleasure, . . . will be obtained from the same event narrated by a poet than if told by a historian,"[51] and the point about the perfecting of reality is made in substantiation. This exaltation of poetry and of verse leads Ruscelli to write a "defence" of the most extravagant kind, one feature of which is the declaration that Italian is superior to all other languages for verse and that Petrarch and more recent Italian poets may be used as models.

PARTHENIO (1560)

A number of the literati whose names had appeared in recent years in connection with Horatian criticism appear again as interlocutors in Bernardino Parthenio's lengthy dialogue, *Della imitatione poetica*, of 1560. Trifon Gabriele, Giovan Giorgio Trissino, Paolo Manuzio, Francesco Lovisini, and Parthenio himself gather together to discuss the matter of poetic imitation and how it differs from rhetorical imitation. In so doing, they pretend to be supplementing the work of Aristotle and Horace, who spoke only of tragedy and the epic and of plot and character in connection with those genres; their own concern will be broader, since they will treat

---

[50] *Del modo di comporre* (1559), p. xix: "cosa grata, uaga, leggiadra, graue, ò piaceuole, & che finalmente ò diletti, ò gioui, ma molto più, che ella gioui et diletti unitamente."

[51] *Ibid.*, pp. xi–xii: "molto più utilità, per tacer la dilettatione . . ., si trarrà da un fatto stesso narrato da un poeta, che da uno istorico, percioche all'istorico si conuiene di narrarlo ueramente come sia seguito, ò bene ò male che sia stato in tutto, ò in parte. Là oue il poeta lo finge, & lo forma nelle parti non buone, quale douerebbe essere stato per esser buono, & perfetto nell'esser suo."

of words, figures of speech, and sententiae (which are common to all genres) and of such general subjects as invention and the universal topics. In his preface, Parthenio defends poetry not only by adducing the customary arguments but by pointing out the multitude of kinds of knowledge which one may derive from such a poet as Homer (the *De Homeri poesi* is echoed here). Besides the knowledge that he imparts, Homer teaches lessons in morality—"What philosopher teaches us better what prudence, what fortitude, what discretion we should use in every slightest action, than in his poems? He makes us wise, prudent, modest, strong, patient, constant, just, good, religious, and holy"[52]—and he shows orators how to write expositions, beginnings, confirmations, amplifications, and so forth. These, then, will be the ends that the poet must pursue. But he will not achieve them if he does not pay attention to the delight that comes from excellence in verse and elocution. It is the latter of these that constitutes Parthenio's central subject.

Parthenio does not wish us to be misled by his title, *On Poetic Imitation*, and insists that he means to present all the precepts of the art not already exhausted by Aristotle and by Horace, "who seems to have kept his feet fixed in the very footsteps of that same Aristotle" (p. 6). But he soon limits his scope by excluding one of the two types of imitation which he distinguished; he will not here treat that kind of imitation which seeks to represent "that certain force, or faculty, that we bear in our soul, that they call Idea,"[53] but rather that other kind which consists in representing the Ideas and the Forms of others. In a word, he is interested in the imitation of other poets, taken as models. A further restriction appears when he makes still another subdivision of poetic imitation. The poet may, on the one hand, imitate the natures and the characters of the persons whom he undertakes to represent; "and this is the end of poetry, which intends to express human actions, and with that expression to instruct and inform the soul, which is its subject and its matter."[54] Imitation of this kind is left by Parthenio to Aristotle. On the other hand, the poet may imitate the words and the figures of speech already used by other poets, and to the problem of how this is properly accomplished Parthenio addresses himself. The major part of the dialogue is devoted to suggestions about how the poet, by long practice, may ultimately come to express himself in a way very similar to that of the model without actually copying or plagiarizing him; and to detailed analysis of the numerous rhetorical "topics" distinguished

52 *Della imitatione poetica* (1560), p. 3: "Qual de' Filosofi meglio ci insegna, qual prudenza, qual fortezza, qual discritione habbiamo da usare in ciascuna minima attione, che ne i suoi poemi? Questo ci fa saggi, prudenti, modesti, forti, patienti, costanti, giusti, buoni, religiosi, & Santi."

53 *Ibid.*, p. 11: "quella certa forza, o uero facultà, la quale portiamo nell'animo, che chiamano idea."

54 *Ibid.*, p. 93: "Et questo è il fine della poesia; laquale intende esprimer le attioni humane, & con quello amaestrare, & informare bene l'animo, che è suo soggetto, & materia."

by Giulio Camillo Delminio, proposed as devices to guide the poet in his imitation.

Throughout Parthenio's treatise, the assumption is implicit that the really important thing about poetry is the diction that it uses. Poetic diction, in fact, is different from that of oratory in several respects. The words used by the orator "must be such that they may be understood by the people and must be drawn from common usage, from that usage which the writers of comedy and the orators have established. Those [used by the poets] must be highly ingenious—I almost said 'bizarre'—and completely alien from habitual use."[55] They must be selected for their qualities of sound as well as of sense (full-sounding words containing "a" and "o" are to be preferred), and compound or complicated words are better than simple ones (p. 80). As he proceeds with this analysis, Parthenio comes closer and closer to the kind of teaching that would be found in the section on diction in almost any standard rhetoric.

It is interesting to note that, in spite of the elaborateness of such a theory as the one just outlined, when its author is called upon to engage in practical criticism he talks in ancient commonplaces. At one point in Book II of the dialogue, Trifon Gabriele, after having refused to comment on living poets, agrees to pass judgment on certain recent Italian poets now dead. This is what he says about Sannazaro: "I have always prized him, and he has always seemed to me grave and sonorous, to have had a fine selection of words, to be of a great and truly poetic nature. . . ." And of Pontano: "Pontano is also very sublime"; and of Fracastoro: "Most ornate and most polished is Fracastoro, and excellent in imagining fables." Navagero is "polished, charming, elegant and full of new, light poetic thoughts, varied and versatile."[56] Such comments as these are consistent with the theory behind them insofar as they bear almost exclusively on diction; but in their effort to characterize the genius of the poet they hark back to a much earlier time, to the days of Pietro Ricci (Petrus Crinitus) or of Lilio Gregorio Giraldi.

A document closely related to the preceding one (through the person of its author and through its rhetorical associations) is Giulio Camillo Delminio's *Discorso sopra l'idee di Hermogene*, published posthumously in 1560. It is a brief treatise which, after a comparison of Cicero's three styles with Hermogenes' types of oratory—the judicial, the deliberative, and the

---

[55] *Ibid.*, p. 34: "Questi deono esser tali, che dal popolo possano esser intesi, & esser tratti dalla communanza, quello, che i Comici & gli Oratori hanno fatto. Quelli hanno da essere ingeniosissimi, & quasi, che non dissi bizarri, & del tutto estratti dalla consuetudine."

[56] *Ibid.*, p. 85: "l'ho sempre prezzato, & emmi sempre paruto graue, & sonoro, hauer hauuta bella elettione di parole, esser di natura grande & ueramente poetica. . . . Molto sublime altresi è il Pontano"; p. 86: "Ornatissimo, & politissimo è il Fracastoro, & eccellente nel finger fauole"; p. 87: "Il Nauaiero polito, & uago, & elegante & pieno di pensieri poetici, noui, & leggiadri, uario, & uersatile."

panegyric—goes on to a brief summation of the various "senses" found in Hermogenes. Only one short section is of interest for poetic theory, a section entitled "Panegirica in Metro," which discusses poetry as a versified type of panegyric oratory; the classification itself is significant. Camillo's notions of poetry are simple and, at the same time, somewhat confused; he says that it is an "imitation of all things," that it contains pleasure and greatness, that it involves the use of verse. Its proper materials are myths about the gods, the supernatural and the superhuman, impossible and incredible actions. Its procedures are the narration of events simply and in detail, the invocation of the muses, and the use of special kinds of words and of figures; the latter it shares with panegyric oratory in general.[57]

Francesco Patrizi would have disagreed with Camillo's classification of poetry as panegyric; for although, in his *Della historia* (1560), he, too, classifies poetry under oratory, he assigns it to the demonstrative and deliberative branches. His dialogue concerns history, and when he classifies poetry, he is expounding Pontano's views on the relationship of poetry to history. According to these views, history is a kind of poetry, but in prose. Both arts treat the same kind of materials, praise and blame their actors, belong to the same branches of oratory; as parts of oratory, they employ similar procedures, "they arouse the passions, they do things with decorum." Their ends are the same: "Both teach, delight, move, profit, adorn, elevate, lower." Their differences are those between truth and probability, prose and verse, natural order and artificial order. Patrizi does not need to identify his sources (or Pontano's) to indicate to what kind of intellectual tradition he belongs; traces of both Horace and the rhetoricians are manifest in his statements. The verbs collected together to define the ends of the two arts provide all the necessary links.[58]

Some of the same principles, applied to a specific literary genre, are operative in Francesco Sansovino's *Discorso in materia della satira* (1560). The dedication presents a brief defence of poetry; then this statement: "the end of poetry consists in nothing else than in withdrawing men from vice, whence it is a gift of God, directing them according to the good orders of nature, His servant, so that they will know their own minds; hence it is that certain poets, wishing to achieve such an end, have written precepts of human life under various forms of verse."[59] Of these divers genres, satire is always a favored one, since it scolds men for their evil-doing. The *Discorso* proper differentiates satire from the other forms on several bases:

---

57 In *Il secondo tomo dell'opere di M. Giulio Camillo Delminio* (1560), pp. 119–21.

58 *Della historia* (1560), pp. 5–5v: "muouono gli affetti, fanno le cose con decoro"; "insignano, dilettano, muouono, giouano, adornano, inalzano, abbassano." Patrizi undoubtedly knew Camillo's work, since he edited Vol. II of Camillo's *Opere* (1560).

59 *Discorso* (1560), p. *3: "il fin della Poesia non consiste in altro, ch'in ritrar gli huomini dal vitio, ond'ella è dono di Dio, indirizzandoli a i buoni ordini della natura sua ministra, accio ch'essi riconoschino la mente loro, di qui è ch'alcuni volendo conseguir cotal fine, hanno scritto precetti della vita humana sotto varie forme di versi."

style (satire uses the humble, low style, rather than the high or the middle), subject matter (which is humble and low, not high and magnificent), the kinds of persons depicted (who are humble, such as servants and sinners, not great), the nature of the imitation (in satire, nature is imitated directly, without adornment or artifice). It will be readily seen that the opposite term in each case is tragedy or the epic, and Sansovino points up the contrast wherever possible. Once again, the insistence is upon diction; this must not differ from the language of prose, must contain neither ornament nor grace, must be instead simple, sharp, witty, and direct. Such a method of describing and delimiting a literary genre by its style, its subject matter, its characters, and its form of imitation (taken in a special sense) falls readily within the context of the tradition that I have been tracing, and Sansovino's little *Discourse* serves as an epitome of many tendencies (pp. *6v–*7).

As a final sample in the present chapter, we may examine those few paragraphs in Benedetto Varchi's *Hercolano* which concern poetry. The dialogue, one of the important documents in the "question of the language," is almost wholly linguistic in content; although it was published only in 1570, posthumously, it was written around 1560, during the years of the Caro-Castelvetro controversy. As might be anticipated, Varchi's approach to poetics is here colored by this specific concern. In one of the pertinent paragraphs (p. 51), he notes that the two components of "poetare" or "poeteggiare" are verse and a certain kind of language present in "fauellare poeticamente." In the second (p. 123), he remarks that whereas other writers practice only one form of eloquence, the poet practices all forms; hence his divinity. The third (pp. 219–20), more extensive, distinguishes seven kinds of poetry by naming the authors who practiced them; the basis of the distinction is not clear, but it would seem that Varchi is merely classifying according to verse forms. The last passage (p. 269), in addition to declaring again that verse is necessary in poetry, contains the following passage:

> The poet, in addition to well-composed and sententious verse, has a greatness, a majesty more divine than human, and not only teaches, delights, and moves, but engenders admiration and wonder in the minds of the listeners, if they are noble and gentle, and in all those who are naturally disposed, for imitation and consequently poetry is (as Aristotle shows in the *Poetics*) most natural for man.[60]

These passages hardly constitute a theory of poetry; at best they display a few common, current preconceptions: poetry is verse, it uses a special kind of language, and it seeks ethical and rhetorical ends.

---

[60] *Hercolano* (Florence, 1570), p. 269: "Il Poeta oltra il verso ben composto, e sentenzioso ha vna grandezza, e maestà più tosto diuina, che humana, e non solo insegna, diletta, e muoue, ma ingenera ammirazione, e stupore negli animi, o generosi, o gentili, e in tutti coloro, che sono naturalmente disposti, perche l'imitare, e conseguentemente il poetare è (come ne mostra Aristotile nella Poetica) naturalissimo all'huomo."

CONCLUSIONS

The materials contained in this chapter have covered a span of approximately fifteen years, from 1546 to 1560, and have included, besides six formal commentaries on the *Ars poetica*, a wide variety of shorter documents on miscellaneous literary subjects. The common basis for their inclusion was the fact that they belonged, in one way or another, to a tradition of poetic theory that I have called the Horatian-rhetorical tradition. The center of this tradition is the text of the *Ars poetica*; but allied to it and mingled with it are a multitude of ideas derived, for the most part, from classical treatises on oratory or on style.

By this period at midcentury, critics and theorists and commentators had developed what might be termed a standard reading of Horace. I do not mean that everybody read him in precisely the same way, but merely that certain interpretations recur with great frequency and that from the maze of suggestions and theories and precepts contained in the *Ars poetica*, a certain number seem to be the favorites of readers and to be cited most constantly. Of these, perhaps the most signally "Horatian" of all is the notion that poetry has as its dual ends to profit and delight. There is no major commentator who does not emphasize this as one of the characteristic features of the Horatian system, and in many cases shorter texts are identified with this tradition basically because of their insistence that "prodesse" and "delectare" constitute the ends of poetry. Indeed, the statement becomes so much a commonplace that it probably has, at times, no really direct connections with the text of Horace itself. This may be one reason why the formula "aut prodesse aut delectare" is so readily expanded to include additional goals (such as the Ciceronian "admiratio") or is crossed with similar statements from other theorists (such as Cicero's "docere, delectare, mouere"). Such expansion and augmentation accounts, in part, for the conflation of Horace with the purely rhetorical treatises, and in part explains the confusion attaching to the purposes of the poetic art. Nevertheless, the predominant tendency is to regard the really important purpose as that of bringing some profit to the reader, and that profit is invariably said to be a moral one. By using sententiae and aphorisms, by demonstrating the common fate of man and the rewards and punishments attached to virtues and vices, by presenting charming allegories which hide eternal truths, the poem teaches man all the lessons he needs to know for proper living. Sometimes, the pleasure resulting from the imitation, or from diction, or from ornaments and episodes retains its full status as a partner or accompaniment of the utility; but more usually it is reduced to the role of a means or instrument for the achievement of that utility. As a device for stirring the emotions of the reader and persuading him through examples, pleasure makes him amenable to the moral teachings that are the real end of the poet.

Certain of the internal components of poems are, according to this standard reading of Horace, in direct relationship to the ends proposed. The whole matter of decorum is extremely important if moral lessons are to be conveyed; in fact, the observance of decorum is itself a form of teaching, since the proper behavior for persons of all kinds should be deducible from the characters and their actions. This is a positive contribution to the achievement of the ends. Most of the components, though, operate indirectly through the pleasure which they afford. Thus the central principle of unity and appropriateness—the two elements are indistinguishable for the Horatians—is a *sine qua non* for the production of pleasure; it is the counterpart, for artistic elements, to decorum, for moral elements. Similarly, imitation is a source of pleasure, but only if it is correctly accomplished and if the object as represented is recognized to be "true."

The other habitual ways of reading Horace consist in the application of a number of distinctions by midcentury universally associated with the text. First and foremost of these is, of course, the trilogy of invention, disposition, and elocution. Certain sections of the *Ars poetica* are now regularly identified as treatments of these three "parts," and when in practical criticism a work is singled out for comment, that comment will almost always revolve about the same three parts. A second trilogy, that of the three styles, is almost equally prominent. It is connected with what Horace says about the vices of diction, becomes the main device for assuring the integrity of the separate literary genres, and is often regarded as auxiliary both to decorum and to appropriateness. That is, a given "style" will entail the speech proper to persons of given social status and to their actions and characters, and it will require figures and ornaments in keeping with the general nature of the subject matter. Finally, the "res-verba" distinction, according to which all considerations relevant to poetry are classified as belonging to the subject matter or to the expression, continues to be applied just as it had been in the earliest Horatian criticism.

A parallel inquiry of equal usefulness for understanding the criticism of the period would be an inquiry into the kind of rhetorical doctrine that was ordinarily associated with Horace. We have already seen some of its constituents, especially with respect to the ends; for if the Ciceronian ends of "admiratio" directed toward the orator himself and of "docere, delectare, and mouere" directed toward the audience are the ones proposed, then a special brand of rhetoric results. It can be seen, strictly in terms of the moral bias of Horace's interpreters and of the construction which they put upon his text, why this type of rhetoric rather than variant possibilities should have been related to him. Cognate ends are the "arousing of the passions" found in so many of the critics (sometimes as an intermediate end) and the imparting of all kinds of miscellaneous information. In fact, just as the conception of the ends is frequently the basis for calling a document Horatian, so the specific nature of the ends is often, in the minds of the critics, the primary reason for developing extended rhetorical parallels. As for the rest of the rhetorical system involved, it is usually of a linguistic character, with the main stress on diction, on figures and styles, and on the "topics" which are curiously transformed into stylistic procedures. Thus of the three traditional parts, elocution is the one accorded the greatest amount of attention and importance—a tendency also notable in the late-classical rhetoricians. When one compares the set of ideas belonging to the reading of Horace with those composing the rhetorical tradition, one finds very close resemblances if not complete identity; one may begin within the text of Horace, as critics of this period did, and end within the context of a standard rhetoric; or one may reverse the process and pass from the *Rhetorica ad Herennium* or from the *De oratore* or from the *Institutes* into the *Ars poetica*. The two traditions are in many very real senses indistinguishable.

But what of Aristotle? This is the period, as I have indicated, when the first persistent attempts are made to connect the *Ars poetica* with the *Poetics*. Especially in the formal commentaries, Aristotle tends to replace the older authorities as a source of illumination and elucidation of the text. The belief becomes current that Horace knew Aristotle's work, used it as his source and guide, meant to do no more than paraphrase it in verse. Of necessity, the ideas in the two works must be the same. This is the basis for the increasing vogue of citing parallels between the two texts; from modest beginnings in Pedemonte, this fashion attains its full expression in such commentators as Maggi, Grifoli, and Lovisini. By the time of Lovisini, parallels are available for almost every passage in Horace that specifically concerns the art of poetry or the composition of poems. If we compare the various lists of parallel passages suggested by the successive commentators, we discover a number of revealing facts. First, certain passages in Aristotle become permanently assigned to given lines in Horace as each expounder borrows from his predecessors. For example, to the opening lines of the *Ars poetica* (ll. 1–23) three passages from the *Poetics* are equated, 1450a38 (on plot as the soul of the poem), 1451b33 (on episodic plots), and 1451a19 (on the fact that unity of plot does not result from unity of hero); to lines 73–88, suggesting styles and meters for various genres, three passages again, 1459b31 on epic meter and 1448b31 and 1449a21 on iambic verse. The same lines in Horace will sometimes suggest other parallels in Aristotle; but certain basic comparisons recur in the glosses of a large number of the writers. There thus comes to be a body of traditional cross references for each section of the Horatian text; to this body, each commentator adds such other parallels as his ingenuity can devise, and indeed one has the impression, occasionally, that the parallels have as their only merit this display of ingenuity.

From this cultivation of parallelism certain advantages accrue to the interpretation of Horace. These are mostly in the form of an enrichment of the understanding of isolated sections of the text. If we take, as a case in point, the first section of Horace's text (ll. 1–13) and compare the glosses of Badius Ascensius and Francesco Lovisini, we may estimate what advance in interpretation has been made during the fifty-year period separating the two commentaries. Badius takes the passage as being, first, a warning against the errors of "soresmos," that is, "mala accumulatione seu aggregatione," and of "coinismos," that is, "vitiosa communicatione, seu commixtione sermonis." Positively, it recommends symmetry, measure, economy, decorum, insistence upon the proper "color" and the integrity of each genre. Badius reduces the meaning to the following "regula":

For any work that is to be composed or written, the poet must so invent the whole subject, so dispose what is invented, so decorate what is disposed that nothing in it will be like a monster or incongruous, but all things will be similar and in agreement among themselves.

Three things thus are necessary at first: The careful consideration and invention of the whole matter; an economy or disposition fitted with deliberation to the materials invented, for the things to be narrated will be placed differently in a poem and in a history; and their embellishment in accordance with their arrangement, in which regard must be had to elegance and decorum.[61]

Lovisini, seeing in the text the problem of limiting the free play of the poet's imagination, begins with Aristotle's distinction (in the *De anima*) between fantasy and opinion; the poet, he says, follows fantasy, "for the poets adopt for themselves the name of poet not because of the verse, but because of the plot and the fiction, as Aristotle testified in the *Poetics*."[62] Horace, he goes on to say, permits the use of figments only to the extent to which "prudence" is observed; the monstrous is never tolerated. "Let all things in a poem therefore harmonize, agree, correspond; let them all regard the aim and the end; let nothing be inconsistent, nothing unsuitable"; so it is that nothing in the *Aeneid* is unfitting to a "summus Imperator," and all things in the *Iliad* and the *Odyssey* serve the moral purposes envisaged.[63] Then, after referring to Quintilian on "coinismos" and drawing a comparison between a mixture of Greek dialects and a mixture of sublime and humble styles, Lovisini compliments Horace for having chosen this as his first precept: "Nor is it by chance that he taught first what the construction of the argument and the plot should be, for, as

61 Ed. Paris, Gerlier, 1500, p. IIIIv: "Compositurus seu cumscripturus quodlibet opus sic rem omnem excogitabit, excogitatam disponet, dispositam ornabit vt nihil monstri simile aut repugnans in eo sit sed omnia sui similia, atque inter [se] quadrantia.

"Tria ergo primum sunt necessaria. Materiae totius excogitatio atque inuentio. Excogitate apta oeconomia seu dispositio. aliter enim in poemate: aliter in historia locabuntur res narrande & disposite exornatio: in qua elegantie & decori habenda est ratio."

62 *Commentarius* (1554), p. 4: "quia poetae nomen sibi asciscunt non propter carmen, sed propter fabulum, & fictionem, ut in poetice testatum relinquit Aristoteles."

63 *Ibid.*, p. 4v: "omnia igitur in poemate sibi conueniant, consentiant, respondeant, scopum, ac finem omnia spectent, nihil abhorreat, nihil alienum sit."

Aristotle established in the *Poetics*, the plot is the soul of the poem."[64] He
then proceeds to the word-for-word explanation of the passage. It is clear
that, whereas Badius' gloss is purely linguistic and rhetorical in character,
speaking only of matters of diction and invention, Lovisini's passes beyond
to considerations of the poetic imagination and of the importance of plot
in the total poetic structure.

As another case, we may juxtapose the readings of Badius and Grifoli on
Ars poetica 114–18. Badius, largely concerned with textual problems, sees
in these lines only a formulation of the principle of decorum and how it is
to be observed; this is solely a question of fitting the proper speech to
personages of different ages, stations, countries, sexes, and so forth. The
statement of the rule is brief: "Seruandum est igitur studiose decorum
personarum pro sua cuiusque fortuna, aetate, ac patria" (p. XXv). Grifoli
starts with this point, stating that Horace here as always is interested in the
decorum of persons and in fitting words to people as well as to things. But
he expands these ideas by bringing into consideration Aristotle's four
requisites for character, all of which Horace treats in the *Ars poetica*;
Grifoli cites the passages in which each of the four is adumbrated. With
respect to all of them, he says, necessity and verisimilitude must be observed
—and he cites *Poetics* 1454a32. For one who reads the Horatian passage
accompanied by Grifoli's remarks, the passage carries with it all the overtones of Aristotle's theories of character and of necessity and probability
and hence (whether or not these associations be correct for the text here
studied) is richer and more suggestive than it was for Badius.

Other passages might be cited to exemplify the claim that through the
cultivation of parallelism with the *Poetics* of Aristotle, critics gave to those
passages a more extensive and a more complex meaning than they had had
for commentators of the preceding generation. But the enrichment stops at
the level of the individual passage. It would not be possible, I believe, to
state that any general change in the interpretation of Horace takes place,
that the total approach to the *Ars poetica* is any different from what it was
previously. The close ties with the rhetorical tradition, the persistence of
basically rhetorical distinctions, the survival of the construction put upon
the text by the earliest commentators, and the fundamental nature of the
text itself prevented any such change from taking place. Moreover, as later
chapters of this study will demonstrate, certain modes of approach to
intellectual problems and certain habits of method practically assured the
continuation of the older approaches. These same modes and habits were
responsible for the fact that, throughout all this extensive comparison and
equation of the *Poetics* and the *Ars poetica*, there was no slightest intima-
tion of the true state of affairs with respect to these two texts: the fact that

64 *Ibid.*, pp. 4v–5: "nec temere primum docuit, qualis esse debeat argumenti, & fabulae
constitutio, quia, ut in poetice auctor est Aristoteles, fabula poematis anima est."

they address themselves to essentially different problems, that they use widely different methods, and that they produce statements of a completely different nature about poetry. For theorists of this period, only the accidental—and sometimes the forced—resemblances between the two were discovered; their real opposition was not even suspected. So it was that Horace could be said to be an imitator of Aristotle, that many lines of his text could be identified with Aristotle, and at the same time the whole of the text could be read much as it had been before Aristotle was brought into the discussion.

CHAPTER FIVE. THE TRADITION OF HORACE'S *ARS POETICA*: III. THE APPLICATION TO PRACTICAL CRITICISM

S O FIRMLY ENTRENCHED an intellectual tradition as the tradition of Horace's *Ars poetica* would not be apt to change with the change of the decades. The habits of interpretation were by 1560 so firmly established that little modification could be expected. Even the way of coupling Aristotle's text with Horace's was a fairly unimaginative procedure. Yet we are not to suppose that the succeeding decades add nothing and modify nothing, nor that the remaining documents to be considered are merely repetitions of the earlier ones. For one thing, the major effort of the century to provide formal commentaries to the *Ars poetica* seems, from this date on, to taper off; and although there will still be some important glosses to the text, they will occur less frequently from now until 1600 than they had in the decade of the fifties. In their place, we shall have to deal usually with shorter treatises, many of which will apply Horatian principles to literary works of current interest.

As a matter of fact, the first two works to be discussed in this chapter are formal commentaries on the *Ars poetica*. One of them is undated, and I include it at this point merely because its author's literary activity fell approximately around 1560. It is an unpublished manuscript, MS BNF II.IV.192, fols. 153²–161v, entitled *Petri Angelii in Quintij Horatij de arte poetica librum annotationes*; its author was Pietro Angeli, who also called himself Petrus Bargaeus. The manuscript is exactly what it pretends to be, a set of miscellaneous notations on Horace's work rather than a complete and thoroughgoing treatment of it. In a number of these notations, Angeli indicates parallels with Aristotle, just as his predecessors had done:

Horace	Aristotle
1	1451a22
14	
34	1456a9
38	1460b15
42	1451a34
82	1449a27
105	1455a23
146	1459a33
150	1451a36
179	1460a11
259	1460a1
333	1449b26
338	1451b1
347	1460b16
465	

The briefness of the list is explained not only by the fragmentary character of Angeli's notes, but also by the fact that he seeks such parallels only incidentally, not as a major intention. In fact, he takes pains to point out how Aristotle differs from Horace on such matters as the history of tragedy and comedy and how superior Aristotle is on such subjects as verisimilitude (fol. 160). For the rest, his annotations are limited to paraphrasing the text, to pointing up the major ideas (such as unity and simplicity of plot or the necessity of deriving the denouement from internal elements rather than from a "deus ex machina"), or to emphasizing certain original interpretations. Among these latter, we might note his distinction (*in re* l. 179) between τὸ πάθος, produced by what is shown on the stage, and τὸ θαῦμα, produced by what is narrated; and his insistence that the five-act division of drama is a means to the resting and refreshing of the audience. He also declares (on l. 318) that the poet, as an imitator, must direct his attention to the general rather than the particular and that this involves a close observance of decorum. He equates Horace's ends of profit and delight (l. 333) with Aristotle's end of "mitigating the perturbations and movements by which the soul is violently affected."[1]

PIGNA (1561)

The second work, Giovanni Battista Pigna's *Poetica Horatiana* of 1561, is not only a full-scale commentary; it is one of the lengthiest and most detailed of the century. Its author apparently starts from the premise that although various of his predecessors had sought a principle of organization for the Horatian text, no one of them had found it. In fact, those who had used the rhetorical terms of invention, disposition, and elocution (such as Pedemonte) had explained successfully the first seventy-two lines of the *Ars poetica*, but then had been obliged to start again with some other system. Pigna sees the whole of the work as organized on another basis:

> The poetics of Horace was written in such a way as to expound first the whole of poetry, treated as still unknown; then to continue with it, after having divided it into its species, to the point where the necessary parts of these same species would be completely analyzed; finally, collecting together these separate elements, to touch again upon the whole of poetry, but treated now as fully known. As not yet known, it must be considered according to matter [rem], words [verba], and the combination of the two [compositionem]. To the matter belong invention and disposition, and the same two also to words. To the composition belong the whole form of the poem and the entire power of the poet. . . . [2]

---

[1] MS BNF II.IV.192, fol. 159*v*: "poëticae finem uidetur statuisse perturbationum ac motuum, quibus animi uehementer afficiuntur mitigationem."

[2] *Poetica Horatiana* (1561), p. 1: "Poetica Horatij ita est conscripta, vt poesim totam, prout est ignota, primo suscipiat: deinde illam in sua genera partitam eo vsque perducat, quousque ipsorum generum necessariae particulae sint absolutae: postremò ex singulis collectis totam rursus poesim perstringat, sed prout iam cognoscitur. Vt tota ignota, consideranda est secundum rem, verba, & compositionem. Rei sunt inuentio, & dispositio: verborum idem pariter. compositionis sunt poematis integra forma, & poetae integrae vires. . . ."

The first half of the preceding paragraph gives the general outline of the *Ars poetica* as Pigna analyzes it; the second half establishes the methodological framework into which he will fit a large part of the text. The "res-verba" distinction, which had been for all commentators (as for Horace himself) an incidental aspect of the total structure, becomes for Pigna the central element of Horace's methodology; even invention and disposition, as the quotation shows, are made subordinate to it.

Pigna organizes most of the text around this "res-verba" distinction. He divides it into sections of a few lines each—the number of divisions has now grown to eighty—and states a precept in summary of each section. The first precept (ll. 1–13) concerns the "inventio rei"; the second (ll. 14–24), the "dispositio rei"; the third (ll. 25–28), the invention and disposition of the words ("de uerbis agit, eodem modo inueniendo, ac disponendo"); the fourth (ll. 29–31), the same with respect to the mixture of styles. The fifth precept (ll. 32–37), on the "poematis forma integra," combines all these elements—invention and disposition of things and words—and proceeds on the basis of an analogy with life; just as the happy life results from the proper admixture of reason and prudence (cf. the *Ethics*), so the perfect poem effects a proper combination of invention (equivalent to reason) and disposition (equivalent to prudence). The analysis continues in this fashion, with a consistent application of the same set of terms. It is not until the twelfth precept (ll. 73–76) that the element of "composition" enters into play, and we discover then that it refers to metrical form rather than to any other kind of "composition": "quae non est elocutio ab Oratore consideranda, sed est carmen" (p. 32); this element accounts for Horace's treatment of the verse forms appropriate to the various genres. For lines 220–50, the forty-first to forty-fifth precepts treat both "res" and "verba" with respect to satyric drama. Precept fifty-four (ll. 309–10), on moral philosophy as supplying the "materia" of poetry, obviously belongs to the same set of distinctions, as do many other precepts throughout the analysis.

One result of Pigna's consistent application of this method is the reduction of almost all of Horace's poetics to a theory of the genres. If material, words, and verse are to be fitted together, some principle of fittingness must be established; this may be the vague notion of appropriateness employed by so many of the commentators, or the more restricted notion of appropriateness involved in appropriateness to genre. Pigna uses the latter principle. This becomes apparent as early as the first precept, which insists that "the different forms of poetry should not be joined together," and it is developed at length in the second, which "refers to the choice of a single *genus* of poetry."[3] Indeed, Pigna forces the Horatian text in order to make it include the four genres distinguished by Aristotle ("caput humanum" representing the epic, "ceruicem equinam" tragedy, "collatas plumas"

---

[3] *Ibid.*, p. 2: "vt diuersẹ poeseos formae simul coniungi non debeant" and "ad solum poeseos genus eligendum refertur."

dithyrambic and lyric poetry, and "atrum piscem" comedy) and to justify this statement of principle: "it is to be understood that those four kinds of poetry can never be brought together in one poem and, in fact, that there is no different method that would be appropriate to all of them."[4] Hence it is, he says, that Horace lays the groundwork for poetry in general in the first lines of his epistle and then passes rapidly to treatment of the individual genres: to the epic with line 42, to the lyric with line 77, to tragedy and comedy with line 89, to satyric drama with line 220, and so forth, in each case considering "res" and "verba" in their relationships to invention and disposition and then "compositio" in connection with all.

A concomitant of this general approach will of necessity be a theory of decorum. Arriving at precept twenty-one (ll. 114–18), Pigna makes and explains the transition:

> Up to this point, I think, we have discussed plot and diction; now comes character . . . which is not expressed for itself but in order to make the plot one which has character. And just as mores are derived from the plot, so are the passions, because when the diction contains character and passion, so too does the subject-matter.[5]

The line of reasoning may not be very clear here, but Pigna apparently means that character and thought (the Aristotelian qualitative parts are referred to here) must depend upon the nature of the plot, and that when they are seen to be proper in the diction, it is a sign that they are correct in the material itself. That is, "oratio morata et perturbata" will be a reflection of "fabula morata et perturbata"—"verba," of "res." When he discusses character, Pigna develops a fairly original and interesting theory. He starts with Aristotle's four requisites for character, which he proceeds to rebuild into a system of his own. All four requisites, he says, are forms of the verisimilar, which itself is of two types: (1) the "easy" verisimilar (because it is easily believed), applicable to well-known persons, and for which "quod decet" is sufficient; (2) the "difficult" verisimilar, applicable to less well-known persons, and for which some kind of "similitudo" is required. Under each type, a personage may be considered by himself or in comparison with others; and the four resulting kinds correspond to the four requisites, thus:

verisimile

facile		*difficile*	
per se	*in collatione*	*per se*	*in collatione*
τὰ χρηστά	τὰ ἁρμόττοντα	τὸ ὁμαλόν	τὸ ὅμοιον

---

4 *Ibid.*, p. 3: "sciendum est, quatuor illa Poeseos genera nunquam in vnum poema posse reduci: etenim nulla esset diuersa ratio illis consentanea."

5 *Ibid.*, pp. 44–45: "Mea est interpretatio hucusque actum esse de fabula, & de dictione: nunc de moribus. . . . qui non absolute traduntur sed vt fabulam moratam efficiunt. & quemadmodum ex ipsa suscepti sunt mores, ita etiam perturbationes: quia vt oratio est morata, & perturbata, ita quoque materia."

Further statements show that τὰ χρηστά is merely a theoretical type of mores and is never really considered in a poem, since no person's actions are of interest of and by themselves; that τὰ ἁρμόττοντα refers to type characteristics, differentiating persons according to station, age, profession, nation; that τὸ ὁμαλόν or "conuenientia" is essentially a principle of self-consistency and is useful especially in comedy; that τὸ ὅμοιον is a matter of opinion or "fama," demanding that known persons be presented in keeping with their reputations, and is proper to both epic and tragedy. Pigna is, of course, completely faithful to his theory of literary genres when he conceives of separate kinds of mores for the separate genres.

To the question of mores (character and decorum) is closely allied, for Pigna, the question of the moral ends of poetry, and this leads him to a seemingly contradictory position. Commenting on lines 311–18 (on the uses of philosophy in poetry), he had approved of Horace's insistence that "the whole of poetry rests upon mores."[6] But a little later, speaking of the "prodesse" and "delectare" of line 333, he argues against the frequent assumption that delight is merely a handmaiden of utility, and he presents a long argument to prove, contrariwise, that the real end of poetry is pleasure. The reconciliation of this conflict is found, I believe, in the notion of the "verisimile." For Pigna, the primary end of poetry is pleasure, but it is accompanied by utility. In order that there may be pleasure, the audience must be convinced of the credibility of the persons and actions involved in the poem, and this credibility is assured by moral verisimilitude. "For if things were treated which were completely alien from truth and which could not really happen, no credibility would attach to them nor would they be followed by that pleasurable remembrance";[7] in support of which Aristotle is cited on the impossible probable. Such credibility is guaranteed by the "fabula morata" (p. 74).

We have seen that, in various places, Pigna calls upon the authority of Aristotle to sustain his arguments. That is, in general, Aristotle's role in his commentary, rather than as an inspirer of the whole Horatian theory. But Pigna does not resist the current fashion of citing parallels; I give the list for the record:

Horace	Aristotle
1–13	1448a4, 1447a14
14–23	[gen.: "Duo sunt, quae ex Aristotelis poetica illis competunt, tum vt ex subiecta materia consistant, tum vt nexu congruenti coniungantur," p. 5.]
	1456a30
	[gen.: "neque enim Hesiodus sub aliquo poeseos genere ab Aristotele reponitur," p. 8.]
	1451b15, 1453a12

---

[6] Ibid., p. 72: "poesim totam positam in moribus."

[7] Ibid., p. 79: "Quòd si à uerò prorsus aliena: & quae accidere non possint tractarentur, nulla eis fides adhiberetur: neque subsequeretur iucunda illa recordatio."

Horace	Aristotle
24–28	1458a18
29–31	1460b3, 1458a18, 1458a21
32–37	1450b34, 1460b17, 1456a18
	[gen.: "Homerum ab Aristotele excusatum," p. 18]
38–41	1460b2
42–45	1447a14, 1449b23, 1448a19(?), 1454a26(?)
46–50	1457b1
52–59	1457b2
73–76	1449a21, 1448a21
79–82	1449a25
83–85	1447a15
89–92	1448a16, 1453a20
93–98	1455b25, 1453a12
104–13	1462a4
114–18	1450a8, 1454a16
119–27	1454a16
128–30	1454a16
136–45	1451a22
149–50	1451a24
153–60	1454a21, 1453a33
179–88	1452b12, 1453b2
189–90	1450b37
191	1452b17, 1454b19, 1454b2
192	1449a16
202–19	1449b7
220–24	1449a19
244–50	[?: "Aristoteles enim Agathonem reprehendit, quòd eius fabulae vulgarium hominum sententiae potius satisfacerent, quam prudentum," p. 67]
260–74	1458b20
275–80	1448a29, 1449a16
295–301	1455a34
333–34	1449b26, 1451b5, 1460b6, 1460a18
338–42	1460a26, 1451a38
347–50	1460b16
351–60	[?: A. on Homer: many virtues, few faults, pp. 80–81]
361–65	1448a4
453–69	1455a34

Although the presence of Aristotle is considerable (less considerable, perhaps, than it might seem, since many of the passages are quoted several times), it has little effect upon the total view of the *Ars poetica*. Pigna seems rather to build his interpretation about the "res-verba" distinction, about a theory of the genres, and about the standard rhetorical notion of the "verisimile." However, he objects to another rhetorical approach, via invention, disposition, and elocution, as a means of discovering the order of Horace's text. His own proposed order is more consistent with his own system. It does not prevent him, nevertheless, from effecting a fragmentation of the text into a number of passages and precepts even greater than that proposed by earlier commentators.

BARTOLOMEO MARANTA (1561)

These positions of Pigna and the even more traditional ones of Robortello and Maggi are attacked openly in a set of six lectures delivered by Bartolomeo Maranta to the Accademia Napoletana, meeting in the convent of San Pietro a Maiella, in 1561. A Latin summary of the first lecture and the actual notes for the other five (in Italian) are now in the Ambrosian Library in Milan, MSS R. 118. Sup. and R. 126. Sup.[8] Maranta devotes all six of his lectures to the first two "precepts" of Horace, the materials contained in lines 1–24—obviously a very extended discussion and one which could not help but bore its listeners; Maranta admits that it did and that he has rewritten the last two lectures to give a more succinct presentation. In fact, the discourses are hopelessly long-winded and repetitious, but they are not without merit. Their initial premiss is itself noteworthy for its time: Maranta declares that the distinction of invention, disposition, and elocution, so universally applied by earlier commentators on the *Ars poetica*, is in no wise appropriate to the poetic art and should not be brought into consideration. Instead, "we believe it necessary that he who wishes to analyze poetics should seek a proper basis of division which would not be applicable to any other art or science."[9] He finds this proper division in Aristotle's *Poetics*, where kinds of poems are differentiated by their means of imitation, and where each poem is divided into qualitative and quantitative parts. Moreover he believes (as others had before him) that Horace set out to treat the same six qualitative parts that Aristotle had distinguished, albeit in a different order, and that "he borrowed from Aristotle almost all the precepts, and especially those which are of greatest importance."[10]

These distinctions from Aristotle enable Maranta to make the point which he regards as his original contribution to Horatian exegesis: the first precept concerns the choice of plot and the unifying of plot, and the second precept is devoted to episodes. Just as Aristotle, according to Maranta, had named three kinds of false unity (unity of person, unity of time, unity of a single war), so Horace gives examples of three kinds of false unity: the multiplex monster, the vision of the man in fevered sleep, and the mixture

---

[8] The manuscripts are anonymous. For my attribution of them to Maranta and a general discussion of the problem, see "Bartolomeo Maranta: Nuovi Manoscritti di Critica Letteraria," *Annali della Scuola Normale Superiore di Pisa*, Serie II, XXIV (1955), 115–25.

[9] MS R. 118. Sup., fol. 117v: "Oportere autem eum qui poeticam partiri cupiat propriam, et quae nulli praeterea arti aut scientiae conueniat, diuisionem quaerere existimauimus."

[10] *Ibid.*, fol. 118v: "ipsa tamen praecepta fere omnia, et praesertim quae maioris sunt momentj ab Aristotele mutuatus est."

of wild and tame beasts. The first of these corresponds to the manifold actions of a single man, which do not constitute unity; the second, to successive but disconnected events, which do not constitute unity; the third, to contemporary but unrelated events, equally without unity. Aristotle's three kinds are thus found exemplified in Horace (fols. 120–23). The second precept, on episodes, demands the major part of the treatment after the first lecture. Maranta decides, on the basis of Aristotle, that the episode must be a quantitative part whose function is to give greater volume to the poem. It is thus never a part of the unified plot, but something added to it and integrated with it. Certain difficult problems arise as a result: How can a quantitative part be integrated with a "formal" or qualitative part? Can extraneous elements appear in the prologue and exode as well as in the "episodes"? How does one distinguish episode from plot itself in such genres as the epic? To such considerations as these Maranta devoted most of his time before the Accademia Napoletana.

It may seem that the debate is trivial, and it is certain that the discussion is too long. But for Maranta the subject warranted all the time and reflection that he could give it, since it was the central problem in any theory of poetics: the constitution of the central, unifying element in the poem—the plot—and the relationship of other parts of the action to it. Maranta apparently believed that if he could decipher Horace's meaning with respect to this problem, he would have the key to the rest of the text. The way in which he uses Aristotle in seeking the solution is in a sense original, for he does not merely cite parallel passages, he does not merely call upon an additional authority; he attempts, rather, to apply the method of Aristotle, as he understood it, to the Horatian text, and this constitutes a considerable innovation. The recognition that rhetorical distinctions do not supply answers to poetic questions and that a specifically poetic method must be used marks a notable departure from the thinking of his contemporaries.

Another unpublished manuscript, this one undated as well, has both theoretical and practical pertinence to the Horatian mode. It is perhaps of even greater interest as an early estimate of Torquato Tasso's *Rinaldo.* This is MS 985 (M.8) of the Biblioteca Comunale at Perugia, and I have assigned it an approximate date of 1561; it is entitled *Tractatus de tragoedia* and is in the form of a dialogue involving such celebrated interlocutors as Cardinal Ranuzio Farnese, Jacopo Sadoleto, Pietro Bembo, Bernardo Tasso, and Annibale Caro.[11] On the theoretical side, the prologue and the dialogue itself touch upon four points in connection with tragedy: the

11 The list of names raises some question about anachronism in the text: both Sadoleto and Bembo died in 1547, at which time Torquato Tasso was only three years old. Such anachronism suggests the possibility that the treatise may have been written at a much later date than that assigned, by somebody whose knowledge of the earlier years of the century was very imperfect.

effect produced, the ends, the pleasure derived from imitation, and the educative function of poets. The following passage demonstrates the attitude with respect to the effect and, to some extent, with respect to the ends:

For what else are we to say of the fact that we very willingly give applause to a mournful poem? that we follow with a pleasant sense of grief the horrible destruction of the most prosperous of princes? that we behold without satiety their unexpected vicissitudes and reversals of fortune? that we are reduced to pity by the pretended complaint of the actors, very pleasurably albeit with pain? that we fill up our eyes with gloomy images? that we cannot satisfy our grief with weeping? that, lastly, we are so regaled by fictional deaths, bereavements, grief, wailing, ruin? if not that we have already accustomed ourselves to wretchedness and failings in the most catastrophic way in the natural course of events, and we have grown so hardened to the sensation of our own calamity, after the pain has healed, that to have the wound now aggravated by one's own hand when it is rough to the touch produces a very agreeable sensation, ameliorated by habit itself. Last of all, so you may not fail to be aware of the ultimate state of the most calamitous exile, there is great pleasure in weeping when a moral man has been overwhelmed by misfortunes that inspire tears.[12]

The effect is here a pleasurable participation in the woes of others (a thesis, incidentally, that explains much of the characteristic quality of Renaissance tragedy), the end is to harden the soul to misfortune and suffering. But the pleasure results also from the artifice of the poet and even more from the fact that the poem is an imitation; things which are disagreeable in life become agreeable through imitation (fols. 103v–104v). "Quanto sunt illa iucundiora ficta quam facta?" (fol. 104v). Because of the presence of such pleasure, the lessons taught by poetry are willingly received—compare the sugar-coated pill—and the utility results, in an almost automatic fashion. Hence the author of the *Tractatus* takes issue with Plato's banishment of the poets and with the severe condemnations of Proclus and of Maximus of Tyre and prefers to adopt instead the opinion of Plato in Book II of the *Laws*. His arguments on the role of poets as educators are the ones commonly used in the defences of poetry.

On the practical side, the author gives extravagant praise to the adolescent Torquato Tasso's *Rinaldo*, of which he has heard a reading. His

---

[12] Perugia, Bibl. com., MS 985 (M.8.), fol. 96v: "Quid enim aliud dicamus esse, quod lamentabili carmini libentissime plausum damus. quod horribiles exitus Principum florentissimorum iucunda conquestione prosequimur? quod inopinatas uicissitudines rerumque conuersiones sine satietate spectamus? quod ad misericordiam actorum ficta querimonia iucundissime quamuis dolenter incondimur? quod oculos moestis imaginibus explere? quod dolorem lacrymis satiare non possumus? Quod denique simulatis funeribus, orbitatibus, luctibus, eiulationibus, vastitatibus tantopere delectamur? nisi quod aerumnosissime natura miserijs ac uitijs iam insueuimus, et ad sensum nostrae calamitatis obducto dolore sic obduruimus, ut sua manu vulnus asperum tactu iam exulcerari iucundissimum sit, ipsa consuetudine mitigatum? Demum vt exilij calamitosissimi conditionem ultimam non ignores, mortali flebilibus aerumnis obruto flere magna uoluptas est. . . ." In referring to this MS, I use the new folio numbers penciled into the codex, which numbers stop at "99"; after that, I have supplied numbers myself.

remarks center largely around the genius of the young poet, his faculties and his knowledge, his familiarity with all poetry and all branches of philosophy. But he also comments on "how diligently he seeks out whatever will please, how acutely he discerns what will teach," and he gives special attention to Tasso's style; such epithets and descriptions as "copious, varied, unhampered, free, sententious, grave, elegant" will sound familiar to the reader who knows the tradition that we have been tracing. Some modicum of the theory—the reference to the ends, for example— pierces through in the practical criticism; but for the most part the latter is satisfied with the facile adjectives for genius and style that had for so long been in vogue.

Sebastiano Erizzo likewise effects a combination of theoretical and practical criticism in his *Espositione nelle tre canzoni di M. Francesco Petrarca* (1562), except that in his case there really is a close relationship between theory and practice. Since he wishes to speak later of Petrarch the poet as having achieved such-and-such effects in his poems, he states all his theoretical ideas in terms of the requisites for the poet rather than in terms of the nature of the poem. His starting point is the statement, from Horace, that mediocrity is not sufferable in a poet; rather must he have a divine and superhuman genius, the components of which will be a natural gift, a knowledge of many things, and the ability to combine the right words in verse. These are all needed if the poet is "to teach and move the listener, and then give pleasure, and awaken in him admiration with his poem."[13] For the natural gift there are no precepts to be given; but on the score of knowledge, Erizzo has much to say. It is essentially knowledge of the natural sciences and of philosophy and, within the latter, of moral philosophy:

... it is necessary that he learn the precepts of all the best arts, for since he has to treat of any subject whatsoever, he should show himself most well versed in that art which treats of the causes of things, of the vices of men, of the pleasures, of pain, of death, of the passions and all the perturbations of the soul, of the honest, of the true good, of all the virtues, of life, of mores, all of which things are contained under moral science.[14]

Its content of moral wisdom makes poetry excellent among all the arts, and the same excellence is found also in its capacity to give pleasure. Pleasure results from the "various ornaments," from the "beauty of the diction," from the harmony of verse. Nor does Erizzo neglect the standard

---

13 *Espositione* (1561), p. 1*v*: "insegnare, & commouere l'uditore, & appresso dilettare, & indurlo à marauiglia col suo poema."

14 *Ibid.*, p. 2: "fa mestieri, che egli apprenda i precetti di tutte le ottime arti, perche douendo di qualunque cosa trattare, in quella peritissimo si dimostri, cio è delle cagioni delle cose, de i uitij de gli huomini, de i piaceri, del dolore, della morte, de gli affetti, & di tutte le perturbationi dell'animo, dell'onesto, del uero bene, di tutte le uirtù, della uita, de i costumi, le quai cose tutte sotto la scientia morale si contengono."

distinctions in his enumeration of its sources; the poem must be of rare and exquisite invention and must have a choice of delightful words.

Before, passing on to the discussion of Petrarch, Erizzo attempts a theory of the genre in which he is specifically interested, lyric poetry. Distinguishing, first, three general kinds of poetry, the expository and narrative (I take it that he has didactic poetry in mind), the fictional, and the mixed, he places lyric poetry in the third category. He then proceeds to definitions of the lyric in general and of the elegy, both of which have a decidedly Aristotelian ring. Of the lyric, "at times it is an imitation of a grave and honest action, and sometimes of a joyous and light one, composed in verses which are not bare, but adorned with rhythm and harmony, so that with its sweetness it may at the same time profit and delight"; of the elegy, "it is for the most part love poetry which revolves about the passions of the soul, and it is an imitation of a complete lamentable action which, feigning the action in [the poet] himself or in another, expresses a melancholy effect."[15] The Aristotelian ring has, at times, Horatian overtones. Lyric poetry is said to be the most pleasing and delightful of all the types because of the elegance of its diction and its special musical qualities.

Petrarch belongs among the lyric and elegiac poets because of his treatment in a modest style of amorous subjects. The weeping and lamenting tone of his poems, the tears and sighs, make him an elegiac. After the classification, the praise; and it contains at once many of the traditional epithets, rhetorical criteria, and Horatian elements. (1) Petrarch's ideas are noble and full of wisdom, his sentiments grave, his style easy and full of an abundance of ornate words. (2) He equals Pindar in greatness, gravity, nobility of spirit, choice of words, and splendor of style and is unique in the imitation of the passions of love. (3) His invention shows the workings of nature and of art, "so abundant, in his style, was the natural facility, so rich, so sweet and full of gayety and loveliness, so rich in figures like precious jewels, and of the most beautiful and most necessary in poems of this kind."[16] (4) His verse is rhythmical and harmonious. (5) The moral sententiae throughout his poems show his mastery of moral philosophy, and the natural philosophy shows his indebtedness to Plato.

Such practical criticism as this shows some progress over the earlier varieties, insofar as some attempt is made to bring into operation the conclusions of the antecedent theoretical thinking. But the progress is still not very great.

[15] *Ibid.*, pp. 3v–4: "alle uolte è una imitatione di attione graue, & onesta, & alcune uolte di giocosa, & lieue, che si compone di uersi non nudi, ma di numero, & di armonia ornati, accioche colla sua dolcezza gioui parimente, & diletti" and "è in gran parte poesia amorosa, che si riuolge intorno alle passioni dell'animo, & è una imitatione di perfetta attione lamenteuole, la quale ò fingendola in se stesso il P. ouero in altrui, esprime malinconioso effetto."

[16] *Ibid.*, p. 4v: "tanto fu larga del suo stile la uena, ricca, dolce, & piena di leggiadria, & uaghezza, copiosa di figure à guisa di care gioie, & delle più belle, & necessarie à sì fatti poemi."

ORAZIO TOSCANELLA (1562)

In the realm of the purely theoretical, again, a document of some interest is Orazio Toscanella's *Precetti necessarii sopra diverse cose pertinenti alla grammatica, poetica, retorica, historia, loica, et ad altre facoltà* (1562). And the interest does not derive from the author's originality; quite the contrary. For Toscanella aims only to simplify other works for beginners and students of his time; in the field of poetics, therefore, he gives reductions and paraphrases of Donatus, Horace, Aristotle, and a section of Minturno. His claim to do so, though, is not completely accurate, for he does not stick very closely to the text that he is treating. For example, much material from Horace, not identified as such, is incorporated into the section entitled "Auertimenti della Comedia da Donato." Such a schoolboy's version of the classics of criticism is interesting in that it represents a kind of vulgate of critical thinking. What such a popularizer as Toscanella chooses to emphasize, what he singles out for quotation or expansion, is significant for estimating the state of criticism at the time.

In the Donatus section, Toscanella collects all of his ideas about comedy —and comedy is taken in the broadest sense of dramatic representation. After a preliminary statement that "comedy was first discovered so that people might moderate their desires through the examples of others and might become better,"[17] Toscanella goes on to such headings as "What persons are introduced in comedy," "What is the subject of comedy," "On sounds (or music)," "On vocal sections," "Why they are called acts," and "How many persons may speak in each scene." Most of these concern the kind of mechanics with which Donatus was occupied, but there are digressions and excursions which add considerably to the richness of the materials. For example, in connection with the subject of comedy he adds a note on the "in medias res" beginning and on the development of suspense in the spectator. When speaking of acts in drama, he gives his conception of imitation: "Comedy consists in imitation, and one who plays the part of a servant imitates as much as he can the comportment of a servant, one who represents a lover imitates a man who is really in love."[18] Like the expositors of the *Ars poetica*, he cites Aristotle (1453*b*1) in reference to Horace's lines on off-stage action. A long section, still in this paraphrase of Donatus, is devoted to the decorum of persons, with extended passages on "convenevolezza," "similitudine," and "egualità," and another to the verisimilitude to be observed in narration. Here, again, several texts from Aristotle are cited as parallel. Clearly, all this is very far from Donatus's text, and it is obvious that the latter has merely been used

---

17 *Precetti Necessarii* (1562), p. 12*v*: "La Comedia primieramente fù ritrouata, accioche le persone moderassero i loro desiderij con lo essempio di altri, & si facessero migliori."

18 *Ibid.*, p. 15*v*: "la Comedia consiste nella Imitatione; & uno, che fa la parte del seruo, imita quanto può gli andamenti del seruo; Vno che rappresenta lo innamorato, imita uno, che sia ueramente innamorato."

as a starting point for the development of a complete collection of statements on poetics, with special reference to the dramatic forms.

In a later section on poetics in general ("Che cosa sia poetica," pp. 57*v* ff.), Toscanella defines the art in a way which reveals the eclecticism of his method: "Poetics is a structure of feigned art and true narration, composed in fitting rhythm, or rather in metric feet."[19] Then, after the division of poems into the narrative, the dramatic, and the mixed, he defines tragedy: "Tragedy is an embracing of the heroic condition in a state of misfortune." (Toscanella is having difficulty in translating Diomedes' "Tragoedia est heroicae fortunae in adversis conprehensio.") "The subject and the material of tragedy are sufferings, tears, hate, murders, poisonings, burnings, bitternesses, poverty, heartaches, sobbings, sighs, dismemberments of small children, downfalls of great houses; movements to madness, betrayals, arms, violence, fury, wrath, etc."[20] In an identical fashion, the definition of comedy is translated from Diomedes and the subjects listed are those which had appeared traditionally in the medieval descriptions of the genre. So for the other genres. What pretends to be a theory of poetics turns out to be merely a compendium of the commonplaces on the art.

Most of what Toscanella gives in the section on Horace is merely a translation of selected lines from the *Ars poetica* strung together to make a fairly continuous exposition. This is preceded by a brief statement of five precepts, which apparently are to be taken as the salient aspects of the text; they all refer to the general principles of composition contained in the first few lines of Horace's epistle. A paragraph on style contains recommendations on invention, disposition, and elocution. When he reaches the point at which he must discuss the ends of poetry, Toscanella presents one of the "tabular reductions" of which he was so fond and which figure so prominently throughout his little manual. I reproduce a part of it here:

On the functions of the poet.

The function of the poet is to:

Delight—		*Profit—*
He who wishes to delight must not depart too much from the truth, but must stand firm within the limits of verisimilitude. In a word, he must mix together:		He who wishes to profit with his poem must be brief and treat only as much as he knows will suffice to make the listener understand what is being treated.[21]

The useful.	*The sweet.*	
So that the poem may delight grave persons, such as mature men, old men, etc., who take delight in utility.	So that the poem may delight the young, who take delight in pleasant things, etc.	

It can hardly be said that here or elsewhere Toscanella offers any interpretation of his basic text; he summarizes, codifies, simplifies, outlines, but that is all. (I shall discuss his treatment of Aristotle's *Poetics* in a later chapter.)

An effort at practical criticism that involves incidental pronouncements on theory was made by Sperone Speroni in his *Discorsi sopra Virgilio*, most of which he probably wrote around 1563–64 but which was still incomplete in 1581, and was published only posthumously.[22] Speroni's central intention is to attack the reputation of Vergil and to prove his inferiority as a poet, both absolutely and in comparison with Homer. To do so, he examines Vergil's performance in the areas of invention, disposition, and elocution. Speroni insists first on the importance of the first of these, which he identifies with plot, and he cites Aristotle on plot as the soul of the poem. Here he finds Vergil at fault in several ways: he does not *invent* anything at all, but borrows both the plot and its disposition from Homer; there are many errors and insufficiencies in the handling of plot and character, which Speroni points out at length and for some of which he suggests corrections. The matter of the poem is itself so slight that one wonders whether Vergil might not have foregone imitation entirely in favor of the cultivation of beauties which were essentially "extra fabulam." In this connection, Speroni proposes his theory on the unity of plot:

[19] *Ibid.*, p. 57*v*: "La Poetica è una struttura d'arte finta, & di uera narrazione; composta di numero conueneuole: ouero di piede metrico."

[20] *Ibid.*, p. 58*v*: "La Tragedia è uno abbracciamento della conditione heroica in stato di disauentura. . . . Il soggetto, & la materia della Tragedia, sono i dolori, le lagrime, l'odio, gli ammazzamenti, ueleni, incendij, amaritudini, pouertà, cordogli, singulti, sospiri, sbranamenti di membra di figliuoli, disgratie di case: mouimenti a pazzia, tradimenti, arme, uiolenza, furore, ira, &c."

[21] *Ibid.*, p. 76:

De gli uffici del poeta.
Vfficio del poeta è
Di

Dilettare,	*Giouare.*
Bisogna, che colui che uuol dilettare, non si parta troppo dal uero: ma stia saldo ne i termini del uerisimile. In somma bisogna, che mescoli insieme	Bisogna che sia breve, colui, che intenda di giouare col suo poema, & tanto tratti, quanto conosca che basti per fare intendere allo ascoltante cio che tratta.

L'utile.	*Il dolce.*
Accioche diletti il poema le persone graui: come gli huomini fatti, i uecchi, &c. che dell'utilità prendono diletto.	Accioche il poema diletti i giouani, che di cose dolci si dilettano, &c.

[22] The date of *ca.* 1563–64 is suggested by Speroni's biographer, Francesco Cammarosano, *La vita e le opere di Sperone Speroni* (Empoli, 1920), p. 164; a letter of 1581 from Speroni to Felice Paciotto, dated 1581, states that the discourses are still incomplete (*Opere* [1740], V, 280–81). The *Discorsi* were first published in the Venice ed. of 1740, IV, 419–579.

Hence it is that the poem must consist of one single action, as Aristotle said, not only because any imitation must imitate one single thing just as any science concerns one subject, but also because if a poem consists essentially in redundant and superfluous ornament, if a poet were to undertake to imitate poetically more than one action, the poem in order to be complete would grow to infinite size.[23]

As for Vergil, Speroni concludes that "Vergil did not possess the poetic art; because with respect to invention, in which the art consists, he does not dare to break away from Homer; for just as the art of oratory resides in invention, so does that of poetry."[24] Without Homer, he says, Vergil would have been nothing at all in plot and in disposition.

Vergil's merit, therefore, is exclusively in elocution. But it is not an absolute merit. Speroni, as we have seen, places the whole essence of poetry in ornament. Another passage may be cited in confirmation: "That poetry consists entirely of ornament may be seen in its figurative modes of speech, which are not used by orators or by historians or even by the art of grammar; it is seen in the sweetness of verse, in the restrictions which it imposes."[25] This leads him to place a premium on two qualities, "ornateness" and "floridity," both of which he finds in Homer, both of which are lacking in Vergil. Vergil's error lies in the fact that he "was concerned with brevity, in which the poet should take no delight if he wishes to delight the reader; for brevity cannot be ornate, and consequently is not pleasurable."[26] The comparison between the two poets is concluded thus:

I return to speak again of the brevity of Vergil and the floridity of Homer. The latter delights properly, pleasantly ornamenting and amplifying his subjects, whence he always abounds in epithets; but Vergil delights through the marvelous, speaking as he does with so much brevity and precision and without affectation. But from the delightfulness of Homer is born joyfulness and gaiety, from that of Vergil is born astonishment and melancholy, which is not proper to the poet but rather to the historian.[27]

23 In *Opere* (1740), IV, 438–39: "di qui nasce che'l poema dee essere di una azione sola, come disse Aristotile, non solo perchè di una imitazione debba essere una cosa sola imitata, come di un soggetto una scienzia; ma anche perchè se'l poema è ornamento redundante e superfluo, se'l poeta togliesse a imitar più di una azione poeticamente, il poema a volere esser perfetto cresceria in infinito." The argument is repeated on p. 534.

24 *Ibid.*, p. 571: "L'arte poetica non era in Virgilio: però quanto all'invenzione, ove l'arte consiste, non osa scostarsi da Omero. che come l'arte oratoria è nella invenzione, così è la poetica."

25 *Ibid.*, p. 534: "Che la poesia sia tutta ornamento, si vede per li suoi modi figurati di dire non usati dalli oratori, e dalli istorici, e dall'arte istessa della gramatica: si vede per la soavità del verso, per li suoi obblighi."

26 *Ibid.*, p. 438: "Fu studioso di brevità, della quale non si de' dilettare il poeta, se vuol dilettar i lettori; perchè la brevità non può essere ornata, e per conseguente non è dilettevole."

27 *Ibid.*, p. 439: "Torna a parlar della brevità di Virgilio, e floridità di Omero. Costui propriamente diletta ornando ed amplificando gentilmente le cose sue; onde sempre abbonde di epiteti: ma Virgilio diletta con la meraviglia, parlando con tanta brevità, e così assegnatamente, come fa, senza affettazione. ma dalla dilettazion di Omero nasce allegria ed ilarità; da quella di Virgilio nasce stupore e melanconia: il che non è proprio del poeta, ma anzi dell'istorico."

So that whereas Vergil may be praised for his brevity and his diction for certain rhetorical effects, these are not qualities which necessarily make of him a great poet. He is likened, indeed, to the "Asiatic" poets whose decoration is not appropriate to their subject matter.

From this process of applying a method of invention, disposition, and elocution there results a fairly consistent poetic. The plot, from invention, must be single and simple (but not too brief) so that a proper amount of ornamentation may be added. The diction must be ornate, but not too much so, lest it be in excess of what is demanded by the materials. If the poet strikes a proper balance between invention and elocution, as Homer did, then he is a great poet and worthy of the highest praise; if he fails in either of these aspects, much as he may be admired for other qualities, he ranks as an inferior poet, as Vergil did. Speroni's insistence upon ornament, upon the florid style, shows that his total approach is rhetorical in its conception of diction as well as in its tripartite division of elements.

MARANTA (1564)

If we had any evidence that Speroni knew Bartolomeo Maranta's *Lucullianae quaestiones* (1564), we might almost think that his discourses on Vergil were written in reply to Maranta. For Maranta's position is the exact opposite of Speroni's, and in the five dialogues contained in the work (so called after Colantonio Caracciolo's villa at Lucullo, near Naples, where the dialogues are set), we find nothing but the most fulsome praise for every aspect of Vergil's work. The interlocutors (they include Scipione Ammirato, Alfonso Cambi, Girolamo Colonna, Giovanni Villani, Gian Pietro Ciccarello, and other members of the Accademia Napoletana) talk most about the beauties produced by Vergil's studied assortments of sounds, about the appropriateness of certain sounds to certain ideas, about effects of onomatopoeia. Their second major concern is with figures of speech and the use of words in general; Girolamo Colonna's original proposal is to defend Vergil on the basis of his diction. For all these matters, an elaborate theory is presented as the conversations develop; the classical rhetoricians are cited in authority, especially Cicero, Hermogenes, and Dionysius of Halicarnassus. Other classical writers are quoted for parallel uses of figures or sounds.

In each of the five dialogues, however, some attention is paid to theoretical matters of broader import, since Maranta apparently wishes to develop a complete theory of the epic—even though much of the generalized material is never applied specifically to Vergil. At least some of the conclusions so presented are reached by comparing the epic with tragedy and comedy, and as a result the theoretical scope of the *Quaestiones* is considerably widened. Aristotle and Horace are the main authorities here, with Plato being used incidentally. The theory evolved is based in large part upon the comparison between the poet and the orator. At times, Maranta states the comparison explicitly, as in Book V: "We are not now comparing oratorical matters with poetic ones; but observing certain rules in the former, as in the very fountainhead, we then apply them to poetic matters, with due respect to the differences."[28] But more usually it is implicit in statements made exclusively about poetics, as in this sentence praising Vergil:

Indeed, to say nothing about the vehemence and the greatness that we see in his sententiae; and how variedly—and always wherever he wishes—he draws away the souls of men, inflames, calms, teaches, impels, excites, diverts, discourages them; and how distinctly and clearly and abundantly and luminously he writes, with respect both to content and to expression; and how also, without ever neglecting brevity, to both matter and form he so adapts all things that if you were to add, or change, or remove anything it would be wholly faulty and less perfect; I shall address myself to the discussion of diction.[29]

The string of verbs describing the effect upon the audience, the "res-verba" distinction, the general terms of praise for the style are all such as would properly belong to a conventional rhetorical estimate.

The poet, as we have seen, is like the orator in the ends he seeks. Maranta insists upon this in Book III also: "The poet proposes as his principal goal to arouse the different passions of the soul and whichever ones he wishes, and to generate them in the souls of those who listen or read. . . . Therefore, as far as this is concerned, the poet and the orator are very close together. . . . Each of them must thus, in the things which are common to both, have recourse to the same devices in order to achieve the goal."[30] Furthermore, the poet shares with the orator the end of admiration, although this is most properly attributed to the epic poet: "the marvelous is more proper to the epic than to tragedy, but it nevertheless belongs to both kinds of poems. . . . Among the principal aims of the poet is to arouse admiration from whatever source he can."[31] From these statements of the ends, the familiar "prodesse" and "delectare" are notably absent; Maranta, here as elsewhere, is

---

28 *Lucullianarum quaestionum libri quinque* (1564), p. 364: "Nos nunc non conferimus oratoria poeticis: sed regulas in illis obseruantes, quasi in proprio fonte proportione seruata, ad res poeticas deinde accommodamus."

29 *Ibid.*, p. 15: "Nam ut omittam, quantam in eius sententijs uehementiam ac magnitudinem uideamus, ac quàm uariè & semper quocunque uult, animos hominum distrahat, incendat, leniat, doceat, impellat, concitet, reflectat, deterreat: ac quàm distinctè & explicatè, & abundanter, & illuminatè, & rebus & uerbis scribat: & cum his quoque breuitatis haud immemor, ita res omnes temperet, ut quicquid aut addideris, aut mutaueris, aut detraxeris, uitiosius & deterius omnino sit futurum: ad orationem meipsum conuertam."

30 *Ibid.*, p. 179: "Poeta preçipuum scopum sibi proponit, ut uarias, & quas uult affectiones animi concitet, atque generet in animis eorum qui se uel audiunt, uel legunt. . . . Igitur quantum ad hoc attinet, Orator & Poeta maximè conueniunt. . . . Debet igitur in re communi utrisque, ad eadem uterque confugere, ut scopum attingant."

31 *Ibid.*, p. 88: "ut admirabilitas magis Epopoeiae conueniat, quàm Tragoediae: tametsi utriusque poematis propria est. . . . Inter praecipuos poetae scopos illud est, ut admirationem undique pariat."

closer to the rhetoricians themselves than to Horace. For similar ends, similar means. The poet will have to pay particular attention to the "proposition" of his poem, which must be simple and unornate and must stand in proper relationship to the plot, just as the orator will use poetic diction in his exordium (p. 179). Both must study the proper handling of "res" and "verba." Maranta equates two rhetorical elements (and he may have in mind two of Aristotle's qualitative parts), sententiae and "oratio," with "res" and "verba" respectively: "The words produce the diction and the things themselves the sententiae. The latter cannot exist without language, that is without words; but the words can exist without sententiae."[32] It is these, indeed, in which he is primarily interested, and he sacrifices the other parts in favor of an abundant discussion of the multiple aspects of words. Like the orator, again, the poet in any given poem works within the framework of one of the three styles; he chooses the proper style for the genre and then the proper words and figures for that style (Book V). Finally, one may analyze a poet's work, as one does an orator's, in terms of invention, disposition, and elocution, and Maranta does not fail to pay passing tribute to Vergil's invention and disposition (p. 96).

There is one lengthy discussion in the work, however, which is specifically germane to the poet, and that relates to truth and verisimilitude and the kinds of plots proper to the epic and to tragedy. Maranta assumes, as we have seen, that one of the ends of the poet is to stir the reader to admiration and that this is done through the use of the marvelous. The marvelous is produced by actions which are "unheard of, new, and completely unexpected."[33] At the same time, however, the poet must be sure never to tax the credulity of his audience; a delicate balance must be maintained between the marvelous and the verisimilar. It is here that a difference arises between tragedy and the epic. For the reader will accept certain things as credible which will be rejected by the spectator, and the spectator will sometimes be more deeply moved by what is narrated than by what is enacted. Therefore, "it is certain that the marvelous, especially when it attaches to those things which cannot really happen, cannot be represented in the same way in drama and in simple discourse where there is no representation of actions."[34] The epic poet may thus cultivate the extraordinary and incredible more freely than the tragic poet, and the latter must take care to relegate certain violent actions ("death itself, massacres, the cooking and eating of human flesh, and others of this kind"[35]) to narrative

32 *Ibid.*, pp. 17–18: "Verba orationem conflant, res ipsae sententias. Hae sine oratione, hoc est sine uerbis esse non possunt: at uerba sine sententijs possunt."
33 *Ibid.*, p. 89: "inaudita, ac noua, & praeter expectationem."
34 *Ibid.*, p. 91: "Constat igitur admirabilitatem, praesertim uerò earum rerum quae fieri nequeunt, non aequè posse in dramatibus effingi, atque in sermone nudo: ubi nulla est actionum repraesentatio."
35 *Ibid.*, p. 90: "Mors ipsa, trucidatio, membrorum humanorum coctio, comestio, & id genus caetera."

passages; in these, however, the "imitative" actions of the messenger or other narrator, his gestures and pronunciation, may considerably enhance the emotional effect. Clearly, all this is an expansion and explanation of Horace's line 179—

Aut agitur res in scaenis aut acta refertur

—but the explanation involves certain ideas about the nature of the audience which bring the analysis close to rhetorical theories. The audience is defined, in this connection, as being made up of "selectissimi viri" whose judgment would be more discerning than that of the "vulgus." It is this audience that sets the standards of credibility and verisimilitude, whose eyes will believe a limited number of actions and through whose ears the proper emotions of tragedy may be aroused and purged.

On the whole, then, Maranta's position remains a rhetorical one. The praise of Vergil which he so generously bestows has as its object the various excellences of Vergil's diction, although compliments are offered in passing to his invention and disposition. Curiously enough, Speroni also admitted in a general way the merit of the diction, but refused all worth and all poetic quality to the other two elements of the trilogy. In Maranta, whatever expansion of theory in the direction of a more complete poetics may be found is left without application to the text of Vergil itself; in Speroni, it is just such an expansion that leads to the denial of Vergil's right to the name of poet.

An even more restricted application of the same principles, with Ariosto as the poet studied, is presented by Lodovico Dolce's *Modi affigurati e voci scelte et eleganti della volgar lingua, con un discorso sopra a mutamenti e diuersi ornamenti dell'Ariosto* (1564). This is really not a treatise at all, but a collection of examples of "selected and elegant words" and of metaphors ("modi affigurati") cited as demonstrations of Ariosto's artistry. The only theoretical statements appear in the preface "A I Lettori," where Dolce says, "Everybody who wishes his compositions to be read willingly and praised by judicious and learned men must without fail try to write in a regulated, ornate, figurative, and artful manner," and where he insists upon the necessity of following the rules. He admits that both ornate and figurative writing find their rules in rhetoric and cites Bartolomeo Cavalcanti's *Retorica* and the *Modi affigurati* as providing examples and suggestions.[36]

To these specimens of practical criticism of the epic and the romance we may add two discussions of comedy, Lodovico Castelvetro's *Giuditio delle*

[36] *Modi affigurati* (1564), p. 1: "Ciascuno, che disidera, che i suoi componimenti siano uolentieri letti e lodati da gli huomini giudiciosi e dotti, dee senza fallo procacciar di scriuer regolatamente, ornatamente, figuratamente & artificiosamente."

comedie di Terentio and his *Parere sopra ciascuna comedia di Plauto.*[37]
Both of these are undated, and I have assigned them arbitrarily to *ca.* 1565.
The *Giuditio* consists of scattered remarks on specific words or lines of
the various comedies of Terence. Castelvetro's main concern is with the
problem of verisimilitude. He reproaches Terence with having neglected to
present the true and the verisimilar, and in all cases these terms refer to
natural rather than artistic probability. For example, it is not "verisimile"
that Pamphilus in the *Andria* should walk from the forum to his house in
complete silence and then begin to shout as he approaches the house,[38]
nor is the line "Ex ara hinc sume verbenas" acceptable since it is not
common to find, on the public streets, altars covered with sacred boughs
(p. 170). These would be, I presume, sins against nature; the remainder of
Castelvetro's strictures apply to sins against art: telling the story in the
prologue, since the comedy should be completely self-contained and have
no need of prior explanation; committing "sconvenevolezze" by assigning
to persons or situations speeches or actions not appropriate to them;
narrating briefly what should be told at length, and vice versa. Rarely
Terence is applauded for a proper solution, as in his introduction of the
parasite in the *Eunuch*; such persons may be used in comedy only as companions to sons of good family whose fathers are far away or to vain and
spendthrift soldiers (p. 174). The tendency of all these remarks is to set up
three criteria—nature, decorum, and the strict rules of art—as guides to
the practicing poet.

The situation is much the same in the *Parere* concerning the comedies of
Plautus. More rules are added by implication: an actor must not address
the audience (p. 8); the stage must not remain empty (p. 9); the "deus ex
machina" ending is not desirable (p. 9), nor is the double ending, which
brings happiness to some and unhappiness to others (p. 14). For the most
part, Castelvetro talks about the plots of the comedies and criticizes details
of construction, again usually in terms of natural probability. On this
score, several new points are made. Of the *Amphytrion* Castelvetro says:
"Next, this action involves kings and gods; but it is not known through
history or through legend; hence it is not a poetic subject"[39]—the implication being the familiar one that, in poems, kings and gods may figure only
in actions already known to the audience. Moreover, Castelvetro raises
moral objections to certain of the actions in the *Asinaria*, indicates the
possibility of sad endings for comedy and happy endings for tragedy. All
these criticisms belong strictly to the Horatian tradition which I have been

[37] The author of the *Parere* is identified in the title of the manuscript (Vat. Lat. 5337) only
as "L. C."; but the editor of the text, Giuseppe Spezi (Bologna, 1868), argues for the attribution to Castelvetro.

[38] In *Opere varie critiche* (1727), p. 168.

[39] *Parere, ed. cit.,* p. 8: "Appresso questa azione è reale e divina, nè appare per historia,
o, per fama; dunque non è soggetto poetico."

tracing, and there are only the slightest reflections of the Aristotelian *Poetics*. This is surprising indeed for one of the century's principal commentators on Aristotle. It may be explained either by assuming that these criticisms were written before Castelvetro began his work of textual exegesis, or by concluding that even a professional Aristotelian theorist could operate, in the domain of practical criticism, in complete independence of the *Poetics*.

Torquato Tasso, himself a sonneteer, provides us with an example of criticism of the sonnet in the same mode. It is his *Lezione sopra un sonetto di Monsignor Della Casa*, written in his youth and recited before the Accademia Ferrarese; I have assigned to it a tentative date of 1565.[40] After a preliminary discussion of nature and art in the poet (Tasso gives precedence to art and indicates how the poet must combine the imitation of models with the following of precepts), he chides the imitators of Casa with having failed to reflect his greatest qualities. "What is marvelous in him, the choice of words and of sententiae, the novelty of the figures and especially of the metaphors, his strength, greatness and majesty, they either do not try to express or are unable to do so in any degree."[41] Tasso will attempt to explain these elements in his lecture. Since they refer exclusively to matters of style, he prefaces his remarks by a distinction of the various styles as seen by Demetrius, by Hermogenes, and by Cicero; then, placing this sonnet in the "magnificent, grand, and sublime" style, he defends Casa's use of this style in the sonnet. Dante's objections are overridden, since if grave and magnificent matters may be used in the sonnet, why not words of the same kind? Tasso here applies the rhetorical distinction between concepts and words: "It is clear that the concepts are the end and consequently the form of discourse, and the words and the composition of the verse are the material or the instrument."[42] Casa's concepts are then analyzed in terms of Demetrius' criteria—with passing reference to Book III of the *Rhetoric* and to Cicero's *Orator*—and the general question of the proper subjects for poetry is raised.

This was a moot question at the time. Tasso shares the position of those who held that profound philosophical and scientific concepts, especially when expressed in proper philosophical terms, are not acceptable in poetry. He praises Petrarch for having reduced Plato's philosophy to terms that were comprehensible to the reader. Two basic conceptions relative to the

[40] Guasti, who edited the *Lezione* in the *Prose diverse* (1875), II, 111–34, gives no indication of its date. According to Solerti, *Bibliografia delle opere minori in versi di Torquato Tasso* (Bologna, 1893), pp. 12–13, the lecture was first published in *Delle rime* (Venice, 1582).

[41] In *Prose diverse*, ed. Guasti, II, 117: "quel che è in lui maraviglioso, la scelta delle voci e delle sentenze, la novità delle figure, e particolarmente de' traslati, il nerbo, la grandezza e la maestà sua, o non tentano, o non possono pur in qualche parte esprimere."

[42] *Ibid.*, p. 119: "chiara cosa è, che i concetti siano il fine e conseguentemente la forma dell'orazione; e le parole, e la composizione del verso, la materia o l'instromento."

poetic art are present here: first, the poet must delight; second, his audience is made up primarily of the common people. With respect to the first:

... since the poet must delight, either because pleasure is his end, as I believe, or because it is a necessary means to bring about utility, as others judge, he is not a good poet who does not delight, nor can he delight with those concepts which bring with them difficulty and obscurity; for a man must weary his mind in order to understand them, and since fatigue is contrary to human nature and to pleasure, wherever fatigue is present no pleasure can in any way be found.[43]

And to the second: "The poet speaks not only to the learned but to the people, as the orator does, and therefore let his concepts be popular; I mean by popular not those which the people uses ordinarily, but such as are intelligible to the people."[44] Judged by these standards, Casa receives a high rating; the concepts in this sonnet are "clear, pure, easy, but of a clearness that is not ordinary, a purity that is not low, an ease that is not ignoble."[45] From these bases, Tasso goes on to an appreciation of Casa's versification, of the sounds he uses, of the figures of speech and their appropriateness to the kind of style employed. The approach remains restricted to various levels of language—to elocution and versification— and never inquires into the possibility of other types of poetic structure and excellence. For this reason, it is related to the Horatian-rhetorical trend, which in the sonnet (where "plot" and "characters" in the strictest sense are lacking) could produce no other kind of interpretation or judgment.

With Benedetto Grasso's *Oratione contra gli Terentiani* (1566) we return to comedy and to Terence. Like Castelvetro's criticism, Grasso's is negative; but it is more severe and it is based on essentially different grounds. Perhaps the starting point for Grasso is his comparison of the poet and the orator. He sees them as having different ends and different procedures:

... just as the orator follows the wide road and goes wandering through the spacious fields of eloquence, never departing from common usage so that at the same time he may show the happy abundance of his speech, so also he tries with every art and diligence to obtain the desired victory. The poet, since he moves toward a different end, issues forth from the common usage of men and in this way he becomes admirable, giving pleasure and attracting the souls of the listeners with the beauty of the words, the sweetness of the rhymes, the variety and the floridity of the figures, in such wise that with the happy representation of charac-

[43] *Ibid.,* p. 124: "dovendo il poeta dilettare, o perchè il diletto sia il suo fine, come io credo, o perchè sia mezzo necessario ad indurre il giovamento, come altri giudica; buon poeta non è colui che non diletta, nè dilettar si può con quei concetti che recano seco difficoltà ed oscurità: perchè necessario è che l'uomo affatichi la mente intorno a l'intelligenza di quelli; ed essendo la fatica contraria a la natura degli uomini ed al diletto, ove fatica si trovi, ivi per alcun modo non può diletto ritrovarsi."

[44] *Ibid.,* p. 124: "Parla il poeta non a i dotti solo, ma al popolo, come l'oratore; e però siano i suoi concetti popolari: popolari chiamo non quai il popolo gli usa ordinariamente, ma tali, che al popolo siano intelligibili."

[45] *Ibid.,* p. 125: "chiari, puri, facili, ma d'una chiarezza non plebea, d'una purità non umile, d'una facilità non ignoble."

ters, gestures, and actions at one and the same time he gives us pleasure, and giving us pleasure he so attracts us that, as if beside ourselves, we are intent upon nothing else but considering the loveliness and perfection of that poem.[46]

According to this statement, the poet produces a kind of Platonic rapture, largely by means of extraordinary diction but also through the proper imitation of actions and characters. The statement is incomplete, however, as far as the ends are concerned; for elsewhere Grasso expands it by intro- ducing the formula "insegna, deletta, e moue" (p. 6) and by citing Plutarch on the uses of poetry in curbing violent passions and in teaching men to bear with equanimity the excesses of adverse or propitious fortune (p. 35). But his real meaning becomes apparent only when he proceeds to condemn Terence for the immorality and the obscenity of his comedies. Quoting Horace on the civilizing function of the earliest poets, who were priests and philosophers, he declares that it was through a desire to please the masses that later poets fell into decadence and that the reading of such poets can produce only blushes and contempt. Terence is one of these: "poets such as this, with the sweetness of their rhymes and the beauty and smoothness of their words, at first delight us; but they leave our souls infected and poisoned by the corruption of their enormous vices and their immoral stories."[47]

On the basis of the quality of the imitation, says Grasso, Terence is again open to criticism. His deficiencies are dual: in the lack of originality and in the nature of the imitation itself. Grasso equates imitation with invention, but only in the narrow sense of "imitation" as borrowing from other poets. To justify his attack on Terence, he develops an elaborate theory of this kind of imitation, which may take any one of three forms: (1) simple translation; (2) the use of different words; (3) an entirely new treatment, different in subject, words, and other ornaments. The last of these itself has three subdivisions: (a) the use of other names, general outline, means and ends, as in Vergil's use of Homer and Cicero's of Demosthenes; (b) the use of the same argument, but with different words, sententiae, and figures, as in Horace's imitation of Vergil's descriptions of rustic life; (c) the use, but in a changed form, of topics, sententiae, and words only, as in

---

46 *Oratione* (1566), p. 7: "si come l'Oratore abbracia la strada larga, e ua uagando per li spaciosi campi di eloquentia non partendosi dalla consuetudine ciuile, a ciò ad un' tempo dimostri la felice copia del suo fauelare. Così ancora tenta con ogni arte, e studio acquistare la desiderata vittoria: el poeta come tende ad un'altro fine, così esce fuori della consuetudine delli huomini, & per questo admirabil' resta, dilettando, e tirando li animi delli ascoltanti con la vaghezza delle parole, la dolceza delle rime, la varietà e la floridezza delle figure, in modo che con la felice representatione delli costumi, gesti, & attioni alle volte in tal modo ci diletta, e dilettando ci tira, che come alienati da noi medesimi ad altro non siamo intenti, quanto che a considerar' la legiadria & felicità di quel poema." Cf. also p. 17 for a restate- ment.

47 *Ibid.*, p. 38: "questi tali poeti con la dolcezza delle rime vaghezza, & lisci di parole al primo ci dilettano, ma lasciano gl'animi infettati, & auelenati dalla corruttela delli vitij enormi, e dishoneste suoe narrationi."

Vergil's borrowings from Lucretius and Ariosto's and Petrarch's borrowings from ancient authors. All the latter forms constitute the perfect art of imitation; but Terence did not possess this art, being a mere translator or at best a borrower of plots without the beauty and excellence that should accompany them. He can thus be credited with no talent for invention. (We may remember Speroni's similar strictures on Vergil.) This deficiency is related to Terence's failings in the other kind of imitation, that which consists in the representation of the actions, lives, and characters of men. The criterion here is resemblance: "one poet comes to be called more excellent than another insofar as he comes closer to what is natural, and this talent of expressing actions and characters and, in describing them, of representing faithfully the nature of things and their decorum, gives life, soul, and eloquence to the poet."[48] But Terence's imitations do not resemble nature, largely because of their immorality and obscenity.

These failures in invention are accompanied by unsatisfactory performance in elocution. Grasso concedes that Terence's diction is familiar and in the low style proper to comedy, that the words and sentences are good (albeit somewhat licentious), but not that he is a truly eloquent writer. For true eloquence demands a diction above and beyond that of the people: "It must use more choice and more beautiful words so that, by delighting with the diction, it will hold with wonder the minds of the listeners; and this thing simple and plebeian speech, because it is lacking in ornament and grace, cannot do."[49] One may wonder how Grasso would reconcile his requirement of florid and eloquent language with his notions about the proper style for comedy; but the problem is neither suggested nor solved. One sees at work, throughout Grasso's analysis, the traditional categories of invention and disposition, the rhetorical ends of teaching, delighting, and moving (accompanied by pleasure, admiration, and a kind of rapture), the moral goals of proper instruction and exemplification, and the current notions about imitation taken in its various senses.

GIOVANNI FABRINI (1566)

In 1566, when most Horatians seemed to be devoting themselves exclusively to practical criticism, Giovanni Fabrini da Fighine published a complete commentary in Italian on the *Opere* of Horace. The final section contained the *Ars poetica* "col comento vulgare" and is remarkable on two scores: it is the first commentary written in Italian and the only one in Italian to be published during the Cinquecento. Since Fabrini is writing his gloss in the vulgar tongue, and since he wishes to make "the two languages

48 *Ibid.*, p. 6: "vn' poeta viene esser chiamato piu eccellente del altro quanto che piu s'accosta al naturale, & questa virtu d'esprimer i gesti, costumi, & descriuendo accostarsi alla Natura delle cose, e il decoro da vita, anima, eloquenza del poeta."
49 *Ibid.*, p. 16: "& vsi parole piu scielte, & leggiadre, aciò con la dolcezza del dir' delettando, tienni ancora con marauiglia gl'animi dell'ascoltanti. La qual cosa non puo il parlar' plebeio & semplice, per esser priuo d'ornamento, & legg adria, operare."

explain each other," he spends much of his time on simple translation or paraphrase of the original; by piecing together the equivalents suggested for each word, one would have a continuous translation of the epistle. Otherwise, he provides the usual identification of historical persons, citation of authorities, and quotation of illustrative examples. Fabrini states at the outset what he thinks to be the content of Horace's treatise: "first it seems to me that in this epistle . . . he teaches the laws of poetry, second that he treats of poetry itself, and finally that he blames and scoffs at those who do not observe in poetry what should be observed by good and true poets."[50] The laws of poetry, he insists, are the same as those taught by Aristotle:

It seems that Horace in this passage [ll. 1–13] imitated Aristotle, or rather, that poetics is one single art which has only one single path from the beginning to the end, and that he who has perfect knowledge of it, wishing to discourse about it, can discourse about it only in one way; for in truth it is seen that Aristotle and Horace have, from the beginning to the end, proceeded at the same pace, with the same order, and with the same arrangement.[51]

The statement that Horace imitated Aristotle is repeated later: "If you wish to see how Horace means that one should proceed [in imitation], place before yourself this poetics of his and the poetics of Aristotle, which it is clear to see that he imitated, and you will know what is to be done."[52] Convinced, as had been so many of his predecessors, that Horace was copying directly the *Poetics*, Fabrini could not fail to point out numerous parallels between the two texts:

Horace	Aristotle
1–13	1450a38, 1455b12
14–23	1451b33, 1451a16, –a23
24–31	1456a25
38–41	1450b35
42–45	1459a29, 1460a1
60–76	1459b34, 1460a1
90–95	1448a14
96–103	1455a30, 1456a33

[50] *L'Opere d'Oratio* (1566), p. 355: "primieramente mi pare, che in questa epistola . . . egli insegni le leggi de la poesia; secondariamente, che tratti de la poesia, e finalmente biasima, e si ride di coloro, che ne le poesie non osseruano quello, che da buoni, e ueri poeti dee essere osseruato." Much of the pagination in this edition is erroneous, and where errors occur I give first the wrong number as printed and then the correct number.

[51] *Ibid.*, p. 355v: "Pare, che Oratio in questa diuisione habbia imitato Aristotile, ouero, che la Poetica sia un'arte, la quale habbia un solo camino dal principio al fine, e che ragionandosene da chi n'ha perfetta cognitione, non se ne possa ragionar, se non in un modo: perche inuerità si uede, che Aristotile, & Oratio hanno dal principio al fine proceduto con pari passo, col medesimo ordine, e con la medesima dispositione."

[52] *Ibid.*, p. 372v [=368v]: "chi ben uuol uedere, come Oratio intende, che si faccia; mettasi innanzi questa sua poetica, e la poetica d'Aristotile, che manifestamente si uede, che egli ha imitato, e conoscerà, come si dee fare."

Horace	Aristotle
104–13	1457a31(?)
119–27	1453b22, 1454a15
146–52	1459a29
153–65	1454a33
179–92	1460a11, 1453b1, 1450b35, 1454a33
193–201	1456a25
347–60	1460b13
361–65	1454b8

In comparison with some of the commentators of the preceding decade, this is a modest list indeed, and it is more significant for the general statement that it seeks to prove than for its own size.

Fabrini's ideas on the Horatian text itself show the curious eclecticism which by this date is commonplace in Italy. Some of these ideas are merely reflections of the old rhetorical tradition. For example, in his preliminary remarks he points out (quoting Aristotle) that the poet is a poet by reason of invention rather than because he uses rhyme; in connection with lines 42–45, that proper disposition is imperative if the audience is to be pleased; on lines 46–59, that elocution may be made more striking by certain devices. Others show a resemblance to more recent emphases on the part of the commentators; he holds (as Maranta had done) that Horace's main concern is with the distinction between plot and episodes, that in fact this division is the basis for Horace's organization of his *Ars poetica* (p. 355v). Elsewhere, he finds solutions in the ancient philosophers. In his gloss on lines 309–22, where Horace is speaking of the poet's wisdom, Fabrini develops the thesis that this wisdom will consist rather in a knowledge of Ideas than in a knowledge of realities:

> For example, if one wishes to write about the duties of a prince, he should not set before his eyes any individual prince as the example from which he would derive the precepts that a prince should observe; for no single prince is so good that he does not have some fault. But Horace wishes that he should have in mind the example or the Idea of the true prince, and that he should write how a prince ought to be according to that Idea or rather that example. . . . his end is to write how a prince should be, even though it is found that no real prince has ever been that way.[53]

There is a strange mixture here of Horace's ideas on decorum, Aristotle's ideas on the universal, and Plato's ideas on Ideas as seen, probably, through Cicero's *Orator*. Cicero's *Brutus* is quoted on the subject of

[53] *Ibid.*, pp. 384v [=380v]–381: "Vno uerbigratia uuole scriuere de l'uffitio d'un Principe. questo tale non si dee proporre innanzi a gli occhi per essempio, donde egli caui i precetti, che dee osseruare un principe: perche nessun principe è tanto buono, che non habbia qualche mancamento: ma uuole, che egli si proponga l'essempio, ouero la idea del uero principe: e scriua, come dee essere un principe, secondo quella idea, ouero quello essempio. . . . il fin suo è di scriuere, come principe dee essere, se bene non si troua, che nessuno mai sia stato tale."

decorum, and Fabrini expands the usual list of topics to include "fortune, age, sex, profession, parentage, nation, and place" (p. 371[=367]); he also makes decorum an equivalent of Aristotle's necessity and probability (p. 375[=371]). Here and there, Fabrini expresses fairly original ideas, as when he finds that tragedy and comedy are comparable in their use of the iambus and in their interchange of styles in certain circumstances (p. 368[=364]); or when, in the perennial controversy on nature versus art, he decides unhesitatingly for the primacy of nature (pp. 383v[=379v], 386); or when he interprets line 128 ("Difficile est proprie communia dicere") in the following way:

> Those matters are called "common" which have never been written down by anybody, for they are in the common domain and anybody can help himself to them. . . . and he speaks the truth, for common material is material without any artificial form whatsoever, in which it is much more difficult to introduce an artificial form than it is to introduce it in a matter which already has some artificial form.[54]

The conception of form and matter provides an illumination (although a questionable one) of this particular passage.

On one subject, the relationship of poems to their audience, Fabrini makes numerous statements which delimit his whole approach to poetry. He apparently has no specific conception of the nature of this audience, for at one place he says that it is composed of both "dotti" and "indotti" (p. 374[=370]), at another—following Horace very closely—of both old and young persons (p. 381v), at still another that the poet has in mind the "popolo" when he writes. But he does have definite ideas about the kinds of things that will affect the audience and what it will believe. It will be more moved by what it sees than by what it hears, but it will reject as incredible certain actions that might be shown to it on the stage. The basis of credibility is again dubious. If, for example, a poet wished to show a mother murdering her children (Medea, obviously), the audience would refuse belief for two reasons: (1) it would not accept the possibility that a mother could actually commit this crime; and (2) it would know that the children so murdered on the stage were of paper, and no belief would ensue (p. 372[=368]). These objections presuppose (1) certain fixed expectations with respect to human behavior and (2) an incapacity, through a lack of imagination, to accept representation for reality. If the same event were narrated, however, the audience would readily give it credence. Without such belief there can be no pleasure for the audience, and hence the "vero" or the "verisimile" is a prerequisite to delight and profit. It is for

[54] *Ibid.*, p. 372 [=368]: "Comuni si chiamano quelle materie, che non sono mai state scritte da nessuno: perche sono del comune, & ciascuno se le puo appropriare. . . . e dice la uerità: perche la materia comune è una materia senza alcuna forma artifitiale, doue è molto piu difficile introdurre una forma artifitiale, che non è introdurla in una materia, che hauesse qualche forma artifitiale."

this reason especially that the poet must observe decorum with the greatest care; if he does, he will please "the educated, because they will recognize the artistry of the writer and will derive pleasure from it; the uneducated, because even if these latter do not know the artistry of the composition, nevertheless they will have pleasure from it because nature in itself, without art, causes things to please whoever sees them whenever they are done with decorum and appropriately."[55] The audience will also find pleasure in the kind of decorations which episodes add to a plot (p. 361v[=357v]) and generally in anything that gives variety to the work: "Variety is a necessary thing and is a great virtue in a poet; for with variety, great delight is given to the listener, and he is made attentive, and he is prevented from being annoyed."[56] Thus, like Horace, although to a greater extent, Fabrini makes much of what may happen within a poem depend upon the likes and the capacity for belief of the audience.

In 1557, Luca Antonio Ridolfi had published at Lyons a *Ragionamento sopra alcuni luoghi del Cento novelle del Boccaccio,* in which Alessandro degli Uberti discussed with Claude d'Herberé various linguistic problems connected with the text of Boccaccio. Some years later (probably around 1567) Lodovico Castelvetro and Francesco Giuntini exchanged letters relating to this *Ragionamento,* which have some bearing on the critical tradition we are here discussing. Castelvetro's *Lettera del Dubioso Academico* answered some of Ridolfi's linguistic objections before passing on to more general remarks on Boccaccio; in these, Castelvetro considerably broadened the whole basis of discussion, making it include both literary and moral issues. On the literary side, his strictures are of two kinds. He objects to a certain number of Boccaccio's stories because in them verisimilitude—and he means exclusively natural verisimilitude—is not properly observed. Everybody knows, for example, that young ladies of good family are carefully guarded by their parents; yet Boccaccio frequently has them meeting with men and he does not tell how this surveillance had been circumvented. Next, Boccaccio does not do all that he might in order to "arouse greater pity in the minds of the readers";[57] he should have treated the sacrament of confession when he was discussing the plague, as a means to awakening in the readers greater compassion for the victims. This objection is closely related to the one which he raises on moral, or rather religious, grounds. He criticizes Boccaccio for his neglect of other sacraments in various of the stories, for attributing to priests actions unbecoming to their office, and

---

[55] *Ibid.,* pp. 374–74v [=370–70v]: "a dotti: perche conosceranno l'artifitio de lo scrittore, e n'haranno piacere; a gl'indotti: perche se bene essi non conoscono l'artifitio de la compositione; nondimeno n'haranno piacere: perche la natura da per lei senza l'arte fa, che le cose piacciono sempre a chi le uede quando elle son fatte con decoro, & conueneuolmente."

[56] *Ibid.,* p. 358v: "il uariare è cosa necessaria, & è una gran uirtu in un poeta: perche con la uarietà si dà gran dilettatione a l'uditore, e si fa stare attento, e si fa, che non gli rincresce."

[57] *Lettera,* undated ed., p. 12: " & muouere compassione maggiore ne gli animi de Lettori."

for similar offences. These criticisms are essentially outside the limits of the Horatian mode as we have defined it. In his *Risposta* to Castelvetro, Giuntini asserts that although Boccaccio's style has many faults, it may nevertheless be defended against some of Castelvetro's attacks. Then he adds objections of his own, all based, again, on violations of natural verisimilitude. In a lengthy discussion of *Decameron* I, 5, he indicates how some of the objections may be met and how solutions favorable to Boccaccio may be found.[58] Both these critics present, in their practical criticism, contacts with the Horatian tradition in their concern with style, with natural probability, and with effects produced by the work on its readers.

Torquato Tasso returns to this series of practical criticisms with his *Considerazioni sopra tre canzoni di M. Gio. Battista Pigna intitolate Le tre sorelle*, to which Pier Antonio Serassi assigned the date of 1568.[59] The little treatise is largely devoted, as so many of these "lezioni" on sonnets were, to the philosophical content of the work studied, here the conception of love found in Pigna's canzoni. But in several excursions Tasso manifests an interest in theoretical matters. At one point, he compares the canzone as a form with the epic; the shorter poem is less perfect than the longer, but it has its own parts corresponding to those of the epic. Both of them are alike in having a "proposition," an "invocation," and a "narration"; the rhetorical source of these terms is at once apparent. In his comparison of Petrarch and Pigna, he again applies criteria derived from the same source. The comparison revolves around the topics of subject matter, language, versification, and "concetti." Petrarch may seem to be superior on the basis of variety of subject matter; but this, says Tasso, is merely an accident of fortune (the death of Laura having provided him with a new body of materials). Petrarch is more prudent in the choice of his subjects, selecting only those which will clearly lend themselves to "ornament and poetic splendor"; whereas Pigna sometimes chooses sterile subjects and overcomes their difficulties through the strength of his genius. In language, Petrarch is more sparing, Pigna bolder since he is striving for grandeur and majesty; the older poet is more apt to expand and dilate his ideas, while Pigna usually confines his to a brief turn of phrase. Petrarch is clear, Pigna sometimes obscure—but gracefully so. The former puts his words together and organizes his rhythms in a delicate fashion, the latter, more roundly and fully. In the variety of "concetti," "drawn from the innermost fountains of the sciences," Pigna is definitely superior; all in all, his poems are like Horace's paintings, which, when seen at close range, give even more pleasure to the viewer than when seen at a distance.[60] Choice and variety of subject matter, paucity or richness in diction, clarity and obscurity, the

[58] *Risposta del Giuntino*, in Castelvetro, *Lettera del Dubioso* (undated), pp. 23–30.
[59] See Guasti, *Prose diverse*, prefatory note to this treatise, II, 73.
[60] *Ibid.*, pp. 81–82, 109–110.

general effect of the versification, these are problems and solutions familiar to the practicing rhetorician.

On the purely theoretical side, Tommaso Correa's *De toto eo poematis genere, quod epigramma vulgo dicitur Libellus* (1569) is different from most of the documents that we have seen thus far in that it develops its theory not with respect to poetry in general but in relation to one of the minor genres, the epigram. A total theory is implicit, but what is said is partial and specific. Correa is much preoccupied with the ends served by the poem and the effects produced by it; and perhaps because of the peculiar character of the epigram as a genre, he sees three different types of relationship between the poem and persons concerned with it. The epigram serves an end, first, with respect to the poet, to whom it brings praise and glory (p. 19), and he must keep in mind these goals when he composes it. Second, it is meant to influence in some way the persons who are its subjects and at whom its praise or blame is directed. At this point more general principles of poetry intervene, in the form of the Horatian idea that the poem must both be useful and give pleasure (p. 22); the utility of the epigram, stated in a general way, consists in the "laus" or the "vituperatio" which it metes out to the persons it treats. This is a part of its very definition: "The epigram is simply a short poem which makes a straightforward mention of something, whether a person or an action; either it is a declaration drawn from what has been stated, in commendation of something, or an expression of censure."[61] The formula appears again in such a series as this: "ad laudem, uituperationem, irrisionem, cauillationem, criminationem" (p. 22).

In order to provide the specific utility for which it exists, the epigram "must show that there is a great baseness present in the vices, an almost divine glory in the virtues; with one single effort it must both moderate the feelings of the soul and render the mores more honest."[62] Third, and perhaps most prominently, it produces an effect upon its general audience, those who merely read about the actions of others but are not involved in them. For this effect Correa has many descriptions, and he repeats them on various occasions. Just as any speech or any poem would presumably do, the epigram "affects and almost seizes upon the most intimate feelings of the soul."[63] The feelings so aroused are ones of pleasure ("voluptas," "delectatio"), of wonder and admiration ("admiratio"), of joy ("gaudio," "laetitia"), and the poem which produces them is pleasant, delightful, praiseworthy ("iucundus," "dulcis," "laudabilis").[64] All these effects are

---

[61] *Libellus* (1569), pp. 25–26: "Epigramma enim nihil est aliud quam breue poema cum simplici rei cuiuspiam indicatione uel personae, uel facti; seu est contestatio deducta ex propositis in commendationem rei alicuius, seu detestationem."

[62] *Ibid.*, p. 23: "demonstret in uitijs summam inesse turpitudinem, prope diuinam gloriam in uirtutibus: una denique, eademque opera & sensus animi leniter afficiat, & mores cohonestet."

[63] *Ibid.*, p. 19: "intimos animi sensus afficiat, ac pene capiat."

[64] See esp. pp. 21, 23, 32, 39, 98.

such as might result from any form of poetry. But they are produced in a special way by the specific qualities of the epigram; its universal and particular qualities are combined in such a passage as the following:

In fact, if it is beautiful, well proportioned and unified, polished and perfect, so that its parts cohere and harmonize among themselves in such a way as to express clearly, briefly, sharply and elegantly any thought, it arouses admiration and produces an extraordinary pleasure. It requires great art, wit, sharpness of talent, becoming brevity, and a certain dexterity and discernment.[65]

Horace's vague recommendations for cohesion and appropriateness are contained in the first sentence, the peculiar characteristics of the epigram in the second. The latter, in combination with the effects they produce, are repeated and expanded a little later: "But in the epigram the brevity delights us, the sharpness arouses us, the harmony seizes us, the thought remains with us, the humor pervades our mind with an incredible pleasure."[66]

Such broad descriptions as these apply to all forms of the epigram; for it is not a single genre, but has many subforms related to it, such as the epitaph, the "naenia, epicedium, monodia, threnus, elogium, aenus, palinodia." These in turn fall into three categories as they conform to one or another of the three kinds of oratory; that is, there are judicial epigrams, deliberative epigrams, and epideictic epigrams (p. 45). In a general way, there are as many different kinds of epigrams as there are subject matters treated in the form: "Tot enim epigrammatum sunt genera, quot et rerum, de quibus texitur" (p. 50). Correa establishes, for each of the kinds, a principle of appropriateness that is merely an application of his general theory: each subject matter will demand a special style (one of the three) and a special verse form (all verses are admissible in the genre).

In true Renaissance fashion, Correa does not fail to include, along with his dicta on the ends of the epigram and the means by which they are achieved, indications about the particular genius of the poet necessary to produce poems in the genre. His initial assumption is Horatian: the poet needs both nature and art to produce the perfect poem. This is translated into two substitute terms which reveal his meaning, "iudicium" and "imitatio." About the first, naturally acquired, he has little to say; about the second, artificially developed, he has many suggestions. Imitation is the imitation of ancient poets; unnecessary for the ancients, it is indispensable for moderns, and no contemporary poet can succeed without it. It operates in this manner:

[65] *Ibid.*, p. 19: "Nam illud si uenustum, aptum connexumque sit, teres, & rotundum, ut inter se ita partes cohaereant, & congruant, ut distincte, breuiter, acute, et ornate sententia exprimatur, & admirationem mouet, & uoluptatem affert, non uulgarem. Multa arte opus est; sale, ingenij acumine, breuitate decora, dexteritate quadam, & iudicio."

[66] *Ibid.*, p. 21: "Sed in epigrammate breuitas delectat, acumen excitat, concinnitas capit, haeret sententia, lepor uoluptate incredibili animum perfundit." For other similar statements, see pp. 23, 24, 25, 32, 39, 49.

We must therefore consider carefully in what way the old poets expressed the feelings of the soul, what they judged to be poetic and what they judged not to be poetic; in accordance with what order, ornaments and figures, what rhythms, length, method, even in particulars, we should adapt our own epigram. . . . In order that we may more easily and properly compose a perfect epigram and more diligently polish it to perfection, it will be very useful for us to compare the various ways in which other poets treated the same subject, so that we may understand in what way these poets achieved proper form, and in what respect another failed; thus we shall become more prudent through the errors of others and by the trials of others we may make trial of our own talent.[67]

Such qualities and procedures as these might of course be assigned to poets practicing in any genre; the argument so far remains general. The epigrammatist must possess in addition the peculiar capacities necessary for his art: cleverness, wittiness, artistry, judgment, and the ability to estimate the nature of the subject matter (p. 23). A particular kind of poetic talent thus becomes the basis for the correct assorting of matter, style, and prosodic form.

Correa's little treatise is an interesting example of the adaptation of the Horatian mode to a specific literary type. Its conceptions of the ends of poetry, of the principles of internal organization, of the poet's talent and method are closely related to the *Ars poetica*. But at every point, and above all in its notions of the three styles, the "res-verba" relationship, the effects produced in the audience, and the personal glory sought by the poet, it extends beyond the basic text and makes contact with the broader rhetorical tradition.

The latter tradition far outweighs the purely Horatian elements in Pietro Pagano's *Discorso sopra il secondo sonetto del Petrarca*, an undated manuscript in the British Museum (Additional MS 33,470), to which I have given an arbitrary date of about 1570. Pagano's main intention is to provide a running commentary on the text, with special attention to the effects produced by words and figures. But he begins with the customary statements about the poet's model (here, Euripides' *Hippolytus*), about the reasons why poets invoke the gods or the muses, about the nature of the action and the classification of the poem. He finds that the action is a single one but not a simple one since it is accompanied by passions. As for the classification, it is derived from Aristotle's *Rhetoric*: "And since every discourse and composition falls, according to the opinion of Aristotle, under one of the three types, demonstrative, or deliberative, or judicial, we shall

67 *Ibid.,* pp. 82, 85–86: "Videndum igitur diligenter est, quomodo ueteres animi sensa exposuerint, quae poetica iudicarint, quae non: quo ordine, quibus luminibus, & figuris, quibus numeris, qua longitudine, qua ratione, & in singulis accommodemus epigramma nostrum" and "Quo facilius, & commodius perfectum epigramma componere queamus, & diligentiam expoliendi adhibere erit utilissimum conferre rem eandem a diuersis poetis explicatam, ut quomodo his assequatur decorum, qua in re ille fuerit mancus, intelligamus: ut in alienis erroribus cautiores efficiamur, et aliorum periculis faciamus de nostro ingenio peri-

say that this sonnet belongs to the judicial kind, and in that part of the assumptive juridical constitution which is called translation of the fault, where guilt is transferred to another person."[68] In the treatment of this kind of subject matter, Petrarch uses the form of expression called by Hermogenes σεμνότης, or the "grave," and his sonnet belongs to the highest level of this form since it speaks of the action of a powerful god. The effect produced is admiration, resulting from an unexpected event (fol. 6v). When Pagano passes from generalities of style to the individual passages of Petrarch's sonnet, he cites Book II of the *Rhetoric* on the figures of speech and points out Petrarch's conformity to the teachings of the rhetoricians. Finally, he indicates how Petrarch achieves the ends of poetry:

> And since poets must delight and profit, we might say that he delights with the poetic fiction, supposing that a powerful god has wounded him with a mortal blow; that he profits, next, because he teaches man that he should take heed not to allow himself to be vanquished by vain and carnal love, lest he should have happen to him what happened to Petrarch; for man can never disentagle himself from that knot. But the profit would be much better shown if one were to give the poem an allegorical and a Christian explanation.[69]

Whereupon Pagano proceeds to offer such an interpretation of the sonnet. The rhetorical tone of Pagano's whole approach is evident, and it is crossed in an interesting fashion with certain medieval practices, such as this closing allegorical interpretation.

What Pagano meant by "the highest level of the grave form" is explained fully in another contemporary document, the *Commentarius in Longinum*, attributed to Franciscus Portus and probably dating from around 1570.[70] The commentary is important since it brings, as it were, a new dimension into the critical tradition that we are here discussing. We have seen throughout the development of this tradition an emphasis upon the three styles and various kinds of relationship established between Horace's theories and this conception of the styles; in more recent years, we have seen the

[68] MS BM Add. 33,470, fols. 5-5v: "Et perche ogni ragionamento, et componimento, casca, secondo l'opinione d'Aristotele, sotto uno delli tre genere, ó Demonstratiuo, ó Deliberatiuo, ó Giudiciale, diremo, che questo sonetto uersa nel genere Giudiciale, et in quella parte della constitutione giuridiciale assontiua, che si chiama translatione del mancamento, quando si transferisce la colpa in altra persona."

[69] *Ibid.*, fol. 15: "Et perche li Poeti deuono dilettare, et giouare, potressimo dire, che diletta con la fictione poetica, con fingere, che un Dio potente l'habbia ferito di colpo mortale; che gioua poi, perche insegna all'huomo, che auertisca che non si lascia uincere d'Amore uano, et lasciuo, che non gli intrauenga quello, che á lui è auenuto, che l'huomo non puo mai suilupparsi da tal nodo. Ma molto piu si mostrarebbe il giouamento, quando si uolesse allegoricamente dichiarare, et christianamente."

[70] On the reasons for the attribution and the objections to it, see "Translations and Commentaries of Longinus, *On the Sublime*, to 1600: A Bibliography," *Modern Philology*, XLVII (1950), 149. I have since found confirmation for the attribution in the existence of Modena Estense MS y.S.3.18, Parte II^a, fols. 1-87. This MS of the *Commentarius* bears Portus' name.

four forms or Ideas of Hermogenes associated with the same theories, giving somewhat more variety and flexibility to critical discussion. What Portus does is to interpret Longinus, now, as a treatise on Hermogenes' "sublime, magnificent, and grave form of expression." Longinus' *On the Sublime* lends itself, of course, to such an interpretation, given its emphasis on the effects produced by diction and figures of speech. Thus, Portus' initial statement in the commentary is a distinction of the four subtypes of the grave style, highest of which is the one that speaks truly of God or the gods. Just as Longinus himself had done, he selects examples indiscriminately from the sciences and the various branches of philosophy, and Aristotle or Cicero may serve to exemplify a given style as well as Homer or Horace. The significant consideration everywhere is the nature of the subject matter treated. Portus also distinguishes three methods for handling the grave or sublime style: clearly and unambiguously, allegorically, and secretly or mysteriously. He comes closest to poetic theory, however, when he states his ideas on words, which come to belong to the sublime form either through their sound or because they are used metaphorically. The poet, who otherwise has much in common with the orator, is distinguished from him on this basis:

They [the poets] may doubtless be freer and more audacious in using words figuratively; orators must be much more diffident. Among poets, the tragic, lyric, and dithyrambic poets are more daring than all the others; to be sure, they seem to aim and strive to make their verse inflated and turgid. Tragic poets achieve this most easily because the persons they introduce are above the ordinary in station; of course, they present on the stage kings and princes, so that, taking the persons into account, the verse must be elevated and more sublime.[71]

At other places, as in the remarks on section 7 of Longinus (p. 293), Portus extends his comparison of poets and orators. This he does on the assumption that the sublime may appear either in prose or in poetry ("sive in soluta oratione, sive in poësi") and that in either case it represents a certain kind of state of soul and produces a similar effect in the audience. His contention with respect to audience is that it should judge not as the ignorant masses do but as serious and wise men do ("non plebeiorum & imperitorum more, sed ut solent graves & sapientes homines," p. 339), that is, in terms of the virtues rather than of the defects of the work. Perhaps one should say rather "the defects of the passage," since nowhere in Portus is there any consideration of works other than as assemblages of passages.

71 Ed. Pearce (Amsterdam, 1733), p. 282: "Sunt nimirum liberiores, & audaciores in verbis transferendis: Oratores multo verecundiores. Inter Poëtas, Tragici, Lyrici, & Dithyrambici audent prae caeteris: illud nimirum spectare, affectareque videntur, ut carmen sit inflatum & turgidum. Tragici facilius id obtinent, quòd personae quas inducunt, habent non mediocrem dignitatem. inducunt nimirum reges, & principes in scenam, ita ut habita personarum ratione necessario tollatur carmen, & fiat sublimius."

He remains close to the text he is explaining, and his poetic theory is limited to a theory of styles, diction, and effects.

The *Lettione* [*sulla favola*] which Baccio Neroni prepared for delivery to the Accademia degli Alterati around 1571 is also restricted, but in a different way; it attacks the proposition, defended by Carlo Rucellai in an earlier lecture, that every plot does not need to comprise recognition and reversal. Hence, it deals solely with aspects of plot. Aristotelian though the problem would seem to be from its statement, it nevertheless is attacked from a Horatian point of view by Neroni. His premisses for the discussion are a mixture of the two authorities:

Plots having been ordered and composed, as are all other things, to some end, undoubtedly those which will be organized in such a way that they achieve the end to which they are directed will be the only ones worthy to be called plots, and the others will not even be taken into account. . . . And it is a certain thing that poets in composing plots have as their end either to profit or to delight, and that for no other reason do they put themselves to this trouble than to be of some usefulness to men. Wherefore when they compose either tragedies or comedies or epic poems they have their eye on this end, and in order to achieve it they use those means which best lead them to it. To do this, reversal and recognition are powerful above all the other parts that are found in these poems, since they are those which are more apt than the others to move the passions, and they seize upon the souls of persons, either delighting them or moving them to disdain or to compassion according to the action that is being represented.[72]

In pursuing his argument, Neroni cites Aristotle's definitions of the two parts; but for the rest, he argues almost exclusively by citing examples from such poets as Homer, Vergil, Sophocles, Euripides, and Terence. His conclusion is that since all genres display the use of recognition and reversal, they are necessary in all genres. Neroni's Horatianism in this lecture is limited to his conception of the ends of poetry.

As an adjunct to Lodovico Dolce's translations of Homer and Vergil, Andrea Menechini published in 1572 an oration *Delle lodi della poesia, d'Omero, et di Virgilio*, a highly inflated and bombastic discourse, which repeats most of the sixteenth-century commonplaces in praise of poetry. It belongs to theoretical criticism insofar as it makes general statements about the ends served by the art, to practical criticism in the later pages where it

---

[72] MS Laur. Ashb. 559, fol. 1: "Essendo le fauole state ordinate et composte, si come tutte le altre cose, à qualche fine, quelle senza dubbio che in tal modo saranno disposte, che quel fine conseguitino, al quale son indiritte, saranno solamente da essere chiamate fauole, et dell'altre non sara da tenerne conto alcuno. . . . Et è cosa per certa, che i poeti nel comporre le fauole hanno per fine, o di giouare, o dilettare, et che per altro non si muouono ad affaticarsi se non per essere di qualche utilita agli huomini, Onde componendo essi, ò tragedie, ò comedie, ò poemi Heroici in tuttj hanno l'occhio à tal fine, per il quale conseguire adoperano que mezzi, che meglio uegli conducono, alche fare sopra tutte le parti che si trouano in tali poemi sono potentissime la Peripetia. et la recognitione, come quelle che sono piu che altro atte à muouere gli affetti, et pigliano gli animi delle persone, ò dilettando, ò mouendo à sdegno, ò à compassione secondo il fatto. che allora si rappresenta."

gives appreciations of Homer and Vergil. The ends, as we might expect, are utility and pleasure. Concerning utility, rather than develop a reasoned argument (since that is neither his method nor his tone), Menechini accumulates in a haphazard fashion as many kinds of usefulness as he can think of. Some of these are historical, such as the civilizing function of poetry in its early days and its use by religion (p. a iv); some are remote from everyday life, such as the everlasting fame or infamy bestowed upon the good or the wicked by the poet (p. b). In a more immediate and more present way, poetry is the "corrector of our life" (p. a ij*v*), largely through the examples which it furnishes us of monstrous things that we must avoid and of desirable things that we must follow. Examples of these kinds are deduced from the actions narrated by the poet, which are much more effective than those told by the historian since they are relieved of dross and imperfection (p. b ij). Through its delineations of characters, poetry will teach us the duties and functions of every kind of man and woman in every phase of life. Especially, it will lead us into paths of virtue, making us chaste and simple, and this it will do better than any other discipline. And so we may ask, thinking of Vergil's excellence:

What philosopher ever taught us more graceful behavior? what orator ever persuaded us more ardently to follow the road to the virtues? what jurist ever ordered us to treat with greater prudence the affairs of state? to regulate with greater wisdom our magistrates? to take more holy counsel in high matters? to help the fatherland with hotter zeal?[73]

All these things it does because of its superior capacity to persuade and because it is accompanied by pleasure.

Menechini does not specify the nature of this pleasure, but he does point out its manifold sources. Principal among them, perhaps, is the imitation contained in poetry, which fills us with incredible delight (how or why we do not know). More directly, we derive pleasure from such technical elements as harmony, rhyme, diction, and maxims; Menechini collects these sources in the following apostrophe to poetry:

Shall I be silent about the delight that is derived from you, when there is no harmony that more sweetly strikes our minds? For what ordered discourse, what eloquent language can be more sweet and more pleasant than a lovely sound and a pure concord of harmonious verses felicitously unrolled? What more elegant and adorned speech can generate in us as much joy as a high composition of beautiful and chosen rhymes, all full and resounding? What is more ingenious and full of greater marvel than a very beautiful subject developed with very ornate

---

73 *Delle lodi* (1572), p. e iv*v*: "Qual Filosofo ci insegnò più gratiosi costumi? qual' Orator ci persuase più ardentemente d'incaminar' alle Virtù? qual Giureconsulto ci diede ordine di trattar con maggior prudenza le cose publiche? di regger con più rara Sapienza i Magistrati? di consigliar più santamente gli alti affari? di aiutar la Patria con più caldo zelo?"

and very lovely words, adorned with the splendor of wise and most grave maxims. sung according to the perfect rule of Music?[74]

Finally, we presumably are pleased at the discovery, within a good poem, of the riches and the treasures of all the arts, sciences, and disciplines.

On the side of practical criticism, the same considerations will of course be prominent. Vergil is praised, for example, for the vehemence, the carefulness, the felicity of his diction, for his abundance of words and their correctness; from these, one obtains the pleasures proper to poetry. I suppose that the same would be true for the gravity of his maxims and the artful disposition of his materials. He would also make profitable reading since he teaches all the lessons that the good poet should teach and since he displays every imaginable kind of knowledge. In every other aspect he is excellent, approaching as close to perfection as any man may do. These judgments of Menechini's are vague and general in character, making no specific reference to texts or parts of them. They come from the application of a small number of topics which belong, almost entirely, to the tradition of the Horatians.

Franciscus Portus, who died in 1581, left behind him (in addition to the *Commentarius in Longinum* already discussed) a number of other unpublished works. Two of these, the *Prolegomena* to Sophocles' tragedies and the *Orationes*, were published together by his son Aemilius in 1584; I presume them to have been written about 1575. Both contain materials pertinent to the present analysis. The title-page of the *Prolegomena* announces that the work contains as well a section on the comparison of tragedy and comedy and another on the relative merits of Sophocles and Euripides. And from Portus' early statement that tragedy and comedy both derive from nature through imitation, one is led to expect some fairly original ideas on the subject. But the hope is soon dashed, for it becomes clear that Portus has in mind no mimetic theory of poetry, but wishes merely to differentiate between tragedy and comedy on the basis of the different kinds of "life" they represent. Man's life is divided into fortunate and unfortunate events; comedy treats the first, tragedy the second. From then on, the distinctions are such as might have been found in Donatus or Diomedes or any of their medieval continuators:

. . . in comedy, the fortunes of men are moderate, their fears [for their safety] are small, the dangers small, the endings are happy; in tragedy, on the other hand, the persons are of great importance, their fears are great, the endings are fatal; in the former the first events are agitated, the last ones calm; in tragedy, contrari-

---

[74] *Ibid.*, p. e iij: "Tacerò il diletto, che da te si prende, non ui essendo armonia, che più addolcisca l'intelletto nostro? perciò che qual' ordinato parlare, qual' eloquente lingua può esser più dolce, ò più soaue, che un leggiadro suono, & puro concento di armoniosi uersi felicissimamente spiegati? Qual' oratione più culta, & più adorna può generar' in noi tanta gioia, che un' alto componimento di uaghe, & scielte rime, tutte piene, & risuonanti? Qual cosa è più ingeniosa, & piena di maggiore stupore, che un bellissimo soggetto spiegato con ornatissime, & leggiadrissime parole, illustrato con splendor di saggie, et grauissime sentenze, cantato con perfetta ragion di Musica?"

wise, the beginnings are joyous and peaceful, the endings disturbed and fateful; and in tragedy the life to be avoided is expressed, in comedy the life to be sought. Finally, comedy invents its subjects, tragedy frequently borrows them from historical truth.[75]

In the comparison between Euripides and Sophocles, the criteria are largely rhetorical. Euripides is said to be less pretentious, hence close to oratory and more acceptable to the popular ear. He is more useful to those who wish to learn how to act, since he is full of maxims and commonplaces. In the arousing of the emotions he is, to quote Aristotle, the most tragic poet of all. Sophocles is always grave, tragic, sublime, grandiloquent; but he tempers gravity with joy, tragic severity with poetic sweetness, and as a result produces great delight through the arousing of pity and admiration, the two feelings proper to tragedy (p. 13).

The second of the *Orationes* is subtitled "Qua Historia, & Historici laudantur." I cite it here not only because it contains, along toward the end, a comparison of history and poetry, but because the terms in which it praises history are almost identical with those familiar in the defences of poetry. Were one to substitute the word "poetry" for the word "history" in the discussion, the rest would be acceptable as an oration on the uses of poetry. The historians, Portus tells us, "set before us examples of lives, characters, exploits, deliberations, and events, upon all of which posterity when it gazes as if at certain pictures, may easily take counsel for both its public and its private affairs."[76] All things in life and in nature are recorded by history, so that we have before our eyes "the things that we must avoid and those that we must follow" (p. 60). We also learn from the reading of history how to form our own characters so that we may ultimately become men, shunning the vices that we see in some, imitating the virtues of others. These effects are not purely intellectual in their origins; we are swayed, moved, impressed by the way in which the history is written: "Who indeed does not take delight in the skilful descriptions of places and regions? Who in reading is not kept attentive by the variety of epochs, the vicissitudes of fortune, the great and important deeds accomplished by various illustrious heroes and placed by the historian almost under the eyes and before the face of everybody?"[77] Aware of the argument that the same things might

[75] *Prolegomena* (1584), p. 12: "in Comoedia mediocres fortunae hominum, parui metus, parua pericula, exitus laeti sunt. In Tragoedia contrà ingentes personae, magni metus, funesti sunt exitus: in illa, turbulenta prima, tranquilla postrema: in Tragoedia contrà, principia laeta & pacata, exitus turbulenti, & funesti: & in Tragoedia vita fugienda, in Comoedia vita expetenda exprimitur. Denique Comoedia fingit argumenta. Tragoedia saepe ab historica fide petit."

[76] *Ibid.*, p. 59: "exempla vitae, morum, factorum, consiliorum, atque euentuum proponunt, in quae omnis posteritas tanquam in tabulas quasdam inspiciens, & publicis rationibus, & priuatis rebus facilè consulat."

[77] *Ibid.*, p. 62: "Quem enim non delectent locorum ac regionum scitae descriptiones? quem in legendo non retineant temporum varietates, fortunae vicissitudines, res maximae grauissimaeque à clarissimis quibúsque viris gestae, ac sub oculos, aspectúmque omnium penè ab historico subiectae?"

be said about poetry or oratory, Portus answers it by declaring the superiority of history to both arts. Poetry is less effective since it relates falsehoods or incredible actions and hence loses the confidence of the reader; the more closely it resembles true history, the better it is. Oratory exaggerates its effects, thereby alienating certain listeners, or it sins by excess of any one of the numerous passions which it seeks to awaken. Philosophy itself, when it wishes to argue effectively on matters of individual character and public affairs, must borrow from history a host of supporting examples. I have previously pointed out (Chapter I, pages 13–16) that a large group of theorists associated history with poetry as a sister art, and the reader may remember that the points of contact indicated were precisely those which Portus here claims for history alone.

ALDO MANUZIO (1576)

After a lapse of ten years, from 1566 (date of Giovanni Fabrini da Fighine's Italian commentary) to 1576, we come again to a formal commentary on the *Ars poetica*, this one in Latin and the work of Aldo Manuzio the Younger. It does not have much new to offer. Most of the remarks on individual passages are the same as the ones made earlier, and frequently they do not go beyond simple paraphrase. In an introductory section, called the "Prolegomena," Manuzio gives initial definitions of poetry, deriving his materials largely from Aristotle (four different texts from the *Poetics* are quoted, 1447a13, 1451b27, 1447a29, 1447b26). He seems to be most intent, here, upon establishing the nature of verisimilitude and the roles of truth and falsehood in poetry. In the body of the commentary itself, the references to Aristotle are slight; the list below gives them all:

Horace	Aristotle
1–23	1451b27
73–88	1449a24, 1459a11, 1459b8, 1460a1, −a5
89–113	1455a31, 1455a27, 1456a2
113–27	1454a15, 1454a30
128–52	1451b27
191–219	1454a37, 1452b16
220–33	1449a19, 1453a4
234–43	1449a19
275–94	1449a15
295–308	1455a33
347–65	1454a30

It will be noted that even in this short list, several of the texts appear twice; one of them, *Poetics* 1451b27, is used three times in all. They are all very general in nature ("Poetry is an imitation," "The poet is a poet by virtue of the imitation and not because he uses verse") and show neither a thorough knowledge of Aristotle nor an intention to make of him a source or a counterpart of Horace.

On the other hand, there are almost as many references to the rhetorical works of Cicero. But here again they are miscellaneous in character and do not go together to make up a rhetorical theory. Manuzio follows the lead of almost all his predecessors in pointing out a parallel between Horace's theories and the oratorical divisions of invention, disposition, and elocution; yet he does so only in passing, in the following sentence: "The sixth precept treats of eloquence in diction; for in the first place he gave his precepts on invention when he said: 'Cui lecta potenter erit res,' then on order, finally on elocution; this the rhetoricians also do."[78] The sixth precept, deduced from lines 46–72, is the last so named; for although Manuzio had begun with an orderly enumeration and stating of precepts, after this one he abandons the method. We shall probably be forced to conclude that in this as in other aspects his commentary is imperfect and haphazard. There is no attempt to distinguish any plan in Horace's work, to impose a general interpretation upon it; the commentary remains a collection of isolated glosses. These tend, for the most part, to be very simple, much simpler than those of the preceding generation of scholars. Sometimes this is an advantage, since unwarranted subtleties are avoided; but at other times the meat of Horace's meaning is missed. For example, the first twenty-three lines are said to contain two precepts: the first, the poet should stick to the subject that he has undertaken; the second, he should avoid descriptions since they would not be in keeping with his serious subject matter. In only a few cases does Manuzio offer interesting readings, as when he declares (against the major part of the antecedent tradition) that the "communia" of line 128 means materials which have already been used by another poet and are hence available for imitation (rather than unused materials open to all comers); or as when he insists, in connection with line 151, that truth is necessary for the poet (else where would the imitation be?), that if he treats only the truth he becomes a historian, and that hence truth must be tempered by falsehood. These few passages relieve only slightly the mediocrity of the text; one misses here the enthusiasm, the scholarship, and the imagination of some of the earlier commentaries.

CONCLUSIONS

Manuzio's commentary is perhaps an unfortunate work on which to end the present chapter, for it leaves an impression of disappointment and a sense of the decadence of a tradition. Perhaps this is in itself significant. For the fifteen-year period under consideration has been distinguished less for its illuminations of the Horatian text than for its expansion and application of the Horatian mode independent of the text itself. While there have been three extensive commentaries, the bulk of the progress in theory has

---

[78] *In Q. Horatii Flacci librum de arte poetica Commentarius* (1576), p. 10: "Sextum praeceptum, de facundia. nam de inuentione primo loco, cum dixit, *Cui lecta potenter erit res*, tum de ordine, postremo de elocutione praecipit: quod etiam rhetores faciunt."

been made in the shorter theoretical articles or incidentally to practical criticism. In the field of practical criticism, this period has contained the first sizable body of pertinent materials and has permitted us to see in what way contemporary critics translated their theory into actual appreciations of works.

Of the specifically Horatian ideas, the one most constantly repeated, developed, and modified by the theorists is the notion of utility and pleasure as the ends of poetry. In a sense, this becomes the hallmark of the mode. Many writers who seem to know little else of the *Ars poetica* emphasize the importance of "prodesse" and "delectare," of the "utile dulci," as the ends to be sought. In these particular years, the stress is probably stronger on utility; writers are concerned with the moral implications of poems and are insistent that they must contribute to the betterment of the individual or of society. They relate to this their preoccupations with truth and verisimilitude; for the general assumption is that moral effects will be properly accomplished only if the audience believes what it sees or reads, and that this belief depends upon the correct admixture of the true or the seeming-true into the ingredients of the poem. The need for the marvelous, the strange, the extraordinary (both to capture the attention of the audience and to give it pleasure) is a complicating factor, and many critics debate the relationship between truth and falsehood, the credible and the incredible. In these debates, the character of the audience enters as a consideration, since the capacity for believing is recognized as varying from group to group. Here, the ground has shifted somewhat from Horace's old man or young man, senator or nut-eating farmer, to the wise against the ignorant, the elite against the masses. It is difficult to see a preference, for Tasso will declare just as loudly in favor of the common people as Maranta does for the "selectissimi viri." For the most part, though, critics at this time seem to have in mind an audience educated at least in two special fields, the rules and requirements of the art of poetry and the eternal laws of decorum.

Considerations of the audience lead us away from the Horatian text strictly interpreted and into the broader rhetorical tradition of which it is by this time an integral part. The explicit comparison between the poet and the orator still serves a number of theorists as a starting point for developing their ideas about the poetic art; for some, the historian replaces the orator or becomes a third writer in the comparison. The more complete these comparisons are, the more nearly the theories propounded take on a special flavor. Thus for many writers there is little perceptible difference between their theories of poetry and the usual doctrine of the rhetorics. They talk constantly about invention, disposition, and elocution; they organize their materials around "res" and "verba"; they construct elaborate systems on the basis of decorum. Only rarely, as in the case of Maranta, does anybody warn against the basic impropriety of such a procedure for the discussion of poetry. One of the most persistent forms of rhetorical approach is via the notion of the effects produced in the audience, and in the years from 1560 to 1567 an even wider variety than had previously existed is introduced into the conception of these effects. Poetry, of course, must move the passions of the audience; but it must also arouse admiration, it must produce a kind of rapture, it must inspire to virtue and create an abhorrence of vice. Thinking of this sort in terms of rhetorical ends was bound to lead to thinking in terms of rhetorical means, and hence we have a growing desire to speak of such parts of a poem as the proposition, the narration, the exordium, and to classify poems as belonging to one or another of the known types of oratory.

Special note must be taken of the attention paid to two sets of ideas, the notion of the fixed styles and the theory of the fixed genres. The first of these goes back to ancient rhetoric, but it was enriched by medieval theorists of poetry; then these Cinquecento critics add certain refinements. As a result, a "style" is now no longer merely a form of diction or discourse; it involves as well certain kinds of actors or personages, certain kinds of actions, a special variety of "thoughts" or maxims, and corresponding effects in the reader or listener. Any poetic genre falls within one of the styles (the traditional Ciceronian three or the four of Hermogenes) and is circumscribed by it from the outset. To the ideas of Donatus and Diomedes concerning the subject matter, the meter, and some of the mechanics of individual genres, critics now bring more subtle conceptions of the style, the kind of figures, the sententiae, the qualitative and quantitative parts, and the specific reactions aroused in the audience. Consequently, these more and more restrict the freedom of the poet as he operates within a given genre, especially if he must at the same time practice the form only as he finds it exploited in the works of his model.

Throughout this theorizing, Aristotle enters much less prominently as a source than he had done in the earlier years. There are still commentators who insist that Horace used Aristotle as his exemplar—Maranta and Fabrini are examples—but there are fewer than previously. For the most part, references to the *Poetics* are scattered and incidental, centering about standard parallels and obvious resemblances, and the main body of theory proceeds independently of them. On the contrary, there is probably somewhat greater use of Plato (this matter will be investigated in later chapters), and we have even seen one reference to Longinus—indications, even if inconsiderable ones, of a broadening of the critical horizon. A few citations of Demetrius' *On Style* and an almost faddish use of Hermogenes would tend to confirm this supposition.

In the domain of practical criticism, the proliferation of documents in these years affords us an opportunity of estimating the state of opinion with respect to a number of literary types and a number of authors, both ancient and modern. We have evaluations not only of the epic, tragedy, and comedy (represented by Homer and Vergil, Sophocles and Euripides, and Terence), but also of such newer forms as the sonnet (Petrarch and Giovanni della Casa) and the verse "romanzo" (Ariosto). It must be said immediately that some of this criticism represents no advance over earlier periods and might have been written at any time during the previous one hundred years; I mean here on the one hand the compliments to the poet's genius, to his faculties and knowledge, to the divine furor as it operates within him; on the other hand, the repetition of those time-worn epithets that had constituted the only evaluative apparatus of a Pietro Ricci or a Lilio Gregorio Giraldi. Most of these epithets refer to style. But this "criticism by epithets" is now a secondary tendency; primarily, writers are making some application—through intention or habit—of the theoretical positions evolved. Frequently they begin, as the theorists did, with a comparison of their author to the orator or the historian and derive judgments from the comparison; Benedetto Grasso affords an example of such an approach.

With even greater frequency (undoubtedly because they regard it as more important) they speak of poets in terms of the ends achieved, remarking upon the peculiar qualities of the delight procured or the effectiveness with which the utility is achieved. This leads some critics (such as Grasso and Castelvetro) to make severe moral judgments, the "utility" here being a negative one and involving improper or unacceptable moral lessons. At times, the objections are on religious grounds; but I believe that these belong rather to the Platonic mode, which I shall be discussing later. For such enthusiastic judges as Menechini, the chief value of the poetry they were considering was in its positive contribution to the moral improvement of its readers. The old medieval justification by allegory still serves as an auxiliary to the discussion of the utilitarian ends of poetry; certain poems whose moral lessons are not immediately discernible are endowed with them by means of an allegorical interpretation.

Just as for the theorists, the problem of verisimilitude was of primary importance for the practical critics. They asked constantly whether the actions and persons represented in a poem were "true to life"; the answer depended upon several criteria: for actions, upon their conceptions of Aristotle's necessity and probability; for persons, upon the laws of decorum. It should be pointed out, again, that for such men as Castelvetro and Giuntini probability was always natural, never artistic; that is, an action was probable because they thought of life as producing actions in the same way, not because it had been made probable by the prior conditions and preparations of the poem itself. As for decorum, the requirements seem to grow more stringent from year to year, until one wonders how a poet, once he had elected to treat a given kind of character, could have done otherwise than to copy in detail the treatments of his predecessors.

Sperone Speroni and Bartolomeo Maranta on Vergil may serve as examples of another typically rhetorical procedure in practical criticism, that is, the inquiry into the invention, disposition, and elocution of their subject poet. Others, of course, did the same, making judgments upon the originality of the poet or upon his skill as an imitator of other poets (both related to invention), upon his arrangement of the parts of his poem, and especially upon his handling of diction. It is sometimes difficult to distinguish treatments of invention, disposition, and elocution from treatments of such qualitative parts as plot and character (associated with invention) and thought and diction (associated usually with elocution); for, as we have seen, theorists and practical critics alike effected a conflation of the two sets of terms. Once again, Speroni supplies us with a typical discussion here, examining in detail Vergil's deficiencies in plot construction and in character development and giving a half-hearted approval to his handling of diction.

I must emphasize the extent to which considerations of sententiae and of diction dominate the practical criticism of this period. The use of epithets describing style was not an accident, for one of the tendencies of rhetorical approaches was to reduce all critical questions to questions of figures of speech and ornaments of diction. Maranta's long *Lucullianae quaestiones* presents an extreme case of analysis and praise of all aspects of style, but there were many others in which the intention was the same even if the results were not so monumental. The whole matter of prosodic excellence is linked to this same brand of criticism, since the sounds of words become as much a subject of investigation as their sense. The position of sententiae, again, is a special one. The seeker after moral usefulness, the lover of philosophical wisdom, the student of mores and character, all found in the little "pearls of wisdom" contained in these maxims one of the most satisfying parts of the poems they read. Hence the praise so frequently bestowed upon the gravity, the variety, the truth of a given author's sententiae. Such statements would, of course, have been equally appropriate to maxims found in orations, in histories, in philosophical writings, or anywhere else; this the critics realized and admitted, but the realization did not deter them. Poems rarely existed for them as complete works of art; in the main, they were content to separate from them this or that component and to judge it independently of the rest.

A final result of the application of rhetorical theories to practical criticism was the habit of judging on the basis of rules and conventions and on the basis of the three (or four) styles. Horace himself had set the pattern for the habit by his remarks on the five-act division of drama, on the three interlocutors, on the "deus ex machina." Critics of the Cinquecento developed and expanded it, and in a writer like Castelvetro we find a multiplicity of rules applied to the comedies of Plautus and Terence. It should not be thought, however, that anywhere nearly so elaborate a procedure is involved here as was later to flourish in French neo-classical criticism; but this is certainly a formative period for that later development. Judgment by asking whether the appropriate style was practiced and exploited in the right way was also popular, and it furnished another compartment into which the practicing critic could neatly fit his remarks and asseverations.

CHAPTER SIX. THE TRADITION OF HORACE'S *ARS POETICA*: IV. THE RETURN TO THEORY

THE LAST GENERATION of critics working in the Horatian mode, covering approximately the last twenty years of the sixteenth century, reverses the tendency of the preceding generation and returns largely to the cultivation of poetic theory. The materials for the present chapter include only a few documents in the field of practical criticism, and these all concern themselves with the sonnet. The theoretical materials, moreover, are still only secondarily devoted to commentary on the *Ars poetica*; only three—possibly four—treatises belong in this category. Instead, theorists produce a large number of short treatises on particular genres—the madrigal, the sonnet, the elegy, comedy, the verse romance—in which they apply Horatian principles to these special forms; they write, besides, on miscellaneous poetic problems and on the relationship of the art to other arts. A partial explanation of the decline in practical criticism may be found in the fact that much of the critical energy of the period was being turned toward the major literary quarrels then raging, and it is only because I have chosen to treat those quarrels separately that materials for this chapter seem so one-sided.

BONCIANI AND PINO DA CAGLI (1578)

One of the miscellaneous poetic problems, that of prosopopeia or personification, forms the object of Francesco Bonciani's *Lettione della prosopopea*, read before the Accademia Fiorentina in 1578.[1] But Bonciani so expands the treatment as to make of his lecture a poetics in little, of which the fundamental principles are simple and few in number. All speech persuades and moves, especially when it is accompanied by such ornaments as verse, harmony, and figures of speech; of the last, prosopopeia is one of the most effective. For it is an imitation and hence marvelous. Bonciani gives several ways in which this figure is an imitation: (1) insofar as animals, inanimate objects, or incorporeal beings are represented as speaking, the poet is imitating because he is not speaking in his own person (Plato's distinction is here being applied); (2) imitation occurs whenever one represents the form, habit, and action of any thing whatsoever (Aristotle's *Rhetoric* is cited in justification).[2] Of the four categories of objects which may be so imitated—the true, the false, the verisimilar, and the impossible—prosopopeia imitates those false objects that are neither verisimilar nor possible; hence it is that the special effect of admiration is added to the persuasion and the moving ordinarily produced by speech. If one ask how

---

[1] On the attribution and the MSS, see my article "Nuove Attribuzioni di manoscritti di critica letteraria del Cinquecento," *Rinascimento*, III (1952), 249–50.

[2] MS Ricc. 1539, fols. 132–34*v*.

it is feasible to imitate things which do not exist, the answer is that we assemble into a nonexistent whole parts which we know from nature: "since we have known various things, our fancy sometimes confuses the natures of these things, making of them a new nature different from all the others as far as the whole is concerned, but similar in the parts."[3] Since the object of imitation is thus something which has never been and cannot be, the audience marvels at it; and because this marvel is accompanied by a process of learning what it had not known before, the audience experiences an extreme pleasure.

Bonciani is quoting Aristotle when he mentions the pleasure which accompanies learning; but he is really preparing the way for the development of an idea that has nothing to do with Aristotle, namely, that the triple end of prosopopeia is to instruct, to delight, and to persuade. When the figure takes the form of animal apologues, as it did in Hesiod and Aesop, it transmits to the ignorant lessons which they need but would be incapable of understanding in any more recondite form. Pleasure, insofar as it graces these stories, is merely a means and an instrument for the achievement of the utilitarian ends. A more philosophical poet, like Dante, will use the figure to express abstract and divine ideas for which no proper words exist in the language. Some poets employ it solely for purposes of delight, but in so doing they incompletely fulfil the purposes of their art; whereas the orators who exploit prosopopeia in order to persuade— through apologues and the invention of supposed persons—are making a much more proper use of it. Poet, orator, and philosopher alike must follow the prime rule of appropriateness in their handling of prosopopeia: all attributes must conform to the nature of the object to which they are assigned; if a place or dwelling is imagined for a person, it must be in keeping with his station; and to each person only such speeches and actions may be given as are in conformity with his character. "This above all is to be observed in every one of our discourses, that evil mores shall not be introduced, and that we should speak with due reverence of things belonging to religion so that these will not supply us with matter for ridicule."[4] In general, the verisimilitude of prosopopeia is comparable to any other, once the initial impossibility has been granted.

Concerning the figure which he is treating (and it has been seen that this figure may sometimes provide the basis for a whole poem), Bonciani thus starts from a general theory of diction, passes on to one of imitation, establishes the relationships of the imitation to nature, indicates the ends for which the imitation is made, and offers recommendations for the

[3] *Ibid.*, fol. 135v: "hauendo noi uarie cose conosciute la fantasia nostra confonde talhora le nature d'esse formandone una quanto al tutto da ogni altra differente, ma simile nelle parti."

[4] *Ibid.*, fol. 139: "questo sopr'ogni cosa è da osseruarsi in ogni nostro parlare, che rei costumi non s'introducano, e delle cose alla religione pertinenti con la debita riuerenza si fauelli, in guisa che elle non ci somministrino materia da cauarne il ridicolo."

internal organization of the work or the part of the work involved. At almost every one of these points, except perhaps the theory of diction, we find him in complete agreement with the many theorists who preceded him in the Horatian-rhetorical tradition.

That popular literary exercise, the defence of poetry, takes the special form of defence of comedy in the *Discorso intorno al componimento de la comedia de' nostri tempi*, which, in 1578, Bernardo Pino da Cagli published as an adjunct to Sforza d'Oddo's *Erofilomachia*; the discourse itself is dated 1572. Pino feels that he must justify comedy against the opinion currently held:

Today, this composition should either be abandoned altogether or else treated with much care and diligence, for it has come to such a state in the opinion of the masses that for the most part they regard it as a simple tale, vain and without profit, and as the work of a low mind, considering not the true artifice present in it and the utility that is had from it, when it is prudently written and treated, but the baseness of certain authors. . . . This results from no other thing than from the false opinion that is held with respect to the end of that type of work; whereas this should be to profit by means of the ridiculous, on the contrary the ridiculous is proposed as the end, to give pleasure alone by means of obscenity and ugliness.[5]

If the masses err in this way, erudite men and certain poets err in another, by a faulty interpretation of Aristotle's remarks on comedy; for the scholars read the *Poetics* as justifying the imitation of low and vile persons, the poets take it as permitting the imitation of vice. The antidote to these positions is obviously the restatement of the proper ends and the correct construction of the Aristotelian text. The ends are Horatian: to give pleasure and profit by means of laughter and without harm to the specta-tors (p. a10v). These ends require a reinterpretation of Aristotle, for vice could under no circumstances generate pleasure, and abject and immoral persons could not possibly provide acceptable moral lessons. Instead, Aristotle meant that the personages of comedy are less noble and less exalted than those of tragedy, being gentlemen and private citizens rather than kings and princes (we return to the medieval differentiation of genres by the station of the actors); and the ugliness he spoke of excluded im-morality, dishonesty, and obscenity and referred only to deformity and disproportion. In fact, the vices, sins, and actions of comedy are less repre-hensible than those of tragedy, where the really monstrous deeds of wickedness occur.

<hr>

5 *Discorso* (1578), pp. a6–a6v: "al dì d'oggi tal componimento si douerebbe ò a fatto lasciare, ò con molto studio, & diligenza trattare, poiche è venuto in tal conditione, & opinione del volgo, che di piu l'hanno per simplice fauola, vana & infruttuosa, & per opera da vile ingegno; considerando non il vero artifitio d'esso, o l'utile, che se ne prende, quando è prudentemente scritto & trattato, ma la bassezza d'alcuni autori. . . . Il che non prouiene da altro, che da la falsa opinione, che si ha del fine di cotal opera: il quale si come douerebbe essere il giouare, col mezzo del ridiculo, cosi per contrario si mette per fine il ridiculo, per piacer solo col mezzo della dishonestade, & della brutezza."

Since it is an imitation of life, says Pino, comedy will change as life changes, but only with respect to its materials. That is, new times will present to the comic poet new mores and new actions as his subjects. But the form will at all times remain the same: "Comedy is a kind of composition which, retaining always the same form, changes from time to time its matter; so that it always had five acts, always its complication and its denouement in order to be good."[6] Its immutable rules for form are found, it would seem, almost entirely in Horace: rules for the handling of the chorus, rules for diction, rules for decorum. The latter are really of two kinds, since they involve the proper "circumstances" for any given action and the proper behavior for any given person. In both, the spectator must have the impression of seeing nature herself represented; and the principal wisdom of the poet will consist in his knowledge of decorum and "circumstances." Indeed, Pino's generalization upon them almost constitutes a definition of comedy: "the whole body of comedy, if we wish to consider it carefully, is nothing else but the matter of divers passions, thoughts, and actions treated in familiar conversations."[7] Each person presented on the stage must be made to speak according to his condition, "with proverbs, maxims, sayings, and ways of speaking" that will be apposite both to the condition of the person addressed and to the circumstances. Finally, all these matters must be expressed in beautiful language, preferably of a metaphorical turn. An Aristotelian of 1578 would have noted in this discussion of the rules an enumeration of the four qualitative parts of comedy, plot, character, thought, and diction; but he also would have noted that the other three are really transformed into functions of thought, that the hierarchy of the parts is destroyed, and that what remains is a moralistic theory of comedy in which the most important thing is the utilitarian value of what is said.

In the same year, 1578, Giason Denores published a short treatise which in a sense reversed the tendencies that I have been discussing. It was entitled *Introduttione sopra i tre libri della Rhetorica di Aristotile,* and since it dealt with the *Rhetoric* rather than the *Poetics,* it might seem not to belong at all in a history of poetic theory. But whereas most of the theorists I have analyzed heretofore had effected an assimilation of poetics to rhetoric, Denores in the present work detaches one whole part of rhetoric from that science and attaches it to poetics. The part at issue is the materials contained in Book III of the *Rhetoric,* which Denores summarizes as including action (by which he means histrionics), elocution, and disposi-

6 *Ibid.,* p. a7v: "E la comedia vna sorte di componimento, che ritenendo sempre la medesima forma muta di tempo in tempo la materia: si che haueua sempre cinque atti, sempre il suo nodo, e'l suo scioglimento per essere bona."

7 *Ibid.,* p. b7v: "non essendo altro tutto il corpo della Comedia, se vogliamo bene considerarla, che materia di diuersi affetti, di pensieri & attioni, trattata con ragionamenti famigliari."

tion. He maintains that, according to Aristotle's conception, only those elements which contribute directly to persuasion—namely, proper and common propositions, examples, and enthymemes—belong to rhetoric; the elements treated in Book III are hence not substantial, and the book really should have been placed elsewhere in the Aristotelian corpus. Why not, then, placed with the *Poetics*? Since action, elocution, and disposition contribute nothing to rhetorical proof, be it demonstrative, ethical, or pathetic, and since they have as their sole purpose to give pleasure, to add beauty, to beguile the listener, their affiliation is clearly much closer with poetics than with its sister art; in fact, they belong primarily to poetics, and their use in rhetoric is accidental. The implication is that the specific domain of poetry is the pleasurable, the amusing, the idle, and that it is not concerned with more serious purposes.[8]

After this case of inverse method, we return to what is an almost perfect example of the rhetoricizing of poetry in Giovanni Andrea Gilio's *La topica poetica* of 1580; the title itself shows that its author wishes to discover rhetorical topics in the art of poetry. In fact, this is the main endeavor of the work: Books II, III, and IV are devoted to a listing of topics (by which he means arguments, passions, bases of demonstration), of figures of speech, and of figures of thought, respectively. More general materials, including a justification of this approach, appear in the dedication and in Book I. In the former, the commonplaces in the defence of poetry are once again collected together, and there is no need to retail them. In Book I, the whole principle of the work is stated: Everything that one says falls under one or several of the three kinds of discourse, the consultative or deliberative, the demonstrative, and the judicial; of these, the first two are more proper to the poet, the third to the orator. It would therefore be well for the poet to know in which type he is going to write, but it is not absolutely necessary; even if he does not, his compositions may be "lovely, and beautiful, ornamented by figures, by topical passages, by beautiful and graceful style, and by the other parts appropriate to well regulated poetry."[9] Clearly, there is no consideration of any "parts" above and beyond diction and possibly thought. There is, however, one prior step that the poet must take before beginning the task of expression; he must discover the materials to be expressed, and he does so through invention, which is, in a way, the most important aspect of poetry. "And when the invention is beautiful, and well conceived, well ordered, and well clothed and well ornamented with words with figures, with topical passages, and with a beautiful style, it may be said to be not only perfect but perfect in the highest degree."[10]

---

[8] *Introduttione* (1578), pp. b*v*, b4–c, g3*v*–g4.

[9] *Topica poetica* (1580), p. 1: "vaghi, e belli, ornati di figure, di luoghi topici, di bello e vago stile, e d'altre parti conueneuoli a ben regolata poesia."

[10] *Ibid.*, p. 4*v*: "E quando la inuentione è bella, e bene intesa, ben ordinata, e ben vestita e bene ornata di parole, di figure, di luoghi Topici, e di bello stile: Si potrà dire non solo perfetta ma perfettissima."

Invention itself is a product of imitation, either of nature, art, or fortune. or of earlier poets taken as models; imitation, in turn, applies to disposition and elocution as well as to invention.

Throughout Gilio's treatise, the Horatian references are numerous, but they are always altered in the direction of a more purely rhetorical approach. For example, Horace's statement of the ends of poetry is expanded from two to four: to delight, to profit, to move or persuade, and to be sweet or agreeable (referring to the "dulcia sunto" of line 99). All would seem to be achieved when words are correctly suited to matter. The subject of variety leads to a discussion of the mixture of styles and of the three styles in general. The quantitative parts distinguished are the proem, the narration, and the invocation. Decorum boils down to the "proportion, correspondence, or conformity that style has with subject matter."[11] All roads thus lead to diction and to the specific topics which Gilio is treating. He shows how the demonstrative, deliberative, and judicial types are used by Dante and Petrarch, how Petrarch and Ariosto may be used as models of style, how native and foreign words may be properly mixed. This limitation of the examples to Italian poets is an interesting feature of the work.

From the dual ends of pleasure and instruction, Torquato Tasso derives as much of the theory of epic poetry as he presents in the *Allegoria del poema* printed with the 1581 edition of the *Gerusalemme Liberata*. The whole passage merits quotation:

Heroic poetry, like an animal in which two natures are conjoined, is composed of imitation and of allegory. With the former it attracts the minds and the ears of men to itself and delights them in a wonderful way; with the latter it instructs them in the virtues or in knowledge, or in both together. And just as epic imitation is never anything else but a resemblance and image of human action, so the allegory of the epic poets is wont to be for us a figuration of human life. But imitation concerns the actions of man which are subject to the external senses, and laboring mainly over these, it tries to represent them with effective and expressive words and ones apt to place clearly before the physical eyes the things represented; nor does it consider characters or passions or the discoursings of the mind insofar as these are intrinsic, but only insofar as they issue forth and accompany action by manifesting themselves in speech and in actions and in deeds. Allegory, on the contrary, concerns passions and opinions and characters not only insofar as these are apparent, but mainly in their intrinsic being; and it signifies them more obscurely, with what one might call mysterious notes, and which can be fully understood only by those who know the nature of things.[12]

---

11 *Ibid.*, p. 10: "quella proportione, corrispondenza ò conformità c'ha lo stile co'l soggetto."

12 *Allegoria*, ed. Perchacino (1581), pp. **1–**1*v*: "L'Heroica Poesia, Quasi Animale, in cui due Nature si coniungano, d'imitatione, & d'Allegoria è composta, con quella alletta à se gli animi, & gli orecchi de gli huomini, & marauigliosamente gli diletta, con questa nella Virtù, ò nella scienza, ò nell'una, [e] nell'altra gli amaestra, et si come l'Epica imitatione altro giamai non è, che somiglianza, & imagine d'attione humana, cosi suole, l'Allegoria de gli Epici, dell'humana Vita esserci figura. Ma l'imitatione riguarda l'attioni dell'huomo, che

Furthermore, Tasso states that since the epic wishes to represent all life, some of its works will depict the life of the soul, or the contemplative life, others the life of the body, or the civil life; the *Odyssey* and the *Divina Commedia* are examples of the former, the *Iliad* and the *Aeneid* of the latter. The whole dichotomy may be figured graphically in the following way:

	Epic poetry	
imitation	allegory	
attracts, delights	teaches virtue	
external actions, appearance	passions, opinions, characters	
clear presentation	obscure presentation	
(all men)	those who know nature of things	
	(soul)	(body)
	contemplative life	civil life
	Odyssey	*Iliad*
	Dante	*Aeneid*

Several points are significant in this analysis: first, the importance placed upon the allegorical interpretation of literature, equal to its importance in the Middle Ages; second, the restricted conception of imitation, which comes to mean a literal and simple portrayal of external actions; third, the division of the functions of the two parts of a poem providing pleasure and utility.

When Tasso was speaking of the epic (as well as writing it), he was occupying himself with the genre that many Renaissance theorists considered the most important of all. When Filippo Massini delivered his lecture, *Del madrigale*, to the Accademia degli Insensati at Perugia in the same year, 1581, he admitted with becoming modesty that he was about to treat the smallest and weakest of all Tuscan verse forms. The object of his lecture was to contest the assertions of Ruscelli and Minturno that the madrigal was a "regulated" poem, to deny the limitations placed upon the form by them, and to indicate how it might be thought of as belonging to the other category of "free" poems. "Regulation," for Massini, involves fixity of subject matter, of style, of metrical pattern; for the madrigal, this means exclusive use of rustic materials (as recommended by Bembo and Minturno), treated in a low style, in eleven or twelve lines rhyming in a set way. Massini contends, on the contrary, that the madrigal is free in all these respects. His authority, in a general fashion, is Aristotle's statement in *Poetics* 1447*b*13, which he paraphrases thus: "the quality of the verse does not distinguish the poem substantially, to use this term; the poem takes its

sono à i sensi esteriori sottoposte, & intorno ad esse principalmente affaticandosi, cerca di rappresentarle con parole efficaci, & espressiue, & atte à por chiaramente dinanzi à gli occhi corporali le cose rappresentate; nè considera i costumi, ò gli affetti, ò i discorsi dell'animo inquanto essi sono intrinseci; ma solamente in quanto fuori se n'escono, & nel parlare, & ne gli atti, & nell'opere manifestandosi accompagnano [l]'attione. L'Allegoria all'incontro rimira le passioni, & le opinioni, & i costumi, non solo inquanto essi apparino; ma principalmente nel lor essere intrinseco, & piu oscuramente le significa con note (per cosi dire) misteriose, & che solo da i conoscitori della Natura delle cose possono essere à pieno comprese."

form and its quality from the quality of the plot or of the thought that one undertakes to write about."[13] Since he thinks of the madrigal as admitting any subject matter, it may thus admit any one of the styles, high, middle, or low. There are, however, preferable practices all along the line. The best subjects are the light ones, "since pleasantness is without any doubt more proper and more fitting to the very agreeable nature of this composition, which however is not at all incapable of gravity."[14] The style should be distinguished, no matter which one it may be:

I should wish then above all else that the madrigal should contain some rare and ingenious thought, and that its elocution should be very pure and artful, and that both thought and elocution in the graver madrigals should be such that they would produce honesty, dignity, majesty, magnificence, and greatness, and in the more amusing ones, grace, suavity, loveliness, sweetness, jokes, and playful expressions.[15]

In the verse form, the poem is "free" to the extent that it does not have a fixed number of lines, that some unrhymed lines are permitted, and that "mezzi versi" may be intermingled with "versi interi." But Massini nevertheless sets up certain rules: it must not contain fewer than five lines and preferably should not have more than twenty; rhymes should not be more than five lines apart. By way of conclusion, he states that, like the canzone, the madrigal is essentially a free form, but that it may be regulated in one of two ways: (1) by accepting and following the form practiced by some other poet, or (2) by evolving one's own rules and then following them consistently (pp. 173–74, 185).

Massini's analysis represents an attempt at liberation from the rule-of-thumb poetizing which had given substance to the late medieval and early Renaissance prosodic treatises; in a broader sense, it belongs to the general contention over freedom and regulation (extending far beyond prosodic matters) which was a permanent concern of Cinquecento theory. We shall meet many other examples of it as we go along. In a minor way, this attempt may be a reaction against some of Horace's specific prescriptions for the drama. But one breaks away from Horace here only to join the ranks of the rhetoricians associated with him in current thinking. The three styles, invention and elocution, the principle of appropriateness of thought and diction, specific effects to be produced by the diction, all these are part of the contemporary tradition.

---

13 In *Lettioni* (1588), pp. 168–69: "La qualità del verso non qualifica, per vsar questo termine, sostantialmente il Poema, il quale prende la forma, e qualità sua dalla qualità della fauola, e del concetto, che s'imprende à scriuere."

14 *Ibid.*, p. 173: "essendo la piaceuolezza, senz'alcun dubbio, più propria, e più proportionata alla natura piaceuolissima di questo componimento, non incapace però affatto . . . di grauità."

15 *Ibid.*, p. 181: "Desidererei poi sopra 'l tutto, che'l Madrigale hauesse 'l concetto raro, & ingegnoso, e l'elocution purissima, & artifitiosa, e che questa, e quello, nei Madrigali più graui, fossero tali, che producessero, l'honestà, la dignità, la maestà, la magnificenza, e la grandezza, e nei più piaceuoli, la gratia, la soauità, la vaghezza, la dolcezza, gli scherzi, e i giochi."

In the same year, 1581, the Plantin press published an edition of Cicero's *De optimo genere oratorum*, with a commentary containing several pages of remarks specifically devoted to poetics; it was written by Giovanni Antonio Viperano, who had published his *De poetica* just two years before. It should be pointed out that the passage at the beginning of Cicero's treatise to which these remarks refer had been used repeatedly by writers on poetry, especially those who were intent upon establishing airtight divisions between the genres, and by scholars working on the text of Horace. Viperano also uses it to set up a system of genres, but in a somewhat different way; indeed, he attacks previous divisions as incorrectly established. His own solution is a strange cross between Aristotle and the rhetoricians. Poetry, he says, is an imitation of human actions, and human actions are of two sorts. Either they are good and virtuous and merit praise, or they are bad and vicious and merit blame. Hence one may classify poems as they provide "laus" for the former or "vituperatio" for the latter. This is, of course, an accurate reflection of Averroës' system. To the laudative poems belong the melic (or lyric) and its derivatives, the epic and tragedy; to the vituperative, comedy. Having thus classified the genres, Viperano then indicates for each one its subject matter (usually persons of a given station in life), its kind of action (happy at the beginning, unhappy at the end, and so forth), its style (a combination of sententiae and diction) and its meter (iambic, hexameter). Unfortunately, most of the materials here are the time-worn ones from Donatus and Diomedes, with occasional additions from Horace, and there is nothing new to be learned from studying them.

As he continues his gloss on Cicero, Viperano takes occasion to insist upon the meaning of the sentence, "Itaque & in tragoedia comicum uitiosum est, & in comoedia turpe tragicum." He argues that, although all poems belong to the genus poetry, they are so distinct one from another that they can under no circumstances be mixed:

... of the forms of poetry, one cannot be associated with another, given the fact that they have a separate and distinct nature. Since then, tragedy imitates the actions of illustrious men and comedy those of humble men, it is improper and faulty and contrary to the nature of either one if comic and humorous matters are brought up in a tragedy, or in a comedy tragic upheavals are employed. . . Nor do comedy and tragedy differ only in the diverse imitation of illustrious and ordinary actions, but also in diction. For tragedy uses a grave and sublime diction, comedy instead descends to the familiar usage of almost pure talk.[16]

---

[16] *In Ciceronis de optimo genere oratorum commentarius* (1581), p. 12: "poëticae formarum altera in alterius consociationem venire non potest, vt quae propriam habeant distinctamque naturam. Quando igitur virorum illustrium actiones tragoedia imitatur, & comoedia humilium, indecorum est, ac vitiosum, repugnansque cuiusque naturae, si aut comicae res & iocosae in tragoedia excitentur, aut in comoedia tragicae perturbationes adhibeantur . . . neque solùm diuersa actionum illustrium & humilium imitatione comoedia & tragoedia differunt, sed etiam oratione. Nam tragoedia graui & sublimi oratione vtitur, comoedia verò ad vsitatam ferè puri sermonis consuetudinem sese dimittit." .

As elsewhere in his thinking, Viperano does not feel that the distinction is complete until he has added "verba" to "res"; this conclusion is borne out by the commentary on the following sentence in Cicero, where he assigns to each of the genres—earlier distinguished on the basis of subject matter—a certain kind of words having a specific and separate tonal effect.

With Roberto Titi's *Locorum controversorum* (1583) we return briefly and fragmentarily to the text of Horace. Titi's work treats a large number of "disputed points" from many ancient authors, pretending to improve upon earlier interpretations, and included are two texts from the *Ars poetica*. The first is lines 408 ff., "Natura fieret laudabile carmen an arte . . . ," which treats the general question of art and nature in the poet. Titi's original contribution is his insistence that even the combination of art and nature is not sufficient and that the poet must possess also "effort, love, exercise, opportunity, time, judgment."[17] The second remark concerns lines 128 ff., "Difficile est proprie communia dicere . . . ," on the use of new and borrowed materials. Titi extends the meaning to a general theory of imitation, with special emphasis on the parts of a model which the poet should imitate. He sees imitation as concerning both "materia" and "verba." The particular passage in Horace refers to "materia" only and (according to Titi) makes the point that the poet should select those passages for imitation which are splendid and noble, which will enable the poet to be brilliant; on the other hand, he should avoid all such as are low and nondescript. The fact that the example chosen to illustrate "low" passages is Catullus leads one to suspect that the criterion being applied is again a moral one.

In 1583, also, Giraldi Cintio's tragedies were collected and published by his son, Celso, and thus the verse "Prologues" to the various tragedies were printed for the first time. They had probably been written many years earlier, but it is impossible to assign exact dates to them. Although there are five prologues containing reflections on poetic theory, the doctrine found in them is consistent and unified and may be reduced to a few major points: (1) The laws of poetry are not immutable, but change with the times, with audiences, with the wishes of the patrons who order them, and with the subject matters that are different from age to age (Prologue to *Altile*, pp. 7–8). An example of such change would be his use of a prologue in each of his tragedies, a practice unknown to the ancients, who used prologues only in comedy. (2) Tragedy does not need to have a tragic ending, but may end happily; when, after turmoil and sadness, a happy ending ensues, the play may be called a tragicomedy. This is the case with his own *Altile* (Prologue, pp. 8–9). (3) The ends of tragedy are to give pleasure and to provide utility, with the emphasis decidedly on the latter. This is the one point most insistently repeated in the various prologues,

---

17 *Locorum controversorum* (1583), bk. II, ch. xxiii, p. 56: "sumptus, Amor, exercitium, opportunitas, tempus, Iudicium." For the second passage, cf. bk. VIII, ch. xxii, pp. 219–20.

the kind of utility varying from prologue to prologue. In *Altile*, for example:

> Vedrete adunque in questa nostra Altile
> . . .
> Quanta inconstanza è ne l'humane cose.
> E che per mal' oprar mai non gioisce
> Vn animo maluagio, e che conuiene
> . . .
> Ch'auenga quel, ch'è statuito in Cielo
> Dal supremo Motor, che il tutto regge,
> Con quella sua ineffabil prouidenza (p. 9).

The lessons: the inconstancy of human affairs; the wicked are never happy; the will of God, expressed through Providence, will be done.

In *Didone*, the same moral as the one taught by the ancient poets who borrowed subjects from Homer:

> E l'esposero in scena, a gli occhi altrui,
> Per purgar l'humane alme col terrore,
> E, con compassion de gli altrui casi,
> Da la vana ridurle à miglior vita (p. 7).

The utility: through purgation of pity and terror, to lead men to a better life.

In the Prologue to *Cleopatra* a statement first about the dual end of dramatic poetry:

> Fra le cose trouate da gli antichi,
> Per insegnare i buon costumi al Mondo,
> Nulla ue n'hà, che piu diletti, e gioui,
> Che le fauole, ben condutte in scena,
> E benche d'esse sian varie le sorti,
> Fra quelle nondimen di maggior loda
> Ottiene la Tragedia il primo luoco (p. 7).

Then the specific moral of this tragedy: that wealth and power are nothing unless accompanied by virtue.

In *Arrenopia*:

> Hor qui vedrete, spettatori, quanto
> Ci apporti danno il non vedere il vero,
> Et il lasciarsi à l'appetito in preda
> E che il non vbedire a suoi maggiori,
> E cagione di scandali, ch'à guerra,
> Inducon spesso i piu potenti Regi (pp. 9–10).

The conclusions: one must see the truth, resist the promptings of appetite, obey one's superiors.

From the Prologue to *Selene*:

> Perche ueggendo indi gli spettatori
> Varie sembianze d'huomini, e di donne,
> Di uarij vffici, & qualità diuerse,
> E di varij costumi, & varie leggi
> Sortir diuersi fini, & uarie sorti;
> Fatti acuti, sapesser da se in tanta
> Varietà di genti, & di costumi,
> Seguir la loda, & ischiuare il biasmo,
> Et ueder, che chiunque uirtù segue,
> Giunge à buon fine, & chi'l mal segue, à reo (p. 9).

The purpose: to demonstrate, via the divers kinds of men and women in the world and the ends they come to, that virtue leads to happiness and vice to unhappiness; and through the demonstration, to make the spectators wary and wise.

There can be little doubt here as to the kind of utility involved and how it is achieved. The stage is a place for examples, in both characters and actions, of proper kinds of behavior—to be followed—and improper kinds —to be shunned. Giraldi, as he enumerates these examples, gives some indications as to how they should be presented—brief remarks on decorum, on the fitting of actions and the general tone to the dignity of the persons, on the inclusion of the action within a single day, on the audience, which is made up of "thousands of people" and must be spoken to in terms accessible to it. Giraldi's own precepts are accessible in this way and show what elements of Horatian theory (with a smattering of Aristotle) he deemed it possible and worth while to address to the pit and the boxes.

TORQUATO TASSO (1584)

From the subtitle of Torquato Tasso's dialogue, *La Cavaletta, overo della poesia toscana* (written in 1584, published in 1587),[18] one is led to expect an illuminating treatment of poetry in the vernacular; and this expectation is further aroused when one discovers that Tasso means to proceed in a practical and deductive fashion by comparing two sonnets, one by Francesco Coppetta and one by Giovanni della Casa. Some illumination, indeed, is provided. But it is a light out of the past, coming largely from two medieval theorists, Dante and Antonio da Tempo, supplemented by Hermogenes' Ideas and the truisms of classical rhetoric.

Tasso's starting point is Dante's definition of poetry as "a rhetorical fiction set to music" ("una fintione Retorica posta in musica"),[19] for which he finds corroboration in Plato's statement from the *Gorgias* that

---

[18] On the date, see Solerti, *Vita di Torquato Tasso* (Torino, Roma, 1895), I, 396.

[19] *De vulgari eloquentia*, II.iv.2. In the edition of P. Rajna (Florence, 1896), p. 129: "fictio rethorica . . . in musicaque posita." In the Trissino translation of 1529, p. c: "una fizione rettorica, e posta in musica."

tragedy is "a deceit in which the deceivers are better than those who do not deceive, and the deceived are wiser than those who are not deceived." Poets, rhetoricians, musicians, actors are all "dissimulators." Aristotle would have called them imitators (except for the rhetorician), but it is clear that Tasso does not mean to speak in the same way as Aristotle. Dissimulation involves, among other things, the hiding of the effects of art itself: "Thus, to hide the deceit, and so to speak the dissimulation of the art, is the highest artistry."[20] Tasso develops at some length the comparisons of the poet with the orator and the musician. Unlike the logician, who uses induction and the syllogism as his forms of argument, the orator uses the enthymeme and the example, and these are the same forms employed by the poet. Generally, anybody who imitates imitates some "example" and hence in a sense argues; even though the argument may not be formally stated, it exists. In poetry, the argument is concealed in some fictional form, and this makes it all the more effective as far as persuasion is concerned. For the poet, like the orator, wishes to persuade; "in truth, through reading of the poets I have been greatly persuaded to honor, to glory, and to virtue, and almost more than by the philosophers themselves."[21] Furthermore, certain kinds of poems are parallel with certain kinds of arguments; the canzone is a reflection of the "divisive" argument, the sonnet of the "compositive" (p. 36v). Finally, both arts are compounded of sententiae and of elocution, of which the latter is the more important in poetry. As for music, it is associated only accidentally with poetry, since the latter may dispense with it; indeed, some of the highest genres do not need it at all, and the fact that some of the lower ones must have it as an additional ornament is a sign of their weakness. Dante's definition is thus now fully explained, and Tasso is able to conclude with respect to poetry in general that "its genus and as it were its matter will be the fiction and its forms will have rhetoric and music."[22] The practicing poet still remains a poet, though, and he must avoid indulging both in sophistic subtleties, which would bring him too close to the rhetoricians, and in excessive and intemperate musical ornament.

With special reference to the sonnet, Tasso holds that it has various forms (by which he means various rhyme schemes) and that each of these is capable of any of the "Ideas" or "characters" of diction. The determining factor in every case is the nature of the subject matter. Thus Coppetta's sonnet, which has a "very noble subject" and a "very grave texture" will require the "most noble" form or character of discourse. In any given sonnet, the style may be mixed, but there will be one dominant style, which

---

[20] In *Rime e prose*, Vol. VI (1587), p. 31: "Il nasconder dunque l'inganno, e per cosi dire, la dissimulatione dell'arte, è sommo artificio."

[21] *Ibid.*, p. 36: "Veramente leggendo i Poeti, molto sono stato persuaso all'honore, alla gloria, & alla virtù, e quasi piu che da filosofi stessi."

[22] *Ibid.*, p. 37: "il genere suo e quasi la materia sarà la fintione e sue forme aranno Rethorica, & Musica."

will set the tone. The poem must end on the dominant, toward which there should be steady progression throughout. The musical terminology is not amiss here, since Tasso has in mind effects of tone—"high-sounding" and "low-sounding" words, and so forth—and their development through the sonnet. In his comparison of the two sonnets, it is largely these effects that he discusses, to the advantage of Casa because he builds properly toward the concluding sonorities, to the discredit of Coppetta because he does not. In this part of the discussion, at least, Tasso is closer to the art of prosody than to the art of poetry; and when he remains within the art of poetry, he is also astride the art of rhetoric.

Girolamo Frachetta attacks directly the problem of the difference between poetry and prosody in his *Spositione sopra la canzone di Guido Cavalcanti, Donna mi prega, &c.* (1585). In spite of its title, the "exposition" is of greater interest as a theoretical than as a practical document; for the sections referring directly to Cavalcanti's poem are, like so many similar works of the century, concerned exclusively with the philosophical content and with detailed speculations on the meaning. Frachetta's thesis is that Cavalcanti's canzone should not be rated as a poem at all, and the demonstration of this thesis leads him into various theoretical questions. He finds it necessary to distinguish, first, between poetry and prosody, and he does so on the basis of their "materia": the matter of poetry is made up of things which can happen, sometimes of things which have happened; whereas the matter of prosody is syllables, vowels, and consonants, combined to make verse. Verse is the form of the work as viewed prosodically and constitutes its internal end; its external end is pleasure. When he raises the question as to whether either of these arts can exist without the other, he finds himself at variance with the opinion of Castelvetro, who had maintained that they cannot. Frachetta's own stand is that the art of poetry cannot exist without versification, but that the art of prosody can exist without poetry. To justify the first of these statements, he interprets Aristotle's text (*Poetics* 1451*b*27) as meaning that the poet is a poet *more* by virtue of imitation than of verse—but that verse is nevertheless necessary. This is in keeping with the nature of the poet and his ends: "the poet, who wishes to be considered by the masses as surpassing the condition of other men (as the ancients especially wished him to be), must speak in that manner which is more exquisite than all the rest, and precisely in the one in which the oracles used to give their answers; and this is without any doubt the manner of verse."[23] In support of the second statement, he declares that since versification is an instrumental science having no essence of its own, it may be attached to other forms besides poetry.

[23] *Spositione* (1585), p. 3: "il poeta, che uuole essere stimato dal popolo trapassar la conditione de gli huomini, come massimamente uoleuan gli antichi, dee fauellare in quella maniera, che è piu isquisita dell'altre, & in quella appunto nella qual si soleuano dar le risposte da gli Oracoli: & questa è senza fallo niuno la maniera del uerso."

The upshot of this argument is that there may be compositions in verse that are not poems, even whole verse genres that are not poetry. The canzone as practiced by early poets was of this kind. How, then, would one distinguish a canzone that was a poem from another that was not? The answer is double: from the style and from the matter. Lyric poems contain matters of various kinds, but above all commendations of one sort or another and amorous themes. But they must not approach commendatory orations or philosophical disquisitions on love in difficulty or subtlety, "because poems were invented to give recreation to men's minds, and not to weary them."[24] Moreover, as compared with these nonpoetic forms, poems have a special kind of style: "they are distinguished mainly by the transformation of the material, which depends upon additions; by metaphors, by allegories, by hyperboles, and by similar colorings and embellishments."[25] Cavalcanti's canzone is not a poem because its subject matter is too obscure, and if Frachetta has undertaken to explain it, it is not because he wished to expound a poem, but merely to shed light upon an obscure work (p. 7).

TOMMASO CORREA (1587)

Tommaso Correa, known to us through his treatise on the epigram, in 1587 published his *In librum de arte poetica Q. Horatij Flacci explanationes.* It was the first of the three complete commentaries on Horace to appear during this "last generation" of Horatian criticism. The immediate impression is one of simplification of the whole approach to the text, as compared with the great complexity of earlier exegeses. This results in part from the reduction in the number of divisions of the text and of accompanying precepts. Whereas Pigna had seen eighty separate rules in Horace, Correa subdivides into only twenty-five sections; instead of Pigna's four separate precepts for lines 73–85, he gives only one, and instead of the six for lines 275–308, one again. The consequence is a sense of more closely knit and better organized exposition. Besides, some of the promiscuous citing of authorities is eliminated; Plato and Cicero are cited a few times each, Donatus with some frequency, and the parallels with Aristotle are whittled down to the following modest list:

Horace	Aristotle
1–23	1450a38, 1451a16, 1450b24
42–45	1450a38, 1449b12
73–85	1449a24, 1459b31
275–308	1450a12
309–32	1447a16

[24] *Ibid.*, p. 7: "percioche le poesie sono state trouate per ricrear gli animi, & non per affaticargli."

[25] *Ibid.*, p. 6: "si seperano principalmente per l'alteratione della materia, laqual depende dalle aggiunte; per le tralationi; per le allegorie; per le hiperboli; & per somiglianti coloramenti, & abbeglimenti."

If these passages be consulted, it will be noted that they contain only the most familiar commonplaces of the Aristotelian text: "The poet is an imitator," "The plot is the soul of the poem," "The plot must be one," and so forth. But these changes do not mean that Correa wishes to make wide departures from the antecedent tradition; rather, he preserves much of the rhetorical machinery which had for so long been a standard feature of the interpretations of the text.

In part, at least, Correa organizes the *Ars poetica* according to the elements of invention, disposition, and elocution. He thinks that the first precept (ll. 1–23) concerns invention and disposition and that the second one (ll. 24–31) treats elocution. Later, the fourth precept (ll. 42–45) returns to disposition. To these three elements he adds, in at least one passage, the rhetorical parts of pronunciation and action (in connection with ll. 99–111). Crossed with this set of distinctions is its constant concomitant, the "res-verba" distinction; but here the treatment is more interesting and more original. For the group of terms appears not only as explicitly stated, but also under various disguises. When he is discussing lines 46–72, where Horace touches upon the invention of new words, Correa indicates that the text here passes from "res" to "verba," "since a poem, like a speech, consists of things and of words."[26] Earlier, in connection with the second precept (already identified as belonging to elocution), the opposition had taken the various forms of "res : verba," "res : dictio," "res : oratio"; later, the sixth precept states it as modified to "res : versus." Clearly, what Correa has in mind is a major juxtaposition of "matter" to "form" and the problem of suiting the latter to the former. The question of decorum, as we shall see, arises in connection with both matter and form.

Alongside these fairly conventional approaches, Correa presents a certain number of personal ideas, which constitute modifications to the standard theory. He seems to regard the materials of poetry as circumscribed and determined in a number of ways. First, as in Horace, by nature: the poet may not mix in his poem parts and elements which are separate in nature, "so that his poem will not resemble a monster made up of various natures in conflict with one another."[27] Second, as in Plato, by the conventions of society: the poet does not have complete freedom of invention since he must not say things which are contrary to the institutions and customs of society (p. 6); for this restriction Correa uses the term "conuenientia." Third, by the rules of the style in which the poet is writing: these are equivalent to a second "nature" whose requirements are as strict as those of the first. Basically, the style should be adapted to the materials; but by a kind of inverse action, certain types of persons, actions, and

---

[26] *Explanationes* (1587), p. 28: "Quoniam poema, vt oratio constat rebus & verbis. . . ."

[27] *Ibid.*, p. 3: "vt non videatur monstrum aliquod ex diuersis inter se pugnantibus naturis conflatum."

thoughts come to be associated invariably with each style. For example, the sublime style:

The highest style contains important personages and excellent actions, to which are to be fitted choice sententiae, which must be expressed with choice words and adorned by rhythmic grouping, as if you were to speak of God or describe heroes, kings, military leaders, governments; but if others are mixed in, such as chariot-eers, sailors, merchants, artisans and others of that kind, it is done so that human society may constitute a kind of complete body. Excellent matters are such things as wars for peace, deliberative councils, trials for selection, the virtues useful for the regulation of life, and great actions. Choice sententiae are those which are remote from common usage, choice words those which are not trite; a rhythmic grouping is one which, through its sounds, almost depicts the thing itself.[28]

Fourth, by the fixed subjects prescribed for the individual genres; this is, in a sense, a refinement and specification of the preceding. Not only is the type of action recommended for each genre ("In tragedy incredible and most horrible actions are related, in comedy actions from the average and common life of men and from their usual behavior"[29]), but for some genres very definite content—largely from traditional sources—is proposed. Thus, in tragedy the plots will revolve about "great and horrible actions, the murders of kings, hopeless situations, exiles, parricides, burnings, armed contests, weepings, wailings, laments, funerals, burial hymns";[30] in the New Comedy, about "loves, marriages, girls sold into slavery who are later found to be free and are recognized by their father, their mother, their brother, their nurse."[31] If to all these limitations one adds the typification of personages imposed by the laws of decorum, characters as well as action become set and almost invariable parts of the work. Indeed, the whole hemming in of the "matter" of poetry is equivalent to a kind of super-law of decorum.

The poet, circumscribed in these ways with respect to his subject matter, finds his great field of activity in the form which he imposes upon it. If one were to ask Correa what the distinguishing characteristics of poetry were, his answer would undoubtedly include primarily those elements

28 *Ibid.*, pp. 14–15: "Genus summum personas graues, & res excellentes continet, quibus lectę sententie accommodandae sunt, & illae proferendae verbis lectis, & numerosa collocatione illustrandae; vt si de Deo loquaris, Heroas describas, Reges, Duces, Ciuitates, quòd si alia admisceantur, vt Aurigae, Nautae, Mercatores, fabri, & huiusmodi id adeo fit, quòd Hominum societas quasi quoddam corpus efficiat. Res excellentes sunt bella propter pacem, Concilia ad deliberandum, Iudicia ad eligendum, virtutes ad vitam constituendam, & actiones. Sententiae lectae, ab vsu remotę communi, lecta verba, quae non sunt trita: numerosa collocatio quae quasi rem ipsam suo sono depingit."

29 *Ibid.*, p. 41: "In Tragędijs atrocissim[ę] res exponuntur, & incredibiles, in Comoedijs res sumptę de media & communi hominum vita, & moribus."

30 *Ibid.*, p. 93: "Res Tragicae grandes, atroces, cędes Regum, desperationes, exsilia, parricidia, incendia, pugnae, fletus, vlulatus, conquestiones, funera, Epicedia."

31 *Ibid.*, p. 95: "In Comoedia noua vt plurimum amores, nuptiae, virgines venditae, quae liberae inueniantur, cognoscuntur a patre, matre, fratre, nutricę."

which he regarded as belonging to the form. Verse would be one of them, inseparably and inescapably connected with any conception of poetry. Therefore, to each type of subject matter the proper verse must be matched. Some genres have verse as their only poetic property; if one were to remove verse from the satire, for example, one would no longer have a poem (p. 79). Another required feature would be a special kind of language or diction. In fact, one reason why the satire is so unstable a poetic genre is that its language is not different from that of everyday usage. The real poet is one who writes metaphorically, who cultivates the figures and the tropes, even though he must not do so to excess or in an inappropriate way (pp. 28–29). Again, poetry is distinguished by the use of an artificial order in place of the natural order found in history and in the narrations of the orator.

The greatest merit of the poet consists in the fact that he departs considerably from the laws of history and disregards the natural order of narration, if one consider the succession of events; for sometimes he passes over the things prescribed by the natural order, pursues those things which it provides, places elsewhere those which it seemed ought to be said in the present. Nor is that law imposed upon him which would make him write a kind of history and collect all things in an orderly fashion. He may of course choose the events, express and embellish some of them, pass over others which he does not deem worthy of mention.[32]

In all this answer, Correa would have little to say about imitation, except for a passing remark about the requirement that the imitation should follow the thing imitated (p. 18) and another indicating that the poet imitates when he introduces other persons who speak for themselves (p. 35). No special essence is contributed to poetry through the fact that it is an imitation; it is merely a particular kind of rhetoric or history.

In keeping with this conception, Correa devotes much of his time to matters of style. He takes pains to define what is meant by the terms "Idea," "character," "stilus," so common in critical parlance, and he does so as follows:

A "character," then, is a diction similar to the thing which it designates, or else it is the effigy and image of the thing, for speech expresses the thing just as colors do in painting. Just as one obtains from wax, when a seal is applied to it, an image in every respect similar to the thing of which the seal is a representation, so the Idea of the thing is expressed in speech; and therefore the form of diction is called "genus" or "stilus," for the word "phrasis" is used to refer to a plain,

32 *Ibid.*, p. 23: "Poetę summa laus est à legibus Historię longe abscedere & naturalem narrandi ordinem negligere, si series rerum spectetur, quoniam, quę naturalis ordo prescribit, interdum negligit, quę fert prosequitur ac quae in pręsentia dicenda videbantur, in alium locum traducit, neque illi ea lex imponitur, vt quasi Historiam scribat, omnia ordine colligat. Habeat sanè delectum rerum, & alia dicat, & ornet, alia prętereat, quę non esse dicenda iudicauerit."

or elegant, or a strange and foreign diction, whereas "stilus" or "character" or "forma dicendi" indicates the general conformation of the diction.[33]

Correa then proceeds to a description of each of the three styles, to an indication of the subject matters to which each is appropriate, and to a statement of the general principle of decorum operative in all matters of style. When, later, he gives his definitions of comedy and tragedy, they are compounded of these elements; he himself says that they differ in three ways, in "the social status of the personages, the manner and quality of the affairs and destinies, and finally in the ending." And then he adds, immediately, a fourth difference: "This being the case, they must necessarily differ in style also."[34] Applied to tragedy, these distinctions lead to the following definition: "Tragedy, then, is an imitation by means of action of an illustrious destiny, with an unhappy ending, and in the grave style";[35] and to comedy, this: "Comedy, then, is a dramatic poem full of activity, with a happy ending, and in the humble style."[36] The elaborate apparatus of distinctions thus produces definitions which are not notably more sophisticated than those of Diomedes and the whole medieval school.

To these questions of matter and of form we may relate what Correa has to say about the audience for which the poem is intended and about the poet who writes it. Audience considerations are not prominent, but they are important beyond their number. The ends of poetry are stated in terms of the audience, in several ways: as the instruction and pleasure of men ("hominum institutio, & voluptas," p. 18); as admiration, admonishment, delight, teaching ("vt spectator admiretur, . . . vt admoneatur, delectetur, doceatur," p. 93). The nature of these ends determines certain characteristics both of matter and of form. Of the many available subjects, the poet chooses those which are most outstanding and excellent, since these will be of greatest interest to his audience (p. 24); he will retain this interest by introducing the greatest possible variety into the materials. No two deaths will occur in the same way, no two cities will be besieged and conquered according to the same pattern, and so forth (p. 40). Moreover, if the "institutio" is to be accomplished, materials must be verisimilar and

---

[33] *Ibid.*, p. 13: "Est autem character dictio similis illi rei, quam notat: siue est rei effigies, & imago, quoniam oratio rem exprimit, vt in pictura colores. Ex cera, vt addita nota exprimitur effigies persimilis ei rei, cuius nota est; sic oratione rei Idea exprimitur, & ideo dicend forma, aut genus, aut stilus dicitur, quoniam phrasis ad elocutionem planam, elegantem, aut peregrinam, & barbaram refertur; stillus, siue character, aut forma dicendi conformationem orationis indicat."

[34] *Ibid.*, p. 91: "Differt Tragedia a comoedia tribus potissimum rebus, personarum condicione, negotiorum, & fortunarum modo, & qualitate, atque tandem exitu. Haec cum ita sint stilo etiam differant, necesse est."

[35] *Ibid.*, p. 92: "Est autem Tragędia imitatio Illustris fortunae per actione[m] exitu infoelici, oratione graui."

[36] *Ibid.*, p. 94: "Est autem Comoedia poema dragmaticum, negotiosum, exitu laeto, stylo humili."

self-consistent (note the references to nature and to decorum); and if the "voluptas" is to accompany it, variety must be cultivated (p. 18). As for form, the great reason for the necessity of artificial order is that by means of it the poet creates suspense. The passage cited previously on artificial order continues thus: "In fact, since the poet makes an effort to detain the auditor as it were against his will and in suspense, he makes his poem varied throughout by the arrangement of the events. . . . For the highest praise of the poet is to hold the listener as if he were a captive."[37] Finally, the pleasure so provided is itself an aid to the achieving of the utility, and the utility involved makes the pleasure more acceptable and more memorable (p. 107).

That Correa is independent of certain parts of the current tradition is attested by his discarding of the notion, in connection with the poet, of the poetic furor. He treats the subject when he is discussing lines 309 ff. ("Scribendi recte sapere est et principium et fons"). "So far," he says, "is the poet from being mad that nobody can write well unless he is wise. Indeed, every good and proper discourse must derive from the knowledge of things."[38] The knowledge in question concerns, for the poet, the rules of decorum—especially with reference to character—and human nature. Since the poet is an imitator, he must express the essence of nature ("exprimit naturae uim," p. 103); this is the opinion of both Plato and Aristotle. For Correa, this knowledge is obtained by study of rules and does not come as a form of inspiration. The poet must of course have an "ingenium" or "facultas" suited to the genre which he means to practice, but even more so must he have such virtues as "prudentia, varietas, efficacia, suauitas" (p. 18). These, translated into terms of his activity, have to do largely with disposition and elocution—with the proper handling of the elements constituting form.

Thus, the major orientations in Correa's commentary are probably more definitely toward the internal relationships of "res" and "verba" than toward the more specifically rhetorical factors so common in the present tradition. These latter are all developed, and in a way only slightly divergent from the ordinary; but the emphasis is elsewhere. One feels, after studying the commentary, that its main preoccupations are with problems of matter and form rather than with the devices and expedients for swaying, influencing, and arousing the audience. Since it is a commentary on Horace, it must of necessity make all the centrifugal movements that are found in the text itself—toward nature, toward conventions, toward the poet, toward the audience. But it manages, in a fairly consistent way, to reverse the

---

[37] *Ibid.*, pp. 23–24: "Nam cum poeta in eo elaboret, vt vel inuitum detineat auditorem, & suspensum, in finem vsque variat poema collocatione rerum. . . . Nam poetę illa summa laus, vt auditorem quasi captiuum detineat."

[38] *Ibid.*, p. 102: "Tantum verò abest, vt furiosus poeta sit, vt bene scribere nemo possit, nisi sapiens. Omnis enim oratio bona, & apta ex cognitione rerum promanet necesse est."

motion of all these and bring them into contact with the central problem of the text as Correa interprets it.

NICOLA COLONIO (1587)

The second of the complete commentaries to appear in this last period was published in the same year as Correa's, 1587. It is Nicola Colonio's *Methodus de Arte poetica,* and its principal distinction is its claim that it perceives—as had never been done before—the true order or "method" of the *Ars poetica.* In his dedication (p. iiiv), Colonio boasts that he has for long years studied Aristotle's "analytic method," and his intention in the present work is to apply what he has learned to the analysis of Horace's epistle. He believes that, by such an application, he has discovered what Horace's principal subject matter is and how it is presented:

> I confess that I was first impelled by this to consider more attentively the subject; then, pondering the particular matters not only carefully but fastidiously— namely, what he teaches, and in what way, and in what order—with the whole method frequently and thoroughly examined in the fashion of an army most beautifully drawn up in order, it seems to me that I have seen that Horace wanted to explain, in this *Epistle to the Pisos,* the universal nature of the poetic faculty (insofar as the law of metrical expression would permit), which he himself, as an especially great poet and adorned with the greatest learning, held contained within his own mind.[39]

What he discovers is that Horace treats the "universal nature of the poetic faculty" not in terms of the general nature of the art, but in terms of the four main genres: epic, tragic, comic, and satiric. Moreover, since the major problem with respect to any genre is the handling of plot, Colonio sees the largest section of the *Ars poetica* as devoted to this problem. His summary to the first two hundred and fifty lines makes this clear:

> To this point, the principal matters of the method of poetics adopted have been explained: whatever the imitation may be, expressing man's life in invented fables, it has four fixed species of plot, and these are the epic, tragic, comic, and satiric plots. He treated these singly, and first of the constitution of the epic plot, which is the most difficult of all because it is composed of many episodes contrived by the poet's genius. And so he taught, in that plot in which one may most easily fail, that unity of plot, which is common to any plot, is what is to be worked on above all else. . . . Along with the fact that what is required especially in a plot is that it be one, he taught briefly both about its order and its language. . . . Just

---

[39] *Methodus* (1587), p. 2: "Hac me fateor primo compulsum, vt rem attentius considerarem; deinde singulis rebus non diligenter modo, sed fastidiose expendendis, quidnam scilicet, & quomodo, quoque ordine doceret, tota Methodo instar exercitus pulcherrime instructi saepius perlustrata, vidisse mihi videor, Horatium vniuersam vim Poeticae facultatis, quam ipse magnus in primis Poeta, & magnis excultus doctrinis, animo comprehensam tenebat, in hoc libello ad Pisones, quantum lex carminis pateretur, explicare voluisse."

as he did for the epic plot, so he treated with respect to the comic and the tragic in what way they differ in matter, diction, and style.[40]

Consistent with this discovery of the general lines of Horace's development, Colonio gives a detailed interpretation of the first part of the *Ars poetica* as a treatise on epic plot. Lines 1–9 treat of plot and episodes, 9–18 of the objects of epic imitation (with the indication, in 14–18, that digressions are a vice and that when they appear, as in the *Orlando Furioso*, they must be condemned). Line 23 is devoted to epic unity, 24–31 to excessive variety as a source of error, 32–37 to knowledge as the source of epic plot. After pausing, in 38–40, to make the essential division into invention, disposition, and elocution, Horace goes on (in 42–45) to discuss epic disposition and the artificial order and then (in 46–56) its elocution. The relationship to epic plot of epic meter is outlined in 73–82, of epic diction in 83–92; the latter problem involves the principle of decorum, and this is applied to elocution in 93–109, to character in 114–18. Horace then speaks of the epic hero (ll. 119–30), of the distinction between old and new epic plots, of the objects of imitation, and once again of epic order; he concludes with further remarks on the juncture of episodes. "To this point," says Colonio after expounding line 152, "[he has treated] of the whole circle of the epic and of composing, distributing, treating, and writing the epic matter and plot."[41] There then follow, according to Colonio, similar sections—albeit abbreviated—on comedy, on tragedy, and on satire.

Within each of these sections, it is clear that Colonio is thinking largely in terms of invention, disposition, and elocution. The reference is explicit in his remark on lines 38–40: "He makes the transition from invention and from composition of the plot to order and to poetic elocution. What could be more consequent than these things and indicate better that they are propounded in a methodical way?"[42] At lines 55–56 he adds: "This is the first part of the method, common to all those who write of poetic invention, disposition, and elocution."[43] But others of the familiar rhetorical distinctions are also present, sometimes in a striking way. So for the "res-

---

[40] *Ibid.*, pp. 39–40: "Hactenus exposita sunt, quae sunt praecipua susceptae Methodi de Poetica: quae cum sit imitatio, exprimens hominum vitam fictis fabulis, certas habet species fabularum quatuor; & sunt fabula Epica, Tragica, Comica, Satyrica. De singulis tractauit, ac primum de constitutione Epicae fabulae, quę est omnium difficillima, quoniam constat ex multis Episodijs, ingenio poetae excogitatis. Itaque, quod commune est omni fabulae vt sit vna, hoc praecipue elaborandum esse docuit in ea fabula, in qua facilius peccari possit. . . . Cum eo, quod in fabula maxime postulatur vt sit vna, docuit breuiter, & de ordine, & de elocutione. . . . Sicut fecit de fabula Epica, sic tractauit de Comica, & Tragica, quomodo differant materia, oratione, & stylo."

[41] *Ibid.*, p. 31: "Hactenus de orbe Epico & materia fabulaque Epica componenda, distribuenda, tractanda, & scribenda."

[42] *Ibid.*, p. 13: "parit transitum ab inuentione, & compositione fabulae ad ordinem & elocutionem Poeticam: quibus rebus quid potest esse magis consequens, & magis indicare haec methodice tradi?"

[43] *Ibid.*, p. 18: "Haec est Methodi prima pars communis omni Scribenti de Poetica inuentione, dispositione, & elocutione."

verba" distinction. Colonio sees it as equivalent to Aristotle's object and means, as the "quas imitantur" and the "quibus imitantur"; the three kinds of things which poets imitate are expressed in the three kinds of language or style (see p. 21 on ll. 83–85). The close relationship between "verba" and "res" is supplied by Nature herself: "So easily in an abundance of subjects Nature herself, without anybody to lead her, if only she is practiced, will glide into the ornaments of speech; moreover, if there is decency in the things themselves that are written, there emerges from the nature of the things even a certain splendor in the words."[44] He does not fail to use, when he wishes to designate the language or style appropriate to a given matter, the rhetorical term "character."

The early statement of an Aristotelian intention prepares us for the discovery, throughout the treatise, of the same kinds of parallels with the *Poetics* which Colonio's predecessors had used; but he cites them in the moderate way current in this latter part of the century. The list follows:

Horace	Aristotle
1–9	1450a34, 1450a38, 1451a4, 1451b27, 1455b34, 1456a12, 1459b28
9–10	1448a5
23	1451a29
24–31	1459b34
73–74	1448b34
79	1448b31
80–82	1449a22
132	1455b15
134	1451b27
140	1451a22
146	1451a20
189–90	1450b25, 1449b12
193–95	1456a26
202–3	1449b28
241–43	1457b6
275–77	1448b34
278–80	1449a15
338–40	1461b11

Except for repeated praise of Homer and certain details in the histories of the genres, Colonio refers to Aristotle mostly on matters of unity, of plot in its relationship to episodes, and of imitation—rather than verse—as constituting the essence of poetry. These are, as we have seen in earlier commentators, the stock topics on which the Horatians sought the authority of the Aristotelians or of Aristotle himself. They do not show any special command of Aristotle's "method" or any particular penetration into the essence of the *Poetics.*

44 *Ibid.,* p. 48: "Ita facile in rerum abundantia ad orationis ornamenta, sine duce, natura ipsa, si modo est exercitata, labetur. praeterea si est honestas in rebus ipsis, quae scribuntur, existit ex rerum natura quidam etiam splendor in verbis."

Nor are Colonio's claims to having made original discoveries with respect to the "method" of the *Ars poetica* substantiated by his commentary. In reality, all that he does is to declare that Horace treated four poetic genres separately rather than poetry in general, and to find an order in the succession of these four treatments. Otherwise, when talking about individual passages, he gives interpretations very similar to those of his predecessors. His finding of the basic analogies in rhetorical theory and of occasional parallels in Aristotle in no way distinguishes him from the common breed of Horatians.

In the year of these two commentaries on Horace, we find, in this period, the first real effort at practical criticism. It is Giovanni Talentoni's *Lettione sopra'l principio del Canzoniere del Petrarca*, read before the Accademia Fiorentina on September 13, 1587, and published in the same year. Like so many other practical essays of the time, it attempts to apply well-stated theoretical criteria to an individual work and to derive evaluative conclusions. It goes beyond the implications of the short title, for the complete title indicates that it will treat the beginning, narration, and conclusion of all kinds of poems, and it touches upon all these in dealing with Petrarch. This same title demonstrates at once the general approach and the general method: an approach via the traditional parts of an oration, a method of deducing from the practice of the ancients a standard of judgment for moderns. Talentoni's investigation will therefore consist of three steps: (1) a discovery of the principles underlying the use of such parts as prologue, invocation, proposition, narrative, and epilogue; (2) an examination of the treatment of these parts by Greek and Latin poets; and (3) a study of Petrarch's *Canzoniere* to see whether or not it conforms to their usage. Since the parts distinguished are rhetorical parts, Talentoni will naturally think of them in reference to their effects upon a prospective audience. In their prologue, for example, the ancient poets "strove to make the listener favorable, to make him attentive to them and aware, and finally to make him well disposed to understand what they say, in the way taught by the rhetoricians."[45] Book III of Aristotle's *Rhetoric* is cited in support. Epic, tragic, and comic poets used prologues for a slightly different purpose—to give the reader or spectator a foretaste of the plot so that he might anticipate what was coming, whereas philosophers used them to prepare their readers for the instruction that they meant to give. Similar reasons are adduced for the cultivation of such other "preliminary" parts as the invocation and the proposition.

Since Petrarch is a lyric poet, Talentoni must analyze some ancient examples of that genre before determining the correctness of Petrarch's

---

[45] *Lettione* (1587), pp. Av–A2: "s'affaticauano in farsi l'uditor fauoreuole, in farselo attento, & auuertito, e finalmente in farselo ben disposto a comprendere il lor parlare, con quella maniera, che c'insegnano i Retori."

procedures; the cases he chooses are Pindar and Horace. He finds that sometimes Pindar wrote merely a "gay proem," and that this was justified by the "demonstrative kind" in which he was writing; Horace sometimes used invocation, dedication, and proposition, sometimes omitted them. As for Petrarch, he "did not depart from this practice of the lyric poets, . . . since once in his canzoni he also merely proposed the subject . . . ; sometimes, he both proposed and invoked; at other times he did neither the one nor the other."[46] The content and the effect of his beginning (Talentoni is speaking of the first sonnet, "Voi ch'ascoltate . . .") are also acceptable, since through his confession of error and his apology for his varied style, "he makes himself known as a good man of high morals, and thus he makes the reader docile, that is, disposed to understand what is treated later."[47] The whole series of sonnets may be considered as a single narration having the following order of materials: the efficient cause of his love, the final cause, the manner, its state of being, its time, place, and name (p. F3). Its epilogue is found in the canzone "Vergine bella," where he warns us not to follow the example of his life.

In the course of this discussion, Talentoni seeks justification for his remarks (and for Petrarch's poems) in more general principles of the art. The end of poetry, he says, is essentially to profit the audience "by introducing into our souls, as Aristotle taught, good mores and by withdrawing them from bad ones."[48] Plato is the second authority for this end; his banishment of the poets was meant to apply only to those who sought pleasure alone, and he gave highest praise to those who taught good behavior and the proper ways of life. Pleasure, to be sure, is to be sought by the poet, but only as an instrument to the working of utility. On this score, also, Petrarch merits praise, for in his epilogue "he makes clear to us that in his rhymes we should enjoy only the sweetness and take from them that utility which is taken from lyric poems, but that we should beware of attaching ourselves to that life which, as he passed through it, caused him to write them."[49] In fact, the moral lessons taught and the subject matter from which they arise constitute a superiority of Petrarch over his compeers—the superiority of the Christian over pagans. The Italian surpasses all Greek and Latin lyricists in the decency ("onestà") of his words and his actions; he speaks as a Christian poet, avowing his shame and confessing his errors in the most proper terms. It will be noted that

46 *Ibid.,* pp. E–E*v*: "Da questa vsanza de' Lirici non si scostò il Petrarca, come uero Lirico, impercioche alcuna volta anch'egli nelle sue canzoni solamente propose il soggetto. . . . Alcuna volta propose, e inuocò. . . . Alcuna volta ancora non fece ne l'vn ne l'altro."

47 *Ibid.,* p. F*v*: "si da a conoscere per huomo costumato, e buono, e perciò si rende l'auditor docile, cioè, disposto a comprender quel, che poi si tratta."

48 *Ibid.,* p. E4*v*: "l'introdur negli animi nostri, come uolle Aristotile, costumi buoni, e ritrargli da' rei."

49 *Ibid.,* "ci viene a significare, che dobbiamo delle rime sue sol goder la dolcezza, e da quelle prendere quell'vtilità, che si prende dalle poesie liriche: ma che guardiamo di non ci appigliare a quella vita, per la quale camminando egli hebbe a comporle."

this "honesty" is one both of matter (Petrarch's emotions and experiences) and of form (his words); in a larger sense, the latter also refers to prosodic form, the sonnet, the canzone, and so forth.

In connection with the larger genres, such as tragedy, comedy, and the epic, Talentoni raises another general question: to what extent are verisimilitude and credibility observed by the poet? The conditions governing these change with the subject matter. They would be widely different for tragedy and comedy, and thus the latter admits a separate prologue, whereas in the former the prologue (which we should call the "exposition") must be made an integral part of the drama.

Credibility involves a believing audience, and Talentoni points out that three matters are to be considered here. First, even the popular audience of comedy recognizes that the play is an imitation and a representation, and that the actors are not real people. Second, it lends credence more readily to tragedy because the events are known through history or legend, whereas the plots of comedy are made up of whole cloth by the poet. Third, the decorum of each of the genres must be respected. In these latter considerations Talentoni comes very close to the commentators on Horace, and the former ones relate him directly to the purest strain of rhetoricians.

FEDERICO CERUTI (1588)

There is a question as to whether Federico Ceruti's *Paraphrasis in Q. Horatii Flacci librum de arte poetica*, published in 1588, should be called a "major" commentary on the Horatian text. For the volume itself is very slight and follows a plan somewhat different from that of its predecessors, printing the complete text first and then adding the *Paraphrase*, which occupies about twenty pages. Besides, much of the material is, in actuality, no more than paraphrase of the original. Yet if the crucial questions be asked—Is there something here in the way of an original interpretation of Horace? Is there a theory of poetry that goes beyond Horace or at least shows a special orientation?—the affirmative answers indicate that the little work at least merits careful consideration. Ceruti does have a theory of poetry, and if it is not complete, it at least contains fairly substantial ideas on what makes good poetry. These ideas are all related to a conception of the audience as the ignorant populace which must be amused, entertained, kept interested, pleased. Essentially, then, a good poem will cultivate those ornaments and those devices susceptible of appealing to such an audience. First of these will be, in such a genre as the epic, the episodes. Ceruti thinks of the central plot of an epic, provided by history and long familiar to the reader, as of minimum importance:

> The epic material, which is like a subject placed at the disposal of all, can be made the writer's own if the epic poet does not dwell on the exact history of the subject proposed, which has practically no importance in the poem; but, disregarding that historical cycle containing what is true in the plot to be treated, he

will seek grandeur and dignity for the poem in those fictitious things called episodes.[50]

What is really important, then, is the unreal material added to the basic story by way of amplification and decoration; this comes from the poet's inventiveness and is a sign of his genius. But if the episodes constitute the "laus Epicae fabulae" (p. 17), they also introduce the primary danger: for the poet, in his eagerness to provide that delight which episodes afford, may invent too many or ones which are not fitting. The monstrous product results. An ornament of another kind is found in the inverted, unnatural, unhistorical order in which the poet narrates his materials; the "exordium," especially, consisting of something which should be said much later but is transferred to the beginning, gives light and luster to the order (p. 18). Still another ornament is contributed by meter and diction. The criterion for the former is appropriateness to the specific genre for which it is used, and hence to the kind of subject matter typical of the genre; for the latter, the same appropriateness to genre and subject. Both, in fact, are regulated by a special kind of decorum: "Materia igitur queque suo carmine, & proprio cum decoro tractetur" (p. 20). All these ornaments, if re-examined, will be found to distribute themselves among the three parts of composition—plot and episodes under invention, artificial order under disposition, meter and style under elocution. This is intentional with Ceruti, who writes in the margin of his remarks on lines 38 ff., "Inuentio fabulae, Dispositio fabulae, Elocutio fabulae."

A good poem, however, is not one which merely pleases its popular audience; the other end—utility—must be served simultaneously. Ceruti believes that the utilitarian purpose of leading men to virtue will be most directly achieved through the introduction of the right kind of sententiae into the work, ones which are brief enough to be easily learned and long remembered (p. 29). Presumably, some instruction in virtue is also contained in the examples presented by perfect heroes, since the poet "expresses the ideal essence of the perfect man."[51] In some genres, also, utility may derive from the development of the plot itself. This may be the case with Old Comedy, which was written "above all for its usefulness in correcting mores,"[52] although Ceruti does not specifically identify the instrumentality of moral correction. Nor does he indicate with precision whether the primordial qualities of unity, self-consistency, verisimilitude, and credibility, each of which is treated in connection with the usual passage in the *Ars poetica*, are related to either or both of these ends. He seems

[50] *Paraphrasis* (1588), p. 22: "Materies epica, quae quasi res omnium usui exposita est; effici propria scribentis poterit; si Epicus poeta non immorabitur in propria rei propositae historia, quae nullam ferè habet in poemate dignitatem: sed circulo illo historiae, continente quod uerum est tractandae fabulae, tamquàm uili neglecto, in rebus fictis, quae Episodia uocantur, amplitudinem, & poematis dignitatem quaesierit."

[51] *Ibid.,* p. 29: "perfecti hominis ideam exprimere."

[52] *Ibid.,* p. 27: "ad mores emendandos adprime utilem."

rather to accept them as a part of the standard doctrine, without attempting to integrate them with his own notions on good poetry. In the same way he accepts the dogma of the decorum of character and the idea that plot is primary in a work as concepts necessarily present in any Horatian commentary, regardless of their pertinence to the commentator's own philosophy of poetry.

Like Massini's lecture on the madrigal earlier in the same decade, Vicenzo Toralto's *La Veronica, o del sonetto* of 1589 deals with one of the shorter, lyric genres. But Toralto would be the last to admit that he was discussing a minor form; rather, he declares that the sonnet is the most difficult of all forms to write, surpassing even the tragedy. The occasion for his treatise is a sonnet by an academician whose pseudonym was "Il Risvegliato," and he spends a portion of his time (and the whole center section of his work) in interpreting this sonnet and others by the same author. The practical criticism involved, however, is concerned exclusively with expounding the hidden meanings to be found in the sonnets, and the treatise remains interesting only for the theoretical positions which it espouses. The matter of hidden meanings is important for Toralto, since he regards every good sonnet as having two sets of meanings, one for the person addressed (this an easy and superficial one), another for the learned and wise reader (this a secret and recondite one). The necessity of combining the two in a single, brief sonnet constitutes the first and perhaps the major difficulty. The second one consists in the prosodic restrictions: limitation to fourteen lines, to fixed rhyme schemes, and so forth. The third, in the necessity of choosing an "easy" subject, since the aim of poetry is to please and there can be no pleasure in grave matters. Among other criteria for the sonnet, Toralto would include the verisimilitude of language, by which he means language such as the person speaking might use to express the emotion involved. That is, a very sorrowful man should speak only in proper terms, not figurative ones, since the latter would not occur to him in his sorrow; but a "grave" sonnet would require metaphorical language, precisely in order to differentiate it from everyday speech. In fact, most of Toralto's preoccupations seem to be linguistic. When he metes out praise to Petrarch, it is because of his variety, and this is in style: "now he raised his style, then lowered it, now made it sorrowful, then pleasant."[53] Variety as a criterion applies to the total work of a poet, not to an individual sonnet, and Toralto demonstrates its presence in Petrarch by citing selected sonnets, each of which represents a different style. One prosodic matter comes in for special attention, and in a way which illustrates a curious effort to relate versification to states of soul; this is the run-on line, or enjambment:

[53] *La Veronica* (1589), p. 19: "hora egli inalzò, hora abbassò lo stile, hora il fece doloroso, hora piaceuole."

... our nature abhors corruption, and on the contrary loves and desires eternity. Thus when we read a sonnet in which every verse represents for us an end [by being end-stopped], that is, corruption, our intellect suffers; and on the contrary, when we read another which has its verses running on into one another, it takes pleasure, for from them it derives an indefinable promise of eternity.[54]

The difficulties of the tragedy are of other kinds. Mostly they concern the invention of the plot and its disposition; from the extent of the treatment, the former would seem to be by far the more important. Invention is circumscribed by many factors. The plot must be true, and it must therefore be historical in origin; but the history must itself be incomplete so that the poet may be free to add episodes of his own contriving, and this he must do without contradicting the history itself. It is only in this one respect that tragedy might be said to be more difficult than the sonnet. The plot, again, should be "magnificent" and "royal" in its personages, "sorrowful" and "fearful" in its effect—the latter apparently a counterpart of Aristotle's pity and fear. Finally, a tragedy must achieve an impression of extreme gravity, and this too has its difficulties.

Toralto has little to say about more general poetic matters. He uses the term "imitation" only for the imitation of models, sees the use of metaphors and other figures as the feature which distinguishes poetry from prose, and insists upon the necessity of both divine inspiration and acquired knowledge for the poet. In passing, he discusses Tasso's works, finding his sonnets inferior to the *Gerusalemme* since they do not imitate as well; in Tasso's heroic poem, the principal qualities are in the diction used to express the borrowed materials.[55]

Another of the shorter lyric genres, the elegy, is the object of Tommaso Correa's inquiry in his *De elegia* (1590). His approach here, however, is broader and more general than in his earlier treatise on the epigram (1569) and proceeds on a somewhat different basis. Before actually beginning the discussion of the elegy, he indulges in a number of generalizations about poetry, and these concern almost equally the poet, the poem, and the audience. Indeed, there is so free a passage from one to another of these topics that at times it is difficult to discover which is being treated. One might state the nearly circular relationship in this way: The poet seeks admiration and praise. He must have, to obtain them, qualities supplied by both art and nature—genius and judgment, precepts and prudence. These qualities will manifest themselves in the poem, both in its over-all structure and in the details. And the poem, when properly constructed, will produce the proper effect upon its erudite and elite audience, which will accord to the poet its praise and admiration. Since this set of relation-

---

[54] *Ibid.*, p. 23: "la natura nostra abborrisce la corruttione; e per lo contrario ama, e desidera l'eternità; leggendo adunque vn sonetto, ch'in ogni verso ci rappresenti il fine, ciò è la corruttione, l'intelletto nostro patisce, ed all'incontro leggendone vn'altro, c'habbia i versi entranti l'vno nell'altro, gode, perche da quelli si promette non sò che di eternità."

[55] The principal passages in Toralto are to be found on pp. 10–30, 37, and 78.

ships obtains, any aspect of a poem may be discussed in itself or with reference to the poet or the audience. Correa does all three, alternately or simultaneously. The following passage on the good poet may serve as an example:

Since indeed the poet seeks admiration and that praise which derives from admiration itself, he must certainly strive to see to it that his poem is admirable, that the artifice is extraordinary, the composition elegant and praiseworthy; and when the reader examines it, he approves the devices, praises the invention, commends the joining of words and rhythms, extols the wit, whatever features it may set forth; he admires the thoughts, expressed in a proper and harmonious manner, and learns to appreciate fully the greatness and excellence of the artifice.[56]

The audience, in this analysis, is the direct opposite of the ignorant crowd, the "plebecula," the "turba inscia et imperita." It is made up rather of men who would be like the ancients in sound judgment, like the poet himself in knowledge of the art. In fact, the best audience would be composed of poets: "That man cannot judge appropriately nor react properly who does not have genius, art, practice and familiarity in poetry, and who is not himself a good poet."[57]

As for the poem itself, it is to be made according to Horace's prescriptions. The three elements to be successfully combined are "res," "verba," and "numeri," and their correct handling is taught by art: "It teaches what subject matter is appropriate, what words, what rhythms, and it sees what connection of words and rhythms is required."[58] The terms "appropriate" and "connection" give the key to Correa's whole conception of poetry. For on the one hand he insists everywhere on the necessity of decorum—in character, in actions, in words, in rhythms—and on the other hand he emphasizes the importance of conjoining things which are compatible by nature and of achieving by their combination a uniform tone and effect. When, after these preliminary matters, he comes to the elegy, he applies the principles enunciated earlier. In a definition which apes Aristotle he says: "The elegy is an imitation of a lamentable action expressed in verses with unequal rhythmic intervals."[59] But the definition would be incomplete for Aristotle, since only "object" and "means" are touched upon, with no reference to "manner" and no equivalent of the purgation (or "effect") clause. The "lamentable action" is part—but only part—of

---

[56] De elegia (1590), pp. 20-21: "Cum enim poeta admirationem quaerat, & laudem, quae ex ipsa admiratione comparatur; eniti certe debet, vt admirabile sit eius carmen, singulare artificium, laudabilis & ornata coagmentatio; quam cum introspicit lector, probat consilia, laudat inuentionem, commendat connexionem verborum, & numerorum, extollit acumen, quaecumque lineamenta praedicat; sententias apte, & concinne conclusas admiratur, artificij magnitudinem, & praestantiam penitus cognoscit."

[57] Ibid., p. 22: "Iudicare congrue non potest, neque honeste sentire is, in quo non sit ingenium, non ars, non exercitatio poetica, & vsus, non sit bonus ipse poeta."

[58] Ibid., p. 6: "Docet quod argumentum conueniat, quae verba, qui numeri, quae verborum, & numerorum coagmentatio requiratur, videt."

[59] Ibid., p. 25: "Elegia quidem est querebundae actionis imitatio, versibus numerorum disparibus interuallis expressa."

the "res"; it comprises such things as the commiserations of lovers, funeral lamentations, and letters. "Res" includes as well the persons concerned in the actions—with all their characteristics and attributes—and nonpersonal elements such as divine providence and fate; I suspect that it also includes the sententiae or thoughts uttered by the characters. Correct development of these matters demands, on the part of the poet, a knowledge of economics and politics, so that he may distinguish public from private affairs, of the characters to be assigned to various types of persons, and of the activities to be attributed to the various kinds of life, the urbane, the rustic, the military. This is, essentially, a knowledge of divers kinds of decorum. Since the elegy belongs to the "low" or simple style, its diction must be "most tender and delicate"

... so that the reader may take delight and admire, and may judge that the most essential feelings have been set forth, and we may be caught by that bright and pure simplicity. In the words, one must strive for a sure and fit propriety of diction, and the words themselves should be varied and elegant, capable of arousing grave, magnificent, noble, distinguished, new and agreeable feelings, and ones which will flow easily into the souls of the readers.[60]

Verse, for Correa, is an essential accompaniment of all poetry, and in the elegy it is even more necessary than elsewhere; it endows the poem with a special essence, makes it admirable and worthy to be read, gives it honor and the assurance of glory for its author. Rhythm is the soul of poetry (p. 54). Correa summarizes his requirements for all poetry, and for the elegy in particular, with a string of nouns: "Varietas, Perspicuitas, Cultus, Proprietas, Venustas, Numerus"; and his estimate of what the effect of the elegy should be with an even more formidable string of adjectives: "candidam, elegantem, laeuem, aequabilem, tersam, mollem, perspicuam, rectam, plenam, rotundam, dulcem, lepidam, puram, venustam, concinnam, variam, floridam, tenui ... et simplicissimo filo perfectam, ... ingenuam" (pp. 29, 43). Matter, diction, and versification must be so combined as to produce a work answering these requirements. From both sets of terms, it would seem that Correa is really more concerned with the poem itself than with its effect upon an audience or with the faculties of the poet. His approach is Horatian in the broadest sense, with the rhetoricians called upon mostly for their distinction of styles and for their teachings on diction and versification.

RICCOBONI (1591)

In 1591, Antonio Riccoboni published three separate works dealing with the art of poetry; two of them concerned Horace's *Ars poetica.* In the first,

[60] *Ibid.*, pp. 29–30: "vt & oblectetur lector, & admiretur, & simplicissime exposita sensa mentis esse iudicet, atque illa simplicitate candida, & munda capiatur. In verbis spectetur dictionis secura, & legitima proprietas, atque verba ipsa sint varia, & ornata, quae sensus gignant graues, magnificos, nobiles, praeclaros, nouos, suaues, & qui facile influant in animos lectorum."

entitled *Dissensio de epistola Horatii ad Pisones*, Riccoboni takes issue with an anonymous "vir doctus" who had declared that Horace's work displayed a complete confusion of subject matters, with no organization or order. Riccoboni counters with the thesis that although the epistle may not show a clear order (it need not, since the epistolary form permits of passage in a random way from one topic to another), it does have a method and an organization. Its ideas, if rearranged, would compose a complete and thoroughgoing dissertation on the art of poetry. Ideally, Riccoboni believes that such an art should have been organized as follows:

. . . first poetry had to be praised, just as Aristotle praised rhetoric before giving its precepts and as many others have similarly done. And since praise for the poet can derive either from nature or art, or from both, this is the reason why such an inquiry had to be broached; and at the same time those should be reproved who wish to seem to be struck by madness, among whom Horace did not wish to be counted. Next, it must be made clear that the work of the poet and his poetry, or the poem, must be something excellent, and that the poet himself should not excel in one single part of the poem, but in the whole work; and that excellence of this kind in invention, in elocution, and in poetic decorum must be sought from philosophy; moreover, that the Greeks were more capable of achieving excellence in poetic matters than the Romans. Further, the end of the poet had to be revealed, the kinds of poems listed. After having explained these latter in general, following the lead of Aristotle, it was necessary, if not for each and every poetic genre, at least for some of the major ones, to examine carefully now the constituent parts, which are six in number: plot, characters, sententia, diction, melody, spectacle, even though all are not proper to all poetic genres. Next the quantitative parts, which are four in number: prologue, episode, exode, choral song, which similarly are not appropriate to all genres. And just as Aristotle at the end of his book treated of the censures brought against poets and the excuses for them, so at the end it would have been necessary to show which errors of the poets should be pardoned and which not, and in what way a sincere judgment of poetic works should be sought and how the bad poets should be avoided by the wise ones.[61]

61 *Dissensio* (1591), p. D4v: "Etenim primum Poetica erat laudanda, ut ab Arist. laudatur Rhetorica ante praecepta, & similiter fit ab aliis multis: quoniamque laus poetae potest prouenire aut à natura, aut ab arte, aut ab utraque, idcirco talis quaestio erat aperienda: simulque reprehendendi illi, qui uolunt uideri furore perciti, in quorum esse numero Horatius nolebat. Deinde ostendendum, poetae opus, & poesim, seu poema rem quandam excellentem esse oportere: ipsumque poetam non in una parte poematis, sed in toto opere excellere debere: atque huiusmodi excellentiam in inuentione, in elocutione, in decoro poetico à philosophia petendam esse: in re autem poetica magis Graecos, quam Romanos excellere potuisse. praeterea erat aperiendus finis poetae: enumerandaque poematum genera. Quibus uniuerse explicatis ad imitationem Aristotelis, si non in singulis poematum generibus, at certe in praecipuis quibusdam oportebat perpendere tum partes conformantes, quae sunt sex, fabula, mores, sententia, dictio, melopoeia, apparatus, quamuis non omnes omnibus conuenientes: tum partes quantitatis, quae sunt quattuor, prologus, episodium, exodus, choricum, non omnibus itidem congruentes; & quemadmodum in fine libri sui Arist. egit de reprehensioni-bus, & excusationibus poetarum, sic denique ostendendum erat, quibus poetarum erroribus esset ignoscendum, & quibus non ignoscendum, ac quomodo de poematibus syncerum iudicium sit requirendum, malique poetae à prudentibus fugiantur."

This program for an art of poetry in part follows Aristotle's order in the *Poetics*, in part adds sections from other works and from the popular defences of poetry.

Riccoboni then proceeds to cut the Horatian text into small pieces and to rearrange the pieces according to the topics outlined in the above plan. For each topic, he indicates parallels with Aristotle wherever warranted. By the time he finishes, every line of the Horatian epistle has been accounted for, and the parallelism with Aristotle is complete. Since this rearrangement itself constitutes a valuable interpretation, I give it below in brief outline form:

		Horace	*Aristotle*
I.	The praise of poetry	391–418	1455*a*33, 1448*b*4,
	art and nature	295–308	1451*a*22
	divinity of poet		
	natural causes		
II.	The necessity of excellence	361–385	1456*a*3, 1456*a*9,
	moral philosophy	32–41	1454*b*8
		309–332	
		285–294	
III.	The ends of poetry	333–334	1448*a*25
	"delectare" primarily	341–346	
	"prodesse" accidentally	73–85	
	the genres		
IV.	The plot in various genres	275–280	
		220–233	
		281–284	
	Aristotle's requirements for plot:		
	(1) order	42–45	
	(2) magnitude	146–152	
	(3) unity	1–13	[General]
	(4) possible	338–340	1460*a*26
		128–135	
	(5) not episodic	14–23	
	(6) admirable, marvelous	136–145	
	(7) simple or complex	[none]	1452*a*12
			1452*b*30
	(8) pathetic	[none]	
V.	Character	119–127	1453*b*22
		114–118	
		153–178	
VI.	Sententia	333–337	1456*a*34
		96–113	

		Horace	Aristotle
VII.	Diction	86–95	
		270–274	
		234–250	
		251–269	
		24–31	
		46–72	
VIII.	Melody	202–219	
IX.	Spectacle	179–188	
X.	Quantitative parts	189–201	1452b19
XI.	Errors of the poets	347–360	[1460b6]
		386–390	
		419–476	

Aside from the mechanical redistribution of segments, Riccoboni has little of interest to offer on the *Ars poetica*. In a preliminary section on epic poetry, he controverts Aristotle's assertion that tragedy is superior to the epic, maintaining instead that since the epic plot is longer and more difficult, it may be considered preferable (p. D2). His insistence that the primary end of poetry is to give pleasure is exceptional, especially in this last decade of the century. So, too, is his wish to find in Aristotle a basis for the organization of ideas about poetry, rather than merely a set of isolated parallels with Horace—a wish infrequently entertained or exploited by the Horatian critics.

Riccoboni's second work of 1591, published three months later in July, is a reply to Nicola Colonio's *Methodus de Arte poetica* (1587); he had either come to know it only after publishing the first or preferred to withhold his rebuttal of Colonio until after he had stated his own position. In his *Defensor seu pro eius opinione de Horatij epistola ad Pisones*, he discusses with Colonio, in dialogue form, the question of the order of the *Ars poetica*. The dialogue does little more than reiterate the positions of the *Dissensio* in a brief and general way. Riccoboni states his stand thus at the beginning of the dialogue:

I have demonstrated that from him [Horace], as from the inexhaustible fountainhead of all doctrine, one may draw if not all the things that pertain to poetry, at least many, which are transmitted in a methodical fashion. . . . I say that not everything is contained in the *Epistle to the Pisos* part for part, but that everything is present there in a general sense, so that it seems that Horace in some way touched upon everything that Aristotle treated.[62]

Colonio's contention that Horace had not treated of plot in general, but

---

62 *Defensor* (1591), pp. 11–12: "ostendi ex eo, tamquam ex uberrimo omnis doctrinae fonte, si non omnia, quae attinent ad Poeticam, ac certe multa, quae Methodice traduntur, hauriri posse. . . . dico non omnia quidem comprehendi in Epistola ad Pisones secundum partem, sed omnia contineri vniuersè, ut omnia quaecunque egerit Aristoteles, quodammodo attigisse Horatius videatur."

only of the plot in specific genres, leads to a long argument over plots and episodes and their interrelationship, in which the opinions of Castelvetro are cited. A long section near the end of the *Defensor* is devoted to an interpretation of line 128, "Difficile est proprie communia dicere," and Riccoboni recommends that the poet should not only prefer materials already exploited by others, but that he should treat them in such a way that their universal applications—in causes, in effects, in modalities of action—will be manifest. By so doing, he will give the greatest possible pleasure to the audience (pp. 31–32).

Five short treatises on literary problems by Giulio Cortese, a Neapolitan poet and academician, were published in 1591 and 1592; they are now usually found with the 1588 or 1592 editions of his *Rime.* Two of them, the *Regole per fuggire i vitii dell'elocutione* (1592) and the *Regole per formare epitafii* (1591), are exclusively rhetorical in content. But the other three, *Avertimenti nel poetare, Dell'imitatione e dell'inventione,* and *Delle figure* (all of 1591), contain theories of poetry and advice for their application to the practice of the art. The *Avertimenti nel poetare* is, in its own way, a very significant document. For it affords us our first encounter, in the present tradition, with a theory of the literary conceit and with the notions of Marinism, gongorism, and euphuism which were to be so prominent in these last years of the century. Cortese distinguishes three elements as important in any kind of poetry, the "concetto," the words, and the sounds. The first of these is defined as "that meditation which the spirit makes upon some object offered to it, of what it means to write about."[63] "Concetto" is thus different from "subject"; the subject is the general material chosen for treatment—arms, love, beauty, madness—whereas the "concetto" is a development of some particular aspect of this subject, through meditation or cogitation, in such a way as to permit expression in words. So considered, the conceit is the soul of poetry. In fact, certain verse genres which do not contain conceits, such as narratives of events, should not be called poetry at all, but rather historical or "casual" verse. Even some lyrics are to be denied the title, such as Petrarch's second and third sonnets, which do not engender any conceit in the mind (p. 2). Basically, the materials for conceits are furnished by the sciences, and hence the poet must be erudite in order to enrich and embellish his poetry. But two dangers attend him here: that of making his conceit too obscure to be understood by the reader (Giulio Camillo's cabalistic poems would be examples of such obscurity), and that of presenting scientific materials in bare, proper terms. Rather, "the conceit will be so drawn from the sciences as not to obfuscate or confuse the eye of the soul, but to instruct and illuminate it, so that the reader will know what it said and not have to guess at what it was trying

63 *Avertimenti* (1591), p. 1: "quella meditatione che lo spirito fa sopra alcuno obietto che se gli offerisce di quello, c'ha da scriuere."

to say."[64] The principle for the other two elements is a simple one. The words must be appropriate to the conceit and the sounds to both. The poet must take particular care to see that the words are adapted to the style in which he is writing and that the sounds are at once fitting to the thought and harmonious among themselves.

In the second treatise, *Dell'imitatione e dell'inventione*, the conceit comes to be, by implication at least, synonymous with imitation. Cortese distinguishes in general two ways of writing, by words which signify directly the intended meaning and by phrases or paraphrases which describe, instead, the action. The first of these he calls simple narràtion (note the parallelism with the distinction concerning "concetti") and the second, imitation. It is imitation in the sense that the description of an action follows, somehow, the procedure of nature herself in establishing the law governing the action. Simple narration may be used to signify an action which is not immediate to the end of the poet; imitation will be used for one which is proximate to that end. Invention, also, has two meanings, since it refers on the one hand to the discovery of new things, new ways, new usages, on the other hand to the production of artificial things in semblance of natural things. In the latter category Cortese places all epic and dramatic plots (which resemble history), all lyric discoursings, with respect not only to the subject matter but also to such ornaments as episodes and epithets. "For," he says, "to invest a substance with a new accident congruous with it, containing a reason or a cause or an explanation, will constitute a very noble invention, and herein reside the riches of poetic compositions."[65]

The very brief *Delle figure*, in addition to a high-flown theory of figures and rules for their use, makes some statements about the reasons for the invention and use of these same figures. Cortese believes that they were invented out of necessity and to give pleasure, the necessity being to make certain ideas understandable, the pleasure being that which the human spirit customarily derives from literary works. In all three treatises, what is notable is a philosophy of linguistics that goes far beyond the usual theories of the styles or of diction, a theory of the conceit, which attempts to distinguish it from its materials in nature, and in general a curious wrestling with the problem of the difference between objects in nature and those same objects as the substance of literary expression.

Some time after 1592, Cesare Crispolti delivered to the Accademia Insensata of Perugia his *Lettione del sonetto*, now found in manuscript in the Biblioteca Comunale of that city. His lecture is a kind of amalgam of materials earlier developed by others. He derives his definition of the

---

[64] *Ibid.*, p. 7: "Sarà dunque il concetto tirato dalle scienze tale che non offuschi, ò ingarbugli l'occhio dell'anima; ma che l'erudisca, & l'illumini, accioche il lettore conosca quello, c'habbia detto, & non quello c'habbia uoluto dire."

[65] *Dell'imitatione* (1591), p. 5: "poiche uestire una sostanza di accidente nuouo congruente, che contenga ragione, ò cagione, ò esplicatione, sarà assai nobile inuentione, & quì stanno le ricchezze delle poesie."

sonnet from Minturno's *Arte poetica Thoscana*, his ideas on its style from Bernardino Tomitano, general notions on the fitting of style to matter from Aristotle's *Rhetoric*, Bembo's *Prose*, and Patrizi's *Retorica*. He also considers and rejects Dante's classification of lyric poetry under the low style, maintaining that a sonnet on a grave matter would demand the grave style. The sonnet, for Crispolti, is the most beautiful and the most difficult of the Tuscan poetic genres; its difficulty results primarily from its small size, in which—as in a small painting—every slightest defect can be seen. In long poems the situation is otherwise:

> In long compositions the poets, no matter how mediocre they may be, usually put many things which, with their beauty and their grace, compensate for other things which are less beautiful and less grave. In this composition, if the thought is happily developed, it moves, arouses, and ravishes the reader as if with a secret miracle. If other compositions must have many parts, this one seeks clarity of style and to join together gravity and pleasantness of diction.[66]

This description of the effect upon the reader has Longinian overtones. The sonnet differs from the epigram in the general tone achieved, and from the canzone in the absence of digressions and ornaments which give to the latter an epic majesty. It shares the subject matter of the other lyric genres —gods, heroes, and loves—and has the same ends as the canzone: to narrate, to pray, to comfort, to praise, and to blame. For all matters, internal construction as well as external effects, Petrarch is to be taken as the model, for his usage is everywhere marvelous. Crispolti's approach is thus essentially traditional. He thinks of the sonnet in terms of subject matter and the styles, of prosodic form and the ends with respect to the reader, of diction and sounds. His solutions for many of these problems come from the rhetoricians.

For Frederico Ceruti, the problem of the available sources is again an important one in his *Dialogus de comoedia* (1593). Since Horace had had little to say specifically about comedy and since Aristotle gave only suggestions, Ceruti was obliged to turn to the perennial source of information on the genre, Donatus. From him he borrowed a definition and the distinction of narrative, dramatic, and mixed manners. His use of Aristotle, however, is of some interest. From him, Ceruti takes the division of qualitative and quantitative parts, and although he desists from a full treatment of the former, he does point out that not only is the poet concerned with supplying them to the poem, but also the actor, the musician, and the architect. Aristotle also furnishes a model for Ceruti's description of the comic protagonist and the comic action: "It [the plot] will then imitate

---

[66] MS Bibl. Com. Perugia 1058 (N. 10), fol. 64v: "Ne i longhi componimenti i Poeti, per mezzani che siano, sogliono porre molte cose, che con la uaghezza, e gratia loro, l'altre men belle, e graui ricompensano. In questo se il concetto è felicemente spiegato, muoue, risueglia, e rapisce altrui, quasi con occulto miracolo. Se gl'altri componimenti deuono molte parti hauere. Questo ricerca la chiarezza dello stile, e che siano insieme accoppiate la grauità, e la piaccuolezza del dire."

only a single action, very agreeable in tone, suitably amusing, concerning private citizens who are neither entirely good nor entirely bad, but who through some imprudence or error (such as happen to men in private life) not unproductive of laughter, pass from a troublesome situation into one where they achieve happiness."[67] Other passages, such as a hint on the nature of the ridiculous (p. 27) and a reference to the dance as a form of imitation (p. 33), may also be traced to Aristotle. For the rest, such recent writers as Pontano, Maggi, and Riccoboni are called upon to authorize and illustrate an essentially rhetorical point of view. The tastes and the pleasure of the audience and the effect which the comedy will have upon it are paramount for Ceruti. He states as the end "to profit through delight and laughter" (p. 15) and sees comedy as a great school for providing examples of ways of life to be followed or to be eschewed. With those who hold that comedy might exert a corrupting influence on the young he disagrees heartily, especially since he sees in his century actors capable of expurgating obscene passages and of pointing up the moral. Many structural features of comedy are determined by the audience. The prologue, peculiar to comedy, exists as a means of obtaining the attention and the good will of the spectators; yet it must not reveal the denouement lest it spoil the suspense. The handling of all aspects of the plot must make it seem credible, even though the audience knows that it has been invented by the poet. Comedies are divided into acts to help the playgoer's memory and to provide intervening periods of relaxation, and the five-act length seems to be naturally adapted to the faculties and the capabilities of the audience. Songs and dances are provided in the *entr'actes* so that no spectator, even the most ignorant who would not understand the goings-on on the stage, will be deprived of some form of entertainment during the performance.

In 1597, Giovanni Talentoni attempted to solve a problem that had long been puzzling his predecessors in the field of poetic theory. Many of them had indicated the marvelous as one of the effects to be produced by the art in general and by the epic in particular and had spoken of the "admiration" which the poem must arouse in its audience. Talentoni's *Discorso sopra la maraviglia*, delivered as a lecture before the Accademia degli Inquieti of Milan, inquired into the nature of the marvelous and the conditions for achieving it; its point of departure was the passage at the beginning of Canto IV of the *Purgatorio*. The approach is only incidentally Horatian; but insofar as it seeks to analyze the effect as one of the passions of the soul, it belongs to the rhetorical tradition so constantly present in the Cinquecento. After an initial statement that the end of poetry is "by

---

[67] In *Dialogi duo* (1593), pp. 24–25: "imitabiturque duntaxat actionem vnam, perplacidam, & risu dignam hominum priuatorum, eorumdemque nec prorsus bonorum, nec prorsus malorum; sed eorum, qui imprudentia aliqua & errore (vt hominibus priuatis solet accidere) non sine risu ex molestia aliqua foelicem statum consequuntur."

means of pleasure to attract men and to lead them into ways of good living" and that the poets do this (according to Strabo) solely by the use of the marvelous,[68] Talentoni indicates that his treatment of the subject will have three parts,

... in the first of which we shall show that admiration is a passion, and to what kind of passion and appetite it should be reduced; in the second, coming much closer to its nature, we shall discover its form, and the subject and the cause from which it springs, and from these things we shall assemble its definition; we shall show that the species into which it is divided are five, and on the occasion of the third we shall treat of laughter and of ridiculous things. Since we shall classify astonishment under some of these species, we shall also speak of it. Having sufficiently explained in this way in the aforesaid two parts its nature and its essence, in the third we shall come to speak of the effects which it produces in those who receive it ..., and finally to inquire into its qualities, that is, whether it be a good or a bad thing.[69]

After having established in the first part that admiration is a passion which, like others, dominates and tyrannizes the soul, Talentoni examines its causes, finding that it springs basically from the unexpected, the unknown, from whatever the patient is ignorant of. In tragedy and comedy, its sources include peripeteia, but exclude accidental events for which no cause may be discovered by the reader or the spectator. The four kinds of the marvelous are related to the four kinds of objects producing it: (1) the inanimate, (2) the animate but nonrational, (3) the animate and rational operating through chance, and (4) the animate and rational operating with intent. As for the effects, Talentoni sees some of them as physiological, especially a kind of helpless amazement in which the functions of both soul and body are arrested. It is important to note for poetics that this sensation is accompanied by pleasure and that hence the poem is capable of effecting its final goal of moral admonition.

One of the few exercises in practical criticism performed by this "last generation" of Horatian critics was Pietro Cresci's *Discorso sopra un Sonetto in lode del celebre luogo di Valchiusa* (1599), delivered to the Accademia degli Uranici in Venice. The sonnet in question was by Marco Cavallo. After preliminary remarks in praise of the sonnet as a genre, emphasizing the perfection achieved in so brief a form, Cresci proceeds to

---

[68] *Discorso* (1597), p. 5: "col piacer allettar gli huomini, e tirargli al ben viuere, nelle fauole sue."

[69] *Ibid.,* p. 6: "nella prima delle quali mostreremo, che la marauiglia è affetto, & à quale specie d'affetto, e d'appetito si debba ridurre: nella seconda, accostandoci molto più alla natura sua, scuopriremo la forma sua, il soggetto, e la cagione, ond'ella nasce, e da queste cose raccoglieremo la sua diffinitione; mostreremo, che le sue specie, nelle quali ella si diuide son cinque, e per cagion della terza tratteremo del riso, e delle cose ridicolose. Ad alcune di quelle, perche ridurremo lo stupore, di lui parimente fauelleremo. Spiegata à bastanza in questa guisa nelle dette due parti la natura, & essenza sua, verremo nella terza à parlar de gli effetti, ch'ella produce in quei, che la riceuono ....; e finalmente à ricercar le sue qualitadi, cioè, s'ella sia cosa buona, ò ria."

a full analysis of Cavallo's sonnet. He does so by discussing in order its invention, its disposition, and its elocution. What he means by these is made clear by his essential statements under each heading. Under invention:

. . . invention, which is nothing other than an imagination of things which are either true or verisimilar, or we might say possible, and which is the main pillar of the great structure of imitation, the base and foundation of the whole poetic art since it is concerned with those same three objects upon which imitation, as if upon its proper seat, rests—that is, imitating nature, or art, or fortune.

Under disposition:

[The author of the sonnet] has, then, so well disposed all things, appropriately placed the words, used the attributes at the right time, developed the thoughts in a beautiful order, scattered the ornaments and the figures with moderation, and has so well observed variety and decorum (essential parts of disposition) that he has certainly achieved its designated end of giving pleasure and of renewing in the minds of the listeners and of the readers the graceful memories of those delightful places.

Under elocution:

And he has similarly succeeded with much felicity in elocution, having judiciously chosen words which are sonorous, grave, clear, proper, circumscribed, and figurative . . . and he has at the same time elegantly filled the whole sonnet with gravity, with clarity, with purity, and with sweetness.[70]

The total critique of the sonnet revolves about these three topics. It is interesting to note, by way of general commentary on the procedure, that the same set of statements might have been made about almost any other work; only the examples or the citations would need to be changed, the judgments would remain the same. This is a characteristic feature of the rhetorical method of analysis in the sixteenth century.

RICCOBONI (1599)

Antonio Riccoboni, who had figured so prominently as an expositor of Horace in the early years of the decade, appears again at its very end with his *De Poetica Aristoteles cum Horatio collatus* of 1599; the work may,

---

70 *Discorso* (1599), pp. B5–B5v: "l'inuentione, la quale altro non è, ch'vna imaginatione di cose, ò vere, ò verisimili, ò vogliam dir possibili, & ch'è colonna principale della gran machina dell'immitatione, base, e fondamento di tutta l'arte Poetica; versando ella intorno quei tre oggetti medesimi, sopra i quali l'immitatione, come in suoi proprij seggi si riposa, cioè, ò Natura, ò Arte, ò Caso immitando. . . . Ha poi cosi ben disposto le cose, collocato conueneuolmente le parole, vsato à tempo gli attributi, disteso con bell'ordine i concetti, sparso con misura gli ornamenti, e le figure, & hà cosi ben seruata la variatione, & il decoro, parti essenziali della dispositione, che certamente n'hà conseguito il dissegnato fine di dilettare, & di rinouellar ne gli animi de gli vditori, ò de' lettori la gratiosa memoria di quei diletteuoli luoghi. . . . Et è con molta felicità parimente riuscito nell'elocutione, hauendo giuditiosamente scelto voci sonore, graui, chiare, proprie, circonscritte, e traslate . . . e hà insieme di grauità, di chiarezza, di purità, e di dolcezza tutto il Sonetto elegantemente ripieno."

indeed, be contemporary with the ones already discussed.[71] In these, Riccoboni had suggested the possibility of reordering the *Ars poetica* according to a more scientific arrangement. In the new work he does just that. Under a number of section headings, which are those of the major divisions of the poetic art, he first places prose passages which are presumably summations of Aristotle's positions, then he quotes *in extenso* the passages from Horace which he deems pertinent. Once again, the whole of the Horatian text passes into the rearrangement. The kind of order which Riccoboni proposes for a scientific treatise on the art of poetry is perhaps of greater significance than the parallelisms between Aristotle and Horace, most of which were by this time completely conventional. I give below the section headings in Latin, a summation of the "Aristotelian" doctrine stated in the prose passages, and the numbers of the lines quoted from the *Ars poetica:*

	Horace
De Natura Poesis	
Poetry as imitation; object, manner, and means. The poet must excel in all parts of the poem.	361–85
Poetry and history, the universal and the particular; imitation through embellishment.	309–32
Ends: profit and pleasure; purgation of pity and fear as the proper pleasure of tragedy.	333–34, 341–46
De Caussis Poesia	
Divine cause: the divine furor.	391–407
Human cause: art and nature.	408–18, 295–308
Natural cause: imitation and harmony. Historical origins and development of tragedy and comedy	275–80, 220–33
Origins of comedy.	281–94
De Generibus Imitationum, & Poesium	
The arts as imitations; definitions of epic, tragedy, comedy.	73–85
De Partibus Qualitatis	
De Fabula. Eight requirements for plot:	
(1) completeness	32–45
(2) magnitude	146–52
(3) unity	1–13
(4) possible (necessity, verisimilitude)	338–40
(5) non-episodic	14–23
(6) marvelous	136–45
(7) simple, complex	[none]
(8) pathetic	[none]
De fabulis non immutandis, aut conuenienter fingendis.	
Traditional plots.	119–35

[71] R. C. Williams, "Italian Critical Treatises of the Sixteenth Century," *Modern Language Notes,* **XXXV** (1920), 506–7, lists a *Praecepta Aristotelis cum praeceptis Horatii collata* under the date of 1592, but I have been unable to find a copy of this work.

De Partibus Qualitatis	Horace
De Moribus. Characters for the main genres; decorum.	114–18, 153–78
De Sententia. Cf. the Rhetoric. The parts of thought. Persuasion.	335–37, 96–113
De Dictione. Kinds of words; two qualities of style; words for each genre.	24–31, 46–72, 86–95, 234–74
De Melopoeia.	202–19
De Apparatu. Not part of the poetic art. Effect from plot, not apparatus.	178–88
De Partibus Quantitatis	
Of tragedy, comedy, epic	189–201
De reprehensionibus, & excusationibus poetarum	
Five sources of blame, three types of excuse.	346–60, 386–90, 419–76

Elements of theory contained in Riccoboni's prose passages are more specifically pertinent to Aristotle than to Horace, and they will be treated subsequently in the appropriate chapter.

In the same year, perhaps even as early as 1598, Camillo Pellegrino wrote his treatise *Del concetto poetico*, returning thus to a subject which had been treated only recently by Giulio Cortese. The latter's discussion, however, seems more philosophical and more sophisticated, even though one of the interlocutors in Pellegrino's dialogue is Giambattista Marino. Pellegrino begins with a conventional position, the distinction of the three styles, which he equates at various places with Hermogenes' Ideas; the different styles are appropriate to different poetic genres. Differences in style, he says, depend upon "subject matter, conceits, words, the disposition of the latter and the colors of the figures."[72] Since this might sound like a description of diction, he finds himself obliged first to define style ("a quality which results from the putting together of the words and the thoughts"[73]) and to distinguish between diction and style: "the former is nothing but the choice and the placing of the words which are images of the thoughts, the latter is a quality which results from the combination of the words and the thoughts."[74] Taken in its broadest sense of "thought," "concetto" is synonymous with "senso, sentimento, sentenza"; it may be defined as "a thought formed by the intellect as an image or resemblance of a real thing, signified by these latter."[75] The specifically poetic "con-

72 In Borzelli, *Il Cavalier Giovanbattista Marino* (Naples, 1898), p. 328: "si cagiona dalla materia, da' concetti, dalle voci, dalla disposizione di quelle e da' colori delle figure."

73 *Ibid.*, p. 328: "una qualità che risalta dalla composizione delle voci e dai concetti."

74 *Ibid.*, p. 329: "quella altro non è che scelta e collocazione delle voci, che sono immagini de' Concetti, e questa è una qualità, che risulta dal Composto delle voci e dai concetti insieme."

75 *Ibid.*, p. 331: "un pensamento formato dall'Intelletto imagine e somiglianza di cosa reale, intesa da quelle."

cetto" is defined in significantly altered terms: "a thought of the intellect, an image or resemblance of true things and of things which resemble the truth, formed in the fantasy."[76]

The poetic "concetto" is defined in this way in order to include the peculiar characteristics of the art. The image produced may be of veri-similar things, since verisimilitude is the proper field of operation of the poet, as compared with the orator, whose province is the true. Besides, the fantasy rather than the intellect is the productive faculty since the poet wishes to give pleasure, not to persuade, and the same imaginative powers involved in the invention of plot are concerned with the formation of "concetti." Indeed, there is a kind of analogy between plot-making and "concetto"-making: just as in tragedy, comedy, and the epic the digressions must bear a necessary and probable relationship to the plot, so in the lyric (which is its preferred genre) the "concetto" must have its roots in the main argument of the poem. This same imagination differentiates the conceit of poetry from that of prose: "Prose in expressing conceits uses pure forms of expression, proper words, and when it uses metaphors and figurative language it uses them rarely and with moderation; whereas verse, with greater liberty and sometimes with excessive boldness expresses its conceits with figures and metaphors distant from literal meanings."[77] The faculty of inventing such conceits springs from nature rather than from art (which is at the basis of ordinary diction) and in this respect is superior to the talent for prose; and (to continue the same analogy) nature is responsible also for the invention which makes plots. Thus Pellegrino is able to say, adapting Aristotle's dictum, that the "concetti" "are the soul and the form of a composition."[78]

We have seen, earlier, Pellegrino's statement that the end of poetry is to give pleasure. This he reiterates at various points; but he does not fail to make a concession which was current in these last years of the century: "considered in itself as an imitation and as a maker of images, poetry has no other end than delight; but as qualified by the civil faculty it will have besides as its end utility and profit, which in any case must make itself felt through the intermediary of the pleasure."[79] The immediate end of pleasure is best served by the diction and the "concetti," which, in a poem, depict the object or the action as if it were before our eyes. In a practical way,

[76] *Ibid.*, p. 332: "un pensamento dell'Intelletto, imagine e simiglianza di cose vere e di cose simili al vero formato nella fantasia."

[77] *Ibid.*, p. 336: "la prosa nello esprimer de' concetti usa modi di dir puri, voci proprie ed usando le metafore, ed i traslati il fa con riguardo e di rado, la dove il verso con più libertà ed alle volte con troppo ardire spiega i suoi concetti con traslati e metafore lontane dal proprio."

[78] *Ibid.*, p. 340: "sono anima e forma di un componimento."

[79] *Ibid.*, p. 340: "la Poesia considerata per se stessa, come Imitazione e facitrice degli Idoli non abbia altro fine che il diletto, ma qualificata dalla Civile facoltà avrà eziandio per suo fine l'utile e il giovamento, il quale in ogni modo converrà che si senta per mezzo del diletto."

these "concetti" seem to be no more than figures of speech; in a series of examples taken from Petrarch, Pellegrino points out how they belong to the general argument of the sonnet, how appropriate they are and how in keeping with decorum, how they correspond to the various Ideas of Hermogenes, and to what extent they contribute beautiful and splendid ornamentation to the poem.

The concluding year of the century presents two works pertinent to the Horation tradition, one of them on a general topic and the other more specific, and both of them by the same writer, Paolo Beni. The first, his *De humanitatis studiis oratio*, is concerned with the broad problem of literary studies and only incidentally discusses the work and the role of the poet. In addition to a conventional praise of the art, he indicates that its usefulness resides in the various precepts and meanings hidden under the fictional veil. But he says nothing about the nature of these precepts or about how the fiction containing them is to be constructed. For Beni, the greatest problem for the poet seems to be that of style—how to provide the just measure of ornamentation so that the style is neither unadorned nor overwrought. Three arts—of rhetoric, of history, of poetry—are involved here, and the poet must see to it that he cultivates his own proper style and not those of the other two:

> Since indeed many things must frequently be taken over into poetry from history and oratory, and not a few in fact from poetry into oratory, it is certainly difficult to retain a just measure in all of them without the utmost degree of care and vigilance, so that the poem does not reproduce the popular exuberance of the orators or the restraint of history, and the speech will not be colored at times excessively by the stylistic colors and pigments of the poets.[80]

The less general treatise is Beni's *Disputatio in qua ostenditur praestare comoediam atque tragoediam metrorum vinculis soluere*, also of 1600, one of the principal documents in the quarrel over verse which achieved such prominence in the last years of the century. Beni's contention is that prose is better than verse for the dramatic genres, and in order to sustain it he develops a fully realized theory of poetry. This theory, in its broadest aspects, is Horatian to the extent that it insists upon pleasure and utility as the ends of poetry, that it places the audience in a determining position with respect to works of art, and that it establishes a central principle of decorum.

Of the two Horatian ends, Beni declares that the really important one is utility, and he sees utility as consisting of moral instruction. The statements are unequivocal. "The function of the poets is to prescribe for man certain

[80] *Oratio* (1600), p. 5: "Cum enim multa saepè ad Poesim ex historia & eloquentia, ad eloquentiam verò ex Poesi non pauca sint referenda; difficile profectò est sine summa quadam industria & vigilantia modum seruare in omnibus, ita ut nec popularem Oratorum vbertatem, siue etiam historiae verecundiam, referat poema, nec Poetarum coloribus ac pigmentis nimis interdum coloretur oratio."

ideal forms and models in relation to the variety of life itself and in a sense place them before his eyes, from which he may regulate his behavior and arrange his life."[81] Or again: "In fact, this is the end proposed by tragedy and comedy, that the spectators may leave them more circumspect, and, learning thoroughly the duties of life, may order their own conduct and may be capable of rendering themselves useful to themselves, to their friends, and finally to the whole country."[82] To such instruction, pleasure serves only as an instrument, the honeyed glass with which the skilful physician makes the bitter potion palatable (p. 4v). In order that the end of moral instruction may be achieved, the poem must possess certain qualities. Above all, it must be completely clear, credible, and verisimilar, and it must observe the laws of decorum; if it does not, the audience will not believe, and where there is no belief there can be no persuasion to emulation or to avoidance of the actions presented. On the side of pleasure, the poet must make sure that attractiveness of the pleasurable aspects of his poem does not grow to such an extent as to constitute an end in itself, to overshadow the utility or even to create an opposite effect. The question of credibility and verisimilitude is related, for Beni, to the peculiar nature of poems as imitations of human actions. This he takes in its narrowest sense of a direct and unaltered representation of life as it really is. For example, since people naturally speak in prose, a poet who made them speak in verse would be departing from nature: "These, therefore, do not follow nature as a guide, they do not observe the law of decorum and of verisimilitude; but they depart from nature and disturb both decorum and verisimilitude."[83] The close relationship of nature (or external reality), decorum (or internal features of the poem), and verisimilitude (which results from a comparison of the poem to nature), is significant.

It is in the light of both ends, utility and pleasure, that Beni makes his case against the use of verse in tragedy and in comedy. We have already seen the essential argument on the score of utility: if verse is unnatural to people speaking among themselves, then the audience hearing them so converse will deny credence to the drama in which they appear. Moreover, the use of verse will so obscure the meaning that the proper lessons will not readily be learned: "since verse may be very difficult to understand, both in itself and because of its unfamiliarity, the result is of course that the audience not only does not take in the total structure and composition of the plot, or even its fictitious characters or the reversal, but it does not even

81 *Disputatio* (1600), p. 1v: "Poetarum munus est homini pro vitae varietate certas quasdam Ideas ac formas praescribere, & tanquam ante oculos ponere, vnde & mores componere possit & vitam instituere."

82 *Ibid.*, p. 3v: "Finis enim Tragoediae Comoediaeque propositus ille est, ut Auditores inde euadant cautiores, ac vitae officia perdiscentes, componant mores, ac sibi, amicis, Patriae denique vniuersae prodesse valeant."

83 *Ibid.*, p. 2v: "non Naturam Ducem sequantur isti: non decorum ac verisimile tueantur: sed a Natura discedant: decorum perturbent ac verisimile."

understand the thought and the diction."[84] On the score of pleasure, verse is undesirable in two ways: it dispels all thought of utility, swaying its ignorant audience through the constant use of rhythm and song; and it so softens the souls of the audience that they become immoral and effeminate. In these ideas, Beni comes very close to Plato in certain passages of the *Republic*, which indeed he cites. The whole condemnation of verse with respect to the ends of poetry is related to a conception of the audience as ignorant, weak, and uncouth—the audience of the vulgar crowd in the pit.

If Beni is willing to admit verse in the nondramatic genres, it is precisely because he conceives of them as addressed to a different audience. The epic poet, he says, writes essentially for himself and the Muses, or "for those who have been exceptionally well educated in the liberal arts" (p. 11*v*). For such as these, the verse is not only a source of a refined enjoyment, but it also helps the reader remember the poem. The case of the lyric is similar. Composed not for the crowd or tumultuous performance, but resulting rather from careful meditation, it may without violating either decorum or verisimilitude cultivate such an additional grace as verse. But for the dramatic genres, given the nature of the audience and the circumstances of performance, only prose is an acceptable medium. All the best features of the dramatic art are enhanced by the use of prose:

. . . in comedy and in tragedy we imitate human actions properly with prose, less properly—nay, even absurdly—when bound by the limits of verse. Therefore prose is to be practiced, verse rejected, . . . since poetry is an imitation of human actions either as they actually were done or as they should have been done, neither of which can be achieved in comedy and tragedy through an imitation bound down by verse.[85]

If prose is used, the audience will understand the events and the thoughts presented, will derive the appropriate lessons from them, and will experience a suitable and a moderate pleasure. Beni's position in the dispute over verse is thus determined entirely by broader considerations of the poetic art.

CONCLUSIONS

It would be futile to reiterate, by way of concluding this chapter, the various ways in which the theorists and the practicing critics of the "last generation" manifested in their writings the standard features of the Horatian-rhetorical tradition. These features should by now be clear, and their appearance in the individual writers has been pointed out in each case.

[84] *Ibid.*, p. 4: "cum enim carmen tum per se tum propter insolentiam sit ad intelligendum perdifficile, fit sanè vt populus non modò vniuersam fabulae structuram & constitutionem aut etiam effictos mores peripetiamue non percipiat animo, sed ne sententiam quidem atque dictionem."

[85] *Ibid.*, p. 2: "in Comoedia & Tragoedia humanas actiones oratione soluta, rectè, carminibus adstricta, minùs rectè, immo praeposterè imitamur. Soluta itaque oratio retinenda, adstricta repudianda est. . . . Siquidem Poesis est imitatio humanarum actionum vel prout gestae sunt, vel certè prout geri debuerunt: quorum neutrum in Comoedia aut Tragoedia efficere potest imitatio adstricta numeris."

It would perhaps be more useful to study in what ways these last years of the century differ from earlier periods, what new directions and what new tendencies may be discerned, what innovations seem to bear the promise of a reorientation of critical thinking.

The existence, in this period, of so many new treatises on individual genres—Pino and Ceruti on comedy, Tasso on the epic, Massini on the madrigal, Correa on the elegy, Talentoni, Toralto, and Crispolti on the sonnet—would seem to indicate the nature of one of these new tendencies. Theorists apparently now feel that what needed to be said about the text of Horace had already been said by earlier generations, that the exegesis and explication of the *Ars poetica* had reached a satisfactory stage; hence the very limited number of such formal commentaries during these years. But what now needed to be done was to discover how the general principles of poetics contained in Horace could be applied to other genres not treated by him or treated only incompletely. If poetics was to be made practical, its theoretical basis must be transformed into clear precepts for the composition of the currently popular genres. To be sure, not only Horatian principles would be so transferred, and we shall see at a later time that many strongly Aristotelian treatises were written during this part of the century.

Under the stimulus of this necessity, the conception of the various genres grows and develops considerably. Thinking about literature in terms of the rules or precepts for specific genres had, of course, long been a standard approach. Some of it is already found in Horace, its tendencies are accentuated in the earliest commentators, and during the Middle Ages it produces such schematizations as the "wheel of Vergil," in which each of the genres involved a specific kind of subject matter, a type of personage, and a style— with all the ramifications inherent in the conception of style. Such a way of thinking is, of course, closely related to the notion of decorum, not as it concerns the behavior of types of personages compared with their counterparts in reality, but as it involves internal relationships within the poem, a notion central in the whole Horatian doctrine. Development of theories of the genres along these lines will thus be a natural outcome of the age-old approaches to the Horatian text.

What particularly characterizes theorizing about the genres in the last quarter of the sixteenth century is the attempt to relate the rules for the specific genre to the audience for which it is intended and the ends which it is meant to serve. Here, again, the tendencies hark back to earlier approaches; but they are now more fully realized and exploited. If the theorist thinks of a type as addressed to a "grave" audience—say the epic or the sonnet—he will associate with it all the multiple qualities by now linked almost automatically with the "grave" style. And they will consist not only of subject matter, persons, and style, but as well of a host of rules and conventions, of prosodic recommendations (the late medieval prescriptions for verse are now aggregated to the other rules for the genre), of descriptions of the general effect to be achieved, and of statements of the ends. For the ends, also, will be adapted to the character of the audience. The major ends of pleasure and instruction are still predominant in the minds of the theorists, with persuasion sometimes added as an auxiliary or a means. Perhaps in these later years the preoccupation with moral instruction is greater than previously. For each genre, now, the problem will be to decide whether its audience is such as to demand utility or delight or both, and what brand of either of these will be acceptable to it. That is, the general theories about the ends of poetry are particularized as the "art of poetry" becomes the "art of the comedy," and so forth. Insofar as the internal workings of the poem are thus brought into relationship with the audience and with audience-oriented ends, this is Horatianism in the best tradition.

If we consider theorizing about the genres as a refinement upon antecedent approaches, then other new directions during these years will be seen to be closely related to it. Throughout the century, for example, the problem of style and of language had been a central one in this rhetorical mode of criticism. Not only had each theory of a genre involved extensive treatment of the particular "style" appropriate to it, but whole theories of poetry had been constructed about differentiations among the three or four styles as they had been found in the analogous rhetorical treatises of Cicero or of Demetrius or of Hermogenes. Now, in these late years, further refinements take place. We have already seen, for example, how Giason Denores would transfer to the realm of poetics all those aspects of rhetoric which had to do specifically with diction; this resulted from his conviction that language, differing in this from the other rhetorical elements whose function was persuasion, had as its peculiar domain the arousing of the passions and the providing of pleasure. This is symptomatic of a growing tendency to regard the distinctive features of poetry as verse and as a special kind of language. Thus Correa saw fit to reverse the usual subordination of style to materials and to see instead an adaptation of materials to the kind of style being cultivated. Perhaps it would not be an exaggeration to say that the emphasis shifts, during this period, from "res" to "verba," that theorists tend more and more to concern themselves with linguistic aspects of the poetic art.

A special manifestation of this tendency is discernible in the preoccupation with the "concetto" as a peculiarly poetic form of expression. Giulio Cortese's theory of the "concetto" as the central organizing element of a poem is the best example. Insofar as he conceives of it as the "soul of poetry," he displaces the emphasis from the Aristotelian "plot" or the "character" of the moralists or the "thought" of the pure rhetoricians. To be sure, the conceit is not a purely linguistic element in poetry, and Cortese, for one, thinks of it as a device for organizing all the materials pertinent to a given feeling or idea. But others, less philosophical in their approach, see it only as a figure of speech and consider it frankly at the level of diction. Indeed, some of the stress upon matters of diction may spring from the fact that theorists believe that the larger matters of poetic form have been satisfactorily solved—or on the other hand that they are insoluble, and hence the poet can do no better than to attend to the virtuoso handling of his medium. I should point out that there is no single statement to this effect and that the tendency is not even implicit in very many documents. But directions and occasional signs in critical thinking lead one to believe that such a hypothesis is tenable.

Such thinking may account for the raising of the question, this time overtly, as to whether the poetic genres are "regulated" or "free." The thesis of regulation, predominant in the early years of the century, when critics were eager to discover exact rules for the composition of each literary type, seems now to be under attack, in part because of the current literary quarrels, which had introduced doubts about such major forms as the epic and tragedy, in part because contemporary poets were practicing successfully a large variety of kinds sometimes in violation and frequently in variation of the accepted rules. Hence, some theorists are willing to propose a doctrine in which genres are broadly characterized by a category of subject matter and a general effect, and to permit great liberty in the working out both of internal poetic structure and prosodic detail. Here, again, the tendencies are little more than incipient, and it should not be thought that Italian critics are about to abandon a "classical" position in favor of the freedoms and excesses of "romanticism." They might, indeed, have done so, had not the influence of French classicism in the following century brought about a reversal of trends. On the whole, these last years of the century mark a broadening, within the Horatian tradition, of the scope of critical inquiry, some loosening of tight systematic distinctions, and occasional prying into the psychological and linguistic factors that underlie a theory of diction.

CHAPTER SEVEN. PLATONISM: I. THE DEFENCE OF POETRY

U NLIKE THOSE RENAISSANCE CRITICS who attached themselves to Horace's *Ars poetica* or to Aristotle's *Poetics* as the basis for their critical thinking, the Platonic critic was essentially a man without a text. I mean by this that he was unable, as were his compeers, to derive his critical doctrine point by point from a central text, to concentrate his efforts of exegesis and commentary and interpretation upon that text, to discover within it all the answers to a host of artistic and technical questions. For there is no Art of Poetry by Plato, no single treatise (the notion of "treatise" is itself alien to the Platonic approach) in which one might find collected the total theory of the philosopher with respect to this specific art, in all its ramifications and all its ultimate deductions. Lacking such a document, the Platonic critic of the sixteenth century was obliged to base his Platonism upon scattered dicta in various dialogues. These dicta were such that they provided a set of general principles about literature without examining in detail their implications for the practice of the art, and the critic who used them possessed rather an all-inclusive attitude toward poetry than a firm body of precepts and rules.

Plato himself had seen the art of poetry not in itself but in relationship to various contexts which required consideration of it. He was interested not in the practice of the art or in the means by which it achieved the beautiful poem, but in how it was related to truth, or to the needs of education in a real or an ideal society, or to the divine forces of inspiration. As these contexts changed, Plato's ideas on poetry—and sometimes his total evaluation of the art—expanded or contracted, became more positive or more negative, took on new orientations. This was, of course, entirely in keeping with his general method. Rather than establishing a separation among the sciences and treating each one in terms of the principles proper only to itself, he chose to preserve at all times the manifold relationships present within an undifferentiated and unanalyzed reality, or at least as many of them as were pertinent to his inquiry of the moment.

Of Plato's various dicta on the art of poetry, the critics of the Renaissance were interested primarily in the following ones:

The divine furor. In several passages of the *Phaedrus* (245A, 265B) and the *Ion* (534), and in a lesser way in other dialogues, Plato had declared that the poet produces not by art but by divine inspiration, that he is moved by the Muses to a state of frenzy, and that when he speaks it is really the voice of the gods and not his own voice that speaks within him. The poet thus mad or possessed is really more than a man, and his works "are not human, or the work of man, but divine and the work of God" (*Ion*, 534). It is for this reason that he is able to bestow immortality upon those whose deeds he sings. The poet who lacks such inspiration and who attempts to write merely according to the rules of art is doomed to failure.

Imitation. Of the various ways in which the term imitation was used by Plato, two especially were found to be eminently useful in Renaissance criticism. First, in Book III of the *Republic* (394 ff.), Plato had divided narration into three types, simple narration, imitation, and a mixture of the two. In the first, the poet spoke only in his own voice, telling a story; in the second, he assumed the person of one or another of his characters, and spoke through the voice of that character; in the third, he alternated between the two procedures. Otherwise stated, imitation in this sense is the equivalent of a dramatic form of presentation. Second, in Book X of the *Republic* (595 ff.), Plato had developed the argument that the poet, as an imitator of appearances rather than of those realities which he calls Ideas, is at several removes from the truth, that he has neither knowledge nor right opinion of the object which he imitates, that hence his imitation is "merely a kind of play or sport" (602). These ideas were used by the Renaissance on the one hand to describe the relationship between imitation and reality, on the other hand to discredit the imitative process.

The banishment of the poets. Since in the *Republic* Plato was primarily concerned with the relationships of poetry to the education of the future citizens and guardians of the State, he had examined the various ways in which the art might be harmful or beneficial as an instrument of instruction. He had concluded that since poetry teaches false tales about the gods, since it tends to render the soul effeminate through its use of soft strains and rhythms, since it is at many removes from the truth through its very nature as an imitation, since it feeds the passions of the soul by providing the occasion for their expression, it should not be granted admission to the ideal State. Rather should the poets, except those who write hymns to the gods and praises of famous men, be banished (Books II, III, X). The point of view is specifically pedagogical and moral, considering as it does the ultimate effects of poems upon the moral fiber of the young. These ideas became in the Renaissance (as they had been at times in the Middle Ages) one of the principal sources of the attack on poetry, and all Renaissance theorists felt themselves obliged to deal with Plato's banishment of the poets, either by way of accepting it or—much more frequently—by way of rejecting it on the basis of other criteria. The defence of poetry in the Cinquecento is largely a reply to Plato.

What the Renaissance frequently failed to realize about Plato's varied positions with respect to poetry was that they do not necessarily represent inconsistencies. Hence much effort was spent in the attempt to reconcile ideas that are irreconcilable only when they are torn from their context of reference and placed in bare juxtaposition to one another. Returned to their contexts, seen in the light of the presuppositions and the conditions which surround them, they are perfectly understandable, consistent, and "true." But it was not in the spirit of Renaissance intellectual method to see ideas in this way, and critics proceeded here as elsewhere by way of fragmentation, separation, and isolation. They were content with the individual dictum—sometimes merely derived from the oral tradition without any reference to the original texts—and with an acceptance or rejection of the dictum by itself. This fact, added to the absence of a central basic text, accounts for the extreme fluidity of the Platonic position in Renaissance criticism. The position is found joined and combined with all other possible attitudes, introduced as an accompaniment or an addendum; when it provides the point of departure for a given theorist, it trails off into some other mode as generalization gives way to the details of the poetic art. In a very real sense, there are hardly any true Platonists among literary theoricians or practising critics of the sixteenth century. And when they are found, they are Platonist in their total philosophical outlook, and this reflects itself in their total approach to poetry.

In the case of Horace, Renaissance critics inherited a tradition of interpretation which had begun in the late-classical period and had persisted, with some additions, through the Middle Ages. For Plato, this was not true. Whereas there had been some use made of his strictures on poetry by churchmen of the medieval period, for the most part his writings became significant documents for literary discussion only with the rise of the great Platonic commentators and philosophers of the Quattrocento. As compared with Horatianism, then, Platonism is a relatively new force in literary theory, relatively unencumbered by an ancient reading, and relatively free for the inquiring lucubrations of the Renaissance mind. Many of the theorists and critics who will appear in the following discussion were not truly Platonists, nor was Plato their immediate source. They belong in the tradition only because they manifest a critical mode or position related to the central problems of Platonism in literature.

QUATTROCENTO DOCUMENTS

Although our concern in the present study is exclusively with Platonism in the Cinquecento, it would perhaps be instructive to examine two typical documents of the Quattrocento, so that we may have some appreciation of the state to which thinking of this kind had advanced before 1500. The first of these is the *De institutione reipublicae* of Francesco Patrizi, Bishop of Gaeta, who died in 1494; the work contains, in Book II, chapter 6, a discussion "De Poetis et eorum virtutibus, & qui legendi, quique ex theatris exigendi sint." Like Plato in the *Republic*, Patrizi is here considering poetry in the general framework of the state, in its possible moral effects on the young. But he tends to disagree with Plato about the banishment of the poets. Citing Cicero and Strabo in support of his thesis, he points out the multiple utilities of the art: The poet, like a first philosopher, leads men to a proper way of life, teaches them what they need to know about the passions and customs of men. He provides the grammarian with the best examples of all kinds of language, especially that which is elegant and ornate and beautiful. Unlike other disciplines, which derive from art, doctrine, and precepts, the functioning of the poet depends upon nature and upon divine inspiration, and hence he is able to combine human and divine matters in his works.

From this general defence of poetry, Patrizi passes to a consideration of the separate genres and their relative usefulness. First, the drama:

> Fictional inventions, which exist partly for utility but partly also for pleasure, are by no means to be repudiated. Children must be taught, and those things which otherwise they could with difficulty conceive, they accept through the enticements of fictions, and they easily bring them to mind, and they allow themselves to be led to virtue much more readily by their meaning. [The story of Hercules.] Stories of this kind instruct the young and make them more disposed to desire praise. . . . However, I do not wish to assume the defence of fictions to the extent of praising all types of them. Indeed, almost all tragedy should be excluded from the best city. . . . It is not without reason that tragedy should be hissed off the stage from every civil spectacle; for it has within it a certain excessive violence mixed with despair which readily changes stupid men into madmen and drives the unstable to frenzy.[1]

Nor does comedy come off much better:

> It does not please me either that comedy should be performed in public spectacles. For it corrupts the mores of men, and makes them effeminate, and drives them towards lust and dissipation. . . . For the plots of comedy for the most part concern adultery and rapes, and the habit of seeing them affords to the spectator the license for changing for the worst.[2]

Comedy may be read by scholars in the privacy of their studies—and essentially for the linguistic interest rather than for the actions represented. Epic poetry, on the other hand, is highly recommended, since it presents the figures of great heroes, with all the virtues they represent. As for satire, it is found to be generally desirable, since it praises virtue and blames vices; but a caution must be expressed in regard to the scabrous and even obscene language which it sometimes uses. In each case, the criterion to which the genre is referred is specifically an ethical one.

---

[1] *De institutione reipublicae* (1534 ed.), pp. xxviv–xxvii: "Fabularum inuentio partim ad vtilitatem, partim autem ad delectationem neutiquam repudienda est. Docendi sunt pueri, & quę vix alioqui cogitare possent, fabularum illecebris accipiunt, & facile in memoriam redigunt, earumque sensu ad virtutem longe magis diriguntur. . . . Eiusmodi fabulae adolescentes instituunt, & promptiores ad optandam laudem reddunt. . . . Non tamen fabularum vsque adeo patrocinium suscipere volo, vt omnes laude afficere velim. Nam tragoedia pene omnis extrudenda est ab optima ciuitate. . . . Nec immerito explodenda est ex omni ciuili spectaculo tragoedia. Habet enim in se violentiam quandam nimiam mistam desperationi, quae facile ex stultis insanos reddat, & leues in furorem compellat. . . ."

[2] *Ibid.*, p. xxvii: "Comoediam . . . in spectaculis etiam recitari non placet. Corrumpit nanque hominum mores, eosque effoeminatos reddit, & ad libidinem, luxuriamque compellit. . . . Comoediarum nanque argumenta, magna ex parte adulteria, & stupra continent, quocirca spectandi consuetudo, mutandi etiam licentiam facit."

One peculiar feature of Patrizi's remarks is his defence of the ancient poets against their banishment by Plato and against their exclusion by Christian apologists. From the point of view of the Christian, the ancient poets rendered a real service to the cause of the true religion by deriding and humiliating the false gods of the pagans: ". . . they ridiculed, by making sport of them in their stories, the very stupid opinions of the people about the gods and their vain and foolish superstitions."[3] Moreover, the wish of the Christian apologist to exclude them as heretical is unfounded, for before the coming of Christ, God was unknown to all men, and the philosophers erred as much as the poets in their ignorance of Him. For these reasons the poets of antiquity should be forgiven their errors and men should be allowed to read them. As we shall discover later, the point of view of the Christian apologist is frequently very close to that of the Platonist and represents a similar approach to literary problems.

Also in the fifteenth century, Antonio Mancinelli published his *De poetica virtute, et studio humanitatis impellente ad bonum*. This is really not a treatise on poetry at all, but a collection of quotations from Greek and Latin poets. Yet the order and arrangement of these quotations is in itself significant, and the prefatory materials state a typical attitude toward the art. The dedicatory epistle quotes the customary ancient authorities on the role of poetry in the betterment of mores—Theophrastus, Strabo—and then defends it against Catholic accusations:

The poets seem, therefore, to be wrongfully damned by certain people, especially on the grounds that they draw away from the Catholic faith those who are unwary. I shall truly show this to be false by the words of the selfsame poets. For we shall find in them the ten commandments of the law, and we shall see that they damn and prohibit the seven deadly sins, and that they likewise teach many of the finest things. . . .[4]

A subsequent section on the "Poetarum Laus" insists on the divine inspiration of poets and the reverence in which they should be held; it also repeats the time-honored examples of the esteem in which certain poets, especially Homer, were held by all antiquity. If they were so regarded, it was because of the contribution that they had made to the civilizing of man; poetry was the first philosophy:

The ancients, in fact, say that poetry is a kind of first philosophy, which brings us from youth to the art of living, which teaches the mores and the passions, which in a pleasant way teaches us our duty. Later writers declare that only the poet is a wise man. For these reasons the cities of the Greeks from the very earliest

---

[3] *Ibid.*, p. xxv: "stultissimas gentium de dijs opiniones, vanasque, ac fatuas superstitiones fabularum ludibrio contempserunt."

[4] *De poetica virtute* (ca. 1490), pp. aiiv–aiii: "Iniuria igitur a quibusdam damnari videntur: praesertim quod a catholica fide remoueant eis inuigilantes. Id equidem ego falsum eorundem poetarum uerbis ostendam. Decem nanque legis praecepta in ipsis reperiemus; septem quoque mortalia uitia illos & damnare & prohibere videbimus. Plurima item quam optima edocere. . . ."

times instructed their children in poetry, assuredly not for its gross pleasure but for its chaste moderation.[5]

Other uses of poetry are adduced in support of the argument. Mancinelli's position is essentially moralistic, placing whatever emphasis it can on the utility of poetry rather than on its pleasure. (It will be noted that the Horatian "utile dulci" is inextricably mingled with the thinking of the Platonists.) When he arrives at the anthology which is the main purpose of his work, he provides a series of headings—religious and ethical for the most part—under which he gives brief prose introductions (themselves quotations from ancient authors) and then pertinent selections from the ancient poets. The ten commandments, the seven deadly sins, and other similar categories furnish the basis of organization for the passages quoted. Clearly, it is the "sententious" quality of poetry that alone is of concern to the editor.

Two distinguished humanists, whose lives span the turn of the century, may serve as a transition to the criticism of the Cinquecento proper. They are Giovanni Francesco Pico della Mirandola and Battista Mantovano. Pico, in a pair of works which date from the late Quattrocento, expresses a point of view which is violently antipoetic in the best neo-Platonic tradition. The first work is his *De studio divinae et humanae philosophiae.* In Book I, chapter VI, he discusses the relationship of the various kinds of ancient writings to divine philosophy, and finds that whereas physics, logic, and metaphysics have some affinity to divine scripture, geometry, arithmetic, and poetry have much less. He cites his own experience, which parallels that of many others: a love of poetry in childhood and early manhood, followed by satiety and complete rejection—

> But after I had devoted myself to philosophy and sacred letters I so completely renounced the delights of poetry that I scarcely opened the books of the poets three times in five years, because I was drawn away from them and felt my soul to be softened by them. But what is more detestable is that most poets mixed into their verses the greatest wickednesses and impurities, which are not only not to be touched by a Christian but are to be utterly expelled by him. You will not easily find many poems, otherwise beautiful, which are not made foul by filthiness and obscenities; for which reason Isidore writes that Christians are forbidden to read the fancies of the poets, because through the delights of their plots they excite the mind to the provocations of lust.[6]

5 *Ibid.*, p. aivv: "Antiqui uerò poeticam primam philosophiam quandam esse perhibent: quae ab ineunte nos aetate ad uiuendi rationes adducit: que mores: que affectiones edoceat: quae res gerendas cum iucunditate precipiat. Posteriores uero solum poetam ipsum sapientem esse asseruerunt. Quamobrem graecorum ciuitates ab ipso primordio eorum liberos in poetica erudierunt: non nude utique uoluptatis sed caste moderationis gratia."

6 In *De rerum praenotione* (1506–7), pp. fv–fii: "Sed postquam ad philosophiam & sacras litteras me contuli adeo illis remisi nuncium ut nec poetarum libros toto quinquennio ter forte aperuerim: quandoquidem ab illis trahi: animum & emolliri sentiebam: Sed quod est detestabilius plerique poetarum turpitudines maximas & obscenitates suis uersibus immiscuerunt. Quae christiano homini non modo attrectanda sed prorsus eliminanda: Nec temerè multos inuenies qui pulchra alioquin poemata spurcitijs libidinibusque non foedauerint: Quare scribit Isidorus ideo christianis prohiberi legere figmenta poetarum quia per oblectamenta fabularum excitant mentem ad incentiua libidinum."

Pico sees in this same corrupting influence of poetry the reason why Plato banished the poets from his republic. In the following chapter, Pico explains why in the early days of Christianity certain very holy men not only made use of pagan literature themselves but recommended its use to others. The circumstances, however, are not now the same, and one should prefer Christian poetry on religious themes; this will have the greatest possible superiority over pagan poetry—the superiority of subject matter—and may be equally eloquent in its language.

The same question is examined again, but in a somewhat different light, in Pico's *Examen vanitatis doctrinae gentium, & veritatis disciplinae Christianae*. In Book III, chapter III of this work, Pico answers the claim that poetry, along with history and grammar, is "useful" for life and leads to happiness. The statement, he believes, is false in its premisses and its conclusions:

... for men derive from the poets occasions for evil not less significant for vice than for virtue, since the poets wrote in different ways, and at one time they let loose the reins of the vices, at another they held them in check, as is easy to see for anyone who takes them in hand; although one may be more prone to virtue than another, and another may be more inclined to narrating or praising the vices.[7]

In order to distinguish poet from poet and passage from passage, the reader must appeal to the philosopher, so that for Pico the whole art of poetics is specifically subordinated to philosophy. In the statement that he is challenging, Pico finds no clear definitions of utility and of happiness, and hence he believes that it is impossible to judge properly of poetry's contribution to either. What he does know is that the poets have frequently, in the past, provided examples for undesirable activity:

... many believe that Epicurus drew from Homer his idea that the greatest good lies in pleasure, that many found the excuse for irreligion in Euripides, that many sought in Alcaeus and Anacreon instigation to impure and lewd loves and to lives of drunkenness, and there are some who hold that precepts of anger were imbibed from Archilochus and Hipponax; and it would take a long time to enumerate the particular cases in which some foolhardy men have fallen on account of those things which they had falsely learned from the poets.[8]

Ethical and religious criteria are inextricably mingled in Pico's judgments

---

[7] In *Opera omnia* (1573 ed.), II, 938: "non minores enim malorum occasiones ex Poëtis, ad uitia quam ad uirtutes trahunt homines, ut qui & uariè scripserunt, & modò uitijs habenas laxarunt, modò eas compescuerunt, ut facilè est uidere si quis eos in manus sumpserit, tametsi alio alius ad uirtutem propensior, & alius alio sit inclinatior in uitia uel narranda, uel extollenda."

[8] *Ibid.*, II, 939: "multi existiment Epicurum ex Homero traxisse summum bonum esse in uoluptate, ex Euripide multos impietatis habuisse occasionem: Impuri & obscoeni amoris, & ebriosae uitę fomenta ab Alcaeo & Anacreonte multos petisse: Iracundiae praecepta ab Archilocho & Hipponacte bibisse, sunt qui uelint, & longum esset percensere singula quibus aliqui praecipites inierunt ob ea quae apud Poëtas perperam didicissent."

of the art of poetry, and, hence, those judgments bear almost solely upon the implications of subject matter for the lives of the reader.

About 1505, Battista Mantovano wrote a letter to Pico in praise of one of his poems; the terms of praise show a clear critical position:

> Since you have written a poem in a scrupulous, eloquent, and learned fashion, I can neither praise nor admire it sufficiently. For it has wit and charm without effeminacy and lewdness, and it gives pleasure not as Flora does, but as Diana; not as Venus, but as Minerva; combining, in the way prescribed by Horace, utility and beauty with pleasure. Obscene and lewd poems, in my opinion, bear the same relationship to true poems as do wanton prostitutes to honest matrons. I, indeed, do not deem a poem to be a true poem and one capable of withstanding every censure unless it be serious, pure, and holy. . . . Nor should we listen to the soft and effeminate poets, for whom nothing is savoury if it is not base, impure, corrupt, and malodorous. . . . This poem of yours is like a river which grows as it flows along, and which the more it advances the more beautiful, the more pleasant, the more grand it appears, which is a sign of a very great talent. It is, I say, the sign of a very great talent, such as does not weaken with exercise, but gathers strength from effort.[9]

Moral and religious considerations are uppermost; but there is also respect for the pleasure to be combined with utility and for the artistic strength of the work, which represents the poet's genius. It is significant that in one of the passages not quoted here Battista cites the verse of Horace (*Ars poetica* 310: "rem tibi Socraticae poterunt ostendere chartae") that indicates that the poet is to use the philosopher as his source.

CINQUECENTO HUMANISTS

In contrast with Pico's passionate abuse of the art of poetry, Lodovico Ricchieri (Caelius Rhodiginus) presents a moderate estimate in his *Lectionum antiquarum libri XXX* of 1516. Book IV of the work is devoted to a defence and discussion of poetry. The defence is made in terms almost identical with those used by Mancinelli: poetry as a first philosophy, as a teacher to youth of a way of life. But Ricchieri also insists on the character of the poet as a good and wise man and makes a case for the priority of verse over prose. In his effort to discern the major usefulness of the art, he develops at length the power of allegory as a pedagogical device; this insistence upon allegorical interpretation relates him at once to a long line of medieval expositors and to his fellow Platonists:

[9] In G. F. Pico della Mirandola, *Epistolarum libri quattuor* (1506–7), p. Fvv: "Poema quod religiose, eloquenter & docte conscripsisti, neque laudare, neque admirari satis possum: Habet enim sine mollitie & impudicitia, salem ac leporem, & delectat non ut Flora, sed ut Diana: non ut Venus, sed ut Minerua miscens, quemadmodum praecipit Horatius dulcedini utilitatem ac pulchritudinem. Poëmata obscoena & impudica sunt iudicio meo inter uera poemata, quales inter probas matronas, forniciariae meretrices. Ego enim poema uerum, & quod omne punctum ferre possit esse non puto nisi sit graue castum, ac sanctum. . . . Nec audiendi sunt poetae molles & effoeminati, quibus nihil sapit nisi turpe, impurum, purulentum, & olidum. . . . Poema hoc tuum simile fluuio, qui currendo crescit quo magis procedit uidetur uenustius, dulcius, grandius, quod est indicium fortioris ingenij. Fortioris inquam ingenij quod exercitio non flacescat, sed laborando uires acquirat."

But if profound matters are veiled and concealed in the outward covering of the fictions, and hidden as in the most secret sanctuaries, you must know that this is invention proper to poetry and among the ancients also that habit of fanciful invention has long since grown strong. . . . With such fictions as these, it seems to me, we should from the start form and, so to speak, "delineate" our youth from tenderest childhood. For this animal, prudent and wise and possessed of reason, whom we call man, wishes, through a kind of internal drive, to know, and is hungry for knowledge; and the poetic fiction is the first stimulus to such learning, especially since it remains unexpressed and vague and seems always to suggest some other matter. Thus all of us, spurred on to it by a kind of natural force, are most avid for what is new, which is experienced by us as most sweet and pleasant and is not lacking in the marvelous.[10]

For all of us, thus, poetry provides a ready and delightful answer to this thirst for knowledge, and especially in youth it may give us the roots of all arts and disciplines. Ricchieri demonstrates his point by giving an allegorical interpretation of the *Aeneid*, insisting on the lessons to be learned from it in this way.

The dangers of such a use of poetry are of course apparent to Ricchieri. If the fictional envelope contains wicked or reprehensible actions, and if the spectator, through youth or ignorance, is unable to penetrate within to the allegorical meanings, what will be the result? Obviously, an undesirable moral conclusion. To prevent it, he says, care must be taken to see that only virtuous plots are presented to the young, and it was such a concern that lay behind Plato's banishment of the poets. But here Ricchieri makes a distinction that became a commonplace among the apologists for poetry:

But with respect to these we must note carefully that the poets are not condemned outright by Plato; since to the degree in which he holds that they should be rejected when they disturb the state and invent shameful things, to that same degree he embraces them and kisses then tenderly when they exhort to moral improvement, celebrating elegantly and eloquently in their praises of heroes or their hymns to the gods.[11]

Plato's ban thus is a limited one, affecting not the whole of the art of poetry but only those practices of it which would lead to undesirable consequences for the state. With these restrictions upon the activity of the poet Ricchieri

10 *Lectionum* (1516), p. 156: "Quod si fabularum inuolucris res profundae conuelantur, obtegunturque, & ferè Sanctariis secretioribus reconduntur, id scire conuenit, esse poetices germanum. Et Veteribus quoque illum irroborasse pridem, confingendi morem. . . . iis uero imprimis tenerior aetas formanda, delineandaáque, ut sic dicam, uidetur, Quoniam animal hoc prouidum, & sagax, ac rationis compos, quem uocamus hominem, intimo quodam impetu scire desyderat, estáque cognationis auidum, Cuius fomentum primum fabula est, eo imprimis argumento, quod indicta inscitaáque alias profert. Sumus autem, ad id nos prouehente naturali quadam ui, nouitatis omnes perauidi, quod praedulcis haec sentiatur, & iucunda, nec admiratione careat."

11 *Ibid.*, p. 158: "Sed in iis illud impense animaduertendum, non damnari prorsum à Platone Poetas, Siquidem quantum ubi perturbant, aut turpia fingunt, reiiciendos putat, tantundem amplexatur, exosculaturáque, si ad bonam frugem hortentur, laudibus heroum aut Deorum hymnis eleganter, facundeáque concelebratis."

would agree, and he sees two agencies as capable of exercising the control, the church and the philosopher. The church, through its canonical decrees, for example, has declared that the good Christian should not read too frequently the fictions of the poets, since through them he becomes stimulated to seek pleasure and, in a sense, is made to "sacrifice to the demons" (p. 160). In a more general way, the writing of the poet and the interpreting of his works should be under the watchful supervision of the philosopher:

... one must have recourse to those who are skilled in philosophy, who administer an antidote, having explained by allegory the outer cloaks of the fables and having used the curative powers of their precepts, by which means (as if by a brake) the enticements of the pleasures are restrained and at the same time the violence of the passions is diminished—which, excited for the most part by reading as by a living example placed before it, forces itself upon the very reason and after having trod upon it succeeds in extending its dominion even farther.[12]

The ideal solution would be a combination of philosophy and poetry, one in which poets were philosophers and philosophers were poets.

Ricchieri's ideas on poetry, moreover, extend beyond the simple consideration of the moral ends to be served. He attacks the problem of imitation and discovers that there are really two types: one in which everything is invented and there is no representation of truth; a second in which the truth is represented in the garb of a fictional narrative. The second is called "narratio fabulosa" and may be treated in either of two ways, by treating profound subjects completely acceptable on philosophical and religious grounds or by admitting reprehensible matters. Once again, the distinction is that between two kinds of subject matter, and obviously the philosopher-critic will tolerate only the first kind (p. 158).

In connection with imitation, Ricchieri does not fail to call attention to the pleasure which we find in accurate representations, even of ugly objects (he is apparently following Aristotle here), a statement to which he adds the warning that we must not allow this kind of admiration to deceive us into accepting everything that we find in poems. He follows Aristotle again in his solution of the problem of art versus nature in the poet and of the differentiation of poets according to their characters; Ricchieri believes in divine inspiration, but he also believes that the characters of men, good or bad, determine what kind of poetry they will write. He reduces questions of art to the types of rhythms used in various genres and to the elements of style proper to poetry. In the latter connection he cites Horace, Cicero, and such rhetoricians as Dionysius of Halicarnassus. On the whole, Ricchieri's position is much more eclectic than that of the other Platonists whom we

---

12 *Ibid.*, p. 160: "... decurrendumque ad Philosophiae non ignaros, Qui antipharmacum propinent, explicatas per allegorias fabulamentorum uelaminibus, adhibitaque praeceptorum salubritate, quibus Voluptatum adlubentia quodam, uelut sufflamine reprimatur, atque item deferuescat perturbationum impetus, qui lectione tanquam exemplo proposito, plerunque concitatior ingerit sese rationi, & illa exculcata latius affectat dominari."

have studied thus far. He goes beyond the usual praise or blame of poetry; but when he does so he finds himself largely outside the Platonic context and is obliged to appeal to other masters.

In his *De incantationibus* (1520), Pietro Pomponazzi displays a much more restricted view of the whole problem of poetics, but one which is essentially favorable to the art. His concern is with two questions, that of the divine furor and that of allegory. For the first, he accepts fully all the ancient statements about the divine inspiration of the poet, about the essential opposition between reason and poetry—the poet really does not *know* what he is writing—about the poets as instruments and interpreters of the gods. For the second, he starts from the assumption that there are important truths hidden under the fables of the poets: ". . . they invent those fables to lead us to the truth and so that we may instruct the un-educated masses, who must be led to the good and drawn away from evil just as children are led and drawn by the hope of reward and the fear of punishment."[13] Poetry has the particular virtue of instructing in abstract matters through the use of material images. It may thus be used or quoted as a supplementary device whenever it is necessary to persuade, because of its capacity "to fortify and caress the minds of the listeners" ("ad firmandum, & animos demulcendum," p. 297). The rhetorical bias of Plato is here very close to the usual theory of the Horatians.

Gasparo Contarini's *De officio episcopi* (which belongs roughly to this period, although its exact date is unknown) is concerned with the role that a bishop should assign to poetry in the education of the young. And the churchman finds that the very rhetorical attractions of which Pomponazzi had spoken constitute the greatest dangers resident in poetry. It is because the poet is divinely inspired, because his works are full of charms and enticements, that he is able to sway the souls of his readers whichever way he will. Hence the young reader, incapable of resisting these influences, should not be allowed to read him. Contarini finds that especially in his own time men err in allowing youth full access to the works of the poets: "he [the bishop] should absolutely not permit the minds of the young, from childhood on, to be corrupted by the lascivious writings of poets and other writers of this kind; for if they drink them in in their tender years, it will be next to impossible for them, in their mature age, to be called back to better moral behavior; in which matter our own time . . . sins greatly."[14] Contarini can see some profit in the reading of certain poets, especially Vergil, but on the whole he deems it better for all men to read Christian

---

13 In *Opera* (1567), p. 201: "nam illa fingunt, ut in ueritatem ueniamus, & rude uulgus instruamus, quod inducere oportet ad bonum, & à malo retrahere, ut pueri inducuntur & retrahuntur, scilicet spe premij, & timore poenae."

14 In *Opera* (1571), p. 425: "non permittat statim ab ineunte aetate puerorum animos corrumpi poetarum, coeterorumque huiusmodi auctorum lasciuiis: quas si à teneris annis imbiberint; impossibile prope erit, vt in maturiori etate ad meliorem frugem reuocentur, qua in re nostris temporibus . . . magnopere peccatur."

writings. Presumably, as so frequently with these antagonists of the art, the term "poet" refers specifically, if not exclusively, to the pagan poets of antiquity, and some, at least, of the objection to them is on theological grounds.

The *Libro de natura de amore* of Mario Equicola (1525) has been studied in connection with Horace's *Ars poetica*. It should be mentioned again, briefly, because of several passing references to Plato's ban on the poets and to exceptions that Equicola would make to the general interdict. Dante, for one, fits the category of those poets who, according to Plato, "draw the ignorant multitude to a knowledge of high matters" (p. 5*v*). The high matters taught by Dante in his hendecasyllables are "what punishment follows the guilt of those confirmed in vice, how one ascends purged to the true glory of beatitude, then the perfect life" (*ibid.*). Another poet whom Plato would have admitted to his republic is Battista Mantovano, who represents the divine nature of the poet required by such theorists as Cicero and Democritus, combined with art as demanded by Horace (p. 37*v*).

If the attack upon poetry and its defence is one of the essential features of the Platonic tradition in criticism, then Francesco Berni's *Dialogo contra i poeti* (1526) in some way fits into the tradition. This may seem a strange classification of the joking and satirical dialogue. But it will be less strange when we realize that Berni proceeds, at least in part, by upholding the contrary of the arguments usually used in the defence; perhaps this might be called reverse-Platonism. The interlocutors make fun of the self-styled madness of the poets, of their overbearing claim to divine inspiration. They should rather be charged with heresy, uselessness, complete lack of substance and solidity; they are venal and obsequious, malicious and immoral, unashamed plagiarists; they are worthy of punishment rather than of praise. Only when they are "good" for something other than the writing of verses should they be tolerated, and even then it is their quality as men and not as poets that is to be appreciated. Berni suggests such punishments as making the poets themselves undergo the adventures which they attribute to their heroes. One should bear in mind, in reading the *Dialogo*, the jocular tone and the satirical intent and make compensatory allowances; but nevertheless a certain serious animus against poets, and on grounds not too dissimilar from those of the unjesting writers, is evident.

Rather than emphasize the moral consequences of the reading of poetry, as most of his contemporaries seemed to be doing, Giovanni Bernardino Fuscano chose to indulge in elaborate praise of the art because of its divine origins. His short treatise, *De la oratoria et poetica facolta*, was really an introduction to the *Stanze sovra la bellezza di Napoli* and was published with the *Stanze* in 1531. Fuscano begins with a general description of the virtues of eloquence, which is a part of poetry, extolling its capacity to seize upon the soul and to confer life upon the dead past. When to eloquence are added the beauties of poetry, especially verse, it achieves its most marvelous form. This is because poetry, unlike all other forms of eloquence and indeed unlike all other arts and sciences, is divine rather than human in inspiration. The poet is like an unconscious instrument in whom and through whom speaks the voice of God; without this voice, the poet is mute. Poetry is defined by Fuscano in this way:

> Poetry is that art which, embracing all other arts, marvelously expresses through definite rhythms, through measured feet, and through grave maxims all that men have done, all that they have ever said and known, under marvelous veils, illuminated by clear ornaments and at the same time adorned by variegated flowers, not without delighting the ears and bringing profit to the mind.[15]

In a separate development he treats of the relationship between the poet and God, implying that it is specifically of the Christian poet that he speaks. He begins with an analogy: God Himself is a poet and all creation is His poem. Of all creatures the poet is most like God in his powers, and this resemblance carries with it a responsibility: the poet must devote all of his God-given powers to the glory, service, and honor of God: "... tempering his voices with the harmony of all the corporeal senses, he must at all times give Him thanks in verses and in hymns, and all the gifts which come to him from His bounty, he must use, spend, and consume in the cult of His glory and in the honor of His majesty; for all that time which is spent otherwise than in thinking of Him must be accounted as lost."[16] Thus it is that the poet always invokes God at the beginning of his compositions, that he is closely akin to the prophet, and that his name itself means to make or to create. Fuscano's approach is still Platonic, and although it emphasizes another of Plato's ideas rather than the idea of the moral utility of poetry, it concludes with a Christianization of the doctrine.

Since he employs the form of the dialogue in his *De liberis recte instituendis liber* of 1533, Jacopo Sadoleto is able to present in a lively way both sides of the argument on the banishment of the poets. Sadoleto himself upholds the affirmative, using proofs that by now have become fairly standard: the divine inspiration of the poets, which causes their works to operate in an irresistible fashion upon the souls of the listeners; their resultant capacity to orient the soul toward good or evil; the necessity, therefore, that they should be supervised by the state and if necessary banished from its walls. On these points Sadoleto is answered by the other interlocutor, Paolo Sadoleto, who declares that he cannot imagine any

---

15 *De la poetica facolta* (1531), pp. Biij–Biijv: "la Poesia è quella che abbracciando tutte l'arti con diffiniti numeri, con misurati piedi, et con graui sententie, quanto l'homini han fatto quanto han mai detto, et conosciuto, sotto merauigliosi uelamenti, da chiari lumi illustrati, et di uarij fiori parimente ornati, non senza dilettar l'orecchi, & giouar l'animo, mirabilmente exprime."

16 *Ibid.*, p. Biijv: "temprando sue voci con l'Harmonia di tutti corporali sensi darli ogn'hor gratie in versi & Cantici, & tutti doni, che da sua larga bontà li ueneno deue per lo colto di sua gloria, & per l'honore di sua Maestà usarli, spenderli, & consumarli, peròche tutto quel tempo, che a non pensar di lui fia speso, indubitatamente se può tener perduto."

reading more useful or more delightful than that of Homer and of Vergil; in Homer, especially, all wisdom and doctrine are to be found, and all other poets have derived from him as rivers from a fountainhead. He extends this toleration of the poets to include even writers of comedy, especially Terence: "What you yourself frequently say, that comedy is the school-mistress of private life and of social behavior, makes me believe that you do not repudiate these poets either."[17] Terence is not only a model for diction and language but may serve as an example of good judgment itself; whereas Plautus is to be recommended solely on linguistic grounds. Paolo concludes that there is some good in every poet and that all should be admitted to the educative process. Jacopo's own conclusion is that, if they are to be admitted, the poets must observe faithfully the proper ethical code, and those who prefer to write trivial, corrupt, or scurrilous verse are by no means to be tolerated. The "good" poets may, along with musicians and those who cultivate the other liberal arts, participate in the education and indoctrination of the young.

If one reduces the general defence of poetry to a defence of a single author, one finds essentially the substance of Nicolò Franco's dialogue, *Il Petrarchista* (1539). In addition to much biographical and anecdotic detail, the dialogue on Petrarch contains a passage presenting the reasons why Petrarch should be imitated. What is said about language and style is not especially pertinent here; it could just as well have occurred in a document in the Horatian mode. But Petrarch is to be admired for his substance as well as for his style, and indeed for his character as a man:

And he should so much the more be always in our hands that he contains within him all knowledge, that every science has some place in his verses. And who can say how many and how great thoughts of divine and human philosophy are hidden in his rhymes? how modest (oh, immortal God!) he is? how clean and pure of every stain of lowness? how gay without lewdness? how religious in his thoughts? how chaste in his mind? how Platonic in his love?... In a word there is nothing in him which does not belong to the divine virtues, to the celestial beauties, to angelic mores, to the most honest love, to the highest humanity, and to ineffable courtesy.[18]

Two remarks: first, there is nothing in this praise that might not also have been found in a typically Horatian document; second, the qualities singled

[17] *De liberis* (1533), p. 108: "Nam quòd comoediam saepe affirmas priuatae uitae & ciuilis consuetudinis esse magistram, speciem habet, ut ego arbitror, hos quoque poëtas non repudiantis."

[18] *Il Petrarchista* (1539), p. 12v: "E tanto piu per le mani si deue hauere, quanto e poi in lui tanta dottrina; che ogni scienza ne i suoi uersi ha qualche luogo. E chi puo dire quanti e quali sentimenti de la diuina, e de la humana philosophia si stieno ascosi ne le sue rime? Quanto e egli (o Dio immortale) modesto? quanto terso, e netto d'ogni lasciua ruggine? Quanto senza lasciuia leggiadro? Quanto e religioso ne i pensieri? Quanto e casto ne la mente? Quanto e Platonico nel suo amore?... Niente in somma e in lui; che non sia di diuine uirtuti, di celesti bellezze, d'angelici costumi, d'honestissimo amore, di somma humanitate, e d'ineffabile cortesia."

out, breadth of knowledge, godliness, and morality, are precisely the same ones that would make a poet acceptable even in Plato's republic.

Mario Equicola presents us, in his *Institutioni al comporre in ogni sorte di rima della lingua volgare*, with a much more completely Platonic work than his *Libro de natura de amore*. Published in 1541, the posthumous treatise is concerned above all with prosodic recommendations for the various lyric forms, for which it leans heavily on the old treatise of Antonio da Tempo. But as a prelude to such discussion, it develops the history of poetry, a lengthy comparison between poetry and painting, a defence of the art, and a praise of both Dante and Petrarch. In almost all phases of this prelude the source is Plato. So for the distinction made, close to the beginning, among the various kinds of verse: the active (under which Equicola classifies tragedy, comedy, bucolic, and satire), the narrative (history, maxims, philosophy, and mathematics), and the mixed (heroic, lyric, and elegiac poetry). So also for the insistence upon divine inspiration. On the matter of the banishment of the poets, however, Equicola disagrees, declaring that it came about only in the *Republic* and only because that work designed a state entirely outside the bounds of human possibility. Elsewhere, he says, Plato praised the poets, and Equicola joins in the praise here: for the delight which they bring to our ears, for the way in which "from our earliest years they invite us, by means of fables, to praiseworthy and great actions" (p. B), for their incitement to virtue. Poetry "teaches us to adorn ourselves with good mores and to hold our passions in check; intent as it is upon giving pleasure and enjoyment and utility to men, it makes accessible for our use the examples of many things, setting before us in a most diligent fashion and with delight the glory of the ancient virtues."[19] More specifically, poetry shows us the fortunes of kings and heroes, indicates how we may temper our passions; thus the fact that it uses myths or fictions is no more to be condemned than a similar use in religious mysteries and parables, and the bad moral examples which it sometimes provides are no worse than those found constantly in life, in history, in the laws. Equicola's comparison of poetry with painting points out that both arts may legitimately "invent" or "feign," provided that in so doing they observe the laws of decorum. His conclusion that poetry is superior to painting is based on two reasons: poetry makes its appeal to the mind rather than to the body, and its products are less subject to destruction. The brief discussion of Dante and Petrarch employs the terms and the attitudes commonplace in Horatian criticism.

TOMITANO (1545)

The *Ragionamenti della lingua toscana* of Bernardino Tomitano (1545) represents the first nearly complete "art of poetry" in the present series of

---

[19] *Institutioni* (1541), p. B: "Ornarne di buon costumi, & rifrenar gli affetti ne insegna. studiosa di far piacere, & dar volutta, & vtile a' mortali, di molte cose gli essempij à nostro vso riduce, diligentissimamente con giocondità delle antiche virtù ne propone la gloria."

Platonic treatises; it also represents the most eclectic and in a sense the most typical studied thus far. If one were to read the three books of the *Ragionamenti* in reverse order, one would find in the third all the detailed treatment of the more particular aspects of the art, a treatment resting largely on Horace's *Ars poetica* and on the rhetoricians but deriving certain essential ideas from Aristotle. The second book deals largely with oratory, but even here the application of oratorical principles to poetry is constantly traced and all the examples are taken from poets; once again, the classical rhetoricians provide the distinctions and the rules. But in the first book, where Tomitano wishes to lay the philosophical foundations for all the art of writing, his source is Plato. And it is Plato appealed to on a much broader basis than was done by most of Tomitano's contemporaries. For rather than begin with one of the favorite dicta (which I have outlined at the beginning of this chapter), he takes as his starting point Plato's general concept of Ideas. Like the painter, the poet and the orator attempt to represent in the medium of their arts some perfect concept or Idea; Ideas are "those simple and spiritual forms . . . which mean nothing else but examples and norms of those things which are born naturally or made artificially, which are absolutely eternal and durable just as all others are born perishable and mortal and may be said to be subject to constant mutation."[20] If the poet is to succeed as a poet, he must therefore be something of a philosopher so that he may know the truths which he is going to imitate.

The relationship of poetry to philosophy is indeed a complicated one. The business of philosophy is the discovery of truth; the business of poetry is the imitation of truth through the medium of fictions. But poetry does not imitate all truth, nor does it serve its ultimate ends in every part of its imitation. Of its two ends, pleasure and utility, it is the latter which involves philosophy. For the utility is both moral and intellectual in character, and it is found in moral and intellectual precepts scattered throughout the work. In order to write such precepts properly, Tomitano insists, the poet must know the philosophical truths from which they spring: "These precepts then will either teach us how to live well and happily, or else they will merely render us wise through some intellectual habit; the latter ones are called contemplative just as the former are called moral, and both kinds are a necessary part of philosophy."[21] Does this mean that the poet must have exact and complete knowledge of all matters, both human and divine? Or does he speak without knowledge and run the risk of Platonic con-

---

[20] *Ragionamenti* (1545), p. 8: "quelle semplici & spiritali forme, . . . che altro non importano che essempi & norme di quelle cose, che nascono naturalmente, ò artificiosamente si fanno: lequali sempiterne del tutto & dureuoli sono, si come tutte l'altre cose nascenti mancheuoli & mortali, & a mutatione di continuo soggiacenti si possono addomandare."

[21] *Ibid.*, pp. 42–43: "Questi precetti adunque ouero ci insegneranno uiuer bene & beatamente, ò che ci renderanno solamente per alcun habito intellettuale saputi, liquali contemplatiui si addomanderanno, come quegli altri morali: gli uni & gli altri de quali sono parte necessaria della philosophia."

demnation on that score? Tomitano takes a middle position: The poet must have knowledge, and the more he knows the more successfully will he write; but it need not be profound and thorough knowledge. "I tell you that the orator and the poet must possess so pure and simple a knowledge of things pertaining to philosophy, that when he remains silent about them he will show that he knows them; and aside from this they will be a guide and norm to him from which he may derive more pleasant and more solid maxims and may give to all that he writes or speaks a greater splendor."[22] Indeed, if the poet cultivates philosophy to an excessive degree, he thereby becomes less good a poet. Tomitano's remarks on Dante clarify his whole position:

I hold therefore that that man is a better and graver poet who with the aid of philosophy will be able to render his compositions more beautiful and more grave, but not that he should for this reason dispute or talk about philosophy. And therefore it is not conceded to you that Dante, although he may be a better philosopher, succeeds in being a greater poet than Petrarch. For Petrarch understood that minimum amount of philosophy which was sufficient to give spirit and solidity to his rhymes; whereas in the matter of beautiful diction, from which the poet derives his name, . . . he was better than Dante.[23]

To this matter of philosophy, also, is related the problem of allegory. The poet knows a basic collection of truths, but instead of expounding them directly he dresses them in the outward fashion of a myth or a fiction. If the reader would derive full benefit from the poem he must penetrate, by means of allegorical interpretation, to the truths within the fable. Tomitano shows how this is done by interpreting the myth of Parnassus and giving an analysis of Petrarch's madrigal "Perch' al viso d'amor portava insegna."

If the poet, as a philosopher in disguise, can be useful to the lives of men, then clearly he should not be expelled from any state. Tomitano meets Plato's ban by two counterproposals: first, the works of the poet should at all times be subjected to the examination and the censorship of the philosophers; second, the poet must both be possessed of knowledge of the truth and must be a man of high moral character. From such a poet, so supervised, no harmful or reprehensible works need be feared (pp. 34, 141–42). He may even tell lies—a practice for which Plato blamed the

---

22 *Ibid.*, pp. 94–95: "dicoui, l'oratore & il poeta douer una cognitione cosi schietta & semplice ritenere delle cose alla philosophia appartenenti, lequali egli tacendole mostrera di saperle, & oltre di questo gli seranno una guida & norma, onde egli piu uaghe & sode sententie ne diriui, & maggior splendore doni à tutto quello, onde egli scriue ò parla."

23 *Ibid.*, p. 240: "Voglio adunque che miglior poeta sia quello & piu graue, che con l'aiuto della philosophia sapra render i suoi componimenti piu belli et piu graui, ma non per questo che egli di philosophia tenzoni ò parli. Et per questo non ui si concede, che Dante quantunque sia maggior philosopho; uenga ad esser piu gran poeta del Petrarca. Percioche il Petrarca quel tanto di philosophia intese, che a recar spirito et fermezza alle sue rime bastaua: la doue che poi nella bella elocutione, dallaquale si denomina il Poeta, come piu à basso ui dirò, fu di Dante migliore."

poets—provided that he avoid the "fraudulent lie," which has no virtue in it, and practice only the "artful lie," which masks a hidden truth. Only in passing does Tomitano mention the divine furor and its manifestations in the poet; apparently he regarded this as an incidental aspect of theory.

In these various remarks on poetry, Tomitano frequently associates it with oratory. The two arts are very closely allied for him as they were for theorists of the rhetorical school. He sees them both as having a similar relationship to Ideas, as seeking the same ends of pleasure and profit, as finding their utility largely in the inclusion of moral precepts, as sharing the same qualitative parts of invention, disposition, and elocution, and as using identical figures of speech. They differ, however, in various respects: oratory tends to emphasize utility, poetry gives more attention to pleasure; the orator uses persuasion as his means of achieving his ends, the poet uses imitation; whereas the one writes in prose, the other writes in verse; and the poet alone makes use of fables and fictions. These theoretical differences do not prevent Tomitano from citing passages from poems as examples of all the rhetorical devices which he discusses; in fact, he tends more and more throughout the treatise to find all his demonstrative materials in Petrarch alone. This means that, in the last analysis, he reduces all the arts using language to a single one, and finds their most interesting and important feature in the language which they use. It is at this point that he comes into closest contact with certain theorists of the Horatian-rhetorical school.

ANTONIO MARIA DE' CONTI (CA. 1550)

To this same period, roughly the middle of the century, must be assigned a group of works by Antonio Maria de' Conti, who called himself professionally Marcantonio Maioragio. Since he died in 1555 and the major part of his career as professor at Milan fell in the preceding ten years, the works published in the *Orationes et praefationes* of 1582 would seem to belong to the period around 1550. On the subject of poetry, Conti has two contributions to make, a theoretical statement in the form of a *De arte poetica* and a number of practical applications in the "prefaces" which were really "praelectiones" to courses of academic interpretation of various texts. Conti's oration *De arte poetica* is not an art of poetry at all, since it makes no inquiry into the nature of the art or into the devices by which poetic excellence is achieved; instead, it offers praise of poetry in fairly conventional terms. Poetry is the most excellent and the most divine of all the arts, since it provides man with a knowledge of things both human and supernatural. Its prime function is educative; as Maximus of Tyre and Strabo have pointed out, it is a first philosophy "which from earliest childhood leads us to an honest way of life, which instructs us in good mores, which calms and rules the disturbed movements of the soul, which

teaches, in the most pleasurable fashion, what things are to be done."[24]
The terms of praise are all old and familiar. As for the Platonic eviction,
there are two great arguments against it: First, one may find in every poet
the most saintly moral maxims, since good poets are also good men and
are the preceptors of life. Second, such great pillars of religion as Augustine,
Jerome, and Ambrose were great readers of poetry and cited it constantly.
Moreover, even Plato argues against himself, since in other works (where
he is not concerned with the perfect state) he insists upon the divinity of
poetry and praises it to the skies. Follows Conti's own extravagant praise:
"By the immortal gods, what sweetness do we not find in the language of
poetry? what harmony? what charm? what loveliness, what cleverness of
invention? what proportion of composition? what gravity of maxims?
what majesty in all kinds of style?"[25] As is so frequently the case, the praise
here given resolves itself into matters of diction and sound, and what
might be considered to be more distinctly poetic qualities are not even
intimated.

A similar set of principles is found applied in the "praelectiones." The
two prefaces to Homer are typical. Homer is, of course, the ocean from
which all knowledge and all literary skill have been derived. He has taught
kings how to be kings, has given the foundations of all the arts and sciences,
and has surpassed even the historians in those lessons which are the proper
contribution of history. His use of mythological tales, blamed by so many,
is to be defended as a device for the presentation of serious materials;
properly interpreted, these tales contain within themselves all kinds of
hidden knowledge. They are the means by which Homer attracts and capti-
vates the "rudes" and the "imperitos," teaching them the greatest
mysteries in the guise of frivolous myths. In so doing, he uses the method
of the theologians, who "frequently use parables and similes for divine
matters, by means of which untutored minds are easily raised from known
things which are apparent to the senses to those which are unknown
and sublime."[26] In so doing, also, he serves the ends of poetry as established by Horace, providing useful instruction in mores and in the good
life.

The second preface, devoted to the *Odyssey* (as the first had been to the
Iliad), stresses what is to be learned from the work about eloquence and
about all the arts; it also quotes Plutarch to the effect that the *Iliad* teaches

24 *Orationes et praefationes* (1582), p. 145: "quae nos ab ineunte aetate ad honestas uiuendi
rationes adducit, quae bonis moribus instruit, quae motus animi turbidos placat, ac regit,
quae res gerendas summa cum iucunditate praecipit."

25 *Ibid.*, p. 148: "Proh Dij immortales, quę suauitas poeticae locutionis? quae concinitas?
qui lepos? quae uenustas? quod inuentionis acumen? quae compositionis harmonia? qui
uerborum splendor? quae sententiarum grauitas? quae denique generum omnium dicendi
maiestas?"

26 *Ibid.*, p. 154v: "sicut etiam Theologi nostri parabolis ac similitudinibus in rebus diuinis
frequenter utuntur, quo rudes animi facilius à cognitis & sub sensum cadentibus rebus ad
incognitas & sublimes extollantur."

above all strength of body and the *Odyssey*, strength of soul (p. 157*v*). In his remarks on Hesiod's *Works and Days*, Conti rests upon the praise given the poet by the greatest philosophers and rhetoricians, sharing their admiration for the precepts and for the apt handling of the "middle" style (pp. 158*v*–162).

Two fairly lengthy prefaces are devoted to Vergil, one to the *Georgics* and the other to the *Aeneid*. The first work is compared with Hesiod and is found to be superior, largely because of the elegance and the clearness of its diction but also because of its erudition. For the *Aeneid*, Conti concentrates on the fourth book. He finds that, if the general aim of the poem is to present Aeneas as the exemplar of piety and fortitude, the particular function of Book IV is to show the evil power of love, the errors and catastrophes to which it leads, so that we may avoid it. For the rest, one may see in the life of Aeneas every virtue in its highest form, presented as a living example and through action rather than description. In a more general way, Vergil is praised for his incredible erudition, for his admirable style and versification, for his use of a poetic rather than a natural order of treatment, and for his proper exploitation of all the rhetorical devices. Once again, as soon as Conti passes from general remarks on subject matter and on the end of poetry to particular consideration of poetic techniques, his text becomes the *Ars poetica* and his method Horatian (pp. 173*v*–177*v*, 178–183*v*).

In another of his works, his *In tres Aristotelis libros, de arte rhetorica explanationes* (posthumous, 1572), Conti reflects other aspects of the current Platonic doctrine. He explains the special sense in which Plato uses "imitation" to describe the representation of things by words (p. 347A) and cites the *Ion* on the divinity of poets (p. 381A). These remarks are found in a context of a commentary on Aristotle and are frequently coupled with similar remarks from Horace. They demonstrate once more the eclectic nature of Conti's approach and the extent to which he uses Plato for a number of purposes.

Sperone Speroni, in his *Discorso in lode della pittura* (undated), is incidentally concerned with the broader meaning of imitation and with Plato's distinction between narrative and dramatic imitation in poetry. He also establishes a hierarchy of nobility on the basis of the subjects imitated and the prosodic means:

. . . all the imitative arts are more or less noble not only according to the thing imitated, which is common to all arts and sciences, but also according to the means and the manner of imitating. Thus if the epic and tragedy and comedy all imitate, as far as the thing imitated is concerned the first two are nobler than the third; but as for the mode or instrument of imitation, tragedy and comedy are not unlike since the one and the other imitates with the iamb. But the epic is indeed different from these because it imitates with the hexameter, a most noble verse. It is quite true that the epic does not imitate as well, speaking absolutely about imitation, as do the other two which are dramatic.[27]

In such a statement as this, of course, there are strong echoes of the distinctions made by Aristotle in chapter 3 of the *Poetics*; but perhaps the assigning of "nobility" on various scores is more specifically Platonic in its implications.

The Platonic element is decidedly secondary in the *In Aristotelis librum de poetica communes explanationes* of Maggi and Lombardi (1550). This is, of course, one of the major Aristotelian commentaries of the century, and it will be treated in detail later on. But Plato appears both as a source for certain ideas in the commentary and as an earlier theorist whose ideas Aristotle either combatted or developed. The latter position is stated clearly in connection with the distinction between narrative and dramatic imitation; Maggi cites Book III of the *Republic* at length "so that we may more easily discover how wisely Aristotle, using the precepts of his teacher Plato, has improved upon them."[28] Occasionally, Aristotle's ideas are seen as being in opposition to those of Plato, as when (in connection with *Poetics* 1460*b*33) Aristotle is said to be answering Plato's attacks on Homer in Books II and III of the *Republic*. Again, in the last lines of his treatise Aristotle is said to be using Plato's argument that the end of poetry is pleasure, although elsewhere Aristotle goes beyond when he states that the end is rather utility through purgation (pp. 277, 299). Most frequently, though, the commentators wish to find parallels and influences. In Maggi's *Prolegomena*, which treats the standard topics relative to any work, one point of investigation is the end of poetry. Insofar as Aristotle holds that the end is, "by imitating human actions, and through pleasurable language, to ennoble the soul," he is spanning the tradition of both Plato and Plutarch, who saw its end as the education of youth.[29] Plato's condemnation of the poets who seek only "voluptas" is thus a limited one, applying to bad poets who would corrupt youth; his general conclusion, like that of Aristotle and Horace, would be that poetry is useful as an educative instrument.

In connection with specific passages of the *Poetics*, the commentators cite Plato's definition of beauty (p. 123), they establish a parallel between the παράδειγμα of *Poetics* 1454*b*13 and Plato's Ideas ("siue natura secun-

27 In *Opere* (Venice, 1740), III, 443–44: "tutte le arti imitative sono più o men nobili non solo quanto alla cosa imitata, il che è comune a tutte le arti e scienzie, ma quanto allo instrumento e modo dello imitare. però se la epopeja, e la tragedia imitano, e la commedia, quanto alla cosa imitata le due prime sono più nobili della terza; ma quanto al modo o istrumento dello imitare non son diverse la tragedia della commedia, imitando l'una e l'altra col jambo: ma sì è diversa la epopeja da esse, perchè imita collo esametro nobilissimo verso. è ben vero che non imita così bene, assolutamente della imitazione parlando, come imitano le altre due, le quali sono drammatiche. ..."

28 *Explanationes* (1550), p. 67: "ut facilius deprehendi possit, quàm doctè placitis Platonis sui praeceptoris Aristoteles utens, in melius ea reformet."

29 *Ibid.*, p. 13: "actiones humanas imitando, suaui sermone animum excultum reddere."

dum se consyderata, non ut in hoc, aut in illo reperta," p. 175), and of course they refer to Plato on the divine furor as antecedent to Aristotle's ideas on the sources of poetic inspiration (p. 187). In all this, it would be very difficult to distinguish anything that might be termed an underlying Platonic position. The text is interesting because of its assumption that Plato is frequently present as a source for Aristotle's ideas and that, contrariwise, Aristotle is frequently concerned with a development or a refutation of his master's poetic theories.

A distinctly Platonic position is indeed visible in a much shorter text of approximately the same time (I date it roughly in the decade 1550–1560), found in several manuscripts: Giovanni Giacomo Leonardi's *Discorso qual sia piu utile al mondo ò l'historia ò la poesia*. Leonardi takes issue with the usual assumption that poetry is more useful than history because it presents ideal models rather than imperfect realities. History, according to this conception, might well incite men to imitate the errors of the great. Leonardi's own opinion is directly opposed:

> ... I always was and still am of the opinion that History is of much greater usefulness to the world than Poetry, since it seems to me that in all things truth carries with it a certain admiration, an impression upon men which gives them a much greater desire to imitate it than do fiction and lies. ... this does not come to pass with invented things, since as fables they give of themselves from the very beginning an impression of the impossible, and one does not heed them with the same attention as the true. Besides the poet, who in large part is desirous of giving pleasure, pays so much attention to this end that at times he forgets to pursue that which he has proposed as his end, that is, utility ... and it results that men, as those who do not understand the secret, or whether what the poet was trying to say is found in the verse, on the surface and in the pleasure, or whether in things difficult to discover, leave aside the intention hidden within the poetry.[30]

Three essentially Platonic ideas are present here: (1) truth is preferable to fiction as a means of teaching men; (2) the poet tends to seek pleasure rather than utility and hence is to be condemned; (3) the meanings contained under the allegorical exterior may not be readily apparent to the reader. Leonardi goes on to say that only good and rare intellects will perceive the hidden meanings, and he concludes with a summation of the various lessons to be learned from history.

[30] MS BNF II. III. 384, fols. 133v–134: "Io nondimeno sempre fui, et sono in opinione che l'Historia torni al Mondo utile molto maggiore che la Poesia, parendomi, che la uerità habbia in tutte le cose una certa admiratione, un' impression negli huomini, che doni loro molto maggiore studio d'imitarla, che la fittione, et la bugia. ... cosi non auuiene nelle cose finte, percioche come fauole danno di se nel principio un' impressione dell'impossibile, et non s'attendono con quella attentione come le uere. Il Poeta poiche è uolto a dilettare in buona parte mira tanto questo che si scorda alle uolte di proseguir quello, che s'hà posto per fine che è l'utile ... fà che gli huomini come quelli che non intendono il secreto, ne quel che habbia uoluto dire il Poeta se ne stia nel uerso, nella superficie, et nella dilettatione, oueramente come di cose difficili à saper l'intention nascosa nella poesia la lascia da un lato. ..."

A letter written by Girolamo Fracastoro to Girolamo Amalteo in 1551 indicates that at that date it was still necessary to protest against a common opinion that poetry was a "madness" ("una pazzia") and that poetic genius was inconsistent with disciplined intellectual activity. Fracastoro declares that, had he been able to live according to his own wishes, he would have chosen to know only philosophy and poetry, since "only these two fields of knowledge with their related materials seem to me to be worthy of man."[31] He quotes Navagero to the effect that without poetic genius, a man cannot indeed be excellent in the mechanical arts nor can he appreciate their beauty. As a case in point, he cites his own works, showing how they combine both scientific and poetic compositions. Fracastoro's argument belongs to the larger position of the anti-Platonists who felt it necessary to defend the art against the charge of madness and irresponsibility.

PATRIZI (1553)

On the other hand, the *Discorso della diversità dei furori poetici* of Francesco Patrizi (1553) lies entirely within a framework of Platonic presuppositions. The problem which Patrizi poses is to discover why different poets excel in different genres. To answer it, he inquires into the various sources of poetic excellence, concluding that to achieve it the poet must possess both the Horatian "ingenium" and the Platonic "furor." Art, in these matters, is of little use, since it will not help to make the poet "rich in all the beautiful images and in all the perfections which can exist in an eloquent man."[32] For "ingenium" two definitions are given: " 'Ingegno' is properly used for an attitude and a readiness of our mind to learn and to discover. ... In still another way, 'ingegno' is taken for a certain disposition and inclination which at times is found in a given man and which makes him incline toward one thing rather than toward another." This is apparently a natural gift in man. "Furor," however, contains certain supernatural elements: " 'Furor' ... as Plato teaches us in the *Phaedrus*, is either natural or supernatural; or, we might say, human and divine ... what is divine descends from Heaven and raises us above the human, and makes us almost semiangels."[33] After having developed at some length the relationship of God, the planets, and the muses to human genius, Patrizi discourses on the possibility that the soul may take certain impressions

31 In *Raccolta*, ed. Calogerà, II, 263: "solo queste due cognizioni con li suoi annessi mi parono degne dell'uomo."
32 *Discorso* (1553), pp. 45–45v: "ricco di tutti i bei concetti, & di tutte le perfettioni, che possano cadere in huomo eloquente."
33 *Ibid.*, p. 45v: "ingegno propriamente si dice, una attitudine, & una prontezza della nostra mente, all'imparare, & al ritrouare. ... In un' altro modo ancora, si prende l'ingegno, per una certa affettione & inclinatione, che tal'hora si troua in alcun' huomo, che lo fa ad una cosa piu che ad un'altra inchinato"; and "Il furore, ... secondo che Platone ci insegna nel Fedro, è ò naturale, ò sopranaturale, ò uogliamo dire, humano, et diuino. ... il diuino, descende da Cielo, & sopra all'esser humano ci inalza, & quasi semiangeli ci rende."

PLATONISM : DEFENCE OF POETRY

from the planets and that the poetic faculty may be one of the impressions
so derived. This assumption leads to the solution of the specific problem:

... the writing of poetry, then, rather on one subject than on another results from
the disposition which the soul, in descending through the other heavens, takes
more from this planet than from that. And according as it is more illuminated by
the rays of Phoebus or of Venus than by Mars or Mercury, it is more given to
sing of amorous matters and the liberal arts than either of war or of the
mechanical arts.[34]

This, then, is the source of "ingegno," of the inclination toward a special
subject matter. "Furor" is a developed state of the same, whose copiousness and abundance results from additional gifts by the muses. A final
problem remains, that of the relationship between these natural or divine
gifts and the purely artificial or acquired powers of learning and practice of
the art. These are regarded as relieving the soul of earthly darkness and
permitting it to see the divine light: ". . . each hour they purify the soul a
little more from its earthly shadow and cause it to be exposed to that
heavenly light."[35] In general, then, for Patrizi the divine furor is necessary
if the poem is to be anything but "cold and stupid" (p. 50v); the particular
kind of poem practised by the poet will depend upon his special gifts; and
even the kind of verse used by him for treating a given matter will be a
function of his inspiration.

I have already had occasion to analyze Alessandro Lionardi's *Dialogi
della inventione poetica* of 1554 (cf. Chapter IV above, pp. 137–38) and to
suggest how both Aristotelian and Platonic elements exist as incidental
accompaniments to an essentially rhetorical theory. The borrowings from
Plato are typical of the period. Thus Lionardi calls upon Plato for the
special meaning of "imitatione" as dramatic representation, as against
"enuntiatione" or narrative representation (p. 76). He calls upon the
Republic, the *Phaedo*, and the *Ion* for the qualities of the poet, which are
said to consist in "copiousness of diction, readiness to discover knowledge
[defined as "perfect erudition and wisdom"], and art [defined as "a judgment reduced to rules for knowing how to invent and imitate well, and at
the same time adorn and enrich the matter"]."[36] Since this definition
involves a conception of knowledge, Lionardi also refers to Plato when he
comes to discuss the kinds of knowledge that the poet must have (p. 82).

34 *Ibid.*, p. 48v: "il Poetare poi piu in una materia, che in un' altra, uiene dall'affettione,
che nel discendere per gli altri Cieli, prende piu da questo Pianeta che da quello. Et secondo
che è illuminata piu da i raggi di Febo, ò di Venere, che di Marte ò di Mercurio, è piu data à
cantare delle cose amorose, & dell'arti liberali, che ò della guerra, ò delle mecanice."
35 *Ibid.*, p. 50v: "ogni hora uanno piu disgombrando l'anima dall' ombra terrena, et à
quel celeste lume la fanno esposta."
36 *Dialogi* (1554), p. 62: "uena del dire, prontezza del ritrouare dottrina [perfetta eruditione
& scienza], arte [un regolato giudicio di saper ben fingere & imitare, & insieme adornare et
arricchire la materia]."

[273]

Finally, he makes the usual references to Plato when moral questions or questions of the lessons taught by poetry are at issue; Book III of t he *Republic* is cited for the opposition to the moving of the passions by poetry (p. 76), and Plato's real meaning is interpreted thus:

Plato does not condemn those passions from which come honest and virtuous desires and effects, but only those which induce vicious longings and activities. This does not mean that the poet should not narrate that which is harmful and to be avoided, since it is necessary for him to relate as well the causes of wicked deeds and blameworthy as of the good and praiseworthy ones.[37]

It would seem, here, that the Platonic criticism is tempered by a theory of the right—even the moral duty—of the poet to treat the whole gamut of the passions. This is a kind of defence of poetry against Plato.

Platonic elements are again secondary in Giovanni Battista Pigna's *Iromanzi* of 1554. The work has as its aim the development of a theory for a new genre, the romanzo, and it founds this theory essentially upon the pattern of the *Poetics*. But when, for example, Pigna speaks of "imitatione" as equivalent to "parlamenti" and of the poet as fulfilling most completely his role of imitator when he presents men conversing (p. 16), he is obviously following the current Platonic tradition. Likewise, when religious pre-occupations lead him to condemn the use of classical mythology and re-commend instead a moderate application of the Christian marvelous, he is at once reflecting the Platonic concern with "a true and proper presentation of the gods" and the later Christian prejudice (itself an outgrowth of Platonic modes of thought) against representation of the pagan gods (pp. 40–41). At other times, however, Pigna places himself in opposition to Plato. His discussion of the true, the false, and the verisimilar results in the conclusion that the poet may feign untrue things, such as the passions of the gods, that certain genres indeed are based upon untrue materials, and that the use of "lies" may even be recommended because of the truths that they may conceal: "So that a lie told by a good poet carries buried within it every form of truth."[38] Plato's ban on the poets is explained rather as a condemnation of certain audiences than of certain poets: "I believe that the reading of the poets is not forbidden to everybody, but only to people who are not capable of perceiving their meanings or of understanding their secrets, such as is the common and ignorant people. . . . For this reason the poets are sent out of the city . . . , since the greater part of the people are not apt for the understanding of poetry." After explaining the four "lies" contained in poetry, Pigna concludes that "these are held to be completely incredible by the ignorant and the material-minded; and

37 *Ibid.*, p. 80: "Platone non riprende quegli affetti, onde ne uengono desiderij & effetti honesti, & uirtuosi, ma quelli, che à uitiose uoglie, & operationi inducono; non però che quello che è noceuole & da fuggirsi, il poeta narrar non debba, essendoli necessario riferir le cause così de' fatti maluagi, & uitupereuoli, come de' buoni, & laudeuoli."
38 *I romanzi* (1554), p. 22: "Tal che vna bugia d'un buon poeta ogni verità sepellisce."

[274]

among those who are judicious they pass as being beautiful and good."[39]

To his essentially Horatian and rhetorical approach Matteo San Martino adds, in his *Osservationi grammaticali e poetiche della lingua italiana* (1555), two arguments springing from Platonic sources. These concern the defence of poetry and the character of the poet. Aside from the usual praise of poetry, based on its englobing of all other arts and sciences, its civilizing function, its antiquity, and its religious uses, San Martino singles it out as the one art devoted to the worship of God and to the betterment of political life. A part of its praise, to be sure, consists in the fact that—of all sciences—poetry alone is of divine origin since it requires the presence of the divine furor (pp. 124–25). At this point, the defence of poetry and the description of the character of the poet are identical. For the distinguishing feature of the poet is that he depends upon a special kind of divine inspiration, without which he cannot possibly excel in his art (pp. 128–29). Indeed, San Martino himself seems to be moved by a basically Platonic aim, since his purpose in writing is to present to future poets: "a simple intellectual form or Idea of the perfect poet, and a solid norm for arriving, by observing it, at such perfection as perhaps nobody could ever achieve."[40]

GRIFOLI (1557)

As its title indicates, Giacopo Grifoli's *Oratio de laudibus poetarum* (1557) is again a praise and a defence of poetry. But it has a special character insofar as it concludes with the Platonic necessity of imposing philosophical restrictions upon poetry. Grifoli's first premiss is that all arts must provide both utility and pleasure and that any art is judged great according as it satisfies both ends. By this standard, poetry is the greatest, since it excels all others in these respects. The utilities of poetry are to be divided into those which it claimed in the past (this is the commonplace allegation of a civilizing function) and those which it may still serve; the latter would seem to be largely political and ethical:

... since the poets so taught us not only the duties of private citizens and those common to the general condition of all men, but also the functions of magistrates, of military leaders, of kings, that no part of human life seems to have been neglected by them; since moreover they bring profit to the human race in many ways and through a multiplicity of actions, in no way did they ever offer us more ample service than in preventing either the virtues of men, or distinguished exploits, or the deeds of the brave from dying in any way. ... now, in fact, the poets

[39] *Ibid.*, p. 31: "mi penso che ad ognuno non sia vietato il leggere i poeti: ma solo alla gente che ne de i sensi loro è capace, ne intendente de i loro secreti; quale è la plebeia, & la ignorante. .... La onde si mandano fuori i poeti della città ...: essendo in esso i piu non atti all' intelligenza della poesia"; and "le quali in tutto per incredibili tenute sono da i rozzi & materiali: & passano per belle & buone tra i giudiciosi."

[40] *Osservationi* (1555), pp. 127–28: "una simplice spiral forma o Idea del sommo Poeta, & una salda norma di peruenir osseruandola a tal perfettione, alla qual forse non fia mai chi arriui."

not only write of the exploits virtuously accomplished by others, but they also teach the offices of virtue and instruct men to do those things which will be the ornaments of the centuries.[41]

This conception of the aim of poetry may also serve as a means of distinguishing among poets; Horace, for example, would be second only to Vergil and would be preferred to Lucretius "because he attends to what is true and proper and is entirely concerned with leading men to a proper life and to true virtue."[42]

If these utilities be present in poetry, why then should Plato have excluded the poets from his perfect state? Grifoli recognizes that for Plato himself there would seem to be contradictions:

Indeed we must believe that that philosopher condemned the teachings of the poets although he himself had called them the fathers of wisdom, or else that he had excluded them as dangerous although he himself affirms that they are the go-betweens of the gods, and while he holds that their poems are not the inventions of men but the gifts of heaven, he nevertheless legislated that they were to be kept, as wicked men, outside the borders of his State.[43]

Grifoli further maintains that, far from being a source of corruption for youth, poems may be used to advantage as a pedagogical device for the imparting of knowledge that would be otherwise inaccessible. The danger lies in the fact that at an early age, readers may be insufficiently wise to interpret the hidden meanings of poetry and may hence be led into error by the trumperies of the superficial statements. The solution lies in the joining of philosophy, which would provide correct interpretations, to the poetry itself:

Thus poetry brings us many sweets by means of which our native abilities may be nourished, but no fewer which—if the best training were not ready at hand— would disturb the mind and would lead it away from proper modes of thinking. Therefore poetry united to philosophy gives pleasure and profit like wine diluted with water. . . . Let this then be the function of the poets, to charm the minds of men with pleasant fables; for it is their business to make known the most famous exploits and to imitate convincingly the characters of all men, so that whoever

41 In *Orationes* (1557), pp. 53, 54–55: "quoniam non modo priuatorum officia, & omnium communis conditionis hominum, sed magistratuum, ducum, regumque munera ita docuerunt, vt nulla pars vitae ab ijs neglecta esse videatur, cum autem multis hi rebus, multiplicique industria iuuent humanum genus, nulla tamen in re commodiores se nobis praebuerunt, quàm quod neque virtutes hominum, neque praeclaros labores, neque fortium gesta vllo pacto mori patiuntur"; and "iam vero poetae non de rebus aliorum modo cum virtute gestis scribunt, sed etiam docent officia virtutum, atque homines instituunt, vt ea faciant, quae sint ornamenta saeculorum."
42 *Ibid.*, p. 56: "qui verum, & decens curat, & totus in eo est occupatus, vt ad rectam vitam & ad ueram virtutem homines perducat."
43 *Ibid.*, p. 59: "est vero credendum illum philosophum doctrinam damnasse poetarum, qui eosdem ipse sapientiae patres appellarit, aut tanquam perniciosos exclusisse, quos idem interpretes deorum testetur esse, & quorum poemata non hominum inuenta, sed munera coelestia esse ducat, hos tanquàm impios arcendos à finibus ciuitatis suae statuisse."

reads or hears them will not only know with the greatest clarity what things are to be done and what ones avoided, but will also be filled with a most joyful feeling of pleasure.[44]

All difficulties thus disappear if the teacher or the philosopher be present to extract the lesson from the poet; the poets are readmitted to the state, where they serve a special purpose because of the pleasurable elements which accompany their art.

The problem of truth, sometimes central in Platonic discussions of poetry, is treated in passing by Annibale Caro in his *Apologia degli Academici di Banchi di Roma* (1558)—his famous reply to Castelvetro's famous attack. In both documents the argument is largely linguistic; but at one point in his reply, Caro has Predella speak thus on the subject of poetic license:

> Don't you know, nevertheless, that where opposite opinions exist the poets may attach themselves to one of them, whether it be the better or the worse? and that in different places they may use now the one, now the other? Don't you know, further, that they may follow not only the opinion of the wise but also the errors of the common people, as when they say that the rainbow drinks? . . . The license of the poets is such that they may use not only opposite opinions, but those which are clearly false and ridiculous, without being blamed for so doing.[45]

Two things are notable here: first, that the poet is not held to logical consistency or to philosophical soundness; second, that the criterion of truth is not necessarily applied to his works.

AMMIRATO (1560)

A still more complete examination of the same questions—of truth, of knowledge, of the ban—forms the subject of Scipione Ammirato's dialogue, *Il Dedalione overo del poeta dialogo*. The dialogue was written in 1560 and presents two interlocutors, Dedalione (identified in the manuscript as Francesco Maria Giordano) and Tiresia (Marino Cosentino); both were members of the Accademia dei Trasformati, which Ammirato founded at

---

[44] *Ibid.*, pp. 60, 62–63: "ita poesis dulcia quidem multa tradit, quibus vegetentur ingenia, at non pauciora, quae, nisi praesto sit optima institutio, perturbent animum, & à recta ratione deducant. quare vt vinum aqua temperatum, ita poesis cum philosophia prodest, & delectat. . . . sit igitur poetarum iucundis fabulis mentes hominum delinire, quorum est & res praeclarae gestas illustrare, atque verisimili poemate cuiusvis mores imitari, vt quicunque legit, aut audit eos, non modo quae sequenda, quaeque fugienda sint apertissime cognoscat, sed iucundissima quoque voluptate capiatur."

[45] *Apologia* (1558), p. 83: "Non sapete uoi nondimeno, che doue sono diuerse openioni, i poeti si possono attaccare à una d'esse, ò migliore, ò peggiore ch'ella sia? & seruirsi anco in diuersi lochi hora di questa, & hora di quella? Non sapete ancora, che non solamente possono seguir l'openione de i dotti; ma gli errori ancora del uolgo? come dicendo, che l'Arcobaleno beua. . . . la licenza de' poeti, è tale; che si possono ualere, non pur de le diuerse openioni; ma de le espressamente false, & de le ridicole; senza meritarne riprensione."

Lecce in 1558–59.[46] There are several sections in the dialogue, corresponding to the various aspects of the problem of poetry; all of them, it will be noted, concern the generalities about poetry with which Platonic discussion was exclusively occupied. As Grifoli had done, Ammirato starts from the apparent contradiction in Plato between the praise of poetry and the banishment of the poets. He sees the banishment as depending upon two things, the incapacity of listeners rather than the vice of poets, the special conditions of the *Republic*. For in the latter work the aim is to consider poetry not in general but rather in its effects upon the education of the youths who will ultimately become the leaders of the state. Now it is at this early age that men are especially unqualified to "understand and penetrate" the lessons concealed beneath poetic expression. The relative character of Plato's ban is to be appreciated in contrast with the absolute ban on sophists:

> Truly Plato drives out all the sophists and from every place; not all the poets, but only those who feign ugly things about the gods and who go about imitating in an intense way disturbed minds. And not from every place, but from the city, that is from the mass of the ignorant and the young, who easily fall into disturbances and who do not penetrate the allegorical meaning of the poets.[47]

This weakness of the audience should not itself be entirely condemned; for it accounts for the fact that, in the Bible, God and the angels are spoken of in certain ways. This is entirely acceptable because of "our small capacity, which is more readily moved to the knowledge of high things through material and common examples than through abstract and subtle ones."[48] The assumption here, apparently, is that the devices of poetry are necessary for the communication of certain ideas to men, young or old; but some safeguards must be offered so that men, young or old, will put the proper construction upon poems and will not be led astray by false interpretations.

The second problem is that of knowledge. Plato had included among his charges against poetry the fact that poets really did not know the subjects about which they wrote, that their poems were at several removes from the truth. Ammirato answers thus: ". . . the poets know nothing about the

---

[46] The dialogue exists in manuscript in MS Bibl. Naz. Florence, Magl. VII, 12 and was published in Ammirato's *Opuscoli* (Florence, 1642), III, 353–94. On the Accademia dei Trasformati, see Eustachi d'Afflitto, *Memorie degli Scrittori del Regno di Napoli* (Naples, 1782), p. 308. On Ammirato's later associations with the Accademia degli Alterati in Florence, see my "Argomenti di discussione letteraria nell'Accademia degli Alterati (1570–1600)," *Giornale Storico della Letteratura Italiana*, CXXXI (1954), 177–78.

[47] In *Opuscoli*, III, 359: "Veramente discaccia Platone i sofisti tutti, & da ogni luogo; i poeti non tutti, ma coloro che degli Dij brutte cose fingono, & gli animi perturbati intensamente vanno imitando. Nè da ogni luogo, ma dalla città, cioè dalla turba de giouani e ignoranti, i quali di leggieri nelle perturbazioni discorrano, & l'allegorico sentimento de Poeti non penetrano."

[48] *Ibid.*, p. 361: "la picciola capacità nostra, la quale più ageuolmente si muoue alla cognizione delle cose alte con gli esempi materiali & comuni, che con gli astratti & sottili."

things about which they write, and still they [are] full of knowledge and wisdom. . . . speaking in terms of the art, he [the poet] really knows nothing as a poet, writing and developing materials under the influence of the divine furor."[49] This divine furor itself, however, constitutes a kind of knowledge, and one which, in the long run, is superior to that obtained through science. That is to say, God and the muses, speaking through the voice of the poet, infuse into his works a kind of superhuman truth which the mind of man alone would be incapable of discovering.

The third problem is that of the ends of poetry. The Horatian assumption of the "utile dulci" is at the basis of the discussion, which revolves about the specific character of the usefulness. Ammirato sees both the body and the soul as suffering ills and as needing remedies. Those of the body are provided by the doctor. Those of the soul are supplied by the legislator, the orator, and the poet. For both body and soul, some device is necessary to make the remedy palatable—the sugar-coating of the doctor's pills, the examples of the orator, the fables and the verse of the poet. It is this that gives the special quality to poetry:

. . . as it was said above that the philosopher in general is concerned with the health of the soul, let us say that when he condescends to minister to it with sweetness, he becomes a poet as distinguished from the other cures. . . . Whence it is necessary to point out that the delight is not to be considered here as a companion to the profit, making two ends for the poet according to which he would truly be held to profit and delight, but it is a consequence of the profit; for the poet wishes first and absolutely to profit, but since he cannot do so without the accompaniment of pleasure, he uses it as a servant of the first.[50]

The poet is thus a philosopher who uses a special instrument to attain the same end: "The philosopher who uses poetry in order to be able to profit does not thereby alter and change his end, even though he takes another means and other ways necessary and appropriate to what he intends to do, but he still follows his principal end, which is to profit."[51]

These various considerations lead Ammirato on the one hand to classify poetry under philosophy and on the other to distinguish the specific uses of the various poetic genres. Philosophy is divided into the contemplative and the active, which subdivide respectively into the natural and the super-

---

49 *Ibid.*, p. 364: "i poeti delle cose che scriuono nulla sanno, & pur tuttauia esser pieni dl dottrina & di sapienza. . . . secondo l'arte parlando, egli veramente niuna cosa sà inquanto poeta, scriuendo & trattando da diuino furore commosso."

50 *Ibid.*, p. 377: "come di sopra si disse il filosofo in genere riguarda la sanità dell'anima, diciamo che quando egli discende à curarla con dolcezza diuenta poeta à differenza dell'altre curazioni. . . . Oue bisogna auuertire, che il diletto non si hà da porre quì per compagno del giouamento, onde s'habbiano à far due fini del poeta, ch'egli veramente sia tenuto di giouare & dilettare, ma và egli in conseguenza del giouamento; perciòche vuole primieramente e assolutamente il poeta giouare, ma non potendo farlo senza la congiunzione del diletto il prende per ministro del primo." Cf. p. 383 on fable and verse.

51 *Ibid.*, p. 378: "il filosofo che per poter giouare prende la poesia, non per questo altera & cangia il suo fine, se ben piglia altro mezzo e altre vie necessarie & proporzionate à quel che intende di fare, ma segue il principal suo, ch'è di giouare."

natural sciences and mathematics (for the contemplative) and into ethics, domestic or family economy, and civil philosophy (for the active). Poetry belongs under the last of these: "If civil philosophy concerns the good of our minds and of our bodies, truly it will concern both of these arts, poetry and medicine; but let us take the matter in a broader sense and say that it concerns equivocally the one and the other medicine, that of the soul and that of the body."[52] The poet here stands in the same relationship to the physician as the legislator does to the surgeon, and "the end of poetics is to introduce virtue into the soul by driving vice out of it."[53] This is done separately by the separate genres. Tragedy ministers to the public person of society, comedy to the private person of the individual. For comedy alone teaches ethics, economics, and perhaps even politics. Such final statements as these constitute Ammirato's ultimate defence of poetry against the Platonic ban. In so doing, it is significant that they remain within the essential presuppositions of Plato's approach, although they find a contrasting answer.

Bernardino Parthenio's *Della imitatione poetica* of 1560 was, as we have seen (Chapter IV, p. 145, a document belonging primarily to the Horatian tradition, since it took "imitation" in the specific sense of imitation of models and developed the techniques for the approximation of another poet's style. It contains, incidentally, two passages related to Platonic modes of thought about poetry. The first is a sequel to the extravagant praise of Homer and the other poets and constitutes a formal defence of the art. Parthenio speaks of the antiquity of poetry, of how it preceded prose, of its invention by the gods; the poets, moreover, are beloved of the gods and inspired by them. If we wish an additional proof, we need only look at the heavens:

. . . if we wish to know that God, wise above all others and prudent above all others, loves poetry, we may understand it either from the harmony of those most holy celestial choirs, which with that ineffable sweetness make sweet the heavens and the divine mind, or from the harmony which we know arises from the most orderly movement of the spheres of heaven, which the divine wisdom wished to be tempered with numbers and with poetic arrangement, joining together to form among themselves such harmony as might calm within us the power of hearing.[54]

[52] *Ibid.*, p. 386: "Se la ciuile riguarda il bene degli animi nostri & de corpi, veramente ella riguarderà amendue questi, cioè la poetica & la medicina; ma prendiamo la cosa più larga & diciamo ch'ella riguarda equiuocamente l'vna & l'altra medicina dell'anima & del corpo."

[53] *Ibid.*: "il fine della poetica è indur nell'anima la virtù discacciandone il vizio."

[54] *Della imitatione poetica* (1560), p. 5: "se uogliamo conoscere, che Dio solo sapientissimo, & solo prudentissimo ama la poesia, comprendiamolo dalla harmonia ouero di quelli beatissimi chori celesti, i quali con quella ineffabile dolcezza addolciscono il cielo, & la mente diuina; ouero dal concento, che sappiamo nascer dal ordinatissimo mouimento delle sfere del cielo, le quali la sapienza diuina uolle, che con numeri, & con ragione poetica temperate fossero tra loro accordandosi in creare tal harmonia che in noi la uirtù del sentire addormenta."

Such a passage as this is doubly significant; it shows the persistence of a habit of regarding poetry in the vaguest analogical terms, as a kind of superior harmony, and at the same time it limits the essence of poetry to rhythm and to musical qualities. In a second passage, Parthenio distinguishes the imitation of which he is speaking from that considered by Plato, so that he may exempt his own from Plato's ban. Plato's imitation, he says, was that of the passions and, hence, involved all kinds of perils as far as truth, religion, and moral education were concerned. His own is merely that of other poets, and far from being blameworthy it satisfies in us our natural instinct to imitate and the delight we take in the process (pp. 15–16).

Two years after the writing of his *Dedalione*, Scipione Ammirato returned, in 1562, to the subject of poetry in *Il Rota, overo delle imprese dialogo*. The particular circumstances of the dialogue explain in part the orientation toward poetry. For poetry enters into the discussion because of a basic similarity with "imprese" (heraldic devices containing a hidden meaning); this is explained by the Bishop of Potenza, one of the interlocutors:

It was an ancient usage among all the wise men to keep, with every care and device, from revealing to all persons the most important doctrines and sciences, so that they would not come to be profaned by the vulgar crowd. And this was the reason why the imaginary fables were invented, under whose outer surface were hidden, by those ancient wise men, all the secrets of the speculative sciences and of the things of nature and all the useful and necessary forms of knowledge which pertain to man. In this way, the ignorant man had the pleasure of the fable and the wise man, penetrating farther within, gathered the fruit contained within it. And since poetry and painting are sisters both born at one delivery, just as poetry began to explain these fictions with words, so also afterwards painting began to depict many things which seemed monstrous but which under these fictions contained many fine secrets.[55]

In the development of these ideas, however, Ammirato passes on to other sources. He finds that both arts need to seek the marvelous—"what rarely happens and is outside the nature of other, ordinary things" (p. 30)—in order to make the proper appeal to their audience. In poetry, the marvelous of subject matter has its justification in Aristotle ("for it presents men as good or bad with greater virtue or vice than ordinary men have"), while that of form is justified by the rhetoricians ("for it uses the figurative, the new, the old, the foreign, the improper, the abbreviated, the extended, and

---

[55] *Il Rota* (1562 ed.), pp. 14–15: "Fu antica osseruanza di tutti i saui guardarsi con ogni studio & ingegno di non palesar le belle dottrine & scienze à tutte le persone in guisa, ch'elle si venissero à profanare dal volgo. Et questa fù la cagione, che si ritrouassero i fingimenti delle fauole: sotto le cui scorze si ricopriuano da quelli antichi saui tutti i segreti delle scienze speculatiue, & delle cose della natura, & tutte le vtili & necessarie cognitioni, che appartengono all'huomo. Di modo che all'ignorante restaua la piaceuolezza della fauola, & il sauio ne raccoglieua, penetrando più à dentro, il frutto di essa. Et perche la poesia & la pittura sono sorelle tutte nate in vn parto; si come la poesia con le parole cominciò à spiegare queste fintioni; così cominciò susseguentemente la pittura à pigner di molte cose, che pareuano mostruose: le quali però sotto esse rinchiudeuano molti belli segreti."

other figures in greater number than does ordinary speech").[56] Horace supplies the basis for the warning against excess in any particular style (p. 31). A final comparison between the "impresa" and poetry concerns their audiences; both must be accessible to the ignorant and pleasurable to the wise, and they must thus be based on common materials which will be readily intelligible. In this sense, comedy is of all poetic genres the one closest to the "impresa" (p. 33).

I have already mentioned, in connection with the *Tractatus de tragoedia* (MS 985 [M.8], Biblioteca Comunale, Perugia, about 1562) how the author's convictions with respect to the utility present in poetry led him to reject the condemnations of such philosophers as Plato. He insists upon the impropriety of regarding either pleasure or utility as the sole end of poetry and considers that both Plato and Aristotle saw the pleasure as serving the utility: "From which it follows that poetry, since it is a diversion, as both Aristotle and Plato hold, is agreeable to those for whom it is employed, and that the technique of the poets has been brought into use as a pleasure, to delight the mind, either to contemplate it as perfect, or at least as next to perfect and as it were mingled with the perfect."[57] It is this function of pleasure as intermediary to utility that constitutes the main defence of poetry, and even Plato himself admits it in Book II of the *Laws*. In essence, poets are educators, and that is their main justification.

One of the interlocutors in the preceding dialogue, Bernardo Tasso, is the author of a *Ragionamento della poesia* delivered before the Accademia Veneziana in 1560 and published in 1562. The *Ragionamento* is a fairly complete Platonic document, touching upon all the main points of current interest. It does not fail to answer those Platonists who interpret the master as having banished the poets; this is sheer ignorance:

He does not exclude poetry in general, but in particular those poets who, by means of the harmony and sweetness of their verses, aroused and inflamed the tender souls of young people to lascivious and voluptuous actions, and by means of the example and of imitation rendered them soft, effeminate, and entirely useless for the good and the improvement of the republic. Nor is this a fault of poetry but of the poet, who like a wicked doctor gives poison instead of medicine.[58]

56 *Ibid.*, p. 30: "percioche fa gli huomini o buoni, o cattiui in maggior uirtù, o vitio, che non son gli ordinarij; e nelle parole; percioche vsa il traslato, il nuouo, il vecchio, lo straniero, l'improprio, l'accorciato, l'allungato, & l'altre figure in maggior numero, che non fa l'oratione pedestre."
57 Perugia, Bibl. Com., MS 985 (M.8), fol. 103ν: "Ex quo consequitur, poesim siquidem ludus est, ut Aristoteli placet et Platoni, iucundam esse quibus adhibeatur, et oblectandis animis artificium poetarum accersitum uoluptatem, uel intueri semper ut ultimum, uel certe tamquam ultimo proximum, quasique cum ultimo temperatum."
58 *Ragionamento* (1562), p. 10: "non la Poesia in uniuersale, ma in particolare que Poeti esclude, i quali con l'armonia, e dolcezza de loro uersi commoueuano, et infiammauano i teneri animi de giouenetti a cose lasciue, e uoluttuose: e con l'essempio, e con l'imitatione gli rendeuano molli, effeminati, e del tutto inutili al benifitio, et a la essaltatione de la republica. Ne questo è difetto de la Poesia, ma del poeta: ilquale a guisa di maluagio medico da il ueleno in uece de la medicina."

The proper function of the poet is indeed the opposite: "by imitating human actions through the delightfulness of plots, through the sweetness of the words arranged in a most beautiful order, through the harmony of the verse, to adorn human souls with good and gentle characters, and with various virtues."[59] This moral and social usefulness is the main element in the defence of poetry, and Tasso finds it both in times past and in times present. He makes the usual statements about the contributions of the poets to the advance of civilization and their present favors. In summary, he asks: "Oh venerable science, which brings pleasure and profit to every kind of person, to every age, to every sex, to every nation, and in every season and in every time, who could ever praise you properly and to the extent to which you merit praise?"[60]

According to Tasso, the poet excels all other men through two qualities, the divine furor and the universality of his knowledge. The first is indispensable and is the sign of the poet's dependence upon God:

... without this extraordinary gift of nature, even though a man may have knowledge of all doctrines; even though through long study he may have learned the law and the art of perfect writing; even though he may have long experience of the things of the world; still it will be impossible that he should turn out to be a good poet. There is no doubt whatsoever but that the perfection of this science has something divine about it, and that for this same reason it should be placed before all others.[61]

Both Plato and Cicero are cited on the necessity of divine inspiration. This does not mean, however, that the poet may rely upon his natural gifts. Tasso develops at length the kinds of knowledge which the poet must possess—all arts and sciences are his prerogative—and cites the cases of Homer and Vergil as the most extraordinary in this respect. This erudition may also be found in the Italian poets (example, Petrarch) and is especially to be appreciated when it is hidden under an allegorical exterior (example, Dante). Probably because a part of this wisdom consists in an understanding of the passions, the poets are able to produce a great emotional effect in their readers, and this is the source of their power both as entertainers and as teachers (pp. 7–8).

It is perhaps interesting that the separate elements of Tasso's theory,

[59] *Ibid.*, p. 12: "imitando l'humane attioni con la piaceuolezza de le fauole, con la soauità de le parole in bellissimo ordine congiunte, con l'armonia del uerso gli humani animi di buoni, e gentili costumi, e di uarie uirtù adornare."
[60] *Ibid.*, pp. 15–15v: "O uenerabile scienza: che ad ogni qualità di persone, ad ogni età, ad ogni sesso, ad ogni natione, et in ogni stagione, in ogni tempo porti piacere e benefitio; chi fie giamai che degnamente, e quanto tu ben meriti lodar ti possa?"
[61] *Ibid.*, p. 12v: "senza questo singolar dono di natura, ancor che altri di tutte le dottrine habbia cognitione; ancor che con lungo studio habbia imparata la legge, e l'arte del perfettamente scriuere; ancor che lunga esperienza habbia de le cose del mondo; impossibil tuttauia sarà, che riesca buon poeta. non è dubbio alcuno, che la perfettione di questa scienza non partecipi di diuinità: e che per questo anco non sia da essere antiposta a tutte l'altre."

taken one by one, are almost identical with the essential doctrines of the Horatian-rhetorical creed: the ends of poetry as pleasure and utility; the complicity of art and nature; the importance of erudition; the moving of the passions. This does not mean eclecticism, but merely current modes of thinking about poetry that are so deeply imbedded that they tend to determine the interpretation put upon any doctrinal source. There is, to be sure, some eclecticism in Tasso: his definitions of the various genres, derived from all the classical and medieval sources, may serve as a case in point. When, however, he wishes to argue the superiority of the epic to tragedy, he returns to Plato, declaring that tragedy appeals only to the people and merely gives delight, whereas the epic gives both pleasure and virtuous instruction to men of mature judgment and dignity (p. 5). Aristotle's arguments for the superiority of tragedy are cited to complete the presentation.

Around 1564, Sperone Speroni, a frequent participator in the literary quarrels of the century, wrote a short fragment on imitation; its editor called it *Dialogo sopra Virgilio: Fragmento*. Two things are noteworthy about this fragment, first its special use of the word "imitation," second its attack upon Aristotle and the intention of the *Poetics*. After reviewing the various meanings assigned to the word, Speroni indicates that it may be applied in an extraordinary way to such a work as the *Poetics*. Nature, let us say, is the first object of imitation, and such poems as the *Iliad* and the *Odyssey* are imitations of it. These poems themselves become objects of imitation, but in two ways: for one, a philosopher may imitate them in an "art," and this is what Aristotle has done in the *Poetics*; for the other, another poet may imitate them, and this is what Vergil has done in the *Aeneid*. The first process, says Speroni, is much less to be praised than the second, which produces "true poetic effects," whereas Aristotle is incapable of practising what he teaches (p. 358). As a practical matter, then, the poet should devote himself to the study of other poets—his models—and should not concern himself with the "rules." Speroni also furnishes a criterion for imitation: that imitation is best which is most like Nature. Thus, if he is to choose between two depictions of a voyage to the Underworld, he will say: "This is now and always has been my judgment, that of these two the better poet ... was the one who made his inferno worse; for evil must be made evil, just as it is, and must not be made good, which it is not."[62] On the whole—and he comes close to a Platonic position here—Speroni disdains imitation and ranks it as inferior to art: "It is a clear fact that imitation is not proper to man, as art is. Therefore art is always conjoined with reason, and imitation is not always so; it is a thing not proper to us, but to rooks and monkeys. ... One can see with a single eye how much

---

[62] In *Opere* (1740), II, 360: "Questo è ora e sempre fu il mio giudicio, quello esser stato miglior poeta di questi due ... che fe piggiore il suo inferno: perciocchè 'l male si dee far male come è, e non far bene come non è."

more worthy art is than either usage or imitation."[63] This last passage indicates that the Platonic opposition to imitation is accompanied by a specific attack on Aristotle's notion that imitation is proper to man.

Lionardo Salviati, who in his abundant critical activity included a translation and commentary of the *Poetics*, shows a strong anti-Platonic bias in his *Trattato della poetica, Lezzion Prima* (1564). Plato's whole philosophy is attacked by Salviati, since his doctrine "does not have as its end, in his works, to teach about Nature . . . , but referring to God the major part of our important actions and the most noble, it tries to fill our minds with pure religion."[64] In the specific realm of poetry, this tendency leads Plato to propose the doctrine of the divine furor and to deny that the poetic faculty is a habit of the mind. It is this denial which Salviati wishes to refute in his lecture before the Florentine Academy. He discusses one by one the arguments offered by the Platonists. First, they claim that the poets write about things which they do not really understand; but all men do this, and it is particularly excusable for the poets because of the brevity of their expression and because of the licenses accorded them. Second, they argue that occasionally a bad poet or a bad painter may produce a single good work, thus demonstrating the power of inspiration; but this may merely show the operation of chance or accident. Third, they contend that the best-trained minds are frequently incapable of writing verse; but just as frequently they are, and in any case all kinds of other influences—the humors, the planets, weather, food and drink—affect the individual's capacities as a poet, in general or at any given time. In conclusion to these rebuttals Salviati says: "I think that I have sufficiently shown so far that poetry is a habit, having demonstrated that from it derive certain operations which usually are regulated and ordered, and which could not in this way, being what they are, derive from anything but a habit."[65]

The affirmative aspect of Salviati's argument is developed further by a classification of the habits. Of the two general kinds, moral and intellectual, the latter subdivides into active and productive, according as it operates within the person acting or within some external matter. This series of distinctions leads to a definition of poetry as "a habit of operating in an external subject, through the reason";[66] no other definition than this is

---

[63] *Ibid.*, II, 365–66: "chiara cosa è, la imitazione non esser propria dell' uomo, siccome è l'arte, però l'arte è sempremai con la ragione congiunta, non già sempre la imitazione: la quale è cosa non pur da noi, ma da cornacchie e da scimie. . . . si può discernere da ciascuno occhio, tanto esser l'arte più gentil cosa, che non è l'uso o l'imitazione."

[64] *Trattato*, MS BNF Magl. VII, 307, fol. 23: "non ha per fine nelle sue opere lo insegnare la Natura . . .; ma riducendo a Dio la maggior parte, e le piu nobili delle azzioni principali, studia di riempiere gli animi di pura relligione."

[65] *Ibid.*, fol. 28: "Assai mi credo io infino a hora hauer mostro la Poesia essere habito, hauendo dimostrato, che da essa deriuano alcune operazioni, che le piu uolte sono regolate, e con ordine, e che da altro, che da habito in cotal guisa, e cosi fatte deriuare non potrebbono."

[66] *Ibid.*, fol. 29: "habito d'operare in subietto esteriore con ragione. . . ."

needed to classify poetry as an art. If further proof be required, Salviati finds it in the exhaustive enumeration of all human actions as resulting from nature, art, violence, intellect, fortune, or chance (the source of the enumeration is said to be Aristotle's *Metaphysics*, Book VIII). He eliminates all of these sources except art, which must thus be the origin of poetry. The anti-Platonic position thus leads him, as he pursues his argument, to adopt what he considers to be an essentially Aristotelian point of view toward poetry and the poet (see below, Chapter XI, pp. 494–97).

An amusing attitude toward the whole idea of the poetic furor is expressed by Lodovico Castelvetro in his *Parere sopra l'ajuto che domandano i poeti alle Muse*; the fragment is undated, but I presume it to be from around 1565. Castelvetro states frankly that the philosophers have never believed in the fiction of the Muses and of the divine furor and that the poets themselves have merely used it as a fraud to impose themselves upon the public: "In truth, Poetry never had its beginning, or its middle, or its end in a divine furor infused by the Muses or by Apollo in the poets, except in the opinion of the vulgar crowd . . .; but the poets, to render themselves marvelous and worthy of attention in the eyes of men, helped and augmented this opinion, calling upon that divine aid and pretending to have obtained it."[67] Given this basic fact about the divine furor (so contrary in its assumptions to Plato's central theory), Castelvetro adopts a realistic attitude toward the conditions and circumstances in which the Muses may properly be invoked by the poet. This leads him to several interesting distinctions with respect to the poetic art. He first divides written works into three pairs: verse and prose, long and short, narrative and dramatic. The Muses will be called upon only in long narrative poems in verse: ". . . the miraculous favor of the Muses, as far as the form is concerned, consists only in helping the writer to make such verses as would be thought impossible, by the masses, as productions simply of human effort, either because of the power of their meaning or because of their beauty."[68] A similar three-way division of subject matters provides these couples: historical and argumentative, invented and observed, difficult and easy. The poet will invoke the Muses only for historical, invented and difficult materials. By "historical" Castelvetro means "that material which we believe to have occurred, or which we give the appearance of believing that it occurred, merely on the basis of the words presented to us by the author, without any other proof." "Invented" materials are those which come "from the mind of the writer," and "difficult" materials,

[67] In *Opere varie critiche* (1727), p. 90: "veramente la Poesia non ebbe mai principio, o mezo, o fine da Furore divino infuso dalle Muse, o da Apollo ne' Poeti, se non secondo l'opinione del Volgo . . .; la quale i Poeti per rendersi maravigliosi, e riguardevoli nel cospetto degli uomini, ajutavano, & accrescevano, domandando quel divino soccorso, e facendo sembiante d'averlo impetrato."

[68] *Ibid.*, p. 88: "il miracoloso favore delle Muse, quanto alla forma, consiste solamente in ajutare lo Scrittore a far versi tali, che l'umana industria non sia creduta dal Volgo atta per se a farli, o per efficacia della significazione, o per riguardo della vaghezza."

those which "contain things which, either because of their past time or for some other reason, it is not verisimilar that the writer could know or understand."[69] In summary, then, the poet may be expected to use the device of the Muses whenever either his form or his subject matter is so extraordinary as to tax the credulity of his audience; invocation of divine assistance will then presumably create a kind of verisimilitude. Such invocation must be used only in a limited way, by poets and for poems that merit it.

GRASSO AND GIRALDI (1566)

As in the case of so many other theorists of this period, it is difficult to distinguish in Benedetto Grasso between the Horatian and the Platonic strains. I have already spoken at some length of his *Oratione contra gli Terentiani* (1566) in connection with the Horatian tradition (Chapter V, p. 177). Perhaps in the present case the distinction could be properly made in this way: as far as the ends of poetry are concerned, the simple assigning of the dual function of pleasing and instructing is essentially Horatian, whereas the condemnation of the art or of specific poets for unsatisfactory serving of the utilitarian end is specifically Platonic. This means, really, that the objection to poetry on moral grounds is taken to have Platonic origins, and Grasso's objections are exclusively moral. He declares that Terence "is not worthy to be read publicly in the schools, since he carries with him . . . a poisonous plague, by which the minds of tender youths, bewitched, become infected and poisoned in the sewer of the vices."[70] Such results are not necessary concomitants of poetry. Grasso sees two factors as producing them, first, the inherent capacity of poetry to dominate the souls of men (something of the Platonic chain of inspiration and the communication of madness is present here), and second, the wilful appeal of poets to the vulgar crowd. In an earlier, more noble age the poets used their art for its highest purposes, addressing themselves as priests and philosophers to the wise men of the community. But later, reflecting a decadence in the art, they tried only "to give amusement to the crowd and to licentious ears."[71] This tendency accounts for Plato's ban, which Grasso endorses wholeheartedly. For the effects produced by Terence's poetry, which should certainly fall under the ban, are like those accompanying a lewd picture:

. . . just as painting, the more close to nature it is, the more it delights the spectators and holds them bound with marvel, so each time it represents for them lasci-

---

[69] *Ibid.*, p. 89: "quella Materia, la quale noi crediamo essere avvenuta, o facciamo vista di credere, che sia avvenuta per le parole sole rappresentateci dallo Scrittore senz'altra prova"; and "dall'ingegno dello Scrittore"; and "che contiene cose, le quali o per tempo passato, o per altro rispetto non è verisimile, che lo Scrittore possa sapere, o comprendere."

[70] *Oratione* (1566), p. 5: "non essere degno publicamente nelle Scuole si legge, portante seco . . . vnà venenosa peste, dalla quale l'animi de teneri fanciulli affascinati nella sentina de vitij s'infettano ed auelleneno."

[71] *Ibid.*, p. 33: "per dar' spasso al volgo, & alle licentiose orecchie."

vious acts, obscene objects, dirty and ugly actions, it moves in us an honest blushing and arouses an unwillingness to look at them. And even if we do look at them, it is rather because we are moved by the artifice of the painter than by the beauty or the novelty of the painting.[72]

Poets and painters, then, will fall into two categories: those who use their art for the proper ends of honest instruction and those who corrupt it to the improper ends of dishonest pleasure. The former are to be accepted and praised, the latter are to be rejected and banished.

Grasso's attack was answered immediately by Lucio Olimpio Giraldi in a *Ragionamento in difesa di Terentio* (1566). I shall not here go into the whole of Grasso's argument, already treated in Chapter V, but shall discuss only the materials pertinent to the present discussion. Giraldi regards Terence as the greatest of comic poets, especially because he is "so excellent a demonstrator of customs and of daily life that nowhere else may one have a more useful and a clearer image of the ordinary way of life, both civil and popular."[73] This general statement provides Giraldi, later, with the basis for his refutation of Grasso's moral strictures. He admits that a poet offering obscene and lewd images would be a dangerous influence upon the young; but he denies that Terence ever does so:

I deny that Terence should be excluded from the schools for having proposed anything less than what was useful for private life; for he was never anything but the most modest writer and representative of every kind of person, and he was so careful that no clever sailor ever avoided the rocks as carefully, while sailing, as he fled from lascivious and obscene words—even though he had before him Plautus, who was very licentious.[74]

Giraldi cites the authority of Sadoleto, who also praised Terence for his avoidance of improper language. Apparently, the critic here is considering only the dangers of language. As for the actions themselves, he believes that even when they seem to be vicious, they contain hidden lessons and precepts and are hence acceptable: "in the comedies of Terence we find examples of honest behavior and of honorable citizens, which teach the reader what is proper to the praiseworthy life and through whose example may be known how much blame is deserved by those who have given them-

---

[72] *Ibid.*, p. 31: "si come la pittura quanto piu s'acosta al naturale, tanto piu gli diletta, e tiene legati, con marauiglia gli riguardanti: Cosi ogni volta gli r'apresenta atti lasciui, figure inhoneste, sporche, & laide attioni, muoue in noi un' honesta erubescentia, & genera un' sdegno di mirarle: Et se pur le mirano, piu presto mossi dal' artificio del pittore, che dalla vaghezza ò nouità della pittura."

[73] *Ragionamento* (1566), pp. 2–3: "così vago dimostratore de costumi, et della vita ciuile, che altronde non si puo hauere di lei piu vtile, ne piu espressa imagine del viuere commune, ciuile & popolaresco."

[74] *Ibid.*, p. 55: "niego, che Terentio sia, da scacciar delle schuole, perche egli proponga cosa meno, che utile alla uita ciuile, perche non fù mai il più modesto scrittore, & rappresentatore di ogni qualita di gente, & fù cosi schifo, che non schiuò mai tanto accorto nocchiero, lo scoglio, nel nauicare, quanto questi ha fuggito (quantunque hauesse hauuto Plauto inanzi molto licentioso) le parole lasciue, & dishoneste."

selves over to a vicious way of life."[75] Indeed, it is of the essence of comedy to provide lessons of this kind; and, rather than being dangerous to youth, it is an indispensable part of early education. Plato's ban on the poets is thus to be considered only as applying to those who displayed wicked acts and words and who created an improper image of the gods; other poets were exempted from it.

Examining Terence's plays, Giraldi finds in them numerous examples of both kinds of actions, wicked ones to be avoided, good ones to be imitated:

> Terence's intention was to show the ugliness of foul things so that men would abstain from them, not so that they would follow them; and to propose to them the praiseworthy and virtuous and honest ones so that they might embrace them and adorn themselves with them. Just as tragedy purges men's minds, through terror and pity, and induces men to abstain from acting wickedly, so comedy, by means of laughter and jokes, calls men to an honest private life.[76]

In sum, then, Terence may serve as a teacher of the very essence of good living. It should be pointed out that, for Giraldi, the position remains definitely Platonic, insofar as the same moral criteria continue to be applied to comedy. He differs from his opponent only in the conclusions which he derives from application of these criteria to Terence. But the difference itself is significant; it shows a much broader moral outlook and an initial tendency to justify rather than to condemn poetic works.

The *Osservazioni sopra Virgilio* of Orazio Toscanella (1566) has little to offer except a conventional defence of poetry in the usual terms; such defences continued to be produced throughout the century and were especially frequent in the works of vulgarizers and popularizers such as Toscanella. The present little treatise is nothing more than a list of the subject matters treated by Vergil, in alphabetical order, with examples of each subject and appropriate citations. In the dedication, he proposes first to indicate why poetry "surpasses all other disciplines in goodness and in dignity" and offers two reasons: "one of which is that from her, as from a mother, all the other sciences issued forth . . .; and the other, that she alone of all the rest of the arts is learned through the divine furor."[77]

---

75 *Ibid.*, p. 58: "nelle Comedie di Terentio, si hanno essempi, di honesti costumi, & di honorate persone, ciuili, lequali dittano à lettori, quello, che conuiene alla lodeuole vita, coll' essempio delle quali si conoscano di quanto biasimo, siano degni quelle, che à vitioso modo di vita, si son date."

76 *Ibid.*, p. 65: "intentione di Terentio è stata, il far uedere la brutezza delle cose sozze, perche gli huomini se ne astengano, non perche le seguitino: & . . . hà proposto loro, le lodeuoli, & virtuose, & honeste, perche le abbraccino, & di esse si adornino, & . . . come la Tragedia purga gli animi col terrore, & colla commiseratione, & induce gli huomini, ad astenersi dal mal operare, cosi il riso, & le beffe nelle Comedie . . . chiama gli huomini alla honesta vita ciuile."

77 *Osservazioni* (1566), pp. *ij–*ijv: "l'una delle quali è, che da lei, come da madre quasi tutte l'altre scienze uscirono . . .; l'altra, che essa sola fra tutto il rimanente dell' arti, per diuin furore s'apprende."

Follow the well-known arguments: all knowledge is to be found in Homer and Vergil—not only fine doctrines, but the most practical suggestions for the conduct of life and for mechanical operations; poetry had early religious uses and was highly honored in antiquity. Consequently, "it is a very fine thing that every elevated mind should devote itself to poetry, in order to acquire the most noble and precious doctrine that may be obtained among mortals, and to ascend to the level of everlasting fame."[78]

In the following year, the same Toscanella published a treatise on the *Arte metrica*, concerned with problems of metrics and extolling the art of writing in verse. Verse is considered to be a necessary part of all poetry, because of the "incredible pleasure" which it affords and because of its power of moving the human passions. As for poetics itself, "it is that art which teaches the decorum, the characters, the style, the way, the passions, and the order which the poet must observe, and in sum, all the artifice that belongs to the best poet."[79] It is hard to see in this anything but the traditional definition of the poetic art, and the emphasis upon decorum and the passions is technical rather than moralistic.

With Frosino Lapini's *Letione nella quale si ragiona in universale del fine della poetica*, we encounter a type of text which will become increasingly prominent during the last third of the sixteenth century, a text combining traditional Platonism with official Christian ethics. The *Letione*, a commentary on Petrarch's sonnet "Lasciato hai, morte, senza sole il mondo," was delivered before the Accademia Fiorentina on May 1, 1567, and the theoretical considerations precede the commentary proper. Lapini starts from the principle that all the arts and faculties have as their end the perfection of man. But since they depend from man's free will, they may be used either to achieve this end or to achieve its contrary, the destruction of man. So with poetry the proper end is "with its delightful and verisimilar fictions presented to us, to profit us much more than would be done if it narrated as does the historian or if it warned and advised us as the moral philosopher does."[80] Tragedy, for example, benefits us by purging our souls of all passions. Thus Sophocles and Euripides always ended their tragedies with useful warnings about human life; thus Aristotle insisted that— among its other requisites—character must be "good." And Vergil intimated, in Book VI, that the divine furor was given the poets so that they might bring to the attention of men many things useful for their lives.

---

[78] *Ibid.*, p. *iiijv: "ottimamente stà, che ciascuno ingegno eleuato, in essa studio ponga, per fare acquisto della più nobile, & pregiata dottrina, che s'acquisti fra i mortali; & per poggiare à grado di nome sempiterno."

[79] *Arte metrica* (1567), p. 1v: "Poetica è quella, che insegna il decoro, i costumi, lo stile, la strada, gli affetti, & l'ordine, che deue osseruare il poeta; & in somma, tutto quello, che d'artificioso pertiene all'ottimo poeta."

[80] *Letione* (1567), p. Bivv: "con le sue diletteuoli e uerisimili fintioni à noi rappresentate molto meglio giouare, che in raccontando come Historico, o amonendo come moral Filosofo non si farebbe."

Such artists and philosophers as these shared a proper conception of the poetic art.

On the other hand, there have always been those artists whose only aim has been "to give pleasure to people, not without damage and harm not only for public and private life, but also for the reverence that is due religion, since they frequently make fun of the things they should revere and exalt."[81] These artists are sometimes read for the elegance of the treatment and the pleasure which men take in imitation (Aristotle is cited as authority here), sometimes for their sensuous appeal. A work of the latter kind

. . . will please and delight, indeed, not because of the power or the art of the poetry, but because of the delight it gives to the appetite eager for such sensuality; by which such appetite is not only not removed and regulated and dominated, as would be done by the good poet who writes to benefit men, but by means of such examples it is called to life and inflamed and invited to do evil and to plunge into vice through imitation and through the evil example observed in others.[82]

Nor is the private life of the poet, which presumably may be purer than his works, any justification; his words, written or spoken, have a power of influence and expansion that renders them dangerous. It is such poets as these whom Plato wished to banish, and justifiably. It is such poetry as this, also, that notable Christian writers have condemned, Saint Paul and Saint Augustine and Savonarola among others. The last of these, for example, distinguishes between the poetry to be prohibited and that to be permitted, and establishes the conditions for the latter:

. . . having damned and driven out of the Christian republic such ruin and pestilential vanity [i.e., poetry intended for pleasure alone], he nevertheless leaves its place, nor does he take away from it its due praises, to that poetry which, following its true end, attends only to the profit of its readers. If this profit is concerned with human and moral matters, he shows that the poetry cannot properly use ornament and other poetic colors which would render it graceful and pleasing. But if it treats high and sublime and divine matters, such as the Christian religion and its mysteries, he affirms that such ornaments (as in truth we see) appear puerile and ridiculous, since high subjects of this kind cannot stand such ornamentation, in itself a weak and vain thing.[83]

81 *Ibid.*, p. Dv: "altro fine non è che dar' piacere alla gente, non senza nocumento, e danno, non solo del uiuer politico e ciuile, ma della reuerentia che alla Religione si debbe, pigliandosi eglino bene spesso in scherzo e in gioco le cose, che reuerire et esaltar douerebbero."

82 *Ibid.*, p. Dijv: "piacerà pure, e diletterà non per la virtù, et per l'arte della Poesia, ma per la delettatione dell' appetito vago di tali sensualità, dalle quali non solo non è rimosso, e regolato, e ribattuto, come il uero Poeta farebbe che per giouare ha scritto . . ., ma con tali esempli ne inanimisce & ne·infiamma, & ne inuita à comettere il male, & attuffarsi nel vitio per la imitatione e per il malo esempio scorto in altrui."

83 *Ibid.*, pp. Div–Divv: "dannata e scacciata dalla Christiana rep. tale rouina, e pestilentiale uanità, lascia pur il suo luogo, ne toglie à quella Poesia le sue douute lodi, la quale seguendo il suo uero fine, all' utile solo attende de suoi lettori; il qual utile se è intorno a cose morali et humane, mostra egli non disconuenirglisi l'ornato, et altri colori Poetici, che gratiato e piaceuole lo rendino; ma se si tratta di cose alte, e sublimi, e diuine, come della Christiana legge, e de' suoi misterij, afferma tali ornamenti apparire (come in verità si vede) cose puerili e ridicole, non patendo tali soggetti alti si fatt'ornamento, per se cosa debile, e uana. . . ."

Lapini recognizes the fact that part, at least, of the blame for the success of "pleasurable" poetry lies with the audience, which is more prone to follow the easy way of its pleasure than the hard way of the utility that it might possibly derive. The end thus comes to lie outside the poet himself and to depend upon those to whom his poem is addressed: ". . . all the blame must be assigned to those who do not allow themselves to be persuaded, because of their wicked disposition in which all good teaching is completely lost."[84]

Lapini's position is thus a curious and a mixed one. Platonic insofar as it starts with a subordination of the art of poetry to moral principles, it becomes strangely rhetorical when it places the effectiveness of poetry in the natural dispositions of the audience and when it undertakes consideration of the poet's life and character. Moreover, these elements are complicated by an essentially Christian severity towards poetic ornament and all artistic elements which might be pleasurable, and by a preference for a kind of poetry whose subject matter might be divine and whose uses would be essentially religious.

The miscellaneous short treatises on critical matters of Lodovico Castelvetro, left in manuscript at his death and published in the *Opere varie critiche* of 1727, contain certain materials of a Platonic character. These treatises were probably written between 1565 and 1571. One of them, entitled *Che cosa abbia la scienza comune, o differente con l'arte*, is generally interesting for its distinction between the sciences and the arts and incidentally displays a tendency (which might also be Horatian) to ascribe moral values and social usefulness to the arts:

Science has two things in common with art and two which are different. It has in common first the solidity of the proofs, because the one and the other proceed by means of demonstrative proofs. Next it has in common the order of the teachings, which in the one and in the other must be complete and perfect. On the other hand, science has this which is different from art, first, that science takes as its subject things which although they may be known do not necessarily lead to action; but Art does not take for its subject things which, when they are known, cannot much more easily lead to action. It has also this that is different, that science tolerates every material, whether it be decent, or useful, or dishonest, or harmful to the world; but art does not tolerate any subject which is not decent and useful to the world.[85]

---

[84] *Ibid.*, p. E: "tutta la colpa è di quelli, che persuader non si lasciano per la mala dispositione loro, nella quale si perde ogni buono ammaestramento."

[85] In *Opere varie critiche* (1727), p. 124: "la Scienza ha due cose comuni con l'Arte, e due differenti. Ha comune premieramente la fermezza delle prove, perciocchè l'una, e l'altra procede con prove dimostrative. Ha poi comune l'ordine de gl'insegnamenti, il quale dee nell'una, e nell'altra essere compiuto, e perfetto. Ha dall'altra parte la Scienza questo differente dall'Arte, prima: Che la Scienza si prende per soggetto cose le quali per sapersi non si possono far venire all'atto; ma l'Arte non si prende cose per soggetto, le quali non possano molto più agevolmente risapendosi venire all'atto. Ha ancora differente questo: Che la Scienza si tollera d'ogni cosa o onesta, o utile, o disonesta, o dannosa, ch'ella sia al Mondo; ma l'Arte non si tollera di cosa, che non sia onesta, & utile al Mondo."

The notion of the arts as necessarily "honest" and "useful" is a first step in the direction of a Platonic subordination of poetry to politics.

A more direct consideration of questions raised by Plato himself is found in the *Chiose intorno al libro del Comune di Platone*, which Castelvetro states to be posterior to his redaction of the commentary on Aristotle's *Poetics*. Here again, as in the following statement, a "usefulness" is assumed for poetry: "Here we see that the utility or the harm that is derived from the epic is the same one that is derived from history, that is, the example."[86] But the whole question is argued in a later passage, and Plato's own solution is rejected; the reference is to the passage beginning "Nihil aliud agere, vel imitari oportet."[87]

In this passage Plato presupposes that poetry was not invented for any other reason than to teach by way of example and that what is found in poetry, whether it be good or evil, can or must be followed by the reader. This is false; for we wish, not that it should teach, but that it should present matters that we can think about and that we may have examples of every kind before us: to frighten the wicked and to console the good, and to give knowledge of the nature of men and women. And for this reason Aristotle said that tragedy, by means of fears and injustices, drove fears and injustices from the hearts of men who heard it, rejecting what Plato says in this passage.[88]

Thus, for Castelvetro Plato's theory would seem to demand that the reader follow, unwittingly and unwillingly, all the examples presented to him by the poet; whereas Aristotle's theory would permit the reader choice and reflection, or rather choice following upon reflection. The basic principle of moral instruction remains, in both, the same; but Castelvetro sees the reader as a more independent and a more intelligent man and the poet as having a greater scope of activity.

CONCLUSIONS

To interrupt this analysis of the "Defence of Poetry" at the present chronological point, about 1570, is not to imply that there was any such interruption in the thinking and writing upon the subject. The defence continues throughout the century, using for the most part the same arguments; so does the attack. But on the one hand, by this date the essential elements of both attack and defence have been established and amply

---

[86] *Ibid.*, p. 209: "Ecco che l'utilità, o il danno, che si trae dell'Epopea, è quella stessa, che si trae dell'Istoria, cioè l'essempio."

[87] Trans. Ficino (Basel, 1546), p. 561.

[88] *Ibid.*, pp. 215–16: "In questo luogo presuppone Platone, che la Poesia non sia trovata per altro, se non per insegnare per Esempio, e ciò, che si truova in Poesia, o bene o male che sia, altri lo possa, o debba seguire. Il che è falso; perciochè è proposta, prima che vogliamo che insegna, per materia da farvi pensamenti sopra, & acciocchè abbiamo esempj d'ogni maniera e da spaventare i rei, e da consolare i buoni, e da conoscere la natura de gli uomini, e delle donne. E perciò diceva Aristotele, che la Tragedia con le paure, e con le ingiustizie scacciava le paure, e le ingiustizie dal cuore de gli uomini ascoltanti, riprovando quello, che dice Platone in questo luogo."

illustrated; on the other hand, after 1570 an increasing number of documents adopt an antipoetic attitude because of their strong Christian bias. This means that while the problem remains the same during the last years of the century, some of the solutions become more extreme and more violent.

This identity of the problem constitutes the principal unifying element for the numerous texts that I have examined so far. Let me state it, briefly, in this way: Should the art of poetry be admitted to society because its products contribute to the good of the state, or should it be proscribed because its works are essentially harmful? Whether the critics take the position favorable to poetry or its opposite, they remain within the same framework of discussion, within the basic assumption that it is proper to consider poetry in this light.

The opponents of poetry start from certain premises which are not always clearly stated and which are sometimes mutually contradictory. They assume that one reason why poetry is dangerous is that it exercises upon the reader or hearer a kind of irresistible power, a superior rhetorical force which sways his passions and imposes upon him the teachings of the poem. The causes of this power are partly divine, partly human. In terms of the ancient poetic of pagan times, the divine cause lies within the gods and the Muses; in terms of a modern Christian theory, within God and the natural talents or inspirations with which he endows certain men. As for the human causes, they consist almost entirely in those pleasurable adornments by means of which the poet beautifies his poem and makes it attractive to his audience. Such an assumption of "irresistibility" would seem to indicate that all men, young or old, wise or foolish, should fall prey equally to the blandishments of the poetic art. Yet a second basic assumption denies this. It holds that poetry, written under the conditions indicated, is dangerous only for certain groups—for the young men and women to whose education it might contribute, for the ignorant masses, for those men who are morally predisposed to wickedness and vice. Others are quite capable of resisting, and hence are out of danger—mature and adult persons already formed by a sound education, the sages of the city who have extraordinary faculties of discrimination, all those men who are morally disposed to goodness and virtue. The differentiating factor here is intelligence; the young and the ignorant cannot understand the true meanings of poetry and are led astray by its false appearances, whereas the old and the wise pierce beneath the illusory surface to the salutary teachings contained within. This involves a third assumption, that all poetry—even the comedies of Terence—is essentially allegorical in character, that what is visible to the eye and audible to the ear is but an imperfect representation of a hidden truth perceptible only by the intellect. The young and the foolish see only the surface and cannot "resist" the pleasurable enticements which it presents; the old and the wise, blessed with intelligence, refuse to be duped by appearances and extract from the core of poetry the most abstruse and recondite teachings.

Because of the dangers presented by the art of poetry to the young and the foolish, several alternatives for combatting these dangers are suggested by critics and philosophers. The most obvious is to forbid, to banish, to condemn poetry entirely. This is Plato's extreme solution in the *Republic*, and it has adherents throughout the years we have been studying. A second solution is to make a choice among poets and poems, admitting some and rejecting others according as they do or do not satisfy accepted standards of a pedagogical, ethical, political, or religious nature. This involves a third possibility, that of placing the whole art under the jurisdiction of a body of arbiters. These might be the elders of the city, and they would then apply political standards; or philosophers, who would see poetry in its relationships with the totality of human behavior; or priests, whose judgments would be based on theological principles involving also an ethical code; or those of the citizens themselves who would be capable of the proper kind of discrimination. Of these groups, it is probably the philosophers who enjoy the greatest favor with Cinquecento theorists, and this is undoubtedly because of the Platonic origins of this point of view and because of the vogue of the notion of the philosopher-king.

Whatever the particular group chosen to hold sway over poets and poetry, the principle of subordination of the art to another discipline is constant throughout and constitutes one of the distinguishing features of the Platonic approach during this century. I have already pointed out, however, that the central assumption of a pedagogical potential is very close to the Horatian notion of utility, whereas the recognition of the corrupting force of sweet ornament takes into account Horace's pleasure. The "utile dulci" is thus present for both lines of critics, as a statement of ends for the Horatians, as a statement of dangers for the Platonists. And while the former debated which of the ends should be predominant or how one might serve the other, the latter sought means of reducing the effectiveness of the pleasure and of directing the application of the utility. A special case must be made for the extreme Christian apologists, such as Lapini, for they tend to admit certain religious uses for certain kinds of poetry, provided that these be carefully limited and circumscribed—as regards both the pleasurable ornaments and the doctrines taught—in the light of firm theological premises.

The critics who defend poetry—not the anti-Platonists, but rather the Platonists who come to opposite conclusions—are concerned with the same basic problem. But they tend to see the circumstances in a different way. As far as they can discover through their historical researches, through their appeal to other authorities such as Cicero, Plutarch, and Strabo, through their own observations, the teachings of poetry are highly desirable and should be encouraged by every society. The testimony of the ancients, historians and philosophers alike, convinces them that in the remote ages of mankind the first contributions to civilization were made by the poets; as a result, poetry became the first of the arts and the sciences and mother of all the rest. They support this opinion on the one hand by citing a restricted number of historical and philosophical texts, on the other hand by pointing to the wealth and diversity of knowledge found in such poets as Homer and Vergil. They themselves seem to recognize in men they have known—and perhaps in their own characters—the softening influences of an art that appeals to men through all kinds of refinements and demands of its audience subtlety both of spirit and of sensibility. They thus argue, as a corollary, that the pleasures of poetry, deriving from its use of verse, a special kind of language, and all the ornaments, should be sought rather than avoided—for their own sake as well as for the contribution that they make to an ultimate utility.

How shall we explain these differences between two groups of men who approach the same problem, on the basis of the same general system of reference, and still come forth with contradictory conclusions? One answer, I believe, lies in the attitude of each group toward the men who constitute the audiences of the poets. The defenders of poetry tend less than their opponents to look upon mankind as corrupt and corruptible. They are willing to admit that the reader or the spectator has enough intelligence to perceive whatever hidden meanings there may be, enough moral stability to be moved or amused by examples of vice without necessarily undertaking to imitate them immediately, enough common sense to recognize that the works of poetry are (after all) fictions. Perhaps they recognize thus in the audience a measure of artistic sensitivity which enables it to enjoy the pleasure of the work without becoming a victim of it and to discern what parts of the work are valid guides to life. Another answer, I suggest, is that the defenders of poetry have, on the whole, a less definitely ethical and political approach to poetry than do their opponents. Although they consent to argue the matter on the grounds proposed by the Platonists, they really do not put much stock in the moral mission of the poet or in the educative function of poetry. They affirm, but without conviction or enthusiasm. Primarily, they are interested in the work of art as work of art, in the problems of its technique and its perfection, rather than in the ulterior ends it might serve. If they argue about these ends, it is because they are driven to do so by the vehemence and the persistence of the attacks; and they argue largely by affirming the contrary of what their opponents had declared. Perhaps a third answer should also be intimated: the defenders of poetry are much less prone to adopt toward their art the official position of the church or the usual suppositions of Christian theology and ethics. They remain to a greater extent within the context of the arguments of classical antiquity, and their loud proclaimings of the beauties and the delights and the educative virtues of poetry constitute, in a way, the triumph of paganism.

CHAPTER EIGHT. PLATONISM: II. THE TRIUMPH OF CHRISTIANITY

D URING THE LAST THIRTY YEARS of the Cinquecento, the principal Platonic ideas on poetry, pro and contra, continue as before. There is little contraction or expansion of the arguments, little diversification of the standard approaches to the problem. At best, one may note an increase in the number of critics and theorists who display an ultra-Catholic attitude toward questions of literature. Some of these are churchmen, and they undoubtedly reflect the conclusions of the successive meetings of the Council of Trent—conclusions which tended to place stringent limitations on the practice and uses of poetry. One may perhaps note this as a general development in the century, a repentance over the pagan excesses of the earlier years and a wish to rival, if not overtake, the strait-laced Puritanism of the reformed churches. In the literary world itself, some such turnabout may be detected in the case of Tasso—there was a modicum of madness connected with it—who first imposed an allegorical interpretation upon his masterpiece, then proceeded to the disastrous "purification" of the *Gerusalemme Liberata* into the *Gerusalemme Conquistata*. Such a purification was in complete keeping with the wishes of those few theorists of whom I shall be speaking.

VIPERANO (1570)

The first of the theorists to be considered in this chapter, Giovanni Antonio Viperano, belongs rather to the defenders of poetry. Or, more specifically, his *De scribendis virorum illustrium vitis* (1570) is a kind of "art of biography," which praises the biographer because he serves the same ends as the poet and describes the techniques common to both. "Of all the arts which teach," says Viperano, "the study of the historians and the poets seems to me to be divine and admirable; for with an almost heavenly power they rescue the deeds of great men from oblivion and from the damage of time, and at the same time sow them far and wide in the memory of all peoples."[1]

The major pedagogical value of history and biography, for Viperano, is in the instruction of princes; but it will be remembered that this was frequently assumed to be the case for certain poetic genres. For both, the education to virtue and the stimulation to glorious actions result from the proper depiction of character, and practically the whole art of biography consists in knowing how to present characters. The ingredients of such a presentation are the ones familiar to the rhetoricians and the Horatians:

[1] *De scribendis vitis* (1570), p. A3v: "inter cetera doctrinarum genera historicorum praecipue studium & poëtarum mihi diuinum, & admirabile videtur: qui coelesti quadam vi clarorum hominum res gestas ab obliuione, & uetustatis iniuria vindicant, simulque in omnium gentium memoriam disseminant."

age, sex, fortune, profession, place of birth, all the others. They must be presented clearly and vividly; *ut pictura historia*: "And just as the painter, in shaping the features of a face, in which the movements of thought shine out, uses all of his powers, so the good writer in expressing the characteristics of the soul, from which the way of life of the person is perceived, will put into such expression all his care and diligence."[2] It would seem, however, that the actions accomplished by the hero of history or of poetry are also important, for the ends are stated, partially at least, in terms of the lessons to be learned from deeds and acts: "Men should be taught to maintain a constancy of spirit in every vicissitude of fortune, not to allow themselves to be carried away by good fortune or to be depressed by misfortune; that there is no dishonor that does not come from wickedness, nor any praise that does not flow from the springs of honor."[3] Such lessons may also be learned, in both arts, from apothegms. History differs from poetry in that it is obliged on all occasions to tell the truth, whereas poetry invents all kinds of fictions (and rhetoric may indulge in expansion and exaggeration). The whole point of view of Viperano is Platonic not only in the assignment of a pedagogical function to the various arts discussed, but, in a more subtle way, in the breaking down of the barriers among these arts and the crediting of all with common ends and common means.

There is little to be added to what has already been said (in Chapter V) about Andrea Menechini's oration *Delle lodi della poesia, d'Omero, et di Virgilio* (1572). It may serve admirably as an example of the close companionship between the Horatian and the Platonic attitudes toward the ends of poetry, and also as a witness to the continuation of the vogue of the "defences of poetry." Menechini cites Plato frequently, in praise of poetry, on the divine furor and the prophetic gift of the poets. He emphasizes especially the superiority of verse over prose in harmony, in persuasive power, in imitative capacity. Imitation itself (and it will be remembered that this is one of the central concepts of the Platonists) constitutes the major effectiveness of poetry: ". . . it excites the movements of our souls, takes possession of our minds, frightening us with examples of monstrous things and delighting us with the image of those things which we desire with every warmth of passion."[4] It is through this capacity to possess the souls of its listeners that poetry achieves its usefulness, that it works miracles, that it arouses men to the contemplation of the general and the universal and frees them from the singular and the particular. Thus it

2 *Ibid.*, p. Cv: "Itaque vt pictor in conformandis lineamentis oris, in quo motus animorum elucent, summam operam consumit, sic bonus scriptor in exprimendis animi moribus, e quibus vitae ratio perspicitur, omne studium suum & diligentiam ponet."

3 *Ibid.*, pp. Dijv–Diij: "Doceanturúque homines in omni fortuna constantem animum tenere, nec in secundis rebus se efferre, nec in aduersis demittere: ac nullam esse ignominiam, quae a turpitudine non proficiscatur, nec laudem vllam quae non ab honestatis fonte emanet."

4 *Delle lodi* (1572), p. a iv–a ivv: "eccita i mouimenti de gli animi, s'insignorisce delle menti, spauentandoci con essempij di cose monstruose, & rallegrandoci con l'imagine di quelle, che noi desideriamo con ogni caldo affetto."

becomes the mistress of all the sciences. These various powers are the consequences of the divinity of poetry: "The divinity of poetry is understood from this fact, that nobody can achieve success in it without celestial breath or inspiration."[5] From the poet, the divine spirit passes to the reader or the listener, making of him a person closer to the gods in his perfection:

Oh holy Poetry! oh highest of divine inspirations! for by purging us of every stain, making us pure and simple, you make our soul shine with its own splendor, and through its proper and natural strength, as also through its intelligence which is the chief and pilot of that same soul, you cause it to obtain from the angels in a single moment whatever it desires.[6]

The praise continues in this tone, now general, now applied to Homer and Vergil—a tone which recalls that of Plato in the dialogues dealing with inspiration and enthusiasm.

The same problem of imitation, but approached from a more intellectual standpoint, is the subject of a brief fragment by Lorenzo Giacomini Tebalducci Malespini; it is without title, and I shall call it *On the Definition of Imitation*. The fragment follows Giacomini's translation of Aristotle's *Poetics* in MS Laurenziana Ashb. 531, and is likewise in the hand of Giorgio Bartoli, and I presume it to be of the same date, 1573. Its content is also related to the text of the *Poetics*, since Giacomini is here trying to distinguish between the definitions of imitation offered by Plato and by Aristotle. By combining the definitions in Books III and X of the *Republic*, Giacomini produces a somewhat strange interpretation of Plato; I have already cited the passage in extenso in Chapter II (p. 62). He assumes that all the uses of the term "imitation" in Plato are identical or at least similar and hence that various meanings can be combined into a single one. This leads him to equate imitation with fable or mythology, to raise the question of whether a fable need be told "in the person of another," to decide that it need not, and to concoct a curious definition of poetry in which various senses of "imitation" and of "fable" are hopelessly confused. Giacomini belongs in the Platonic tradition in the sense that he continues the discussion of one of the main ideas associated with that tradition by contemporary theorists and that he presents a kind of commentary or interpretation of the text of Plato.

AGNOLO SEGNI (1573)

In fact, Giacomini's little passage on imitation (if indeed it be his) may be more closely indebted to another work of 1573 than to his own translation of the *Poetics*. That work is a set of lectures delivered by Agnolo Segni

---

[5] *Ibid.*, p. b ij$v$: "Et di qui si comprende la diuinità della Poesia, imperò che alcun non può conseguirla senza fiato, ò inspiration celeste."

[6] *Ibid.*, p. b iij$v$: "Ò santa Poesia, ò ben somma inspiration diuina; poiche purgandoci da ogni macchia, rendendone casti, & semplici, rilucer fai l'anima col proprio splendore, & per la natural, & propria diligenza sua, come ancor per la sua mente, che è capo, & auriga di essa anima, in un subito momento la fai conseguir da gli Angeli ciò, che ella disidera."

to the Accademia Fiorentina; in their original form they were six in number, although Segni reduced them to four in 1576. The original lectures are now to be found in the Biblioteca Laurenziana, MS Ashb. 531 (the one which contains Giacomini's works); the published form appeared post-humously in 1581.[7] In keeping with the traditions of the Accademia, Segni must limit himself to a discussion of Petrarch, and he chooses to speak of the canzone (No. CXXVII) beginning "In quella parte dove Amor mi sprona." But only a few paragraphs of the lengthy *Lezioni* are devoted to the poem; the rest is an essay on imitation, on Platonic principles, meant to serve as prolegomena to the analysis of Petrarch. In itself, the essay is one of the most extensive, most thoroughgoing, and most valuable Platonic documents of the century.

Seen in its narrowest sense, Segni's group of lectures may be taken as an attempt to justify lyric poetry as a proper genre and Petrarch as a poet. But in its broadest sense, this justification requires a complete theory of poetry, of imitation, and of all the literary genres, and it is to that theory that Segni addresses himself. The first lezione establishes a general Platonic system, involving the need for the search, in any field of knowledge, for the "highest good," discovering that in most disciplines it is found in the intellect but that in poetry it is found in the divine furor, asserting that the genus of poetry is imitation. The second lezione defines imitation, establishes its relationships to false discourse ("orazione falsa") and to fable ("favola"), and inquires into the objects of such an imitative fable. The third studies the kinds of imitation, both without and within poetry, and explains in what sense Plato found imitation bad and why he banished the poets from the Republic. The fourth investigates the instruments of imitation, including the necessary instrument of verse, and arrives at preliminary definitions of poetry, poetics, and poem. In the fifth, seeking to discover the ends of poetry, Segni examines the various kinds of arts (with respect to their ends), the faculties to which they are addressed, and the various ends which might be assigned to poetry. Finally, in the sixth (after a lengthy summary of the preceding five lezioni), he reaches the discussion of Petrarch; but since this immediately involves him in an elementary theory of the lyric, little if anything is said about the poem in question.

Segni's first definition of poetry (in the fourth lecture) is: "An imitation of human and divine things, by means of fable-making discourse, in verse, according to the divine furor." In the last lecture, this definition is expanded and completed by the addition of the formula "to the end of purging human minds of their emotions."[8] A gloss on this definition will reveal Segni's main ideas about the art of poetry. He means, by imitation, a

---

[7] See my "Nuove Attribuzioni di manoscritti di critica letteraria del Cinquecento," *Rinascimento*, III (1952), 247–49.

[8] MS Laur. Ashb. 531, fol. 74v: "Immitazione de le cose humane, et de le divine con orazione favolosa in versi secondo il furor divino"; and fol. 88: "à fine di purgare gli animi humani da loro affetti."

number of things. He does not exclude the simplest Platonic meaning of "to speak in the person of another" (fol. 53); but this is too limited a meaning and it would eliminate most of the writings of the lyric poets—for example, Petrarch. It indicates an accident of poetry, not an essential differentia. In its most general meaning, to "imitate" is to make one thing resemble another (fol. 54), to fabricate one thing—an "idolo," an "immagine," a "fantasma"—in likeness of another which is its "essempio" or "essemplare." The "idolo" gives an appearance, a representation of its object, and poetry is concerned with the making of such images. As an art of imitation, poetry enters into the whole broader schematism of imitation which Segni borrows from Plato. Since it uses discourse, its words imitate concepts just as its concepts imitate things (fol. 86v). The general process of imitation is found everywhere in the world: God imitates himself in man (see Scripture), nature imitates the world of ideas, art imitates nature, men imitate each other (fols. 32–33). In a word, the whole Platonic chain of relationships—from universal Ideas to particular concepts or objects to representations of those concepts or objects—is constituted by a series of imitations.

The particular realm of poetry involves imitations of special kinds and many cautions with respect to them. Its materials are not "true" things, such as those which go into the making of history and science and the arts, but rather "false" things; for it imitates things which, without being true in themselves, create a semblance or a likeness of truth. These are called "fabula" by the Latins, "favola" by the Italians, "mythology" by the Greeks. Segni, in this analysis, apparently collapses the materials of poetry with the instrument of their expression. As he himself states (attributing the distinction to Plato), it is the language (the "orazione") of poetry which is false, and hence poetry is a false imitation:

> Of these two kinds of language, the true, which narrates the truth of things exactly as they were done or are done or as they are, does not belong to poetic imitation or to poetry, but it is proper either to history or to one or another of the sciences. Hence, the other part remains for poetic imitation and for poetry: to make images out of false language and out of fable; and consequently poetry is this—false language which makes images, that is, which makes false things and things invented by itself in resemblance to the true, which language is called mythology by the Greeks and "favola" by us and by the Latins.[9]

In another context, however, he distinguishes false plot from false speech: "The fable is thus always lying and falseness, but it is divided into two; one

---

[9] *Ibid.*, fol. 56: "Di queste due orazioni la vera, la quale narra la verità de le cose appunto come sono state fatte ò si fanno ò come elle sono, questa non appartiene à la poetica immitazione, ne à la poesia, ma è propria ò del istoria, ò d'una ò d'un altra scienzia: adunque l'altra parte resta al'immitazione poetica et à la poesia, il far idoli con l'orazione falsa et con la favola; et diremo la immitazione poetica essere il far idoli con la orazione falsa et con la favola; et conseguentemente la poesia essere questo, orazione falsa la quale fa idoli, cio è fa le cose false e finte da lei somiglianti à le vere, la quale orazione mithologica è chiamata da Greci, et da noi favola et da Latini."

is the false language, as Plato says . . . , which contains within itself false things, whatever they may be; the other is those false things themselves and particularly false actions, not true but invented."[10] Segni thinks that herein lies the difference—or one of the differences—between Aristotle and Plato on imitation: Aristotle considered the actions themselves, not the words, as the plot or "favola."

In a general way, Segni attributes to Aristotle the same meanings for imitation as to Plato. He argues that because Aristotle divided imitation into three manners—narrative, dramatic, and mixed—and because these were the three manners which Plato had given to "mythology," then imitation and mythology must be the same thing. Aristotle is made the authority for the statement that the objects of imitation are not restricted to human actions but include characters, passions, and thoughts as well (fol. 59), while Plato indicates that the gods also may be treated. Segni feels that these statements are necessary, first to justify the inclusion of lyric poetry (which has no actions), second to permit the kind of loose description of the object, in his definition, as "human and divine things." In that same definition, the means of imitation are said to be "fable-making discourse" (a concept which we have already examined) and verse. Verse is demanded by the common conception of poetry, by Plato (explicitly) and by Aristotle (implicitly); it is the "necessary matter" for the realization of the "form":

Thus poetry is a composite of imitation and of verse, in which the imitation is its essence and not the verse; but not for this reason can it be poetry without verse, which is necessary to it as its proper matter, just as a body is necessary to man, and not just any body, but a particular body and a particular matter: but to the soul and to the form corresponds, in poetry, the imitation, just as the language corresponds to the body and to a certain kind of body, and not any language whatsoever but this fixed one, that is, metrical language or language made in verse.[11]

The last member of Segni's original definition—"according to the divine furor"—is meant to indicate the main efficient cause of poetry. Nature and art are also efficient causes; but nature, in the Platonic system, is identifiable with divine inspiration, and art is secondary because it is powerless without nature. For Segni, it is the presence or absence of the divine furor which accounts for the goodness or badness of poetry.

When, in order to complete his definition, Segni adds the formula "to the end of purging human minds of their passions," he is providing his

[10] *Ibid.*, fol. 57: "È adunque sempre menzogna la favola et falsità, ma si divide in due, una è la orazione falsa come dice Platone . . ., la quale contiene in se cose false, qualunque elle si sieno: l'altra è le stesse cose false, et particolarmente l'azzioni false non vere ma finte."
[11] *Ibid.*, fol. 72v: "Cosi la poesia è il composto di immitazione et di verso, dove la immitazione è l'essenza di lei, et non il verso, ma non pero puo essere poesia senza il verso, il quale è necessario à lei come propria sua materia, si come al huomo è necessario il corpo, et non qualunque corpo, ma un corpo tale, et una materia tale, ma al anima et à la forma risponde ne la poesia la immitazione, si come al corpo, et tale corpo risponde l'orazione, et non qualunque orazione, ma questa determinata, ciò è l'orazione metrica, ò fatta in versi."

statement of the final cause. This may seem to be a nod to Aristotle; but the formula is much more than a paraphrase of the purgation clause in Aristotle's definition of tragedy. For Segni, working in a Platonic context, the ends of poetry are varied and complex. As an imitative art, it appeals to the senses, which are both deceived and satisfied by it; it does not appeal to the reason. If there is another part of the soul to which imitation is germane, it is the appetitive faculty, for the appetite transforms itself into the object of its desire. In a word, poetry addresses itself to the irrational and hence the inferior parts of the soul. According to Plato, the end of poetry is to alter the appetite and to fill it with passions; if these are good, the poem will be good, and vice versa. But according to Aristotle, the end is just the opposite: to remove the passions from the soul by means of purgation. After lengthy examination of the nature of this effect, Segni concludes that it consists in the removal, not of pity and fear themselves, but of their opposites, and that a similar purgation of opposites takes place in the other genres. He states that the end of poetry is "the purgation from the mind of various noisome and blameworthy passions, brought about through the means of other better passions" ("la purgazione del animo da diversi affetti noiosi et biasimevoli col mezzo d'altri affetti migliori condotta à fine," fol. 82). He does not, however, fail to take into account other suggestions of the possible ends: Aristotle's, that it is the plot; Horace's, that it is pleasure and utility; Proclus', that it is similarity to the original. In a final summation, he attempts to distinguish among these rival ends and to admit all of them into a total conception of poetry:

We have explained several ends for poetry: the plot as the form and soul and the end of the other parts: the moving of the passions and purgation as operations of the whole; the passions that are moved and the purgation, ends insofar as they are works which remain as made. Pleasure as an accident of the end is also called an end and is placed among the ends. But because when one speaks about the end, one means that end which is the end of the whole and not of the parts of the thing proposed, and because also the works made by the operations are an end and purgation is an end of the passions previously aroused, it follows that the true and ultimate end of poetry and of the poem is the purgation of our minds of their passions, as we said above according to Aristotle. And I mean always by this name of purgation not the operation of purging which is in the agent, but that of the patient and of the subject purged.[12]

---

[12] *Ibid.*, fols. 83–83v: "Habbiamo esplicati piu fini de la poesia, la favola come forma et anima, et fine del altre parti: il mover gli affetti et il purgare come operazioni del tutto: gli affetti mossi et la purgazione, fini come opere che rimangano fatte: il piacere come accidente del fine, ancora egli fine s'appella et si pone tra' fini. Ma perche quando e' si ragiona del fine, e' s'intende di quello che è fine del tutto et non de le parti de la cosa proposta: et perche ancora l'opere de le operazioni sono fine et la purgazione è fine de gli affetti mossi inanzi: seguita che de la poesia et del poema il fine vero et ultimo è la purgazione degli animi nostri da loro affetti, come noi dicevamo disopra secondo Ar.e et intendo sempre per questo nome purgazione, non l'operazione del purgare la quale è ne lo agente, ma quella del paziente et del suggetto purgato."

The seeming duality of approach, involving an admixture of an incidental Aristotelianism to a basic Platonism, is present throughout the work. We have seen it in the concept of imitation, in the insistence on verse, in the idea of purgation. At times, Segni thinks that the two ancient philosophers are in precise agreement; at others, when they disagree, he finds the means of reconciling them by a more inclusive theory which embraces both. Occasionally, where Aristotle fails to define a term, Segni assumes that he adopts and shares Plato's use of it. When Aristotle says (*Poetics* 1454*b*11) that the tragic poet's portrayals must represent men as more remarkable than they really are, Segni interprets this as calling for a representation of Platonic Ideas of character and the passions (fol. 63). The distinction of poetry into four species, epic, tragic, comic, and lyric, is found in both philosophers, and it depends upon the division of the three manners of imitation: the epic is mixed, tragedy and comedy are dramatic, the lyric is narrative. (It is a further division of lyric poetry that permits Segni to discover the proper classification of Petrarch as a writer of encomia and of threnes.) From Aristotle Segni borrows the notion that poetry is superior to history because it is more universal; from Plato, the judgment that it is inferior to philosophy because of its very particularity (fol. 90). On the whole, the general structure of ideas and the framework of reference in Segni are Platonic: poetry exists in a Platonic world of imitations, it is made possible by the presence of the divine furor, it pursues a goal of moral betterment for the spectator.

At the beginning of his discussion of the utility of poetry in his *Apologia dei dialogi*, written around 1574–75,[13] Sperone Speroni seems to be espousing a position opposite to Plato's in the *Republic*. For he answers Plato by pointing out the political usefulness of the art:

> If it is a good thing to purge the errors of a single man through repentance, it is undoubtedly much better to connect in their natural order our particular arts with that general art of the state, and to subordinate the former to the latter, as is proper. For from the preservation of that order arises the determination not only to do no evil . . . , but to refrain from any actions which might appear legitimate to this or that individual, but which are in opposition to the best behavior of the whole body of the citizenry.[14]

It is this notion of a social usefulness, according to Speroni, which led Aristotle to include the purgation clause in the definition of tragedy. We note here that although Speroni sees virtues in the use of poetry for social instruction, he nevertheless wishes to subordinate the art to the higher art

13 See Speroni, *Opere* (1740), V, 209, 364, 365, for letters useful in dating the *Apologia*.
14 In *Opere* (1740), I, 355: "se egli è bene purgar gli errori di un uomo solo per penitenza; è senza dubbio assai meglio tener congiunte nel loro ordine naturale le nostre arti particolari colla comune della repubblica, e quelle a questa, come è ragione, subordinare. con ciò sia cosa che da questo ordine conservato nasce il consiglio, non solamente di non far male . . . ma di astenersi d'alcune vili operazioni, che pajon lecite a questo e quello, ma son diverse al decoro della adunanza cittadinesca."

of politics. When he goes on to discuss specific genres, especially comedy, he discovers that such forms may do as much harm as good—that they may be "schools of vice" as well as "schools of virtue." He must therefore conclude that the state should restrict the kinds of poetry that it allows men to write and to publish, and that essentially all public or political poetry should have a religious intention:

It is the duty of every well-ordered city to portray in verse, as elegantly as it knows how and without admitting any other fables, all of the favors that God has granted it . . . ; to praise the deeds of the citizens who were victorious in just wars . . . ; and to sorrow over the death of those who did not merit death. . . . If it does so, its poems will not turn out to be comedies, or tragedies, or epics, but hymns, canticles, and psalms, useful, decent, and religious. If these poems are accompanied artistically in the presentation by music, song, and dance . . . , there is no woman or child who, having heard them one single time, will not retain them pleasurably in the memory for the rest of his life.[15]

The conclusion is that of Plato; it reflects the general circumstances and tone of the *Apologia*, a work written in old age as a repentance for youthful sins. Perhaps some of the religious afterthought of which I have been speaking is already present here.

LORENZO GAMBARA (1576)

The next two documents are definite examples of such public repentance. The first is the *Tractatio de perfectae poëseos ratione* of Lorenzo Gambara (1576); its subtitle is in itself significant: "tum ostenditur, cur abstinendum sit à scriptione poëmatum turpium, aut falsorum Deorum fabulas continentium. Ac quàm late pateat campus ad pulcherrima alia poëmata edenda." Gambara admits that he had spent his youth in the writing of profane poetry and that he was now determined to the necessity of burning these same poems. For they had served neither of the two ends legitimate for poetry: the singing of the glory of God and the salvation of man's soul. Instead, they had merely been manifestations of his own desire for worldly fame (one is reminded of the conversations between St. Augustine and Petrarch in the *Secretum meum*). In writing them, he had been pursuing false appearances, false gods and lying muses, because the only real truth had not yet been apparent to him. The misguided Gambara is here like the poet of Plato, who represents semblances only and is never able to see Truth. He thus agrees with the banishing of the poets by the pagan philosophers (Plato, Dio, Suetonius, and Plutarch are cited) and with the con-

---

15 *Ibid.*, p. 357: "egli è officio di ogni cittade bene ordinata ritrarre in versi quanto più sappia elegantemente, senza altre favole, tutte le grazie che le son fatte dal Signor Dio . . .; lodar le geste de' cittadini in guerre giuste vittoriosi . . .; e condolersi alla morte de chi era degno di non morire. . . . ciò facendo, riusciranno li suoi poemi non commedie, non tragedie, non epopeje, ma inni, cantici, e salmi, utili, onesti, e religiosi. li quai poemi, accompagnandosi con bella arte nelli spettacoli al suono, al canto, ed al ballo . . ., non sarà donna o fanciullo, che quelli uditi una sola volta, volentieri tutta sua vita non li abbia sempre in memoria."

demnation by the church fathers (Clement of Alexandria and Basil, for example) of any works which introduced heresy, magic, or moral wickedness.

Gambara himself will base the whole discussion of the art of poetry on the foundation of Christian theology. Seen in this light, the obscene and wicked fables of the poets and the licentious images of the painters are the work of Satan, designed to make men revolt against reason and develop the habit of sin. Moreover, the poet who adds to a Christian poem either the myths of antiquity or improper moral actions creates a work as ridiculous as Horace's monster:

> But if he who joined a human head to a horse's neck ought to be laughed at, certainly he who joins to a Christian neck, that is a poem, a hydra's head in the form of a vile conflux of filthy wantonness is greatly to be lamented, for his salvation, along with the salvation of many others, is either already to be deplored or is fast approaching the point where it will have to be deplored. And indeed the hydra's head and all other prodigies and chimeras were invented by us according to our powers, since we filled our writings with so many monstrosities, that even if there were no peril for our honor and decency, there certainly would derive from them a considerable peril for our faith so long as our minds were darkened when submerged in these shadows, and distracted completely from heavenly things to the constant pursuit of vanities.[16]

If the writing of such works is reprehensible, the reading of them is full of dangers: our senses are depraved, we are excited to vice, or if we have already sinned we are moved to sin again rather than to repent our former errors. The ultimate consequence is heresy. Hence, there is no doubt that the Christian reader should avoid all the literary monuments of antiquity, in spite of the fact that certain church fathers may seem to have authorized them.

In place of these monuments, the Christian poet will provide works representing not only a new theology and a new ethic, but also a new poetics. For Aristotle's *Poetics* based on Homer and Horace's *Ars poetica* based on Vergil can be of no use to him; they merely provide rules for the imitation of unacceptable models. Gambara is willing to admit, with St. Augustine, certain beauties of art and of style in the ancient poets; but their content is such as to render them inadmissible to the Christian state. If the wise ancient philosophers who wrote arts of poetry based them upon these works, it is only because they had not yet had the privilege of seeing the light of Truth:

16 *Tractatio* (1576), pp. 11–12: "Quod si . . . qui humano capiti ceruicem equinam adiungeret ridendus esset, sane qui Christianę ceruici, hoc est poëmati caput hydrę, faedarum nempe libidinum colluuiem apponit, magnopere deflendus est, cuius salus, cum salute plurimorum aut deplorata sit, aut non procul est, cum sit deploranda. Et hydrę quidem caput, ceteraque portenta, & chimera[e] pro viribus effingebantur à nobis, cum scripta tot monstris oppleremus, vt nisi honestati periculum ac pudicitię fuisset, certe fidei non leuis erat iactura dum mens nostra his tenebris offusa cęcabatur, atque à cęlestibus ad inania celebranda curuabatur omnino."

. . . but although they have understood that poetry has been instilled in us by nature, and that it therefore resides in the imitation of truth, still, when once the fountain of nature had been troubled and their vision was overcast by a cloud of error, because they had not achieved the greatest virtue in poetry, they chose finally what seemed right to themselves.[17]

The Truth that was lacking to them was of course that of Christian revelation, and without it they could not possibly discover the truth about poetry:

Now, since they were neither enlightened by the light of faith, nor so lived by the light of nature as to give glory to God; and since, moreover, sin had introduced into the world the errors of the false gods and the many common ideas about them; and since indeed they had neither read nor understood the holy Scriptures, nor had they read or understood something in them would they have believed them, or even had they believed something in them would they have dared to make it public out of fear; and finally, since they did not see among their countrymen absolutely anybody endowed with those virtues which even the light of nature requires in the formation of a perfect man, they themselves invented certain men for whom descendance from the gods or their exploits or the supposition that they were numbered among the gods won a certain esteem, stimulating others to imitate them. But we have already indicated with what manifold error![18]

The new poetry, the Christian poetry, must have principles essentially different from the old. Perhaps, in a sense, the ends will be the same, since it too will seek to delight and profit; "imitation" and "doctrine" are the two ends proposed for poetry, and it is the function of the poetic faculty "to see whatever is appropriate to the imitation of each action, passion, character, by means of beautiful language, in order to improve life and to live well and happily."[19] But whereas the old poetry was content, for its subject matter, with the necessary and the probable (following Aristotle's recommendation), the new poetry must content itself with nothing less than the truth. Whereas the old pagan poets derived their model of the perfect man from error, through invention and fiction, the new poets will find theirs in truth, through pious meditation and the teachings of theology.

17 *Ibid.*, p. 22: "quod & si, à natura Poësim nobis inditam, ac proinde in veritatis imitatione sitam esse intellexerunt, naturę tamen fonte turbato, & caligine errorum oculis offusa, quod in Poesi rectissimum erat, non assequuti, quod sibi tandem rectum visum est, elegerunt."

18 *Ibid.*, p. 22: "Cum enim nec fidei lumine illustrarentur, neque pro naturalis luminis ratione ita viuerent, vt Deo gloriam tribuerent; falsorum autem Deorum errores, promiscuasque de illis opiniones peccatum inuexisset in Mundum; nec vero Diuinas scripturas legissent, aut intellexissent: nec si quid legerant, aut intellexerant crediddissent, aut tamen si quid crederent, auderent propter metum pronunciare: denique cum apud suos neminem ijs omnino virtutibus pręditum cernerent, quas ipsum etiam naturę lumen requirit in homine perfecto efformando, ipsi per se aliquos effinxere: quibus vel ortus ex Dijs, vel res gestę, vel in Deorum numerum conficta relatio illis quidem existimationem conciliarent, ceteris autem adderent calcar ad imitandum. Sed quam multiplici errore, iam diximus."

19 *Ibid.*, p. 24: "vt poëtica facultas sit videndi quodcunque accommodatum sit ad imitationem cuiusque actionis, affectionis, moris, suaui sermone ad vitam corrigendam, & ad bene beateque viuendum."

Thus the old criteria of "prudentia, varietas, efficacia, suavitas," will be replaced by two only, "modestia" and "veritas," sufficient in themselves to assure the achievement of the ends. The strength of the word of God will be more efficacious than all the rhetorical devices and all the prodigies of the ancient poets and their modern imitators. The lives and deeds of the martyrs will supply materials having all the required characteristics; using them, one may write

... the epic without adulation and without damage to the truth; tragedy presenting the praise of the Christian religion; satire without bitterness, permitting the poets to inveigh against heresy and against the vices with the greatest sincerity, but without violating charity. A vast field is thus opened for writing all kinds of poems without falsehood, without ineptitudes, without causticness, without foulness, but with faith, majesty, graveness, penetration, charity.[20]

To a degree the new poetry has already been attempted. But Gambara condemns those who have chosen sacred subjects only to mix them with profane matters and to treat them in profane meters; Marot, Beza, Buchanan come under the ban for this reason. Only those poems devoted to the spreading of the faith, to the publishing of holy crusades, to the conquest of Jerusalem, will be found acceptable and will be admitted to the Christian Republic.

I have dwelt at some length on Gambara's theories for two reasons: First, they represent the complete Christianization of the Platonic point of view. The Republic having been transformed into the Christian Republic, everything that Plato had said about poetry in relation to the former is restated in terms of the latter. The treatment of the gods or of God, the relationship to truth or to Truth, the role in education, all these come in for consideration. Second, these theories are an early statement of a doctrine which was to be developed at some length in the following century, not only in Italy but in France as well, the doctrine of the Christian epic. Gambara adumbrates, in 1576, the characteristics of that new literary genre.

It must have been shortly after its publication that Cardinal Sirleto sent a copy of Gambara's treatise to Francesco Panicarola, for in 1576 Panicarola wrote a letter to Sirleto thanking him for the work and adding his own remarks to the discussion; the letter is preserved in MS Vat. Lat. 6531 and is dated "Di Bologna li .8. di Settembre 1576." Panicarola reveals an interesting filiation among writers sharing the same point of view toward poetry; he speaks of Gambara as his friend and states that his master was Antonio Possevino, who in 1593 was to write a treatise *De poësi et pictura*

[20] *Ibid.*, p. 27: "epopeia sine assentatione, aut veritatis damno; Tragica cum Christianae religionis commendatione; satyrae sine amarulentia, dum in haeresim, vitiaque Poetę sincerissimi salua charitate inuehuntur. Ad cetera denique Poemata scribenda latissimus patet campus, sine falsitate, sine ineptijs, sine mordacitate, sine faeditate, sed cum fide, maiestate, grauitate, acumine, charitate."

ethnica. All three writers were Jesuits and reflected the teaching of the order; Panicarola makes specific reference to the decree of the twenty-fifth session of the Council of Trent, 1563, condemning obscene works of art. He is enthusiastic over Gambara's burning of his own poetry and hopes that other poets—and especially painters and sculptors—will destroy their works. The whole tenor of his letter is that he wishes to see Gambara's principles for poetry applied to the other arts; it is especially important that painting and sculpture should be subjected to control and censorship since the images they present affect the senses even more violently than do those of poetry. On the thesis of the close similarity between poetry and painting, which he finds stated by the best philosophers, he proposes that just as an Index has been established for books, so also one should be set up for works in the other arts. What he is most eager to insure is the limitation of any works which might be obscene or libidinous in their materials. The principles upon which such restriction would rest are suggested by Panicarola, who calls upon the authority of the ancient saints and upon the suggestions made in the Decree of the Council of Trent. Clearly, the letter has no pretentions of being an exhaustive treatment of its subject; it merely extends Gambara's arguments to the other arts. It is useful as an illustration of the spreading of this ultra-Christian point of view, as a representation of the kind of thinking current within a certain restricted milieu.

When, in 1576, Agnolo Segni revised for publication his set of lectures to the Accademia Fiorentina, he made those excisions necessary to reduce the series from six to four lectures. He died in the same year, and the *Ragionamento sopra le cose pertinenti alla poetica* was not published until 1581. A comparison of the two texts[21] shows no really essential differences in poetic theory. Although he cuts out some of the basic philosophical material (such as the general outlines of a Platonic theory of the "summo bene" at the beginning of the first lecture) the general position does not change. Nor does it differ as a result of curtailment of some passages presenting specific arguments. In its broad lines, the point of view toward the art is the one outlined earlier in this chapter. At certain points there are significant alterations of the text; but their importance should not be overstressed. Thus the addition to the definition of poetry of the words "and spirit"—"it is an imitation of human and divine things, by means of fable-making discourse, in verse, according to the divine furor and spirit"[22]—merely brings in another of the terms which had been frequently used in the original version. The expansion, at a later place, of the final clause of this definition so that it reads "to the end of purging human minds of their emotions and of harmful passions,"[23] may be intended only to stress a

21 See my "Nuove Attribuzioni di manoscritti di critica letteraria del Cinquecento," *Rinascimento*, III (1952), 247–49.

22 *Ragionamento* (1581), p. 44: "ella è imitazione delle cose humane, & delle diuine con orazione fauolosa in versi secondo il furore, & spirito diuino."

23 *Ibid.*, p. 58: "à fine di purgare gli animi humani da' loro affetti, & dalle passioni nociue."

utilitarian end which had always been recognized. In any case, the gloss upon the total definition need not be revised, nor was it by Segni, in the light of these alterations. His general vision of poetry as an art intermediate between philosophy and history[24] still obtains, and Plato remains the dominant master, who explains and complements the terse and elliptical Aristotle.

Some of Segni's ideas were certainly known to Lorenzo Giacomini by 1576, for he had a copy made of the original lectures of 1573. Yet it is difficult to see any direct reflection of them in his own lectures *Della nobiltà delle lettere e delle arme*, read to the Accademia Fiorentina in 1576. His problem in the three lectures is to discover the relative worth of letters and of arms; early in the first lecture he outlines his procedure: "... it will be necessary ... to discuss virtue in general, both active and contemplative, and, since the virtues are habits of the soul, to discuss the soul and its capabilities; and moreover happiness, for the virtues are the causes of happiness."[25] This outline describes the general character of the discussion, which throughout remains vague and abstract and only occasionally approaches the specific problem of literature and of poetry. I have indicated in Chapter I its general conclusions: those branches of "letters" which constitute the contemplative sciences would be superior to arms, whereas the ones which merely lead to the kind of action represented by arms would be inferior to them. The general supposition is that philosophical disciplines which determine the ends and the modes of action take precedence over it, whereas ancillary sciences—including poetry—which merely serve the ends of action are less meritorious. Giacomini, remaining within his generalizations and considering poetry only in terms of the ends served, represents one of the typical Platonic attitudes toward the art.

The Accademia Fiorentina also heard, two years later, in 1578, Francesco Bonciani's *Lettione della prosopopea*. (I have analyzed its Horatian elements in Chapter VI.) From Plato Bonciani borrowed above all certain ideas on imitation. He sees imitation in the broader sense as any representation of a person or object; in the more specific sense, "when anybody, in his speech, introduces a third person who speaks in his own person ... , there is nobody who does not know that this is an imitation. One imitates also in relating partially the form and the character and the action of any person whatsoever."[26] These preliminary distinctions allow him to classify the figure in which he is interested, prosopopeia, as an imitation. Along

---

[24] See above, chap. i, p. 31 and n. 61.

[25] MS B.N. Paris, Fonds italien 982, fol. 2: "sarà necessario ... ragionare della virtù in vniuersale, et della attiua, et della contemplatiua: et poiche le virtù sono habiti dell'anima, ragionare dell'anima et delle sue potenzie; et della felicità ancora; poiche sono cause della felicità." See also above, chap. i, p. 18 and n. 29, for an earlier discussion.

[26] MS Ricc. 1539, fol. 132v: "quando altri nel suo ragionamento introduce un terzo, che'n sua persona fauelli ... niuno è che non sappia questa essere imitatione: Imitasi ancora nel riferire partitamente la forma, e l'abito, e l'attione di che che sia."

with other Platonists, he defends poetry on the basis of its civilizing function in antiquity; but he makes the argument specific by insisting that one of the devices used by the wise men of early times to educate and domesticate primitive peoples was the animal apologue, a form of prosopopeia. This form seems to him to fit ideally the requirements for poetry, since it presents a pleasurable exterior—an imitation—under which is concealed a serious lesson useful to the audience.

In a short passage of a very considerable work, the *Uniuersales institutiones ad hominum perfectionem*, Filippo Mocenigo considered briefly the problem of the regulation of the arts. The work was first published in 1581, and the passage in question is Contemplatio V, Pars II, Cap. XIIII, entitled "De artium omnium, ac de Magistratuum, qui artibus praeficiuntur, fontibus." Starting from a division of the arts into the perfect ones and the imperfect ones, the former being those which create, by means of the artistic activity, a product which remains, the latter being limited only to the activity, Mocenigo sees the imperfect arts as having as their sole end an appeal to one or several of the senses. They may be productive of no effect beyond that upon the senses, or they may be applicable to some further use. In some cases, the appeal to the senses may result in pleasure for a spectator rather than for the person engaging in the activity, or in addition to the latter's pleasure. Such arts as the dance, choral singing, singing and instrumental playing, belong to the latter category, whereas tragedy, comedy, and other poetical works combine such pleasure of the spectator with a higher function. This would seem to be the building of character and of moral strength. Both the pleasurable aspects of art and its educative possibilities demand that the magistrates of the city intervene to control it; they must "drive out the useless and indecent arts, as well as the indecent uses of the arts, according as will be established by the laws."[27] Plato's suggestions in the *Republic* are here echoed in an incidental way.

GIROLAMO FRACHETTA (1581)

In the same year, 1581, Girolamo Frachetta published a work which enters much more fully into the Platonic current than the last few which I have been discussing; this was his *Dialogo del furore poetico*, whose interlocutors were Frachetta himself, Giovan Battista Pona, Prospero Bernardo, and Luigi Prato. The problem of the dialogue is double: to discover whether Plato's theory of the divine furor is reconcilable with other things which Plato himself has to say about poetry, and to ask whether the theory itself is tenable. Two interpretations of Plato are presented in connection with the first problem, one asserting that all Plato's statements about the art of poetry are consistent, the other insisting that it is impossible to accept at the same time the doctrine of the divine furor and the banishment

---

27 *Institutiones* (1581), p. 529: "expellere inutiles, ac inhonestas artes, necnon inhonestos artium vsus, prout legibus sancitum erit."

of the poets. Pona is the champion of the affirmative, and his argument may be summarized in this way: Plato does believe completely the theory of the divine furor; the poet writes not through natural causes but through a divine inspiration coming to him from God via the muses. If at the same time he banishes the poets from his Republic, it is because of the special conditions of the Republic and because of certain characteristics of poetry. When the poet speaks under the influence of the furor he can speak only the truth, and this should be desirable in any state; but he may speak this truth in the guise of an allegory which, because it is not intelligible to the young and the ignorant, would thus not be desirable. The Republic, accepting only what is perfect and wishing to use poetry for pedagogical purposes, could not admit poetry of this kind. But poets also speak, at times, for themselves, on the basis of their purely human capacities; and at such times they may err and may introduce lies into their poems. They may seek the pleasure of their audience, especially through such forms as tragedy and comedy, and in so doing they may depart from the mission assigned to them by the state. Any of these contingencies would disqualify them from participation in the labors of the Republic. Pona insists that Plato's statements are to be taken absolutely: the ban affects all poets and all poetry, it was necessary in the conception of the Republic, and it is entirely defensible in the light of a belief in the divine furor.

Through most of the *Dialogo*, Frachetta himself takes the negative position. He cites Castelvetro and other scholars to the effect that Plato could not really have believed in divine inspiration. For divine inspiration would mean truth and truth would mean good poetry, and good poetry could not possibly be excluded. The ban, however, applies only to bad poets and certain fictions and lies that must be considered bad poetry; these things were not only not true, they were not even verisimilar, and neither Plato nor his readers accepted them as such at the time. Being bad and false, they could not result from the divine furor; hence, either the ban is unjustified or the divine furor is itself a fiction. Frachetta chooses the latter alternative. Throughout this argument, he contrasts the position of Aristotle with that of Plato, using the former in support of his own points of view. In the later pages of the dialogue, other interlocutors intervene and carry the major part of the conversation, and they conclude by stating that Aristotle's theories of poetry not only are more acceptable to the reason but are also more in keeping with Christian theology and the views of a Christian reader. (I shall treat these discussions of Aristotle in a later chapter.)

In addition to its comparison of poetry and history, already studied (Chapter I, p. 15), Lionardo Salviati's dialogue *Il Lasca* (1584) is interesting for its attack upon the art of poetry from a Platonic point of view. The comparison of the two disciplines, which begins innocently enough, ends with a condemnation of poetry on all scores; the attack, indeed, springs from principles stated in the first stages of the argument. Among other distinctions, poetry and history are differentiated on the basis of their ends: that of poetry is to "purge our souls of the passions and assure that our behavior will be proper"; that of history is "prudence."[28] But there is some doubt about this difference, for the epic poem seems also to have "prudence" as its goal:

It seems necessary to admit that the proper end of epic poetry, which is commonly conceded to be the most magnificent form, is equally prudence and the good of the state; and I said the "proper" end because the other forms of poetry, just as all the arts, are governed in some way or other by the needs of the city. . . . But in such cases it is a secondary or derivative end. . . . Whereas it seems that the work of the epic poet concerns the good of the republic by primary intention . . . by purging the passions and by correcting manners it makes itself useful to the city, but accidentally and not through primary concern.[29]

The essence of the argument here is that, in the special case of the epic, poetry serves accidentally an end which falls in the domain of ethics and essentially an end which falls in the domain of politics. The important question, and the one upon which the attack will later be founded, is this: Is poetry capable of properly serving its end, whether it be ethical or political?

Il Deti, the interlocutor who is responsible for presenting the argument, believes that poetry is incapable of so serving its end. As compared with history, it has the weakness of not carrying conviction: "For history is believed as true, and poetry is held to be a fiction. . . . the poem moves us more than history does, but the emotion ends with the reading. History on the contrary does not by any means arouse us so much as poetry does, but it leaves us persuaded, a thing which, in my personal belief, is not brought about by a poem."[30] As for the pleasure involved in poetry, it is brief, passing, and costly in the sense that it involves a great loss of time. Worse still, it is accompanied by a corrupting influence on character and behavior:

When poetry puts forward the virtues, no benefit results; for since we quickly recognize them as false, we do not found our actions upon those good examples.

28 *Il Lasca* (1584), p. 11: "il fine il purgar gli animi dagli affetti, e renderci ben costumati"; and for history, "il fine la prudenza."

29 *Ibid.*, pp. 11–12: "del poema eroico, che per lo piu magnifico si reputa comunemente, par da concedere, che il diritto fine sia la prudenza altresì, ed il ben esser del comune. e ho detto il diritto: imperciochè anche l'altre guise di poesia, si come tutte l'arti, sono ordinate per alcuna delle maniere de' beni della città. . . . Ma il cotale si è fine conseguente. . . . Ma l'opera dell'Eroico il ben della repubblica par che riguardi di prima intenzione. . . . col purgarsi le passioni, e col dirizzarsi i costumi, si fa vtile alla città, ma per conseguente, non di primo riguardo. . . ."

30 *Ibid.*, p. 31: "Perchè la Storia si crede cosa vera, ed il poema si tien per finzione. . . . il poema ci commuoue piu, che la Storia: ma il commouimento cessa con la lettura: La Storia per lo contrario non ci sollieua a gran pezza quanto la Poesia, ma lasciaci persuasi: cosa che dal poema, secondo che credo io, non s'adopera."

On the contrary, by showing us vice the poet frequently does us much harm. For vice is completely the prey of the passions, and these passions constitute properly the power of the poem: it excites them, it works upon them, it exercises its force over them, it is with respect to them that poetry excels. Nor is damage of this kind compensated by blame or punishment of vice [within the poem]; for our desire, without wishing to hear out the argument, seizes suddenly upon what pleases it and accepts it for true; but when unpleasant things are involved, it has recourse to reason and says, "These are mere stories, what's the use of thinking about them?" The pleasure is in the imitation, the beauty of the verse, the sweetness of the song, the excitement of the dance; all these are sulphur and pitch which augment the fire and the flame; all are ready to harm.[31]

It will be noted that if the presentation of the virtues is inefficacious while that of the vices is capable of producing undesirable effects, it is because of inherent weaknesses of the audience, which tends to be led by its appetites rather than by its reason. Another weakness of this same audience consists in its inability to reason about what it sees; hence the relationship of the false objects of poetry to truths of reality, through verisimilitude, escapes it, and it does not learn the intended lessons. Such a conception of the audience—the young and the ignorant—is common among the Platonists, but Salviati generalizes it in such a way as to lead to a complete condemnation of the art of poetry. The state as such is not involved in the same way as it is in the *Republic*—a special kind of commonwealth with specific functions reserved for poetry—but the governing disciplines of politics and ethics are brought to bear upon the judgment of the art of poetry. In the light of these disciplines, Salviati decides (through his interlocutor, Il Deti) that one should completely abandon poetry in favor of the superior art of history.

Since Torquato Tasso himself had indicated, in the *Allegoria del poema* affixed to the 1581 edition of his *Gerusalemme Liberata*, that he meant the allegorical aspects of his poem to have an educative function (see Chapter VI, p. 206), his critics and commentators were not long in applying such criteria to his epic. One commentator, Scipione Gentili, made a few remarks of this character in his *Annotationi sopra la Gierusalemme Liberata di Torquato Tasso* (1586). As a result, his commentary on stanza I presents the following theory of the ends of poetry:

31 *Ibid.*, pp. 39–40: "La Poesia del metterne auanti la virtù, niun guadagno ne puo lasciare: conciosia che per falsa riconoscendola noi prestamente, sopra quei buoni esempli non facciam fondamento. Per lo contrario, col dimostrarne il vizio, spesse fiate ci nuoce assai il Poeta. Perocchè il vizio è in tutto in preda agli affetti: e questi affetti sono propriamente lo sforzo del poema: quelli eccita, quiui s'adopera, in quelli esercita la sua possanza, in questa parte sormonta la Poesia. Ne col biasimo, ne col gastigo si fatto danno si puo ricompe[n]sare: poscia che l'appetito senza voler vdire il discorso, subitamente, prende quel, che gli piace, e come vero il riceue: ma verso lo spiaceuole ricorre alla ragione: e dice, queste son fauole: che fa luogo il pensarci? Il piacere della imitazione, la vaghezza del verso, la dolcezza del canto, il solleuamento del ballo, son tutti zolfo, e pece, che crescono lo'ncendio, e la vampa: tutti stanno per nuocere."

But what is more important is the fact that the true and proper end of the poet is no other that to profit by introducing the virtues and extirpating the vices from the souls of the citizens. He brings this about by purging them of those passions from which a great proportion of adverse events are born and depend. This purgation was indeed known and praised by Plato, who called it καθαρμόν; to say nothing of Aristotle, who put it in his definition of tragedy as the proper final cause of the latter.[32]

The conflation of Plato and Aristotle, so familiar in the century, is here presented in a highly abbreviated form.

The whole theory of purgation is developed at great length by Lorenzo Giacomini in his *Sopra la purgazione della tragedia* (1586); but since much of the text concerns the interpretation of Aristotle, I shall treat it at a later time. There is, however, one sense in which the discussion is pertinent in the present context, and that is insofar as purgation, for Giacomini, is related to the utilitarian ends of poetry. Indeed, he sees the introduction of the purgation clause in Aristotle's definition of tragedy as a direct answer to Plato, an attempt to counteract the banishment of tragedy and the tragic poets. Giacomini distinguishes two ends for poetry: one, which we might call Aristotelian, is the making of the poem according to the principles of the art; the second, which is "Platonic" in a vague way, is the use of the poem for other purposes, "whose consideration with respect to their causes belongs to the politician who forms the state or who governs it."[33] When, therefore, he forms his own definition of poetry, he includes in it two phrases which state these ends, "made according to the poetic art" and "proper for purging, for teaching, for giving recreation or noble diversion."[34] And when he seeks to identify the four causes of poetry, he sees the final cause (according to Aristotle) as including "purgation, teaching, rest from the cares and from the affairs of life, and finally the diversion of the mind in the intelligent man, which is found in the perfect and joyous knowledge of the excellence of the work."[35] (The same ends are also applicable to painting and sculpture.)

These distinctions provide Giacomini with a satisfactory solution to the debate about pleasure and utility; his is a compromise position:

. . . we say that poetry should be used not for one single end but for many,

---

[32] *Annotationi* (1586), p. 3: "Ma cio che piu importa, s'è che il vero e dritto fine del poeta non è altro, che di giouare inserendo le virtu, e sterpando gli vitij dagli animi de' cittadini. Il che conseguisce col purgargli di quelle passioni, che gran parte dalle cose auuerse nascono e dipendono. La quale purgatione fu etiandio cognosciuta e lodata da Platone, dimandandola καθαρμὸν. per tacere di Aristotile, il quale la mise nella definitione della Tragedia, come per causa finale di essa propriamente."

[33] In *Orationi e discorsi* (1597), p. 33: "la consideratione de quali per le loro cagioni pertiene al politico."

[34] *Ibid.*, p. 33: "fatta secondo l'arte poetica" and "atta a purgare, ad ammaestrare, a dar riposo, o nobile diporto."

[35] *Ibid.*, pp. 33–34: "la purgatione, l'ammaestramento, il riposo da le molestie, e da negotii de la vita, e finalmente il diporto del animo nel huomo intendente, che è gioconda, e perfetta cognitione del eccellenza del opera."

according to the different kinds of poems and of listeners, all of which ends we include under the name of profit; for the rest and relaxation of the mind from its affairs and labors, and the noble diversion of the mind through the knowledge of the exquisiteness of the work—along with Aristotle we classify these as profit, along with purgation and teaching. Those first two ends are common to all kinds of poetry, but one of them belongs to intelligent men, the other indeterminately to everybody. The last two are proper to special kinds of poetry, since purgation takes place only where strong passions are expressed, and it is certain that some poems do not have the power to benefit virtue and to improve character.[36]

Some indication of the specific ways in which the last kinds of utility are effected is found later in the discourse, where Giacomini points out that we see, in poetry, how calamity falls to the lot even of the great and that we learn wherein true happiness is to be found (p. 46). For all these reasons, he concludes that the politician, far from exiling the poets, "should accept tragedy as profitable to the city if it is used properly and at the right time and in moderation; for if it were used too frequently it would not effect purgation, or else it would bring about a purgation that was neither useful nor necessary."[37] Once again, within the framework of Platonic presuppositions, Giacomini arrives at conclusions divergent from those of his opponents, conclusions that he considers to be integral to the philosophy of Aristotle.

GIASON DENORES (1586)

The juxtaposition of Plato and Aristotle, or rather their fusion and confusion, is again characteristic of Giason Denores' *Discorso intorno à que' principii, cause, et accrescimenti, che la comedia, la tragedia, et il poema heroico ricevono dalla philosophia morale, & civile, & de' governatori delle republiche* (1586).[38] But more striking still in this text is the extent to which the whole art of poetry is reduced to the service of its utilitarian ends. Whereas most theorists are content to make general statements about these ends, Denores insists upon seeing in every part and every feature of the poem a specific device for the achievement of these ends, in each case determined by them. His final summary makes his point clear: " . . . we have already clearly shown that most of the parts of tragedy, of comedy,

36 *Ibid.*, p. 34: "diciamo essa douersi vsare non per vn fine solo, ma per molti secondo la diuersità de poemi, e deli vditori, i quali fini tutti comprendiamo sotto nome di giouamento, poiche & il riposo, e l'allentamento del animo da negozij, e da le fatiche, e'l nobile diporto de la mente per la conoscenza de la esquisitezza del opera, con Arist. al giouamento riduciamo, si come anco la purgatione, e l'ammaestramento. quei due primi fini sono a tutte le poesie comuni, ma vno pertiene a gli huomini intelligenti, l'altro indeterminatamente a ciascuno; gli altri due s'appropriano a speziali poesie, poiche la purgatione non ha luogo, se non doue si esprimono gagliardi affetti, & alcuni poemi è certo non hauer forza di giouare alla virtù, e di migliorare il costume."
37 *Ibid.*, p. 51: "douere il Politico accettare la Tragedia come gioueuole a la Città, se conueneuolmente, & a tempo, e con misura è adoperata: perche il troppo frequente vso, o non purgherebbe, o farebbe purgatione non vtile, ne necessaria."
38 See above, chap. i, p. 26, for a brief discussion of this text.

and of the heroic poem—change of fortune, reversals, recognitions, character, thought—practically serve no other purpose than this utility."[39] The general statement is, of course, present—present on almost every page of the work—and it takes various forms in various contexts. It is present in the discussion of the origins of poetry, where certain men of high genius directed the art, after its natural beginnings, "to the public benefit and utility, to which according to reason and according to the sayings of the wise all the arts and the professions of men who lead civilized lives in the cities must be directed."[40] Present, necessarily, in the definition of poetry, a definition modeled on Aristotle's definition of tragedy and containing this final clause: ". . . in order to purge them [the listeners], by means of pleasure, of the most important passions of the soul, and to direct them to good living, to the imitation of virtuous men, and to the conservation of good republics."[41] Present, in a modified way, in the definitions of the various kinds of poetry. The modification comes about through the assignment of each genre to a specific audience, in a special kind of state, and needing a particular kind of indoctrination. Thus, comedy will have as its end "to purge the spectators, by means of pleasure and the ridiculous, of those troubles which disturb their peace and their tranquillity through the falling in love of wives, daughters, and sons, through the deceit and treachery of servants, pimps, nurses, and others of their kind; and to cause them to love private life and to wish to preserve that well-regulated popular republic in which they live."[42] Tragedy will seek "to purge the spectators, by means of pleasure, of terror and of pity, and to make them abhor the life of the tyrants and of the most powerful men."[43] And the heroic poem will have as its goal "to inflame the listeners to the love and the desire to imitate the magnanimous and glorious exploits of great persons and of good and legitimate princes, and to make them content to live under their state, and to abhor the dominion of tyrants and to wish to preserve that well-regulated monarchy in which they live."[44]

[39] *Discorso* (1586), p. 43: "gia habbiamo apertamente fatto uedere, le piu parti della tragedia, della comedia, & del poema heroico, la tramutation di fortuna, le peripetie, le agnitioni, il costume, la sentenza non tender quasi ad altro, che alla utilità."
[40] *Ibid.*, p. 1v: "al beneficio, & alla vtilità publica, alla quale per ragione, & per sentenza de' sauii deono hauer la mira tutte le arti, & profession d'huomini, che uiuono accostumatamente nelle città."
[41] *Ibid.*, p. 36: "per purgargli col mezzo del diletto da' piu importanti affetti dell'animo, & per indrizzargli al ben viuere, alla imitation degli huomini virtuosi, & alla conseruation delle buone republiche."
[42] *Ibid.*, p. 36v: "per purgar gli spettatori col mezzo del diletto, & del ridicolo da que' trauagli, che turbano la loro quiete, & tranquilità per gl'inamoramenti delle mogli, delle figliole, de' figlioli, per gl'inganni, & tradimenti de' seruitori, de' ruffiani, delle nutrici, & di altri simili, & per fargli inamorar della vita priuata a conseruation di quella tal ben regolata republica populare, nella quale si troueranno."
[43] *Ibid.*, p. 36v: "per purgar gli spettatori per mezzo del diletto dal terrore, & dalla misericordia, & per fargli abhorrir la uita de' tiranni, & de' piu potenti."
[44] *Ibid.*, p. 37: "per accender gli ascoltanti all'amor, & al desiderio d'imitar l'imprese magnanime, & gloriose de' gran personaggi, & de' buoni, & legitimi principi, & per fargli contentar di uiuere sotto il loro stato, & abhorrir la Signoria de' tiranni a conseruation di quella tal ben regolata monarchia, nellaquale si troueranno."

Since each of the genres has a special message for a separate group of people, its content and its construction will be determined by that message. For example, the heroes of the epic, because they are presented as models to be admired and imitated, must be perfect in every respect; but those of tragedy and comedy, because their vices and failings are to be punished as warnings to the spectator, should be midway between the absolutely good and the absolutely bad. Denores develops at length the reasons why, in these characters, absolute goodness or absolute badness would defeat the purposes of poetry. Similarly, the materials of poetry must be presented in such a way as to engender the marvelous, for this brings about pleasure and pleasure is the instrument of utility. In tragedy and comedy, the marvelous is achieved through the accomplishment of the change of fortune within the brief period of time (twelve hours) allotted to the poet. The rapidity of the change in itself provides lessons:

Who then of the spectators would not be inflamed to a desire for private living, seeing many times in these plays that in so brief a period of time every trouble of private citizens may be changed into the greatest happiness? and who would not hate the tyrannical life of the more powerful, seeing and considering that every form of their greatness almost in the blinking of an eye may be turned into extreme ruin, into exile, death, and murder?[45]

The more leisurely adventures of the epic hero show that even the life of the perfect man is full of uncertainties and hence less to be desired than a private existence; they also serve to illustrate even more vividly his numerous virtues. Thus the episode, the particular form which the marvelous takes in the epic, is itself a pedagogical device. So also, in all forms, are the other constituents of plot as Aristotle distinguishes them: recognition and reversal. Both help to produce the marvelous and both enable the poet to bring about the reward of the good and the punishment of the wicked. A perfect plot will combine all these elements in such a way as to communicate a simple and intelligible moral and political lesson (Denores illustrates his meaning by showing how excellent epics or tragedies could be drawn from Boccaccio's tales about the Conte d'Anversa, Gismonda, and Rosciglione). One requisite for perfection will always be the capacity of the materials to "riceuere . . . la moralità" (p. 29v).

Following Aristotle's order in the *Poetics*, Denores then passes on to the other qualitative parts. Character, with which he associates decorum, was introduced into all forms of poetry "especially to generate in the minds of the spectators or of the listeners a knowledge and experience of human actions. . . . for who will ever say that it is not also useful to him to understand all these qualities and conditions of men, and to distinguish the good

[45] *Ibid.*, p. 17: "Chi è dunque de' spettatori, che non si accenda al desiderio della vita priuata, riguardando spessissime volte in queste rappresentationi, che in cosi breue giro di tempo ogni trauaglio de' priuati si riuolga in somma letitia, & che non abhorisca la vita tirannica de' piu potenti, vedendo, & considerando, che ogni loro grandezza quasi in vn batter d'occhio si possa riuolger in estrema ruina, in essilio, in morte, in vccisioni?"

from the bad, in order to know himself and the ways of human life?"[46] This is a separate end, served by a separate part of the poem. Thought, which he translates by "sentientia" and "discorso," has (curiously enough) a utility of a different kind, insofar as it may be of service to those of the citizenry who devote themselves to the study of eloquence. Diction and verse, finally, contribute to the production of the marvelous; besides, when they are properly adapted to the character and the station of the personages, they enhance the verisimilitude and hence the power of persuasion of the work.

Every part of a good poem will therefore be included in the poem because it makes a contribution to its utility; it may serve either the general end of moral instruction or some particular end peculiar to itself. Moreover, the handling of each part by the poet will be judged proper or improper as it corresponds or fails to correspond to the needs of the lesson. All the criteria for the poem will necessarily be linked to ethical and political considerations. Indeed, Denores insists that "as a good moral and political philosopher" Aristotle treated only those forms of poetry which derived their principles from moral and civil philosophy. He himself, applying the same principles, declares that such forms as the tragicomedy and the pastoral are not worthy of attention since they are monstrous as artistic compositions and, more damaging still, they cannot possibly teach the kinds of lessons which are the province of poetry. Their authors are not poets; at best, since they seek only the pleasure of their audience and not its profit, they are like sophists who pursue a false and deceptive form of their art. Throughout this analysis, Denores holds tenaciously to his principle of the social usefulness of poetry, never doubting it to be true, never seeking to answer those who had raised doubts about it. The principle is axiomatic, no defence is needed. He applies it to every aspect of the art and every part of the poem; and since he does so within the skeleton of the arrangement of Aristotle's *Poetics*, he achieves a kind of complete Platonization of the latter document, limited only by the limits of the problem: the usefulness of poetry in the state.

TOMMASO CORREA (1586–87)

In contrast to Denores' work, Tommaso Correa's *De antiquitate, dignitateque poesis & poetarum differentia* (1586), is entirely conscious of its Platonism and seeks a position that will at once explain Plato's favorable statements about poetry and justify his banishment of the poets. It begins with a defence of poetry composed of all the traditional elements: its ancient dignity, its noble rank among the arts, its status as a first philosophy bringing wisdom and manners to uncouth peoples. But immediately,

---

[46] *Ibid.*, pp. 30–30ν: "per generar specialmente negli animi de' spettatori, & degli ascoltanti cognition, & esperienza delle attioni humane. . . . chi dira mai, che non gli sia anchora utile il comprender tutte queste qualità, & condition d'huomini, & distinguer le buone dalle cattiue, per cognoscer se stesso, & la prattica del uiuer nostro."

a distinction: not all poets are worthy of such praise. It belongs only to those poets whom Plato called "the ministers and interpreters of the gods" and should be denied to those who sing vacuous verses appreciated only by the vulgar crowd. To explain these differences among poets, Correa appeals to a metaphysical principle of the three levels of existence in the human soul. The highest of these is celestial and divine, representing the existence of God in man, removed from all corruption by the senses and the body. The middle level is the peculiarly human one, representing a combination of the highest and the lowest things in man's nature, of the divine and the bestial; it is the realm of the mind, of reason, of knowledge. The lowest level is the dark region of the body and the senses, where man is close to the lower animals; it is dominated by visions, phantasies, appearances. To each of these levels, says Correa, corresponds a category of poetry and a kind of poet.

The divine furor is responsible for the first and most excellent class of poetry. It denotes the presence of God in man and is the expression of his highest capacities. This is that furor or afflatus of which Plato spoke. From it comes all such poetry as celebrates the great deeds of our ancestors and serves to render us and our progeny more perfect. The poetry of the prophets and the seers, that of sacred letters and religious writings, belongs in this category:

> In this kind of poetry were active almost all those holy prophets whose works we have in sacred letters, who in part predicted many future things, in part revealed to mortals many things about God and about heavenly matters, in part celebrated excellent deeds, in part exhorted men by divine warnings to religion and to the other virtues, in part deterred them from vices. All these things those men have done, inspired and impelled by a heavenly spirit, and deservedly these things are referred to this first kind of poetry.[47]

The second species, inferior in many ways to the first, is the product of the human faculties of reason: "... it knows the nature of things, and takes delight in honest deeds and sayings, and concerns finite things."[48] It is a kind of philosophical and moral poetry, providing knowledge, admonitions to virtue, warnings against vice; examples of it are furnished by Tyrtaeus, Theognis, Empedocles, Nicander, and Lucretius.

To the lowest form, dark and ignoble because it springs from opinion and visions, belongs all such poetry as has its basis in imitation. Aristotle devoted his *Poetics* exclusively to this type, and Horace most of his *Ars poetica*. Imitation itself is divided into two kinds:

[47] *De antiquitate* (1586), p. 679: "In hoc genere poeticae versati sunt omnes fere illi sacri vates, quorum monumenta in sacris litteris habemus, qui partim futura multa prędixerunt; partim de Deo, rebusque celestibus multa mortalibus aperuerunt: partim excellentia facta exornarunt; partim monitis diuinis ad religionem, caeterasque virtutes adhortati sunt, partim à vitijs deterruerunt. Quae omnia illi afflati, & instincti caelesti numine fecerunt, & merito, ad hoc primum poeticae genus referuntur."

[48] *Ibid.*, p. 682: "cognoscit naturam rerum, & honeste factis, & dictis delectatur, & res in numerum includit."

. . . a kind of true and exact imitation which renders each and every thing exactly as it is; the second, contrived and invented, expresses each thing, not as it actually is, but as it appears to be, or else can appear to the many. From this there arises one form of poetry which has rested upon opinions about true things, and, by putting forth a likeness very close to those [things] and distinct, is completely adapted to the imitation of the truth. The second form, which, by following only that which seems and appears to be, sets before their eyes not the true likeness, but a kind of simulated appearance of the likeness, is completely adapted to pleasure. The former alters nothing by imitation, the latter inflates slight defects to huge dimensions, restores the listeners by the kind of language and the variety of harmony, completely changes the feelings of men and the nature of things, because it renders them by imitation not as they actually are but as they can seem to be, since it is a kind of sketchy outline, not a finely wrought conception of things.[49]

Correa goes on to say that the first two types are not only approved but are highly recommended by Plato; whereas the third is accepted insofar as its first subdivision is concerned, rejected and excluded and banned in its second subdivision. For the end of the first two categories is instruction; but the end of the third is pleasure. Correa seems to accept these distinctions as he sees them in Plato, and to see in them an adequate explanation of Plato's "contradictions."

The same Correa published, in 1587, his *In librum de arte poetica Q. Horatij Flacci explanationes* (already analyzed in Chapter VI, p. 215). Since his purpose here obviously was to provide a commentary on Horace, the problems of poetry are seen from a special point of view; Plato enters only incidentally and in an illustrative capacity. There are, however, several points of interest with respect to Plato, and perhaps even one modification of the theory presented in the *De antiquitate*. Plato is first called upon in connection with the remarks on *Ars poetica* 1–23, where Correa sees above all a principle of propriety or "conuenientia." This propriety is of various kinds, and among them there is a "Platonic" kind: "Indeed Plato also in Book IV of the *Republic* affirms that the poets are not permitted to say whatever they wish, but he teaches that they must observe the law of propriety. There exist in fact certain circumscribed limits beyond which they may not pass, lest things be said contrary to the accepted norms of life and

---

[49] *Ibid.*, pp. 682–83: "Imitatio quaedam vera & recta quę talem vnamquamque rem effingit, qualis ipsa est; altera simulata, & ficta vnamquamque rem exprimit, non qualis ipsa est, sed qualis videtur, aut multitudini videri potest. Hinc existit vna forma poeticę, quae veris de rebus opinionibus nixa est, & germanam illarum, & expressam similitudinem proponens tota ad imitationem veritatis accommodatur. Altera, quae sequens id tantum quod videtur, & apparet, non similitudinem veram, sed quamdam simulatam speciem simili- tudinis ante oculos ponit, ac tota ad voluptatem comparatur. Illa nihil immutat imitando, hęc ad ingentem magnitudinem extollit exigua mala, auditores verborum genere & concentus varietate recreat, commutat animos hominum, & naturam rerum, quia non quales sunt, sed quales videri possunt effingit imitando, cum sit adumbratio quaedam, non subtilis rerum cognitio."

of mores."[50] Correa seems to imply that in the Horatian context the preoccupations of Plato, largely religious and ethical, are reduced to a political and social level. So in his statement of the ends of poetry the Platonic elements of instruction of the young and formation of character are attenuated to the traditional rhetorical "vt admoneatur, delectetur, doceatur" (p. 93). But he passes from attenuation to denial when he discusses the subject of the poetic furor. It will be remembered that in the *De antiquitate* Correa had situated the operation of the poetic furor in the highest reaches of poetic activity, as a manifestation of the presence of God in those poets who wrote religious and prophetic poetry. In the present work, however, he all but denies the existence of such divine intervention. Commenting on lines 309–10, where Horace is speaking of the necessity for knowledge, Correa writes:

> Since he had touched upon the argument that, according to the opinion of Democritus, the poet became a poet through nature and through a kind of furor, in this twentieth precept he declares whence springs every praiseworthy poem having decorum. Knowledge, he says, just as it is the mother, the fountain, and the origin of all things meriting praise, is also the nurse of poetry. And so far is it from the truth that the poet is "furious," that nobody can write well unless he has knowledge. In fact it is essential that every good and proper form of writing should derive from a knowledge of things.[51]

The difference between this text and his own treatise is undoubtedly explained by the fact that in the latter he had denied the existence of the furor in the second and third levels of poetry and had asserted that Horace himself was concerned only with the lowest of these levels. But part of the explanation may also be found in the circumstance that Correa is here no longer in the realm of the purely theoretical; he is providing a commentary on what he regards as an essentially practical treatise.

LORENZO GIACOMINI (1587)

As its title indicates, Lorenzo Giacomini's oration *Del furor poetico*, delivered before the Accademia degli Alterati in 1587, is also devoted to the problem of poetic inspiration. And in a sense it reaches the same practical conclusion as had Correa in the *Explanationes*, and for the same reasons. For Giacomini recognizes immediately the practical consequences of assuming that the divine furor exists: if it does, then art and principles and practice are useless; if it does not, then the poet must address himself to his

---

[50] *Explanationes* (1587), p. 6: "Nam etiam Plato in iiij. de Rep. negat permitti poetis dicere, quicquid voluerint, sed spectandam esse conuenientiam docet. Nam quidam sunt circumscripti termini, vltra quos egredi, fas non est, ne aliena à vitae institutis, & moribus dicantur."

[51] *Ibid.*, pp. 101–2: "Quia natura, & quasi quodam furore poetam fieri attigerat ex sententia Democriti hoc xx. precepto declarat vnde effiorescat laudabile & decorum carmen. Est inquit sapientia, vt omnium laudandarum rerum mater fons, & origo, sic etiam est poetae altrix. Tantum verò abest, vt furiosus poeta sit, vt bene scribere nemo possit, nisi sapiens. Omnis enim oratio bona, & apta ex cognitione rerum promanet necesse est."

art with greater seriousness and application. After presenting the conventional arguments for the divinity of poetry, Giacomini points out that this theory involves a separation of poetry from the other arts; for, whereas all the other arts would have particular principles and fixed subjects, poetry would have neither. He sees no reason for making this distinction. Poetry, he says, may be defined simply as "a fable expressed in verse," and both fable (or plot) and verse may be produced separately. Moreover, the concept of divinity destroys all art, all merit and praise for the poet. If not by the furor, how then are poems produced? Giacomini's answer is simple; it involves instead a theory of the humors:

The man who wishes to rise to the heights of poetry or of eloquence or of philosophy has need of temperate spirits, inclining rather towards the cold ones, in order to think, investigate, discourse, and judge . . . ; to continue in such operations, he seeks an abundance of humors neither weak nor easily dissipated, but stable and firm, which move through vigorous and powerful imaginations; but in order to execute well in conformity with the idea conceived within himself, he needs warmth so that the expression may be effective.[52]

These latter "heated" spirits are the ones that give the effect of "estasi, rapimento, furore, smania"; it is because of them that the soul, "fixed and intent upon an operation, forgets every other object, and does not even remember itself or what it is doing."[53] Such concentration by the poet may in a sense be called a furor and divine:

. . . if by furor we mean that fixation of the soul upon the Idea, or if we denote that internal incitement and movement, born not of individual reasoning and judgment but of the natural disposition of the instrument to which it is united, then there will be furor in the poet, and it will be called divine not without reason since it proceeds from Nature, which is the daughter of God, and from an excellent Nature: I mean the human soul combined with a subject having that temperament.[54]

But this furor has nothing to do with an individual act of inspiration on the part of God, with a special favor accorded to given men (and only the poets) at given moments in their lives.

The mechanism of poetry is thus essentially a natural one for Giacomini.

---

52 In *Orationi e discorsi* (1597), pp. 59–60: "l'huomo che al altezza de la Poesia o del Eloquenza, o de la Filosofia dee salire, per pensare, inuestigare, discorrere, e giudicare, ha bisogno di spiriti temperati, che inclinino nel freddo . . .; per continuare in queste operationi, ricerca copia di spiriti non deboli, ne facili a risoluersi, ma stabili, e fermi, che muuon con vigorosi, e potenti fantasmi, ma per bene eseguire secondo l'idea in se conceputa, ha bisogno di calore, accioche con efficacia esprima."

53 *Ibid.*, p. 60: "affisata & intenta ad vna operatione di ogni altro oggetto si scorda, ne pure si ricorda di se stessa, ne quello che faccia."

54 *Ibid.*, p. 61: "se per furore intendiamo quel affisamento del anima del Idea, o vero se denotiamo quel incitamento, e mouimento interno, nato non da proprio discorso, e giudizio ma da naturale proprietà del instrumento al quale è vnita, harà luogo il furore nel poeta, e sarà non senza ragione detto Diuino, poiche procede da la Natura, che è figliuola di Dio, e da Natura eccellente dico dal anima humana a soggetto di tal temperamento congiunta."

He explains the power that the art has over its listeners or spectators not by an appeal to supernatural intervention but by two natural causes. One is sympathy, that movement of the soul by which men identify themselves with the passions of others. In the case of poetry, this identification is favored and augmented by a second cause, the delight which comes to men, through their senses, from imitation. The poet wishing to produce these effects operates on the basis of principles (the ends proposed) and upon a special subject matter (the words and ideas employed in the construction of the poem). His is a work of art rather than of nature; the poet possessing completely the principles of his art will succeed better than one who has merely a natural inclination or instinct toward it. This is true for all the arts, and the fact that a man of talent becomes a poet rather than something else is a result of various circumstances and accidents. In some cases, and only for short poems in the minor genres, precept and principle may be replaced by imitation (which I take to mean imitation of the works of others). But this can never be a sufficient means of achieving perfection in the major poetic forms. In order to become an excellent poet a man must possess "those natural virtues of the soul, intelligence, judgment, docility, and memory";[55] besides, he must know everything about all subjects, and Giacomini presents a long list of the sciences in which he must be expert, including the whole range of arts and disciplines.

Giacomini thus occupies a very special place in the ranks of those who discussed the inevitable Platonic question of the divine furor. He does not believe in it; there were others who did not. But he sees in poetry the kinds of effects usually attributed to such a furor and investigates them in order to find some other explanation. That explanation is a completely natural one in which the innate qualities of the poet, supplemented by what he has learned about his own art and about others, and taking into account the natural capacity of the audience to be moved by poetic means, produce the pleasurable excitement and enthusiasm which result from poetry. It is also an "artistic" explanation in the sense that it tends to ascribe all causes and their effects to the art of the poet rather than to the accidents of divine intervention.

JACOPO MAZZONI (1587)

The two parts of Jacopo Mazzoni's *Della difesa della Comedia di Dante*, written around 1585 and published respectively in 1587 and 1688, are in a sense complementary to Giacomini's oration insofar as their Platonic elements are concerned. For whereas Giacomini had centered his attention upon the question of the divine furor, Mazzoni is interested in the other two major Platonic problems: the definition of imitation and the ends of poetry, the latter involving the banishment. I have already discussed at some length (Chapter I, pp. 24–26) those aspects of Mazzoni's work that relate to his

---

[55] *Ibid.*, p. 70: "quelle naturali virtù del anima Ingegno, Giudicio, Docilità, e Memoria."

classification of poetry. It springs in part from a distinction which he finds in Book X of the *Republic*, concerning the three kinds of objects that lend themselves to the activity of the arts. These are Ideas (which are contemplated), Works (which are made), and Images (which are made by imitation). In this connection, Mazzoni finds it necessary to define imitation, and the first attempt produces this statement:

Since, then, we see that the artifice of the arts of making [i.e., those which produce an object, such as the bit of the bit-maker] is directed toward something other than mere representation or mere resemblance, therefore we shall say that they cannot be called imitative. But those arts which have as their object the Image ["idolo"], have an object that has no other end, in its artifice, than to represent and to resemble; therefore they were properly called imitative.[56]

The kind of image or idol imitated by poetry "has its origin in our artifice and is born of our fancy and of our intellect through our choice and our will."[57] This statement immediately raises the question of Plato's seeming use of the term "imitation" to mean only a dramatic representation. Mazzoni concludes, after due analysis, that Plato also admitted other forms of representation as imitations, but that he wished to indicate the superiority of dramatic representation to narrative; imitation is thus the genus for all poetry.

To Plato also Mazzoni ascribes a correlative principle: imitation is correct and proper when it represents things exactly as they are, and it is an error of the poetic art to imitate them in any other way or with dissimilarity.[58] A further restriction upon the imitative arts is introduced at a later point in the discussion, and this is the unity of the object that leads to the unity of the work:

... the proper nature and the excellence of the Image ["idolo"] which is the object of the imitative arts is that it should be of one thing and only one thing; this is not true either of the Work or of the Idea. . . . The Image which is their object will be all the more worthy and excellent as it represents better that one thing in imitation of which it is made. . . . They limit themselves only to the representation of the unity of the thing which they wish to resemble.[59]

---

[56] *Della difesa*, Pt. I (1587), sec. 10: "Perche adunque veggiamo, che l'artificio dell'arti facitrici viene indirizzato ad altro, che al solo a [sic] rappresentare, & al solo rassomigliare, però diremo, ch'elle non si poteano nomare imitatrici. Ma quell'arti, c'hanno per oggetto l'Idolo, hanno vn'oggetto, che non hà altro fine nel suo artificio, che di rappresentare, e di rassomigliare, però furo debitamente imitatrici appellate."

[57] *Ibid.*, sec. 15: "hà l'origine dall'artificio nostro, la quale suol nascere dalla nostra phantasia, e dal nostro intelletto mediante l'elettione, e la voluntà nostra."

[58] *Ibid.*, secs. 20–28; also secs. 45–46. The same ideas are discussed again in chaps. 1 and 58 of Book III.

[59] *Ibid.*, pp. 644–45: "la propria natura, e l'eccellenza dell'idolo oggetto dell'arti imitanti è, ch'egli sia d'vna cosa sola d'vno, il che non auuiene dell'opera, ne dell'idea. . . . l'Idolo oggetto loro sia tanto più degno, e più eccellente, quanto che rappresenterà meglio quella cosa sola a imitatione della quale è fatto. . . . si ristringono solamente a rappresentare l'vnità della cosa, che vogliono rassomigliare."

These notions with respect to imitation stand in close relationship, for Mazzoni, to Plato's ideas about the ends of poetry. If, ideally, poetry should have as its object only the truth, practically it is also required to imitate the false, the possible, and the credible, and the latter is indeed its best object. For poetry appeals to an audience of common and ignorant men and cannot hope to present to them the same materials as would the sciences, or in the same way. It is thus that Mazzoni classifies the art under the rational faculty of sophistics: "Poetry is a sophistic art because of imitation, which is its proper genus, and because of the credible, which is its subject, and because of pleasure, which is its end; since being under that genus, and concerning that subject, and because it seeks that end, it is frequently constrained to admit what is false."[60] One should, however, distinguish this "sophistic" from another one which has no relationship to the truth and to true philosophy, and which deliberately engages in the telling of lies. To this latter kind belongs a species of poetry which is not real poetry and which has no place in the state; this is the kind that Plato banished. For in addition to its end of pleasure, springing from good and perfect imitation, poetry also serves another end, that of relaxation from labor; since it does, it also falls under the civil faculty and under the jurisdiction of politics. When this second end is improperly satisfied, the philosopher has the right to expel poetry from the state. The two ways of considering poetic pleasure are distinguished as follows:

In the first way, pleasure is the end of that poetry which was placed under the blameworthy type of sophistic, for it is such as brings disorder to the appetite through excessive delight, making it in every way rebellious to reason and bringing at the same time harm and danger to virtuous living. . . . But qualified by the civil faculty, we shall necessarily have to say that that kind of poetry which was placed under the praiseworthy type of sophistic, that is, under that which orders and subordinates appetite to reason, and considered as a game authorized by the civil faculty, has utility as its end.[61]

Plato, says Mazzoni, recognizes this kind of utility in the *Laws*, and, indeed, we may interpret the *Republic* as distinguishing three kinds of poetry as bringing separate utilities to three classes of people: epic poetry, which teaches virtue and glory to soldiers through the examples of great heroes; tragedy, which presents to princes and magistrates and men of

---

[60] *Ibid.*, sec. 60: "la Poesia è arte Sophistica, e per l'imitatione, che è il suo genere proprio, e per lo credibile, che è il suo soggetto, e per lo diletto, che è il suo fine, poiche per esser sotto quel genere, per esser intorno a quel soggetto, e per rimirare quel fine, viene astretta molte volte a dar luogo al falso."

[61] *Ibid.*, secs. 73–74: "Nel primo modo [il diletto] è fine di quella Poesia, che fù collocata sotto alla Sophistica degna di biasmo, poich'ella è tale, che disordina l'appetito con smoderato diletto rendendolo in tutto ribello dalla ragione, e recando insieme nocumento, e danno al viuere virtuoso. . . . Ma se si considera questo diletto, inquanto ch'egli è regolato, e qualificato dalla facoltà ciuile, ci bisognerà necessariamente dire, ch'egli sia indirizzato all'vtile, e conseguentemente, che quella specie di Poesia, che fù riposta sotto la Sophistica lodeuole, cioè sotto quella, ch'ordina, e sottopone l'appetito alla ragione, considerata come gioco qualificato dalla facoltà ciuile habbia per fine l'vtile."

power the terrible cases of the fallen great, so that they may seek moderation and remain submissive to the laws; and comedy, which consoles the middle and lower classes for their mediocre fortune by showing them actions which end happily (sec. 80).[62] These various types of utility are achieved through the arousing of the passions, and hence the further question arises as to whether it is legitimate to proceed in this fashion. Plato condemns all arousal of the passions in Books II and III of the *Republic*, as does Proclus. But Mazzoni contends that the method of poetry is acceptable here, provided that the proper passions be properly moved; and he says that Plato's true intention was to condemn the stimulation of certain passions while allowing others to be exploited in the proper circumstances. Book VII of the *Laws* is cited in support of the latter contention.

Part II of the *Difesa* repeats many of these ideas, develops some of them, and seeks to apply them practically to the defence of the *Divina Commedia*. The whole argument over imitation, for example, is reopened and expanded. New distinctions are added: The poet does not imitate when he speaks in his own voice—or, if he does, it is to an inferior degree. But imitation is nevertheless present whenever events are related that did not really happen, since verisimilitude is an imitation of the truth (pp. 133–34). Mazzoni treats the question of the passions, of virtue and vice, at great length in Book IV, where he is discussing mores and character in Dante's poem. He sets up a contrast between the position of Plato, who does not admit any representation of wickedness or of bad character, and that of Aristotle, who admits the whole range of passions. Both seem to him to be "right"; for Plato's point of view is supported by reason and Aristotle's by the practice of the poets (see Chapter I, p. 25 for a translation of the passage). The difference between the two is explainable to Mazzoni (as I have already noted) by the fact that Plato is speaking in terms of an ideal republic where there is no need for the poets "since its citizens learned everything that was necessary in the civil education instituted by him, and moreover lived with the obstinate wish not to allow any kind of pleasure to enter into that Republic, knowing that pleasures are linked together in such a way that one necessarily draws another after it."[63] Whereas Aristotle's state was a practical one following the common practice of men. As for those critics who attempt to defend poetry on the basis of allegorical interpretations, Mazzoni rejects their argument:

. . . this defence should not be admitted as a good one, since there is too great danger that honest things will come to be expressed in ugly and dishonest words. Without doubt, appetite, by its nature inclined to evil, would stop at the outer

---

62 The usefulness of tragedy and comedy is discussed later in Bk. II, chap. 9.

63 *Della difesa*, Pt. II (1688), p. 5: "essendoche i suoi Cittadini imparauano tutto quello ch'era necessario nella educatione ciuile instituta da lui, e nel resto viueuano ostinati di non voler lasciar entrare in quella Republica sorte alcuna di piacere, sapendo, che i diletti sono di modo insieme concatenati, che vno si tira dietro l'altro necessariamente."

covering as at a thing adapted to its pleasure, and in this way it would rather receive harm from the apparent meaning than benefit from the hidden one.[64]

There is everywhere in Mazzoni's lengthy work a consciousness of the moral problems raised by the art of poetry, undoubtedly because these were the problems raised by some of the critics of Dante. And his appeals to Plato for answers to some of these questions are a part of his determination to seek, in any source whatsoever, the means of defending Dante. I shall indicate the particular character of that defence at the appropriate time.

The range of Platonic "topics" is somewhat extended in the *De re poetica libellus incerti auctoris* (1588), which I have attributed to Federico Ceruti (see Chapter I, p. 11). For not only does Ceruti touch upon such matters as the furor, the defence of poetry, the ban, and the kinds of imitation; he also appeals to Plato for assistance in his classification of the art, which is indeed one of the most interesting contributions of his little treatise. He declares that Plato divides poetry into two kinds:

. . . one which he calls θεωρική, the other πρακτική; the former treats of God, of the celestial creatures, of heaven, of the constellations, of the stars, and of divine things; the latter, instead, of men, of animate beings, of countries, cities, mores, laws, in a word, of all things human insofar as it is proper and possible to do so. From which division we conclude readily that the material of poetry is very vast and extends everywhere, and that it undertakes to treat in verse all human and divine matters.[65]

Ceruti's willingness to accept the inclusion of divine matters among the subjects of poetry indicates his general position: he is a defender and an apologist, and he selects from Plato those texts and passages which provide praise for the art of poetry. Thus in his first chapter, "De poetices vtilitate ac dignitate," he includes Plato among the writers who have declared poetry to be "not only pleasant and useful for young people, but indeed necessary," and he cites the *Minos* on the poets as "interpreters of the gods, so long as they use poetry chastely and modestly to direct the minds of the young to every virtue."[66] The art itself is divine, and Ceruti traces its

---

[64] *Ibid.*, p. 22: "Ma questa difesa non si deue ammettere per buona, essendoche troppo gran pericolo è dell'honesta, ch'ella venga dichiarta [sic] con brutte, e dishoneste parole. E senza dubbio l'appetito inclinato per sua natura al male si fermarebbe nella scorza di fuori, come in cosa appropriata al suo diletto, e in questo modo più tosto riceuerebbe nocumento dal senso manifesto, che giouamento dall'occulto."

[65] *De re poetica* (1588), pp. 9–10: "vna, quae θεωρική altera, quae πρακτική vocatur; illa de Deo, de coelitibus, coelo, syderibus, astris, rebusque diuinis; haec autem, de homine, de animantibus, regionibus, ciuitatibus, moribus, legibus, denique de rebus omnibus humanis, quoad licet, & fieri potest, pertractat. Ex qua diuisione facile colligimus, poetices materiam amplissimam esse, & per omnia vagari; & quae res diuinas, & humanas carmine tractandas suscipiat."

[66] *Ibid.*, p. 1: "non modo iuuenibus iucundam, & vtilem; sed etiam necessariam esse ducant" and "interpretes deorum appellat, modo poeticen castè, & pudicè ad formandos animos ad omnem honestatem, iuuenibus tradant."

origins to Moses, Noah, Abraham, and other holy men who used it for religious purposes. In fact, the term "divine" appears in almost every description of the poet or of the content of the art offered by Ceruti (v. p. 6 for several examples). It follows almost necessarily that the ends of the art will be useful ends, and Ceruti multiplies his statements of its utility. In Chapter VII, "Quod sit poetae officium, et quis finis," he states the ends thus: "to teach men by means of precepts and instructions, to bring them to wisdom, to drive the shadows of ignorance from the minds and souls of men is a difficult and sublime thing which requires labor and industry."[67] The formulation is more specific in Chapter XI, "Quantum ex poetices facultate emolumentum percipiatur" (I give the chapter titles because they reveal so much about the general approach):

Two extremely important things happen to those who are taught by poetry: for first, indeed, it serves by that restraint of the soul and it teaches that no man should accuse his own fortune harshly and boldly; and, on the other hand, it opens the way to magnanimity, by means of which you may so prepare your mind against all the accidents of fortune that you will not be dejected, or perturbed, or excessively moved by anything.[68]

Earlier in the same chapter Ceruti points to the special efficacy of poetry in this kind of instruction, since its pleasurable aspects have a ready appeal to the young. For these reasons, he believes that poetry is eminently useful to the state (v. Plato in Book II of the *Laws*) and that far from being banned from the state, it should be encouraged and cultivated. If one ask why Plato should have condemned it in the *Republic*, the answer is that he condemned only evil and wicked poets, not the art as a whole (p. 16). In order to escape such blame, the poet must praise virtue, decry vice, follow decorum, and provide the kinds of instruction which will serve its ends.

The other topics are treated in a fairly perfunctory manner. It is notable that when Ceruti discusses the nature of the poet in Chapter VI ("Poeta naturane, an arte, an vtraque fiat"), he makes no mention of the divine furor, putting the question rather in terms of the Horatian art-versus-nature. He mentions the divine afflatus only in Chapter IX, where he uses it to explain the powerful effect which poetry has upon the minds of its audience. As for imitation, he reflects the Platonic tradition only in the distinction of narrative, dramatic, and mixed representation; but he does so in such a way that he might easily be reflecting Aristotle or the ancient, anonymous tradition of the rhetoricians. In general, he is a theorist who

---

[67] *Ibid.*, p. 8: "pręceptis, & institutis homines docere, ad sapientiam erudire, ignorantiae tenebras ex hominum mentibus, atque animis depellere, arduum quiddam, & sublime est, & quod magnum requirit studium, atque industriam."

[68] *Ibid.*, p. 17: "Duo pręclara illis contingunt, qui poetica instituuntur: primum enim ea moderatione animi famulatur, docetque, nulli moleste, ac temere fortunam exprobandam; alterum viam struit ad magnanimitatem, qua ad omnes fortunę casus ita componas animum, vt non deijciaris, ac conturberis, nihilque commouearis."

has Plato's writings fairly constantly in mind, but who selects from them those dicta that would seem to rank him with the anti-Platonist defenders of poetry rather than with the Platonic objectors.

Giovambattista Strozzi (the Younger) concerns himself with a much more restricted subject in his paper *Se sia bene il servirsi delle favole delli antichi*, delivered before the Accademia Fiorentina in 1588. For the "favole" of which he speaks are the ancient myths concerning the gods, and his inquiry centers about the possibility or the desirability of Christian poets' using these myths in modern times. The work thus belongs to the literature that considers poetry from a religious point of view. Strozzi's first care, therefore, is to summarize the arguments of those who would deny the use of that mythology. These men, he says, argue that no religion can permit the publication of myths contrary to its own beliefs, that the Christian religion especially outlaws all fables, that these fables cannot possibly produce the effects desired by poetry because they are known to be false and incredible, and that they cannot but have a harmful effect upon the ignorant multitude. But such arguments, Strozzi insists, do not carry conviction, and critics like Castelvetro have already refuted them. He himself proceeds to counter them. First, he says, the Christian religion does not specifically ban the use of fables and even admits such mythical personages as nymphs and fates. Second, even though these myths are recognized as being entirely false, they may still be effective in poetry, and not only because they give pleasure, but also because they may arouse a whole variety of emotions. This comes about because the actions represented are what move the audience, not the names of the persons performing the actions. Third, the multitude remains in no danger from contact with these pagan tales; for no Christian, however simple, will ever take the pagan gods to be true and real, and hence his religious beliefs will not be imperiled. Since these myths are now so widely disseminated as to be known by all, it would be ridiculous and impossible to try to exclude them. Hence, Strozzi finds it expedient to establish norms for their proper use. They should be introduced only into nonreligious poems, whether their subject be ancient or modern; in religious poems they are presumably replaced by God, the angels, and other supernatural beings. He concludes: ". . . let us use the myths and the mythical personages not as principal subjects for poems but as intercalation, as ornament, as passing reference in the descriptions of times, in comparisons, in examples, in order to delight, to give recreation to the minds, to cause men to marvel; and let us always direct the whole to our own profit and that of others."[69]

It is perhaps stretching a point to include within the Platonic tradition

<hr/>

[69] In *Orazioni et altre prose* (1635), pp. 137–38: "servianci delle fauole, e de fauolosi non per suggetto principale, ma per framesso, per condimento, per passaggio nelle descrittioni de tempi, nelle comparationi, negl'esempli, per dilettare, per recrear gl'animi, per eccitar marauiglia, e'l tutto indrizziamo sempre à giouamento nostro, e altrui."

Giovanni Mario Verdizzotti's treatise *Della narratione poetica* (1588). It might perhaps have been just as well classified among the rhetorical documents studied in Chapter VI. I have placed it here since it belongs (vaguely perhaps) in the long series of discussions about the kinds of imitation and their subdivisions. Verdizzotti is not interested, as were Plato and so many others, in the major classification of narrative, dramatic, and mixed modes of representation; he is concerned exclusively with narration. This he divides into four kinds: the direct ("retta"), the semidirect ("quasi retta"), the oblique ("obliqua"), and the semioblique ("quasi obliqua"). In direct narration the poet himself relates events with all their accompaniments; in semidirect narration, he introduces another person who relates such events, as, for example, when Aeneas tells his story in Books II and III of the *Aeneid*. In oblique narration, things are said to have been said by a third person who is not himself introduced as a speaker. And in semioblique narration no person at all is introduced, but stories are told by means of depictions in painting, sculpture, embroidery, and so forth. Alongside this classification, Verdizzotti makes a number of remarks which indicate clearly his conception of the art of poetry. The method of direct narration is that of the historian or orator; but poetry differs from these

... in the manner of discourse, which is in verse, with a greater and freer abundance of figures, of thought as well as of words, than is found in either of the other two; and in the excess in quality of the virtues and of the vices and of all the other things which he explains and demonstrates in the actions of the persons introduced in his poem, as for example an excessive strength, an excessive wickedness, an excessive prudence, an excessive madness, love, beauty, of places or of persons, and other things of this kind meant to arouse the marvelous which accompanies the particulars.[70]

Semidirect narration is peculiarly poetic in quality, since it is "all imitation" —so much so that it may not be used by the historian or the orator. So also for the semioblique form, purely poetic since it is imitative. It is such narratives as these that give the poet his particular character and his works their special charm. Verdizzotti cites the case of Vergil's summary, at the beginning of the *Aeneid*, of what was to take place:

... this is a kind of artistic narration and one which is completely poetic since it is proper to the poet alone; for he is not allowed to pass beyond the limits of the single action which he proposes to treat. If he observes this rule, the action will be treated by him as a poet, not as an historian. For this manner of proceeding is the only thing which distinguishes him from the historian and the orator; and

---

[70] *Della narratione poetica* (1588), pp. 5–6: "per la maniera di dire, che è in verso, con maggior e piu licentiosa copia di figure, sì di sentenze, come di parole, che non ha lo stile di questo, ò di quello: & per l'eccesso in qualità delle virtù, e de i vitij, & di tutte l'altre cose, che egli spiega, e dimostra nelle attioni delle persone introdotte nel suo poema: come sarebbe à dire, vna eccessiua fortezza, una eccessiua viltà, vna eccessiua prudenza, vno eccessiuo furore, amore, bellezza, di luoghi, ò di persone, & altre cose di questa sorte per far nascer la merauiglia accessoria de i particolari."

through this way of proceeding we may learn how to constitute the true definition of the poetic art.[71]

The poetic art would thus seem to consist, for Verdizzotti, in four qualities: imitation, the representation of a single action, an abundance of figures and ornaments (including verse), and a superior or excessive degree of all the characteristics represented by the poet. Such a definition as this, as I have already intimated, is very close to the formulations of the rhetoricians and of the Horatian theorists.

GIOSEPPE MALATESTA (1589)

Although it belongs primarily to the documents concerning the dispute over Ariosto, Giuseppe Malatesta's *Della nuova poesia* (1589) is sufficiently involved in the discussion of the ends of poetry to merit treatment here. Through much of the dialogue, the main interlocutor, Sperone Speroni, insists so constantly that the end of poetry is delight alone that one wonders whether other possible ends will be considered at all. He defines the subject matter of poetry as "all pleasurable things treated through imitation" and explains the "dilettabili" in this way: ". . . although Poetry with a generous hand takes of all things, nevertheless these are useful to her or not to the extent to which they are pleasurable or not."[72] Art must direct all its dogmas and precepts toward the achieving of this pleasure (p.110), and "the end of poetry, if we are to speak the truth, is nothing else but delight."[73] Monsignor Dandino, however, raises the question of utility, and this leads to a full-scale consideration of the ends of poetry. Speroni recognizes the possibility of three solutions: (1) utility as the end, served by pleasure; (2) utility and pleasure as joint and equal ends; (3) pleasure alone as the end. To the first he objects that "giovare" would not be an end peculiar to poetry since it would be shared by other arts; that this would presuppose the possibility of poetry without delight, whereas no such exists; and that the presence of imitation, the form and soul of poetry, necessarily involves the presence of pleasure. To the second he objects that it is impossible for a single thing to have more than one end. The third solution is thus the proper one, and he contends that all the means of poetry are proportioned to the end of pleasure. Aristotle, Quintilian, and Cicero, he says, all support this theory.

71 *Ibid.*, pp. 11–12: "questa è vna specie di narratione artificiosa, & tutta poetica: come solo propria del Poeta; alquale non è lecito passar i termini dell'vnica da lui proposta attione. Laquale esso così facendo vien da lui trattata, come poeta, non come historico. Percioche questa maniera di fare è quella sola, per laquale egli si distingue dall'historico & dall'Oratore: & per questa via di procedere si uiene in conoscimento di constituire la vera diffinitione dell' arte poetica."
72 *Della nuova poesia* (1589), pp. 109–10: "tutte le cose dilettabili trattate con imitatione" and "se ben la Poesia con ampia mano piglia da tutte le cose, nondimeno elle tanto fanno, ò non fanno per lei, quanto sono delettabili, ò non sono."
73 *Ibid.*, p. 119: "il fin della Poesia, secondo il vero parlando, non è altro, che la dilettatione." See also p. 150.

Does this mean that the end of utility is to be completely denied to the art of poetry? In the course of the discussion, Malatesta admits not only that useful ends may be served, but also that they are desirable. He first admits that "giovamento" or "documento" may be an accidental concomitant of the pleasure, all the while insisting that a poet may do harm and still be a good poet. The second admission is more serious: at times, he says, arts may have two ends, one intrinsic and the other extrinsic; so for poetry, "which proposes for itself, indeed, a proper end, which is to imitate elegantly in order to delight; but frequently another extrinsic end follows this one, namely that of profit."[74] The poet achieves his proper end through pleasure only; but he may also participate in the general end proposed by Aristotle for all the arts, that is, to help men to achieve human happiness:

> Whence Poetry, which is not the least among the arts, wished to have a part along with the others in this happiness of ours, and, therefore, resolved to bring profit to the human species insofar as that was possible, she conceived the idea of directing that pleasure of hers in some way to our utility and profit; and thus by means of imitation, of fiction, and of verse, which naturally delight us, she tried to unroll before us such things and subjects as might bring us a considerable utility. . . . under the outer bark of the fables are hidden and covered many mystical and allegorical meanings, all directed toward our good and instruction.[75]

Follows a conventional praise of poetry—with a caution, however, that the poet should not allow such concerns to take precedence over his primary end, which is to give pleasure. Inevitably, before the conclusion of the dialogue, the question is asked why Plato should have banished the poets if they are useful in the ways indicated. Scipione Gonzaga undertakes the explanation. After examining the usual arguments, he presents his own conclusion about Plato: ". . . his intention is not to wish that the poets should be exiled and driven out absolutely as poets, but only with respect to the guardians."[76] The fault is thus in the weakness of the audience, not in the poetic art; and the passage ends with a long defence of the latter. Malatesta's position thus develops from one in which there would seem to be no evidence of Platonism, through one in which the Horatian thesis is essentially approved (as interpreted by certain theorists, at least), to one in which Plato himself is made to be a defender of the utility of the art.

---

[74] *Ibid.*, p. 189: "la qual si propon bene un fin proprio, che è di imitare acconciamente; per dilettare, ma a questo segue molte uolte un' altro fine estrinsico, che è del giouamento."

[75] *Ibid.*, p. 190: "Onde la Poesia, che pur trà le Arti non è infima, volle auer parte, come le altre, in questa beatitudine nostra, & perciò risoluta di giouare, in quanto per lei si potesse, alla specie humana, imaginossi d'indrizzare in qualche modo quella sua dilettatione all'vtilità, & giouamento nostro, & così con la imitatione, con la fintione, & col verso, che naturalmente ci dilettano, si sforzò di andarci spiegando cose, & soggetti tali, che potessero apportarci non picciola utilità. . . . sotto alla scorza delle fauole stanno uelati, & coperti molti sensi mistici, & allegorici tutti indrizzati a nostro prò, & ammaestramento."

[76] *Ibid.*, p. 256: "animo suo non è di uoler, che i Poeti siano fuggiti, & discacciati assolutamente come Poeti, ma solo per rispetto delli custodi."

Unlike his fellow Jesuits, Gambara and Panicarola, Francesco Benci spoke out in praise of poetry in two of his *Orationes*, published in 1590, Numbers VI and VII, both entitled "De laudibus poëticae." He does not understand how anybody can attack an art which is "mother of all the virtues and all the arts, sole parent and mistress of our duties and our mores."[77] Rather would he praise it for its service to mankind in the past— "it taught men to moderate their passions, restrain their desires, control their impulses; to hate the vices and embrace the virtues; to have knowledge and wisdom of all things"—and for the ends which it still pursues; for the poets

... are totally dedicated to the praise of good deeds and the blame of bad ones, by the magnification of any glory and infamy whatsoever; and by doing these things they both introduce the virtues into the souls of men and draw out of them the vices, to their very roots; and they produce men wholly lacking in greed, and wholly deserving of every honor and praise.[78]

The effectiveness of poetry, ascribable to its pleasurable accompaniments and to the ease with which it is remembered, is enhanced in certain cases by the knowledge that the events recounted are true—so for the Old and the New Testaments, which have religious as well as ethical uses. For all these reasons, Benci believes that Plato's ban was meant to affect only false poets who used the art as a disguise for their wickedness and that Plato himself recognized and recommended the pedagogical possibilities of the art.

In the *Oratio VII*, Benci passes on to a comparison of poetry with its sister arts of painting, music, and divination. As compared with the first, poetry is definitely superior: painting merely gives a visual image of things, to which poetry adds character, attitudes, disposition, and the deeds, words, and counsels of men, as well as the sound of the actions presented (p. 110). Music moves the passions; but poetry does so better, since its verses not only move the soul but "impel men to every kind of virtue, deter them from vice, and are very efficacious in exercising and sharpening their minds."[79] Poetry is thus itself a kind of divine force, as useful for the inculcation of piety and religious observance as for the direction of our mundane lives. Benci's praise of the art is thus complete and unreserved, and indeed he commends it warmly for that quality which its Platonic opponents most frequently denied it, its service of religion.

[77] *Orationes* (1590 ed.), p. 88: "in procreatricem illam virtutum omnium & artium, in vnicam officiorum morumque parentem & magistram contumeliose inuehuntur."

[78] *Ibid.*, pp. 89, 94: "coërcere cupiditates, impetus frangere, detestari vitia, amplexari virtutes, rerum denique omnium . . . cognitionem ac scientiam tenere"; and "Toti sunt in benefactorum commendatione, maleficiorum vituperatione, gloriae cuiuslibet atque infamiae amplificatione: quod cum faciunt, & virtutes in animis inserunt, & vitia radicitus extrahunt: & homines omni carentes cupiditate, omni honore ac laude dignissimos efficiunt."

[79] *Ibid.*, p. 112: "homines ad omne virtutum genus impellunt: deterrent à vitio, & in excitandis acuendisque ingenijs nimium quantum valent."

ANTONIO POSSEVINO (1593)

With Antonio Possevino's *Tractatio de poësi et pictura ethnica, humana, et fabulosa collata cum vera, honesta, et sacra,* we rejoin the ultra-Catholic, Jesuit tradition of Gambara and Panicarola, and we encounter one of those documents which, if they do not dominate the last years of the Cinquecento, at least give them a special character. The treatise, published in 1593, is also in a sense a reply to Benci, whom it mentions. And while it contradicts Benci, refusing to accept his praise of the Greek and Latin poets (the ones whom Possevino calls "ethnic"), it does not go so far as Gambara and Panicarola in their condemnation of the whole art of poetry. Possevino's position is simply stated: he approves of the art because of its potential utility; but this must be manifested always in glorification of Christianity, which means that only Christian poetry is acceptable; thus all the poetry of pagan antiquity is condemned and discarded. Although he begins with a statement of his intention to treat both poetry and painting (announced also in the title), Possevino devotes himself almost exclusively to poetry, only the last six chapters bearing upon the ends and techniques of painting. The two arts, he says, are alike in their ends, different in their means:

> The whole effect of poetry and of painting is reduced to two things, teaching and delighting; and what poetry achieves by means of narrations, episodes, eulogies, tropes, and other such means, painting also achieves, which by using colors, catches the ideas from things themselves, or else as these should be, [and] by which ideas it imitates lines, light, dark, and background.[80]

Of these two ends, the primary one is instruction, and to it the poet should bend all his effort; pleasure is secondary. The specific lessons taught are variously stated:

> . . . through a knowledge of natural things and of mores, and through a demonstration of the virtues, men are made in some unknown way to be greater and more excellent; and . . . from both of these things are derived a greatness of soul against adversity and against the weaknesses inherent in human affairs, strength against the fear of death, temperance against lustful desires, constancy in the Catholic religion against all heresies.[81]

From Lucretius one may learn lessons "on the contempt for death, on avoiding love, on controlling the desires, on calming the emotions and achieving tranquillity of the soul; about sleep, about the rising and setting

---

[80] *Tractatio* (1593 ed.), p. 1v: "tota vis Poeseos, atque Picturae duobus absoluitur docendo, & delectando; quodque, Poesis efficit narrationibus, episodijs, encomijs, tropis, & eiusmodi alijs; idem Pictura facit; quae coloribus vtens, ex ipsis rebus, aut quales hae esse deberent, capessit notiones, quibus lineamenta, lucem, vmbram, recessus imitatur." (Page numbers represent my own counting.)

[81] *Ibid.*, p. 3v: "è rerum naturalium cognitione, morumque, ac virtutum explicatione homines efficiantur, nescio quo modo, maiores, atque elatiores: & . . . ex vtraque re animi magnitudo contra aduersa, rerumque humanarum imbecillitatem, fortitudo contra mortis timorem, temperantia contra libidinem, constantia Catholicae Religionis contra haereses comparetur."

of the stars, about the eclipses of the sun and the moon"—and so forth.[82] Man will therefore learn from poetry divers lessons which fall into the general categories of ethical, religious, and scientific.

The fact that the lessons are of so many kinds leads Possevino to a conception and a classification of poetry that are not conventional for his century. In the first place, he rejects the idea that imitation is necessary for poetry. Rather than accepting the authority of Aristotle, he turns to Lambin, who declares that the distinguishing features of poetry are not only imitation, but also rhythm, figures, certain kinds of extraordinary words, and the divine genius of the poet. The purpose of Possevino's rejection of imitation is to permit the inclusion, among the kinds of poetry, of compositions in verse which are not necessarily imitations but which serve the ends already noted. Possevino proceeds to his classification by two steps. First, he cites Plato's division of poetry into true and false, the true poetry being that which delights by teaching decent things and which has a laudable subject matter, the false being that which insinuates obscene and wicked things by means of its attractions. It is this latter kind, incidentally, which Plato is said to have banished from his *Republic* (p. 3). True poetry then subdivides into the following categories: (1) divine, of which Moses and David may be proposed as the best examples; (2) natural, represented by Empedocles, Lucretius, and Fracastoro; and (3) moral, exemplified by Phocylides and Pythagoras. The last category also includes economic and political poetry and all such genres as tragedy, comedy, the epic, the lyric, and the epigram when they are made to lead to virtue and to exclude vice (p. 3). It will be noted that this is a mixed classification, based partly upon subject matter and partly upon effect.

Obviously, the only poetry which Possevino cares to condone is the true, and his preferred category is the religious. Sacred poetry is the best of all: Moses, David, the Psalmists.

. . . the other poems, which consist only of fanciful wrappings, are fables rather than poems. . . . Moreover, the utility of every honest form of poetry is great and great its advantage for learning things, so that he spoke true who called it the nurse and the teacher of the minds of the young. Certainly the very movement and rhythm of the verses, since it attracts the soul, so impresses itself upon the memory, making the mind receptive through its diversified charm, that it causes the mind almost never to forget what it has perceived so well. Moreover, it also incites to the praise of God's work and is a great solace for setting aside one's cares.[83]

82 *Ibid.*, p. 11: "de morte contemnenda, de amore fugiendo, de coercendis cupiditatibus, de sedandis animorum motibus, de mentis tranquillitate comparanda, de somno, de ortu, obituque syderum, de Solis, & Lunae defectu. . . ."

83 *Ibid.*, p. 3v: "vt reliqua Poemata, quae tantum ex fabulosis inuolucris constant, fabulae potius sint, quàm Poemata. . . . Ceterum honestae omnis Poeseos ingens vtilitas est, atque ad res ediscendas percommoda: vt vera dixerit, qui eam adolescentis animi nutricem, & alumnam vocauit. Certè ipse carminum flexus, & numerus, vt animum allicit, sic memoriae

Possevino is hard put to it to find modern examples of the kind of poetry which he recommends; but he nevertheless cites and quotes a number of sacred poems, songs, epigrams, elegies, and epics written in recent times. Above all he admires, in the category of epics, the *Triumphus Christi ascendentis in caelum* of Macarius Mutius, which he reprints *in toto* as an example to future poets.

It will be remembered, however, that Possevino's primary interest in this treatise is in "ethnic" or pagan poetry, and hence he does not fail to inquire to what extent that poetry is acceptable and useful to Christians. He finds in the ancient poets certain passages stating that there is only one God and rejecting the numerous pagan gods; these would be useful. He finds it possible, through allegorical and Christological interpretations, to discover in the Greeks and Romans certain adumbrations of the Christian mysteries and to transform an ode of Pindar or a song of Sappho into a religious poem. Most of all, he extracts from the works of antiquity innumerable passages—proverbs, "centones," speeches—which contain the kind of moral instruction of which he approves.

This procedure, by selection, by extraction, by interpretation, exemplifies what Possevino states theoretically to be the proper use of the ancient poets. In Chapter IV, "Usus qualis, ac fructus è poetis ethnicis. Adduntur cautiones," he outlines that theory, introducing it thus:

> In truth we must say first that from most of the pagan poets may be learned many things which pertain to the investigation of natural phenomena and to the forming of character. Similarly, from them may be derived the style and the correct use of words either of Greek and Latin or of the other languages. But one must know how to choose and apply generally cautions which were taught by the pagans themselves, but still more profoundly and solidly by the church fathers, with respect to this matter.[84]

The theory is stated in a number of precepts: (1) one must choose carefully the authors to be read; (2) one must be prepared to resist the false teachings of the pagan poets, to remove their errors, to turn them to our own purposes; (3) rather than translate the obscene poets and surround them with critical apparatus, one should expurgate them and publish selections only; (4) from the good poets one should select passages on such useful matters as descriptions of wars, comparisons, honest and grave sententiae. In a general way, the criteria are religious orthodoxy and moral acceptability: whatever would seem to praise or even recognize the pagan gods is

---

haeret, variaque iucunditate mentem permulcens facit, ne penè vnquam ea, quae rectè percipit, obliuiscatur. Quin & incitat ad laudanda Dei opera, magnoque est ad remissionem curarum leuamento."

[84] *Ibid.*, p. 3*v*: "Id vero ante omnia fatendum est, è plerisque Poetis Ethnicis multa intelligi posse, quae ad rerum naturas vestigandas, & ad mores efformandos pertinent: Stylum item, ac verborum proprietatem siue Graecae, ac Latinae; siue aliarum linguarum ex ijs posse comparari: delectum tamen eorum habendum, & cautiones omnino adhibendas, quas ipsimet Ethnici, sed altius, atque solidius Patres hac de re docuerunt."

to be excluded, whatever might seem to prophesy Christianity may be retained; whatever is lewd, obscene, demoralizing must go, whatever tends to inculcate the proper moral lessons may remain. Two lesser criteria are also present: we may read those parts of ancient works which contain useful linguistic and stylistic models and those which impart information about the natural world. In terms of these criteria, Possevino makes a rapid examination of the principal writers of antiquity and provides for each a criticism and a commentary.

These latter ideas demand a modification of my original statement that "all the poetry of pagan antiquity will be condemned and discarded." Condemnation and discard will apply only to the poems as wholes, or to certain poets from whom nothing may be salvaged. For most works, carefully selected sections or lines will be salvable and what Possevino proposes is a kind of anthology or *morceaux choisis* of Greek and Roman writings. A few works may be totally conserved, but only when surrounded by the proper commentaries, which will assure correct interpretation. In a word, those remnants of ancient literature which correspond to the doctrinal, ethical, scientific, and stylistic principles of the Christian critic—who is also a Christian theologian—will be permitted the modern reader. The basic Platonism of the approach is apparent; indeed, this fundamental way of looking at poetry in a context of theological and ethical standards is much more significant, in the case of Possevino, then the fact that he occasionally refers to the divine furor. It is also apparent in his review of ancient and modern writings on the art of poetry itself, in which he lauds or condemns theorists on the basis of their conformity to his own standards.

Allegorical interpretation of the kind suggested by Possevino for religious reasons and by other defenders of poetry for other reasons is judged to be entirely inexcusable by Fabrizio Beltrami in his *Sopra l'allegoria del poeta nella sua favola*. The treatise, found in manuscript in MS D. VII, 10 of the Biblioteca Comunale of Siena and accompanied by a letter dated June 22, 1594, is an answer to statements made by Francesco Patrizi and Jacopo Mazzoni on the subject of allegory. The denial of all allegory by Beltrami is based upon several simple premises: poetry is written specifically for the common people, who would be incapable of penetrating beneath the surface to seek out hidden meanings; allegory supposes an impossible external action and a possible internal action, whereas the general theory of poetry admits only the possible; the admission of allegory involves permission of a plurality of actions, which is against the poetic art. Plato is cited as the authority for the first of these premises; in the *Gorgias*, says Beltrami, Plato declared that "Poesia est res popularis," and similar statements are to be found in the *Phaedo* and in Book X of the *Republic*. In Book II of the latter, moreover, Plato prohibited all things said in the form of fictions, either allegorically or nonallegorically. The reasons are clear: not only will no two men ever come to the same interpretation of a given work, but rarely will anybody be found who will have the necessary intellectual qualities to find a proper meaning:

... if we were to seek this credibility of poetry in allegorical meaning, we should be forced to confess that poetry, insofar as it is an imitation, was not given to us as a pastime, as Plato said; since allegory demands acuteness of mind, profundity of learning, variety of knowledge, a most happy memory, and, finally, exquisite judgment in order to fit the allegorical sense to the literal sense. And this effort is fatiguing even to men having these qualities; how much more so will it not be to those who are moderately educated, or to those who are completely ignorant? And that these latter are the audience of the poets is confirmed by Plato in Book II of the *Republic* and by Strabo in the first Book.[85]

Thus the ignorance or the incapacity of the audience, so frequently alleged as an argument against the art as a whole, is here adduced specifically as an argument against allegory.

For the second of the premisses the authority is Aristotle. If poetry is an imitation of an action, one of its conditions is that this action be necessary, probable, credible—and not only in the intrinsic meaning but also in its superficial expression. We cannot, therefore, accept the basic assumption of allegorical writing, that is, that something which appears on the surface as being impossible and untrue should be, within, both possible and true. For the third premiss the authority is partly Aristotle but mainly the reason (thus completing the trilogy of Plato, Aristotle, and the reason, invoked at the beginning). Allegory, say some (and the commentary of Eustathius on the *Iliad* is cited), may be present either in the main plot—which constitutes the soul of the poem—or in the episodes, principal or secondary. But whether it occurs in the one or in the other, it amounts to a second action, and thus the unity of action required by reason is destroyed. Hence it was that Aristotle did not even mention the possibility of allegory in the *Poetics*, and by his silence condemned it. Plato on the audience, Aristotle on credibility, and the reason on unity of action all unite to outlaw a system of interpretation (and perhaps of writing) that is upheld in vain by such critics as Patrizi and Mazzoni, by such poets as Tasso in the *Allegoria* appended to the *Gerusalemme Liberata*.

TORQUATO TASSO (1594)

Tasso himself is the author of a treatise on epic poetry in which many of the problems debated by Possevino, Beltrami, and others of the period are

[85] MS Bibl. Com. Siena D.VII, 10, fols. 64v–65: "quando si ricercasse questo credibile ne senso allegorico, saremmo forzati confessare, che la poesia inquanto è immitatione, non ci fusse stata data per passatempo, si come si diceua da Plat. ricercando l'Allegoria, acutezza d'ingegno, profondità di dottrina, uarietà di scienze, felicissima memoria, e finalmente giuditio esquisito in saper accomodare il senso allegorico al senso letterale; e questo ricerca anco fatica in cosi fatti huomini; quanto maggiore la ricercherà ne' mediocremente letterati, o negl' idioti afatto? e che questi sieno gl'ascoltatori de' Poeti, e Plat. nel 2°. della rep. e Strabone nel primo lo confermano."

POETIC THEORY

treated in some detail. The *Discorsi del poema heroico* was not published until 1594, but it was probably written between 1575 and 1580; it repeats, in many respects, the materials included in the *Discorsi dell'arte poetica* of 1587. The Platonic reference is perhaps most distinct in Tasso's consideration of the ends of poetry. I have already pointed out in Chapter I (p. 32) that in classifying poetry among the arts he subordinated it to politics because he regarded utility as the primary end, pleasure as auxiliary. In a general way, the highest end of poetry is "to benefit men through the example of human actions," and Tasso would therefore define poetry as "an imitation of human actions made for the instruction of life."[86] More particularly, epic poetry instructs great men, who seek to conform to its examples, in "the forms of strength, of temperance, of prudence, of justice, of faith, of piety, and of religion, and of every other virtue."[87] It should thus be defined as "an imitation of an illustrious, great, and powerful action, made by narrating with the highest form of verse, in order to move men's minds through the marvelous and to bring profit in this way."[88] Indeed, the end will be differently stated for each genre: tragedy will purge by means of terror and pity; comedy will use laughter to make men ashamed to do ugly things.

There is a sense, however, in which the functions of the poet are more noble than the mere providing of examples or demonstrating of actions. Like the theologian, he is a maker of images presented for the contemplation of men; this makes of him a kind of theologian—rather of the mystical than of the scholastic strain: ". . . the act of leading men to the contemplation of divine things and of arousing them in this way by means of images, as the mystical theologian and the poet do, is a much more noble operation than teaching by means of demonstrations, which is the function of the scholastic theologian."[89] For this reason the poet should be held in high esteem, and his art should occupy a more elevated position than that assigned to it by such divines as St. Thomas. His high calling imposes certain obligations. For one, he must treat only the truth, seeking novelty in form and detail rather than in matter. For another, he must avoid the use of the pagan marvelous and employ only that authorized by Christianity. Here again, the close relationships between the poet, the theologian, and the legislator are apparent:

. . . the most excellent poem is proper only to the most excellent form of govern-

86 *Poema heroico* [1594], pp. 6–7: "giouare à gli huomini con l'essempio dell'attioni humane" and "imitatione dell'attioni humane fatta per ammaestramento della vita."
87 *Ibid.*, p. 1: "le forme della fortezza, della temperanza, della prudenza, della giustitia, della fede, della pietà, & della Religione, e d'ogni altra virtù."
88 *Ibid.*, p. 14: "imitatore d'attione illustre, grande, e perfetta fatta, narrando con altissimo verso, affine di muouere gli animi con la marauiglia; e di giouare in questa guisa."
89 *Ibid.*, pp. 29–30: "il conducere alla contemplatione delle cose diuine & il destare in questa guisa con l'imagini come fà il Theologo mistico, & il Poeta è molto più nobile operatione, che l'ammaestrar con le demostrationi com'è officio del Theologo scolastico."

ment. This is the monarchy; but the monarchy cannot be properly governed with a false religion. The true religion is therefore proper to the best monarchy, and where there is false piety or false worship of God there can be no perfection in the prince or in the principality. Therefore poems must also participate in this same imperfection, but the fault is not that of the poetic art but of politics, not of the poet but of the legislator. We conclude, therefore, that no poem is to be praised which is excessively full of prodigies.[90]

The only marvelous that is really acceptable is the Christian marvelous, since actions attributed to God and his ministers—even though they are improbable or impossible—become verisimilar through faith. The opinion of the multitude, to whom poetry is addressed, will accept such actions as true: "One and the same action may therefore be both marvelous and verisimilar: marvelous if one consider it in itself and hemmed in by natural limitations, verisimilar if one consider it separated from such limitations with respect to its cause, which is a supernatural force capable of and accustomed to producing such marvels."[91] This credibility of the Christian marvelous is an additional reason why the epic poet—who seeks always credibility—should by preference choose a Christian subject. He must not use the most sacred of these, nor those of recent times. All other conditions of subject matter derive from these original bases. In all this theorizing of Tasso there is, moreover, a hidden Platonism, to the extent to which he sees behind every poem or every part of a poem an Idea which the poet seeks to imitate through the happy combination of matter and form.

Like Tasso's treatise, Sperone Speroni's *Dialogo dell'historia*, published only in 1596, probably goes back to a much earlier date; I have been unable to find any grounds for assigning an approximate date to it. The *Dialogo* also has certain points of doctrine in common with Tasso. One similarity is in the classification of the art, for Speroni too places it, along with logic, grammar, and rhetoric, under rational philosophy. He also sees it as essentially useful to the state and in the service of politics. Most important of all, he insists that the subject of poetry is truth, not falsehood, and that it derives its materials (as does history) from annals:

. . . a fable is thus not a lie, as it would seem to be from the meaning of the word itself, but without any doubt the truth, not merely natural and pure and simple

90 *Ibid.*, p. 35: "l'eccellentissimo poema è proprio solamente della eccellentissima forma di gouerno. questa è il Regno, ma il Regno non può esser' ottimamente gouernato con falsa religione. Conuiene adunque all'ottimo Regno la vera religione, & oue sia falsa pietà, e falso culto d'Iddio, non può essere alcuna perfettione nel Principe, ò nel Principato: però i poemi ancora participano dell'istessa imperfettione, ma il difetto non è dell'arte poetica, ma della politica, non del poeta, ma de' legislatori, conchiudiamo dunque, che non si debba lodare alcun poema souerchiamente prodigioso."

91 *Ibid.*, p. 37: "Puo esser dunque vna medesima attione, e merauigliosa, e verisimile, merauigliosa riguardandola in se stessa e circonscritta dentro à i termini naturali, verisimile considerandola diuisa da questi termini nella sua cagione, laquale è vna virtù sopranaturale possente, & vsata à far simili merauiglie."

truth, standing on its own . . . , but the truth adorned and decorated by certain images which are marvelous imitators of the behavior of the reason, or of the ways of saying or believing things common to some part of the world which in other parts would be held as impious or reputed to be impossible.[92]

Simple truth is found in the annals; noteworthy truth is the matter of history; and noteworthy and marvelous truth is the subject of poetry. What is more, this marvelous aspect is less the product of the action itself or of the persons involved in it than the product of the words, metaphors, epithets, and other decorations used to present them. Poetry rapidly becomes a form of rhetoric. We should note, however, that Speroni encounters the Platonic tradition at several points—political usefulness, ends, truthfulness—without specifically calling upon the authority of Plato or discussing his text; rather, the definite references and borrowings involve Aristotle's *Poetics*.

Almost at the end of the century—so healthy is the tradition—Diomede Borghesi supplies us with another example of the extravagant "defenses of poesy" which had been so frequent in the early years of the Cinquecento and which were to continue as a favorite literary exercise in the Seicento as well. This is his *Oratione intorno a gli onori, et a' pregi della poesia, e della eloquenza* of 1596. Borghesi bases his praise of poetry primarily on the fact that the poetic art is a gift of nature and that natural objects are more excellent than all others. It is the divine furor, without which no amount of industry will avail the poet, that constitutes the natural foundation of the art, the divine furor "which is breathed into our souls miraculously by infinite providence."[93] A second source of eulogy is found in the witness of innumerable philosophers, kings, generals, and others who have either practised the art themselves or praised those who did. For poetry, in spite of what the ignorant may think, contains under the beautiful exterior sound counsels and useful instructions. Both poetry and eloquence are joined in a third form of appreciation, the superiority of their language and reasoning to those of the common people. For all these reasons, Borghesi believes that Plato's ban upon the poet was a restricted one and that the whole art was not blamed for the misdeeds of those who practised it badly; these latter are the wicked and unscrupulous versifiers who wilfully corrupt an innocent citizenry. The citation of poets by Christians, even by the church fathers, and the many religious uses of poetry may be taken as proof that this is a proper interpretation of Plato's meaning. Borghesi's paean of praise comes at the end of his oration: "Poetry, by means of which the

---

[92] In *Dialoghi* (1596), p. 394: "fauola adunque non è menzogna, come ella par nel uocabulo, ma uerità senza fallo, non natural solamente, & pura, & semplice, & per se stante . . . , ma uerità lauorata, & intagliata di alcune imagini imitatrice merauigliose del decoro della ragione, ò del usanza del dirsse [sic], & credere uolgarmente in alcuna parte, del mondo cose, che altroue sarebbono empie tenute, ò riputate impossibili."

[93] *Oratione* (1596), p. 10: "il qual ne gli animi nostri dall'infinita prouidenza miracolosamente si spira."

mover of the stars is duly celebrated, is the unique imitator of all things, the moderator of unbridled passions, the teacher of high-minded behavior, the producer of noble actions, the arouser of virtue, the dispenser of praise, the guardian of honor, and the immortal conservator of the memories of other men."[94]

It is perhaps fortunate that the last of the texts to be analyzed in this chapter should represent so typically one of the dominant forms of Cinquecento Platonism. The text is Paolo Beni's *Disputatio in qua ostenditur praestare comoediam atque tragoediam metrorum vinculis soluere* (1600), already studied at some length in Chapter VI (p. 244). It is a typical document in the sense that Beni maintains throughout a fundamentally Platonic attitude—considering poetry in the context of ethical and political criteria —while starting always from an opposite assumption: the ethical and political effects will be desirable. A purely personal note is added in the theory that these effects are desirable (at least for tragedy and comedy) as long as the poems are written in prose, but that undesirable consequences result from the writing of the same forms in verse. It is this latter note that constitutes the originality of the work.

I have already indicated that Beni assumes that the real end of poetry is utility through moral instruction and that pleasure is ancillary to this end. To the passages already cited may be added others which clarify and specify the position. The statement on the relationship between pleasure and utility also reveals Beni's conception of the audience to which tragedy and comedy are addressed:

> For honest utility, . . . not pleasure, is the common and proper end of tragic or comic imitation. Pleasure indeed was sought and obtained in tragedy and comedy with this purpose: that, since naked precepts for living joined with philosophical severity are received and borne with difficulty by the people, they should be seasoned and tempered with a kind of pleasure and agreeableness, as if with salt. . . . Thus certainly the good writers of comedy and of tragedy, in imitation of the expert medic who tempers with sweetness the bitterness of a medicine which would otherwise be distasteful to the palate of the patient, season and mix with pleasure the regulations and precepts for life, in order that—by fooling the palate of the masses as it were revolted—they may give them useful lessons in an agreeable way.[95]

---

[94] *Ibid.*, p. 20: "la Poesia, con la qual degnamente si celebra il mouitor delle Stelle, è singolare imitatrice di qualunque cosa, moderatrice di trasandanti affetti, insegnatrice di generosi costumi, producitrice di nobili operationi, solleuatrice di virtù, dispensatrice di lodi, albergatrice d'onore, e dell'altrui memorie immortal conseruatrice."

[95] *Disputatio* (1600), pp. 4–4v: "Etenim honesta vtilitas . . . non voluptas est germanus finis ac proprius Comicae aut Tragicae imitationis. Voluptas enim in Tragoedia & Comoedia eo consilio quaesita & comparata est, vt quoniam nuda vitae praecepta philosophicae seueritati admista difficilè excipiuntur a popularibus aut sustinentur, voluptate quadam ac iucunditate tanquam sale condiantur ac temperentur. . . . Sic sanè bonus Comicus & Tragicus periti instar Medici qui Pharmaci amaritudinem dulci temperat, ac fastidiosum aegroti palatum fallit, vitae officia atque praecepta voluptate condit ac temperat, vt vulgi palatum quasi nauseantem fallens, vtilitatem illi cum suauitate propinet."

For such an audience as this, an excess of pleasure can only be dangerous, and Beni takes a stand very close to that of Plato: "They [verses and song] soften our souls and destroy all the sinews of manliness; finally, in the guise of liberal education they can bring us much harm and evil."[96] Thus, the question is raised as to whether the whole art should be condemned because of these potential dangers. Beni cites Cicero's *Pro Archia* for a moderate position and then passes on to a discussion of Plato's banishment of the poets. He believes that if we read Plato well we will find that he disapproves only of certain genres and that in sum his argument authorizes that of Beni himself:

> If one read him more carefully, he will understand that he is not hostile to the lyric poets or to any others who are not bound by the law of imitation, especially since their verses seem to be adapted to singing the praises of the gods. He might easily have restored to his favor Homer and the epic poets, whom indeed he praises on many scores, wherever they had both used imitation more moderately and had corrected certain things which seemed to be in opposition to decency and virtue. In fact, he became so indignant against the tragic and comic writers because they put that constant imitation through verses and songs so completely to the use of voluptuousness and brutality that in the end he both repudiated the poems and ordered that the poets themselves leave his state, as if he intended to put them completely beyond the pale. And this was because they lulled the ear with rhythm and verse and harmony, and delighted the senses deprived of reason, finally exciting to admiration the mob gathered in the theater; but not only did they not direct men's minds towards prudence and temperance, but with such means they were not even capable so to direct them.[97]

This vice is above all apparent in comedy, where a variety of meters and melodies, in combination with all the claptrap and machinery of the stage, leads to ethical results that are directly the opposite of those sought by the art; Comedy herself, in a long soliloquy, confesses her sins and, in essence, blames them upon the use of verse. Beni's is thus a kind of Platonism which holds one attitude toward poetry in verse and the opposite attitude toward poetry in prose, and which thus bends the texts of Plato to its own purposes. This was not by any means an infrequent situation in the Cinquecento.

---

[96] *Ibid.* p. 15v: "sed tamen mollire animos nostros, neruos omnes virtutis elidere: denique per speciem liberalis eruditionis multa nobis afferre mala & detrimenta."

[97] *Ibid.*, pp. 16–16v: "si quis attentiùs eum perlegat, intelliget non lyricis infensum esse aut si qui sunt alii qui imitationi haud astricti sint: cum praesertim horum carmina diuinis laudibus canendis . . . accommodata uideantur. Cum Homero etiam Heroicisque poetis, quos etiam in multis laudat, facilè rediisset in gratiam vbi & temperatiore imitatione vsi essent, & in primis nonnulla quae cum honestate ac virtute pugnare viderentur, emendassent. verùm in Tragicos & Comicos, quoniam perpetuam illam imitationem metris & cantibus ad lasciuiam seuitiamue inflecterent totam, sic exarsit vt tandem & illorum poemata repudiauerit, & poetas ipsos, è sua Rep. excedere iusserit tanquam si aqua illis & igni interdictum vellet: idque quia versu, rythmo & harmonia mulcerent quidem aures, & expertem rationis sensum delectarent, confluentibus denique in theatrum turbis admirationem mouerent; ad prudentiam verò & temperantiam non modò non informarent animos, sed ea ratione ne informare quidem possent."

CONCLUSIONS

During the last thirty years of the Cinquecento, the documents of literary theory belonging to the Platonic tradition show in certain respects striking similarities with those of the preceding years, in other respects innovations and departures. Perhaps the most constant element is the praise or defence of poetry, usually couched in the most general terms and originating in a vague enthusiasm for the art. Such writers as Menechini, Correa, Benci, and Borghesi add little in the way of arguments to those that had been adduced by a Boccaccio two centuries earlier. One might even say that their orations or treatises reflect little of the critical sophistication which had, nevertheless, developed during the intervening years. In spite of the great erudition resulting from the innumerable commentaries, debates, and discussions of the sixteenth century, their own writings display a kind of charming naïveté—which has the one disadvantage of sounding, always, somewhat trite and unoriginal.

As for the particular questions that at all times formed a part of the Platonic attack or the Platonic defence, these change very little. The critics continue to discuss the great issues—imitation, the divine furor, ethical and political ends—in much the same terms. But perhaps here there is a shift in the balance of interests, for the question of imitation (probably under the influence of the abundant discussions of Aristotle's definition and its uses) ceases to be as exciting as it had been to earlier generations of theorists, and the question of the divine furor is either taken for granted or gives way before a more naturalistic conception of the poet's talents and of his modes of operation. Contrariwise, the consideration of poetry in terms of its relationships to the state and to ethical instruction increases rather than decreases. For all these problems, there is much less direct reference to the texts of Plato themselves, to the point that it is sometimes difficult to distinguish whether a critic actually has a Platonic basis for his point of view or whether he starts from vague and anonymous positions of heterogeneous origin. By this late date theie comes to be a κοινή of Platonic ideas, present universally but unspecifically in the minds of men; and it is to this common fund that reference is made by the critics rather than to the dialogues themselves. Such references remain fragmentary and scattered, just as the literary citations before them had been, because of the fundamentally unsystematic attitude of the critics. That is, Plato remains a collection of passages concerning the poetic art—passages extracted from many dialogues—rather than a philosopher having a total system in the light of which his various ideas on poetry were developed.

If the ethical and political connotations of the art of poetry tend to predominate in these years, it may be because there is present in the consciousnesses of the critics a stronger idea of the state. It is true that, beginning with the earliest writings that I have considered, there were suggestions that the art of poetry was subordinate to the art of politics and that the politician should exercise a role of direction and censure with respect to the poet. But these were theoretical in tone and showed always the direct impact of the Platonic texts. In such writers as Denores, now, the whole problem has an air of immediacy and of reality not earlier sensible. I hesitate to say that this phenomenon results either from a broader awareness on the part of critics of the contemporary developments in political theory or from their observations of current politics. But the critical treatises themselves, unless I am mistaken, give increasing prominence to political implications and a lesser role to ethical instruction; the emphasis is less on "character building" and more on the consequences to the state of the practice of the art of poetry as a whole or of certain of its forms. As a rather surprising corollary, theorists are now less prone to banish or expel the poet from the state and more prone to seek ways in which the practice of his art can be controlled and turned to the advantage of the body politic. It is only in the cases of the extreme Christian theorists that the wish to condemn and exile the art is expressed with increased vigor.

The Platonic position, as I have already remarked, carried with it from the start admirable possibilities for exploitation by Christian theorists, and the first steps in such exploitation were taken by writers of earlier years. This application of Platonic methods and ideas to the Christian attack upon poetry reaches its culmination in the years after 1570. Gambara, Panicarola, Possevino see the whole art in the theological context of Catholicism—and a brand of Catholicism that condemns all forms of pleasure in the severest terms. Such an art as poetry, combining pleasure with utility or using pleasure as an instrument of utility, is immediately suspect because of the very presence of pleasure. It must either be prohibited *in toto*, or all such parts of it as cannot be salvaged for purposes of Christian indoctrination must be put under the ban. This may mean the exclusion of certain genres or certain poets or of whole ranges of poems having unacceptable subject matters or teaching undesirable lessons. An especially reprehensible body of poetry will be that produced by poets who were themselves not Christians, since in their works will be found not only vicious moral incitements but also the praises and the beauties of false religions. All pagan antiquity is the object of such a condemnation. Even in less rabid theorists, whose point of view is not specifically that of the church, the desirability of reading, consulting, or citing the Greek and Roman poets is brought into question. Giovambattista Strozzi's lecture is an example of this kind of thinking. I wish to emphasize again that such thinking is far from setting the tone for late Renaissance attitudes toward poetry. It exists to its maximum degree in a small number of sectarian theorists; but it has an influence upon others as well and helps determine the general orientations of theory.

Both the school of political reference and the school of Christian interpretation were joined in a common point of departure, their contempt for the public to which they assumed that poetry was addressed. For if poetry is politically dangerous, it is because the men who will read or hear it are disposed rather to act upon its malevolent insinuations than to follow its salutary lessons. And if it carries with it dangers to religion, it is because the men whom it affects are too weak in their faith or too susceptible to the blandishments of other beliefs to remain Christians unscathed. In both cases, these men are presented by the critics as of the lowest classes, hence ignorant and morally weak, hence under the domination of their senses uncontrolled by reason. Far from being the art of the élite, poetry is the art of the masses. It writes the kind of poems it does and in the ways it uses because it wishes to appeal to these masses, to sway them, to pander to their low tastes, to instruct them if it can. But this instruction itself is a doubtful thing, granted the recalcitrance supposed to characterize these men. Even the possibility that they may be appealed to indirectly, through allegory, is now subjected to serious doubt—again because of their weakness of intellect and their lack of education. Here, the Platonic tradition, insofar as it subjects the whole art of poetry to the considerations of a specific audience, comes very close to the tradition of Horace and the rhetoricians. It comes closest of all, probably, in such a writer as Mazzoni, who diversifies his audience into various classes, establishes for each class a special utility to be sought by the poet, and then assigns a given poetic genre to each such utility.

There are, in fact, many other points of contact between the Platonic tradition and those of Horace and Aristotle. The Platonic ends, as these critics see them, are practically indistinguishable from those that they find in Horace's *Ars poetica*. Utility and pleasure, equal or unequal, dominant or subordinate. The tendency of the Platonists is to declare that the two are unequal in importance, that utility is dominant, that pleasure is its instrument; and this is true even for those who believe that the art serves desirable ends in a satisfactory way. With Aristotle, the *rapprochements* become increasingly numerous and distinct. The theory of imitation moves closer to an Aristotelian solution; the question of utility is with greater and greater frequency answered by means of reference to the theory of purgation. Doubts raised by Plato are solved by Aristotle; attacks made in the name of the *Dialogues* produce defences based on the authority of the *Poetics*. If this is the general position of the Platonists, it is because from the very outset it is an intermediate position, both philosophically and in point of time. The position grew and developed in an intellectual milieu that had already fully accepted Horace's dicta on many of the problems of the poetic art. It raises questions which had already been answered to a certain extent, or for which answers might be found by a re-examination of the Horatian text. Moreover, it raises only a limited number of questions —those which I have sought to trace in the last two chapters—and leaves untouched the vast body of accepted doctrine that the Horatians had developed for all the practical aspects of the art. This doctrine will not be easily displaced. As the sixteenth century advances, a younger text, Aristotle's *Poetics*, comes to vie with Plato's dialogues for domination in matters theoretical—at least insofar as the theory of poetry is concerned. This text, like Horace's, is seen to have, above all, practical uses and applications, suggestions for the poet in the practice of his art, for the critic in the practice of his profession, for the public in its reading and understanding of poetry. But it is also seen to supply answers to many fundamental and abstruse problems—problems which had been raised by Plato, answers which in some few cases confirm Plato's own findings but which in most cases contradict and deny them. The weakening of the Platonic tradition is a concomitant of the solidification of Horatian doctrine and of the growing authority of Aristotle's *Poetics*.

CHAPTER NINE. THE TRADITION OF ARISTOTLE'S *POETICS*: I. DISCOVERY AND EXEGESIS

THERE IS NO DOUBT but that the signal event in the history of literary criticism in the Italian Renaissance was the discovery of Aristotle's *Poetics* and its incorporation into the critical tradition. Whereas Horace's *Ars poetica* had continued to influence critical thinking throughout the Middle Ages, and whereas Plato's miscellaneous ideas had entered into consideration with the coming of humanism, the text of the *Poetics* became available only at the very end of the fifteenth century and became generally known only toward the middle of the sixteenth. Thus, it appeared at a time when a way of thinking about literary matters, derived from the texts known earlier and from the whole rhetorical tradition associated with Horace, was firmly established in the minds of men. It was necessarily read and interpreted in keeping with that way of thinking, and in its turn it changed and modified the body of existing attitudes. The history of the Aristotelian tradition in the Cinquecento will thus be a narrative of the give and take between habitual modes of thought and a fresh text presenting extraordinary and surprising ideas.

If the dates themselves are fundamentally important, the states of mind current in the successive periods are of even greater significance. By the turn of the century, several mutations had taken place which throw the appearance of the *Poetics* at that precise moment into peculiar relief. On the one hand, by 1500 the "spirit of the Renaissance" was full blown. Italy had produced remarkable masterpieces in the fields of painting, sculpture, and architecture; and in the special domain of literature she was engaged in active production both in Latin and in the vulgar tongue. These works of original artistry had been accompanied, since around 1450, by a notable activity in the fields of theory and criticism: universities, academies, scholars in their studies, all had addressed themselves to the problem of ascertaining whence these works acquired their beauty or their quality or their worth. Naturally, the answers were first sought in the ancients, and the study of Horace and of Plato was renewed and extended. The arrival of Aristotle among the company, with a text previously unexplored and unexploited, promised new possibilities for solving the remaining problems.

On the other hand, the text of the *Poetics* was published (first in Latin and then in Greek) at a time when Aristotle's repute in the scholarly world was not of the highest. His method, regarded as too severe and too "scholastic" and too closely linked to the medieval tradition of the church, had been abandoned in favor of the more attractive and more facile discoursings of Plato (as he was then interpreted). In any case, the rigorous construction and logic of Aristotle's treatises was neither understood nor esteemed, and few men of the Italian Renaissance would have been capable of analyzing or applying it. To be sure, the vogue of Aristotle (especially of such works as the *Ethics*, the *Politics*, the *De Anima*, the *Rhetoric*, and the treatises on natural history) continued throughout the sixteenth century: witness the large number of editions and commentaries, of university courses devoted to interpreting him, of discussions of all kinds. But he was no longer the Master, the Philosopher, the tyrant who imposed method as well as doctrine. His authority was frequently questioned, he was openly attacked by some, and the methods and conclusions of his rivals were upheld against him. Even more serious was the fact that his best expositors and champions were often men of insufficient training and improper intellectual habits (I have spoken of them in Chapter II), and, hence, the interpretations that they offered were woefully insufficient. Thus the appearance of the *Poetics* was essentially an anachronism: the newest, most exciting, and most promising text of Aristotle came to light at precisely the time when men were least prepared to read and understand it correctly.

It should be said, in defence of the Renaissance reader, that the text of the *Poetics* was not—is not—easy to understand. Incomplete in the form in which we have it, it is highly condensed, and the subtlety and rigorousness of its structure become apparent only after the most searching study and in the light of a method discoverable only through analysis of the whole Aristotelian corpus. For the Renaissance reader, the procedure was even more difficult. He had before him a text in many places corrupt, a text which has been much improved by the labors of modern scholarship but in which conjecture and uncertainty are still present. Moreover, it was a text which borrowed its examples and its illustrations from a literature still very imperfectly known, either as to content or to form, and these examples must have provided little clarification for him. If to these circumstances are added the hazards of badly printed texts and inadequate translations, it will be seen that his difficulties were indeed almost insuperable. Hence the necessity, after discovery, for the tremendous effort of exegesis to which the Cinquecento dedicated itself.

I hesitate, even in our time, to propose an interpretation of the text against which the problems and the solutions of the Renaissance may be reflected; the matter is still in great dispute. But perhaps the following general statement would be acceptable. If there has been, in recent years, a recrudescence of interest in the *Poetics* as a guide to the theory and practice of literary criticism, it is because critics have seen in it, more than in any other theoretical document, a treatise which concentrates its attention upon those qualities of the work of art itself which make it beautiful and productive of its proper effect. Aristotle is at no time neglectful either of the audience in whom this proper effect is produced or of the natural reality which is represented in the artificial work of art. But his aim is neither to analyze audiences nor to study nature. He wishes to discover how a poem, produced by imitation and representing some aspect of a natural object—

its form—in the artificial medium of poetry, may so achieve perfection of that form in the medium that the desired aesthetic effect results. His points of departure are two: one, a general conception of aesthetics which comprises such elements as the end of poetry, the nature of imitation, the relationship of artificial to natural objects, the relationship between the work and its contemplator, and the general criteria for artistic achievement; the other, a body of materials (the literature of Greece as he knew it) which he analyzes in the light of this aesthetic to discover how poets have achieved or have failed to achieve the perfection of which their art is capable, and from which he obtains suggestions as to how, in the past, the various forms and genres have been successfully practised. The analysis of the works thus becomes a verification of the aesthetic, just as the aesthetic had provided the initial means for the analysis. The suggestions with respect to the past are never solidified into rules or dogmas, and hence the critic of the future may find in them guides and indications for the analysis of other poems, differently conceived and executed, but nevertheless relatable to the same aesthetic insofar as they belong to the same art.

In anticipation of the ways in which the Renaissance was to read the *Poetics*, two things should be noted about the theory as I have outlined it: First, as concerns the audience, Aristotle at all times bears in mind the presence of a contemplator who sees or reads and appreciates the poem. Statements about the "effect" of which I have spoken may be made either in terms of the kind of reaction within an audience or of the structural particularities within the work which produce that reaction. In either case, the audience is considered in a general way; it is a general and universal one, and never particularized through race, time, place, class, or personal idiosyncracies. It is composed of men sharing the common feelings and experiences of all mankind, having the common conviction that actions spring from character and that events spring from causes, susceptible of enjoying the pleasures afforded by the imitative arts, and capable through their sensitivity and their habits of reading of distinguishing good works from bad. Otherwise, it has no distinctive qualities as an audience. Hence the position of the *Poetics* is not a rhetorical one, because nowhere is the poem made to be what it is in order to have a particular effect of persuasion upon a particular audience; moreover, nowhere does the "character" of the poet enter as a structural element in the poem.

Second, as concerns natural reality, Aristotle at all times maintains a sense of the relationship between the natural object which lies behind the imitation and the artificial object which is the product of the imitation. But this does not mean that the latter is good as it conforms to the former or bad as it fails so to conform. The criterion is not one of resemblance, of faithfulness, of "realism," of "imitation" in its narrowest sense. This means that the requirements of "necessity" and "probability" are not derived from natural verisimilitude or from the way in which things usually happen in an ordered universe. Rather, they are expressions of relationships of a strictly structural character, which assure the proper integration and order of the component parts of the work. Since they are, in a way, like the laws of nature—wherein actions spring from character and events spring from causes—they on the one hand establish the imitative relationship between the poem and its object in nature and on the other assure the intelligibility of the work to the audience and its capacity to feel the desired effect.[1]

How, then, did the men of the Renaissance, first coming into contact with the text of the *Poetics*, read that text? What kind of text, what kind of translations, what kind of commentaries were first available to them, and what was the nature of their interpretations of these documents?

I do not think it useful here to speak of the existence of a medieval translation of the *Poetics* into Latin, recently published,[2] since as far as we can discover that translation was completely unknown during the Renaissance. Nor is it necessary to retail the first fragmentary and passing allusions to the *Poetics* found in the writings of the humanists,[3] since these display merely a knowledge of the existence of the work without any indication of the way in which it was understood. Instead, I wish to pass immediately to a discussion of Averroës' commentary on the *Poetics*. Written in Arabic in the twelfth century, translated into Latin by Hermannus Alemanus in the thirteenth, it was first published in Venice in 1481 under the title of *Determinatio in poetria Aristotilis*. It was reprinted in 1515 and several times thereafter. It was thus that Averroës' commentary was made available before Giorgio Valla's Latin translation of 1498 or the Aldine Greek text of 1508 and was the first instrument by means of which the scholars of the Renaissance could gain an apprehension of the content of Aristotle's text.

THE AVERROËS PARAPHRASE

It would be difficult for any writer of classical antiquity to be less well served, for his presentation to the modern world, than was Aristotle by Averroës and Hermannus. It is clear, from the printed version of their text as we have it, not only that Averroës had before him a garbled version of the *Poetics* but that he himself was incapable of understanding completely the materials with which he was working. He did not know the Greek works to which Aristotle refers for his examples (only the names of Homer and Aesop, among Greek poets, seem to be familiar to him), and the illus-

---

1 For fuller statements of this interpretation of the *Poetics*, see various articles in *Critics and Criticism: Ancient and Modern*, ed. R. S. Crane (Chicago: University of Chicago Press, 1952), especially those of R. S. Crane, R. P. McKeon, and Elder Olson. See also Elder Olson, "The Poetic Method of Aristotle: Its Powers and Limitations," in *English Institute Essays, 1951* (New York: Columbia University Press, 1952), pp. 70–94.

2 *De arte poetica, Guillelmo de Moerbeke interprete*, ed. E. Valgimigli (Bruges-Paris: Desclée de Brouwer, 1953).

3 Cf. Remigio Sabbadini, *Il Metodo degli Umanisti* (Florence: Le Monnier, 1922), pp. 71–74; also Lane Cooper and Alfred Gudeman, *A Bibliography of the Poetics of Aristotle* (New Haven: Yale University Press, 1928).

trations were meaningless to him. He did not have any idea of the literary forms of which Aristotle speaks, with the possible exception of the epic, and the whole of the treatise must have seemed to him to exist in a kind of vacuum. He did know certain kinds of Arabic poetry, and he saw in them certain similarities to the works which Aristotle was describing. Moreover, he was aware of a rhetorical tradition in his own literature, concerned largely with tropes and figures and rhetorical devices, and these too he assimilated to the text of Aristotle. Indeed, his intention as stated at the outset is to discover to what extent the *Poetics* is applicable to his own literature: "Our intention in this edition is to determine how much of Aristotle's book *On Poetry* is concerned with universal rules common to all nations or to most; for most of what is found in this book either consists of rules proper to their poetry and their usage [i.e., of the Greeks] in Greek poems, or they are not found in Arabic poetry, or they are found in other languages."[4]

The cross between misunderstanding on the one hand and an intention to "Arabize" on the other brings about several immediately visible consequences in Averroës' *Determinatio*. In the first place, it leads him to omit many passages, sometimes fairly long ones, from the translation that forms the basis of the commentary. I think it useful to indicate here which passages are actually translated; to do so, I have numbered the passages in Hermannus' translation and given the equivalents in the *Poetics*.[5] The gaps will speak for themselves:

1	1447a8	16	24–27
2	12–13	17	1449a21–28
3	15–16	18	31–36
4	18–28	19	1449b9–13
5	28–1447b8	20	24–28
6(?)	1447b9–13	21	31–34
7(?)	16–23	22	36–1450a7
8	23–29	23	1450a7–14
9	1448a1–5	24	15–23
10	11–12	25(?)	23–37
11	14	26	37–1450b4
12	24–25	27	1450b4–8
13	1448b4–12	28	8–13
14	12–19	29	13–16
15	20–24	30	16–21

[4] *Determinatio* (1481 ed.), p. f: "Intentio nostra est in hac editione determinare quod in libro poetrie aristotilis de canonibus uniuersalibus comunibus omnibus nationibus aut pluribus cum plurimum eius quod est in hoc libro aut sunt canones proprii poematibus ipsorum & consuetudini ipsorum in ipsis aut non sunt reperta in sermone arabum aut sunt reperta in aliis idiomatibus."

[5] A question mark after the number of a passage indicates that the parallelism is so vague as to make exact identification impossible; after a reference to the *Poetics*, that the limits of the passage being paraphrased are unclear.

31	22–24	70	17–22
32	25–32	71	23–26
33	35–40(?)	72	31–25
34	1451a6–15	73	1455b12–(?)
35	16–19	74	24–29
36	23–24	75	33–1456a3
37	30–35	76	1456a3–7
38	36–1451b11	77	25–(?)
39	1451b15–19	78	33–34
40	27–33	79	35–1456b2
41	33–39	80	1456b2–8
42	1452a12–18	81	8–19
43	22–23	82	20–21
44	29–33	83	22–34
45	33–36	84	35–38
46	36–1452b3	85	38–1457a6
47	1452b9–13	86	1457a6–10
48	14–18	87	10–14
49	25–27	88	1457a14–18
50	30–32(?)	89	18–23
51	1453a7–12	90	23–30
52	22–23	91	31–1457b6
53	23–26	92	1457b6–12(?)
54	30–36	93	33–35
55	1453b1–8	94	1458a1–3(?)
56	8–15	95	18–26(?)
57	15–22	96	1458b1–11
58	27–31(?)	97	11–15
59	1454a13–15	98	1459a15–30
60	16–27	99	1459b8–12(?)
61	33–36	100	17–21(?)
62	1454b1–2(?)	101	1460b2–5
63	8–14	102	6–7(?)
64	15–18	103	13–17(?)
65	19–21	104	23–25(?)
66	30–31	105(?)	1461b16–17
67	1454b36–1455a4	106(?)	1461a16(?)
68	1455a4–6	107	1461b22–25
69	12–15	108	[no equiv.]

A study of the passages in Aristotle omitted by Averroës-Hermannus shows both misunderstanding and "Arabizing" at work. Many of them (more than in any other category) are passages in which Aristotle had cited or analyzed specific works by Greek authors, and these were, of course, incomprehensible to Averroës, especially when Aristotle had spoken of specific details of plot or character (e.g., 6, 7, 9–10, 10–11, 11–12, 16–17, 35–36, 36–37, 38–39, 39–40, 53–54, 54–55, etc.). In another group are passages in which Aristotle had spoken of such specifically dramatic elements of tragedy as the constitution of the plot, the tragic hero, recognition, reversal, the "deus ex machina," the quantitative parts; since Averroës had no notions of dramatic poetry, these sections were completely meaningless for him (e.g., 1–2, 17–18, 32–33, 41–42, 46–47, 48–49, 49–50, 50, 62, 72–73, etc.). A third set is comprised of passages in which Aristotle had treated the very essence of poetry as an art of imitation; since Averroës' conception of poetry (as we shall see later) was an entirely different one, he could have no comprehension of such ideas as that of imitation itself, of necessity and probability, of truth and historical truth as related to imitation, of the distinctions among object, manner, and means (e.g., 3–4, 11–12, 20–21 42–43, 102, 103–4, 104–7). Contrariwise, Averroës felt quite at home in discussions of diction and rhetorical figures, and the most continuous single part of the *Poetics* translated by him is that represented by passages 79 to 91.

The intention to "Arabize" leads, in the second place, to the replacing of Aristotle's examples by examples from Arabic poetry. Besides, many fresh examples are added. It is difficult, from the bare translation, to discover what kinds of Arabic poetry Averroës has in mind. But some of the names mentioned and some of the descriptions help to establish the general categories. It is clear that he excludes the Koran from the general classification of poetry; it is the "liber sanctus" (p. gii) and is carefully differentiated from poetry: "Most hyperbolical figures of this kind are found in Arabic poetry, but in the book of the Most High, that is, the Koran, none such are found."[6] It is also clear that he excludes certain religious writings, called the "Sermones Legales" and apparently very close in content to the Old Testament: "You will find several stories of the kind mentioned here in the Books of Laws, since of this kind are the laudatory tales which incite to praiseworthy actions; for instance, Joseph and his brethren is an example from history and there are other similar incidents as examples in accounts of the past; these are all called hortatory exempla."[7] Once again, the distinction is carefully made: "And you will find many examples of this kind, all of them in the Scriptures of the Laws since poems in praise of virtue [i.e., tragedies] are not to be found among the poems of the Arabs; and they are not found in our times except in the legal writings."[8] If these are excluded specifically, other kinds of writing are excluded merely because they do not exist among the writings of the Arabs: all dramatic genres and

---

[6] *Determinatio* (1481 ed.), p. gᵛ: "tales iperbolici sermones quamplurimi inueniuntur in poematibus arabum sed in libro altissimi id est in alkoratio [sic] nihil."

[7] *Ibid.*, p. f vii: "tu reperies plures representationum incidentium in sermonibus legalibus secundum hunc modum cuius fecit mentionem cum talia sint sermones laudatiui instigantes ad opera laudabilia: ut quidem inducitur de historia ioseph et fratrum suorum & alia similia de narrationibus gestorum preteritorum que nominantur exempla exortatiua." Cf. p. f viiᵛ on the story of Abraham.

[8] *Ibid.*, p. f viiᵛ: "Et tu reperies multa ad modum omnium istorum in scripturis legalibus cum carmina laudatiua uirtutum non inueniantur in poematibus arabum & non inueniuntur in hoc nostro tempore nisi in legibus scriptis."

such lengthy narrative poems as the epic. The poetry which Averroës knew consisted therefore exclusively of shorter works, narrative or lyric in general form and embracing such matters as encomia or eulogies, satires, elegiac or love themes, laments and songs of joy. Within this body of known materials, he tried to find examples of the literary phenomena which he thought Aristotle was describing and discussing, with greater or less success according as parallelisms did or did not exist between Arabic and Greek poetry.

In a positive way, we may say that the theory of poetry found in the *Determinatio* differs from that found in the *Poetics* in three striking ways: (1) Averroës conceives of poetry as a representation or manifestation of the truth, in which the notion of "imitation" is essentially lacking; (2) he thinks of the end of poetry as exclusively ethical, seeking to inculcate virtue or to discourage vice in the reader; (3) he sees this end as achieved specifically through the affective devices of rhetoric—the figures, mainly—rather than through the total effect of a poetic form. I shall expand somewhat on each of these points in order to indicate the precise nature of Averroës' position.

Perhaps the simplest approach to Averroës' general conception of poetry is through his initial statement that "sermones poetici sermones sunt imaginatiui" (p. f). From what follows, it is clear that "imaginatiui" means something like "composed of or productive of images," something like "figurative." The next sentence, "Modi autem imaginationis & assimilationis tres sunt," confirms this through the establishment of the equivalence between "imaginatio" and "assimilatio"; moreover, it indicates without a doubt that these formulas are meant to translate *Poetics* 1447a15–16 and that "imaginatio" and "assimilatio" are translations of μίμησις. But whereas Aristotle had gone on to distinguish three kinds of differences among imitations, according to object, manner, and means, Averroës discerns three kinds of figures: (1) an "assimilatio rei ad rem," which may take the form either of a simile using "quasi" or "sicut" or of a metaphor based on a proportional relationship; (2) an "assimilatio conuersa" in which a comparison is "reversed" (you say that the sun is like a woman rather than that a woman is like the sun); and (3) a combination of the other two. Since synonyms for "assimilatio" are "transumptio," "translatio," and "similitudo," and since Averroës refers the reader to Aristotle's *Rhetoric* for further information, it is clear that the notion of imitation has been reduced to that of figurative expression.

The consequences of this construction put upon the term "imitation" are apparent throughout the work. It should be pointed out that "imitatio" does appear as a term, but always in a meaning consistent with that already given. When Averroës comes, shortly afterward, to a listing of the three means of imitation in poetry, he gives them as "sonus" (harmony), "pondus" (rhythm), and "assimilatio"; the last is equivalent to diction, and an

imitation or representation in diction is said to be "in sermonibus repre-
sentatiuis seu imaginatiuis" (p. f*v*). When he wishes to state the natural
causes of poetry, he gives the first as man's natural practice of "assimilatio
rei ad rem: & representatio rei per rem" and he cites as evidence the usefulness in teaching of such "assimilationes" as examples and comparisons
(p. f2*v*). In a more important way, when he is confronted with the necessity
of treating the parts of plot (which is a much larger "imitative" form than
any he could conceive), he is obliged to replace translation by paraphrase,
to substitute for the ideas of the original those which agree with his own
conceptions. Reversal and recognition (translated by "circulatio" and
"directio") are both figures of speech, both may be found together in a
brief narrative passage such as the one cited from a poet called Abyraibi
(pp. f vi–f vi*v*). Action or plot itself has no more specific meaning than
"res" or subject matter, although the word "actio" is at times used; unity
of action is violated in certain Arabic poems of praise, for example, when
"some matter worthy of praise presents itself, such as a fast horse or a
precious sword, [and] they digress from the main theme and they linger too
long on the praises of the matter which has offered itself for praise."[9]
Similarly, the notions of knot and denouement (translated by "carmen
consecutiuum" and "dissolutio" or "disiunctio") are made to pertain to
lyric poetry and may be illustrated by short citations (cf. p. gii).

Further evidence that the concept of imitation has, for Averroës, anything but its Aristotelian meaning is found in his insistence that poetry must
treat only what is true. There are echoes here, of course, of Aristotle's ideas
on probability and on historical truth; but essentially the ideas are reversed
and an opposite conclusion is presented. Thus when he is translating
Poetics 1451*a*35 ff., he makes this categorical statement:

. . . representations which are made through untrue and extraordinary figments
are not the poet's business. And these are the ones which are called proverbs and
exempla, and they are those which are found in the book of Aesop and in similar
fabulous writings. For it does not belong to the poet to speak of anything except
things which exist or which can possibly exist. . . . For the maker of extraordinary
proverbs and fables invents or fabricates entities that simply do no exist as a
matter of fact and he gives them names. But the poets give names to things which
exist. . . .[10]

The same thesis is developed more specifically with respect to tragedy,
which he calls the "ars laudatiua" or the "carmen laudatiuum":

9 *Ibid.*, p. f v: "quando occurrerit eis aliqua materia laudandi: ut aliquis equus strenuus
aut ensis preciosus digrediuntur a proposito: et immorantur nimis in laudibus materie que
optulit ad laudandum."

10 *Ibid.*, p. f v*v*: "representationes que fiunt per figmenta mendosa adinuenticia non sunt
de opere poete. Et sunt ea que nominantur prouerbia & exempla: ut ea que sunt in libro
Isopi et similibus fabulosis conscriptionibus: ideo quod poete non pertinet loqui nisi in rebus
que sunt aut quas possibile est esse. . . . fictor ergo prouerbiorum adinuentiuorum et fabularum adinuenit seu fingit indiuidua que penitus non habent existentiam in re: & ponit eis
nomina. Poete uero ponunt nomina rebus existentibus."

... the things from which the imitative representation is selected must be things existing in nature, not things invented or imaginary, for which terms are fabricated. For the songs of praise [i.e., tragedies] have as their intention the improving of those actions which spring from the will; when therefore they are possible and almost real, they contain a greater capacity for persuasion or poetic credibility, which moves the soul to follow something or to reject it. In actions, however, which do not exist in nature, [this capacity] is not present.[11]

Imitation is no longer the process of presenting something that is *like* nature; it is the process of presenting nature.

The reason for this, the greater credibility of that which is and its greater persuasiveness, is contained in the last paragraph quoted; if the poem is to produce ethical action through persuasion of its audience, and if persuasion depends upon a conviction of truth, then only true subjects will be admitted to poetry. The end is action, the means persuasion, the materials truth. We may take this as a statement of Averroës' other two fundamental concepts of the art of poetry. With respect to the end of moral action, his statements are once again unequivocal. Paraphrasing *Poetics* 1448a1, he writes: "Those who represent and those who imitate intend by means of their imitations to instigate to certain actions which spring from the activity of the will and to prevent certain other actions; whence those things which they seek through their imitations will of necessity be virtues and vices."[12]

Later in the same passage he rephrases the intention in such formulas as "propter ostentationem decentis aut indecentis," "assecutio decentis & refutatio turpis," "laus bonorum et uituperatio malorum," "approbatio decentis & detestatio turpis." The various literary genres come to be named and judged in the light of their service of these ends. Tragedy ("ars laudandi") and comedy ("ars uituperandi") will be acceptable forms since both praise and blame contribute to the end of virtuous action; the definition of tragedy, for example, is modified to contain this clause: "It is an imitation, I say, which generates in men's souls certain passions which temper them toward pitying and fearing and to other similar passions, which it induces and promotes through what it makes virtuous men imagine about honesty and moral cleanliness."[13] (It should be remembered that Averroës knew no dramatic literature and conceived of these two forms as

11 *Ibid.*: "ut sint res a quibus sumitur imitatiua representatio res existentes in natura non res adinuenticie siue figmentales quibus ficta sint nomina. Carmina namque laudatiua intentionem habent promouendi actiones uoluntarias: quando ergo fuerint possibiles & quasi reales amplius incidit per eas sufficientia persuasiua seu credulitas poetica motiua anime ad assequendum aliquid aut ad refutandum ipsum. Rebus autem non existentibus in natura non ponuntur...."

12 *Ibid.*, pp. fv–f2: "representatores et assimilatores per haec intendunt instigare ad quasdam actiones que circa uoluntaria consistunt et retrahere a quibusdam erunt necessario ea que intendunt per suas representationes aut uirtutes aut uicia."

13 *Ibid.*, pp. f3–f3v: "Representatio inquam que generat in animabus passiones quasdam temperatiuas ipsarum ad miserendum aut timendum aut ad ceteras consimiles passiones quas inducit & promouet per hoc quod imaginari facit in uirtuosis de honestate & munditia."

short poems resembling eulogies and satires.) But love poems, since they lead only to vice, will not be acceptable:

But the species of poetry which they call elegy is nothing but an incitement to acts of copulation which they conceal and adorn with the name of love. And therefore it is necessary that children should be restrained from the reading of such poems and that they should be instructed and exercised in poems which incite and incline to fortitude and liberality.[14]

After pointing out what virtues are pursued by Arabic poetry, Averroës insists that the Greeks always seek to teach in their poetry and that didactic materials are included in it "insofar as they intend by them [their poems] to convey didactic illustrations and precepts for the following of the virtues and the rejecting of the vices, or for any other good things which may be done or known."[15] The end of poetry is thus instruction—for what may be learned, but especially for the actions that may be taken in the light of learning. Because of this emphasis, it is essentially moral instruction.

With respect to the rhetorical means by which such moral instruction is achieved, we have already seen that the principal one will be figurative language. If we think of poetry as consisting in imitation and of imitation as essentially a process of "assimilatio" or metaphor, then whatever power the art has must be found in the rhetorical effectiveness of such metaphors. Averroës states the case fairly clearly, again deforming the text of Aristotle, in connection with his treatment of recognition and reversal. It will be remembered that he had reduced both to the status of figures of speech; to explain their effectiveness he says this, after pointing out how they should be mixed within the individual poem:

For it is proper that odes, that is songs of praise [Aristotle's tragedies], through which one seeks the instigation to the virtues, should be made up of representations of the virtues and of representations of things causing fear or bringing sadness, from which follows some emotion, such as the misfortunes falling upon good people without relationship to their merits. Through these indeed the exciting of the soul to the reception of the virtues is made powerful. . . . Certainly these representations stir up men's souls and make them quick to the reception of the virtues.[16]

---

14 *Ibid.*, p. f2: "Species uero poetrie quam elegiam nominant non est nisi incitatio ad actus cohituales quos amoris nomine obtegunt & decorant. Ideoque oportet ut a talium carminum lectione abstrahantur filii & instruantur & exerceantur in carminibus que ad actus fortitudinis & largitatis incitant & inclinant."

15 *Ibid.*, pp. f2–f2v: "inquantum intendunt per ea tradere documenta & precepta ad sequendas uirtutes aut respuenda uicia aut quaslibet alias bonitates operabiles aut scientiales."

16 *Ibid.*, p. f vii: "Oportet enim ut ode id est carmina laudum per que intenditur instigatio ad uirtutes composite sint ex representationibus uirtutum & ex representationibus rerum incutientium pauorem & contristantium ex quibus sequitur perturbatio: ut sunt infortunia incidentia bonis praeter merita ipsorum: per haec enim uehemens fit incitatio anime ad receptionem uirtutum. . . . He nempe representationes exacuunt animas & festinas reddunt eas ad receptionem uirtutum."

Further consequences of this basically rhetorical attitude are seen throughout the work.

We may take as a striking example the handling of the six qualitative parts of tragedy. These are the terms which he uses as equivalent to Aristotle's:

plot	"sermones fabulares representatiui"
character	"consuetudines"
thought	"credulitas"
diction	"metrum"
spectacle	"consideratio"
song	"tonus"[17]

As I have already pointed out, there is in Averroës no conception of plot or action as such; thus "sermones fabulares representatiui" really refers to the whole of the poem rather than to a specific part. The next two parts are for Averroës the most important: "the major parts of laudatory songs are 'consuetudines' and 'credulitates.'"[18] He states the reasons for this judgment: "For tragedy is not a part which represents men themselves as they are individuals present to the senses; but it is representative of their honest ways of living and of their praiseworthy actions and of their beliefs which render them happy. And 'consuetudines' include actions and characters."[19] It is the third of these parts, "credulitas," which has the most specific rhetorical implications. Averroës defines it as "the capacity to represent a thing as being thus or as not being thus." Then he goes on to explain:

And this is similar to that which is attempted in rhetoric in the declaration that a thing exists or does not exist; except that rhetoric seeks to do this through a persuasive composition and poetry through an imitative composition. . . . And the difference between a preceptive poetic composition which incites to beliefs and a preceptive one which incites to ways of living is that the latter incites to accomplishing and doing something or to renouncing and avoiding something; whereas a composition which incites to belief incites to nothing else but the acceptance or the rejection of the notion that something is or is not, not to the active seeking out or refusal of the thing itself.[20]

---

[17] *Ibid.*, p. f3*v*.

[18] *Ibid.*, p. f iiii: "partes maiores carminis laudatiui sunt consuetudines et credulitates."

[19] *Ibid.*: "Tragedia enim non est pars representatiua ipsorummet hominum prout sunt indiuidua cadentia in sensum: sed est representatiua consuetudinum eorum honestarum & actionum laudabilium & credulitatum beatificantium. Et consuetudines comprehendunt actiones & mores."

[20] *Ibid.*: "Et hoc est simile ei quod conatur rethorica in declaratione quod res existat aut non existat nisi quod rethorica conatur ad hoc per sermonem persuasiuum & poetria per sermonem representatiuum. . . . Et differentia inter sermonem poeticum preceptiuum & instigatiuum ad credulitates & preceptiuum & instigatiuum ad consuetudines est quoniam ille qui instigat ad consuetudines instigat ad operandum & ad agendum aliquid aut ad recedendum & fugiendum. Sermo uero qui instigat ad credulitatem non instigat nisi ad credendum & fugiendum aliquid esse aut non esse sed non ad inquirendum ipsum aut respuendum."

There are many curious things about these statements, but perhaps the most significant aspects are these: (1) "plot," "character," and "thought" are not parts of poems at all, but separate kinds of poetic compositions; (2) these kinds are divided into two larger classes, both of which produce ethical ends through rhetorical means, but one of which leads to knowing while the other leads to doing.

It should by now be clear what the reader of the late fifteenth or early sixteenth century would learn about Aristotle's *Poetics* from reading Averroës' *Determinatio* in the translation of Hermannus Alemanus. He would derive from it only the vaguest notions about the text: some of the main terms (but often misused and misapplied), some of the central ideas (but as frequently as not deformed), the most general theoretical distinctions. He would be led, contrary to the intention of Aristotle himself, to think of poetry as a didactic instrument proceeding to moral instruction through rhetorical devices. Of these, the most important would be the figures of speech and other ornaments. Poetry, in this view, comes to be identical with rhetoric, and with the kind of limitation to diction and figures associated with the Alexandrian rhetoricians. None of the distinctively Aristotelian concepts of poetry remains clear and discernible.

THE VALLA TRANSLATION (1498)

The first great step forward in the presentation of Aristotle's *Poetics* to the modern reader came with the publication, in 1498, of Giorgio Valla's translation into Latin. According to E. Lobel's *Greek Manuscripts of Aristotle's Poetics* (p. 25), Valla used as the basis for his translation the manuscript now in the Biblioteca Estense at Modena, Estensis gr. 100. The translation, which preceded any publication of the Greek text, is in general a good one. For the first time, it gave to a larger public than was able to consult the few available manuscripts of the Greek original an accurate idea of what was contained in the text. It is by no means a perfect translation; it could not be, given the state of the manuscript on which it was based and the state of Greek scholarship at the time. For the modern reader, it offers the additional difficulties of a solid presentation, with no paragraphing or division into chapters, and of a completely capricious punctuation; these are undoubtedly the responsibility of the printer rather than of Valla himself. But still, it is a good translation and, above all, a notable advance over everything that had preceded it. I should like, in the following pages, to emphasize the following points with respect to it: (1) the degree to which it rendered properly the key terms of the *Poetics*; (2) the degree to which it rendered correctly most of the text, including certain central passages; (3) the kinds of errors which it made as a result of the imperfections of the Greek manuscripts; and (4) those errors which were actually errors of translation, and the reasons behind them. Again, my purpose will be to indicate what kind of general idea a reader of this translation might have of Aristotle's *Poetics* during the years from 1498 to 1536 (when Pazzi's translation took its place beside it).

The key terms of the "Poetics." The satisfactory character of Valla's rendering of the key terms is not only apparent but even striking to one who has read the Averroës version. Not only that, but Valla, in a sense, established the tradition of the Latin terms that were to be used in the translations of his successors and by the later commentators. Thus, with respect to the general nature of poetry, μίμησις becomes "imitatio" and μιμοῦνται becomes "imitantur"; the three means ῥυθμῷ καὶ λόγῳ καὶ ἁρμονίᾳ are rendered by "rhythmo & oratione: & harmonia"; the distinction of means, object, and manner of imitation, τῷ ἐν ἑτέροις..., ἢ τῷ ἕτερα, ἢ τῷ ἑτέρως, is translated by "genere in alienis [there is some ambiguity in the translation here], aliena, aliter"; the "effect" of poetry (δύναμις) appears as "vis" and the imitation of characters, passions, and actions (καὶ ἤθη καὶ πάθη καὶ πράξεις) as "mores: & affectus & actiones imitantur." With respect to the qualitative parts of tragedy, the terms used are "fabula" for plot, "mores" for character, "animi sententiae" for thought, "dictio" for diction, "conspectus" for spectacle, and "melopoeia" for song (I shall speak later of the difficulties involved in the use of "animi sententiae" and "conspectus"). One of the parts of plot, ἀναγνώρισις, is expressed as "recognitio" and the effects of pity and fear resulting from tragedy—φοβερὰ καὶ ἐλεεινά—as "miseratio" or "commiseratio" and "formido." For the "complication" and the "denouement" of plot (δέσις, λύσις), Valla uses "ligatio'" and "solutio."

A certain number of miscellaneous terms are equally well translated: πράττοντας and δρῶντας = "peragentes, agentes"; τὴν σύστασιν ... τῶν πραγμάτων (1450*b*23) = "rerum complexum"; θαυμαστόν = "mirificum"; τὰ πάθη = "affectus"; εἰκονογράφους = "pictores simulacrorum"; ἐκ συλλογισμοῦ = "ex ratiocinatione"; τὸ πρέπον = "decorum"; πεπληγμένη = "implexa" and παθητική = "passiva"; φιλάνθρωπον = "humanum"; κατὰ τὸ ἀνάλογον = "iuxta proportionem"; εὐφυΐας = "ingenii"; διηγηματικήν = "expositricem"; ἄλογα = "rationis expertes." And so on for many other felicitous solutions. To have presented in this way, to the reader of the beginning of the Cinquecento, a large number of the Latin terms that were to become standard in the translations and commentaries of the *Poetics* was already a considerable achievement for Giorgio Valla.

The translation in general. But Valla's achievement was more extensive. In most cases, he solved correctly the problems of syntax presented by the original, giving as a result a text which for the most part made sense—and the right sense. This is difficult to demonstrate, except by an extensive comparison of the original and the translation. I can only invite the reader to compare the translation with the original text.

Errors resulting from the text. In spite of these excellences in Valla's translation of 1498, there were a large number of errors and inadequacies. These were of two kinds, those occasioned by the corruptness of the manuscripts which he was using and those resulting from his own misunderstandings. With respect to the manuscripts, they presented many lacunae, haplographies, misreadings, and these were reproduced in the later *editio princeps* (1508); hence we are able to discover the state of Valla's manuscripts through the edition of 1508 as well as through our modern editions. For in many cases, and in spite of the brilliant conjectures and emendations of modern scholars, the text remains imperfect. Indeed, in almost every passage of Valla's translation where major difficulties are found, one may find the explanation in some imperfection of his original text.

1447a28. Valla: "Epopoeia orationibus tenuibus: aut metris. Hisque siue inuicem inter se miscendo: siue uno aliquo genere utendo metrorum ad hoc usque tempus." Valla's difficulties come from the presence in the MS of the word ἐποποιία after Ἡ δέ and from the absence after μέτρων of the word ἀνώνυμος, which is a conjecture of Bernays confirmed by the Arabic version.

1448a15. Valla: "circa leges pergas." 1508 reads: τοὺς νόμους. ὡς πέργας. The passage gave infinite trouble throughout the sixteenth century. ὥσπερ γάρ is a conjecture of Vahlen.

1448a25. Valla: "in quibus & quo modo." καὶ ἅ lacking in the text.

1450a16. Valla: "Tragoedia namque est imitatio non hominum sed actionis & uitae & felicitatis &· infelicitas in actione est & finis actio quaedam est non qualitas...." Valla's text lacked, after εὐδαιμονίας, the words καὶ κακοδαιμονίας·ἡ δὲ εὐδαιμονία, a Vahlen conjecture.

1452b25. Valla: "partes tragoediae quibus utendum: Antea diximus." The words ὡς εἴδεσι were lacking from 1508 (and from Pazzi, 1536); they have been supplied subsequently from other MSS.

1455b27. Valla: "unde transitus est ad infortunium." The MSS lacked, after εἰς εὐτυχίαν, the words συμβαίνει ἢ εἰς ἀτυχίαν, supplied by a Vahlen conjecture and from other MSS.

1455b31. Valla: "ligatio quidem quae prius gesta & pusionis acceptio rursus ipsorum quod est apetita morte adfinem usque." There is a lacuna in our text which was still longer in Valla's.

1455b35. Since ἁπλῆ . . . ἡ δέ was lacking from Valla's text, his kinds of tragedies did not include the "simple."

1456a2. Valla: "Quarta porro aequabilis," since 1508 reads τὸ δὲ τέταρτον rather than the modern conjectural reading; the passage is still corrupt.

1457a2. Valla: "tam in extremis quam in medio," translating καὶ ἐπὶ τῶν ἄκρων καὶ ἐπὶ τοῦ μέσου, which now is excluded from the text by editors.

1460b15. Valla: "duplex error est. unus non recte praeoccupare: sed aequum in utramlibet partem prouoluere quod in qualibet sit arte peccatum." Valla's translation is garbled for two reasons: because certain words now conjectured for the text were lacking and because his text included, after μὴ ὀρθῶς, a repetition of κατὰ συμβεβηκός, thus leading to a haplography.

1461a27. Valla: "unde factum est crus nuper fabrefacti stanni & aereas ferro elaboratas: unde dicitur ganymedes ioui uinum miscere non bibentibus uinum." The garbled translation results from the fact that in Valla's MS, as in 1508, the two phrases beginning with ὅθεν εἴρηται and ὅθεν πεποίηται were inverted.

These are by no means the only cases of imperfect translations ascribable to an imperfect text (others may be found, for example, at 1454b2 and b14, –55b15 and b33, –56a10, 11, and 17, –56b8, –57a7, –60a11, –61b28). But they may serve as examples of the kinds of difficulties which the Greek text presented and of the kinds of confusion and misunderstanding which were necessarily reflected in the Valla translation. For the reader of the time, they merely served to make more difficult and enigmatic a document whose philosophical difficulties were already almost insuperable.

Actual errors of translation. Some of these are of the simplest kind and are easily explained: the terms signified objects which Valla did not know and hence he had no idea as to their proper rendering in Latin. These are mostly technical terms of the poetic art. He did not know what gnomic poetry was and translated τῶν νόμων at 1447b26 as "legum"; πάροδος and στάσιμον as parts of the chorus are given as "accessus" and "statiua" (–52b17). Whereas he consistently gives the proper equivalent for ἀναγνώρισις as "recognitio," he just as consistently mistranslates περιπετεία as "petulantia" (e.g., –52a17) or as "procacitas" (e.g., –59b11). It is not surprising that ἁμαρτία should have troubled him; he translates it as "flagicium & scelus" (–53a16). In other cases, proper names gave him trouble: thus καρκίνῳ (–55a27; preceded by τῷ in 1508) becomes "cancrum," Λάϊος (–60a30) is "iolaus," and Πινδάρου (–61b35) is "darium," giving the completely misleading "talis fuit erga darium opinio."

In another category, and a far more extensive one, come those terms whose general meaning he understood clearly enough but for which, at given places in the text, he gave unacceptable equivalents. That is, he failed to seize the shade of meaning required by the context. This came about for two reasons: one, because he did not fully understand the text at specific points; two, because he lacked a knowledge of the possible range of meanings for a word, of its nuances and its implications. For example: πάθος is usually properly rendered as "affectus"; but it is also so rendered at –52b10, where one needs something equivalent to "pathetic event," and at –53b18, where one needs "actual pain." λύειν is usually correctly given as "soluere"; but at –53b22, it should be "change" or "modify." ἦθος is character; but at –60a10, it needs to be "a person having character," and the total phrase "uirum aut foeminam aut morem aliquem" becomes ambiguous. οἱ γραφεῖς may mean "scriptores"; but at –48a5 it means "painters."

Other cases are more serious, since they involve terms whose understanding is essential for the total interpretation of the *Poetics*. Such terms as "necessity" and "probability," for example, are fundamental. Valla regularly gives "necessarium" for ἀναγκαῖον; but he just as regularly gives "aequum" or "aequitas" or even "modestia" for εἰκός (cf. –51a27, –51a36, –51b8), and these do not render the notion of probability. Aristotle's four terms for the four requisites of character are χρηστόν, ἁρμόττον, ὅμοιον, ὁμαλόν. The third and fourth find satisfactory equivalents, I think, in "simile" and "aequabile." But "frugalem" and "concinnum" were hardly capable of giving the reader the notions of "goodness" and "likeness" (I should point out, in passing, that the exact sense of the terms is still in dispute). In discussing the types of action, Aristotle uses the phrase εἰδότας καὶ γινώσκοντας; Valla interprets the first epithet as "idiotas planeque uulgares," thus deforming the sense (–53b28); shortly afterward, he translates εἰδότας ἢ μὴ εἰδότας (–53b37) as "cernentes: aut non cernentes." Numerous other examples of the same kind might be cited.[21]

For another category of "mistranslations" Valla should perhaps not be blamed. For they do not constitute errors of translation. Rather, they consist in the choice of unfortunate Latin equivalents—unfortunate in the sense that they had associations and implications which might lead the reader to assign to Aristotle meanings that he did not intend. Thus for σπουδαίους ἢ φαύλους at –48a2 Valla gives "probos: aut improbos," restricting unnecessarily the distinction of moral character. At –48b25, "speciosas & speciosorum" emphasizes excessively the attitude of others towards actions and persons. At –49b8 and –50b13, the rendering of καθόλου by "in totum" fails to get across the notion of generality which is needed. At –49b17 (cf. the first example above) Valla's translation for τραγῳδίας... σπουδαίας καὶ φαύλης is "tragedia honesta & uili," which again over-emphasizes the moral implications. The use of the word "insignes" at –50a5 adds to the definition of character an inappropriate element, and at –50a19 it introduces an unfortunate distinction of moral merit. At –55a18, the translation of δι' εἰκότων by "per decorem" not only loses the meaning of verisimilitude, but it makes dangerous allusion to a current theory which should not be confused with Aristotle's text.

---

21 *Poetica*, tr. Valla (1498). Cf. φιλομετρίαν (–48a11) = in carminis tenuitate; φθαρτική (–52b11) = corruptiua; ὡς εἴδεσι (–52b14) = tanquam speciebus; ἐπιεικεῖς (–52b34) = modestos & aequos; φιλάνθρωπον (–52b38) = homini amicabile humanumque; χορηγίας δεόμενον (–53b8) = egetque adminiculo uerum; τερατῶδες (–53b9) = monstrosum; μιαρόν (–53b39) = scelestum; δι' ἀπορίαν (–54b21) = ex ambiguitate; σημεῖον (–56a15) = coniectura; ἄνευ διδασκαλίας (–56b5) = citra doctrinam; τὸ κύριον (–58a23) = proprium; ὀγκωδέστατον (–59b35) = turgidissimum; παραλογισμος (–60a20) = absonum; πάθη τῆς λέξεώς (–60b12) = dictionis sunt passiones; ἡμαρτῆσθαι (–60b29) = hallucinari; ἀμιμήτως (–60b32) = sine imitatione.

Finally, one must consider, in addition to the isolated terms already studied, those longer passages which present unsatisfactory translations. There are many of these. They are explained by the presence of the types of words just examined, but also and particularly by deficiencies in Valla's comprehension of construction and of syntactical difficulties. The result is a passage which fails to give a clear and precise meaning. Some of these are fairly short; so the version of –50*b*4, "id autem est uerbis complecti posse agitantia & concinnantia"; of –50*b*35, "item ad honestum & animal"; of –53*b*30, "est sane agere. quidem ignorantes sed ignorantes agere quiduis siue posterius recognoscendo amiciciam"; of –54*a*21, "est quidem mos fortis: sed nec dum mulieri congruus fortem ipsam aut grauem esse"; of –54*b*34, "quia iuxta dictam est hallucinationem. licet namque non nihil est ingerere." Some of them are longer. So for –59*b*26–30, collapsed into the following sentences: "Quantitate & in quae seiuncta diuiduntur. Haec sunt ut uero oportet coniectare: & quae constructas fabulas uereri oporteat & unde fuerit opus tragoediae post haec quae nunc dicta sunt nobis dicendum erit." So also for –59*b*26 ff.: "quod sit expositio est partes multas facere terminatas quibus suis eius aceruus poematis augetur. Proinde id habet bonum ad magnificentiam & mutare auditorem & agressus admittere inaequalibus episodiis." There are, in all, some twenty passages of this kind throughout the translation.[22]

I should not fail to point out that in addition to these "actual errors" of translation, there are many passages in Valla which I should characterize as "questionable" or "doubtful." In these, because of ambiguities of meaning or because of unclear constructions the reader might easily be led to understand the text in a way which was not intended. Or he might not understand it at all. The reader's difficulties would be further enhanced— and his distance from the original text increased—by the fact that in the whole section on diction (chapter 22) the textual examples are omitted and that in the section on replies to criticism (roughly –61*a*12 ff.) the Greek examples are given without translation. Therefore, in spite of Valla's really considerable contribution and of the many qualities of his translation, his reader would not find in it a perfectly satisfactory introduction to Aristotle's *Poetics*. He had the *Poetics* for the first time in a reasonably accurate form; but he also had before him a form which could easily lead to the many problems and discussions and insurmountable difficulties that were to plague the exegetes throughout the sixteenth century.

THE ALDUS TEXT (1508)

In 1508, ten years after the Valla translation, the first Greek text of the *Poetics* appeared, in a volume published in Venice by Aldus and entitled simply *Rhetores in hoc volumine habentur hi*, followed by a listing of the

---

[22] Cf. also the translations of –53*b*35, –55*a*35, –56*b*3, –56*b*9, –56*b*33, –58*b*12, –59*a*21, –60*a*26, –60*b*3, –60*b*32, –60*b*36, –61*b*13, –62*a*6, –62*a*9, –62*a*17.

texts included. There is no prefatory or explanatory material. The text, based on manuscripts then in Italy, is a reasonably good one, and it was long to remain the basic text for the *Poetics*; it was copied or adapted or corrected by most of the sixteenth-century editors. It is possible that the editor of the text may have been Joannes Lascaris; such, at least, was the thesis of Margoliouth, who credited Lascaris with the greatest single contribution to the editing of the *Poetics*.[23] If one compares this text with a modern edition, one finds many errors of spelling, many lacunae, and of course the same difficulties which have led to the conjectures and the exclusions of recent editors. But these are largely imperfections of the manuscripts and not failures of the editor of the printed text. Essentially, Aristotle's text is presented in a usable form, and to the growing group of humanists and scholars it offered the possibility of controlling Valla's translation, of preparing generally more satisfactory translations, and of proceeding to better editions and to intelligent exegeses.

For the next thirty years, there is practically no activity in the tradition of Aristotle's *Poetics*. Such texts as are found treat the *Poetics* in passing, alluding or referring to it in connection with other problems. It is hardly an exaggeration to say that study of the document, if we are to go by the extant works, was at a standstill for almost a third of a century. An example of the passing references to the *Poetics* may be found in Pomponio Gaurico's commentary on Horace, *De arte poetica* (*ca.* 1510).[24] In a work which is essentially a paraphrase of Horace, we suddenly come upon this phrase in the section on tragedy: "praecipue quum uult spectatores ad misericordiam commouere" (p. Aiii). The phrase, if it refers to Aristotle at all, does so only in the vaguest way and might be the result merely of hearsay rather than of a knowledge of the text. In an almost contemporary work, Vittore Fausto's *De comoedia libellus* (1511), the citations are more specific. Fausto takes directly from the *Poetics* the assertion that comedy imitates the ridiculous ("Hoc etiam Aristoteles comprobauit, inquens, quod in turpitudine ridiculum est comoediam imitare," p. AA3) and he cites it on the origins of comedy ("quemadmodum Aristoteles in poeticis ait: quoniam Epicharmus comicorum antiquissimus poeta illinc [of Sicily] esset oriundus," p. AA4; this refers to *Poetics* 1448a33).

In Lodovico Ricchieri's *Lectionum antiquarum libri XXX* (1516), the references are still more extensive.[25] For the most part Ricchieri is working

---

[23] For indications of the basic manuscripts, see D. S. Margoliouth's edition of the *Poetics* London: Hodder and Stoughton, 1911), pp. xv, 95–97; also Vahlen's edition (Leipzig, 1885), p. xi; and E. Lobel, *Greek Manuscripts of Aristotle's Poetics* (London: Oxford Univ. Press, 1933), pp. 31–32. Margoliouth, who ascribes the Aldine text to Lascaris, makes this judgment on it: "Lascaris's emendations constitute an important epoch in the history of the Poetics. . . . a number will be retained so long as the Poetics is studied; and it is probable that the contribution of Lascaris to the text is the greatest which any one scholar has made" (p. 97).

[24] See above, chap. iii, pp. 88–90, and n. 41 for a study of this text and for its date.

[25] See above, chap. ii, p. 57 for this work.

in the Platonic tradition. But when he speaks of the origins of poetry, he gives as equivalent to the Latin "ex rudi principio" the Greek ἐκ τῶν αὐτοσχεδιασμάτων, which may derive from *Poetics* 1449*a*9, and then he gives the following explanation, translating fairly closely *Poetics* 1448*b*24 ff.:

Indeed, from this basis of imitation, whence poetry had its origin, art was disengaged and as an art was subdivided and issued in several component parts. For the inclination to imitate was revealed according to the nature and the character of each writer. The more worthy ones proposed to imitate fine and honorable actions, but the lower and baser ones chose conformably vile and ignoble actions; just as some from the start undertook poems of blame while others sang hymns and praises.

There is also possibly some reflection of *Poetics* 1448*b*9, on the pleasure derived from the imitation of ugly objects, in the following passage:

For that work of art arouses admiration whose portrayal seems to be coherently handled for the representation and depiction of the images of things. In the same way, indeed, we praise a lizard or a monkey depicted in conformity with the truth, not because of their beauty, which we know to be non-existent in such animals, but because of the resemblance.[26]

Pietro Pomponazzi's *De incantationibus* (1520), first published in the *Opera* of 1567, contains a short passage which cites the Averroës paraphrase of the *Poetics*. It is a defence of poetry as an instrument of education:

For the mode of expression in the laws, as Averroës says in his *Poetry*, is similar to that used by the poets; for just as the poets do, they invent fables which, according to the literal meaning of the words, are nor possible, but within they contain the truth, as Plato and Aristotle frequently point out. For they tell untruths so that we may arrive at the truth, and so that we may instruct the vulgar crowd, which must be led toward good action and away from wicked action.[27]

Such a passage as this is especially interesting for several reasons: it shows to what extent Aristotle, in these years, was still read through Averroës,[28] and it demonstrates with what ease Plato and Aristotle were spoken of as assigning the same pedagogical role to poetry.

[26] *Lectionum* (1516), p. 162: "Ex hac uero imitandi ratione, unde Poesis ortum ducit, diuulsa, disparataáque Ars est, ac abiit quodammodo in membra plura. Nam pro cuiusque natura, & moribus imitandi studium proferebatur, honestiores enim pulchras honestasáque actiones sibi imitandas proponebant. Tenuiores autem, humilioresáque Viles itidem, & ignobiles, & primo quidem uituperationem complexi, Sicuti hymnos alii, & Laudes concinnarunt"; and p. 160: "Verum Artificium parere admirationem, quo expressio congruenter uidetur pertractata adumbrandis, informandisáque rerum imaginibus. Nam & eodem ferè modo Lacertam, aut Simiam commode ad Veritatem pictam laudamus, non utique ex pulchritudine, quam esse nullam in eiusmodi animalibus scimus. Sed ob similitudinem."

[27] In *Opera* (1567), p. 201: "Sermo enim legum, ut inquit Auerrois in sua poësi, est similis sermoni poëtarum, nam quanquam poëtę fingunt fabulas, quę, ut uerba sonant, non sunt possibiles, intus tamen ueritatem continent, ut multotiens Plato & Aristoteles referunt: nam illa fingunt, ut in ueritatem ueniamus, & rude uulgus instruamus, quod inducere oportet ad bonum, & à malo retrahere."

[28] The Averroës paraphrase and the Valla translation had been reprinted together in 1515.

Apropos of Averroës, it should be mentioned that a new Latin translation of his paraphrase of the *Poetics,* that of Abram de Balmes, was published in 1523. Balmes' translation was based, however, on the fourteenth-century Hebrew translation of Todros Todrosi, and there is not much evidence to indicate that it was used extensively by Italian commentators. The earliest extensive exploitation of the *Poetics* in Italian among the documents we shall examine is found in Giovanni Giorgio Trissino's dedication of his *Sophonisba* to Pope Leo X, dated 1524. Trissino first calls upon the text of Aristotle for a general distinction between tragedy and comedy:

... knowing also that tragedy, according to Aristotle, is to be preferred to all other poems, since it imitates by means of harmonious language a virtuous and perfect action, which should have magnitude; and just as Polygnotus, an ancient painter, imitating in his works, made the bodies better than they were and Pauson worse, so tragedy as it imitates makes the forms of behavior better and comedy, worse. And therefore this comedy moves to laughter, a thing which is related to ugliness, since what is ridiculous is defective and ugly. But tragedy moves to pity and fear, with which—and along with other teachings—it brings pleasure to the listeners and utility for human living.[29]

At the very end of the passage, inevitably, the Horatian "utile dulci" is introduced. Trissino then proceeds to an apology for his use of Italian rather than Latin and of his use of unrhymed verse; and for both the justification is found in Aristotle. The defence is curious and the interpretation of Aristotle garbled:

... since tragedy has six necessary parts, that is, plot, characters, words, discourse, representation, and verse, it is clear that, having to be presented in Italy, [the Sophonisba] could not be understood by all the people if it were composed in another language than Italian. And furthermore the ways of behavior, the sententiae, and the discourse would not provide universal utility and pleasure if they were not understood by the listeners. Hence, in order not to deprive it of the possibility of representation, which (as Aristotle says) is the first of the parts of tragedy, ... I chose to write it in this language.[30]

---

[29] *Sophonisba* (1524), p. aijv: "sapendo etiandio, che la Tragedia, secondo Aristotele, è preposta a tutti gli altri poemi, per imitare con soave sermone una virtuosa, e perfetta actione, la quale habbia grandeza; e come Polygnoto antico pictore nele opere sue imitando faceua e corpi di quello che erano migliori, e Pauson peggiori, cosi la Tragedia imitando fa e costumi migliori, e la Comedia peggiori, e per ciò essa Comedia muove riso, cosa che partecipa di brutteza, essendo ciò, che è ridiculo, difettoso, e brutto, Ma la Tragedia muove compassione, e tema, con le quali, e con altri amaestramenti arreca diletto agli ascoltatori, et utilitate al vivere humano."

[30] *Ibid.,* p. Aiij: "hauendo la Tragedia sei parti necessarie, cioè, la favola, e costumi, le parole, il discorso, la rappresentatione, et il verso; Manifesta cosa è, che hauendosi a rappresentare in Italia, non potrebbe essere intesa da tutto il popolo, s'ella fosse in altra lingua, che Italiana composta; & appresso e costumi, le sententie, et il discorso, non arrecherebbono universale utilitate, e diletto, se non fossero intese da gli ascoltanti. Si che per non le torre la rappresentatione, la quale (come dice Aristotile) è la prima parte de la Tragedia ... elessi di scriverla in questo Idioma."

Trissino's confusion springs either from his identification of "plot" with "representation," or more probably from a faulty reading of *Poetics* 1450*a*14, where "spectacle" is listed first among the qualitative parts. He defends the absence of rhyme, also on the basis of the *Poetics*, declaring that speeches which move to pity must themselves be expressions of suffering, and that such expressions are spontaneous and intolerant of such restrictions as that provided by rhyme (p. Aiij*v*).

Parts I to IV of the *Poetica* of the same Trissino, published in 1529, occupy a remarkable position in the history of Aristotle's *Poetics* (Parts V and VI, based entirely upon the *Poetics*, were published posthumously in 1563, and they will be treated in a later chapter). What is remarkable is that Trissino, knowing the *Poetics* as he did, should have proceeded almost without reference to it in the composition of his own *Poetica*. His sources are, instead, the rhetoricians and such writers on prosody as Antonio da Tempo. He cites the *Poetics* twice, first in a passage preliminary to his study of diction:

> I say then that poetry (as Aristotle said before me) is an imitation of the actions of man, and since this imitation is made by means of words, rhymes, and harmony, just as the painter's imitation is made by means of design and colors, it would be well before coming to this imitation to treat of that with which this imitation is made, that is of words and of rhymes, leaving harmony or song aside, since the others are capable of producing the imitation without song, and since the poet considers these two and leaves song to be considered by the singer.[31]

From then on, Trissino in these four parts treats only diction and rhyme. His second reference to Aristotle, indeed, is occasioned by his treatment of the choice of words, when he speaks of foreign words: "These are especially to be used in heroic poetry, where variety of languages, as Aristotle says, is sought."[32] The allusion is probably to *Poetics* 1459*a*10.

In Aulo Giano Parrasio's *In Q. Horatii Flacci artem poeticam commentaria* (1531, posthumous) we have the first of those numerous commentaries on Horace which were to develop the parallelisms between the *Ars poetica* and the *Poetics*. In this case (as I have already pointed out[33]), the parallels are few in number, and in most cases the statement of the Aristotelian position is such that one thinks immediately of Averroës rather than of the *Poetics* itself. So, in Parrasio's introduction, for the statement "Obseruauerunt eam mortales, quod harmonia & rythmus natura nobis tributa

---

31 *La poetica* (1529), p. ii*v*: "Dico adunque, che la Poesia (come prima disse Aristotele) è una imitazione de le azioni de l'homo; e facendosi questa cotale imitazione con parole, rime, et harmonia, si come la imitazione del dipintore si fa con disegno, e con colori, fia buono, inanzi che ad essa imitazione si vegna, trattare di quello, con che essa imitazione si fà, cioè de le parole, e de le rime; lasciando la harmonia overo il canto da parte; perciò, che quelle ponno fare la imitazione senza esso, e di queste due il Poeta considera, e lascia il canto considerare al Cantore."

32 *Ibid.*, p. iiii*v*: "e queste specialmente stanno bene ad usarsi ne lo heroico, nel quale la varietà di lingue, come dice Aristotele, si ricerca."

33 Cf. chap. iii, pp. 96–100.

sunt" (p. 1*v*), which refers to Averroës, p. f2*v*, and for another, "Erit ergo boni poetae ante omnia ideam futuri sibi poematis statuere, & quod periti faciunt architecti, breui quasi tabella totius operis imaginem ante oculos proponere" (p. 6*v*), which may refer to Averroës, p. g*v*. In the same introduction, however, there is at least one passage which seems to go back directly to the *Poetics*. Beginning with a rapid history of poetry before Homer, Parrasio continues:

> The latter [Homer], having put together all that was previously dispersed, gave to poetry a single and definitive body, and it is to be marveled at that no imitation—not even a dramatic representation—might be contrived which did not have a counterpart in his work. With his own might he introduced into his works the subjects of comedies, tragedies, dithyrambs, and of all kinds of poems.[34]

The next statement, however—"All poems are either dramatic, or narrative, or a mixture of these"[35]—could come as well from Plato or from the current Horatian tradition. In the line-by-line commentary on Horace there are no references to Aristotle. But late in the text, in connection with vss. 318 and 408, there are two brief passages which again are closer to Averroës than to the *Poetics*: on p. 68*v*, Parrasio says, "Nihil enim aliud est poesis nisi imitatio uitae & morum, quae hominis propria est, facitque ut vel hac una differt a caeteris animalibus," with which compare Averroës, p. f2*v*: "istud proprium est homini respectu ceterorum animalium. Et causa in hoc est quum homo inter cetera animalia delectatur in assimilatione rerum quas iam in sensu percepit & in earum representatione seu imitatione." And on p. 78 he says "Si enim . . . poetica nihil aliud est, quam imitatio naturae," with which compare Averroës, p. f*v*. As in other contemporary documents, the text of the *Poetics* itself is reflected only slightly; Averroës continues to dominate the scene.

PAZZI'S TEXT AND TRANSLATION (1536)

The general situation will be changed, however, after the publication in 1536 of Alessandro de' Pazzi's Greek text and Latin translation of the *Poetics*. Pazzi's own statements in the dedication indicate that he had prepared the volume in Rome in 1524; the dedication itself is dated 1527, and the publication was posthumous, Pazzi (or Paccius) having died in the intervening years. For the contemporary reader, Pazzi's volume must have had two especially attractive features. For the first time, it offered text and translation together, separated from the other works with which both had previously been printed; and for the first time it presented them in a small, portable, inexpensive format, contrasting with the sizable tomes of earlier

---

[34] *Commentaria* (1531), pp. 2–2*v*: "Hic complexus quicquid antea diuisum fuerat unum poeticae corpus perfectum fecit, & admirandum, ut nulla imitatio ne ritu quidem dragmatico effingi possit, quę non in illo eluceat, ui sua comediarum, tragoediarum, dythiramborum, omniumque poematum argumenta suis operibus inseruit."

[35] *Ibid.*, p. 2*v*: "Poemata omnia aut actiua sunt, aut enarratiua, aut ex his mista."

editions. These reasons probably explain why the volume was rapidly reprinted in Basel, in 1527, and in Paris, in 1538. As for the text and translation themselves, both represent advances over their predecessors. The progress is perhaps less notable in the case of the Greek text, where there was little to add, on the basis of available manuscripts, to Lascaris' distinguished contributions in the Aldine edition. Pazzi used three manuscripts, one of them in the Vatican (now Vat. gr. 1400), and from them he derived a certain number of useful emendations to Lascaris' text. But it was the translation which really rendered the greatest service to Pazzi's contemporaries. It is, generally, far superior to Giorgio Valla's. I should not say that it is always and unfailingly better; some of Valla's errors are repeated, some of his correct solutions are spoiled, and the basic difficulties of the available Greek manuscripts still continue to be reflected in the translation. But for the most part, Pazzi's work is more accurate and more readable; it has a much greater clarity of construction and is less dense and elliptical, and its sentence divisions and punctuation assist the reader in making sense out of the *Poetics*. As an example of the kind of improvement achieved, we may compare the two translations of the crucial passage in which tragedy is defined (*Poetics* 1449*b*24):

Valla: Est igitur tragoedia imitatio actionis probae atque consumatae magnitudinem iucunda oratione obtimentis citra quamlibet speciem in particulis agentium nec de comissorum pronuntiatu de miseratione & pauore terminans talium disciplinarum purgationem. suauem ac oblectabilem in quam orationem habentem rhythmum & harmoniam & melos quod autem citra species id per metra quaedam dumtaxat perficitur sicut porro alia per melos. Verum quia faciunt agentes imitationem. primo quidem si particula tragoediae aliqua sit uisus ornamentum esse necesse est inde melopoeiam & dictionem in his siquidem imitationem conficiunt. Dictionem uero ipsam uoco metrorum compositionem ut melopoeiam uim omnem habet manifestam at quia actionis. est imitatio. agitur autem ab aliquibus agentibus. quos qualitate aliqua insignes esse necesse est moribus atque animi sententia propter haec enim quod actiones qualitate insignes esse dicamus uis tulit naturae actionum binas esse causas animi sententiam & morem unde assecuntur & uoti impotes fiunt. est uero actionis fabula imitatio (p. r ii*v*).

Pazzi: Tragoedia est imitatio actionis illustris, absolutae, magnitudinem habentis, sermone suaui, separatim singulis generibus in partibus agentibus, non per enarrationem, per misericordiam uerò atque terrorem perturbationes huiusmodi purgans. sermonem suauem appello, in quo numerus, harmonia, & melos inest: id uerò separatim genere dictinctum: cum metro tantum quaedam absoluantur, quaedam rursum melodia. Quoniam uerò tota imitatio in actione uersatur, primum quidem apparatum ipsum, partem Tragoediae ponere necesse est, mox melodiam, & dictionem; utpote ex quibus imitationem conficiant: dictionem appello illam quidem metrorum compositionem: melodiam, cuius omnino uis per se ipsa satis apparet. Sed quoniam actionis imitatio est, agiturque ab agentibus quibusdam, quos tum moribus, tum sententia tales esse omnino oportet, sicuti quoque & actiones aliquas esse tales dicimus: manifestum est harum actionum duas esse causas, sententiam, & mores: per quas planè uel uoti compotes, uel minime compotes omnes fiunt. Ad haec actionis imitatio fabula est (p. 9v).

Pazzi's translation immediately became standard for the *Poetics*; not only was it reprinted at least a dozen times during the century, in Italy, France, and Switzerland, but it was taken as the basis for such important commentaries as those of Robortello and Maggi.

LOMBARDI AND MAGGI (1541)

The next event in the history of Aristotle's *Poetics* in the Cinquecento involves three men and two important documents. The event is the first public lectures on the *Poetics* of which we have accurate records; the three men are Bartolomeo Lombardi, Vincenzo Maggi, and Alessandro Sardi; and the documents are, first, Sardi's notes on Maggi's lectures, dated 1546, and the *Explanationes* published by Maggi, for himself and Lombardi, in 1550. The story is rather complex; I reconstruct the chronology roughly as follows:

In December, 1541, Bartolomeo Lombardi began the public exposition of the *Poetics* at Padua. But shortly afterward he died, leaving among his papers: (a) a text and translation of the *Poetics*; (b) a "Praefatio" to the work, addressed to the Accademia degli Infiammati of Padua; and (c) extensive notes on the work, later incorporated into the *Explanationes*.[36]

The lectures were continued by Maggi, and apparently with considerable success. As witness, we may consult the letter which Benedetto Varchi received from Cosimo Rucellai on December 17, 1541:

> I am greatly desirous of having those lectures, few or many as they may be, which Maggi gave on Aristotle's *Poetics*; wherefore I pray you, if you have them, to send them to me as soon as you possibly can, and as carefully written as is possible. If you don't have them, try to get a copy of them from some friend of yours, and then send them to me. In a word I desire greatly to have them such as they may be; although I have heard that they are divine.[37]

In 1543, Maggi became professor of philosophy at Ferrara, where he again expounded the *Poetics*.

Among those who heard Maggi's lectures at Ferrara was the young

[36] For the date of Lombardi's lectures, see F. V. Cerreta, "An Account of the Early Life of the Accademia degli Infiammati in the Letters of Alessandro Piccolomini to Benedetto Varchi," *Romanic Review*, XLVIII (1957), 253, 264. See also Maggi's introduction to the *Explanationes* (1550), p. *ij on Lombardi's lectures, interrupted by his death; and p. 27 on Lombardi's contributions to the volume. The "Praefatio" is printed in the same volume, pp. 1–11.

[37] Letter of Cosimo Rucellai (from Florence) to Benedetto Varchi (in Bologna), dated "Di Firenze adì 17. di Dicembre 1541," printed in the *Prose Fiorentine*, Pt. IV, Vol. I (Florence, 1734), p. 42: "io desidero assai di avere quelle o poche, o assai lezioni, che elle fussero, che fece sopra la Poetica d'Aristotile il Maggio; per la qual cosa vi prego, che se l'avete, me le mandiate quanto prima potete, e più diligentemente scritte, che sia possibile; se non l'avete, cerchiate da qualche vostro Amico averne copia, e dipoi me le mandiate. In somma grandemente desidero di averle quali elle si siano, benchè ho inteso son divine."

Alessandro Sardi, who was later to become the author of several erudite works.[38] His notes on these lectures are dated "15 Cal. Februarj MDXLVI" and are preserved in the Biblioteca Estense at Modena as MS.a.Q.6.14. In spite of the late date of these notes, I see no reason for believing that they do not represent the lectures substantially as Maggi began to give them in 1541, since in them Maggi declares that his interpretation is still based on that of Lombardi. Even with their date of 1546, however, Sardi's notes constitute the earliest extant commentary on Aristotle's *Poetics*.

In 1548, before Maggi was able to publish the *Explanationes* on which he had been working, Francesco Robortello published his own *Explicationes*, which thus became the first published commentary. Maggi was of course furious, and he took occasion to attack Robortello in a section of his manuscript entitled "Obiectiones quaedam aduersus Robortelli explicationem in primum Aristotelis contextum," stating his objections and indicating Robortello's errors and omissions.

Finally, in 1550, the joint work of Lombardi and Maggi appeared under the title *In Aristotelis librum de poetica communes explanationes*. I am assuming that this text represents a much later state of Maggi's thinking, and hence I shall discuss it under the date 1550.

Meanwhile, we may suppose that Lombardi's "Praefatio" was published essentially as he wrote it and analyze it at this point. As a preface to a commentary on Aristotle's *Poetics*, these pages are remarkable above all for the fact that they have nothing to do with the text or the ideas of the *Poetics*. Except for a brief passage near the end (p. 10) where Lombardi divides the *Poetics* into "prooemium" and "narratio," indicates its subject matter, and exclaims upon the excellence of the work and its superiority to all others on poetics, the "Praefatio" might just as well serve as an introduction to any other work on the art of poetry. Lombardi's ideas are completely traditional. He is interested in two problems: the relationship of poetry to the other arts and disciplines, and the defence of poetry. With respect to the first, he insists upon the fact that all other disciplines are present in poetry, and he shows one by one how the materials of the other sciences are also the materials of poetry. This is done for grammar and especially for rhetoric, which treats of the same subjects and uses the same devices; Homer and Vergil, for example, are full of rhetorical topoi, just as the works of the rhetoricians are full of examples from the poets. Similarly for logic, all of whose parts are found in the exposition of the poet and in the speeches of his personages, including the syllogism and paralogism. All natural philosophy has been treated by the poets, and indeed philosophy is a necessary appanage of the poet. The demonstration continues for theology, music, astrology, geography, the prophetic arts, physiognomics, moral philosophy, painting, and medicine.

[38] On Sardi, see the life written by Girolamo Ferri and published with Sardi's *Numinum et Heroum Origines* (Rome, 1775).

In another development, Lombardi adopts Averroës' classification of "Demonstrativa, Dialectica, Sophistica, Rhetorica, Poetica" and seeks the distinctions to be made between poetry and each of its sister-disciplines. The five arts are divided into two groups. The first, containing Logic, Dialectic, and Sophistic, produces dissertations which attempt to convince by argumentation and the use of the syllogism; all three are branches of "logic." The second, containing Rhetoric and Poetics, does not really belong to logic; it uses more popular devices, such as the example and the enthymeme, and its materials are largely political. Having accepted this classification, it is not surprising that Lombardi should propose a definition of poetry which is much closer to Aristotle's definition of rhetoric than to anything found in the *Poetics.* "Poetry," he says, "is the faculty of discovering whatever is appropriate to the imitation of any action, passion, or character, by means of harmonious discourse, for the purpose of correcting our way of living and of leading to a good and happy life.[39]

Lombardi's defence of poetry is based in part on the moral utility indicated in this definition. Poetry is superior to philosophy since it proposes, through the imitation of an action, to correct moral behavior by pleasurable means ("morum cum uoluptate correctione," p. 6). Its purpose is to lead us to a good and happy life ("ad bene beateque uiuendum comparatam," p. 9) by teaching us to love the virtues and to hate the vices ("uirtutes ut amplexemur, uitia ut auersemur," p. 8). These considerations lead Lombardi to answer Plato's ban of the poets, and he does so by insisting that Plato had in mind not the art as a whole but only certain passages in Homer. The rest of the defence derives from the universality of subject matter of poetry—and of the poet's knowledge—and from its antiquity. Only in passing does Lombardi mention that it springs from two natural causes (and he cites Aristotle). In general, the whole argument is related to the current discussions in the Platonic tradition, to the conception of the ends as proposed by Horace, and to the ideas of the classical rhetoricians. Aristotle figures only in the most incidental way.

Later in the sixteenth century, it became a commonplace to say—in explanation of the deficiencies of the *Poetics*—that the text represented merely a set of lecture notes by Aristotle; hence its incompleteness, its inconsistencies, its lack of order. The same is really true of those notes which Alessandro Sardi took on Maggi's exposition of the *Poetics* at the University of Ferrara in 1546, except that these are the notes of a student rather than of the lecturer. They must represent only imperfectly the spoken word of the master, still less satisfactorily the written notes from which he was speaking. One senses, in reading them, an abridgment of the numerous quotations, an elimination of much of the source material, many inade-

---

[39] *Explanationes* (1550), p. 9: "Poetica est facultas uidendi quodcunque accommodatum est ad imitationem cuiusque actionis, affectionis, moris, suaui sermone, ad uitam corrigendam, & ad benè beateque uiuendum comparata."

quacies of the language. Nevertheless, these notes are a completely remarkable document in the history of modern literary criticism. Remarkable, first, by its date: as was pointed out, the lectures given in 1546 probably were very close in content to the ones that Maggi began giving in 1541; hence by all odds the earliest extant commentary on Aristotle's *Poetics*. Remarkable, also, by its approaches to the *Poetics* and by its solutions to the problems raised.

The text as we have it in MS.a.Q.6.14 of the Biblioteca Estense at Modena is incomplete; it provides a commentary on the *Poetics* from the beginning through 1453*b*11 (i.e., to the end of what would later be Maggi's seventy-third "particella"). Whether this is because the lectures themselves stopped at that point, or because Sardi did not hear the rest, or because the remaining notes have not come down to us, we can only surmise.[40] The word-by-word gloss was preceded by a general introduction, devoted by Maggi to a general discussion of the art of poetry, of the nature of Aristotle's treatise, and of the latter's title. At no point is the treatment as complete and extended as it was to be in Maggi's later published *Explanationes* (1550); first, because an Italian student taking notes in Latin on a lecture in Latin was bound to abbreviate and condense as much as possible; second, because Maggi's thought and his erudition were undoubtedly much less fully developed at this point than they were to be almost ten years later. As an example of the differences, we may take Maggi's statements about the word "Dithyrambica" in Pazzi's translation of Aristotle's second sentence (1447*a*14).

In the notes, folios 8*v*–9, the whole of the gloss occupies about one small page; I give here the whole of the text:

Dithyrambica. in graeco habetur διθυραμβοποιητικὴ. id est. dithirambopoetica uno uerbo. Ideo interpres non est fidelis. Aristoteles autem miro artificio hoc uerbo composito usus est. quia dithyrambi maxime gaudent nominibus compositis, et nominibus longis. Ideo etiam philosophus de ipsis loquens usus est nomine longo, et composito. Horatius enim tum loqueretur quo pacto nomine nouo uti debemus utitur ipse nouo nomine Inuideo cum loquatur de nouitate. Ita philosophus hic loquens de Dithyrambicis nominauit nomine composito, et longo. Plato L. 7. de legibus dicit ambiguum esse an saltatio Bacchica, quae est

---

[40] In his edition of Sardi's *Numinum et Heroum Origines*, Girolamo Ferri prints two documents of interest for the history of these notes. One of them, a list of unpublished works of Sardi, includes the following passage: "le Lezioni manoscritte del Maggio, del Guarino, e di altri miei precettori in tre Volumi in quarto" (Ferri, p. xlviii). The other, from which the first passage had been quoted, is a testament bequeathing the same works to Gio. Francesco Serragli: "Al Sig. Gio. Francesco Serragli Medico l'opere d'Ippocrate, e di Oribasio, Plinio *de re Medicinali*, l'Istoria Naturale di Plinio *appostillata da me*, il Commento sopra Detti di Stefano Aqueo, e le *Lezioni manoscritte del Maggio, del Guarino*, e di altri miei Precettori, legati alla Romana in tre Volumi in quarto" (Ferri, p. lii). Sardi's handwriting, notorious among scholars at the Estense, is practically undecipherable. To this date, I have succeeded in transcribing only a portion of the MS, and the analysis I give is based on that partial transcription.

ista, sit saltatio: quia [fol. 8v] saltationes erant in duplici differentia, quae imi-
tabantur res bellicas, in quibus ostendebatur agilitas: et etiam saltationes urbanae
et modestae ad bonos mores. Et quia saltationes istae in honorem Bacchi erant,
propter uinum. nec urbanae, nec militares, ideo inter saltationes eas non rediget.
In Phaedro autem de dithyrambis loquitur. et Arist. L. 3. Rhet. ubi dicit proemia
esse similia in Dithyrambis demonstratiuis, id est libera quae nihil cum re conueniant. et Diony: Halicarnasseus ubi de mutatione, ubi modos saltandi esse
dicit tres, Doricos, lyricos, et Phrigios: quandoque graciles etiam. et quandoque
ad imitationem dithyramborum. Et idem fl. 167 examinat dithyrambicum Pindari.
In istis transitur ab una musica in aliam musicam. Aristopha. in Nebulis, quo
pacto nubes alant aliquos deridet Dithyrambicos poetas Vbi multa de illis agit
commentator. et etiam alibi in ornithiis deridet eos Aristophanes quod sint multa
uerborum, et nullum sententiarum habeant. Inde uerba Dithyrambicorum diuersa,
et absque sententia. De his [illegible] in libro de poetis: et de nomine eorum et
quia erant in honorem Bacchi nunc nos iis non utimur (fol. 9).

As against this relatively short passage, the commentary in the 1550 work
fills one and one-third closely printed folio pages. Many of the same
materials appear, but in a different order (pp. 34–35). Maggi now repeats the
explanation of Aristotle's use of a compound noun, so appropriate to the
genre which it signifies (omitting, however, the citation of "inuideor"
from *Ars poetica* 56); this is much expanded and other examples are
offered. Next follows the allusion to *Rhetoric* III, in very similar terms.
In place of the brief "In Phaedro autem de dithyrambis loquitur," he
quotes two separate passages from the *Phaedrus*. He then gives, in rapid
succession, passages from *Rhetoric* III, the *Problemata*, and *Politics* VIII,
and references to Lycophron, Dionysius of Halicarnassus, Demetrius of
Phaleron, Menander, and the commentator on Aristophanes. Finally, he
discusses the relationship between dithyrambic poetry and Bacchus,
quoting at length from Book VII of Plato's *Laws*. The purpose of this
display of erudition is to define the name of the genre, to describe it as
fully as possible, and to collect opinions about it from ancient authors.

Maggi's procedure in this passage is typical of what he does throughout
his spoken commentary on the *Poetics*. He brings to bear, upon each word
or phrase that merits remark, all the erudition that he has been able to
accumulate. His erudition is very extensive, perhaps remarkably so for so
early a date in the century; it covers the whole range both of Greek and
Latin writers and includes many texts which had been made available only
since the beginning of the century—the space of a generation. In the first
ten pages of the notes, for example, Sardi records references to authors as
diversified as the following: Plato (*Laws, Phaedrus, Cratylus, Sophist,
Phaedo, Timaeus*), Aristotle (*Prior Analytics*, both *Rhetorics, Posterior
Analytics, De Anima, Physics, Problemata, Ethics*, as well as commentators
on several of these texts), Plutarch, Hermogenes, Dionysius of Halicarnassus, Ammonius, Aphthonius, Diomedes, Simplicius, Suidas, Cicero
(*De Oratore, De Finibus, Tusculan Orations*), and Quintilian. The list for

the whole of the set of notes would be much longer. In using these ancient authors for the exposition of his text, Maggi was merely applying the familiar technique of the scholarly gloss; more specifically, he was adapting to the *Poetics* the devices of elucidation which had been for so long used in connection with the *Ars poetica*.

Throughout, the consideration of the *Poetics* in the light of the *Ars poetica* is completely explicit. In his opening sentence, Maggi declares his intentions; after stating that he means to rely on Lombardi's notes, he continues: "... and we shall observe this order: we shall say how Aristotle and Horace agree between them, and what Aristotle said that Horace omitted, or what Horace said that Aristotle omitted; and who did better."[41] He passes immediately (according to the canonical order) to an examination of the titles of the two works, asking why Aristotle should have called his merely *De poetica* whereas Horace called his *De arte poetica*, and these considerations lead him far into the discovery of the basic difference between the two works. The same is done at other points where a parallel examination of Horace seems appropriate. What Maggi is doing is really very simple: he takes as a basis for his discussion that work of literary theory which his audience knows best, and to it he compares, *pari passu*, another work which he himself is in a sense introducing into the canon of public literary discussion; the reference is from the known to the unknown. In so doing, however, he is making history; he is establishing the tradition of the confronting of Aristotle and Horace which will last to the end of the century and beyond.

This does not mean that Maggi conceives of the two works as identical. Instead, his initial opposition of their titles leads him to discover a fundamental difference between them. Stated in a succinct formula, it is that "the philosopher [Aristotle] treats of the thing in itself and Horace of precepts and almost nothing at all of the thing."[42] Thus Aristotle calls his treatise *De poetica* because "considering the knowledge of poetry, he speaks of poetics so that we may know its parts both quantitative and qualitative." In other words, "because Aristotle's intention was to treat of the knowledge of poetry, since the art is taken from the thing, and because according to nature it [the thing] precedes, he entitled his book for that very same thing."[43] But Horace's title, *De arte poetica*, is a clear recognition of his intention to include those precepts and rules that would teach the poet how to write a poem: "Horace, who writes only a little of the thing and more of the art, justly gave the title 'de arte,' as if he were to

---

41 MS Modena, Bibl. Estense, a.Q.6.14, fol. 1: "et hunc ordinem seruabimus. quid concordent inter se Aristoteles et Horatius dicemus: et quid dixerit Aristoteles, quod omisserit Horatius: uel quid dixerit Horatius quod omisserit Aristoteles. Et quis melius fecerit."

42 *Ibid.*, fol. 3: "philosophus de re in se; et de praeceptis agit Horatius quasi nihil de re."

43 *Ibid.*, fols. 3-3v: "respiciens ad cognitionem poesis, dixit de poetica, ut cognoscamus partes, quantas, et quales . . . quia Aristotelis intentio erat agere de cognitione poesis, quia ars sumitur a re: et quia secundum natura praecedit, de ista re inscripsit librum."

speak of the laws which the poet must observe."[44] The philosopher, in sum, writes a "method" whereas the poet writes an "art." Maggi repeats this opposition, very briefly, when he glosses the first two words of Pazzi's translation (fol. 5).

As a result of the difference in intention, the content of the two works is also different. The *Ars poetica*, adding precept to knowledge and art to method, will comprise a larger variety of materials than the *Poetics*. Maggi divides it into three sections, points out how it treats both poetry and the art of poetry, distinguishes it from the *Poetics*:

> Whence with respect to his book you will see that it is divided into three parts. In the first he writes of what poet [?]; in the second, of poetry; in the third he teaches the precepts of poetry. At the beginning he speaks to him who wishes to be a good poet; Aristotle says nothing about this. Horace, when he says "Pictoribus atque poetis quidlibet audendi semper fuit aequa potestas," is speaking of poetry; because like Plutarch in the book *Quomodo pueri debeant uidere poetas*, he says that poets are like painters. On the other hand, [he speaks] of precepts in "Humano capiti," etc.[45]

The *Poetics*, being a methodical treatise, will be differently composed and will have another kind of order. Maggi sees it as having two parts, which may be designated as the "proemium" and the "tractatus" or as the "principium" and the "narratio." The "proemium," brief as it is (it is made up of only the first sentence), has many functions to perform and is subdivided into many parts:

A. Genera et partes
1. Genera
2. Partes
   a. De poesi in se
   b. De generibus
   c. De fabula
   d. De partibus qualibus et quantis
   e. De omnis quae pertinent ad hanc materiam
B. Modum quae uult seruare in tractandis propositis (fol. 5)

The "tractatus" is subdivided into only two parts:

A. De poesi
1. De conuenientia Epopeiae, Comoediae, et Tragoediae . . . et aliarum artium quae conueniunt in hoc, quod sint imitationes
2. Differentia tria inter has
3. De inuentione poesis
B. [Treatment of the individual kinds] (fol. 7*v*)

---

[44] *Ibid.*, fol. 3*v*: "Horatius qui modicum de re, plura de arte scribit, merito inscripsit de arte, quasi diceret de legibus quas seruare poeta debet."

[45] *Ibid.*, fol. 3: "Vnde circa scripta ipsius uidebitis ipsa diuisa in tres partes. in prima quem poetam [illegible] scribit: in 2. poesim: in 3. tradit praecepta poesis. In principio loquitur eum qui uult esse bonus poeta. Aristoteles nihil de hac dicit. Horatius quando dicit pictoribus atque poetis quidlibet audendi semper fuit aequa potestas, loquitur de poesi. quia ut plutarchus in libro quomodo pueri debeant uidere poetas: dicit poetae esse similes pictoribus agit autem de praeceptis Humano capiti etc."

Clearly, and in spite of his designations, Maggi sees in the *Poetics* a philosophical rather than a rhetorical order.

This establishment of differences between Aristotle and Horace and this distinction of Aristotle's method do not, however, prevent Maggi from assigning to his poetic theory the same ends for poetry that might be found in philosophers of widely different approaches. The naming of the ends is found first in Maggi's definition of poetry: "We say consequently upon Aristotle's principles that poetry is an imitation of the actions, passions, and characters of men themselves, in pleasant speech, to the end that men may be led to proper conduct."[46] The "art" will be the art of making the imitation in such a way that "men will be enticed to proper conduct" ("ut homines alliciantur ad bonos mores," fols. 3v–4). Although each of the genres may have a specific end, they have a common end in the production of moral improvement. As Maggi distinguishes the "end" of tragedy from those of comedy, he uses two meanings of "end" as he repeats various medieval commonplaces. First, "end" is taken as equivalent to "denouement": ". . . for no matter how much tragedy and comedy may seem to differ, they agree nevertheless in the end. Comedy may have a sad beginning and a happy ending, and tragedy just the opposite." The passage continues by distinguishing the other ends: "Yet not for this do they differ in end, because they bring men to proper conduct through divers ways. Comedy laughs at bad and wicked men so that we may flee them; Tragedy extols illustrious men and the best characters so that we may follow them."[47] Sweetness of language is considered a rhetorical device which makes the lessons of poetry acceptable.

It is this same identification of the moral end that enables Maggi to classify poetry under moral philosophy. Antecedent traditions had provided him with two major alternatives for the classification: the medieval logicians and Averroës suggested a subsuming under logic, Plato and Plutarch and Cicero a subsuming under moral philosophy. Maggi accepts both suggestions and tries to reconcile them:

Nevertheless we say that poetics must be classified under moral pholosophy; for Plutarch says that the poet teaches proper conduct, and Cicero also says so. But in what way can it be classified under the moral [philosophy] if Averroës puts it under logic? If poetics be considered according to the way in which it goes about imitating actions, characters, and passions, because it has to do with language and depicts actions, characters, and the passions of men by means of language, it is concerned with logic. Because it is concerned with words and

[46] *Ibid.*, fol. 3v: "Nos dicimus consequenter ad principia Aristotelis quod poesis est imitatio actionum, passionum, et morum ipsorum hominum sermone suaui ad hoc ut homines trahantur ad bonos mores."

[47] *Ibid.*, fol. 4: "quia quamuis tragoedia, et comoedia uideantur differre: conueniunt tum in fine licet comoedia principium triste, et laetum finem habere, e contra autem tragoedia. non tamen in fine differunt, quia redducunt homines ad mores bonos per diuersos modos. Comoedia deridet malos, et uiles, ut ab eis effugiamus. Tragoedia uiros extollit claros, et mores optimos, ut eos sequamur."

λόγος, it is language. But it is under the moral because of this reason, because it considers its end as being conduct; for this reason, it is classified as moral.[48]

Regarding both classifications as justifiable, Maggi goes on to point out that Petrarch is a moral philosopher because he teaches how lovers should love; that poets who treat wicked matters are "cacopoetae" and should not be read ("nec legendi sed cohorrendi," fol. 4v); that Plato's and Cicero's demand for the teaching of good conduct is reflected in Horace's "Aut prodesse uolunt, aut delectare poetae." The Platonic and Horatian traditions of the end of poetry are thus allowed to direct the reading of Aristotle.

In an exactly similar way, this first commentary on the *Poetics* reads into it, from earlier critical positions, the requirement that poetry be in verse. If the object of imitation is actions, passions, characters, the means is sweet language and verse ("sermo suauis" and "carmen," fol. 4). The laws of poetry are reduced to those "which we must use in composing verses" ("quibus uti debemus in componendis carminibus," fol. 5). So, too, the meaning assigned to "fabula" is traditional and rhetorical. Discarding the meanings suggested by Terence, Horace, and Cicero, Maggi adopts the whole of Aristotle's argument from the *Problemata*, assuming that what he says there is applicable to the poetic "fabula":

But now we understand by "fable" that which stands in the place of a true example, which is like a certain exemplum. Aristotle in the *Problemata* (particula 18, probl. 3) asks why in their orations orators take greater pleasure in examples and fables than in enthymemes and reasonings, and he advances these three reasons. Because examples are more familiar and pleasant, they are quickly learned and on that account they are more acceptable. Also because fables are particular things, but reasonings are universal things which are more remote; but fables are closer to us, therefore we learn more speedily. And the second reason, because that thing is said to be more readily believed by us, which is confirmed by judgment, which is present in examples. The third reason, because we learn more readily things that are similar, and because examples and fables are similar. Therefore we enjoy the things more. With respect to this, when Aristotle there says expressly that a fable is like an example, we thus here understand by fable an image of some thing, and thence fables are like a picture of the thing which is being treated.[49]

[48] *Ibid.*, fols. 4–4v: "tamen dicimus quod poetica debet redduci sub philosophia morali: quia Plutarchus dicit poetam docere bonos mores. quod etiam Cicero dicit. quo pacto autem debetur [?] redduci sub morali: si Auerrois eam sub logica ponit? Si poetica consideretur ratione qua uersatur ut imitetur actiones, mores, et passiones. quia uersatur circa sermonem et pingit sermone actiones mores et passiones hominum uersatur circa logicam: qui[a] uersatur in uerbis et λόγος est sermo. sub morali autem est quia ea ratione, quia respicit finem mores esse. ea ratione ad moralem redducitur."

[49] *Ibid.*, fols. 5v–6: "Fabulam autem nunc intelligimus id quod est loco exempli ueri, quod est ueluti quoddam exemplum. Aristotel. in problematibus particula 18. probl. 3. quaerit quare in orationibus oratores magis delectentur exemplis et fabulis, quam Entimematibus et rationibus. et has tres rationes affert. Quia exempla sunt magis familiaria, iucundia, cito addiscuntur, ideo gratiora sunt. Etiam quia fabulae sunt res particulares: rationes autem uniuersales quae sunt magis remotae: uiciniores autem fabulae, ideo magis discemus cito. et .2. ratio quia haec res dicitur magis credi a nobis, quae est existimatio confirmata: quod in exemplis est. .3. ratio quia nos addiscimus libentius similia, et quia exempla et fabulae sunt similes. Ideo res magis gaudemus. Quo circa cum Aristoteles ibi exprese dicit quod fabula est uelut exemplum. Ideo hic per fabulam intelligimus imaginem alicuius rei, et ideo fabulae sunt ueluti pictura rei de qua agitur."

In the first of these cases, the meaning is derived from old ways of thinking about poetry; in the second, from old ways of talking about rhetoric.

Maggi's developments are, indeed, apt to be more extensive on such traditional matters as these than on ideas which are new because they are particularly germane to Aristotle's *Poetics*. For some of the latter, the treatment is brief to the point of being disappointing; topics which later became the great cruxes of Aristotelian discussion are here passed over without a flurry. We may take as an example the definition of tragedy. Maggi states that Aristotle defines tragedy first, before the other genres, because it is the most excellent of all, that he includes its qualitative and quantitative parts as promised in the "proemium," and that the definition meets all requirements by stating genus and differentiae. His glosses on the individual words are extremely short. "Imitatio" is said to indicate the genus, the rest of the definition the differentiae. "Illustris" means merely "ad differentiam uulgarium." (There is no gloss on "actionis," since action had been discussed previously.) "Absolutae" means "perfectae, quia debet esse una tota actio integra." On "magnitudinem," he merely remarks that this is the magnitude of the action, the imitation. For "sermone suaui" and "separatim" he refers to a later commentary. "Enarrationem" is clarified by the phrase "vt in epopeis." The only extensive notes are on "misericordiam," where Maggi compares the purgation of pity and fear to that purgation of which Aristotle speaks in Book VIII of the *Politics*, the purgation of passions from the soul through music. The pleasurable aspects of the effect are indicated in the sentence: "And purgations are exaltations of the soul along with pleasure" ("Et expurgationes sunt sublationes animae cum uoluptate," fol. 44). Maggi interprets the effect of purgation as the driving out from the soul, through the spectacle of strong passions, of those same passions, leaving the soul provided with more desirable ones: "...they are purged and liberated of such passions, and thus they are made strong and constant" ("expurgantur, et liberantur a talibus affectibus, et ita redduntur fortes et constantes," fol. 44). Maggi thinks that this is the best of several suggested interpretations. It might be noted at this point that in the 1550 *Explanationes* he studies the whole matter much more thoroughly, and arrives at an essentially different conclusion.

Even this partial analysis of Sardi's notes on Maggi will serve to show their distinctive features. Maggi begins the long tradition of explicating the *Poetics* by placing it in two contexts, Horace's *Ars poetica* and the rhetorical tradition. He brings to it the same kind of erudition that had long been called upon for the elucidation of other classical texts. But because he does use old methods and refers to old ways of considering poetic problems, he is bound to miss much that might have been new for a fresh reader of the *Poetics*. He sees in it at times distinctions, definitions, and conclusions which belong rather to other systems, even if at other times he is scrupulous about trying to discover Aristotle's own system. He is, of course, faced with insuperable difficulties: a difficult text, philosophically, in poor philological shape, in an only moderately satisfactory translation, full of terms and conceptions that had not previously attracted the attention of the scholars. His great merit, in this situation, was having tackled the problem, pursued it with great diligence through at least a decade, and produced a number of valid conclusions. What he did in his lectures set the pattern for Aristotelian commentary throughout the century and provided for later theorists an initial interpretation on the basis of which they might elaborate their own studies.

All these materials were of course "unpublished" in 1541, the date under which they have been treated. But they were "public" in the sense that Lombardi's "Praefatio" had been delivered as an opening lecture before the Accademia degli Infiammati (Robortello was to make a similar use of his preface, recited before the Accademia Fiorentina in 1548[50]) and that Lombardi's and then Maggi's lectures were actually a form of publication. Between this date and 1548 the uses of the *Poetics* in critical documents are sparse and incidental.

One of these documents is of especial interest since it constitutes an early application of Aristotelian principles and terminology to practical criticism. It is a set of notes on a speech or conversation about Dante by Girolamo Benivieni, preserved in the Biblioteca Marucelliana, MS A.137. The notes are undated; I assign them without proof to *circa* 1540, since Benivieni died in 1542. In them, Benivieni passes judgment on the *Divine Comedy*. First, he praises the unity of structure, and in so doing he uses terms all of which are borrowed from Aristotle's definition of tragedy; I give the text in Italian, italicizing the significant phrases:

... quanto all'*anima di questa compositione* che e, senza dubbio, la inuentione, o, *la fauola,* chi punto sottilmente bada, ageuolmente scorge, hauere Dante *imitato un sol ' fatto,* non dico un sogno, anzi uno desto, et auueduto uiaggio, che egli altra uolta hauea trapassato, e fu questo *di conueneuole grandezza, proportionato, e finito,* narrando di se quello, che alcune altre fauole, narrano di altrui, *con ornato parlare,* e profitteuole alli ascoltanti.[51]

Despite such traditional elements as the identification of "favola" with "inventione" and the final "profitable to the listeners," the description has a note of freshness supplied by the intention to apply Aristotle's definition to an actual critical judgment. One other phrase in the notes, "egli tutto Poeticamente passa, per uia d'Imitatione" (fol. 138*v*), may have

---

50 See MS BNF II.IV.192.

51 MS Marucelliana A. 137, fol. 134*v*. In translation: "as for *the soul of this composition* which is, undoubtedly, the invention or *the plot,* he who looks at all carefully will easily discover that Dante has *imitated a single action,* I do not say a dream but rather a voyage made while awake and aware, which he had taken at a previous time; and this was *of proper magnitude, proportioned, and complete,* narrating about himself what certain other plots narrate about others, *with embellished language,* and profitable to the listeners."

Aristotelian origins. For the rest, Benivieni insists on the utility of Dante's poem, which, like those of the best and most ancient poets, "under a pleasant veil, with the beauty of Poetry, . . . impresses upon those who enjoy his poem the highest mysteries of Christian philosophy."[52] He praises the variety and multiplicity of ideas in Dante, his treatment of the sciences and the liberal arts, and his many wise sayings, pointing out finally how both Petrarch and Boccaccio had imitated him.

Another contemporary piece in Italian, Giovambattista Giraldi Cintio's dedication to his *Orbecche* (written in 1541 but published in 1543), complains of the impossibility of using the *Poetics* rather than doing so. It may well reflect the attitude of readers in general before the publication of the great commentaries. Giraldi is speaking of the difficulty of writing tragedy in his time:

And although Aristotle gives us the method for composing them, aside from his native obscurity, which, as you know, is extreme, he remains so obscure and full of so many shadows because we do not have the authors from whom he derives his authority and the examples for confirmation of the orders and the laws that he imposes on writers of tragedies, that one understands with difficulty I will not say the art that he teaches but the very definition that he gives of tragedy.[53]

Bernardino Tomitano's *Ragionamenti della lingua toscana* of 1545 makes extensive use of the *Poetics*, but withal it is not an Aristotelian treatise; rather, as has been pointed out, it is a little bit of everything (see Chapter VII, pp. 264–67). Tomitano tends to develop individual sections of his dialogue by paraphrasing earlier works or by translating from them directly; and as Plato, Horace, and various rhetoricians pass through his hands, so also does Aristotle. There is a long section in Book III which follows the *Poetics* closely. It develops the difference between orator and poet as a difference between persuasion and imitation; but then it adds the further differential of verse and rhyme. It lists the kinds of poetry approximately as Aristotle had done and repeats his distinction of object, manner, and means of imitation (p. 226). The poet is defined as "an imitator of human actions who arouses admiration in the listener"[54]—obviously a mixed definition. It is followed by this statement:

In this definition we are led to understand that poetry is an imitation; and since an imitation is related to him who acts in life as a shadow is to bodies, it is necessary that, actions themselves being of two kinds, good and bad (since all human

[52] *Ibid.*, fol. 136: "sotto piaceuole uelame, con la uaghezza della Poesia, ne imprime . . . in coloro, che sono del suo Poema uaghi, i piu rileuanti misterij della Cristiana filosofia."

[53] *Orbecche* (1543), p. 2: "Et anchora ch'Aristotile ci dia il modo di comporle, egli oltre la sua natia oscuritade, la quale (come sapete) è somma, riman tanto oscuro, & pieno di tante tenebre, per non ui essere gli auttori, de quali egli adduce l'auttoritadi, et gli essempi, per confirmatione de gli ordini, & delle leggi, ch'egli impone à gli scrittori d'esse, ch'affatica è intesa, non dirò l'arte, ch'egli insegna, ma la diffinitione, ch'egli dà della tragedia."

[54] *Ragionamenti* (1545), p. 227: "imitatore de gli atti humani con merauiglia di chi l'ascolta."

[384]

actions prove to be distinguished on the basis of vice and of virtue), similarly every imitation should turn out to be like a real action, or better, or worse.[55] This ethical distinction is what leads to the difference between tragedy and comedy. But when Tomitano wishes to develop the difference, he does so in terms which go back to the rhetorical classification of the literary genres according to subject matters or passions:

This imitation is based on our common human passions, on the events of fortune, on the qualities of the mind and of the body. As for the passions, tragedy imitates hopes, desires, despair, weepings, memories of deaths, and deaths; comedy, suspicions, fears, sudden passages from good to evil and from evil to good, rescues, happy human lives and human beings. Sapphic poetry brings forth tender thoughts and magnificent eulogies; the hendecasyllable, humble and low concerns; the elegy, tears and signs; odes, precepts, customs, memories, loves, and praise of others; sermons, discourses necessary for happy living; satire, condemnations of vicious living and rewards for virtues; the heroic style, illustrious and magnanimous feats.[56]

Similar distinctions are made for the Italian genres.

When Tomitano develops his ideas on the "manner" of imitation, he follows *Poetics* 1448a25 fairly closely; but when he expands the passage by adding examples of his own, he shows that he has not understood at all the implications of narrative and dramatic "manner": "Thus Michelangelo and Titian," he says, "might possibly imitate the same thing, but nevertheless in different ways; which difference may equally well be seen in Petrarch and in Dante."[57] The section of the *Ragionamenti* based on Aristotle concludes with a passage on the natural causes of poetry. The whole section is of interest since it reveals how a scholar of 1545 used the letter of the text of Aristotle without understanding its spirit, and how he sought elucidation in more familiar texts and traditions.

The same kind of eclecticism is apparent in Lilio Gregorio Giraldi's *Historiae poetarum dialogi*, a set of ten dialogues variously dated from 1541 to 1545 and published in 1545. Giràldi wishes primarily to list the Greek and Latin poets and provide a biographical compendium of the known

[55] *Ibid.*, p. 227: "Nellaqual diffinitione si da à comprendere, che la poesia sia imitatione: & perche l'imitatione è tale rispetto à colui che opera, quale l'ombra à i corpi; per questo è necessario, che operandosi in due maniere ò bene ò male (come che tutte le attioni humane uengono ad esser differenti per conto del uitio & della uirtu) similmente ogni imitatione o simile adiuiene, ò migliore, ò piggiore dell'effetto."

[56] *Ibid.*, p. 228: "E questa imitatione fondata sopra gli affetti della nostra humanita, sopra i casi della fortuna, sopra i beni dell'animo & del corpo. Quanto à gli affetti, imita la Tragedia le speranze, i desii, le disperationi, i pianti, i mor[t]al ricordi, & le morti, La Comedia i sospetti, le paure, i subiti mouimenti dal bene al male, & dal male al bene, le saluezze, le uite & gli humani contenti. Dolci pensieri partorisce & magnifiche lodi il Saphico: humili & basse cure lo Endecasillabo: lagrime & sospiri la Elegia: precetti, costumi, ricordi, amori, & lode d'altrui le Ode: discorsi al uiuere beatamente necessari i sermoni: uituperi del uitioso uiuere, & premi delle uirtu le Satire: gesti illustri & generosi l'heroico stile. . . ."

[57] *Ibid.*, p. 229: "cosi Michel'agnolo & Titiano potranno per auentura imitare l'istessa cosa, nondimeno dissomigliantemente: laqual differenza comprender si puo medesimamente nel Petrarca e in Dante."

facts relating to them. He includes as well the standard defence of poetry, a discussion of the poetic furor, and a certain amount of theoretical material. Plato, Horace, Cicero, Donatus are freely drawn upon, and almost necessarily—at this date—there are a number of references to Aristotle. At the outset, Giraldi lists Aristotle first among the writers "qui de poëtis scripserunt"; he cites him on the origins of poetry (p. 6) and for his insistence that the plot, not verse, makes the poet: "Aristotelis est sententia, poëtam ex fabulis potius esse, quàm ex carminibus" (p. 84). In Dialogue III, he deplores the loss of the original two books of the *Poetics*.[58] It is not, however, until he comes to the discussion of tragedy and comedy, in Dialogue VI, that he makes any substantial borrowings from Aristotle's text. There, after giving Diomedes' and Theophrastus' definitions of tragedy, he cites Aristotle on the antiquity of the genre and then gives his definition, in a translation that does not correspond to any of those published before 1541 and hence may be his own or may represent some manuscript version: "Est ergo Tragoedia imitatio studiosae & perfectae actionis, magnitudinem suaui oratione habentis, separatim ab unaquaque specierum agentium in particularis: & non per annunciationem, sed misericordia quadam & timore perficiens talim affectionum purgationem" (p. 672). There are short quotations from Aristotle's explanation of the definition and a discussion of the qualitative and quantitative parts.

When he comes to comedy, Giraldi again cites first a traditional Greek definition, then those of Donatus and Cicero, finally that of Aristotle: "Comoedia est imitatio improbioris quidem, non ad omnem tamen malitiam, sed turpitudinis quaedam est ridicula particula" (p. 677); the translation is again unknown. Ultimately, after citing Aristotle's definition of the ridiculous, he concludes: "It is seen from these words that the philosopher implies that comedy was invented to give pleasure to the people"[59]—a conclusion by no means justified by the text. Giraldi's method is the same as that of many of his contemporaries. He takes pieces out of the *Poetics*, transports them to his own work; they there stand alongside other pieces borrowed from other works, neither changing them nor changed by them. There is nothing even vaguely suggesting an "interpretation" of Aristotle.

In Parrasio's commentary on Horace of 1531 there had been some introductory allusions to the *Poetics*. Fifteen years later, in 1546, the *Ecphrasis in Horatii Flacci artem poeticam* of Francesco Pedemonte (published posthumously by Puresius) made the first full-scale use of the *Poetics* as a source of parallels to and explanations of the *Ars poetica*. Moreover, it gave fairly extensive quotations of the text in Greek. There are some thirty

---

58 *Historiae poetarum* (1545), p. 313: "duo primùm de ea facultate uolumina composuit, quae temporum, ut uidemus, iniuria periere. Mox alterum uolumen edidit, quod dimidiatum imperfectumque nunc in studiosorum manibus habetur."

59 *Ibid.*, p. 677: "Videtur ex his uerbis Philosophus innuere, Comoediam inuentam esse ad oblectandos populos."

such parallel passages (as I have indicated in Chapter IV). They are drawn from widely separated sections of the *Poetics* and demonstrate a fairly complete knowledge of the text. Pedemonte achieves a better fusion of his borrowed materials than was the case with his immediate predecessors. For example, he assigns to the first thirteen lines of the *Ars poetica* the subtitle "De idea concipienda," suggesting that Horace means to demand that the poet have a conception of his total "form" before setting to work; on the one hand, this conception is likened to a Platonic Idea, and on the other the process of representing it is described by Aristotle in the term "imitation": "This also [the preconception of the Form] comes about in every art, especially in painting, molding, and sculpturing, which indeed seem to Aristotle to proceed in the same way of imitation as does poetry."[60] This same requirement explains why Aristotle demands the complete form having beginning, middle, and end ("miniméue totum ipsum, quod [ut inquit Aristoteles] ex principio, medio, ac fine constat, absoluetur," p. 4), and why he should have proposed Homer as the model most closely resembling nature (p. 4*v*.) In such a case as this, Pedemonte attempts to clarify a text of Horace by studying what seem to him to be related ideas in Plato and in Aristotle.

In general, the passages from Aristotle which Pedemonte uses fall into categories. First, those of historical interest: he cites numerous texts on the origins and development of tragedy and of comedy, somewhat fewer on the origins of the epic and on the excellence of Homer as an epic poet. These are for the most part without critical interest. Second, those which concern general principles of the poetic art: the notions of necessity and probability and the differences between poetry and history (pp. 52–53); the poet's need for knowledge, especially of a philosophical kind (pp. 36*v*, 57); the necessity that the poet should himself first feel what he hopes to convey to others (p. 16); the requirement of appropriateness, related to Horace's "decorum" (p. 15*v*); the conception of the poem as having a proper magnitude and thus of its resemblance to a beautiful animal (p. 16); and the idea of the inevitability of the work's structure, of the presence and place of each of its parts (p. 25). In a third classification come those passages which pertain to the handling of the separate genres. Most of these pertain to tragedy and comedy, although there are a fair number for the epic and some for satire. What Horace has to say about tragedy, for example, is elucidated by citations from the *Poetics* of its definition and explanations of that definition; on the comparison between tragedy and comedy and tragedy and the epic; on the use of iambic verse; on unity through action rather than through the choice of a single hero; on the creation of the tragic effect through reading only, without recourse to spectacle and stage presentation; on the kinds of plot; and on the mixture of tragedy with

60 *Ecphrasis* (1546), p. 3*v*: "sic itaque in omni arte, pingendi maxime, fingendi, atque sculpendi; quae quidem eodem imitationis tramite cum poesi Aristoteli incedere uidentur."

satire (mostly, pp. 29–32). What results from all this is undoubtedly a conception of the art of tragedy much richer and much more detailed than the reader might obtain from Horace alone. But it still remains doubtful whether there is any interpretation of Aristotle's text or any awareness of the special character of his theory of tragedy.

Several passages in Pedemonte, finally, should be singled out for the witness they give to the position that Aristotle's *Poetics* was attaining at this state. The first of them, a part of the commentary on *Ars poetica* 179–88, asserts that Aristotle's notions were inferior to Horace's since Horace came at a later date and represented a more refined taste: "Since he [Aristotle] handed down the norms for the poetic art without departing from the models supplied by ancient poetry, whereas this poet [Horace] —and this is a matter of the greatest importance—assessing the poems of his predecessors and contemporaries, accepts certain things while rejecting others."[61] Nevertheless, Aristotle's dicta are to be taken as laws; and, in addition to the usual "asserit" or "inquit" or "autore Aristotele," we find such formulas as "statuisse" and the final categorical statement that the precepts of the art are to be found only in Aristotle and in Horace, "who taught the rules which it would never be possible to transgress" ("qui regulas docuerunt, quas transgredi nequaquam licitum foret," p. 60). Before the time of the great commentaries, then, the *Poetics* had achieved a position of authority equal to that of the *Ars poetica*—and this was no small feat, considering the reverence for the latter document throughout the late Middle Ages and the humanistic period.

ROBORTELLO (1548)

The first of the "great commentaries" to be published was that of Francesco Robortello, the *In librum Aristotelis de arte poetica explicationes* of 1548. Robortello apparently prepared his own Greek text, using as a basis the Aldine text of 1508 but correcting it by consulting manuscripts; two of these were in the possession of the Medici family, and Robortello frequently argues for the superiority of their readings. He used the Pazzi translation; but again he corrected it, and a collation of the two Latin versions shows many slight variations in detail. For the history of literary criticism in the Renaissance, however, Robortello's great importance lies in his commentary, the first extensive one to be printed. It not only was an epitome of the earlier scattered interpretations of the *Poetics*; it also in many ways made new suggestions which determined the future tendencies in the reading of the text.[62]

---

61 *Ibid.*, p. 31*v*: "Quippe ille ab antiqua poesi non discedens artis poeticae normas tradidit; hic autem uates, quod quidem permultam interest, cum maiorum tum iuniorum poemata perpendens quaedam admittit, quaedam uero non probat."

62 I have given an extensive analysis of the commentary in an article, "Robortello on the *Poetics*," in *Critics and Criticism: Ancient and Modern*, the argument of which is summarized above, chap. ii, pp. 66–68. In the following pages, I extract from the article its essential points.

The essential direction of Robortello's analysis of the *Poetics* results from his conception of the ends of poetry. There seem to be three ends: First, the dual Horatian end of pleasure and utility: "Poetry, if we consider it carefully, bends all its efforts toward delighting, although it also does profit."[63] Besides, there is the Aristotelian end of imitation: "And since this imitation or representation is produced by means of discourse, we may say that the end of poetry is language which imitates, just as that of rhetoric is language which persuades."[64] All the ends are brought together in such a passage as the following (commenting on 1448*b*4): "Poetry thus sets a double end for itself, one of which is prior to the other; the prior end is to imitate, the other to delight."[65] Profit is here included as an unexpressed concomitant of delight.

The nature of the pleasure derived from poetry is specified in a passage from Robortello's prologue:

> There is, indeed, for men no greater pleasure, truly worthy of a man of refinement, than that which is perceived by the mind and by thought; it frequently happens that things which arouse horror and terror in men as long as they are in their own nature, once they are taken out of nature and represented in some form resembling nature, give great pleasure. . . . What other end, therefore, can we say that the poetic faculty has than to delight through the representation, description, and imitation of every human action, every emotion, every thing animate as well as inanimate?[66]

Two salient features of this passage must be emphasized; first, the pleasure is achieved *through* imitation, which thus becomes an intermediate end; second, the imitation is not only of human actions and passions (as in Aristotle) but of all kinds of objects as well. The nature of the utility derived from poetry is much more explicitly indicated; once again, the key passage is found in the prologue:

> For, just as poetic readings and imitations are of various kinds, so they bring to men a multiple utility. If, on the one hand, the reading (or performance) and imitation consist in the virtue and the praise of some excellent man, people are incited to virtue; if, on the other hand, vices are represented, people are strongly

---

[63] *Explicationes* (1548), Prologue, p. 2: "Poëtice, siquis diligenter attendat, omnem suam vim confert ad oblectandum, & si prodest quoque."

[64] *Ibid.*, p. 2: "Et quoniam imitatio, & repręsentatio hęc per orationem fit; dicimus in poëtice finem esse, sermonem imitantem, sicut in rhetorice sermonem persuadentem."

[65] *Ibid.*, p. 30: "Finem enim duplicem habet sibi propositum poëtice, alterum altero priorem: Prior est imitari. Alter vero est, oblectare."

[66] *Ibid.*, p. 2: "Nulla verò inter homines maior voluptas, quae quidem liberali homine digna sit, quàm quae mente, & cogitatione percipitur; imò saepè contingit, vt quae horrorem, & terrorem incutiunt hominibus, dum in propria natura sunt, extrà naturam posita in quapiam similitudine, dum repraesentantur; multum oblectent. . . . Quem igitur alium finem poëtices facultatis esse dicemus, quàm oblectare per repraesentationem, descriptionem, & imitationem omnium actionum humanarum; omnium motionum; omnium rerum tùm animatarum, tùm inanimatarum?"

deterred from those vices, and they are driven away from them with much greater force than if you were to use any other form of persuasion.[67]

From this and other passages[68] it is clear that the utility is essentially an ethical one, achieved through rhetorical means; men discover through poetry man's common fate, they learn what characters and events are worthy of dread and commiseration, and they achieve the capacity to moderate their own passions when adversity strikes.

In these passages on the various ends of poetry, it becomes clear that the end of imitation is an intermediate end, producing beyond itself either pleasure or utility of the moral kind so completely outlined. It is soon clear not only that the different ends of pleasure and utility are achieved by different means but that they result from different parts of the poem itself. Moreover, each separate kind of utility has its source in a separate poetic element. Neither is the pleasure a concomitant of the utility, nor is the utility a resultant of the total structure of the poem. Rather, Robortello proceeds by a fragmentation of the work and an analysis of what each fragment contributes toward one of the separate ends. The case is especially clear with respect to utility. Moral betterment derives from three separate sources: there are lessons from the fortunes of men, there are lessons from the characters of men, there are lessons from maxims or sententiae. Let us take the fortunes of men first. The conclusion that fate strikes all men equally, that men pass quickly from happiness to unhappiness, is deduced not from a study of men's characters but from the contemplation of the actions in which they are involved; hence it is related to the plot or the "fabula" of the play. The representation of such a plot on the stage is a powerful moral instrument: "This representation is very powerful in moving and rousing the souls of men to anger and rage, on the one hand, or, on the other hand, in calling them back to gentleness and in softening them, now exciting them to pity, to sorrow and tears, now to laughter and joy."[69]

The effectiveness of the representation depends, however, upon the resemblance of the imitation to life; if the imitation is "as if it were the thing itself" ("quasi rem ipsam," p. 3), it will produce its full effect. Hence the criterion of truth to life and credibility enters as a fundamental consideration in any discussion of the actions of the poem. The problem is a

---

[67] *Ibid.*, p. 3: "Recitationes autem, & imitationes poëticae vt sunt multiplices, ita multiplicem afferunt hominibus vtilitatem; Nam si recitatio, atque imitatio virtutum fit, & laudum praeclari alicuius viri; incitantur homines ad virtutem: Si rursus vitia repraesentantur, ab his homines multum deterrentur; maioréque quadam ui repelluntur, quàm si alia quauis hortatione vtaris."

[68] *Ibid.*, pp. 53, 102, 165–66, 211.

[69] *Ibid.*, p. 3: "Magnam autem habet vim huiusmodi repraesentatio in commouendis, & inflammandis hominum animis, tum ad iram, & furorem; tum ad mansuetudinem reuocandis, & emolliendis, tum concitandis ad commiserationem, ad fletum & lacrymas; tum ad risum, & laetitiam."

real one and a difficult one; for, essentially, poetry differs from the other arts of discourse in taking for its subject matter things which are not true:

Since, then, poetics has as its subject matter fictitious and fictional discourse, it is clear that the function of poetics is to invent in a proper way its fiction and its untruth; to no other art is it more fitting than to this one to intermingle lies. . . . In the lies used by the poetic art, false elements are taken as true, and from them true conclusions are derived.[70]

If from these fictional elements an impression of truth is to be obtained, the *plot* itself must contain actions belonging to one of three kinds: "For poetics speaks only of those actions which exist, or which can exist, or which do exist according to what men used to think"[71]—i.e., the true, the possible, the traditional. The true is the best: "we should try, if it is at all possible, to treat true actions."[72] The possible or probable is next best— "but, if not, we should invent new ones according to the probable."[73] Insofar as a poet uses a true plot, he does not invent, and hence his work resembles the activity of a historian; his true poetic activity, as we shall see, bears upon elements other than the plot. If he creates in accordance with probability, then he is an inventor on the level of plot as well.

The whole range of possibilities is summarized by Robortello in his commentary on *Poetics* 1460b7:

The things, actions, and persons which a poet imitates are either true or invented. If true, they either exist now or did exist, or they are living or died long ago. If they exist and are living, the poet imitates them in two ways, either as they are commonly said to be or as it appears they are. If they are neither living nor exist, but died long ago, they are still imitated in these two ways, either as general opinion reports them to have been or as it appears they were. If the persons are invented by the poet himself, he imitates and expresses them as being what it is fitting and proper that they should be.[74]

It will be noted that Robortello omits, from this apparently exhaustive set of distinctions, the notion of imitation of things as they are. This is not accidental. "True" is equated with "said to be" and "seem to be" rather than with "are" for the simple reason that the realm of the poet is, after all, the fictitious. If he treats things as they are, then he trespasses upon the

---

[70] *Ibid.*, p. 2: "Cum igitur poëtice subiectam sibi habeat pro materie orationem fictam, & fabulosam; patet ad poëticen pertinere, ut fabulam, & mendacium aptè confingat; nulliúsque alterius artis proprium magis esse; mendacia comminisci, quàm huius . . . in poëticis mendaciis principia falsa pro veris assumuntur, atque ex his verae eliciuntur conclusiones.'

[71] *Ibid.*, p. 2: "Nam poëtice loquitur de iis tantum rebus, aut quę sunt, aut quae esse possunt. aut quas uetus est apud homines opinio, esse."

[72] *Ibid.*, p. 219: "danda est opera, vt si fieri possit, circa veras actiones versemur."

[73] *Ibid.*, p. 219: "Sin minus, nouas ex verisimili confingamus."

[74] *Ibid.*, p. 290: "res, actiones, & personę quas imitatur, poëta, aut verae sunt, aut fictae. Si verae, aut sunt aut fuerunt, vel enim viuunt; vel iamdiu interierunt. Si sunt, ac viuunt duplici modo has imitatur poëta, aut quales aiunt vulgò esse, aut videntur esse. Si non viuunt, neque sunt; sed iamdiu interierunt, imitatur etiam has duplici modo; aut quales rumor est fuisse, aut quales videntur fuisse. Si personae fictae sunt ab ipso poëta, eas imitatur; exprimitque, quales esse conuenit, & oportet."

domain of the historian. It is by this line of reasoning that Robortello arrives at his interpretation of Aristotle's τὰ δυνατὰ κατὰ τὸ εἰκὸς ἢ τὸ ἀναγκαῖον (1451a38); at his own theory of the possible, the probable, and the necessary; and at his central doctrine of credibility as determining the moral effect of the action. The true is credible, hence moving; the verisimilar is moving only insofar as it resembles the true. The whole argument is presented in the passage expounding 1451b15:

> Tragedy has as its purpose to arouse two of the major passions of the soul—pity and fear. Now it is much more difficult to arouse these than others which agitate in a more pleasant way, such as hope, laughter, and others of this kind. For men by their very nature are prone to pleasant things but averse to unpleasant ones; they cannot, therefore, easily be impelled to sorrow. It is thus necessary for them first to know that the thing actually happened in such and such a way. Thus if a tragic plot contained an action which did not really take place and was not true, but was represented by the poet himself in accordance with verisimilitude, it would perhaps move the souls of the auditors, but certainly less. For, if verisimilar things give us pleasure, all the pleasure derives from the fact that we know these things to be present in the truth; and, in general, to the extent that the verisimilar partakes of truth it has the power to move and to persuade. . . . If verisimilar things move us, the true will move us much more. Verisimilar things move us because we *believe* it to have been possible for the event to come about in the way specified. True things move us because we *know* that it did come about in the way specified. Whatever virtue is thus contained in verisimilitude is derived totally from its relationship to truth.[75]

This passage relates credibility to verisimilitude and verisimilitude to truth.

Other terms relevant to the action in a poem are treated elsewhere. The false and the impossible are never acceptable: "The poetic faculty rejects those things which are absolutely false"; and "as often as poetry errs in its imitation and fails to preserve what is necessarily true, or else verisimilar, and instead tries to express something which is impossible and completely unbelievable."[76] The necessary is the same as the true, consisting of those things which had happened or been done; as a critical term, it must then

---

[75] *Ibid.*, p. 93: "Habet sibi propositum tragoedia mouere duas maximas perturbationes animi commiserationem, & metum; multò verò difficilius est, has mouere, quàm reliquas, quae iucundius perturbant, qualis est spes, risus, & huiusmodi. sunt enim suaptè natura homines ad iucundas res proni; ab iniucundis autem alieni; non facilè igitur ad luctum possunt impelli. necesse est igitur, vt sciant prius rem ita cecidisse; quod si fabula tragica actionem contineat, quae non acta sit, neque sit vera; sed ab ipso poëta fuerit efficta secundum verisimile; commouebit fortasse animos audientium, at minus certè. nam verisimilia si nos oblectant, oblectatio omnis inde prouenit, quòd in veris inesse ea scimus; & omnino quatenus verisimile veritatis est particeps vim habet mouendi, ac persuadendi . . . si nos verisimilia mouent, multo magis vera mouebunt. Verisimilia nos mouent, quia fieri potuisse credimus, ita rem accidisse. Vera nos mouent, quia scimus ita accidisse, quicquid igitur vis est in verisimili, id totum arripit à vero."

[76] *Ibid.*, p. 284: "patet poëticen facultatem . . . reiicere ea, quae prorsus sunt falsa"; and p. 292: "quotiescunque poëtica in imitatione peccat; neque seruat, necessarium, ac verisimile, conaturáque exprimere aliquid, quod impossibile sit; praeteráque omnem fidem."

have the same meaning as the "true" and refer not to real existence but to possibility and opinion. The possible consists of those things which can be done (τὰ δυνατά) and subdivides into the necessary and the probable. If to this subdivision we add another one, that affecting unnatural and incredible objects (for these in certain circumstances are admissible into certain poems), we get another exhaustive distinction as follows:

Duplici modo fingere, & mentiri poëtas:
1. in rebus secundum naturam (the possible)
   (a) τὸ ἀναγκαῖον (the necessary)
   (b) τὸ εἰκός (the probable)
2. in rebus praeter naturam (the impossible)
   (a) quae receptae iam sunt in opinionem vulgi (the traditional)
   (b) non antè unquam auditis, aut narratis ab alio (the newly invented)

The impossible or the false, because it is incredible, has no place in poetry, no persuasive power, no possible moral effect. But it is occasionally admitted when the poet can succeed in giving it a semblance of credibility (p. 87).

In many of the passages in which Robortello speaks of the utility springing from the actions of poems, he speaks of representation or performance (rather than merely of imitation) and of the effect upon spectators (rather than upon readers). This is because he considers the art of imitation really two arts, a *poetic* art concerned with the writing of poems and a *histrionic* art concerned with their performance. The division of functions is clear in his commentary on *Poetics* 1449*b*31:

It should be noted, in fact, that the imitation in tragedy may be considered in two ways, either insofar as it is scenic and is acted by the actors or insofar as it is made by the poet as he writes. If you think of it in terms of the poet who writes, then we may say that the principal end of tragedy is to imitate the nature of souls and the characters of men through written words, through which description it is possible to discern whether men are happy or unhappy. If you assume it to refer to the actor as he acts, then we may say that the greatest and most powerful end is that very action as a result of which men are judged to be happy or unhappy. In the writing and the imitation of the poets some such order as the following is established, if you follow nature; *character,* from which comes *happiness* or *unhappiness.* But in the action on the stage of the actor as he recites, in this way: *action,* from which comes *happiness* or *unhappiness.*[77]

[77] *Ibid.,* p. 58: "Notandum verò . . . tragoediae imitationem duplici modo considerari; aut quatenus scenica est, & ab histrionibus agitur, aut quatenus à poëta fit scribente. Si quatenus à scribente poëta intelligas, dicimus primarium in tragoedia finem esse imitari, habitum animi, & mores hominum per orationem scriptam; ex qua descriptione homines cerni possunt an felices, an verò infelices sint. Si quatenus histrio agens eam refert, sumas . . . dicimus maximum, ac potissimum finem esse ipsam actionem, ex qua homines diiudicantur aut felices, aut infelices. In scriptione & imitatione poëtarum talis ordo constituitur, si naturam sequaris. MORES, ex quibus FELICITAS, aut INFELICITAS. In actione verò scenica recitantium histrionum, huiusmodi. ACTIO. ex qua FELICITAS, aut INFELICITAS."

In the light of these ideas, one of Robortello's most puzzling statements about poetics becomes significant. In *Poetics* 1450*a*10, Aristotle indicated that the six parts of tragedy (plot, character, thought, diction, song, and spectacle) might be distributed thus among the constitutive elements of poetry: three to the object, two to the means, and one to the manner of imitation. Robortello provides such a distribution, and in it, plot (which in the Aristotelian text must be one of the objects of imitation) becomes the one part belonging to the manner of imitation; the manner is dramatic, what is acted is the action or plot, hence the plot is the part of tragedy belonging to the manner of imitation. He even goes on to demonstrate how that part of the means especially germane to stage presentation—spectacle or apparatus—is in a sense the end of tragedy and contains all the other parts within itself.[78]

The second kind of moral utility, the lessons learned from the characters of men, comes specifically from the depiction of character. In the distribution of parts already mentioned, Robortello assigns to the object of imitation the three parts of thought, character, and diction. The characters as depicted serve as moral examples to mankind; hence, they must be well chosen, must present no wicked persons except when one means (as in comedy) to expose them to ridicule. These considerations lead him to interpret as he does Aristotle's distinction of "better," "worse," and "like" characters. He takes "better" as meaning "superior to those who live in our times," the heroes of epic and gnomic poetry and the kings and heroes of tragedy. "Like" refers to characters who resemble men of our own times and who appear in dialogues and in epic poems. "Worse" means those who are morally base; but it may also mean those who are of low station in life. Indeed, all along the line the distinction tends to become social rather than moral. The process is especially clear in the case of the tragic hero, who must be of high station if his fall from happiness to unhappiness is to produce the desired effect (pp. 20, 132–33).

Just as in the case of action no moral utility can be achieved unless the action itself is credible or is made credible, so in the case of character a basis of credibility must be established. The problem is perhaps more complicated than it is with action; indeed, all four of the requirements for character that Aristotle indicated in 1454*a*15 ff. become, in the hands of Robortello, separate means to credibility. "Goodness" becomes conformity to type characteristics; the audience will accept readily only those persons who conform to type. "Appropriateness" is interpreted as the theory of

---

[78] *Ibid.*, p. 57: "Probat verò alia quadam ratione esse sex, per tres videlicet notas illas differentias, quae in principio libri appositae fuerunt, & declaratae. Sunt autem hae, οἷς. ὡς. ἃ. Per primam differentiam scilicet οἷς, quae instrumentum significat velut quoddam. Per secundam differentiam scilicet ὡς; quae modum significat, ex quo imitatio diuersitatem sumit. Per tertiam differentiam scilicet ἃ quae subiectam materiem significat, in qua versatur imitatio tragoediae. Ex prima differentia duae existunt partes, APPARATVS, MELODIA. Ex secunda vna pars tantum. FABVLA. Ex tertia; tres partes. DICTIO, MORES, SENTENTIA."

decorum, according to which a complex of traits was assigned to each person in accordance with the circumstances surrounding him. Here again, the audience holds these expectations with respect to the person and will find him credible when they are realized. "Likeness" is taken to mean the observance, for traditional or historical persons, of the conception of character established for them. They must conform to the accepted opinion held by the audience. "Consistency" refers especially to persons newly invented by the poet; these must be constant throughout if the audience is to believe in them (pp. 167–69).

This distinction between new and traditional characters is fundamental. We have already seen a similar distinction at work with respect to action: "true" actions, as they should be or seemed to be (note the traditional element), fall into the category of the necessary; "invented" actions into that of the probable or verisimilar. So for character:

If, therefore, the persons are real and the actions in themselves and the outcome of the deeds related are true, then the characters of the persons must be expressed by the poet according to the necessary, that is (as Averroës correctly explains it), according to truth. If the persons are fictitious, their characters will have to be expressed according to the verisimilar, that is (as the same Averroës interprets it), according to the opinion of the majority.[79]

These various statements about action and character assume that both truth and verisimilitude are within the jurisdiction of the audience, that the individual character or action is submitted to the judgment of the spectator or the auditor. The assumption is made more specific in connection with Robortello's treatment of the passages on the epic. He says:

In epic poetry, just as in the others, this is the first thing that must be attended to: that the words used should have nothing about them that is incongruous or contradictory, but that they should in every respect agree among themselves and fit properly together. For, whenever either the period of time in which the action is done or the place or the person or the manner is not congruous, these things do not satisfy reason, nor are they acceptable to the mind of the readers or the hearers.[80]

Such a passage as this indicates that the really important consideration in any poem is the relationship among words—rather than among characters and actions—that the goodness of the relationship is determined essenti-

[79] *Ibid.*, p. 175: "Si igitur personae verae sunt, & facta ab ipsis, euentaque rerum, quae narrantur, vera sunt; debent tunc personarum mores exprimi à poëta, secundum necessarium. hoc est (vt aptè declarat Auerroës) secundum veritatem. Si nouae sint personae, illarum mores exprimendi erunt secundum verisimile. hoc est (vt idem interpretatur Auerroës) secundum plurimorum opinionem."

[80] *Ibid.*, p. 286: "In poësi Epica, sicuti etiam in aliis illud in primis videndum, ne sermones habiti absonum aliquid habeant, aut repugnans. Sed ab omni parte consentiant inter se, & quadrent; Quotiescunque enim aut spatium temporis, quo res gesta fuit; aut locus, aut persona, aut modus, non constat; non quadrant rationi, neque cum legentium, aut audientium mente conueniunt."

ally by the reactions of the audience, and that the only internal criterion is one of a vague "fittingness" or "congruity" of all the words in the poem.

It is perhaps in this sense that diction, along with sententiae and character, becomes for Robortello one of the objects of imitation; this is just as remarkable as that plot should be assigned to the manner. The poetic faculty "produces ethical discourse [conficitque orationem moratam]" (pp. 291–92) and both character and thought (sententiae) contribute to the production of this discourse; in this sense it is an end or an object rather than a means of imitation. A special form of diction, the speech made by a character in a poem, is even more clearly an object of imitation for Robortello. As in the cases of action and character, it produces a special kind of effect upon the audience, an effect of persuasion which, in addition, arouses the emotions (p. 198). As for action and character, also, the persuasive and emotional qualities of speeches will depend upon the credibility of these speeches; they must closely resemble "true" speeches made by "real" people. Verisimilitude will bring about credibility.

In summary, then, the various kinds of utility which men derive from poetry come separately from various parts of poems: from plot, the spectacle of man's happiness or unhappiness springing from his actions; from character, the example of man's happiness or unhappiness springing from his character; from sententiae, the statements which will persuade the spectator to action or dissuade him from it, which will demonstrate truths to him and move him to imitation or revulsion. These are not, perhaps, entirely separate, since the sententiae become the final expression of the lessons from both action and character. In all cases, utility will result only from a belief of the audience in the truthfulness of the poem, and that, in turn, will depend upon the degree to which the poem is made probable and verisimilar.

Since Robortello's system is analytical in the sense that specific effects result from separate causes, we may expect that his treatment of pleasure will follow the same pattern. Pleasure itself will not be subdivided into a number of kinds, but separate parts of the poem will be distinguished as providing different aspects of the "voluptas" produced by poetry. Moreover, these will usually be different from the parts providing utility or will be special subdivisions of these parts. The whole problem of pleasure will be complicated by several considerations: (1) it must be derived from subjects which are in themselves not pleasurable (in the case of tragedy); (2) the audience will tend to prefer inartistic to artistic pleasures; (3) the things done for the achievement of utility essentially militate against the achievement of pleasure.

Since truth itself lies outside the domain of poetry, pleasure will be associated with the credible. However, credibility in itself is not enough (as it is for utility); some subjects will readily be "believed" by an audience,

[396]

but they will not as readily be "liked." Hence there arises a distinction between genres such as comedy, where the subject matter itself is pleasurable, and tragedy, where it is not pleasurable; men will naturally prefer the former to the latter. Hence, also, bad poets will make concessions to the mob in the form of such devices as the happy ending for tragedy (p. 142). The distinction between the pleasure of tragedy and the pleasure of comedy is found in the following passage:

... the pleasure which is obtained from tragedy is that which imitation provides. The power that this imitation has in delighting our souls may be sufficiently recognized from the fact that even horrible things, if they present themselves in some imitative expression, attract us to them and bring us delight and pleasure. ... Such is therefore the pleasure that is derived from tragedy. Nor is that which comes from comedy unlike it, insofar as comedy contains imitation. The latter, therefore, pleases because it imitates in a joyous fashion the ridiculous actions of men; the former because it imitates in an artistic fashion the sorrow, the lamentation, and the calamity of mortal men. Now if you should ask which is the greater pleasure of the two, I should dare to affirm that the one deriving from tragedy is much greater, for it pervades our souls more deeply and touches us in a more unusual way, and that imitation is accomplished with somewhat greater effort. Therefore, to the extent that we know it to be more difficult to express that imitation, to that extent—if it be successful—we regard it with greater admiration, and we obtain from it a greater pleasure.[81]

I have cited this passage at length because it contains an elaboration of what are, essentially, the three bases of pleasure for Robortello: imitation, the *difficulté vaincue*, and admiration.

Of these three bases, perhaps the most important is admiration, that feeling of wonder and amazement which comes from the spectacle of the unexpected, the extraordinary, the marvelous. If this is an essential ingredient of pleasure, then a crucial question is raised: Is not the marvelous the exact contradictory of the credible, and would not the pleasure arising from it exclude the possibility of utility? Robortello works out the difficulty in a way entirely consistent with the previous *données* of his system. The marvelous is indeed in conflict with the credible. Hence it must be kept to a minimum in those genres where credibility is most essential (e.g., comedy) and may attain a maximum in other genres, where, because they

---

[81] *Ibid.*, p. 146: "Sed respondeo; voluptatem, quae capitur ex tragoedia, esse eam, quam parit imitatio. quantum verò habeat haec vim ad oblectandos animos, vel inde satis cognosci potest. quòd etiam horribilia, si imitatione aliqua expressa sese nobis obtulerint; delectationem, voluptatémque afferunt. . . . Talis est igitur voluptas quae ex tragoedia percipitur. Nec dissimilis huic est, quae ex comoedia prouenit quatenus imitationem continet. Haec igitur oblectat, quòd festiuè imitatur ridiculas actiones hominum, illa quòd artificiosè imitatur moerorem, luctum, calamitatémque mortalium. Quòd si quaeras vtra maior voluptas, ausim affirmare, quae ex tragoedia prouenit maiorem multò. altius enim peruadit animos, rariusque nobis contingit; maioréque quadam vi fit imitatio illa; quantò igitur difficilius exprimi eam posse scimus, tantò magis, si exacta fuerit, admiramur; maioremque capimus voluptatem."

are narrative rather than dramatic, credibility is of lesser importance. This is especially true of the epic (cf. p. 87). In such a genre as tragedy, the problem for the poet is to reconcile the credible with the marvelous, and this he does through the use of a number of specific devices (cf. pp. 328, 45, 121). In the last analysis, the poet is virtually permitted to discard all concern for credibility in order to exploit all the available means of achieving the marvelous and the pleasure connected with it.

The pleasures arising from imitation, the *difficulté vaincue*, and admiration are largely attached to parts of the poem different from those which produce utility; they come from episodes, from recognition and reversal rather than from the principal action of the plot, from secondary characters rather than from the hero, from elements of diction independent of the ethical speeches, from gratuitous descriptions. This does not mean that the other "essential" parts of the poem do not give pleasure. It merely means that, in keeping with his analytical tendency, Robortello seeks as often as possible to find separate causes for the pleasure and the utility derived by the audience. Pleasure will contribute to the achievement of the ultimate utilitarian goal of the work (if such a subordination indeed exists) only by making the poem as a whole enjoyable to the audience. The total effect upon the audience will be one of moral betterment accompanied by pleasurable sensations.

The constant conclusion of any individual discussion, in the preceding pages, with such terms as "persuasion," "moral betterment," "effect upon the audience," "pleasurable sensations," should point clearly to the essential character of Robortello's system. It is a rhetorical system, in which Robortello sees the poem as seeking a specific effect of persuasion upon a specified audience and obtaining that effect through the potentiality of each of the parts of the poem to move the audience in a separate way. The character of the audience is thus involved as an ingredient. It is an audience of the élite, not the "vulgus"—not the "rough and ignorant crowd of men" that demands such cheap satisfactions as those found in the double ending of tragedies (pp. 145–46). It is, moreover, an audience made up of good men only, an audience which will sympathize with the tragic hero and will be capable of experiencing the effects of purgation and of moral betterment. Robortello develops his idea at length in the commentary on 1453a5, "a man like ourselves":

Fear is aroused, indeed, when we behold someone like ourselves who has fallen into misery. Aristotle means like the auditors themselves, almost all of whom are judged to be good; or else he speaks only of the good ones. For it is out of their souls that the rule for writing tragedy is derived, nor must any poet ever be mindful of the wicked, but he must adapt everything he writes to the nature of good men. Good men, then, when they see evil things happen to some good man, fear—since they understand that he is like themselves and that they are like him—lest a like thing at some time befall them, since they live in equivalent circumstances.[82]

Finally, we know that the audience is possessed of a large amount of knowledge and a large number of expectations, all of which contribute to the constitution of its canon of credibility: what is true, what is traditional, what is a matter of opinion, what is probable and verisimilar—all these are known only by reference to the audience, and only by consulting the audience do we know whether they have been achieved.

I have already pointed out, in Chapter II (pp. 66–68), the consequences of this shift from a poetical system to an almost completely rhetorical system and the implications of a methodological order. The reader is referred to that discussion.

THE ROBORTELLO TREATISES (1548)

To his commentary on Aristotle, Robortello added—"so that nothing belonging to the poetic art might be lacking"—a paraphrase of Horace's *Ars poetica* and a group of short treatises on satire, the epigram, comedy, humor, and the elegy; these were published in a separate part of the volume containing the *Explicationes*. The latter group especially would seem to hold great promise of an Aristotelian approach applied to genres not treated fully by Aristotle, for Robortello declares that "in iis scribendis Aristotelis methodum seruauit: & ex ipsius Libello de arte Poetica principia sumpsit omnium suarum explicationum" (half-title page to the separate part). The promise is not, however, fulfilled. Robortello does indeed cite from the translation of the *Poetics* those passages which are pertinent to the particular genre being treated. But for the development of the theory he is usually content to seek elsewhere, in other writers of antiquity, the materials not found in Aristotle. There is, of course, no guarantee that these materials will in any way develop Aristotle's thesis; they merely supplement it with a miscellany of information.

The treatise *De satyra*, first in the group, establishes the pattern. Satire, like all other kinds of poetry, imitates human actions, and it does so by means of rhythm, diction, and harmony. Imitation, not verse, is its distinguishing feature; for a history in verse would still be a history. Paraphrasing Aristotle in this way, Robortello goes on to the distinction between actions which have happened and actions which might happen. But when, soon, he wishes to treat the "manner" of satire (finding no direct indication in the *Poetics*), he shifts to Athenaeus (*Deipnosophistae*, Bk. XIV, §§ 28 ff.), cites his subdivisions of lyric and scenic poetry, and finds satire in the latter

---

[82] *Ibid.*, p. 128: "Metus verò concitatur, cum intuemur aliquem nobis similem, in miseriam esse lapsum. Similem auditoribus ipsis intelligit Aristoteles; qui ferè omnes boni censendi sunt, vel de bonis tantum loquitur. nam ex eorum animis norma sumitur scribendę tragoediae; neque vllus debet poëta improbos vnquam respicere, sed totam suam scriptionem accommodare ad bonorum naturam. Viri igitur boni, cum immerenti alicui viro bono aliquid mali vident accidisse, metuunt, quòd similem illum sibi, seque illi esse intelligunt, ne idem sibi aliquando accidat, quia pari viuunt conditione."

group. Various authorities are then cited on the antiquity of the form. Satyrs, fauns, and sileni are distinguished, again on the basis of many authorities. Robortello next attacks the problem of the personages of satire; he finds information on satyrs in Julius Pollux and Dionysius of Halicarnassus. As for the subject matter of this genre, Robortello returns to Aristotle, excludes the terrible and the pitiable, decides that satire, like comedy, must treat the ridiculous. The people at whom it pokes its laughter are "ambitiosos, auaros, ingratos, prodigos, periuros, rapaces, adulteros, adulatores, loquaces, stolidos, amatores, ineptos, irreligiosos, parricidas, desides, inertes, parasitos, & qui huiusmodi sunt" (p. 30); the list resembles those traditionally cited in discussions of comedy. Next, the qualifications of the satiric poet: he must be versatile, skillful, keen, sharp-witted, eloquent; but he must also be good and honest: "for seeing that he examines the vices of others, he himself must possess such a way of life as may not justly be criticized by anybody."[83] There follows a long section on "maledicentia" and on the poets of antiquity who have used it well or badly; on the good to be gained by proper use of satirical blame; and on why Horace called his satires "sermones."

In all this, there is occasional quotation of the *Poetics* and an occasional attempt to extend what Aristotle said about comedy to the sister genre of satire. But nowhere is there any intention to apply, in a fundamental way, the principles underlying Aristotle's treatment to a genre which he had not treated.

The procedure in the *De epigrammate*, which follows ("ex Aristotelis Libro de Poetica; magna ex parte desumpta"), is somewhat different. Robortello announces at the beginning that he will treat three subjects: the kind of poetry to which epigrams belong, their subject matter, and what practices are to be followed or avoided in writing them. These subjects are then treated in the order given. For the first, poetic genres are divided into two groups, the longer forms (tragedy, comedy, epic, dithyramb, and "legum poesis" or divine poetry) and the shorter forms (satire, epistle, and sylva). The epigram, in a strange way, may belong to either group; for just as a tragedy or a comedy is a small part of an epic, so the epigram is a small part of any of these forms. The genres may be further divided into those having "imitation" or direct speech and those having no imitation but only "narration." The first section ends with a discussion of the origins and etymology of the epigram. So far, no word of Aristotle. In the second section, Robortello states that the matter of the epigram will in each case be one that would be appropriate to the genre of which it would be a smaller "part." So for the tragic epigram, in a passage where the text of the *Poetics* is reflected indirectly:

It is proper for tragedy to treat serious matters that have about them much to

---

[83] *Paraphrasis* (1548), pp. 30–31: "qui cum optimè aliorum vitia perspiciat. ipse tamen talem ineat vitae rationem, quae à nullo, iurè reprehendi possit."

evoke pain, pity, and no little wonder, as Aristotle abundantly explains in the *Poetics.* Sorrow is produced by all horrible things, such as floggings, wounds, murders; pity is produced by these same things if they happen to a man who does not deserve them or if they come about between relatives, as between a mother and her son or between brothers. Events arousing admiration are those involving accident, such as when the statue of Mitys at Argos, falling down, killed him who had killed Mitys. All these things are susceptible of the most beautiful descriptions.[84]

Epigrams written on deaths and funerals will belong in this category. For comedy, also, Robortello cites Aristotle (1449a31); the epigram related to it will use a "materia conuitiosa & ridicula" (p. 37) for the purpose of laughing at vice and condemning it. "Nor does the epigram differ from comedy in anything except in the form and in the way of treating the materials; the latter is more diffuse and proceeds by dialogue, the former is shorter and proceeds by a kind of simple narration."[85] Similar comparisons are provided for epigrams related to amatory verse and to the epic. In the third section, the positive recommendations concern such elements of style as "venustas," "suauitas," and acuteness, as well as the kinds of words to be used, while negatively Robortello condemns the use of acrostics and Greek words. Things, in the epigram, should not become the servants of the words, and the poet should never indulge in excess or superfluity. A final sentence urges the poet to follow Robortello's method, to read the ancient poets, and to practise writing.

The treatise *De comoedia* would seem, outwardly, to be more nearly "Aristotelian" than the others, for almost all the materials of which it is made are direct quotations or paraphrases of the *Poetics.* But with few exceptions they are passages from that text dealing with tragedy, in which the word "comedy" has been substituted for the word "tragedy" or in which the passage has been taken over unchanged as equally applicable to both genres. Some adjustments, of course, had to be made. The treatise is most interesting for the light it throws on Robortello's conception of a dramatic genre and for some of its interpretations of the text of Aristotle. Robortello begins by reporting from the *Poetics,* in brief form, the fundamental distinctions with respect to the end of poetry, its three means, its objects, and its manners. For the objects, a first difference: comedy "differs from the others in the subject matter which it treats; for it imitates those actions of men which are more lowly and more common; and in this it

---

[84] *Ibid.*, p. 36: "Tragoediae quidem proprium est tractare res serias, quae in se multum doloris, & commiserationis habeant, neque parum admirationis, sicuti copiosè explicat Arist. in Poët. Dolorem afferunt omnia atrocia, vt verbera, vulnera, caedes; Commiserationem afferunt eadem ipsa, si viro immerenti accidant; aut si inter consanguineos, vtpotè inter matrem, & filium, vel inter fratres. Admirabilia sunt fortuita, vt Argis statua Mityi collapsa eum peremit, qui Mityum peremerat; Recipiunt enim haec omnia pulcherrimas descriptiones."

[85] *Ibid.*, p. 37: "neque vlla in re epigramma differt à comoedia, praeterquàm forma, et ratione tractandarum rerum, Illa enim fusius, ac per collocutionem; Hoc autem breuius, atque simplici quadam narratione."

differs from tragedy, which imitates those which are more excellent."[86] From Aristotle come also the developments on the natural origins of comedy, its history and improvement, supplemented, however, by Plutarch and Donatus on the distinctions between Old and New Comedy. For the discussion of the qualitative parts, Robortello again merely adapts the treatment of tragedy in the *Poetics*. In such a passage as the following, for example (paraphrasing *Poetics* 1449*b*31 ff.), it is only the substitution or the addition of the word "comoedia" which makes the text in any way especially pertinent to comedy:

Non potest recitari comoedia vlla, si non adhibeatur Melodia (quia ita obtinuit vsus) & apparatus, vt res in scena, tanquàm in vrbe, aut oppido aliquo geri videatur; Ergo necessariae sunt hae partes. Melodia, Apparatus; multò verò magis necessariae aliae, quia sine iis ne scribi quidem potest comoedia; Nam scripturo comoediam prius necesse est excogitare rem, quae scribenda est; Ea continetur fabula. sed rursus oportet fabulam, quia imitatur esse moratam; & exprimere exactè diuersorum hominum mores; & ideò necessaria altera pars. MORES. nam non omnis oratio Morata; qualis est Mathematicorum, Medicorum, Physiologorum, Dialecticorum. Verùm quia necesse est animi sensa exprimi per orationem; ideò necesse alteram addere partem, quae est. SENtentia. Sed quia sententia verbis constat; ideò necessariò additur etiam alia, quae est. DICTIO" (pp. 44–45).

The central section of the treatise is occupied by an orderly discussion of the "rules" and conditions of the qualitative parts, a discussion which leans heavily upon Robortello's own interpretations in his commentary on the *Poetics*, but which also appeals to later sources such as Horace. For the parts "sententia" and "dictio," most of the materials are drawn from Aristides, and for "apparatus" from a whole series of Latin writers on the theater. Donatus is the authority on the quantitative parts and on the division of comedy into five acts.

The *De comoedia* is in a sense the most disappointing of the supplementary treatises. We would be curious to discover how a theorist of 1548 would have constructed a theory of comedy, but we find instead merely a transfer of familiar ideas and passages, with only the most passing and the most perfunctory adaptations to the special conditions of comedy.

Aristotle's *Rhetoric* and Cicero provide the majority of the materials for the short treatise *De salibus*. As its title suggests, it has no particular reference to any poetic genre; indeed, its interest is rhetorical rather than poetic, as Robortello indicates in his first sentence: "Of the rhetorical faculty, which has many and ample parts, it seems to us that hardly anything remains to be explained except these two matters: first, what aims at delighting and lightening the souls of the listeners, that is, wit and clever sayings; then, those things that aim at a form of discourse and at the embel-

[86] *Ibid.*, p. 41: "differt etiam comoedia ab aliis materie rerum subiectarum, quas tractat; nam imitatur actiones hominum humiliores, & viliores; & ideò differt à tragoedia, quae praestantiores imitatur."

lishment of speech."[87] The treatment is thus exclusively rhetorical, except for such kinds of wit as may be used in certain poetic types, and the whole document is unrelated to the fortunes of the *Poetics* in the Renaissance. Indeed, the work seems to be a fragment of a larger treatise on rhetoric.

In the last of the short treatises, *De elegia*, the *Poetics* appears again only in a most incidental way; since Aristotle had not treated the elegy specifically, Robortello was obliged to turn to other sources. Unable to adapt Aristotle's theory to this genre, he took refuge in a conventional treatment of the "origo, finis, materies, artificium" of the elegy. For each topic, he sought solutions in a variety of ancient authors (Athenaeus, Proclus, Cicero, Horace are prominent among them). He sees the elegy as a poem which may treat almost any subject matter and whose kind and category vary with variations in subject matter. A funeral elegy belongs to auletic poetry; one which describes laws belongs to the "poesis legum"; others which treat of war, mores, philosophy are of doubtful classification. In a general way, all elegies are related to the epic since their "imitation" is "mixed," containing both narration and dialogue. They are neither too high nor too low in style, use a variety of devices, create an effect in which the pathetic is accompanied by an air of antiquity.

We may conclude our discussion of the addenda to Robortello's *Explicationes* of 1548—actually it is the first item in the supplementary volume—with his *Paraphrasis in librum Horatii, qui vulgo de arte poetica ad Pisones inscribitur* (see above, Chapter IV, p. 118). Just as the "paraphrase" is little more than that, so the uses of Aristotle's *Poetics* are the traditional ones for the period: Robortello cites the *Poetics* in about a dozen passages, in each case showing how it says the same things that Horace had said or corroborates his statements. The choices seem to be haphazard. Several of the texts concern matters of metrics (1459b31, 1449a23), others refer to the history of tragedy and comedy (1449a2, –19), still others to the treatment of character (1453a17, 1451b11, 1454a16). In the latter connection, Horace's "sibi constet" is explained by the ὁμαλόν of Aristotle (1454a25). Some random distinctions are borrowed from the *Poetics*: the fact that epic is a narrative form (1460a5), the uses of lies and paralogism (1460a18), the interdict on the "deus ex machina" (1454a37). In none of this is there any interpretation of Aristotle, except insofar as the allegation of equivalence is a kind of reading of the text. In one passage of the *Paraphrasis*, Robortello seems to interpret the *Poetics* as saying the opposite of what it says, insisting that meter is necessary for poetry;[88] but this is consonant with

---

[87] *Ibid.*, p. 51: "Ex Rhetorica facultate, quae multas et amplas partes habet; nihil iam ferè nobis videtur reliquum, quod explicemus, praeter duo haec. Primum ea quae ad oblectandos, & releuandos animos auditorum spectat: Sales scilicet & acutè dicta. Deinde, quae ad locutionis genus, & ornamentum sermonis spectant."

[88] *Ibid.*, p. 6: "vt enim poëma aliquod dicatur, non tantum imitatione opus est, sed etiam metro; non quidem quòd metrum absque imitatione poëtam vllum efficiat; Sed & ipsum requiritur tamen, ne nimium soluta sit oratio, sicut etiam in Poët. innuere videtur Aristoteles."

his theory, expressed in the *Explicationes*, that the best kind of poetry is a composite of imitation and verse (cf. p. 90).

THE SEGNI TRANSLATION (1549)

Bernardo Segni had the distinction of publishing, in 1549, the first translation of the *Poetics* in a modern vernacular—his *Rettorica et poetica d'Aristotile*. He paid tribute in his introduction to the recent advances in the understanding of the text, Pazzi's work on the text itself, Robortello's text and commentary. His debt to the latter was probably more considerable than he admitted, since he seems to have based his Italian translation on Robortello's Latin translation rather than on the Greek. In any case, Pazzi was not his source, because passages present in Pazzi and lacking in Robortello are also lacking in Segni's version (cf. Segni, p. 278, Pazzi, p. 6v, Robortello, p. 20). On the whole, Segni's translation is a good one; it is clear and readable, and it is accurate within the limitations of the available texts. He made no effort to correct errors or to supply lacunae, and hence at the really garbled spots in the text he makes no better sense than had his predecessors. But for the unlettered public of his day his contribution must have been most welcome, giving them for the first time the opportunity to read the *Poetics* in Italian. The volume was reprinted at Venice in 1551 and again, in the series of the *Autori del ben parlare*, in 1643.

Besides the translation, Segni provided a brief explanatory introduction and a set of commentaries on the individual chapters. The introduction is concerned with comparing the arts of poetry and of rhetoric, probably because Aristotle's *Rhetoric* occupies the larger part of the volume. But there is nothing Aristotelian about the comparison. Segni finds the two "faculties" alike in that they achieve their ends by using language "which has spoken discourse, and character, and the other desirable features capable of rendering the diction beautiful."[89] Both use the same kinds of arguments—enthymeme, example, and amplification—as means of proof and demonstration, although poetry tends to make greater use of the example. Both are capable of treating any subject, although poetry "imitates more worthy persons and more celebrated actions" than does oratory (p. 273). The ends are the same for both; they are the traditional "to move men's minds" and "to delight them," otherwise stated as "to profit" and "to give pleasure." Segni attempts to evaluate the two arts on their capacity to give pleasure; poetry, because of its beauty, is definitely superior here. This beauty results from imitation "represented to us in action," from a special diction and figurative speech, from meter and verse, from great and delightful materials, from universality in virtue and in vice, and from the general fact that the art is divine and derives all its goodness from nature rather than from art. As for utility, it is difficult to judge of the

[89] *Rettorica et poetica* (1549), p. 272: "che habbia discorso, & costume; & l'altre conuenienze atte à far bella la locutione."

comparative effectiveness of poetry and of rhetoric since, in modern times, we do not see either of them in public performance. Poetry is even less frequently performed than oratory, which may be heard in the pulpit. Hence the effectiveness of purgation, its capacity to bring to our minds "tranquillity and freedom from every perturbation" (p. 275), cannot be properly measured.

In the commentaries on the individual chapters Segni proposes to give brief paraphrases first, "so that those who are less learned may understand some part if not all of it" (p. 280). He will then expound difficult points in the text. Such interpretation as is found here seems again to come largely from Robortello, who, declares Segni, "has in such wise made this work clear that no obscurity now remains in it."[90] But Segni's total theory of poetry is less complete and less systematic than Robortello's. He frequently seeks explanations and parallels in Horace, and he is not averse to citing Italian works to illustrate the theories expounded (thus Boccaccio's stories are given as examples of poems written in prose [p. 281]). His division of the *Poetics* into twenty-two sizable chapters is an improvement over the unbroken texts of Pazzi and Robortello's 270 fragments. It enables the reader to get a much clearer idea of the general order of Aristotle's text.

As for that order, Segni believes that when Aristotle declares that he will treat first things first, he means that he will give definitions of the individual genres before attempting a general definition of poetry and that this determines the general scheme of the *Poetics.* Following the text chapter by chapter, Segni presents a number of separate interpretations which are of interest because of their originality or because they go counter to the accepted tradition. He states, in connection with chapter I, that it is not possible to give a universal definition of poetry for the same reasons that Aristotle adduced for the impossibility of defining the state (referring to the *Politics*). On the moot question of the meaning of λόγοις ψιλοῖς, he offers the correct reading of "prose," whereas many Renaissance commentators refused to admit the possibility of prose as a medium for poetry. Yet he adopts Robortello's conclusion that the best poetry joins verse to imitation. Still relative to the same chapter, he makes significant remarks on the ways in which painting may imitate mores. When, on chapter II, he distinguishes the two natural sources of poetry, he again lists them correctly as imitation and the pleasure derived from imitation, unlike many of his contemporaries who insisted that meter was one of the natural sources. The effect of purgation (chapter V) is said to be a moral and a psychological one:

When we see similar cases which have happened to excellent people, we support our own calamities more easily; or rather we learn how to bear them. And in this way if we are wrathful or intemperate, we come to purge our souls of such

90 *Ibid.,* p. 280: "di tal' sorte ha fatto aperta questa opera, che nessuna oscurità più ci resti."

passions, considering those perils and those evils which befall him who is wrapped up in vice and him who is involved in the passions; from which consideration it is inevitable that very great pleasure results.[91]

As he passes on to the qualitative parts of tragedy, he adopts for them Robortello's division, assigning "apparatus" and "music" to the instrumental parts, plot to the material, and language, thought, and character to the final. It will be noted, however, that whereas the division is the same as Robortello's, the categories are different, instrumental replacing means, material replacing manner, and final replacing object. By the same token, the division of Aristotle is altered to fit another Aristotelian form of analysis, but not the one being employed at this point in the *Poetics*.

In those sections of his commentary which relate to Aristotle's specific remarks about the tragic form, Segni leans more heavily than elsewhere upon parallels from Horace and upon traditional materials inherited from the Middle Ages. Thus, for example, his commentary on *Poetics* 1453*b*1, ἐκ τῆς ὄψεως, includes a citation of Horace's "Nec pueros coram populo Medea trucidet" (l. 185), and Aristotle's remarks on the "deus ex machina" bring forth the obvious quotation from the *Ars poetica* (l. 191). Similarly, when he discusses the tragic hero, Segni distinguishes him, in conventional fashion, as a "principe" excellent and great for his "beni di fortuna"; tragic heroes would thus be separated from the "privati" of other genres (p. 308). On the whole, however, such references are rare; and because of its brevity and conciseness Segni's commentary seems to be dealing much more directly with the meaning of the text than did the glosses of his contemporaries. For this reason, as well as because it was written in Italian, it must have shed considerable light upon the *Poetics* for a large reading public.

LOMBARDI AND MAGGI (1550)

The second of the great published commentaries was that of Bartolomeo Lombardi and Vincenzo Maggi, *In Aristotelis librum de poetica communes explanationes* (1550). As has already been pointed out, this was a work of long elaboration, in which the role of Lombardi ceased at an early date and for which, in its final form, Maggi was undoubtedly largely responsible. The arrangement is special in the sense that after each section of text and translation (the *Poetics* is divided into 157 sections) there is a paragraph entitled "Explanatio" and then the usual "Annotatio." The text and translation are essentially those of Pazzi; but where the commentators wish to emend the text they place an asterisk before the doubtful passage, and when they

---

[91] *Ibid.*, p. 294: "ueggendo noi simili casi auuenuti in persone eccellenti, più ageuolmente comportiamo le calamità nostre; ò uero impariamo à sopportarle. Et in tal' modo se noi siamo iracundi, ò intemperati uenghiamo à purgar' l'animo di tali affetti; considerando quei pericoli, & quei mali, che incontrano à chi è ne' uitij rinuolto, & à chi è fitto nelle perturbationi: dalla qual' consideratione è forza, che ne risulti piacer' grandissimo."

wish to propose an alteration of the translation they mark both text and translation with a dagger. The same symbols are then used in the annotations to explain the changes that they propose. The "Explanationes" are given as the work of Lombardi and Maggi; they contain first a kind of paraphrase of the preceding text, then a first commentary of a textual and literary character. This commentary is continued in the "Annotationes," prepared by Maggi, usually in a much expanded form. In both explanations and annotations, linguistic matters and questions of translation bulk large; for many sections, indeed, this is the only kind of commentary provided. Nevertheless, there is a very extended treatment of all problems involved in the interpretation of the *Poetics*. Moreover, since Maggi had a thorough knowledge of the other works currently consulted on the art of poetry—Horace, Plato, Aristotle's *Rhetoric*, the other Greek and Roman rhetoricians—and since he himself had some well-developed conceptions of the art, we find in his annotations a completely consistent theory of poetry—not Aristotle's, but his own.

The cornerstone of this theory, as needs must be, is his conception of the end of poetry, a dual end borrowed from Horace: teaching and pleasure. The earliest statements in the "Prolegomena" (an important section for the discovery of Maggi's views) emphasize the utilitarian end. Thus: "The end of poetry itself is, by imitating human actions in delightful discourse, to render the soul refined" ("Finis autem ipsius Poesis est, actiones humanas imitando, suaui sermone animum excultum reddere," p. 13). The utilitarian end is a moral one, variously described in the same "Prolegomena": poetry attempts to embellish the human soul with the best possible moral dispositions ("optimis moribus sibi expoliendum proponit") and to produce proper moral action ("ut bonos mores inducant," *ibid.*). The moral end is variously stated for the various genres—for tragedy, to purge the soul of its passions ("illa nos ab animi perturbationibus expurgari" and "perturbationes ex animis auferendo"); for the epic, to praise the deeds of great men ("praeclara illustrium uirorum gesta uersibus exornando"); for comedy, to make fun of the vices ("uitia irridendo," *ibid.*). In the course of the commentary, these ideas are considerably expanded and clarified. The restatements bring with them the use of terms long associated with other critical traditions. Horace's "Aut prodesse uolunt, aut delectare poetae" is quoted in connection with the pleasure to be derived from recognition and reversal (p. 111), and the meaning of "prodesse" is defined in connection with Aristotle's τὸ φιλάνθρωπον:

By φιλάνθρωπον he means that which expresses good character and which leads to proper living in society. . . . Thus when Aristotle says οὔτε γὰρ φιλάνθρωπον, οὔτε ἐλεεινὸν, οὔτε φοβερόν ἐστι, it is as if he were to say that it is neither profitable nor does it bring pity or terror. And the poets attempt above all to bring profit to humankind, and those examples of action are useful to the society of men in which the worst men fall from happiness into unhappiness, since through these the human race is taught and abstains from wicked deeds.[92]

Having established the end of moral utility for all poetry, Maggi is careful to seek, in the various parts of tragedy, the particular ways in which that end is achieved. Purgation, as we have already seen, is the particular kind of utility produced by the genre. In discussing its operation, Maggi takes sides on an issue that was beginning to be much debated: whether tragedy, through purgation, actually removes pity and fear from men's souls or whether it removes, through their intermediation, other less desirable passions. Maggi argues for the latter interpretation, holding that men would be worse off if pity and fear were expelled from their souls:

Therefore it is much better, by the intervention of pity and terror, to purge the soul of wrath, through which so many violent deaths come about; of avarice, which is the cause of almost an infinity of ills; of lust, thanks to which the most harmful of wicked deeds must frequently be suffered. For these reasons I have no doubt whatever that Aristotle was unwilling to make the purgation of terror and pity from the human soul the end of tragedy; but rather, to use these for the removal of other disorders from the soul, through which removal the soul comes to be adorned with the virtues. For once wrath is driven out, for example, kindness takes its place. . . . [93]

Maggi cites the *Politics* in support of his position; he concludes, at a later point, that "the purpose of tragedy is to purge the human soul of disorders; once these are expelled, men emerge at peace and essentially better."[94] The moral utility contained in purgation is a function of plot; other kinds derive from the handling of mores. Of the four requisites of character, Maggi concludes that the first, goodness, has a pedagogic utility. "Good" character in the personages of tragedy will lead to improvement of character in its spectators: "For this reason we judge that in this section Aristotle accorded the first place to goodness of character, so that he might admonish the poets most strongly to be especially attentive to their expression."[95]

92 *Explanationes* (1550), p. 153: "Per φιλάνθρωπον intelliget idem, quod moratum, quodque ad societatem humanam conducit. . . . Aristoteles igitur cùm dicit οὔτε γάρ φιλάνθρωπον, οὔτε ἐλεεινὸν, οὔτε φοβερόν ἐστι, idem est, ac si diceret, nec prodest, nec misericordiam, timoremúe habet. at in primis humano generi poetae prodesse student, Prosunt autem humanae societati exempla, in quibus pessimi uiri ex felicitate in miseriam labuntur; quoniam his instruitur genus humanum, & à sceleribus abstinet."

93 *Ibid.*, p. 98: "longè igitur melius est misericordiae & terroris interuentu expurgare animum ab Ira, qua tot neces fiunt: ab Auaritia, quae infinitorum penè malorum est causa: à Luxuria, cuius gratia nefandissima scelera saepissime patrantur. His itaque rationibus haudquaquam dubito, Aristotelem nolle Tragoediae finem esse animam humanam à terrore, misericordiaúe expurgare; sed his uti ad alias perturbationes ab animo remouendas; ex quarum remotione animus uirtutibus exornatur. nam ira, uerbi gratia, depulsa, succedit mansuetudo. . . ."

94 *Ibid.*, p. 110: "Officium uerò Tragoediae . . . est humanum animum à perturbationibus expurgare: quibus extrusis tranquilli, ac seipsis meliores homines euadunt."

95 *Ibid.*, p. 170: "hac ratione arbitramur Aristotelem hac in parte primum locum bonis moribus concessisse, ut poetas potissimùm admoneret de illis exprimendis magis esse sollicitos oportere."

Goodness consists in the highest possible degree of manifestation of the virtues (cf. p. 175 on the procedure of painters), in such a way that the actors in a tragedy may serve as models for the audience ("debent exemplar facere," p. 175). In a similar way, that particular kind of tragedy which Aristotle calls ἠθική (1456a1) is taken to mean one "imitating and expressing good mores, and those which contribute to proper living in human society" ("imitans exprimensque bonos, & humanae societati conferentes mores," p. 195); Maggi derives the interpretation from the earlier φιλάνθρωπον. In all these passages, it is difficult to assign an exact meaning to "mores"; but it seems clear that Maggi means by the term, rather than the "character" or the "disposition to moral action" of Aristotle, a form of action itself, judged as "good" according to an accepted ethical code.

A similar set of distinctions and developments is offered by Maggi with respect to the other end, pleasure. The assumption throughout, I believe, is that the "voluptas" afforded by poetry is an intermediate end to the achievement of the moral utility, although there are few specific statements to this effect. Such a clear statement comes near the end, in the commentary to *Poetics* 1462b3:

> But in these words Aristotle seems to say that the function of the poet is to give pleasure, and that this should be considered the end of poetry. Yet since in the definition of tragedy he had said that it purges the disorder of the soul by means of pity and terror, purgation and not pleasure must be considered to be the end. . . . in such matters there may be many ends, of which one is regarded as greater than another. We thus concede that the poets have as their end to produce pleasure, but that they wish in a more important way to bring profit by adorning men with the virtues.[96]

The elements of a poetic work which give pleasure to its audience are mostly the plot and the diction. Hence the necessity that the plot of tragedy should be a known plot, based on the argument that what is known gives greater pleasure than what is unknown. Maggi is explaining *Poetics* 1457b19:

> Just as the image of a thing gives greater pleasure to one who knows the thing previously than to one who does not, since one who knows the thing learns and reasons, so one who knows previously that action which the poet imitates will learn and reason that this is the imitation of that action. . . . thus he who knows the action of which the plot is an imitation experiences a greater pleasure than he who does not know it, since the latter is incapable of deducing [the identification of the action] from it. . . . for those plots which give the greatest pleasure

---

96 *Ibid.*, p. 299: "his enim in uerbis Aristoteles dicere uidetur, poetae munus esse uoluptatem afferre, eamque poeticae finem statuere. uerum cùm in Tragoediae definitione dicatur, quòd interuentu misericordiae, & terroris animum perturbationibus expurgat: igitur huiusmodi expurgatio finis. non autem uoluptas statuenda erit. . . . rei eiusdem multi possunt esse fines; quorum alter altero magis intenditur. concedimus enim poetas scopum habere uoluptatem inducere, magis tamen uirtutibus exornando prodesse uelle."

(other things being equal) are to be preferred to others which are less enjoyable.[97]

Maggi himself recognizes the contradiction that exists between this statement (pleasure from knowledge) and the earlier statement that recognition and reversal, as parts of plot, produced pleasure out of the unknown (pleasure from ignorance). In this latter connection, he is led to examine the whole question of the derivation of pleasure from the essentially painful events of tragedy. Rejecting the explanation of Alexander of Aphrodisias— that we rejoice at seeing ourselves exempt from the sufferings of others—he proposes rather that the "pleasure" of tragedy results from the fact that it is natural and human for men to feel pity:

> We feel sorrow by reason of the heart, which contracts beyond its normal state at the spectacle of piteous events, but in fact we do [at the same time] feel joy because it is human and natural to have pity. . . . Since therefore it is human and natural for men to feel pity, it will also be pleasurable and most delightful. . . . For pleasure and pain concern different objects; pain to be sure will be a pleasure to the heart, since it is a movement contrary to nature precisely towards that which is constrictive; whereas pleasure is a movement of the soul towards that which is natural for it and born with it.[98]

The pleasure associated with tragedy will thus come from certain kinds of plots, from certain parts of plot, such as recognition and reversal, and from the emotion of the spectator involved in his sympathy for the fate of the personages. Maggi takes this last kind as an answer to Plato's condemnation of the "voluptuous" aspects of poetry. Assuming from the start that the *Poetics* is a defence of the art against such attackers as Plato (cf. p. 37), Maggi asserts that the cultivation of "voluptas" is a fault of certain poets, not of the art as a whole, and that Aristotle specifically answers the objection by assigning to the pleasure of tragedy an intermediary role in the achievement of purgation and hence of moral utility (cf. "Prolegomena," p. 13).

Pleasure may come, as well, from other features of the poetic work. From the chorus, which provides the possibility of relaxation ("cantus choricos ad relaxandos animos audientium," p. 149). From the episodes, which are to be considered as ornaments to the plot rather than parts of it. As a matter of fact, it is because of the desirability of such ornamentation that

---

97 *Ibid.*, p. 134: "sicut imago rei magis eum delectat, qui rem prius nouit, quàm qui non nouit: quoniam qui rem nouit addiscit, & ratiocinatur: ita quoque qui prius eam actionem nouit, quam imitatur poeta, discet. & ratiocinabitur hanc actionis illius imitationem existere. . . . is utique, qui actionem nouit, cuius fabula imitatio est, maiori uoluptate afficietur, quàm is, qui eam ignorat, quoniam de ea ratiocinari non potest. . . . nam fabulae, quae magis delectant (caeteris paribus) aliis minus gratis sunt praeferendae."

98 *Ibid.*, pp. 112–13: "Dolemus itaque ratione cordis, quod à specie rei miserabilis uisae ultra naturam suam constringitur: laetamur uerò, quoniam humanum, ac naturale est miserere. . . . Cum igitur misereri humanum, atque hominibus naturale sit, uoluptuosum etiam erit, ac periucundum. . . . Voluptas itaque ac dolor diuersa respicient. nempe dolor gratia cordis erit; quoniam motus praeter naturam est, ad id scilicet, quod angustum est: uoluptas uerò erit animae motus ad id, quod ei naturale connatumúque est."

the poet—as compared with the historian—chooses a relatively meager plot, which he then proceeds to magnify and adorn with episodes.

Since it is the poet's aim to amplify the action and to strengthen it with every ornament, he will adorn the subject most wonderfully with digressions, and he will separate and rejoin one thing with another in such a way that the action, through the episodes, will appear more beautiful and clear. For it is not the poet's end to express the action in an arid and meager way, but to place it before our eyes in an ornate and elegant fashion.[99]

The total conception of the plot—brief in tragedy so as to avoid satiety ("satietatem parit," p. 257), extensive and varied in epic for the pleasures of magnificence ("ad oblectandum varietate accommodatur," *ibid.*)—is itself determined by this end of pleasure. Furthermore, in different genres the plot will end differently—happily or unhappily, similarly for all persons or diversely for the wicked and the good—in order to create different kinds of pleasure: "It is necessary that the pleasures [voluptates] which come from tragedy and from comedy should be different and appropriate to each separately."[100]

Finally, but by no means as a minor cause, pleasure will be provided by the language, the diction of poetry. One of the principal differences between poetry and rhetoric, aside from the fact that the latter persuades while the former imitates, resides in the superior ornateness of poetic diction ("poeticam elocutionem esse pluribus illustratam ornatibus," p. 237). One of the main consequences of this demand for ornament is Maggi's insistence that verse is essential for poetry. Since this runs counter to certain clear affirmations of Aristotle, Maggi is obliged to develop a complicated theory of the ingredients of true poetry. He distinguishes three degrees: (1) the true poets, who both imitate and use verse; (2) those who imitate without using verse, and who are also poets; (3) those who do not imitate, and who are called poets merely because they write in verse (p. 57). Of these, the first are the only real poets. Maggi reinforces his theory by declaring that meter is one of the natural causes of poetry (with the assertion that "cùm . . . Poetica ex imitatione & carmine constet," p. 74), and that the phrase "suauem sermonem" in the definition of tragedy is again a demand for the inclusion of verse: "From this text one concludes most clearly that verse is an intimate part of poetry and included in its very nature."[101] Such a conception almost necessarily brings with it the further theory of the appropriateness of verse to subject matter. Each genre will be written in a form of verse light

---

[99] *Ibid.*, p. 251: "cùm poetae propositum sit, quam amplectitur actionem, omnibus eam ornamentis fulcire, egressionibus uerò mirum in modum rem exornet, & rem à re disterminet ac seiungat, iure factum fuit, ut actio episodiorum interuentu pulchrior, ac perspicua magis appareret. non enim poetae munus est aridè ac ieiunè res exprimere, sed ornatè, ac expolitè eas ob oculos ponere."

[100] *Ibid.*, p. 160: "uoluptates, quae ex Tragoedia, Comoediaque proueniunt, diuersas, ac unicuique accommodatas esse oportere."

[101] *Ibid.*, p. 100: "Ex hoc contextu colligitur manifestissimè, carmen esse quid intimum Poesi, in eiusque natura claudi."

or grave according to the nature of the materials treated. In the epic, for example, "the verse must be proportioned to the subject treated, and since heroic matter is grave and magnificent, it requires a meter by its very nature stable and ample."[102]

Having adapted so much of Aristotle's *Poetics* to his own notion of the dual end of poetry, instruction and pleasure, Maggi is inevitably led to develop in considerable detail two further matters, the nature of the audience and the demands which it will make on the poetic work. For Maggi, as later for Castelvetro and other theorists, the poet's audience is not the few but the many, not the élite but the "vulgus." He states so specifically with respect to tragedy:

Add to this the fact that tragedy is performed for the pleasure of the populace and of the crowd in general, and moreover that such a multitude does not know that sort of plots. For even if they may be known to one or another of the spectators, because the poet has in mind the people in general he will pay no attention to those few, even if he might give them great pleasure.[103]

In a curious way, this "generality" of the audience becomes a basis and a justification for the "universality" of poetic subject matters.

The argument runs thus: If the poem is to have its proper effect, especially as concerns moral instruction, it must be accepted as "true" by its public. Maggi insists upon this on several occasions, and most particularly in connection with Aristotle's remarks on the "impossible probable" (*Poetics* 1460a27):

. . . because his end is to teach proper conduct, whether this be introduced into men's souls by false narratives or by true narratives, his desire is fulfilled. But since a poet cannot accomplish this purpose unless he obtains the belief of his audience, he follows common opinion in this respect.[104]

Acceptability to common opinion, rather than "truth," is the criterion; for the poet may invent things which are essentially "untrue," provided that he does so in a way which makes them seem probable:

. . . falsehoods of the kind that are told by the poets, insofar as they are received in the opinion of the crowd, are held to be verisimilar and true. Therefore if a certain poet were to imagine something new, it will be said to be acceptable to the opinion of the crowd. Since the crowd admits as true similar things and things

102 *Ibid.*, p. 259: "carmen debere rei, qua de agit, proportione respondere. & quoniam heroica materia grauis est, & magnifica, iccirco ex sui natura stabile, atque amplum metrum requirit."
103 *Ibid.*, p. 135: "Adde, Tragoediam in populi, ac uniuersae turbae gratiam fieri, eiusmodi autem multitudinem fabulas eas ignorare. Quanquam igitur unus, aut alter eas optime calleat, poeta tamen populum respiciens, de paucis illis, etiam si magis eos delectet, non erit sollicitus."
104 *Ibid.*, pp. 267–68: "quòd ei propositus finis est, bonos mores instituere: quos siue ueris, siue falsis narrationibus in hominum animos inducat, uoti compos efficitur. sed quoniam id poeta praestare non posset, nisi ei fides adhiberetur, iccirco uulgi opinionem sequitur."

which for a long time cannot have been done, then it will accept as true what is but recently invented.[105]

It is thus not necessary that the materials of poetry be "true"; the only requirement is that they be acceptable as such to the common crowd which constitutes the audience of poetry.

Moreover, acceptability may result from various qualities of the materials: (1) From what is "natural." Maggi seems to mean by this those aspects of any action or character which seem to be inherently present in it: "To express things according to verisimilitude and necessity is nothing else but to express them taking into account the nature of those things. Nature indeed is a kind of universal."[106] (2) From what is "verisimilar." This does not always correspond to everyday truth, but it is nevertheless acceptable to the mind. "For many things happen customarily to mortals which are not verisimilar, and every day the senses experience what is contrary to the reason. And still this is reasonable; for since verisimilar things are not necessary, and may come to pass in some other way, it is verisimilar that certain things should happen contrary to verisimilitude."[107] The distinction here is apparently between what reason would demand as constituting normal action and what actually does happen in life—between the "rational" and the "probable."

(3) From what is "necessary." This is an internal factor; according to necessity, certain circumstances of action and of character, presented among the *données* of the poem, must lead to expected consequences in the later development of the work. "This is called the necessary *ex positione*, when one thing being posited, it is necessary that another should follow."[108] But even here a criterion of universality is present, since the consequences "most usually" resulting from the given circumstances are the ones to be used by the poet: "He warns us that we should contrive those conclusions for our plots which follow upon the actions necessarily or for the most part, not those which follow rarely."[109] These somewhat vague distinctions are clarified slightly by the example which Maggi develops. He assumes that

---

105 *Ibid.*, p. 131: "id genus falsa, quae à poetis dicuntur, quoniam in uulgi opinionem sunt recepta, pro uerisimilibus ac ueris habentur. Quòd si quispiam poeta nouum aliquid finxerit, id etiam uulgi opinione receptum dicetur. quoniam si similia & quae longè minus fieri nequeunt, tanquam uera uulgus, admittit: etiam quòd recenter est fictum, tanquam uerum recipiet."

106 *Ibid.*, p. 131: "Exprimere autem res secundum uerisimile & necessarium, nil aliud est, quàm eas exprimere habita ratione illarum rerum naturae. natura uero quidpiam uniuersale est."

107 *Ibid.*, p. 201: "nam multa mortalibus usu uenire non uerisimilia, praetérque rationem omnem in dies ipso sensu comprobatur. idque rationi consonum est. nam cùm uerisimilia necessaria non sint, aliter quoque fieri possunt: igitur uerisimile est, praeter uerisimile nonnulla fieri."

108 *Ibid.*, p. 126: "Id autem ex positione necessarium dicitur, cùm uno posito, necesse est aliud sequi."

109 *Ibid.*, p. 121: "nos admonet, ut fines eos fabulis faciamus, qui aut necessariò, aut in plurimis, non autem qui rarò huiuscemodi actiones sequuntur."

we are given certain characters for a father and a son and a proposal for the marriage of the son; certain reactions will have to follow:

We say that such-and-such actions must necessarily follow; for these things which preceded having been established, the poet must see to it that others come about. Otherwise the comedy will not be properly made. . . . if the father proposes a marriage to the son, it is verisimilar that the son should consult a household servant or a friend concerning the way to avoid his father's proposal. If, therefore, the poet introduces the son consulting a servant, he will then rest on verisimilitude. . . . But if the poet introduces a father, who, in order to bring about the marriage of his son, tries to use the offices of the servant, it will immediately result from necessity that the servant should, for example, necessarily deceive the old man.[110]

But the distinction is still not very useful; at best we see in verisimilitude an approximation of what traditionally happens, in necessity a development from stated *données*. (4) Acceptability depends in part on conformity to the reason. Maggi's commentary is a fairly close paraphrase of *Poetics* 1460a27: "He enjoins that in the total composition of the poem there should be no part which might seem to contain anything absurd or contrary to reason, but that all should be made with a maximum of reason. This is the same as if one were to say that everything should present itself as verisimilar or necessary."[111]

(5) Most clearly and most convincingly, acceptability by the audience will result from the presentation of type characters according to the requirements of decorum. The relationships are fairly simple here: if the audience is to derive from the poem the proper utility in the form of moral instruction, it must be willing to accept as "true" the characters presented, and it will do so if these correspond to recognizable, traditional types. The people presented in poems are exemplars of good behavior: "Since they [the poets] imitate the best people, when they present their behavior they must make exemplars of it, that is, they must express the highest probity of character in those persons whom they undertake to imitate."[112] Maggi relates the παράδειγμα of his text at this point (1454b13) to Platonic Ideas of character, "Nature considered in itself, and not as manifested in this or

110 *Ibid.*, p. 126: "id sanè dicitur esse necessarium, ut sequatur. constitutis enim illis, quae praecessere, poeta id efficere cogitur: alioqui Comoedia probe facta non esset. . . . ut pater filium de nuptiis tentarit, uerisimile sanè est, filium consulere seruum domesticum, uel amicum, quomodo possit patrem eludere. Si igitur poeta filium consulentem seruum inducit, ueri-simili tunc innititur. . . . Quòd si pater inducatur à poeta, qui ut ad exitum nuptias filii deducat, serui opera uti uelit, hoc statim exoritur necessarium, ut scilicet seruus necessariò senem eludat."
111 *Ibid.*, p. 267: "Praecipit quoque, ut in uniuersa Poesis constitutione nulla sit pars, quae aliquid absurdi, ac praeter rationem continere uideatur, sed omnia summa cum ratione facta sint. hoc autem perinde est, ac si diceret omnia praeseferre uerisimile, aut necessarium oportere."
112 *Ibid.*, p. 175: "quoniam praestantiores imitantur cùm mores exprimunt, debent exemplar facere, hoc est in moribus summum probitatis illius personae, quam sibi imitandam proponunt, exprimere."

that particular object" ("natura secundum se consyderata, non ut in hoc, aut in illo reperta," p. 175). These Ideas, however, rapidly become the collections of traits habitually associated with certain types; a servant will be gluttonous and will think only of food; his master will think only of honor and glory (p. 115); a king must do and say those things proper to a king (this constitutes another kind of "universal"). "The meaning is that the poet deals with the universal. For if he introduces a king as saying or doing a given thing, what he says or does must belong to those things which are usually or necessarily attributed to kings."[113] In a still more general way, a man must not have feminine characteristics (Ulysses should not be presented as weeping), and a woman should not show virility of soul (example, Menalippe, p. 171).

Because the ends of pleasure and utility must be achieved in an essentially common audience, and because this audience provides certain criteria of universality, generality, and truth, the activity of the poet in writing the poem comes to be fairly well restricted. The great field of liberty remaining open to him is that of ornamentation through a variety of episodes added to the plot and through ornateness of diction—in a word, the field of the pleasurable elements of the poem. Contrariwise, the plot itself must be one known or acceptable to the audience, the characters must conform to traditional types, and the needs of instruction must be kept constantly in mind. At times, as in the case of necessity, an internal and structural criterion results from these demands of the audience; but more frequently the criterion is imposed from without. Thus Aristotle's remark on the usual time of tragedies is transformed into a rule for both tragedy and comedy ("unico solis circuitu, uel paulò longiore exprimere *debet*," p. 93) on the basis of audience demands for credibility.

Since then tragedy and comedy . . . attempt to approach as close to truth as is possible, if we were to hear things done in the space of a month presented in two or at most three hours, in which time certainly a tragedy or a comedy is acted, the thing will absolutely produce an effect of incredibility. [Thus if a messenger is sent to Egypt and he returns within an hour:] what spectator indeed, if after one hour this man returning here is seen introduced on the stage, will not whistle and hiss the actor off the stage and judge that an action lacking in all reason was contrived by the poet?[114]

113 *Ibid.*, p. 131: "sensus est, poetam circa uniuersale uersari. quoniam si regem quidpiam, aut dicentem, aut facientem inducit, debet id ex iis esse, quae regibus ut plurimum, aut necessariò contingunt." Cf. p. 272: "Poeticae enim scopus est rerum ideas . . . exprimere. ueluti si regem exprimit, regis ideam referre, quantumq̀ue in rege desyderari posset, id omne illi tribuere. . . . rectitudo enim Poeticae est, quae fieri possunt sectari in quacunque re, qua de agit. quòd si ab eo quod fieri potest recedat, à propria sua rectitudine recedet."
114 *Ibid.*, p. 94: "Cùm igitur Tragoedia atque Comoedia, . . . propè ueritatem quoad fieri potest, accedere conentur, si res gestas mensis unius spatio, duabus, tribusúe ad summum horis, quanto nimirum tempore Tragoedia uel Comoedia agitur, factas audiremus, res prorsus incredibilis efficeretur. . . . quis profectò spectator, si post horam hunc redeuntem illinc, in scenam introduci uideat, non exibilabit, explodetq́ue, & rem à poeta omni prorsus ratione carentem, factam praedicabit?"

The system of ideas encountered in Maggi's *Explanationes* shows two complementary tendencies: first, a wish to explain Aristotle's text in terms of its own order and its own intellectual structure; second, an almost inevitable tendency, at this period in criticism, to complete the explanations by reference to other documents and, hence, to give the whole of the theory a decidedly un-Aristotelian cast. With respect to the first, Maggi is at some points more successful than his predecessors. The interpretation of "necessity" may again be cited as an example, since it conceives of the term as designating an internal relationship in the poem, just as Aristotle does. Again, when he assigns the various qualitative parts of tragedy to object, manner, and means, Maggi makes a more correct distribution than Robortello had done: for the means, "melopoeia, dictio"; for the manner, "apparatus"; and for the object, "fabula, mores, sententia" (p. 104). He shows here a much keener apprehension of Aristotle's basic meaning.

On the other hand, he cannot resist the temptation of other ideas current in the thinking of his time. So, as we have seen, he ascribes to the *Poetics* the ends of utility and pleasure, with which he was familiar through Horace, and cites Horace as his authority. From Horace also, and from the long rhetorical tradition associated with him, he borrows the theory of decorum and of the types of character and human behavior. The same rhetorical tradition provides him with a number of remarks on tragedy and comedy which come ultimately from Donatus and Diomedes rather than from Aristotle. Thus the moral distinction between "better" and "worse" forms of character is turned into the familiar social distinction between "reges & heroas" for tragedy and "uiles, moriones, seruos, ancillas, scurras" for comedy (p. 64)—otherwise stated as "uenerandis, atque potentibus" against "humiliores, puta rusticos, seruos, id genus homines" (p. 77)—and the two genres are further differentiated by the unhappy ending of the one and the happy ending of the other (p. 160). Indeed, when Maggi presents a summary of Aristotle's ideas on the qualitative parts of tragedy, he collects a group of terms which might easily be found so assembled in any standard rhetorical treatise: "Dicitur igitur ab Apparatu, uel regia, uel sumptuosa: à Dictione, metrica, elegans, ornata: à Musica, suauis: à Sententia, euidens, grauis, affectibus referta: à Moribus, morata: à Fabula simplex, uel perplexa" (p. 101). The conventional association between poetry and verse leads to the long argument justifying verse that we have already noted. Homer is praised for his proper handling of invention, disposition, and elocution (p. 79). The answers to critical objections are organized around the old "res-verba" distinction. And so on for other rhetorical ideas. From Plato, Maggi derives the conception of character types as παραδείγματα or Ideas, the theory that poetry may serve in the education of youth (he does not fail to explain away Plato's banishment of the poets), certain ideas on the nature of beauty (p. 123).

This is not, however, pure eclecticism. Maggi does have a theory, centering about his notion of the dual end of poetry; and most of what he offers in the way of interpretation tends to orient the *Poetics* in the direction of that theory. He is not led, however, to a total deformation of Aristotle's text, and in at least a few respects his commentary presents the best light on the *Poetics* to date.

In the same volume as the *Explanationes*, Maggi published two other works, his commentary on Horace's *Ars poetica*, called an *Interpretatio* (treated in Chapter IV, pp. 119–22), and his treatise on comedy entitled *De ridiculis*. I have already pointed out that his main interest in the first of these was the establishment of parallels between the texts of Aristotle and of Horace and that his array of such parallels was the most extensive yet prepared. Naturally, some of the theory elaborated in the *Explanationes* is repeated in connection with Horace's text, which Maggi regards as stemming directly from Aristotle. The "res-verba" distinction figures prominently, and Maggi tends—perhaps more than in the *Explanationes*—to identify "res" with elements of plot and with the end of utility and "verba" with diction and with the end of pleasure. Hence, the ends distinguished are also the same and they are similarly related to the various parts of the poem. The essence of character is once more found in decorum. Maggi again interprets necessity as an interconnection of the parts of the poem, and he regards as digressions all those episodes which are meant to give a variety and magnitude to the plot. All these matters are stated more succinctly —and with less philosophical justification—in the *Interpretatio*, which must be considered essentially as an appendix to the commentary on Aristotle.

A similar judgment may be made on the little treatise *De ridiculis* which, in the 1550 volume, comes between the *Explanationes* and the *Interpretatio*. Maggi means it as a supplement to Aristotle, for he notes that comedy requires two elements, a certain kind of plot structure and the ingredient of the ridiculous, and that Aristotle treats only the first of these. Before offering his own theory of the ridiculous, Maggi examines those of Cicero, Quintilian, and Pontano. His own theory, unfortunately, is very unsatisfactory, since it does little more than collect the passages from the *Poetics* which refer to the ridiculous and attempt to explain them by citation of other authors. Thus, after quoting Aristotle's definition, "peccatum, & turpitudinem ac deformitatem quandam esse sine dolore," he points out that the ridiculous may be of the body or of the mind, and he cites examples of the latter from Cicero. A third kind may come from circumstances ("ex rebus"). Plato's *Sophist* is consulted for a definition of "turpitudo." Various examples of the ridiculous springing from "res" and from "verba" (note the persistence of the distinction) are cited. Maggi sees the need in comedy for the same kind of admiration which he had required in tragedy and in the epic, achieved in part through variety and novelty. "Risus à turpitudine citra dolorem cum admiratione dependet," he insists (p. 307).

And as for the various genres treated by Horace, comedy as well requires the gifts of nature and the skills of art on the part of the poet.

GIACOPO GRIFOLI (1550)

The middle year of the century was also marked by the publication of another extensive commentary on Horace, Giacopo Grifoli's *In artem poeticam Horatii interpretatio* (see above, Chapter IV, pp. 122–27). Unlike Maggi, Grifoli is primarily interested in the text of Horace, and he uses Aristotle as a means of clarifying and expounding the *Ars poetica*. In a few places—and a considerable number of Aristotelian passages are used by Grifoli—his remarks and applications constitute an interpretation of the *Poetics* and are hence of interest to us here. Generally, there is the tacit assumption that Aristotle and Horace are not only talking about the same things, but that they are saying the same things. Hence, it is just as proper to read Aristotle in terms of Horace as it is to read Horace in terms of Aristotle. In the second place, since Grifoli seeks in Aristotle primarily a means of discovering the order and sense of Horace's text, he is most attracted by those sections of the *Poetics* which present neat categories and numerical divisions. Two such sets of distinctions appeal to him most forcefully: the six qualitative parts of tragedy and the four requisites of character. Not only does he see in the six parts the essential ordering principle of Horace's text, but he interprets them in the light of that text. Grifoli takes "fabula" to be the whole of the work, and to consist of two elements, "res" or the materials and "verba" or the instruments of expression; the other five parts are then distributed thus:

All these things indeed happen on the stage, whose external presentation does not in any way clash with the materials themselves. Rather is it a kind of instrument, since imitation occurs also in the spectacle and the melody, according to the laws of plot. In truth, diction and character and thought are the materials [res] which are proposed for imitation. Now if we *read* a tragedy, spectacle and melody are no more parts of it than delivery and memory in the orations of the ancients when they are read.[115]

We should note here the crossing of imitation with the "res-verba" distinction, the parallelism with rhetoric, and the strange division which puts melody (considered as actual singing) among the "means" and diction among the objects of imitation (this is the same division suggested by Robortello). The same division is repeated, perhaps more clearly, in connection with lines 319–22 of the *Ars poetica*:

We said from the beginning that there are six parts of tragedy: plot, character,

115 *Interpretatio* (1550), p. 82: "omnia enim haec versantur in scena, quae quidem speciem habet à rebus nihil abhorrentem: est enim velut instrumentum, nam ex apparatu, & melodia sunt imitationes vt fabulae ratio postulat. dictio verò, mores sententiae res sunt, quae ad imitandum sunt propositae. verum si tragoediam ipsam legamus, non magis apparatus & melodia sunt illius partes, quàm in antiquorum orationibus, quae leguntur, actio, & memoria."

diction, thought, spectacle, and melody. Of these the last two are as it were the instruments of imitation, the middle three are the subjects proposed for imitation. The first, then, contains in itself the manner of imitation, since the plot is a composition of all the things in a tragedy and since the imitation must be made in that manner and in that order in which the plot itself has been composed.[116]

As for the four requisites of character, Grifoli begins by generalizing them into a set of criteria for language ("verba"): ". . . without language, indeed, it will be difficult to determine whether the moral quality, the appropriateness, the similarity, and the constancy of character have been observed or not."[117] The very terms used indicate Grifoli's understanding of the requisites: "officium," "proprietas," "similitudo," "constantia." He explains them in full at several later points. Commenting on lines 114–18, he cites Aristotle's Greek terms and then proceeds to define them:

> This means that we should see to it in the first place that there should be characters which are good, then that they should be appropriate, then that they should be similar, finally that they should be uniform. These qualities are different from one another, for—to speak briefly—the first concerns the moral quality, the second appropriateness, the third similarity, and the fourth constancy of character. In the first, nobody errs except through wickedness; in the second, he errs who goes counter to his own dignity; in the third, he who departs from his proper kind; in the fourth, he who does not remain constant to himself.[118]

Grifoli thus reduces Aristotle's four requisites to (1) a rule of moral goodness, (2) a rule of decorum, (3) a rule of conformity to type or tradition, and (4) a rule of self-consistency. By so doing, he brings them into harmony with his interpretation of the *Ars poetica*. Moreover (pp. 42–43), he especially assigns the fourth quality, τὸ ὁμαλόν, to characters newly invented by the poet, since the nature of traditional characters will have been well established by earlier poets.

These matters of character and the rules associated with them belong to the "res" of poetry; they affect "verba," however, since they are the

---

116 *Ibid.*, p. 97: "Diximus à principio sex esse partes tragoediae fabulam, morem, dictionem, sententiam, apparatum & melodiam: quarum postremae duae sunt tanquam instrumenta imitationis, tres mediae subiectae sunt, & propositae ad imitandum. Prima verò continet in se modum, cum fabula sit compositio rerum omnium in tragoedia, & eo modo, & ordine imitandum sit, quo composita sit ipsa fabula."

117 *Ibid.*, p. 12: "officium porro, proprietas, similitudo, constantia morum seruetur nec ne, sine oratione vix constare poterit."

118 *Ibid.*, p. 39: "id est vt videamus, vt mores primum sint, qui boni sunt, tum qui consentanei, deinde qui similes, postremo qui aequabiles. differunt enim haec inter se, quod ut paucis agamus, primum genus est officij, secundum est decori, tertium similitudinis, quartum constantiae: in primo nemo peccat sine scelere, in secundo qui contra dignitatem suam, in tertio qui à suo genere discrepat, in quarto qui sibi non constat." Cf. p. 40: "τὸ δὲ ἁρμόττον postulat, vt naturae quisque suae consentiat: vt vir, quae sunt viri: mulier, quę sunt mulieris agat. τὸ ὅμοιον δὲ, vt non discrepet à sua conditione, vt seruus seruo non sit dissimilis, neque mercator mercatori. τὸ δὲ ὁμαλὸν vt in omni actione sibi constet."

material for which words are used. Grifoli justifies his insistence on the primacy of "res" by quoting Aristotle to the effect that the poet is a poet through imitation, not through the use of verse. But imitation becomes invention and this in turn becomes plot and character, which are more important than verse because they make a greater appeal to the audience. The whole nature of the transformation of Aristotle's thesis is seen in such a passage as the following: "The poet indeed, as Aristotle himself affirms, insofar as he imitates is a poet of actions, not of meters. Therefore, an excellent invention—and a structure of the plot in which character is diligently observed—holds the audience much more than would verses poor in content and presented on the stage with great solemnity."[119] Moreover, Grifoli sets up a single criterion of Nature for these subject matters, making probability and necessity dependent upon it: "Tragedy cannot support anything which is not appropriate to Nature. And even though it is not the function of the writer of tragedy or of comedy, as Aristotle says, to relate those things which actually happened, nevertheless they must relate them in a way that they might probably or necessarily have come about."[120] Nevertheless, the Nature to be imitated is not a commonplace and visible one; just as Maggi does, Grifoli refers to the Ideas of Plato as the norms which the poet—like the painter—should attempt to represent. Once again, Plato and Aristotle are brought together as providing a single object for the poet's study, the Form or the Idea; and Grifoli also indicates a parallelism between them on the purgation of such passions as pity and fear (pp. 96, 37).

There is, in all this, a kind of total interpretation of the *Poetics*. It becomes a text in which poetry appears as a "natural" object, seeking on the one hand to present the perfection of the highest forms in Nature, the Ideas, and on the other hand to conform to a more commonplace Nature as represented by the traditional practice of the poets and by the laws of decorum. That is, an ideal of beauty is proposed to the poet, but it is accompanied by an ideal of verisimilitude, which prevents any wild flights of the imagination. Everything that he does is reduced to rule and precept.

In 1550, also, Lodovico Dolce published his *Osservationi nella volgar lingua*, of which the first three books are exclusively linguistic and grammatical; the fourth treats of poetry only by way of introducing a lengthy discussion of prosodic questions relevant to the various genres. In the treatment of poetry, one might say that Dolce begins at each step with Aristotle but rapidly moves in the direction of the current rhetorical

---

119 *Ibid.*, p. 98: "Poëta enim (vt idem testatur Arist.) quatenus fingit, rerum est poëta, non metrorum. Inuentio igitur insignis, & fabulę constitutio, in qua ratio morum diligens habeatur, magis capit spectatores, quàm versus inopes rerum & magno cum pondere missi in scenam."

120 *Ibid.*, p. 15: "Atqui Tragoedia ferre nihil potest, quod non sit naturae consentaneum. Et quamuis tragici non sit, vt inquit Aristoteles, nec item comici ea dicere, quę gesta fuerint ea tamen illi dicenda sunt omnino, quae fieri potuisse verisimile sit, aut etiam necessarium."

theory. So for the definition of the art: "That Poetry, a heavenly gift, is nothing else but imitation is taught to us by Aristotle in a single and proper definition; for the function of the poet is to imitate the actions of men; and the end is to delight the soul of the reader under pleasant veils of moral and useful inventions."[121] Here the "slipping" is from imitation to invention and from a notion of imitation as the end to the more readily comprehensible pleasure and utility. So also for the idea that imitation, not verse, makes the poet:

But let nobody think that all those who write in verse are worthy of this title of Poet. For in addition to the variety of knowledge which this faculty requires, it needs invention, order, artifice, and words; which things—each one by itself and all together—are so difficult and so necessary that they are acquired only with great sweat, and if one of them is lacking, the dignity of the Poet is in large part decreased. But none is more so than imitation, which does more to make him a poet than artifice and words. For it is possible for any mediocre mind to find some noble invention; but to display it with those ornaments and beauties which are proper to the function of the Poet is given to few; and these few are the good Poets.[122]

In this passage, Dolce reduces all his ideas to terms of invention, disposition, and elocution (slightly disguised); and although he seems at first to mean that imitation-invention is the most important ingredient of poetry, he ends up by saying that imitation-elocution is really the crux of poetic excellence. In later passages, he emphasizes increasingly the fact that the real art of the poet lies in his handling of words and of verse; and Dolce is thus justified in devoting his book on poetry to such matters of composition.

In 1550, finally, Jacob Mantino's translation of Averroës' commentary on the *Poetics* was added to the two already available, those of Hermannus Alemanus and of Abram de Balmes. Like the latter, Mantino's was based on the Hebrew translation of Todros Todrosi (1337). Both translations from the Hebrew were to enjoy some circulation during the coming decade, Balmes' being reprinted in 1560 and Mantino's in 1562. The significance of the shift away from Hermannus and toward the new versions lies in the fact that the latter tend to omit most of Averroës' materials based upon Arabic

---

121 *Osservationi* (1550), p. 87v: "La Poetica, celeste dono, niente altro essere, che imitatione, c'è con propria e una difinitione insegnato da Aristotele: percioche l'ufficio del Poeta è di imitare le attioni de gli huomini: e il fine sotto leggiadri ueli di morali & utili inuentioni dilettar l'animo di chi legge."

122 *Ibid.*, pp. 87v–88: "Ma non pensi alcuno, che tutti coloro, che uersi scriuono, siano degni di questo titolo di Poeta: percioche oltre la diuersità delle dottrine, che questa faculta ricerca, ella ha mestiero di inuentione, di ordine, d'artificio, e di parole: lequali cose, ciascuna da per se, e tutte insieme, sono tanto difficili e necessarie, che non senza molti sudori s'acquistano: e mancandone l'una, è scemata in gran parte la dignità del Poeta: ma niuna è oltre alla imitatione, che maggiormente lo faccia Poeta di quello che fa l'artificio e le parole. Percioche ad ogni mediocre intelletto è conceduto il poter trouare alcuna nobile inuentione; ma quella spiegar con quegli ornamenti e bellezze, che all'ufficio del Poeta conuengono, è dato a pochi: e questi pochi sono i buoni Poeti."

literature, and the work seems therefore to be closer to its distant Greek original.[123]

CONCLUSIONS

The first half-century—or slightly more—of the history of Aristotle's *Poetics* in modern times is thus a period of tremendous progress in the knowledge and the interpretation of the text. We must constantly bear in mind the fact that as the end of the fifteenth century approached, only a few humanists knew the text at all, having read or consulted the available manuscripts. A somewhat larger group of scholars might have read Averroës' commentary, extant in a number of manuscripts and printed in 1481; but from it they would have obtained a very imperfect idea indeed of the content and orientations of Aristotle's theory. Beginning with Valla's translation into Latin in 1498, a whole series of documents soon became available to the Renaissance reader: the Greek text of 1508, the reprint of Valla and Averroës in 1515, Erasmus' Greek text of 1532, Pazzi's text and translation of 1536 (reprinted 1537 and 1538), and finally Segni's translation into Italian of 1549. With these documents at hand, it was soon possible to undertake the serious study and exegesis of the *Poetics*; especially after the appearance of the Pazzi volume does activity of this kind seem to increase, as witnessed by the public lectures of Lombardi-Maggi beginning in 1541 and by the first two of the great published commentaries, Robortello's in 1548 and Lombardi-Maggi's in 1550.

The first result of this diffusion of texts and commentaries was the increasing number of passing references to the *Poetics* in works of many kinds. It became necessary to consider and cite the dicta of Aristotle on the art of poetry, just as it had long been necessary to reckon with the opinions of Horace, of Plato, and of such rhetoricians as Cicero |and Quintilian. Such consideration of Aristotle was usually brief and fragmentary, tending to limit itself to a few passages which the writers found eminently useful; from it we can derive no general statements about the way in which the *Poetics* was read in this early period. The second result of the diffusion was undoubtedly more significant: Aristotle came to be considered an authority on poetry equal in prestige to Horace. If such "equality" was possible, it was because the cumulative wisdom of the time found in Aristotle's *Poetics* essentially the same theory of the poetic art which it had come to attribute to Horace's *Ars poetica*. Thus, in the period which we have been studying, we discover the growth of a habit and of a procedure, that of establishing parallelism between the two texts. This was done at first for separate passages, in the passing references of which I have spoken; it was

[123] For a modern edition of the Mantino translation, see Friedrich Heidenhain, *Jahrbücher für class. Philologie*, Supplementband XVII, 1889, pp. 354–82. See also the discussion by Jaroslav Tkač, "Über den arabischen Kommentar des Averroes zur Poetik des Aristoteles," *Wiener Studien: Zeitschrift für klassische Philologie*, XXIV (1902), 70–98.

later done, and in a constantly more elaborate way, for the totality of the two texts. Naturally, it appears in its most complete form in the successive commentaries on Horace: Parrasio's of 1531, Pedemonte's of 1546, Maggi's and Grifoli's of 1550. In all these, the procedure is to search in Aristotle for clues to the meaning of Horace, whether they be to single lines or passages or whether they be to the general organization of the epistle.

I have studied, in earlier chapters, the effects of this search on the understanding and the elucidation of the *Ars poetica*. As has already been obvious in the present chapter, the partnership with Horace was not without its dangers for Aristotle. For it meant that many readers—specialists in Horace and others—came to the *Poetics* determined to find in it the doctrine which they had long associated with the *Ars poetica*. This they did without difficulty, for there are sufficient similarities of subject matter and enough accidental likeness of detail to facilitate the discovery of "parallels." It should be said, in exculpation of those who yielded too easily to the temptation, that the temptation was very great indeed. The first half of the Cinquecento was deeply concerned with all problems of poetic theory, and the discovery of a new treatise by so revered a writer as Aristotle was bound to elicit much attention. Naturally, the first impulse was to find the known in the unknown, to read Horace into Aristotle. On the other hand, this impulse prevented or delayed for a long time the discovery of what Aristotle was actually doing and saying in the *Poetics*. Even the "great commentaries" on the *Poetics* published during this period (and later as well), directly concerned though they were with the text and its exegesis, show the results of this tendency. They may not specifically seek identity of theory; they may even attempt to read Aristotle for his own sake. But, nevertheless, the old habits of mind and the old accepted ideas are there, and what is produced in the way of theory is much closer to the standard Horatian rhetorical tradition than to any distinctively Aristotelian analysis.

CHAPTER TEN. THE TRADITION OF ARISTOTLE'S
POETICS: II. THE FIRST THEORETICAL APPLICATIONS

I N THE YEARS following the middle of the century, the tendencies
observed in the first half are continued and accelerated. This is generally
true in all branches of criticism, for as the documents accumulated, as
more new materials became available, as the partisan spirit grew, there
was a multiplication of discussions, of pamphlets, of treatises. If one were
to prepare a statistical curve of Cinquecento criticism, on a purely quantitative basis, one would note a sharp rise in the years following 1550. The
writings relative to Aristotle's *Poetics* would provide no exception. There
is no "great commentary" until 1560, when Vettori's appeared. Nevertheless, the editions of and commentaries on Horace, short independent
treatises on a variety of poetic matters, and miscellaneous materials
become constantly more numerous, and with them the Aristotelian tradition expands and develops.

CONTI AND SPERONI (CA. 1550)

I shall discuss first three documents which are not dated and which I
place roughly at the middle of the century for want of better evidence. The
first two are by Antonio Maria de' Conti (called Maioragio), who died in
1555. His very brief *De arte poetica* appeared as "Oratio XXIV" in the
collected *Orationes et praefationes* of 1582. The oration, as I have pointed
out (Chapter VII, p. 267), is primarily devoted to a defence of poetry and a
rejection of Plato's ban; but it uses the *Poetics* as a part of this defence and
—more important still—derives from it statements about imitation and
about the history of poetry. Conti refers to *Poetics* 1447b1 to confirm his
defence of poetry: "Aristotle himself intimates that poetry is the same
thing as wisdom and philosophy, when he numbers among poems the most
learned and most elegant dialogues of Plato, in which are treated the most
important matters both divine and human."[1] In a later passage, Conti
collapses together a brief early history of poetry. He begins with "imitation" as a "cause" or "origin" (coupling it immediately with meter), proceeds to the division of poetry into species (comic, tragic, epic, melic, and
dithyrambic), concludes with the differentiation between poets of high
moral character and those of low moral character and between their
divergent products.[2] Conti thus chooses some of the ideas from the *Poetics*

---

[1] In *Orationes et praefationes* (1582), p. 145: "quod autem poetica sit eadem quae sapientia
seu philosophia, innuit etiam Aristoteles, qui doctissimos & elegantissimos Platonis dialogos,
in quibus maximae quaeque res & diuinae, & humanae tractantur, inter poemata con-
numerat."

[2] *Ibid.*, p. 146*v*. The full text reads thus: "Aristoteles poesim ex imitatione primo natam
fuisse censet, quoniam imitandi studium sit ab ineunte aetate cunctis hominibus innatum,
qua in re à belluis homo differat. qui igitur ad metrum natura procliues fuerunt, eos ait
poesim primo protulisse, ex quodam imperito rudique principio, atque ex subita ac fortuita

most frequently cited by his predecessors, those which might throw light on the beginnings of the art and its earliest history.

Conti returns to Aristotle and imitation in his *In tres Aristotelis libros, de arte rhetorica explanationes*, published posthumously in 1572. There are a few scattered passages in the commentary on Book III that are of interest for poetic theory. In the first one, Conti argues for the antiquity of poetry and for the fact that it preceded oratory, basing his argument on Aristotle's statement that it is an imitation; this he proceeds to support by citing the *Cratylus* to the effect that words themselves are imitations and that imitation is natural to man. Then, again, the brief history of poetry:

> Whence from the imitation contained in words were born many arts, such as the epic, which expresses in hexametric verse the wars and the deeds of kings, generals, and leaders; and the histrionic art, which includes comedies, tragedies, satires, and mimes, and which represents through the medium of words the characters and the lives of men of every age, class, and condition.[3]

As he had done previously, Conti assimilates Aristotle to Plato; but when he speaks of the literary types he moves in the direction of the medieval definitions and of a theory of literature based above all on decorum. In later passages he states that one of the important differences between oratory and poetry lies in the ornate language of the latter (this is because poetry comes from a divine furor, p. 381A); he repeats his assertion that imitation is the essence of poetry (" & Horatius egregium poetam uocat doctum imitatorem," p. 406A); and he distinguishes those poets who please only on the stage from those who also please when they are read (p. 415B). In all these statements about imitation, Conti shows no understanding of the peculiar meaning given the term in the *Poetics*; he chooses rather a Platonic meaning and one that can be applied to passages separated from the whole of the text.

Sperone Speroni is also concerned with the problem of imitation in his *Discorso dell'arte, della natura, e di Dio*, but in a much broader and more philosophical way. It is difficult to say whether his doctrine is primarily Platonic or Aristotelian, as elements from both seem to be intermingled. Speroni's premiss is that art imitates Nature just as Nature imitates God

---

dictione. sed deinceps ex hac imitandi ratione, quasi in plura membra diuisa poesis multas in species abijt, atque ita poetę dicti sunt alij Comici, alij Tragici, alij Epici, alij Melici, alij Dithyrambici, alij alio nomine. nam pro cuiusque natura & moribus imitandi studium proferebatur. honestiores enim poetae res egregias & praestantes, & laudabiles actiones sibi canendas proponebant. itaque in regum & deorum conuiuijs uirorum excellentium laudes, resque praeclarè gestas heroicis carminibus concinebant, ut ad eas imitandas iuuenes excitarentur, & alacriores redderentur. qui uerò abiectiori essent animo. uiles etiam & humiles actiones canere coeperunt, atque hunc & illum irridere, salibusque inuadere. unde postea comoedia atque Satyra nata est."

[3] *De arte rhetorica* (1572), p. 347A: "quare à uocis imitatione natae sunt artes plurimae, ut epica, quae regum, imperatorum, ducum res gestas & bella carminibus exametris exprimit, & histrionica, quae comoedias, tragoedias, Satyras, mimos amplectitur, & cuiuslibet aetatis, ordinis, conditionis hominum mores & uitas uoce repraesentat."

in operation. He seeks the conditions under which art imitates Nature and finds, first, that art always seeks to resemble Nature as much as possible. But complete resemblance is not possible since the object of art is not the real object.

And this comes about because the subject upon which art operates is an actually true thing; therefore no substantial form can be introduced into it, but everything that is added to it is an accident which resembles the substance as much as it possibly can. . . . Art therefore has for subject the being in action, so to speak, and insofar as it is in action and must remain in action, just as it was before, after the form which the artifex will have impressed upon it.[4]

Consideration of the triple relationship among God, Nature, and art leads Speroni to inquire into their relative nobility and to decide that it follows the order in which they have been named:

Thus since art imitates Nature, but is not Nature herself—for the painting is not a man, but his image and imitation—but imitates her, since it operates in a subject which was made by Nature and in this subject art and Nature are joined, the latter making it, the former presupposing it to be already made; and Nature is more noble than art, since the less noble always seeks to resemble the more noble; the same is to be said about Nature and God.[5]

Speroni is clearly inquiring into a metaphysical and aesthetic problem when he examines imitation, a problem of a far different order than that posed by Conti. The text of the *Poetics*, if it is present at all, is present only in a remote way.

Imitation is once again the subject of discussion in the *Lettione decima*, published by Giovanni Battista Gelli in 1551 in a volume entitled *Tutte le lettioni*. But in Gelli we encounter the same kind of discussion as in Conti. The lecture is devoted to the arts of painting and poetry (it ends with praise for Giotto, Dante, and Petrarch), both of which are arts of imitation. Gelli cites Aristotle (*Poetics* 1448b4) on the reasons why imitation is pleasurable to man, adding to these arguments the notion (from *Rhetoric* III.1) that man imitates by speaking words and by using his voice, "since words are nothing but an imitation of concepts, and since the voice serves for nothing better than for demonstrating the passions of the soul."[6] He

---

4 *Discorso* (1740 ed.), III, 365: "E ciò avviene, perche il subietto, intorno al quale si adopra l'arte, è cosa vera in effetto; però in essa non può introdursi alcuna forma sustanziale, ma ogni cosa, che vi si aggiunge, è accidente, che alla sostanza, in quanto puote, si rassimiglia. . . . L'arte adunque ha per subietto lo ente in atto, per dir così, ed in quanto egli è in atto, ed in atto de' rimanere, come era prima, dopo la forma, che vi arà impressa l'artefice."

5 *Ibid.*, p. 366: "Dunque come l'arte imita la natura, ma non è essa natura; perciocchè la dipintura non è uomo, ma sua imagine ed imitazione; ma imita lei, perciocchè ella opera in un subietto, il quale è fatto dalla natura, ed in esso si aggiungono arte e natura, questa facendolo, quella già fatto presupponendolo; e la natura è dell'arte più nobile; perciocchè sempre al più nobile cerca il men nobile di assimigliarsi: così è da dire della natura e di Dio."

6 *Tutte le lettioni* (1551), p. 358: "Non essendo altro i nomi, che imitation de concetti; ne seruendo la voce a cosa alcuna meglio che a dimostrare gli affetti de l'animo."

then returns to direct translation or paraphrase of Aristotle on the pleasure derived from learning and on the pleasure derived from contemplating representations of essentially unpleasant objects.

Two years later, in 1553, Giason Denores published his *In epistolam Q. Horatij Flacci de arte poetica* (see above, Chapter IV, pp. 128–29). Denores is less interested than were some of his predecessors in the mere listing of parallels between Horace and Aristotle, although there is a small number of cross references in the course of his commentary. Thus, for example, he cites Aristotle on the resemblance of the iamb to common speech (p. 34), on the proper size of animals (p. 69v), on artistic and nonartistic errors (p. 125v). But there are several major questions of poetic theory for which he recurrently appeals to the *Poetics*, and they are the same ones that were troubling his contemporaries. One was the problem of imitation. We see a first reflection of it in his statement that invention is the "soul" of poetry: "de inuentione, hoc est de ipsa quasi anima, & constitutione poematis" (p. 5v). We see it reflected again, in what may seem to be an extraordinary way, in his discussion of figurative language. Denores wonders why metaphors and similes are pleasurable and discovers that it is because they are imitations which teach; Aristotle's whole argument is then brought to bear on the question:

I should hold then that metaphors produce in all men greater admiration and pleasure than do proper terms for the same reason for which we judge that poetry delights more than history, that is, because poetry imitates. Imitation, moreover, affects and delights all men equally. . . . For, since all receive learning easily, by means of imitation and resemblance, of matters from the knowledge of which they then derive the greatest pleasure, it is certain that metaphors are most pleasurable, not only because they generate knowledge in us via resemblance and imitation, but also because they produce pleasure in us out of that knowledge.[7]

These ideas are not basically different from those expressed by certain writers studied in the last chapter, notably Maggi, Grifoli, and Dolce. The passage just quoted introduces the second of the problems for which Denores consulted Aristotle, that of the relationship between poetry and history. He sees one difference in the distinction between things as they actually happened and things as they might happen ("Non, ut gestae sunt, sed ut geri potuerunt," p. 32), and quotes Aristotle in corroboration. Another distinction is between truth and what may be added to truth—provided that verisimilitude be observed: "For it is not simply that the historian differs from the poet only because one uses verse and the other

---

[7] *In epistolam* (1553), pp. 23–23v: "Ego autem uel ea potissimum ratione existimarem translata maiorem afferre apud omnes admirationem, & uoluptatem, quàm propria, qua etiam magis oblectare poesis historia iudicatur, hoc est, quia imitatur. imitatio autem omnes pariter afficit, atque delectat. . . . Quare cum ex imitatione, & similitudine facile omnes disciplinas percipiant, ex quarum postea cognitione summam capiant iucunditatem: certum est translationes esse gratissimas: tum quia per similitudinem, & imitationem pariunt in nobis cognitionem; tum quia ex cognitione pariunt uoluptatem."

prose, but also in this, that the historian adds nothing to the truth and takes nothing away from it; the poet adds and removes many things, but what he presents is verisimilar."[8] Aristotle is again cited on history and on verisimilitude.

Denores' third problem is that of the end of tragedy and the purgation of pity and fear. It is significant that his problem arises in connection with *Ars poetica* 333, in the gloss on "prodesse." He quotes the definition and then comments:

> For, since the end of tragedy relates to softening and as it were purifying the passions of the soul, because it aims, apparently, at inculcation of the right way of living and [thus] at a practical effect, we must say that it is not only proper for the poet to express things relevant to living, but that this is his main object. . . . On this subject, when Aristotle says that it is proper to poets to treat above all those matters of a universal kind, so that they will present them not such as events were on a particular occasion but as they should have been, does he not perhaps openly say that this end should be assigned to them—to embrace in their poems the various species and the various functions of daily life? This is nothing other than to express things relevant to living.[9]

The transition is easy, for Denores, from the purgation of pity and fear, to moral usefulness, to the instruction in proper living which constitutes for him the end of poetry. Aristotle is readily reduced to Horace. As for the achievement of this end, the question arises partially in connection with Horace's remarks on off-stage action (ll. 179 ff.). Denores identifies those actions which should not be shown on the stage with those which bring pity and fear to the spectator, which are incredible or miraculous, or which are wicked (p. 64). He summarizes: "Tria igitur sunt tantummodo referenda, non autem agenda in scaena, quae terribilia sunt, & miserabilia; quae fieri non possunt; & quae obscaena sunt" (p. 64v). Rather should pity and terror be produced by the composition of the plot (*Poetics* 1453b1). This consideration leads Denores to conclude that the epic is superior to tragedy as a genre since it requires less in the way of external machinery and appeals to the ear rather than to the eye, and that those tragedies are most perfect which most closely approach the epic form (pp. 65–67).

What is most striking, perhaps, about Denores' use of Aristotle is his wresting of the texts from their original reference and their application to widely different materials. This is evidence not only of a lack of respect

---

8 *Ibid.*, p. 56v: "Neque enim solum differt à poeta historicus carmine, uel soluta oratione; sed quòd alter ueritati nihil addat, ac nihil detrahat; alter plura addat, ac plura detrahat, uerisimilia tamen."

9 *Ibid.*, pp. 117–17v: "Quare cum finis tragoediae referatur ad leniendos, & quasi expiandos animorum motus, quod ad recte degendae uitae institutionem, & utilitatem uidetur spectare non solum dicendum est poetis etiam esse proprium idonea uitae afferre, sed hoc maxime. . . . Ad haec cum Aristoteles in rebus uniuersi generis maxime uersari proprium poetis esse dicat, ut non quales aliqui fuerint, sed quales esse debuerint ab his referantur, nonne aperte indicat munus hoc esse illis assignatum, ut uarias in eorum poematis ciuilis uitae species, & officia complectantur, quod nihil quicquam esse putandum est, quàm idonea uitae dicere."

for the text of the *Poetics*, but of a complete indifference to careful thinking
or to proper distinctions. A modicum of similarity—a word—is enough for
Denores, not only to establish parallels but to set up elaborate arguments
and to reach definite conclusions.

BENEDETTO VARCHI (1553-54)

Benedetto Varchi's *Lezzioni della poetica*, delivered before the Accademia
Fiorentina in late 1553 and early 1554 and published in 1590, constitutes a
kind of art of poetry. The philosophical derivation of the lectures is complex, but I think it no exaggeration to say that the principal basis of
organization is found in the *Poetics*. In a preliminary lecture, Varchi concerns himself first with the classification of the art (see Chapter I, pp. 7-9)
and then proceeds to such general matters as the end of poetry. Varchi sees
the end of poetry as that shared by all arts and sciences, "to make man
perfect and happy" ("fare l'huomo perfetto, e felice," p. 574); but it
differs from others in that it uses imitation to achieve this end. We find,
therefore, a distinction between "end" and "function": "The end of the
poet is thus to make the human soul perfect and happy, and his function is
to imitate, that is to invent and represent, things which render men good
and virtuous, and consequently happy."[10] The particular objects imitated
by the poet are the actions, passions, and moral characters of men (p. 574),
and hence the poet must be thoroughly versed in ethics and in politics.
Although we begin here with an Aristotelian principle of imitation, it is
rapidly reduced from the role of "end" to that of "function"; and since
the "end" becomes one of moral improvement, the art is soon identified as
a branch of moral and civil philosophy. Nevertheless, it obtains its efficacy
from the power of imitation over men's souls (cf. Aristotle), and imitation
becomes an essential part of the definition of poetry which Varchi compounds: "Poetics is a faculty which teaches in what ways any action,
passion, or character should be imitated; by means of rhythm, discourse,
and harmony, all together or separately, in order to remove men from
vice and incite them to the virtues, in order that they may achieve their
perfection and beatitude."[11] Again the framework of the definition is vaguely
Aristotelian; but its content has been so changed as to make of the art of
poetry an entirely different one from what Aristotle intended.

Even the meaning of "imitation" becomes fluid, and in his gloss on the
above definition Varchi soon gives it another sense. Speaking of art and
genius, he declares that genius would not be sufficient for poets "unless

[10] *Lezzioni* (1590 ed.), p. 576: "è adunque il fine del Poeta far perfetta, e felice l'anima
humana, e l'vffizio suo imitare, cioè fingere, e rappresentare cose che rendono gl' huomini
buoni, & virtuosi, e per conseguente felici."
[11] *Ibid.*, p. 578: "La poetica è vna facultà, la quale insegna in quai modi si debbe imitare
qualunche azzione, affetto, e costume; con numero, sermone, & armonia, mescolatamente,
o di per se, per rimuouere gli huomini da' vizij, & accendergli alle virtù. affine, che conseguano
la perfezzione, e beatitudine loro."

they were to make use of imitation, that is, in their own compositions to go about imitating the compositions of good poets, for in that way it would be like using art; indeed, nothing can be done of greater usefulness than to consider the works of the perfect masters."[12] This is imitation in the meaning so frequently given to it in the Renaissance. Nevertheless, its use in this way does not prevent Varchi, almost immediately, from speaking of the kinds of imitation as narrative, dramatic, and mixed (pp. 579–80), of object, manner, and means, and from quoting Aristotle to the effect that imitation, not verse, makes the poet. One sees, in his distinction of the kinds of poets, the same ideas that Maggi had expressed: the poet may be considered "most narrowly" as one who practises both imitation and verse, "properly" as one who uses imitation only, without verse, and "commonly" as one who uses verse only, without imitation. Varchi himself believes that verse is a necessary ingredient of poetry, and he so construes *Poetics* 1448*b*20 as to make it an argument for his position. In these multifarious ideas on imitation, we note that Varchi, like so many of his contemporaries, had clearly in mind the content of the *Poetics*; but he freely combined it with the content of other texts and other traditions, leading sometimes to patent contradictions.

The ideas presented thus far are contained in the introductory lecture to Varchi's series. In the *Lezzione prima*, of December, 1553, he returns again to the discussion of imitation, this time taking as a point of departure *Poetics* 1448*a*1 (on the objects of imitation) in order to develop his theory that the poet imitates three objects: actions, passions, characters (pp. 602–3). The *Lezzione seconda*, devoted specifically to epic poetry, raises the question of the relationship between imitation and object, and the answer is found in the demand for the necessary, the possible, or the probable. Here again the utilitarian end directs the poets in their choices:

They are not to write of human actions in the way in which they were done, but in that way in which it was either possible, or verisimilar, or necessary that they might be done. . . . Poets must not consider in the main how things are done by men, but how they should be done, although many things are permitted to them even outside nature; and even outside the reasonable or the verisimilar, so that they may bring not only greater utility for this mortal life but also greater delight and admiration to men.[13]

These general considerations lead to judgments on Homer and Vergil—

---

[12] *Ibid.*, p. 579: "se già non si seruissero dell'imitazione, cioè andassero ne' componimenti loro imitando i componimenti de' poeti buoni, perche in tal caso è come si seruissero dell'arte, anzi non si può far cosa di maggiore vtilità, che andar considerando l'opere de' maestri perfetti."

[13] *Ibid.*, pp. 616–17: "non hanno à scriuere l'azzioni humane in quel modo, che fatte furono, ma in quel modo, nel quale era o possibile, o verisimile, o necessario, che si facessero. . . . i poeti non deono considerare per lo piu come le cose si fanno da gli huomini, ma come fare si douerebbono, ancora che si conceda loro molte cose, eziandio fuori della natura, non che del ragioneuole; o uerisimile, accioche possano arrecarne non solo piu vtilità alla vita mortale, ma ancora maggior diletto, e ammirazione a gli huomini."

judgments in which the theoretical positions are almost entirely absent. Homer is great because of his extensive knowledge and because of the good characters and customs he presents; Vergil is great because of his erudition, his eloquence, his gravity (pp. 617–20). The *Lezzione quarta*, on tragedy, quotes Aristotle's definition *in extenso* (reflecting still the imperfect state of text and translations in the transition to the last clause, "non per modo di narrazione, ma mediante la misericordia, e il terrore," p. 657). His commentary on the definition is of interest in many ways. He interprets "graue" as referring to great and illustrious persons—"Kings, Generals, and other such persons" (p. 658)—whose actions are grave, high, worthy, and of great moment, and as distinguishing tragedy from the low persons and ordinary actions of comedy. He gives to "perfetta" the function of distinguishing good tragedies from the earlier imperfect ones and from the action of the epic, which because of its many episodes is less perfect. To "purgazione," of course, he gives the meaning already noted; it indicates the end of tragedy, that of "leading men, through virtue, to their perfection and beatitude" (p. 660); but he takes the clause as referring not only to pity and fear but to all the passions. The commonplace lessons to be learned from tragedy are then retailed. The rest of the lecture treats the qualitative parts in the order listed by Aristotle. With respect to character, he does not fail to add to what he says by way of commentary a complete treatment of the various types and the characteristics which need to be attributed to them according to the laws of decorum.

It is thus apparent that, while Varchi organizes his set of lectures around the *Poetics* and follows its order in many of the detailed developments, he is constantly led away from the position of the *Poetics* by his knowledge of other texts. More frequently than not, he ends up with a theory whose real support would be found in Horace, not in Aristotle. It is for this reason that his lectures are significant. Unlike the official commentaries on Horace or on Aristotle, he is not seeking parallel passages, he is not looking for corroboration of one text by the other. Rather, he is attempting an original treatment whose basic source is Aristotle. But the weight of the established tradition is too heavy, and at every juncture it causes him to veer away in the direction of accepted positions.

Two letters to Varchi from Pietro Angeli, of November and December 1553, return to the question of imitation and challenge particularly Varchi's belief that the dialogue, as a form of imitation, was to be considered a genre of poetry.[14] Angeli believes that to hold this view is to interpret badly the passage in the *Poetics*. Rather, he says, the ends are so different as to separate the dialogue completely from poetic forms. He declares that Pietro Vettori is also of his opinion and that Vettori's interpretation of the *Poetics* will confirm their agreement.[15]

[14] Cf. Varchi, *Della Poetica* (1553), printed in the *Lezzioni* (1590 ed.), pp. 580–82[=81].
[15] In *Prose Fiorentine*, I, 66–68, 68–70.

Like Varchi's *Lezzioni*, Alessandro Lionardi's *Dialogi della inventione poetica* (1554) are an attempt at an original formulation of certain theories with respect to the art of poetry. But whereas Varchi begins with Aristotle, Lionardi begins with Horace and the rhetorical tradition. I have indicated in Chapter IV the kind of theory which he develops. His use of Aristotle is incidental and in most cases reflects the thinking of his contemporaries; it revolves largely about the question of imitation and verisimilitude. As for others, imitation for Lionardi is identified with the "invention" of the rhetorical scheme: "[The poet] is not a poet because of verse, but because of the plot, that is, because of the quality of the invention and imitation."[16] But the meaning of imitation is not clear, especially in such a sentence as this: "It is true that the most perfect poem is the one which is made up of fiction, of imitation, and of verse."[17] Nor is the meaning helped by this statement: ". . . all this [the poet's varied knowledge] belongs to the imitation, feigning, and description of persons, operations, and accidents."[18] The text of Aristotle is more accurately represented in the assertion that "the plot may stand without the characters, since it carries with it the actions,"[19] but this too is obscured by the discovery that "favola" means not only plot but also "fables" or even "falsehoods." This becomes apparent when, after distinguishing three kinds of "favole," Lionardo defines the second kind which is proper to poetry:

That "favola" which is called poetic imitation is a shadow and image of the truth, that is a narration and exposition of verisimilar things. And the tragic or heroic poem is made up of truth and of verisimilitude together. . . . And thus it comes about that the poet relates the causes of events sometimes by means of history, sometimes by means of fable. . . . just as it is vicious for the historian to tell fables or false things, so it is also improper for the poet to depart from imitation and from the use of fable.[20]

Yet, at a later point Lionardi does not hesitate to require of the poet—especially the tragic poet—the use of true materials:

[Tragedy] follows verisimilitude in all things . . . , tries to imitate some other past action described by somebody else. But that imitation will be best which is founded on the truth, and which will be decorated and enriched with many veri-

16 *Dialogi* (1554), p. 14: "non è poeta per li uersi, ma per la fauola, cioè per la qualità dell'inuentione & imitatione." See also p. 30: "essendo lo scriuere poeticamente null'altro, che imitare le attioni de gli huomini, se il Poeta non si servisse ancora di questa guisa di parlare, sarebbe imperfetta la inuentione, ò imitatione."
17 *Ibid.*, p. 15: "È il uero che piu perfetto poema è quello, che si fa di fintione, d'imitatione, & di uerso."
18 *Ibid.*, p. 23: "tutto ciò appartiene all'imitatione, fintione, & descrittione delle persone, dell'operationi & accidenti."
19 *Ibid.*, p. 58: "la fauola puo stare senza i costumi, apportando seco l'attioni."
20 *Ibid.*, p. 63: "Ombra & imagine di uero poi è quella fauola che è chiamata poetica imitatione, cioè narratione & ispositione di cose uerisimili. Et il poema Tragico & Eroico fassi di uero & di uerisimile insieme. . . . E perciò auiene che il poeta racconta le cause de gli auenimenti, hora per istoria, hora per fauola. . . . come è uitioso all'istorico il narrar fauole ò cose false, cosi ancora al poeta si disconuiene il partirsi dalla imitatione et dalla fauola."

similar things. . . . And just as art succeeds best when it is aided by nature, so the verisimilar is worth much more every time that it has for its assistance and basis the truth.[21]

Aristotle's preference for the impossible probable to the improbable possible is to be taken seriously as a guide to poetic composition (p. 67).

The sequence of ideas associated with imitation and verisimilitude, confused as it may sound, does have a certain consistency. Imitation is invention; as such, it is the invention of what is not true, of fables, and this is the proper domain of the poet. However, the poet will err if he "invents" too freely. The closer he stays to the truth—especially in such serious genres as tragedy and the epic—the better his work will be; and where the truth cannot be strictly observed (historical and actual truth), the verisimilar or the probable should take its place. Such a theory, of course, has only surface similarities with the doctrine of the *Poetics*, and although the latter is frequently cited, its sense is just as frequently distorted and obscured.

GIRALDI AND PIGNA (1554)

A whole group of important documents belonging to the year 1554 is concerned with the controversy between Giovambattista Giraldi Cintio and Giovanni Battista Pigna over the romance form. Pigna's treatise, *I romanzi*, was published first; but Giraldi Cintio answered by publishing his own, in which he declared that Pigna, who had been his pupil, had seen Giraldi's treatise many years before and had plagiarized its ideas. In fact, Giraldi dates his treatise, *Discorso intorno al comporre dei romanzi*, "MDXLIX adi XXIX di Aprile" and the accompanying *Discorso intorno al comporre delle Comedie, et delle tragedie* "In Ferrara a di XX. di Aprile. MDXLIII." (A companion treatise, *Lettera ovvero discorso sopra il comporre le satire atte alle scene* is also dated 1554, although it was not published until the nineteenth century.) There followed letters and denials, accusations and counteraccusations.[22] Without prejudice to either side of the case, I shall treat Giraldi's discourses first because of the earlier dates which they bear—even though these may be falsified dates.

Giraldi's discourses belong to the history of Aristotle's *Poetics* in a rather curious way. Basically, they are modeled upon the *Poetics*, taking their essential points of departure in it; one of them, the discourse on tragedy (dated 1543), even claims to be the first exposition of Aristotle's text. Yet

[21] *Ibid.*, p. 64: "segue in tutto il uerisimile . . ., si sforza di imitare qualche altra d'altrui descritta & passata attione. Ma miglior fia quella imitatione, che sara fondata sopra il uero, & che fia ornata, & arricchita di molti uerisimili. . . . Et come l'arte riesce meglio quando ella è aiutata insieme dalla natura, così il uerisimile assai piu uale qualunque uolta ha per suo aiuto & fondamento il uero."

[22] A group of letters relevant to the controversy is to be found in a sixteen-page brochure, without date, title page, or other identifying information (British Museum, 11826.d.42). The third letter, by Giraldi, is dated 1554 and gives the reasons for publishing the others. The pamphlet was apparently prepared by Giraldi to substantiate his case against Pigna. See below, chap. xix, p. 957, on the dates of the first two letters.

the theory that Giraldi develops with respect to the romance finds itself at every point in overt opposition to Aristotle, and he presents it in three sections devoted respectively to invention, disposition, and elocution. Moreover, the conclusions which he reaches on such matters as the end of poetry are constantly those of the Horatian tradition. Perhaps the fundamental reason for a difference of theory between the *Poetics* and the *Discorso intorno al comporre dei romanzi* is Giraldi's contention that there are two kinds of poems, those in which there is a single unified action (the kind treated by Aristotle) and those in which there is a multiple action unaffected by requirements of unity (as exemplified by the romance). This conception leads to a rephrasing of the definition of plot—and incidentally of poetry—so as to account for the two types: "The plot should be based on one or several illustrious actions, which he [the poet] imitates appropriately by means of pleasant discourse in order to teach men honest living and good character, for this is the end that every good poet must seek";[23] and "since Heroic Poetry is nothing else than the imitation of illustrious actions, the subject of such compositions will be one or more illustrious actions of one or more famous and excellent men, which the poet will imitate by means of words accompanied by rhythm and by sweet language."[24]

The opposition to Aristotle inherent in these definitions is explicitly stated later in the text: "The laws given by Aristotle apply only to the forms of poetry which are of one single action; and . . . all poetic compositions which contain deeds of heroes are not included within the limits that Aristotle has set for poets who write poems having a single action."[25] Giraldi clearly means to separate the romance from the epic. Once he has done so, the way is clear for the establishment of a whole new set of requirements and conditions, and these are such as would not be admissible for the epic. The first is multiplicity of action: the poet may relate many actions of one hero—indeed, all those included in a long lifetime—without making the poem too long for the audience's pleasure (see p. 21). Rather, the multiplication of actions and ornaments will increase the variety of the poem and hence the delight of the audience: "This diversity of actions brings with it variety, which is the condiment of pleasure, and gives a wide field to the writer to add episodes, that is, enjoyable digressions, and to

23 *Discorso intorno al comporre dei romanzi* (1554), pp. 8–9: "la quale fauola uuole essere fondata soura una o piu attioni illustri, lequali egli imiti conueneuolmente con parlare soaue per insegnare a gli huomini l'honesta uita, et i buoni costumi, che questo si dee preporre per fine qualunque buono Poeta."

24 *Ibid.*, pp. 10–11: "perche la Poesia Heroica non è altro che imitatione delle attioni illustri, sarà il soggetto di tali componimenti una, o piu attioni illustri, di uno o di piu huomini chiari, & eccellenti, che con le uoci, accompagnate col numero, & con la dolcezza imiterà il Poeta."

25 *Ibid.*, p. 22: "le leggi date da Aristotile non si stendono, senon alle Poesie, che sono di una sola attione; & . . . tutte le compositioni Poetiche, che contengono fatti di Heroi, non sono chiuse tra i termini, c'ha messo Aristotile a Poeti, che scriuono Poema di una sola attione."

introduce therein events which can never happen (without some suspicion of blame) in poems which are made up of a single action."[26] Another way of obtaining multiplicity of action is by recounting many deeds of many heroes.

As a second general new requirement, the poet will add to the action or actions a large number of ornaments or "fillers" ("riempimenti"). Giraldi gives several lists of such ornaments: on page 26:

. . . amori, odij, pianti, risa, giuochi, cose graui, discordie, paci, bruttezze, bellezze, descrittioni di luochi, di tempi, di persone, fauole finte da se, & tolte da gliantichi, nauigationi, errori, mostri; improuisi auenimenti, morti, essequie, lamentationi, recognitioni, cose terribili & compassioneuoli, nozze, nascimenti, uittorie, triomphi, singolari battaglie, giostre, torneamenti, cataloghi, ordinanze, & altre simili cose.

On page 43: "amori, auenimenti improuisi, cortesie, giustitie, torti, liberalità, uitij, uirtù, offensioni, difese, inganni, insidie, fede, lealtà, fortezze, dapocaggini, speranze, timori, utili, danni"—and the passage continues: "and other such episodes or digressions which are most numerous and which can introduce, along with the linking together and the disposition of the work, so much variety and so much pleasure that the poem will become most lovely and most delightful."[27]

A third general requirement is that the poet interrupt the flow of the action as a means of obtaining suspense and of removing satiety ("leuare la satietà," p. 42) from the reader. Whereas the epic poet may tell his story in a continuous fashion, the writer of romances should break up the narrative as much as possible. The many digressions and disturbances of the natural order will be means to this end.

Any Aristotelian conception of "unity of action" has thus been completely rejected. But Giraldi realizes that some way must be discovered for holding the poem together, and he proposes two devices: verisimilitude and decorum. There is also a general principle of order or disposition, stated in the rhetorical terms of proposition, invocation, and narration. By verisimilitude Giraldi means credibility, by disposition he means a believable order of events; the two are closely linked in such a statement as the following:

And because poetry is all imitation, and alone imitation and verse make the poet, and because this imitation as far as the subject of the poem is concerned relates to the actions, the poet must be extremely careful that the actions which he takes for subject and foundation of the structure of his work carry with them,

---

26 *Ibid.*, p. 25: "Però che porta questa diuersità delle attioni con esso lei la uarietà, laquale è il condimento del diletto, & si da largo campo allo Scrittore di fare Episodij, cio è digressioni grate, & introdurui auenimenti, che non possono mai auenire (senon con qualche sospetto di biasimo) nelle Poesie, che sono di una sola attione."

27 *Ibid.*, p. 43: "& altri tali Episodij, o digressioni, iquali sono piu che molti, & possono indurre insieme con la legatura, & con la dispositione dell'opera tanta uarietà, & tanto diletto, che diuerrà il Poema uaghissimo, & piaceuolissimo."

both in the disposition and in the other parts, so much verisimilitude that it will not be incredible, and that one part of the work will depend from another in such wise that one will come after the other either necessarily or probably.[28]

The same principles of disposition and verisimilitude apply to the digressions as well as to the main subject of the poem:

And in these digressions the poet must be very watchful to treat them in such a way that one will depend from the other, and that they will be well joined with the parts of the subject which he has undertaken to relate with a continuous thread and a continuous chain, and that they will bear verisimilitude with them (insofar as this is possible in poetic fictions). For if these digressions were made in any other way, the poem would become faulty and displeasing, whereas it delights and pleases when they are seen to come about in a way that they appear to be born along with the subject itself.[29]

There are, of course, no specific recommendations for the achievement of this order, this linking, this over-all disposition. The principle is no more precise than the Horatian dogma which it obviously reflects in such a statement as this: "... giving with these [digressions] to all the parts the proper size and the appropriate ornament, with such proportion that out of it all will come a regulated and well-composed body."[30]

As for the principle of verisimilitude, it will also be related to that of decorum. Just as proper order leads to a kind of credibility, so a proper handling of characters and situations produces another kind of credibility. The problem is complicated, however, by the fact that the poet must relate what is untrue and incredible in order to please his audience; the marvelous is an essential ingredient of his work. Giraldi resolves the difficulty in several ways: first, by a distinction between major subject and digressions —the major subject must be true, the digressions may be false (pp. 50–51); second, by admitting that certain false stories and episodes have come to be accepted as verisimilar through their exploitation by earlier poets (p. 55). Verisimilitude is thus essentially a matter of action or plot; decorum may also be a matter of plot, although primarily it concerns character and thought. Giraldi's description is very broad: "In these things as in the

---

28 *Ibid.*, p. 54: "Et perche la Poesia è tutta imitatione, & solo la imitatione, & il uerso fa il Poeta, & perche essa imitatione quanto al soggetto del Poema, è intorno alle attioni, deue hauere grandissimo riguardo il Poeta, che le attioni, ch'egli si piglia per soggetto, & per fondamento della fabrica della opera sua, portino con esso loro, & nella dispositione, & nelle altre parti tanto del uerisimile, che non rimanga priua di fede, & che una parte cosi dall'altra dipenda, che o necessariamente, o uerisimilmente l'una uenga dietro l'altra."

29 *Ibid.*, p. 25: "Et deue in queste digressioni esser molto aueduto il Poeta in trattarle di modo, che una dipenda dall'altra, & siano bene aggiunte con le parti della materia, che si ha preso a dire con continuo filo & con continua catena, & che portino con esso loro il uerisimile (quanto s'appertiene alle fittioni, Poetiche . . .). Perche, se queste digressioni si facessero altrimenti, diuerrebbe il Poema uitioso & increscieuole, come diletta, & piace quando elle si ueggono nascere tali, che paiano nate con la cosa istessa."

30 *Ibid.*, p. 26: "dando con esse a tutte le parti la debita misura, & il diceuole ornamento, con tale proportione, che se ne ueda riuscire un regolato, & ben composto corpo."

others, the poet must always keep an eye on decorum, which is nothing else but what is proper to places, times, and persons. . . . decorum is merely the grace and the appropriateness of things, and it must be considered not so much with respect to actions as to the speeches and the responses that men make to one another."[31] As such, decorum once again approaches the general Horatian principle of appropriateness. Insofar as it relates to the depiction of character, decorum has a peculiarly normative function. It shows people not as they are, but as they should be; and it provides object lessons by displaying the necessary accompaniments, fair or foul, of virtue and vice:

The poet, imitating illustrious actions in his fictions and visualizing them not as they are but as they should be, and accompanying appropriately the things which vice carries with it with honor and pity (for this belongs no less to the heroic poet than to the tragic poet, when the matter justifies it), purges our souls of similar passions and arouses us to virtue, as we see in the definition that Aristotle gives of tragedy. And thus it is that, in addition to verisimilitude, what is praiseworthy and what is honest must be considered everywhere in the work.[32]

In this passage, two Aristotelian ideas take on new forms. The notion that the poet, unlike the historian, relates such events as *could* happen (*Poetics* 1451b5) is transformed here into an ethical requirement that the poet present what *should* be. And the effect of purgation indicated in the last clause of the definition of tragedy becomes a statement of an ethical end—to make us better by demonstrating the results of vice.

The principle of appropriateness involved in decorum raises the question —a constant one in all theories of decorum—as to the criterion by which appropriateness is judged. Usually, the expectations or the demands of a given audience are involved. Here, Giraldi does not hesitate: the audience is a contemporary one, and Italian. The poet follows the customs and manners of his own time, not those of his model or even those of the period which he is depicting; Vergil's practice may serve as an example here (p. 58). If this is the general rule for poets, it is because they wish to satisfy a contemporary audience, "in order to profit and delight at the same time, satisfying the men of that age in which they are writing."[33] As a matter of

31 *Ibid.*, p. 63: "Et in queste cose, come nell'altre, il Poeta dee sempre hauere l'occhio al decoro; ilquale non è altro, che quello, che conuiene a i luochi, a i tempi, alle persone. . . . il decoro non [è] altro, che la gratia & il conueneuole delle cose; & si dee egli considerare, non pur quanto alle attioni, ma quanto al parlare, & al rispondere, che fanno gli huomini tra loro."

32 *Ibid.*, p. 59: "imitando il Poeta, col suo fingere, le attioni illustri, & proponendolesi non quali sono, ma quali esser si debbono, & accompagnando conueneuolemente le cose, che portano con esso loro il uitio, con l'horribile & col miserabile (che ciò non è meno del Poeta Heroica, che sia del Tragico quando la materia il richiede) purga gli animi nostri da simili passioni, & ci desta alla uirtù, come si uede nella difinitione, che da Aristotile della Tragedia. Et di qui è, che oltre il uerisimile è da considerare in tutta l'opera il lodeuole, & l'honesto."

33 *Ibid.*, p. 58: "per giouare, & dilettare insieme, sodisfacendo a gli huomini di quella età, nella quale scriuono."

fact, the whole difference between Aristotle and the theory of the romance may be stated as a difference of time: Aristotle's *Poetics* is based on the practice of the poets of his time and of earlier centuries; Giraldi's is similarly derived. The rules for the romance

... should be left within those limits established by those poets who have, among us, given authority and reputation to that kind of poetry. And just as the Greeks and the Latins have derived the art of which they have written from their poets, so also we must derive it from our own, and follow that form which the best writers of romances have given us.[34]

The poet who writes a romance is thus independent of the rules of Aristotle and of Horace and needs to consider only the practices of his predecessors in the same genre—all of whom are relatively recent. The audience will thus prefer a form which is close to it, within which it will recognize its own mores. Moreover, that form will achieve its ends with special efficacy if it uses as one of its means the religion of its contemporary audience. Giraldi praises Boiardo and Ariosto for having added the embellishment of Christianity,

... which arouses a marvelous attention, and causes the reader to be joyous over the fortunate adventures of those who are of the same faith as he is, and to be sorrowful when the contrary happens, and to be always in a state of suspense, waiting for his God to provide relief from the difficulties and the harms which they suffer at the hands of the unfaithful. This is a thing which is also well adapted to the terrible and the pitiful, which two things are not the least in importance in compositions of this kind.[35]

It is difficult to reconcile, with such statements as these, another affirmation of Giraldi: the subject of a poem "must be pleasing in every age, not only to the learned but to all men of that language in which he writes."[36]

In most of the passages previously cited, there are indications of the ends which Giraldi proposes for the poet. These are Horace's ends of utility and pleasure, assimilated to Aristotle's text by the same method that we have seen elsewhere in Giraldi. There is a kind of division of labor among the parts of the poem for the service of these ends; Giraldi states it overtly in his discussion of elocution: "just as utility belongs to the sententiae and to

---

[34] *Ibid.*, p. 45: "ma si deuono lasciare tra que termini, tra quali gli hanno posti, chi ha data tra noi auttorità, & riputatione a queste specie di Poesia. & come i Greci et i Latini hanno tratta l'arte, dellaquale hanno scritto, da i loro Poeti, cosi la debbiamo anco noi trarre da i nostri, & attenersi a quella forma che i migliori Poeti de i Romanzi ci hanno data."

[35] *Ibid.*, p. 11: "laqual cosa desta marauigliosa attentione, & fa che si allegri il lettore de i felici auenimenti di coloro, che sono della medesima fede, della quale egli è: & si dolga de i contrarij, & stia tuttauia con l'animo sospeso in aspettando che dal suo Iddio uenga prouisione alle inconuenienze, & a i danni, che patiscono da gli infedeli. Cosa ch'è anco molto atta al terribile & al compassioneuole, lequali due cose non tengono le ultime parti in simili compositioni."

[36] *Ibid.*, p. 15: "si che possa piacere in ogni tempo, non pure a i dotti, ma a tutti gli huomini di quella fauella, nella quale egli scriue."

the things which are treated, so the words—in addition to the expression of the idea—entirely serve pleasure and delightfulness."[37] In terms of Aristotle's qualitative parts, utility would come from plot, character, and thought, and pleasure from diction; in terms of the rhetorical division of invention, disposition, and elocution (around which he organizes his own treatise), utility would derive essentially from the first two, pleasure from the third. The latter division really involves also the "res-verba" distinction. Following the total line of relationships, we see that the utilitarian end of moral improvement is achieved by the arousing of pity and fear (even in the romance), which depends for its effectiveness on verisimilitude of subject, upon proper disposition of the parts, and upon a general credibility springing from the audience's sense of contemporaneity, of decorum, and of common interest with the heroes of the poem. Pleasure, on the other hand, depends upon the total composition of the work, upon the marvelous introduced by means of digressions, upon variety resulting from innumerable ornaments, and above all upon diction. (Giraldi regards elocution as the "soul" of the poem; see pp. 160–61.) On the whole, the treatise presents the physiognomy of a work which begins with certain Aristotelian conceptions of the tragedy and the epic, which it treats in the mould of the habitual rhetorical distinctions, and from which it derives conclusions which are primarily Horatian.

At the beginning of his *Discorso intorno al comporre delle comedie, e delle tragedie*, also published in 1554, Giraldi Cintio declares that this is the first vernacular treatise on comedy and tragedy and that thus far "nobody has set his hand to the exposition of Aristotle's *Poetics*."[38] If the date which he gives at the end, "In Ferrara a di XX. di Aprile. MDXLIII," is authentic, his claims are justified, at least insofar as published treatises are concerned. In any case, the treatise follows very closely the order of the *Poetics* and in many places is little more than a translation. The commentary, however, as we should now expect, at every point finds in Aristotle Giraldi's own theory of poetry, which becomes clear as the exposition develops. It consists of little more than an application of the principles already discovered for the romance to the genres of tragedy and comedy. Giraldi's remarks may be divided into two categories, those which concern the common characteristics of the two dramatic genres and those which concern their differences. Of the common characteristics, the most salient is the end pursued; it is in all cases to teach good behavior; "both of them intend to introduce good manners" ("amendue intendono ad introdurre buoni costumi," p. 207). The means to the achievement of this end are two, the imitation of an action and language accompanied by verse; both of these contribute to the moving of the audience's passions, and from this

[37] *Ibid.*, p. 99: "come il giouare è delle sentenze, et delle cose, che si trattano; cosi le uoci oltre l'espressione del concetto sono tutte del piacere et della uaghezza."

[38] *Discorso intorno al comporre delle comedie, et delle tragedie* (1554), p. 202: "ne alcuno habbia ancora messo mano ad isporre la Poetica di Aristotile."

movement comes the desired moral effect, "since the power of moving the tragic passions rests only upon imitation, which is not separated from verisimilitude, and since things in themselves cannot move the passions without words which are properly put together and in verse."[39] Apparently the moral lesson results from the sympathy which the audience feels for the actors, from its sense of justice and humanity. But it also results from a reasoning process by which the spectator puts himself in the place, let us say, of Oedipus the King: "The spectator, in an unexpressed deduction, says to himself: 'If this man, because of a fault committed unwittingly, has suffered as much harm as I now see, what would happen to me if I were perchance to commit this sin voluntarily?' and this thought makes him abstain from mistakes."[40]

Imitation is thus equivalent to verisimilitude, and this in turn is necessary for the participation of the audience in the action. The poet presents actions as they should be, as they appropriately come about, as they are in their most general and universal aspects (p. 226). But—as in the case of the romance—verisimilitude is local and contemporaneous: "In selecting or forming for himself these illustrious actions, ... it is good to have them such as the times in which the poet is writing desire them according to verisimilitude, with respect to the reasonings, the mores, the decorum, and the other circumstances relative to persons."[41] The difference between verisimilitude and necessity is indicated by an example: a courageous man will *necessarily* seek to avenge an insult, and it is *verisimilar* (or *probable*) that he will do so in an open, rather than in an underhanded, fashion (p. 245). The ultimate appeal in matters of verisimilitude is to what would happen in everyday life:

Be sure that the persons introduced on the stage do not do or say in public things that they would not verisimilarly do or say at home; and be certain that what would be blameworthy if done at home, according to honest rules of action, is also blameworthy on the stage. ... things must be composed and represented as they would be done according to verisimilitude.[42]

Giraldi, of course, thinks of verisimilitude and decorum in terms of an

[39] *Ibid.*, p. 209: "non stando la forza del mouere gli affetti Tragici, senon su la imitatione, che non si parta dal uerisimile, & non mouendo le cose da se gli affetti senza le uoci acconciamente, & numerosamente insieme giunte."

[40] *Ibid.*, pp. 217–18: "lo spettatore con tacita consequenza seco dice, se questi per errore commesso non uolontariamente, tanto male ha sofferto, quanto uedo io hora, che fia di me, se forse uolontariamente commettessi questo peccato? & questo pensiero il fa astenere da gli errori."

[41] *Ibid.*, p. 218: "nello eleggersi, o formarsi queste attioni illustri, cosi dette, non perche siano lodeuoli, o uirtuose, ma perche uengono da grandissimi personaggi, non è senon bene hauerle tali, quali le ricercano uerisimilmente i tempi, ne iquali scriue il Poeta, quanto a i ragionamenti, a i costumi, al decoro, & alle altre circonstanze della persona."

[42] *Ibid.*, p. 284: "auertiate, che le persone introdutte nella Scena, non facciano, o dicano quello nel publico, che uerisimilemente non farebbono, o non direbbono in casa; & che teniate certo, che quello che in honesta attione sarebbe uituperoso a fare in casa, sia anco uituperoso nella Scena. ... cosi si debbono, & comporre, & rappresentare, come uerisimilmente si farebbono."

audience; he excludes obscene and plebeian matters, which please only "sausage-makers and similar kinds of people" (p. 219), and insists that the poet must try to please only "the good judges" (p. 285). But please the audience he must, since this is one of the fundamental requisites for all poetry; without pleasure, the participation of the audience in the action and the consequent moral instruction are both impossible. When he deems it necessary, Giraldi goes counter to Aristotle in recommending devices that will be more pleasurable to the audience. Thus he does not hesitate to suggest a diluted form of tragedy with a happy ending, designed for presentation to his audience (pp. 221–22).

The other precepts relevant to common characteristics are largely close reflections of the Aristotelian text. Plot in both tragedy and comedy must be complete ("perfetta") and of a proper magnitude ("debita grandezza"); but proper size is quickly translated into length of performance (despite Aristotle's warning), with minima of three hours for comedy and four for tragedy—lest the audience be disappointed (pp. 203–4). Verse is required for both forms, and Giraldi seems to be conscious of no discrepancy between this requirement and Aristotle's theory (p. 205). Both imitate an action and limit the time of that action to a single day (pp. 205–6). In both dramatic genres, the plot is the end toward which the other parts contribute (p. 207); and such parts of the plot as knot and solution must be carefully contrived, without recourse to such artificial means as the "deus ex machina" (pp. 211–13). For both—and here the departure from Aristotle is radical—a double plot is preferable to a single one; the "good" and "bad" characters and their rewards and punishments will provide additional enjoyment to the audience.

It is in the treatment of the difference between the two genres that the force of the antecedent tradition makes itself most clearly felt. Joined to this is the concern for the pleasure of the contemporary audience. We have already seen that Giraldi ascribes to tragedy and comedy the common end of moral instruction. He derives from Aristotle, as well as he can, the different emotional effects by means of which they proceed; tragedy works through terror and pity, comedy through pleasure and merry jokes (p. 208). These are produced by different kinds of action: tragedy presents death and horrible events, comedy the activities of everyday life. The kinds of actions themselves have moral implications:

Tragedy through horror and compassion, showing what we should avoid in life, purges us of the disturbances in which the tragic characters have become involved. But comedy, by setting before us what we should imitate, through passions, through temperate feelings mixed with play, with laughter, with derisive jests, calls us to a proper way of living.[43]

43 *Ibid.*, p. 219: "la Tragedia coll'horrore, & colla compassione, mostrando quello che debbiam fuggire, ci purga dalle perturbationi, nelle quali sono incorse le persone Tragiche. Ma la Comedia col proporci quello, che si dee imitare con passioni, con affetti temperati mescolati con giuochi, con risa, & con scherneuoli motti, ne chiama al buon modo di uiuere."

But if in Aristotle tragedy and comedy involved particular kinds of plot structure, in Giraldi the differences between those kinds tend to be diminished. Thus the happy ending is recommended for both forms, and Giraldi proudly declares that he has used no other type in his own tragedies. He admits that this goes against Aristotle and that it favors the audience; he has used the happy ending

. . . exclusively to serve the needs of the spectators, and to make them [the tragedies] more pleasing on the stage, and to conform better to the usage of our times. For even if Aristotle says that this is a way of catering to the ignorance of spectators, since the other side nevertheless has its partisans I have thought it better to satisfy him who must listen, at the risk of lesser excellence (supposing that Aristotle's opinion be accepted as the better), than with a little more grandeur to displease those for whose pleasure the plot is put on the stage. For it would be of little use to compose a slightly more praiseworthy plot if it were to be distasteful when acted on the stage. Those terrible plots (if perhaps the minds of people in the theater abhor them) may be used in written works; and those with a happy ending in works to be acted on the stage.[44]

Principle—as he understands it—gives way to expediency.

Just as rapidly and as wittingly, the distinction between "better" and "worse" moral characters is made into a distinction between higher and lower classes; that is, a similar transformation takes place with respect to plot and to character. The personages of tragedy, fitted to an "illustrious and royal" action, are kings, heroes, nobles; those of comedy, participating in a "plebeian and civil" action, are men and women of the people; "and therefore Aristotle said that comedy imitated worse actions; not that he meant that it imitated the wicked and the guilty, but the less illustrious, who are worse insofar as nobility is concerned if they are compared with royal persons."[45] The personages of comedy are even less dignified than the average citizenry; they are "servants, parasites, prostitutes, cooks, pimps, soldiers, and finally almost every kind of plebeian folk who are to be found in the city"[46]—all those who had long figured in the traditional lists.

If these differences are to be found among the objects imitated, there will be corresponding differences among the means of imitation. Tragedy may still use rhythm (bodily motion) and melody (choral song) as means supple-

[44] Ibid., p. 221: "solo per seruire a gli spettatori, & farle riuscire piu grate in Scena, & conformarmi piu con l'uso de i nostri tempi. Che anchora che Aristotile dica, che cio è seruire alla ignoranza de gli spettatori, hauendo pero l'altra parte i difensori suoi, ho tenuto meglio sodisfare a chi ha ad ascoltare, con qualche minore eccellenza (quando fusse accettata per la migliore l'openione d'Aristotile) che con un poco piu di grandezza dispiacere a coloro, per piacere de quali la fauola si conduce in Scena: che poco giouerebbe compor fauola un poco piu lodeuole, & che poi ella si hauesse a rappresentare odiosamente. Quelle terribili (se gli animi de gli spettatori forse le abhoriscono) possono essere delle scritture: queste di fin lieto delle rappresentationi."

[45] Ibid., p. 203: "& però fu detto da Aristotile, che la Comedia imitaua le attioni peggiori. Non che ci uolesse significare, che imitasse le uitiose & le ree, ma le meno illustri, lequali sono peggiori, quanto alla nobilità, se si conferiscono colle reali."

[46] Ibid., p. 215: "serui, parasiti, meretrici, cuochi, ruffiani, soldati, & finalmente quas ogni sorte di gente popolaresca, che si troui nelle città." V. pp. 271–75 for other listings of persons and for the characters to be associated with various types.

mentary to verse; but comedy now uses neither (p. 205). If verse is the universal accompaniment of diction, it is not used in the same way in the two genres. Comedy admits of no rhyme, whereas tragedy should mix rhymed with unrhymed sections, rhyme being useful especially in the choruses and in those "moral" parts where a lesson is specifically stated, "so that they may be more easily received in the mind of the listener" ("accioche piu ageuolmente siano riceuute nell'animo di chi ascolta," p. 234). The diction itself will necessarily be appropriate to the actions and the persons depicted. "The speech of tragedy should be great, royal, and magnificent, and figurative; that of comedy simple, pure, familiar, and appropriate to men of the people."[47] Giraldi develops his ideas on the special circumstances which require a more or less noble diction than that employed for the rest. One senses, throughout the discussion, the presence of the theory of the styles, and also the rules of decorum in character and in diction as they were applied to the examination of Terence's comedies.

The third of Giraldi's treatises, bearing the date 1554 but published much later, is entitled *Lettera ovvero discorso sopra il comporre le satire atte alle scene.* It is relatively short, and its shortness permits one to perceive, even more clearly than in the case of the previous treatise, the extent to which its organization depends upon the outline of the *Poetics.* Giraldi conceives of the dramatic satire, "proper for the stage," as a genre combining the characteristics of both tragedy and comedy. Thus the definition which he gives for it and the detailed remarks on the definition attempt to combine the materials found in Aristotle—and in his own treatise—on the other two dramatic genres: "Satire is an imitation of a complete action, of suitable length, combining the mirthful with the grave, in pleasant language, the components of which are in part combined in a single place, in part divided, presented on the stage in order to move men's souls to laughter and to an appropriate terror and pity." And the gloss; the remarks made on imitation and on the complete action are the same as those on all other kinds of poetry.

"Of suitable length"—separates it from complete works which are short, such as epigrams, odes, elegies. . . . "Mirthful and grave at the same time"—this shows its difference from comedy and from tragedy, of which the first is composed to be pleasing, the other to be serious. . . . "In pleasant language"—this divides it from works written in prose, for it favors verse just as much as do the other two types already mentioned.[48]

[47] *Ibid.,* p. 264: "quel parlare della Tragedia uuole esser grande, reale, & magnifico, & figurato: quello della Comedia semplice, puro, famigliare, & conueneuole alle persone del popolo."
[48] *Lettera ovvero discorso,* in *Scritti estetici* (1864), II, 134–35: "La satira è imitazione di azione perfetta di dicevole grandezza, composta al giocoso ed al grave con parlar soave, le membre della quale sono insieme al suo luogo per parte, e per parte divise, rappresentata a commovere gli animi a riso, ed a convenevole terrore e compassione. . . . Di dicevole grandezza—la separa dalle cose perfette, ma che sono picciole, come epigrammi, ode, elegie. . . . Insieme giocosa e grave—la fa diversa dalla comedia e dalla tragedia, delle quali la prima è composta al piacevole, l'altra al grave. . . . di parlar soave—il quale la divide dalle cose scritte in prosa, perchè ella così ama il verso, come l'amano l'altre due già dette."

The remainder of the gloss explains the appearance of "numero, armonia, canto" together or separately; the dramatic character of the genre; and the "appropriate" terror and pity, to be distinguished from the stronger passions of tragedy. For the satire, Giraldi demands the unhappy ending which he had not deemed necessary for tragedy, an action limited to one day and having the same quantitative and qualitative parts as the other dramatic forms. The qualitative parts are treated in this order: (1) "l'apparato," or spectacle; (2) "il ragionare" (language, including necessarily verse); (3) "melodia," or the music of the choruses; (4) "sentenza" (the verbal expression of concepts); (5) "costume," or character; and (6) "favola." There is very little here that goes beyond the text of Aristotle, although some of the points of view noted in the other treatises reappear here in its interpretation.

Giraldi Cintio's group of treatises is highly representative of the activity around the *Poetics* in these middle years of the Cinquecento. They are original treatises rather than commentaries, treating three dramatic genres which Giraldi regards as traditional and one narrative genre which he considers to be new. They are patterned on the *Poetics*, following its general outline and repeating many passages and many principles. For the traditional genres, they accept without question much of Aristotle's theory; for the new one, they declare the independence of modern forms of the rules established before such forms came into being. Throughout, however, the acceptance of Aristotle is only superficial, for the theorist is constantly led to alter—sometimes drastically—Aristotle's principles by his own adherence to another set of principles which is essentially Horatian and rhetorical.

I romanzi of Giovanni Battista Pigna, also published in 1554, belongs to the group of original treatises based on Aristotle as did Giraldi Cintio's three discourses. Whether Pigna learned what he knew about the romance from Giraldi or whether Giraldi plagiarized Pigna is indifferent; Pigna's work presents an essentially independent theory of the romance. It is based on Aristotle in a somewhat different way from the others. For although Pigna declares that Aristotle has been his guide in everything that he has said on the romanzo (p. 65), he does not follow the order of the *Poetics* as Giraldi had done. He seems to state the problem this way: Given the fact that Aristotle does not treat the genre of the romance, what may one derive from his theories of history, tragedy, comedy, and the epic that will be useful in defining the conditions and the excellences of the new genre? His method everywhere reflects this statement. He proceeds by finding similarities in the romance to one or another of the genres and by transferring to the romance the apposite statements. He must use this method since the only genre closely resembling the romance, the epic, is nevertheless considerably different, and the same rules do not apply to both (p. 68). This is a fundamental tenet of his position: "the rule will be discovered whereby one will be required to write in a way proper to the romance ["Romanzeuolmente"]; and that this kind of writing has a form of its own, in part agreeing with the others [Greek and Latin epics], in part not; and that given this foundation it is not to be blamed for the fact that it is different from the other forms in many respects."[49]

The principal differences between the romance and the epic will be in the object of imitation, which Pigna calls merely "imitazione." The general rules of imitation apply equally to both; but the epic is based on the truth and the romance is not:

There is this single difference, that the basis of their imitation [i.e., of the romances] is not the same as that of the epic; for the epic uses a true event as the basis for a probable one. By true I mean derived either from history or from fable, that is, true in actuality or supposed to be true. These others [romances] have no concern whatever with the truth.[50]

In this respect—and here the cross reference to other genres appears—the romance is like comedy, which invents its own subjects. But not entirely, since the romance does treat known and "true" subjects. It may mix a large ingredient of falsehood with the true and in any case must make its materials acceptable as verisimilar (pp. 20–21). Next, there is a difference in the kinds of persons selected for treatment. Here, the romance will rather resemble the *Odyssey*, which mixes "high" and "low" (royal and pastoral) personages, than the *Iliad*, which represents only the "high." It will thus have a "mixed" action, accompanied necessarily by a double ending; like the *Odyssey*, "each romance will be such through a great variety of infinite fortunes, and in the rank of the persons it will also be of two kinds, but it will tend toward the highest rather than toward the lowest, and almost every one of its actions will be illustrious."[51]

The general structure of the action will also be different, for whereas the epic presents one action of one man, the romance will relate many actions of one man. The problem of unity of the poem without unity of action necessarily arises, and Pigna solves it in a way which may not be thoroughly satisfactory since it is essentially "impressionistic":

The romances readily devote themselves to several deeds of several men, but ... they concern especially one man who should be celebrated over all the others. And thus they agree with the epic poets in taking a single person, but not so in

[49] *I romanzi* (1554), p. 15: "la regola si scoprirà, con cui Romanzeuolmente scriuer si richieda: & come tale scrittura habbia vna forma da per se, parte con l'altre conueniente, & parte nò: & come per lo posto fondamento non sia degno di biasimo, se in molte cose dall'altre s'allontana."

[50] *Ibid.*, pp. 19–20: "Euui questa sola differenza; che il fondamento della costoro imitatione non è con l'Epico vn' istesso: percioche l'Epico sopra vna cosa vera fonda vna verisimile. & vera intendo ò per historie, ò per fauole: cio è ò in effetto vera, ò vera sopposta. Questi altri alla verità risguardo alcuno non hanno."

[51] *Ibid.*, p. 24: "tale per molta varietà di casi infiniti sarà ciascun Romancio. il quale ne gradi delle persone sarà etiandio di due sorti. ma piu alle supreme mirerà, che all'infime: & quasi ogni sua attione sarà illustre."

taking a single action; for they take as many of them as seem to be sufficient. The number is "sufficient" when they have put the heroes in all those honorable perils and in all those major actions which are sought in a perfect knight; and in this way endless adventures are avoided. . . . And to finish the poem as soon as we have arrived at that goal which we have selected, the order of nature will help; for when all the attributes are present in matter, motion ceases.[52]

A final difference of subject matter between the romance and the classical epic lies in the use of religion. The gentiles were permitted to invent fables based on their religion and to use them as ornaments for their poems, whereas Christians are not (p. 14). Nevertheless, the Christian poet may use saints and devils, miracles and other supernatural acts, insofar as they agree with the beliefs of his audience, which he is much more apt to please in this way than by the introduction of an antiquated pagan mythology (p. 41).

I have already touched upon the handling and organization of these materials in connection with the problem of unity. Pigna notes other important differences. The epic poet presents a continuous narrative, whereas the poet of romance interrupts his story from time to time, pretending to sing it in portions before his hosts (p. 14). Thus the narrative of the epic will be straightforward and direct, while that of the romance will wander, digress, retrace its steps—just like the knights who are its heroes:

Even if it does not observe the epic order, this does not mean that it does not have a rule of its own, which is the following: . . . It breaks off the narrative either when the time for an interruption presents itself, or when it does not. When it does, the mind of the reader remains at rest, from which he derives contentment and therefore pleasure, since he remains in presence of a completed action . . . When the time does not present itself, the mind remains in suspense, and from this there arises a desire which is a source of pleasure.[53]

Similarly, the romance will be longer. There is no need for its plot to be perceptible in one glance, and it is better to err by excessive length than to disappoint the reader by excessive shortness. One may even consider that the proper length for each canto is what one may sing or hear in a single sitting. The cantos should be connected to one another by moral discourses.

52 *Ibid.*, pp. 25–26: "i Romanzi si dan bene à piu fatti di piu huomini, ma . . . vn huomo specialmente si propongono: il quale sia soura tutti gli altri celebrato. & cosi con gli Epici concorrono nel pigliare vna sola persona. ma nel prendere vn sol fatto non è cosi: percioche tanti ne trattano, quanto lor pare essere assai. Et assai è, ogni volta che in tutti quegli honorati pericoli, & in tutte quelle maggiori attioni posto gli hanno, che à vn perfetto cauagliere si ricercano. & cosi il gire in infinito si toglie. . . . & quanto al finire il poema tosto che arriuati siamo à quel segno, à che mirauamo; seruasi l'ordine della natura. percioche presenti che sono gli habiti nella materia cessa il moto."

53 *Ibid.*, p. 45: "se bene l'ordine Epico non osserua, non è che vna sua regola non habbia: la quale è questa. . . . Tralascia ò quando il tempo dà che s'interponga, ò quando nol dà. Quando il dà, l'animo di chi legge, quieto rimane. dal che ha contentezza, & perciò piacere: restando egli con vna cosa compiuta. . . . Quando nol dà, l'animo resta sospeso. & ne nasce perciò vn desiderio che fa diletto."

And this discourse will be moral so that by means of virtue it will invite us to be better, and so that it will serve its purpose, which is to inflame us to praise-worthy action through pleasure; whence arises a certain affection which makes us attentive, and through attention we become capable of absorbing the material, and ultimately benevolent toward the poet.[54]

The romance, generally freer, will use more numerous descriptions and comparisons than the epic (p. 51), and although both are necessarily written in verse, the verse form is not the same (p. 15).

In their totality, these differences between the romance and the epic do not represent merely the adaptation to two sister genres of the same set of principles. Rather, as we pass from Aristotle's theory of the epic to Pigna's theory of the epic and the romance we see certain major changes in orientation—from a theory directed toward the beauty of the work itself to one seeking a particular kind of pleasure and of moral instruction for a given audience; from one concerned with the structural unity of the poem to another recommending variety, multiplicity, diversity, discontinuity; from one deriving its criteria from within to another seeking criteria in a miscellany of external factors. The movement in these directions is even clearer when one considers the broad context of theory in which Pigna places his treatment of the romance. The development of his thought on the dual end of utility and pleasure may be taken as an example. He gives a lengthy explanation of why we derive pleasure from the representation of sad and tearful events, and in this explanation Aristotle's remark about the pleasure accompanying knowledge plays only a minor part:

The profit arises from learning about the tenor of human life and about how uncertain is prosperity; and it teaches us especially about the opposite fortune. This nevertheless gives pleasure, since knowledge is a perfection, and since therefore the soul rejoices, finding its proper form. And it is a natural thing to wish to know, and that which is natural and which occurs gives us pleasure. And for the same reason we have another delight, which consists in being so moved by these great changes of fortune that we take pity on those who suffer them. For pity comes to man of itself and is therefore natural.

To explain pleasure from painful events, a physico-physiological theory is offered:

The consideration is diverse, since it is the natural movement of pity which delights us and a movement of the heart that is not natural which saddens us. For when the heart is compressed, sadness results, as dilatation produces joy. If then joy comes about through dilatation, how can pity ever give us pleasure, since it produces the shrinking of the heart in the opposite direction? It is nevertheless necessary that these humors [spiriti] should expand; otherwise they will not comfort us; and this will come about at the very same time in which they are being

---

[54] *Ibid.*, p. 46: "Et sara questo discorso morale; accioche per mezzo della virtù meglio c'inuiti; & accioche stia nel suo proponimento, che è con diletto à lodeuoli cose infiammarne. dal che nasce vna certa affettione, che attenti ne rende: & d'attenti capaci della materia, & finalmente beneuoli verso il poeta."

compressed. For in part restricted and in part set free, they will give us partly pleasure and partly uneasiness. Pleasure, because it is a human thing to have pity on the afflicted, aside from the fact that it consoles us to see that we ourselves are free from the evil, in which there is still another pleasure. Uneasiness, because feeling sorrow is outside of nature, aside from the fact that it disturbs us to transfer to ourselves, by the imagination, the suffering of others.[55]

Pigna presents here a kind of compendium of current thinking on the causes and nature of aesthetic pleasure. In other passages, he studies the artistic devices which may produce that pleasure. The ornateness of the narrative style, for example, produces novelty, hence the marvelous, hence an intense pleasure (p. 17). A strict observance of decorum, presenting to the audience types which it knows and recognizes, makes possible the pleasure of recognition (p. 20). Those plots which teach most about human life will be the most pleasurable, because of the delight accompanying knowledge (p. 24). Verse is required at once because it is more enjoyable than prose, being more artistic, and because it assists in the communication of the moral lesson (pp. 53–54).

Very few of Pigna's statements take issue with Aristotle, since for the most part he believes himself to be in agreement; the differences consist in added ideas which essentially alter Aristotle's thought. So for the distinction between poetry and history:

And although both of them, not without some profit, are delightful, they are nevertheless different and of unequal value. For the historian remains always with the particular, pursuing a perpetual similarity rarely changed; and the poet seeks the universal, removing monotony through constant variety. And there are many other things which make a notable difference between them, so that the poet charms and teaches more than the historian.[56]

[55] *Ibid.*, pp. 28–29: "il giouamento nasce dall'apparare il tenore della vita humana, & quanto instabile sia la prosperità: & dal contrario massimamente c'insegna. Ciò tutta uia fa diletto: essendo la scienza vna perfettione; & rallegrandosi perciò l'anima che il suo sugello ritroui. & natural cosa è il voler sapere: & quello che è naturale & che viene, ne dà piacere. & per questa istessa ragione vn'altro diletto habbiamo, che è nell'essere da questi grandi mutamenti talmente commossi, che pietà ci venga di chi loro sottoposto si troua. percioche la misericordia viene all'huomo da se, & è perciò per natura. . . . il rispetto è diuerso; essendo il moto naturale della misericordia quello che ci diletta; & il moto del cuore che naturale non è, quello che ci attrista: percioche compresso ch'egli è, contristatione ne nasce; come allegrezza dalla dilatatione. Se adunque l'allegrezza è per mezzo della dilatatione, come ci porgerà mai diletto la misericordia, poscia ch'ella ha lo stringimento del cuore in opposito? Bisogna tutta uia che essi spiriti s'allarghino: altramente non ci conforteranno. & ciò auerrà in quel tempo istesso che comprimeransi: percioche parte ristretti & parte slargati, parte piacere & parte noia ne daranno. Piacere, quanto che humana cosa è l'hauer compassione à gli afflitti. senza che ne consola il vedere che siamo fuor del male, in che è vn'altro. Noia, quanto che il rincrescimento è fuor di natura. senza che ne disturba il trasferire con l'imaginatione in noi stessi l'altrui dolore."

[56] *Ibid.*, p. 2: "& quantunque ambe non senza qualche giouamento sien diletteuoli; sono nondimeno diuerse, & di pregio disuguale. percioche l'historico stà in sul particolare con vna perpetua similitudine alterata di rado: & all' uniuersale mira il poeta togliendo col sempre variare la satietà. & molte altre cose vi sono che differenza notabile vi fanno: & tale, che questo alletta & insegna piu che quello."

From the particular and the universal the passage is made to monotony
and variety, and thence to greater pleasure and instruction. A more striking
case, perhaps, is found in the treatment of the four requisites for character.
Pigna assumes immediately that characters are either traditional or new
(i.e., invented) and that Aristotle's four requisites are divided between these
two types. All four are forms of verisimilitude, but some are natural and
others are "by reference." These distinctions give the following schema:

	Verisimilitude		
New characters		Traditional characters	
(*finta*)		(*tolta*)	
Appropriateness		Similarity	
(*convenevole*)		(*simile*)	
By nature	By reference	By nature	By reference
Christón	Armótton	Ómalon	Ómion

The terms "by nature" and "by reference" are explained thus:

> By reference: referring the one whom I am treating to the opinion in which he
> is held in histories or in fables, I will depict him primarily as fierce or pleasant, as
> prudent or bold, as deceitful or just. . . . By nature: considering the habits as
> confirmed dispositions of the soul, I will make any person throughout the work
> and to the very end such as I have established him to be from the beginning.[57]

Verisimilitude is thus defined in terms of consistency of character ("by
nature") or of faithfulness to a tradition ("by reference"), and Aristotle's
four requisites are reduced to these terms.

A special feature of *I romanzi* is its insistence on the pleasure that the
audience takes in the *difficulté vaincue.* A number of passages point to this.
But Pigna notes that it is not always appreciated and that there is perhaps
a difference between those who admire ingeniousness—a select group—and
the popular taste which is less discriminating. So tragedies will be "demonstrative of greater wit" ("di maggior ingegno dimonstratrici," p. 2), but
will appeal less to popular taste than the romance. Still, even in the romance
form the difficult solution will be the best. A new subject involving new
characters will be less admirable than the traditional ones, since the poet
will not, in handling them, be under the constraint of the accepted story
and of the decorum of known personages, "which, because it is less easy
to do, always shows greater virtuosity."[58] As a general thing, pleasure
comes from the spectacle of the poet's triumphs: ". . . the more narrow is
the field in which our genius is restricted, the more difficulty is seen there;

[57] *Ibid.,* p. 34: "Per relatione; se referendo colui di ch'io tratto, all'opinione in che egli
è nelle historie ò nelle fauole, ò fiero ò piaceuole, ò circonspetto ò temerario, ò insidiatore
ò giusto principalmente il dipingerò. . . . Per natura; se mirando à gli habiti che sono dispositioni confirmate, tale qual da principio haurò stabilito alcuno, il farò essere per tutta
l'opera infino alla fine." See below, p. 468, for a similar schema resulting from the text of
Pigna's *Poetica Horatiana* of 1561.
[58] *Ibid.,* p. 20: "che perche disagiosamente si fa, mostra tutta uia piu virtù."

and . . . difficult things happen rarely; and they are therefore more beautiful and of greater efficacy, since this grows by opposition to its contrary."[59] It is for this reason—and we may again see an adaptation of Aristotelian principles—that tragedy is to be considered superior to the epic:

> Restriction gives it all its excellence, since it is limited in its action, not disposing of a plot in which great events come together; and in the matter of digressions, since it cannot permit itself many or varied ones, lest the composition turn out to be disproportionate; and in time, having only the space of one day or of a day and a half in which the whole action must be concluded; and in its pleasure, which is deprived of an important element, brought about more easily by a narrator than by a chorus.[60]

Pigna's treatise is significant, finally, for the extensive sections devoted to practical criticism. All of Books II and III is occupied by an examination of Ariosto's works, the comedies as well as the *Orlando Furioso* (although primarily the latter). In this examination, Pigna is not really seeking a judgment of the works, for the judgment is admitted from the start: the *Orlando Furioso* is the best romance ever written, and Ariosto's comedies, especially the *Cassaria*, are the best in the language. Rather, he wishes to discover in the *Orlando* the authority for the precepts he has given in Book I; indirectly, praise will fall upon the *Orlando* as the source of all the best examples and precedents. A certain amount of Pigna's material may be neglected, since it is biographical or deals with Ariosto's fame. But his indication that the form of the plot is determined by the works of Boiardo and Homer needs to be noted. So also the fact that the digressions are in part explained by the wish to glorify the Este family, for it is also a justification; and Pigna takes it for granted that such external reasons do constitute justifications of the form of the plot. He declares that Ariosto is supreme both in the essence and in the accidents, and, from an earlier statement (p. 15), we know that the essence or substance is the plot and the accidents are the digressions. The analysis of plot consists in asking which of the four types of plot are to be found here—and Pigna finds them all—in examining the treatment of the quantitative parts, in studying the use of knot and denouement. It is clear from the analysis that Pigna thinks of the *Orlando Furioso* as made up of many whole plots and that each of the separate "actions" constitutes a "plot." This is consonant with his theory of the multiplicity of plot in the romance. So that while the machinery of

[59] *Ibid.*, pp. 36–37: "quanto piu stretto è il campo, in che l'ingegno nostro è ridotto, che tanta piu difficoltà ui si vede: & . . . le cose difficili di rado auengono; & sono perciò piu belle & di maggior virtù, accrescendo ella contra il suo contrario."

[60] *Ibid.*, p. 37: "la strettezza tutta l'eccellenza le dà. essendo ella angusta nell'attione, per non hauere vn fatto, in cui gran fatti concorrano: & nelle digressioni, percioche non può pigliarne molte ne varie, accioche sproportionato non venga il componimento: & nel tempo, hauendo ella solo lo spatio d'un giorno, ò d'un giorno & mezzo, in cui tutta la cosa conchiuda: & nel piacere, che d'una gran parte manca, la quale dal narratore piu commodamente nasce, che dal choro."

the Aristotelian text is applied, the theoretical basis is fundamentally different in Pigna. He applies a criterion of unity to the poem—but only insofar as it is possible or desirable in the romance: "in the end everything is properly conducted with beautiful unity, to the extent that this kind of poetry admits of unity."[61] The problem of unity involves the problem of digressions, and Pigna praises Ariosto for the use of episodes which properly mix the grave and the light, the calm and the disturbed, the active and the passionate. Decorum is everywhere correctly observed, in the transfer to the *Orlando* of traditional materials, in the use of contemporary events, and in the expression. Finally, events and episodes are accompanied by moral overtones and by possibilities of allegorical interpretation which serve the end of utility.

In this discussion of the *Orlando Furioso*, Pigna uses the term "imitation" in three separate senses which demonstrate with especial clarity his habits in the use of terminology. Since the plot depends upon Homer and Vergil, it contains "imitations" of them. A second kind of imitation occurs when men are presented "as they should be," either through narration or through dialogue. Dialogue itself is a kind of imitation, in the Platonic sense which distinguishes imitation from narration (p. 80). The Aristotelian sense appears earlier in the text: "The plot is an imitation of an action" ("Favola è imitatione d'una attione," p. 15); but in the definition which follows, Pigna clearly gives it a restricted meaning: "To imitate is to use the verisimilar according to that form which is most proper in the matter undertaken."[62] Imitation as direct or dramatic representation is also fully treated in the early sections of the text (p. 16). Although he assigns so many meanings to the word, Pigna makes no attempt to define or distinguish, and the reader must derive the proper meaning from the context. A similar case, although not nearly so extensive, is found with respect to the word "favola" (pp. 15, 92).

The examination of Ariosto's comedies (pp. 105 ff.) presents interesting solutions to the question of why one comedy, the *Cassaria*, is superior to another, the *Suppositi*. Seven reasons are offered: (1) the denouement derives more successfully from the preceding action; (2) the denouement does not depend upon external signs; (3) the *Cassaria* is more verisimilar; (4) the comedy succeeds in conducting a more difficult plot; (5) it has more of pleasantness in it and less of sadness; (6) its devices are newer, causing increased admiration and greater pleasure; (7) the episodes are more immediately derived from the knot and solution and more closely linked to them. In these seven points, Pigna once again raises questions found in the *Poetics*, although his applications and conclusions are not necessarily

[61] *Ibid.*, p. 101: "alla fine ogni cosa con vaga vnità per quanto questa poesia patisce, è debitamente guidata."

[62] *Ibid.*, p. 15: "Imitare è pigliare il verisimile secondo quella forma, che nella proposta materia piu conuiene."

Aristotelian. But he does more: judging that works may be evaluated by comparison with their contraries, he compares the *Cassaria* with the "best tragedy that one might read." This is the result:

In this [tragedy], we will see royal life expressed, in the *Cassaria*, the life of the people; the one excellent in long discourses, the other in brief repartees; on the one hand, the operation of fortune, on the other, of cunning; in the former, grave teachings and majesty and sorrows and infinite anguish, in the latter, delight and joy and playfulness and many warnings about private life.[63]

Here, Aristotle is absent, and we return once again to the juxtaposition of tragedy and comedy familiar throughout the Middle Ages. A final reason for preferring the *Cassaria* to the *Suppositi*, and one which should not surprise in the context, is its superior morality (p. 107).

Pigna devotes the third book of *I romanzi* to a study of the style of the *Orlando Furioso*. His method is new and prophetic. He takes one hundred passages from the romance and shows the successive stages in the composition of the text; in each case, he gives the reason why Ariosto preferred the last version. In this study of variants, the comments concern such matters as grammar, phonetics or sound, proportion and symmetry, prosody, clarity, ease of construction, ambiguity, appropriateness to matter and to nature, and ornament. The point of view is thus almost entirely grammatical and rhetorical.

LOVISINI (1554)

The year 1554 was thus extraordinarily rich in short works on the poetic art that bore in one way or another the stamp of Aristotle's *Poetics*. It also was the year of publication of a major commentary on Horace, Francesco Lovisini's *In librum Q. Horatii Flacci de arte poetica commentarius*, which made the customary comparisons between Aristotle and Horace. But in regard to the history of Aristotle's *Poetics* in the Cinquecento, Lovisini's work is much less rewarding than its contemporaries. Although it discovers an extraordinarily large number of parallels between Horace and Aristotle (see Chapter IV, pp. 130–32 above), for the most part it does little else than cite the selected text from the *Poetics* and give a translation of it. Moreover, since by this time many of the parallels have become commonplace and traditional, not much is to be learned from a mere examination of the juxtaposed passages. It would be difficult to say what Lovisini's general interpretation of the *Poetics* was, aside from the fact that he found in it many passages that conveyed the same meaning as Horace's *Ars poetica*, perhaps so many that one might insist that the total meaning of the two texts was the same. There are a few points at which what is said about a

---

[63] *Ibid.*, pp. 106–7: "in essa la vita reale espressa si vedrà; & nella Cassaria la popolaresca. In lunghi discorsi l'una: l'altra in prontezze strette eccellente. Di là la fortuna: di qua l'astutia. In quella documenti graui & maestà & dolori & angoscie infinite: in questa diletto & gioia & piaceuolezze & auertimenti domestici assai."

passage in Aristotle reveals the construction which Lovisini put upon it. So for the early commentary on lines 1–13 of the *Ars poetica*, where we find how Lovisini understands imitation:

Poets follow the imagination, not opinion, since they call themselves poets not because they write in verse but because of the plot and the fiction, as Aristotle has set it down for us in the *Poetics*. And therefore all those who imitate the image or the appearance of things by means of art, as do many sculptors and painters, are poets, as Plato's Socrates affirms in the *Symposium*, through the fact that they give pleasure by their invention and imitation of things.[64]

The sense of "imitation" is here composed of its meaning in the *Poetics* plus its meaning in Plato, with emphasis on the latter. Furthermore, the Platonic (and Horatian) element is further emphasized in the next sentence: "Indeed, in these matters we must establish a rule: not all poetic figments are to be approved, but only those which derive rather from prudence than from freedom of creation."[65] The presence of prudence, with its moral and political connotations, indicates the direction taken by the interpreter. Lovisini again expresses the same ideas in connection with *Ars poetica* 146–52, when he cites *Poetics* 1451a36 (p. 34v). For lines 119–27, on character, Lovisini necessarily refers to Aristotle's four requisites: then he makes the following distinction between ὅμοιον and ὁμαλόν: "There is a difference between ὅμοιον, καὶ ὁμαλόν, that is, similar and uniform; for similarity refers to those about whom others had written previously, and uniformity to those about whom we alone are writing. We must observe constant uniformity in a personage whom we are ourselves introducing, so that he will always be himself."[66] This is the distinction between traditional and newly invented characters which we have just seen developed by Pigna, but with differences in the understanding of the requisites. Lovisini also attempts to answer one of the questions about the *Poetics* which was already much debated, the meaning of "one day" in the remark on the duration of the tragic action. Here he accepts Robortello's demonstration that an "artificial day" (i.e., twelve hours) was intended (p. 40).

In a few places at least, Lovisini seems to wish to oppose some point of theory offered by Aristotle. In *Poetics* 1454a28, Aristotle had given examples of a number of characters who were improperly treated. Lovisini takes exception to several, claiming that Menelaus seems to him to be an

---

[64] *Commentarius* (1554), p. 4: "Poetae phantasiam, non opinionem sequuntur: quia poetae nomen sibi asciscunt non propter carmen, sed propter fabulam, & fictionem, ut in poetice testatum relinquit Aristoteles. & iccirco quicunque rerum effigiem, & simulacra arte imitantur, ut mechanici plerique artifices faciunt, poetae sunt, quemadmodum in symposio Platonis Socrates affirmat, propterea quòd fictione, & rerum imitatione delectantur."

[65] *Ibid.*, pp. 4–5: "Verum his modus statuendus est: neque enim omnia poetarum figmenta probanda sunt, sed quae à prudentia potius, quàm à sola fingendi libertate proficiscuntur."

[66] *Ibid.*, p. 29v: "discrepant inter se ὅμοιον, καὶ ὁμαλόν, idest simile, & aequale, nam similitudo ad eos refertur, de quibus alij etiam scripserunt, aequalitas ad eos, de quibus nos tantum scribimus, perpetuam aequalitatem seruare debemus in ea, quam inducimus, persona, ut sit sibi constans."

example of admirable probity and that Iphigenia does display the necessary uniformity of character. Such differences of judgment might result from the fact that Lovisini had different texts in mind or that he interpreted in a different way Aristotle's requisites (p. 54v). On the subject of necessity and probability, the disagreement apparently springs from the fact that Lovisini believes necessity to be natural necessity, that is, the inevitable realization of events. Hence he says: "Horace required of the poet only the law of verisimilitude, Aristotle that of necessity as well. But it seems to me that our author understood the matter better. Indeed, so far are poets from expressing the law of necessity that sometimes they invent things which are not even verisimilar."[67] It is to be noted that Lovisini in no sense regards Aristotle as an authority whose opinion is to be preferred to that of Horace.

As for the important matter of the end of poetry, finally, Lovisini hides his disagreement under a verbal distinction. Wishing to reconcile Aristotle with Horace, he uses the term "munus" or "finis" for Aristotle and "officium" for Horace:

Munus and officium. These two words may either signify the same thing or tv different things [so distinguished] that "munus" means the end sought by tue poet. Indeed the "finis" and the "officium" are different. The "officium" of the poet is to imitate, since ποίησίς έστι μίμησις, as Aristotle says in the Poetics. But the "finis" is instead to profit and delight.[68]

The distinction is clearly between function or operation and end, with Horace as providing the real definition of the latter.

Matteo San Martino's Osservationi grammaticali e poetiche della lingua italiana of the following year, 1555, belongs primarily to the history of Horace's Ars poetica, although certain passages are relevant to the fortunes of Plato's ideas (see above Chapters IV and VII, pp. 138, 275). Only incidentally does it concern Aristotle's Poetics, and then almost exclusively for the interpretation of imitation. In his highly heterogeneous definition of poetry, San Martino of course includes imitation as an element; the times would not have permitted him to do otherwise: "Poetry is a beautiful fiction which, restricted within harmonized rhythms and imitating human actions, by means of pleasure brings profit to the listener." In what immediately follows, however, he shows the importance he attributes to

67 Ibid., pp. 66v–67 (the latter page misnumbered 65): "Horatius uerisimile tantum, Aristoteles etiam necessarium poetis proposuit. at melius sensisse uidetur hic n[o]ster. nam tantum abest, ut poetae necessarium exprimant, ut ea aliquando, quae uerisimilia etiam non sunt, comminisci uideantur."

68 Ibid., p. 61v: "Munus, et officium. duae hae dictiones uel idem significant, uel diuersa: ut munus finem poetae innuat. differunt enim inter se finis, & officium. officium poetae est imitari. nam ποίησίς έστι μίμησις, ut ait in poetice Aristoteles. finis uero prodesse, & delectare."

imitation: "So that imitation is its secondary and not its principal part."[69] From such a passage as this it would seem that the "principal part" would be the pursuit of pleasure and utility. Yet, at a later point, the writer insists that "the final intention of the poets consists in imitation, and all must practice it according to the doctrine of Aristotle and of Cicero, that is, by means of diction, number, and harmony."[70] Here again there is uncertainty, since one wonders what is meant by the "doctrine of Aristotle and of Cicero." In any case, it is fairly clear that the ends of poetry are Horatian and that imitation has some intermediary function in the achievement of those ends. Further light is thrown on the problem in San Martino's statement on the relationship of poetry to reality:

> He [Aristotle] says also that since the poet is an imitator, or another designer of images, he must always imitate one of three things, either things as they were, or as they appear and are said to be, or as it is proper for them to be, provided that all poets make their imitations, according to what was said, of diction, number, and harmony, either separately or together.[71]

In both these passages, I have translated by "diction" the original "componimento," which is stated to mean something like "the disposition or arrangement of ornate speech" (p. 158). As San Martino uses this and the accompanying terms "numero" and "concento" or "harmonia," not only do they signify the means of imitation indicated by Aristotle, but they also carry with them the stress on rhetoric and on prosody which will be his principal concern in the treatise. Aside from these passages, the *Poetics* is used only rarely.

SIGONIO (1557)

Another kind of activity affecting Aristotle's text is represented, in 1557, by Carlo Sigonio's *Emendationum libri duo*. For besides the editions and commentaries of the text, we frequently find philological and philosophical discussions in shorter critical miscellanies devoted largely to textual exegesis. The sections on the *Poetics* in Sigonio's book are answers to suggestions by Robortello or statements of open disagreement with him. Before proceeding to the study of individual passages, Sigonio expresses his opposition to Robortello's way of dividing the text; his own suggestion is an interesting one for the total conception of Aristotle's plan:

---

69 *Osservationi* (1555), p. 130: "la Poetica sia una uaga fittione che fra harmonizzati numeri ristretta, imitando l'humane attioni, con diletto gioui a chi l'ascolta; Si che la imitatione è sua parte secondaria, e non principale."

70 *Ibid.*, p. 146: "consistendo la final intentione de i Poeti nella imitatione, che a tutti exercitarla conuiene secondo la dottrina d'Aristotele, e di Cicerone, cioè con Componimento Numero, & Concento."

71 *Ibid.*, p. 184: "Dice ancor che essendo il Poeta imitatore, o come aitro disignator de imagini, che una di tre cose conuien che sempre imiti, o le cose come furono, o come appaiono e che si dicono, o come esser gli conuiene, pur che tutti fanno la loro imitatione secondo che è detto, di Componimento, Numero & Harmonia o separatamente o congiuntamente."

In my judgment this book is to be divided not into three parts, but into six. For in the first he treats not only the definition of poetry, but also its origin and its growth. But origin and growth do not belong at all to the definition. There follow then two other parts, one on tragedy, the other on the epic. The fifth part concerns questions and answers about poetry, which comes afterwards in his division since it is a separate subject from tragedy and the epic. In the last book he compares tragedy with the epic; this may properly be called a sixth part because it is detached from the discussion of tragedy and the epic.[72]

For the rest, Sigonio's "emendations" offer his opinion on some of the texts which gave the greatest difficulty to his contemporaries:

On 1447a15, "Quid sit αὐλητική, & κιθαριστική." Sigonio draws three conclusions from the text: (1) there are some kinds of auletic and citharistic poetry which do not imitate at all; (2) they use harmony and rhythm (dance) only for their imitation, excluding speech and meter; (3) Aristotle meant them as examples of kinds of poetry which imitate without speech (pp. 148v–50).

On 1447b24–28, "Quid sit Poesis Nomorum. Persas non esse iocosum comoediae nomen." The text presents two difficulties. First, what is meant by "gnomic" poetry—or, more properly, how should one interpret "νόμος" in the text? Sigonio's suggestion is that it has nothing to do with laws but rather is a counterpart to comedy in the same way that the dithyramb is a counterpart to tragedy. The first two express "little" matters, the last two "great" matters. The νόμος would thus be a form of comic poetry, and Sigonio cites the texts of ancient authors who condemned it as such. The second difficulty comes from Robortello's reading at 1448a15 of νόμους ὡς Πέρσας; hence the statement about "Persas" in the heading of the paragraph. Sigonio uses the term as synonymous with νόμος and offers no emendation to the text (pp. 149v–50v).

On 1448a20, "Quid sit μιμεῖσθαι ἐν τοῖς αὐτοῖς." Sigonio rejects Robortello's explanation that the phrase ἐν τοῖς αὐτοῖς referred to the men whose actions were imitated. He declares that it should rather be interpreted as signifying the means of imitation, discourse, harmony, and the dance. Here as before he uses the word "saltum" as equivalent to Aristotle's ῥυθμός (pp. 150v–51).

On 1448b4 ff., "De causis naturalibus poeseos." Another moot point. Robortello had seen the two "natural causes" of poetry as the instinct toward imitation in man and the pleasure which he derives from imitation.

---

[72] *Emendationum libri duo* (1557), p. 148v: "Meo enim iudicio liber hic non in tres, sed in sex partes distribuendus est. primum enim non solum de definitione poeseos agit, sed etiam de origine eius, & incremento. origo autem, & incrementum nihil ad definitionem pertinent. Sequuntur deinde aliae partes, una de tragoedia, de epopoeia altera. Quinta est de quaestionibus, & dissolutionibus poeticis. quae ab eo in sua diuisione praeterita est, cum tamen à tragoedia, & epopoeia separata materia sit. extremo libro tragoediam cum epopoeia comparat. quae sexta pars appellari, cum à disputatione de tragoedia, & epopoeia auulsa sit, merito potest."

Sigonio chooses rather to adopt the position of Averroës that the two causes are (1) imitation and (2) rhythm plus harmony; one cause would thus be imitation, the other the means of imitation. Rhythm itself is dual, being composed of meter and the dance. Sigonio gives his version of Aristotle's arguments thus:

> The means indeed are three in number, comprising harmony and rhythm; for rhythm is divided into two, dance and meters. Meters, then, he says, are constituent parts of rhythms. He does not offer proof, though, that the means of imitation are natural to us, because he thought this sufficiently clear from the fact that he had proved imitation itself to be natural to us.[73]

On 1449b25, "'Ηδυσμένῳ λόγῳ quid sit, non esse intellectum." Sigonio thinks that λόγῳ should be translated by "Rationem, modum" and that the whole phrase means "modo suauitatis pleno." The means he considers to be music, harmony, and rhythm, with music ("melos") having the special sense of meter (pp. 153v–54).

On 1449b25, "Quid sit χωρὶς τῶν εἰδῶν non esse intellectum." At this point, Sigonio believes, Aristotle is using "melos" in a broader sense of harmony and rhythm. He thinks that the whole passage in the definition of tragedy is meant to indicate that there were certain parts of a tragedy recited with music and dance, certain others without them (pp. 154–54v).

On 1450a10, "Partes tragoediae intellectas non esse." Rejecting Robortello's distribution of the six qualitative parts of tragedy among object, manner, and means of imitation, Sigonio proposes his own division which he defends thus:

> For the tragic poets imitate plot, character, and thought as their subject matter; they imitate with diction and song as means, and song includes harmony and rhythm. The third element, manner, is the stage onto which the actors are introduced, which Aristotle calls *ornatus aspectus*. . . . the means of imitation are two, diction and song; the manner, one, embellishment of visual spectacle; the objects, three, plot, character, and thought.[74]

It would be difficult to affirm that, on the whole, Sigonio's emendations represent an advance over Robortello for the interpretation of the passages discussed. His over-all division of the text and his distribution of the qualitative parts are superior; but some of the individual exegeses move backward rather than forward.

In 1559, the *Poetics* appears in a role which it frequently played during

---

[73] *Ibid.*, p. 152v: "instrumenta uero tria sunt, harmonia, & rhythmus. nam rhythmus in duo diuiditur, in saltum, & metra. metra enim, inquit, particulae sunt rhythmorum. Non probat autem instrumenta imitationis esse nobis naturalia, quia satis perspicuum putauit ex eo, quòd imitationem ipsam nobis esse naturalem probauit."

[74] *Ibid.*, p. 155: "Nam tragici imitantur fabulam, mores, & sententiam, ut materiam, imitantur autem dictione, & melopoeia, ut instrumentis, melopoeia uero harmoniam, & rhythmum comprehendit. Modus autem tertius est scena, in qua agentes inducunt, quem Aristoteles uocat ornatum aspectus. . . . quibus imitantur duo sunt, dictio, & melopoeia. quomodo, unum, aspectus ornatus: quae, tria, fabula, mores, & sententia."

the Cinquecento, that of a source of theory on the art of history. The document in question is Dionigi Atanagi's *Ragionamento de la eccellentia et perfettione de la historia*. Atanagi's theoretical treatment of history follows two separate lines, one emphasizing the differences between poetry and history and one displaying their similarities. It is for the first of these that Aristotle is the principal source; for the second, Atanagi refers largely to the tradition of Horace and of the rhetoricians. After a defence of the art as a means to Platonic elevation of the soul, Atanagi defines history as "a narrative of things done as they were done, with praise or with blame, according to persons, places, and times, and including the deliberations, the causes, and the events."[75] Then he proceeds to the comparison with poetry, from which I cite the salient passages:

History is different from poetry, not because the latter is written in verse and the former in prose, as is commonly believed by those who think that everything that is written in verse is poetry. For although verse is proper to the poetic faculty, nevertheless it is not verse but imitation that makes poetry; and that this is true is shown by the fact that there are also poems which are composed in prose. . . . Therefore the true difference and divergence between them lies in this, that poetry imitates and history does not. . . . Poetry takes a single action of a single man and all its other actions are accidental. History takes several actions of several men; and although it is not denied that history also at times treats a single action . . . , nevertheless its proper function is to treat several and diverse actions. The poet concerns himself with the universal, attending to the simple and pure idea of things; the historian deals with the particular, representing things as they are, like a painter who draws from nature. The historian thus relates things done, as they were done; the poet relates them as they should be done necessarily or as they might verisimilarly and probably be done. The poet, once he has undertaken to imitate somebody, keeps him always and everywhere exactly the same as he was when first introduced. . . . The historian keeps men constant or varies them, as he takes them from life, depending on whether he finds them constant or unstable and varied. The order of poetry is certain, connected, and linked, since because of the interrelationship of its actions it makes one out of many, one toward which it directs all the others as servants and domestics serve a mistress; and this by means of the episodes, which by their nature and property always concern the plot, which is the substantial part and as it were the form and soul of the poem. The order of history is for the most part uncertain, disjoined, and fortuitous, since its actions are not similar and linked but separate and diverse; neither does one depend from another nor do they relate to a single end.[76]

75 *Ragionamento* (1559), p. 3v: "La historia è una narration di cose fatte, come elle son fatte, con laude, ò con uitupero, secondo le persone, i luoghi, e i tempi, co i consigli, con le cagioni, & con gli auenimenti."
76 *Ibid.*, pp. 4–4v: "La historia è differente de la poesia, non perche questa in uerso, & quella in prosa si scriua, come uolgarmente si crede; stimando, che tutto ciò, che in uerso è scritto, sia poesia. Percioche se bene il uerso è proprio de la poetica facoltà, nondimeno non il uerso, ma la imitatione fa la poesia, & che ciò sia uero, si ritruouano de le poesie anco in prosa tessute. . . . Adunque la uera differenza, & diuersità loro è in questo, che la poesia imita, la historia nò. . . . La poesia prende una sola attione, d'un'huomo solo, l'altre tutte

Back of each one of these comparisons there lies some principle derived from the *Poetics*. If one were to abstract from the passage the sections relevant to poetry alone, one would have a fairly complete statement of Aristotle's basic theory. But in some cases at least, this theory will have taken on a flavor peculiar to Atanagi's text, as in the indication that "necessity" refers to things as they "should be" and probability to things as they "might be." As the process of opposition continues, Atanagi breaks away from the Aristotelian text, and the basic principles become more exclusively Horatian.

It is also Horace who presides over the somewhat lengthy study of the resemblances between the two arts of poetry and history—Horace augmented by general notions derived from the rhetoricians. Both are narrative, but poetry alone uses invocation. Both practise the demonstrative and the deliberative types of rhetoric, and therefore both praise the virtues and blame the vices and both introduce consultations and speeches. Nor is the judicial type excluded, although history uses it more frequently. Both observe prudence and decorum, both wish to teach, delight, and move—and above all to produce utility. They describe many peoples, places, customs, laws, present great variations of fortune, practise digressions and many rhetorical devices. Both must attempt a visual representation of what they are saying, so as to make it live for the audience. Although he disagrees with Robortello on the matter of the classification of history and would make it a part of moral philosophy rather than of rhetoric, Atanagi seems to agree in seeing in history an art prior to poetry—whatever is true in poetry comes to it from history (pp. 4v–7v).

Atanagi's *Ragionamento* is not at all extraordinary, for the times, in its facile combination of various theoretical traditions. It is perhaps unusual in the extent to which it keeps them separate for separate purposes and in the completeness with which each is represented in a small compass.

Like Sigonio's *Emendationes*, Cristoforo Rufo's *Antexegemata*, published in Padua in 1559, is a collection of commentaries on isolated

sono per accidente. La historia piu, & di piu huomini; & come che non si nieghi, che la historia, anch'ella tratti alcuna uolta una attion sola . . . nondimeno il proprio officio suo è di trattar piu, & diuerse attioni. Il poeta opera intorno a l'uniuersale attendendo a la semplice, & pura idea de le cose. L'historico intorno al particolare, rappresentando le cose, come elle sono, quasi pittor, che ritragga dal naturale. L'historico adunque narra le cose fatte, come elle son fatte. Il poeta le narra, ò come elle dourebbono necessariamente, ò come elle potrebbono uerisimilmente, & probabilmente esser fatte. Il poeta, poi che s'ha proposto la imitatione d'alcuno, egli il mantien sempre, & per tutto in quel modo stesso, che egli l'ha da prima introdotto. . . . L'historico come prende gli huomini, cosi ò gli mantiene, ò gli uaria, secondo che gli truoua, ò costanti, ò instabili, & uariati. L'ordine de la poesia è certo, congiunto, & concatenato, percioche ella per l'affinità de le attioni ne fa una di molte, a la quale come a donna indirizza tutte l'altre, come ministre, & seruenti, & cio col mezzo de gli episodij, i quali di loro natura, & proprietà sempre riguardano a la fauola, che è la parte sostantiale, & quasi la forma, & l'anima del poema. L'ordine de la historia il piú è incerto, disgiunto, & a caso, percioche le attioni in essa non sono simili, nè congiunte, ma separate, & diuerse: ne l'una dipende da l'altra: ne risguardano ad un medesimo fine."

passages. They are largely linguistic and philological in character, although some do represent interpretations of texts. As they relate to the *Poetics*, they state disagreements with such earlier commentators as Robortello and Maggi.

On 1456*b*3, ἀπὸ τῶν αὐτῶν εἰδῶν. The initial difficulty at this point results from the text, which is still defective. For the reading which he had, Rufo disagreed with Robortello's version, "ad naturam rerum," and proposed instead "ex iisdem earum rerum propriis locis." His whole interpretation of the passage reads as follows: "I think that he meant that, whenever the occasion presents itself in tragedies and comedies . . . for compassion to be aroused or a certain horror produced or for something to be amplified or proved or made acceptable to the mind, all these things should be derived from the very situations proper to these actions."[77]

On 1456*b*8, εἰ φανοῖτο ἡδέα. Again, difficulties of text, and Rufo supports his own reading against that of Maggi. He interprets the passage (which still gives difficulty) as meaning that there must be a difference between the language of tragedy and that of oratory. His commentary throws light on his conceptions of both arts:

It has been said, indeed, that in order to arouse the emotions of the soul, the tragic poet may seek his arguments in the same places in which the orator seeks them. But there should be a certain difference between them; for it is indispensable that the art of the tragic poet should be most secret and that his words should not reek of precepts or of doctrine. But in the orator it is proper that the art and the teaching should be clear, in such a way that by the force of oratory what he says has manifest luster and is set out in a clear light. Indeed, what function will the orator be judged to have served if some things seem to be pleasantly and agreeably expressed and delivered, but if his speech nevertheless is not judged to be productive of this pleasure?[78]

The comparison of the two arts and the notion that tragedy secretly works toward the same moral ends are of interest here.

On 1451*b*29, κἂν ἄρα συμβῇ γενόμενα ποιεῖν. The disagreement is again with Robortello, on the question of whether the poet may imitate events which have actually happened and still remain a poet. Rufo judges that he may, providing that such events satisfy his criteria of verisimilitude and probability (p. G7).

---

[77] *Antexegemata* (1559), pp. G5–G5*v*: "voluisse censeo, si quando contingat, vt in tragoediis & comoediis . . . misericordia mouenda sit, aut horror quidam incutiendus, aut amplificandum, aut probandum & suadendum aliquid, ex iisdem earum rerum propriis locis eae res omnes comparandae erunt."

[78] *Ibid.*, p. G6: "Dictum quidem est ad ciendas animi motiones ex iisdem locis peti argumenta posse a tragico, ex quibus a rhetorico petuntur. ceterùm inter vtrunque debet interesse, quòd tragici ars sit occultissima oportet, nec praecepta aut doctrinam aliquam redoleant eius dicta. At in oratore artem & doctrinam conspicuam esse decet, ita vt constet vi denique orationis ea, quae dicat, splendescere atque illuminari. Etenim quodnam munus praestitisse censebitur orator, si suauiter aliqua & iucundè expressa elataáque fuisse appareant, eius tamen suauitatis non iudicetur effectrix oratio?"

On 1453a32, καὶ τελευτῶσα ἐξ ἐναντίας τοῖς βελτίοσι καί χείροσιν. Rufo interprets the passage as meaning that the great and praiseworthy men in the *Odyssey* undergo a fate opposite to that of the wicked (p. G7v). On 1453b13, ἐν τοῖς πράγμασιν ἐμποιητέον. Rufo insists that the pleasure of tragedy must come from the action itself and not from the spectacle (p. G8).

On 1461b23, ἢ ὡς βλαβερά. Robortello is again rejected, since Rufo believes that Aristotle meant by βλαβερά those things which are harmful to morality (p. Hv).

On 1462b13, φανερὸν ὅτι κρείττων ἂν εἴη μᾶλλον. This time it is with Maggi that Rufo disagrees, denying that Aristotle wished to indicate a superiority of tragedy over epic in the achievement of the end proposed (p. H2).

On 1452b11, πάθος δ'ἐστὶ πρᾶξις φθαρτική. Robortello's translation of πάθος as "perturbatio" and his reference of the passage to the spectators are contested. Rufo declares instead that Aristotle meant to refer to the personages of the tragedy and to some extreme ill that they might suffer (p. I3).

On 1453a9, ἀλλὰ δι' ἁμαρτίαν τινά, τῶν ἐν μεγάλῃ δόξῃ ὄντων καὶ εὐτυχίᾳ. Disagreeing again with Robortello, Rufo interprets the passage as meaning that the tragic hero must be of those "who enjoy great fame and a prosperous and abundant fortune" ("qui magna sunt in opinione, lautaque & secunda fortuna," p. I5).

Rufo's work belongs to the long and slow process concerned with improving the text of the *Poetics* and especially with suggesting, passage by passage, better interpretations. His suggestions are sometimes more acceptable than those of his predecessors, and this alone gives him a certain distinction in the elaboration of the process.

VETTORI (1560)

In 1560, Pietro Vettori published the third of the "great commentaries" on the *Poetics*, the *Commentarii in primum librum Aristotelis de arte poetarum.* (The phrase "in primum librum" appeared traditionally in such titles because of the assumption that additional books, now lost, had once existed and had contained Aristotle's theory of comedy and of the other genres.) Vettori's work followed the usual plan: the Greek text, divided into small fragments—there are two hundred and twelve of them in Vettori's division—was given first, followed by a translation into Latin, followed by Vettori's commentary on each fragment. Vettori's Greek text was the best to date, based as it was upon the available editions and upon an ancient manuscript (Vahlen believes that it was the Parisinus gr. 1741[79]); his Latin translation was also his own. In a general way, he was more interested in the philological and textual questions raised by the *Poetics* than his prede-

[9] Vahlen (1885 ed.), p. viii.

cessors had been, less interested consequently in imposing a poetic theory of his own upon the reading of Aristotle. Much of the commentary is exclusively linguistic; certain of his questions and suggestions have been taken up by modern editors. For example, his doubts about the position in the text of 1452b14–31 were later shared by Ritter and subsequent scholars.

It is perhaps because of this close philological attention to the text that Vettori is frequently more faithful to the spirit of the *Poetics* than were his contemporaries. Early in the text for example, in connection with 1448b19 on the natural origins of poetry, he summarizes these two natural sources as (1) the instinct to imitate and (2) the pleasure which men derive from imitation. He makes of the naturalness of rhythm and harmony a third cause (p. 34), whereas Maggi (p. 71) had insisted that this was one of the two sources indicated by Aristotle (Robortello [p. 30] had earlier rejected this last interpretation, which he had found in Averroës). At 1449a30, Vettori insists that both comedy and tragedy imitate "the actions of men" (p. 47), departing from the positions of Lombardi and Maggi, who defined imitation as "the expression of the actions, characters, and passions of human beings,"[80] and of Averroës, who held that poetry was an "imitation of Nature" (fol. fv). A really significant difference from Robortello and Maggi is found in Vettori's assignment of the qualitative parts of tragedy to object, manner, and means. It will be remembered that the two earlier commentators had placed plot under manner, spectacle and song under means, and diction, character, and thought under the objects.[81] Vettori, commenting on 1450a8, correctly distributes diction and song to the means, spectacle to the manner, and plot, character, and thought to the objects (p. 62). In other less extensive developments, he shows proper insights into the meaning of the text: in connection with the definition of tragedy, 1449b23, he sees clearly that the purgation included by Aristotle constitutes the "end" of tragedy (p. 56); in connection with Aristotle's criticism of the character of Menelaus in Euripides' *Orestes* (1454a29), he shows correctly that the "plot could very well have been brought to conclusion without the dishonoring of so great a hero; . . . indeed, the plot was not established in the beginning in such a way that this would be the necessary consequence."[82] What is interesting here is that Vettori understands clearly Aristotle's criticism as based on structural considerations; he does not criticize the character because it failed to follow the traditional portrayal, as later critics frequently did (cf. Castelvetro [1576 ed.], p. 327). Such passages as these demonstrate a comprehension of some of the basic orientations of the *Poetics*.

All of Vettori's interpretations are not, however, so fortunate as these. In

---

80 Maggi and Lombardi, *Explanationes* (1550), p. 34.

81 See above, chap. ix, pp. 394 and 416.

82 *Commentarii* (1560), p. 146: "sine tanta nanque clari viri turpitudine fabula ad exitum commodè perduci poterat. . . . neque enim à principio res ita constitutae fuerant, vt hoc inde sequi necesse foret."

many cases, the force of the tradition as already established is irresistible, and he makes repeated and ingenious attempts to fit Aristotle's text into that tradition. The most notable example of this effort is found in Vettori's remarks, throughout the commentary, on the relationship between poetry and verse. His basic and immutable contention is that verse is necessary for poetry, and he bends his interpretation of the *Poetics*, at numerous places, to justify that contention. This is done for the first time in the remarks on λόγοις ψιλοῖς at 1447a29; Vettori states his position:

In order to declare completely how I feel about this matter, I hold that one of those elements which make true poets of some men is metrical discourse. Nobody can call himself a poet in the proper sense of the word, even if he imitates and expresses what he wishes in an excellent fashion, unless he uses this form of discourse.[83]

There would thus seem to be, for Vettori, three indispensable elements of poetry: imitation, verse, and excellent expression. On the basis of this assumption he condemns those modern writers of comedy who have written it in prose (p. 12). Consonant with the same position, Vettori interprets the ἡδυσμένῳ in the definition of tragedy (1449b25) as implying meter— "numerum concentum & metrum" (p. 55). He argues again, in connection with 1450b13, that the passage confirms his earlier thesis that poetic diction necessarily involves verse (p. 77).

A second example of Vettori's yielding to tradition may be found in his wish to reduce poetics to a kind of rhetoric. There are many examples of this, but perhaps the position may be sufficiently clear if we examine those passages treating the end of poetry with respect to its audience. The first occurs in the commentary on the first sentence of the *Poetics*, where Vettori says that the species of poetry were invented "to purge us of the vices and to delight us."[84] The statement becomes more distinctly rhetorical when, in the definition of tragedy, he states that purgation is achieved in tragedy by "putting before our eyes misfortunes which necessarily move our souls."[85] Specifically, purgation is said to be an answer to Plato's banishment of the poets for their moving of the passions:

Aristotle, on the contrary, judges that these feelings are useful if they are moderated. Nevertheless, since at times they could spill over in such a way as to be completely irrepressible, it is necessary to provide a remedy for this evil. The remedy is found when somebody purges them in advance and takes away from them what is excessive in quantity and dangerous. This is done most conspicu-

---

[83] *Ibid.*, p. 12: "Vt autem penitus, quod sentio, de hac re, testificer, arbitror alterum eorum, quae reddunt aliquos propriè poetas, esse orationem metricam. nec posse quempiam vere vocari poëtam, quamuis imitetur: eximiéque exprimat, quod vult, nisi vtatur hac oratione"; cf. p. 18: "primo ipsum λόγον cum dixit, poeticam orationem, id est certis mensuris illigatam intellexisse"; and p. 23, where Vettori claims that prose is not acceptable for the poet: "remotamdue ipsam penitus existimo ab officio poëtae." Also p. 52.

[84] *Ibid.*, p. 2: "cum inuenatae sint nobis à vitijs purgandis atque oblectandis."

[85] *Ibid.*, p. 56: "ponens ante oculos casus, qui necessario moueant animos nostros."

ously indeed by tragedy, which sets bounds to all the passions and teaches how far one may go. In fact, tragedy devotes itself to this end and heals the violence and the outbreak of all the passions by means of two of them which it arouses and moderates through the actions which it presents on the stage, i.e., by means of pity and fear.[86]

Moreover, the verbs used in later repetitions of these formulas are ones constantly found in rhetorical treatises: "ad timorem *iniiciendum,* & ad misericordiam *mouendam* accommodatos," "ad metum *iniiciendum,* & ad misericordiam in animis spectatorum *excitandam*" (p. 101); "timoremque magnum *incutere* animis eorum" (p. 134). So for the parts of tragedy. Recognition and reversal make for tragedies which "vehementer *capiant* animos hominum, ac *ducant* ipsos quò *velint*" (p. 69); spectacle "*allicit* ad se animos" and has power to "*capere* sine dubio animos spectatorum" (p. 78). The need for verisimilitude is dictated by the fact that both tragedy and comedy must "sumere materiam ... *aptam ad persuadendum*" (p. 96); their actions are those which "magis *aptae* sint *ad persuadendum*" (p. 97). Vettori states the whole position very clearly in this passage, again in connection with verisimilitude: "In fact, the end of the poets is to obtain the belief of the listeners; for which reason poets must adapt themselves to their judgment and express those things which are apt to persuade."[87]

These rhetorical orientations are apparent in Vettori's theory of the nature of the poet's audience and of its expectations. The audience of tragedy is made up of "the multitude seated in the theater" (p. 183). The poet must strive to please it: "I say that nothing must be brought upon the stage which would go counter to the wish and the desires of the spectators. Since the poets seek to please them, the very opposite effect would result [from any such unacceptable materials]."[88] The poet must strive to move it in various ways; he will use surprise "to provoke in the minds of those who hear this marveling and this fear";[89] he will use episodes for the sake of elegance and pleasure (p. 244) and especially to avoid monotony and tedium for the spectator (p. 251). Above all, he will use probable materials in order to gain credibility: "For the poetic art is in subjection to the beliefs of the listeners, and it attempts to insinuate itself, with every

---

86 *Ibid.,* p. 56: "contra vero Aristoteles iudicat motus hos temperatos esse utiles: veruntamen quia aliquando ita effunderentur, vt nulla ui reprimi possent, opus esse huic malo remedium adhibere: remedium autem esse, si quis antea ipsos purget, ac quod nimium importunumque est in illis, tollat. Hoc verò praeclare facere tragoediam, quae modum adhibet omnibus perturbationibus: docetque quatenus progrediendum sit: ipsa enim incumbit huic rei, & curat impetum, exultantiamque perturbationum omnium ope duarum, quas factis, quae in scenam inducit, excitat, moderaturque, id est misericordiae & metus."

87 *Ibid.,* p. 260: "finis enim poëtarum est adipisci assensum eorum qui audiunt: quare accommodare se debent ad eorum iudicia, & ea proferre, quae sint apta ad persuadendum."

88 *Ibid.,* p. 122: "nihil inquam afferri debere in scenam, quod contra voluntatem & desideria sit spectatorum: cum enim poëtae placere studeant ipsis, contrarium inde penitus sequeretur."

89 *Ibid.,* p. 163: "efficere in animis eorum qui audiunt hanc admirationem ac pauorem."

means possible, into their minds, seizing upon all means useful for this purpose and rejecting their opposites."[90]

The rhetorical bent expresses itself, finally, in Vettori's emphasis upon a special poetic diction. We have seen earlier that he regards this as one of the distinguishing features of the art and as necessarily involving the use of verse. In his commentary on 1450*b*13, he specifically states that diction is not the same for prose and for poetry: " . . . not all words are proper in the same way to both kinds; for the poets have certain words which are properly their own, which are only little used in prose."[91] When this demand for verse and a special diction is reduced to terms of the poet's genius, it becomes its distinctive quality, "since it is proper to the poetic faculty to embellish diction with words and to bring to it all the beauties of this kind."[92] In certain parts of the poem, then, as Aristotle suggests, the poet will cultivate all the "flowers" and "beauties" of diction.

Besides the insistence on verse and the tendency toward rhetorical interpretation, a certain number of miscellaneous elements appear in Vettori as a result of the prevalent critical tradition. For one thing, he interprets Aristotle's "better, like, or worse" as meaning "better than men of our times [nostra aetate], or worse, or similar" (p. 20; cf. "nunc" on p. 22). In connection with character, again, the personages of tragedy are said to be those of highest birth while comic persons are of middling condition (p. 24); the nature of the tragic hero is clarified in this later passage:

. . . he should not be a man of the people, or some lowly person, but one of the number of those who have a great name and are rich and favored by fortune with all advantages. This is not in opposition to the fact that he [Aristotle] does not wish this same person to be provided with an extraordinary virtue. For he approves his being excellent in praise and in esteem, even though honor and glory are usually the companions of virtue. Indeed, he is speaking in terms of the judgment of the multitudes, who admire the appearance of virtue more than virtue itself and false more than true glory.[93]

Vettori's distinctions among characters are social, whereas Aristotle's had been moral. Similarly, Aristotle's four requisites for character take on the contemporary meaning: "good" becomes morally good ("for this is useful to life, for those who watch, when they see these qualities praised in

---

[90] *Ibid.*, p. 291: "seruit enim ars poëtarum opinionibus eorum qui audiunt: studetque insinuare se omni ratione, qua potest, in animos ipsorum, captans quidquid ad hoc aptum est, reiiciensque contraria."

[91] *Ibid.*, p. 77: "quamuis non omnia verba eodem pacto conueniant vtrique generi: habent enim poëtae sua quaedam propriaque verba, quae non magnopere vsurpantur in prosa."

[92] *Ibid.*, p. 264: "Cum facultatis poëtarum sit ornare verbis orationem: omnesque huiuscemodi concinnitates adhibere."

[93] *Ibid.*, p. 123: "ut non sit vnus e populo, & obscura aliqua persona, sed è numero eorum aliquis, quorum magnum nomen est: quique opulenti sint, atque à fortuna omnibus commodis ornati. Non repugnat autem, quod ipsum uirtute aliqua praestanti praeditum esse non vult: eundem tamen laude & existimatione excellentem probat, quamuis uirtutis comes honor ac gloria plerunque sit: loquitur enim ex opinione multitudinis, quae admiratur magis imaginem uirtutis, atque inanem, quàm veram gloriam."

the plot and accepted with approval, are impelled to imitate those deeds which spring from these characters, and they try to become just such persons"[94]); "appropriate" refers to decorum and such considerations as the sex of the personage; "like" means like the characters of the century being depicted; and "constant" means self-consistent (pp. 144–45).

For matters other than character, also, Vettori calls upon traditional interpretations. The meanings assigned by Aristotle to "imitation" are crossed with those found in Plato, and true imitation is identified with the dramatic manner (p. 26). Tragedy is said to "purge" other passions besides pity and fear (p. 57), and thus the notion of an effect proper to a given genre is lost. All statements concerning necessity and probability reveal that these are understood in the context of nature; thus a man wounded in the heart "necessarily" dies (p. 81) and things which could "probably" happen are those which common opinion admits to be such (p. 94).

On the whole, while it cannot be said that Vettori presents a general theory of poetics at variance with that of Aristotle—I think indeed that there is no general theory contained in his commentary—it is nevertheless true that many individual interpretations derive from current thinking about poetry rather than from insights into the *Poetics* itself. However, Vettori makes many contributions to the text and to the translation, his remarks are sometimes original and acceptable, and the very fact that he does not impose upon Aristotle a total theory of his own is perhaps a distinguishing quality of his work.

Little need be added to what has already been said (Chapter V, pp. 156–57) about Pietro Angeli's *In Quintij Horatij de arte poetica librum annotationes*, except to put it in chronological place (around 1560) among the commentaries on Horace which made use of the *Poetics*. Angeli, as his references to Aristotle indicate, used one of the editions of Vettori's commentary; but these references do not permit us to determine exactly whether it was that of 1560 or that of 1573. If it were the latter, then of course our treatment of him here and in Chapter V would have to be moved to a later date.

PIGNA (1561)

Like Angeli's work, Pigna's *Poetica Horatiana* of 1561 is a commentary on the *Ars poetica*; but it is a full-scale one, presenting on each one of the eighty "precepts" found in Horace a lengthy explanatory remark. The correspondences which Pigna found between Horace and Aristotle have already been summarized (Chapter V, pp. 160–61); at the present time we may look more closely at the particular construction which Pigna puts upon the *Poetics*. As might be expected, there are many points at which his

94 *Ibid.*, p. 143: "hoc enim uitae prodest, nam qui spectant cum haec in fabulis laudari, plausuque excipi vident, ad ea facta imitanda excitantur, quae ab illis moribus proueniunt: conantúrque & ipsi tales euadere."

references to Aristotle give no hint as to how he understood him. Such, for example, are his remarks on language (pp. 10, 12, 23) and on meter (p. 32) and his distinction between artistic and nonartistic errors (p. 16). But there are three broad subjects on which Pigna offers a rather extensive interpretation of the *Poetics*: (1) imitation, (2) necessity and probability, and (3) character.

The passages on imitation concern everything from the nature of imitation itself to the six qualitative parts of tragedy. Commenting on the first lines of Horace, Pigna avers that poetry and painting are both imitations and that both, seeking beauty, treat the better, the like, and the worse (p. 2). The object of imitation is defined as one action of one man; the reason is that "we must judge in the case of a poem as we do in human affairs, in which our understanding embraces a single action more readily than when it is directed towards several ends."[95] The magnitude of a poem (p. 56) is similarly related to our capacity for understanding—the whole must not surpass our ability to remember—as well as to our willingness to attend to it—the whole must not be negligibly small. In a general way, different objects of imitation produce different effects, and this gives the basis for the distinction among the genres: tragedy produces horror, comedy wit, and the epic admiration. The effect of each genre is proper to itself; but somehow (since this is a commentary on Horace) the effect of tragedy becomes identified with its utilitarian end. Pity and terror are aroused and the minds of the spectators are "purified" of them:

... [tragedy] does not purge for the reason that we become [in consequence] more circumspect and that those emotions teach us the tragedy of human life and repress the pride in our individual lives, but rather because, while we are attracted by that spectacle, our wearied mind is refreshed and ceases its burdensome thoughts; so the soul throws off every care and so it is purified.[96]

Whatever Aristotelian elements there might be in these topics related to imitation are stated, more so than in Aristotle, in terms of effects upon the audience.

Much more closely related to the text of the *Poetics* is what Pigna has to say about necessity and probability, although such a reference as the first one—"They [the digressions] will be coherent whenever they are necessary or probable"[97]—is little more than an allusion to a vague current generalization. His main treatment of the matter concerns Horace's "sixtieth precept" (ll. 338–40), where he finds Horace saying that verisimilitude is a

95 *Poetica Horatiana* (1561), p. 8: "Ita uerò in poemate statuendum, vt in rebus humanis, in quibus vna actio contemplatione nostra commodius amplectitur, quàm si plures fines posceret."
96 *Ibid.*, p. 76: "non purgat, quia cautiores, euadamus: & permotiones illae nos humanae vitae calamitatem edoceant, & superbiam nostrae premant. Sed quia dum illo attrahimur spectaculo, aegra mens reficitur, & cessat à duris cogitationibus: ita vt animus omni solicitudine exuatur: itaque purgetur."
97 *Ibid.*, p. 5: "Erunt autem cohęrentia, quoties aut necessaria, aut verisimilia."

condition of our pleasure as spectators. This accounts for Aristotle's statement that the impossible verisimilar is preferable to the incredible true. Pigna identifies Aristotle's necessity with Horace's verisimilitude; but his gloss on *Poetics* 1451*a*37 shows that he himself is thinking of necessary and contingent actions:

> Indeed those words καὶ τὰ δυνατὰ κατὰ τὸ εἰκὸς ἢ τὸ ἀναγκαῖον must be understood in this sense: that εἰκὸς is used for the contingent and ἀναγκαῖον for the necessary; and εἰκὸς is not distinguished because it is verisimilar, but because it is proper to things which may either happen or not happen. Indeed δυνατὰ at that point are verisimilar things, and of these some are contingent, others necessary. For at times the truth is necessary, as in history, at times verisimilitude, as in poetry.[98]

The terms of the *Poetics* are thus interpreted in the light of other theories of Aristotle, not in the light of his poetic theory. It might be appropriate at this point to indicate that Pigna frequently refers to other works of the Aristotelian corpus: to the *Rhetoric*, the *Ethics*, the *Politics*, the *Posterior Analytics*, the *Meteorologica*.

The most extensive and detailed treatment of materials from the *Poetics*, however, is given in connection with character. Following Aristotle, Pigna states that both character and passions are derived from plot; but Aristotle's four requisites for character are justified in terms of verisimilitude, consistent with Pigna's general position. A special schematism is provided for the relationship of the four requisites to verisimilitude and to the separate poetic genres. First, verisimilitude is divided into two kinds, one for things which are easily believed, the other for things which are believed with difficulty. The former includes known things, and the requisite for it is propriety, in itself or by comparison; the latter includes unknown things, and the requisite for it is resemblance, in itself or by comparison. Thus the following diagram results:

	Verisimile		
facile		*difficile*	
quod decet		similitudo	
(notioris)		(ignotius)	
per se	in collatione	per se	in collatione
χρηστόν	ἁρμόττον	ὁμαλόν	ὁμοιον
	(personarum qualitas)	(similes)	(opinione)

It then follows that Aristotle's χρηστόν would be the appropriateness of a woman's character to her nature as a woman, and his ἁρμόττον would be the appropriateness of the same character as compared with that of a child

---

98 *Ibid.*, p. 79: "nam verba illa καὶ τὰ δυνατὰ κατὰ τὸ εἰκὸς, ἢ τὸ ἀναγκαῖον ita sunt intelligenda vt εἰκὸς dicatur de contingenti, & ἀναγκαῖον de necessario, atque εἰκὸς non distinguitur; quia sit uerisimile, sed quia sit de eis, quae possint accidere, & non accidere. Siquidem δυνατὰ ibi sunt uerisimilia. quorum alia contingentia alia necessaria: est enim necessarium modo uerum, vt in historia: modo verisimile, ut in poesi."

or of a woman from another country. Aristotle's ὁμαλόν is consistency of character with itself throughout the work, whereas his ὅμοιον demands the resemblance of such a personage as a prince to the character which opinion ascribes to him. Pigna believes that the first quality, χρηστόν, is mentioned only to make the distinction exhaustive, "for we never consider any person in action by himself."[99] With respect to ὁμαλόν and ὅμοιον, Pigna sees them as serving different genres. In such poems as tragedy and the epic, ὅμοιον must be observed, since the heroes are traditional; but this is not true for comedy, where all persons are invented and where hence only ὁμαλόν applies (pp. 46–47). Both qualities, moreover, are needed by the orator and the historian. At a later point, finally, commenting on Horace, lines 153–60, Pigna affirms that ἁρμόττον must be considered especially with respect to the age of characters and that this is the most difficult of all its applications (p. 53).

Many of the same principles appear in Pigna's *Gli heroici*, also published in 1561; indeed, the second work constitutes a clarification of the first insofar as its dealing with concrete cases provides examples of the principles. *Gli heroici* is a short treatise meant to introduce and explain Pigna's own heroic poem on the fall of Alfonso da Este in a tournament; the poem follows in the same volume. His choice of the subject was dictated, he says, by the fact that it contained in their proper form the "seven circumstances of all civil operations": a person, an action, relationship to great persons, an instrument, a place and occasion, a mode for the action, and an end (pp. 9–10). As a heroic poem, or an epic, this work will possess some qualities common to all poetry, some features peculiar to the epic, and some characteristics which it will share with the related form of tragedy. So for the most part the statement that it contains "one single action of one illustrious person" is general in its application, except that the "illustrious" relates it specifically to tragedy and the epic (p. 11). Similarly, the particular relationship of his *Heroico* to truth classes it among the serious genres:

... this imitation consists in "coloring" a verisimilar thing upon a true one. In comedy and in certain other poems it is sufficient that the thing should be said in a verisimilar way, even if there is no truth present. But in heroic poetry . . . and in tragedy it is necessary to have a foundation of some true thing, since it is not reasonable that a great event should have occurred to some great and famous gentleman without being widely known.[100]

In Pigna's poem, the true event is the fall of Alfonso from his horse; the verisimilar consequence is that the guardian angels, headed by Mars,

---

[99] *Ibid.*, p. 45: "nunquam tamen personam vllam in actionibus solam consideramus."

[100] *Gli heroici* (1561), p. 11: "questo imitare è sopra una cosa uera colorire una uerisimile. nella comedia & in certi altri Poemi basta che la cosa si dica uerisimilmente, ancora che non ui sia uerità alcuna. ma nella Poesia Heroica che in un sol nome è detta Epopeia & nella tragedia è necessario che ui sia il fondamento di cosa uera. non essendo ragioneuole, che sia occorso un gran fatto di qualche gran Signore segnalato che diuolgato non si sia."

should have interceded with God for his life. This latter action constitutes the "imitation." It will be noted that the action as described contains elements both of tragedy and of the epic: first, there is a mutation of fortune which relates it to tragedy; second, there is a perfecting of the actual events which relate them to the epic. The emotional effects are equally mixed: pity and terror accompanied by the desire for honor (on the part of common men) and the desire for magnanimity (on the part of the great). "And thus in addition to the emulation of illustrious actions, which will be the principal passion, pity and fear will touch our hearts every time we read a heroic poem having tragic elements."[101] Finally, the action combines elements of the active and the contemplative lives; the active life is more proper to illustrious persons, the other to private citizens. Thus Pigna's poem leans more towards the active, which is both heroic and tragic (pp. 65–66).

Tragedy differs from epic in the limits of time, and these in turn are imposed by the willingness of the audience to believe:

... the epic is longer than tragedy, since the accidents of things of this world may change all of a sudden, so that these may easily be contained in the space of one day. And they thus become useful for the stage, which does not admit too much passage of time since it is not proper that an action of many days should be represented in four hours. ... And since a man may not, in so short a time, show that he has something divine in him, nor can he in one single day give an account of his greatness of soul, not less than a month is required to set forth the life of a great prince. This is not too long, since a composition made in this way is to be read, not to be listened to by a waiting spectator.[102]

The nature of the action itself and the circumstances of its presentation to an audience will thus determine whether it is fit for epic or for tragedy. Regardless of the genre, the poet uses certain devices, common also to the orator, to present his materials; these are such rhetorical means as the enthymeme, the example, the deduction, the conclusion. These are all adapted to the capacities of the audience: "One considers men in general, insofar as these must be able to comprehend what is contained in the poem."[103]

It is clear from what Pigna says in the three books of *Gli heroici* that theory has been made to serve two purposes, to provide the basis of the

101 *Ibid.*, p. 14: "Et cosi ancora oltre alla emulatione delle attioni illustri, che sarà l'affetto principale, la pietà & lo spauento, ci toccheranno il cuore, ogni uolta che leggiamo una Poesia Heroica, c'habbia del tragico." V. p. 76.

102 *Ibid.*, p. 14: "è piu lunga l'Epopeia della tragedia: perche gli accidenti delle cose del mondo possono uariare in un subito di modo, che essi si rinchiudono facilmente nello spatio d'un giorno: & uengono a seruire alla scena che non comporta troppo tempo per non essere il douere che una attione di molte giornate sia rappresentata in quattro hore. ... Et perche non cosi tosto l'huomo dimostra hauer del diuino, ne puo in un di solo dar conto del suo grand'animo, non ui uuol meno d'un mese a dichiarare la uita d'un supremo Principe. il che non è di troppo lunghezza douendosi leggere cosi fatto componimento, & non stare ad udirlo come spettatore."

103 *Ibid.*, p. 23: "si riguarda l'uniuersale de gli huomini: in quanto che essi hanno da esser capaci di cio che si contiene nel Poema."

poem itself and to justify, after the fact, certain features of that same poem. In this way the "theoretical application" of Aristotle's *Poetics* is two-edged. But it is at best a vague and general application, since most of the Aristotelian principles taken over are now hardly recognizable. One is aware of their presence in certain formulas, and one realizes that they are there especially because one has seen them earlier in the *Poetica Horatiana*.

MARANTA (1561)

In 1561 also, but some time after the publication of the *Poetica Horatiana*, Bartolomeo Maranta undertook to expound the *Ars poetica* to the members of the Accademia Napoletana; the lectures are now found in MS R.126.Sup. of the Biblioteca Ambrosiana.[104] If these discourses have a place in the present chapter, it is because Maranta seeks to cast some fresher light on the interpretation of Horace by referring at length to the *Poetics*. He concerns himself only with the first two "precepts" of Horace, which he interprets as treating the relationship between plot and episodes. The interpretations of Robortello, Maggi, Vettori, and Pigna are all rejected as inadequate. Instead, Maranta suggests that we must define carefully the meanings of "plot" ("favola") and "episode." Plot, he says, has three meanings in Aristotle; it is, first,

. . . one formal part among the six. . . . it does not differ at all from the universal except in the addition of names; for the universal, the plot, and the principal action of the whole poem are all one and the same thing. . . . In the second way, plot is the same thing as the tragedy or the comedy or the epic or any other poem, that is, the whole aggregate of the universal and of the episodes. . . . The third way of the plot is that which concerns the action proper . . . ; in this meaning plot is restricted solely to the true episodes, that is, to all that part of the poem which begins from the first chorus and ends in the last chorus.[105]

Maranta's disagreement with his predecessors consists in the fact that they regard episodes as external to the action, whereas he can admit of no part of the poem as external to the unifying plot. The distinction he makes is between episodes which belong to the general "story" and those which are integral to the plot; he has this to say about plot and episodes in the *Aeneid*:

In this way, we can say that the universal contains within itself a sum of epi-

104 See my article, "Bartolomeo Maranta: nuovi manoscritti di critica letteraria," *Annali della Scuola Normale di Pisa*, Serie II, XXIV (1955), 115–25, for the dates of these discourses and the attendant circumstances. The MS now being discussed is No. VI in the article mentioned.

105 MS Ambr. R.126.Sup., fols. 128v–29: "una parte formale delle sei . . . non differisce punto dall'vniuersale se non per la aggiuntione de nomj. perche l'vniuersale la fauola, e la principal attione di tutto il poema sono tutte una cosa medesima. . . . Nella 2ª maniera Fauola è quello medesimo che la Tragedia o uero la comedia o la epopeia o altro poema cioè tutto l'aggregato della vniuersale e delli episodij. . . . La terza maniera della Fauola e quella che uersa circa la attione propria . . . in questo significato la fauola si ristrigne solo nelli ueri episodij cioè in tutta quella parte del poema che comincia dal primo coro et finisce nell'ultimo coro."

sodes, considering, however, those episodes which truly belong to the principal action of the whole poem, but not to the plot which the poet has undertaken principally to write. And these episodes are the most appropriate when taken from within the action for they are like a part of the principal action and they are truly necessary; the others are indeed drawn from within, but they are not considered as parts of the principal action.[106]

In these passages, Maranta seems to be distinguishing one kind of plot which contains the whole of a story in general terms and the episodes proper to it; a second kind which specifies this story in terms of a single action and named characters, and the episodes proper to it; and, finally, plot as a qualitative part of a tragedy or an epic. In the last sense, the "episodes" are the sections between the choruses of a tragedy, for example.

The preceding remarks constitute the substance of Maranta's second discourse. In the third, he repeats Aristotle's recommendation that the poet find the universal plot, the "modello," then add names to it, then supply the episodes. The dominant principle of construction is unity and the plot must be so knit that the removal of any episode would spoil the whole structure. Unity must exist independently of episodes. There seems to be some wavering and inconsistency when, later in the same discourse, Maranta declares that the episode is a quantitative part (adding "volume" to the poem) and that as such its addition to plot constitutes a combining of formal and quantitative elements. In the fourth discourse, Maranta gives further details on the definition and use of episodes. The episode, he says, "does nothing else but extend and augment the plot and the universal by telling how what is summarized in the universal has come about. . . . its nature and its end is none other than to tell the way in which the complication and the solution of the plot are brought about."[107] The plot is thus the "immutable, invariable, eternal" story, the episodes are the variations which a poet can bring to that story. It is clear that Maranta is here speaking in terms of traditional, accepted stories and of their particular treatment by successive poets.

The fifth and sixth discourses do little more than repeat and expand the discussion of the same materials. In its totality, the manuscript belabors in a repetitious and monotonous way Maranta's ideas about plot and episode. But this is perhaps its chief worth. For it gives very extended consideration to what he considers to be the most important aspect of the poetic art, and

106 *Ibid.*, fols. 129v–30: "A questo modo noi potremo dire che l'uniuersale contenghi dentro di se somma di Episodij pigliando pero quelli episodij che sono ben del fatto principale di tutto il poema ma non della fauola presa principalmente a scriuersi dal poeta; Et questi episodij sono gli più proprij presi da dentro l'attione perche sono como parte della attione principale; et sono ueri necessarij: li altri si dùcono bene da dentro ma non hanno consideratione di parti della principale attione."

107 *Ibid.*, fol. 146v: "non fa altro che dilatare et accrescere la fauola et l'universale con dire il modo che quello che nell'universale si dice sia accaduto. . . . non sia altro la sua natura et il suo ufficio senon dj dire il modo con el quale si fa la connessione et la solutione della fauola."

it seeks its solutions for this aspect in the text of the *Poetics*. Maranta's reading of Aristotle is frequently closer and more adequate than were his predecessors', although it has some notable failings. At any rate, his presentation of the lectures to the Accademia Napoletana must have seemed new and informative—if boring.

During the same months of 1561, Maranta wrote for Giovanni Villani a clarification of some of the points made in his lectures; the manuscript, in Latin, is now Ambrosianus R.118.Sup., fols. 117–24v. The additions to his statement of theory are significant. Most important of all is his rejection of the usual way of dividing and interpreting the *Ars poetica* by seeking in it the parts corresponding to invention, disposition, and elocution. His rejection is on Aristotelian grounds: "We believe that he who wishes to divide poetics must seek a division proper to it and which does not belong to any other art or any other science."[108] The distinction rejected, belonging to rhetoric, cannot be of any possible use for poetics. In its place, Maranta will try to apply the divisions of the *Poetics* to the *Ars poetica*.

[Aristotle] seems to divide the *Poetics* itself according to the variety of means by which the imitation is made. As for the imitation, indeed, having enumerated the kinds of poems, . . . and omitted the last three of these, . . . we may easily adapt it to the latter three by using a kind of similarity derived from the first three types. He divides the first three very carefully into parts. . . . Then there are two kinds of parts: some, like ideal forms or species, are present in the whole of the poem and can be revealed in it rather in potentiality than in actuality, whence they are properly called "potentials," if I may use that term. . . . The others are the parts which Aristotle calls quantitative because they divide the same poems into parts "actually" existing; these have also come to be called "integrating" parts since by means of them the body of the poem is brought together and made into a whole, just as the body of an animal by means of the members. . . . A perfect master of poets must reveal all these six parts one by one, which is what Horace indeed accomplishes, albeit not in the same order that Aristotle used.[109]

The consideration of the first qualitative part, plot, brings Maranta back to his constant theme: the discussion of "fabula," of the conditions for unity, and of episodes. Here he makes another important remark, too

---

108 MS Ambr. R.118.Sup., fol. 117v: "Oportere autem eum qui poeticam partiri cupiat propriam, et quae nulli praeterea arti aut scientiae conueniat, diuisionem quaerere existimauimus."

109 *Ibid.*, fols. 118–18v: "poeticam ipsam a uarietate instrumentorum quibus imitatio perficitur partiri uidetur: imitationem uerò enumeratis poematum speciebus . . . omissis uero tribus posterioribus . . . ex tribus prioribus per similitudinem quandam acceptam facile ipsis accommodare possumus; tria priora diligentius in partes scindit. . . . Sunt autem partium duo genera: aliae quidem ueluti formae siue species sunt in toto poemate quae potentia potius quam actu in ipso ostendi possunt quam obrem potentiales ut hoc verbo utar merito appellantur. . . . Aliae sunt partes quas quantas appellat Aristoteles quia in partes actu existentes eadem poemata diuidunt, has etiam integrantes appellare consueuerunt quia ex ipsis ueluti corpus animalis ex membris poematis corpus coalescit et totum fit. . . . optimus autem poetarum institutor has omnes sex partes sigillatim ostendere debet quod quidem exequitur Horatius tam et si non eodem ordine quo Aristoteles usus est."

frequently missed by his contemporaries: the plot is an imitation not of men but of human actions, of the fortune and misfortune that is found in such actions (fol. 118v). Again, the principle for choice and exploitation of a plot is its unity, and Maranta summarizes the three kinds of false unity listed by Aristotle as that of person, of time, and of a single war (fol. 120). Horace's first two "precepts," to return to the original argument, concern unity of plot and its relationship to episodes.

CONCLUSIONS

The years 1550 to 1561 are marked by several developments in the history of Aristotle's *Poetics*. Not many of these are new, since critics and commentators early established the main lines of discussion with respect to the text. But some of the emphases are marked and significant, and the tradition takes on new general lines. These may perhaps be more clearly seen if we consider three questions: (1) the uses to which the *Poetics* was put during these years, (2) the range of problems connected with it, and (3) its relationship to other critical modes.

Some of the "uses" of the *Poetics* are already familiar to us. To seek within it as many passages as one could find to parallel the text of the *Ars poetica* was a game discovered early in the century; in the present period the game continues to be played, although perhaps with less vigor and imagination. The tendency is now less to accumulate increasingly large numbers of parallels and more to investigate in detail the similarities between selected points of theory. Maranta's study of plot and episodes may serve as an example here. Another favorite use is for confirmation or refutation of Plato's ideas, the former for such problems as the meaning of "imitation," the latter for the perennial question of the ban put upon the poets in the *Republic*. Here again there seems to be some slackening of activity—or at least in the texts studied this is an incidental rather than a dominant preoccupation. The procedure, indeed, may be generalized: critics continue to use Aristotle as an incidental authority in the exposition of all kinds of theories; a passage here, a fragment there, will be used for the illustration of specific points in a miscellany of systems, rhetorical, poetical, and historical.

Something newer, something that really gives the tone to this decade, is the exploitation of the *Poetics*—if only occasionally—in original treatments of the art of poetry, themselves based essentially on other principles. When Benedetto Varchi, in his *Lezzioni della poetica*, takes Aristotle as a starting point for a theory which turns out to be of an entirely different kind, he is making just such use of him. Newer still is the type of activity which consists in using the *Poetics* to provide an order and a framework for new theories of the genres. Thus Giraldi's treatises on tragedy, comedy, and satire take their suppositions from the Aristotelian text, on which they frankly admit that they are modeled. Both Giraldi and Pigna do the same thing when they develop their theories of a genre unknown to Aristotle, the romance. But here there is a basic difference of procedure, since they must start with the admission that only a part of Aristotle's theory will be applicable. The extent to which each will depart from the dogma will depend first upon the way in which he reads the *Poetics,* second upon the degree of independence which he is willing to accord to the new genre—an independence involving its fundamental similarity or dissimilarity to the epic. Many factors—some of which were later to constitute arguments in the "quarrel of the ancients and the moderns"—must here be taken into consideration. In any case, the *Poetics* becomes more immediate and more contemporary when used in this way. The same is true whenever it contributes to the theory of a new genre, even though the contribution may take the form only of isolated precepts or miscellaneous remarks.

One should give special attention, finally, to the use of the *Poetics* as a basis for practical criticism. For as the century wears on and as abstract theories become commonplace modes of thought, all kinds of works, both old and new, come to be examined and judged in the light of those theories. In the 1550's, perhaps, the effort is more distinctly toward examination than toward judgment; for the problem is to discover what kinds of statements can be made about works by employing the terminology, the distinctions, and the general approaches of the *Poetics.* These statements are at first largely descriptive. They relate to such matters as the identification of the parts of a poem, the discovery of character, the summation of the plot and its episodes. They make affirmations with respect to the unity of the plot and the decorum of the characters. In a word, critics are at work testing the ways in which the text of the *Poetics* may be useful for practical criticism. It will be some time before evaluations will be attempted on the basis of the same text, since the derivation of criteria from principles is a long, difficult, and subtle process.

By "the range of problems connected with the *Poetics*" I mean, as distinguished from the subjects just discussed, the kinds of treatment to which the text itself was actually subjected. With some of these, again, we are already familiar. There was only one major commentary during these years, that of Vettori in 1560. Aside from it, however, there were the partial examinations of the text by such writers as Sigonio and Rufo. In all these there seems to be increased attention to philological, linguistic, and textual problems, and many useful suggestions are made for the improvement of the text. Both Vettori and Maranta work with the text at close range, the one primarily as an erudite professor concerned with the text itself, the other as a popular expositor (literature was his hobby rather than his profession) interested in correcting interpretations and in restoring the Aristotelian tradition. The latter way of handling the text, in public lectures before an academy of distinguished amateurs, seems also to be one of the newer emphases of this period: from the universities (witness

Lombardi and Maggi in the 1540's) the *Poetics* passes to the academies (witness Maranta and Varchi in the '50's and '60's), thus to a wider and less specifically professional audience.

But while attention on the text becomes fixed more closely and while its audience grows, its universality seems to be contested. This results largely from the attempt to apply it to new genres or to the new exploitation of old ones. The scope of the *Poetics*, for example, is narrowed specifically when such a theorist as Giraldi doubts its applicability to the romance. Such a limitation may have serious consequences, for the authority of Aristotle in matters literary is contested and the probability is suggested that there may be forms for which rules must be sought elsewhere. Likewise, when the same Giraldi declares that the double plot is preferable, in modern tragedy, to the single one demanded by Aristotle, he implies that as art changes the principles of Aristotle may no longer be applicable. Hence the principles themselves come to be linked with certain works and certain times—and cease to be principles. Despite such restrictions, the influence of the *Poetics* continues to grow in certain ways. It still remains the source for much new theory about new poetic genres, and in such a writer as Atanagi its main orientations are applied to the art of history. One should thus not see diminution during these years, but rather a complication of attitudes and the raising of some healthy doubts.

As for the relationship of Aristotle's theories to other critical modes, few changes are to be noted. Horace continues to be the dominant authority on poetic questions, and the most frequent assimilation of Aristotle's text is to the statements of the *Ars poetica*. It would not be an exaggeration to say that in most cases Aristotle is read with Horace in mind and that the uncertainties of the former are solved by reference to the relative certainties of the latter. In some cases the procedure is reversed, and difficult passages in Horace are illuminated by citation of the *Poetics*. As usual, we find that Horace is coupled with—and sometimes not distinguishable from—the rhetorical tradition; I mean, of course, in his bearing upon the interpretation of Aristotle. One still thinks of invention, disposition, and elocution as the essential divisions of the art of poetry, and Maranta's vehement protest against this kind of thinking assures us of its currency. Perhaps this is the most striking way in which the Middle Ages continue to exert an influence upon the interpretation of the *Poetics*. Almost equally prominent, though, is the medieval conception of the literary genres. For many of the commentators, the abstract and partial statements found in Aristotle are "completed" by the addition of the whole collection of medieval precepts for the genres: subject matter, kinds of characters, type of action and of ending, style, tone. Pigna provides us with an example here. Related to the same tendency is the insistence upon decorum, which perhaps combines all of the influences already mentioned. This leads increasingly to an emphasis upon social distinctions when Aristotle had made ethical distinctions, and upon ethical distinctions which derive rather from tradition than from the needs of a particular poem.

Among critical modes which had more recently become current, the one most usually associated with the *Poetics* is that of Plato's ideas on imitation. Since imitation was one of the central doctrines of the work, it was only natural that Plato's texts should be called upon for elucidations and for supplementary ideas. Otherwise, little influence of Plato is felt in the interpretations of Aristotle. Aristotle himself becomes one of the main sources of light on the *Poetics*; the other works, especially the *Rhetoric*, are studied more and more intensively, and some of the theorists present complete sets of cross references to the whole of the Aristotelian corpus. These are not always happy or useful; but they indicate a realization of the usefulness, for an understanding of any one work of Aristotle, of studying his other writings. Finally, during the years under examination, there is an increasing desire to ask questions about the relationship of Aristotle's theory to Christian subject matters and Christian attitudes toward the art of poetry. No polemic is as yet engaged. In the years to come, however, when practical criticism becomes more diversified and when the great literary quarrels develop, these considerations will have significant effects in the whole development of Cinquecento criticism.

CHAPTER ELEVEN. THE TRADITION OF ARISTOTLE'S POETICS: III. THE VERNACULAR COMMENTARIES

OF THE VARIOUS TENDENCIES just outlined, those that gained the greatest prominence in the years now to be studied were the newer rather than the older ones. The *Poetics* becomes, in a sense, a more "popular" document; formal and erudite commentaries in Latin, searching linguistic analyses, tend to give way to treatments which will be accessible to a larger and less professional audience. Again, within limits, the older modes will continue to be practised. But there will be more numerous academic discourses, many practical applications, a certain number of vulgarizations. These will culminate in the two great vernacular commentaries, Castelvetro's in 1570 and Piccolomini's in 1575, with Piccolomini's Italian translation coming in the intervening years, in 1572.

TOSCANELLA (1562)

Given these general trends, it is perhaps significant that the first work in the present group should be Orazio Toscanella's *Precetti necessari* of 1562. This is a frank work of vulgarization, as were all those of its author. In his preface, Toscanella states that he is merely presenting simplifications of certain basic texts for the benefit of beginners and students; the printer, Avanzo, makes a similar statement: "ho fatto imprimere l'arte poetica d'Oratio Flacco. L'arte poetica d'Aristotile: L'arte breue del Lullio: Vna parte del poeta del Minturno . . . " (p. *4). The digest of Aristotle's *Poetics*, for it is no more than that, occupies pages 80–89. Toscanella prepares a kind of catechism for the text, mentioning topics and then summarizing—in shorthand form—what Aristotle has to say on those topics. The technique may be seen in these opening lines of the treatment:

> Che cosa sia poesia. La poesia considerata in uniuersale è IMITATIONE: hor con questa, hor con quella cosa secondo la diuersità delle poesie. Che cosa habbia per genere la poesia. La poesia ha per genere l'imitatione. Differenza della imitatione. La Imitatione è differente in tre termini. Nel Modo dell'imitare. Nelle cose, che si imitano. Nelle cose con che si imita (p. 80v).

Moreover, when even so simplified a statement might not be fully understood, Toscanella reduces the ideas to tabular form. On the whole, the digest must have been of no value to the serious Aristotelian; but it is highly interesting as an indication of what the schoolmaster of 1562 would have told his pupils about the *Poetics*.

The digest is interesting for other reasons. We can see in it a typical reading of the *Poetics* for this period, a compendium of the solutions which had been reached for all the difficult problems of the text. There is a kind of scholastic undertone to the treatment, a wish to proceed by way of genus and differentia and to make progressive subdivisions, which Toscanella undoubtedly thought appropriate to the handling of an Aristotelian text. If we merely take the text in the order of presentation, we find some of the typical solutions of which I have spoken. The means of poetry, as exemplified by the epic, may be verse (of one kind or several kinds in the epic) or prose. The objects at times determine the genre, at times do not; thus men "better than others" are found in tragedy and the epic, men "like ourselves" are found in comedy, and the "worst" men in any one of the three (p. 81v). On the natural bases of imitation, Toscanella gives the correct reading: "Imitation, which is most natural. The deriving of pleasure from imitation."[1] His translation of the definition of tragedy displays all the contemporary uncertainty, resulting especially from the imperfect state of the text:

Tragedy is an imitation of a virtuous perfect action. Which has magnitude, with pleasant speech, separately in each one of its species, in the parts of those, who are performing actions. Pleasant speech is that which has number, harmony, sweetness. Conducting the PASSIONS not by means of narration, as the epic poem does, but by means of pity, fear.[2]

When he comes to distributing the six parts of tragedy among object, manner, and means, Toscanella adopts, if imperfectly, the system of Robortello. Apparatus and music are the "instrumental" parts; character, elocution, and discourse are the "final" parts (i.e., those which are imitated). The plot should represent the means; but Toscanella calls it rather "the subject or material part, since it gives the invention." Its parts, he says, are reversal and recognition—no mention of knot and solution. Definitions of some of the other parts are equally strange: elocution is the "composition of the verses" and discourse is everything which "shows or does not show some 'sentenza'" (p. 83).

The pleasure derived from tragedy, through pity and fear, results from the learning of a moral lesson: "The pleasure of tragedy results from pity and from fear; for when the spectators see such terrible misfortunes happening to such great persons, they learn to suffer patiently their own calamities, or to bear them. So that the pleasure springs from the LEARNING."[3] The treatment of plot and episodes is highly instructive, showing as it does the tendency to think in terms of a theme rather than of an action as constituting the unity of plot. Toscanella uses the example of Vergil, whose single

[1] *Precetti necessari* (1562), p. 82: "Imitatione, la quale è naturalissima. Il pigliarsi piacere dalla imitatione."
[2] *Ibid.*, p. 82v: "La Tragedia è Vna imitatione d'attione uirtuosa perfetta. Che habbia grandezza, con parlar soaue, separatamente in ciascuna sua spetie, nelle parti di coloro, che uan negotiando. Parlar soaue è quello, che ha Numero. Armonia. Dolcezza. Conducendo gli AFFETTI non per uia di Narratione, come fà il poema heroico: ma per uia di Misericordia. Timore."
[3] *Ibid.*, p. 83v: "Il piacere della Tragedia risulta dalla misericordia, & dal timore: perche uedendo li spettatori casi cosi terribili, successi in persone cosi grandi; imparano a comportar patientemente le calamità sue, ò a supportarle. Tanto che il piacere nasce dallo IMPARARE."

action is constituted by "the exploits of Aeneas after he came to Italy" (p. 83v); the other matters are said to fall outside the poet's intention and to constitute digressions. These are "all those things which the poet treats when he departs from the matter undertaken, which digressions, however, must not be entirely unrelated to the matter proposed, but must have in part an appropriateness to it. "[4] Toscanella's translations of the passages on the tragic hero and on the nature of pity and fear both show a basically sound understanding of the text. (I italicize significant words.) On the tragic hero: "Those pass into misery who are not excellent either for virtue or for justice; not for their vice nor for any iniquity, but *for some error committed by them*; who are placed in glory and in prosperity of fortune."[5] On the effects of tragedy: "Pity concerns him who is not worthy, that is him *who should not fall into misery*, and so forth. Fear concerns him *who is like us*; for we fear lest a similar thing should happen to our own selves."[6]

The solutions with respect to the four requisites for character are less felicitous. The principal difficulty lies in Toscanella's inability to distinguish among them. He says that "goodness" ("bontà") consists in the assigning of good characters to good people; that "appropriateness" ("conuenienza") involves assigning the proper kind of speech to men and to women, according to the characteristics of their sex; that "resemblance" ("similitudine") concerns the passions, which must always express the basic character of the person; and that "constancy" ("ugualità") requires uniform presentation of the person's desires throughout the play (p. 85v).

At the end of the digest we find a number of miscellaneous precepts for tragedy and the epic, some of which reveal essential interpretations. The epic poem, for example, is said to contain numerous plots (p. 87v). The episodes of tragedy must be varied, since satiety would result from too much similarity. Epic verse is characterized by stability, swollenness (but not of the blameworthy kind), a variety of languages, and the use of metaphors. Narrative imitation—and he here opposes Aristotle—is the most excellent kind. All forms of speech must be based upon reason. So far as doctrine is concerned, these remarks are no more miscellaneous than the rest of the work. It presents no organized or systematic interpretation of Aristotle's *Poetics*; but isolated translations and commentaries reveal important interpretations of the passages involved.

While Toscanella's thumbnail summary presents the *Poetics* in a volume

[4] *Ibid.*, p. 84: "tutte quelle cose, che tratta il poeta partendosi dalla materia incominciata; i quai digressi però non uogliono essere in tutto lontani dalla materia propostasi; ma hauere in parte conuenienza seco."

[5] *Ibid.*, p. 84v: "Quei passino in miseria, iquali ne per uirtù, ne per giustitia sono eccellenti: non per uitio loro, o per iniquità; ma per qualche errore commesso da loro, che in gloria, & prosperità di fortuna posti sono."

[6] *Ibid.*, p. 85: "La Misericordia è intorno a chi non è degno; cioè à chi non douerebbe cadere in miseria, &c. La Paura, è intorno à chi ci è simile; perche dubitiamo, che il somigliante non interuenga à noi medesimi."

which also contained the other essential treatises, Bernardo Tasso's *Ragionamento della poesia* (published in 1562, but probably delivered before the Accademia Veneziana in 1560) attempts to combine Aristotle's theory with various others in order to make an elaborate defence of the art. Essentially, Bernardo's sources are these three: the elements of the Boccaccian defence of poesy, the allegations of universal knowledge found in such texts as the *Vita Homeri,* and Plato's ideas on the divine furor (see above, Chapter VII, pp. 282–84). In this context, Aristotle plays only a minor role. He is corrected and clarified with respect to the distinction between poetry and poetics; poetry, says Tasso, is "the universal material of the whole poem," while poetics is "the art which teaches the poet how to arrange well and according to rule this material which in itself is confused."[7] Strictly in passing, Aristotle provides a definition of poetry as "an imitation of human actions" ("una imitatione de le attioni humane," p. 4). He provides, much more extensively, the six poetic genres which Tasso distinguishes: comedy, tragedy, epic, auletic, citharistic, and dithyrambic. But the definitions of these types and descriptive statements about them come from elsewhere. Aristotle is contradicted, again, on the matter of his preference for the tragedy over epic; for Tasso, the epic is to be preferred because its writer never has to suffer from the inadequacies of actors (p. 5). In spite of its limitations for his own purposes, the *Poetics* is regarded by Tasso as eminently useful for the practising poet, especially in this generation. Before its discovery, the art of poetry had to be laboriously deduced from the reading of the poets themselves:

. . . now the poetics of that most famous philosopher, which teaches the art of writing poetry with such orderliness and in such detail, so long buried in the dark shadows of the world's ignorance, and happily translated into the Latin language and perfectly expounded and interpreted by the erudite Robortello and by our most judicious M. Vincentio Maggio and by the excellent M. Pier Vittorio, conducts us like a sure and dependable escort along the difficult roads of poetry.[8]

The same Bernardo Tasso figures as an interlocutor, as the principal authority on tragedy, and as a subject of praise in the anonymous *Tractatus de tragoedia* found in the manuscript at Perugia, Biblioteca Comunale 985 (M. 8). The praise accrues to him through the character and the recent poetic achievements of his son Torquato. (On the treatise and its date, see above, Chapter V, p. 163 and Chapter VII, p. 282.) As far as Aristotle is

---

7 *Ragionamento* (1562), p. 3*v:* "la poesia è la materia uniuersale di tutto il poema: e la poetica l'arte, che a bene, et regolatamente essa materia da se confusa di disporre insegna al Poeta."

8 *Ibid.,* pp. 9–9*v:* "hora la poetica di quel famosissimo filosofo, laqual con tanto ordine, et si particolarmente insegna l'arte del poetare tanto tempo ne l'oscure tenebre de l'ignoranza del mondo sepolta, e felicemente ne la latina fauella tradotta, e perfettamente dal Erudito Robortello, dal nostro giuditiosissimo M. Vincentio Maggio, et dal Eccellente M. Pier Vittorio isposta, et interpretata, quasi sicura, e fidata scorta per le difficili strade de la poesia ci ua conducendo."

concerned, the main problems of the treatise are two: How does it happen that we find pleasure in the artistic representation of objects which are themselves distasteful? And how can we justify the practice of an art which was condemned by Plato? Aristotle gives answers to both questions. It should be noted at the outset that, in general, the appeal to Aristotle is understood to be a departure from an earlier way of solving problems about poetry. Trissino (author of the *Sophonisba*) and Bernardo Tasso are assigned the opposing points of view: "the one [Trissino] urges a narrower [definition of poetry, one] scrupulously subjected to the injunctions of Aristotle; while the other thinks, more liberally, that it should be defined according to the judgment of the multitude, its perceptions of nature, and the examples supplied by poets."[9] With respect to the first of the questions the answer is found in the pleasure which men take in imitation. There is no direct reference to the *Poetics* but the position is essentially that of Aristotle:

> For who does not know how much delight is present in the imitation of things! we all drink in with our minds a certain joyfulness that, by nature's principles, is intimately involved with our faculties, so that with incredible pleasure we see the representations of things and the semblances of persons and images of the truth and as it were the forms of actions copied through imitation. . . . For what extreme of pleasure is it, if not this, that vices bring us when presented in a play and produced on the stage—vices, however, that in the very truth of life are rejected by the most discriminating minds and eyes and ears?[10]

Imitation supplies the answer to the second question as well, for the pleasure that it assures to the contemplation of objects and actions makes it possible to use them as devices of instruction. Imitation coats the pill. One may thus contradict the strictures of Plato and Proclus by emphasizing the usefulness of poetry in education. This, of course, has nothing to do with the *Poetics*, although the anonymous author seems to make a direct transition from Aristotle's views on imitation to these other views on pedagogy.

Carlo Sigonio's *De dialogo* of 1562 is Aristotelian in another of the ways noted in the preceding chapter. It applies what it considers to be the system and the principles of Aristotle to a literary form not treated by him, the dialogue. In so doing, it necessarily reveals a reading of the *Poetics*. Thus, our problem in discussing it is to discover what kind of a reading it implies

[9] Perugia, Bibl. Com. MS 985 (M.8), fol. 100: "alter angustiorem, et religiosa cogit praeceptionibus Aristotelis deuinctam, alter dissolutius iudicio multitudinis, naturae sensibus, poetarum exemplis definiendam putat."

[10] *Ibid.*, fols. 103v–4: "Quis autem ignorat quanta insit in rerum imitatione suauitas! omnes iucunditatem quamdam e naturae principijs implicitam sensibus animo imbibimus, ut cum incredibili uoluptate spectemus et exempla rerum, et simulacra personarum, et ueritatis imagines, et actionum quasi figuras imitatione simulatas. . . . Quid enim est illud, nisi hoc est, quod in ludum, et scenam prolata uitia tantum oblectationis afferunt! quae tamen in ipsa uitae ueritate fastidiosissimis animis oculis auribus respuuntur?"

and to summarize the character of the precepts for dialogue ostensibly derived from Aristotle. Having no basic text to work with, Sigonio must proceed by analogy, and he starts from a supposition that the dialogue is like three other forms: poetry, oratory, and dialectic. It is like poetry in that it is an imitation; like oratory in that it uses prose rather than verse; like dialectic in that its "res," "those things which demand reason and inquiry,"[11] is the same.

Before we can proceed with the analysis, we must point out that Sigonio uses "imitation" in several meanings. The first is un-Aristotelian. Imitation is common to the poet and the orator. It consists, basically, in copying the style of another writer. When this consists merely in the imitation of language and figures and a way of speech, it may serve a writer's own ends, but it is an improper pursuit and is to be condemned. When, instead, it makes the writer assume the personality of his model and write in such a way as to be mistaken for the model, it is properly done and is to be praised. Amazingly enough, Sigonio cites Plato's condemnation of the poet who always speaks in his own person and Aristotle's rejection of Empedocles as a poet as arguments in favor of this kind of imitation. The second meaning is Platonic; it refers to the dramatic manner as distinguished from the narrative and the mixed. The third meaning is not clearly defined, but it seems to be related to the sense given it in the *Poetics*. The genus of poetry, oratory, and the dialogue is imitation; other forms, such as history and the epistle, come under the same genus. This would seem to indicate that wherever persons and actions are presented or represented in arts of discourse, imitation takes place. At the same time, the term is roughly equivalent to "feigning" or "invention." Thus Silius Italicus and Lucan may be classified as poets because "they described these wars as poets, not as historians. And they achieved this by feigning episodes at will and by interweaving the deliberations of the gods and goddesses with the meetings and discourse of men, and by seeking elsewhere gay narratives of events and pleasant descriptions of places."[12] The test of good poetry is good imitation; if the poet fails by going "counter to the laws handed down to us by the great master"[13]—for example, by treating all the actions of a whole war rather than a single action of a single man—he will be a bad poet.

Since the dialogue belongs to the same genus as poetry, Sigonio will seek a definition of it by examining the same differentiae as Aristotle had considered for poetry, "a rebus, ab instrumentis, a modis" (p. 10). The "res," as we have seen, are the same as those of dialectic; the "instrumentum" is prose; the "modus" combines narrative, dramatic, and mixed, as one may

---

11 *De dialogo* (1562), p. 13: "ea, quae . . . ratione & disquisitione egent."

12 *Ibid.*, p. 3v: "bella haec non historicorum, sed poetarum more descripserint. Id quod episodiis pro arbitratu fingendis, & deum, dearumque consiliis, & hominum concionibus intexendis, atque festiuis rerum narrationibus, & iucundis locorum descriptionibus aliunde petendis consequuti sunt."

13 *Ibid.*, p. 4: "contra leges a summo doctore traditas."

see in Plato's dialogues. The definition thus has but few resemblances to that of poetry, which Sigonio gives as follows:

The matters which the poets represent by imitating he finds to be the actions of men of grave or of light character or of those in between; the instruments which contribute to the imitation are speech, harmony, and rhythm; the manners of undertaking the imitation: when they use continuous narration, or introduce [the personages] as performing the action, or when they use both manners. And thus, when he [Aristotle] came in turn to the treatment of tragedy, he concluded from these principles that tragedy is an imitation of those actions which are undertaken by grave men, using verse, harmony, and rhythm, conducted by the presentation only of persons in action.[14]

In such a statement as this, Sigonio remains fairly close to the text of the *Poetics*. When he adapts it to his own purposes, he does not attempt to deform it. Indeed, he soon departs from Aristotle, by declaring, for example, that the proper style for the dialogue is the "middle" style of the rhetoricians (p. 14), or that the fundamental problems in the handling of the dialogue are decorum and verisimilitude (p. iii).

Indeed, his total theory of the dialogue is really a theory of decorum. The form is to be praised insofar as it obeys the laws of verisimilitude and of decorum, through the observation of which every form of imitation is made perfect (p. 18). "For in fact, what else need be prescribed with respect to this form besides the fact that it is based at once in observation of persons, times, places, and causes, and in keeping one's attention on them?"[15] Even in his dedication, Sigonio insists that all matters relative to the dialogue "must obey above all else the laws of decorum and of verisimilitude; there was never anything more difficult in all the arts than to accomplish these ends, even in the judgment of the most learned men."[16] Essentially these laws, which reduce to one, have as their end convincing the reader of the truth of what is being said. They concern two elements of the dialogue: the man speaking and the language in which he speaks. For the man speaking, verisimilitude of character according to poetic requirements gives the assurance of truth:

This poetic verisimilitude is of such power and such a nature that when it is present it causes the thing which is invented not to seem so. Rather will that seem

14 *Ibid.*, p. 10: "Res, quas poetae imitando simularent, aut grauiorum, aut leuiorum hominum, aut qui his interiecti essent, actiones esse inuenit; instrumenta, quae ad imitandum afferrent, orationem esse, concentum, & rhythmum; modos ineundae imitationis, cum iidem aut perpetua uterentur narratione, aut quasi agentes inducerent, aut utrunque. Itaque cum deinceps ad tractationem tragoediae descendisset, ex his principiis tragoediam imitationem esse conclusit earum actionum, quae a grauibus susciperentur hominibus, uersu, concentu, rhythmoque, ac sola personarum inductione initam."

15 *Ibid.*, p. 18: "Quid igitur hoc de genere praecipiendum est aliud, nisi utrunque in personarum, temporum, locorum, & caussarum consideratione, atque animaduersione esse positum?"

16 *Ibid.*, p. iii: "quae decoro in primis, & uerisimilitudini seruiant, quibus tuendis officiis nihil in omnibus artibus fuit unquam uel doctissimorum hominum iudicio difficilius."

invented which is in strong contrast to the true and which achieves no resemblance to truth, that is, whatever is in disagreement with persons, times, and places and either contains no causes why it should be done as it is or contains improbable causes.

The same passage contains the explanation of verisimilitude (or decorum) in language: "Just as in fact not every man can do every thing, so it is not verisimilar that any one man should speak in every kind of discourse. And for the reason that there is no action except in time and in place, it is necessary that whatever is the case in given circumstances be also expressed in the manner of speech."[17] The whole position is later summarized in a single formula: "Poetic decorum is involved both in the imitation of the characters of men and in the creation of appropriate speech."[18] This statement is followed immediately by a reference to Aristotle's four requisites for character. In the remainder of the treatise Sigonio seems to pass imperceptibly from "mores" to "morata oratio"—a natural transition since the same basic law applies to both.

What starts as an attempt to apply Aristotelian distinctions to a new genre thus becomes little more than an expression of the current theory of decorum in literature. Clearly, Sigonio still writes at a time when the implications of Aristotle's method are not clear, when it is easy to pass from one critical context to another, when there is no notion at all of methodological rigor.

The next document in our chronology, however, displays rigorous method of another kind, the method of the philologists. This is a letter from Pietro Vettori to Bartolomeo Maranta, dated "Florent. XIIII. Kal. Ianuar. CIƆ IƆ LXII" (i.e., December 19, 1562). It is a reply to an earlier letter in which Maranta, after praising Vettori for his achievement in his commentary on the *Poetics*, expressed disagreement and asked clarification on several points. The passages involved in the discussion, found in chapters I and II, concern the distinctions among the arts as "mimetic" and "poetic"; here are Maranta's questions and Vettori's answers:

Should not all the arts mentioned by Aristotle, such as flute-playing, the dance, painting, sculpture (*Poetics* 1447a13–28), be considered as "poetic" arts? They should not, since although they use one or several of the means used by poetry, they do not use the distinguishing means of discourse.

If they are not "poetic" arts, why does Aristotle include them at this

---

[17] *Ibid.*, p. 18v: "Hoc autem poeticum eius est potestatis, atque naturae, ut cum adest, efficiat, ne res, ut est ficta, sic uideatur. ficta autem uidebitur, quae a uero longe abhorrebit, nec ueritatis ullam similitudinem consequetur, idest, quae cum personis, temporibus, & locis discrepabit, & caussas nullas, cur ita factum sit, aut certe non probabiles continebit. Vt enim non quicunque homo quancunque rem agit, sic non est uerisimile, quencunque hominem in quocunque sermone uersari. et quoniam actio nulla est nisi in tempore, & loco, propterea quod in re est, id etiam oratione exprimatur necesse est."

[18] *Ibid.*, p. 20: "Iam uero decorum poeticum cum in imitandis moribus hominum, tum in conuenienti affingenda oratione uersatur."

point? He does so because, like poetry, they are mimetic arts; and this in spite of the fact that the mere use of one of the means does not necessarily constitute imitation.

Is not the use of any one of the means of poetry in a given work a sufficient reason for classifying it as "poetry"? No; the presence of discourse ("oratio") is absolutely essential. Indeed, if diction is present (accompanied, adds Vettori, by verse) in a work which imitates, we will have a poem.

The crux of the whole matter, says Vettori, is the distinction between μίμησις and ποίησις, between all the arts on one side and the poetic arts on the other. Once we understand the basic difference, the disputed passages in Aristotle become clear; thus a philological distinction provides the basis for important philosophical developments.[19]

MARANTA (1563–64)

Bartolomeo Maranta raised these questions with Vettori at a time when he was himself engaged in a study of Aristotle's *Poetics*, not in order to publish a commentary as Vettori had done, but apparently for a series of lectures which he was preparing. It is quite possible that these were meant for delivery to the Accademia Napoletana, as a pendant to the series on Horace's *Ars poetica*. Four of the lectures (or sketches for them) are preserved in MS R.118.Sup. of the Ambrosiana; they date from the years 1563–64. I shall treat these in their order of generality rather than attempt to discover and observe a chronological arrangement.

The first of the discourses (fols. 125–32v) purports to discover Aristotle's central intention, but it soon drifts into other related problems. Aristotle's purpose, says Maranta, is "to reduce to a method the rules and precepts of the poetic art, by means of which the poet may become perfect."[20] This he attempts for two reasons: because he recognizes the importance of poetry in human life and sees the extent to which the art is badly practised; and because he wishes to complete his philosophical system. Such reflections as these bring Maranta to a study of the relationship between the philosopher and the poet; he finds that they are one and the same thing. The same definition applies to both their pursuits: the science of divine and human things ("scientiam rerum diuinarum et humanarum," fol. 125v). The poet, like the philosopher, treats—and teaches—all manner of arts and sciences, and this is especially true of the moral sciences: ". . . they omit nothing pertaining to moral precepts, to the art of ruling cities and houses; their works are full of the precepts of prudence, justice, fortitude, and temperance."[21]

---

19 In *Epistolarum libri X* (1586), pp. 107–9.

20 MS Ambr. R.118.Sup., fol. 125: "ad methodum redigere regulas et praecepta artis poeticae, quibus optimus fieri poeta possit."

21 *Ibid.*, fol. 126: "nihil omittunt quod ad praecepta morum pertinet, quod ad artem regendarum urbium et domuum; plena sunt omnia praeceptorum prudentiae, iustitiae, fortitudinis, temperantiae."

If there is a difference between the two, it is one which redounds to the credit of the poet and makes him superior to the teacher. Since he uses examples rather than naked propositions, his works appeal to the senses rather than to the mind; they are therefore more apt to move the passions and to affect the reader. Maranta summarizes his argument thus:

... not only do they [the poets] teach things as do the others [the philosophers], but they make them more powerful through examples. Indeed, the poets teach them better because more clearly, since, as they move the passions and display the habits, they place the things themselves before our eyes in such a way that we seem to see them and to touch them. But the pure philosophers, when they treat a discipline by abstracting it from its matter, weary the mind and the capacity to understand, whence it comes about that they drive their listeners or their readers away from knowledge. Therefore the ancient sages said that poetry is much more useful for this reason, that by penetrating, through the sweetness of diction, into the soul even of him who does not wish it, it makes itself accessible to a greater number of men; whereas unadorned philosophy reaches few men.[22]

Maranta bolsters his argument that poetry is more useful as an instrument of teaching by citing many ancient authors. In the course of the discussion we learn that poetry is especially apt for appealing to simple men, since it uses—instead of the definitions and demonstrations of philosophy—such readily understandable devices as examples and imitation.

By this time, Maranta has departed considerably from his original project of discussing Aristotle's purpose. The next step in the argument at the same time brings him back to Aristotle and removes him farther in the direction of Plato. The new argument reflects Aristotle's statement (*Poetics* 1451b5) that poetry is more philosophical than history. The poet treats the universal, the historian the particular. But Maranta has some difficulty in reconciling this statement with the notion that poetry works through examples, which are always particular. He resolves the difficulty by declaring that the poet really depicts the Idea—the perfect and complete expression of any virtue or vice, for example—by presenting an individual manifestation; thus Achilles displays all possible aspects of strength and fortitude. In so doing, the poet serves the greatest end of poetry, which is the inculcation of the virtues.

In a final step of his argument, Maranta recognizes a conflict between two ends which he has distinguished for the art, that of teaching through examples and that of delighting through diction. Clearly, the double Horatian end has been influencing his thinking throughout. He decides,

22 *Ibid.*, fol. 126v: "cum non solùm res doceant ut illi sed exemplis corroborent. Melius etiam quia significantius cum in mouendis affectibus explicandisque habitibus poetae res ipsas ita ob oculos ponant ut intueri ac tractare illas uideamur. At nudi philosophj cum disciplinam tradant à materia abstrahendo mentem et intelligendi uim fatigant, unde fit ut audientes uel legentes a rerum scientia auersos reddant: quare ob hanc rationem multo utiliorem poeticam esse antiqui sapientes dixerunt quia cum ob dictionis suauitatem in animos uel nolentium illabatur, multo pluribus hominibus communis fit: at simplex philosophia paucorum est hominum."

ultimately, that all traces of contradiction can be removed by distinguishing between poetry and the poet, between the art and the artist. The art and the precepts appropriate to it have as their aim the pleasure of the audience:

In fact, it is Aristotle's purpose in this little book to set down the rules by means of which simple and clear philosophy may be adorned so as to make it seem most pleasurable to all men. Whence we have concluded that we should not expect from the art of the poets philosophical teachings, since these are obtained from philosophy itself, but instead the rules through which we may compose, using the probable lie, little fables in which philosophy itself is hidden; for which reason pleasure itself is the end of the art.[23]

But the poet seeks something else. He wishes to profit men, to teach them virtue, to impress philosophical precepts upon their minds ("imprimere philosophica praecepta in hominum animis," fol. 132). This he does by employing pleasurable devices as instruments for moving their souls, so that they may be purged of the passions, returned to tranquillity, and led thus to the highest degree of happiness. The poet's goal is completely utilitarian.

In the first of these discourses, then, Bartolomeo Maranta finds that the *Poetics* is close to Horace in the ends which it establishes for poetry and close to Plato in its conception of the object of imitation. In the second (fols. 109–14v) he addresses himself to the problem of Aristotle's philosophical method and the general organization of the *Poetics*. He finds that one may describe the philosophical method as an orderly passage from the universal to the particular, and that this in turn determines the organization: Aristotle will treat first those things common to all forms of poetry, then the peculiar features of the individual genres. Again, the terminology used, "communia" and "propria," is vaguely reminiscent of Horace. Maranta thinks that the "communia" may be reduced to four general headings: (1) "... in what ways all species of poems are alike, and in what ways they differ." From these come genus and differentia, which in turn give the definitions. The genus is imitation. (2) "On the origin of poems and why different kinds of them were invented." (3) "On the growth of these poems and how, from a formless state, they reached perfection." (4) "In what way tragedy and the epic are alike or how they differ from each other."[24] After these general statements, Aristotle passes on to the treatment of the individual genres.

[23] *Ibid.*, fol. 131v: "Est enim Aristotelis mens in hoc libello tradere regulas quibus philosophia simplex et aperta, ita exornari possit ut iucundissima omnibus uideatur. . . . Ex quo colligimus ab arte poetarum nos non expectare debere philosophica documenta quia haec habentur à nuda philosophia sed tamen regulas, quibus uerisimili mendacio fabellas componamus in quibus lateat ipsa philosophia: quare finis artis est ipsa oblectatio."

[24] *Ibid.*, fols. 113–13v: "Ac primum eorum est ut doceat in quibus omnes poematum species conueniant, et in quibus differant. . . . Secundum agit de origine poematum et quam ob rem diuersa eorum inuenta sint genera. . . . Tertium de incremento horum poematum, ac quomodo ad perfectionem ex informibus deuenerint. . . . Quartum ac postremum docet in quo tragoedia & epopoeia conueniant in quoúe discrepent inter se."

As he develops this general scheme of the *Poetics*, Maranta makes several distinctions which are of interest for the interpretation of that text. He is very early obliged to decide what is meant by δύναμις (1447a9), and after excluding any reference to the end of poetry ("which is to purge the minds of men of the vices"[25]) he argues that it means

. . . the formal and, so to speak, the specific nature of each poem, by which one differs from another; indeed, when we know the definition of each, we know wherein consists their proper essence [vis], in virtue of which essence, for example, tragedy is so distinctly tragedy that the name of any other kind of poem would not be fitting for it.[26]

This is, I believe, a fairly keen understanding of the term. Shortly afterward, subsequent to remarks on the importance of plot, he says that Aristotle treats tragic plot in a series of ten precepts. The attempt to reduce Aristotle's discussion to a set of numbered precepts recalls a similar effort on the part of the commentators on the *Ars poetica,* an effort by this time commonplace. It had not yet, however, gained currency among the students of the *Poetics.* Maranta's ten precepts, reduced to their simplest form, concern these topics:

1. Proper magnitude; easy to remember without excessive brevity.
2. Unity; a single action directed to a single end.
3. Universality; verisimilar actions, but not particular ones since these are the object of history.
4. Necessary and verisimilar connection of episodes.
5. Pity and terror, produced by incredible events since these excite greater admiration.
6. Complex rather than simple plot.
7. Quantitative parts of tragedy.
8. The proper character for tragic personages.
9. Simple plot: the passage of a single person from good to bad fortune.
10. Rules for the pitiable and the terrible.

These careful recommendations for plot, says Maranta, are essential since plot is the soul of tragedy and since the slightest error in its handling will mean the ruin of the whole poem.[27] In a final section of the manuscript, separate from the rest, Maranta makes a distinction with respect to the genus of poetry. He had earlier declared that the genus was imitation; but he now realizes that poems are also classified under such terms as "effictio," "poesia," "poetica." Of these, the term which most needs to be separated

---

[25] *Ibid.,* fol. 110: "δύναμιν hoc loco non puto referri ad finem poeticae artis qui est ut expurget a uitijs animos hominum."

[26] *Ibid.,* fol. 110: "formalem ut sic dixerim ac specificam naturam cuiusque poematis qua alterum ab altero differt; nam cognita uniuscuiusque diffinitione scimus in quo uis propria eorum consistat ob quam uim uerbi gratia tragoedia ita est tragoedia ut aliud ei poematis nomen conuenire nequeat." Note that it would be possible to translate "vis" as *effect;* I have avoided doing so because of the danger of reflecting the spirit of certain modern translations.

[27] *Ibid.,* fols. 110v–11.

from imitation is "effictio," and Maranta separates them on the basis of their generality; every imitation is a "making" but not every "making" is an imitation. Imitation is thus the more "proximate" genus and the one in terms of which kinds of poems are to be defined.

Finally, it should be noted that in several of the marginalia to this manuscript Maranta indicates that his position is opposed to that of Vettori. There are three such places, marked in the margin by the phrase "Contra P. Victor." The first is the discussion of δύναμις already noted (fol. 110); the second, his contention that κατὰ φύσιν refers to the method of exposition, beginning with universals and passing on to particulars (fol. 112); the third refers directly to the correspondence with Vettori (already studied) on Aristotle's reasons for listing various arts at the beginning of the *Poetics*. Maranta contends that two of the kinds of "poetry" enumerated at 1447a13, auletic and citharistic, really belong to poetry—rather than to the more general category of imitations—but that they use rhythm and harmony alone without discourse (fol. 114). Unfortunately, the manuscript ends abruptly shortly after this point, and we are deprived of Maranta's particular views on these genres.

The fragments included in the second discourse seem to be of especial interest for their interpretation of the method and order of Aristotle's text, for their distinctions with respect to several terms, and for the way in which they reflect the philological and philosophical disagreements between two contemporary humanists.

At the beginning of the third discourse (fols. 100–107), Maranta announces that he means to give a brief summary of the contents of the *Poetics*, and that is precisely what he does. Most of the interesting ideas are repeated from the discourses which we have already analyzed. There are occasionally, however, passages which reveal a significant attitude toward the text. After speculating on the probable contents of the missing third book, Maranta sees a five-part division of the first book: poetry in general, tragedy, the epic, resolution of objections, and the relative merits of tragedy and the epic. Somewhat later, Maranta remarks on the way in which the definition of tragedy is constituted and how the genre is treated: "He puts together the definition of tragedy in part out of what he had said about poetry in general, in part from the things that he is about to say; and after having explained the parts and the differentiae of the definition, beginning with the definition itself he seeks out the parts of tragedy, especially those which he calls 'formal.' "[28] As is the case with most of his contemporaries, Maranta provides revealing explanations of the requisites of character. "Goodness" is moral goodness, necessary if the poem is to

---

[28] *Ibid.*, fol. 101: "partim ex his quae in genere de poesi dixerat partim ex his quae mox est dicturus colligit Tragoediae definitionem. rursusque explicatis partibus et differentijs definitionis ex ipsa definitione uenatur partes Tragoediae praecipue illas quas formales appellat."

achieve its utilitarian end of ethical improvement; "likeness" may refer either to the nature and habits of the persons introduced or to a resemblance to the customs of the times involved in the action (fol. 103v). Among the features differentiating tragedy from epic is the fact that the former appeals to the eye, the latter to the ear; hence tragedy must be more verisimilar, less marvelous, "for the eyes consent less readily to those things which are said to be against the reason than do the ears."[29] Otherwise, Maranta repeats such ideas as those already expressed on imitation as the genus of poetry, on the five proofs of the priority of plot, on unity and magnitude, on the universality of poetry (as compared with history), and on the pedagogical uses of purgation.

There is some question as to whether the last of the discourses (fols. 133–39v) really belongs to the same series; for it is in Italian rather than in Latin and makes no claim to being related to the text of the *Poetics*. It treats largely of the form and the excellences of the *Aeneid*. But it does so in Aristotelian terms, repeating many of the ideas found in the other fragments and clarifying some of them. One may consider it as developing Aristotle's—and Maranta's—ideas on the epic just as the other discourses had discussed fully problems relevant to tragedy. Perhaps because it is in Italian, perhaps because it takes into consideration some forms of contemporary Italian literature, this little treatise strays somewhat farther from Aristotle and displays strong leanings toward the current Horatian tradition. The objects of imitation are distinguished on the basis of social classes: "illustrious men, great leaders and princes and kings and such like; or . . . very inconspicuous men and of low condition; or intermediate ones between these two extremes."[30] All these are presented rather as they should be than as they are, in accordance with an Idea of human action. The three objects gave rise, in antiquity, to three groups of poets: those who wrote tragedies and epics, those who wrote comedies, and those who wrote mimes. In modern times, in the Kingdom of Naples itself, all three levels are found; tragedies and comedies are written by recognized authors, while the "low" kind is found in farces, in the "Gianni," "Venetiani," and "Mattoccini," as well as in macaronic prose narratives.

With respect to the epic itself, Maranta thinks that Aristotle is perhaps mistaken in his preference for tragedy. The epic, being more varied in its episodes and its digressions, in its reversals and its recognitions, being longer and more pleasant and more marvelous, is on the whole more difficult to achieve. Hence, it is perhaps better. In any case, Vergil is the greatest of all poets in any language and in any form, with the possible exception of the Prophets. Within the epic form, Maranta sees the same

---

[29] *Ibid.*, fol. 106: "quia oculi non ita assentiuntur his quae praeter rationem dicuntur ut aures."

[30] *Ibid.*, fols. 133–33v: "huominj illustri gran maestri et prencipi et Re et similj ò . . . huomini uilissimi et di bassa conditione. O, tra questi duo estremi, mezzani."

qualitative parts that Aristotle had discerned; its quantitative parts are proposition, invocation, and narration. Its pedagogical ends are achieved on the one hand by the action—"from those heroic deeds one is fired in such a way that he, too, is incited to become like their doer, and thus the fruit of poetry is gathered"[31]—on the other hand by the characters, since these represent the perfect expression of given virtues. Maranta's general conclusion on the *Aeneid* is that it has one plot, of one man, in one time, engaged in one action with a beginning, a middle, and an end, that its separate parts are irremovable and unchangeable. These would seem to constitute Aristotelian criteria applied to a single work, and they are prophetic of some of the arguments which were to be adduced during the literary quarrels of the '70's.

Bartolomeo Maranta's one published work of literary criticism, the *Lucullianae Quaestiones* of 1564, is greater in bulk than all the unpublished writings taken together. Its general orientation is rhetorical and Horatian (see above Chapter V, pp. 171–74), and such Aristotelian elements as there are appear incidentally to a long-winded discussion of stylistics and metrics. They reduce, almost all of them, to considerations relative to the tragic plot, its conditions and effects; but there are some applications to the epic form since Maranta is engaged in the study and praise of Vergil. Again, the interpretations of Aristotle echo those found earlier in the manuscript discourses. But since his problem is Vergil, he concentrates on three essential questions: the comparison of tragedy and the epic; the sources of the tragic effect; and the bases of verisimilitude. On the first, he compares the two genres with respect to their qualitative and quantitative parts, to their length, to their manner (dramatic versus narrative); for all these, Aristotle is the source. On the subject of the marvelous, which is more properly produced by the epic than by the tragedy, he goes considerably beyond the *Poetics*; "admiratio," he says, must be produced by all poets at all times, but it falls especially in the domain of the epic. This is because, as a narrative form, it appeals to the ear rather than to the eye and may thus treat more incredible matters (pp. 88, 133). The need to astonish the audience necessarily involves consideration of the effects of tragedy as compared with those of the epic and, above all, of verisimilitude. Maranta at various times cites Aristotle on pity and fear, and he elaborates on the nature of the tragic plot and the tragic hero (p. 125). In this connection, he makes some important remarks on the nature of "fear." Starting from Aristotle's τὸ ὅμοιον (*Poetics* 1453a5), he sees two kinds of "likeness" to the tragic hero. The first is our common humanity with the persons of tragedy; we think of ourselves as subject to the same calamities and the same death. The second is a resemblance among us on the basis of one or several of the elements which constitute decorum: fortune, age, sex, pro-

---

[31] *Ibid.*, fol. 135v: "da quelle prodezze si accende di si fatta sorte che si incita anco egli a diuenire simile a quello et cosi si coglie il frutto della poesia."

fession, character, and so forth (p. 124). Here again the transition from the *Poetics* to the rhetoricians is almost imperceptible.

Maranta's study of the tragic hero is important to him insofar as he wishes to discover whether Aeneas does or does not fit Aristotle's description. With it in mind, he attempts to analyze more closely the conditions for the tragic action. If pity and fear are to attend the tragic personage, he must be of high station and enjoy great esteem; otherwise, his misfortunes will not produce the proper effect. Maranta accepts Aristotle's notion of the "intermediate" situation (1453a7) and he properly interprets ἁμαρτία as involving an error; but he adds an idea of his own which he recognizes as being non-Aristotelian: the error may be that of persons other than the hero "qui in magna sunt existimatione, & auctoritate" (p. 126). A number of tragedies are cited in proof. Besides, he introduces a distinction between the action, which may be wicked, and the intention, which may not; an essentially good hero who commits, unwittingly, a wicked deed may thus be considered as "intermediate." As for Aeneas, he would in no wise qualify as a tragic hero because he is perfect and cannot err.

Un-Aristotelian, again, is Maranta's thesis that the effects of tragedy may be achieved not only by the plot and character but by all the lesser elements—diction, sententiae, melody, chorus, setting. For Aristotle, these would contribute to the effect; for Maranta, they may produce it almost independently. In keeping with his rhetorical bent, he asserts that the function of sententiae is to arouse the passions, "such as anger, terror, pity, fear" (p. 18).

These passions will be aroused, however, only if the audience believes, only if verisimilitude is achieved. Aristotle is cited:

Aristotle wrote that if two actions were to offer themselves to the poet, one of which indeed could happen but was not verisimilar, the other of which could not really happen but was nevertheless credible, the poet would accept and choose the one which had an apparent truth, even though it belonged to the number of those which cannot naturally happen under any circumstances.[32]

One of the interlocutors goes on to explain that verisimilitude is a matter of audience opinion and that the difficulty lies in reconciling this with the marvelous: "The poets seek nothing else but the assent of the listeners and they try with all their energies to force men to give credence to marvelous actions. And herein lies the greatest difficulty for the poet."[33] The solution to the problem lies partly, as it did for Aristotle, in the choice of extra-

[32] *Lucullianarum quaestionum libri quinque* (1564), p. 89: "Aristoteles tradit, ut si duae res sese poetae obferant, altera quae fieri quidem possit, sed uerisimilis non sit: altera quae fieri reuerà nequeat, credibilis tamen: capiat atque eligat poeta eam quae apparentem habet ueritatem, etiam si ex eorum numero sit quae naturaliter fieri nullo modo possit."

[33] *Ibid.*, p. 89: "poetae nihil uenantur, praeter assensum eorum qui audiunt: atque omnibus neruis contendunt, ut assentiri homines cogant admirabilibus rebus: atque in hoc uersatur maior poetae difficultas."

ordinary events that really occurred, those catastrophes visited upon certain great and noble families (p. 133).

Maranta's total contribution to literary theory is about equally divided between Horatian and Aristotelian elements. It is Horatian in the lectures devoted to the *Ars poetica* and in the *Quaestiones*; it is Aristotelian especially in the other set of lectures, but also in the *Quaestiones*. Throughout, he establishes and reaffirms the parallelism between the two theorists; or, in any case, he introduces the one into a context primarily reflecting the other. He frequently shows a good understanding of his texts, and his interpretations are sometimes superior to those of most of his contemporaries.

SALVIATI (1564)

While Maranta was preparing (and perhaps giving) his lectures on Aristotle for the Accademia Napoletana, Lionardo Salviati was writing the First Lecture of a series of three to be known, collectively, as the *Trattato della poetica*. The *Lezzion prima* was delivered before the Accademia Fiorentina in December of 1564.[34] It is heavily Aristotelian in tone, not only because of the multiple reference to other works of the Stagirite—the *Metaphysics*, the *Ethics*, the *Topica*, the *Posterior Analytics*, the *Physica*, the *De caelo*—but also because of the method which Salviati everywhere attempts to apply. Salviati believes that answers to his questions are to be found only in Aristotle, and as he traces the early history of the arts he sees the beginnings of order and clarity in Aristotle's works—

. . . until at last Aristotle—descended upon earth, I believe, through divine pity in order to liberate us from the fog of so long ignorance—reduced the truths pronounced at first by those first philosophers, not indeed by chance but confusedly, in a scattered way, and as it were stammeringly, to a marvelous order; and reduced divers members to an incredible clarity, as if to an artful body proportioned with ineffable mastery.[35]

If such answers are to be reached in the realm of poetics, an equally rigorous method must be used.

Salviati conceives of this method as involving, basically, two procedures: the careful use of definitions and the application of the device of the four causes. Everything must be defined, including definition itself. A definition (see the *Metaphysics* and the *Organon*) is "that reply which would be given by whoever was asked, not about the word, but about the essence of some

---

34 I am indebted, for the indication of the whereabouts of this MS, to Peter Brown's "Il Discorso sopra la Ginnastica degli Antichi attribuito al Cav. Lionardo Salviati," *Annali della Scuola Normale Superiore di Pisa*, Serie II, XXVI (1957), 4; Brown gives a complete description of the MS. The second lecture, as far as I know, was never written. The so-called Third Lecture was merely a copy, made in 1566, of a part of this First Lecture.

35 MS BNF, Magl. VII, 307, fol. 7: "infino che Aristotile finalmente disceso, credo, in terra per diuina pietà a liberarne dalla nebbia di cosi lunga ignoranza, le uerità da quei primi filosofi, non pure a caso, ma in confuso, e sparsamente, e quasi balbettando prima pronunziate in ordine marauiglioso, et in chiarezza incredibile, quasi in un corpo proporzionato con indicibile maestria et artifizioso diuerse membre ridusse."

Universal and of some universal substance, completely properly, but in such a way that there be no part in it which is not operant, nor any part lacking that might operate in it."[36] The first term of which we need a definition, as we approach the subject of poetry, is art itself, and Salviati (see the *Metaphysics*) defines it as "an external Principle of operation, to be differentiated . . . from Nature; because nature . . . is a principle of action in itself."[37] Otherwise stated, it is a "habit of operating in an external subject by means of the reason."[38] The latter definition requires a full differentiation among the possible kinds of habits and among their sources. Salviati (see the *Ethics*) derives the habits from two kinds of intellect, the higher intellect and the reasoning power, and he classifies them under art, prudence, and science:

. . . he [Aristotle] derives from the former [the higher intellect] all the habits which concern themselves with necessary and eternal things, from the latter [the reason] all those which exert themselves only on contingent things. To this group belong, without any doubt, prudence and art; which two habits are different from one another because prudence treats of those actions whose effect remains in the agent, but art directs those whose effects pass over into some foreign matter.[39]

All the arts, and poetry among them, induce perfection in some object outside of the agent himself.

The introduction of the concept of habit obliges Salviati to pursue two further arguments. First, he must answer the Platonists, who maintain that poetry is not a habit but an inspiration, a product of the divine furor. This he does by presenting various rebuttals—it is philosophically wrong to think that God, completely perfect, would operate in an individual; where furor is present, judgment is lacking; the claims of the poets are not reliable—and by insisting that, in accordance with his method, he is seeking a surer and more predictable origin: " . . . we are looking for the cause, or rather the principle, which most of the time does not fail." And again: "But we are seeking for the principle which, not once in a while, but most of the time is a principle. And this must definitely be habit." [40] Furor, in

36 *Ibid.*, fol. 11v: "la risposta, che si darebbe da chi fosse richiesto, non del uocabolo, ma dell'essenza d'alcuno Vniuersale, e d'alcuna uniuersal sostanza proprijssimamente, ma in tal guisa, che parte alcuna non ui sia che non operi, ne alcuna uene manchi, che operare ui potesse."
37 *Ibid.*, fol. 15: "Principio esteriore d'operare; a differenza . . . della Natura; percioche la natura . . . è principio d'azzione in se stesso."
38 *Ibid.*, fol. 14v2: "Habito d'operare in subbietto esteriore con ragione." (There are two folios bearing the numbers 14 and 15 each; this is the second 14.)
39 *Ibid.*, fol. 142: "da quello tutti gli habiti, che sono dietro alle cose necessarie, ed eterne, da questo fa uenire tutti quelli, che nelle contingenti s'adoperano solamente. Ciò sono la Prudenza, et l'Arte senza dubbio ueruno. I quali due habiti perciò sono tra loro differenti, percioche la Prudenza in quelle delle azzioni si raggira, l'effetto delle quali si rimane nell' agente; ma l'Arte dirizza quelle, i cui effetti in alcuna materia forestiera trapassano."
40 *Ibid.*, fol. 18: "noi cerchiamo della cagione, ò uogliam dir principio, che le piu uolte non falla"; and "Ma noi cerchiamo del principio, che non alcuna uolta, ma le piu uolte è principio. E ciò conuiene, che sia l'habito fermamente."

a word, cannot be accepted into the category of universal causes, whereas habit can. Second, he must discover what kind of habit is present in poetry. To do so, he divides the habits into moral and intellectual, the intellectual into habits of doing and of making, and classifies poetry under the last of these (fol. 29). This makes it possible for him to declare that the art of poetry "is capable of counsels and of precepts, and can very well be acquired by an excellent mind through human industry."[41]

A related argument considers the various other sources to which poetry might be attributed. Salviati makes an exhaustive classification of all operations as coming from nature, art, violence, mind alone, fortune, and chance; then he sets out to show that poetry cannot properly be assigned to any of these except art. Not to nature, since nature has its principle in itself, whereas all poems have their source in the poet. Not to fortune or chance, since the poet makes his poem according to design. Not to violence, since this is always contrary to the will. Not to the mind alone, since this is only rarely the source of poetry; hence it cannot be a principle. Thus poetry is an art: "it has in itself all the qualities which are universally required for the existence of art."[42] As an art, it contains the three necessary operations: speculation, before anything is done: the operation of the artist; and the work itself. Its matter is the matter of art, consisting solely in contingent and corruptible matter.

With respect to that other Aristotelian device, the analysis of the four causes, Salviati makes his own assignment of causes. In so doing, he reveals at once how many of his presuppositions come from sources other than Aristotle and how uncertain is his own method. The final cause, he says, is to "bring profit to our minds through pleasure" ("il giouare a gli animi con diletto," fol. 34); this is identical with what Horace has to say in lines 333 and 343. The efficient cause is "the intellect invested with this habit" (i.e., the habit of the art; "l'intelletto di questo habito riuestito," fol. 34). It is when he comes to the material cause that he finds difficulties. For other critics, such as Vettori, have considered as instruments those elements which he himself regards as the matter, that is, language, harmony, and rhythm. Of these, language is indisputably the most important: "not rhythm and music, but significant words, both according to the truth and according to Aristotle's opinion, are firmly of the essence of poems. Words then . . . , according to the authority of Aristotle, are the most general material of all poetry."[43] Salviati finds no philosophical impropriety in considering a single element as now material, now instrument.

41 *Ibid.*, fol. 29: "d'auertimenti, e di precetti è capace, e con humano studio da eccellente ingegno puo molto bene conseguirsi."
42 *Ibid.*, fol. 31v: "ha in se tutte le qualità che all'essere dell'Arte in uniuersale sono richieste."
43 *Ibid.*, fol. 34v: "non il rimmo, e la musica, ma le parole significanti, e secondo la uerità, e secondo l'opinione d'Aristotile, sono della essenza delle poesie fermamente. Sono dunque le parole . . . secondo l'autorità d'Aristotile, materia generalissima di tutta la Poesia."

Finally, the formal cause consists in the "invention"; he takes the *Iliad* as his example: "in that greatest poem, the form is that invention which makes it different from every other poem which is not this very same one."[44] As he recapitulates his findings with respect to the causes, Salviati merely repeats what he had said earlier for three of them; but on the subject of final cause he finds it important to make a further distinction. This consists in differentiating an ultimate from an immediate end. "The end," he says, "is to profit with pleasure; I do not say the most proximate end, because this is without doubt the form and the work itself, . . . but I am speaking of the ultimate end of the poet."[45] The *Physica* and the *De caelo* are cited as the basis for this distinction.

Salviati's ties with an un-Aristotelian critical past are further attested by his repetition of the standard, conventional defence of poetry. He traces the beginnings of society, the civilizing role of the arts, their relationship to the sciences. Among the arts, poetry appeals to the highest faculty, the intellect, and hence is close to the contemplative operations of philosophy (fol. 9). Poetry is, moreover, supreme among the arts because it serves the highest end, the health and the well-being of the mind. Once more, Aristotle confirms the conclusion: his belief that tragedy purges the mind of its disturbances shows that poetry is concerned only with the mind (fol. 35*v*). On his own, Salviati raises some further interesting questions about the art: whether poetry can exist in the poet's mind without being written down or put into words; whether, if this were true, the real matter of poetry would be the feelings expressed rather than the words used to express them; whether, following the same line of argument, poetry would not pass from the arts of making to the arts of doing, and ultimately become a part of prudence. But the answers, rather than being given here, are promised for the subsequent lectures.

Two treatises of Sperone Speroni, one a set of discourses on Vergil and the other a dialogue on Vergil, probably belong to this same year, 1564.[46] As far as Aristotle is concerned, Speroni finds in the *Poetics* useful suggestions with regard to plot and the unity of plot, to imitation in general, and to verisimilitude. Speroni declares that the *Discorsi sopra Virgilio* will treat its subject "according to the art taught by Aristotle and Plato"[47] and that the first of its teachings establishes the primacy of plot: " . . . it is the first thing made by the poet; . . . and this must be woven in such a way that the events follow on one another in almost a natural order, and one should not see in it the poet's will that it should be made in this way;

[44] *Ibid.*, fol. 35: "in quel sommo poema la forma è quella inuenzione, che lo fanno diuerso da ogni altro poema, che esso stesso non sia."

[45] *Ibid.*, fol. 35: "il fine il giouare con diletto; non dico il fine piu propinquo, percioche questo senza fallo è la forma, e l'opera medesima . . . ma parlo dell'ultimo fine del poeta."

[46] See the reasons offered by the editor of the 1740 edition of the *Opere*, II, 419 and 356. Also Fr. Cammarosano, *La Vita e le Opere di Sperone Speroni* (Empoli, 1920), p. 164.

[47] In *Opere* (1740), IV, 425: "secondo l'arte da Aristotile e da Platone insegnata."

for if one does, the poem becomes affected rather than verisimilar."[48] Verisimilitude is thus a product, in part at least, of a seemingly natural order of the events. Although we are not so told, we may perhaps assume that it is this "natural order" itself which guarantees the imitative quality of poetry. Poetry is an imitation, it is the plot which imitates human actions; all parts not belonging to the plot are digressions or accidents. Speroni's reasons for insisting upon the unity of plot are not, however, thoroughly Aristotelian. The first is, for "an imitation must be of one single imitated thing, just as a science is of one subject." The second is not, since Speroni argues that the main reason for requiring unity is to provide, through a highly simple and reduced plot, the occasion for much amplification and ornamentation, "for if the poem consists of unnecessary and superfluous ornament, if the poet were to undertake to imitate poetically more than one action the poem, in order to be perfect, would have to grow to infinite length."[49] A poem constituted of more than one action would be possible but imperfect, for the poet would not be able to "decorate" it completely in every one of its parts without making it over-long and tedious. Hence the preference for the simple over the complex plot: "Thence it arises that double or triple comedies and tragedies are not beautiful, as simple ones are; for they are less ornate and more obscure, and this removes some of the beauty."[50] In such an argument as this, Aristotelian *loci* and terms are present; but the whole tendency and conclusion are different.

Imitation is the topic, once again, of the fragmentary *Dialogo sopra Virgilio*; but it is a strange kind of imitation which becomes farther and farther removed from Aristotle's. The *Poetics* itself is an "imitation" of Homer's two epic poems, which thus become its "nature." A philosopher writing on poetics bases his work on poems just as a poet writing poems bases them on nature. But the poet may also use other poems as his "nature," and Vergil should be praised for "imitating" Homer as he did; indeed, it is better to imitate other poets than to heed the instructions of philosophers in their arts of poetry. Speroni goes so far as to suggest that "imitation," since it is not based on the activity of the mind, is not really a human activity. It is more proper to monkeys and to children than to man. Art, on the other hand, is properly the province of man, for it is the disciple rather than the enemy of reason. Clearly, Speroni is thinking, here,

48 *Ibid.*, p. 425: "Però è la prima cosa fatta dal poeta; . . . e questa bisogna che sia in modo tessuta, che le cose succedano quasi per ordine naturale l'una dall'altra, e non vi si veda volontà del poeta, che così li paja di fare: perchè diventa non verisimile, ma affettato il poema."

49 *Ibid.*, pp. 438–39: "perchè di una imitazione debba essere una cosa sola imitata, come di un soggetto una scienza"; "ma anche perchè se'l poema è ornamento redundante e superfluo, se'l poeta togliesse a imitar più di una azione poeticamente, il poema a volere esser perfetto cresceria in infinito."

50 *Ibid.*, p. 534: "di qua viene che le commedie e tragedie doppie, o triple, non son belle, come le semplici, perchè son meno ornate, e più oscure; il che lieva della bellezza."

of imitation as a kind of copying or physical mimicry, rather than as the essence of the artistic process.

In the following year, 1565, Speroni discussed another Aristotelian problem, that of purgation, in a letter to Alvise Mocenigo dated February 26, 1565. He recognizes two current interpretations of purgation, one insisting that it concerns only the two passions of pity and fear, the other that it admits other similar passions. He adopts the latter, "ut liberemur ab *hujuscemodi* facinoribus," and he gives his reasons:

. . . the Aristotelians must be of this opinion, explaining the definition that Aristotle gives of it in the *Poetics* by using the words spoken to us by Plato in Book VIII of the *Laws*, where in fact he talked of the tragedy of Canace and Macareo. And he says that those dishonest acts, and the death of him who commits them, are shown so that one will learn to avoid them; and this is truly the proper way of understanding Aristotle.[51]

Speroni interprets his opposition as holding that purgation achieves its effect through the forming of habits; thus, it would accustom people to pity and fear through repeated exposure to them. He believes that the latter theory also implies a limited usefulness for tragedy and comedy; both would be acceptable only in a state where the government was popular rather than monarchical. Tragedy, showing the misfortunes of the great, would convince the people that their rulers are not gods and that their own station in life is preferable; comedy would teach other "popular" lessons. Both, in such an analysis, become instruments used by the governors—in an indirect and hidden way—for the good of the governed. Throughout the discussion, Platonic overtones are apparent, and Aristotle is forgotten.

Giovanni Fabrini da Fighine's commentary on Horace's *Ars poetica,* in Italian, appeared in 1566 (see above, Chapter V, pp. 179–83). Like its predecessors, it made numerous comparisons between Horace and Aristotle; like them also, it assumed that Horace was following Aristotle and that the content and order of the two treatises were essentially the same. But whereas some of the other commentaries revealed, incidentally, an interpretation of Aristotle, there seems to be none discernible in Fabrini. His constant practice is merely to cite similar passages, prefacing each quotation from the *Poetics* by some such formula as "questo medesimo dice Aristotile nel testo lvi," or "secondo Aristotile ne la poetica al cxxxi. testo" (references throughout are to Maggi's divisions in the edition of 1550). Nor is one any more rewarded by a quest of the topics in Aristotle that were of especial interest to Fabrini; he was interested in everything. Perhaps the more detailed and practical topics appear with greater fre-

---

[51] In *Opere,* letter CCXLII, V, 175: "di questa opinione deono esser li Aristotelici, esponendo la definizion, che ne dà Aristotile nella poetica con le parole detteci da Platone nell' ottavo *de legibus;* ove appunto egli parla della tragedia di Canace e Macareo; e dice che queste cose disoneste, e la morte di chi le commette, si rappresentano, perchè si impari a lasciarle stare: e questa è veramente la bona intelligenzia di Aristotile."

quency, merely because they are closer to the stuff of Horace's work than the more abstract and theoretical considerations—perhaps, also, because Fabrini's Italian commentary was addressed to a more popular and less erudite audience. At times his translations are interesting, since the terminology reveals the extent to which he is thinking of Horace rather than of Aristotle. Thus, for example, he translates 1451*b*27 with the formula "i poeti sono denominati piu da *l'inuentione*, e da la *perfetta narratione* de le fauole, che dal comporre in uersi" (p. 355, italics mine); and he paraphrases 1455*b*23 thus: "diuide la poesia d'Omero in due parti, in fauola, & episodi. cioè, in *digressioni*" (p. 355*v*; italics mine). Again, 1448*a*16 is translated: "la comedia, e la tragedia sono differenti tra loro; perche questa imita cose *piu eccellenti*, & quella *piu humili*" (p. 364; italics mine). All in all, Fabrini's commentary has little significance for the history of the *Poetics* in the Renaissance, except as another document relating it to the *Ars poetica* and seeing it essentially in terms of the later work.

To about the same period belongs an anonymous manuscript (Siena, Biblioteca Comunale K.IV.36) ascribed by another hand to "Lottino," dedicated to Giovan Francesco Stella and Dionigi Atanagi, and having as its general theme the one indicated in the title, *Intorno alli episodij de' poeti nelle poesie*. I have placed it *circa* 1566 because it treats of the general relationship between plot and episodes that Maranta had discussed in his lectures and because it seems to share the preoccupations of those authors who, around 1566, were debating the merits and demerits of Terence. Lottino starts from Aristotle, in whose works he finds authority for stating that the episodes are to plot as accidents are to substance:

... in fact, it [plot] is nothing else but the substantial part of the poem. But just as nature in her compounds works in such a way that the substantial parts are served by those which are accidental, so the poet causes his plot to be served by the episodes.... This came to pass because the number of principles from which all things in the world had their origin was so small, that it was necessary that not only the principles but things themselves (by resemblance to the principles) should be mixed and intermingled with one another. None of these things could ever have been truly distinguished from another, nor be called one thing, if all the other parts were not regulated and commanded by one single part, as by its principal form.... In this same way, the good poets have proceeded in the linking of the episodes with their plots, in which no episode is found that is not united to them and derived from them in such a way, that it is not possible to divide it from them effectively or even—except by those who are very expert in the matter—to distinguish it from the plot.[52]

52 Bibl. Com., Siena, K.IV.36, fols. 1–1*v*: "elle in somma non è altro che la parte sustantiale del poema. Ma si come la natura ne suoi composti fa sempre, che le parti sustantiali siano da quelle seruite, che in esso si ritrouano accidentali; cosi il poeta fa, che la sua fauola sia da gli epissodij seruita. ... Il che è auuenuto, percio ch'il numero de principij, da quali tutte le cose del mondo hanno hauuto origine, è stato cosi piccolo; ch'egli è stato di bisogno, che non pure i principij, ma le cose stesse a simiglianza di quelli si siano infra loro mescolate, et

Lottino seems here to be seeking metaphysical justification for the close connection of episodes with plot; at the same time, he states an evaluative principle for that connection. As his argument continues, however, it becomes clear that he means by plot not the assemblage of events peculiar to the individual poem, but rather the whole complex of traditional materials associated with a given story. From these, he says, the poet selects those elements which are "excellent" and "singular," which will give to the poem "efficacy" and "admiration," "clarity" or "beauty." Such a process means a reduction of the basic materials to be included in the poem and the possible danger of meagerness. It is to prevent this that the poet introduces episodes. Harking back to Aristotle again, Lottino declares that the addition of episodes is more feasible in the epic than in tragedy and comedy, since the dramatic forms are more restricted in time—"into their operation they cannot put more space of time than those few hours during which they must be presented to the people."[53] A final theoretical consideration regarding plot is again derived from Aristotle; it concerns the division of the "represented" plot into complication and solution. For Lottino, this plot is itself preceded by another, the "narrated" one, which apparently consists of those expository parts at the beginning of the drama which recount the completed parts of the action.

These principles are carefully applied to the discussion of Terence's *Eunuch*, which is interspersed with the theoretical sections of the short treatise. Episodes were added to the central plot, says Lottino, because without them the comedy would have had insufficient size and insufficient beauty; they augment the plot pleasantly through probable actions (fol. 3*v*). Several dicta from the *Poetics* are compounded into this conclusion on the episodes: " . . . they are all substantial parts of the plot, no one of which—nor of the others like them—could be transposed or removed without causing damage to the plot; and the poet makes them, through verisimilitude, so necessarily follow one from the other, always observing the decorum of persons, that nothing is left to be desired."[54] Decorum itself is clearly respected in the presentation of all personages and the ordering of all parts of the plot is such that verisimilitude and propriety are at all times respected. Hence, for Lottino the *Poetics* becomes the

---

trapposte: ciascuna delle-quali non haurebbe mai potuto uera distintione dall'altra hauere, ne una esser chiamata; se da una sola parte, come da sua forma principale, non fusse stato dato regola all'altre, et comandato. . . . In cotal modo sono i buoni poeti proceduti nel collegamento de gli epissodij con le fauole loro: nelle quali ui se ne troua alcuno per si fatta maniera ad esse unito, et da esse deriuato; che non che con effetto diuiderlo; ma non si puo pure; senon da quelli, che ne sono ben pratichi, conoscerne la differenza."

[53] *Ibid.*, fol. 2*v*: "queste nella operation loro non posson mettere più spatio che quelle poche hore, nelle quali elle debbono essere al popolo rappresentate."

[54] *Ibid.*, fol. 4: "son tutte parti sustantiali della fauola: delle quali, et delle altre à lor simiglianti, non si potrebbe trasporre, ò leuar alcuna, che non ne uenisse danno alla fauola: et il poeta le fa con uerisimili così necessariamente seguitar l'una dall'altra; il decoro delle persone sempre seruando; che non si puo piu oltre desiderare."

source for both theoretical and practical statements in criticism and a source from which he makes relatively few departures.

The place of Aristotle in Frosino Lapini's *Letione nella quale si ragiona in universale del fine della poesia* (1567) is quite different. For in this lecture, delivered before the Accademia Fiorentina on May 1, 1567, the dominant influence is Plato; it is he who gives the essential orientation to a work which declares that the end of poetry is the inculcation of virtue in man (see Chapter VII, pp. 290–92). There are some references to Aristotle, but rather to the *Physics* and the *Ethics* than to the *Poetics*. From the Aristotelian approach in general, Lapini derives his identification of the material, formal, and final causes of poetry:

We conclude therefore that since the material of the poet is the plot, under which are veiled and enclosed all the subjects taken by him for explanation, and since the form is the imitation, it follows that the end must be different from these. Nor is this pleasure alone, which is felt as very great, as accidental, in the outer shell and surface of the beautiful invention of the plot, but mainly the utility enclosed within the meaningful and moral subject, veiled by the plot in the same way that the mysteries were hidden and covered in the sacred ceremonies.[55]

Here, whereas the approach may be Aristotelian, the conclusions are surely not those of the *Poetics*, wherein all the causes are differently defined. The conception of moral utility as the end determines Lapini's interpretation of catharsis; moral betterment is achieved when the soul is purged of its passions (p. C). It also determines how he understands "goodness" of character, which he takes to mean honor and virtue, necessary if the personages are to serve as exemplars for better living. Lapini cites Vettori's gloss as corroborating his own and Horace's "utile dulci" as containing the same conclusion. The need for heightened goodness of character is further emphasized by the nature of imitation itself. Imitation is always meant to be pleasant and beautiful, and these effects are achieved by representing any object—even a low person or action—as more nearly perfect than it would normally be. When a virtuous person is concerned, the heightening will bring him near to moral perfection, and the ends of the poem will be completely realized.

CASTELVETRO (1570)

The year 1570 was marked by the publication of the first of the "great commentaries" in Italian and hence the first in any European vernacular. This was Lodovico Castelvetro's *Poetica d'Aristotele vulgarizzata et sposta*, printed first in Vienna in 1570 and later, in a revised edition, in Basel in

---

55 *Letione* (1567), pp. Eij–Eijv: "Conchiudiamo adunque che sendo la materia del Poeta la Fauola, sotto la quale sono velati & racchiusi tutti i soggetti presi da lui a dichiararsi, & la forma sendo la imitatione, ne segue che diuerso da queste conuien che sia il fine: ne ciò sia il solo piacere, che per accidente nella scorza, e superficie della vaga inuentione della fauola si sente grandissimo ma l'Vtile principalmente, racchiuso nel sensato, e morale soggetto, velato dalla fauola, non altrimenti che i misterij erano nelle sacre cerimonie ascosi, e coperti."

1576.[56] Castelvetro follows the usual pattern for such commentaries; his work is divided into six major "Parti," each of which is divided into "Particelle," and for each "Particella" we are given a section of the Greek text, a brief statement of the "Contenenza" or content, a "Vulgarizzamento" or translation, and then the long "Spositione" or commentary. The passages themselves are fewer in number and longer than in Castelvetro's predecessors, totaling fifty-six in all. Castelvetro differs from his predecessors, also, in his attitude toward Aristotle and the text of the *Poetics*; whereas they were respectful and subservient, he declares his doubts about the theory and proposes to develop his own. The *Poetics* as we have it, he says, is "a first rough form, imperfect and unpolished, of the art of poetry, which it is probable that the author preserved so that it might serve him as a collection of notations and of brief reminders, in order to have them at hand when he might wish to compile and compose the complete art."[57] His own purpose is more ambitious:

I have tried . . . to render the art of poetry clear, showing and displaying not only what was handed down to us in these few pages by that greatest of all philosophers, but also whatever should or could be written for the full benefit of those who might wish to know how one should go about composing poems correctly and how one should judge properly whether those already written do or do not have what they ought to have.[58]

Aristotle will be used, therefore, partly as a point of departure, partly as an opponent. Our immediate problem, here, is to discover what happens to Aristotle's theory in the process of adaptation and of refutation.

It would perhaps not be too bold to say that, in general, Castelvetro transposes the whole of the analysis from the world of art to the world of reality. Let us say, by way of explanation, that Aristotle in the *Poetics* considers the special qualities of poems as works of art (rather than as natural objects), that he analyzes those characteristics of objects which affect their usability in works of art (rather than their natural qualities), that he takes into consideration only those capacities of men which affect

---

[56] Castelvetro died in 1571, and the second edition is posthumous; it was prepared by friends on the basis of the author's manuscripts. There are numerous variations between the texts, even in the direct translations of Aristotle. Questions arise about the authenticity of the changes and which text to use as a basis for study. I have used the 1576 edition as probably representing Castelvetro's final thinking on the text of Aristotle and on poetic theory.

[57] *Poetica d'Aristotele* (1576 ed.), p.)()(3: "vna prima forma rozza, imperfetta, & non polita dell'arte poetica, laquale è verisimile, che l'autore conseruasse, perche seruisse in luogo di raccolta d'insegnamenti, & di brieui memorie per poterle hauere preste, quando volesse compilare, & ordinare l'arte intera." See my article, "Castelvetro's Theory of Poetics," *Critics and Criticism: Ancient and Modern*, ed. R. S. Crane (Chicago: University of Chicago Press, 1952), pp. 349–71; the present treatment is, in large part, abstracted from the article.

[58] *Poetica d'Aristotele* (1576 ed.), p.)()(3: "ho tentato . . . di far manifesta l'arte poetica, non solamente mostrando, & aprendo quello, che è stato lasciato scritto in queste poche carte da quel sommo philosopho, ma quello anchora, che doueua, o poteua essere scritto per vtilita piena di coloro, che volessero sapere, come si debba fare a comporre bene poemi, & a giudicare dirittamente, se i composti habbiano quello, che deono hauere, o no."

the intelligence, the appreciation, and the evaluation of works (rather than all their characteristics as men). That is, works and objects and men are viewed always with respect to the special conditions of the art of poetry. In Castelvetro, any idea of "special conditions" tends to be lost; works are treated as if they were natural objects, objects themselves remain unchanged as they pass into the work, and men are men.

Perhaps the crux of the matter lies in Castelvetro's determination to remove the principal emphasis from the poem to the audience. Such a transformation means that all aspects of poetry are considered not in terms of the artistic exigencies of the poem itself but in terms of the needs or demands of a specifically characterized audience. Castelvetro's audience is thus limited and restricted, and it comes to be composed of the "common people": " . . . poetry was invented for the pleasure of the ignorant multitude and of the common people, and not for the pleasure of the educated."[59] Since the élite and the educated are thus rigorously excluded, certain qualities of mind are denied the audience:

... poetry [was] invented exclusively to delight and give recreation, I say to delight and give recreation to the minds of the rough crowd and of the common people, which does not understand the reasons, or the distinctions, or the arguments—subtle and distant from the usage of the ignorant—which philosophers use in investigating the truth of things and artists in establishing the rules of the arts; and, since it does not understand them, it must, when someone speaks of them, feel annoyance and displeasure.[60]

This audience will be almost completely lacking in imagination and will believe only the evidence of its senses: "Nor is it possible to make them believe that several days and nights have passed when they know through their senses that only a few hours have passed, *since no deception can take place in them which the senses recognize as such.*"[61] In matters not reducible to the senses, it will be incapable of going beyond what historical fact it knows—"We cannot imagine a king who did not exist, nor attribute any action to him."[62] It is immediately clear that any poet writing for such an audience would have to select as his objects such actions and characters

[59] *Ibid.*, p. 679, l. 35: "la poesia fu trouata per diletto della moltitudine ignorante, & del popolo commune, & non per diletto degli scientiati." For this text, I give page and line numbers, since the lines are numbered by the publisher.

[60] *Ibid.*, p. 29, l. 36: "la poesia sia stata trouata solamente per dilettare, & per ricreare, io dico per dilettare & ricreare gli animi della rozza moltitudine, & del commune popolo, il quale non intende le ragioni, ne le diuisioni, ne gli argomenti sottili, & lontani dall'vso degl'idioti, quali adoperano i philosophi in inuestigare la verita delle cose, & gli artisti in ordinare le arti, & non gli'ntendendo conuiene, quando altri ne fauella, che egli ne senta noia, & dispiacere." See also p. 25, l. 30.

[61] *Ibid.*, p. 109, l. 27: "Ne è possibile a dargli ad intendere, che sieno passati piu di, & notti, quando essi sensibilmente sanno, che non sono passate senon poche hore, non potendo lo'nganno in loro hauere luogo, il quale è tuttauia riconosciuto dal senso" (italics mine).

[62] *Ibid.*, p. 188, l. 25: "non ci possiamo imaginare vn re, che non sia stato, ne attribuirgli alcuna attione."

as would be acceptable to the audience, that the choice of the objects would be determined to a degree by the audience, and that the objects would be chosen on the basis of their natural characteristics.

But that is not all. The physical comfort and the convenience of the audience need to be considered. We are speaking, says Castelvetro (p. 53, l. 27), of poems presented before an assembled crowd; we must not ask the crowd to assemble for a poem so short that it would not be worth its while, nor must we expect it to remain beyond a certain limit of physical endurance:

... the restricted time is that during which the spectators can comfortably remain seated in the theater, which, as far as I can see, cannot exceed the revolution of the sun, as Aristotle says, that is, twelve hours; for because of the necessities of the body, such as eating, drinking, excreting the superfluous burdens of the belly and the bladder, sleeping, and because of other necessities, the people cannot continue its stay in the theater beyond the aforementioned time.[63]

Finally, this audience has as one of its characteristics the capacity to be pleased by certain things and to be displeased by others. One of the bases for pleasure and displeasure is knowledge: the audience takes pleasure in learning, "especially those things which it thought could not come about"; contrariwise, it dislikes stories from which it cannot learn anything, those which present commonplace events and rapidly lead to satiety (p. 553, l. 9). Another is its hopes ("volontà"): the audience is pleased by events which happen in accordance with its wishes, displeased by those which do not (*ibid.*). Finally, the audience will relate the events of a poem to the fortunes of its own life; it will enjoy seeing the good happy and the wicked unhappy, since the case of the former will lead it to expect happiness from its own goodness and the case of the latter will give it a sense of security and justice. On the other hand, if the good are unhappy, it will experience fear and pity, and if the wicked are happy, it will feel envy and scorn; but these will be only temporary displeasures, since they will give way to feelings of self-righteousness and of justice, which will be ultimately pleasurable (pp. 121, l. 34; 122, l. 21). These additional characteristics of the audience not only restrict further the poet's choice of objects; they also limit his art, for he must now make plots and conceive of characters in certain ways, conform to certain wishes for the length and ordering of his work.

Throughout the above passages, Castelvetro has taken it for granted that pleasure alone is the end of poetry. This is his explicit position everywhere. He finds Aristotle in agreement with him and sees the utilitarian notion of purgation (as he interprets it) as a contradiction on Aristotle's

---

[63] *Ibid.*, p. 109, l. 21: "il tempo stretto è quello, che i veditori possono a suo agio dimorare sedendo in theatro, il quale io non veggo, che possa passare il giro del sole, si come dice Aristotele, cio è hore dodici. conciosia cosa che per le necessita del corpo, come è mangiare, bere, diporre i superflui pesi del ventre, & della vesica, dormire, & per altre necesstia non possa il popolo continuare oltre il predetto termino cosi fatta dimora in theatro." See also p. 57, l. 11.

part: "For if poetry was invented principally for pleasure, and not for utility, as he demonstrated in the passage where he spoke of the origin of poetry in general, why should he now insist that tragedy, which is a part of poetry, should seek utility above all else? Why should it not seek mainly pleasure without paying attention to utility?"[64] He explains purgation as an answer by Aristotle to Plato's banishment of the poets on moral grounds; here, insists Aristotle, is a moral use for poetry (pp. 9, l. 4; 116, l. 24; 272, l. 15; 697, l. 13). The utility lies in the diminution of the passions of pity and fear in the audience or their expulsion (pp. 117, l. 16; 299, l. 12). But if purgation is admitted as a utility, it is only incidental to the real end of pleasure:

> Those who insist that poetry was invented mainly to profit, or to profit and delight together, let them beware lest they oppose the authority of Aristotle, who here [*Poetics* 1459a21] and elsewhere seems to assign nothing but pleasure to it; and if, indeed, he concedes some utility to it, he concedes it accidentally, as is the case with the purgation of fear and of pity by means of tragedy.[65]

As a matter of fact, Castelvetro believes that purgation itself may be considered as a source of pleasure; thus, he affirms that "Aristotle meant by the word ἡδονήν [1453b11] the purgation and the expulsion of fear and of pity from human souls," and he goes on to explain how it can be pleasurable: " . . . it comes about when, feeling displeasure at the unhappiness of another unjustly suffered, we recognize that we ourselves are good, since unjust things displease us, which recognition—because of the natural love that we have for ourselves—is a source of great pleasure to us."[66] It is significant that in this discussion Castelvetro places the end of poetry within the audience in such a way that the end, too, becomes an external force operating upon the composition of the poem.

If the end of pleasure and its achievement are related to certain characteristics of the audience, the means by which the end is to be achieved are similarly related. Here the main consideration is the lack of imagination on the part of the audience. In sum, the argument runs as follows: the audience will derive pleasure only if it identifies itself with the characters

---

[64] *Ibid.*, p. 275, l. 30: "Percioche, se la poesia è stata trouata principalmente per diletto, & non per vtilita, come egli ha mostrato la, doue parlò dell'origine della poesia in generale, perche vuole egli, che nella tragedia, la quale è vna parte di poesia, si cerchi principalmente l'vtilita? Perche non si cerca principalmente il diletto senza hauer cura dell'vtilita?"

[65] *Ibid.*, p. 505, l. 38: "Coloro, che vogliono, che la poesia sia trouata principalmente per giouare, o per giouare, & per dilettare insieme, veggano, che non s'oppongano all'autorita d'Aristotele, il quale qui, & altroue non par, che le assegni altro, che diletto, &, se pure le concede alcuno giouamento, gliele concede per accidente, come è la purgatione dello spauento, & della compassione per mezzo della tragedia."

[66] *Ibid.*, p. 299, l. 12: "Aristotele intese per la voce ἡδονήν la purgatione, & lo scacciamento dello spauento, & della compassione dagli animi humani . . . è quando noi, sentendo dispiacere della miseria altrui ingiustamente auenutagli, ci riconosciamo essere buoni, poi che le cose ingiuste ci dispiacciono, la quale riconoscenza per l'amore naturale, che noi portiamo a noi stessi ci è di piacere grandissimo." The passage goes on to discuss additional, secondary pleasures.

and the events; this identification is possible only if the audience believes in their reality; its belief in their reality will depend upon the credibility—the verisimilitude—of the presentation. It is here that imagination enters. If the audience were endowed with great capacities of imagination, it would "believe" things far removed from the conditions of "real life"; since it is not, it will "believe" only what seems to it to be in the realm of its own experience, to be "true." It is this general argument which leads Castelvetro to interpret as he does Aristotle's remarks on necessity, probability, and verisimilitude. He divides the whole realm of possible actions according to the following schema (see p. 184, ll. 39 ff.):

I. Possible actions, *which have actually happened*
   A. Natural
      1. According to the course of nature
      2. Contrary to the course of nature (i.e., monstrous or miraculous happenings)
   B. Accidental
      1. Resulting from chance or fortune
      2. Resulting from the will of men
II. Possible actions, *which have not yet happened*
   A. and B. as above

Now Category I, since it includes accomplished actions, is essentially the province of history; it corresponds to Aristotle's τὰ γενόμενα and is limited to particular actions, performed by specific persons. Actions of this kind are essential in tragedy and epic, which, since they deal with royal persons, cannot dispense with a historical basis; the audience is incapable of imagining kings who did not exist, etc. But no poem may be composed entirely of such actions, since it then would be a history and not a poem at all. Comedy, of course, needs no component of historical events, since its persons and their actions are private and obscure.

Category II, on the other hand, is coequal with Aristotle's τὰ δυνατά; it is the realm of the universal, since the actions are possible for many persons; it is thus the realm of poetry. All poems must possess some component of actions which have not actually happened. But whereas in the first category the question of credibility does not arise, in the second it is of primary importance. In order that credibility (and hence verisimilitude) may be assured and that the ingredient of the marvelous, also necessary if any pleasure is to occur, may be present, the following three requisites are established for possible actions:

(a) They must be similar to those actions which have actually happened.
(b) They must be similar to those actions which had the least probability of happening, but which did actually happen.
(c) The parts or parcels of such actions must individually be similar to those parts of actions which happened in various cases to various people.

With respect to credibility, then, it may be assured by several means: first, by the use of a historical basis for the action in certain genres; second, by a close adherence, in invented actions, to the conditions of "real" or "true" actions. At this point, the expectations of the audience again impinge upon the poet in a very important way, for the audience is the touchstone of natural probability, and it will believe whatever conforms to its conceptions of reality. In part, its conceptions are formulated in terms of decorum, of traditional traits to be assigned to characters of given types, and of conventional actions. Castelvetro equates these at once with the ἁρμόττοντα of Aristotle and the Horatian decorum.

All degrees of probability as Castelvetro conceives them are natural probability rather than aesthetic probability; that is, probability in a work is established not by reference to the conditions of the work itself or to preliminary statements within the work, but by reference outside the work to the operations of nature. This is especially clear in the example he uses for distinguishing between necessity and verisimilitude. Actions of both kinds are possible, hence admissible into poetry. If a man is wounded on the head, it is "verisimilar" or probable that he will die; hence the poet may represent his death. If a man is wounded in the heart, it is "necessary" that he die; hence the poet may represent his death (p. 188, l. 1). Similarly for actions springing from character, all of which are really matters of decorum (p. 330, l. 40). In all such considerations of historical truth or natural probability or necessity and verisimilitude, the primary aim is not the imitation of nature for the sake of making the poem resemble nature but rather the resemblance to nature for the sake of obtaining the credence of the audience.

If the problems connected with the objects represented in poetry and with its audience are largely problems of "nature," so—in an indirect way —are the problems connected with the making of the work of art. The challenge is not to produce a beautiful work of art through the ordering of all the parts to an artistically perfect structure. Questions of beauty rarely concern Castelvetro. Rather, it is the task of the poet to find some way of entertaining the audience while he keeps it convinced that what it sees (or reads) is true, that is, some way of striking a proper balance between the probable and the marvelous. As we have seen, the first means to the achievement of this end is the proper selection and assorting of materials. A second means to convincing and amusing the audience is the disposition of these materials in accordance with the unities of time, place, and action. We have already noted that the physical comforts of the audience and its lack of imagination have to be taken into account by the poet; these two factors lead, respectively, to the unities of time and of place. With respect to time, the clearest statement is found in the comparison of tragedy and the epic:

Now, just as the perceptible end of tragedy has found its proper compass within the revolution of the sun over the earth without going beyond this limit, in order to put an end to the discomfort of the audience and the expense of the actors, so the perceptible end of the epic has found its proper compass in being able to be extended over several days, since neither the discomfort of the listener nor harm or expense connected with the reciter took this possibility away from it.[67]

Besides, the action before its eyes will take place on a single spot, the stage. Hence two unities: " . . . tragedy . . . must have as its subject an action accomplished in a small area of place and in a small space of time, that is, in that place and in that time where and when the actors remain engaged in acting, and not in any other place or in any other time."[68] Ideally, the invented action should occupy no more time than a real action, and this time should not exceed the time of performance; the place should remain unchanged and be contained within the space visible to a person who himself did not move.

As for the unity of action, which for Aristotle is the only important one and which for him is the very essence of the work of art, Castelvetro's treatment is highly revelatory of his general attitude toward poetics. To begin with, he denies any necessity—in the nature of things—for limiting a poem to a single action; as so frequently, he takes issue sharply with Aristotle here:

> For there is no doubt that, if in history one may relate in a single narrative several actions of a single person, . . . in poetry it will be possible in a single plot to narrate without being blamed for it several actions of a single person, just as similarly in poetry one may relate without being blamed for it a single action of a whole people, for history does this with much praise. . . . And, indeed, in poetry not only a single action of a whole people may be narrated, but even several actions of a people. . . . And even if it were conceded to poetry to relate many actions of many persons or of many peoples, I do not see that any blame should come to it for this reason.[69]

Moreover, the presentation of a double or even a multiple plot would more readily serve the end of pleasure sought by the poet:

[67] *Ibid.*, p. 534, l. 1: "Hora, si come il termine sensibile della tragedia ha trouata la sua misura d'vn giro del sole sopra la terra senza passare piu oltre, per cessare il disconcio de veditori, & la spesa de rappresentatori, cosi il termine sensibile dell'epopea ha trouata la sua misura di potere essere tirato in lungo per piu giornate, poi che ne disagio d'ascoltatore, ne danno, o spesa del recitatore non gliele toglieua."

[68] *Ibid.*, p. 109, l. 17: "la tragedia . . . conuiene hauere per soggetto vn'attione auenuta in picciolo spatio di luogo, & in picciolo spatio di tempo, cio è in quel luogo, & in quel tempo, doue, & quando i rappresentatori dimorano occupati in operatione, & non altroue, ne in altro tempo."

[69] *Ibid.*, p. 178, l. 23: "Perche non ha dubbio niuno, che, se nell'historia si narra sotto vn raccontamento piu attioni d'vna persona sola, . . . nella poesia si potra sotto vna fauola narrare senza biasimo piu attioni d'vna persona sola. si come parimente nella poesia senza biasimo si potra narrare vna attione sola d'vna gente, percioche l'historia fa cio con molta lode. . . . Et non solamente pure nella poesia si potra narrare vna attione d'vna gente, ma anchora piu attioni d'vna gente. . . . Et, se le si concedera la narratione di molte attioni di molte persone, o di molte genti, non pero veggo, che biasimo alcuno le debba seguire." The argument rests upon an analogy between poetry and history which Castelvetro develops at great length.

... we should not marvel at all if several actions of one person or one action of a people or several actions of several persons delight us and make us attentive to listen, since such a plot carries with it, through the multitude of the actions, through the variety, through the new events, and through the multitude of persons and of the people, both pleasure and greatness and magnificence.[70]

Why, then, does Aristotle insist upon unity, and why does Castelvetro recommend it? The reason is different for the different genres. For tragedy and comedy, unity of action is a consequence of the unities of time and of place; it would not be possible to crowd into a restricted space and into twelve hours more than one action; indeed, sometimes one of these plays will contain only a part of an action.[71] For the epic, where this "necessity" does not exist, unity of action is sought for two other reasons: first, because such a unified plot is more "beautiful," less likely to satiate the spectator with an abundance of different things (see pp. 179, l. 16; 514, l. 29), and, second, because such a plot demonstrates the ingenuity and the excellence of the poet (see pp. 179, l. 24; 179, l. 16, and 504, l. 23). What is symptomatic about this position, especially in a commentary on the *Poetics*, is its abandonment of any concern with the structural or formal beauties of the work and its insistence upon two such nonartistic considerations as the comfort and character of the audience and the glory of the poet.

Many of these lines of argument, in fact, point to a conception of the art of poetry essentially different from Aristotle's. A first major difference appears in Castelvetro's assimilation of this art to the art of history. Their kinship is so intimate, he says, that if we possessed an adequate art of history, it would be unnecessary to write an art of poetry, "since poetry derives all its light from the light of history."[72] Indeed, Aristotle's work is to an extent vitiated by the fact that he did not base it upon an adequate art of history, and most of the precepts which he presents would have been more adequately and more appropriately developed in an art of history. The two arts differ in two respects only: history presents events which actually happened, poetry those which have not occurred but which might occur, and poetry uses verse whereas history uses prose (see pp. 115, l. 41; 190, l. 1). Otherwise, they are so much alike that poetry may be defined as "a resemblance or imitation of history" ("similitudine, o rassomiglianza d'historia," p. 28, l. 19). Poetry is certainly more like history than it is like painting, and Aristotle errs with others in making the latter comparison.

---

[70] *Ibid.*, p. 179, l. 18: "non sia punto da marauigliarsi se piu attioni d'vna persona, o vna attione d'vna gente, o piu attioni di piu persone ci dilettassono, & ci rendessono intenti ad ascoltarle, portando seco la fauola per la moltitudine dell'attioni, per la varieta, per gli nuoui auenimenti, & per la moltitudine delle persone, & della gente & piacere, & grandezza, & magnificenza." See also pp. 504, l. 36; 692, l. 31.

[71] *Ibid.*, pp. 179, l. 4; 504, l. 19. Castelvetro thinks of the "action" as the whole of the traditional or historical story, not as the plot of thei ndividual work of art.

[72] *Ibid.*, p. 5, l. 21: "prendendo la poesia ogni sua luce dalla luce dell'historia."

Castelvetro was so completely dedicated to the analogy between poetry and history that he failed to construct, as most of his contemporaries were doing, a parallelism between poetry and rhetoric—and this in spite of the essentially rhetorical character of his own system. Aristotle's notion of imitation as introducing differences between an object in nature and that object as represented in a work of art is completely absent; none of the implications of the Aristotelian concept of imitation is present. For the object in nature is also the object in art, and the art which most readily treats of "nature" by means of words, history, is the one which provides all the essential distinctions.

Some of these matters are further discussed, if briefly, in Castelvetro's *Chiose intorno al libro del Comune di Platone*, a work which dates from the period of the *Poetica*[73] but which was first published in the *Opere varie critiche* of 1727. The sections of the *Republic* which deal with poetics are naturally of unusual interest to Castelvetro. He finds that Aristotle contradicts Plato's statement that poetry is meant to teach by example and that we must of necessity follow its examples. Rather, we are at liberty to accept or reject its teachings, since it teaches "through materials about which we may think, and so that we may have examples of all kinds, both to frighten the wicked and to console the good, and to learn the nature of men and of women." The aim is still to teach, in this context, but the audience may react against the examples rather than follow them blindly. This, in essence, is the meaning of purgation: " . . . therefore Aristotle said that tragedy, by means of fears and injustices, drove out fears and injustices from the hearts of the men listening, refuting what Plato says in this passage."[74] Again on purgation, Castelvetro proposes an alternative theory in which like would purge like: "Perhaps Aristotle . . . said that tragedy purged those same passions by means of those same passions because they constituted a purification and a proving of man, just as Plato relates . . . that the perils proposed are a fire for man."[75] Castelvetro's explanations of Plato depend upon an understanding of Aristotle, as his explanations of Aristotle depend upon an understanding of Plato.

Somewhere between 1570 and 1572 an author variously referred to as Anselmo or as Ridolfo Castravilla wrote an attack upon Dante entitled

---

73 A passage on p. 215 of the *Opere varie critiche* indicates that the commentary is posterior to that on the *Poetics*.

74 In *Opere varie critiche* (1727), pp. 215–16: "per materia da farvi pensamenti sopra, & acciocchè abbiamo esempj d'ogni maniera e da spaventare i rei, e da consolare i buoni, e da conoscere la natura de gli uomini, e delle donne. E perciò diceva Aristotele, che la Tragedia con le paure, e con le ingiustizie scacciava le paure, e le ingiustizie dal cuore de gli uomini ascoltanti, riprovando quello, che dice Platone in questo luogo." The reference in Plato is to p. 561 of the Ficino translation in the Basel edition of 1546.

75 *Ibid.*, pp. 226–27: "Forse Aristotele . . . disse, che la Tragedia purgava quelle medesime affezioni con quelle medesime affezioni, poichè erano affinamento, e paragone dell'uomo, siccome racconta . . . Platone, che i pericoli proposti sono il fuoco dell'uomo."

Discorso nel quale si mostra l'imperfettione della Comedia di Dante. This
was the work which started the great controversy over Dante, and I shall
treat it in detail in a later chapter. But since the attack is based upon principles which claim to be Aristotelian, it is of interest here to see how Castravilla (who has never been successfully identified) understood the text of
the *Poetics.* It is important to note that this is a full-scale examination of a
great modern work, an examination that takes its approach and its criteria
from Aristotle, and that it is one of the earliest practical studies to do so.
Castravilla writes in rebuttal of Benedetto Varchi's claim (in the *Hercolano,*
1570) that Dante's poem was superior to Homer's. He first asks whether
the *Divina Commedia* is a poem at all, establishing the principle that a poem
must contain a plot which is the imitation of an action—an Aristotelian
principle:

> Aristotle declares this in his *Art of Poetry* in several places, and especially in
> the beginning of that book, where he states that all kinds of poems are imitations,
> and in the passage below where he adds that those who imitate imitate persons in
> action: and farther below he says that the plot is an imitation of an action. From
> this passage one concludes that a poem is a plot . . . , except for the fact that a
> poem is not a poem until it is expressed in meter, which is its outer garment, and
> that the plot is an imitation of an action even in the mind of the poet and before
> it has been expressed. For this reason Aristotle said that the plot was like the soul
> of tragedy.[76]

Two interesting comments are included here: first, plot as an imitation
exists prior to any expression in the form of a "poem"; second, making it
into a poem involves necessarily the use of verse. Castravilla next asks
whether Dante's work may properly be classed as an epic poem, applying
to it Aristotle's yard-stick that an epic poem must be "an imitation of
heroes" (fol. 77*v*). Before he proceeds to an analysis of the *Commedia,* he
establishes a set of requisites for a good plot; these are attributed to
Aristotle and constitute a digest of parts of the *Poetics:*

> It should be verisimilar: for without this the poem would fall short of its end,
> and would remain deprived of all force and vigor;
> Second, it should be clear and easily remembered, that is, such that it can be
> seen at a glance and remembered in a single turn of the memory;
> Thirdly, it must be one, that is, include one single action and that a whole one,
> that is from the beginning to the end;

[76] I quote this treatise from MS Vat. Lat. 6528, fols. 76–84; see fol. 76*v*: "Ilche declara
Aristotele nella sua arte poetica in piu luoghi, e maxime nell'exordio di quel libro, doue pone
che tutte le spetie delle poesie sono imitatione, et in quello che poi sogiugnie che quelli che
imitano, immitano persone agenti: et più di sotto dice che la fauola e imitatione d'attione.
dal qual luogo si ritrae che poema è fauola . . .; senonche il poema non e poema sinòche non
è espresso col metro, che e la sua ueste, e la fauola è imitatione d'attione etiam nella mente
del poeta, e prima ch'ella sia espressa. Pero dicea Aristotele che la fauola era quasi l'anima
della tragedia." There are numerous Latin words and expressions throughout the text.

Plots will be beautiful if they are dramatic, that is if the persons introduced act and are in continuous action;

if they are simple, that is if they contain actions of a single thread;

if they have body and a proper size, for beauty cannot exist in little subjects;

if they have recognition and reversal which break forth from the subject probably or necessarily, in some marvelous fashion;

if they contain within the argument itself the marvelous, the terrible, the pitiable, and the moral;

if they do not have too many episodes, and if these are connected in such a way with the argument that they seem to be members born along with the body, not that were added to it.

if it has a beautiful knotting and a beautiful solution which comes out of the action itself.[77]

Castravilla's idea of plot seems to be a proper one—surely more correct than that of Castelvetro—and his digest of the requisites shows an understanding of the essential problems as Aristotle raises them.

NERONI (CA. 1571)

To approximately the same period (I have assigned them roughly to 1571[78]) belong three discourses by Baccio Neroni, probably prepared for delivery to the Accademia degli Alterati. They all deal with matters discussed in the *Poetics* and at times present interpretations of that text. One of them is entitled *Se il verso è necessario nella poesia*, and Neroni's answer to the question is a strong affirmative. This is of course in opposition to the *Poetics*; the author is therefore obliged to prove his position and to find a suitable interpretation of certain passages in Aristotle. He presents twelve distinct (and numbered) arguments: (1) Verse gives importance to subjects which are in themselves unimportant; it adds majesty, greatness, the marvelous, and by delighting the audience achieves the end of poetry: "This is a manifest sign that poets must necessarily use verse, as men who

---

[77] *Ibid.*, fols. 78v–79: "Che la sia uerisimile. che senza questo il poema caderebbe dal suo fine, e resteria spogliato d'ogni forza e uigore.

"Secondo uuol essere conspicua e ramemorabile cioe tale che si possa uedere in un girare d'un guardo e ricordarsene in una uolutione di memoria.

"Item debbe essere una, cioe comprendere una sola actione, e quella tutta cioe dal principio sino al fine.

"Le fauole saranno belle, se saranno dramatiche, cioè se le persone indotte s'opereranno, e saranno in continua operatione se saranno semplic[i], cioe se conteneranno actioni dun sol filo se haranno corpo e grandezza giusta; perche ne piccoli argumenti non puo esser beltà.

"Se haranno peripetia et agnitione, che erumpino uerisimilmente, o necessariamente dalla cosa in alcun modo amirabile.

"Se haranno nell argumento stesso l'admirabile, il terribile et il misericordieuole, el morale.

"Se non haranno troppi episodij e quelli saranno connexi talmente con largumento che pareranno membri nati col corpo non sutiui apposti.

"Se hara bello nexo e bella solutione che erumpa dalla cosa."

[78] See my "Argomenti di discussione letteraria nell'Accademia degli Alterati (1570–1600)," *Giornale Storico della Letteratura Italiana*, CXXXI (1954), 178.

treat mostly of vain things and of little importance, and such that they need to help them by means of the style, a thing which they cannot better achieve in any way than through verse."[79] (2) Even in poems treating important subjects, such as tragedy and the epic, verse is needed, along with all the ornaments of style; without them: "it is clear that these [poems] will remain a cold thing and a simple narration of a fact, and I am positive that such works will never be read in prose because without verse they would give no pleasure at all."[80] (3) The situation is different for histories, where the reader is interested in learning the facts; but in poems, which are imitations of true things, we need "the sweetness and the pleasantness of verse, by which the readers are most highly attracted."[81] (4) Such imitations of history as the *Amadigi* were neglected because they were in prose; this explains why Bernardo Tasso put this work into verse. (5) Even Aristotle argues for the necessity of verse:

... when Aristotle says that to compose any matter at all in verse does not make the writer become a poet ..., it is a clear sign that the proper poetic style is that which is contained in verses. Nor are works that are written in prose to be called poetry even if there be imitation in them, which is most important in poems. ... he [Aristotle] said that if somebody were to write in prose and to imitate some action according to probability, as is required in poems, he should not for that reason be called a poet, as one who understood that in poetry verse is necessarily to be required.[82]

This represents, of course, a considerable twisting of Aristotle's meaning. (6) Were this not true, Boccaccio, who imitates most excellently, would be called a poet. (7) Tragedy is poetry, and it is in verse. (8) Verse is needed in lyric poetry, which would be uninteresting without it. (9) One might think that comedy, which treats of low matters in a low style, might dispense with verse; but comedies having it are always more highly praised. (10) Universal usage has given the name "poet" only to those who write in verse. (11) When Aristotle uses the phrase λόγοις ψιλοῖς in connection

[79] MS Laur. Ashb. 559, fol. 1v: "Ilche è segno manifesto, che necessariamente i poeti deuono usare il uerso, come coloro che per lo piu trattano di cose uane, et di poca importanza, talche hanno bisogno di aiutarle con lo stile ilche per altra uia meglio conseguire non possono che mediante il uerso." The folios of the MS are unnumbered, and I have merely given a separate pagination to each of the discourses.

[80] *Ibid.*, fol. 2: "chiaro è che esse rimarranno una cosa fredda, et una semplice narratione d'un fatto, et mi rendo sicuro che tali opere mai saranno lette in prosa, per che senza uerso non darebbono piacere alcuno."

[81] *Ibid.*, fol. 2: "la suauita, et piaceuolezza del uerso dalla quale sono sommamente alletati i lettori."

[82] *Ibid.*, fol. 2v: "dicendo Aristotele che il comporre qualsi uoglia cosa in uersi non fa che il compositore diuenti poeta ..., è segno manifesto che il proprio stile poetico, è quello che da uersi è contenuto. Ne l'opere scritte in prosa poesia douersi chiamare, ancorche in quelle sia l'imitatione che è importantissima ne poemi. ... non per questo disse che se alcuno componessi in prosa et imitassi qualche attione secondo il uerisimile come si ricerca ne poemi, egli ne douesse essere chiamato poeta, come quegli che intese necessariamente nelle poesie ricercarsj il uerso."

with the epic (*Poetics* 1447*a*29),[83] he does not mean prose but rather language without rhythm and harmony. (12) In his definition of tragedy, again, the phrase ἡδυσμένῳ λόγῳ denotes "that language in which were present harmony, rhythm, and verse."[84] Neroni concludes his argument by insisting that if verse is required in tragedy and the epic, it is also to be demanded in all other poetic genres.

It is clear that the principles behind Neroni's argument include the necessity, if poetry is to be pleasurable, of certain stylistic and prosodic ornaments, the traditional identification of poetry with verse, and the conviction that Aristotle is the final authority. This last being true, he must follow the lead of his predecessors in giving to every doubtful passage in the *Poetics* a meaning that fits his own theoretical position. The two passages studied in the last two arguments were among those most frequently debated.

Another of Neroni's discourses is entitled *Che la fauola è di maggiore importanza nella poesia che i costumi.* Once again, the argument is very systematically pursued and Aristotle is the main authority; but this time Neroni agrees throughout with his source—or, rather, his use of it does not involve any extensive deformation. The discussion is repetitive, but one may distinguish these essential points: Plot and character are the most important parts of poetry. Neroni presents a philosophical defence of his contention that plot is the more important of the two: " . . . plot is of greater importance in poems than character because the plot exists in poems as the substance upon which all the other things [*var.*: qualities] rest as accidents, the fact being that the substance is not resident in any other subject but is itself the subject of all the accidents."[85] As Aristotle points out, plot can exist without character but character cannot exist without plot; the plots of *Iphigenia in Tauris* and the *Aeneid* are analyzed in proof. Not only is plot the substance of poetry, it is also the end:

The plot is the end and the purpose of every poem, for the end of poetry is imitation, but actions are imitated primarily, thus the plot. Besides the end is action and not a quality of action, as is said in the *Poetics* and in the first book of the *Ethics*, and this excludes character which, because it consists of accidents and of qualities, cannot be the end.[86]

It is plot which gives form to any poem—the form which is the end of any maker—and as such it is the most noble and the most important of its

83 See above, p. 363, for the difficulties with the text at this point.
84 *Ibid.*, fol. 3v: "quella oratione, nella quale era l'Armonia, il ritmo, et il uerso."
85 MS Laur. Ashb. 559, fols. 1–1v: "la fauola è di maggiore importanza ne' Poemi che i costumi non sono peroche la fauola è ne' Poemi à guisa della sustanza su laquale sono appoggiate tutte l'altre cose [*var.*: qualità] come accidenti; sendo che la sustanza non è posta in altro suggetto ma è lei il suggetto di tutti gl'Accidenti."
86 *Ibid.*, fols. 1v–2: "La fauola è il fine e l'intendimento d'ogni Poema peroche il fine della Poesia è l'imitatione, ma si imitano principalmente le attioni adunche la fauola; oltreche li fine è attione e non qualità d'attione come si dice nella Poetica e nel primo dell'Etica il che esclude i costumi, iquali perche sono accidenti e perche sono qualità non possono esser fine."

parts. Poems are praised or blamed for the success or failure of their plots, as Neroni demonstrates by citations from Aristotle, by references to the condemnation of the *Canace*, to Aristotle's praise of Homer, to the high esteem for Vergil and the contempt in which many critics hold the *Orlando Furioso*. Whereas character is multiple, plot is one and its unity brings it beauty and perfection; these qualities result from the fact that it may be seen in its totality in a single glance, and that it may be easily remembered. It is hence the principal source of pleasure in its reader or audience, and this is because actions are more pleasing than their accompanying circumstances. Besides, it is through the plot that a poem achieves its particular effects: " . . . the poem achieves its end to the degree to which it has a plot well adapted and proper to the moving of pity or terror or to receiving whatever other thing is desired by the author; for the moving of the passions in every poem is brought about properly by the plot, since this consists in reversal, recognition, and perturbation."[87] Other reasons are suggested for the superiority of plot over character and over all other parts of the poem. Neroni's conclusion presents, suddenly, a striking analogy between his consideration of plot and his conception of the place of poetry as subordinate to politics among the sciences: "in this case, it [plot] is the architectonic part and that which commands all the others, in no wise less than does politics over all the other arts and sciences."[88]

The last of the Neroni lectures, although it bears no title, might well be called *Che ogni fauola ha la peripetia, et la recognitione,* for it is a response to the negative of the same proposition presented by Carlo Rucellai. Neroni's reply is made at the request of the Reggente of the academy. What he has to say about recognition and reversal again represents, if not a distortion, at least a very loose understanding of Aristotle on the subject. If reversal, he says, means a change of status, then all forms of poetry necessarily will have it, since tragedy and comedy and the epic all represent a change of fortune from happiness or unhappiness to its contrary. Likewise, in every poem somebody or something is recognized. Of far greater significance are Neroni's remarks on plot, which in a sense continue those of the preceding discourse. But he now emphasizes a utilitarian end not even suggested in the other writings:

And it is a sure thing that poets, when they compose plots, have as their end either to profit or to delight, and that they expend a great effort for no other reason than to be of some utility to men. Wherefore, when they compose either tragedies or comedies or heroic poems, in all of them they have their eye on this end. To achieve it they use those means which best lead them to it; and to

---

[87] *Ibid.,* fol. 3: "in tanto ha il Poema conseguito il fin suo quanto ha la fauola ben' accomodata e conueniente à muouer la misericordia od il terrore o à riceuere qual si uoglia altra cosa desiderata dall'Autore percioche il muouer degli affetti in ogni Poema à propriamente cagionato dalla fauola, consistendo cio nella Peripetia Recognitione e perturbatione."

[88] *Ibid.,* fol. 4v: "è in questo caso la Architettonica e quella che comanda a tutte l'altre niente meno che si faccia la ciuile a tutte l'altre arti e scienze."

do this, of the parts which are found in such poems certain ones are powerful over all others: reversal and recognition. These are the ones which are apt, more than anything else, to move the passions, and they seize the minds of persons, delighting them or moving them to contempt or to compassion, depending upon the action which is then being represented.[89]

Like his theory of verse, this passage shows Neroni's adherence to the Horatian tradition. But even here he insists on essentially Aristotelian ideas; and, in general, his faithfulness to the text and the principles of the *Poetics* is exemplary for his time.

PICCOLOMINI'S TRANSLATION (1572)

In 1572 appeared the third of the translations of the *Poetics* into Italian, the second (after Segni's) to be issued separately and independently of a commentary. This was Alessandro Piccolomini's *Il libro della Poetica d'Aristotele*. It had been prepared, Piccolomini tells us, as a part of the work on his annotations to the same text, already completed; but fearing delays (and indeed the *Annotationi* were not to appear until 1575), he publishes his translation alone, accompanied only by a prefatory epistle containing a theory of translation. Piccolomini makes no direct mention of Castelvetro's "vulgarizzamento," although it would be surprising if he did not know it; in fact, one may detect throughout his translation an effort to make it as different as possible from that of his immediate predecessor. When one compares the two, one finds the following essential differences: Piccolomini's translation is always a little longer and more diffuse than Castelvetro's, since he is more intent upon making the meaning clear through translation alone, without relying upon a commentary. For example, his "Particella 5" (he uses Maggi's divisions) as compared with the last sentence in Castelvetro's "Particella Terza" (= *Poetics* 1447a26):

Castelvetro: Ma con lo stesso numero rassomigliano senza harmonia certi ballatori, percioche questi per figurati numeri rassomigliano anchora & costumi, & tormenti, & attioni (p. 15).

Piccolomini: Col ritmo stesso poi disgiunto dalla melodia imitan' alcuni di coloro, che son' instrutti nell'arte del saltare. conciosia cosa che questi tali col mezo di ritmi accompagnati da figurati mouimenti, cerchino d'imitare i costumi, gli affetti, & le attioni de gli huomini (p. 10).

Whereas Castelvetro, in such a passage as this, preserves the denseness of the original, Piccolomini substitutes phrases for words and achieves a

---

[89] MS Laur. Ashb. 559, fol. 1: "Et è cosa per certa, che i poeti nel comporre le fauole hanno per fine, o di giouare, o dilettare, et che per altro non si muouono ad affaticarsi se non per essere di qualche utilita agli huomini, Onde componendo essi, ò tragedie, ò comedie, ò poemi Heroici in tuttj hanno l'occhio à tal fine, per il quale conseguire adoperano que mezzi, che meglio uegli conducono, alche fare sopra tutte le parti che si trouano in tali poemi sono potentissime la Peripetia. et la recognitione, come quelle che sono piu che altro atte à muouere gli affetti, et pigliano gli animi delle persone, ò dilettando, ò mouendo à sdegno, ò à compassione secondo il fatto, che allora si rappresenta."

clearer final meaning. Moreover, he frequently uses words ("imitare" rather than "rassomigliano," "affetti" rather than "tormenti") that seem to convey a meaning closer to the original. For another example, we may compare his "Particella 11" with Castelvetro's "Particella Sesta" (*Poetics* 1448a1):

Castelvetro: Hora, poi che i rassomiglianti rassomigliano coloro, che fanno, & è di necessita, che questi sieno o buoni, o rei, percioche i costumi quasi sempre accompagnano questi soli, conciosia cosa che tutti *gli huomini* sieno differenti di costumi per maluagita, o per bonta, egli è di necessita rassomigliare i migliori, che noi, o i piggiori, o i cosi fatti, secondo che fanno i dipintori. Et certo Polignoto effigiaua i migliori, & Pausone i piggiori, & Dionigi i simili (p. 34).

Piccolomini: Hor perche coloro, che imitano, imitan persone, che qualche cosa facciano, & queste tai persone, ò buone, ò ree fa di mestieri, che siano: conciosia cosa che à queste due sole (si può dir) qualità del buono, & del reo, ogni costume dell' huomo segua, & si riferisca; come che per la virtù, & per il vitio, gli huomini nei lor costumi differiscan tutti: è necessario per questo che ò di persone migliori, ò di peggiori, di quali communemente noi siamo; ò di cosi fatte si faccia l'imitatione; si come vsan di fare li Pittori ancora. posciache Polignoto più belle le persone di quello, ch'ordinariamente sono; & Pausone più brutte, & Dionisio simili ad esse, soleuano depingendo rappresentare (p. 11).

It is certain that the second makes better sense than the first to the reader, who is obliged to a lesser degree to puzzle over terms and constructions. It may also, at certain points, represent the Greek text more accurately. We should find it useful, in this connection, to juxtapose the solutions proposed by the two men for certain crucial passages, i.e., passages which gave the sixteenth century more trouble than the rest of the text:

At 1447a29, the λόγοις ψιλοῖς (so critical because of the debate over prose and verse) is translated by Castelvetro as "con parlari nudi" (p. 17), by Piccolomini as "sciolta da misure di versi" (p. 10); the latter permits us to conclude that poetry may be written in prose.

At 1448a11, for ψιλομετρίαν (related to the same problem) Castelvetro gives "intorno a parlari, & a *nudi versi*" (p. 41) and Piccolomini "intorno al parlare, & *allo stesso verso, da per se solitariamente preso*" (p. 11); the latter is a kind of paraphrase, but it attempts to explain the meaning of "nudi."

At 1448b18, on the pleasure which accompanies imitation, Castelvetro translates badly by "& tutti si ralegrano delle rassomiglianze" (p. 63). Piccolomini expands to "L'altra [cagion] è poi, l'esser parimente naturale all'huomo il sentir piacere, & diletto dell'imitatione (p. 13)." The first version allows Castelvetro to find another factor as the second "natural cause," whereas Piccolomini is committed by his to the more correct interpretation.

At 1449b10, σπουδαίων is translated by Castelvetro as "de nobili" (p. 107), permitting the sociological interpretation; by Piccolomini as "di graui, & illustri persone" (p. 16), in which ethical as well as social elements are present.

At 1452*b*38, φιλάνθρωπον gives Castelvetro's "non è *gratiosa a gli huomini*, ne compassioneuole, ne spauenteuole" (p. 265) and Piccolomini's "ne di *commouimento humano*, ne di compassioneuole, ne di temibile" (p. 27), a better rendering of the much-discussed term.

These few examples show to what extent Piccolomini's translation may claim a greater fidelity to the original than Castelvetro's, which frequently is allowed to take on that form most useful for Castelvetro's private theories about poetry. At times, however, Piccolomini (perhaps because of his wish not to repeat Castelvetro) will adopt a less satisfactory solution—for example, in his translation of μίμοι as "ridicolose imitationi" (p. 10) instead of the more simple "mimi." Both translators, it should be noted in passing, are still faced with the problems of an imperfect text, and here they are almost equally unsuccessful; one may examine their attempts to deal with *Poetics* 1447*a*28 (Castelvetro, p. 17; Piccolomini, p. 10), 1447*b*22 (p. 18 and p. 10), 1449*b*26 (p. 113 and p. 25), and several others.

ELLEBODIUS (CA. 1572)

The date of 1572 is the most exact one that can be assigned to the *In Aristotelis librum de Poetica paraphrasis* of Nicasius Ellebodius (Nicaise Van Ellebode) contained in Ambrosian MS R.123.Sup., fols. 68–91*v* and accompanied by a set of "Notae in primum Aristotelis librum de Poetica" (fols. 92–110). The date results from a letter, apparently accompanying the manuscript, sent from Pressburg on February 22, 1572, asking the correspondent to show the manuscript to Riccoboni and to Paulo Manuzio. Throughout, the manuscript shows Ellebodius' Italian connections. It refers to earlier texts and commentaries printed in Italy, especially the Aldine edition of 1508 and Vettori's *Commentarii* of 1560; it derives many good readings for the text of the *Poetics* from an old codex said to be in the possession of Giovanni Vincenzo Pinelli; and it calls upon the authority of Michael Sophianos of Chios who had studied and later taught in Padua. Indeed, most of Ellebodius' connections are Paduan; he himself had studied there, and in addition to Sophianos his literary relationships seem to have been closest with Vettori, Riccoboni, and Pinelli. This work by a Belgian, probably written in Pressburg, may thus properly be considered to belong to the Italian tradition ot the Cinquecento, through its origins, its intellectual ties, and its ultimate destination.[90]

[90] On Ellebode (also written Ellebaudt), see the article in the *Biographie Nationale de Belgique*, VII, 554; also Adolfo Rivolta, *Catalogo dei Codici Pinelliani dell'Ambrosiana* (Milano: Tipografia Pontificia Arcivescovile S. Giuseppe, 1933), pp. xxiv, xlv, lxxxviii. Also Jean Noël Paquot, *Mémoires pour servir à l'histoire littéraire des dix-sept provinces des Pays-Bas* (Louvain: Imprimerie Académique, 1765), I, 659. On Michael Sophianos, whose main published work was a translation of Aristotle's *De anima*, see Emile Legrand, *Bibliographie hellénique (XVᵉ et XVIᵉ siècles)* (Paris: Leroux, 1885), II, 168–76, and the various indices to Legrand's volumes.

Ellebodius' work is remarkable in several ways. In the "Notae" he suggests numerous improvements of the Greek text, either from the Pinelli manuscript or from suggestions by Sophianos, some of which have found their way into the modern text through the conjectures of recent scholars (see, for example, in the edition of J. Hardy, the variants on pages 33, 43, and 53). These are frequently supported by citation of other texts which show a considerable erudition in Greek and Latin sources. The paraphrase itself, which is sometimes merely a running translation, sometimes an expansion and development of the original work, is reasonably accurate and faithful to the intentions of the original. Ellebodius sees these intentions as contained in the following program: ". . . so that we may understand under what genus poetry is placed, what conception we should have of it, both how it differs from other arts in the same genus and how its forms differ among themselves, what were its beginnings and development."[91] He attempts to remain as closely Aristotelian as he can, even to the extent of seeking clarification for both text and ideas in other works of Aristotle, and he refers much less frequently than do his predecessors to the rival critical school of the Horatians. Nonetheless, there are two major points on which he departs quite markedly from what we must now consider to be the meaning of the *Poetics*.

The first of these is on the use of verse in poetry. For Ellebodius, poetry is impossible without verse; and, as so many of his fellow-commentators were doing, he interprets all apposite passages in the *Poetics* to corroborate this view. The initial statement comes in connection with 1447*a*28:

> The epic uses in imitating only bare language, that is verse without modulated . . . sound, and dancing; and it either mixes with one another several kinds of verse, or it uses one form of verse alone. . . . now this must be conceded, that language limited by poetic numbers cannot be absent from the epic or from any kind of poem; surely without this poetry can in no wise imitate. Moreover, imitation is so essential that the very name of poetry chiefly resides in it, nor indeed can it subsist without it; in the light of which remarks neither can verse without imitation, nor imitation without verse, be made into epic, or into poetry of any sort.[92]

Whenever, later in the text, any crucial phrase appears, he finds authority for giving to it a meaning in keeping with this position. Even the most

---

91 MS Ambrosianus R.123.Sup., fol. 68: "ut cui generi subijciatur poesis, quae eius sit notio, quo modo cum ipsa a ceteris, quę sunt eiusdem generis, tum eius formę inter se differant, quae initia, progressusque poeseos sint, intelligatur."

92 *Ibid.*, fol. 68*v*: "Epopoeia nudam tantum orationem, hoc est uersus sine modulato . . . sono, et saltatione adhibet in imitando, siue misceat inter se plura uersuum genera; siue una carminis forma utatur. . . . nunc hoc concessum sit, orationem quae poeticis numeris adstricta sit, neq. ab epopoeia, neq. ab ullo poematis genere abesse posse. quippe sine qua imitari poesis nullo modo potest. imitatio porrò ita necessaria est, ut in ea potissimum poeseos nomen sit positum, nec sine ea cohaerere sanè possit. quocirca neq. carmen sine imitatione, neq. imitatio sine carmine epopoeiam, aut omnino poesin efficitur." The text of Aristotle is corrupt at this point through the presence of the word ἐποποιία.

cautious and faithful of Aristotelians were thus unable to shake off the traditional association between poetry and verse.

The second point of distortion (if we may call it that) is Ellebodius' insistence that purgation produces moral instruction, which in turn serves the political ends of those who govern the state. Again, he is far from being alone in this contention, and the effects of both Platonic and Horatian ways of thinking are abundantly apparent. This meaning is first read into the *Poetics* at the point at which the *Paraphrasis* is dealing with the explanation of the definition of tragedy:

The last part of the definition is formulated in such a way that the usefulness of tragedy is made clear: tragedy brings to the state a utility which indeed is the very greatest, even for those who rule over citizens, and is to be sought out at all costs. For the error must be refuted by those who believe that tragedy was devised for no useful role for the citizenry, but merely for the worthless pleasure of the eyes and the ears.

After arguing that, in general, it is the duty of the rulers to make the citizens morally better, Ellebodius continues:

Virtue moreover, since its effect is especially to hold in check the turbulent movements of the soul and to restrain them within the bounds of moderation, and since tragedy, more than that, curbs these emotions, it must surely be granted that tragedy's usefulness to the state is extraordinary. For it causes two troublesome passions, pity and fear—which draw the soul away from strength and turn it toward a womanish weakness—to be regulated and governed by the soul with precise moderation.

The way in which this is done and the character of the lessons learned are those consecrated by a long line of texts:

For when we see repeatedly on the stage the most bitter sorrows of kings and princes and blameless (?) men and other most cruel misfortunes, we observe the fickleness of human affairs, and we are taught how to bear with moderation every change of fortune. And thus the soul is hardened by habituation, and those things which it formerly feared in the highest degree, it begins almost to hold in contempt.[93]

[93] *Ibid.*, fols. 72–72*v*: "Extrema definitionis pars est posita, ut usus tragoediae ostendatur; quem affert reip. qui quidem maximus est, et ijs qui ciuitates regunt, uehementer expetendus. coarguendus enim error eorum est, qui ad nullam partem utilem ciuitatibus, qui ad inanem dumtaxat uoluptatem oculorum, et aurium tragoediam comparatum putant. . . . uirtus autem, cum potissimum id agat, ut animi motus turbidos ratione coerceat, et mediocritatis regionibus includat, tragoedia porrò hos motus comprimat, concedatur profecto, singularem eius esse in rep. utilitatem. facit enim ut duae affectiones importunae, misericordia, et timor, quae auocant à fortitudine animum, et ad muliebrem ignauiam abjiciunt, temperentur et definita animi moderatione gubernentur. nam spectandis in scena identidem regum et principum uirorum inte . . . bus, acerbissimis doloribus, et alijs asperrimis casibus perspicitur inconstantia rerum humanarum, et ad omnem fortune commutationem moderate ferendam erudimur. itaque duratur consuetudine animus, et quae antea summe metuerat incipit penè contemnere." Cf. fols. 77–77*v*: "est autem munus tragoediae per miserationem, et timorem has ipsas affectiones ex animo abstergere quare fabula ita facienda est ut res formidabiles et miserabiles inducantur. nam hoc tragoediae est proprium."

Ellebodius concludes, therefore, that the Platonic exiling of tragic writers from the city was a mistake, for the pedagogical usefulness of purgation is an answer to any charge of moral harmfulness. Later, in the notes to the same passage (fol. 96), he develops the analogy with the gladiatorial spectacles, used to accustom young men to blood and wounds and to incite them to military valor.

A number of miscellaneous translations or notes in the *Paraphrasis* are of interest as they confirm or contradict current thinking about the matters which they treat. Ellebodius' view both of character and of the effects of tragedy depends upon his conception of catharsis. He translates φιλάν-θρωπον as "communis humanitatis sensu" (fol. 77v) and glosses it thus: ". . . it generally means the sorrow by which the soul is affected through the misfortunes of others; for nature causes man, from the mere fact that he is a man, to be sorrowful at the troubles of men."[94] Demosthenes, Cicero, Horace, and Hermogenes are cited as authorities. The accompanying effect of fear gives the usual difficulty; he believes that it takes place when the tragic hero is similar in virtue to the mass of men ("cum is qui uulgo hominum uirtute par est," fol. 77v).

The matter of similarity is again involved in Ellebodius' understanding of the third of the requisites for character, τὸ ὅμοιον (1454a23), translated by "similes." This implies a representation of character either as it actually was in the person imitated or as tradition has made it out to be (fol. 82). The requisite is thus closely related to the general problem of verisimilitude, since here too opinion and current conceptions must be respected: "One must take care lest anything be related which is unacceptable to the opinion of men; wherefore those things should be preferred which cannot be done, if only they are probable, to those which can indeed be done, but do not seem to be credible."[95] In a sentence such as this, the last part is the translation of Aristotle, while the first part adds an interpretation which shows the general critical bent of its author. If now we work backward through these various statements we find that credibility will make possible an identification with the tragic hero, who is like ourselves, that this will enable us to feel the tragic emotions, and that as these latter are purged we will become morally better.

Another concatenation of readings of the same kind occurs in Ellebodius' work on the passages dealing with character. Initially, he uses the terms "probi" and "improbi" to differentiate the objects of imitation at 1448a2. Then, when he comes to the four requisites for character, the same term "probi" is used for the first requisite, "good," in spite of the difference in

[94] *Ibid.*, fol. 100: "communiter dolorem significat, quo afficitur animus ob alterius res aduersas. nam natura fert, ut homo hominis ob hoc ipsum, quod homo est, incommodis doleat."
[95] *Ibid.*, fols. 87v–88: "Danda etiam opera est, ne quid afferatur, quod ab hominum opinione abhorreat. quamobrem praeoptanda sunt quae fieri nequeunt, modo probabilia sint, ijs, quae fieri quidem possunt, sed tamen credibilia non uidentur."

the original Greek terms (fol. 82). Moral goodness is taken to be necessary because, in tragedy and the epic, the hero teaches virtue in a positive way through the excellence of his own character. He becomes, in a way, a "specimen" or exemplar. It is for this reason that the commentator adds to Aristotle's idea of the heightening of portrayal the reason already given: "Although characters are to be portrayed as similar, nevertheless it is necessary, like the painters, to add something to them, each in its own kind, whether the poet imitates good or less good characters . . . so that they may appear as examples of the virtues and the vices."[96]

On the whole, the *Paraphrasis* of Ellebodius constitutes an extraordinary example of works of its kind: it shows with what vigor the Italian critical tradition imposed itself upon writers of other countries and how closely they remained linked to it. As far as Aristotelianism is concerned, the work presents some remarkable features in the correction and commentary of the text, along with some cases in which, unfortunately, the vigor of the tradition led to a perpetuation of misreadings and misunderstandings.

GIACOMINI (1573)

Another translation of the *Poetics* into Italian, following closely upon Castelvetro's and Piccolomini's and emphasizing the growing activity in the vernacular, was prepared by Lorenzo Giacomini Tebalducci Malespini in 1573. It was never published and exists today in MS Laur. Ashb. 531, fols. 1–38, written by Giacomini's secretary, Giorgio Bartoli, and dated at the end, "Fine A Laude Di Dio à di 28 d'Ag° 1573."[97] Giacomini was neither a scholar nor a professor; he was a distinguished amateur, most of whose literary activity centered about the meetings and the chores of the Accademia degli Alterati. This fact may account in part for the principal merits of the present translation. Giacomini does not copy any of the earlier vernacular translations, although borrowings from both Castelvetro and Piccolomini—in turn of phrase and in choice of words—are frequent. One might say that he combines the best features of both, the conciseness of Castelvetro (which also brings Giacomini's text closer again to the original) and the superior terminology of Piccolomini. His language is terse and direct and his words seem to the modern ear to be closer to those of common speech than were his predecessors'. His main aim is always simplicity, and he frequently achieves it. It might be instructive to compare him with Castelvetro, using the same passages that were quoted for the comparison with Piccolomini. On *Poetics* 1447a26:

Castelvetro: Ma con lo stesso numero rassomigliano senza harmonia certi

96 *Ibid.*, fol. 104: "Etsi mores affingendi sunt similes; tamen instar pictorum addere illis aliquid in suo cuiq. genere oportet, siue bonos siue minus bonos mores poeta imitetur . . . ut uirtutis, uitijq. specimen appareant."

97 For a more complete account of this MS, see my "Nuove Attribuzioni di manoscritti di critica letteraria del Cinquecento," *Rinascimento*, III (1952), 245–46.

ballatori, percioche questi per figurati numeri rassomigliano anchora & costumi, & tormenti, & attioni (p. 15).

Giacomini: et il ritmo solo senza armonia usano i ballatori; perche questi mediante i figurati ritmi imitano et i costumi et le passioni et le azzioni (fol. 1v).

On *Poetics* 1448a1:

Castelvetro: Hora, poi che i rassomiglianti rassomigliano coloro, che fanno, & è di necessita, che questi sieno o buoni, o rei, percioche i costumi quasi sempre accompagnano questi soli, conciosia cosa che tutti *gli huomini* sieno differenti di costumi per maluagita, o per bonta, egli è di necessita rassomigliare i migliori, che noi, o i piggiori, o i cosi fatti, secondo che fanno i dipintori. Et certo Polignoto effigiaua i migliori, & Pausone i piggiori, & Dionigi i simili (pp. 33–34).

Giacomini: Ma perche gli imitanti imitano agenti, et necessario è questi essere, ò buoni, ò cattivi, perche i costumi quasi sempre questi accompagnano soli, perche per la virtu et per il vizio quanto à costumi tutti sono differenti ò migliori che secondo noi ò peggiori, ò ancora tali necessario è imitare: come i pittori Polignoto migliori Pausone peggiori, et Dionisio simili ritraeva (fols. 2–2v).

The first of these passages shows the return to brevity and the choice of words which are in almost every case more current; the second, along with the same qualities, some of the confusion which might have been avoided if Piccolomini's suggested versions had been adopted.

Giacomini experiences the same difficulties with the text itself as did his predecessors. But in at least one case, the definition of tragedy, he supplies a word which none of his predecessors had included and which immediately clarifies one of the major problems of the text:

Giacomini: È adunque la tragedia imitazione d'azzione virtuosa [vars.: studiosa; spudea] et perfetta, che habbia grandezza con orazione condita in disparte ciascuna de le specie ne le parti, *di negozianti*, et non per narrazione: ma per misericordia et terrore conducente à fine la purgazione di cotali passioni (fol. 7; italics mine).

The translation is still confused and unclear and on the whole inferior to Piccolomini's; but the inclusion of "di negozianti," furnishing for the first time the proper opposition to "et non per narrazione," is a notable improvement. In a marginal gloss on the same passage, Giacomini also makes a clarifying statement about the meaning of σπουδαίας, for which he had offered three variant translations: "An action which is 'studiosa' or 'spudea' is to be distinguished from that action which is done in play in the reposeful moments of life."[98] In another passage, the best in the *Poetics* for the understanding of necessity and probability (1454a34), Giacomini's translation is superior because of its completeness and its clarity:

Castelvetro: Hora fa bisogno cosi ne costumi, come anchora nella constitutione delle cose cercare o quello, che è di necessita, o quello che è di verisimilitudine, &

98 MS Laur. Ashb. 531, fol. 7: "Azzione studiosa spudea si contradistingue da la azzione che si fa per gioco nel riposo de la vita."

che si faccia questo dopo questo o per necessita, o per verisimilitudine (p. 320).

Piccolomini: Hor' egli fa di bisogno, che nei costumi, si com'ancor nella fauola, & nel connettimento delle cose, si cerchi sempre, ò il necessario, ò il verisimile, & che l'vna cosa segua doppo l'altra ò necessariamente, ò verisimilmente (p. 31).

Giacomini: Ancora bisogna ne' costumi, si come ne la constituzione de fatti sempre cercare, ò il necessario, ò il verisimile, si che il tale tali cose dire ò fare, ò necessario sia ò verisimile, et questo dopo questo farsi, ò necessario, ò verisimile sia (fol. 20).

This is, as far as I know, the best translation of the passage to be found in Italy in the sixteenth century. One should not, however, exaggerate Giacomini's merits; on many of the difficult passages (such as those wherein Piccolomini was better than Castelvetro) he has no contribution whatsoever to make.

On the margins of several folios, Giacomini gives, in addition to alternative translations, notes which tell us how he understood the text; there are only four such places, and we may look briefly at them all.

On folio 3*v*, a note about the natural causes of imitation. Giacomini tries to reduce to syllogistic form two of the arguments in the text. The first is on pleasure in general, and is presented in tabular form:

Passion	Cause of the passion	Subject
a. pleasure	b. learning	c. seeing the images

"In seeing of images there is learning, in learning there is pleasure; therefore in the seeing of images there is pleasure." The second is on the pleasure deriving from images of objects which are in themselves distasteful:

Passion or predicate	Subject and cause	Effect and sign
a. pleasure	c. things made with imitation	b. images of ugly things

Things made with imitation are the cause why the images of ugly things give us pleasure; and these are a sign of their cause, that is, the things made with imitation give pleasure. This is demonstrated as follows: The images of ugly things give us pleasure, the images of ugly things are things made with imitation; therefore things made with imitation give us pleasure.[99]

---

[99] *Ibid.*, fol. 3*v*:

"Passione	Causa de la passione	subietto
a. Diletto	b. Imparare	c. veder le imagini

Nel veder l'imagini è l'imparare, nel imparare è diletto. adunque nel veder le immagini è diletto.

Passione ò predicato	Subietto et causa	Effetto et segno
a. Diletto	c. Cose fatte con imitazione	b. immagini de le cose brutte

Le cose fatte con imitazione sono causa che le immagini de le cose brutte ci danno diletto; et queste sono segno de la loro causa, cio è le cose fatte con imitazione danno diletto. dimostrasi cosi Le immagini de le cose brutte ci danno diletto, le immagini de le cose brutte sono cose fatte con imitazione, Adunque le cose fatte con imitazione ci danno diletto."

On folio 4, continuing the same discussion, Giacomini analyzes the syllogistic form of the deduction by which we recognize objects as they are represented by images. After reducing the argument to a syllogism, he says: "It is in the second figure, and good because it can be converted, the major premiss saying 'Whoever has these properties is this example . . . ' or without converting as follows: 'This example alone has these properties.' The middle term will thus be the properties common to the image and to the example which alone has all of them."[100] Such passages as these reveal the way in which men of the time were accustomed to practice textual analysis and commentary.

On folio 4v, we find a lengthy discussion of the passage on Homer as the model for the dramatic genres (1448*b*34). Giacomini is here concerned with clarifying the meaning of the text, its terms and its implications. "When Aristotle says first that Homer imitated virtuous things dramatically, he means that in his imitations of virtuous actions he showed the design for tragedy."[101] "Dramatically" is thus to be taken as meaning "in the way of drama" and is further explained by the formula, "that is, to introduce persons who act among themselves and who talk with one another."[102]

On folio 17, Giacomini reduces to tabular form all the ways in which plot may be constituted:

Plot is divided according to	the action	one	
		many	
	the agents	simple,	if the agents are on one side
		double,	if in the plot there are two sides, contrary and opposed
	fortune	simple,	if fortune and the state of affairs is the same from the beginning to the end
		reversed,	if it has a mutation of fortune and of state[103]

---

100 *Ibid.*, fol. 4: "E ne la seconda figura et buono perche si puo convertire, la maggior dicendo Chiunque ha queste proprietà è quello essemplare . . . ò senza convertire cosi Quello essemplare solo ha queste proprietà. il mezzo adunque sarà l[e] proprieta comuni à la immagine et à lo essemplare che solo le ha tutte."

101 *Ibid.*, fol. 4v: "Dicendo Aristotile prima che Omero imitò le cose virtuose dramaticamente vuole dire che ne le sue imitazioni de le virtuose azzioni mostrò il disegno de la tragedia."

102 *Ibid.*, fol. 4v: "a uso di drama . . . cio è introdur persone che tra se negozino et parlino l'uno con l'altro."

103 *Ibid.*, fol. 17:

"la favola si divide o	da l'azzione	una	
		molte	
	da gli agenti	semplice—se gli agenti sono una parte sola	
		doppia —se ne la favola sono due parti contrarie et nimiche	
	da la fortuna	semplice—se la fortuna et lo stato de le cose è uno et il medesimo dal principio à la fine	
		piegata —se ha mutazione di fortuna et di stato."	

This is interesting as a synthesis of fairly widely separated passages, and again as an indication of the total approach to the text.

In a general way, Giacomini's translation is symptomatic of the lively interest in getting the *Poetics* into Italian and of the resultant tendencies in technique—tendencies toward greater conciseness, toward simpler language, and toward the use of terms more like those of common speech than like those of the philosophers or the Latinists. In a sense, it is unfortunate that the work was not published, for such later Italian translations as the reprint of Piccolomini's (1575) and even such Latin versions as Riccoboni's (1579) might have been better for having known it.

The same manuscript contains a folio (39–39*v*) immediately following the translation of the *Poetics* which discusses the meaning of imitation and the definition of poetry (see above, Chapter II, pages 62–63); it may readily be taken as a further note on the text. In it, Giacomini displays some of the less admirable aspects of his literary method. He assimilates Aristotle's imitation to Plato's mythology and fable and extends the parallel to the three forms indicated for each. Similarly, in an interpretation of "favola," he allows the meaning of "lying" found in Plato to color his interpretation of Aristotle, producing thus a definition of poetry in which lying and falseness—in speech at least—are a necessary element.

Another Florentine manuscript, Magl. IX, 125 of the Biblioteca Nazionale, folios 23–26, contains a document by Francesco Bonciani which belongs to the same year and to the activities of the same Accademia degli Alterati. It is his *Parere intorno alla risposta del primo argomento del Castravilla*.[104] Here again the materials are purely theoretical and relate directly to the interpretation of the *Poetics*. For Bonciani is intent upon disproving Castravilla's first argument in the *Discorso*, which for present purposes is reduced to the following form:

> Every poem is a plot;
> Dante's *Commedia* is not a plot;
> Therefore Dante's *Commedia* is not a poem.[105]

The rebuttal involves a close analysis of both terms, poem and plot, as they appear in Aristotle and, hence, some fundamental questions about the total meaning of the *Poetics*. Bonciani offers three arguments in refutation of the statement "Every poem is a plot." (1) Plot cannot be predicated of a poem either as its material or as its form:

> If the plot is to be "said" or (to use the proper terms) predicated of the poem, it must be predicated either as material or as form . . . but it is not predicated as

---

104 See my "Nuove Attribuzioni . . .," *Rinascimento*, III (1952), 253–54.
105 MS BNF Magl. IX, 125, fol. 23:
"Ogni Poema è fauola
La Commedia di Dante non è fauola.
Adunque la Comedia di Dante non è Poema."

material because then the comparison of Aristotle (who says that the plot is the soul of tragedy), derived from a substituted proportion, would be bad. . ... The soul is not the material of the animal, hence neither is the plot the material of the poem. [Nor can it be predicated as the form:] because the form is not predicated substantively but rather by denomination. . . . Just as we cannot say that the animal is a soul, so we cannot say that the poem is a plot.[106]

In this argument, the same kind of logical analysis used by Giacomini is again applied. (2) The second argument depends upon a translation of 1447a13—a bad translation—which Bonciani renders thus: "The epic, tragedy, comedy, dithyrambic poetry, and the greater part [la maggior parte] of the poetry fitted to zithers and to flutes agree in this, that they are imitations."[107] From this use of the phrase "the greater part" Bonciani deduces that there are some parts of some kinds of poems which are not imitations, "and if there is no imitation there is no plot, whence is constituted the following argument: every plot is an imitation, some poems are not imitations, therefore some poems are not plots; or rather, not every poem is a plot."[108] This is the contradictory of Castravilla's original proposition. (3) For his third argument Bonciani refers to *Poetics* 1447b13, which he interprets as meaning that those who use verse alone, without imitation, may also be called poets. "It seems then that Aristotle admits that one may be called a poet even if he does not imitate; therefore not every poem is a plot, contrary to the proposition."[109] In the last two arguments especially, Bonciani's Aristotelianism seems to be shaky, and he surely does not contribute to a better understanding of the text.

Bongianni Gratarolo's *Difesa di Dante* [undated, but *ca.* 1573][110] relates again to the controversy started by Castravilla; but it is more concerned than was Bonciani's *Parere* with answering specific objections and making a detailed defence. Some of its answers involve denying the authority of Aristotle, upon which Castravilla had based his attack, and Gratarolo finds his best denial in a general question about the worth of the *Poetics*. Fairly early in the manuscript (MS Vat. Lat. 6528) he refers contemptu-

106 *Ibid.*, fols. 24v–25: "Se la fauola si debbe dire ò (per parlare co' termini proprij) predicare del Poema, ò la si debbe predicare come materia, ò come forma . . . ma la non si predica, come materia, perche cattiua sarebbe la comparatione d'Aristotele (che dice la fauola essere l'anima della tragedia) cauata dalla proportione commutata. . . . l'anima non è materia dell' animale, adunque ne anco la fauola è materia del Poema. . . . perche la forma non si predica in sustantiuo, ma denominatiuamente . . . come . . . non si puo dire l'animale è anima, cosi non si puo dire il Poema è Fauola."
107 *Ibid.*, fol. 25: "la epopeia, la tragedia, la commedia, la dithyrambica, et la maggior parte della poesia accomodata alle cithare et alle tibie conuengono in questo che sono imitatione."
108 *Ibid.*, fol. 25v: "e se non u'è imitatione non u'è fauola perche si constituisce questo argomento ogni fauola è imitatione, qualche Poema non è imitatione, adunque qualche Poema non è fauola, o uogliam dire Non ogni Poema è fauola."
109 *Ibid.*, fol. 26: "Pare adunque, che Aristotele ammetta, che uno si possa chiamare Pceta, ancorche non imiti, et pero non ogni Poema è fauola contra alla Propositione."
110 See M. Rossi, *Filippo Sassetti* (Città di Castello, 1899), p. 77, n. 4; also below, chap. xvi, pp. 841–42.

ously to "that little note-taker and paper-spoiler of Aristotle's *Poetics*" ("quel Notaiolo, o sfogliaccio della poetica d'Arist.," fol. 90). Later he defends his remark in a complete statement: "Other universal Aristotelians also, and especially your Castelvetro, confess that this is not a work reduced to perfection by its author, but merely a set of notes in which he put down things as they came to him, in order to treat them fully later with his usual orderliness (in which he surpasses all others) in some perfect book."[111] Gratarolo offers historical and literary proofs of the incompleteness of the *Poetics* and asserts that, because of the many poetical matters that it leaves in doubt, we cannot follow it literally on those that it does treat. He himself makes only one important theoretical statement, which consists in reducing all poetry to two basic types, tragic and comic; the reduction, he says, would be perfectly clear if we possessed the whole of Aristotle's treatise. The raising of one's voice against Aristotle was to become increasingly frequent as the great literary quarrels of the century developed.

SASSETTI (CA. 1573)

Still related to the same controversy and belonging approximately to the same period—these were the years of the initial flush of excitement—is Filippo Sassetti's *Sopra Dante*, found in MS VII, 1028 of the Biblioteca Nazionale, Florence.[112] It is an Aristotelian document in several ways, first because its essential organization follows the order of Aristotle's qualitative parts, second because it presents at the beginning a long discussion of theoretical matters found in the *Poetics*. The examination of the *Divina Commedia* comes only later. Moreover, the discussion has a remarkable feature in that it attempts, from a kind of practical point of view, to see how Aristotle's theories may be adapted to the circumstances of the present time and what modifications must be made when one passes from fifth-century Greece to sixteenth-century Italy. Aristotle is the master, although his teaching is not correctly understood at all times; Plato is called upon for certain ideas; but Horace has disappeared.

Sassetti really has his own theory of poetry, which results in a particular interpretation of the *Poetics* in many places. In general, he believes that the art has two ends, one of them internal—this is the imitation of human actions—the other external—this is the moral usefulness to the audience: "I say an end within the art of poetry because ultimately it seeks the profit

111 MS Vat. Lat. 6528, fol. 92*v*: "anco degli altri Aristotelici catolici, e specialmente il uostro casteluetro, confessano ch'ella non è opera ridotta à perfettione dall'Authore. ma solamente un memoriale nel quale esso metteua giu le cose secondo che gli soueniuano per distenderle poi co' suoi ordini soliti (ne quali soprauanzaua tutti) in alcun libro perfetto." The reference to Castelvetro is to the *Poetica*, p.)()(3 in the 1576 edition; see n. 57 above.

112 The treatise was published by Mario Rossi in the *Collezione di Opuscoli Danteschi inediti o rari*, Vols. XL–XLI (Florence, 1897), pp. 37–118. On the date, see Rossi, *Filippo Sassetti*, p. 19, n. 6.

of the human species and this is, we might say, the ultimate end which terminates, as in a thing outside the poet's work, in the soul of the readers or of the listeners who are the end to which this utility is ordered."[113] The poet's end is thus succinctly stated as "imitation for profit" ("lo imitare a giouamento," fol. 2*v*). It should be noted that this is not the Horatian end —pleasure is omitted—but one which seems to be Sassetti's own. In this connection Sassetti makes his first adaptation to modern times. The utilitarian end, he says, will vary according to the needs of different peoples at different times; so at carnival, comedies and masquerades are presented and on holy days one sees representations of the Passion. The poet, then, serves different ends by the choice of different objects, "now grave actions and full of high marvelousness, now light ones worthy of jests."[114] "Grave" and "light" are not absolute qualities of the object, however, since Sassetti thinks that each is magnified in the direction that it takes away from the middle; grave actions are made more grave, low ones more humble and abject. This in a sense constitutes one kind of imitation, the second kind residing in such actions as one sees done every day. Sassetti believes that the former kind is still practised in Italy, and he cites Alamanni's *Avarchide* as an example of "better" actions and Pulci's *Morgante* as an example of the worse; he is unable, however, to discover any case of imitations of the "like." With respect to the "better," finally, Sassetti thinks that one must, almost of necessity, seek such characters in ancient times, "whose men are always magnified and celebrated as more virtuous than those of the present century"[115]—a passage which gives us his interpretation of *Poetics* 1448a18.

Similar considerations lead to Sassetti's redefinition of the epic hero for modern times; and since this is done in terms of virtue rather than of position or of military prowess, we are suddenly brought back to a proper reading of Aristotle on the tragic hero.

Now if heroic virtue is virtue, generally considered, which in perfection exceeds that which is commonly found, we must believe that, just as extraordinary strength is a heroic virtue, so also is extraordinary prudence; and the same for every other disposition of the mind . . . so that today in the place of the heroes we should not put those of illustrious lineage who are renowned in war, but, wishing to take cognizance of the change, generally those who through their virtue are far and away superior to virtuous men. . . . In a word, let us not be led into thinking that instead of the heroes there come now only men valorous in war, but rather all

113 MS BNF VII, 1028, fol. 2*v*: "dico fine dentro all arte della poesia percioche egli ultimamente si ricerca il profitto del genere humano e questo è come si dice il fine vltimo il quale termina come in cosa fuori dell opera del poeta nell anima de lettori o degli ascoltanti che sono il fine a cuj è ordinata quella vtilità."

114 *Ibid.*, fol. 3: "hora attioni graui e piene di alta marauiglia hora le leggieri e degne di beffe."

115 *Ibid.*, fol. 3*v*: "gl huomini de' quali sono sempre magnificati e celebrati come piu uirtuosi di quegli del secolo presente."

those who through their virtue, whatever it may be, are greatly admired by other virtuous men.[116]

The same may be said for the epic action. For whereas tragedy presents actions "which happen every day to the human race" ("che auuengono tutto giorno al genere humano," fol. 4), the epic seems to treat only war; but since heroic deeds of the kind treated in ancient epics no longer occur, "we need to find men who could properly accomplish actions similar to those which the ancients supposed to have been done by such heroes [as Achilles, Ulysses, Hector, Aeneas]."[117]

Almost everything that Sassetti has to say about action and plot is in the nature of a commentary on Aristotle, and most of the clarifications tend to show how plot may achieve its proper pleasurable effects. Two ideas seem to be predominant: that of verisimilitude and that of the marvelous. The first is essential: "if one were to recount simply an action which did not bear credence with those who listened to it, it would not in any way move their soul, which is poetry's effect."[118] Sassetti insists on this at various places; ultimately he explains what verisimilitude is and how it is to be obtained:

A probable proposition is verisimilar, so that in order to know the nature of the latter it is necessary to know that of the probable. Those things are probable which are in agreement with the opinion of all men or of most or of the wisest, so that truth is of no concern in this matter of verisimilitude. It is indeed true that false things are lacking in probability, and consequently in verisimilitude, whenever impossibility is made to accompany them. . . . The probable is not determined by the possible because there are many possible things which are not probable. . . . Since, then, verisimilitude depends upon the opinions of men, it is absolutely necessary that, as these change, the probable should also change.[119]

116 *Ibid.*, fols. 4v–5: "Hora se la virtu eroica e uirtu generalmente considerata che di perfettione sourasta a quella che uulgarmente si ritroua, stimar si dee che sicome la sourastante fortezza è eroica uirtu, cosi ancora sia la sourastante prudenza; e dogni altro habito il somigliante . . . in maniera tale che hoggi in luogo degli heroj non si douranno porre da noj coloro che di sangue illustre sono di nome nella guerra, ma uolendo rendere il cambio generalmente coloro che per la uirtu loro sourastanno agl huominj virtuosi di gran lunga. . . . ensomma non ci lasciamo dare ad intendere che in luogo degli eroi succedano solamente gl huominj nella guerra ualorosi ma tutti coloro che per la uirtu loro qualunque ella si sia sono dagl'altri uirtuosi grandemente ammirati."

117 *Ibid.*, fol. 4v: "percio habbiamo bisogno di trouare huominj da quali stieno bene essere adoperate attioni a quelle somiglianti che gl antichi fingeuano essere fatte da que' tali.'

118 *Ibid.*, fol. 5: "chi raccontasse semplicemente una cosa laquale non hauesse credenza appresso coloro che lascoltano ella di niente mouerebbe lanimo loro che à leffetto della poesia."

119 *Ibid.*, fol. 10v: "Verisimile è una propositione probabile di maniera che per sapere la natura desso bisogna sapere quella del probabile. probabili sono quelle cose le quali sono secondo l'oppenione di tutti o de piu o de piu saggi di maniera che la uerita in questo affare del uerisimile non adopera cosa nessuna. egli è ben uero che le cose false mancano del probabile e conseguentemente del uerisimile ogni uolta che in compagnia loro si aggiunga limpossibilità. . . . non si determina giai l probabile dal possibile conciosia cosa che molte cose sieno possibili le quali probabili non sono . . . stando adunque il uerisimile con loppenione degl huomini egli è al tutto di mestieri che secondo che esse si mutano si muti ancora il probabile."

The last sentence transports us again into modern times; just as the super-stitions of antiquity have been replaced by the teachings and precepts of Christianity, so the notion of what will be probable and verisimilar in poetry is affected by this change. Again, if what is verisimilar lies within the bounds of credibility, the marvelous lies beyond them. Sassetti dis-cusses the latter largely in connection with the complex plot, which, because it contains recognition and reversal, is more apt than the simple plot to make the audience marvel. Simple plots place before our eyes only such things as anyone might readily imagine to have happened; in complex plots, the human intellect is led to expect one event, but another happens instead. This is a source of pleasure, "because marvelous things as such are pleasing" ("perche le cose marauigliose come tali sono gioconde," fol. 6). The need for these features of plot is more urgent in tragedy than in the epic, since the general conditions of the epic are such as to facilitate the achievement of the marvelous:

For these [tragedies] are limited to a small action and to one place where it must happen, whereas the epic plot is longer and spreads out over more territory and embraces various sites and places where it occurs; and since it must be nar-rated and not acted it carries with it greater possibility of moving the passions and of appearing marvelous, because what has really happened, even a thing marvelous in itself, will lose none of its power when it is recounted, whereas when it is acted—since the imitation cannot take place in it without great likeli-hood of being recognized as false—clearly the deed will leave us cold.[120]

The conclusion would seem to be that circumstances which permit the marvelous to be disguised give to it the kind of credibility that the verisi-milar has; but when it must be presented forthright, it is best presented through such acceptable devices as recognition and reversal.

In the last passage cited, Sassetti extends the principle of the unity of action to include a unity of place; the unity of time is stated in Aristotle's terms. But nowhere does he call them "unities" (except of action), nor does he emphasize them to the extent that Castelvetro had done. His notion of unity of action is loose; after excluding the actions of one person, he clarifies thus: " . . . it is circumscribed by the continuation of one and the same affair, such as a voyage, an acquisition of some thing, or even a war carried to its conclusion by a valorous captain."[121] Aristotle's

120 *Ibid.*, fol. 6: "auuenga che esse si determinano a piccola attione e a un luogo doue ella debba seguire, la doue lepopeia ha la sua fauola piu lunga e piu per costa si distende et abbraccia diuersi siti e luoghi doue ella accaggia e douendo essere raccontata e non rappre-sentata apporta seco maggior facilita nel muouere e mostrarsi marauigliosa conciosia cosa che quello che ueramente sara accaduto cosa per se marauigliosa nell essere raccontato non perdera niente della sua forza; doue che nell essere rappresentato per non hauerui luogo limitatione, senon con grandissima euidenza dessere falso [cognosciuto manifestamente: added] il fatto cadra nel freddo."

121 *Ibid.*, fol. 5v: "si circonscriue dalla continouatione dun medesimo negotio come un viaggio, un acquisto di qualunche cosa opure una guerra tratta a fine da un valoroso capi-tano."

ideas of causality and of inner determination are lacking, as they are in Sassetti's contemporaries. He has some difficulty in deciding to what extent the plot and the poem are consubstantial—this was an issue much debated in the current controversy over Dante—and he concludes that they are not; plot is argument, the bare action summarized in a few words, to which must be added the episodes if one is to have the whole poem (fol. 5). In spite of such looseness, he insists firmly that the important part of any poem is the plot and that this is particularly true of tragedy. As a result he condemns those who, like Seneca, forget that they are poets and become rhetoricians, the danger that threatens epic poets above all others:

... since all their affair consists in a work of words, they come to resemble orators more than do dramatic poets who, if they have fine actions at hand, spend their time uttering many *sententiae*, as Seneca did in his tragedies, and they cover up the main action in such a way that it disappears and is not considered as its proper object (the mind running after the truth of these *sententiae*).[122]

Sassetti's one extensive call upon Plato is on the matter of imitation. He conflates Plato's notion of imitation with the Aristotelian concept—or rather, he replaces the latter by the former, and imitation here comes to have the meaning of dramatic manner. This leads to some confusion in the use of the term. Elsewhere, however, the major guide to the judgments on Dante is Aristotle; we shall see what those judgments were in a later context.

DEL BENE (1574)

Early in 1574, the Accademia degli Alterati, which figures prominently in the literary life of these years, devoted several sessions to a debate over the need for the poet to imitate actions rather than characters or passions.[123] One of the discourses, Giulio Del Bene's *Che egli è necessario à l'esser poeta imitare actioni*, is preserved in MS Magl. IX, 137, folios 69–80r, of the Biblioteca Nazionale in Florence. The debate arose for two reasons: first, because some commentators on Aristotle declared that the three objects, action, character, and passion, were equally important; second, because others declared that a poem might still be a poem even if it imitated only character or passion. Del Bene's stand is clear: the only essential object of imitation is action, and it is essential in all forms, lyric as well as narrative and dramatic. Most of what he has to say is direct quotation or paraphrase of the *Poetics*, accompanied at times by interpretative remarks. His willingness to rely on the *Poetics* stems from his admiration for Aristotle and

---

[122] *Ibid.*, fol. 24v: "consistendo tutto il caso loro in opera di parole e uengono ad assomigliarsi piu agl oratori che i rappresentatiuj poeti non fanno i quali se hanno belle attionj alle mani e s'occupano in proferire molte sentenze come Seneca fece nelle sue tragedie e ricuoprono lattione principale in guisa che ella sparisce e non è considerata correndo l'intelletto dietro alla verita di quelle sentenze come al proprio oggetto suo."

[123] See my "Argomenti di discussione letteraria," *Giornale Storico della Letteratura Italiana*, CXXXI (1954), 180.

his conception of his method, "since he not only drew the precepts of the art out of nature, as an admirable observer of its secrets, but he also considered it principally in all the poems that had been written up to his time, the best and the most perfect of which were [those of] Homer, no less good as a poet than he [Aristotle] was as a philosopher."[124] The double reference to nature and to the poet-model will be increasingly important in the later Renaissance.

Del Bene's argument is simple and, for the most part, remains close to that of the *Poetics*. He sees the end of poetry as pleasure, but limited to the special pleasure which is proper to each poem ("quella delettatione quale e propria del poema," fol. 71v). Three elements—beauty, purgation, and the marvelous—seem to contribute to pleasure, although this is not clearly stated and we must derive it from such passages as the following: "All the beauties and the delights and the purgations which poems produce, all depend upon the plot and the actions which are contained in it, and by means of which the poet achieves his end"; "The marvelous is a most beautiful part of the poem, when something happens in it beyond the expectations of the listener; for men marvel at new things and at those contrary to their opinion, and they take pleasure in them."[125] The main source of pleasure, however, is the imitation of an action; without it there is no pleasure and no poem. Hence the inevitability of action and of plot: "Poetry in truth will be nothing but the imitation of actions, and it will be necessary for the poet, in order to be a poet, only to imitate actions."[126] These statements lose some of their clarity, however, when we discover what meanings Del Bene associates both with imitation and with plot. The former comes to mean a dramatic representation, as it had in Plato, and the poet is said to be imitating only when he writes in this way (fol. 72v); "plot" takes on some of the overtones of "fiction," and the kinds of action are consequently restricted: "Not of every kind of thing, but of those actions which are not true but verisimilar; and because these are made in this way, being feigned, they merit the name of 'favola'; and therefore little or no difference is found between poetic imitation, fiction, and plot."[127]

124 MS BNF Magl. IX, 137, fol. 71: "il quale hauendo, non solo i precetti di essa tratti dalla natura, come speculatore mirabile de suoi secreti, ma anchora hauendo cio principalmente considerato in tutti i poemi che furono fino al suo tempo, et i migliori et piu perfetti fra i quali fu homero non meno buono poeta che egli filosofo si fosse."

125 *Ibid.*, fol. 71: "tutte le bellezze, et i diletti, et li purgamenti [corrected to "le purgationi"] che fanno le poesie tutte dependono dalla fauola et dalle actioni che in essa si contengono, et mediante le quali il poeta consegue il suo fine"; and fol. 73: "Bellissima parte è della poesia lo ammirabile quando in essa qualcosa fuori della espettatione di chi lascolta adiuiene, perche gli huomini delle cose nuoue et fuori della loro opinione si marauigliono et ne pigliono diletto."

126 *Ibid.*, fol. 70: "altro ueramente non sara la poesia che imitatione di actioni; et al poeta sara necessario solo per esser poeta di imitare le actioni." Cf. fol. 69v.

127 *Ibid.*, fol. 70: "Et non dogni sorte cosa, ma di quelle actioni che uere non sono ma uerisimili; et questa per esser cosi fatte, sendo finte, meritono il nome della fauola, et però poca a nulla differentia si ritroua fra la imitatione poetica, la fintione et la fauola."

We find thus that a poem is an imitation, an imitation is a dramatic representation of a plot, a plot is an unreal but probable action. This goes for all poems, including the less "perfect" ones found in the lyric genres; the difference is that the latter are exclusively "narrative" (the poet recounting the actions of men), whereas the epic is "mixed" and tragedy and comedy are "dramatic." All are alike in that their actions must be at once marvelous and verisimilar; we may suppose that in all of them—although the statement as made is restricted to the dithyramb—the kind of necessity which springs from character will be required: " . . . he feigns and describes and imitates them [actions] not as they were, but as it was necessary that they should be, being done by such men."[128] Del Bene shows how ancient lyric poets and writers of pastoral eclogues really did imitate actions and makes an incidental defence of Dante (who constantly introduced people speaking and acting) and of Ariosto (even though his action is multiple) and of Petrarch (who imitated actions in a different way in each genre that he practised). In the light of these convictions, Del Bene contradicts certain common notions about the arts in general. Not only are all poets necessarily imitators of actions, but so are all other artists. To say that a painter, for example, imitates characters or passions is nonsense, for the latter can be imitated only through action. The historian narrates actions, the painter depicts them, the poet imitates them.

Giulio Del Bene also delivered before the Alterati, in 1574, a lecture entitled *Che la favola de la comedia vuole esser honesta et non contenere mali costumi* (MS BNF Magl. IX, 137, fols. 47–58*v*).[129] The subject being what it was, he was led much farther afield than in the other lecture, not only into consideration of the ends proposed for poetry by Horace and Plato but also into reflections on the nature of man (both as the object of poetry and as its audience) and on the nature of art. Throughout, however, matters seem to be decided by reference to the *Poetics*. As the object of poetry, man provides more actions and characters for comedy than he does for tragedy and the epic, for low and ordinary men are more numerous than exalted and extraordinary ones. This is the way of nature, which creates more frequently what is commonplace than what is rare and excellent. Hence, there are many more examples of comedy to study, many fewer of tragedy and the epic (fols. 47–47*v*). As the audience of poetry, however, man seems to demand what is rare and excellent. He prefers what is beautiful to what is ugly, what is honest to what is dishonest. Indeed, he can derive no pleasure from the morally ugly and reprehensible; the actions of comedy, "if they were dishonest, would not move to laughter, but rather to disdain and accusation and shame, because for the most part men are ashamed of dis-

---

[128] *Ibid.*, fol. 74: "non quali furono, ma quale era necessario che elle fussero sendo di cotali huomini le finge et descriue, et le imita."

[129] See note 123 above.

honest things as badly done and by vicious persons."[130] Or again, "a dishonest action does not produce joy, but hatred and shame."[131] Our first conclusion then is that morally dishonest actions will fail to please their audience, specifically because of its nature as an audience.

Similar generalizations result from Del Bene's thoughts on the nature of art. He sees it first as a device by which nature is perfected, a device "to imitate nature and render it more perfect" ("imitare la natura, et quella rendere piu perfetta," fol. 48); this means that whatever the subject matter, humble or exalted, art will depict it in a superior degree. For the subject at hand, comedy, it means that even common objects will be presented "in estremo grado et exquisite" (fol. 55). Moreover, the artist is to blame if he does not treat nature in this way, for he has complete freedom of choice in what he does. This distinguishes the poet from the historian:

> And all the more so must the poet do this than the historian, that the latter is really constrained to recount actions just as they happened according to the truth, the former, as they should have been or as it is verisimilar that they must have been; whence he has the choice, and by art and by nature he is driven to what is honest and to virtue, to follow always what is best as the most useful and the most delightful thing, in order best to achieve his end.[132]

The free choice of the poet, in connection with his striving for perfection, is further emphasized in this passage:

> And since this art of poetry, so excellent, operates upon its subject not through necessity but through choice, shall we believe that its artist, being able to select an honest subject and one which concerns honest actions, will choose among so great a multitude of subjects as are those of comedy rather one which is dishonest and dishonorable than one which is honest and gentle, having the freedom to take the one and the other?[133]

What subject is ultimately preferred will depend upon the poet's conception of the end of his art. Here he has two alternatives: He may think of the ends proposed by Horace, pleasure and utility; if he does, he will have to choose the honest subject, for its opposite would neither teach the right

---

130 MS BNF Magl. IX, 137, fol. 53: "se fussero dishoneste, non mouerieno a riso, ma si bene a sdegno et a riprensione, et à uergogna auuenga che delle cose dishoneste per lo piu gli huomini si uergognino come cose mal fatte e da persone uitiose."

131 *Ibid.*, fol. 55v: "la dishonesta, non partorisce allegrezza ma odio et uergogna."

132 *Ibid.*, fol. 54v: "E tanto maggiormente debbe far questo il poeta che lo Historico, che questi è pur costretto à raccontare le actioni qualli elleno sono state secondo il uero, quelli, quali doueuono essere ò quali è uerisimile che esser debbino, onde egli ha la eletione, et da larte et dalla natura a l'honesto, et alla uirtu e spinto, a seguire sempre il meglio come cosa piu utile et piu diletteuole per meglio conseguire il suo fine."

133 *Ibid.*, fol. 48v: "Et questa arte tanto eccellente della poesia non per necessita ma per eletione operando nel suggetto, crederremo noi che potendo eleggersi lartefice di essa un suggetto honesto et di honeste ationi egli sia per scerne in cosi gran multitudine come son quelli della comedia piutosto [uno] dishonesto, et uituperoso che [uno] honesto et gentile sendo in suo arbitrio di pigliare luno et laltro?"

moral lessons nor (given the nature of man) afford any real pleasure (fol. 51*v*). The end of teaching, to show men good mores and to induce emulation of them, is constantly repeated through Del Bene's pages. Or the poet may think of the ends proposed by Aristotle, the moving of the audience to pity and fear by tragedy, to laughter and contentment by comedy. Again, only the honest subject will achieve these ends, for the audience will find no pleasure in what is basically immoral.

Difficulties and doubts about these matters are solved by an artistic consideration, the way in which the poet interprets Aristotle's grouping of moral characters. There are three groups, the high, the middle, and the low; the low contains the personages of comedy. But we would err gravely were we to equate "lowness" with vice, "since he himself interprets it, saying that the actions of tragedy are actions of illustrious men, those of comedy not of vicious men, but of men who are humble and low in family and in intellectual capacity; not meaning the 'worst' through some vice that might be in them, but through the low and base concepts of their mind."[134] Another passage from Aristotle may also be appealed to here, the one in which he distinguishes the four requisites of character (*Poetics* 1454*a*15); the requisite of "goodness" must be taken to mean moral goodness—in every kind of poem, including comedy—"honesty" and "virtue" to the exclusion of ugliness, vice, dishonesty, wickedness (fol. 56). Such characters are excluded, moreover, by the artistic demands for the handling of plot and of character. The argument on plot may be stated thus: To produce joy and contentment in the audience the action of comedy must end happily; but a happy ending for wicked people fails to produce the desired effect; hence the poet, if he wishes his plot to be properly complicated and resolved, must avoid the inclusion of wicked people (fol. 54). If this is unavoidable (e.g., Aeneas' Dido), such persons must be admitted only to the episodes and not to the central plot (fol. 55). Corroboration of this thesis is found in the fact that when poets actually do introduce bad characters, they always punish them in the denouement, thus creating an effect different from that proper to comedy (fol. 50). The argument on character is similar: Since all poets imitate men not as they are but as they should be— Achilles represents the perfect Idea of strength, Ulysses of prudence— character must show an improvement upon nature in the direction of virtue and honesty (fol. 55).

It is only when these artistic conditions are met that dramatic works achieve the end of purgation, which they seek. Del Bene offers several possible interpretations of this effect:

... tragedy arouses fear and pity in the breasts of the listeners, in order to liber-

---

[134] *Ibid.*, fol. 49: "interpretandolo lui stesso, dicendo; queste della Tragedia ationi di huomini illustri, quelle della comedia, non di huomini uitiosi, ma humili et bassi di sangue et di intelletto. non intendendo i peggiori per alcuno uitio ch'in loro sia ma per i bassi et uili concetti d'animo."

ate and purge them of these same passions of fear and pity. .... it seems that the end of the comic poet is to delight and to move to laughter and gaiety . . . in order to purge them of the pleasure that they take in similar low actions and of the laughter that necessarily arises from them; or perhaps in order to purge them through the laughter and the pleasure that they feel in comic actions, so that when later they see or hear other real ones of the same kind, they will no longer be moved to laughter or take delight in them.[135]

The poet who violates these moral and artistic requirements by treating wicked persons—especially if he treat them publicly on the stage—should suffer the banishment recommended by Plato. In its totality, then, Del Bene's theory goes beyond that of the *Poetics* in seeking elsewhere (in the nature of man, in the nature of art) the principles upon which the poet works; but it returns to Aristotle for such artistic recommendations as will enable him to make poems conforming to those same principles.

In the same year the same academy heard Francesco Bonciani's *Lezione sopra il comporre delle novelle*. This was the kind of Aristotelian exercise of which we have already seen several examples, an attempt to treat a genre not mentioned in the *Poetics* in terms of the same critical system. Bonciani proceeds in an orderly fashion, following Aristotle's text quite closely as he attempts to discover the particular rules and precepts of the novella. And just as Aristotle had appealed constantly to the practice of Homer, so Bonciani uses Boccaccio as his principal model. Certain of Bonciani's presuppositions about poetry in general color the way in which he treats the short story. He turns Aristotle's statement about the delight found in imitation into a statement that imitation removes the pain from learning, relieves the ills of man's life, and allows him to distinguish between true and false pleasures (p. 162). This view will later determine Bonciani's understanding of purgation; since man's life is so full of annoyances and troubles, such literary works as the novella will have as their end to drive out sorrow and replace it by joy (pp. 183–84). I say "literary works" advisedly, since Bonciani refuses to classify the novella as poetry for the simple reason that it is in prose. All poetry, he says, must be in verse; the best interpreters of Aristotle give to the word λόγος the exclusive meaning of verse. Furthermore, far from accepting the theory that imitation is the genus of poetry, he declares that poetry contains imitation as a part, residing in its plot which is the summation of its action (he likens it to an "argument"). Hence we arrive at a definition of poetry in which verse is perhaps

---

135 *Ibid.*, fol. 55v: "la tragedia, muoue timore et la misericordia ne petti delli auditori, per questi medesimi liberare et purgarli da questi medesimi affetti di timore et di misericordia. . . . pare che il fine del poeta comico sia, il dilettare et mouere a riso, et allegrezza . . . per purgarli del diletto che in simil[i] ationi uili si piglia, et del riso che da esse necessariamente nasce. o forse perche, purghino per il riso ò per il piacere che essi sentono per le ationi comiche, et altre poi ueramente ueggendone ò udendo, non piu si mouino a riso, ne di esse si rallegrino."

a more essential element than imitation, although this he specifically denies (p. 174).

The novella will differ from other genres in its objects, its manner, and its means. Bonciani's definition of the objects changes as he thinks of one kind of novella or another, and the refined distinctions which he makes tend to obscure the issue. The general object of literary works, of the novella as well as of the epic, tragedy, and comedy, is human actions. But the men who perform these actions are either virtuous or vicious, and virtue or vice may be depicted either as it is or in a supreme degree:

> But because it is seen that people usually maintain a certain middle ground, in virtue as well as in vice, and that nevertheless our mind can conceive the Idea (so to speak) of wickedness or of goodness, never found in their supreme degree in any one person, hence it comes about that not only may we imitate men endowed with that virtue or that vice as we see them every day, but moreover those who exceed them considerably, who for this reason come to be called "better" or "worse."[136]

Aristotle's ethical distinction is thus transformed into a difference of degree, with "better" or "worse" applying either to virtue or to vice and "like" meaning the everyday way in which these manifest themselves. The novella, especially since Boccaccio, imitates any one of these objects. But because its actions, when they resemble those of tragedy and the epic, may be handled in the ways indicated by Aristotle, Bonciani finds no need for discussing them and, instead, concentrates his attention on those stories which are like comedy. These present "light and foolish" actions (p. 176), ones which fall into the general category of the ridiculous (p. 169). Another division must be made here; for anybody may be ridiculous, the great and the poor as well as those in between. Since we should not laugh at the great and should pity the poor, only men of the middle station will be proper objects for this kind of novella. But not all:

> That sort of persons, then, who without being completely crazy smack (rather more than less) of folly, will be imitated by novelle. . . . One should imitate in these men of vulgar stripe not their ordinary actions, since all of theirs are foolish, but those which are completely out of kilter. . . . One may say that all those who, thinking themselves possessed of great wisdom and sagacity, lay themselves open

---

[136] My references to Bonciani are to the edition published in the *Prose fiorentine* founded by Dati, Pt. II, Vol. I (Florence, 1727). For the present passage, v. pp. 164–65: "Ma perchè e' si veda, le persone ordinariamente osservare una certa mezzanità, così nella virtù come nel vizio: e nondimeno può l'intelletto nostro immaginarsi l'idea (per dir così) della malvagità o della bontà, che in niuno in così supremo grado si ritruovano; di quì è, che non solo si possano imitare gli uomini, di quella virtù o vizio dotati, come tutto il dì si veggiono; ma quegli ancora, che di gran lunga gli trapassano, i quali perciò migliori o peggiori ne vengono a essere chiamati." See also p. 178: "Le azioni . . . sono da due maniere d'uomini adoperate, o da' virtuosi o da' malvagi, i quali in due modi si possono considerare, o con quella bontà e cattività, che sono per l'ordinario, onde simili da Aristotile sono chiamati: o veramente nel supremo grado di ciascuno di questi abiti."

to deception, should be imitated by our novelle; and all the more so when they have greater wit, for the marvelous appears even more in these.[137]

Wickedness and vice must also be excluded; they bring sorrow to men and give examples of bad behavior, and hence they can never produce the laughter that is the end sought.

After some hesitation, the question of the manner is resolved in favor of the "mixed"—narrative interrupted by speeches and dialogues among the personages. The hesitation results from doubts as to whether dialogues which tell a story, such as Lucian's, should properly be considered as belonging to the genre, and hence whether a purely dramatic manner is acceptable. Bonciani decides that it is not (pp. 165–70). As for the means of imitation, his answer is unequivocal. None of the three means proposed by Aristotle, rhythm, harmony, and verse, appears in the novella; it uses instead a fourth means, prose, and thus falls outside the general category of poetry: "For the novelle use discourse which is unmetered and in prose, as is known by the authority of all writers, whereas poems always employ verse."[138]

The specific recommendations for the handling of the form also have the *Poetics* as their admitted source. Definitions of the qualitative parts follow the text closely, except that Bonciani adds to the definition of plot this short clarification: "It is that brief summary which we find written at the beginning" ("è quel brieve raccolto, che nella fronte loro scritto troviamo," pp. 184–85). Magnitude of plot in the novella is contrasted with that of tragedy and comedy, the latter determined by considerations which echo closely those of Castelvetro:

But because tragedy has to be acted, it must in part adapt itself to the spectators, who cannot remain for several days at a time in the theater; nor would it be at all verisimilar that an action which took many days to do should be represented in just one. For these reasons tragic poets are obliged to include the whole action within one revolution of the sun; and it seems that the same must be said about comedies, since these use the same means as tragedies.[139]

137 *Ibid.*, p. 206: "Quella sorte adunque di persone, che non essendo però pazze affatto, sentiranno, anzi che nò, dello scemo, sarà dalle novelle imitata. . . . Deesi adunque in questi uomini di grossa pasta imitare, non le loro ordinarie azioni, comecchè tutte le loro sieno sciocche, ma quelle, che sono al tutto fuor di squadra"; and p. 208: "si può dire, che tutti coloro, che di molta saviezza e sagacità stimandosi, fanno luogo allo 'nganno; dalle nostre novelle debbono essere imitati: e allora viepiù, che essi maggiore ingegno avranno; imperocchè in questi maggiormente la maraviglia apparisce."
138 *Ibid.*, p. 173: "imperocchè le novelle si servono dell' orazione sciolta e 'n prosa, siccome per l'autorità di tutti è noto, laddove le poesie adoperano sempre il verso."
139 *Ibid.*, pp. 186–87: "Ma perchè la tragedia si dee rappresentare, e bisogna ch'ella in parte s'accomodi agli aspettatori, i quali non possono stare parecchi giorni per volta ne' teatri: nè manco averebbe del verisimile, che un opera, in molti dì condotta, in un solo si rappresentasse; onde i tragici sono costretti a chiudere in un girare di Sole l'azione tutta quanta: e 'l medesimo pare, che si debba dire delle commedie, poichè esse adoperano lo stesso modo delle tragedie."

The frank admission, on the one hand that the needs of the spectator must be considered, on the other hand of the poet's "obligations," should be noted. Like the epic, the novella is unlimited in time and hence achieves greater verisimilitude than either of the dramatic forms; at the same time, it more readily admits the marvelous since it is addressed to the ear (p. 188). Its popular actions may be freely invented by the storyteller, who is restricted only by the laws of decorum and of verisimilitude and by the admonition to use only those episodes which are necessary. Bonciani finds in Aristotle a basis for listing nine different kinds of plots, all of which he illustrates by examples from Boccaccio. The style of the short story will be the ἰσχνός, or "humble and minute," because "novelle being in prose and containing actions done by ordinary persons who are somewhat ridiculous, they clearly cannot use appropriately that grandness of speech which tragedy and the epic would use."[140] As for the quantitative parts, they will be three in number (combining various suggestions from Aristotle): a prologue, presenting the characters and the circumstances; an "embroiling" ("scompiglio") or knotting which complicates the action; and an "unfolding" ("sviluppo") or unknotting which brings on the conclusion.

Giovambattista Strozzi delivered a similar lecture, also in 1574, before the Accademia Fiorentina, attempting to apply the principles of the *Poetics* to the lesser form of the madrigal. His *Lettione sopra i madrigali* was published posthumously in 1635. The definitions and the descriptions which he develops are all within an Aristotelian framework, although they frequently record conclusions which we should have to consider as heterodox. After a general definition of poetry as "an imitation of an action in verse" ("Imitatione d'Attione in versi," p. 160), he inquires into the kinds of actions which may constitute the proper subjects for the madrigal. There will be two kinds: human actions, especially those revealing character and passions, and actions attributed to nonhuman or inanimate things. Since human actions are really the more important, the genres which treat them—epic, tragedy, comedy—will be the great poetic genres; such a form as the madrigal, however, may permit itself

... a representation and description of those things which, even if they are lacking in speech, may nevertheless be put before the eyes of others by assigning action to them; and this is the proper function of the poet, for he must not merely describe things as they are in fact (for this is proper to others), but it is necessary for him to imitate them in such a way that he will to a certain extent depart from the truth.[141]

140 *Ibid.*, p. 210: "essendo le novelle in prosa, . . . e contenendo azioni fatte da persone ordinarie, che abbiano del ridicolo; chiara cosa è, che elle non potranno usare acconciatamente quella grandezza del favellare, che la tragedia e l'epopeja userebbono."

141 In *Orazioni et altre prose* (1635), p. 161: "vna rassomiglianza, e descrittione di quelle cose, che se bene mancano del discorso, si possono tuttauia mettere altrui dauanti à gl'occhi col dargli operatione, il che è proprio offitio del Poeta, perciòche egli non dee semplicemente descriuere le cose come elle stanno appunto, perche questo ad altri appartiene, ma fà à lui di mestiero per sì fatta maniera imitarle, che e' venga in qualche parte à partirsi dal vero."

The apologue and the descriptive poem come to be, in a strange way, the opposites of "things as they are." Lyric poems in general may treat everything in the world; but they tend to leave the grand subjects to the grand genres and to exploit rather those which are "pleasant and small," such as love. This will be the case of the madrigal.

Poetry needs verse as well as imitation; the two are indispensable. Therefore, according to Strozzi, Aristotle requires verse in his definitions of tragedy and the epic. Differences among kinds will relate to subject matter, manner, and the type of verse. On the basis of such differences we may constitute a definition of the madrigal: "The madrigal is an imitation of a pleasant, small action, made by way of narration, with verses in rhyme which are not restricted in their number and kind of rhymes."[142] When it does not imitate human actions, it attributes action to objects through metaphorical description. In any case, it will have a plot (if that be the correct translation for "favola" here) and hence necessarily character and discourse (for διάνοια) and language. Its parts will thus be the same as those of the grand genres, if reduced and less perfect. But their order of importance will be disturbed, even to the extent of introducing a rivalry between plot and language for first place; for "he who would place [language] before it [plot] would perhaps not depart from the truth."[143] Choice of words and texture of verse may thus, in Strozzi's opinion, legitimately be the primary concern of the madrigal poet, especially since the form is so brief that every word must be made to count. So prosodic and rhetorical matters demand close attention, and Strozzi offers specific advice with respect to them. The totality of his theory shows a reorientation away from Aristotle and toward the old-fashioned rules for language and versification.

It is perhaps to the years 1574–75 that we should assign Sperone Speroni's *Apologia dei dialogi* (see Chapter VIII, pp. 304–5), which in addition to defending his dialogues expresses his ideas of the moral and political utility of poetry. These relate to Aristotle in that the purgation clause is interpreted as referring to such moral utility; but it is, according to Speroni, a very imperfect instrument for the purpose. The problem is the correct behavior of the whole citizenry:

Aristotle was well aware of that behavior when in the definition of tragedy, besides certain other pleasurable circumstances which are proper to that poem, he added in opposition that useful component, whence it might be called "civil," saying as follows: *ut purgemur ab huiuscemodi.* . . . This means that on seeing a tragedy man is purged of two passions which are not very useful to citizens, that is, horror and commiseration. . . . But if Aristotle wished to purge two such passions by means of tragedy, passions which seem to have something political

142 *Ibid.*, p. 172: "Il Madrigale è imitatione d'attione gentile picciola, fatta per via di narratione con versi in rima, non sottoposti à numero, nè à maniera di rimare."
143 *Ibid.*, p. 173: "e chi ancora glie le antiponesse, non si dipartirebbe forse dal vero."

about them and which are without doubt human, his suggestion was not so good as it should have been.[144]

Speroni objects because he believes that such spectacles as the death of gladiators would serve the same purpose more effectively. He thinks that in fact tragedy was invented for another purpose—"to teach citizens to be quietly content with their humble lot and not to try to elevate it by bringing on the ruin of their fatherland"[145]—and that Aristotle failed to mention this end in his definition of tragedy. For comedy, too, he distinguishes desirable and undesirable ends, by reference always to political criteria:

If I once said that in the laughter of comedy the wearied mind is rested and that such repose is useful to it, I say it now again; and I say again that it is one thing to laugh in the theater for an hour or two, another to write in order to make people laugh on purpose; the former gives repose and is necessary, the latter is an indecorous labor and an antisocial activity.[146]

I take it that in the latter category Speroni would include satirical and humorous and obscene poetry. Throughout, it is clear that he is carrying over into discussion of Aristotle the general Platonic prejudices that inform his thinking at this point of his career.

PICCOLOMINI'S COMMENTARY (1575)

The second of the "great commentaries" in the vernacular, Alessandro Piccolomini's *Annotationi nel libro della Poetica d'Aristotile*, was published in 1575, although its author had declared in the preface of his translation (1572) that the annotations were already complete. Coming as late as it does, his commentary reflects an advanced state of work on the text, at least in the sense that it can discuss and accept or reject all the multitude of interpretations that had already been suggested. Piccolomini announces that he will say nothing about those passages for which he finds the remarks of Maggi and of Vettori satisfactory; but he frequently disagrees with them, as he does with Robortello and Scaliger and Castelvetro. Indeed, some of his most revealing and original pages were written under the stimulus of such disagreement. This does not mean that his approach is essentially controversial or fragmentary. For he does have a personal inter-

---

[144] In *Opere* (1740), I, 355–56: "Ben si accorse di tal decoro Aristotile, quando nella difinizione della tragedia, oltre alcune altre sue dilettevoli condizioni, che sono proprie di quel poema, soggiunse contra quella dell'utile, onde civile si nominasse, così dicendo: *ut purgemur ab huiuscemodi*. . . . il qual vuol dire che nell'aspetto della tragedia si purgò l'uomo di due affetti non molto utili a' cittadini, ciò sono orrore e commiserazione. . . . Ma se Aristotile purgar volendo colla tragedia due tali affetti, che assai par che abbiano del civile, umani son senza dubbio, non fu sì buono come dovea. . . ."

[145] *Ibid.*, p. 356: "per insegnare alli cittadini di star contenti quietamente alla loro umile condizione, e non tentar d'innalzarla con la ruina della lor patria."

[146] *Ibid.*, p. 357: "se io già dissi, che nelle risa della commedia riposa l'animo affaticato, e che gli è utile un tal riposo; torno anche a dirlo; e ridico che altro è ridere in un teatro una o due ore, ed altro è scrivere per far ridere a bello studio. quello è ozio e necessità; questo è fatica indecora ed incivile operazione."

pretation of the *Poetics*—one might say, even, his own theory of poetry—which determines how individual passages and their commentators will be considered. Some of this theory is explicitly stated in the "Proemio," which precedes the main body of the work; much of it is found in the individual glosses. For these, Piccolomini uses the numbers and the text of Maggi's *Explanationes*. Unlike Maggi and the earlier scholars, however, his interest is almost not at all philological or textual; it lies rather in the production of a consistent and complete reading of Aristotle.

One of the cornerstones of the theory expressed in the "Proemio" is Piccolomini's conception of the ends of poetry. This is stated as early as his announcement of his general program for the work; he will treat poetry's "form, its end, and its material, and the profit and the pleasure which it brings to the world."[147] The relative importance of profit and pleasure is included in the definition which comes soon after: "Poetry is nothing but an imitation, not only of things either natural or artificial, but mainly of human actions, characters, and passions, done mostly by means of language and of diction, taken universally, in order to give pleasure and by giving pleasure ultimately to benefit human life."[148] These ends of pleasure and utility—with the pleasure made to serve the utility—will be explained and developed repeatedly throughout the text. Good poems will be distinguished from those which merit the Platonic charge of effeminacy and corruption, "those imitations so made that they would be made for a single end, either voluptuous and vain pleasure which was its own end and termination and served no purpose, or instead such pleasure as would bring damage to our lives by rendering our manners effeminate and corrupt, or by some other means."[149] Rather than so doing, poetry must be subordinated (according to Aristotle in the *Ethics*) to the architectonic art of politics, and it must serve these various specific ends:

... through the imitation of virtuous men and the expression of their praise, we come to be aroused and excited to virtue, in order to be like those whom we hear celebrated. On the other hand, if we hear vices and wicked actions expressed through poetic imitation and, as they are expressed, reviled and vituperated, we immediately begin to dispose ourselves to flee and to hate vicious actions, much more incited to do so by such imitations than we would be by direct and personal admonition, no matter how effective.

Similarly, if we see horrible tragic events acted on the stage, a great part of our

147 *Annotationi* (1575), p. ††4v: "la forma, il fine, & la materia sua, & il giouamento, & il diletto, ch'ella reca al mondo."

148 *Ibid.*, p. ††5: "la Poesia non sia altro, che imitatione non solo di cose, ò naturali, ò artifitiose; ma principalmente d'attioni, di costumi, & d'affetti humani: fatta col mezo principalmente del parlare, ò ver della locutione nel lor' vniuersale, à fine di dilettare, & dilettando finalmente giouare alla vita humana."

149 *Ibid.*, p. ††5v: "quelle così fatte imitationi, che si facessero à solo fine, ò di voluttuoso, & vano diletto, ch'in se stesso finisse, & terminasse, ò non seruisse à nulla; ò ver di diletto tale, che ò con effeminare, & corromper' i costumi nostri, ò in qual si voglia altra maniera, fusse alla nostra vita per recar danno."

insolence, our temerity, our arrogance, our audacity, our pride disappears in us through this means; and seeing the miseries and the perils to which are subject not only men of middle and low condition but even those who through their power and greatness are used to being happy, . . . we come to moderate our sorrow over the misfortunes which do happen and which can happen every day. Likewise the wrath, the envy, and the other passions which usually are fomented in us through the fact that we do not know well the inconstancy of fortune and the fragility of all worldly things, all these come to be tempered within us.[150]

Piccolomini here collects all the uses previously proposed for tragedy. He will frequently make such compendia; and, to a degree, his work presents a summation of ideas about poetry current in his time.

If we follow through the commentary this guiding principle of utility, we shall see how it affects the interpretation of various separate passages. Primarily, it determines how Piccolomini will understand purgation. He states his theory in connection with *Poetics* 1449*b*24, after repeating what he had said about the priority of usefulness:

. . . since man cannot enjoy and obtain any more useful thing than the possession of true tranquillity of the spirit, from which cannot be separated his virtuous living; and moreover, since this tranquillity cannot be spoiled except through the fault of the passions of the soul, hence it arises that on no other thing have the philosophers so exerted themselves, in order to make the soul peaceful, as on the attempt to purge it of those passions.

Developing, then, the theories of the Stoics and the Peripatetics and repeating (from the *Rhetoric*) Aristotle's classification of the eleven passions, all natural and all moderated by reason, he goes on to the specific uses of purgation, which profits men

. . . by means of the compassion and the terror and the fear which it brings to others with those events and those misfortunes which it represents. For when we see the bitter misfortunes and the unhappy accidents with which the world is so full, . . . we come as we see these things to moderate our hopes, and through the vanity that we see in these hopes, we temper also our joys, considering how fragile is their basis. . . . Although tragedy takes into account the nature of the crowd, it has undertaken, for the profit which it intends to bring to it, to purge

---

[150] *Ibid.*, p. ††7: "con l'imitation degli huomini virtuosi; & con la spressione delle lodi loro, veniamo ad infiammarci, & ad escitarci alla virtù, per diuenir simili à quelli, che celebrar' vdiamo. se i vitij, & le scelleratezze dall'altra banda sentiamo con poetica imitation' esprimere, & esprimendo vilipendere, & vituperare; subito cominciamo a disporsi alla fuga, & all'odio delle vitiose attioni; molto più incitati à questo da cotali imitationi, che da quanto si voglia efficace, & aperta particolar' ammonitione.

"Medesimamente se recitarsi in scena veggiamo horribili auuenimenti tragici, vien per questo à mancar' in noi gran parte dell'insolentia, della temerità, dell'arrogantia, dell'audacia, & superbia nostra. & vedendo le miserie, & li pericoli, à che son sottoposti, non solo gli huomini di mediocre, ò di bassa conditione; ma quegli ancora, che per la potentia, & grandezza, soglion' esser felici . . .; veniamo a moderare il dolore negli infortunij, ch'accascano, ò accascar tutto 'l giorno possono. Vien parimente à mitigarsi l'ira, l'inuidia, & gli altri affetti, che dal non ben conoscere l'instabilità della fortuna, & la fragilità delle cose mondane, fomento riceuer sogliono."

POETIC THEORY

the souls mainly of the excess of those passions which have as their object evil
and fear, more than all the others, since these more than all others disturb our
lives.[151]

The function of such purgation (which is more useful when it relates to
fear than to pity) is thus multiple, in line with the multiple usefulness of
poetry in general. The theory is completed in the glosses on other passages.
On *Poetics* 1453b11, two new ideas are offered: pity must not be the pity
of the participants in the action, but of the spectators (thus reaffirming the
orientation toward the audience); and pleasure accompanies these passions
because we learn about man's fate and such learning is delightful (pp. 208,
211). On 1449b31, Piccolomini disagrees with Maggi on the meaning of
"ethical tragedy"; for him, any poem is "costumato" which is "entirely
composed in a way to be instructive and to excite to honesty and to
virtue."[152] On 1459a27, Piccolomini tells us that any pleasure connected
with poetry is extrinsic, its intrinsic end being profit; indeed, pleasure
merely serves this ultimate end: "To this utility pleasure is given for company, as a servant and companion, so that man may more willingly allow
himself to receive that usefulness."[153] On 1450b24, he disagrees with Castelvetro's statement that pity and fear may be produced separately in separate
tragedies; when the drama is properly constituted, both will be produced
together. Other passages might be cited. Throughout, the conviction that
moral instruction is the real end of poetry determines the reading of single
passages in the *Poetics*.

Any such idea involves, of course, a definite conception of the nature of
the audience. We have already seen it referred to as the "multitude" (a
term used repeatedly), and we are ultimately told why poetry appeals
especially to the crowd:

. . . like epic poems, tragedies are written mainly to benefit and to give pleasure
to the multitude. For people who are educated and judicious and friends of virtue
and all forms of knowledge do not need, in order to be taught and benefited, to

151 *Ibid.*, pp. 101–3: "non potendo l'huomo gustare, & conseguir maggior' vtilità, che in
posseder' vna vera tranquillità dell'animo, da cui non può star separata la virtuosa vita sua;
& d'altronde non potendo riceuer macchia questa tranquillità, se non per colpa delle passioni
dell'animo, di quì è, ch'in cosa alcuna non si son tanto affatigati i Filosofi per render tran-
quillo l'animo, quanto in cercar di purgarlo da quegli affetti. . . . col mezo della compassione,
& del terrore, & timore, che reca altrui, con quegli auuenimenti, & casi, che rappresenta.
Conciosiacosache vedendo noi gli acerbi casi, & gli infelici accidenti, dei quali è ripieno
talmente il mondo . . .; veniamo in veder queste cose, à moderar le nostre speranze; & per
la vanità, che veggiamo in esse, temperiamo ancor le allegrezze, considerando in quanta
fragilità sian poste. . . . quantunque hauendo riguardo la tragedia alla natura della moltitudine, habbia ella nel giouamento, che recarle intende, preso à purgar principalmente gli
animi dal souerchio di quegli affetti, che han per oggetto il male, & il timor più di tutti gli
altri, si come più di tutti inquieta la vita nostra."
152 *Ibid.*, p. 107: "tutto composto in modo, che sia atto à instruire, & ad escitare all'
honesto, & alla virtù."
153 *Ibid.*, p. 372: "alquale vtile è dato per compagnia il diletto, come ministro, & compagno,
accioche più voluntieri l'huom si ponga à riceuer quel giouamento."

have the teachings and recommendations which are given to them seasoned with pleasure, as must necessarily be done in order to teach the multitude.[154]

The audience is thus the same as Castelvetro's, and indeed we find Piccolomini speaking of the needs of this audience, and of how they affect the conditions of tragedy, in terms almost identical with those of the earlier commentator. Tragedy must be confined within an artificial day "since those three or four hours which are allowed to the imitation and the performance must represent the time of a whole day, in order to free the spectators of the tedium and the boredom and also the discomfort which would result for them if the performance lasted all day."[155] The division into acts is a device for adjusting the time of performance to the time of the action, with the intermissions accounting for the difference; in this way verisimilitude is saved and, incidentally, change of settings and periods of rest for the actors are made possible (p. 182).

But in one important way, Piccolomini's audience is unlike Castelvetro's: it has imagination. It knows that an imitation is not reality and that it should not expect an imitation to be identical with reality. This is perhaps Piccolomini's most original contribution to the theory of poetry.

I suppose . . . that the spectators of tragedies and comedies have an awareness and knowledge of the fact that the things that are done and said on the stage do not happen there and then as true things and without any feigning, but that they are imitations of things which have already happened or which could happen differently. . . . Therefore, we must not imagine that the cause that might diminish the pleasure of the spectators would be the happening, on the stage, of something that would make them realize that it was not really taking place there, but only as a fiction; but the cause would rather be the lack of resemblance which is required of the imitation.

Actors on the stage, as they walk and talk, cover less space than people in real life; asides are not heard by other actors; but these things do not matter:

. . . these and other similar things do not offend the spectators at all, nor do they in any way disturb their pleasure. This is explained simply by the fact that although these things really go beyond verisimilitude, nevertheless they are rendered necessary by art itself. . . . just as imitation is not truth itself, but is lacking in some part of truth (for if it were not so lacking it would not be an imitation, but the real thing), so also it is necessary that in imitating, certain things should be done which do not accord completely with the truth of the things imitated.

154 *Ibid.*, p. 415: "così le tragedie, come gli epici poemi, si compongon principalmente per giouare, & dar diletto alla moltitudine. Conciosiacosache alle persone perite, & giuditiose, & amiche delle virtù, & delle scientie, non faccia di mestieri per instruirle, & per giouar loro di condire col diletto gli ammaestramenti, & gli auuertimenti, che si dian loro; come è necessario di farlo per instruire la moltitudine."

155 *Ibid.*, p. 97: "douendo quelle tre, ò quattro hore, che si concedono all'imitatione, & rappresentatione; rappresentar' il tempo di tutto vn giorno, per liberare gli spettatori dal tedio, & dal fastidio, & ancor dall'incommodità, che seguirebbe loro, se tutto 'l giorno durasse la rappresentatione."

... The spectators ... grant and concede to the imitators everything far from the truth that the art of imitation necessarily brings and requires.[156]

We should distinguish several important ideas here: the audience never makes the mistake of thinking that it is seeing reality; it recognizes important differences between the world of reality and the world of art; it admits the necessity of certain unreal things in works of art; and it grants the poet the license of introducing such things. There is thus present a concept of artistic necessity which has nothing to do with the natural necessity which most commentators emphasized. Piccolomini describes it thus in another context:

... if at times the poet should be forced by the course of the plot and by some legitimate consideration not to observe completely some one of the aforementioned conditions [i.e., the requisites of character], being unable to escape such violation in order to achieve something which might be more important, he will deserve pardon and excuse and it will not be counted against him as an error.[157]

An audience so endowed with imagination will be ready to accept the verisimilar instead of the true as the proper subject for poetry. Poetry becomes a kind of leveler of differences among men; for whereas in life a thing may be pleasant to some, unpleasant to others, in poetry it will please all. If pleasure is to ensue from its representation, it is not important that the audience should be convinced of its truth, but it is important that the audience believe in the probability of the action. Resemblance to truth, not truth itself, is the real criterion (pp. 68–71). But there are certain difficulties in this principle. For if we accept the proposition that pleasure is a function of credibility and that credibility, in turn, is a function of closeness to the truth, then we shall soon be driven to the conclusion that true subjects will ultimately be those which are most effective. This is indeed the argument that Piccolomini pursues, and he is led to the inevitable deduction.

156 *Ibid.*, pp. 23–24: "io suppongo ... che gli spettatori delle tragedie, & delle commedie, habbian notitia, & conoscentia, che le cose, che si fanno, ò si dicon nelle scene, non accaschin quiui allhora, come vere, & senza fintione alcuna; ma che siano imitationi delle già accadute, ò che accascar potessero altrimenti. ... La causa dunque, che possa offuscare il piacere degli spettatori, non s'ha da stimar, che sia l'accader qualche cosa in scena, per la quale eglin possin' accorgersi, che ella quiui, non veramente ma fintamente accaschi: ma la causa di questo sarà la mancanza della somiglianza necessaria all'imitatione. ... queste, o altre così fatte cose, non offendon punto gli spettatori, ne conturban punto il piacer loro. Il che, non d'altronde procede, senon perche, quantunque queste cose trapassin veramente il verissimile; nondimeno son recate necessariamente dall'arte stessa. ... si come l'imitatione non è lo stesso vero, ma in qualche parte mancante da esso; posciache se punto da quel non mancasse, non sarebbe l'imitatione, ma la cosa vera; così parimente fà di mestieri, ch'alcune cose imitando si facciano, le quali con la verità delle cose imitate, pienamente non concordino. ... gli spettatori ... tutto quello, che lontan dal vero reca, & richiede necessariamente l'arte dell' imitare, donano, & concedono agli imitatori."

157 *Ibid.*, p. 222: "se alle volte il poeta sarà sforzato dal corso della fauola, & da qualche legittimo rispetto, à non osseruar' à punto alcuna delle dette conditioni, non potendo per saluar qualche cosa ch'importi più, fuggir tal' inosseruantia; meriterà egli perdono, & scusa & non gli sarà attribuito per errore."

Much of the discussion occurs apropos of *Poetics* 1451b19, on the subjects of tragedy, and is a development of Aristotle's suggestions. Piccolomini establishes a proportion between the degree of our belief and the intensity of our passions: " . . . when the actions of others are offered to our soul and to our knowledge, they are apt to awaken in us passions proportionate to their quality. . . . Hence it is that the degree of vehemence of the passions will correspond to the degree of certainty of such offerings and cognitions."[158] The essential ratio is "certainty : vehemence"; on the basis of it, we may suppose a scale of increasing credibility accompanied by increasing violence of the passions, hence, of increasing delight. Piccolomini explains that a case we know as false will affect us only during the time of reading, as a result of the force of the poet's words or of his appeal to the imagination; intellectual examination will soon banish the impression. One which we know to be true will produce a deeper and more lasting effect. So for tragedy:

. . . if some image of a tragedy were to be based on persons of whom we not only had no certain knowledge or even belief, but held the opinion that they were entirely invented, this tragedy would be placed at so low a level of perfection that only with the greatest difficulty could it legitimately retain the name of tragedy; whereas if it were based on persons known with clear and definite certainty, in this case (as far as its subject matter is concerned) it would be at the highest level of perfection, and would consequently merit the absolute name of tragedy above all others.[159]

Piccolomini therefore leans toward the "known" rather than the "new" subject for tragedy. This is in spite of the fact that the intrinsic truth or falseness of a subject, its possibility or impossibility, are not a proper consideration for the poetic art. But its credibility is, and this depends upon the audience; Piccolomini distinguishes carefully between possibility as a quality of the action itself and credibility as a function of the audience's knowledge and beliefs about it (p. 392).

These considerations lead Piccolomini at times to reject the theories of his predecessors, at times to accept some of the most traditional explanations. He rejects Castelvetro's notion that tragic subjects must be historical and that history is an art prior to poetry. He thinks that Scaliger is wrong in maintaining that the epic poet sets out to depict a hero perfect in some

[158] *Ibid.*, p. 150: "nell'offerirsi all'anima nostra, & alla nostra cognitione gli altrui fatti, son' atti, à suegliar' in noi affetti proportionati alla qualità di quelli . . .; di qui è, che secondo il grado di così fatti offerimenti, & cognitioni nella certezza loro, sarà parimente il grado degli affetti nella vehementia d'essi."

[159] *Ibid.*, p. 152: "se sopra persone, delle quali, non solo, non s'habbia notitia, ò creduta, ò certa, ma s'habbia opinione, che sian totalmente finte . . . sarà formata qualche immagin di tragedia; in così basso grado sarà ella collocata di perfettione, ch'à gran fatiga potrà ella ritener legittimamente il nome di tragedia. doue che se sopra di persone, per chiara, & per risoluta certezza note, sarà fondata; in tal caso si trouerà per quanto appartiene alla materia sua, nel suppremo grado di perfettione; & meriterà conseguentemente sopra tutte l'altre il nome assoluto di tragedia."

virtue or other, since this would imply the use of action to demonstrate character—"an opinion that is not very Aristotelian"—whereas character really exists for the purposes of the action (p. 96). One is thus surprised to find that his ideas of verisimilitude involve an expectation on the part of the audience that characters will always behave according to type; the imitation will be lacking in resemblance "if indications of generosity appear in an old man, or signs of temperance in a very low servant, or of shame in a prostitute, or of great knowledge in a maidservant, and so forth."[160] The old laws of decorum are made equivalent to the audience's conceptions of probability. In fact, Piccolomini's explanation of the four requisites of character derives from what he believes about verisimilitude and about the ends of poetry. He is careful to point out that characters are "good" not in order to serve as moral examples to the spectators, but so they may arouse pity and fear; they are "endowed with virtue and with praiseworthy qualities, and deserving of happiness, and consequently unworthy of those misfortunes."[161] But "appropriateness" for the same good characters means that their good qualities are proper to the type which they represent, according to the laws of decorum: "rank, calling, sex, or other circumstance" ("la qualità, la conditione, il sesso, ò altra circonstantia," p. 219). "Similarity" refers to the characteristics commonly assigned to a known personage; it is distinguished from appropriateness in this way:

... the requirement of appropriateness concerns the universal, as if to say that this character belongs to a prince, that one to a subject, this one to a man, that one to a woman, and so forth, without considering this or that particular person; and the requirement of similarity concerns the particular or the singular, as if to say what character it is proper to give to one who has to represent Achilles, ... seeking to form and to qualify the persons in the plot similar to the character of those who are being represented, according to the knowledge and the reputation associated with them.[162]

"Constancy," for Piccolomini, is not a separate requisite, but merely another aspect of similarity; he considers the possibility of distinguishing between them by saying that similarity applies to characters already treated by earlier poets, constancy to the new ones whom the poet might invent; but he sees difficulties in this theory.

160 *Ibid.*, p. 23: "se appariranno in vn vecchio inditij di liberalità, ò in vn vilissimo seruo inditij di temperantia, ò in vna meretrice, di pudicitia; ò in vna ancilla, di gran dottrina, ò simili."
161 *Ibid.*, p. 218: "di virtù, & di lodeuoli qualità dotate, & meriteuoli di felicità, & per conseguente indegne di quelli infortunij."
162 *Ibid.*, p. 220: "la conditione del conueneuole, riguarda l'vniuersale; com' à dire, che quel costume conuenga ad vn principe, quello ad vn suddito, quello all'huomo, quello alla donna, & simili, senza considerar questa particolar persona, ò quella; & la condition del simile riguarda il particolare, ò ver' il singolare. com' à dire, qual costume conuenga di porre in vno, che habbia da rappresentar' Achille ... cercando ... di formare, & qualificar le persone nella fauola simili di costume à quelle, che si rappresentano, secondo la notitia, & la fama, che sene tiene."

A similar persuasion about character produces Piccolomini's stand toward the factors which differentiate literary forms one from another. He takes issue, first, with the commentators who have held that "better" and "worse," relating to the objects of poetry, mean of higher or of lower social station; the distinction is an ethical one: "Aristotle is obviously speaking of goodness and badness with respect to virtue and to vice, whence man obtains absolutely the quality of being good or bad."[163] This difference would in itself be insufficient to constitute two species of poems. Nor would it be adequate to bring into play such factors as age, wealth, health (these are components of decorum), for genres must be differentiated by greater factors still; the only one capable of doing so is social rank or station: "Those qualities are sufficient to do it which diversify man's life and his status from the very foundations, such as the difference between persons of illustrious and dominating station and persons of middling station and of private and subordinate condition; this diversity makes tragedy different from comedy."[164] Thus, on the reading of *Poetics* 1448a1 Piccolomini disagrees with his predecessors; but the necessity of finding a basis for distinguishing among genres ultimately leads him to adopt their essential position. He goes so far as to declare that Aristotle's definition of comedy at 1449a31 is incomplete and imperfect because it includes only one differentia, "the worse," and that not the essential one. A proper definition would call for the imitation of "civil and private persons, and ones placed in a middling station" ("persone ciuili, & priuate, & in mediocre, stato poste," p. 90).

These distinctions are directly related, for Piccolomini, to the ends of purgation and to the whole problem of credibility and of the effect upon the passions. The audience, composed as it is, will not believe in the happiness of heroes unless they are of high estate: " . . . it does not seem to the mass and to the multitude that a person of private and low condition, no matter how virtuous and happy he may be, should be called happy, since they include among the most important parts of happiness the power and the capacity of a man to determine and to be able to do what he wants, and this they believe to be found in princes."[165] Such credibility is essential if the proper effects are to be produced; hence the sharp line drawn between tragic and comic subjects:

. . . those actions which have to draw from our soul the two tragic passions will

163 *Ibid.*, p. 45: "euidentemente parla Aristotele della bontà, & malitia rispetto alla virtù, & al vitio, donde prende assolutamente lo huomo la qualità ò del buono, ò del reo."

164 *Ibid.*, p. 45: "quelle qualità, che posson dai fondamenti diuersificar la vita sua, & lo stato suo; son bastanti a farlo come à dir, trà persone d'illustre, & signoreggiante stato, & persone di stato mediocre, & di priuata, & soggetta conditione; la qual diuersità rende differente la tragedia dalla commedia."

165 *Ibid.*, p. 195: "non par' al volgo, & alla moltitudine, ch'vna priuata, & bassa persona, quanto si voglia che virtuosa, & felice sia, si debbi domandar felice; ponendo lor frà le principalissime parti della felicità, la potentia, & facultà di nominare, & di poter fare ciò che l'huom vuole; il che stiman' essi, che sia nei principi."

have need of greater credibility than will those which must elicit such agreeable passions [as those of comedy] and ones which are so close to nature and to our sensibility. . . . since the circumstances and the actions which are imitated in comedies are based on persons of civil and middling status, . . . no sooner have the spectators understood the argument of the plot than they readily believe that it could have taken place. . . . It is necessary, in order to bring credibility to the plots of tragedies, to attribute those imaginary actions to real persons, and the names should be used in order to cause in the minds of the spectators that form of false deduction which we have seen.[166]

For comedy, then—and there is a parallelism here to the decorum of characters—actions will be credible because they are commonplace; in fact, they will be most credible when they are such actions as have frequently been used by poets, "the avarice of old men, the tricks of prostitutes, the prodigality of young men, the cheating of servants, the madnesses of lovers, the boastings of soldiers, the lies of pimps, and so forth";[167] the world, in a word, of Plautus and Terence. For tragedy, the lack of the commonplace quality will be compensated by the knowledge that the persons were real.

Another of the cornerstones of Piccolomini's theory—and this again fixes him firmly in the current tradition—is his insistence that verse is a necessary part of the perfect poem. He remains closer to the letter of the text than did many of his contemporaries on the interpretation of λόγοις ψιλοῖς (1447*a*28). This means, he says, "speech not measured by verse, but made in prose" ("il parlare non misurato dal verso, ma fatto in prosa," p. 21). Poetry may thus be written in prose, and the presence of imitation will be its distinguishing characteristic. But Piccolomini introduces the matter of the two natural causes of poetry as a means of establishing a hierarchy of perfection. One of these causes is the pleasure which man takes in imitation; the other is the pleasure which he naturally finds in rhythm and song (p. 20). If we interpret the *Poetics* in this way, then it becomes possible to say that the poem which adds verse to imitation will be more perfect than one which does not. Piccolomini takes this position, after Maggi and Vettori, whom he cites; he declares that ποίησις is most properly taken to mean "that imitation . . . which would be made with speech measured by verse" ("quella imitatione . . . che col parlar misurato dal verso, si facesse," p. 20). Verse, as a consequence, becomes "not that element which contributes essentially to the making of the true poet, but

---

[166] *Ibid.*, pp. 142–43: "di maggior credibilità haran bisogno quelle attioni, che han da trar dal nostro animo quei due tragici affetti, che non n'han bisogno quelle, che così piaceuoli affetti, & amici alla natura & al senso nostro, n'han da cauare. . . . essendo i casi, & le attioni, che si fingon nelle commedie, fondate in persone di ciuile, & mediocre stato . . .; non prima gli Spettatori comprendono l'argomento della fauola, che facilmente si fà lor credibile, che possa essere stato. . . . fà di bisogno, che per recar credibilità alle fauole delle tragedie, si attribuischin quelle immaginate attioni à persone vere, & li nomi si prendin di esse, per far nascer negli animi degli Spettatori quelle forma di paralogismo, che hauiam veduto."

[167] *Ibid.*, p. 90: "auaritia di vecchij, inganni di meretrici, prodigalità di gioueni, fraudi di serui, pazzie d'innamorati, vantamenti di soldati, bugie di ruffiani, & simili."

only to making him perfectly so."[168] The question arises immediately, as it was to arise with increasing prominence during the latter years of the century, about the use of verse in comedy. Piccolomini's answer contradicts his general position on verse. He thinks that the comic poet (and the dramatic poet in general) can make himself heard, via the actor, through prose as well as through verse; that the example of Greek and Latin drama is inconclusive, since ancient verse was so different from Italian; that there is no Italian verse adapted to comedy; that Italian audiences prefer prose to verse, deriving a greater pleasure from it. Hence, he believes that ultimately tragedy in Italian, as well as comedy, will be written in prose (pp. 25–28).

There are a number of passages, such as the one on prose, in which Piccolomini presents better readings than those of his fellows. He solves correctly the difficulty with respect to the arts of the flute and the zither (1447a15) by pointing out that these are meant to be examples of imitation, not of poetry (p. 8). He shows how wrong Castelvetro was in taking 1447a16 as an indication of the species of poetry, whereas it is really a listing of the differentiae (pp. 9–10). He declares, in connection with 1450a15, that Robortello erred in maintaining that character might be the principal part of the play as read, plot of the play as acted; instead, one must at all times regard plot as the essential form of the imitation (p. 115). With reference to 1450a12, he properly distributes the qualitative parts among the categories of object, manner, and means (p. 120). Castelvetro is taken to task for his whole conception of the unity of plot, both for holding that it was not necessary in the epic and for making it depend upon the auxiliary considerations of time and place (pp. 132–36).

On the negative side, Piccolomini makes his own mistakes. His great difficulties with the manner of imitation spring in part from ambiguities in his use of the term "imitation" (pp. 52–57). He offers debatable ideas about episodes removable without damage to the work (p. 156) and about the relationship of hamartia to ignorance (p. 197). But, on the whole, he makes improvements on his predecessors in the reading of the text, especially on Castelvetro whom he was most eager to controvert. His theory of poetry, although it is independent and frequently far from Aristotle, is less extreme than that of Castelvetro.

SASSETTI ON PICCOLOMINI (1575)

Not long after the publication of Piccolomini's *Annotationi*, Eleonora di Toledo de' Medici, a member of the Accademia degli Alterati, asked the academy to prepare a judgment on the new commentary. The request was made early in August, 1575, and the judgment was presented to the meeting of August 16th; although signed by the "Accademici Alterati," the *Dis-*

[168] *Ibid.*, p. 72: "non è quello, che essentialmente concorre à far' il vero poeta; ma solo à farlo perfettamente tale."

corso containing it was the work of Filippo Sassetti.[169] Sassetti charges Piccolomini with imperfections of translation, with failure to explain certain difficult passages, and with errors of statement. It is interesting to note that in the last category fall some of those items of theory that I have pointed to as most original with Piccolomini. First, Sassetti rejects the hypothesis that the distinction among the genres is essentially one of social status; rather, one must understand Aristotle as establishing the difference on the basis of virtue and vice. But Sassetti has his own way of interpreting "better," "like," and "worse": " . . . if we imitate the good and the bad in the way in which we see them every day, without inventing anything beyond, we will imitate the 'like'; but if we add perfection to the goodness that we find commonly or most frequently, and imperfection to the vices, we will imitate the 'better' and the 'worse.' "[170] There are thus only two kinds of character, good and bad; but either may be imitated in an ordinary or in a superlative degree. Second, Sassetti discards Piccolomini's opinion that verse is not necessary for poetry and that one may admit the existence of "perfect" and "imperfect" poetry, distinguished on this basis. He himself thinks that verse is indispensable, and he reads *Poetics* 1447a28 in the light of this conviction (p. 63). Finally, he disagrees completely on the matter of comedy in prose, citing the practice of the ancients and of Ariosto and insisting that Aristotle demanded verse in all poetic forms.

A much more complete and revealing expression of Sassetti's ideas on Piccolomini—as well as on Aristotle and on the theory of poetry—is found in the marginal notes to his copy of the *Annotationi*, which may be consulted at the Biblioteca Nazionale in Florence. He himself dated the reading of Piccolomini between August 29 and September 18, 1575, just a few weeks after the preparation of the judgment for the Alterati. A few, but not many, of the marginalia concern matters of translation; for example, at 1451b5 Piccolomini has translated in a way which would make it seem that Aristotle is comparing universal things with particular things, rather than poetry with history, and Sassetti claims that the text will not permit this (p. 139). For the most part, however, Sassetti objects to what seem to him to be misunderstandings by Piccolomini, and his objections spring from an essentially different way of reading the *Poetics*. The central question is Aristotelianism. He has certain disagreements with Piccolomini on the nature of the poetic faculty and on what Aristotle was trying to do in the *Poetics*. Whereas Piccolomini had classified it as a "habit" which gives precepts for the poet, Sassetti insists that a habit does not give precepts and that hence it should rather be called a "method" (p. ††7v). Again, he

169 See my "Argomenti di discussione letteraria," *Giornale Storico*, CXXXI (1954), 182–83, and M. Rossi, *Filippo Sassetti*, pp. 98–100.

170 Ed. F.-L. Polidori, in the *Nozze Riccomanni-Fineschi*, p. 61: "imitando i buoni e' rei in quella guisa che tutto 'l giorno si veggono, senza fingere più oltre, si imiteranno i simili; ma se aggiugneremo alla bontà che comunemente e per lo più si suole ritrovare, perfezione, e imperfezione a i vizii, si imiteranno i migliori e' peggiori."

believes that Piccolomini is wrong in setting out (p. ††5) to treat poetry universally:

... it is nothing unless considered in its species, from each of which in turn the precepts must be derived, and not from that general "poetry" which has no nature of its own. And therefore, Aristotle never used that term, but rather when he wishes to name the genus (so to speak) of poems, he does not say that it is poetry, but imitation.[171]

He takes no exception, however, to Piccolomini's statement that Aristotle meant to give "leggi, precetti, regole, & ammaestramenti" (p. ††7v), and he apparently conceived of the *Poetics* in the same general way (v. p. 28).

These general doubts about method lead Sassetti to disapprove of Piccolomini's definition of poetry and of his conception of its objects, its means, and its manners of imitation. Several things are wrong with the definition: it mentions only one of the means, language, and omits the other two; it includes accidental differences, such as the imitation of natural or artificial objects; it adds to "human actions" the unessential elements of "characters" and "passions," which do not belong in the definition (p. ††5). As for Piccolomini's statement of the end of poetry in his definition, "dilettare, & dilettando finalmente giouare alla vita humana," Sassetti raises no objection at this point; but later, in his own statement of the four causes of poetry, he limits the "final" cause to pleasure:

... considering pleasure also with respect to the imitator, I think that it is necessary to say that it is the final cause, for he who imitates imitates for the pleasure that he takes in doing it, ... whence one might say that the efficient cause of poetry was the poet himself; the formal, imitation; the material, verse; and the final, pleasure.[172]

With respect to these same causes, he challenges Piccolomini's assertion that the actions are the "matter," although not without falling into ambiguity himself; " ... because the imitation of an action is nothing but the plot, which Aristotle said was the soul and the end of tragedy."[173] The problem of the end remains unresolved.

Disagreement on the objects of imitation centers about Piccolomini's repeated stand that "better" and "worse" were not a differentiating factor

---

171 All references are to the copy of the *Annotationi* in the Biblioteca Nazionale, Florence, call number Postillati 15. For the present passage, see p. ††5: "ella non è nulla se non considerata nelle sue spetie, dalle quali à una à una si debbono cauare i precetti, e non da questa comune Poesia, che non ha natura propria, e però Aristotile non se ne serui mai, anzi quando uuole nominare il genere (per dir cosi) delle Poesie, non dice, che sia la Poesia, ma l'imitatione."

172 *Ibid.*, p. 65: "considerato anche il diletto quanto all'Imitante, credo, che sia necessario dire, che egli sia causa finale; auuengache chi imita imita per il diletto, che prende ... onde si potrebbe dire, che la causa efficiente della Poesia fusse lo stesso Poeta la formale l'imitatione la materiale il uerso, e la finale il diletto."

173 *Ibid.*, p. ††5v: "perche l'Imitatione d'attione non è altro che la fauola, laquale Aristotile disse essere l'anima, e'l fine della Tragedia."

among the genres and that to them must be added the element of social status. This Sassetti denies emphatically, stating that the position of Castelvetro and Piccolomini is completely false (p. 44). In his note to the commentary on 1448b24, he says:

It appears that we may conclude from this text that the difference of characters is an essential difference, and not an accidental one as Piccolomini wishes. . . . Not only does Aristotle hold this to be an essential difference, but the one which is more important than all the others. Nor can it be said that here the station of the persons is to be understood; for the words of the text are clear, and Piccolomini makes them even clearer through his explanation.[174]

Moreover, these are to be taken as differences in character, in virtue and vice, rather than in degree; when Aristotle compares the poets to the painters, he means that both groups make similar ethical distinctions among their objects (p. 45). On the related question of the "goodness" of character (Piccolomini had limited it to "good" people), Sassetti offers some distinctions of his own. He rejects as artistically unsound the notion that the wicked may be introduced provided that they are punished; at 1454a15 Aristotle "speaks in universals, requiring that all the persons who are imitated should be good, each one, however, only as much as his rank permits, with this reservation however that if it were necessary to invent a bad person, he should not be made good"[175]; and in tragedy, where "goodness" must be accompanied by a fall to misfortune, the personage is given only average goodness in the action which the tragedy imitates (p. 218). All in all, on the objects of imitation, Sassetti tries to restore the ethical distinction in place of the social one and to clarify some of the misunderstandings about character.

On the means of imitation, he passes over Piccolomini and returns to the earlier commentators: his general thesis is that verse is a necessary component of poetry. The possibility of greater or less perfection in poetry, depending upon the presence or absence of verse, is denied in a passage which is also interesting for its general remarks on method:

. . . this division of poets into perfect and imperfect seems completely useless and outside Aristotle's intentions; first because the imperfect poets, if they belong under a species of poetry, should have been mentioned by Aristotle, and if they are not, it results that we should not mention them either; next, art never considers any but the perfect form of that thing which it treats; finally, if this same Piccolomini's explanation is correct, that the two universal causes of poetry are

---

174 *Ibid.*, p. 74: "Da questo testo pare, che si possa cauare, che la diuersita de Costumi è differentia essentiale, e non accidentale, come uuole il Piccolomini. . . . non solo Aristotile stima questa essere una essentiale differenza, ma quella che piu uaglia, che tutte le altre; Ne si puo dire, che qui s'intenda dello stato delle persone, perche le parole del testo son chiare, e più le chiarisce il Piccolomini con la sua spositione." See also p. 203.

175 *Ibid.*, p. 221: "parla in uniuersale uolendo che tutte le persone che s'imitano, sieno buone ciascuna però quanto comporta il grado suo, con questo riguardo tuttauia che se fusse necessario fingere vno cattiuo non si faccia buono."

imitation and verse, it follows that no poetry can ever exist without verse, because no effect can ever come into being without all its causes.[176]

The argument runs thus: the means are three, language, rhythm, and harmony, and rhythm includes verse; *Poetics* 1448*b*20 is cited as the authority, although Aristotle's meaning is stretched by the implication that verse is necessarily a part of rhythm (p. 72). Sassetti would thus demand verse in all genres, including comedy; he quotes Castelvetro and Horace against Piccolomini (p. 26), admitting, however, that reason is sufficient without authority; the authorities, he says, are on his side, beginning with Aristotle. He rejects Piccolomini's statement that the imitation is made "con le attioni," since this would make action a means (p. 52). As long as all three means are present in a poem, its basic conditions will be fulfilled; there is no requirement that they all be used simultaneously (p. 39).

The marginalia relevant to the ends of poetry concern two subjects, purgation and credibility. We have already seen that the end of pleasure belongs to Sassetti's definition of poetry; he argues for it, in a roundabout way, by maintaining that Aristotle's remarks on the pleasure found in the imitation of unpleasant objects are meant to stress the greater pleasure to be found in the representation of pleasing objects (p. 69). He does not anywhere indicate specifically that there is an additional end of instruction. But when he comes to speak of purgation, he characterizes it as the end of tragedy, meanwhile correcting Piccolomini (p. 103) on habituation as giving moral effectiveness to tragedy; if purgation is really an intrinsic end, then it must produce its effect through quality and not through quantity. The passions purged by tragedy are pity and fear. But Sassetti contradicts Piccolomini's contention that the more important of the two is fear; this is un-Aristotelian. For Aristotle, he says, frequently speaks of pity without mentioning fear, implying that the former may be produced alone in any given tragedy; this is because it is a passion proper to our feelings about the "better," whereas fear concerns only the "like." The whole argument is given in this passage:

> We should note, on this text, that it is not always true that those things which move us to compassion also move us to fear, and this for many reasons. First, because many times we have compassion for one who may have lost a thing which we do not possess, whence we cannot be afraid of losing it ourselves. And another because fear is for those like us . . ., whereas compassion can fall upon those who are not like us. Lastly, because, while we are feeling compassion for the misfor-

[176] *Ibid.*, p. 20: "questa diuisione de Poeti in perfetti, et imperfetti pare al tutto uana, e fuor della mente d'Aristotile. prima perche i Poeti imperfetti, se sono sotto una spetie di Poesia, doueuano essere mentouati da Aristotile e se non sono, resta che anche noi non debbiamo farne mentione; di poi l'arte non considera mai se non la perfetta forma di quella cosa, che ella tratta: In ultimo se è buona la spositione del medesimo Piccolomini che uuole che le due cagioni uniuersali della Poesia sieno l'imitare, e'l uerso, ne segue che non possa mai trouarsi la Poesia senza'l uerso perche niuno effetto puo mai nascere senza tutte le sue cause."

tunes of someone, we do not have time to think about our own, but we continue to think about that evil which he is suffering. Therefore, since tragedy must always move compassion, as it seems that Aristotle supposes when he constitutes the personage fitted for tragedy, and since it is not always necessary that fear should follow compassion, one must conclude that tragedy principally arouses and purges compassion.[177]

Sassetti clearly sees factors of personal involvement as influencing the effect of tragedy.

On the other hand, credibility depends rather on the quality of the poem itself than on the knowledge of the audience, and Sassetti attacks Piccolomini's subtle differentiation between comedy and tragedy on this score. His is an interesting position. He sees the situation as distinct from that in painting, where our pleasure is related to the knowledge of the subject, "whereas poetry makes us entirely capable of the things which it recounts, nor is it necessary that we worry our brain to ascribe this action to that given person; for poetry tells us sufficiently who the person is who does that action, whence we derive a universal pleasure not dependent upon individuals."[178] This would make the art more self-sufficient, less rhetorical, in its general operation. However, Sassetti still finds a need for the poet to attend to credibility; in tragedy, he must use known names in order to make the marvelous actions of "better" heroes acceptable to the audience; in comedy, where credibility is just as important, he avoids the use of known names to keep from falling into the kind of personal criticism which is proper to satire (p. 143). Indeed, this matter is related to two essential considerations about art: How much should nature (or history) be allowed to supply to the poet? And how much do particularities of the audience affect the work of the poet? Sassetti tackles these problems in his marginal note to Piccolomini on *Poetics* 1454a10:

. . . it seems that Aristotle, when he says that the poets derived the plots for their tragedies not from their own art but from fortune, is scolding them as men who are not willing to use the power of their art but have recourse to fortune. When they do so, they submit to a very uncertain thing, because it might be that none of those terrible misfortunes which are demanded in a tragedy have ever happened

177 *Ibid.*, p. 105: "E da notare in questo discorso, che non sempre è uero, che quelle cose che ci muouono à compassione ci muouano à timore per molti rispetti vno perche molte uolte noi habbiamo compassione, che uno habbia perso una cosa, la quale noi non habbiamo, onde non possiamo hauer paura di perderla noi, e l'altro perche il timore è de simili . . ., la doue la compassione puo cadere ne non simili, in ultimo perche in mentre che noi habbiamo compassione a' casi d'uno non habbiamo tempo di poter pensare a' nostri, ma perseueriamo in considerare quel male, che colui patisce, perloche douendo sempre la tragedia muouer compassione, come pare che supponga Aristotele quando constituisce la persona atta alla tragedia, e non essendo sempre necessario, che alla compassione seguiti il timore si debbe conchiudere, che principalmente la tragedia ecciti, e purghi la compassione."

178 *Ibid.*, p. 147: "la doue la Poesia ci fa interamente capaci delle cose che ella racconta ne ci fa di mestiere d'applicare col nostro ceruello questa attione à quella tal persona, perche la Poesia a bastanza ci dice, chi è colui, che faccia quell'attione onde si caua il diletto uniuersale non applicato à indiuiduj."

to those men whom a people consider to be famous. Hence poets, if they wished to follow things which have actually happened, could not compose tragedies. Moreover, it might well not be proper for the poets of all nations to use with equal opportuneness the misfortunes which happened to those ancient Greeks, not only because of the great disparity in time, which is a reason why the customs and the opinions of men vary so greatly, but as well because of the diversity of places and of laws, also a cause of very great difference in humors.[179]

The answer would seem to be that the poet makes his plots, rather than taking them from history or legend, and that when he does so, he takes into account the characteristics and the beliefs of his own potential audience.

In a number of the remaining marginalia Sassetti corrects Piccolomini on specific points of interpretation. These concern largely plot (what is meant by simple plot, p. 166; unity of plot in the epic, p. 377; invention of plot, p. 250; the tragic act on the stage, p. 175) and character (what is meant by σπουδαίας, p. 104; how a tragedy may be "ethical," pp. 114, 115, 116; the real difference between the third and fourth requisites for character, p. 220). These contribute less than do the others to an original Sassettian theory of poetry and an individual interpretation of Aristotle. Nevertheless, theory and interpretation do exist even in these scattered fragments. Sassetti sees the *Poetics* as providing a method that should be used by the poet to the fullest extent. He believes in a strict Aristotelianism of approach, but one contained within the text of the *Poetics* and not dependent upon reference to other works of the corpus; he thus frequently reproaches Piccolomini with erroneous reading. For the art itself, pleasure rather than instruction is the end, and it is achieved by artistic devices (verse is one of them) which themselves produce pleasure, or which operate upon the passions, or which fit the particular needs of the audience. We shall have an opportunity, under a later date, to discover whether these same tendencies manifest themselves in Sassetti's own commentary on the *Poetics*.

CONCLUSIONS

The period from 1562 to 1575 thus presents a fairly distinct character to the student of the Aristotelian tradition during the Renaissance. These are years marked by a growing activity in the translation of and commentary on the *Poetics* in Italian; the major documents are Castelvetro's and Piccolomini's extensive works, and the vernacular translation of Giacomini

---

[179] *Ibid.*, p. 216: "pare, che Aristotile dicendo che i Poeti non dalla propia arte, ma dalla fortuna cauauano le fauole per le loro tragedie gli riprenda, come quegli che non si uoglion ualere della forza dell'arte, ma ricorrono alla fortuna, al che fare si sottopongono à una cosa non ben certa, perche potrebbe essere, che in quegli huomini, che uno popolo stima famosi, non fusse mai accaduto alcuno di questi casi si terribili, che n'una tragedia si ricercano, onde i Poeti se uolesson andar dietro alle cose accadute non potrebbon comporre tragedie; auuenga che possa molto bene non conuenirsi, che i Poeti di tutte le nationi si seruano cosi acconciamente de casi auuenuti à quegli antichi greci; non solo per la disparità dell'età si lunga, che è cagione, che i costumi, e pareri degl'huomini si uarijno tanto, ma ancora per la diuersità de luoghi, e delle leggi, che è anco questa causa di grandissima differenza d'humori."

brings the number to three. Besides, the continued effort toward vulgarization is apparent. Orazio Toscanella presents a digest in his *Precetti necessari* of 1562 and Giovanni Fabrini is much concerned with the *Poetics* in his Italian commentary on Horace. This was in keeping with—and indeed was partly stimulated by—the heightened intellectual life of the Italian academies. In various cities, these groups of gentleman-critics and of amateur literati worked very seriously with literary problems, one of the most prominent of which was the discussion of the *Poetics*. The Accademia degli Alterati stands out among them for the number and the intensity of these discussions, as well as for the quantity of manuscripts which have survived; but one should not overlook the contributions of Maranta to the Accademia Napoletana, of Lapini and Strozzi to the Accademia Fiorentina, of Bernardo Tasso to the Accademia Veneziana. The removal of the *Poetics* from the scholar's study and the university lecture-hall to the open disputes of the academies was a considerable factor in the growth of knowledge about it. One direct consequence is such a work as Giacomini's translation.

There are other consequences. One of them is the repeated attempt to adapt Aristotle's principles to genres which he had not treated or to later works: Bonciani wrote his discourse on the novella and Strozzi his lecture on the madrigal for presentation to academies, as did Maranta his reflections on the *Aeneid* as an epic. Sigonio's Latin treatise on the dialogue is of the same kind, but was not intended for public presentation. Another is the fact that many of the documents coming within this period tend to include consideration of Italian works, and even contemporary ones, as examples or as sources of theory. The most striking case, perhaps, is the *Divina Commedia*; the growing polemic, in its early years, frequently gives rise to academic speeches. Petrarch and Boccaccio are examined, and a certain number of sixteenth-century poems are subjected to analysis. Furthermore, there is an occasional attempt to introduce contemporaneity into the interpretation of the *Poetics* itself, as Sassetti did in several documents.

Concomitant with this growth in activity in the vernacular, there is a decline in the amount of work being done in Latin. No single new Latin translation or commentary is published during these years, although Vettori's compendious volume was republished in 1573. Nicasius Ellebodius was the only writer to attempt a paraphrase and commentary, and this, perhaps significantly, remained unpublished. So did Maranta's lectures, treating both the general content of the *Poetics* and certain specific problems. This does not mean that the scholars were no longer working on Aristotle, for we have traces of correspondence and controversy in the exchanges between Maranta and Vettori and between Ellebodius and Sophianos; but these did not bear fruit as they had in the past.

Perhaps this turn toward the present, toward Italian literature, toward

the amateur academies, accounts in part for the fact that Plato and Horace
tend less to dominate conversation about Aristotle than they had in previous years. This tendency should not be exaggerated. For our study has
shown that comparison among ancient authorities continues to be a
favorite form of elucidation, that both Horace and Plato are still called
upon constantly for solution of the most difficult problems in the *Poetics.*
But the favorite game of parallelism seems to be played less vigorously,
and there is a growing desire to find solutions to Aristotle within Aristotle,
either within the one central text or by reference to the rest of the corpus.
There are, as there had always been, attempts to discover and apply an
Aristotelian method, to speak in terms of the four causes and to insist on
syllogistic analysis—these not always with great success. One has, however, the sense of a fairly fresh approach, probably because the gentlemen
of the academies were less limited by the tradition of the universities than
their predecessors had been.

As for the interpretation of the *Poetics* itself, certain problems persist,
others tend to disappear, new emphases make themselves felt. Of the old
problems, the most perennial is the text, and we may ask whether any
forward steps were made by a group of men who were not primarily philologists. I think that the answer is affirmative, especially if we recall some
of the excellent conjectures of Ellebodius and his friend Sophianos (unfortunately not published and hence unavailable to the reading public).
These men were, of course, philologists connected with universities; but
some of their contemporaries also made, on occasion, useful suggestions
for the improvement of the text. More important still, they made definite
progress in the translation of the *Poetics.* The three successive versions are,
I believe, successive ameliorations, if we take as our criteria clarity, con-
cision, and the use of a language which is neither cant nor jargon. In the
Latin of Ellebodius as well, we find good solutions, although these are
frequently lost in the context of the paraphrase.

The issue of interpretation remains very much alive. In at least two cases,
those of Castelvetro and Gratarolo, the authority of Aristotle and the
general validity of the *Poetics* are challenged. Do we need, they ask, to take
this man and this document as necessarily infallible? And they proceed
from there to quite complete rejection. But this is not a general tendency,
and without being as explicit in Aristotle's defence as was Giulio Del
Bene, most critics of the period still assumed that he was infallible and
went on to the important business of discovering what he meant. Part of
that discovery consisted in the reiterated controversy over given words and
phrases, much of it now conducted in Italian and discussed in public
sessions. Such stock passages as those containing the words μίμησις,
ποίησις, ἁμαρτία, λόγοις ψιλοῖς, such central notions as purgation, verisimilitude, plot, and the four requisites of character continue to arouse
interest and debate: and if they do so, it is because they are regarded by

men of this period as the fundamental issues of the *Poetics*. I think that it is possible to generalize with respect to their findings, admitting always that there was never any unanimity and that the generalization represents no single theorist. Poetry comes to be distinguished from imitation as a species from its genus, and the poetic imitations are separated from non-poetic. But poetry—in spite of a few dissenters and subtilizers—remains inextricably linked with verse, and the argument as to whether verse is required in all genres, especially comedy, is usually decided in the affirmative. There is some clouding of all these terms, especially of imitation, by reference to Plato.

The ends of poetry remain what they have been throughout the century, pleasure and instruction, sometimes with pleasure standing as an end in itself, more usually with pleasure subordinated to the utility of moral exemplification and preachment. Here purgation enters, for, taken as it was to mean the expulsion of undesirable passions—pity and fear and others —it provides the most effective means for achieving usefulness. It is still the answer which Aristotle gave to Plato, but less prominently than before; discussion centers more directly on the passions concerned and the ways in which purgation works. Questions of plot and of character are made to relate to the ends of poetry. For if pleasure is to be given to an unruly audience of the "vulgus," plot must be made of certain known materials and organized in certain convenient ways. It is thought of largely as a kind of scenario or "argument" to which episodes are added for purposes of amplification and adornment—episodes which may be considered integral or removable, depending on the decision of individual theorists. In spite of quotations about the "soul of tragedy," there is no organic conception of plot as the organizing element of the poem, from which nothing can be removed. But we should note in this connection that there is at least one trace (in Piccolomini) of a notion of artistic necessity, which would demand that elements of plot be present or absent for "artistic" rather than for "natural" reasons. Verisimilitude and the marvelous are also related to the capacities of plot to achieve its ends, the first establishing the conditions of belief—hence, of moral effect—in the audience, the second creating the possibility of a strong effect upon the emotions and hence of pleasure. Similar considerations affect ideas about character, and Aristotle's four requisites are studied over and over again in the desire to make them serve the purposes of credibility and moral instruction. So are his "better," "like," and "worse," although in this case there is more controversy, relevant to the decision as to whether these involve an ethical or a social distinction; most critics opt for the latter, but there are many nuances in their reasons for doing so.

Perhaps the most subtle way in which an enduring Horatianism manifests itself is in the twisting of the *Poetics* to make of it a set of precepts for the poet who would amuse and instruct an audience of the multitude.

Castelvetro is, of course, the prime example of this, since his theory is so completely directed to the masses. But he is not alone; in almost every theorist, one may ultimately see the audience as the primary determinant of the poem's content and form. Audiences differ. Piccolomini's is more imaginative and intelligent than Castelvetro's. But all are ever-present in a system that continues to be rhetorical in its essential workings. Once this basic position has been taken, it is less necessary than it had been (not long since) to rise to the defence of poetry or to compare it—and its merits—to the other arts. Utility has by this time been established for each specific audience, and now the job is to see how art may serve this utility. The superior appeal of poetry, because of its accessibility to the senses and the passions, is often stressed; but the defensive, even apologetic tone is no longer needed. From Horace and the rhetoricians, again, stem the complex and numerous components of the theory of decorum, which still informs much of the thinking about character, about plot, and about credibility as related to both.

One has the impression, on the whole, that the total interpretation of Aristotle in these years is less rigid and more fluid, perhaps more vigorous, than it had been in the years immediately preceding. It remains to be seen whether this impression is justified by the events of the following years, when the influence of the current literary polemics made itself strongly felt on the interpretation of Aristotle.

CHAPTER TWELVE. THE TRADITION OF ARISTOTLE'S *POETICS*: IV. THE EFFECT OF THE LITERARY QUARRELS

T HE EFFECT of the current literary quarrels upon the interpretation of the *Poetics* had already begun to be perceptible in the materials studied in the last chapter. Only one quarrel had been involved, that over Dante's *Divina Commedia*. In the years to come, this polemic will continue to influence the thinking of the theorists, and to it will be added two other major literary debates: that over Tasso and Ariosto (implicating the whole theory of epic poetry) and that over Guarini's *Pastor Fido* (necessitating a re-examination of the whole theory of dramatic poetry). Immediately after 1575, the most prominent is still, of course, the quarrel over Dante; the others enter the picture at broadly spaced intervals. All this activity reflects increasingly the successive "vulgarization" of the *Poetics*, its spread into constantly broader circles of discussion. From Florence the dialogue ranges outward, as other academies and other cities begin to participate.

To be sure, old problems are not forgotten and traditional solutions continue to be offered. In fact, some of the first documents that we shall have to study in the present chapter will echo the sounds of an earlier generation—works by philologists, in Latin, with rather more interest in Horace than in Aristotle—and such works will appear constantly throughout these years. The only major published commentary of the decade is Riccoboni's, and it is in Latin. Alongside it, we shall find several manuscript translations and commentaries in Italian, manifestations of the growing excitement within the academies.

The old tradition is clearly represented by Franciscus Portus' *In omnes Sophoclis tragoedias* Προλεγόμενα, published posthumously by his son Aemilius in 1584, probably written around 1575. One feels, indeed, that Portus is returning to the early Horatian commentaries of the beginning of the century, in spite of his frequent citation of Aristotle; some of the passages in the *Prolegomena* are direct translations of the *Poetics*, but they are followed by explanations which have a distinctly medieval flavor. We may take as an example his treatment of the *Ajax*. In one paragraph he collapses much of the content of the early chapters of Aristotle:

Tragedy, comedy, and indeed every form of poetry is derived from nature and from it receives its origin. In fact, man is born for imitation and adapted to it, as can immediately and easily be seen in children themselves, who learn by means of imitation to do whatever they do. Now men imitate either happy or sad things. For human life revolves almost entirely about these two pivots, I mean fortunate and unfortunate events. And thus those first men, some of them applying themselves to the former, others to the latter according to the difference of their talents, tried to express them by means of imitation. This came about at first by chance, as even Aristotle affirms. Then, the matter having come to the attention of those who were more skilled and more capable through the sharpness of their genius, both comedy and tragedy gradually grew and made progress, first modest, then considerable. It is believed that its origin springs from divine things.

Except for the last sentence, the paragraph is entirely out of Aristotle, and so is the following section on the origins of tragedy and its quantitative parts. But then Portus continues with an array of distinctions that recalls Donatus and Diomedes and Badius:

While there are other differences between tragedy and comedy, this is the principal distinction: in comedy the circumstances of men are middling, the fears small, small the perils, the endings happy; in tragedy on the other hand the persons are mighty, the fears great, the endings mournful. In the one, the first events are disturbed, the last are serene; in tragedy instead the beginnings are happy and peaceful, the endings are violent and sad. And in tragedy is portrayed the kind of life to be avoided, in comedy the kind to be sought. Lastly, comedy invents its subjects, tragedy often seeks them in historical truth.[1]

In the same prologue, Portus draws up a comparison between Euripides and Sophocles; in it, rhetorical criteria alternate with references to Aristotle. Euripides is praised for being more accessible to the ears of the people, more like an orator, more capable of inducing to action. This is because of the many sententiae and commonplaces which he uses and because of his skill in disputation. It is for his skill in moving the passions that Aristotle calls him τραγικώτατος, taken as meaning "aptissimus ad mouendos affectus." To Sophocles are applied such epithets as "grauis," "tragicus," "sublimis," "grandiloquus"; but he always tempers gravity with gaiety, severity with the sweetness of poetry. This gives pleasure. But he also arouses the tragic emotions of pity and wonder (translating οἶκτος, καὶ θαῦμα) and these vie with pleasure in the general effectiveness of his tragedies (p. 13). The use of the Greek phrase and its translation by "misericordia, & admiratio" (for the two tragic emotions) makes one wonder how clearly Portus, at this point, had the text of the *Poetics* in mind.

[1] *Prolegomena* (1584), p. 11: "Tragcedia, Comoedia, atque adeò omnis poësis à natura fluxit: & ab ea suum ortum accepit. homo enim ad imitandum natus, aptúsque est: id, quod etiam in ipsis statim infantibus facilè cerni potest, qui imitatione discunt agere quaecunque agunt, imitantur autem homines res vel laetas, vel tristes. Vita enim hominum in his quasi duobus vertitur cardinibus, secundis (inquam) rebus, vel aduersis. Primi itaque illi homines alij has, alij illas pro diuersitate ingeniorum, sequuti, eas imitando exprimere sunt conati, casu primùm hoc accidit vt Aristoteles etiam testatur: deinde re notata ab iis, qui erant solertiores, & ingenij acumine valebant, vtraque res, Comoedia, Tragoediáque paulatim creuit, & progressus primùm modicos, deinde magnos fecit. Ortus eius à rebus diuinis manasse creditur"; and p. 12: "Inter Tragoediam, & Comoediam cum alia intersunt, tum illud in primis est discrimen. in Comoedia mediocres fortunae hominum, parui metus, parua pericula, exitus laeti sunt. In Tragoedia contrà ingentes personae, magni metus, funesti sunt exitus: in illa, turbulenta prima, tranquilla postrema: in Tragoedia contrà, principia laeta & pacata, exitus turbulenti, & funesti: & in Tragoedia vita fugienda, in Comoedia vita expetenda exprimitur. Denique Comoedia fingit argumenta. Tragoedia saepe ab historica fide petit."

In 1576, the *In Q. Horatii Flacci librum de arte poetica commentarius* of Aldo Manuzio the Younger was added to the long list of such studies. It made the customary allegations of parallelism between Horace and Aristotle, but in surprisingly modest number (see Chapter V, p. 194). In the commentary itself there is very little of interest for the study of Aristotle. Manuzio prefaced it, however, by prolegomena in which he considers essentially one problem—the relationship between imitation and poetry—and here he does draw upon the *Poetics*. After an initial definition of poetry as an imitation using language and the additional means of rhythm, harmony, and meter, singly or together, he states that poetry may exist without verse—thus taking his position in the current quarrel. He thinks that Aristotle admits poetry with and without verse and that Plato's dialogues may thus be called poetry. He finds five genres enumerated by Aristotle, the epic, tragedy, comedy, the dithyramb and the gnome; and the question arises as to whether the last two contain imitation. Manuzio derives the answer from a series of distinctions about the dithyramb; the dithyramb, he says, sings the praises of Bacchus:

... now praises are either true or false; if they are true, it is a history and not an imitation; if they are false, what imitation can there be without the image of truth? A double answer suggests itself. For first, as concerns that part of imitation "which is made through λόγος," I concede that when true things are narrated, there is no imitation; about the false things I do not feel in the same way. For false things are either verisimilar or they are such as cannot happen. Every imitation is drawn from the verisimilar ones, nobody imitates those which cannot be done. But if with verisimilar things true ones are occasionally intermingled, the imitation ceases to exist insofar as true things are being narrated. Still, it does not cease to be poetry because of that, but since it continues to treat verisimilar things, it takes its name from the imitation. The fact is not that in tragedy and the epic there is no place for the true, but verisimilar things are more numerous than true ones. ... I therefore believe that the dithyramb is a poem because it consists of praises of Bacchus, some of which are true but the majority of which are verisimilar.[2]

Other demands of the definition are satisfied because the dithyramb also uses meter, rhythm, and harmony. The same argument is then applied to gnomic poetry. Manuzio reiterates the same ideas on truth and verisimili-

2 *Commentarius* (1576), pp. **-**v: "nam laudes aut uerae sunt, aut falsae. si uerae, historia est, non imitatio: si falsae, quae potest esse sine imagine ueritatis imitatio? Duplex occurrit responsio. nam, quod attinet primum ad eam partem imitationis, quae λόγῳ fit; concedo, cum uera narrantur, imitationem non esse; de falsis, non idem sentio. sunt enim falsa aut uerisimilia, aut quae fieri non possunt. ex uerisimilibus omnis ducitur imitatio: ea, quae fieri non possunt, imitatur nemo. quod si uerisimilibus admiscentur interdum uera; desinit esse imitatio, quatenus uera narrantur; nec tamen poesis non est ob eam caussam, sed, quia uerisimilia persequitur, ab imitatione nomen capit. non enim aut in tragoedijs, aut in epopoeia nihil ueri locum habet: sed uerisimilia plura, quam uera. ... Opinor igitur Poema esse, dithyrambum, quia constet ex Bacchi laudibus nonnullis fortasse ueris, plerisque tamen uerisimilibus."

tude in connection with lines 1–23 of the *Ars poetica*, on imitation as the distinguishing mark of the poet in connection with line 151 (pp. 2 and 35). Throughout, Manuzio reflects the concern of his contemporaries with the problem of truth; but he differs from many of them in admitting the possibility of poetry without verse.

Plato rather than Horace provides the point of departure for Lorenzo Gambara's *Tractatio de perfectę poëseos ratione* (1576). As has already been pointed out (Chapter VIII, pp. 305–8), it is a document which Christianizes Plato in order to make an appeal for a new Christian poetry. Aristotle enters the argument in several capacities. First, he is the authority for the preference for what is verisimilar and necessary to what is true, and this preference is turned by Gambara to his own purposes. Whoever portrays the perfect model of man, he says, departs from the truth and moves in the direction of what might be. The poetic art becomes one of meditation and actions are used as episodes: "A vast field is opened to pious and Christian writers, not for inventing, but for meditating piously many things and for drawing them from the springs of theology—things which are most useful and pleasant for the persuasion of human minds and well adapted moreover to receiving the narration of events inserted as episodes."[3] Aristotle's conception of poetry is thus completely reversed. Second, the *Poetics* gives as the natural causes of poetry the desire to imitate and harmony and rhythm; Gambara uses these as demonstrations of the precedence of Biblical writings over those of the Gentiles. Finally, Aristotelian elements enter prominently into a rather complex statement of the ends and workings of poetry:

... they set down a double end for poetry, the one imitation, the other instruction, so that the poetic power lies in seeing whatever may be adapted to the imitation of any action, passion, character, in pleasant language, for the amendment of life and for the promotion of a good and happy life. But if in imitation we must have regard for what we imitate, and why, and with what means, and in what manner, certainly ... the rule for every proper imitation must be sought in the very truth of the actions, and in actions of men gloriously accomplished, and in solid virtues.[4]

Here Aristotle's distinctions with respect to poetry are deliberately set aside in favor of rules which would further its didactic ends.

---

[3] *Tractatio* (1576), p. 23: "pijs & christianis scriptoribus latissimum patere campum ad multa non confingenda, sed piè meditanda, & ex theologię fontibus haurienda, quae vtilissima, iucundissimaque sint permouendis humanis ingenijs, rerum autem narrationi, interpositis illis tanquam episodijs, valde commoda."

[4] *Ibid.*, p. 24: "Duplicem porro finem Poëtices statuunt, imitationis alterum, alterum Doctrinae: vt poëtica facultas sit videndi quodcunque accommodatum sit ad imitationem cuiusque actionis, affectionis, moris, suaui sermone ad vitam corrigendam, & ad bene beateque viuendum. At si in imitatione spectandum est quid, quare, quo, & quomodo imitemur, sane ... ex ipsa rerum veritate, & rebus hominum praeclarè gestis, solidisque virtutibus petenda erit omnis rectissimae imitationis ratio."

ORAZIO CAPPONI AND TORQUATO TASSO (1576)

The next set of documents to be examined returns specifically to the *Poetics*. It consists in a set of remarks on Piccolomini and on Castelvetro by two writers, Orazio Capponi and Torquato Tasso, who were engaged in 1576 in a correspondence about these very questions. Of the two manuscripts by Orazio Capponi, the first, his *Censure sopra le annotationi della Poetica d'Aristotele del Rever.ᵐᵒ Monsig.ʳᵉ Alessandro Piccolomini*, is found in the Biblioteca Comunale of Siena, MS C.VI.9, folios 50–53v; I have assigned to it the date of 1576.[5] It contains a series of separate paragraphs on passages in Piccolomini which Capponi refers to by "particella" and page numbers; the general method is similar to that of Sassetti's *Discorso*. Capponi usually rejects Piccolomini's ideas in the particular passages studied, agreeing rather with those of Maggi, Vettori, or Robortello, or proposing his own solutions. Two major topics preoccupy him: whether "good" and "bad" (for persons imitated) constitute specific differences among genres, and whether the plots and characters of tragedy need to be previously known. Both were discussed by Sassetti. On the first, Capponi states firmly that by the distinction between good and bad objects Aristotle meant to establish a specific differentia (fol. 50v). He refers to 1448a16, on tragedy and comedy:

> Why then did Aristotle include it at this place, where it seems indeed that he is treating the specific differences which exist between these imitations? And there is no doubt that these differences of instruments, of things, and of the manner are specific. Why then should we want to say that they do not differentiate these two poems specifically? And if there were another specific difference between them which consisted in the things imitated, why would Aristotle not have mentioned it here?... And if there is another which does not consist in imitating the better or the worse with respect to character, we shall reprove Aristotle as one who enumerated only three of them for us, and not all of those that he should have.[6]

The question of how such goodness or badness is made known to the audience involves Capponi in a discussion of new and traditional plots and characters. He tries to steer a middle course between the conflicting views previously expressed. When both plot and persons are known, he says, the poet must conform in every way to the accepted opinions about them, lest his imitations appear false. When they are newly invented, their goodness or badness of character must be made apparent not only through their

5 See my "Nuove Attribuzioni . . .," *Rinascimento*, III (1952), 257–59.

6 MS Bibl. Com. Siena C.VI.9, fol. 51: "Perche dunque l'ha numerata Arist: in questo luogo doue par pur che tratti delle differenze specifiche che si ritrouano fra queste imitationi? e non è dubbio che queste differenze d'istromenti, di cose imitate, e del modo non sieno specifiche. per qual cagione dunque voliam dire che non diuersifichino specificamente questi due poemi? e se altra differenza specifica fusse fra loro che consistessi nelle cose imitate perche non harebbe fatto qui Aris: mentione?... E se altra ce n'è che non consista nell'imitar i migliori o peggiori in quanto a costumi riprenderemo Arist: come quello che n'habbia annouerate solamente tre, e non tutte quelle che deueua."

own choices and actions within the tragedy but also by expository reference to their past actions. Here the various devices of the dramatist's art must be used (fol. 53). Capponi's general position is that if characters are known, their actions must also be known through history. He thinks that Aristotle was arguing inconsistently when, at 1451b19, he declared that a tragedy might exist with no known personages in it; such a tragedy would be less perfect than one presenting known persons (fols. 52–52v).

Throughout, one of Capponi's main preoccupations is plot. He argues for Robortello and against Piccolomini on the interpretation of "a single action" and on the relationship of episodes to it. Aristotle's statement, at 1451a30, that all arts imitate a single thing seems to him to be a cogent refutation of those who would argue for multiplicity of plot or action (fol. 52). He points out, further, that a single episode is of necessity less moving than a whole plot: "If they are moved to compassion on hearing Oedipus' weeping, coming to see through it how he fell from a happy state into misery, they will also purge and diminish the other passions. . . . It is true that it will move and purge very little, since the interweaving of the whole action is not present."[7] This is a shrewd observation. On other passages his views are less acceptable. So for his agreement with Maggi and Vettori that the "one actor" of early tragedy must have been the one who expounded the plot (fol. 51v) and for his misunderstanding of Aristotle on spectacle at 1453b1.

The area of discussion is somewhat enlarged in Capponi's letter to Lionardo Salviati, dated September 27, 1576, and now found in the Ambrosian Library, MS Q. 113. Sup., folios 155–58. Capponi is apparently answering a request by Salviati for remarks which he might use in his own commentary on the *Poetics*; hence he remains less closely attached to Piccolomini (although some of the comments are repeated) and expresses more clearly his own opinions about Aristotle. He is also more directly concerned with textual matters (as in his notes on 1453b26 and 1448b37) and with general questions on the order of parts in the *Poetics* (as in his doubts whether 1454a3 ff. should appear where it does in the text). Some of the problems in the *Censure* reappear, approached now from a different angle. So for the question of "goodness" as a requisite of character; Capponi believes, after comparison of passages, that Aristotle means to require it of all characters, not only the one upon whom pity falls. He is willing to admit "bad" characters when they are necessary for the conduct of the tragedy (fol. 156). His discussion of unity of plot in tragedy involves considerations of both time and place in an interesting way. Challenging Aristotle's statement (1459b22) that the difference between tragedy and the

---

[7] *Ibid.*, fol. 52: "Se si moueranno a compassione nel sentir il pianto d'Edippo venendo a veder per questo com'egli di stato felice sia caduto in miseria purgheranno ancora gl'altri affetti, e li diminuiranno. . . . è ben uero che poco si mouerà, e poco si purgherà per non ui essere l'intessimento di tutta l'azzione."

epic in length and complexity of plot results from the difference between a dramatic and a narrative form, he maintains that the tragic plot may be just as complicated, that events which occur off stage may readily be narrated, and that such events are just as much "imitations" as those actually represented. The real difference, he says, is in the length of time involved, and he expresses surprise that Aristotle did not emphasize it further. Moreover, it is probable that the difference in place is also important:

> Perhaps it could be said that, while the epic can contain actions which are done in very remote places, and tragedy on the other hand can contain only those nearby, it would not be verisimilar to receive, within a matter of hours, information about other deeds. Therefore the epic may contain a greater diversity of episodes because in very remote places more diverse actions may take place than in those nearby.[8]

Capponi thus seems to be moving toward Castelvetro's position, if for different reasons. He disagrees with Aristotle, again, on the difficulty of perceiving a very small plot (1450b39). The smaller the better, in fact, for a small plot (unlike a small animal) would have fewer parts and their relationship would be easily perceptible. Finally, he thinks that at 1451a36 Aristotle is begging the question which he sets out to prove. We should note in this letter the serious attention paid to the text and its interpretation as well as the willingness to question the authority and the method of Aristotle.

In this letter to Salviati, Capponi speaks of having written to Torquato Tasso on the same day. Perhaps the subject was again Aristotle, for we have a letter from Tasso to Capponi, dated 1576, in which he speaks of his objections to Castelvetro, objections which he planned to state in a projected treatise.[9] Tasso's jottings have come down to us in a manuscript which is also at the Ambrosiana, and which was published in 1875 under the title of *Estratti dalla Poetica di Lodovico Castelvetro*. Using his copy of the 1570 edition of Castelvetro, Tasso makes extracts from it and to them appends his expressions of approval or disapproval. Most of these are brief, some are quite pungent; some, also, concern themselves with Aristotle directly. From them emerge Tasso's ideas on a number of central poetic questions. He rejects, first, Castelvetro's thesis that the materials of poetry and history are the same: "If the material of the poem were that of history, it would be the very same thing, and therefore it would not be 'similar.' Answer that one! Besides the poet would deserve no praise for

---

8 MS Ambrosiana Q.113.Sup., fols. 156v–57: "Fortasse dici posset, quod cum epopeia continere possit actiones quae in remotissimis locis gestę sunt. Tragedia autem eas tantum quae in uicinis alias non esset uerisimile spatio horarum resciri. Idcirco maiorem dissimilitudinem episodiorum potest continere cum in remotissimis locis magis diuersae fiant actiones quam in uicinis."

9 In *Lettere*, ed. Guasti, I, 195–96.

it, since he would have made no effort to invent it. This is a better reason."[10] If one thinks correctly about imitation, one will have the answer about the materials, for "the imitation required of poetry cannot be called imitation directly; but it can be called a rivalry of the poet with the arrangements of fortune or with the course of mundane affairs."[11] As for the end of such imitation, Tasso believes that it is restricted to pleasure (without utility) and that Aristotle meant to treat only such poems as are performed in the public square "for the pleasure of the people" ("per diletto del popolo," p. 285). Hence he quarrels with Aristotle for having introduced the whole question of purgation and for having treated it as he did, without proof and without cogent arguments.

Aristotle contradicts himself; for having said earlier, where he is seeking the origin of poetry, that its end is pleasure, he now directs tragedy toward utility, that is, the purgation of souls; of which utility no account at all must be taken, or at least not so much that because of it all the other kinds of tragedies, which do not have it, will be rejected. And if indeed we are to have some consideration for utility, why not of another kind of utility? as in those tragedies which contain the passage of good men from misery to happiness, which confirm the opinion that the people has about God's providence. And so forth.[12]

The whole argument is quickly summarized in a later passage: "you will see that the end of the poet is pleasure and that poetry is not an imitation of history. Read the text and the commentary; you will find inconsistency in Castelvetro."[13]

Tasso finds Castelvetro most unsatisfactory on matters of unity, especially when he advocates kinds of unity other than that of plot: "Note that it seems that Castelvetro holds that several actions may become one through the unity of time, of place, of person, not merely through dependency. This is most false."[14] The same epithet "falsissimo" is applied to Castelvetro's contention that all tragedies and comedies have double plots; this comes, says Tasso, from a false supposition that a variety of personages necessarily means a multiplicity of plots. He believes that the whole

10 In *Prose diverse*, ed. Guasti, I, 280: "Se la materia del poema fosse quella dell'istoria, sarebbe quell'istessa, e perciò non sarebbe simile. Rispondi tu a questa. Oltre di ciò il poeta non ne meritarebbe lode, perchè non si sarebbe faticato a trovarla. Questa è miglior ragione."

11 *Ibid.*, p. 284: "La imitazione richiesta a la poesia non si può chiamare direttamente imitazione; ma si può appellare gareggiamento del poeta e della disposizione della fortuna, o del corso delle mondane cose."

12 *Ibid.*, pp. 283–84: "Aristotile contraddice a se stesso, perchè avendo detto di sopra, là dove cerca l'origine della poesia, che 'l suo fine è 'l diletto, ora drizza la Tragedia a l'utilità, cioè a la purgazione degli animi; della quale utilità o non si deve tenere conto alcuno, o almeno non se ne deve tener tanto, che per lei si rifiutino tutte l'altre maniere di Tragedie, che ne son prive. E se pur dell'utilità s'ha d'aver considerazione; perchè non d'altra sorte d'utilità? come di quelle Tragedie, che contengono la mutazion de' buoni di miseria in felicità; le quali confermano l'opinione, che ha il popolo, della provvidenza di Dio, ec."

13 *Ibid.*, p. 290: "vedrai che 'l fine del poeta è 'l diletto, e che la poesia non è imitazion dell'istoria. Leggi il testo e 'l comento: troverai contrarietà nel Castelvetro."

14 *Ibid.*, p. 282: "Nota, che par che 'l Castelvetro voglia che più azioni possano divenir una per l'unità del tempo, del luogo, della persona, non solo per la dipendenza. Falsissimo."

difficulty may be solved by admitting the possibility of greater or less
simplicity within unity and that this will explain why the epic, while still
unified, is more complex than other forms (p. 294). On the epic specifically
(the form which interested him most personally), he states that it is capable
of greater magnificence, of a more marvelous quality, than other forms
(p. 289); by "magnificence" he means essentially the ornaments of language, justified in the epic by several of its peculiar conditions. Vergil
would thus seem to be superior to Homer as an epic poet: "Homer,
particularizing, was concerned with what is proper to poetry in general,
that is, imitation; Vergil, universalizing, had in mind what is proper to the
epic, that is, the magnificent."[15]

BALDINO (1576)

The most curious document of the year 1576 returns us to Aristotle
himself, presenting as it does a translation of the *Poetics* into Latin verse.
This is Bernardino Baldino's *Liber de arte poetica Aristotelis versibus
fideliter, et latine expressus*, published in Milan. The phrase "Liber de
arte poetica" in the title prepares us, in a way, for the general form and
tone of the translation; for Baldino makes of the *Poetics* a kind of Horatian
art of poetry, complete with an invocation to the muses and not without
an occasional anachronism such as reference to a Roman actor. At times
the original text is followed fairly closely, at others there are rapid sum-
maries or complete gaps. A general idea of Baldino's technique may be
had from the following lines, corresponding to the beginning of Aristotle's
text:

> Plura loqui nobis opus est, artemque poesis,
> Et genera, & uires; quo gratas texere pacto
> Fabellas deceat uatem, qui ducitur arte;
> Et quae membra sibi, quas culta poetica dotes
> Vendicet ars; ac cuncta tuo natura tenore
> Educam; notumque prius caput eloquar artis.
> Sunt imitatores alijque, aliique poetae.
> Vt qui cantat epos, tenui nec uoce tragoedus,
> Comicus & tenuis, dithrambique inclytus author;
> Atque alij, quibus est plectrum, queis tibia in usu.
> Vt propriis Helenes expressa coloribus ora
> Sunt Zeusi; caput ut Veneris depinxit Apelles.
> Hique uel à ritu docti, uel ab arte magistra.
> Roscius in scenis ut uerbis, gestibus, ore
> Voces, & gestus effinxit, & ora uirorum,
> Sic rhythmis, sic harmonia, sic uoce canora
> Assimilant aliis alij se, ceu citharoedus,
> Tibicenque aliique uelut queis tibia cordi.

15 *Ibid.*, p. 291: "Omero, particolareggiando, ebbe riguardo a quel che è proprio della
Poesia in generale, cioè l'imitare. Virgilio, universaleggiando, mirò al proprio dell'Epopeia,
cioè al magnifico."

It is clear that while the meaning of the text is given fairly accurately now and then, the exigencies of the verse and the desire to create a given poetic tone preclude the possibility of any careful distinctions of meanings. Sometimes, instead, the translation reflects all the current misconceptions about the sense of the text. We may take as an example the verses presenting the distinction between tragedy and epic:

> Inter epos, tragicumque poema hoc conuenit; ambo
> Reges, magnanimosque duces, genus atque Deorum
> Complectuntur; epos metris sed pergit eisdem
> Ad calcem: uariique pedes, numerique cothurnis
> Aptantur: tragicosque dies amplectitur una
> Actus: sed plures aeneis tenditur annos:
> Vtraque se quamuis extenderet ante poesis.
> Sed quas coepit epos sublime, recepit & omneis,
> Insuper ac alias inflata tragoedia partes.
>
> (Pp. B2–B2v; for 1449b7)

Or those which translate the definition of tragedy:

> Nunc mihi de tragicis est rebus sermo futurus.
> Nobilis, et nitido spectanda tragoedia cultu,
> Est grauis, egregiique actus imitatio, certos
> Ad fines porrecta, breui neque margine pressa:
> Cui musaea mele, cui mixta locutio rhytmis,
> Addita; quaeque metu, pietateque pectora flectit;
> Fluctibus ut uariis animos exoluat, & aestu.
>
> (P. B2v; for 1449b24)

Baldino's translation may be taken as a curious and unique exercise, reflecting a kind of accumulated popular tradition with respect to the *Poetics*, but making no serious contribution either to the translation or to the exegesis of the text.

SASSETTI (1576)

Filippo Sassetti's earlier work with the *Poetics*, both on Piccolomini's *Annotationi* for the Accademia degli Alterati and in his marginalia to the same book, may be considered as preparation for his own translation and commentary of Aristotle. He began to work on this in 1575 and probably interrupted it the following year; the manuscript (untitled, but commonly called the *Sposizione della Poetica*) is in the Biblioteca Riccardiana, MS 1539.[16] Sassetti made little more than a beginning on what was to have been a compendious volume, for the fragment of forty-five pages which we have goes only from the beginning of the *Poetics* to 1449a2 and includes as well a fairly long preface. Such as it is, it is full of original ideas on the *Poetics* and constitutes a clarification and expansion of what Sassetti had said in his earlier writings. Rather than taking the early commentators as its

16 See M. Rossi, *Filippo Sassetti*, pp. 25–26.

point of departure, it develops an independent analysis, discussing its predecessors only when necessary.

˙ Perhaps the distinguishing feature of Sassetti's approach is his determination to find an Aristotelian method for the analysis of Aristotle. Whereas others had been content to elucidate the *Poetics* by occasional reference to the *Ethics*, the *Politics*, and the *Rhetoric*, Sassetti goes instead to the *Organon* (and even to the *De partibus animalium*) for statements on such matters as the constitution of definitions, the inductive method, and the criticism of syllogistic structure. Hence, while others had been content with discovering the order of the parts of the text, he wishes rather to determine the philosophical reason for their presence in the treatise. Such a wish may have been prompted by his dissatisfaction with the method of Piccolomini and by his hope of improving upon all his predecessors; Castelvetro, for example, is severely chided for his logical deficiencies (fol. 115v). This does not mean that Sassetti proves in every respect to be a sound Aristotelian, for some of his solutions are doubtful; but his attention to method does result in many excellent interpretations.

This attention allows us to understand why he wrote the kind of preface he did for his commentary. For the preface seems at first reading to be a kind of Platonic statement of the didactic and political ends of poetry. Not only different genres, he says, but poems within each genre are distinguished by the kinds of persons they imitate, and these persons are paradigms of goodness or badness or of the middle state between the two. So for goodness: "one poem will imitate valorous men of high enterprise, placing before us the idea of the proper knight, of the true captain, and the form of the true king and lord, representing in each one of these kinds of men that character from which perfect teachings may be derived, with no possibility of learning any ugly thing from that work."[17] Sassetti maintains that we read all kinds of poetry for the pleasure which they afford; but some make us laugh, others make us weep. We must wonder, then, whether all kinds are good at all times and in all places. Sassetti answers that this depends upon the general state of happiness in the country:

This matter must be decided according to the various conditions in which men find themselves. For if some country abounds in great happiness, whence the citizens derive the highest joy, and if the souls of the good men must be in such wise habituated that in the midst of joys they realize that they can fall into misery, to such as these it might well not be good to show pleasurable spectacles which would distract their minds so considerably from believing that that good fortune might some time change, as every well prepared heart should do.[18]

17 MS Riccardiana 1539, fol. 81v: "luno imitera huomini ualorosi e dalto affare proponendoci l'idea del propio caualiere, del vero capitano, e la forma del uero Re e signore; fingendo in ciascuna di queste maniere dhuomini quel costume onde perfetti ammaestramenti possano trarsi; senza che cosa laida possa in quell opera appararsi."
18 *Ibid.*, fol. 82: "ma in cio debbe deliberarsi secondo i varij stati ne quali gl huomini si ritruouano; peroche abbondando alcuna terra di grandissima felicita donde ne cittadini somma letitia deriua e douendosi talmente assuefare gl animi de buoni che nelle allegrezze

The opposite would hold true for unhappy states. Now while it is the function of the poet to produce the desired effects, he neither decides which effects are wanted nor does he know by what precepts they may be achieved. He therefore needs to receive advice from two experts whose decisions are prior to his own: the magistrate or the prince who will tell him what effects are good for his contemporaries—politics thus becomes the reigning art—and the preceptor of poetics who will tell him how to achieve the effects in exactly the correct degree. Aristotle falls into the third category, and the *Poetics* "contains nothing but the precepts and the instructions to poets on how to compose their poems well."[19] Sassetti establishes a hierarchy among the three arts: "the order among these three arts will be such that politics will be the noblest and the most important, as the one that commands; after it will be poetry; and in the third place will be put that faculty which shows poets in what way they must compose their poems."[20]

The first function of Sassetti's preface is thus to separate the determination of the ends from the writing of poems on the one hand and from the setting down of precepts on the other hand. Its second function is to discover what method Aristotle uses in writing the *Poetics*, and for light on this Sassetti turns to the distinction of methods which he finds in Galen. Galen, he says, had described three possible methods: a method by definition, which defines its object, analyses the definition into parts, and then treats each of the successive parts; a method by composition (the opposite of the first), which by division discovers each of the component parts of an object and then combines them into a conception of the whole; and a method by resolution, which proceeds from the knowledge of an end to the discovery of the means to its achievement. As an example of the first (or analytical) order, Sassetti cites Galen's own works on the medical art; of the second (or synthetic) order, Aristotle's treatises on natural objects and his *Organon*, which moves from nouns and verbs to syllogisms and demonstrations; of the third (or resolutive) order, Galen's writings on the curative art, Aristotle's *Ethics* and certain of the logical treatises which move from a knowledge of the syllogism and of demonstration to a study of their necessary components. The case is thus clear for the *Poetics*:

... since it has no other purpose than to explain the things which are necessary for their composition [i.e., of poems], and since I showed that this is found by means of the method of resolution, it is clear that in this treatise the precepts will

---

stimino di potere cadere nelle miserie a costoro facilmente non istara bene il mostrare i piaceuoli spettacoli i quali tanto maggiormente distrarrebbono lanimo loro dal riputare che possa quella fortuna per alcun tempo cangiarsi come pensare dourebbe ogni bene preparato petto."

19 *Ibid.*, fol. 82*v*: "in esso altro non si contiene che precetti e ammaestramenti a Poeti per che bene compongano le loro Poesie."

20 *Ibid.*, fol. 83: "tale adunque sara lordine tra queste arti che la Politica sara la piu nobile e la principale come quella che comanda; dopo a lei sara la Poesia; e nel terzo luogo si riporrà quella faculta, che dimostra a poeti in che maniera deono comporsi le Poesie."

be given through the method of resolution, insofar as the principal purpose is concerned. But because it is necessary, if we wish to write this or that poem, to know what it is and what it is good for, the demonstration of which is a result of definition, it was therefore necessary in the first part of this book to use the method of definition, which is itself necessarily preceded by the divisive method; for no definition can be obtained without the latter.[21]

As Sassetti sees the *Poetics*, its main problem in the early chapters is that of definition; before giving the precepts for the correct composition of poems, precepts which constitute the "art," it must seek the definition of poetry by inquiring first into its matter and its form, then into the combination of the two. The initial section, up to the definition of tragedy, will treat "of poetry in general and in itself" ("della poesia insomma e di per se," fol. 87v), after which it will discuss the species with respect to their natures, omitting for the time being their subject matter and other differentiating factors. Afterward will come the detailed treatment of each kind. This, says Sassetti, is the same method as that which Aristotle followed in the *Categories*, essentially a search for the genus through induction, passing from less universal to more universal considerations, then a discovery of the differentiae and the constitution of the species. Sassetti keeps this plan constantly in mind as he comments on the successive passages of the treatise. Thus, the first sentence is said to contain the "general proposition" of the work; the second is an indication of the genus; the third lists the three differentiae; the fourth (1447a18), as it distinguishes the three means of poetry, makes possible the later definitions of the separate species. When he comes to the point (1448a24) at which Aristotle summarizes the three differentiae, he digresses from his orderly commentary on passages and reduces the materials to tabular form, as follows:

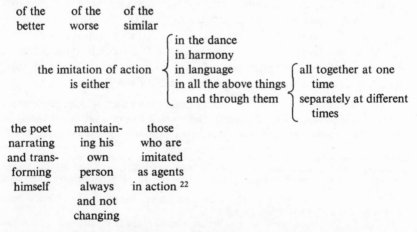

of the better	of the worse	of the similar		
the imitation of action is either		in the dance in harmony in language in all the above things and through them		all together at one time separately at different times
the poet narrating and transforming himself	maintaining his own person always and not changing	those who are imitated as agents in action [22]		

21 *Ibid.*, fol. 84v: "non hauendo altro intendimento che lo spianare le cose che a comporle si ricercano; et hauendo io dimostro che cio si ritroua per mezzo della resolutiua disposizione

Sassetti maintains that the definition of every poetic species may be derived from this table, and he offers some examples. But he qualifies Aristotle's treatment by insisting that it covered only the "perfect" species: ". . . it should be clearly noted that since in this book the precepts of true and perfect poems are given, only those things are considered in it which belong to these poems, and the precepts for them are given."[23] Thus Aristotle should not be blamed for his failure to treat so "imperfect" a form as the pastoral.

If he is to treat poetry completely, Aristotle must include in his method a consideration of all four causes. Sassetti believes that he does. The elements entering into the definition provide two of the causes, the material and the formal; the others will come along later, and we shall thus have all four causes

. . . which (because poems are inventions of our intellect which imitates nature) will be four just as the causes of natural things are four, which are composed of matter and of form and have the efficient cause which made them and the end for which they were made. [These will all be found in poems:] . . . since these also have that element which, in proportion, corresponds to matter and that which corresponds to form, which are the imitation common to all kinds and the differences . . . these are causes which are in poetry just as matter and form are in natural things.[24]

---

manifesta cosa che in questo trattato i precetti saranno dati con la resolutiua dispositione; quanto appartiene allo intendimento principale; ma perche e bisogna a voler comporre questo o quel poema sapere quello che egli è et a quello che egli è buono il che dimostrare è effetto della diffinitione però e stato di mestieri nella prima parte d'esso libro adoperare la diffinitiua dispositione alla quale necessariamente ua innanzi la diuisiua non si potendo senza essa procacciare alcuna diffinitione."

22 *Ibid.,* fol. 115: "de migliorj de peggiori de simili

			⌈ nel ballo	
			nella armonia	
			nell oratione	
l'imitatione d attione e o		⟨	in tutte le	⌈ tutte insieme in
			sopradette	vno stesso
			cose e per ⟨	tempo
			queste	separatamente
			⌊	⌊ en diuersi tempi

| narrando e tra-
mutandosi il
poeta | conseruando la
sua persona
sempre e non si
mutando | come adoperanti
enfaccendati co-
loro che simi-
tano." |

23 *Ibid.,* fol. 108v: "egli si dee bene auuertire che dandosi in questo libro i precetti delle poesie uere et perfette quelle cose solamente in esso si considerano che a queste si appartengono & sene danno i precetti."

24 *Ibid.,* fol. 118v: "lequali (percioche sono le poesie inuentioni dello intelletto nostro che imita la natura) saranno quattro sicome quattro sono le cagioni delle cose naturali. le quali sono composte di materia e di forma, et hanno la causa efficiente che le fece, el fine per il quale esse furono fatte. . . . hauendo esse ancora quello che proportionatamente risponde alla materia e quello che alla forma; che sono l'imitatione comune a tutte quante; e le differenze . . . lequali sono cagioni che sono nella poesia si come la materia e la forma sono nelle cose naturali."

As for the efficient and the final causes, Sassetti finds them in the paragraph on the natural origins of poetry (1448b4). To distinguish them, he must divide the paragraph differently from Maggi (whose divisions he normally follows), breaking it after the parenthetical section ending with πρῶτας. In this way the natural disposition to imitation becomes the efficient cause and the pleasure derived from imitation becomes the final cause. The relationship between the two is stated by Sassetti as follows:

Since this power [of imitation] is one of the cognitive ones, which operate for pleasure or for utility or for what is honest, it follows that one or several or all of these things moved it [the human mind] to generate poetry. But because Aristotle says that the cause was the joy that every man finds in things which imitate, it follows that pleasure is the end which moved the human mind to create poetry, even though this pleasure may be such that it can include the useful and the honest. . . . poems must be used which are composed in such a way that they delight us and bring profit to us honestly.[25]

In the last parts of this passage, Sassetti allows himself to be influenced by the theory which produced his preface, and there may be some doubt about the solidity of his own method at this point.

Applying these various methodological distinctions to the text of the *Poetics*, Sassetti discovers to us his own interpretation of the text. In the light of what earlier commentators had done with it, he is obliged to decide whether imitation is the genus of poems or whether another genus, "poetry," is interposed between imitation and the individual species. He rejects his predecessors and affirms that the genus is imitation; as for poetry, it will be "a name given to its single species considered altogether, without its having any proper differentia or any proper nature which is distinct from each one of these species in a way that they would possess one differentia more than it; and imitation will be the true genus whence the essence of the species is derived."[26] Object, manner, and means are the differentiae which divide the genus. In connection with them, Sassetti makes the following philosophical statement on their function in the "art":
". . . but because those things by which one species is different from another are those of which they are composed, and these are the same ones which divide the generic nature, hence it is that one may say that the three differentiae named, through which one kind of poem is different from another, are

25 *Ibid.*, fol. 119v: "essendo questa potenza una delle cognoscitiue lequali si muouono per il diletto o per l utile o per l honesto egli ne seguita che una di queste tre cose o piu o tutte siano state quelle che l hanno mossa allo ingenerare la poesia; ma perche Aristotile dice che questa e stata il rallegrarsi ciascuno delle cose che imitano e ne seguiterà che il diletto sia il fine che mosse l'intelletto humano a creare la poesia auuenga che questo diletto sia tale che e possa comprendere el utile el honesto. . . . adoperare si deono le poesie in maniera disposte che elle ci dilettino e ci giouino honestamente."
26 *Ibid.*, fol. 89v: "uno nome posto alle spetie singolari dessa tutte insieme considerate senza che ella habbia una propia differenza o una propia natura laquale sia diuersa da ciascuna desse spetie perche elleno abbondino duna differenza piu di lei e limitatione sara il vero genere donde lessenza delle spetie si piglia."

the ones which divide the imitation."[27] In such judgments as these the methodological concern is paramount.

When he comes to the actual discussion of the differentiae, Sassetti finds himself on much more controversial ground. Means, object, and manner had been interpreted in many ways, and he must decide among them; and almost everywhere he makes decisions of a partisan nature which are not justified by the *Poetics* itself. So, for example, with respect to the means. He translates the terms for the three means as "nel ballo; nell oratione; e nell armonia" and provides a lengthy discussion of all three. The meaning of λόγος especially troubles him, and after examination of his predecessors, he decides that it must include the concept of verse (fols. 94–94ν); no poetry is possible without verse. Hence, at a later point the translation becomes "ballo, melodia, verso" (fol. 100), and all the passages which traditionally aroused dispute—1447a28, 1448a11—are interpreted in such a way as to corroborate his thesis.

The difficulty with respect to the objects of imitation is to know what is meant by "good" and "bad," by "better," "worse," and "like." Sassetti takes a strong position against Piccolomini on this point, insisting that these distinctions do constitute a substantial differentia, capable of distinguishing one genre from another. He proposes his own theory that, however one interprets the terms themselves, they must be taken as referring "to actions, and not to the condition in which men have been placed by fortune."[28] Therefore, any theory which ascribes to them a distinction of status or station or condition will be false, and Sassetti disagrees both with Piccolomini and with the earlier commentators. He finds a solution rather in his contemporary Agnolo Segni, whose lectures he must have heard or read in their original form (1573)—unless, of course, he had access to the revised version before its publication:

I find much more probable the opinion of messer Agnolo Segni, who believes that by the "better" Aristotle here meant the heroes, who are not called "better" because they were masters of the others but because—since it was thought that they descended in some way from those false and lying gods—it was probable that in them were to be found greater vigor both of mind and of body, joined with greater prudence, than were to be found in men of Aristotle's time.[29]

27 *Ibid.*, fols. 90ν–91: "ma perche quelle cose per lequali una specie è dall altra diuersa sono quelle delle quali elle si compongono e questo sono le medesime che diuidono la natura generica di qui è che dire si possa le tre nominate differenze per lequali luna poesia e differente dall altra; sono quelle che diuidono l'imitatione."
28 *Ibid.*, fol. 107ν: "ha riguardo alle attioni; e non allo stato nel quale sono gli huomini stati posti dalla fortuna."
29 *Ibid.*, fol. 103ν: "molto piu uerisimile giudico io che sia loppinione di ms. Agnolo Segni il quale per i migliori crede che fussono intesi qui da Aristotele gl'eroi i quali non sono chiamati migliori perche e fossono signori degl'altri; ma perche stimandosi che e discendessono in qualunque maniera da quegli Dij falsi e bugiardi; uerisimile era che in loro fusse e maggior uigore d'animo e di corpo aggiunta con maggiore prudenza che negl huominj del secolo dAristotile non si ritrouaua." Note that in a letter of 1573 (MS Riccardiana 2438 bis, Pt. III) to Lorenzo Giacomini, Sassetti speaks of Segni's lectures: "egli stesso studia la Poetica leggentela il segni con bella frequenza" (fol. 2).

Social station here seems to be replaced by qualities of body and of soul rather than by the accident of divine descent, although Sassetti does not go so far as to make of it an ethical distinction. "Likeness" would differ from the other two terms by referring to the present century; for it is possible to imitate virtuous and good actions as well as wicked and bad ones in our own time (fol. 104). In any case, Sassetti reiterates his insistence that these differences must be considered in actions (fol. 103v).

On the subject of the manner, Sassetti runs afoul of the old Platonic use of "imitation" to mean dramatic representation, and all his care for method does not enable him to untangle the knot. He discards Castelvetro's notion that there is a "modo similitudinario" in addition to the three manners usually distinguished, as he discards Piccolomini's refinements on the mixed manner. But he cannot see how a poem can be an imitation—and hence a poem—if the poet speaks constantly in his own person. The dithyramb is pure narration; it becomes an imitation only because its other two means, harmony and the dance, are added. And a work such as Vergil's *Moretum*, spoken entirely by the poet, cannot rank either as poem or as epic (fols. 107–112v).

We must regard some of Sassetti's failures as deriving from the deficiencies of his own method and from the pressures of tradition. Others, such as the lengthy wonderings over the use of ἐποποιία at 1447a29, are ascribable to an erroneous reading of the text, which the state of scholarship in his time did not permit him to correct. On the whole, however, his commentary must be regarded as one of the most remarkable of the period—especially because of his careful study of method—and we can only regret that he did not push it beyond the first few chapters of the *Poetics*. His promises to treat utility as an end in connection with purgation and the pure narrative form in connection with the dithyramb remain unfulfilled.

In 1578, Francesco Bonciani delivered before the Accademia Fiorentina his *Lettione della prosopopea*, now found in three manuscripts in the Biblioteca Riccardiana. This differs from other works of its kind in treating, rather than a literary genre, a rhetorical figure used in various genres. Orators, poets, and philosophers alike represent inanimate objects and animals as human beings, and such representations constitute the figure called prosopopoeia. Aside from its connections with Horace and Plato (see Chapter VI, p. 201 and Chapter VIII, p. 310), this lecture belongs to the Aristotelian tradition by virtue of its development of a theory of imitation for this figure. Imitation, according to Bonciani, may be of four classes of objects: the true, the verisimilar, the false, and the impossible; of these, prosopopoeia imitates impossible things and those false things which are not verisimilar. Since this imitation generates pleasure—the marvelous teaches us things we did not previously know—Bonciani is able to constitute thus his definition of prosopopoeia: "An imitation of impossible things, in an appropriate way, made in the simple narrative mode, or the mixed, or the dramatic, in order to teach or to delight or to persuade."[30] He is careful to point out that imitation, here, does not mean dramatic representation but has rather that broader sense given to it elsewhere by Aristotle, especially in the *Rhetoric:* "a person by means of words represents the form and the nature of a thing and gives it motion."[31] The imitation of the impossible itself becomes possible through the workings of the imagination, which combines known parts into an unknown and unnatural whole. "In an appropriate way" in the definition is explained by an example: one must not animate objects which, in their natures, are too far distant from animate things, as Petrarch did with his sighs. Other kinds of appropriateness are demanded within the figure, and they seem to be related either to decorum or to verisimilitude. Of the three ends mentioned in the definition, pleasure is the servant of instruction, although it is sometimes used alone by the poets, as persuasion (by means of prosopopoeia, of course) is by the orators. Bonciani thus constructs a kind of "little poetics" around the figure of speech which he has chosen to elucidate.

All the preliminary materials accompanying the editions of Sforza d'Oddo's comedy, *L'Erofilomachia, ouero Il duello d'amore & d'amicitia,* bear the date of 1572, and the exact date of August 1, 1572 is found at the end of Bernardo Pino da Cagli's *Discorso intorno al componimento della comedia de' nostri tempi,* which is printed with it. I am treating the *Discorso* at the present place, however, because I have found no edition of it earlier than 1578. The *Discorso,* in the midst of a discussion which is essentially Horatian in its sources and theory, calls upon Aristotle for enlightenment on two matters, the distinction between tragedy and comedy and the limitation of the comic subject. For Bernardo Pino, the basic difference between the two dramatic genres lies in the social status of their subjects, and he interprets Aristotle in this light:

Comedy must not be the imitation of men who are more unfortunate or wicked, as would seem to be indicated by the word φαυλοτέρων which means viler and lower men, but of persons low and abject in comparison with those who are introduced in tragedy; for in tragedy princes and kings and other persons of highest station are introduced . . . and in comedy men of humble condition are introduced, such as gentlemen and private citizens.[32]

---

30 MS Ricc. 1539. fol. 134: "Imitatione di cose impossibili in maniera conueneuole fatta nel modo narratiuo semplice o misto, o nel rappresentatiuo a fine d'insegnare, o dilettare, o persuadere."

31 *Ibid.,* fol. 134v: "altri con parole ritragga la forma, e l'abito d'una cosa, e mouimento le dia."

32 In *L'Erofilomachia* (1578 ed.), p. A9: "non debbe esser la Comedia imitatione de huomini piu tristi, o piu ribaldi, come par, che noti la parola, φαυλοτέρων, che vuol dire huomini piu vili, & piu bassi, ma di persone in comparatione di quelle, che sonno introdotte nella Tragedia, bassi & abietti, essendo in essa Tragedia introdotti, Prencipi & Regi, & altre persone de grandissimi stati . . . & nella Comedia, introducendosi huomini di humile conditione, come sono Gentilhuomini, & Cittadini priuati."

The point is restated later (p. b), and Pino adds the judgment that the actions of tragedy are, in the last analysis, more wicked than those of cómedy, whose heroes are not necessarily characterized by greater vices, greater crimes, or worse actions; they are merely of inferior station. The question thus arises with respect to the kind of "badness" to be attributed to comic characters, and again Pino gives Aristotle's answer:

... even if Aristotle in the *Poetics* says, almost openly, that the subject upon which the whole argument of comedy rests is vice (called by him κακία), such vice is not as a result totally that which is the contrary of virtue, but rather that which is opposed to beauty, that is, ugliness or deformity. ... vice cannot, by its nature, generate any praiseworthy or fruitful pleasure.[33]

The nature of this ugliness and a definition of comedy are developed more specifically in the following passage:

Nor by "ugly" are we always to understand what is dishonest and obscene, for by themselves such words as "obscene" and "dishonest" always have the meaning of evil; but we must take as ugly that which does not have its parts in proportion and in a proper relationship. ... Comedy is therefore an imitation of persons and of actions lower and more abject than those which are described in tragedy, and it must move to laughter and to pleasure just as tragedy moves to pity and to terror.[34]

Pino's Aristotelianism is thus mixed; it is fairly correct in its understanding of the ridiculous and the ugly, it is wrong in its affirmation that the differences between tragic and comic characters are exclusively social differences.

RICCOBONI (1579)

Antonio Riccoboni's work on the *Poetics*, constituting in its totality the last of the "great commentaries" in Latin to appear in the Cinquecento, resembles Piccolomini's in that it was published in two stages, translation first, then commentary. Riccoboni had professed the *Poetics* at Padua, and in 1579 he added to a volume which also contained his translation of the *Rhetoric* the following items related to the *Poetics*: a prefatory notice entitled *Quomodo ars poetica sit pars logicae*; a brief set of *Variae quaedam lectiones*; a translation into Latin, accompanied by marginal topical headings; and a treatise *De re comica*. The lengthy commentary was not to appear until 1585. But the preliminary notice of 1579 examines the argu-

---

[33] *Ibid.*, p. A11: "se bene Aristotile nella Poetica, quasi alla scoperta dice, che'l soggetto in cui s'appoggia tutto l'argomento della Comedia è'l vitio da lui detto κακία, tal vitio non è perciò totalmente quello, che è contrario alla virtù, ma quel che s'appone [sic] alla bellezza, cioè la brutezza, ò deformità. ... il vitio non puo di sua natura generare piacere alcuno lodeuole, & fruttuoso."

[34] *Ibid.*, pp. A9v, A10v: "Ne per brutto si dee sempre intendere il dishonesto & l'osceno, che per se stesse tali parole d'osceno, & di dishonesto, hanno sempre significato di male: ma per brutto l'ha da prendere, quel che non ha le sue parti proportionate, & corrispondenti. ... E adunque la Comedia, vna imitatione da persone & di cose piu vile & piu abiette, che non si descriuono nella Tragedia, & debbe muouere al riso e al piacere, come la Tragedia alla misericordia & a l'errore." The text is very bad throughout and full of typographical errors.

ments of those who had previously studied the relationship of poetry to logic: Bartolomeo Lombardi, who had maintained that poetry uses both the enthymeme and the example, just as rhetoric does; and Iacopo Zabarella, who, in his *Logic,* had held that poetry teaches by using examples of things or actions (rather than words) and that any art which does so belongs to logic. Riccoboni is astonished at the latter argument, since he believes— and he cites Aristotle as his authority—that all argumentation takes place in the words which express things rather than in the things themselves. He agrees with Zabarella on one point—poetry uses syllogism and paralogism—but he would revise the position by saying that its purpose is "to teach the use of reasoning powers in imitation."[35] A comparison with rhetoric helps him to delimit further the role of poetry: "Poetry indeed has certain things in common with rhetoric, certain others proper to itself. The common ones are sententiae, character, and diction; the proper one is plot."[36] One of the functions of sententiae is to present arguments; but according to the *Poetics,* this function is more properly a part of rhetoric, as are the other tasks of appealing to the passions and of augmenting and diminishing. The only way in which poetry will properly belong to logic is through its one distinctive element, plot. Now Aristotle indicates that recognition and reversal are beautiful parts of the plot, that recognition involves a kind of syllogism which is proper to the art of poetry; this art is consequently a part of logic. Riccoboni concludes:

For although it has many things which do not belong to logic, nevertheless it is sufficient that in some outstanding aspect it may be called logic; just as also is the case with rhetoric, which contains not only the demonstrative discourse through which it is assigned to logic but also character and passions and moreover language and the order of its parts; nevertheless it is said to be a part of logic because of one device of demonstration. Similarly poetry, in addition to sententia which it has in common with rhetoric, treats not only plot whose most important part, which is called recognition, needs the syllogism, but also character and diction and harmony and spectacle; nevertheless because of one form of reasoning which is employed in plot construction, and instruction in whose use is pertinent in the extreme to the plot itself, it seemed to the great philosopher Averroës and to others that it should be called a part of logic.[37]

35 *Aristotelis ars poetica* (1579), p. 378: "docere vsum ratiocinandi in imitatione."

36 *Ibid.,* p. 378: "Ac Poetica quidem habet quaedam sibi communia cum Rhetorica: quaedam propria. Communia sunt, sententia, mores, & dictio. propria est fabula."

37 *Ibid.,* pp. 382–83: "Nam tametsi multa habeat, quae non pertinent ad Logicam: tamen suffict, ut in aliqua re praecipua appellari Logica possit; quemadmodum etiam euenit Rhetoricae, quae non solam continet oratoriam demonstrationem, propter quam reducitur ad Logicam, sed simul mores, & affectus, & praeterea elocutionem, ac partium dispositionem: tamen dicitur pars Logicae propter unum artificium demonstrationis. Sic Poetica praeter sententiam, quam ipsa habet cum Rhetorica communem, non unam fabulam tractat, cuius praecipua pars, quae dicitur agnitio, indiget syllogismo; sed mores quoque, & dictionem, & harmoniam, & apparatum: tamen propter unam ratiocinationem, quae fit in fabula, cuiusque usum docere ad ipsam potissimum spectat, videtur ab Auerroe maximo philosopho, & ab aliis fuisse pars Logicae appellata."

The reference to Averroës indicates his continued influence, even late in the century, on the interpretation of the *Poetics*.

`The "variae lectiones" are few in number and not of any great originality. Riccoboni merely justifies his choice, at various difficult points in the text, of one of the solutions proposed by his predecessors, and he does so largely to explain why he translated as he did. Sometimes his decisions are good, as when he discards the troublesome ὡς πέρσας at 1448a15; elsewhere they are bad, as when he adopts ἀμφοτέροις at 1447a20 in place of διὰ τῆς φωνῆς and translates it by "alij autem vtrisque" (p. 386). Their total effect upon the translation is small. Riccoboni's translation is itself characteristic of his times, for it constitutes a kind of vulgarization of the Latin text. He makes every effort to render his version accessible to the reader. Marginal notations summarize the content of the adjacent passages— the kind of notations that readers of earlier translations and commentaries had to write in for themselves—and provide a sort of running index. Moreover, they frequently raise the problems which were most discussed by the commentators; for example, opposite the sentence (at 1447a28) "Epopoeia vero solum sermonib. nudis, vel metris," Riccoboni writes "Quidam exponunt, uel, pro Idest," thus raising the moot question about prose and verse. Immediately afterward, the margin bears this query: "An Epopoeia possit fieri soluta oratione," making the same question even more specific (p. 386). At times conveniently numbered lists are added to the margins, and wherever feasible Riccoboni inserts references to works cited. The text is broken up into major sections, according to Riccoboni's own division, unnumbered but clearly titled. Paragraphs and sentences are also so broken up, sometimes with the addition of numbers, to produce an almost tabular effect. For example, the definition of tragedy appears as follows (p. 392):

1. Est igitur Tragedia imitatio.
2. actionis probae,
3. & perfectae,
4. magnitudinem habentis,
5. suaui sermone,
6. separatim singulis formis in partib. agentib.
7. & non per enarrationem,
8. sed per misericordiam, & metum inducens talium perturbationum purgationem.

Many of these mechanical devices were dropped when the text was reprinted in 1587, but some of them were expanded and exploited.

I think that we may state thus Riccoboni's principles for the translation: To achieve a Latin version simpler and more readable than those heretofore available; to adopt, by means of the translation itself, a firm stand on as many of the disputed questions of the text as possible; to render apparent the order, the parts, and the method of the original work. The first of these ends is obtained through a number of devices. Riccoboni simplifies Latin word order in such a way as to make it almost as straightforward as Italian word order; he eliminates all flourishes of style, all farfetched words, all useless attempts at variety and sonority; he adopts a uniform terminology which eliminates ambiguity and doubt. The results of this effort may be seen in a comparison of the following passage (1447a18) as it is handled by Maggi and by Riccoboni:

Maggi, p. 39: Vt enim coloribus, atque figuris pleraque quidam aemulantes imitantur, hi quidem arte, consuetudine illi, nonnulli etiam uoce: ita quoque & in dictis artibus accidit. etenim omnes imitationem exercent, numero dico, sermone, harmonia; hisque uel separatim, uel promiscue.

Riccoboni, p. 386: Vt enim, & coloribus, & figuris multa imitantur aliqui effigiem exprimentes, partim quidem per artem, partim vero per consuetudinem; alij autem vtrisque: sic in dictis artibus omnes quidem faciunt imitationem in numero, & oratione & harmonia; atq. his separatim, aut mixtis.

Latinity has suffered, but something more palatable to the Italian reader has been achieved. For consistency of terminology, we may take the case of the crucial words βελτίονας and χείρονας, which Aristotle uses for "better" and "worse" at 1448a4 and –a17. Maggi translates by "meliores" and "deteriores" at the first place, by "praestantiores" and "humiliores" at the second (thereby prejudicing the interpretation); whereas Riccoboni uses "meliores" and "peiores" throughout.

As for the second of the main objectives—to make the translation a kind of interpretation—we have seen that Riccoboni is at times obliged to resort to his marginalia for clarifications. Thus at 1448a4, having translated ἢ καθ' ἡμᾶς by "quàm secundum nos," he explains in the margin: "... secundum nos id est quàm homines praesentis aetatis, uel quàm homines communes, quales nos sumus" (p. 387). This, of course, leaves the choice to the reader; at other points the stand is much clearer. On page 405, two of the requisites for character are explained in the margin: "Similitudo refertur ad eos de quibus alij scripserunt," "Aequalitas ad eos, de quibus nos primum scribimus." In the text itself, the renderings may seem unremarkable; but in such a passage as that on the tragic hero, the words that I have italicized constitute decisions on much-debated issues:

Est autem talis, qui neque virtute praestat, & iustitia. Neque propter vitium, & prauitatem *mutatur in aduersam fortunam,* sed *propter errorem aliquem.* Eorum, qui sunt *in magna existimatione,* & *fortunae prosperitate,* cuiusmodi Oedipus, & Thyestes, & qui *ex talibus familijs* illustres uiri sunt. Necesse enim est egregie se habentem fabulam simplicem esse magis, *quam duplicem,* vt quidam dicunt (p. 401).

The third objective, concerning order and method, is largely reached by means of the mechanical devices already mentioned, the main one of which is the breaking up of the text into short, numbered sentences.

For his *De re comica* (expanded and republished in 1585 as the *Ars comica*), Riccoboni had before him the example of Robortello's *De comoedia*, printed as an adjunct to the 1548 commentary on the *Poetics*; he could also consult, on a more limited subject, the *De ridiculis* which Maggi added to his own volume in 1550. But whereas Robortello spends most of his time in a paraphrase of the *Poetics*, making a few alterations to adapt its principles to comedy, and in a retailing of the traditional saws about the form, and whereas Maggi leaves these things aside in order to write a treatise on laughter, Riccoboni addresses himself to the task of constructing a new art of comedy. He bases it on Aristotle's statements about poetry in general as well as about tragedy and the epic, and it springs from his total conception of Aristotle's method in the *Poetics*. That is, he attempts to apply Aristotle's basic distinctions to the treatment of the comic genre (his statement of intentions is quoted above, Chapter II, p. 53) and to devote a single chapter to each of the major subjects: the origin of comedy, its definition, its qualitative parts, its quantitative parts, and the ridiculous. It should be pointed out here that the conception and the application of the method are less well developed in 1579 than they will be in 1585.

Riccoboni seems to take as his point of departure the "laus : vituperatio" distinction of Averroës, which permits him to classify hymns and encomia, then tragedy and the epic, under "laus," iambic songs and comedy under "vituperatio." Comedy belongs in a subcategory of forms which blame by means of the ridiculous. It is defined in fairly rudimentary terms: "Comedy is defined as an imitation, which is made by means of language, the dance, and harmony, through the mode of action, of a matter consisting of that vice which moves to laughter."[38] As Riccoboni elaborates his gloss on this definition, he reveals his position on one of the current debates, concerning the means of imitation. He states that prose is not acceptable in comedy. Distinguishing between usage, which authorizes prose, and reason, which does not, he argues that verse is necessary in all poetic genres, "not because verse constitutes the nature of poetry, but because it is its proper instrument or vestment."[39] He holds that any poem in prose is a defective poem; for comedy, moreover, prose is too weak an instrument and fails to command an audience assembled in the theater.

Riccoboni's discussion of the qualitative parts revolves largely about plot ("fabula" is defined as "the composition of the materials, which imitates actions performed outside of the stage," "Fabula est rerum compositio, quae actiones extra scenam habitas imitatur," p. 442). And for plot he establishes eight requisites:

38 *Ibid.*, p. 438: "Definitur Comoedia, vt sit imitatio, quae fit sermone, saltatione, harmonia, per modum actiuum, in materia eius vitij, quod mouet risum."
39 *Ibid.*, p. 439: "non quòd versus constituat naturam poesis, sed quia sit proprium instrumentum, uel uestimentum eius."

1. Debet esse tota;
2. Debet congruentem magnitudinem habere;
3. Debet esse una;
4. Debet esse verisimilis;
5. Non debet esse episodica;
6. Debet esse admirabilis;
7. Debet esse implexa;
8. Debet esse affecta, vt moueat laetitiam, & molestiam (pp. 442–45).

The list of requisites recalls the lists of criteria for plot currently being applied in the literary quarrels. For Riccoboni, the oneness and the wholeness are among the primary considerations, and they are conceived of in a way which shows his indebtedness to Castelvetro. A comic action may be thought of, he says, as a larger one which contains all the events of many days, or as a smaller one which contains only the events of the last day. The comic plot is restricted to this "totum parvum"—which nevertheless is complete and has a beginning, a middle, and an end (p. 443). It is essentially the audience (and here we recognize Castelvetro's arguments) which imposes these restrictions upon the plot:

It must have a suitable magnitude, in order to be neither too small nor too large but adapted to viewing in that time which the spectators can easily support. For one must take into account the ease of the public, and the people must leave the theater after a number of hours because of their human needs. And thus one must maintain that the time proper to the comic plot is of one or two hours, nor should it exceed twelve hours.

Riccoboni then provides the most succinct statement we have so far encountered of the "three unities"—one which makes unity of action depend upon the other two: "It must be one.... Moreover the time of twelve hours and the narrowness of place does not permit a multitude of actions in comedy."[40] He distinguishes three kinds of verisimilitude: universal verisimilitude (those things which might happen to many persons), particular verisimilitude (which must nevertheless be treated in a universal way), and a verisimilitude which consists in the giving of names befitting the qualities of character. The "admirabilis" or "marvelous," a quality usually associated with tragedy and the epic, has a peculiar function in Riccoboni's conception of comedy; on the one hand, through our marveling at some ridiculous deception, we are purged of that same kind of deception; on the other hand, our marveling at wickedness teaches us not to fall into similar forms of wickedness (p. 445). The dual poetic ends of purgation and moral instruction are thus both served by the marvelous.

[40] *Ibid.*, p. 443: "Debet congruentem magnitudinem habere ut nec perexigua, nec permagna sit, sed accommodata ad eius temporis prospectum, quod fert commodum spectatorum, cum ratio commodi popularis habeatur, & necesse habeat populus post aliquot horas de theatro propter humanas necessitates discedere. Itaque tempus fabulae comicae accommodatum necesse vnius, aut duarum horarum, nec duodecimam praeterire censendum est.... Debet esse una.... Tempus autem duodecim horarum, & angustia loci non permittit in Comędia multitudinem actionum."

POETIC THEORY

Just as the requisites for plot are all drawn from the *Poetics*, so the four requirements for character are adapted to comedy. "Goodness" of character becomes "badness"—such qualities as harshness, obsequiousness, boastfulness. It is apparent that Riccoboni thinks of "goodness" as a general term for the virtues. The second requisite—appropriateness—includes all the usual components of decorum. And the third—likeness—may be understood in two ways: either as meaning a conformity to the literary tradition associated with a given character, or as implying (for present-day personages) a conformity to the conventions of comic types—Pantaleone, Gianni, Graziano. "Consistency" is a warning against any change in character throughout the course of the play (pp. 446–47). Riccoboni represents, regarding character, a kind of average position for the period, with all its doubts and hesitations. What he says about the remaining qualitative parts and about the quantitative parts repeats the *Poetics* without interpreting it.

On the subject of the ridiculous, Riccoboni is somewhat more original. He begins, of course, with Aristotle's statement, to which he adds a definition of laughter derived from a "very learned man": ". . . it is a sign of joy which the soul makes through the dilatation of the heart coming from the liberation of the spirits, which can no longer be contained as the image of happy things triumphs."[41] Such a definition, of course, departs from the materials of the *Poetics*, and Riccoboni admits that his sources on the ridiculous are Aristotle's *Rhetoric*, Cicero, Maggi, and Castiglione. He finds it useful to enumerate, in a way not unlike that of Aristotle treating the tragic plot, the kinds of wickedness that will arouse laughter in comedy; each springs from a kind of deception:

1. One that comes from ignorance of those things that people ordinarily know;
2. one that comes from false opinion;
3. one that comes from misunderstanding, or from a turning of events against their author;
4. one that comes from the trickery of another or from accident (p. 456).

In spite of such adventures as these into other topics and other sources, Riccoboni follows closely the text of his model, creating thereby the first "ars comica" of the century to be based so closely on Aristotle. For Riccoboni, however, it was merely a first attempt, and just as the translation of 1579 was to be supplemented by the full commentary on the *Poetics* a few years later, so the *De re comica* was at the same time to benefit from his broader understanding of his basic text; the *Ars comica* of 1585 becomes a much more learned document.

DELLA POETICA (CA. 1580)

The Biblioteca Nazionale in Florence possesses, in its manuscript Magliabechi VII, 437, an anonymous translation of and commentary on

---

41 *Ibid.*, p. 453: "signum laetitiae quod facit animus per dilatationem cordis ex spirituum resolutione, qui vincente imagine rei laetae contineri non possunt."

[588]

the first part of the *Poetics*, entitled simply *Della poetica*. I have not yet been able to assign even an approximate date to the work, although its method of procedure and its central preoccupations would lead me to place it around 1580. It is essentially a paraphrase, giving either parts of the Greek text or sections of an Italian translation followed by more or less extensive explanatory remarks. The fragment covers the text from the beginning to 1450*a*7, then (since there is apparently one folio missing) from 1450*a*18 to 1450*b*4, where it ends abruptly. Such parts of the translation as we have are clumsy and confused, and it would not be unfair to say that its author usually does less well than his predecessors; there are no passages in which he makes a decidedly superior suggestion. On the other hand, his commentary is a very typical one for the period, wrestling with all the current problems; and in many cases his arguments and analyses are original—if not always completely convincing.

Linguistic matters—questions of meaning, of syntax, and of punctuation—occupy a fair proportion of the commentary. The author's speculations about meanings of words reflect the uncertainty which still prevailed, even toward the end of the century, over the sense of the text. Many of the meanings assigned affect directly the interpretation of the *Poetics*. Thus if μιμουμένους at 1448*a*23 is said to mean "istrioni" (fol. 11*v*) and if πράττοντες at 1449*b*31 means "mimi" (fol. 33*v*), one will necessarily think of the tragedy as acted rather than as written, and the nature of the object of imitation may be misunderstood. Similarly, if αὐτοσχεδιασμάτων at 1448*b*23 is taken as meaning "in rude verses" ("co' versi rozzi"; the author specifically rejects "allo improviso" as a translation, fol. 21), then the identification of poetry with verse is further stressed. The author's purely lexical difficulties are exemplified by the word λευκογραφήσας at 1450*b*2, translated by "se dipingesse in bianco" and glossed with "come dipingere in un muro bianco" (fols. 20–20*v*). Elsewhere in the work interpretations depend upon syntactical matters; so at 1447*a*29, ἤ is taken to be a "corrective" copulative with the force of "or rather." The author insists at length upon this meaning, citing a passage from the *Nicomachean Ethics* in corroboration; for upon it depends in large part his thesis that verse is indispensable for poetry. At least one excellent suggestion is made for punctuation, that of separating δρώντων at 1449*b*25 from the rest of the sentence, making possible an independent phrase in the translation, "di coloro che negotiono in scena"; but the author does not go far enough in reorganizing the sentence, and the last part of the definition still reads "et facendo la purgatione di tali passioni non per narratione, ma per misericordia et paura" (fol. 32). The imperfect readings in the Greek text still account for many hesitations, and long passages of the paraphrase are devoted to their explanation.

In a brief prologue, the author of the paraphrase tackles two problems, the old distinction among "poema," "poesia," and "arte poetica," and the essential content and organization of the *Poetics*. The "arte poetica," as a treatise on the art, will have to offer a definition of poetry, one which will define the species by giving the genus and the differentiae; it will also have to analyze completely the differences. The author believes that the task of definition is accomplished in the first part of the *Poetics*, which is to be taken rather as a "propositione" than as a "proemio," since it does not attempt to gain the reader's attention. Because the work fails to define "imitation," an integral part of the later definitions, the author does so himself (relying, he says, upon Plato): "Imitation then is an assimilating of one thing to another and of a false one to a true."[42] In the paraphrase itself, the author (who here resembles Sassetti) is very sensitive to the kind of methodological questions raised in the prologue. He divides the work into a proposition (extending to 1447a28) and a narration and finds that the first part indicates that Aristotle will treat of poetry—rather than of the "art"—and that the whole of the *Poetics* will offer precepts for the poet. It will pass from the universal to the particular, which is the proper order of science as Aristotle himself distinguishes it in the *Posterior Analytics* and the *Physics* (fol. 2v). The universals are ones which are most known to nature, least known to men; but men already know the particulars from which they derive: "Thus if Aristotle begins from universals, he assumes that the reader of the *Poetics* already knows comedies, tragedies, the epic, and dithyrambs and the other species of imitations; whence one concludes that it is necessary to have heard and read the poets, otherwise one cannot approach this study."[43]

The author is especially interested in the constitution of definitions. He points out carefully how Aristotle first establishes the genus of poetry, then its differentiae, and—much later—how the definition of tragedy is derived from preceding universals about genus and differentiae (fols. 4, 30v). He warns the reader against taking Aristotle's statements on comedy at 1449a31 as a definition: ". . . this can be seen because many things are lacking which should enter into its definition; he does not do this when he defines tragedy, but rather does not omit any single thing."[44] At 1449b31 he calls the attention of the reader to the passage from definition to discussion of the component parts and the reason why Aristotle now proceeds to the latter: ". . . for we then know well a whole when we know all its parts, which parts make it what it is."[45] Contrariwise, he warns us not to

42 MS Magl. VII, 437, fol. 1: "L'imitazione dunque è un assimigliare una cosa ad un'altra et una falsa ad una vera."

43 *Ibid.*, fol. 3: "cosi se Arist: incomincia dagl' uniuersali, presuppone, che allo auditore della Poetica gia siano [note] le comedie, le tragedie, l'epopeia, e dithirambicj, et l'altre specie d'imitatione. onde se ne caua che sia bisogno hauere udito e letto de Poetj, altrimenti non si puo accostare à questa lettione."

44 *Ibid.*, fols. 26–26v: "questo si puo uedere, perche ci mancono molte cose, le quali douerrebbono entrare nella sua diffinitione, il che quando diffinisce la tragedia non fa cosi, anzi non lascia cosa ueruna indietro." Cf. fol. 31.

45 *Ibid.*, fol. 33v: "perche all'hora si sa bene un tutto, quando si conoscono tutte le sue parti, le quali parti sono quelle che la fanno quale."

take as a treatment of parts something which is not (fol. 36). Finally with respect to method, he distinguishes between Aristotle's a priori and a posteriori arguments (fol. 19), again with a view to keeping his reader constantly aware of how the text is organized and presented.

As was the case with Sassetti, however, these scruples about method do not prevent the author from reading the *Poetics* pretty much as his predecessors had done. The definition of imitation was, as we have seen, one of the "universals" most needed for the understanding of Aristotle's text; yet he does not hesitate to take it over directly from Plato, without inquiry into its appropriateness to the particular circumstances of the *Poetics.* Moreover, he declares that μῦθος or "favola" is necessary for imitation, and this permits him to identify poetry with mythology (following Plato) and to find in this identification the reason for Aristotle's insistence upon "fiction." He does not, however, fall into the usual confusion over the various possible meanings of the word "imitation," excluding from Aristotle's use the designation of a dramatic manner (fol. 1, margin). He sees imitation as one of the two natural causes of poetry; but the other one, he says, is rhythm, not the pleasure found in imitation. Taking issue with the position (found also in Sassetti's manuscript *Sposizione*) that one of these constitutes the final cause of poetry, the other the efficient, he argues that both of them must be called efficient causes (fol. 14). The case is clear for him: "these two natural causes are made up of imitation and rhythm, because imitation and rhythm are natural in us and poetry is composed of imitation and of rhythm; for rhythm is in verse, which is a part of poetry along with imitation."[46]

The last of the preceding assertions is in line with the author's constant affirmation that poetry and verse are inseparable; every relevant passage in the *Poetics* is interpreted in this sense, as they had so frequently been by his contemporaries. From the very beginning, when the means of imitation are identified, language is said to imply verse: "quando dice oratione intende sempre metrica" (fol. 3v); the phrase later becomes "parlar' metrico" (fol. 5v). If a general statement is needed, we may find one in connection with 1447b14: "But we must not think therefore that the poet can be a poet without verse, because it is one of his differences through which he becomes different from those who imitate without verse."[47] Metrical language thus becomes the means by which poetry is distinguished from kindred imitations.

If the author treats the means in a somewhat conventional way, he is more original in his treatment of the objects of imitation. These are

[46] *Ibid.*, fol. 14v: "queste due cagioni naturali siano fatte dall'imitatione et dal rhithmo, perche l'imitatione e'l rhithmo sono in noi naturali, et la poesia è composta d'imitatione et di rhithmo, perche il rh[i]thmo è nel uerso, che è parte della poesia insieme con l'imitatione."

[47] *Ibid.*, fol. 7v: "Ma non bisogna però pensare che il poeta possa essere poeta senza 'l uerso, perche è una sua differenza per la quale si fa differente da quelli che imitano senza 'l uerso."

identified as "passions, characters, and actions" (fol. 3v). In order that
we may know what these are, the author gives us a set of examples:
"The passions are fear, hope, love, and the like; the characters, strong,
generous, audacious, just, unjust, prodigal, temperate, intemperate; the
actions, to perform an act of fortitude, an act of timidity, and the like."[48]
Aristotle's three-way division of the objects is interpreted as follows: men
"better" than ourselves are "heroes and sons of the gods and semi-
gods"; men "worse" than ourselves are "the very avaricious or the very
stupid or the very unfortunate" men of comedy (fol. 9); but we are not
told who are "like" us.

While purgation is specifically identified as the end of tragedy, no such
statement is made about the ridiculous as the end of comedy. On both of
them, the author makes fairly extensive remarks. Having said that purgation operates by "putting pity and fear into the souls of the listeners," he
is obliged to explain his meaning:

... pity can be good and bad, and so also fear; for we are afraid of certain things
which it is a virtue to fear. Tragedy, therefore, puts into our breasts the good pity,
by which we drive out pitilessness, cruelty, and other similar passions which are
contrary to the good pity. In the same way, by driving out from our breasts
certain passions which make us insolent, we get used to being afraid; whence, if
terrible and horrible things happen to us, we have formed the habit of being
afraid, and so they do not give us so much fear. In the second book of the
Rhetoric, Aristotle teaches us how to remove bad passions from our breast by
putting in good ones.[49]

The effects of purgation are thus indirect, and they make permanent changes
in the moral well-being of the spectator. The ridiculous is not considered
in terms of its effects—except for the general one of laughter—but the
author concerns himself rather with distinctions among the terms used
by Aristotle at 1449a33 ff. and with separating the ridiculousness of the
spirit from that of the body. The latter opposition is also derived from
Plato, in the Laws (fol. 27v).

Perhaps the most elaborate set of distinctions in this anonymous
paraphrase of the Poetics relates to the qualitative parts of character and
thought. The initial distinctions will be clearest if we assume, on the part
of the author, a separation between the world of reality and the world of

[48] Ibid., fol. 5v: "Le passioni sono il timore, la speranza, l'amore et similj: i costumi,
forte, liberale, audace, giusto, ingiusto, prodigo, temperato, intemperato: l'ationj operare
un'atto di fortezza, uno atto di timidità & simili."
[49] Ibid., fols. 32v–33: "la misericordia puo esser' buona et cattiua, cosi la paura, perche
si ha paura d'alcune cose, le qual' temendo è uirtù, la tragedia adunque ci mette nel petto
la misericordia buona, con laquale noi scacciamo l'impietà la crudeltà, et simili altre passioni,
lequali sono contrarie alla misericordia buona, cosi scacciando dal petto alcune passioni che
ci fanno essere insolenti, ci aue[z]ziamo hauer paura onde se ci sopraggiungono cose terribili,
et spauenteuoli, habbiamo fatto l'uso nell'hauer' paura, et cosi non ci danno tanto spauento.
Nel secondo della Rethorica Aristotile ci insegna cauar' le cattiue passioni del petto, metten-
doci le buone."

art, which becomes later a separation between things and words. The true actions of reality are represented by the feigned actions of a tragedy. Actions are performed by agents, and insofar as agents have habits of the soul which determine their actions, they have character; in the work of art, character will be manifested through language, and this is the "character" or "orazione morata" of tragedy. Agents also have habits of the soul which account for their reasoning and their speech, and when these are expressed through language in the work, they become the "thought" or "dianea" of tragedy (marginalia to fols. 34v–35). Another way of making the distinction is to refer character and thought to the appetitive and the intellective principles of the soul, which combine in the production of any action. These principles give, respectively, character and thought (now called "intelligenza") and the author summarizes thus their relationship to action: "The plot is the composite of the actions, intelligence is the act of the intellect, as in speaking and taking counsel, character is in appetite. If there are actions in tragedy, it is necessary that these two principles be there."[50] An agent will be "prudent, imprudent, sagacious, malicious, stupid or wise or ignorant" as these qualities are present in his "intelligence" and manifest in his actions. Throughout the discussion, the author makes underlying assumptions of a philosophical kind which determine his attitudes toward art and nature and toward the specific problems of the *Poetics*.

Plato rather than Aristotle is the main topic of study in Girolamo Frachetta's *Dialogo del furore poetico* of 1581; but since Aristotle is used as a rebuttal to Plato's various charges against the poets, some general ideas about the *Poetics* emerge. Moreover, Frachetta examines and rejects certain interpretations of Castelvetro and Maggi and otherwise shows himself in touch with the Aristotelian tradition. Unlike most of those who pitted Aristotle against Plato, Frachetta's principal concern is not with the uses of poetry for moral education, but rather with its relationship to the truth. Plato had condemned poetry for not representing the truth; Aristotle says that it has no business with the truth. For the poet is supposed to use as his material things as they "should be," not as they "are," and thus "we can in no wise, if we want to rely on Aristotle, designate as a good poet one who undertakes to describe in verse true things exactly as they are."[51] Indeed, we should not call him a poet at all, since truth is different from probability and possibility. This is apparently only a tentative position in the dialogue, for later the interlocutors argue that Aristotle

[50] *Ibid.*, fol. 35: "La fauola è il componimento dell' ationi, l'intelligenza è l'atto dello intelletto, come discorrere consigliarsi. Il costume è nello appetito. Se nella tragedia sono le ationi, è necessario che ci siano questi duoi principij."

[51] *Dialogo* (1581), p. 29: "noi non potiamo in modo niuno, se ci uogliamo appoggiare ad Aristotele, appellar buon poeta colui, che si prende a descriuere in uersi le cose uere per l'appunto come elle sono."

does permit the use of known events and real people in poetry. They go so far as to admit that the completely or even the partially invented plot, in epic or in tragedy, would be less desirable than that which was based on the truth: "... since the material of tragedy is things which can come about, things which have already happened will be by far a more suitable material than those thought up or imagined by the poet"; Aristotle's statements on the epic lead us to conclude that "without doubt it is much better if they are true than if they are not."[52] Thus, the difference between poetry and history resides less in the nature of the matter than in the way of handling it:

... the historian must write of things which happened in that exact manner in which they happened, without altering them in any detail no matter how small or without inserting the slightest bit of his own invention; whereas the tragic or the epic poet, taking an event which occurred, must not recount it in the way in which it happened, but he must strive by means of eliminations and much more of additions and otherwise to polish it up and to make it as noteworthy as he can.[53]

The art of poetry in this way becomes a kind of superior art of rhetoric, whose main function is to adorn and augment.

Frachetta touches, of necessity, upon the ends of poetry as seen by Plato and Aristotle, and here he finds the two authorities in distinct opposition. Aristotle, he says, proposes only one end for poetry and that is pleasure, "to give delight and recreation to the minds of everybody, and especially of the common people; and if the poet sometimes benefits us, he does so by supererogation and as if by accident."[54] He points out (with acute historical insight) that those who have found the double end of pleasure and utility in Aristotle have merely been concerned with making him agree with Horace. If pleasure is the only end for Aristotle, why then does he include purgation in the definition of tragedy? Frachetta's answer is the standard one: this is done in order to contradict Plato, and the very passions which Plato had attacked seem to be recommended by Aristotle:

... as if he wished to say that horrible and pitiful things not only do not make us fearful and pitying, as Plato thinks, but rather bring about the exact opposite. Nevertheless it must be understood that they do this accidentally, since through the events of this kind which are placed before us we become accustomed, and

---

52 *Ibid.*, p. 86: "essendo materia della tragedia le cose aueneuoli, di gran uantaggio piu conueneuol materia saranno le cose già state, che le pensate o immaginate dal poeta"; and "senza fallo molto meglio è se son uere, che se non sono."

53 *Ibid.*, p. 88: "l'histori[c]o dee scriuere le cose accadute in quella istessa guisa per l'appunto, che elle accaddettero, senza uariare in alcuna cosa, da quanto che ella sia; o senza trametterci entro pur un puntino di suo trouato. la oue il poeta tragico, o l'epopeico pigliando un fatto auenuto, non nel modo, che' succedette, dee raccontarlo; ma dee sforzarsi con isminuimenti, & assai piu con aggiunte, & con altro, di ripulirlo, & di renderlo ragguardeuole il piu, ch'ei può."

54 *Ibid.*, p. 90: "dilettare, & ricrear gli animi di ciascuno, & spetialmente del uulgo. Et che se'l poeta alcuna uolta ci gioua, ciò faccia per sopra derrata, & quasi per accidente."

little by little we free ourselves of such passions. And Aristotle's mind was so intent upon this matter, and he was so preoccupied with it, that he did not take care to include pleasure in that definition, even though he held it to be the principal and almost the only end.[55]

In the light of this interpretation, Frachetta brands as ridiculous Maggi's notion that Aristotle wishes to include the purgation of anger, avarice, debauchery, and so forth. When he comes, finally to consider whether Aristotle would or would not admit the presence of the divine furor in the poet, Frachetta expounds Aristotle's metaphysics to show that he would necessarily think of the poet's operations as natural, linked to the body and to the humors, and susceptible of a "divine" influence only in so far as the heavenly bodies which cause alterations in the humors may be said to be divine.

CARRIERO AND BULGARINI (1582)

The *Breve et ingenioso discorso contra l'opera di Dante* of Alessandro Carriero (1582) is divided into two distinct sections, the first entirely theoretical in nature, the second devoted to a discussion of the *Divina Commedia*. In the first, the *Poetics* supplies not only the essential theoretical basis but also the general plan of organization. However, Plato is frequently consulted on points of detail and the doctrine shows many similarities to the current Horatian mode. Carriero is a lover of distinctions, and he tries everywhere to refine upon the divisions suggested by his authorities. In its general outlines, his treatise examines successively these matters: the ends of poetry; the narrative and dramatic manners, divided respectively into three and four kinds; the qualitative parts; the comparison of poetry with history; the use of verse; comedy and tragedy; the mixed manner, divided into eight kinds; and the comparison of tragedy and epic. The comparison with history serves to place and delimit the art.

Carriero starts from Aristotle's differentiation between truth on the one hand and verisimilitude and necessity on the other; this is accompanied by a difference in order of presentation of the events. The second major difference lies in the treatment by the historian of many actions, by the poet of one only. This does not prevent the poet from being universal; for if he recounts the actions of one man, he does so in such a way as to emphasize the general qualities of that man—for example, Ulysses: "nor indeed should he be considered as he was; but leaving aside the circumstances and the minute particularities of the individual, one should pass

---

[55] *Ibid.*, p. 92: "Quasi dir uolendo, che le cose horribili, & compassioneuoli, non che ci faccino tementi, & misericordiosi, come uuole Platone; ma adoprano innanzi tutto il contrario. Il che non dimeno si dee intendere, che faccin per accidente, in quanto che per i casi di questa fatta, che ci son porti dauanti, noi ci auuezziamo, & a poco a poco ci liberiamo da cotai passioni. Et a questo hebbe tanto Aristotile l'animo inteso, & ne fu in guisa sollecito, ch'ei non si curò di mettere in detta definitione il diletto. tutto che egli lo hauesse per principale, & quasi per solo fine."

on to the universal, in order to make this man prudent and shrewd as he is wont to be perfectly described by the philosophers."[56] The third difference (supplied by Lucian) lies in the writer's attitude toward his subjects; the historian must not indulge in excessive praise, since this would be a departure from the truth, whereas the poet may make any changes he wishes in words or in deeds. Finally, the historian has many actions and hence he does not need to resort to the use of episodes; but the poet, restricted to a single action, must invent and imagine many episodes in order to fill out and adorn his poem. It is here that his admirable genius is displayed (pp. 12–18).

The distinction between truth and verisimilitude accounts, in a way, for the primary end of poetry; for the poet depicts "things as they should be" in order to exert a moral influence on his audience: ". . . whence we understand clearly that this is the function of the poets, i.e., to treat various and divers forms of civil life in their poems; this brings not a little profit to those who read and consider them with care. Indeed, poems are not only profitable to private persons but also to public ones, and to cities themselves."[57] Tragedy may prevent civil wars through the example of the miserable end of wicked persons, comedy maintains the calm and the happiness of the citizenry. In all this, pleasure is the instrument: "Thus the poets, having utility as their aim, in order to lead men to obtain it more easily, first endeavor to give pleasure to the readers and auditors of their poems by means of every grace of poetic ornament."[58] The audience is not otherwise specified than by its designation as the "vulgo" (p. 52).

Kinds of poems are determined jointly, for Carriero, by their audiences and their subject matter and their ends. He divides narrative poetry into three kinds, called historical, moral, and dogmatic. The historical sings the famous deeds of illustrious ancients; the moral treats subjects which have reference to the instruction of the citizenry; and the dogmatic teaches both the divine and the natural mysteries. Of the four kinds of "active" or dramatic poetry, the first, the mime, imitates the thoughts, the actions, and the gestures of any person whatsoever; because of its obscenity, it is not to be tolerated in a republic. Satire scolds wicked people and their vices—essentially unpleasant things—in order to arouse laughter and to generate hatred for these same vices. But comedy imitates pleasant things;

---

56 *Breve et ingenioso discorso* (1582), p. 16: "nè già quale egli sià stato considerar si deue, ma tralasciate le circostanze, & minute particolarità dell'indiuiduo passar si deue all'uniuersale, per formar quest'huomo prudente, & accorto, quale egli suole esser descritto perfettamente da i Filosofi."

57 *Ibid.*, pp. 1v–2: "da che chiaramente si comprende questo esser l'ufficio de Poeti, cioè di trattar uarie, & diuerse guise della uita ciuile ne i lor poemi: il che apporta non mediocre giouamento à chi con diligenza li legge, & li considera: Anzi le Poesie non solamente giouano alle persone priuate, ma anco alle publiche, & alle Cittadi stesse."

58 *Ibid.*, p. 2v: "Cosi i Poeti hauendo per suo scopo l['] utile, per indur' à conseguirlo più facilmente gli huomini, prima s'ingegnano con ogni uaghezza d'ornamenti Poetici di porger diletto à Lettori, & Auditori de i lor Poemi."

its purpose is to make people laugh; and it may be defined as "an imitation of the worst men, which by discovering their uglinesses and their obscenities induces laughter in the spectators."[59] Its subjects are common people of ordinary condition, city dwellers, peasants, soldiers; they are never illustrious or heroic. The latter characteristics are reserved for tragedy, defined by Aristotle as "the imitation of a great and illustrious action, made completely, and sweetly written with its parts separate and distinct, setting forth and calming the troublesome accidents which happen in it, not through narration but by means of pity and of despair."[60] (The translation of the definition illustrates how completely it still baffled those who were not expert Aristotelian scholars.) When, much later, he comes to the subdivisions of the mixed manner he finds that it contains eight kinds: epic, melopoeia, elegy, dithyramb, iamb, epigram, hymn, and epithalamium. Of these, only the epic is treated at length, and that for two reasons, because Carriero could find much material on it in Aristotle and because it was pertinent to his discussion of Dante. Its essential characteristic, as compared with tragedy, is its length and complexity; through the variety of its episodes and the pleasantness of its digressions, it prevents the boredom and the lassitude of the reader (p. 50).

For the handling of the qualitative and the quantitative parts, Carriero has little to suggest besides what he had found in the *Poetics*. He does insist that verse is necessary in all forms of poetry—a commonplace in his day—if perfection is to be achieved; poems which imitate without verse are of an inferior order (pp. 18–19). The general rhetorical turn of his theory becomes apparent in the handling of the parts of poetry. Plot is more important than character because to it belong such elements as recognition and reversal, "which are wont in the highest degree to move within our souls various and divers passions, and to fill them with wonder, and at times to affect them violently and to carry them away in any direction whatsoever."[61] Sententiae are of two kinds; some of them relate directly to the central subject, and these follow political precepts; others are outside the subject, and these are handled rhetorically. In comedy, sententiae concern matters of "economy," the government of one's possessions and one's family. If decorum is needed in character (in all forms of poetry) and if all parts of the plot require verisimilitude, it is because the achievement of the ends of poetry, "the teaching of good manners and of refined character,"[62] depends upon the belief of the audience. The poet must, therefore,

59 *Ibid.*, p. 9: "una imitatione de gli huomini peggiori, che co'l iscoprir le loro brutture, et oscenità s'induca il riso ne gli Spettatori."

60 *Ibid.*, pp. 27–28: "è imitatione d'un' attione grande, & illustre, compitamente fatta, e dolcemente descritta con le sue parti separate, e distinte, dichiarando, & acquetando i trauagliosi accidenti, che ui concorrono non per uia di narratione, ma per mezzo di misericordia, e di sgomento."

61 *Ibid.*, p. 10: "i quali massimamente sogliono muouer ne gli animi uarii, e diuersi affetti, e di merauiglia ingombrarli, e tall'hora uiolentarli, & rapirli in qual si uoglia parte."

62 *Ibid.*, pp. 51–52: "il documento di buone creanze, e di costumi gentili."

at all times follow the opinions of the people. In this way, Carriero's theory is just as Horatian in its theory of the achievement of the ends of poetry as it- is in the statement of those ends.

The copy of Carriero's *Breve et ingenioso discorso* which belonged to Bellisario Bulgarini is now in the library of Harvard University; it contains Bulgarini's marginal notations, some of them expressing ideas that he was later to develop in his attack on Carriero. His marginalia seem to have two purposes: to condemn some of Carriero's theoretical conclusions and to state some of Bulgarini's own positions. He blames Carriero for not considering Plato's banishment of the poets and for trying to reconcile Plato with Aristotle (p. 2). Referring to Carriero's three subdivisions of narrative poetry, he believes that they tend to make a poet of any versifier, "against Aristotle's opinion and against reason" ("contra l'opinion d'Aristo: e contra la ragione," p. 3). Carriero's statements about the effects of recognition and reversal, which "carry the soul away," would be more appropriate to the orator than to the poet (p. 10) and his distinction between the poet and the historian with respect to the expression of praise is a false one. For if the poet were to reveal his own feelings about a character he would on the one hand destroy the verisimilitude of his poem, on the other he would speak in his own person and would thus cease to imitate (p. 16). On more specific matters, Carriero completely mistranslates and misunderstands Aristotle's definition of tragedy (p. 28), and his own definition of comedy is false because it misconstrues the meaning of "worse" (p. 9).

A few of Bulgarini's own suggestions refer to general matters of poetic theory, such as his insistence that certain poetic genres, like the lyric, the elegy, the epigram, do not need to have a plot (p. 10). But for the most part he is interested in correcting Carriero on the three major forms, tragedy, comedy, and the epic. He agrees that the poet should not invent new plots for tragedy out of whole cloth, truth being a necessary ingredient; but it is possible to think of "new" plots as those which are true, but which the tragic poets have not previously treated. These are permitted to the poet. When old plots are used, the complication and denouement must be altered according to Aristotle's recommendation (p. 34). Bulgarini admits the possibility of tragedies with happy endings and says that some do exist (p. 39). He has doubts about Aristotle's requirement of the unified plot:

Nor must the poet be prevented from including in his poem several and divers actions, provided that they are well interconnected and interdependent; let Ovid's *Metamorphoses* be an example of this, which although they are of many and divers actions are still praised. But Aristotle approves principally the poem in which the single plot is found, because the genius of the poet who has undertaken to imitate such a plot is perhaps demonstrated more fully as he varies it and conducts it pleasurably to a proper size.[63]

63 Harvard copy of Carriero, *Breve et ingenioso discorso* (1582), p. 15: "Nè al Poeta si

Multiplicity of plot is especially desirable in comedy, where the double plot is to be preferred to the single; example, Terence's *Andria*. Carriero errs when he uses Plautus' *Amphytrion* as an example of a double comedy; Bulgarini cites the opinion of those who regard this play as a monster because it combines tragic and comic characters and actions, and of those who think it is a tragedy (p. 21). His main concern with comedy centers about its end and its object. He would distinguish comedy, which moves to laughter, from satire, which moves to indignation (p. 4). The objects of comedy are not, as Carriero wishes, obscene and wicked persons, but rather good men of middling condition; Aristotle's "worse" should be understood as meaning the condition of fortune, not the quality of the mind—or at least, he says, this is the opinion of the best interpreters of the *Poetics* (p. 9). He thinks that the happy ending of comedy will be much more pleasurable if it is preceded by grave disturbances and not merely by ridiculous events (p. 22). Concerning the epic, Bulgarini speaks only of its greater length, which results from the fact that it may be recited in a number of sittings and does not depend upon the comfort of an assembled audience, and of the fact that it is not necessarily better adapted to the production of the marvelous than is tragedy (pp. 50–51).

There is little pertinent to the present discussion in Giordano Bruno's *De gl'heroici furori* (1585), since it is essentially a set of dialogues devoted to the amatory poets and to an analysis of the various passions of love. But in the first Dialogue his interlocutors digress to make an attack upon the "regolisti di Poesia" who examine and reject the great poets according to the rules of Aristotle. Bruno holds that those rules were meant only to give a representation of Homer's poetry or of epic poetry like Homer's, "and not to teach others who could well be different in talent, art, and inspiration, equal, similar, and greater, of diverse genius."[64] Poetry does not spring from the rules, he says, but rather the rules from poetry; Homer does not follow them, he is their source. Moreover, such rules are good only for those who are more capable of "imitating" than of inventing, and they were set down by one who was not a poet at all. (It is interesting to see this meaning given to the verb "imitate.") They are useful only for those who have no individual genius. It is not by setting up criteria of this kind that we recognize the true poet, but rather through his singing in verse, by means of which he comes to delight or profit or to do both at

---

dee uetare il comprender nel suo poema più, e diuerse azzioni, purche se sieno infra di loro ben colligate, e dependenti; siancene essempio le Trasformazioni d'Ouidio: che pur essendo di molte, e diuerse azzioni uengon lodate. Ma Aristotile approua maggiormente il Poema, nel qual si troua la fauola una, perche, nel uariarlo, e condurlo con delettazione a conueneuol grandezza, si dimostra perauentura più l'ingegno del Poeta, che una tal fauola s'è presa ad imitare."

64 *De gl'heroici furori* (1585), p. A.2.v: "et non per instituir altri che potrebbero essere con altre vene, arti, et furori; equali, simili, et maggiori, de diuersi geni."

once (p. A.3). There follows an attack upon the "poor pedants" of the time who exclude certain writers from the ranks of the poets because they have failed to observe one of the prescribed rules. Bruno's stand is of course anti-Aristotelian, and it has traces both of Platonic and of Horatian influences.

PATRIZI AND TASSO (1585)

Another anti-Aristotelian document of the same year (1585) is Francesco Patrizi's *Parere in difesa dell'Ariosto*; but this time the attack upon Aristotle is the direct result of the publication of the first work in a new literary polemic, Camillo Pellegrino's *Carrafa*. We can thus see the immediate impact upon Aristotelian theory of one of the great literary quarrels. If it is a negative impact, it is because Pellegrino had used Aristotle's rules to attack Ariosto's *Orlando Furioso*; now, rather than interpreting the rules in another way in order to defend and justify Ariosto, Patrizi says that the rules themselves are without value. His conclusion involves a general reappraisal of the *Poetics*—and, incidentally, of Horace. The point of view is unequivocally stated; Pellegrino was wrong

... in taking the poetical teachings of Aristotle as comparable, in this matter, to the clear, proper, and firm principles of the sciences; for those of Aristotle are neither proper, nor true, nor sufficient to constitute a scientific art of poetry, nor to form any poem whatsoever, nor to judge it; nor are they made according to the practice of either the Greek or the Latin poets.[65]

Having made this comprehensive statement, Patrizi proceeds to attack Aristotle on three grounds: his failure to make proper distinctions, his failure to produce proper definitions, and the lack of conformity between his precepts and the practice of the best poets. Other arguments appear with lesser emphasis. The best example of Aristotle's insufficiencies in the field of distinctions is his failure to treat adequately the term "imitation," because the meanings which he and Plato assign to the term amount to four or more, and his first task should have been to discover the meaning proper to poetry. Since he did not do so, how can he pretend to have developed a useful and scientific approach to the art (pp. L8v–M)? Another example is the confusion among the terms used to designate epic poetry; Aristotle does nothing about it, and this is a sign both that his knowledge of Greek was imperfect and that he did not actually know the whole of Greek epic literature (pp. L6–L7). The inadequacy of definitions is a corollary of the lack of distinctions. Since the prior definitions of imitation, of poetry, and of the heroic poem have not been supplied, we can make no sense of such a definition as this: "The epic poet was an imitator of the

---

[65] *Parere* (Ferrara, 1585), p. L5v: "in prendere gli insegnamenti poetici d'Aristotele pari in questo affare, a i principi chiari, e propri, e fermi delle scienze; non essendo questi di Aristotele, ne propri, ne ueri, ne bastanti à constituire arte scienziale di poetica, ne à formar poema alcuno, nè à giudicarlo. nè sono fatti secondo l'uso de' poeti nè Greci, nè Latini."

actions of illustrious persons" (p. M); for we know neither what a poet is nor what an imitation is.

Patrizi sees Aristotle as having formed for himself an Idea of epic poetry; unfortunately, it is one which is in no way related to the epics that we know. He says that all poems are imitations; but this is obviously not true. For the works of Orpheus, of Homer, and of Hesiod contained no imitations, and indeed none were to be found before the advent of tragedy, comedy, and the other dramatic genres. (It is clear that Patrizi is using "imitation" in one of the Platonic senses, that of dramatic representation.) Moreover, Aristotle asserts that plot, not verse, makes the poet; whereas it is clear from the practice of the poets themselves that there are many poems which have no plots and many plots which are not poems (p. M). In the case of the epic, if we were to apply the definition just given along with the restriction to a single action, we should get very strange results indeed:

> ... if a poet were to take for imitation not actions, as it says, but one single action ... of Caligula the Emperor, a most illustrious person, who, having led his army in formation to the shore of the ocean, had the signal for battle given by the trumpets and shouted that they should gather all the shells and shellfish that were on the shore; or when Domitian caused the flies that were going through the air to be captured and shut up in a paper prison; I do not know, I say, whether these poets and poems should be called "heroic."[66]

This is, of course, a *reductio ad absurdum*, as well as a misunderstanding of what is meant by a single action. Patrizi challenges the necessity for unity of plot and even the requirement that poems must in all cases have plots; the practice of Lucretius, of Vergil in the *Georgics*, of Lucan—all epic poets—is cited in support of his thesis. More damagingly still, Homer's great epics have no central unified action, but are composed rather of a multitude of episodes. Similarly, Patrizi calls into question everything that Aristotle has to say about the requisites for character. In the first place, these are not only common to all poetic genres, but they are even the same requirements as those set up for the historian and the panegyrist. In the second place, they are false. Goodness? But Homer, the perfect example, presents many wicked people, and of all his gods and heroes only one, Nestor, is absolutely good. He also violates in many places the demand for appropriateness. Likeness? The precept, which is both Aristotelian and Horatian, is very shaky; for it requires the likeness of persons to their counterparts in history or reputation, and how are we to establish the character of the counterparts when history is so uncertain and public

---

[66] *Ibid.*, pp. M–M*v*: "s'un poeta togliesse a poetare, non azioni, come ella dice, ma azione vna sola . . . di Caligola Imperadore, illustrissima persona, il quale condotto l'essercito suo in sul lito dell'Oceano in ordinanza, fece dar nelle trombe il segno di battaglia, e gridare che si raccogliessero tutte le conchiglie, e calcinegli ch'erano in sù'l lito. ò quando Domiziano facea a prendere le mosche che per l'aria andauano, e a chiuderle in vna prigion di carta; non sò, dico, se questi poeti, e poemi, sariano Eroici da chiamarsi."

opinion so variable? Finally, the demand for constancy (Horace's "sibi constet") is belied by our common human nature and is everywhere violated by Homer, from whom Aristotle derived his theory (pp. M7–M8v).

Aristotle's Idea of the epic poem is thus without basis in any such poems existing before him. It will not stand the examination of the reason, and, hence, there is no reason why it should be set up as a standard for later epic poets. Patrizi's rejection is complete; it prepares, in a way, the development of his own theories at a later date.

Patrizi's objections were answered, point for point and with great firmness, by Torquato Tasso in his *Discorso sopra il Parere fatto dal Sig. Francesco Patricio, in difesa di Lodouico Ariosto* (1585). What Tasso most objected to in Patrizi was the general anti-Aristotelian position, and hence his own *Discorso* becomes a serious defence of Aristotle. Starting with Patrizi's initial statement (quoted above), he affirms that the opposite is true: "Aristotle's principles are proper, and true, and sufficient to teach us the art of poetry and to form poems, and to show us the way in which to judge them."[67] Then he proceeds to show in what ways the principles are "proper," "true," and "sufficient." They are proper in the sense that they are not common to any of the other imitative arts (such as painting and sculpture) or to any of the other arts of discourse (such as dialectic and rhetoric). "Besides this, they have those conditions which are appropriate to proper ones, since they are the first by nature and the clearest; and they are those by which all the other propositions of poetry may be demonstrated, and they are capable of separating poetry from every other species or genus of imitation."[68] The argument on "truth" is less cogent. Poetry, says Tasso, is not concerned with distinguishing true from false (this is the field of dialectic), but rather with imitating truth; or rather, it imitates verisimilitude which is itself a kind of truth. Aristotle's principles are not false since they consider verisimilitude and truth. As for their being "sufficient," Tasso insists that "no other one is needed, nor is there any species of good poetry which cannot be discovered through the differentiae that Aristotle sets down and for which correct judgment cannot be given in the way that he teaches us."[69] He insists, moreover, that it is not the business of the preceptor of the art to derive his precepts from usage, but rather "by considering the reasons why some of the things used merit praise and others blame, to separate the ones from the others, and to teach how to choose

---

[67] *Discorso* (1585), pp. 100–101: "i principij d'Aristotele sono proprij, e veri, e bastanti ad insegnarci l'arte della Poesia, & à formar i poemi, & a mostrarci la maniera di giudicarne."

[68] *Ibid.*, p. 101: "hanno oltre di ciò quelle conditioni, che si conuengono a' proprij, percioche sono primi per natura, e sono piu chiari. E son quelli, co' quali si posson dimostrare tutte l'altre propositioni della Poesia, e possono separar la Poesia da ciascuna altra specie, ò genere d'imitatione."

[69] *Ibid.*, p. 102: "non ce n'è necessario alcuno altro, ne c'è alcuna specie di buona poesia, che non possa ritrouarsi con le differenze, le quali pone Aristotele, e darsene dritto giudicio in quel modo, ch'egli c'insegna."

the good from the bad in the same way that this has come about in medicine."[70]

As for the principles themselves, Tasso re-establishes poetry under the genus imitation, for all its species imitate, even those which do not have plots, and the name of "poet" itself means "imitator." A part of his argument here consists in removing poetry from the genus music, where others might wish to put it because of its use of verse. But verse is not an adequate basis for distinction among genres, the poet is a poet through imitation, and even if both genera were possible places of classification, imitation, as the more noble and the more necessary one, should be chosen. For the rest, Tasso defends both the definitions and the distinctions which he finds in Aristotle, and he defends Homer's epics. Patrizi's attacks seem to him unjustified, his readings of the *Iliad* and the *Odyssey* incorrect. Tasso's own final estimate of Homer reveals in a significant way his attitudes toward the art of poetry: ". . . all his poetry is nothing else but a praise of virtue, according to the testimony of the great Basil himself; whence he has risen above death and above envy."[71]

RICCOBONI (1585)

The skirmish between Patrizi and Tasso over the position of Aristotle, as I have just outlined it, may serve as a prelude to the publication in 1585 of Antonio Riccoboni's "great commentary" on the *Poetics*. After having published in 1579 a first set of materials on the *Poetics*, including a translation into Latin and the *De re comica* (see above, pp. 582–88), Riccoboni added to these a full-scale commentary and a revised version of the treatise on comedy. These appeared separately, without the translation, in a volume entitled *Poetica Antonii Riccoboni poeticam Aristotelis per paraphrasim explicans, & nonnullas Ludouici Casteluetrij captiones refellens. Eivsdem ex Aristotele ars comica.* The volume contained, in addition to the works, only a dedication and a very brief index. After a short introductory section, "De natura poeticae," the commentary itself presented (in fifty numbered paragraphs) a much briefer analysis of the *Poetics* than those of Riccoboni's immediate predecessors; he wished to treat Aristotle's ideas in general rather than philological questions of the text.

To a degree, Riccoboni's commentary is polemical in tone, since he reacts not so much against Castelvetro's errors of interpretation as against the general tone of disparagement with which Castelvetro had treated the Aristotelian text. His own commentary is written in the spirit of one who believes that the text provides the ultimate answers on all matters related to the art of poetry. Before embarking on an analysis of the in-

[70] *Ibid.*, p. 102: "considerando le cagioni per le quali alcune delle cose vsate meritano lode, altre biasimo, separar l'vne dall'altre, & insegnar à sceglier il buono dal cattiuo in quel modo, ch'è auenuto nella medicina."

[71] *Ibid.*, pp. 116–17: "tutta la sua poesia, altro non è, ch'una lode della virtù per testimonio del gran Basilio istesso: la onde hà superata la morte, e l'inuidia."

dividual passages, however, Riccoboni presents his general ideas on the art (in the section called "De natura poeticae"), and these, for the most part, have nothing to do with Aristotle. He means to treat of the art of making poems rather than of poems themselves. For when he seeks the genus of "poetics," he says that it is either an art or a faculty or an organic habit ("organic" is taken as equivalent to "instrumental"): an art in the general sense that it seeks, in a given matter, the causes through which an end may be achieved; a faculty insofar as it is a discipline; and an organic habit because it serves something else as an instrument. In the last sense, it belongs to rhetoric, both because it makes use of sententiae and because one of its most beautiful devices, recognition, is produced by enthymeme or syllogism. The differentiae of the art are four in number: its end, its function, its subject matter, and the way in which the subject is treated. As he discusses the differentiae, the reason for the multiple genus becomes apparent; and as he works especially with the end, the solutions of other philosophers are rejected in favor of Aristotle's.

Surveying the various ends proposed for poetry, Riccoboni concludes that they are five in number: (1) utility, (2) pleasure, (3) utility and pleasure jointly, (4) imitation, (5) the plot. The first three are found in Horace; arguments in support of the first are found in Zabarella, who makes pleasure an instrument of utility, and in those critics who interpret Aristotle's purgation as a form of utility; common opinion, corroborated by statements of Cicero, approves the second. The fourth is argued most effectively by Scaliger; but it is the fifth which is in Aristotle, and which Riccoboni adopts. Against the other positions, Riccoboni maintains that the first, utility, is proper to the philosopher as an end and is sought by the poet only *per accidens*; that the second, pleasure, leads to such extremes as Plato's ban on the poets, since it may fly in the face of good mores and may justify wickedness and obscenity; that the third, utility and pleasure jointly, is impossible because the two ends are mutually exclusive; that the fourth, imitation, fails to account for many poems which have no imitation. Only the fifth, plot, is fully acceptable; for this is an internal end, common to all poems, and having as a necessary consequence the pleasure which is always attributed to poetry. Hence, one may properly state the end as "fabulosa delectatio" (p. 4).

When, however, Riccoboni attempts to show how the fifth end agrees or disagrees with each of the others, his distinctions lose their sharpness. There is agreement with the first insofar as the plot may be useful through its moral lessons; disagreement, because this is a utility *per accidens*. Good poetry need not be useful. In this connection, he studies the question of purgation in Aristotle, with some interesting results. His general conclusion is that whatever is useful in purgation is an end *per accidens*, for the following reasons:

For tragedy in itself leads men to pity and to fear, and by the very structure of the events it causes the spectators, who feel discomfort as they see misery unjustly visited upon others, to recognize that they themselves are good, and they learn that no hope is to be placed in the course of human affairs; and we shall understand that this is the pleasure appropriate to tragedy. But at the same time, through frequent example and by placing before their eyes many cases of misfortunes, it causes the spectators to become strong and magnanimous, and in this way they also derive utility. Indeed, by habituation to pity and terror, they purge pity and terror, that is, they temper and moderate them. And in this way they become, not excessively pitying and timid as Plato believed, . . . but rather magnanimous and strong.[72]

The construction of the plot has, *per se*, pleasurable consequences; the utilitarian results are accidental. Riccoboni's thesis agrees with the second proposal for the end, since the plot is followed by pleasure; but rather than expressing the end of pleasure overtly, it includes it tacitly. Moreover, since other things beside poetry give pleasure, to say that pleasure is the end is not sufficiently specific and proper. On the third proposal, agreement insofar as plot gives both utility and pleasure, the one *per accidens*, the other *per se*; disagreement, because Riccoboni's thesis makes a distinction between them. On imitation, finally, a similar acceptance of plot as an imitation; but again he distinguishes, saying that imitation is a genus which includes many other species besides poetry, whereas plot is a single species.

The other three differentiae are treated summarily. The "munus" or function is to imitate in verse, the subject matter is human actions, and these are handled in such a way as to become useful for the plot. Having made these various distinctions, Riccoboni is now in a position to define poetics as an art, as a faculty, and as an organic habit: "Poetics is the art of executing plots; or the faculty of imitating in verses; or the organic habit of seeing, in human actions, whatever is suitable for fashioning a plot."[73]

Most of the significant passages in the commentary itself are developments of the principles stated in this introductory section. If we take the end of "fabulosa delectatio," we find important glosses concerning both the origins of poetry and the nature of plot. In connection with his second chapter (1448b4 ff.), Riccoboni separates the origins of poetry into divine

[72] *Poetica* (1585), p. 5: "Etenim Tragoedia per se adducit homines ad misericordiam, & metum, atque ipsa rerum constitutione efficit, vt spectatores ex alterius miseria iniuste exorta molestiam percipientes se bonos agnoscant, & in rebus humanis spem ponendam non esse condiscant; quam esse propriam voluptatem Tragoediae intelligemus: sed simul fit, vt frequenti exemplo, & crebra miseriarum ante oculos subiectione spectatores magnanimi, & fortes efficiantur, atque hoc modo adiuuentur. Nam per consuetudinem misericordiae, & terroris, perpurgant misericordiam, & terrorem, id est, temperant, & moderantur. Itaque non nimis misericordes, & timidi, vt Plato existimabat, . . . sed potius magnanimi, & fortes efficiuntur." References to the commentary are to the second pagination of the volume; the first, in smaller type, is used for the translation.

[73] *Ibid.*, p. 7: "vt Poetica sit ars fabularum conficiendarum; vel facultas versibus imitandi: vel habitus organicus videndi in actionibus humanis, quod appositum est ad fabulam conformandam."

and natural (or human), and further subdivisions give the following schema:

Origins

	Human	
Divine		
"furor divinus"	"natura"	"ars"
(cf. Plato)	"imitatio" "harmonia"	"ars poetica"

Now in this schema all the elements under human origins are productive of pleasure: "imitatio," because it is the genus under which plot is found, "harmonia," because it supplies verse and the other pleasurable accompaniments, and the "ars poetica" (as we have seen), because it furnishes the way of making the plot correctly. In a general way, harmony "was given to men by nature so that they might bear the labors of human life."[74] We may even ask, therefore, whether there is not here a suggestion of one of the utilities springing from artistic pleasure. This would be perfectly consistent with Riccoboni's usual derivation of utility, naturally but *per accidens*, from the pleasure of poetry. So much for the end of "delectatio." But since this is "fabulosa," and since the plot is the internal end of the poem, the excellence and pre-eminence of plot among the qualitative parts must be established. This is, of course, done by Aristotle; Riccoboni, as he comments on 1450a15, multiplies the arguments, and among others he insists that that part of a poem which most vigorously attracts our minds is the most excellent. Plot satisfies this criterion since it contains the elements of recognition and reversal. If we remember that the same elements are at once the most beautiful and the most pleasurable, we may then establish some such series of effects as the following: the plot (because of recognition and reversal), gripping the soul most effectively, hence producing the greatest pleasure, hence achieving the proper end of the art.

Consideration of plot always involves consideration of the objects imitated insofar as these are human actions. Riccoboni, on this matter, makes several departures from the thinking of his contemporaries. First, he declares that the action of tragedy need not be based upon history or upon legend; it is sufficient that some similar example be found among events which have occurred (p. 52). This is a sort of verisimilitude. Next, he constructs (in various passages) an elaborate system of verisimilitude, which we may again represent by a schema:

Objects of
Imitation

Natural		Supernatural	
"facta"	"ut fieri	contrary to	according to
(= history)	potuerint"	common opinion	common opinion
	according to necessity	according to verisimilitude	

[74] *Ibid.*, p. 19: "data est hominibus à natura ad humanae vitae labores tolerandos."

In each major category, one of the alternatives is eliminated; history, not poetry, treats those events which have actually happened; and supernatural events which have no acceptance in public opinion are not usable. Of natural objects, those "which could come about" are the proper province of the art; they are divided, in turn, into necessary objects and verisimilar objects, and Riccoboni explains the distinction by examples. A man wounded in the heart must die: the cause-and-effect relationship is, in nature, necessary and inescapable. A man wounded in the head may die: there is a probability, but no necesssity, that the effect will follow on the cause. Of actions which run counter to nature, the poet will choose only those which most men would believe. It should be noted that belief includes traditional belief, perhaps as its main ingredient. For a poet must present the characters and actions of great heroes as tradition has brought them down to his public; otherwise he sins against verisimilitude. Finally, with respect to the objects, the poet treats them universally and thus achieves another kind of verisimilitude:

Poetry treats universal things; that is, it considers single facts universally or as they might have come about through many causes and in many ways. For instance, the deed of Orestes when he killed his mother Clytemnestra, was a particular deed; nevertheless, the poet considers it in a universal way, as it might have happened through numerous causes and in numerous ways. And poetics is concerned precisely with this universality, in order to invent causes and ways at discretion according as they seem capable of providing greater pleasure.[75]

Consistently with the general position, universality itself is regarded as a source of pleasure, and the end of pleasure directs its operation.

It would seem, then, that the actions chosen and represented in a poem are above all such as will contribute to the pleasure of its audience. But this is not exclusively true; for in Riccoboni's view, the pleasures of plot are always followed by some utility. Various moral lessons are learned. Above all, actions which are terrible and pitiable will bring about the purgation of fear and pity, itself an accompaniment of the correct pleasure: "In fact, in tragedy one must not seek every pleasure, but the proper one; and since the poet must bring about pleasure through imitation, out of pity and fear, this must be achieved by the actions."[76] However, utility seems to spring more directly from another part of the object, character. That is why the poet must have an eye to the beauty of the characters (the phrase "de spectanda morum pulchritudine" appears in the title of Section

[75] *Ibid.*, p. 44: "Poesim tractare vniuersalia, id est, in vniuersum considerare singularia, quatenus scilicet plurimis de caussis, & plurimis modis euenire potuerunt; vt singulare factum fuit Orestis, cum Clytemnestram matrem interfecit. id tamen in vniuersum consideratur à poeta, quatenus plurimis de caussis, & plurimis modis potuit euenire; & in hoc vniuersali versatur poetica, vt caussas, & modos ex arbitrio fingat, prout affere posse maiorem delectationem videantur."

[76] *Ibid.*, p. 66: "Non enim omnem in Tragoedia oportere voluptatem quaerere, sed propriam; &, quoniam ex misericordia, & metu per imitationem poetam efficere oportet voluptatem, id in rebus efficiendum esse."

XVIII), which means that each passion must be represented in its best, or most complete, or supreme manifestation. For each passion is to serve as an example for the men who witness it, and the role of imitation is to embellish and enhance (p. 80). Of the four requisites for character, Ricco-boni singles out propriety for special recommendations which are no more than the standard rules of decorum. Presumably, a kind of verisimilitude is obtained by giving to each personage the characteristics of his type. One of the kinds of tragedy, the "morata," is actually written for the purpose of presenting good characters, and in it character is more important than action.

Although the greater part of Riccoboni's commentary centers about the objects of imitation, he does have some things to say about the means. Here it would appear that his concern is with pleasure rather than with utility. With most of his contemporaries, he proclaims the necessity of verse in poetry; but his reasons are somewhat different. Verse, he says, is the proper instrument of poetry because it contributes to verisimilitude:

That this has the greatest importance for the verisimilitude of poetry is seen in this fact: since poetry itself requires an ample and elevated tone of voice, in order that the audience may hear it readily (because it is scarcely probable that men should speak to one another in prose in a tone so high and so ample as to be intelligible to the spectators—unless those who speak be either deaf or stupid, and thus obliged to raise their voices), verse then is particularly adapted to this purpose, because it is proffered with elevation and amplitude of the voice, almost half sung, and is the opposite of the low and humble tone of prose.[77]

If verse is "verisimilar" in tragedy because it lends itself to the loud recita-tion of a public performance, Riccoboni does not tell us how it would be justified in other more intimate genres; he merely calls upon Aristotle, who authorizes it as the proper instrument of all poetry (p. 13). Of the three means, only "oratio" (or metrical language) will appear in all genres; "saltatio" (or the dance) will appear in some, "harmonia" (or choral music) in the same ones or in others.

Riccoboni's commentary reintroduces a certain amount of restraint into the study of the *Poetics*. It is the shortest of the great commentaries for two reasons: it eliminates all the philological and most of the historical materials which had cluttered up its predecessors. In a way, this makes it less useful. Secondly, it insists on removing the oversubtleties of a Castel-vetro, on returning to the text, and on reading it fairly simply and directly. To be sure, this is frequently done by referring to outside sources, especially

[77] *Ibid.*, pp. 13–14: "quodque valere plurimum ad verisimilitudinem Poesis ex eo perspici-tur, quia cum ipsa vocis postulet elationem, & amplitudinem, vt commode à populo audiri queat, quemadmodum parum verisimile est, vt homines soluta oratione tam elate, & ample inter se colloquantur, vt à spectatoribus intelligantur, nisi illi, qui loquuntur, aut surdi, aut stulti sint, qui vocem extollere necesse habeant: sic ad eam rem maxime accommodatus est versus qui cum elatione, & amplitudine vocis, ac dimidio quodam cantu profertur, & sub-missioni, atque humilitati solutae orationis oppositus est."

Horace, for clarification. But in certain notable aspects it does return to Aristotle. The most striking of these is the attempt to re-establish the plot as the end of the poem, according to Aristotle's own statement, and to combat the specious arguments of those who argued otherwise. This attempt is spoiled somewhat by Riccoboni's eagerness to reconcile his own position with all the others. Such a preoccupation is, of course, typical of the thinkers of his century.

SALVIATI (1586)

In 1586, Lionardo Salviati completed his work on the first of four parts of a major translation and commentary of the *Poetics* in Italian. He had been engaged on the project for at least ten years by this time. The manuscript, some of it in two copies or drafts, is in the Biblioteca Nazionale in Florence. Of the sections for which we have two copies, one is a short note entitled *Delli interpetri di questo libro della Poeticha*; we may regard it as a kind of prolegomenon to the rest, since in it Salviati examines the earlier scholarship on the *Poetics*. Beginning with Averroës' commentary, which suffers from the differences between Greek and Arab customs, he reviews the translations of Valla and Pazzi and then the later commentaries. Of these he thinks that Vettori's is the best—"it seems that little more light can be desired on this work"[78]—and that Castelvetro's is not entirely acceptable, although he does credit Castelvetro with the best translation into Italian. Throughout his own commentary he finds many occasions to reject Castelvetro's solutions, whereas he frequently praises those of Robortello, Maggi, and Vettori.

Salviati's translation and commentary (a title-page added later calls it *Poetica d'Aristotile parafrasata e comentata*) extends from the beginning of the text through 1449b9, thus treating most but not all of the first five chapters of modern editions. All the initial definitions and distinctions are handled, but unfortunately the commentary stops before the definition of tragedy and its development. Salviati divides the text into short sections, numbering 320 in all; only the first fifty are covered in the extant manuscript. For each "particella" he gives the Greek text, then a translation into Italian, then a "parafrasi," which is an extended and expanded translation, and finally the "comento." Index reference numbers are generously interspersed in the translation, providing the link with sections of the commentary bearing the same numbers. The translation is Salviati's own. It is closer to Castelvetro than to Piccolomini, especially in its conciseness and in the use of certain constructions. But Salviati, who seems to be using Castelvetro as a starting point, attempts to find more current and more accurate terms and in general to achieve a clearer version. We may compare their versions of Aristotle's statement on the object of comedy, both to

[78] MS BNF II, II, 11, fol. 372: "poco piu auanti pare che di lume a questo libro possa desiderarsi."

indicate how Salviati works and to show what difficulties were still besetting the translators. The passage is *Poetics* 1449*a*31:

> *Castelvetro*: Hora la comedia è, come dicemmo, rassomiglianza de piggiori, non gia secondo ogni vitio. Ma il rideuole è particella della turpitudine. Percioche il rideuole è vn certo difetto, & turpitudine senza dolore, & senza guastamento, come, per non andare lontano per essempio, Rideuole è alcuna faccia turpe, & storta senza dolore (1576 ed., p. 91).

> *Salviati*: Ma la commedia è si come habbiam detto imitazione di piu cattiui certamente non gia secondo ogni cattiuità, ma del brutto è il ridicolo parte, percioche il ridicolo è una certa fallenza, et bruttezza senza dolore et non corruttiua, come di fatto il ridicolo uiso brutto alcuno, e trauolto senza dolore (fol. 350).

Since he has tried to be brief in the translation and to remain as close as possible to the Greek text, Salviati uses the paraphrase as a means to clarification; thus the above passage is expanded as follows:

> *Parafrasi*: Ma la commedia, come addietro dicemmo è imitazione di persone piu cattiue che le moderne comunali non sono. Cattiue dico non però in ogni maniera di cattiuità: percioche non ogni maniera di cattiuità è ridicola, come uuole essere quella della commedia: ma solamente alcuna parte della bruttezza, o uogliam dir la cattiuità è ridicola: percio che il ridicolo tra le cose, che stanno male, e tra le cose brutte è solamente quell'errore, e quella bruttezza, che non arrecano, ne dolore, ne graue danno a chi l'ha, come, per darne pronto esempio, è ridicolo alcun uiso brutto, a trauolto, che sia senza dolore (fol. 350v).

The commentary itself is quite extensive, perhaps as extensive as Castelvetro's. Frequently, it calls upon examples from contemporary Italian literature, discusses the opinions of earlier scholars, attempts to point out the major divisions and subdivisions of the *Poetics* as well as to provide glosses on individual words and phrases.

In the preliminary materials as well as in the commentary itself, Salviati reveals fully his attitude toward the text on which he is writing. It is a curious and complicated one. Rather than sharing the skepticism of some of his contemporaries, he judges the *Poetics* to be

> . . . a precious book, and not only most useful but necessary to anyone who wishes to write poetry properly; for in it there are most wonderful teachings and most subtle considerations, compressed in marvelous brevity; whence, as Maggi says so well, one may derive greater benefit from this book alone—so small and so ill-treated—than from all the volumes which have been written about this art by the ancients or by the moderns up to our day.[79]

But one must not take it to be a perfect book, for it is limited both in method and in content. In method, by the fact that Aristotle is not writing

---

79 *Ibid.*, fols. 6v–7: "prezioso libro e non solo utilissimo, ma necessario a chiunque uoglia dirittamente poetare. Peroche ci hanno bellissimi ammaestramenti, e sottilissime considerazioni, ristretti in marauigliosa breuità. Onde, come ben dice il Maggio, maggior profitto si puo ritrarre da questo cosi picciolo, e mal trattato libro solo, che da tutti i uolumi, che d'antichi, o moderni dietro a questa arte infino a hoggi sono stati composti."

about a science and hence does not need to observe the same rigor of exposition that would be required in a scientific treatise. Thus in the very first sentence he speaks of the composition of the plot, which is only one part of a poem, whereas a "proem" of this type should treat only general matters (fols. 30v–32). In content, by the fact that Aristotle does not mean to treat the whole of the art of poetry but only those parts of it which pertain to six genres: epic, tragedy, comedy, dithyramb, and auletic and citharistic poetry. His principles would therefore not be applicable to such kinds as the mask, the epithalamium, the parody, the satire, and to such poems as Petrarch's *Trionfi* and Boccaccio's *Amorosa Visione* (fol. 252). This means that he did not consider all the possible differentiae of imitations, and his art remains a partial one. Moreover, Aristotle based what he had to say upon the literature available in his time; he studied only a part of that literature, for he wanted to investigate two kinds of poetry, the magnificent as represented by the epic and tragedy, the low as represented by comedy.

All these restrictions mean that if we are to make of the *Poetics* a useful art of poetry we must supplement it in various ways. We must appeal to usage, to authority, and to reason. "Usage, again, when it does not cause any harm, brings with itself not a little authority, and it must be revered and observed as law, especially if it is confirmed by a very long period of time and by the authority of wise men."[80] Usage is invoked as one of the justifications for the insistence upon verse in all forms of poetry. Authority, in this same statement, is of two kinds: it is the practice of the poets and it is the theory of the "wise men," undoubtedly the writers of arts of poetry and the critics. Reason tells us what is "reasonable"; for example, if rhyme is an accompaniment of song, it must not be used in those parts of poetry which are not sung; hence, it would not be reasonable to include it in the spoken parts of a tragedy (fol. 345v).

Finally, by way of reservation, Salviati occasionally points to the corrupt state of the text and its incompleteness. He thinks that some passages have been interpolated by a "corrector" (e.g., 1448a1), that others are not in their proper place (e.g., 1448b4), that in still others the disagreements among the manuscripts make the determination of the proper text impossible. The text he used was, of course, less satisfactory than our own, and in many cases he devotes lengthy discussions to problems which have since been solved or eliminated by better readings.

Salviati distinguishes three major divisions in the *Poetics*, the prologue or proposition, the treatise itself, and the epilogue. The treatise in turn subdivides into four major sections as it examines four problems: poetry in general; two special kinds of discourse (I presume that he means the

80 *Ibid.*, fols. 137–37v: "L'usanza ancora, quando alcun male non cagioni, porta seco medesima non picciola autorità, e si dee riuerirla, e come legge osseruarla massimamente se da molto lungo spazio, e dall'autorità de' saui huomini è confermata."

magnificent and the low); criticisms and defences of the poet; the priority of tragedy over the epic (fol. 15). The end of Aristotle in this work is "to teach how to make the poem and to give its rules; since he wishes to derive these rules from the definitions of the species of poems—and will do so, as will be clearly seen in the course of the work—he will give the latter [definitions] first."[81] In the achievement of this end, one may distinguish, as it were, qualitative parts of Aristotle's presentation; these are "demonstrative or declarative," "narrative," "definitive," "instructive," "dubitative," and "confirmative." For example, the narrative parts will be those in which he traces the origins and development of the divers species; the "definitive," such sections as the definition of tragedy; the "instructive," all the parts containing precepts; the "dubitative," those in which accusations and defences are offered; the "confirmative," ones in which "the precepts are reinforced through the comparison of tragedy with heroic poetry."[82] Such an enumeration of parts implies an analysis of Aristotle's method and order, which Salviati approves in a general way in the following statement: "And this is the order which may be required of a book which does not treat the secrets of philosophy, not only the resolutive, definitive, compositive, and divisive methods over which Robortello exerts himself so much without advantage for the present work."[83] These are the same distinctions of method that we discovered in Sassetti a decade earlier; they appear early in Robortello (pp. 4–5), who attributes them to Philoponus' commentary on *Posterior Analytics* II.

To the interpretation of the *Poetics* Salviati brings three basic suppositions, and these color everything that he has to say in his commentary. (1) Poetry is an imitation of verisimilar objects; this supposition involves him in a lengthy debate over the nature of imitation, over verisimilitude, and over the identification of the objects. (2) It is an imitation in verse; this supposition requires much sleight of hand in the reading of Aristotle. (3) Its ends are to profit and to please; this supposition introduces many extraneous elements into the consideration both of matter and of form in poetry. As we examine these suppositions in turn, we shall discover to what an extent Salviati departs from Aristotle in his attempt to use them as a basis for understanding the *Poetics*.

(1) For Salviati a poem is "an imitation of the verisimilar expressed through ornamented language" ("imitazione del uerisimile espresso col fauellar condito," fol. 10). But to define imitation is not so easy a matter,

---

81 *Ibid.*, fols. 41–41*v*: "d'insegnarne fare il poema, e di darne le regole, le quali regole percioche dalle difinizioni delle spezij del poema uuol ritrarre, e farallo, si come nel processo dell'opera si uedrà manifesto, prima quelle ne darà."

82 *Ibid.*, fol. 42*v*: "i precetti si fortificano col paragone della tragedia per rispetto all' heroico."

83 *Ibid.*, fol. 42*v*: "E questo è l'ordine, che da un libro, che non tratti i segreti della Filosofia puo richiedere, non i cotanti metodi risolutiui, diffinitiui, compositiui, e diuisiui, ne' quali il Rubertello senza pro di questa opera cotanto s'affatica."

since he finds many meanings and much confusion both in Plato and in Aristotle. He thinks that the meanings in Aristotle reduce to two. The first attaches to simple narration, wherein "the poet imitates, that is, expresses or represents continuously anything whatsoever, either actions, or characters, or persons, or places, or seasons, or tempests, or battles or anything else that can fall under imitation; and he does this without introducing anybody who speaks."[84] This is an acceptable form; what is not acceptable is for the poet to intervene himself, giving judgments and making speeches, for here no imitation is present. The second kind is present when persons are introduced as actors and speakers; this is imitation in the Platonic sense. Further light is thrown upon the term by the comparison which Salviati makes between poetry and history. History is an imitation, for it represents the kinds of things listed; but it is less an imitation than poetry because it does so less vividly. We may thus distinguish, within poetry itself, between two kinds of imitation, one of which represents the principal action in a general way (this is universal), the other of which is found in particular parts:

Then it receives particular imitations especially in the parts in which either bodies, or sounds, or times, or movements or other things compounded of these are feigned by the poet; in which either characters or thoughts of the mind or passions which are not true but verisimilar are depicted in this special way; wherever by comparison, diminution, augmentation, distinct narration, we are made almost to touch with our hands the things invented by the poet, and they almost to appear visibly in their verisimilar form.[85]

These kinds of partial imitation are found separately in different poets: Dante imitates by descriptions, Petrarch by character, Euripides and Vergil by thoughts of the mind, Vergil by passions, Homer by comparison, Terence by diminution, Lucan by augmentation, Ariosto by distinct narration. In the latter contexts, imitation seems to consist in the enhancing or the heightening of the materials by the use of rhetorical devices.

This impression is confirmed by Salviati's remarks on imitation in the lyric. Since the lyric has no action or plot, it will not display that kind of imitation which accompanies narration; hence, it will not conform to the requirement that a "poem" be imitative throughout. But that is not necessary, for "poetry is present whenever one makes with verse any poetic imitation whatsoever, no matter how brief and compressed, as a part or a

[84] *Ibid.*, fol. 68: "il poeta imiti, cioè esprima, o rappresenti sempre mai che che sia, o azzioni, o costumi, o persone, o luoghi, o stagioni, o tempeste, o battaglie, o cheunque altro cader possa sotto l'imitazione. E questo faccia senza indurr' alcuno a parlare."

[85] *Ibid.*, fols. 70v–71: "Appresso particolari imitazioni riceue spezialmente nelle parti, ouunque, o corpi, o suoni, o tempi, o mouimenti, o altre cose di queste mescolate dal poeta si fingono, ouunque ò costumi, o concetti di mente o passioni non uere, ma uerisimili in un cotal modo si dipingono: ouunque comparando, diminuendo, accrescendo, partitamente recitando, ci si fanno le cose trouate dal poeta quasi toccar con mano, quasi nella lor forma uerisimile uisibilmente apparire."

parcel of a composition which may not be a poem."[86] It will thus be possible to find imitation, and hence poetry, even in the minute sections—wòrds or phrases—of works which are not imitations in the more general sense. Salviati here comes close to the position of Averroës, who saw imitation essentially in the rhetorical figure; and he departs radically from the position of Aristotle. He expresses the same idea in a modified way when he says that "imitation is thus only of appearances, of appearances I say which are the objects of those same senses to which imitation has as its end to show itself."[87] If we compare poetry with nature, then, we find that in nature the cause-and-effect relationship is as follows:

$$objects > senses > [pleasure]$$

whereas in poetry it is as follows:

$$objects > appearances > imitation > senses > [pleasure].$$

The objects may be actions, in which case the imitation informs the whole work and makes it a poem; or they may be things, in which case the imitation is fragmentary and partial and produces poetry only occasionally.

There are two further consequences of this theory of imitation. First, on the general relationship between imitation and poetry, Salviati holds that imitation is essential and that we have poems or parts of poems according as we have one or the other kind of imitation. But imitation itself is not sufficient. He discusses Aristotle's statement that imitation makes the poet: "For if one had to take that statement absolutely, it would follow that every imitator should be called a poet and every imitation a poem. Similarly, painters and monkeys would be poets, and statues, masks, and puppets would be poems." What must be added is verse, which does not in itself make the poet but which is a necessary adjunct to imitation: "Nor is it enough to say that imitation is the form of the poem; for in order to make the composite, form in itself is not sufficient, but there must also be the matter and not every matter but the proper matter which (speaking of the extrinsic one) in poetry is verse."[88] Second, in any conception of the ends of poetry, imitation must be reduced to its proper importance. Salviati finds that there are four ends for poetry, stated in ways which come closer and closer to the definition of the art as he sees it:

[86] Ibid., fols. 244v–45: "ogni hora si poeti, che si faccia col uerso qualunque poetica imitazione, sia pur quanto si uoglia breue, e compresa, come parte, o come particella da un componimento, che poema non sia."

[87] Ibid., fol. 276: "È adunque l'imitazione solamente dell'apparenze, delle apparenze dico, che oggetti sono di quei sensj, a i quali ell'ha per fine il mostrarsi."

[88] Ibid., fol. 131v: "Percioche se assolutamente douesse prendersi quella sentenzia, ne seguirebbe che ogni imitatore poeta, et ogni imitazione poema dir si douesse. Cosi poeti sarebbono i dipintori, e le scimie, e poemi le statue, le maschere, e i fraccurradi. . . . Ne uale il dire l'imitazione è la forma del poema: percioche a fare il composto non è la forma da per se stessa sofficiente, ma ui uuol la materia, e non ogni materia. ma la materia propria, la qual (parlando dell'estrinseca) nella poesia si è'l uerso."

Artists have two ends: one of them proximate, and that is the work itself; the other ultimate, and that is what follows upon it. The proximate end of the poet is truly to imitate, the ultimate to bring profit and pleasure, which is the same as saying to offer utility and enjoyment by imitating. . . . The poem, therefore, has mainly four ends: To imitate; to imitate with verse; to profit and delight by imitating; to profit and delight by imitating with verse. The first is the proximate general end, the second the proximate special, the third the ultimate general, the fourth the ultimate special.[89]

In this analysis, imitation becomes an element in a composite of ends rather than a simple end in itself.

Poetry is an imitation, but of verisimilar objects. Its objects, we have seen, are not merely actions or characters but also a large variety of things, animate and inanimate. We have seen what some of these things are (compare also fol. 202v). It is possible, moreover, to classify them, and Salviati's classification gives a first answer to the relationship between objects and imitations. The poet may imitate objects which are true or false, and in the latter category those which are probable or improbable. But true objects are improper to poetry, since they come from nature and do not demand invention; the poet cannot be a poet without invention. Those which are false and improbable are also excluded, because they prevent the poet from achieving his end, "which is to move the passions along with profit and delight; this cannot be achieved by the imitation of the improbable."[90] The assumption is that emotion depends upon belief and belief upon probability. Hence the third category, of false (or invented) objects which are probable, is the only one left for the poet, and it is this one which Aristotle considers exclusively (fol. 77). Salviati also suggests the sources of our notions of the probable: "It cannot be denied that the probable is found either in nature, or in the sempiternal Idea, or in the mind of the poet, or in the universal, and being found there it is clear that it can be imitated."[91] The poet invents his subject by taking probable materials and fashioning them into a likeness of truth; he disposes them in a proper order; and he expresses them in words (the rhetorical elements of invention, disposition, and elocution are clearly present). Of all these things he is—unlike the historian—maker and creator:

. . . the poet in his work makes everything himself. . . . the poet, inventing what does not exist, and in such a way that it is formed equal to that which exists or

[89] *Ibid.*, fols. 151-51v: "gli arteficj hanno due fini, un vicino, e cio è l'opera stessa, uno ultimo, che è cio che ne segue. Prossimo fine del poeta è ueramente l'imitare: ultimo l'arrecar giouamento, e piacere, che il medesimo uiene a dire, che porgere utilità, e dilettazione imitando. . . . Ha adunque il poema quattro fini massimamente. Imitare. Imitar col uerso. Giouare, e dilettare imitando. Giouare, e dilettare imitando col uerso. Il primo si è prossimo fine generale, il secondo prossimo speziale, il terzo, ultimo generale, il quarto, ultimo speziale."

[90] *Ibid.*, fol. 76: "il quale è di commuouere con profitto, e diletto il che l'imitazione del non uerisimile non puo adoperare."

[91] *Ibid.*, fol. 76v: "negar non si puo, che'l uerisimile, o uogliam dir nella natura, o nell'Idea sempiterna, o nella mente del poeta, o nell'uniuersale non si ritruouj, e ritrouandosi è manifesto, che si puo imitare."

even better, by himself makes the matter, by himself disposes it; and not content with this, since he must make it appear as it were in the mantle of speech, he does not wish to borrow the latter, either, from somebody else; but he forms a new and excellent one by himself, so that no part shall find a place in his work that he himself has not made.[92]

Verisimilitude is the resemblance of what the poet produces to the world of reality; insofar as it is "better," it resembles the world of Ideas; and the process of creating or inventing such resemblance is called imitation.

(2) Poetry is an imitation in verse. Salviati has established, in passages already examined, the necessity for verse as the proper matter of poetry (and he has called this the "extrinsic" matter to separate it from the "intrinsic" matter or "subject matter" or the objects as imitated). He recognizes the philosophical (and Aristotelian) principles concerning form and matter in imitation:

... the imitation is of the form alone; so long as this is expressed by the imitator, it is of no importance through what matter or with what instrument he presents it to us. And since the matter of the thing imitated and the matter of that which imitates must be different, this difference ought to be, as the logicians say, not specific but of number. For it would be important not that the same sort of language, but that the same words arranged in the same way, should not be used.[93]

But his argument for verse is not based on principle; it consists in a triple appeal to artifice, to pleasure, and to usage. By "artifice" he means the skilful use of the potentialities of language; this is pleasurable because it reveals the greatness of the poet's genius, and moreover it serves to "magnify" the poem. Pleasure itself is a part of the end—or one of the ends—and insofar as verse adds an element of pleasure to the poem it is desirable. The usage of the best poets in the past should convince the poet that verse is indispensable.

These arguments are not without their difficulties. On the one hand there are such works as Sannazaro's *Arcadia*, which is to be blamed for not being entirely in verse rather than for mixing verse with prose. On the other hand, Boccaccio's *Decameron*, although it is a plot and should require verse, is so good in prose that one would not wish it otherwise: " . . . perchance no composition either of the moderns or of the ancients

[92] *Ibid.*, fol. 167: "il poeta nella sua fabbrica fa da se ogni cosa. . . . il poeta fingendo quel che non è, et in maniera, che al par di quel, ch'è, o ancor meglio è formato, da se medesimo fabbrica la materia, da se medesimo la dispone, ne contento di cio, quella douendo fare quasi col manto della locuzione apparire, ne anche quella uuol da altrui torre in presto, ma una nuoua, et eccellente se ne forma da per se, acciò niuna parte nella sua fabbrica non da lui fatta, habbia luogo."

[93] *Ibid.*, fol. 136v: "l'imitazione è della forma solamente, la qual pur che dall'imitatore uenga espressa, nulla rilieua per uia di qual materia, o di quale strumento auanti ce l'appresenti. E posto che la materia della cosa imitata, e di quella che imita esser douesse differente, si fatta differenza harebbe a essere, come dicono i loici, non ispecifica, ma di numero: che importerebbe non che la stessa maniera di locuzione, ma le medesime parole nel medesimo modo ordinate non si douessero adoperare."

was ever made so graceful and so beautiful: and woe to the author if he had made it in verse!"[94] Salviati solves the dilemma by stating that the fault is with respect to the species, but that the particular work is excellent; nevertheless, one senses the ascendency of taste and preference over the dictates of principle and argument. The problem of comedy is especially thorny. If it is a poem, it must have verse: Aristotle never permits, in any passage of the *Poetics*, the use of prose. One might think that the popular actions of comedy and its homespun conversations would demand the medium of prose; but instead, poets have invented a kind of verse particularly suited to its needs, and this always appears. Piccolomini's arguments for prose are rejected, and Salviati develops a thorough case for the use of Italian verse in Italian comedy. He summarizes it thus:

> The law that it must be made in measured language is given to all comedy, not to the Greek language or any other; and the reason on which the aforementioned law is based is common to all languages: this is artifice, which, even if it did not afford utility and profit to the listener, if only it did not bring harm and damage to him, should not be neglected, lest the author be deprived of praise and of the privilege of his title. And if one makes verse in the way that has been indicated, it will bring no unpleasantness and no harm to the ears and to the mind of the spectator.[95]

Salviati obviously has in mind not only his principle about verse but also his conviction (stated in another context) that "Art is one and has a certain form of its own and a firm essence from which it must not be removed."[96] In a perfectly consistent way, he maintains that verse does not necessarily involve rhyme. There is no justification for rhyme in Italian tragedy, and, indeed, reason tells us that the use of rhyme in any spoken verse is an improbability (fol. 345v).

(3) The ends of poetry—its ultimate ends—are utility and pleasure. In his initial statement about the four causes (see Chapter II, p. 49 above), Salviati declares that the final cause "is concerned with mores" ("è intorno a' costumi," fol. 13). Nevertheless, he neither subordinates pleasure to utility nor does he insist that utility must always be present. Instead, he seems to neglect the "concern with mores" almost completely and to talk largely about the pleasure to be found in the various genres. Two considerations relate to the kind of pleasure resulting from a given literary

---

[94] *Ibid.*, fol. 140v: "niun componimento ne da' moderni, ne da gli antichi si grazioso, e si bello fu fatto per auuentura: e guai all'Autore, se l'hauesse fatto in uersj."
[95] *Ibid.*, fol. 189v: "La legge, che in legata locuzione debba farsi è data alla commedia non alla greca lingua, o ad altra: e la ragione sopra la quale la predetta legge è fondata a tutte le lingue è comune: cio si è l'artifizio, il quale, come che utile, o giouamento all'uditore non recasse, solo, che noia, o disutile non gli arrechi, per non ispogliar l'autore della lode, e del priuilegio del suo titolo non douerrebbe trascurarsi. E chi farà il uerso nella guisa, che s'è detto, niun fastidio, e niun danno all'orecchia, et all'animo dello spettatore porterà."
[96] *Ibid.*, fol. 69: "L'arte è una, et ha una sua certa forma, et una ferma essenza, onde trarla non conuiene."

form: the audience for which it is written and the objects which it represents. The end of comedy, for example, is pleasure alone—the pleasure which comes from laughter (fols. 146, 200). It has nothing to do with teaching, with using other people's lives to better our own, although this has sometimes been ascribed to it as an end; at best, it avoids presenting positively harmful examples (fol. 355). Its audience is of two kinds: some men (the common people) care only about their laughter and their pleasure; others (the educated men) are more discriminating:

. . . since pleasure is sufficient for men, they care about nothing else, nor are they bothered by the obscenities, or the lack of verisimilitude, or the other errors of the art, or the improprieties and the impertinences of which these plots [in the "commedie di zanni"] are everywhere full, so long as the laughter and the pleasure last continuously. Grave men also find extreme pleasure in them, because of their admirable imitation; but on the other hand, they feel greater annoyance at the absurdities and the other defects than if this were not so. From the striving for pleasure nothing but praise can come to these plots, because pleasure must be said without any doubt to be the end of comedy.[97]

The same is true for certain "joyous writers" in Italian, such as Berni, whose works give even greater pleasure to the "giudiziosi" and the "discreti" than they do to ordinary men: " . . . they are heard with greater pleasure by men of merit because they recognize in them, better than the multitude, the beauty of the sayings, the grace of the witticisms, the sharpness of the conceits, and the appropriateness of the language."[98]

In order to achieve this effect, to please this audience, comedy must treat men of low social station. Salviati insists throughout that the difference between comedy and tragedy is not a difference between vice and virtue, or badness and goodness, but uniquely between common and illustrious people. This is the "specific" difference:

For the fact that the persons are good or bad in a given tragedy or comedy will make them more or less commendable, indeed, or more or less perfect; but it will not make them change species. For if popular subjects were taken, no matter how much "better" the persons of such a story were made to be, we should not have a tragedy; and on the contrary, if kings were taken for the imitation, even if their actions were as abominable and as wicked as possible, from such a

97 *Ibid.*, fols. 145v–46: "gli huomini bastando loro il diletto, di niente altro hanno cura ne fa lor noia le sconce cose, ne'l mancamento del uerisimile, ne gli altri errorj dell'arte, ne le sconueneuolezze, e le scede, di che per tutto ripiene sono quelle fauole: pur che continuo il riso duri, e'l piacere, il quale eziandio i seueri huominj grande ui gustano oltr'à misura, per l'ammirabile imitazione di coloro: ma degli assurdi all'incontro, et degli altri difetti senton maggior la noia, che se questo non fosse del cercare il diletto, altro, che lode a quelle fauole non potrebbe uenire: impercioche il diletto il fine della commedia senza alcun fallo è da dire."

98 *Ibid.*, fol. 298: "sono . . . da' ualent' huomini con piu diletto ascoltate, quanto eglino meglio, che'l uolgo la bellezza de' mottj, la grazia degli scherzi, l'acutezza de concettj, e la proprietà della fauella dentro ui riconoscono."

plot—provided it were set forth as a dramatic representation—no other poem than a tragedy would ever result.[99]

Hence, all the passages in Aristotle that make an ethical distinction between goodness and badness are explained away or are interpreted in such a way as to justify Salviati's basic contention. Unfortunately, we do not have his remarks on tragedy, on the effect of purgation, and on the specific pleasure to be obtained from that form. But his judgment of Dante is revealing; he holds that Dante writes for "wise men" rather than ordinary ones, that he therefore chooses a highly noble subject, magnifies it in every way, and by so doing gives to his audience marvelous and extraordinary pleasure (fol. 168*v*). We do know that the effects of compassion and terror result from the spectacle of the misfortunes of illustrious men, just as those of laughter are produced by the spectacle of men who are "ridiculous through their condition" ("ridicoli per la loro condizione," fol. 209).

Salviati's definitions of poetry and of its kinds reflect his attitudes toward imitation and its objects, toward the use of verse, and toward the essential end of pleasure. We have already seen poetry defined as "an imitation of the verisimilar expressed through ornamented language" (fol. 10). The presence of verisimilitude and the use of language both establish a relationship between poetry and rhetoric, since rhetoric treats of both; some knowledge of rhetoric is thus prior to the practice of poetry. Besides, insofar as "costumi" are involved, there will also be a link with moral philosophy. But Salviati refuses to follow Castelvetro in establishing a priority of history over poetry. The reasons are clear: although history is also an imitation, if to a lesser degree than poetry, its object is the true and not the verisimilar; neither the imitation of the truth nor the use of prose would satisfy the basic conditions of poetry, and hence history is essentially different from it. The notion of fiction, of falsehood, of the lie is contained in such terms as μῦθος and λόγος, and these inevitably accompany poetry (fols. 70–70*v*, 76*v*). By definition, then, poetry is more closely akin to rhetoric and to moral philosophy than to history. The definition of comedy is modeled on Aristotle's definition of tragedy: "Comedy is a representation of a low subject, having a happy ending and magnitude, with ornamented language, with the ornaments sometimes separated, giving recreation to the soul by means of laughter and of witticisms."[100] It is

[99] *Ibid.*, fol. 200*v*: "Percioche l'essere, o buoni i personaggi, ò cattiui d'una qualche tragedia, o commedia, le farà bene piu, o meno commendabili, o piu, o men perfette, ma cangiare spezie non gia. Conciosia cosa, che se soggetti si prendano popolareschi, facciansi quanto si uuol migliori le persone di cotale argomento tragedia mai non s'haurà, et all'incontro tolgansi Re ad imitare, sien pur quanto si uogliano abbomineuoli, e scelerate le loro operazioni, di cotal fauola, se per maniera di rappresentazione si distenda, altro poema, che tragedia non uscirà giamai."

[100] *Ibid.*, fol. 351: "La commedia è rappresentazione di basso, e sollazzeuole auuenimento hauente fine, e grandezza con fauellar condito, coi condimenti alcuna uolta in disparte, per uia del riso, e delle piaceuolezze l'animo ricreante."

notable that no ethical end is here stated for comedy, as was so frequently done in this period; but otherwise the definition shows many incomprehensions of the *Poetics*.

Throughout his commentary as we have it, Salviati indicates his independence of the earlier students of the text. He examines their positions in the light of his own theory, accepting or rejecting accordingly. That theory is difficult to describe succinctly. It has some elements of a rhetorical theory, such as the concern for the audience and for certain problems of language; but it is not completely oriented in these directions. It discards the contemporary supposition that poetry has moral instruction as its end; hence, the Platonic or the Horatian element is much reduced. It remains close to Aristotle on some points, but frequently—as on the matter of verse, of imitation, of the objects—is far distant from him. One can only regard it as highly eclectic, as perhaps not fully achieved, but as seeking nevertheless a clarification of Aristotle's text and a removal of accumulated error.

One should not conclude, from Salviati's position, that it represented a general tendency in the period. For the next document to be studied, a short pamphlet by Lorenzo Parigiuolo entitled *Questione della poesia* (1586), takes a clearly anti-Aristotelian stand. Its central thesis is that verse makes the poet. We have seen most of the apologists of recent years maintaining that verse was an essential ingredient of poetry, along with imitation, but we have not seen them discarding imitation. That is precisely what Parigiuolo does. He rejects Aristotle's proposition that imitation, not verse, makes the poet, and this constitutes the first point in his program for the work:

> We shall therefore first deny Aristotle's proposition. In addition to this we shall prove that verse makes poetry, not imitation. From this it will follow that the writers of verses without imitation are true poets, contrary to Aristotle's deduction. Finally, we shall remove the accessory that is made to all this, that when the poet speaks in his own person he is not a poet and that one who speaks through the mouth of another is a poet.[101]

"Aristotle's proposition" is disposed of rapidly, merely by saying that he offered no proof for it and that of all the writers of antiquity, only Plutarch accepted it. For the rest, the basic distinction is Cicero's: oratory is in prose, poetry is in verse. Parigiuolo states only one condition: "I do not say, though, that the poet (by which I mean the good poet) is made by verse alone . . . ; but by good verse, which can be written only through

[101] *Questione della poesia* (1586), pp. 6–7: "Si neghera dunque prima la proposta d'Aristotele. Oltre accio si prouera che il verso fa la poesia non la imitatione. A questo seguitara che i compositori di versi senza imitatione sono veri poeti contra la consequenza di Aristotele. Vltimamente si torra via la giunta, che vi si fa, che il poeta fauellando in persona sua non sia poeta, e sia quello che per bocca d'altri fauella."

miracles of nature, not without art, and eloquence, and a knowledge of universal things."[102] Imitation may also be included in the poetic faculty; but it is accidental, its use depending upon the ends sought by the poet. The ends are simply stated: all composers of poetry "have directed their road to the end of profiting others, but along different routes according as certain things were pleasant to and appropriate to their minds and their powers."[103]

In many other ways Parigiuolo returns to the tradition of the beginning of the century. Etymologizing on the principal terms connected with the art, he finds that one of them is "fingo" and that this means both "to feign" and "to form"; hence the question of fiction, which brings on a consideration of allegory in poetry: " . . . for the poet, this will be 'to feign' and simulate parables and stories and other similar things in order to delight and profit others with those fictions, under which are always hidden a thousand fine secrets about nature and about customs."[104] This, of course, repeats one of the essential arguments in the early defences of poetry. But Parigiuolo adds the caution that one must introduce no such fictions into religious, Christian poetry, with which fables of the pagan gods must not be intermingled: Horace, in his *Ars poetica*, forbids such monstrous compositions. Many others of the standard arguments for poetry are introduced. Indeed, the extent to which Parigiuolo is retrogressing to a distant time is indicated by his final use, as a definition for poetry, of the Latin formula, "Poesis est cuiuslibet rei versibus comprehensa dictio" (p. 19). All these arguments, it should be noted, are offered as contradictions to Aristotle and as proofs that the concept of imitation is unnecessary in any consideration of the art of poetry.

DENORES (1586)

The position of Aristotle in Giason Denores' *Discorso intorno à que' principii, cause, et accrescimenti, che la comedia, la tragedia, et il poema heroico ricevono dalla philosophia morale, & civile, & da' governatori delle republiche* (1586) is indeed a curious one. As we have already seen (Chapter VIII, pp. 316–19), Denores is primarily concerned with the relationship between poetry and moral and civil philosophy and with the various pedagogical ends served by poetry. To this extent he is a Platonist. He believes that the end of pleasure, everywhere present, is auxiliary and accessory— that instruction follows upon pleasure. Insofar as he holds that the devices capable of producing pleasure are defined and described in the *Poetics*, he

---

102 *Ibid.*, p. 8: "Non dico pero che semplicemente il verso basti a fare il poeta intendendo del buon poeta . . . ma il buon verso, il quale far non si puo se non per miracoli di natura, senza arte, & eloquenza, e cognitione delle cose vniuersali."

103 *Ibid.*, p. 9: "hanno . . . drizzato il lor camino al fine di giouare altrui, ma per diuersa strada, secondo che piu le cose a gli animi, & alle forze loro aggradano, e si confanno."

104 *Ibid.*, p. 13: "per la parte del poeta, sara fingere, e simulare parabole, e nouelle, & altre simili cose per dilettare e giouare altrui con quelle fittioni sotto le quali stanno sempre coperti mille bei secreti & ammaestramenti di natura, e di costumi."

is an Aristotelian. This means that he goes to Plato for a statement of the ends of poetry, to Aristotle for information about its means. The means themselves work in two ways: some of them, such as character and sententiae, produce instruction directly; others, such as plot and diction, produce pleasure directly and instruction ultimately. One may summarize the total situation in this way: The poet himself, wishing to benefit mankind, seeks as his goal instruction about ethics or about nature; hence he turns to Plato for an indication of the proper ends. But realizing that his audience, which seeks only pleasure, must be moved and delighted before it will learn, he turns to Aristotle for precepts of the art.

If pleasure is the means, or at best an intermediate end, all matters pertaining to it will be fully discussed in the *Poetics*. For according to Aristotle, one of the two bases (and the earliest) for the origin of poetry was the wish to give pleasure through imitation; the other (coming later) was the wish to be useful to the public (p. 1*v*). Art itself is the reduction to method and precept of those devices by which poets have succeeded in pleasing their audiences. For Denores, as he considers the sources of pleasure, all reduce to one word, the marvelous—"la marauiglia." Each of the devices used in the poem must be capable of causing wonder and admiration in the audience. "Therefore every poem is founded on the marvelous. For if this were not so, it would not engender in our minds that pleasure which the audience desires."[105] The marvelous depends, in part, upon the selection of the materials by the poet; to achieve it, he must avoid all those matters which are well worn, familiar, commonplace. But it depends, in greater part, upon how they are handled, for therein lies the artistry of the poet. First and foremost, of course, is the handling of plot, and Denores sees each element of plot-construction, as well as the totality of its form, as contributing to the arousing of admiration. Every plot consists in a change of fortune (the two poles being prosperity and adversity), and this change must be contrived in an unexpected and extraordinary way; for example, in comedy: "it consists in this, that a man of low estate finds himself in some predicament, and it does not seem that he can ever get himself out of it; nevertheless, the poets, following the orders of the law-givers, arrange this kind of poem in such a way, through their inventions, that although in the beginning he is in trouble, at the end however he achieves a most happy conclusion."[106] Wonder grows as the audience sees these things accomplished within the limited time of twelve hours. For tragedy, the conditions are almost identical, even if the situation is reversed:

[105] *Discorso* (1586), p. 16: "Pertanto è fondato ogni poema nella marauiglia. Percioche se non è tale, non partorisce negli animi nostri quel diletto, che si propone l'auditore."

[106] *Ibid.*, pp. 16–16*v*: "consiste in questo, che trouandosi vn huomo di bassa fortuna in vna qualche molestia, non pare, che possa mai rileuarsi da quella, nondimeno i poeti, seguendo gli ordini de' legislatori, acconciano con le loro inuentioni si fattamente questa tal poesia, che se ben nel principio egli è in disturbo, all'vltimo tuttauia sortisce felicissimo fine."

. . . while some powerful man is in a state of the highest happiness, it does not seem, because of his great power and authority, that he can ever fall into misery. Nevertheless, the poets, through their most skilful plots, weave the tragedy in such a way that although in the beginning he is in a state of extreme contentment and prosperity, at the end, however, he falls into many misadventures. Such marvelousness is rendered even greater by the very brevity and shortness of time, since it is necessary that the poet bring about this great transmutation from good to bad fortune within one revolution of the sun.[107]

In the epic, similarly, a great prince is returned to a state of good fortune.

A plot will be still more marvelous if, to the kinds of "revolution" already indicated, it adds the devices of recognition and reversal. For both of these go counter to our expectations, surprise us, fill us with wonder not only at the turn of events itself, but at the poet's skill in putting them together in this way. The episode may also be added to the list of marvelous devices; for the poet displays both his genius and his inventiveness when he "finds" those episodes which, in a verisimilar way, extend a plot to its correct proportions (pp. 17v–21). Verisimilitude and the proper handling of time are two considerations which must everywhere be observed in these matters. From such passages as his discussion of Vergil, it is apparent that Denores gives to "verisimilitude" the meaning of "natural probability"; such phrases as "per natura" and "contraria alla ragione" are used as criteria for actions. As for time, not only does the limitation for tragedy and comedy permit the display of the poet's powers while the freedom of the epic gives scope to his invention, but somehow the varying lengths are adapted to the differing moral lessons. The king in a tragedy may quickly fall into misery; but it will take a long time for the hero of an epic to regain his lost position. Indeed, since the moral lesson is the ultimate end, it will never be omitted from judgments on the effectiveness of plot. Denores' way of combining means and end may be exemplified by his remarks on the usefulness, for tragedy, of Boccaccio's novella on Rosciglione's wife (*Decameron* IV, 9); it has a plot

. . . which can equally well receive both the change of fortune, and the reversal, and the recognition, and the revolution of one single day, and the morality; by which it is demonstrated that these furtive and illegitimate loves are discovered at last and receive as punishment, through these secret ways from eternal providence, desperation and death.[108]

---

[107] *Ibid.*, pp. 16v–17: "essendo qualche potente huomo in vna somma felicità non pare per la sua gran potenza, & signoria, che possa mai trabocar in miseria, nondimeno i poeti, hauendo la mira alle cose predette, tessono con le loro prudentissime fauole la tragedia in tal guisa, che quantunque nel principio egli sia in vna suprema contentezza, & prosperità, all'vltimo nondimeno cade in molte disauenture. Vna tal marauiglia si rende ancho maggiore dalla medesima breuità, e strettezza di tempo, essendo necessario, che il poeta faccia risultar questa gran tramutatione dalla buona fortuna alla cattiua in vn giro di Sole."

[108] *Ibid.*, p. 29v: "laquale parimente puo riceuer, & la tramutation di fortuna, & la peripetia, & l'agnitione, & il giro di vn sol giorno, & la moralità, per la quale si dimostra, questi amori furtiui, & non legitimi essere finalmente discoperti, & riceuer per queste occulte vie dalla prouidentia eterna per castigamento la desperatione, & la morte."

The devices of the marvelous contribute to the achievement of the pedagogical ends.

·Diction and verse constitute another qualitative part capable of producing the marvelous. In comedy and tragedy the audience is astonished
by the fact that verse can so completely resemble prose and that it can so
well be adapted to the conditions of the personages. In any genre, the use
of figures of speech will in itself be pleasurable. Denores thinks of diction
in terms of the "figures," or the traditional styles, each of which is adapted
to particular kinds of subject matters.

The marvelous of words in all these poems, but especially in the heroic and
the tragic, consists in this, that they are accompanied by poetic figures and forms
of speech and raised above the way of speaking of private persons, so that the
language appropriate to the condition of their illustrious persons has in itself a
certain royal dignity and grandeur which stems from the choice of the words and
from the artful ordering and succession of the same. The figure of lowness, next,
must be used for comedy, since it is the imitation of the actions of private
citizens.[109]

It is interesting to note that whereas on matters of plot Denores appeals
to the authority of Aristotle, on questions of style he attaches himself to the
medieval tradition.

The two remaining qualitative parts, character and what Denores calls
"sententia," present their moral lessons in an even more direct way. He
speaks of character and decorum as affording great delight because the
poet presents, via imitation, all the imaginable types and nationalities and
the good and the bad in each. He does so specifically in order that his
audience may obtain knowledge of the various types, each of which will be
delineated in accordance with the laws of decorum. The special language
to be used for this delineation is called "oration morata." Here it is another
tradition—the rules of decorum of the rhetoricians—that is called upon to
provide a basis of procedure for the poet. The rhetorician is also uppermost in Denores' mind when he considers the utility of sententiae, for these
arguments and appeals to the emotions are no more than so many lessons
in eloquence (p. 32v).

If such parts as plot and diction are marvelous and hence produce
delight, and such others as character and thought achieve a moral end
more directly, there is no formal or structural criterion which would determine the relationship among all these parts. Aristotle's "if one wishes the
poetic composition to be beautiful" (1447a10) is not represented in any

---

109 *Ibid.*, pp. 35–35v: "La marauiglia delle parole in tutti questi poemi, ma sopratutto
nell'heroico, & nel tragico, consiste in questo, che siano con figure, & con maniere di dir
poetiche, & inalzate dal modo di ragionar delle persone priuate, a tal che il parlar secondo
la conditione delle sue persone illustri habbia in se una certa dignità regia, & grandezza,
che deriua dalla eletion delle parole, et dalla prudente ordination, & continuation delle
medesime. La figura poscia dell' humilta douera essere accommodata alla comedia, essendo
ella imitation delle attion de' priuati."

way, and there is no substitute for it. The only general conception that would permit one to see a given poem as a totality is the conception of its moral lesson, and indeed genres themselves are distinguished on the basis of such a conception. Tragedy, for example, must teach an ethical lesson of a specific kind, having the required social and political implications. Hence, whatever the particular form of its plot might be—revolution, recognition, reversal—its general form must always be the same: it must have an unhappy ending, else the lesson will not be taught. In the same way, its personages must be public figures of illustrious rank; social position, not character, is the only basis of distinction which Denores finds in Aristotle, and he believes that Aristotle also meant to imply the necessity of the unhappy denouement. Moral character enters, to be sure, but because it is an accompaniment to the social station necessary to arouse the proper passions. Moderately good men, in high station, who fall rapidly into misery and a final state of misfortune will arouse the passions of pity and terror; and these were the only ones useful and necessary for Greek tragedy, which aimed at preparing the citizens for military life and for the defence of their country (pp. 10–14v). Hence, purgation itself, as a pedagogical instrument, takes the form required by the lesson.

The definitions of poetry itself and of the various genres (some of which we have already seen in Chapter VIII) are little more than combinations of the various elements that produce the moral lesson—although they have the external form of Aristotelian definitions. One need only compare them with such definitions as we have in the *Poetics* to discover how basically different is Denores' total orientation. His general definition of poetry is modeled on that of tragedy found in the *Poetics*:

Poetry, then, is an imitation of some human action, marvelous, complete, and sizeable, which has in itself a change of fortune either from prosperous to adverse or from adverse to prosperous, which is presented to the listeners through language in verse, either in narration or in dramatic form, in order to purge them by means of pleasure of the most important passions of the soul, and to direct them toward good living, toward the imitation of virtuous men, and toward the conservation of good republics.[110]

The same general pattern is followed in the definition of comedy. By the very abundance of elements which he includes, and by their specificity, Denores shows on the one hand the eclecticism of his sources, on the other his failure to grasp the essence of an Aristotelian definition:

Comedy therefore will be the representation of a pleasant action of private persons, between the good and the bad; which through some human error of

110 *Ibid.*, p. 36: "E dunque la poesia rassomiglianza di vna qualche attion humana, marauigliosa, compita, & grande, che habbia in se tramutation di fortuna; ò dalla prospera nell' auuersa; ò dall'auuersa nella prospera, che si propone agli ascoltanti con parlar in versi; ò narrando; ò rappresentando, per purgargli col mezzo del diletto da' piu importanti affetti dell'animo, & per indrizzargli al ben viuere, alla imitation degli huomini virtuosi, & alla conseruation delle buone republiche."

POETIC THEORY

stupidity, beginning from hardship, ends in laughter and happiness; in the space
of one revolution of the sun; composed in short verses and with low words; in
order to purge the spectators, by means of pleasure and of the ridiculous, of
those hardships which disturb their calm and tranquillity, through the love affairs
of wives and daughters and sons, through the deceits and treacheries of servants,
pimps, nurses, and others of that kind; in order to make them become enamoured
of private life; for the conservation of that well-regulated popular republic in
which they will find themselves.[111]

In such a definition as this, one may work back from the Platonic statement
of the ends, through the medieval enumeration of the kinds of subjects,
through rhetorical elements of verse and style, to certain Aristotelian requirements for the constitution of the poem; but even these latter are
warped by extraneous considerations. In this sense, the definitions of
Denores are symptomatic of his total method: a generous eclecticism in
which all other ingredients are made to serve two general aims, the achievement of ends whose statement derives from Plato, through means whose
conditions are outlined in Aristotle's *Poetics*.

There are striking affinities between Denores' general point of departure
and that of Lorenzo Giacomini in his lecture *Sopra la purgazione della
tragedia*, delivered before the Accademia degli Alterati in 1586. For Giacomini also, there is a duality of ends, consisting in an immediate end of
beauty and pleasure and an ultimate end of Platonic instruction (on the
latter, see Chapter VIII, pp. 315–16). Giacomini himself states it this
way:

The end of the poet, as a poet, is to construct the poem correctly according to
the rules, and the end of the tragic poet is to form the tragedy according to the
general idea of the art—the tragedy which, like any poem, may be used for many
ends, whose consideration with respect to their causes belongs to the politician
who forms the city or who governs it.[112]

The first of these is the proper end of the art, "which is the poem itself"
("il quale è lo istesso poema," p. 33); as he deals with it further, Giacomini
indicates that it is also the formal end. He defines poetry as "an imitation,
in figurative language reduced to verse, of a human action; ... made

111 *Ibid.*, pp. 36–36v: "Sara per tanto la comedia rappresentation di una attion piaceuole
di persone priuate fra buone, & cattiue, che per qualche errore humano di sempietà, comin-
ciando da trauaglio, finisce in riso, & in allegrezza nello spacio di un giro di Sole, composta
con uersi corti, & con parole humili, per purgar gli spettatori col mezzo del diletto, & del
ridicolo da que' trauagli, che turbano la loro quiete, & tranquilità per gl'inamoramenti delle
mogli, delle figliole, de' figlioli, per gl'inganni, & tradimenti de' seruitori, de' ruffiani, delle
nutrici, & di altri simili, & per fargli inamorar della vita priuata a conseruation di quella
tal ben regolata republica populare, nella quale si troueranno."
112 *Orazioni e discorsi* (1597), p. 33: "il fine del poeta in quanto poeta, è il fabricare il
poema con retta ragione, & il fine del poeta Tragico è secondo l'idea del arte formare la
Tragedia, la quale si come ogni poema per molti fini può essere adoperata, la consideratione
de quali per le loro cagioni pertiene al politico, che forma la Città, overo la gouerna."

[626]

according to the poetic art; proper for purging, for teaching, for giving recreation or noble diversion."[113] Now the human action imitated, in terms of the four causes, is the formal cause, the material cause is language, the efficient cause is the poetic art, the final cause is that indicated in the last part of the definition. The form itself must be beautiful and pleasurable, and indeed it achieves directly one of the ends, that of "recreation or noble diversion." Hence it is that "the poet always aims to make the work delightful, and therefore he invents the plot out of marvelous things . . . , he forms the verse which flatters our ear, he uses chosen words, he adorns the diction with strange and wonderful forms of speech."[114] There is thus, for Giacomini, a proper area for the operation of an art of poetry—based on the *Poetics*, we may assume—and this is the creation of the beautiful form according to the rules.

But Aristotle also provides for him the best statement of the pedagogical ends, and this is in the purgation clause, which is the subject of his lecture. He is moved to consider it at length because of the many difficulties of interpretation and because of the three alternative meanings proposed by earlier commentators. The first theory holds that tragedy purges only the two passions of pity and fear, causing the men in its audience to be less fearful and less pitying. The second theory holds, instead, that the opposites of these passions are purged—envy, hate, wrath, joy, confidence. According to the third theory, tragedy moderates all the passions through the spectacle that it gives of the instability of human affairs, makes us accept our own misfortunes with greater equanimity. Giacomini's theory is none of these. He believes, in a general way, that the passions are purged by exteriorization, that a man who suffers any given passion within his soul will suffer it less as he gives it outward expression, as, for example, through weeping. Moreover, this lightening or purgation of the soul is accompanied by a feeling of pleasure. A tragedy presents just such an opportunity for exteriorization. Giacomini likens its effect to that of medicinal purgatives which drive out certain humors from the body, provided that the purgatives have some natural appropriateness to the humors. Tragedy presents vividly before our eyes the spectacle of terrible and pitiable events. As we see misfortunes impending over men like ourselves, we fear for their safety; when misfortune actually occurs, we are compassionate. Hence as we feel these passions in sympathy with others, our souls are relieved of them (pp. 36 ff.). At the same time, the spectacle is full of moral teachings.

To this seemingly divided poetics, divided between two ends of pleasure and utility, between a formal cause and a final cause, Giacomini gives

[113] *Ibid.*, p. 33: "imitazione con parlare fauoloso ridotto in versi di azzione humana . . . fatta secondo l'arte poetica, atta a purgare, ad ammaestrare, a dar riposo, o nobile diporto."
[114] *Ibid.*, p. 35: "il poeta intende sempre far l'opera dilettevole, e perciò finge la favola di cose maravigliose, . . . forma il verso, che ci lusinga l'orecchio, usa sceltezza di parole, adorna la favella di maniere di dire pellegrine e mirabili."

unity by making pleasure a necessary condition of purgation. That is, the form of the poem itself produces not only the pleasure but also the utility. He expresses this notion elaborately in a passage which offers at once a psychology of aesthetic pleasure and a statement of utilitarian ends:

... the spectator of the tragic act, although he knows as long as he has recourse to his intelligence for assistance that what is represented is not true, nevertheless fooled by the artful imitation accompanied by flattering sweetness, especially when present objects strike his view and create within his imagination phantasms capable of moving it, feels within himself fear and compassion and weeping, and in addition to the pleasure coming from the lightening of his spirit which he achieves while it is operating according to these passions, he feels still other pleasures. First, tragedy pleases by teaching the action represented, since learning is among the things which are joyful by their nature; it pleases through the marvelous, demonstrating that a thing not believed can readily come to pass; it is delightful through the imitation. . . . To these delights it is not improper that we should add in order three others, even though they are somewhat external and remote. One is that since compassion is an act of virtue, and since every operation according to virtue or resembling virtue is by its nature joyful, the compassion of tragedy can bring delight also in this respect. . . . The second is, that it informs us that we indeed are free from such grave misfortunes, which cannot do otherwise than give us pleasure and joy. The last is the learning of salutary lessons. . . . [115]

Giacomini's ideas on purgation are not derived exclusively, it will be clear, from the *Poetics*; he refers also to the *Politics* on the effects of music, to Plato on poetry in general, and to a theory of the passions and of their effects upon the soul. These elements are welded into a doctrine which uses Aristotle to defend the poet against Plato, and which achieves an almost complete identification of the pleasures and the utilities of poetry.

TASSO (1586–87)

It is another of the questions raised by Aristotle in the *Poetics*, that of truth and verisimilitude, that occupies Torquato Tasso in his *Risposta al Discorso del Sig. Oratio Lombardelli*, also of 1586. And although this work sets out to contradict Lombardelli, essentially it develops a thesis of its own

[115] *Ibid.*, pp. 240–41: "lo spettatore dell'atto tragico benchè conosca quello, che si rappresenta, non esser vero, mentre all'intelletto ricorre per aiuto, nondimeno ingannato dall'artifiziosa imitazione da lusinghevole dolcezza accompagnata, massimamente quando oggetti presenti feriscon la vista, e crean nella fantasia fantasmi possenti ad alterarla, sente in se timore, e compassione, e pianto, ed oltre la compiacenza dell'alleggerimento dell'animo, che mentre secondo questi affetti opera, egli consegue, prova ancora altri diletti. Primieramente piace la tragedia insegnando l'azione rappresentata, poichè lo imparare è tralle cose per natura gioconde, aggrada colla maraviglia, proponendo la cosa non creduta poter agevolmente avvenire; è dilettevole per l'imitazione. . . . A questi diletti non è disdicevole, che accompagniamo in ischiera tre altri benchè alquanto esterni, e remoti. Uno è, che essendo il compatire atto di virtù, essendo ogni operazione secondo la virtù, o alla virtù somigliante, per natura gioconda, può anche per questo riguardo la compassione della tragedia apportar diletto. . . . L'altro è, che ne fa conoscere, che pur da sì fiere disavventure siamo liberi noi, il che non può non ci porgere piacere, e gioia. L'ultimo è l'apprendere documenti salutevoli. . . ."

[628]

with respect to necessity, probability, credibility, and the marvelous. Much of what Tasso has to say is of course influenced by his intention to defend his own poem, and the thesis becomes a justification of his own practice. Throughout his argument, he uses the art of history as a point of comparison with the art of poetry (answering Lombardelli's views), and the following conclusions result from the comparison: History and poetry differ essentially in the absence and presence of imitation. Tasso has some difficulty with the term, since, at times, he tends to use it as meaning dramatic representation. But in a broader sense it seems to mean the vivid placing of things and actions before our eyes, and this occurs in poetry; whereas history gives merely a simple narrative of events. One consequence of this distinction is that the customary statement to the effect that history treats the truth and poetry treats verisimilitude is not valid. For Tasso, both arts are equally concerned with the truth. In fact, he sees truth as a necessary foundation for poems in whatever genre, and the hierarchy which he establishes descends from genres which are based entirely on the truth to those which represent it only slightly. He puts it this way:

... all poems have some foundation of truth, some more and some less, according as they participate more or less in perfection. We must nevertheless note that just as the whole structure is not the foundation, so perchance the whole action does not need to be true, but it must leave its part to the verisimilar, which is proper to the poem.[116]

Thus tragedy and the epic would be the highest genres, being wholly founded on the truth; comedy and the pastoral would be the lowest, since they have no foundation in truth. Tasso thinks little of poems whose only truth is a truth (or reality) of cities and countries; somewhat more of those which present true (or real) persons as well; and most of those whose actions are true in the sense that they are historically verifiable.

Since poetry is not merely a retailing of historical facts—or a falsification of them—other elements must be added. The "mode" and not the "matter," he says, distinguishes poetry from history (p. 9). For one thing, the poet must organize his materials according to necessity and probability; for another, he must give them a proper form. Perhaps Tasso reduces both of these to one procedure: "That is not a poem to which form is lacking, in which things and events are not well composed together."[117] We are not told of what necessity and probability consist. But we do know that the poet must add something to the truth (otherwise there would be no opportunity for his "invention") and that the marvelous is a necessary ingredient. "The poem reaches the highest degree of perfection when these

---

116 *Risposta* (1586), p. 18: "tutti i poemi habbiano qualche fondamento della uerità, chi piu, e chi meno, secondo che piu, e meno participano della perfettione; dee nondimeno hauersi auertenza, che si come tutta la fabrica non è fondamento, cosi per auentura tutta l'attione non dee esser uera, ma lasciarsi la sua parte al uerisimile, il quale è proprio del poema.'

117 *Ibid.,* p. 10: "quello non è poema, à cui manchi la forma, nel quale le cose, e gli auenimenti non siano ben composti insieme."

two things [the marvelous and verisimilitude] are joined together, and they may be conjoined in various ways."[118] He thinks of the marvelous as consisting of those events which do not enter into natural probability. How, then, can they be credible and acceptable in the poem? The answer is in the beliefs, even the faith, of the audience. For Christians believe the miracles of the Bible, know them to be true even though they are improbable. This is the only kind of credibility which the poet seeks:

. . . from Cicero we may deduce that the credible belongs rather to the orator, because it is a part of the probable; but the verisimilar belongs to the poet, who frequently does not seek to persuade, if only he can please, nor does he care whether things are believed, but that they should give pleasure; nor does he so much avoid lying as the inappropriateness which may be in the lie, and he seeks to hide it or at least to color it in many ways, so that even if it is known, at least it will not be blamed; and if the poet ever takes the credible into consideration, I believe that he does not consider it *per se* but *per accidens.*[119]

There seems to be much confusion in these terms and in the general position. Perhaps we can clarify it in this way: The poet, at his best, takes a historically true subject. He develops it by the addition of elements that seem to flow "necessarily" and "probably" from the given materials. These may be inconsistent with natural probability and with normal credibility; but to the extent to which they contribute to the totality and the beauty of the poetic form, and hence give pleasure, they will be acceptable. In spite of Tasso's protestations, the element of belief in the audience seems to remain an important factor, and "truth" may as well be something which the audience believes to be true as something for which there is historical evidence.

Some further clarification of these points is given by Tasso in his little pamphlet entitled *Delle differenze poetiche*. It was written sometime after 1585, in response to Orazio Ariosto's *Difese dell'Orlando Furioso dell' Ariosto*, but was not published until 1587. In the final pages of the work, where he is discussing the relationship of episodes to plot, Tasso throws light on the meanings which he attaches to necessity and verisimilitude. He does so by proposing an analogy to nature, in which there are no "episodes" but in which everything is necessary, i.e., in which all the parts have a fixed order and interdependency. A similar order would be desirable in poetry, but it is impossible:

118 *Ibid.*, pp. 14–15: "all'hora il poema è nella somma perfettione, che queste cose insieme s'accoppiano, e si possono in piu modi congiungere."
119 *Ibid.*, p. 19: "da Cicerone si può raccorre, che'l credibile appartenga piu all'Oratore; perche egli è parte del probabile, ma il uerisimile è del poeta, il quale molte uolte non cerca di persuadere, pur che diletti, nè si cura, che le cose sian credute; ma che elle piacciano: nè tanto fugge la menzogna; quanto la sconueneuolezza, ch'è nella menzogna; e cerca d'occultarla, ò almeno colorirla in molti modi: accioche, s'ella è pur conosciuta, non sia almeno biasimata: e se'l poeta hà mai consideratione al credibile, io stimo, ch'egli no'l consideri per se, ma per accidente."

... art also would like to demonstrate conclusively its riches and its ornaments and reduce all the parts of the poem to an almost certain order and give to each one the necessary dispositiorr and dependency. But not being able to attain such perfection, it sometimes does in a verisimilar way that which it is not permitted to it to do necessarily.[120]

Verisimilitude, in this context, appears to imply a looser connection of parts than that required by necessity; but it must not be so loose that removal of the part could be effected without spoiling the whole structure.

Tasso's concern with these matters is incidental in the pamphlet. His main problem is twofold: to justify the value and the usefulness of the *Poetics* in a general way, and to insist that Aristotle's ways of distinguishing between genres (these are the "differenze poetiche") are the only proper ones. On the first score, he denies all of Orazio Ariosto's assertions; here is his total estimate of the *Poetics*:

... we do not have, in any work which has been written in any of the three finest languages, any greater light on the art of poetry than in this one. We must not take poetic teachings more willingly from any other, nor allow ourselves to be deceived by false persuasions or by apparent reasons; for every little error that is committed in the principles, as we go beyond, becomes very great toward the end. Thus, Aristotle's principles remain sound and not thrown to the ground.[121]

The principles of which he speaks are the definitions, the bases of similarity, and the differentiae of the species—primarily, the distinction of the object, manner, and means of imitation.

On the interpretation of this distinction, Tasso is usually more rigorist than his contemporaries. For whereas they are frequently willing to admit that objects may be distinguished on a number of bases—rank of persons, or their moral character, or the way in which they are intermingled—and that a number of genres is possible within each manner, Tasso reduces severely the possibilities: the only valid basis of characterizing objects is the general nature of the total action, as illustrious or as popular, and hence only two genres are possible under each manner of imitation. As a consequence, for example, tragedy will present an illustrious action, and even if popular persons take part in it, it will still be a tragedy. The dramatic manner will admit of only two genres, tragedy and comedy; any mixture of the two in a tragicomedy or a comitragedy would be impossible, since it

---

[120] *Delle differenze poetiche* (1587), p. A7: "l'arte vorrebbe anch'ella dimostrar à proua le sue ricchezze, & gli ornamenti; & ridurre tutte le parti del Poema sott'ordine quasi certo; & dare à ciascuna dispositione, & dependenza necessaria ma non potendo peruenir à tanta perfettione; fà verisimilmente alcuna volta quel, che non l'è conceduto di fare necessaria-mente."

[121] *Ibid.*, pp. A4v–A5: "non habbiamo in opera, che sia stata composta in alcuna delle tre lingue più belle, maggior luce dell'arte Poetica, che in questa: non debbiamo prendere gli ammaestramenti Poetici più volentieri da alcun' altro, ne lasciarsi ingannare da false per-suasioni; ò da ragioni apparenti: imperoche ogni piccolo errore, che si commette ne' principij, procedendo oltre, diuiene grandissimo verso il fine: rimangano dunque i principij d'Ari-stotele saldi, & non gettati in terra."

would violate the essential nature of either action. The narrative manner will also give two forms, serious epics like the *Iliad*, the *Odyssey*, and the *Aeneid*, and comic epics like the *Margites* and the *Moretum*; again, mixtures of the two are unthinkable in Aristotelian terms. This integrity of the essential action is a condition of and product of the unity of plot. But Tasso insists that unity does not mean singleness of action; rather, unity implies a multiplicity of things to be unified, and in a poem this multiplicity is constituted by all the various elements which contribute to the realization of the central action.

In some ways, Tasso's view represents a return to Aristotelianism. It sets aside some of the irrelevant subtleties on which others were insisting, it proclaims the primacy of unity of plot and the adequacy of Aristotle's distinctions with respect to object, manner, and means of imitation. In other ways, it is less sound methodologically. For the dictum against mixture of different kinds of actions is little more than Cicero's principle of the purity of styles; and the notion of unity out of multiplicity goes back to certain ideas of Plotinus on harmony in music. Tasso admits his use of some of these external sources, which are basically irreconcilable with the stern Aristotelianism that he is advocating.

CONCLUSIONS

During the years we have been discussing, the effect of the literary quarrels made itself felt upon the Aristotelian tradition in a real if only an occasional way. I mean that there was no continuous and growing body of polemical materials whose vital arguments involved interpretation and reinterpretation of the *Poetics*; yet in such works as those by Bulgarini, Carriero, Patrizi, and Tasso the current literary quarrels brought about fresh and significant appraisals of what Aristotle had said. In fact, these works make more of a contribution to the study of Aristotle than they do to the furthering of the literary debates.

Something of the polemic spirit manifested itself in the estimates of Aristotle's worth as a writer on the art of poetry. Once Aristotelian arguments had been used in defence of Dante or of Ariosto, it was natural that those who wished to attack these Italian poets should, as at least a part of their attack, deny the validity of Aristotle's principles. Such was the case with writers like Patrizi and Lombardelli. They were answered, in turn, by the vigorous defences of a Tasso or a Salviati. The importance of the whole procedure is that, as in the preceding decade, the question of Aristotle's merits leads to a much more searching analysis of his text, in the broadest terms. The minute exegeses of earlier times—which had already accomplished most of what they were to achieve in this century—tend to be replaced by the over-all view of the text, its principles, its arguments, its relationship to poetical realities. Two broad orientations with respect to the text now result. First, the attention to Aristotle's method (we have seen examples of it in Chapter XI) continues to provide some of the most original ideas. As it motivates Riccoboni, Sassetti, or the anonymous writer of the Magliabechi MS VII, 437, it leads to fruitful discoveries of principle and useful interpretations of detail. Second, a new criterion appears with frequency: How useful is the *Poetics* as a guide to the poet who wishes to write today? The theoretical approach, perhaps under the impact of the quarrels, gives way to a much more practical attitude. Should Ariosto, one asks, have followed the demands of Aristotle in the *Poetics*? To what extent? Are ancient principles valid for modern times? Will Tasso be well- or ill-advised to respect these principles? And what about a man who wishes to write a tragicomedy? The questions are put on two levels, on the level of theory (as we have seen in recent pages) and on the level of actual performance (as we shall see in the later chapters on the quarrels).

These diversified orientations may account in part for the nature of the documents written during these years. Certain types of work are conspicuously absent; there is only one major commentary in Latin among the printed volumes of the period, none in Italian. Three lesser commentaries are written in Italian—two of them never continued beyond the early chapters—but none is published. These seem to be the result of the great academic activity of the '70's; but not only has public interest waned, the authors themselves lose courage and enthusiasm—or go off into other adventures. Riccoboni is the only universitarian to publish a Latin translation of the *Poetics*; no new one appears in Italian. In a similar way, the academic discourse or lecture is much less often encountered. So is the commentary on Horace, in which discussion of Aristotle might play a secondary part; I think only of Aldo Manuzio the Younger, in whose work Aristotle's part is very secondary indeed. What we do have is a highly miscellaneous group of works, some of them connected with the polemics, others presenting independent views of highly varied subjects.

Since the great commentaries are few in number, we find in this period, rather than total analyses of the text, discussions of detailed points isolated from their context in the *Poetics*. In this sense, Lorenzo Giacomini's lecture on purgation is typical. The main problems discussed continue to be the same ones—after all, it is still the same text—but some new suggestions are made for interpretation. Theorists still have great difficulty with the notion of imitation; but although many meanings are given the term, Aristotle's are not so often confused with Plato's. Increasingly, writers see as one of the necessary components of imitation a kind of heightened and vivid portrayal which appeals to the senses rather than to the intellect. The complicated matter of the interrelationship of truth, verisimilitude, and necessity draws much attention. Most critics believe that the object must be a true one if credibility is to result, that verisimilitude is a kind of second-best truth. But they interpret necessity variously as referring to a cause-and-effect sequence in nature, or as indicating an artistic quality of poems which justifies the way in which certain devices are handled. Aristotle is sometimes challenged on his requirement that plots be unified; but more usually the problem is how they should be unified—to what extent "double" and "multiple" plots are permissible, in what way episodes may be integrated into the whole. Such theorists as Tasso, in their insistence on a high degree of unity, are perhaps most representative of the period. There is at least one statement, by Riccoboni, which recognizes the existence of three unities.

On some major issues there is relative unanimity of attitude. Almost everybody thinks that verse is inseparable from poetry, and (just as before) many ingenious interpretations of the *Poetics* are offered to prove it. In the same way, almost all the critics are in agreement that the ends of poetry, either immediately or ultimately, are utilitarian. The moral intention of the poet may be realized in the general form which he gives to his story, in the characters he presents, or in the dicta which constitute the sententiae. This theory determines, for the most part, the way in which the four requisites of character are understood; or at least the first, that of "goodness," is generally given an ethical meaning. Aristotle is juxtaposed to Plato on this matter of moral instruction, and both the statements of the ends of poetry and the discussions of purgation are seen as answers to Plato's banishment. None of these is a new idea; all echo the earliest expressions of the Aristotelian tradition in the sixteenth century.

More generally, Plato seems to be less omnipresent than he was in former times. So do Horace and Cicero and the rhetoricians. For the documents studied here, while they make the customary references to other authorities, are more closely concerned with the problem of interpreting Aristotle in and for himself. This may result in part from the fact that the work of comparison and conflation has long since been done, in part from the concentration upon specific passages of the *Poetics* itself. The question now is agreement or disagreement with Aristotle's principles —and the element of disagreement should not be overlooked in such writers as Capponi and Parigiuolo—for the purpose of discovering the truth about the art of poetry. Aristotle is the guide. But he is not infallible, and writers now feel justified in setting up their own theories against those of the master. The commentary on commentaries is much less conspicuous, the study of Aristotle himself more direct. It is perhaps this kind of spirit which gives rise to the last great defences of Aristotle in the closing years of the century.

WEST POINT
The Men and Times of the United States
Military Academy

ALSO BY THOMAS J. FLEMING

HISTORY

One Small Candle
The Pilgrims' First Year in America
Affectionately Yours, George Washington
A Self-Portrait in Letters of Friendship
Now We Are Enemies
Beat the Last Drum

FICTION

All Good Men
The God of Love
King of the Hill
A Cry of Whiteness

West Point

The Men and Times of the United States Military Academy

*

THOMAS J. FLEMING

19 69

William Morrow & Company, Inc.

New York

Acknowledgments

NO BOOK of this dimension could be completed without the help and cooperation of many persons. I would like to take this opportunity to thank Egon Weiss, Director of the United States Military Academy Library, and his former assistant, William G. Kerr, who did their indefatigable best to make all the resources of their fine new library available to me. Equally helpful was J. Thomas Russell, Chief of the Special Collection Division of the Library. I owe an equal debt of gratitude to Lieutenant General James B. Lampert, who was the Superintendent of West Point when I began the book, and to Major General Donald V. Bennett, his successor; both offered me every conceivable cooperation, with complete freedom to make my own discoveries and draw my own conclusions about West Point, past and present.

The same generous spirit of cooperation was displayed by Lieutenant General Leslie Groves, head of the Association of Graduates, who first approached me with the possibility of writing a biography of Sylvanus Thayer, an idea that broadened into this full-scale history of the Academy. Even more helpful was Colonel Thomas M. Metz, secretary of the Association of Graduates, whose friendliness and tireless energy opened numerous doors and files for me. Were it not for the research assistance of two Army wives, Cindy Adams, the editor of the Sylvanus Thayer papers, and Lenora Cross, whose knowledge of library and Army procedure was invaluable, this book would probably never have reached even a semifinished state. I must also express at least as much gratitude to my wife Alice Fleming in her role as a combination researcher-counselor who spent more weekends than I like to remember in the basement of the USMA Library playing Mrs. Xerox. Finally my secretary, Kay Daffron, who suffered through the innumerable versions of the manuscript, solving my atrocious handwriting, bad spelling and tendency to forget first names. For editorial counsel I wish to thank Fulton Oursler, Jr., and Hobart Lewis of the *Reader's Digest,* who not only provided the funds that sustained this project but also devoted many thoughtful hours to helping me shape the manuscript, especially the section on the Civil War.

The members of the West Point faculty who took extra pains to pro-

[v]

vide me with materials and hours for interviews are too numerous for me to name individually here. I would like to express special gratitude to Colonel E. V. Sutherland, head of the English Department, and Colonel Samuel Hays, Director of the Office of Military Psychology and Leadership, for being especially generous. At the same time I wish to make it clear that in the best West Point tradition I take full responsibility for everything—facts as well as judgments—in this attempt to see West Point in the context of the American experience.

THOMAS J. FLEMING
New York, N.Y.

Contents

Illustrations appear following
pages 72, 136, 232, 296

School of the Future

I

THE SLIM, SINEWY young officer leaped from the unsteady deck of the Hudson River sloop to the welcome solidity of West Point's North Wharf. The sentry on duty snapped to attention. The officer's trim blue coat with gilt buttons, his white trousers, were the summer uniform of the U.S. Corps of Engineers. The gold epaulets on his shoulders made him a major—a fairly momentous rank in the minuscule Army of the United States of America in 1817.

Crisply the new arrival ordered the sentry to have his trunk sent up to the Superintendent's office. He turned and strode up the steep path from the wharf. There was a grim, almost unhappy, expression on his finely featured, angular face—the expression of a man about to perform an unpleasant duty.

It was July 28. Brackanack, Crow's Nest, and the other rugged humps of the Hudson Highlands loomed greenly against an azure sky. The summer sun beat down upon the mighty Hudson gliding serenely around the massive outcropping of ancient rock that Washington and his generals had made a key bastion of the War for Independence. Rock and river, timelessness and time, the ironies of unstable men attempting to find something solid in which to anchor their lives—a continental nation attempting to build here beside this first-discovered, primal flow a new kind of fortress, that would survive, surmount, even conquer time— Thayer thought of none of these things. He was not a man given to poetic symbols. But the place was heavy with them, nonetheless. Here was the where the Revolution, with its dream of equality for all men, came close to foundering through the treachery of a great soldier who sold his honor for enemy cash, where the name Benedict Arnold became a synonym for traitor. Irony within irony that here the new nation was hoping to mold generations of soldiers in a new tradition that demanded both intellectual and emotional loyalty to a political system in prickly conflict with military habits of mind.

Swiftly Major Thayer crossed the almost treeless "Plain," noting several groups of young men in unfamiliar grey uniforms and round soft leather caps standing or strolling idly. There were new buildings—two big sturdy affairs, barracks, no doubt. But there would be more than enough time to inspect them later. Now was the time to begin and end the most difficult part of this unwanted duty. Ignoring curious eyes and turning heads, he strode straight to the door of a low-roofed salt-box that had long been the office of the Superintendent.

Thirty-two-year-old Sylvanus Thayer had arrived to take over the United States Military Academy.

He knew that the man he was replacing would become his enemy for life. Thayer and Acting Superintendent Alden Partridge had been fellow students at Dartmouth. Thayer had been a cadet when Partridge was an assistant professor at West Point. Years later, Thayer was to characterize Partridge as "a bundle of deceit and hypocrisy, artful and plausible as he was revengeful and malevolent." Small wonder that Thayer was tense. This was no routine transfer of command.

In the Acting Superintendent's cluttered office Thayer could see at a glance that Partridge had not changed. He still had the twitchy air of a man about to ride off in all directions. Few characters in history better exemplify the old adage about deceptive appearances. Partridge looked twice as soldierly as the lean, ascetic Thayer. The Acting Superintendent had the bold, hawk-nosed stare of a born martinet. Rarely did he appear in public without a resoundingly martial uniform, complete with flamboyant sash and clanking sword. He loved to drill the cadets personally, and was passionately devoted to artillery practice, which he also supervised in person. That was the trouble with Partridge. He saw himself as a kind of one-man faculty. Worse, he was incapable of following a schedule. He did whatever occurred to him. A nice day? Drill and artillery practice! Raining? A lecture on military engineering—a subject that he was barely qualified to teach. Above all, he had to be doing something. He was a veritable *reductio ad absurdum* of the energetic American.

At a distance of 150 years, Partridge is a ludicrous figure. (Even the cadets had a somewhat contemptuous nickname for him—"Old Pewter.") But there was nothing funny about him when Sylvanus Thayer confronted him on that hot July afternoon in 1817.

Partridge's defiant scowl made it clear that he knew what Thayer's arrival meant. For over a year his position at the helm of America's fledgling military academy had been under fire from a wide circle of critics. But it was doubly galling to find himself superseded by a man who was his junior in rank. Thayer's majority was by brevet—an honorary title only. In any matters connected with military seniority, such as choice of quarters on a post, position in a review, Partridge outranked Sylvanus Thayer because he had received his commission two years ahead of him. Moreover, this "brevet major," as Partridge undoubtedly addressed Thayer with cutting sarcasm, had been his pupil, his faculty assistant.

There was no need for introductions. Thayer, exhibiting that superb self-control that was to become his most notable trait, quietly told Partridge he had been ordered to relieve him. Knowing the explosive nature of the man, Thayer seems to have made a conscious effort to do nothing that might possibly arouse Partridge. When he demanded to see the orders, Thayer quietly handed them over.

Captain Alden Partridge
West Point
On receipt of this you will deliver to Major Sylvanus Thayer, U.S. Engineers, the command of the post of West Point and the superintendence of the military academy.

J. G. Swift, Brig. Genl.

For Partridge the signature was the bitterest part of the order. Swift had been his protector against Presidential criticism, boards of inquiry, faculty sniping. Had Swift turned against him too? Partridge simply could not believe it. Curtly he told Brevet Major Thayer where he would be quartered for the night and stalked out, leaving the new Superintendent without a shred of information about the current situation at the school.

The next morning Thayer found Partridge still in possession of the Superintendent's quarters. When Partridge told him that he would be leaving for his home in Norwich, Vermont, "in a day or two," Thayer left him alone and began an inspection of the post. What he found was not reassuring. There was only a handful of cadets on duty. Most of the 213 young men on the rolls had left for an apparently unlimited vacation. They were to return only when and if they received a written order—although the government regulations clearly stated that the school year was to begin in September. More appalling was Thayer's discovery that the five most prominent members of the faculty were under arrest.

President James Monroe had visited West Point in late June, and the professors, totally disgruntled with Partridge's helter-skelter way of running the school, had handed the Chief Executive a long memorandum detailing the "ill effects" and "ruinous tendency" of the "arbitrary" administration of Captain Partridge. Among the professors were Jared Mansfield, the man who had laid out the main street of Cincinnati, Ohio and mapped much of the Northwest Territory; Andrew Ellicott, one of the country's leading mathematicians; and Claudius Crozet, a brilliant young French engineer whom Thayer himself had met in Paris. General Swift had shown Partridge the accusing memorandum, and Partridge had retaliated with a barrage of countercharges and an order for the professors' arrest.

In his quarters on this same first day of Thayer's tenure, Partridge was far from giving up the fight. He was still convinced that Swift would defend him as he had done so often in the past. Coolly, without even mentioning the change in command, he wrote to Swift in New York:

I have the honor herewith to enclose you the charges and specifications preferred by me against Professors Mansfield and Ellicott . . . I also enclose you charges and specifications against Mr. Berard, teacher of French . . . I request that the charges against all those persons may be attended to in a proper manner . . . I leave here in a day or two for Norwich, Vermont . . .

In great haste,

Yours with the greatest respect,
A. Partridge

The same day Thayer wrote a letter of his own to Swift, reporting that he had assumed command of the post and informing his superior officer that Partridge had placed the cream of the faculty under arrest. "I hope these gentlemen will be either released from arrest or their places supplied by other instructors before the end of the actual vacation," was his somewhat plaintive closing.

Thayer's position was complicated by his genuine friendship and high regard for Swift. He felt that Swift had compromised himself—and possibly the entire Corps of Engineers—by his championship of Partridge in the face of so much criticism. Years later he would tell Swift: "I appreciated the purity of your motives. Then, as always, you were activated by noble and generous feelings and a high sense of duty." With this for background, it is not hard to imagine the shock Thayer received when he returned in May 1817 from a two-year tour of European study and travel, under direct orders from the Secretary of War to take over West Point, and found Swift still defending Partridge. The truth had been instantaneously, painfully clear. The government had lost confidence in Swift and gone over his head, issuing orders to a subordinate officer in the Engineers without even bothering to inform him.

Thayer decided to say nothing to Swift about the orders he had received in France. He knew Swift had defended Partridge because he honestly believed Partridge was the right man in the right place—and because he was determined to keep the sticky hands of the politicians out of the Engineering Corps, which included West Point.

But consideration for Swift was not the only reason Thayer remained silent. As he told Swift later: "From having known (Partridge) a great deal better than you did, I felt a strong disinclination to be stationed at West Point." Thayer was human. He had no desire to inherit a monumental mess which he strongly suspected was beyond the power of any single individual to set straight. Thayer was not alone in his "disinclination." Other Engineers, such as the brilliant William McRee, with whom Thayer had toured Europe, had been offered West Point and respectfully declined. Fresh from meeting with the best military minds in Europe, ambitious young men such as McRee and Thayer were eager to tackle the thousand and one engineering challenges of their young, undeveloped country. Retiring to the primitive society of the Hudson Highlands to ride herd on a gaggle of unruly youths when the bustling, booming worlds of Boston, New York, Philadelphia, and Washington beckoned to their talents was hardly an appealing prospect. But a sense of duty was rooted deep in Sylvanus Thayer's New England character. He had waited patiently in New York while Swift accompanied President Monroe to West Point in a last vain attempt to rescue Partridge, hoping, as he later said, "that the President, after a personal inspection, would consent to revoke the order and let Partridge remain." But the order had not been revoked, and without a word of complaint or a moment of hesitation, Sylvanus Thayer had accepted responsibility for the future of West Point.

The dispersal of his students and the arrest of the academic staff were by no means the least of Thayer's worries. Conferences with the various professors over the next two days made it clear that the school also lacked anything that could be even charitably described as a regular course of study. Cadets had been taught according to accidental abilities

and talents and the whims of Captain Partridge. Although he had resigned his professorship of engineering and was technically no longer a
member of the faculty, Partridge regularly organized groups of cadets
into special classes and taught them himself, monopolizing the school's
few scientific instruments and frustrating those professors who were
attempting to create some sort of academic system. The regulations
specifically stated that cadets were to be accepted only in September.
Partridge accepted arrivals at any time of the year and graduated others
with equal carelessness. Usually the captain's favorites won his recommendation for commissions, with small regard to their academic standing
or accomplishments.

Clearly, if West Point was to begin a school year in September 1817,
there was a staggering array of decisions to be made and work to be
done. Thayer wasted no time. On August 1 he sent his first communication to the faculty, recommending "that each professor should make out
a particular program for his own department, specifying the branches to
be taught, the time required for each, and the books which shall serve as
guides." Thayer went on to suggest in rough outline a daily pattern for
the school—classes to run from eight o'clock to twelve-thirty or one
o'clock in which the "principal studies" would be covered, followed by
classes in the nonscientific branches, such as French and drawing, from
two to four o'clock. He assured the faculty that the arrangement of
cadets into regular classes would be "rigidly observed" and that no cadet
would be received hereafter "except during the regular period of admission." Nor would any cadet be allowed to pass to the next higher class
"unless regularly admitted thereto at the general examinations"—thus
ending another unfortunate Partridge precedent. Thayer ended his
memorandum with a modest plea: "I have thus given you the outlines of
my hasty and desultory reflection on some of the means of better organizing the instruction of this institution, not with an idea that the opinions
here advanced are the most correct, but with a view to invite a discussion of the subject and to elicit your opinion thereon. The business is new
to me and I rely with pleasure on the superior judgment of the learned
professors . . ."

The same day Thayer sent a crisp letter to George Graham, the
Acting Secretary of War. It covered a copy of a report he had sent his
friend Swift, "not knowing," as he explained, "whether it was expected
that I should correspond directly with the War Department on the concerns of this institution." The young major was still determined to tight-

rope-walk across the widening chasm between the War Department and his immediate superior. He asked Graham to station a quartermaster at West Point and supply him with enough funds to make urgently needed repairs and to buy "considerable supplies of instruments, stationery, etc., for the ensuing term . . . I request particular instructions which may inform me how far I am authorized to order expenditures; to what objects and to what amount my powers are limited."

Three days later he wrote again to the Secretary of War, urging him to issue an order for all cadets to return on September 1 to begin the fall term. Writing from New York, to which he had returned, probably to arrange for the translation of some badly needed French textbooks, he ended his letter with a clear-eyed summation of his attitude toward his new responsibility. "I shall repair again to West Point in four or five days to resume the duties of superintendent altho' I cannot say under the most favorable auspices. I enter upon them, however, with alacrity and with a zeal which shall know no bounds, in full confidence that the government will grant me every necessary aid and that I shall be permitted a free and direct correspondence with the War Department on all the concerns of the military academy."

Back at West Point, Thayer was heartened by a long, carefully detailed letter from the Acting Secretary of War, assuring him of the government's enthusiastic support. Most significant were the words: "As superintendent of the military academy you are amenable to, and subject only to the orders of the President thro' this department; and all communications in relation to the academy are to be made thro' you." Thayer must have breathed a small sigh of relief when he read this. It meant he at least did not have to worry about doing his job with Partridge lurking in the background, whispering calumnies into Swift's too receptive ears.

Thayer was equally pleased by the vigor with which Acting Secretary Graham urged him to select officers from the Army to instruct the cadets in tactics and to solve such problems as supplying the cadets with clothing. Under Partridge, uniform costs had been outrageously high, causing "much discontent among the friends and parents of the cadets." The Secretary also urged him to begin immediately dividing the cadets into classes, assigning studies and hours of attendance for each class, selecting books and generally taking a firm hold on the multitudinous details of getting the school into motion.

Meanwhile Thayer was grappling with another problem. Tavern-keepers, small merchants, and other tradesmen in the vicinity bombarded the new Superintendent with an appalling list of debts run up by cadets. Even more alarming was information Thayer unearthed in New York about cadets who sold their pay accounts in advance in order to raise money for vacations in the city. Not only were these young men cheating themselves—since the vouchers were sold at tremendous discounts—they were also plunging headlong into dissipation hundreds of miles from home while their trusting parents thought they had placed them in the care of a wise and benevolent government. Thayer asked Graham to adopt immediately a regulation prohibiting cadets from receiving pay from anyone except the paymaster at West Point. Again the Secretary gave Thayer his full support and approval.

Before the end of August, Thayer was reporting a new plan of study for the Academy and urging the need for additional French teachers to handle the new courses, which were built around textbooks he had bought in Paris. He also appointed a temporary instructor of tactics and a professor of artillery, and directed the faculty to prepare a schoolwide examination for the returning cadets. Most of them were back on the post by the last week in August, and Thayer was more than a little dismayed by what he saw. Many of them were mere boys. By act of Congress, the admission age had been lowered to fourteen—much too young, in Thayer's opinion—and Partridge had apparently accepted some of even more tender years. Off duty they had a slovenly, undisciplined look. They eyed the new Superintendent warily, and there were rumors that those who had enjoyed Partridge's favor were vociferously condemning Old Pewt's dismissal.

But Thayer was hardly inclined to let this worry him—until the afternoon of August 29. He was at his desk, perhaps studying faculty recommendations for the forthcoming examination, when his concentration was disrupted by fantastic cheering and bedlam from the direction of the cadet barracks. He ordered the post adjutant to find out what was causing the disturbance.

Before the adjutant could return with an answer, Sylvanus Thayer found out for himself. There in the doorway of the office was none other than Alden Partridge. Drawing himself up, he haughtily informed Thayer that he had returned to West Point to prepare himself for the forthcoming board of inquiry which (he assumed) was to investigate the charges and countercharges between him and the professors. He therefore demanded the right to reoccupy his former quarters, which Thayer had assigned to Captain David B. Douglass, assistant professor of mathematics. Quietly, politely, Thayer said no.

Partridge vehemently repeated his demand. As senior officer to Douglass, he had a right to the quarters under Army regulations. Grimly controlling his temper, Thayer again said no. Partridge stormed out.

That night Sylvanus Thayer must have awakened more than once, wondering if he had dreamed the whole thing. But the nightmare continued into the morning. Back came Partridge to Thayer's office to demand once more his old quarters. Again Thayer refused. Partridge thundered that he had the power to seize the quarters if Thayer insisted on refusing them. As the senior officer of Engineers present, Partridge argued, he had a legal right to the Superintendency of the Academy.

Thayer quietly replied that if Partridge should take such a step, he would immediately surrender all responsibility for command of the post. Within the hour Partridge ordered the corps paraded and stood by beaming while Lieutenant Charles Davies read an order announcing that Captain Partridge was reassuming command.

The cadet corps' answer was a tremendous cheer.

In his quarters Sylvanus Thayer sat down and wrote a letter to the Secretary of War:

I have the honor to inform you that Captain A. Partridge of the Corps of Engineers has returned to this post and has this day forcibly assumed the command and the superintendence of the academy. I shall, therefore, proceed to New York and wait your orders.

Without a word to anyone, Thayer mailed this letter and went straight from his office to the West Point wharf, where he hailed the first sloop heading for New York.

Why did he do it? Those cheers from the cadet ranks were grim proof that the influence of Alden Partridge would not easily be eradicated from West Point. His haphazard favoritism had obviously won the affection of the boy cadets. If Thayer had attempted to resist Partridge's usurpation, the whole corps might well have mutinied, forcing a mass court-martial and the probable collapse of the Military Academy. Thayer was well aware that the Academy had many enemies in Washington. So he stifled his inclination to challenge Partridge to a personal struggle for power.

In New York, he promptly notified General Swift—by letter. It is interesting that Thayer avoided a face-to-face confrontation with him.

Was it because he was still not sure whether Partridge had come with Swift's secret backing? Thayer quickly found out the truth.

The moment Swift heard the news, the dwindling friendship he still felt for Alden Partridge evaporated. He ordered his aide-de-camp, George Blaney, to leave immediately for West Point with Sylvanus Thayer. In Blaney's pocket were orders for Alden Partridge's arrest.

Up at the Academy, meanwhile, Partridge was composing a long letter to Swift, explaining why he had taken charge. He also drew up an equally lengthy set of charges against Thayer and called for his prompt arrest. "I wish you not to believe that I intend to attribute to Major Thayer any improper motives in his conduct in this case," Partridge wrote. "You know the opinion I have always expressed to you concerning him and it will require the most cogent reasons to induce me to alter it."

Partridge then fired what he hoped was his best and shrewdest shot. "I would now observe, sir, that I consider it of the greatest importance both to yourself, to myself, and to the military academy that you should come up and take upon yourself the superintendence of the institution until difficulties here are all adjusted."

A year before, Swift had resided briefly at the Military Academy and smothered a rising storm of protest against Partridge. Old Pewt was obviously hoping the same trick would work twice.

He was wrong. Down in New York, Swift was writing to Thayer: "Captain Partridge was at my quarters a few days since and informed me of his intention of going to Washington and to West Point. I advised him not to go to either place and I am astonished at the folly and error of his conduct."

Up at West Point around the same time, Blaney was demanding the surrender of Partridge's sword and placing him under arrest. Thayer, who returned to West Point with Blaney, remained in the background. But he made sure that Swift's order of September 1 was read to the Corps of Cadets:

Brigadier General Swift has been informed that Captain Partridge has assumed the command of West Point—this unmilitary and unauthorized act has caused the arrest of Captain Partridge.

An implicit obedience of the orders of Major Thayer is expected from every cadet—disobedience will be punished by immediate dismission.

The next day Swift arrived to reinforce his authority personally. On his heels came a spate of angry letters from the War Department, ordering Partridge's arrest and imprisonment on Governors Island and demanding a copy of the orders Swift had given to both Partridge and Thayer.

The affair inevitably got into the New York newspapers, which ran lurid stories about the "mutiny" at West Point. Thayer and the professors interrogated a number of the cadets, attempting to find out just how mutinous they had been. They were astonished to discover that when Partridge had left the post in July, he had told several cadet leaders that Thayer was only a temporary replacement, taking over so Old Pewt could enjoy a vacation in his native Vermont. Partridge may have actually planned to return and oust Thayer; more likely, however, he was still convinced that Swift would come to his aid and restore him to power. His seizure of command was probably an act of impulse and anger—one more example of his instability.

After placing Partridge under arrest, Swift returned to New York. The prisoner stayed at West Point another five days, using as an excuse the steamboat schedule and the labor of collecting his furniture and papers. On the evening of September 10, several cadets came to Thayer and asked permission for themselves and a number of friends to leave their barracks after tattoo to greet some comrades expected on the steamboat from Albany. Thayer gave them a long, cool stare. He knew that Alden Partridge was leaving on the same boat. It was obvious that the cadets wanted to say good-bye to Partridge as riotously as they had greeted him.

A more impulsive man might have snapped a curt refusal and berated them for their deception. But Thayer was determined to do nothing that might give Partridge a chance to unleash his rabble-rousing invective against him personally. The moment he let the struggle for control of the school become a man-to-man combat, chaos would erupt. Quietly, pretending to know nothing, he gave his permission.

A half hour later, Lieutenant John Wright arrived with another request. Could the band march to the wharf and strike up a few tunes to greet the returning young warriors? Wright was Partridge's nephew. (Old Pewt had a habit of handing out jobs to relatives. For a while the cadets were fed by one Isaac Partridge, another relation.) Why Wright wanted the band was all too obvious. Commanding officers often received "the honors of music" when leaving a post. But Thayer was not going to let Alden Partridge, under arrest for defying the orders of his general and his government, enjoy such a privilege. His answer to Wright was a stern *no*.

To make sure the erratic Partridge did not attempt some sort of farewell confrontation, Thayer himself left the post an hour or so before his antagonist's scheduled departure. The next morning several professors came to Thayer with the lurid details of Partridge's leave-taking. The cadets had swarmed down to the dock, shouting and cheering him and vowing they could not wait until he returned, cleared of all charges against him. Right behind them, adding to the tumult, marched the post band. In direct defiance of Thayer's orders, Lieutenant Wright had ordered them out to give Captain Partridge a send-off worthy of a brigadier general at least.

Thayer instantly summoned Wright to his office and ordered him to leave West Point before the day was over and report himself to General Swift in New York. Watching Wright, still defiant, stomp away to his quarters, Sylvanus Thayer must have brooded for a moment. It was easy enough to get rid of obvious troublemakers like Wright, but how was he going to root out the disaffection and disloyalty that Partridge had implanted deep into the cadet corps itself? On September 9 he had told the Secretary of War that he had reason to believe "the bad spirit which has been excited among the cadets will subside by the exercise of prudent and vigorous measures."

Partridge's wildly unmilitary farewell was certainly grounds for second thoughts. Could Thayer turn these unruly boys into soldiers equally skilled in science and military arts? Could he mold this disorganized academy into another Ecole Polytechnique, the school whose teachers and graduates had made France the premier scientific nation of the world? On that September morning, after Alden Partridge's departure, Sylvanus Thayer must have wondered.

II

PARTRIDGE AND HIS influence were by no means the only reasons for Thayer's doubts. The U.S. Military Academy was an uneasy compromise between young America's suspicion of a standing army and the nation's obvious need for soldiers skilled in the art and science of war. We tend to think somewhat smugly that the twentieth century is the era when war and science have blended. But it was no less true in the eighteenth and nineteenth centuries.

It took some knowledge of mathematics and physics to aim and fire a cannon successfully. It required even more book learning to become a good military engineer. Without engineers an army was little more than an organized mob. They had the mathematical training, the military education to construct forts and redoubts, to position artillery, to plan defensive positions—and to give invaluable advice on how to attack an entrenched enemy. Few soldiers were more important to George Washington than the French Lieutenant Colonel Louis Duportail, who commanded the engineers in the Continental Army. From the construction of the Delaware River forts, which almost starved the British Army out of Philadelphia, to the creation of the bastion at West Point to control the Hudson, to the siege of Yorktown, Duportail and his little corps of specialists were the technicians of the American Revolutionary War effort.

But in the early years of the nation, earnest recommendations from President Washington and his former commander of artillery (and first Secretary of War) Henry Knox to found a school that would create American engineers and artillerymen got nowhere. Congressional military thinking was dominated by the myth of the heroic militiaman who could supposedly seize his musket and become overnight a terror on the battlefield.

As the century ended, various other Americans, notably Alexander Hamilton, repeatedly urged the formation of a military academy. But Congress still declined to do more than edge a little closer to the idea by expanding the tiny corps of artillerists and engineers (less than 100 men) stationed at West Point, and creating the rank of cadet. The politicians fondly hoped that nature would take its course and older officers would instruct eager juniors. But no books were purchased, and when the commanding officer attempted to teach both officers and cadets, the officers mutinied and burned down the schoolhouse.

Things drifted for several years; then Secretary of War James Mc-Henry revived Hamilton's plan for a military academy, combining it with the suggestions of a talented French officer, Louis de Tousard, who had fought for America in the Revolutionary War and might with some justice be called the forgotten founder of West Point. Adams approved the idea, but he was soon a lame duck, defeated by Jefferson who had opposed the idea of a military academy the first time he heard about it, when he was serving as Secretary of State in Washington's Cabinet.

Jefferson was not so leery about military power, once he was commander in chief. So often misrepresented in his historic feud with Hamilton as an impractical idealist, Jefferson was the first of America's great pragmatic politicians, combining vision and know-how. He wanted a national university, and as the foremost apostle of progress in America he wanted that university to teach science, not the musty classics that prevailed at other American schools. But the tug of sectionalism was too strong for Congress to agree even on where such a school should be situated, much less what it should teach. Jefferson, therefore, decided that he would smuggle his national scientific school into the nation under the guise of a military academy. But opposition was still so strong that Congress would only agree to authorize the President to organize a corps of engineers which "shall be stationed at West Point . . . and shall constitute a Military Academy."

The law could not have been more vague or hesitant. It specified ten cadets for the Corps of Engineers and forty for the artillery, but there was not the slightest attempt to set up standards of selection or even to discriminate on the basis of age. One cadet, John Lillie, was ten years and seven months old. Another had a wife and several children. The school had exactly two professors, Captain William Amherst Barron, a graduate of the British School of Artillery at Woolwich, and Jared Mansfield. Barron taught mathematics; Mansfield, "natural and experimental philosophy," which today we would call physics. In the fall of 1802, Francis de Masson arrived to teach French and topographical drawing.

The Academy was fortunate in the choice of a Superintendent. Jefferson persuaded Jonathan Williams, a relative of Benjamin Franklin and one of the nation's outstanding scientific figures, to accept the job. But Williams was simultaneously head of the Corps of Engineers, and since he had no interest in the details of superintending the school, this gave him a perfect excuse to all but ignore it and range up and down the East Coast planning fortifications and pursuing other duties that flowed from this second title.

When Cadet Sylvanus Thayer arrived at West Point in 1807 after four years at Dartmouth (where he was graduated first in his class), it was not Superintendent Williams who greeted him but Captain Joseph G. Swift, the Academy's first graduate (1802). It was he who issued Cadet Thayer the uniform of that era, a long-tailed blue coat, single-breasted, with eight flat, eagle-stamped buttons and a high collar. Thayer was undoubtedly pleased by the uniform. He had always had a strong interest in things military. His Dartmouth classmate and best friend, George Ticknor, later told how "he was the only person in college who took the *National Intelligencer* (printed in Washington), and he took it because it contained the amplest accounts he could get of the movements of Bonaparte and his armies—all of which, and especially those of the earliest campaigns in Metz, he seemed to know by heart."

But Thayer must have been dismayed by the textbooks Swift handed him. They included Hutton's *Mathematics*—a book Thayer had used teaching grade school back in Washington, New Hampshire—and Enfield's *Natural Philosophy,* which he had covered at Dartmouth. The course of study was haphazard, to say the least. Mornings were devoted to mathematics, the early afternoon to French and drawing. It must have been somewhat unnerving for Lieutenant Alden Partridge, commissioned the previous year (as a first lieutenant—the first of many favors Swift bestowed on Partridge), to have a student as keen as Thayer in his mathematics class. About the only subjects in the curriculum that were new to Thayer were the rather rudimentary studies in artillery and in the theory and practice of fortification.

Physically the school itself was even more unimpressive. Joseph G. Swift left in his diary a vivid description of how it looked. A single stone building stood "on the western margin of the Plain." Four hundred rocky feet above it were the ruins of old Fort Putnam. Beside the Academy building was the small frame salt-box house used as a headquarters by the post commander. It perched on the edge of a long deep indentation known as Execution Hollow. The name was another relic of Revolutionary days, and had nothing to do with summary punishments of cadets. On the other side of the Hollow, which ran down the center of the present-day parade ground, was another Revolutionary relic, the "Long Barracks" in which cadets and most enlisted men were quartered indiscriminately. A half dozen officers' houses, a small hospital building, a tailor shop, were scattered at various points about the Plain. To the northwest, below the Plain near the river, were the moldering military stores of the U.S. Army—largely guns, equipment and brass cannon captured from General John Burgoyne at Saratoga in 1777—in two long yellow buildings. At the opposite end of the reservation in the northeast angle of the Plain (not yet named Trophy Point) was Fort Clinton, a dilapidated work of Revolutionary War engineers Duportail and Kosciusko, containing four 24-pounder cannon and a magazine filled with powder "many years of age."

The whole school had a faintly comic-opera air about it. Surrounded by crumbling forts and ancient rusty equipment, using out-of-date textbooks, West Point would have driven a modern college graduate to despair—or demonstrations. But the rest of the country was not in much better shape. It took 24 days for a letter to get from Washington to New Orleans, if it got there at all. The roads were so abominable that intelligent men traveled by water whenever possible. When President Jefferson journeyed from his Monticello mansion to the muddy, unpaved streets of Washington, D.C., he ploughed through mud up to his axle wheels, floated his carriage across swollen rivers and prayed that his horses would not drown or collapse. America was raw, rough, huge. Over the violent objections of many who thought that the original thirteen colonies should develop their own resources before expanding, President Jefferson had doubled the size of the nation with the Louisiana Purchase. The country was rich in land, but poor in almost everything else—not merely underdeveloped but undeveloped.

Without material resources, the West Point of Thayer's cadet days turned to another resource—brain power. The American Philosophical Society, founded by Benjamin Franklin in 1743, was flourishing mightily in 1807, laying the foundations for America's future scientific preeminence. Superintendent Williams decided that the idea—that of an organization to serve as a central clearinghouse for the latest and best in scientific research and discovery—could be applied with equal success to military knowledge. The Military Philosophical Society was formed, and promising cadets such as Sylvanus Thayer were invited to join, but the Society's roster also included such distinguished names as DeWitt Clinton, then Mayor of New York as well as a noted amateur scientist, Chief Justice John Marshall, and Robert Fulton of steamboat fame. Under Williams' astute presidency the Military Philosophical Society was no mere debating club. Meetings were held on the first and third Monday of each month. Among the subjects discussed were breech-loading cannon, just being developed in Europe, the careers of professional soldiers such as Kosciusko, and plans for a general map of the United States and a survey of the nation's coasts.

Aside from this mental exercise, which was entirely outside the curriculum, the Military Academy had little to offer Sylvanus Thayer. It admitted as much. On February 23, 1808, less than a year after he entered, he was commissioned a second lieutenant in the Corps of Engineers. An order to survey sites and plan defenses for a number of harbors along the Connecticut and Massachusetts coast occupied him for the next year.

Less than a month after Thayer left West Point, Superintendent Jonathan Williams sent a report on the current state of the Military Academy to Washington. It was not encouraging. He pointed out that by law the Corps of Engineers was limited to sixteen officers. With almost two thousand miles of coastline to supervise, it was impossible for them simultaneously to run a military academy, as the original plan for West Point had proposed. He criticized the government's tendency to appoint gifted men such as Jared Mansfield to the West Point faculty and then to yank them out and send them off for several years at a time on engineering projects elsewhere.

Williams urged the government to make up its mind once and for all that it was running a school. If it was to be a national school, it should be under the immediate direction of the President and there should be a first-class academic staff. Finally, he recommended moving the school to Washington, D.C. Otherwise it would remain "a foundling, barely existing among the mountains and nurtured at a distance out of sight, almost unknown to its legitimate parents."

Congress did nothing, in spite of the obvious drift toward war with Great Britain over her callous disregard for American rights on the high seas. Worse, Secretary of War William Eustis was a Massachusetts man mesmerized by Bunker Hill and Lexington into a belief that militia was the backbone of the country's strength. He could see no use for a national nursery for professional soldiers and quietly proceeded to starve the Military Academy by cutting off the flow of cadet appointments.

West Point's slow disintegration must have been obvious to Sylvanus Thayer when, after a year of fortress-building in New England, he was reassigned to the school as a junior instructor in mathematics. Superintendent Williams was spending even more of his time in New York. The best of the school's mathematics teachers, Swiss-born Ferdinand Hassler, had left to begin a survey of the American coast. Swift was building forts along the northeast coast. Lieutenant Partridge was now head of the Mathematics Department and, in the absence of the Superintendent, was already assuming many of the prerogatives of the post commander. Thayer remained at West Point until November 1810, watching the school drift and the number of cadets dwindle to 47. He was undoubtedly delighted to be reassigned to Colonel Williams in New York. To an ambitious young man with a first-class education, West Point must have been a Siberia during these years. More important, there was work to do in New York. Fortifications were rising rapidly on Governors Island and other key points in the vast harbor. War with Great Britain was now considered almost inevitable.

The "War Hawks," men of Thayer's generation led by John C. Calhoun and Henry Clay, fired by dreams of seizing Florida and carving up Canada, used British insults at sea as a pretext for shoving a reluctant President Madison and an uncertain nation into a "second American revolution."

This rhetoric inspired some congressmen to take a closer look at the American Army, and they did not like what they saw. Hastily, they decided it was long past time that the nation had a decent military academy, and promptly passed a bill that, considering the feverish atmosphere in which they labored, was surprisingly good. The Law of 1812, as it came to be called, expanded West Point's faculty, providing professorships in engineering, mathematics and natural philosophy, and specified that each cadet would require a degree from the "academical staff" in order to graduate. It increased the number of cadets to 250, and stipulated that an applicant be decently trained in reading, writing and arithmetic. The law also called on the Superintendent to add regulations as he saw fit, organize the cadets into companies, and put the cadets into camp for three months each year, where they would apply their military lore in daily practice.

The law arrived at West Point just in time to rescue the school from oblivion. The stalling tactics of Secretary of War Eustis had reduced the Academy to the vanishing point. After a hasty graduation to meet the needs of a war-expanded army, the school consisted of Captain Partridge and one lone cadet. A half dozen more arrived before the year 1812 was out, but the graduating class of 1813 was also a party of one. Then President Madison, awakening to imminent disaster, junked Eustis, and the new Secretary of War issued a flood of warrants drastically escalating the student body. But these young men were rushed through and graduated with little more than a year of training. Neither the 71 pre-1812 graduates nor the 35 half-baked wartime products could prevent the second American revolution from becoming a fiasco from the first shot. The Regular Army, starved by inept Secretary of War Eustis, was utterly incapable of coping with the hundred thousand raw militia Congress called up for a six months' campaign—time enough, in their rosy opinion, to drive the British off the continent of North America. Thayer, promoted to first lieutenant, had a chance to see at first hand what a nation could expect from untrained amateurs on the battlefield. He was ordered to join the "Army of the North," concentrating at Plattsburg, New York, under Revolutionary War hero Henry Dearborn, who had heretofore never commanded anything larger than a regiment. By the time this army began its advance toward Canada, it had already heard the disgraceful story of General William Hull's surrender at Detroit without firing a shot. Hull handed over 2200 men to a besieging Canadian force of some 2000.

Next had come the disaster of Queenstown Heights, in which 600 American regulars seized a strong position on the Canadian side of the Niagara River, only to be wiped out when New York State militiamen refused to reinforce them on the ground that their military service did not require them to leave the state. The news of these setbacks considerably cooled the ardor of Dearborn's army, and young Thayer had the mortification of personally observing a similar military performance on his own front. Crossing the La Colle River on November 20, Colonel Zebulon Pike, with some 600 men, seized an enemy blockhouse. A few moments later a brigade of New York militia came charging down the road, heading for the same objective. The two groups of Americans opened fire on each other, and by the time the British advance guard appeared on the scene the American line was in chaos and they were thrown back across the river in a single charge. Dearborn promptly announced that his invasion of Canada was over, turned his army around, and retreated to winter quarters.

The following spring Thayer served as aide-de-camp to General Wade Hampton, who had been given command of the right division of the northern army. Hampton was another do-nothing general. He let the British burn Plattsburg, although he was in sight of the blazing buildings, and then proceeded to quarrel bitterly with James Wilkinson, who had relieved the unsuccessful Dearborn.

The second invasion of Canada in 1813 ended as fecklessly as the campaign of 1812. Joseph G. Swift, who served as Chief Engineer, summed up what was wrong in a bitter lament: ". . . Everything in a most disgraceful and deplorable condition; no plan of campaign studied or definitely fixed; the enemy's position unknown and the St. Lawrence unexplored; supplies deficient through neglect or incompetency of the War Department; expense of transportation enormous, that of a single field piece costing over a thousand dollars; our troops mostly recruits and sick from eating contract provisions."

The following year, even this farcical performance was topped by the ragbag militia army assembled to defend the nation's capital. After a one-volley "battle" at Bladensburg, Maryland, they fled in terror before a British force less than half their number, and the redcoats marched leisurely to Washington and put the White House and other public buildings to the torch. West Pointer Walker K. Armistead saved Baltimore from a similar fate by dueling the British fleet to a standstill at Fort McHenry—and incidentally inspiring Francis Scott Key to scribble some historic verses by the rockets' red glare.

In the North, there was some small consolation for a professional soldier. Brigadier General Winfield Scott and 1300 regulars won a solid victory at Chippewa in a frontal assault against 1500 British. At West Point, Alden Partridge decided that the unorthodox gray uniform worn by Scott's men was a badge of honor and immediately ordered some for himself and the entire cadet corps. Then, toward the end of January 1815, came news of Andrew Jackson's stunning victory against 7500 British regulars in New Orleans. The nation went wild, parading by torchlight through the streets, hailing a new military hero. Less than a month later word arrived that a treaty of peace had been signed at Ghent, Belgium, by American and British commissioners, two weeks before the redcoats died by the hundreds before the muzzles of Jackson's frontiersmen.

Recovering from a bout of fever contracted while working on fortifications around Norfolk, Sylvanus Thayer took his own long look at the war. No matter if the country was on a veritable jag of victorious jubilation, thanks to Andrew Jackson; from a soldier's viewpoint, the war as a whole had been a disgraceful national performance. Again and again, untrained militia had proven to be totally undependable on the field of battle. Officers and men alike had repeatedly shown themselves incapable of carrying out planned attacks. Battle after battle had been lost because commanders bickered, failed to obey orders, were incapable of organizing the complicated machinery of army movement and supply.

West Point graduates, on the other hand, had distinguished themselves repeatedly. One out of every five had been promoted for exceptional service in the field. Of William McRee, '05, with whom Thayer had forged a close friendship during his service on the Canadian front, Winfield Scott later remarked: "In my opinion and perhaps that of all the army, he combined more genius and military science with high courage than any other officer who participated in the War of 1812." It was McRee's fortifications at Fort Erie that baffled the attacking British. Likewise, the work of Captain Eleazer Derby Wood at Fort Meigs farther west in the Ohio Territory enabled William Henry Harrison to survive a British attack there on the fifth of May, 1813. Captain Joseph Gilbert Totten was the man who built the forts at Plattsburg that helped stop the formidable British invasion in September, 1814. Not a single fort constructed by a graduate of West Point was captured by the enemy.

Graduates had also shown a fighting spirit that unfortunately was never communicated to most American generals. Wood and James Gibson, '08, died at the head of their sortieing columns, which routed the British besiegers at Fort Erie. When General Hull surrendered Detroit, Lieutenant William Partridge, '06, younger cousin of Alden Partridge, staggered from a sickbed to protest the disgraceful collapse. When Hull insisted on surrendering, Partridge broke his sword in pieces and flung it at his commander's feet.

President James Madison, who had witnessed the American disaster at Bladensburg which led to the burning of Washington, was among those who were convinced that West Point's 106 graduates had more than proved their worth. But Sylvanus Thayer felt he and his classmates were still largely amateurs, struggling to make do in a nation that had no real military tradition or organization. During his convalescence, a new idea slowly gripped him: only by going abroad and studying at first hand the science, the advanced weapons and the techniques that underlay the professional armies of Europe, could American officers hope to create an army worthy of the name.

On March 23, 1815, Sylvanus Thayer, his health restored, arrived in Washington, hoping to find his old friend Joseph G. Swift, now a brigadier general and head of the Engineering Corps. He was disappointed. Swift had already left for New York. Thayer sat down and wrote his friend a letter, summing up his months of meditation.

Dear General:

I hastened my departure from Norfolk as soon as the state of my health would admit in the expectation of meeting you here. But having arrived too late, I am under the necessity of troubling you with a letter in order to obtain your consent and aid in bringing about a scheme which I have long cherished in my mind and for the accomplishment of which I deem the present a most favorable moment. This scheme is no other than a furlough to visit France for my professional improvement. I need not dwell on the advantages which the Corps or the government would derive by sending abroad in time of peace a portion of its officers. I know that you view the subject in its proper light and it only remains to select those individuals who by their endowments, natural and acquired, are the best calculated to collect in their travels useful information and afterwards to employ their acquisitions most usefully in the services of government. Should I be happy enough to be ranked among this class by your partiality, I am persuaded you will most cheerfully promote my wishes. A letter from you under cover to me at this place to the Sec'y of War approbating my object and stating your opinion of me as an officer, will, I have no doubt, have the desired effect.

Swift's answer was prompt and, for young Thayer, delightfully positive. Swift had already discussed with Secretary of War Monroe the proposition of sending officers abroad and had learned that the government, in a passion of parsimony now that the war was over, would send only two engineers. "However," Swift wrote, "I decided in favor of

Colonel McRee and yourself." Their mission was to be twofold. Swift described it in another letter to the Secretary of War. ". . . our officers should gain a knowledge of the European military establishments, their fortifications, mil'y schools and military workshops; to those objects I presume the enquiries of Colonel McRee and Captain Thayer would be diverted, and also to the collection of rare books, maps, plans, and instruments for the military academy."

On June 10 Thayer and McRee sailed on the frigate *Congress,* which was, somewhat ironically, carrying William Eustis abroad, where he would take up his duties as Minister to Holland. The man who had tried to wreck West Point and the man who was destined to save it seem to have gotten along quite amiably on their long voyage—hardly surprising, since Eustis was a born politician. The main subject of conversation on shipboard was probably not the Military Academy but Napoleon Bonaparte. Shortly before they sailed, word had reached America that Napoleon had bolted from Elba and seized power in France once more. Napoleon devotee Thayer must have been almost desperate with excitement as the *Congress* plowed stolidly across the wide Atlantic. Would he, after all, have a chance to see the greatest captain in history at the head of his armies? In the English Channel off Dover, Thayer found to his vast disappointment that the answer was no. Eight days after they had left America, their pilot informed them, the Duke of Wellington had shattered Napoleon's last dream at Waterloo.

Thayer and McRee found Paris chaotic—swarming with British, Prussian, and Russian armies of occupation; the populace convulsed with grief for their fallen hero; the puppet king, Louis XVIII, and his Royalists determined to take revenge on all those who had rallied to Bonaparte's standard in his hundred days of power. The young American officers had letters of introduction to the Marquis de Lafayette and dozens of other European dignitaries, but these were, for the moment, of little use. "America's old friend, Gen. Lafayette," Thayer wrote, "has shared the fate of all those patriots and men of principle who are not either imprisoned or banished and has once more retired from the political world . . . The military schools are suspended and their buildings occupied as barracks. The Allies possess all the depots, arsenals and military workshops which have not been destroyed and occupy all the fortresses . . ."

It was months before Paris settled down to something resembling normal life. But the two young American officers had plenty to do. The schools may have been closed but the bookstores were still open, and they spent long hours roaming the shelves, selecting in the end over a thousand books for the Military Academy library. Most of the faculty of the famed Ecole Polytechnique were still in Paris, although many members were in disgrace with the Bourbon regime. Thanks to the friendship of General Simon Bernard, one of Napoleon's talented engineers, the Americans managed to meet many of them. They also met Claudius Crozet, a most unhappy graduate of the Ecole and an ex-engineer of the French army, who was under a Bourbon ban for having switched from Napoleon and then switched back in the wake of the great man's meteoric return from Elba. Aside from their help at the Ecole, Crozet and Bernard must have fascinated the two Americans with their reminiscences of Napoleon. Bernard had been his aide-de-camp, and Crozet often told in later years how at Waterloo bad roads and other difficulties had prevented him from bringing up the reserve ammunition that might have saved the day.

There was a small but lively American colony in Paris, revolving around the suave American Minister to France, Albert Gallatin. Colonel Winfield Scott, the hero of Chippewa, was also there, making his own European tour. Thayer and McRee were frequent guests at the Gallatin house, and the Swiss-born minister with his many European contacts undoubtedly smoothed the young officers' paths in many directions.

In America a new luminary, William Crawford, was now Secretary of War. A big, energetic Georgian, Crawford had been a prominent senator for years and was believed by many to be on his way to the Presidency. He was determined to make a name for himself in the War Department and he went to work with even more than his customary vigor. One of his first conclusions was Swift's inadequacy as Chief of the U.S. Engineers. It was no reflection on Swift personally. Crawford probably felt Swift was simply too young (thirty-three) for the vast responsibilities involved in fortifying the coast, running the Military Academy, and supervising the Corps of Engineers. Crawford had preceded Gallatin as Minister to France, and it was there, no doubt, that he got the idea that America needed an engineer with European training to act as a sort of supervisor of the Corps. Now, when Crawford learned that Bernard was available and willing to emigrate, he quickly persuaded President Madison to hire him.

Swift and the Corps of Engineers exploded. In Paris, Thayer got a long letter from Christopher Van Deventer, chief clerk in the War Department, condemning Bernard's appointment in the bitterest possible terms. "I need say but little to expose the evils to the service and the wrongs to engineer officers which will flow from this system of withdrawing confidence from American talent and exposing it exclusively in the presumption of adventurers."

Writing to Swift from Paris, Thayer exhibited a much milder point of view. He assured Swift that he was "consoled . . . by the belief that it is beyond the power of that hon'ble Secretary to disgrace us." He also assured his chief that General Bernard was "a most worthy gentleman. At least his appearance corresponds with his character which is that of a most amiable man and officer of distinguished talents. I am disposed to believe that his conduct will be extremely conciliating and that he will avoid any interference with the Corps."

Swift did not agree. Bernard's appointment became for him the signal for a running feud with Secretary of War Crawford and the War Department. More than anything else, this explains Swift's peculiar intransigence in face of Crawford's attempts to remove, or at least control, Partridge's slipshod command at the Military Academy. Swift ignored repeated hints that he should go to West Point and take personal charge of the deteriorating situation. In his mind, the Bernard appointment merged with attacks on Partridge as part of an overall scheme to humiliate and degrade the Engineering Corps.

It is hard for us at this distance to realize how intensely the American Engineers felt themselves a body apart from the rest of the Army. Van Deventer's letter to Thayer gives us a glimpse. "The nation have uniformly made this Corps (the Engineers) an exception from the censure bestowed on the army; and all parties seem to unite in acknowledging the necessity of educating the most promising youths in the country to the higher grade of the military profession. Whenever the army has been assailed for ignorance and deficiency in science, the Corps of Engineers have always been excepted. To it the friends of a respectable army have constantly pointed as proof of the usefulness of well educated officers."

In Washington, Secretary of War Crawford's irritation with affairs at the Academy grew more intense. He stonily rejected Partridge's claim to be the legal Superintendent; it was based on a letter that Partridge had apparently drafted himself and persuaded outgoing Secretary of War

James Monroe to sign. "No officer," Crawford informed Swift, "as long as the law remains as it is, can 'be the superintendent of the institution but the principal officer of the Corps of Engineers or the next in command of that Corps in case of his absence.' " Swift persisted in letting Partridge run the school, and more and more of the Secretary's wrath focused on the Chief of Engineers. Writing to Professor Mansfield on the seventh of October, 1816, Crawford again denounced the idea that "a person residing at a distance from the Academy" could control it, and even more tartly condemned the idea of letting a man pose as Superintendent, Partridge style, when the law "excluded" him. "There seems to have been formed a systematic plan . . . to introduce regulations in direct hostility with the organic laws of the Academy."

Swift summoned a court of inquiry in a vain attempt to dissipate the charges the faculty was making against Partridge. Since it was held under Swift's aegis and Partridge was still the only man Swift could see in the job, the court predictably exonerated Partridge of serious wrong-doing, but it reprimanded him for a wide variety of misconduct and poor judgment. He allowed enlisted men stationed on the post to cut wood on the public lands and sell it for a profit. Refractory cadets were confined to a "black hole"—a pit some eight feet square with a wooden lid—and the captain persistently gave cadets commissions without bothering to make them pass a graduation examination.

Partridge's highly unrealistic approach to discipline was evident in testimony he himself introduced. Cross-examining one of the cadets, he asked him to describe how the corps received him when he returned from a visit to Washington. "They expressed great joy," the young man said, "by illuminating the barracks and huzzahing." He also introduced an endorsement of his regime, written by the corps adjutant, Cadet Thomas Ragland, and signed by 109 cadets. Already Partridge was attempting to use popularity with immature boys as a substitute for achievement.

Unimpressed by Partridge's exoneration, Secretary of War Crawford made grimly clear what he expected from the Academy. He wanted general examinations twice a year, a four-year course for each cadet with no exceptions, annual inspections by a Board of Visitors, and an absolute end to commissioning cadets without an examination. He also ordered Swift to make his headquarters at West Point and become Superintendent in fact as well as in name. Swift obeyed for a few months but was soon down in New York again, working on Engineering Department affairs.

At West Point, Partridge resumed the reins and proceeded to pursue the same headstrong course that had brought him to the brink of disaster the previous year. Once more the professors erupted with a flood of complaints that brought President Monroe to the Academy for a personal inspection. Crawford had already written to Thayer ordering him home, so the President's visit was really more an afterthought to confirm Partridge's unfitness. "I do not think much of your Captain Partridge and would prefer to see Major Thayer in his place," the President told Swift. Swift humbly replied that the President's wish was his command. But even then he did not really believe that the change would take place. He knew nothing of the explicit orders already sent to Thayer in Europe. But he did know "that engineer officers deemed the superintendence of the Academy as a species of schoolmaster's place," and he was sure that Thayer, if he was offered the job, would turn it down as his friend McRee had done before him.

Sylvanus Thayer, however, had received not an offer but an order. The sea of clashing policies and personalities into which he sailed might have been a harrowing prospect for a young man of thirty-two. But Thayer's European tour had broadened him immensely. Months of meeting diplomats and generals had given him a polish and confidence that made him ready for the job. More important, his visits to France's Ecole Polytechnique, his conferences with the professors and students of that world-famous school, had confirmed and intensified Thayer's conviction that young America needed these same technological and scientific resources if the nation was to prosper. In mid-October, he told his sister why he had taken the job, in words that reflected the depth of his commitment. "I had a solemn duty to perform and was determined to perform it whatever were the personal consequences to myself."

III

THE FIRST STEP in Thayer's revitalization campaign was a general examination for every cadet in the Academy. By the end of September, 1817, the faculty had completed this arduous chore, and Thayer was writing to Acting Secretary of War George Graham, transmitting a list of forty-three cadets, almost one-fifth of the current enrollment, with serious academic deficiencies. "Twenty-two of these gentlemen have been here more than three years and some of them much longer without having advanced beyond the first year's course," Thayer wrote. "The remaining twenty-one have been here more than two years, and some of them three and four years, without having made any progress whatever in the course of studies."

Thayer was determined to be fair, however. He and the academic staff leaned over backward lest any one of these young men be penalized for the inadequacies of Partridge's regime. Twenty-two of these deficient cadets were, therefore, allowed to resume study in the first year's course. Twenty-one others, however, were recommended for removal "as their longer stay is deemed injurious to the institution."

"Most of them," Thayer wrote, "are deficient in natural abilities and all are destitute of those qualities which would encourage a belief that they could ever advance through the four years' course of studies. The public money would be wasted, therefore, by retaining them here any longer." Thayer also took this opportunity to get rid of two young South Americans who had been carried north by Commodore Horace Porter on a cruise from Chile and dumped at the Academy. "These lads are extremely deficient in the first rudiments of education, reading, writing, and orthography. They manifest no desire to learn and accordingly make no progress. They are besides extremely troublesome as they cannot be made to observe any of the police regulations. They have been advised, admonished, and punished but entirely without effect. They are real nuisances and should be removed."

Thayer's recommendations were supported by a simultaneous letter from the entire academic staff. West Point now settled down to its first school year under its new Superintendent. The classroom system Thayer constructed was based on his observations of the Ecole Polytechnique. Each class was divided into small sections. The head of the department taught the first section, which included the most gifted cadets and moved at a faster pace than other sections. The goal was a course of studies in which a man could advance and grow according to his abilities. There was no need to hold back the brighter cadets in the name of fairness to the slower ones. But the less gifted were guaranteed a chance to learn at least the essentials of the subject under study.

These were revolutionary ideas in 1817. At Harvard, Yale, and the other colleges of Thayer's era, the lecture delivered to the class en masse was the basic educational tool. Everyone studied the same course, at the same pace. Thayer's Dartmouth classmate, George Ticknor, who had gone to Germany to study its educational system during the same years Thayer had been in France, criticized this intellectual uniformity, declaring that its result was "a great deal of idle time, since the principle is for those who are best able and disposed to study, to wait for the rest."

Thayer was determined to maintain the closest possible check on each boy's progress. On October 11, 1817, he issued the following order: "The professors, assistant professors and teachers of the military academy will hand in every Sunday to the superintendent a written report . . . The report shall designate those cadets who have neglected their lessons or shall not have made suitable progress in their studies and also those who shall have conducted improperly in the recitation rooms or academics. These reports will be consolidated and forwarded with the police reports for the information of the War Department. When it shall appear that any cadet has been habitually inattentive to his studies, he will be struck from the rolls of the military academy."

Discipline on the post became strict and swiftly enforced. The cadets were ordered to forward to the Superintendent the names and addresses of their parents or guardians. Charles Floyd of Georgia refused to obey this seemingly painless order. The order was repeated, and again Floyd refused. He was probably trying to stop Thayer from informing his father that he was one of the poorest students on the rolls and his conduct had "evinced a spirit . . . intractable and . . . repugnant to subordination and good discipline." On the thirtieth of September, Floyd was dismissed.

Thayer was equally determined to create at the Academy a spirit of absolute fairness, a rule of law in which exceptions were made neither for Partridge-style favoritism nor the influence of powerful friends. His first test came in mid-October with a letter from Swift informing him that Thomas Pinckney of South Carolina had asked permission to detain his son Edward at home until the fifteenth of October because of the dangers of traveling in unhealthy weather. Pinckney was one of the most important men in the country—a former governor, congressman, Minister to England, Revolutionary war hero. Alas, his son Edward apparently had failed to inherit his father's gifts; he was among the cadets who had already been at the Academy for more than the regulation four years with no progress, and was recommended for dismissal. Unflinchingly, Thayer wrote General Pinckney, explaining the new regime and regretfully informing him "that the resignation of your son will be accepted to take effect from the date of this letter.

"In communicating this advice I have the satisfaction to state that the personal deportment and moral conduct of your son while a member of this institution has always been very commendable."

Organization, principles, discipline—all these were vital, but they did not guarantee educational success. The Academy was desperately short of textbooks. The few they had were in French, and the knowledge of that language, even among members of the first class, was painfully inadequate. With only one French professor to teach more than 150 cadets each week, Thayer again wrote to Washington, urgently requesting the power to appoint an assistant professor of French. A volley of letters went to New York, galvanizing Captain John O'Connor, who was translating Gay de Vernon's *A Treatise on the Science of War and Fortification*. This three-volume tome had been revised by a board of distinguished French marshals and engineers before it was, by order of Napoleon, adopted at the Ecole Polytechnique.

Tall, heavily built Claudius Crozet, struggling to teach engineering in a language he had been speaking less than six months, was another of Thayer's problems. But Crozet's pupils were even more worrisome. Edward Dearing Mansfield, the son of West Point professor Jared Mansfield, has given a graphic glimpse of the classroom situation in his memoirs of his student days at West Point. "Professor Crozet was to teach engineering but when he met the class he found not one of them fit to learn engineering. There were branches of science and its affiliations essentially necessary to engineering which they had never been taught. What was he to do? All he could do, obviously, was to supply these preliminary studies before he could commence in his own department.

In other words, he must begin by becoming a teacher of mathematics and drawing."

Such deficiencies could not be blamed entirely on the students. As Mansfield wrote: "Among these preliminary studies was descriptive geometry . . . We doubt whether at that time more than a dozen or two professors of science in this country knew there was such a thing . . . Perhaps this is not surprising when we reflect that this new application of geometry was scarcely thirty years old."

Crozet, attempting to repair this total ignorance of descriptive geometry, was confronted by another problem: there was no textbook either in English or in French. A true soldier of Napoleon, Crozet refused to admit defeat. He consulted, Mansfield tells us, the "carpenter and painter," and *voilà,* he had a blackboard. It was not the first one used in America, or even at West Point, but it was one of the first half dozen and it struck the new cadets as proof of the professor's genius.

Mansfield wrote an unforgettable portrait of the Frenchman at work during Thayer's first crucial year: "We now see Crozet with his blackboard before him, chalk in hand, an animated intellectual face, about to teach his class a new science, without a textbook. With extreme difficulty he makes himself understood. With difficulty his class comprehend that two planes at right angles with one another are to be understood on the same surface of the blackboard, on which are represented two different projections of the same object. But at last it is done. The professor labors with inexhaustible patience and the pupils are pleased to receive into their minds entirely new ideas."

New ideas! This was Sylvanus Thayer's dream for West Point and America. But this steady, if somewhat tantalizing, progress had to be halted for an unpleasant necessity—the court-martial of Alden Partridge. A board of officers headed by General Winfield Scott assembled at West Point on October 23, 1817. Partridge was charged with neglect of duty and unofficerlike conduct, disobedience of orders, and mutiny. The court heard an array of witnesses, including Thayer, until November 11, and then handed down its sentence. Partridge was found guilty of disobedience of orders but cleared of mutiny as such. He was sentenced to be cashiered. However, the court recommended clemency "in view of the zeal and perseverance which the prisoner seems uniformly to have displayed in the discharge of his professional duties up to the period of August 1."

Swift, ever faithful to his concept of the Engineering Corps as a breed apart, went to Washington and persuaded President Monroe to accept this plea and permit Partridge to resign. Reluctantly the President agreed. If Swift thought he could soothe Partridge by this last gesture of friendship and thus end for good his unfortunate link to West Point, the Chief Engineer was wrong. Old Pewt promptly lodged a set of charges against Thayer and Swift, accusing his protector both of graft and waste in the new buildings erected at West Point during the years 1815 to 1817. President Monroe dismissed the charges as beneath official notice, and Partridge went home to Norwich, Vermont. But Thayer knew West Point had not heard the last of him. Partridge had dreamed of making himself the permanent Superintendent of West Point. A man whose lifetime ambition had exploded in his face was not likely to forget or forgive those who had pricked his bubble.

In a letter to Swift, Partridge promised he would found a military school of his own that would soon put West Point in its shadow. He added a bitter vow: "You may rest assured the business will not rest (if my life is preserved) until the whole scene of iniquity . . . relative to the affairs of West Point be fully developed . . . I am near 33 years of age, and should I live to be 70, this subject shall never . . . be abandoned unless justice be done."

For the time being, however, Partridge was *hors de combat*. Thayer concentrated once more on the multitude of daily problems he faced at West Point. He had organized the corps into two companies, one for tall, the other for short cadets. To increase their self-reliance and better prepare them for their future careers, he announced they would act as their own officers. At first the honor was distributed on a rotating basis. At the same time Thayer searched the Army lists for a competent professor of military tactics—an Army officer who would be able to take charge of cadet discipline and give them all they needed to know on the strictly military side of their education.

Early in December, Thayer must have been heartened by news from Washington: a hard-driving young congressman from South Carolina, John C. Calhoun, had become Secretary of War. One of the "War Hawks" who had led the country into conflict with England in 1812, Calhoun had felt humiliated by the wretched performance of the American Army in the field, and he tackled the job of creating a sound peacetime army with refreshing zeal. He inherited problems even more crushing than Thayer's. His department had a war debt of fifty million dollars to pay off. An economy-crazy Congress was determined to reduce the Army to the vanishing point. Paradoxically, this made West Point all the more important in the new Secretary's view. If quantity was out of the question in the government's plans for the Army, there could be no substitute for quality. No more would the Military Academy be a foundling in the mountains, much less a rejected child starved by callous parents.

Thayer and Calhoun were soon corresponding, with enthusiasm and respect high on both sides. At the end of 1817, Thayer ordered another series of examinations. He wanted to see how well his system was working. The results were more than satisfactory. Thayer's letter to Calhoun on January 31, 1818, is a landmark in West Point's history.

Sir,

I have the honor to enclose herewith a class-roll of the cadets of the military academy. On which the cadets are arranged in their respective sections in the order of their relative merits as determined by the academic-staff at the general examination which commenced on the 15th of December and continued seven hours each day until the third of January. The cadets were examined by sections in order that the academical exercises might suffer no interruption. The instruction being conducted by acting assistant professors selected from cadets. The examination was highly satisfactory, except that many were found deficient in the French language, a deficiency which is mainly to be ascribed to the want of a suitable number of teachers in that department.

In addition to a rigid examination (in which demonstrations and operations were performed on the blackboard) the class-reports (of which one is herewith enclosed) have contributed not a little to make known individual merit by recording the degree of knowledge which each cadet evinces of his lesson at his daily recitations. The emulation excited by the class-reports and by the merit rolls has produced a degree of application to study which is believed to be unexampled at this institution. This emulation is still increased by the expectation which has been encouraged that the merit-rolls will be printed and perhaps published in the Army Register from and after the next general examination.

Competition and rewards meted out with absolute impartiality—these were essential, in Thayer's view, to create the kind of spirit needed by an educated soldier. Calhoun agreed. On February 10 he wrote Thayer:

It affords me pleasure to witness the progress of the institution under your superintendence, and to express to you my approbation of the measures you have adopted to promote its improvement and to secure to it the reputation which it ought to possess with the nation.

As publishing in the Army Register, the names of those cadets who are distinguished for attainments and meritorious conduct, may inspire an attention to study and create emulous exertion, you will report to this Department annually, in November, for that object, the names of those who have most distinguished themselves in the examination, not exceeding five in each class, specifying the studies in which they excel.

But Calhoun was also a politician, and not even he could prevent the first small clash between Washington's ways of doing business and Thayer's high ideals. In that same month of February the new Superintendent was dismayed to learn that Edward Pinckney had been reappointed by order of the President. Thayer apparently wrote a cautious private protest to his friend Christopher Van Deventer, chief clerk in the War Department, who sent him a frustrating reply: "I should have answered your late favor but not having anything to communicate to explain the restoration of Cadet Pinckney, of course was silent— whenever I can communicate anything useful to you or the institution, I shall certainly do it; and shall especially be careful to prevent as far as representation can do it the introduction of any measure which may be injurious to our military alma mater."

Thayer gritted his teeth, swallowed Pinckney (he flunked out again within a year) and went back to work. Before the end of that same month he had submitted to the Secretary of War a twenty-four-point program for the reorganization of the Military Academy. Primarily, Thayer sought government approval and ratification of changes he had already made. But he also urged that the Academy should be distinct from the Corps of Engineers. He called for an instructor in military tactics to be selected from the Army and attached to the academic staff.

Other changes illustrate the constant forward thrust of Thayer's mind. Regulations already called for the faculty to constitute an academic board. He specified that the board's duty would be "to fix and improve the system of studies and instruction." In his remarks on this point he added that the board "is intended to be equivalent to Conscil (sic) de Perfectionment of the French Polytechnique school." Elsewhere

Thayer urged that the age limit for admission be raised from fourteen to sixteen. "The principal study of the cadets during the two first years of their course is mathematics, and the experience of the professors has proved that most young men at the age of fourteen are neither sufficiently matured nor sufficiently grounded in the previous studies to proceed to the higher and abstruse parts of that science." Thayer also suggested that an added requirement for new cadets should be a knowledge of English grammar. An appalling number of applicants were apparently deficient in this fundamental. On the other hand he saw no need to expand the Academy—250, the number of cadets specified by the Law of 1812, was sufficient.

Thayer also worried over the public image of the school. The Chief Engineer, he suggested, should be named the Inspector of the Academy. More important, "four scientific men" should be selected by the President of the United States and constitute the Board of Visitors with the Inspector as chairman. Each year this board should attend the general examinations and "report accurately" to the War Department the progress of the institution.

One other proposition reveals Thayer's thinking about West Point's purpose. A provision of the law then in force called for cadets to "sign articles of obligation to remain five years in service." Thayer recommended dropping this requirement, "as it has never been carried into effect and is not calculated to produce an equal effect." West Point, in Thayer's view, would not create scientists and engineers simply for the Army. With Congress talking of slashing the army to 6300 men there would not be enough commissions to go around anyway. West Point's peacetime function was to supply a vast and growing America with the trained men it needed to build bridges, canals, highways; to dredge harbors and rivers; and to provide a reservoir of expert soldiers who could step into a wartime army's ranks without difficulty or disruption.

Thayer had one more change in mind, too important to include in his twenty-four propositions. It required a separate series of letters between him and Calhoun and Swift. According to the current regulations, Thayer pointed out, the cadets were to be encamped at least three months of each year. This was out of the question under the present schedule since it was not possible to camp and go to school simultaneously. On the other hand, regulations provided for an annual vacation from mid-July to the end of August. This, Thayer thought, should be eliminated. "It is the unanimous opinion of the academic staff . . . that a general vacation is not only unnecessary, but highly injurious to the cadets and to the institution. The cadets being supplied at the academy with everything necessary to them, have no occasion to go home for supplies of clothing and money as is the case with students at our colleges . . . Much the greatest portion of the cadets did not visit their homes during the last vacation but flocked, as usual, to New York and other cities, there to indulge in dissipation and to contract disease, vices, and debts. Many were there detained some months either by disease or on account of debts. Others were put in jail and several of the young gentlemen I have not heard of since . . . I am therefore fully of the opinion that the annual vacation ought to be abolished."

Instead, Thayer suggested that the cadets go into camp immediately after June examinations and remain there until September. During this period furloughs could be granted to a limited number at the discretion of the Superintendent. This twelve-month regime would give the cadets the right balance between academic and military experience. It would also be wise, Thayer suggested, to order all incoming cadets to report on June 1 so they, too, could participate in a summer of camp, which would convert them into soldiers before they became scholars. Vacancies left by those who fell by the wayside in preliminary examinations or under the rigors of camp life could be filled in time to begin classes in September.

By regulation, drills were eliminated at West Point from November 1 until April 1 because of the severe weather. As the time for reinstituting drills drew near, Thayer finally selected an instructor of tactics, Captain John Bliss of the 6th Infantry. He was, Thayer said, "peculiarly well qualified to fill that important station." Thayer had seen Bliss in action during the War of 1812 and had admired the spirit of discipline he inculcated in his men. Alas, the new Superintendent was soon to discover that an officer skilled at handling Regular Army enlisted men was not necessarily suited for disciplining high-spirited gentlemen cadets.

But Thayer, for the moment, was laboring under a more immediate difficulty. As Superintendent of the Academy he was required to entertain any and all important visitors who passed through West Point. He had to do this out of his own pocket. "While receiving brevet pay (as a major) and double rations," he wrote to Swift, "I have found my expenditures, although regulated by the most rigid economy of which I was capable, to exceed my means of payment." Then, under the pressure of the Congressional economy wave, the paymaster of the Engineering Corps was instructed to cease paying brevet compensation or double rations to the commanding officer of West Point. "It is with extreme regret that I am reduced to the necessity of representing to you my pecuniary embarrassments," Thayer wrote to Swift. "To you who are perfectly well acquainted with the extraordinary private expenses to which the superintendent of the military academy is necessarily subjected unless he would consent to live in a style which would degrade the station which he holds, I need say nothing more than to request you will have the goodness to inform me whether any additional compensation will be allowed."

Swift's answer to this was silence. At the same time Thayer learned to his considerable chagrin that Congress had no intention of acting on his recommendations for the Academy in the current session. These and other minor vexations, such as the government's persistent refusal to establish a quartermaster at West Point with sufficient funds to make repairs on buildings and improve the grounds in keeping with a "national institution," undoubtedly inspired Thayer's letter of May 12, 1818:

Believing that I shall not have it in my power hereafter to be useful in any considerable degree to the military academy, I request the War Department will be pleased to have me relieved of the command of this post and the superintendence of the institution.

In case this request should be granted I would wish to obtain a furlough for the purpose of visiting my relations whom I have not seen for many years.

The second paragraph may also have had something to do with Thayer's decision. With his brother Nathaniel dead and his father growing old, he was the man in the family, and his sisters bombarded him constantly with pleas for letters, visits, advice, and, occasionally, money. But more probable is the conclusion that the letter was a calculated move on Thayer's part in the delicate game of politics he was forced to play with Washington. There is nothing better than a resignation to test one's value with superiors. The resignation was firmly refused, and, soon after, the Secretary of War approved most of the changes in regulations Thayer suggested, including the abolition of vacations and the summer encampment.

In June came the first examination of the Thayer regime, and on July 24, 1818, the first regular graduation. Twenty-two cadets won the recommendation of the academic board for warrants as second lieutenants in the United States Army.

The rest of the corps went into summer camp. Here the cadets were under the stern hand and unrelenting eye of Captain Bliss. Their days were spent in drill, weapons training, tactics, and more drill. Since there were no horses on the post, for artillery practice the cadets had to harness themselves to the field pieces and haul them around the plain under the scorching sun. It was not the sort of summer the cadets had expected to spend, and it was hardly surprising that most of their resentment should have focused on Bliss.

By the time classes began again in September, more than one cadet's temper was at the boiling point. Bull sessions in the barracks recalled the easygoing Partridge days. But Bliss kept up the pressure. Thayer, delighted with his work, had already begun to evolve the concept of making the instructor of tactics a Commandant of Cadets, fully responsible for all aspects of post discipline. A cadet letter of September 28, 1818, gives a revealing glimpse of the Bliss regime:

At daylight in the morning we are called up by the drum beating in the barracks. We must be up in a minute to answer to our names or else be reported and have to sweep about two hours. In about thirty minutes after, the drum beats for drill at which they keep us two hours, then form and go to breakfast. At eight o'clock go to recite—dismissed at eleven. At twelve go to recite French. At one, dinner. At four drill again, two hours as before, then supper. At nine p.m. the roll is called again and five minutes afterward the lights must be out . . . The only time we have for recreation is about a half hour at noon and Saturday afternoon; at these times even cannot go off the Point—without getting permission from Captain Bliss.

Four hours of drill on top of a rugged classroom schedule was considerably more than Thayer himself had envisioned in his original schedule for the Academy. However, he permitted Bliss to continue afternoon drills after November 1, probably because a large number of cadets had arrived on the old September 1 date for admission. To the holdovers from Partridge's regime this was an added goad.

On November 22 the explosion took place. A cadet from Maryland, Edward Lloyd Nicholson, misbehaved in the ranks. Bliss, enraged, ordered him to his quarters. The cadet did not move fast enough, and Bliss seized him by the collar, dragged him out of the ranks, and treated him to a torrent of drillmaster's oaths.

Two days later, five cadets presented themselves to Thayer in his office. They coolly announced they were a committee selected by the corps to condemn Captain Bliss for a long list of outrages, culminated by his "attack" on Cadet Nicholson. To back them up they presented the Superintendent with a "round-robin" petition signed by 179 members of the corps.

Thomas Ragland was the spokesman for the five-man committee. He had been adjutant of the corps under Partridge and one of Old Pewt's favorites. He had also been one of the ringleaders in the riotous greeting and farewell Partridge had received when he seized command. The other committee members were Charles A. R. Vining, Charles R. Holmes, Nathaniel W. Loring, and Wilson M. C. Fairfax. All but Holmes had stood high in Partridge's favor. But Thayer had not allowed this association to interfere with his impartial rule of merit. Ragland and Fairfax had just been appointed acting assistant professors—the highest reward the faculty could bestow on good students. Loring was cadet captain of the second company.

There was no doubt that these were talented young men. Among the signers of the petition were Edward D. Mansfield, the old professor's son; Andrew J. Donelson, nephew of Andrew Jackson; William H. Swift, younger brother of General Swift. But Thayer did not allow either gifts or prominence to alter his vision of reality. This round-robin petition was a holdover from the Partridge regime. Old Pewt had actually encouraged this form of communication between cadets and faculty. By using it, the young men left no doubt that they were asserting their preference for the slack discipline of earlier years. But they were young, and Thayer restrained his first impulse to hit them with the full weight of his authority. Quietly he told them that any cadet who had a grievance could have a hearing with the Superintendent. But he would not tolerate anything as unmilitary as round-robin petitions. The committee was dismissed with a warning not to make the same mistake twice.

The very next day the five ringleaders were back, this time with a set of charges against Captain Bliss. Cadet Ragland, again the spokesman, backed up his stand with another round-robin petition plus a threat that unless Thayer took them seriously the entire corps was prepared to mutiny. Ragland was a cocky, outspoken young man. His work as post adjutant had apparently given him the illusion that he could treat the Superintendent and other members of the faculty as if they were equals.

Grimly Thayer ordered Ragland and his four friends to get off the post within six hours. They were to retire "to the places of their respective guardians where they would remain until further notice." Thayer then published an order to the corps denouncing round-robin petitions as "not only in a military but in a civil point of view, a crime of the first order."

As a soldier Thayer was certainly right in pointing out the unmilitary nature of the round-robin approach to discipline. But calling a petition a civil crime was an exaggeration that suggests he was far more disturbed by this new defiance than his icy demeanor showed. The five ringleaders departed, but not until they had collected another letter signed by 108 members of the corps, attesting "deepest regret" at their departure. "We feel the same resolution which called forth that noble exertion of soul and made you offer your individual welfare in our behalf . . . We pledge our sacred word to aid you in the common cause," the signers declared. It was clear to Thayer and everyone else that this was only the opening round in another duel for control of the Military Academy.

Thayer's position was rendered somewhat more delicate by Swift's recent resignation as Chief of Engineers. To Walker K. Armistead, the new Chief of Engineers, Thayer wrote a long letter on November 30, outlining the whole incident. He did not waste words.

The pretty general dislike of the young gentlemen to Captain Bliss arises in part from his strict discipline forming as it does a complete contrast to that of former times and is in part incident to the unpleasant situation which he fills, he being the person charged to watch over and report their conduct and to inflict the punishments for all minor delinquencies. But the radical cause of the disturbances to which the military academy is liable is the erroneous and unmilitary impressions of the cadets imbibed at an inauspicious period of the Institution when they were allowed to act as tho' they had rights to defend as a corps of the army and to intrude their voices and opinions with respect to the concerns of the acdy. So long as these impressions shall remain, the acdy shall be liable to combinations and convulsions and the reputation of the Institution and of the officers connected with it be put in jeopardy. Notwithstanding these proceedings . . . I am happy in being able to assure you that there has been no positive act of mutiny or disorder and that the operations of the Institution have not been interrupted for a moment. But as reports may be spread calculated to injure all concerned, I hope the Secretary of War will think proper to direct one of the principal officers of the Corps of Engineers to repair to this place as soon as possible in the capacity of an inspector . . .

The five dismissed ringleaders retired to New York, where they wrote a long letter to Secretary of War Calhoun. From there they proceeded to Washington, where they handed up an even longer document attacking the entire Thayer administration. With any other President or any other Secretary of War, Thayer might have been in serious trouble. But Monroe and Calhoun gave him their unqualified personal backing. A Court of Inquiry appointed by Armistead also reported in favor of the Superintendent. "The course pursued by the cadets," Calhoun wrote, "is highly reprehensible throughout the whole transaction and particularly objectionable on the part of the young gentlemen who composed their committee—the redress of military grievances must never be extorted or obtained by combinations which are alike mutinous."

As for Captain Bliss, Calhoun concluded from reading the list of charges preferred against him by the cadets, attested in many cases by individual letters, that he "does not appear to possess sufficient command of his temper." The Secretary ordered him transferred.

The dismissed cadets, meanwhile, laid their grievances before Congress. This produced a resolution in the House of Representatives calling upon the Secretary of War to lay before the next session of Congress a copy of the rules and regulations of the Military Academy along with a report "whether any and if any, what legislative provisions are necessary for the more convenient organization and government of said academy; the better to secure a strict obedience to all proper orders and a suitable respect for the rights of those whose duty it may be to yield obedience."

Thomas Ragland, for his part, demanded a court-martial, which convened at West Point on the twenty-ninth of May and then promptly adjourned because its members did not feel they were empowered to try cadets under the current Army regulations. The Attorney General of the United States, William Wirt, was asked for an opinion, and he declared in favor of court-martial, maintaining "that the corps at West Point form a part of the land forces of the United States and have been constitutionally subjected by Congress to the rules and articles of war and to trial by courts-martial." The court-martial reconvened again on the twenty-third of September, 1819, and after hearing a long and passionate defense by Ragland again declared itself incompetent to try cadets. Annoyed, President Monroe ordered the court dissolved and flatly stated he upheld his Attorney General: "The professors, teachers, and cadets are governed by the rules and articles of war." The President ordered the entire institution to assemble and hear a reading of the January 15, 1818, letter from Secretary of War Calhoun, emphatically restating this principle.

By now, almost a year had elapsed since Thayer had ordered Ragland and his associates off the post. Deciding they had been sufficiently punished by their twelve-month suspension, Monroe ordered them reinstated. But their class had already been graduated and they had utterly failed to dislodge Thayer. Bitter, they resigned in a body and went back to Congress to prosecute their case—in vain. A committee of the 16th Congress held lengthy hearings and concluded on April 11, 1820, that Thayer, Calhoun, and Monroe were all above reproach.

Thus Superintendent Thayer survived what may justly be called another attempt at mutiny by the spirit of Alden Partridge. Even when Congress found in his favor, Thayer knew attacks of this sort were by no means over. He had made not just five enemies but five enemy families —fathers, mothers, brothers, cousins, often people of power and influence, who were convinced that Sylvanus Thayer was an unjust tyrant.

But for the moment Thayer had emerged from his battle with Ragland and company enormously strengthened. The Attorney General's decision became one of West Point's disciplinary cornerstones. Never again could a West Pointer claim he was neither a soldier nor an officer but a "gentleman cadet" with a peculiar set of rights he could assert whenever he chose. The military nature of the school was reconfirmed by the reaction of the War Department to a new spate of complaints by Professor Mansfield in 1819. Mansfield groused: "we need less military and more civilian influence here." He wanted to have more say in running the school. He also obviously disliked Thayer's fondness for things French, and made wry comparisons of West Point to "Academies of despotic countries." Secretary of War Calhoun ignored the Professor, and he dwindled into sulky silence. By the end of 1819 it was abundantly clear to everyone at West Point that Sylvanus Thayer was the man in charge.

IV

AS WEST POINT moved into the new decade, Thayer's vision of what the Academy could become moved steadily closer to reality. He found an ideal instructor of tactics in Captain William C. Worth, a hero of Chippewa, a man who looked and acted every inch a soldier. The cadets nicknamed him "Haughty Bill," and even the most recalcitrant had to admit Worth's swagger added a touch of glamor that made the drill and discipline side of his military regime more bearable.

In the classroom Professor Crozet had mastered the English language and most of the cadets had acquired enough French to read the text-books. The competition for positions on the rolls of General Merit became keener with each year. In a letter to Secretary of War Calhoun, Thayer explained how a cadet's standing was achieved:

Each branch of study pursued at the institution is represented by a multiplier or number corresponding with the importance of the branch and the time bestowed in its acquisition—the numbers which were originally adopted and are still employed for this purpose are

For the course in mathematics   .2
Natural and experimental philosophy   .2
Engineering   .2
Military exercise and conduct   .2
French language   .1
Drawing   .1
Whole course of studies   .1

Each individual's knowledge in any one of the above-mentioned branches is expressed by a fraction of the number representing the value of that branch and his total or general merit by the sum of all the fractions which express his knowledge in the several branches in which he is examined.

To render this explanation more clear, I will take as example Cadets John C. Holland, Clark Burdine, and David Wallace who are the third, fourth, and fifth on the roll of General Merit of the third class. Their relative knowledge in mathematics was expressed by the following fractions, viz.— that of Cadet Holland by .80—Cadet Burdine, .90—Cadet Wallace, .85. These decimals being multiplied by .2, the representing of the value of mathematics in the course, gives for Cadet Holland, .160—Cadet Burdine,

.180—Cadet Wallace, .170—again the relative knowledge of these gentlemen in the French language which was expressed as follows, that of Cadet Holland by .95—Cadet Burdine, .70—Cadet Wallace, .50, which being multiplied by .1, the number representing the value of the French language in the course and added to the former products become,

Cadet Holland .160 plus .95 equals .255
Cadet Burdine .180 plus .70 equals .250
Cadet Wallace .170 plus .50 equals .220

Thus Cadet Holland who is below Cadets Burdine and Wallace in mathematics, is placed above them on the roll of General Merit in consequence of his much superior knowledge of the French language.

Thayer made only a few modest additions to the school's physical plant. In response to the law of 1812, General Swift had built a new mess hall, an academic building and two barracks running in a line from west to east along the southern edge of the present parade ground. Three stories of stone with a slate roof, the barracks became "South Barracks" when another barracks, four stories high with the same spare functional style and slate roof, was built at right angles to it, becoming, predictably, "North Barracks." Thayer, acutely conscious of the hostile eye of Congress, attempted no major building programs. He brought running water into the basement of the barracks by drawing on a mountainside reservoir through iron pipes and built for himself the comfortable quarters that successive Superintendents have continued to use. He added four small stone houses facing the beautiful upriver scenery, the beginning of present-day Professors' Row. The new importance of the school, which brought a flood of visitors and involved the Superintendent in heavy entertaining, and an expanded faculty made these additions absolute necessities. Also badly needed and eventually added was a larger cadet hospital, to the south of the barracks area. Around the Plain he planted trees, many of which still stand today.

Inside the barracks, life remained as spartan as it had been in Thayer's cadet days. The would-be lieutenants still slept two to a narrow room on mattresses thrown on the bare floors. The only heat came from small fireplaces, and reminiscences of those days tell of studying on winter nights wrapped in blankets, numb feet pressed against the fender around the fire. Aside from the money these minimum accommodations saved (the Academy was soon able to report that it was educating cadets for one-half the cost at England's military academy, Woolwich),

Thayer obviously understood the value of shared hardship in creating a spirit that would animate West Pointers for the rest of their lives. How well it worked can be seen from the speeches of graduates in later years, in which they invariably recalled with pride the freezing rooms, the mediocre food, drilling on the Plain when it was covered with ice.

Discipline remained severe. No cadet was permitted to receive money from home. They had to live on their pay, ten dollars cash a month, from which large amounts were regularly deducted for such items as uniforms, swords, blankets. Thayer worked over the cadet schedule until almost every minute of their fifteen-hour day was devoted to study, drill, policing their rooms, or some other kind of useful work.

Minutely as he attempted to control and motivate the average cadet, Thayer was always ready to change the rules to let a gifted boy move ahead at his own pace. Dividing each class into sections permitted this kind of progress—but only up to a point. A particularly brilliant student could find even the first section holding him back. A good example was Joshua Baker of Louisiana, a mathematical genius who was allowed to study on his own and recite to the professors in private sessions held before daybreak.

Thayer drove himself with the same relentless dedication he expected from his faculty and students. He arose each day before reveille and usually took a walk around the post. More than one drowsy sentry was startled to see the Superintendent's slim figure striding past in the pre-dawn murk, wrapped in the cloak that was the only heavy garment he wore, even in the bitterest weather. He would then supervise the morning parade and return to his quarters for breakfast. From seven to eight o'clock he received cadets in his office.

It was in this hour that Thayer created his reputation for knowing with almost preternatural skill the most minute details of every cadet's personal affairs. Requests for excuses from duty were answered without a moment's hesitation by the exact number of delinquencies on the petitioner's disciplinary record. A permit to buy new shirts or shoes from the post store would bring an instantaneous frown. "You are in debt $5.20 already, sir," Thayer would say, and the delinquent would go wandering off to class, trying in vain to figure out how Thayer remembered the misdeeds and debts of every cadet in the corps.

Actually Thayer had a secret, which one of his professors, Albert E. Church, revealed many years later. Thayer had hired an energetic young

Irishman, Timothy O'Maher, as his clerk. In the back of Thayer's desk
was a series of deep pigeonholes. Each month, or week if necessary,
O'Maher prepared memoranda on each and every matter relating to an
individual cadet. These were pasted upright in the pigeonholes, and when
a cadet appeared before him Thayer had only to glance casually downward to get a complete reading on the young man's current standing in
the corps.

Thayer would seem to have deliberately encouraged this omniscient
personal image among the cadets. He was determined not to make Partridge's mistake of sentimental fraternization, of addressing the cadets as
"my young friends." The disastrous results of this approach were grimly
apparent during Thayer's first three years. But his knowledge of each
cadet as an individual was by no means limited to O'Maher's memoranda. Every Saturday between two and three-thirty, every instructor
teaching a section of a class presented himself to the Superintendent and
submitted a written report showing the progress of each pupil in his
section.

The instructors were received in Thayer's "private office"—not the
same one in which he saw cadets. Thomas Jefferson Cram, a cadet from
1822 to 1826 and later an assistant professor, recalled these sessions.
"Colonel Thayer was particular in his inquiries of the instructor, not
only into the proficiency of acquisition of the pupil but also of his
deportment during the recitations. In this way the superintendent obtained a pretty accurate insight into the moral deportment and mental
acquirement of every cadet."

Thayer was also in the habit of inspecting the cadets' quarters during
the course of the school year, often in the company of distinguished
visitors. On these occasions he would always introduce the young men
by name, with unerring accuracy. Often they would chat for a few
moments. "By these visits," Cram said, "we were most favorably impressed with the superintendent's kindly disposition towards us."

There were other times when Thayer could unbend. Many thought he
was at his best when greeting new cadets. He met every young applicant
personally, shook his hand, and gave him a searching interview. He
made "the young strangers . . . feel themselves at once at home and
many expressed their delight afterwards at the questions he asked them
about their homes, surroundings, etc." Since these boys were not yet
soldiers, the Superintendent let them get away with things no cadet

would have dared to do or say in his presence. A lanky Kentuckian named Henderson K. Yoakum struggled up the long steep hill from the dock one hot June day and arrived at the Superintendent's office gasping for breath, pouring sweat. Randolph B. Marcy, who was in Yoakum's class, described what happened next.

"Unlike most of the cadets on their first introduction to (Colonel Thayer) he was not in the slightest degree abashed, but felt entirely self-possessed, and taking a chair close to the colonel, and looking him attentively in the face, said, 'Old man are you Colonel, or Captain, or whatever-you-call-um Thayer?' The Superintendent calmly replied, 'I am Colonel Thayer, sir.' 'Wall now look-a-yere, Kern,' said Yoakum 'this yere hill o yourn am a breather; if it ain't damn me.' "

Yoakum not only survived to graduate, but wrote a notable history of Texas. Thayer undoubtedly told the story of his entry as a good joke, because it survives in the Academy's annals in several versions.

Though he carefully concealed it from his cadets, Thayer had a first-rate sense of humor. Cram recalled one encounter with his strapping Irish servant Patrick Murphy: "Pat knew how to be a good servant but was addicted to ruling the roost upstairs while the cook (Molly) was omnipotent below. One day, the Colonel with a friend was overlooking the fitting down of new carpeting in the hall of his quarters. Pat was exceedingly officious in the operation but could not, with all his pretensions, make the figures match, and was standing nonplused with one foot on the end of the new piece when the Colonel, grown quite weary with Pat's bungling, taking hold of the piece, said, 'Get your big Irish splay foot off the carpet.'

"Pat rushed away and on passing the Colonel's friend said in an undertone, 'Big splay foot, is it, and by Jazzas, I've worn his booths many a time it is.'

"The Colonel's quick ear caught the reply." Instead of a stern reproach (which any cadet would have received for such a wisecrack), Thayer and his friend "both roared with laughter at the Irish wit."

But many cadets found no humor in Thayer's stern dictum: "Gentlemen must learn it is only their province to listen and obey." Still others disliked the tough discipline and rougher language of the tactical officers. One complained that Haughty Bill Worth, in distributing his reproofs, "descends to scurrility sometimes." This smoldering discontent exploded one winter night in December, 1821. The cry of "fire" sent cadets scrambling from their beds to man the primitive post pumper. The mess hall was ablaze, and before they could put it out, most of the roof was demolished. Only then did the firefighters and their officers notice a loaded cannon, dragged from the artillery park during the pandemonium, and aimed at Superintendent Thayer's house. The slow match had burned out before it reached the powder.

Thayer slapped some suspects under arrest, but the culprits were never found. The incident only toughened Thayer's trend toward iron discipline. But he tried to make this discipline systematic and impartial. He saw that a personal contest between him and the cadets would be continuous chaos. Thus he moved two tactical officers, Lieutenants Zebina J. D. Kinsley and Henry W. Griswold, into the North and South Barracks, but they reported to Commandant Worth, not the Superintendent. It was Worth and his assistants who enforced the rules, meted out the punishments. Thayer entered the picture only as a court of last resort, in the chain of command.

One incident made clear his determination to avoid the policeman's role. A cadet was invited to a dinner across the river. He sought permission from Superintendent Thayer and it was refused for good and sufficient reasons. The young man decided the meal was too tempting to resist and "ran it" that night, got by the sentries, and rowed himself across the river. Imagine his shock when he sat down at the table and there, sitting opposite him, was Sylvanus Thayer himself. Frozen with horror, the young man waited for the words of condemnation to fall. Instead, Thayer was utterly charming and passed the evening making expert small talk with the benumbed delinquent. After dinner the cadet hurriedly made his excuses, slipped out of the house, and rowed frantically back to West Point. Once more he eluded the sentries and stumbled, trembling, into his room. The next day he waited with resigned dread to hear his name read out at parade. But nothing happened, either that day or for the cadet's next two years at West Point. Only much later did he learn that the Commandant of Cadets and his assistants had received a stiff reprimand from Thayer for permitting such escapades.

Another explanation was given by Albert E. Church, who was a cadet and a professor under Thayer: "With all his strictness and apparent coldness on duty, he had a heart as big as breast could hold." More than once, Church said, he had seen Thayer "interpose a saving hand" to save a cadet who had yielded to impulse and broken a regulation that put him in danger of expulsion. Only when there was a "vicious motive" behind the misdeed—and Church obviously felt Thayer knew the cadets well enough to make this judgment—would he invoke the supreme penalty.

With these tactical instructors living in the barracks, Thayer began the evolution of West Point's honor system. They—and the cadet officers—were responsible for reporting cadets who disobeyed the regulations. These reports, soon nicknamed "the skin list," were forwarded to the Commandant of Cadets, who held hearings in his office each day. At these hearings it was assumed that a cadet, as a gentleman and man of honor, would answer truthfully any and all direct questions. If the Commandant was satisfied with the cadet's excuse or explanation, he erased the report in the presence of the cadet. If the Commandant upheld the report, the cadet had the right to make a written appeal to the Superintendent. The advantages of this system, as Thayer pointed out in a letter to the Secretary of War, were immense. Besides inculcating a profound sense of honor in the cadets, it made it unnecessary to investigate every report as if it were a judicial case with witnesses to be summoned and facts to be determined—obviously an impossibility for the school's tiny staff in the first place. Where any substantial doubt existed, all a cadet had to do was deny a report—and it was forthwith cancelled.

From the beginning, however, Thayer understood clearly that his problems in running West Point were by no means solely internal. Do what he could, or might with the school, it was a national institution and its students came to him through political appointments. It was, inevitably, a prime target for political sniping. The Partridge affair, followed by the political infighting of the dismissed Partridge ringleaders, increased this susceptibility. In March, 1820, around the time that Congress was hearing the last gasp of protest from Ragland and his friends, a resolution was offered in the House of Representatives to abolish the Academy and end "this retreat for the pampered sons of the rich." The sharp rise in the number of cadets dismissed or turned away for lack of learning or bad conduct also increased the number of attacks upon West Point in local newspapers and state legislatures. The public at large simply did not know what to believe. The remoteness of West Point made the place mysterious to the man in the street—adding spice to the swirl of rumor and calumny emanating from the politicians. Thayer decided to do something about it.

In the summer of 1820 the corps boarded Hudson River steamboats, which landed them at Staten Island. From there they crossed to New Jersey and marched in easy stages all the way to Philadelphia, where they put on a spanking show for the admiring citizens of the City of Brotherly Love. The trip was a success, and the following year Thayer ordered an even more elaborate expedition to Boston. The cadets traveled by steamboat to Albany and from there marched through Lenox, Springfield, Leicester, Worcester, Framingham, and Roxbury to the Athens of the North. In town after town they were greeted with cheers, celebrations and exclamations of amazement at the precision of their marching and drilling. Boston welcomed them with militia escorts, public dinners, and dances and parties at night. By day they drilled on the Common and one afternoon marched out to Quincy, where they heard a speech from the venerable former President, John Adams.

From Boston they marched to Providence for more feting and then to New London, where they took a steamboat to New Haven. They spent another day of drills and parades there and then sailed to New York, where there was a reception for the whole corps at City Hall. Not until September 26 did the cadets return to West Point. They had been over two full months on the road and were very tired young men. But they had done what Sylvanus Thayer wanted them to do—shown the average voter in the most populous part of the United States that the public was getting more than its money's worth at West Point.

The Military Academy's fame was, in fact, spreading throughout the country. When Thayer first arrived, the number of cadet warrants was seldom filled. Friends of the Academy in Washington often had to go out looking for young men willing to chance West Point. By 1823, the number of applications for the hundred-odd places open each year at the Academy had swelled to over a thousand. A letter from former cadet Andrew Jackson Donelson, introducing an 1823 appointee from Tennessee, informed Thayer: ". . . I have learned with a great deal of pleasure that your exertions have extended the course and given more perfect organization of the school. It is more popular in this section of the country than it has ever been before." Donelson went on to tell Thayer with obvious pleasure that one of the Academy's fiercest Congressional critics, Newton Cannon (better known as the "Tennessee Cannon"), had not been reelected. The letter itself is a tribute to the impartiality with which Thayer administered the school. Although Donelson had failed to graduate, he obviously held no personal grudge against the Superintendent.

It is probably no accident that during these same years there began to flow into the Academy a number of exceptional young men, some of whose names would later be written large in American history books. Perhaps the most important, though not as publicly famous, was a small, somewhat scrawny lad from Virginia, who arrived on July 4, 1820. Oddly, as he no doubt explained to Superintendent Thayer in his introductory interview, he had come to West Point primarily to study drawing. He did not seem to have a particular interest in soldiering. But Thayer swiftly recognized in the young man something more important —a glowing intelligence. Dennis Hart Mahan stood at the head of his class for four consecutive years at West Point. The moment he was graduated Thayer requested him to be detailed to the Academy as an assistant professor in mathematics. Like Alfred Mordecai, one of West Point's most noted Jewish graduates, who was a year ahead of Mahan, he had already been teaching the slower sections as a cadet instructor.

Between Mahan and Thayer there soon grew an almost paternal bond. This son of a simple Irish carpenter obviously needed a second father; Thayer, in his middle thirties, was at that age when a man begins to yearn for a son. This bond was to keep Dennis Mahan at West Point for over forty years and make him Sylvanus Thayer's spiritual heir as well as the intellectual father in his own right of generations of American military leaders.

In 1822 came Albert Sidney Johnston, destined to be one of the South's most glamorous generals in the Civil War. From the moment he arrived, he was a leader in his class. Though he was only nineteen, a fellow cadet described him on their first meeting as "a full-grown man of commanding figure and imposing presence." Johnston was one of those cadets who excelled in the military side of academy life and early won the admiration of Commandant Worth. Although he was also a good student, Johnston had a misadventure in his final year's examination, which is a good example of how well Thayer and the academic board knew each cadet as an individual.

Johnston prepared himself for the examination to the best of his ability; he did not, however, have time to cover two mathematical problems. Since other cadets left many more than this number unprepared, betting on the laws of probability and a close study of previous examinations to get them through, Johnston was not overly concerned. To his consternation, on the day of the exam the first question put to him was one of the two neglected problems. A cadet could decline to answer once without failing, but two strikes were out. To Johnston's horror, the next question put to him was the second unprepared problem. He was ordered to take his seat. "Gentlemen," he said before sitting down, "I wish to state that these two problems are the only ones on which I am not prepared to recite."

"You will take your seat, sir," said Superintendent Thayer.

Johnston went back to his room and wrote a letter to the Board of Examiners, challenging them to give him a rigorous examination on the entire course. Major Worth went to Thayer and backed up the cadet's request with a warm recommendation for him as a soldier. Thayer recalled Johnston for a long and searching examination, which he passed with scarcely a flaw. He was promptly recommended for a commission, and graduated eighth in his class.

In the summer of 1824 another young Southerner arrived with an air of command about him. He was from Mississippi and his name was Jefferson Davis. Though he swiftly became a leader in his class, he was a perennial problem to Thayer. There was a stubborn, rebellious streak in the boy that constantly got him embroiled with the school authorities. In the dusty, yellowed pages of the "Record of Delinquencies" for Davis' years, there is a stream of charges—such as absent from quarters after taps, cooking in quarters, spitting on the floor, candlesticks out of order, making unnecessary noise in study hours, foul clothes not in clothes bag. Similar charges appeared beneath the names of many other cadets, but very few were credited with "improper conduct, firing his musket from the window of his room."

Davis had a particularly keen hatred for Lieutenant Kinsley, the assistant instructor of tactics. In this he was not alone. Kinsley was known among the cadets as "Old Detestation" for his zeal in enforcing regulations in the barracks and on the parade grounds. One day Kinsley was lecturing on small bombs and mortar shells. Davis picked up a crude version of a hand grenade and, while Kinsley was not looking, lit the fuse, then casually asked: "What should I do with this, sir?"

"Run for your lives!" Kinsley screamed and led a stampede out the door.

Davis, with a cool smile, carried the still sputtering bomb over to the window and tossed it out.

Young Jeff was also one of the first cadets to be court-martialed for frequenting a tavern at Buttermilk Falls, some two miles from the Point, run by one Benny Havens. A veteran of the War of 1812, Benny seems to have drifted by degrees into entertaining cadets, first out of conviviality, later for profit.

During the first eight years of Thayer's regime most of the cadets in search of liquid nourishment or additional food to supplement the mediocre messhall fare "ran it" to Gridley's Hotel, which was only a few steps away from the southern boundary of the post with only a board fence for a barrier. Thayer did everything in his power to stop these visits, sending tactical officers again and again to Gridley's and making life extremely uncomfortable for the owner. Meanwhile, he launched a campaign in Congress to appropriate enough money to buy the place. In 1825 he ostentatiously began building a new hotel (which would not be completed until 1829) on Trophy Point. Gridley panicked and sold out for $10,000. As Albert E. Church, of the class of 1828, said, "What was Gridley's loss was a great gain to Benny Havens O! . . . from this time he became an institution for many years of wide renown . . . To his house there was at once a rush and for years after he had a monopoly on the business."

One advantage of Benny's was its distance. Tactical officers were less likely to make the two-mile hike to catch a thirsty cadet. But they did it often enough, and on Sunday, the thirty-first of July, 1825, they caught Jeff Davis and five others at Benny's bar, downing porter and hard cider. They tried to explain to the tactical instructor, Captain Ethan Allen Hitchcock, that a rainstorm had drowned out their tent and they had wandered to Benny's only in search of shelter. But Hitchcock said that they all suffered from "a certain wildness of countenance which is produced oftentimes by the use of ardent spirits."

A court-martial was convened, and each cadet made a written and a spoken defense. Davis' plea on his own behalf was extremely eloquent. He made his first appearance as a strict constructionist, arguing that although cadets knew in a general way that visits to Benny Havens' were prohibited, no such order had been officially promulgated. Moreover, he argued that he did not believe malt liquors, cider, and porter were "spiritous." "It is better," he declared at the end of his plea, "that a hundred guilty should escape than one righteous person be condemned."

The court did not agree with him and found Jeff and his five companions-in-crime guilty as charged. They were all sentenced to be dismissed from the corps, but Davis fortunately had two good friends in Commandant Worth and Captain Hitchcock. They interceded for him on the basis of his soldierly talents, and Thayer acquiesced, permitting the sentence to be suspended and ordering Cadet Davis and one of his companions, Cadet Hayes, to be returned to duty.

Davis was apparently unimpressed by this clemency. Not long after, he was back at Benny Havens' once more with a fellow cadet when a lookout bellowed a warning: "Old Hant"—the cadet nickname for Major Worth. Davis and his companion leaped up and dashed out the back door into the pitch-black night. Running pell-mell along the cliff above the Hudson, Davis tripped and went headlong into space. Miraculously, about forty feet down some outgrowing trees broke his fall. His companion peered over the edge and called out in a trembling voice, "Jeff, are you dead?"

Up from the blackness floated Cadet Davis' mocking laugh.

By the time he limped back to the Academy, however, Davis was no longer so jolly. He had a broken arm and internal injuries that kept him in the hospital for several weeks. But because he was never identified by the raiding tactical officers, no charges were lodged against him.

The year after Davis arrived to give Thayer gray hairs came another young man from the South who was a source of consolation to the idealistic Superintendent. Robert E. Lee was the son of Revolutionary War hero Light-Horse Harry Lee, the man who gave Washington his farewell salute, "First in war, first in peace, first in the hearts of his countrymen." Young Lee was a strikingly handsome boy with dark flowing curls, a proud dignified bearing, and limbs so perfectly proportioned, according to one of his classmates, they seemed to have been turned out on the lathe. He was an excellent student, always first or second in his class, and his conduct was impeccable. Not a single charge was lodged against him in the "Record of Delinquencies" during his four years at the Academy. Eventually he became known among his fellow cadets as "the Marble Model," but there was never any rancor in this nickname. Joseph E. Johnston, who was his classmate, said of Lee years later: "We had the same intimate associates that thought as I did, that no other youth or man so united the qualities that win warm friendship and command high respect. He was the only one of all of the men I have known that could laugh at the faults and follies of his friends in such a manner as to make them ashamed without touching their affection for him, and to confirm their respect and sense of his superiority."

Flattering as it was for Thayer to see an influx of exceptional young men, they also created new problems. They were, above all, not very amenable to West Point discipline. Because so many of them came from influential families, they were prone to appeal over Thayer's head to the Secretary of War and even to the President. There was a constant flow of letters during these years between the War Department and Thayer, informing him that the President or the Secretary of War had decided because of a certain cadet's "youth" or because his previous conduct had shown no "vicious traits" that the offender be reinstated. Each of these cadet victories weakened Thayer's position, and so in 1825 he decided to institute another disciplinary measure, which has become a basic part of the West Point system. Henceforth the number of demerits lodged against a cadet in a given year would play a part in computing his class standing. This innovation also placed an effective answer in Thayer's hands when a cadet's family or friends complained about the supposed injustice of his dismissal for bad conduct.

The cadets resented the demerit system, which made discipline more systematic. They resented even more another Thayer decision that ended an Academy tradition. Each July 4 there was an outdoor banquet at which the cadets drank quantities of champagne. In 1825 the celebration turned into a near riot, climaxed by most of the corps seizing Commandant Worth, flinging him on their shoulders, and snake dancing with him back to the barracks. Thayer decreed that there would be no more alcohol served to cadets on the post for any reason. The cadets retaliated by increasing their trips to Benny Havens'. They also came up with an ingenious gambit to beat Thayer's honor system: They drank with their faces averted from one another. If caught in a raid and called upon to testify, they could say that in a strictly literal sense they had not "seen" Cadet So-and-So drinking.

Throughout the early months of 1826 this spirit of defiance grew steadily worse. That summer Thayer became so concerned about it, he made a special trip to Washington in the hope of obtaining a private interview with President John Quincy Adams. Unfortunately, the President was out of town and Thayer had to content himself with telling his troubles to Secretary of War James Barbour.

The malaise continued through the last months of 1826, and on Christmas Eve reached an explosive climax. The trouble began when Jeff Davis and a number of Southern friends announced to the corps that they were prepared to reveal "the mysteries of eggnog." Cadet Davis and two others were to get the necessaries from Benny Havens. Thayer and his staff caught wind of the plan, and the tactical officers were ordered to stay up all night to keep order. Thayer made sure the cadets knew about the arrangement, but the young fire-eaters were in no mood to be intimidated. They smuggled in the mixings, and in the dark of the morning of December 25 invitations were sent out. Robert E. Lee and Joseph E. Johnston declined, but dozens of others accepted and crowded into No. 5 in the North Barracks, which was designated as the barroom. Davis was out extending invitations in the South Barracks when someone told him Captain Hitchcock was on the prowl. He went dashing back to the GHQ and charged into the room, shouting, "Put away that grog, boys, Old Hitch is coming—"

Captain Hitchcock had already arrived. "Mr. Davis, you're under arrest," he snapped. "Go to your room."

Davis obeyed. It turned out to be the best order he ever received. A few minutes later, when Hitchcock attempted to confiscate the eggnog, the hosts in room No. 5 rebelled. One cadet pulled out a sword and chased Hitchcock back to his room. When the captain called for reinforcements, the tactical officers who came on the run were met by a barrage of stove wood and stair railings, chair backs, anything detachable. Windows were smashed, insults flung into the dawn, and a full-scale mutiny was soon under way. Davis' roommate, Walter Guion, lost his head completely, seized a pistol, and attempted to shoot Captain Hitchcock. Fortunately it misfired. Guion and other cadets then formed a "Helvetian league," primed their muskets, and vowed to defend themselves to the death against the Bombardiers, should the tactical officers turn these regular army ruffians loose on them. It took more than two hours to restore order, and when it was over, every tactical officer on the post was covered with bruises and cuts from the bombardment. The North Barracks was almost completely wrecked. Thayer called a Court of Enquiry, which summoned almost every cadet in the corps for long, tough hearings. Nineteen cadets were finally dismissed. But Davis, though kept under arrest and issued a reprimand and a fistful of demerits, was spared again.

Psychologists might be tempted to read into such conduct an instinct for rebellion that Jefferson Davis was later to exercise on a national scale. After the Civil War some vengeful anti-West Pointers did indeed try to trace Davis' disloyalty to his education under Thayer. They maintained that the future leader of the Confederacy had derived not a little encouragement from one of his textbooks at West Point, *On the Constitution,* by a disunionist legal philosopher named Rawle, who taught that the states had a natural right to secede. Davis himself denied that he ever studied Rawle, and West Point defenders, paging through old archives, reported that the book had been used for one year early in Thayer's regime, largely for want of an alternative text. When James Kent, New York State's great Supreme Court justice, sometimes called the American Blackstone, published his *Commentaries,* which sternly rejected the idea of secession, Thayer immediately snapped up copies for his cadets. Only in this century has the Rawle canard been totally laid to rest in the most definitive possible way. An examination of James Kent's journal for June 3, 1828, reveals him to have been a member of West Point's Board of Visitors. After listening to the cadets recite on constitutional law, he noted, "They appeared to be masters of the first volume of my *Commentaries.*" The cadet who shone brightest in discoursing on the principles of this rock-ribbed Unionist was Jefferson Davis.

Ironically, the Christmas riots occurred in the same year that saw the beginnings of a religious revival at West Point. As the officer of a national institution, Thayer maintained a strict neutrality in the field of religion. He did insist that every cadet attend chapel each Sunday, but this was as far as he went. Among the cadets the prevailing attitude ranged from religious indifference to downright hostility. It was an era when the conflict between science and religion was becoming steadily more acute, and West Point was the first school in America to have a curriculum dominated by science. Cadets usually brought their schoolbooks to the chapel and studied during the sermon. No cadet or professor ever knelt during the religious service.

In 1825 a new chaplain arrived. His name was Dr. Charles Pettit McIlvaine. Young and vigorous, he was an inspiring preacher with a missionary spirit, and he immediately went to work to change the school's secular atmosphere. He found resistance formidable. McIlvaine spent a full year at West Point without discussing religion with a single cadet.

Then, in 1826, a boy came to McIlvaine in search of consolation after the death of his father. McIlvaine gave the bereaved cadet a tract on Christianity, which he asked the cadet to leave in the barracks after reading it. The tract fell by accident into the hands of Leonidas Polk, one of the leaders of the class of 1827. Some of the claims made in the tract intrigued young Polk, and he recalled that the chaplain had deposited with the quartermaster a number of volumes on the Christian religion. He took out one called *The Evidences of Christianity* by Olinthus Gregory of the Royal Military Academy, Woolwich, England. The book was a series of letters written in response to a request from a friend. Drawing upon the best writings of several authors and piecing these excerpts together in logical sequence, Gregory presented both the evidences of Christianity and its doctrines and duties. Cadet Polk was much impressed, since Gregory "often—as in miracles—instituted comparisons between religion and the sciences."

Polk appeared at McIlvaine's house one Saturday afternoon not long after finishing Gregory. He was by now a deeply troubled young man, and he poured out the story of an inner conversion, against which he had struggled in vain. McIlvaine calmed the boy and prayed with him. In a long conference he resolved many of the difficulties still troubling young Polk, and let him talk out what he feared most—the ridicule of his comrades. What should he do, Polk asked the chaplain? McIlvaine suggested that Polk immediately step out from the corps and take his stand. Young Polk took a deep breath and agreed.

The next day was Sunday, and the cadets trooped into chapel as always, to sit there, arms folded, staring into space or reading their textbooks while McIlvaine preached on for the better part of an hour. Then, as the chaplain turned back to the altar to complete the service, an astonishing (for the rest of the corps) event took place. Quietly, deliberately, Leonidas Polk assumed a kneeling position.

Writing to his brother, William Polk, he described his feelings: "This step was my most trying one," he said, "to bring myself to renounce all of my former habits and associations, to step forth singly from the whole corps acknowledging my convictions of the truth of the holy religion which I had before derided and was now anxious to embrace, and to be put up, as it were, a mark for the observation of others; were trials which unaided by the consolations of the Bible, humble and fervent prayer, and above all the strong hand of Him who is all powerful to shield and protect all such as do earnestly desire to make their peace with Him, I should have sunk under."

Leonidas was well named. He more than held his own in the heated discussions that now erupted in the barracks. Soon a number of other cadets were seeking conferences with Chaplain McIlvaine, who began holding regular prayer meetings in his home. These increased so rapidly in attendance, it was necessary to shift the services to the chapel. There, forty days after his first conference with Cadet Polk, McIlvaine baptized Polk and William B. Magruder.

Polk's conversion was profound and lasting. He eventually left the Army and entered the Episcopal church. He was later ordained a missionary bishop in the South, presiding over the states of Alabama and Mississippi, the Arkansas Territory, and the Republic of Texas.

The religious revival begun by McIlvaine did not end when he departed from West Point in 1827. The cadets themselves carried on his work for several years. Leonidas Polk, for instance, led a praying squad in the prison, the only unoccupied room in the barracks. From the beginning Sylvanus Thayer, while maintaining his strict personal neutrality, gave the movement his warm approval. "The Colonel," Polk wrote home, "is very well disposed toward religion and has kindly granted us permission to attend . . . nightly meetings for purposes of worship."

Helpful as this new influence was in the life of the school, Thayer knew it only affected a minority of the cadets. He thus continued to believe that the school's discipline and moral tone would remain erratic as long as Washington undermined his authority by reinstating dismissed cadets. Alexander Macomb, the new chief of Engineers, was particularly careless on this point. Macomb was one of the first graduates of West Point, and although he was officially an Engineer he had made his reputation in the Army outside the Corps. He was an excellent organizer, a chief-of-staff type, but he lacked Thayer's passion for academic excellence and was inclined to keep one eye on the political weathervanes. Thayer decided to make another effort to reverse this trend. His source of hope was the news that his old roommate from Dartmouth, George Ticknor, was one of the Academy's Board of Visitors for the year 1826. Here, at last, was a chance for Thayer to exert his personal influence on a report that was made directly to the President. Eagerly he wrote his old friend, urging him not to fail to appear.

V

HAPPILY FOR HISTORY, Ticknor wrote a series of letters to his wife which gave a superb picture of Thayer and West Point in action. The Board of Visitors was, as usual, impressive. Besides Ticknor, there were three naval commodores; a clutch of senators, including Martin Van Buren, already a power in New York State politics; and General Sam Houston, who was elected president. The first day, Ticknor wrote:

Precisely at nine o'clock, the whole staff of the academy assembled at Thayer's house in full uniform. I was presented to them, and when this little ceremony was over . . . all were presented to the rest of the board of examiners . . . We went forthwith to the examination which was extremely thorough. Thirteen young men under the screw four hours on a single branch and never less than four on the floor, either drawing on the blackboard or answering questions every moment so that each one had above an hour's work to go through; and, as I said, in a single branch. It was the lowest section of the upper class, but no mistake was made, except by one cadet. Of course, it was as nearly perfect as anything of the kind ever was. The manner, too, was quite remarkable. The young men do not rise when they answer; they are all addressed as Mr. So-and-so; and when the drum beat outside for one o'clock, Colonel Thayer adjourned the examination while a cadet was speaking, so exactly is everything done here. We dined at Cozzens's and the examination was continued in the afternoon till seven o'clock.

My residence at Thayer's is extremely agreeable; that is the little time I pass there. He seems to feel toward me just as he did nineteen years ago, just as if we had never been separated. The house is perfectly quiet and there is a good deal of dignity in the sort of solitude in which he lives, and without any female attendant, yet with the most perfect neatness, order, and comfort in all his arrangements. There is nothing at all, either repulsive or stiff in his manner to the officers and teachers under him, or to the cadets. All the members of the board seem to have the most thorough admiration for him.

June 10th

I delight exceedingly in the exactness with which everything is done here. The morning gun is fired exactly at sunrise, though I am free to say I sleep well enough to hear it rarely, and as there never seems to be the least noise in Thayer's house. The first thing I hear is the full band, when precisely at six, the maneuvering being over, the corps of cadets begins its marching. I get up immediately and when Thayer comes home at half-past six from parade he brings me your letter. You will hardly believe how welcome his step is to me and how I have learnt to distinguish it from that of his Adjutant, his Orderly, or his servants, none of whom ever gives me my letters. I sometimes think he takes pleasure in doing it himself—at any rate, he always calls me by my Christian name when he brings them. Breakfast precisely at seven; then we have all the newspapers, and a little before eight o'clock, Thayer puts on his full-dress coat and sword and when the bugle sounds we are always at Mr. Cozzens's, where Thayer takes off his hat and inquires if the president of the board is ready to attend at the examination room; if he is, the commandant conducts him to it with great ceremony, followed by the board. If he is not ready, Thayer goes without him; he waits for no man.

In the examination room, Thayer presides at one table surrounded by the academic staff; General Houston at the other, surrounded by the visitors. In front of the last table two enormous blackboards, eight feet by five, are placed on easels; and at each of these boards stand two cadets, one answering questions or demonstrating and the other three preparing the problems that are given to them. In this way, if an examination of sixteen young men lasts four hours on one subject, each of them will have had one hour's public examination on it; and the fact is that each of the forty cadets in the upper class will tonight have had about five hours' personal examination. While the examination goes on, one person sits between the tables and asks questions, the other members of the staff and the board join in the examination frequently as their interest moves them. The young men have that composure which comes from thoroughness, and [they] unite to a remarkable degree ease with respectful manners to their teachers . . .

Yesterday (Sunday) afternoon I stayed at home and had a solid talk of three hours with Thayer concerning his management of this institution from the time he took it in hand. It was very interesting, and satisfied me more and more of the value and efficiency of his system . . . There is a thoroughness, promptness, and efficiency in the knowledge of the cadets which I've never seen before, and which I did not expect to find here. The consideration of this and of the means by which it is produced is, of course, very gratifying to me and will, I hope, come to account and be useful hereafter.

June 15th

We had something a little out of the ordinary course today. A section was brought up for examination, and before it was begun, a young man from

New Orleans stood up respectfully enough and began to read a paper, but in so low a voice that it was not distinctly heard. Thayer asked him very politely what he was doing. R. replied that he wished to make a communication to the academic staff and the board of visitors. Thayer told him to bring the communication to him that he might judge whether it was suitable. R. immediately carried it to him. Thayer received it with great politeness and laid it on the table but did not open it, for, with his usual tact, he felt at once that if there were anything indecorous in it he must punish him the moment he should read it, and he did not like to proceed so publicly. He waited, therefore, until the day's work was over and then opened and read it before the visitors. It set forth that his teacher was prejudiced against him, and marked him much too low, and that he desired to be examined by the head of the department and did not care how strictly. It was perfectly respectful. When therefore, he was called up this morning, your old friend Lieutenant Davies examined him very kindly and very patiently about half an hour. The result was no more favorable than the result of his recitations . . . I was sorry for him but I was delighted with the management of the whole affair throughout which there was an obvious desire to do him an entire justice and save him from mortification as much as possible.

June 17th

Thayer is a wonderful man . . . With all this labor, and the whole responsibility of the institution, the examination, and the accommodation of the visitors on his hands, he is always fresh, prompt, ready, and pleasant; never fails to receive me under all circumstances with the same affectionate manner; and seems, in short, as if he were more of a spectator than I am. I do not believe there are three persons in the country who could fill his place; and Totten said very well the other day when somebody told him—what is no doubt true—that if Thayer were to resign he would be the only man who could take his place—"No; no man would be indiscreet enough to take the place after Thayer; it would be as bad as being President of the Royal Society after Newton."

June 21st

The last section of the lowest class was examined ten hours in mathematics, and a finer set of young men, more manly, more prompt, more interested, I never saw. Their only desire was to have enough investigation, for as they know, they are to be ranked according to their appearance now, and feel that they are not deficient in knowledge, their great desire is to have an opportunity to show themselves. Three persons, since the examination began, have come forward in the room, declared that they were dissatisfied with the investigation into their acquirements, and asked to be put on trial again. The request was granted in every case—in one the cadet gained by it, and in the other two he remained where he was. This is the first instance I ever heard of in which a whole body of young men, like the cadets here, was evidently eager to be examined; for everywhere else the only question is how they may avoid an examination.

As the educator on the Board of Visitors, Ticknor was given the job of writing the report—something Thayer no doubt anticipated. In a letter to his old friend on the twelfth of October, 1826, Thayer reported that he had read the final draft during his summer visit to Washington. "I read your report with the most lively satisfaction. It is the only complete and accurate exposition of our system I have ever seen and I wait with impatience for its publication."

Thayer gives a glimpse of the struggle going on between him and Macomb. "I was told by the Department that it [the report] would be handed to the printer so soon as copied, but I fear the delay has been intentional."

Elsewhere in the letter he told how the Secretary of War "apologized for the errors into which he had been led by General Macomb and promised that all regulations should hereafter be inforced, etc., etc., for all of which we are indebted to the firmness and independence of the late Board of Visitors. But the Sec'y rarely looks into the details of his department and habitually yields to the suggestions of the chiefs of bureau. My only hope, therefore, rests upon the success of the proposition to separate the academy from the Corps of Engineers. Until this be done, the genius of evil will continue to afflict us."

Thayer was by no means helpless in this struggle between politics and principles. Over the years he had built up a wide circle of influential friends. He did it not merely by making West Point the country's first and foremost school of science. At least as important as his professional accomplishments were Thayer's personal qualities. Thomas J. Cram, who was often a guest at Thayer's dinner parties, recalled them as the time that "the host showed himself to the best advantage socially; his graceful, courteous politeness to every guest present was remarkably winning; his tact in leading the conversation in a manner without showing off self, into channels that would elicit something from every gentleman present, was perfect and made all easy and contented with themselves."

Thayer's years in France had also made him something of a gourmet and a wine connoisseur. He kept a first-rate cellar beneath his Superintendent's quarters. "Between the opening and closing of the navigation of the Hudson," Cram wrote, "by which almost the only access to West Point was then had, gentlemen of distinction came from every part to visit the academy and on arriving at the post were sure to be noticed by Colonel Thayer with a manner that evinced his hospitable propensity as well as the urbane side of his character. I with others of my young fellow officers had opportunities of being present on many such occasions and it was a source of great satisfaction and pride to us to witness how perfectly at home our superintendent would be with the statesman, the lawyer, the physician, the divine, historian, poet, scientist, merchant, and, indeed, with every branch, he seemed to possess and to be ready to exhibit when called upon, an unlimited knowledge of the particulars as well as the general intimacy with the principles of the subject under discussion. I never knew, nor to my knowledge did anyone else know him to be at fault upon any question of civil or military history—ancient or modern. His knowledge of the biography of men distinguished in literature, science, and the military profession was astonishingly extensive and accurate."

Aside from the entertaining he did himself at West Point, Thayer had another potent source of social influence right across the river at Cold Spring. This was the home of Gouverneur Kemble, owner of the West Point Foundry and a power in New York State, both economically and politically. Joseph G. Swift was Kemble's associate in creating the Foundry, which built the first railroad engine in the United States and for decades supplied the entire Northeast with "everything iron." It also dominated the armament industry in the United States, making almost all the heavy cannon for the United States Government from its early days to the end of the Civil War.

Kemble was an old friend of Washington Irving and in his younger days had been a leading member of a coterie of lively New Yorkers who often assembled at his family mansion on the Passaic in New Jersey. When marriage, death, and the other inevitabilities of life dispersed the group, Kemble retired to Cold Spring and built a magnificent mansion near his factory, which became New York's loss and West Point's gain. Every Saturday night Kemble played host on a grand scale, drawing to his table distinguished men from every walk of life. Colonel Thayer and the rest of the West Point faculty had a standing invitation and Thayer rarely failed to take advantage of it. Erasmus D. Keyes, who often attended when he was an instructor at the Academy and kept up his acquaintance in later years, called Kemble's guests "the choicest company of men I have known socially." Among them were Winfield Scott, Martin Van Buren, historian George Bancroft, and "many foreigners of distinction from various countries and numerous other men who were distinguished in government and for their learning and good breeding."

The chief danger, according to Keyes, was "of eating too much. . . . The wines were good, especially the port and sherry." But the conversation was what drew men to Kemble's table. The discussions "embraced every subject that claims the attention of civilized man—the policy of governments, the habitudes engendered by climate, race, and occupation; the laws and rights of various nations and ages; sculpture, painting, architecture, and all the vast domain of science, history, politics, parties, civil and military biographies, poetry, and manners." The only subjects seldom debated were "religion and matrimony." There was a standing rule, hardly needed, thanks to the "urbanity of the guests," that everyone was allowed without interruption to state his own opinions.

But in 1826 neither Kemble nor his friends, nor, probably, any other group of politicians in the United States could have gotten Thayer the changes he wanted in West Point's status. Thayer's position was essentially defensive and he was well equipped to fight from that stance. When West Point was attacked in Congress there was seldom any difficulty in finding friends to issue energetic replies. But getting things done on West Point's behalf was another matter. This required the kind of assiduous politicking that only an inhabitant of Washington could undertake, and in 1826 and 1827 there were few politicians inclined to give much thought to West Point. The capital was almost totally absorbed by the civil war raging between President John Quincy Adams and Congress. Adams had won the highest office when the 1824 election was thrown into the House of Representatives, though his opponent, Andrew Jackson, had actually outpolled him among the voters. Bitter Jackson supporters in Congress blocked every move the Adams administration tried to make. Adams did not help himself by absolutely refusing to play politics with political appointments or any other aspect of the government.

Thayer had undoubtedly hoped for strong support from Adams; he was, after all, a Massachusetts man, born in Thayer's hometown of Braintree. Moreover, the President's domestic policy espoused a vigorous program of "internal improvements," recommending construction of roads and canals, the exploration of the interior and the Pacific Northwest coast, and the passage of laws promoting the arts, sciences, and literature. West Point graduates would be called upon for key roles in such a program. But Congress all but threw it back in the President's face. Even such loyal supporters of West Point as John Calhoun leaned to the Jackson side, using his powers as Vice-president to fill half the Senate committees with anti-administration men.

Thayer did his best to arouse Adams to action. In the summer of 1827 he made another trip to Washington. This time he got to see Adams. The President recorded the interview in his diary, and it makes most enlightening reading:

Colonel Thayer, the superintendent of the academy at West Point, came to make, as he said, a confidential communication relating to the condition of that institution. The annual report of the visitors this year is highly favorable as it has been heretofore. He said this was correct so far as the examination of the visitors extended, which was only to the studies of the cadets and their acquirements in science. But, he regretted to say, the moral condition of the institution was not so favorable; that a habit of drinking had become very prevalent among them and that unless something effectual could be done to repress it, the academy instead of proving a seminary of accomplished education would usher into the world a large proportion of its pupils even then vicious and prone to ruin and destruction.

The President asked Thayer if these practices had been of long standing.

He said not in much extent; that the classes being arranged according to their merit, the head of each class possessed an influence almost boundless over his associates; that heretofore the heads of the classes have usually been distinguished for their good conduct as much as for their talents; that the reverse has happened with the class now recently graduated; that a young man from this district was at the head of the class, but with fine talents was of very loose morals, much addicted to drinking, avowing it as a right to be asserted and maintained by every youth of spirit and encouraging and stimulating others to the same practice. This has now become so common that no small number of the cadets are in danger of dating their ruin from their connection with the academy.

The Colonel spoke also of the practice of trying the cadets by court-martial as very objectionable, the superintendent being required to prefer the charges against the culprit and thereby placed in the attitude of a party against his own pupils and the court-martial consisting of officers and instructors at the academy, always parties when the charges are for violations of the discipline of the academy as they almost always are.

Adams asked Thayer to put the substance of his suggestions in writing and leave it with him. On August 14, Thayer returned and left a manuscript copy of a revised set of regulations for the Academy. Again he urged the President to end the practice of trying cadets by court-martial. Adams noted in his diary that the new regulations were "under examination and must be deliberately considered." But whether it was simply a case of indecision or whether Adams was too embroiled in his struggle with the Jackson forces, nothing came of Thayer's pleas.

Thayer was no doubt mildly cheered by the departure of Alexander Macomb from the Engineering office. In 1828 he became commanding general of the United States Army—a post that paradoxically gave him less influence over Thayer. Succeeding him as Chief of Engineers was Charles Gratiot, a man Thayer knew well both as a friend and a first-class scientific engineer. But before he could begin to rejoice over this change, a far more momentous transformation convulsed Washington—the Presidential election of 1828. Sweeping in on a tidal wave of votes that buried John Quincy Adams was the champion of democracy, the foe of aristocracy and privilege, Andrew Jackson.

For Sylvanus Thayer and West Point the change could be summed up in one word: trouble.

VI

PRESIDENT JACKSON'S ATTITUDE toward West Point is best indicated by a remark he made to his friend Joel Poinsett. "The military academy was established for the sons of Revolutionary officers who died poor." As a soldier Jackson had been continually embroiled in feuds with his superiors; his military experience had been confined almost entirely to volunteer armies fighting irregular battles where discipline was not as important as raw courage. Moreover, Old Hickory's hostility to "privilege" inclined him to cast a cold eye at the Military Academy, since those with a good preliminary education had a far better chance of staying through Thayer's rugged course.

Earlier historians have attributed much of Jackson's hostility to Thayer's treatment of his nephew Andrew J. Donelson, who supported the Partridge mutineers. But as we have seen, Donelson's letters to Thayer show no hostility over his cadet experience. He sent a brother and several other relatives to the Academy. Another theory has been suggested by William H. C. Bartlett, who was graduated in 1826 and was a professor at the Military Academy for almost forty years. In an interview with George W. Cullum, one of West Point's first serious historians, Bartlett blamed Jackson's bad opinion on George Wurtz Hughes, who was dismissed by Thayer in 1827 only a few days before graduation for getting into a brawl with one of the tactical officers. According to Bartlett, Hughes went to Washington and devoted himself to poisoning Jackson's mind against Thayer. Whether it was Hughes or the several Donelson relatives who fell by the wayside will probably never be known. It may well have been neither, since there were plenty of other influences at work in Old Hickory's mind that more than explain his antipathy to Thayer's system.

Cadets soon discovered that appeals to Washington brought dramatic reprieves, even from decisions of a court-martial board. Francis H. Smith, Superintendent in later years of the Virginia Military Institute, was at West Point from 1829 to 1833 and recalled how "reinstatements of cadets followed so rapidly upon their dismissal" that Thayer "was driven to the necessity of asking no courts-martial but sent each case requiring extreme discipline to the War Department for its decision and action."

Just how completely discipline escaped from Thayer's control can be glimpsed from a story Smith told about his roommate Willoughby Anderson, who had gone once too often to Benny Havens' and "was found under the influence of what Benny so liberally supplied to cadets." Thayer recommended him for dismissal and the Secretary of War agreed. When the order from Washington arrived dismissing Anderson, Thayer gave him thirty minutes to leave West Point. Smith, understandably distressed, rushed to the Superintendent's office and pleaded in his behalf. He asked the privilege of calling a meeting of the class to make an appeal for clemency. Thayer refused. Smith retired to the barracks and summoned a council of war. Together with Henry du Pont, of later industrial fame, and other class leaders, Smith composed a letter of appeal to President Jackson. Another member of the class, Robert McLane, gave Anderson a letter of introduction to his father, who was Jackson's Secretary of State.

In Washington, Secretary McLane quickly wangled Anderson into the White House, where he handed Jackson the cadet's letter. It was, Smith says, "an earnest appeal to the old hero in behalf of a son of a gallant soldier of the War of 1812 and was adroitly framed to touch the tender feelings of the great man." Jackson read it without a word of comment then turned to Anderson and growled, "Who wrote this letter?"

"I don't know, sir."

"Have you not read it?"

"No, sir."

"Go back to West Point and report for duty. And tell the young man who wrote this letter if he don't look out I will have his ears cut off."

Who should reappear at this critical juncture but Alden Partridge. Retiring to his native Vermont, he had made good his threat to found a rival military school. He called it the American Literary and Scientific and Military Academy, but it remained pitifully obscure while Thayer's West Point blossomed into national fame. Nevertheless, Partridge never ceased lobbying against West Point and calling for its abolition. As a replacement, he recommended a series of local military schools around the country. Now with Jacksonian hostility to West Point overt, Partridge rushed to fan the flames. In March, 1830, he published a pamphlet in Washington, D.C. entitled, "The Military Academy at West

Point Unmasked or Corruption and Military Despotism Exposed."

The tract did not live up to its title. Partridge was as disorganized as a writer as he had been as a superintendent. His diatribe consisted of three rambling, repetitious appeals, the first to the members of Congress, the next to the President of the United States and the third to the American people, warning them that West Point was spawning a "military aristocracy." He told the congressmen, "There is not on the whole globe an establishment more monarchial, corrupt and corrupting than this." He told the President that Thayer's treatment of the cadets was "tyrannical, unjust and even barbarous." His final volley to the people of the United States revealed Partridge's basic hostility to the idea of West Point teaching anything but essentially military subjects. The school was, he said, "effeminate and pedantic" and its emphasis on scholarship inevitably destroyed whatever spark of manliness might have been flickering in "the sons of politicians or influential men" who won appointments. Finally, Partridge descended to complete rabble-rousing, urging the people to act and save their sons from becoming "the mere pack horses of military service."

That same year, in the House of Representatives, a Tennessee politician named David Crockett laid Resolution Number Seven before the Congress. It called West Point "not only aristocratic but a downright invasion of the rights of the citizens and a violation of the civil contract called the Constitution." Crockett went on to claim that those who were educated at the Academy were "generally the sons of the rich and influential who are able to educate their own children, while the sons of the poor, for want of active friends, are often neglected or if educated at the expense of their parents or by the liberality of their friends are superseded in the service by cadets educated at the West Point Academy." Whereupon Crockett resolved, "for the foregoing reasons, that said institution should be abolished and the appropriation annually made for its support discontinued."

Jackson's first Secretary of War, John H. Eaton, stood up manfully for the Military Academy in this barrage of brickbats. Chief Engineer Gratiot also rallied to Thayer's side. "Since the appearance of Partridge's pamphlet, I do not perceive that his object has had the least success," he wrote. "It is spoken of by none but such as entertain a lively interest in all matters which concern you. The publication is treated, as far as I can ascertain, with disgust; and the motive of the

Old South, the first cadet barracks, erected in 1815. There was no running water and cadets slept on blankets stretched on the bare floor. Running water arrived (in the basement only) in the 1820's. Beds were introduced in the 1840's. *U.S. Military Academy Archives.*

West Point around 1838. The cadet corps numbered 250. Visitors came and went by steamboat or Hudson River sloop. The isolation bred nasty rumors and hostility to the school in Washington, D.C. *U.S. Military Academy Archives.*

Sylvanus Thayer, "Father of the Military Academy," painting by Professor Robert Weir, Department of Drawing. Thayer's seventeen-year reign as Superintendent (1817-33) transformed West Point into the foremost engineering school in America. "With all his strictness and apparent coldness on duty, he had a heart as big as breast could hold," said a professor who served under him. *U.S. Military Academy Archives.*

Cadet uniforms about 1840. George Pickett, Class of 1846, refused to wear the high strangulating leather collar, and amassed dozens of demerits for his defiance. *U.S. Military Academy Archives.*

West Point in the 1850's. Note the horses, introduced in the early 1840's. The breach between Southern and Northern cadets was widening at this time, in spite of Superintendent Robert E. Lee's reminders that the corps was "a band of brothers." *U.S. Military Academy Archives.*

writer seems to be well understood by the community at large in or out of Congress. Your friends concur in the belief that the allegations set forth in the pamphlet are not worthy of notice and that they should pass by unregarded."

Academically, during these same years West Point continued to grow. Many of the original faculty had died or gone elsewhere. Crozet had left for the University of Virginia in 1823. He was succeeded first by David B. Douglass, then, in 1830, by Dennis Mahan. Thayer never wavered in his enthusiasm for the young Virginian. After Mahan had spent two years as assistant professor (1825–26), Thayer arranged for him to receive the same invaluable experience he had won at a similar age— study and travel in Europe. Mahan's tour, in fact, was even longer and more thorough than Thayer's. From January 1, 1829, to March 10, 1830, he studied at the Military School of Engineers and Artillerists at Metz, then the premier school of its kind in Europe. Mahan came home imbued with the same passionate desire Thayer had known —to bring the best science of Europe to his young country. There was no better place to communicate this knowledge than West Point, and in 1830 he resolved to devote the rest of his life to the Academy.

Almost a match for Mahan was Charles Davies, professor of mathematics and first popular teacher of his subject in America. Davies had been a Partridge supporter, but that indiscretion did not stop Thayer from recognizing his talent. Davies had the knack of making the abstruse clear. Thayer's troubles with French textbooks inspired Davies to write a series of mathematics texts for his classes. Their fame spread rapidly and they were soon standard in schools all over the nation. In some places they were still being used at the turn of the century.

Edward H. Courtenay, who had been graduated first in the class of 1821, became professor of natural and experimental philosophy, succeeding the venerable Mansfield, who resigned in 1828 and died soon after. Of Courtenay, Francis H. Smith said many years later: "There never was a clearer-minded or more faithful teacher—or a more modest one. Well do I remember the hesitating manner with which he would correct the grossest error on the part of a member of his section—'I hardly think so.'" No doubt with Thayer's approval, Courtenay used the latest French textbooks.

Among the assistant professors were men such as Lieutenant Edward C. Ross, whom Smith called "the best teacher of mathematics I ever knew." It is a testament to Thayer's broad-minded administration that Ross found a place on his faculty. As Smith recalled, when Ross sketched a demonstration upon the blackboard "every line appeared as if it had been printed, so neat was he in the use of his chalk pencil. But when he commenced to explain he would twist and wiggle about from one side of the board to the other, pulling his long whiskers and spitting out in inordinate volumes his tobacco juice. The class was as ignorant when he closed as when he began. We copied word for word what was written, well knowing that on the next day the first five would be called upon to make the discussion." But the next day Ross "commenced his power as a teacher. In a series of orderly questions he would bring out the points of the discussion step by step, sometimes occupying half an hour with each cadet, and when the three hours of recitation were over we knew the subject thoroughly. He was an expert in his power of questioning a class. He did this without note or book and gave such earnestness and vividness to his examinations that he kept his class up to the highest pitch of interest all the time."

Smith mentioned a gambit Ross pulled on him during his plebe year January examination. "I was the first called upon and explained my work step by step and exhibited my result. His only remark was, 'It's all wrong, sir.' My confusion may be imagined. I trembled like an aspen leaf."

Frantically Smith rubbed out his work and began all over again. He went through it all a second time, "rigidly examining each step in my process," and reached the same result. "I became desperate," Smith said, "and in this state I said to him in a firm but nervous tone, 'My result is right, sir.'

" 'It is right and was right before,' Ross snapped. 'Why didn't you stick to it?'

"This," Smith said with some irony, "was not altogether a legitimate way of making the young algebraist self-reliant, but it was Ross's way and as such I record it."

Cadet learning in French had made strides since Thayer's early days, with Claudius Berard at the helm of this expanded department. Though not many cadets acquired a speaking knowledge, they read novels such as *Gil Blas* fluently and were able to handle all the current French scientific works. At one point Thayer meditated on adding Spanish to the curriculum but he eventually decided against it because he felt the cadets could not spare the time from the ever-widening field of science.

Thayer was, however, aware of the dangers of an education too narrowly scientific and he encouraged, in 1826, the organization of a Dialectic Society, which debated and discussed the subjects of the day. He also expanded somewhat the course in ethics, history, and philosophy taught by the chaplain.

By now West Point was world-famous. English travel writers journeyed up the Hudson and reported their impressions. Almost all of them were favorable, though one found that the cadets seemed to lack the high spirits of the young noblemen at Woolwich, England's military academy. Long articles in English and French magazines discussed the virtues of Thayer's system. Year after year, Boards of Visitors heaped praise on West Point. Distinguished Americans such as former President James Monroe wrote to Thayer, asking his advice on matters military and educational. But none of these consolations made the antics of Andrew Jackson and his political henchmen any easier to endure.

The situation began rumbling toward an explosive climax in 1830. We are indebted for many of the details to the appearance in the cadet corps of another young man whom later years would bring fame: Edgar Allan Poe. After two years in the Regular Army disguised as "Sergeant Major Perry," Poe won an appointment to West Point and was enrolled in the corps on July 1, 1830. Alas for this moody and unstable artist, he chose (or was chosen by) two roommates whose conduct perfectly illustrated Thayer's concern about the collapse of the Academy's discipline. One was Thomas W. Gibson of Indiana, the other Timothy Pickering Jones of Tennessee. Jones lasted exactly six weeks; he was tried on November 15, 1830, before a general court-martial, for "gross neglect of his academic and military duties," found guilty, and dismissed on December 31, 1830.

It is Jones who, in interviews after Poe became famous, told many lurid tales about the poet's drunkenness at West Point, as well as of his intense aversion to mathematics. Actually Poe stood seventeenth in a class of eighty-five after the first term's examination, no mean record. Moreover, Thayer's struggle against the demon rum had courts-martial sitting almost continuously throughout the fall of 1830, and cadets were dismissed for merely having liquor in their possession. It is unlikely that Poe could have escaped a similar fate if, as Jones later asserted, he was frequently thrown into the post prison, uncontrollable from too much whisky.

Jones had no political influence. His court-martial was upheld in

Washington. Thomas W. Gibson was another matter. His chief interest in life seems to have been evading or breaking the regulations. In the course of eighteen months he was court-martialed no less than four times for major offenses, found guilty each time and dismissed, only to be reinstated by the Secretary of War. One of his boon companions (and no doubt Poe's) was George W. Featherstenaugh, who was finally dismissed by a court-martial for no less than ninety-five different offenses, ranging from arson to playing the zither in his room on Sunday.

With such companions, Poe inevitably came to look with jaundiced eye on the stern self-discipline and unrelenting effort called for by Thayer's system. Everyone who knew Poe at the Academy recalled him as a brilliant student. Even when he neglected his work he was capable of preparing himself in the section room while other cadets were reciting. But brilliance was not enough at Thayer's West Point. A young man had to respond to the moral challenge or he would inevitably falter. And for those who listened to the wrong voices in the corps, to rebels and troublemakers such as Gibson, it was difficult, if not impossible, to see Thayer's larger meaning and purpose.

This, in part at least, explains what happened to Poe. His case was complicated by his strange, ambivalent relationship to his guardian John Allan. In November, Poe was writing hopefully to Allan: "I have an excellent standing in my class—in the first section in everything—and have great hopes of doing well. I have spent my time very pleasantly hitherto—but the study requisite is incessant and the discipline exceedingly rigid—I am very pleased with Colonel Thayer, and indeed with everything at the institution."

But just after the December examinations Poe received a bitter letter from Allan, telling him that he was "finished with him." His guardian had by accident seen a critical letter Poe had written about him to a third party in the previous summer. This news apparently was all Poe needed to destroy his fragile morale. He replied with a long violent letter to Allan, dredging up all their grievances and misunderstandings. He concluded by declaring it was impossible "to put up with the fatigues of this place" and announced his intention to resign. For this he needed his guardian's written permission. "It will be useless to refuse me this last request," Poe wrote, "for I can leave the place without any permission . . . From the time of writing this I shall neglect my studies and duties at the institution."

The young poet proceeded to do exactly that. He was absent from evening parade on January 8, 9, 15, 20, 24, and 25; from reveille call on January 8, 16, 17, 19, 21, 25, and 26; from class parade on January 17, 18, 19, 20, 24, and 25; from guard mounting on January 16; and from church parade on January 23. He also stopped attending classes from January 15 to 27.

On February 8 he was court-martialed for "gross neglect of duty" and dismissed. His roommate, Thomas W. Gibson, was tried and convicted in the same court-martial for "going beyond cadet limits," no doubt to Benny Havens'.

Poe went his tragic way, having first collected subscriptions from his classmates to publish a book of poems, which they all expected would be an assault on the Military Academy. They were puzzled and considerably annoyed when it appeared without a word of such censure in it. There is no record that anyone at West Point was impressed by such lyrics as "To Helen" and "Israfel." But then, neither were the critics of the day. Poe made no attempt to appeal his dismissal. On March 10 he wrote to Thayer for a letter of introduction to friends in Paris that might enable him to gain a commission in the Polish army. "A certificate of standing in my class is all I have any right to expect," he said. "Anything farther . . . would be a kindness which I should never forget." There is no record of a reply from Thayer.

If all the failures had submitted as respectfully and quietly as Poe, Thayer would have had no problems. Instead, the worst offenders, such as Gibson, seemed to have the most powerful friends. Secretary of War Lewis Cass cancelled Gibson's February 8 court-martial. Gibson was court-martialed twice more for "drinking or otherwise partaking of intoxicating liquors" and each time reinstated. Finally, in the fall of 1831, he turned to arson. He began by collaborating with Cadet Robert Allen in setting fire to a building near his barracks on October 17. Allen set the fire, and Gibson disabled all the pumps in the vicinity of the barracks. The building was "consumed to its bare walls." While under arrest on this charge, Allen persuaded another friend, Alexander Wolcott of Connecticut, to set fire to another building, an icehouse, which was badly damaged. When Wolcott was arrested, Gibson proceeded to persuade him to desert and both were caught at the steamboat landing. Not wanting to confuse matters, Thayer had Gibson tried for the second case of arson and for collaborating with Wolcott in an attempt to desert. Both were found guilty and dismissed from the Academy. Wolcott was sentenced to a month of solitary confinement at Fort Columbus in Newport harbor. To Thayer's amazement, the Secretary of War set aside this verdict, reduced Wolcott's sentence to mere dismissal, and reinstated Gibson once more. Thayer immediately convened another court-martial, which tried Gibson for his first act of arson. He pleaded not guilty to everything but disabling the pumps. This time his dismissal stood.

Exercising the luxury of hindsight, some might see in Thayer's troubles with the cadet corps proof that he had gone too far in creating an almost superhuman system that practically forced young men of spirit to become insubordinate. There is no doubt that Thayer tended at times to overuse the weapon of dismissal. In 1824, for instance, John Quincy Adams had to soothe several irate congressmen who complained about Thayer's abrupt expulsion of a young man who declined to strip naked for West Point's physical examination. During the ten central years of Thayer's reign, less than two in five of the students found qualified to enter West Point eventually graduated, and dismissals (as distinguished from failures) exceeded one in four.

Perhaps the saddest result of Thayer's unbending discipline was the failure of his nephew Jonathan Moulton, son of his sister Dorcas. Leaning over backward lest he be accused of showing favoritism to a relative, Thayer never relaxed his stern Superintendent's demeanor with the boy—although he confessed to friends that "he had set his heart" on Moulton entering the Army. The young man soon began to suspect that his uncle was persecuting him. In the spring of 1831, Moulton debouched to Washington without leave to see if he could persuade the Secretary of War to rewrite the regulations and place him solely under the orders of Captain Hitchcock, Commandant of Cadets.

Chief Engineer Gratiot had the good sense to write Thayer and ask what he should do. Thayer told him to order Moulton back to West Point "on pain of dismissal with disgrace." Enraged, Moulton returned and resigned. Thayer sent for him and for the first time threw aside his Superintendent's role. He tore up the resignation and burned it. But the boy was too bitter to be impressed by this gesture. The next day he returned with another resignation, plus a threat that he would again take his troubles to Washington if it was not honored. A saddened Thayer had to admit defeat. "He gave me good advice on how to meet the world," Moulton said, "and bade me go. I never wrote to him for twenty years, but after that we became fast friends."

No judgment should be passed on Thayer's system, however, without considering the special problems he confronted in his era. An expanding, booming America encouraged more than a few young men to identify rebellion with independence. A glance at the history of Harvard during the years of Thayer's Superintendency at West Point is illuminating. For instance, 1823 was known in the Yard as the Rebellion Year. The senior class rioted constantly in the Commons, dropped cannonballs from upper windows, poured buckets of ink and water on disliked professors. Bonfires with billets of wood loaded with gunpowder were another popular form of protest. Historian William Prescott lost an eye in a Harvard brawl, and one tutor went through the rest of his life with a limp as a result of an assault from student rioters. A series of rebellions at the University of Virginia was climaxed in the 1840's by the murder of a professor, and a campus patrolled by armed constables.

The diary of the Reverend Dr. Ashbel Green, President of Princeton, has the following entry: "January 19, 1817. A very serious riot commenced, with the manifest intention of preventing the usual religious exercises of that sacred day . . . A great deal of glass was broken; an attempt was made to burn the out buildings, and the bell was rung incessantly." Discussing Princeton's six rebellions between 1800 and 1830, President Green intoned: "The true causes of all these enormities are to be found nowhere else but in the fixed, irreconcilable hostility to the whole system established in this college . . . a system of diligent study, of guarded moral conduct and of reasonable attention to religious duty."

Thayer's troubles with his students were, in short, not much different from those of other college presidents of his time. Like them, he insisted on discipline. Unlike them, he could justify his system by the unarguable fact that he was training men for military careers.

But by the end of Jackson's first term, Thayer was evidently growing weary with his losing fight. His disenchantment is evident in a letter he wrote to Swift in February, 1832, replying to his old friend's plea on behalf of his nephew Julius Adams, who was in deep academic and disciplinary trouble.

Nothing can be done for him by the authorities of the academy . . . The only source of hope is in the President who is in the habit of dispensing with the most important regulations of the academy in favor of his friends, in spite of the academic authorities and the Secretary of War himself. I do not see why he will not be as likely to yield to any solicitations from the friends of Cadet Adams as to those of others in behalf of their relations. The chances of success would, in my opinion, be as three to one.

Even more alarming to Thayer was the discovery in the summer of 1832 that three cadets, Henry Waller, John F. Lee, and Edward Robinson, had written to the Secretary of War for extensions of their leaves of absence, and without even consulting the Military Academy, Lewis Cass had said yes. Thayer wrote Cass a furious protest:

I consider it due not less to the interests of the military academy than to the office confided to me by the government to present a respectful but earnest remonstrance against these instances of interference by the Department with the proper duties of the superintendent of the military academy. In the first place I beg leave to remark that all communications from cadets to the War Department are required by the 145th par. of the academy regulations to be passed thro' the superintendent. I would also represent that the rules which govern in the granting of furloughs and leaves of absence were framed with the particular view to reward and encourage meritorious conduct and cannot be departed from without prejudice to the institution.

An even more direct clash between Thayer and the Jackson administration came in the fall of 1832 when Old Hickory was running for President again. As with most strong Presidents, there were those who loved him and those who hated him, and few in between. The political turbulence reached deep into the cadet corps, and was a source of serious concern for Thayer and Commandant Hitchcock. One night a cadet from New York, H. Ariel Norris, crept out of his tent (it was during the last week of the summer encampment) and planted a hickory pole in the middle of the parade ground. Friends of Old Hickory were doing this all over the country, but Thayer was infuriated at this intrusion of partisan politics into the Military Academy. Moreover, Norris was a friend of Thomas W. Gibson and had a long record of courts-martial and reprimands. In 1831 he had been caught playing cards with Gibson. Both had been dismissed and promptly reinstated by Jackson. This time Norris was court-martialed for being absent from his tent at tattoo and also at reveille on the following morning.

By now Norris had become something of a professional in the court-martial game and he coolly pleaded guilty to the "specifications" and not guilty of the charge. The court found him guilty of both and sentenced him to be dismissed. Within the month Norris was back at the

Academy, reinstated by Jackson on the basis of a fantastic quibble—that the regulation under which Norris was tried prohibited a cadet from leaving his room in the barracks after tattoo and not his tent in camp. "The prisoner, therefore, pleaded correctly . . . guilty of the specification and not guilty of the charge and the finding of the court that he was guilty of the charge was illegal and ought to be set aside," Jackson wrote. Norris was soon strutting about the post announcing he could do anything that he pleased. Regulations be damned!

Thayer did nothing until after the November election, which Jackson won by another landslide, burying Thayer's best hope, John Quincy Adams, for good. Faced with four more years of Jackson, Thayer summoned Commandant Hitchcock to his office for a momentous conference. "We agreed," Hitchcock recalled in his memoirs, "that the evil influence was spreading. He noticing it chiefly in the growing neglect of study, while I observed it principally in the tendency to disorder . . . I asked Colonel Thayer's permission to go to Washington and see the President personally . . . He answered at once that he would give me an order for it . . . Colonel Thayer directed me to say to the President that if the regulations were not such as he approved, he should cause them to be modified till they should meet with his approbation; but that in all events it was absolutely necessary that the rules should be enforced, for the value, if not the existence, of the institution depended upon it."

Hitchcock left immediately for Washington and on November 24 obtained an interview with President Jackson. The results were not auspicious. The moment the Norris case was mentioned, Jackson flew into a volcanic rage, "Sylvanus Thayer," he bellowed, "is a tyrant! The autocrat of all the Russias couldn't exercise more power."

"Mr. President, you are misinformed on this subject and do not understand it," Hitchcock said.

Jackson calmed down, but insisted that "Norris had only done what the people in New York and everywhere else were doing." Hitchcock replied, "The people of New York and everywhere else may do many things which the students at West Point cannot be permitted to do." Jackson ended the interview by asking Hitchcock to tell Chief Engineer Gratiot to see him at once.

Meanwhile, at West Point, Thayer was writing a long letter to Secretary of War Cass:

I am aware that a direct and unofficial communication to the Secretary of War on a public matter is informal and unusual but trust that the peculiar circumstances of the case will plead my apology. From what has occurred during the present year, and especially from the nature of certain recent orders to which I need not allude particularly, I am led to believe that there is something at this institution which does not altogether meet with the President's approbation, but I am at a loss to conjecture whether the dissatisfaction, if such really exists, relates to persons or things. If it be the former, I need not point out the proper remedy and have only to say that I have nothing to ask or to deprecate with respect to myself. Fourteen successive annual Boards of Visitors have been sent to attend the general examination and to inquire into the administration of the institution. Many of the members of these boards were known to come here with strong prepossessions against the institution. Others were also known to be confidential friends of President Jackson. All will, I am sure, do me the justice to acknowledge that I afforded every possible facility for these investigations and that they had access to all sources of information on the spot. Beside these annual visitations, frequent inspections have been made by the Inspector of the academy and other high officers of the government. Has a single abuse or act of maladministration during these fourteen years been presented to the notice of the government by either of the authorities I have named? If so I am utterly ignorant of it. I am certain that the President is too just and generous to pass sentence of condemnation on anyone without a hearing or to have formed unfavorable opinions with respect to the administration of the academy from information derived from interested or prejudiced sources. My mind is, therefore, at ease on that score. Some persons, I am told, are of opinion that the regulations are too rigid. I can indeed concede that many, if not most persons might arrive at that opinion by a bare perusal of the regulations and by considering them in the abstract. But I flatter myself that that opinion is confined principally to those who have not witnessed their operation and the spirit and manner in which they are administered . . . I would respectfully propose that as a preliminary step, several, not less than three discreet persons having the entire confidence of the President, be sent to West Point to examine and discuss the whole matter and report their opinions . . . If this or any similar measure be adopted, I entrust that it may be so without delay. You know better than I can tell you that any regulations however perfect in themselves and however well administered by the authorities here are incapable of producing the desired result so long as the impression continues (and I assure you that the impression is deep and general) that they do not meet with the full approbation of the Executive, or while it is believed that a dismissed cadet can get reinstated whether by the influence of powerful friends or by direct and personal application to the President.

With this letter on his desk, Lewis Cass proceeded to blunder into a matter of relatively minor discipline involving Cadet Frederick A. Smith. One of the top men in his class, Smith had been blamed by Commandant Hitchcock for giving an unauthorized serenade to a lady on the post. Smith received a number of demerits and promptly wrote in protest to the Secretary of War. "With respect to the penalty of the offense," he admitted, "it being a few marks opposite our name, the charge may appear to you to be made upon trivial grounds, but when you reflect that those marks materially affect our character abroad and our place in the class here, they will perhaps appear sufficiently to justify our using all honorable means to cancel them—especially when unjustly given."

Smith's basic complaint was the way Hitchcock had made the accusation against him—on suspicion bolstered by very little evidence. All Smith had to do to cancel the report was to deny it, but he maintained that it was unjust to be accused at all when the evidence was so circumstantial. Cass sided with Smith. "The proceedings in relation to him have been erroneous," he wrote Thayer. Here, apparently without recognizing it, the Secretary of War was striking at the heart of the honor system that Thayer had set up as the bulwark of the school's discipline.

Incredibly, the day before Cass handed down his decision on Smith, he wrote Thayer a long letter assuring him that both he and President Jackson were entirely satisfied with him as Superintendent. The letter is particularly interesting if we recall that little more than a month before it was written Jackson had called Sylvanus Thayer a tyrant.

There is not in the mind of the President the slightest shade of unkindly feeling toward you. I speak to you with the utmost candor, and I say that I do know. He has the greatest respect for you and he has expressed it to me many times. His ideas concerning some of the principles of the government of the institution are known to you, but they impute no blame to yourself. These principles are founded upon the regulations, and I assume their operation may be traced to the era of the liberty of the academy. I did in fact and yet entertain similar notions though probably not to the same extent. Though I must confess to you that within a short time and in consequence of conversations with persons in whose judgment and views I placed much confidence, and particularly General Eaton, my questions have been somewhat weakened. But these impressions, when strongest, were not associated with the least doubt of your conduct and capacity, and in justice to myself, I may add of your peculiar fitness for the very arduous and responsible office you hold. I need not tell you what I've always thought and said of your qualifications and course. My public reports are correct evidences of my opinion upon that subject.

I will deal with you with all frankness. The state of affairs at the academy is good. Temporary difficulties have disappeared and I imagine when they existed they were greatly overrated. Dismiss the whole subject from your mind.

If Cass thought he could satisfy Thayer with this kind of syrupy doubletalk, he got a severe jolt in January 1833, when Chief Engineer Charles Gratiot placed a twenty-eight-word letter from Thayer on the Secretary's desk:

I have the honor to tender my resignation as superintendent of the military academy and to request that I may be relieved with as little delay as practicable.

Cass's first reaction was mild panic. He ordered Gratiot to tell Thayer that the resignation will "be acted on at the proper time but that he cannot recognize the principle which would seem to be advanced by your resignation that an officer possesses the right to decline a service which constitutes a legitimate part of his duties." This was more doubletalk and Cass knew it. On March 14 Gratiot wrote again, informing Thayer that his resignation was accepted—but that he would not be relieved until the close of the general examination in June.

It was over, and Thayer's first reaction seems to have been a sigh of relief. The seventeen-year accumulation of worry and responsibility was at last removed from his shoulders. Answering a letter from his old friend Swift, he said: "The change altho' delayed some years too long, will, as I flatter myself, prove to be an advantageous one as far, at least, as regards my health, purse, and comfort." Washington had given Thayer the choice of building fortifications either in New York or Boston and he had chosen Boston. He was going home.

The West Point faculty was by no means as happy as the Superintendent. To some, West Point without Thayer seemed an impossibility. Commandant Hitchcock, in a spasm of idealistic fervor, sent in his resignation as well. But Thayer prevailed upon him to withdraw it for the good of the school. If both the Superintendent and the Commandant of Cadets left simultaneously, the breach might well disrupt the entire corps.

Thomas Cram and other faculty members attended a "spontaneous meeting at which complimentary resolutions were unanimously passed expressive of our regret . . . and closing with a resolution that a committee of three be appointed to immediately wait on Colonel Thayer to request him to sit for his full-size portrait and for himself to choose the artist; the cost of the picture to be borne by voluntary subscription of the professors and officers then serving under his Superintendency."

"In a few hours," Cram said, "every professor and officer at the post had cheerfully subscribed to bear his proportion of the cost of the painting." The committee then called on Thayer and read him the resolutions. By now his first feelings of relief and freedom had passed. The committee's words summoned up for him all the strands of friendship and loyalty and common endeavor he had shared with these men in the years they had all given to West Point. Thayer almost lost control of himself. "For some seconds—with eyes full of tears [he] could not reply." But he soon recovered his usual firmness and said: "Gentlemen, you and all others connected with this mark of friendship must well know that from the bottom of my heart I thank you and them: but I will make you a formal reply if one of you—of your own choosing—will come to me early this evening."

That evening Lieutenant Nicholas Tillinghast, one of the delegates, called on Thayer in his quarters. "This action of my friends," he told Tillinghast, "must not be made public nor allowed to go any farther: the expression of any approbation or disapprobation from officers in respect to a commanding officer about being relieved is unmilitary and contrary to the spirit of military discipline: and were approbation to be allowed in my own case, it would reflect badly upon my friends as well as upon myself and might be made to react upon all of you with grave consequences. Therefore, I must ask your committee to destroy the resolutions and the subscription list."

Final examinations came soon after. The class of '33 performed handsomely. Somewhat ironically, Frederick A. Smith was its star. For the first time there were separate examinations in civil and military engineering. After more than two decades of peace there was a growing interest in having West Pointers perform many of the internal engineering chores being undertaken by more and more state governments.

The president of the Board of Visitors, Joel R. Poinsett, casually remarked at dinner that they were the best examinations he had ever heard—and that it was difficult for him to conceive how the class as a whole could have done so well without knowing beforehand the subjects upon which they would be examined. Poinsett was something of a Jackson man, but he was also a fairly good friend of Thayer's. Probably the remark was, as Poinsett later claimed, intended as a compliment, but when a member of the faculty reported it to Thayer he went into thoroughly characteristic action.

An order was sent at once to Dennis Mahan, telling him to prepare by the afternoon session of the board a full synopsis of the subjects in his whole course. The class was also ordered to reappear en masse, and when the curious young men assembled, Colonel Thayer explained why Mr. Poinsett's remark forced him to take this unusual action. Although Poinsett mumbled apologies, Thayer insisted that the injury done to the Academy and to the class could only be repaired by a thorough reexamination over the whole course. Francis H. Smith, who was one of the cadets, recalled how "the examination was resumed and continued with the deepest interest, each member of the class feeling that an appeal was made to his honor as well as his pride; and when it closed, the highest compliments were extended to it by the president of the board and the other members of the board which fully compensated for the severe ordeal through which we had passed."

On July 1, when the class was graduated, every member came to Thayer's office to shake hands and say a personal good-bye to him. As for the Superintendent, he was more than satisfied with the kind of farewell he had said to the Board of Visitors. He made it clear to everyone that he wanted no "honors of music" or any other fanfare when he departed. Alden Partridge's riotous farewell was still a living memory to him. As the days passed, he made a habit of strolling casually down to the dock to greet the night steamboat to New York. It was a habit shared by many on the post, and since the boat's timing was somewhat irregular there was always a circle of officers standing there in the twilight, having a pleasant chat.

One night Thayer appeared as usual and stood talking for several minutes while the steamboat docked, landed a few passengers and cargo, and then hooted its farewell warning. It was the signal Sylvanus Thayer had been awaiting. He held out his hand and said, "Good-bye, gentlemen." Quickly, quietly, he shook their hands and stepped aboard the boat, leaving the officers on the dock frozen in silent astonishment. Not a word was spoken as the deckhands pulled up the gangplank, hauled in their lines, and the long white boat churned away into the gathering darkness. Sylvanus Thayer had said good-bye to West Point in his own inimitable fashion.

Band of Brothers

I

MAJOR RENÉ E. DeRUSSY was Thayer's replacement as Superintendent. The son of a Revolutionary War sailor who had won a commission for gallant conduct under John Paul Jones, DeRussy was born in the West Indies and had graduated from West Point in 1812. He thus had no contact whatsoever with the Thayer era, and was much more in sympathy with Jackson's conviction that Thayer's rigid discipline bordered on the tyrannical and was the real source of cadet misbehavior. An urbane man of polished manners, DeRussy attempted to remove the aura of aloof dignity that Thayer had built into the Superintendent's image. He regularly invited cadets to his house for tea, where they conversed as equals with him, his charming wife and other members of the faculty. Another social amenity introduced—or at least permitted—by the new Superintendent was a ball at the end of the summer encampment.

Cadet Peter Hagner of South Carolina, in a letter to his father on August 29, 1833, expressed a fairly widespread opinion when he wrote: "A ball took place on last evening. It was quite well attended there being about 120 ladies and easily twice as many gentlemen, including our class. It really did me good to see Major DeRussy dancing and waltzing away as young as any of us . . . It occurred to me that it would be rather difficult to find Colonel Thayer lowering his dignity so far as to go to a cadets' ball, much less to dance at it."

The post band was another DeRussy preoccupation. On March 19, 1834, young Hagner was telling his father how the new Superintendent had completely reorganized it. "Major DeRussy is very desirous to have a good band, believing that good music tends to lead the thoughts from bad to good reflections and purify the ideas. It is very certain that while one is listening to good music he is not apt to be plotting anything bad. He wishes also no doubt to render our stay here as agreeable as possible so far as is consistent with his duty."

Almost inevitably, these pleasantries increased in scale. Two years later, Cadet Isaac Ingalls Stevens of Massachusetts was writing to his father, describing the most recent cadet ball: "We made use of the mess hall which was decorated in fine style. Our band was present and their performances served to increase their reputation. The ball was continued until after 3 o'clock but I did not remain after half past one. It was estimated that nearly 600 visitors were present . . ."

DeRussy showed his consideration in other unprecedented ways. On July 31, 1834, Peter Hagner told his father: "The weather was so warm as to incapacitate many of us for duty . . . The Major was obliged to order the sentinels to be taken off post during the warmest part of the day by the direction of the surgeon, a thing which has never been done before on account of the heat."

In these efforts to produce a change of mood and manner, DeRussy seems to have gotten practically no cooperation from the faculty. There is little sign of a conciliatory spirit in the following letter to Thayer from Dennis Mahan, who was already emerging as the school's dominant figure. "We are going on here *tant bien que mal,* but I am sorry to say with an overproportion of the latter . . . Some of the officers have applied to be relieved and of those ordered to relieve them no one seems to consider himself bound to show by his conduct that a measure which is really pernicious can be made even tolerable."

DeRussy and his prime backer, President Jackson, soon found out that neither bands nor balls nor tender loving care prevented unruly young Americans from "plotting anything bad." High on their list of problems was the perpetual temptation to "run it" to Benny Havens', which had by now achieved the status of a West Point institution. Neither Thayer nor DeRussy could do much to cure the real reason for Benny's popularity—the atrocious cadet mess. Modeled on army field rations, it was basically beef—boiled, roasted, or baked for dinner, cold sliced or smoked for breakfast and supper, and beef soup twice a week. No wonder cadets were willing to risk clouds of demerits and even expulsion to sample Benny's buckwheat cakes, oysters, or roast turkey, washed down by a mug of hot flip.

More than a few undoubtedly came just for the flip, which was Benny's specialty. His recipe was recalled in later years by one lip-smacking old graduate as follows: Place eggs, well beaten, sweetened and spiced, into a mixture of ale, and heat by plunging a red hot iron or "flip dog" into it. If the iron was left in just long enough, the result had a delicious caramel-like flavor. A second too long and the drinker got the taste of ashes. Benny knew just how long to leave the dog in the pitcher.

To all this Benny added the bonus of his Irish wit, plus a perpetually boyish ingenuity. The cadets rarely had any money, and he was a master at juggling credits and creditors. He frequently used the barter system— one of the favorite items of trade being blankets, which the cadets requisitioned during cold winter days, and smuggled out for a night of fun and food at Benny's.

Benny's appeal did not diminish when the corps got the impression that the Superintendent and the President were inclined to be lenient toward those who rolled up too many demerits.

By 1838, Benny was ready to be immortalized in song. An Army doctor named Lucius O'Brien stopped off at West Point to visit his friend, first classman Ripley A. Arnold. Cadet Arnold seemed to have no difficulty making numerous visits to Benny's emporium, where he and O'Brien consumed quantities of flip. O'Brien, ordered to the Southwest to help the 8th Regiment fight Indians, became so fond of Benny that he proceeded to dash off some verses to the tune of "The Wearin' o' the Green":

> Come, fill your glasses, fellows, and stand up in a row,
> To singing sentimentally, we're going for to go;
> In the army there's sobriety, promotions very slow
> So we'll sing our reminiscences of Benny Havens, oh!
> Oh! Benny Havens, oh!—oh! Benny Havens, oh!
> So we'll sing our reminiscences of Benny Havens oh!

Other verses saluted ladies of the Empire State, of the "orange clime," and of the Army. Successors to O'Brien as Benny's bards added verses commemorating events in Academy and U.S. history, totaling at least thirty-seven, and estimated by some to exceed sixty.

Even before Benny added music to his charms, the disciplinary situation at the Academy had deteriorated so badly that Superintendent DeRussy was forced to call for reinforcements from Andrew Jackson. He got it in the form of a curt Presidential Order, read to the Corps of Cadets one evening parade in the summer of 1835:

I had hoped that a lenient system of administration would be found sufficient for the government of the Military Academy, but I have been disappointed and it is now time to be more rigorous in enforcing its discipline. If the young gentlemen who are sent and educated there by their country will not demean themselves as they are required to do by the regula-

tions, they must suffer the prescribed punishments. Hereafter, therefore, the
sentences of courts-martial will, when legal and regular, be confirmed; and
the punishment will be remitted only in cases recommended by them or
where the circumstances may appear so very favorable as to justify such a
measure.

But the members of the institution must make no calculations on a
favorable result. Let them look to their obligations and fulfill them faithfully.
Unless they do, they must expect to be visited by adequate punishments.

Thus DeRussy and Jackson were forced to eat their policy in public.
Equally mortifying to the Jacksonians was a report from the House of
Representatives' committee on military affairs which was laid upon the
table on May 17, 1834. This document summed up the whole wave of
criticism begun by the Partridge pamphlet in 1830 and which now included condemnations from the state legislatures of Ohio, Tennessee
and South Carolina.

Declaring itself to be "a deliberate investigation of the origin and
history of the Military Academy, of its system of instruction and discipline, and of its effects upon the character of the army and the nation,"
the report was a complete vindication of Thayer and his system. The
committee declared that the discipline to which the cadets were subject
was "a judicious combination of military and paternal rule." Striking at
the claim that the Academy was a nursery for the sons of the rich, it
pointed especially to the regulation limiting the allowance of money
from parents and guardians and the duty of each cadet to keep his room
in "a state of perfect cleanliness and order." The committee argued that
these regulations strongly indicated the desire of the framers to introduce an equality in dress and expenditure and to foster a feeling of self-
reliance and independence, both of which were certainly "destructive of
false pride and of all exclusive or aristocratic pretensions." The report
went on to point out that the monthly pay of the cadet, including the
daily rations allowed him by law, amounted to $28.20. But when deduc-
tions were made for his food, clothing, books and other necessities, the
balance that any cadet received in cash seldom exceeded $4.50 a month.

As for the charge that the Academy wasted the public money, this
"vague impression . . . of a heavy and unreasonable expenditure" was
refuted by a close study of West Point's account books. From 1802 to
1821, the annual cost to the country for each cadet was $555.50. From

1823 to 1833, the cost per cadet, thanks to Thayer's careful pruning, dropped to $421.55. The committee closed the report with a ringing encomium: "Our whole army possesses now far more of the public respect and confidence than it did not many years since. It is the great distinction of the Academy at West Point that it has contributed largely and effectually to this elevation of the character of the military establishment."

As Jackson's second term ran out, he seems to have lost interest in West Point. Lewis Cass left the Cabinet to become Ambassador to France, and Benjamin Butler became acting Secretary of War. DeRussy seized the opportunity to commit himself completely to the ranks of the disciplinarians. On October 20, 1836, he wrote a long letter to Butler urging him to enforce without hesitation the sixty-seventh Regulation of the Academy Rule Book, which called for the immediate expulsion of any cadet who passed the 200 mark in demerits. "It is not overrating its importance," wrote the Superintendent, "to say that without its rigorous enforcement good order and discipline cannot be maintained." He went on to urge the Secretary of War to end the habit of reinstating dismissed cadets. "With the chances of escape from punishment, the temptation to the commission of delinquency is necessarily increased; and it may be safely affirmed that the leniency extended for the safety of one had in the end caused the destruction of many who without such a hope of escape held up before them might have persevered in the correct course." In summation he wrote a sentence that could easily have come from the pen of Sylvanus Thayer. "Whatever of benefit the country at large and the army in particular may have derived from this institution, may be traced to its discipline." Butler replied that as far as he was concerned the regulations "will be enforced with strict impartiality and inflexible justice."

The letter was a somewhat pathetic gesture, and the way the cadets celebrated the New Year on January 1, 1837, proved it was much too late. They dragged the reveille gun from its place at the flagstaff into the narrow "area" between the North and South barracks, and fired it. "The effect was great," writes John Bratt, '37, in his diary, "only four windows on the west side of N. Barracks escaped having their eyes put out." While tactical officers staggered around wondering if the world had come to an end, six cadets used their engineering know-how to hoist the gun to the fourth floor of the shattered barracks, where they again tried to fire it. Almost certainly, it would have blown out the wall of the barracks, and perhaps collapsed the building. John Sedgwick, one of '37's more levelheaded leaders, fortunately was able to stuff his handkerchief in ahead of the powder charge, and the match sputtered in vain.

By now a new President, Martin Van Buren, was on the scene. Although the dapper politician from Kinderhook, New York was a Jackson disciple, he had his own ideas about West Point. He had met Thayer at Gouverneur Kemble's soirees and admired the tough-minded Yankee and the school he had created. If he inherited any illusions about how to run the Academy, the explosion on New Year's day blew them away. It was obvious, even to the cadet corps, that DeRussy's administration was in a state of collapse. Richard S. Ewell, who entered in '36, told his family it was "going downhill with increasing velocity." Van Buren ordered his Secretary of War to find a new Superintendent.

The Secretary was Joel Poinsett, the man whom Thayer had chastened at his last Board of Visitors examination. Far from resenting this treatment, Poinsett remained a fervent admirer of Thayer and he immediately launched a campaign to reappoint him. But Thayer demurred. He had no great wish to spend the rest of his life at West Point. Moreover, the Academy's position vis-à-vis Washington was far from secure, and Thayer undoubtedly felt that his return would only invite a fresh barrage from those partial to Partridge and his Jacksonian friends. He wisely declined to stake the survival of the school on his own political standing. So Poinsett reluctantly looked elsewhere.

No doubt leaning heavily on Thayer's advice, he chose Major Richard Delafield, who had topped the order of merit when he graduated in 1818 and thus became the first man to win this coveted prize in Thayer's reorganized Academy. A pudgy, energetic soldier with a large nose and bustling manner, Delafield emphatically restored the Thayer regime. He clamped down hard on the night walkers heading for Benny Havens', and forbade civilians in the area to sell food to the cadets. The orders were so forcibly and frequently repeated, one boy wrote home that it was impossible to get a pie baked within five miles of the Academy. Delafield also toughened the examinations, which had slid into the general slough created by DeRussy's compromising spirit.

A sensible man, Delafield improved the school's basic facilities. He imported iron bedsteads, so that cadets no longer slept on blankets spread on a bare cold floor. He also replaced their flickering candles with oil lamps and tried hard to improve the mess hall fare. Above all, he never gave a thought to his popularity. He was always bouncing around the post making surprise inspections, and making sarcastic comments on what he was not supposed to see. While grimly conceding, in Richard Ewell's words, "it is better for the institution that the Superintendent should have a character for strictness," few cadets could muster much fondness for Delafield and his ways. They dubbed him "Dickey the Punster."

General Horace Porter told, years after it happened, how cadets ruined one Delafield innovation. From a tour of duty studying European armies, the Superintendent had picked up the idea of wearing the overcoat in a roll over the shoulder at ceremonies under arms. The West Point overcoats did not lend themselves to making smooth rolls. Moreover, it was the cadet fashion at the time to disdain wearing them. This combination inevitably persuaded the corps to try some impromptu tailoring. One cadet cut off his cape, another amputated his sleeves, a third his skirt, while a fourth decided a pair of trousers made a trimmer, more military roll. To keep them tight and shapely, all the rolls were sewn shut.

As adjutant, Porter was responsible for daily inspection of the guard. Of course, he never ordered the overcoats to be unrolled. All went well until a Russian officer visited Delafield. The next morning, the Superintendent, anxious to show his guest the latest practice he had imported from abroad, sent out an aide to Porter with an order to unroll the overcoats.

Terror numbed every brain. There was no hope of evasion. The rolls had to be unripped in ranks with the bayonet and one man put on an overcoat without sleeves, another without a cape or skirt, while another dragged a pair of gray trousers over his shoulders and the guard began to pass in review before the Superintendent "as ragged as Falstaff's army." The band was so convulsed with laughter that the only musician able to play was the bass drummer. In a fury, Delafield broke Adjutant Porter on the spot.

The normal cadet inclinations to try beating the game were not the only reason why Delafield's tough new broom was necessary. As the 1830's came to a close, the Military Academy found itself under new and more incisive criticism from Congress. Ironically, the seeds of the

trouble could be found in the lavish praise of the 1834 committee report, which noted that the Academy sent forth "numbers annually, competent to superintend the construction of those chains of internal improvements which are to be the eternal bonds of our national union."
The congressmen were calling attention to the numerous West Pointers
who were using their engineering skills to help build railroads, bridges,
canals, reservoirs for the burgeoning young nation.

Railroading was the most exciting field, and here the man with the
star quality was George W. Whistler, of the class of 1819. Father of an
even more famous Whistler, this brilliant young man was the leader of a
team of West Pointers who laid out the Baltimore and Ohio, America's
first railroad. From there he went on to plan the Baltimore and Susque-
hanna, the Paterson & Hudson (subsequently the Erie), the Western of
Massachusetts (now the Boston & Albany), and smaller railroads
around Providence, Rhode Island, and Stonington, Connecticut. Eventually Whistler ran out of challenges in the United States and accepted a
golden offer from the Tsar of Russia; he laid out Russia's first railroads
and soon found himself tackling bridges, docks, fortifications—practically every imaginable engineering problem in the vast reaches of the
Tsar's domain. Overwork and the cruel Russian winter finally killed
him, in 1849.

Equally impressive was the number of West Pointers who went on to
academic careers in the new colleges that seemed to be springing up
everywhere. In the two decades following Thayer's departure, West
Pointers filled forty chairs as professors of mathematics and sixteen as
professors of civil engineering.

Soon schools, state and city governments, and private corporations
were bidding fiercely for their services, dangling salaries that ranged
from five to sixteen thousand dollars a year—startling sums in an era
when the annual pay for second lieutenant in the elite Engineers was
$700. West Pointers resigned from the Army by the dozen. This would
have caused little or no comment, since the tiny Regular Army did
not have enough openings for all the graduates if they chose to stay in
the service, anyway. But from 1835, the country found itself involved in
an ugly little war.

In Florida, the Seminole Indians violently resisted government efforts
to move them to so-called Indian lands, farther west. Like so many
American wars, the conflict began with a shocking defeat which sent a

shudder through the nation. On December 28, 1835, Major F. L. Dade and his small command of 117 men were ambushed by over 700 Seminoles and Negroes. Only three enlisted men, all wounded, escaped the slaughter. Four West Pointers, a captain and three lieutenants, were among the slain. The war was to drag on for another decade. Out of the twenty officers killed in battle, thirteen were West Pointers.

But Congressional critics, pointing to the numbers of graduates still resigning from the Army to pursue lucrative civilian careers, saw a new opportunity to rip into the Military Academy. In 1837, another committee was appointed by Congress to investigate West Point, and its conclusions were radically, alarmingly different from the high praise heaped upon the school in 1834. The committee chairman, F. O. J. Smith of Maine, found practically nothing to his liking. He blasted the high failure and dismissal rate and used the Academy's conduct roll to prove what he called "the moral inefficiency of the institution." Smith submitted a bill recommending the remodeling of West Point into a "school of practice." Out would go courses in mathematics and engineering, anything that smacked of higher learning. If an individual wanted to combine a military career with a college education, let him pay for his book learning himself, Smith argued. Meanwhile, "all the grades of office in the Army" would be open to the "free and honorable competition of all classes of citizens." Colleges across the country, Smith averred, would rush to teach military arts and sciences. Smith's colleagues in Congress were not inclined to agree with him. His bill languished.

II

AS THE DECADE of the 1830's dwindled, there began to appear on the cadet register more names that would later resound in history. From Ohio, in 1835, came a slender, volatile sixteen-year-old with a strange name—William Tecumseh Sherman. Always full of cheerful chatter, Sherman was nicknamed "Cump" by his classmates. As his best friend he chose a grave twenty-year-old Virginian, who was in almost every respect his exact opposite. Built like a rock, silent, solemn George H. Thomas was nicknamed "General Washington" by William S. "Rosy" Rosecrans, a brilliant sophomore from Ohio. Sherman nicknamed him "Old Tom," and for four years the two were almost inseparable. Among many reasons for their close relationship was the way the burly Thomas handled an upperclassman who had come into his room and begun issuing absurd orders, typical of a tradition of hazing plebes that was just beginning to flower. "Get out of this room," said Thomas, "or I will throw you out that window." The upperclassman got out, fast.

Sherman was never a model cadet, though his keen mind had no difficulty with West Point's mathematics and engineering courses. He stood fourth in his class academically, but the 380 demerits he amassed in four years (in contrast to Thomas' 87) reduced him to number six. No doubt this was in part a symptom of the slack discipline of the DeRussy era. In the class ahead of Sherman another leader, Edward Otho Cresap Ord of Maryland, was a mathematical prodigy, but he stood 193 in conduct, only eighteen from the bottom, which reduced his standing in the class to twenty-one. Rosecrans, reminiscing about Sherman in later years, said:

He was always ready for a lark and usually he had a grease spot on his pants from clandestine night feasts. He was the best hash maker at West Point. Food at the table was cheap and poor and we stole boiled potatoes in handkerchiefs and thrust them under our vests; we poked butter into our gloves and fastened them with forks to the underside of the table until we could smuggle them out of the dining room as we departed. We stole bread and when we got together at night 'Old Cump' would mix everything into hash and cook it on the stew pan over the fire. We ate it hot on toasted bread. We told stories and at this too Sherman was the best. We would all risk expulsion by going down to Benny Havens at night to eat oysters.

Not once was Sherman chosen to be a cadet officer—a post which always went to the most military among the corps. Yet West Point had made its mark on Sherman in other ways. Writing to Ellen Ewing, the girl who would later become his wife, he spoke contemptuously of a graduate who was planning to resign and study law. "No doubt you admire this choice but to speak plainly and candidly, I would rather be a blacksmith. Indeed the nearer we come to that dreadful epoch, graduation day, the higher opinion I conceive of the duties and life of an officer of the United States Army and the more confirmed in the wish of spending my life in the service of my country. Think of that!" Hungering for action in the fading Seminole War, Sherman passed up a chance to choose the highly prized Engineering Corps and asked for a commission in the artillery instead.

From the lofty eminence of a first class man in 1839, Cump Sherman had barely noticed the arrival of another Ohioan in that year's plebe class. Hiram Ulysses Grant had even more trouble with his name than Sherman. The first of his two christening names had swiftly been forgotten by his family. Father, mother, all his friends, called him Ulysses. But when his uncle tacked his initials in brass on his trunk a few days before he left for West Point, the old name was revived and the boy saw that the initials spelled H.U.G. Hypersensitive, and with no real desire to go to West Point in the first place—his father, Jesse, had selected the school because the education was free and expected his son to resign as soon as possible to pursue a profitable civilian career—Ulysses had begged his uncle to change the initials. Otherwise he would be the laughingstock of the Academy.

His uncle good-naturedly rearranged the brass tacks to read U.H.G., without mentioning it either to his mother or father. But a clerk in the U.S. War Department compounded Grant's problems. As he rode east by steamboat, stage and railroad, his name was forwarded to West Post as U. S. Grant. Blissfully unaware of the confusion, the lad signed himself on the post's adjutant's register, "Ulysses Hiram Grant." But he soon learned that the older cadets, scanning the names of incoming plebes posted on the bulletin board in North Barracks, had seized on his name as the funniest of the lot. U. S. Grant, they roared. United States Grant. Uncle Sam Grant—Uncle Sam! They decided it was even funnier

when they found the new boy to be small, round-faced, a mere 5′1″ and
weighing only 117 pounds—a total opposite to the lank, lantern-jawed
Uncle Sam who was the cartoonists' symbol for shrewd, cunning, ag-
gressive America. "A more unpromising boy never entered the Military
Academy," was the way William Tecumseh Sherman remembered
Grant.

Son of a sweet, loving mother who had never scolded him at home,
Ulysses Grant found West Point an appalling place. He was not old
enough or strong enough to handle plebe hazing in George Thomas'
summer fashion. He also had no talent whatsoever for the spit-and-
polish soldiering demanded of him. He was sloppy in dress and habits,
and having spent most of his Ohio life on a horse's back, his feet found
it impossible to follow the drum beat of drill, to stay smartly in step. All
day long the new cadet lived in a storm of belittlement.

"Salute. Salute. Stand up straight there, MISter Grant—You're an
animal—Throw out your chest—Say Sir—Shut your trap—Can't you
hear the drum—Salute—Eyes front—Who's your tailor—Keep step,
MISter Grant—Put out that light—You're a hell of an Uncle Sam—Pull
your chin down, MISter Grant—You're a beast—Send him home—
Salute—Pull that belly in, MISter Grant—Does your mother know
you're out—You're a beast—Who in God's name sent that THING
here—Left, right, left, right. Now you've got it, can't you keep it—
Whose calf is that—Salute—You're an animal—Salute—Salute,
salute . . ."

But there was another side to "Uncle Sam" Grant, and his fellow
plebes saw it one day and never forgot it. A big hulking cadet named
Jack Lindsay contemptuously shoved Grant out of his place in line at
squad drill. The son of an Army colonel, Jack had numerous friends on
the Academy staff and this gave him, in his opinion, the right to be an
overbearing loudmouth. Quietly, Grant told Lindsay not to do that
again. The big fellow sneered and repeated the performance. With one
punch Grant flattened him. Thereafter his classmates stopped laughing
at "Uncle Sam" and soon had shortened the nickname to a good-natured
"Sam," which he bore without complaint for the rest of his life.

During his first encampment that summer, Grant had a curious psy-
chic experience. General Winfield Scott, the magnificent six-foot-four
hero of the War of 1812, arrived to review the troops. Watching Old
Fuss-'n-Feathers, as Scott was called because of his fondness for splen-

dor, small, underweight Sam Grant suddenly had what he later called a "presentiment" that some day he would stand in Scott's place, reviewing the cadet corps.

Another man Grant found fascinating was Captain Charles F. Smith, Commandant of Cadets. Later he would say he considered Smith and Scott at that point in his life, "the two men most to be envied in the nation." The Pennsylvania-born Smith was the very model of a soldier, straight as a pine, superbly mustached, beloved by the corps for the justice with which he administered Delafield's rigid discipline.

West Point's physical beauty was a homesick boy's only other consolation. To a cousin Grant wrote that it was the "prettiest of places . . . The most beautiful place I have ever seen . . . I do love the place—It seems as though I could live here forever if my friends would only come too . . . Now this sounds romantic and you may think it very easy; but I tell you what, Coz, it is tremendous hard."

He was soon collecting demerits by the bushel. To the same cousin he wrote with wry humor, "I came near forgetting to tell you about our demerits or black marks. They give a man one of these black marks for almost nothing and if he gets 200 a year they dismiss him. To show how easy one can get these, a man by the name of Grant, of this state, got eight of those marks for not going to church. He was also put under arrest so he cannot leave his room perhaps for a month; all this for not going to church."

Except for French, Grant found the West Point course of studies rather easy. In later years, his roommate Rufus Ingalls said: "In his studies he was lazy and careless. Instead of studying a lesson he would merely read it over once or twice; but he was so quick in his perceptions that he usually made very fair recitations even with so little preparation. His memory was not at all good in an attempt to learn anything by heart accurately and this made his grade low in those branches of the study which required a special effort of the memory. In scientific subjects he was very bright and if he had labored hard he would have stood very high in them."

Grant was bored. Although Ingalls was a steady patron at Benny Havens', Sam Grant made the trip only once. He sat in his room reading romantic novels when he should have been declining French verbs. In December, 1839 he found a new interest—reading debates in Congress about another bill to abolish the Military Academy. The homesick youngster grasped this possibility as the answer to his prayers. "I saw in this an honorable way to obtain a discharge," he later said, "and read the debates with much interest but with impatience at the delay." Like previous bills, this one got nowhere and Sam Grant drifted through his first year to find himself number 27 among the 60 boys left in the opening day class of 73. It was not a performance to cheer about and it certainly did not please his father, who was fiercely ambitious for his oldest son.

Then came news that Superintendent Delafield had introduced a radical change in the curriculum—horses. Sam Grant's heart leaped up. Riding was above all things his supreme pleasure, his best skill. As a toddler in his father's tannery he had wandered carelessly between the hoofs of waiting horses, swung from their tails. Everyone in the village of Georgetown, Ohio had stories to tell about the remarkable way in which horses seemed, as his mother said, "to understand him."

But first Grant had to survive a change of roommates that put him in cahoots with George "Dragon" Deshon, one of the best students in the class—a straight-faced Connecticut Yankee who had an equally impeccable record on the conduct rolls. Only Grant and a few close friends knew that Deshon was a fearless forager, famed for his ability to procure food for midnight feasts. After graduation, Deshon abandoned the army to become a Catholic priest, and founded the most progressive and enlightened religious order in the Church, the Paulists. But in his cadet days, he was decidedly among the unconverted. Unable to buy pies or fowl from nearby farmers because of Superintendent Delafield's get-tough policy, Deshon coolly stole them—from Superintendent Delafield. One night Sam and the Dragon were roasting one of the Superintendent's turkeys in their little fireplace when the door swung open and there stood the officer of the day, Lieutenant William N. Grier. The two boys leaped to attention, elbow to elbow in front of the fireplace. The room was redolent with roasting turkey. But Grier, just returned from fighting Choctaw Indians in the West, had not yet imbibed the disciplinary ambitions of Major Delafield. Putting on the sternest possible face, Grier solemnly inspected the room while the cadets carefully shifted positions to keep between him and the turkey. He departed after inspecting every square inch but the fireplace.

That same September came a change in the cadet uniform that gave Sam Grant and the rest of his classmates some moments of mirth. Third classman John Pope, son of a prominent Illinois politician, had come back from his furlough with pantaloons that buttoned down the front—flies, as this new departure was eventually called, were the newest fashion in male dress that year. Major Delafield, in love with efficiency, promptly gave the new idea his blessing and ordered the post tailor to dress the whole corps that way. The ladies on the post reacted with horror at so bold a recognition of the male anatomy. Mrs. Delafield reportedly told the major that "cadets thus dressed should not come in person to the house." But the major ignored the female bombardment and the style soon became regulation in the corps, and throughout the entire Army.

Meanwhile, Grant made friends: "Pete" Longstreet of the junior class, tall, athletic, fiercely military; lumbering, bearish Simon Bolivar Buckner of the incoming plebe class. They were both big, aggressive men and their attraction to the stumpy Grant would have mystified an outsider—until he saw Sam Grant on horseback. Though other cadets remembered him in later years as "tiny-looking" upon a horse, Longstreet regarded him as "the most daring horseman in the Academy." Plebes often went to the riding hall just to watch him. Egbert Viele later recalled "it was as good as any circus to see Grant ride . . . There was a dark bay horse that was so fractious that it was about to be condemned . . . Grant selected it for his horse. He bridled, mounted and rode it every day at parade; and how he did ride! He handled the refractory creature as a giant would a child. The whole class would stand around admiring his wonderful command of the beast and his graceful evolutions." The Academy riding-master invariably allowed Grant to break the bad horses that Delafield, with his mania for economy, was constantly buying for the corps.

Another thing that his fellow cadets never forgot was Grant's unshakable poise. Blackboard recitation, which made even such imperturbable types as George Thomas turn pale and quake, never bothered Grant in the least. One day at the blackboard he proved his poise could survive maximum stress. A cadet named Gardiner had brought into the engineering class a huge heirloom watch, some four inches in diameter. It was being passed from hand to hand when the assistant engineering professor, Lieutenant Zealous B. Tower, arrived. Sam Grant found himself with the watch in his hand and he hastily stuffed it into the bosom of his coat and buttoned it down.

A few moments later, four cadets including Grant were sent to the board to work out problems. Grant finished his figuring, put down his chalk and began to explain what he had done. Suddenly—bong, bong, bong, the old watch in his coat began striking the hours. One cadet later said it sounded like a Chinese gong. Lieutenant Tower thought the noise was coming from the hall, but when the door was closed the bongs only got louder. Furious, Tower began hunting under desks and in closets. While the rest of his class strangled to suppress their mirth, Grant calmly continued his mathematical recitation. Eventually Sam outtalked the alarm and sat down. Professor Tower never did figure out where the clangor originated. But the corps never forgot Sam Grant's iron nerves.

In his studies Grant remained in the middle of the class, finishing twenty-first among thirty-nine survivors. He amassed 290 demerits in his four years, making him a middle man in conduct as well. But his horsemanship made him the most memorable figure on graduation day. A part of the senior class exercises was a drill in the riding hall. Visitors, professors and cadets crowded the stands as the horsemen wheeled, brandishing huge cavalry swords, one by one leaped the bars, and finally drew up in a line down the middle of the long tanbark-covered floor. A moment of silence, then the riding-master strode to the jumping bar, lifted it higher than his head, and barked, "Cadet Grant."

Among the spectators cadets hastily whispered, "He's on York." This was the huge sorrel Grant had tamed the year before. To the extreme end of the hall went the slim cadet on the big horse. James F. Fry, a plebe that year, never forgot the sight as Grant came thundering toward the bar. Faster, faster, then soaring from the ground "as if man and beast had been welded together" to set an Academy jump record that stood for at least 25 years.

As Sam Grant wended his way west to Jefferson Barracks on the outskirts of St. Louis, where he would marry the sister of his first class year roommate, Fred Dent, he left behind him two cadets who were just emerging from the torment of plebedom—George B. McClellan of Pennsylvania and Thomas J. Jackson of Virginia. It would be hard to imagine two more opposite personalities. McClellan was a boy genius, admitted to the Academy when he was only fifteen years and seven months old. The minimum age regulation was suspended in his case, thanks to his mental ability and superb physique. As one of his classmates, Dabney H. Maury of Virginia, put it, he bore on his "charming countenance every evidence of gentle nature and high culture." The son of a socially prominent Philadelphian, McClellan had already spent two distinguished years at the University of Pennsylvania and was accepted by the entire school, even the Southerners, as a natural aristocrat.

Jackson was at the opposite end of the social scale. An awkward, shambling constable from the hills of western Virginia, he caused hysterics among the upperclassmen when they saw his homespun clothes, coarse wool hat and a pair of saddlebags stained with horse sweat hanging from his round shoulders. An orphan, Jackson's learning scarcely qualified him for a grammar school diploma. Dabney Maury felt a twinge of sympathy for his fellow Virginian (he also said later that he was impressed by Jackson's "cold bright gray eyes" and remarked, "That fellow looks like he has come to stay"). Maury approached Jackson "to show my interest in a fellow countryman in a strange land." He got the shock of his life. Far from accepting the proffered friendship, Jackson, Maury said, "received my courteous advances in a manner so chilling that it caused me to regret having made them."

Jackson's withdrawn, surly manner was, of course, defensive, a product of his terrible insecurity. A few weeks later, during summer camp, Maury tried again. Lolling on his cot with fellow plebe A. P. Hill, he noticed Jackson and some other cadets were policing the ground. Lifting his tent wall, Maury mockingly called to Jackson, "You there, you missed these cigar butts. If you don't do a better job you'll be in trouble around here." Jackson's reply "was a look so stern and angry as to let me know that he was doing his job." Ever the gentleman, Maury was troubled by this misunderstanding and went to Jackson to apologize. "Mr. Jackson," he said, "I find that I made a mistake just now in speaking to you in a playful manner—not justified by our short acquaintance. I regret that I did so."

Jackson gave Maury an even stonier look. "That is perfectly satisfactory, sir," he said.

The mortified Maury returned to his tent and announced: "In my opinion, Cadet Jackson of Virginia is a jackass."

But the gaunt countryman who "could add up a column of figures but as to vulgar or decimal fractions, it is doubtful if he had ever heard of them," soon impressed the entire corps with his burning determination to survive. He kept a notebook in which he wrote mottos and sayings to keep up his morale. The one he counted on most was, "You may be whatever you resolve to be." He lived by these words, says one of his biographers, "as a scientist follows a formula. He assumed literally that he could be what he resolved to be—by concentration, strain, sweat, endurance." As his fellow plebes watched with amazement, he studied night after night into the dawn, piling coal high on his grate just before lights went out at ten o'clock so that after taps he could stretch on the floor in the firelight and dig at mathematical problems, the very terms of which were a puzzle to him.

His unfeigned academic misery touched the heart of one third class cadet. Traditionally third classmen were the bane of plebes' existence, but William H. C. Whiting forgot such minor matters in admiration for Jackson the fighter, and began to tutor him privately. "The General," as he was first called, in a mocking reference to Andrew Jackson, became "Whiting's plebe." To the ends of their lives cadets carried memories of Jackson during that first year, struggling over problems at the blackboard, his face wet with perspiration, the chalk spreading over his uniform, his cuffs wrinkling as he wiped his streaming forehead. He literally fought his way through every recitation, ending almost inevitably among "the immortals"—the tailenders of the class. But he survived, standing fifty-first among eighty-three members in June.

McClellan, on the other hand, found the Academy's academic studies almost ridiculously simple. For this sort of cadet West Point was a different kind of challenge. There was no fear of the academic disgrace that terrified Tom Jackson, but there was the question of manhood. Thanks to the happy survival of a letter young McClellan wrote to his sister Fredericka, we are able to be almost literally present at the moment when the transformation of boy into soldier took place. The letter begins with a mournful paean of self-pity:

> . . . I sometimes . . . get so homesick and want to see you all so very, very much—that I have been on the point of "packing up my traps" and starting for home . . . I am as much alone as if in a boat in the middle of the Atlantic, not a soul here cares for or thinks of me—not one here would lift a finger to help me; I am entirely dependent on myself—direct myself and take the blame of all my mistakes, without anyone to give me a word of advice. . . . If I were "found" on account of my age, I would be delighted to get home—

He then goes on to discuss alternative plans—the study of law, particularly prominent in his mind. Suddenly the letter breaks off—the plebe was called to drill. When he returns he continues in an entirely different tone:

I expect to—I forget what—as I was there called off to drill. I have just this moment returned and feel so much encouraged by my successful endeavors to do better than all the rest that I feel like an entirely different person. I am to get a musket this afternoon and will be on post about next week . . . You can't imagine how much more in-spirited I feel since I have acquitted myself handsomely at this morning's drill. It is strange how some little circumstance like that can make so great a difference in one's feelings —before drill I felt in low spirits—homesick—and in doubt as to my competency to go through here with credit, but now how different. I feel in high spirits and know that I am able to go through here and do my duty as well as anyone who ever did go through here. I know I can do as well as anyone in both my studies and my military duties. If this state of mind continues I will be able to stay here for four years—though I am still very anxious to see you all.

McClellan soon stood first in his class in mathematics and close to the top in other subjects. Tom Jackson, meanwhile, toiling fiercely by midnight firelight, painfully, like a man climbing a sheer rock wall, edged up into the middle, and by the time he reached the end of senior year, stood seventeenth in the order of general merit. Classmates remarked that if the course had been two years longer, Jackson would have graduated at the head of the class.

He made friends, too, his frosty reserve thawing as his confidence grew, but even his friendships were chosen in a highly individual way. He preferred lower-ranking cadets—not a common practice—as long as the men shared his fondness for long walks and talks on serious subjects. If anyone in the corps was sick or in trouble, Tom Jackson was among the first to volunteer his aid. But there was a ferocity in him that sometimes appalled his classmates. One day Tom found his own clean musket gone and another in its place, inexcusably dirty. Jackson had marked his own musket so he could identify it and with the aid of the cadet captain they soon discovered it in the hands of another cadet. Jackson angrily demanded that the thief be court-martialed, insisting he should be discharged from the Academy. Pleas from his classmates finally persuaded him to settle for less drastic action.

Another Virginian who graduated with Tom Jackson in 1847 spent his four years moving steadily downward in class standing. His name was George E. Pickett. Debonair and self-willed, he had his own ideas about discipline and was constantly in trouble. He refused, for instance, to wear the stiff leather collar which made it impossible for a cadet to throw his head back and laugh heartily. Pickett constantly appeared in a soft collar, and every time a tactical officer spotted him, his list of "crimes," as demerits were called in those days, grew longer. No one thought much of the unusual way Pickett had entered the Academy in the first place. He had taken up residence in Illinois and persuaded a prominent Virginian who had emigrated there to wangle an appointment for him from the local congressman—a gaunt, obscure son of the plains named Abraham Lincoln. Though Pickett graduated at the very foot of his class, the congressman maintained a lively interest in his appointee, writing him letters of encouragement and advice and following his military career in the years after graduation.

III

DURING THESE SAME YEARS, West Point's faculty, under the leadership of Dennis Hart Mahan, senior member of the academic board, chose the best of Thayer's "sons" to head its departments. William H. C. Bartlett, '26, became professor of natural and experimental philosophy in 1834. Albert E. Church, '28, became professor of mathematics in 1837, and Frederick A. Smith, '33, took over the new Department of Practical Engineering in 1841. They were to be the nucleus of West Point's intellectual vigor for the next twenty years. The reigning spirit was undoubtedly Mahan, who insisted on adding to his title of Professor of Civil and Military Engineering the words—"and of the Art of War." Brilliant as were his scientific gifts—his *Course of Civil Engineering* was a leading textbook in the United States for several decades—Mahan's influence on history bulks larger as a theorist of war.

Speed, or, as he called it, "celerity," was the essence of Mahan's tactical concepts. "No great success can be hoped for in war in which rapid movements do not enter as an element." Another key word was information. "Too often a general has only conjectures to go on and these based upon false premises . . ." Among Mahan's other points was the importance of assuming the initiative and directing one's maximum effort against the enemy's weakest point. With a ferocity that belied his mild professorial manner, he urged them to give a defeated army no rest. Frederick the Great and Napoleon, he pointed out, never fought for paltry towns and villages, but to destroy utterly all means of further resistance. He also warned them that an officer must inspire confidence and emulation; all troops are brave when their leaders set them the example. A great general, he insisted, was a man who simultaneously was loved, esteemed and feared by his troops.

A strange figure, this diminutive, intense Irishman whose acid tongue and violent temper could terrify the unprepared cadet. At home whole days passed without his saying more than good morning and good night to his wife. The mind that Sylvanus Thayer discerned so early was constantly at work on new insights, new projects. He was also frequently the spokesman for the Academy in its defense against continued criticism in Congress and elsewhere.

Jacksonian Democrats persisted in asking why America needed West Point, why the money spent there was not distributed to the states to train militia. The minutemen philosophy still had strong support throughout the country. Each year when Congress came to vote the annual appropriation for the Academy there were new blasts of criticism and demands for its abolition. The constant furor forced West Point supporters to make changes in both cadet selection and length of service.

In 1838, Congress decided to make every graduate agree in advance to serve four full years in the Army after graduation instead of the single year previously required—and often waived. In 1843, Congress took the nomination of cadets out of the hands of the Secretary of War. The practice of funneling all appointments through the executive branch had been a prime irritant among the legislators. To soothe their anguished cries, during the 1830's the Secretary of War began as a matter of course to do his utmost to find at least one West Point nominee from each Congressional district. The practice was regularized by the act of March 4, 1843; henceforth Congress had the sole right to nominate cadets.

But criticism of the Academy continued. Throughout the 1840's it rose ominously until it reached a kind of crescendo in the vote on the West Point appropriation for the year 1845. Congressman Hale of New Hampshire moved as a substitute for the regular bill a provision for abolishing the institution after the thirtieth of June, 1844. Congressman Dana of New York rose to support it and in a scathing speech raked the Academy with a verbal fusillade that summed up all the things that West Point's enemies found wrong with the place.

First and foremost, Dana scored the Academy "as an aristocratic institution" both in its nature and character. "Out of a population of eighteen or twenty million about one hundred individuals are annually selected as the exclusive recipients of the national bounty," he fumed, and proceeded to heap scorn on the way Congress chose cadets. "When we examine the roll of cadets and compare it with the lists of members of Congress, we find such a coincidence of names as I cannot attribute wholly to accident; there must have been some relationship between them to produce such a striking family likeness." Next Dana denounced the "monopoly of military commissions" held by West Point graduates.

"No man, whatever may be his talents or qualifications or his thirst for military fame can get into the Army unless he enter through the gate of the West Point Academy, the only portal open to ambition." This monopoly made the cadets "proud and vain." He concluded they were "a military nobility," and looked with "scorn and contempt" on the multitude which was returned by the latter with "feelings of envy and detestation." What else, he demanded, explained the "ill feeling that exists between West Point and the country."

Finally, Dana maintained that West Point's monopoly produced "positive evils" in the Army. There was a lurking antagonism between the graduates and the older commanding officers in the Army, most of whom were nongraduates. Even worse was the effect on the enlisted man who, "excluded from promotion, has no incentive to bravery or good conduct."

In his peroration Dana revealed his basic allegiance. "The main reliance of this country for defense is and ever must be the militia." But throughout the country, particularly in New York State, the militia hated West Point. "If war should occur and the Army and militia be brought in contact, the most disastrous consequences might ensue from their dissension." Dana, therefore, called upon his fellow congressmen to join him in abolishing "an expensive, extravagant and anti-democratic institution of little use, the occasion of many controversies between the officers and of discontent and degradation to the soldiers."

The appropriations bill carried by a single vote. Next year? The friends of West Point shuddered at the prospect.

But men and events many hundreds of miles from West Point and Washington were moving toward a confrontation that would change the nation's attitude toward the Military Academy. On December 29, 1845, the Republic of Texas entered the union as the twenty-eighth state. Mexico, still smarting over the loss of this immense territory in 1835, regarded the annexation as an act of war and rejected American efforts to negotiate a settlement. Skirmishing soon broke out along the Rio Grande between Mexican troops and Americans under the leadership of General Zachary Taylor. On May 11, President Polk went before Congress and demanded a declaration of war. After thirty years of peace, thirty years in which West Point had graduated more than a thousand officers, Thayer's graduates were about to meet the soldier's best—perhaps only—test, the battlefield.

IV

CONGRESSMAN DANA'S DESCRIPTION of the Army that fought the Mexican War was accurate enough. A rich proportion of the younger officers were West Pointers. The commanding generals, the regimental colonels, were almost all nongraduates, products of the War of 1812 and decades of Indian fighting along the frontier. Lieutenant Sam Grant's 4th Regiment, commanded by Colonel William Whistler, brother of the West Pointer who was already in Russia building the Tsar's railroads. Colonel Whistler was sixty-five and a drunk. Commander in Chief Zachary Taylor was an Indian fighter who totally ignored military etiquette and punctilio, wandering about camp in blue jeans and a big palmetto hat, chewing tobacco and talking about the crops on his Louisiana plantation. Lieutenant Colonel Ethan Allen Hitchcock, Thayer's ex-Commandant of Cadets, noted in his diary as he rode out with Taylor that his three colonels were total incompetents; Whistler could not give the simplest command, and the other two were incapable of maneuvering a brigade or disposing one for battle.

Colonel Whistler found Lieutenant Richard H. Graham of the class of 1838 bringing a small case of books along in the wagon train. "That will never do, Mr. Graham. We can't encumber our train with such rubbish as books," wheezed the old war-horse. Another officer, asked if it was all right to bring a small keg of whiskey. He explained that he was not feeling very well and required a "stimulant."

"Oh," grunted Colonel Whistler, "that's all right, Mr. Hoskins, anything in reason. But Graham wanted to carry a case of books."

With such senior officers one might reasonably expect the young West Pointers to acquire a distinct sense of superiority, which could readily lead to insubordination. But nothing of the sort seems to have happened. West Point's critics reckoned without the effect of Thayer's system of tactical instructors. These men served as a bridge between the corps and the Army. This and the intense esprit de corps of the old Army combined to make Academy graduates as proud of their Regular Army commissions as they were of their West Point backgrounds.

Between the regulars and the volunteers, however, there did at first seem to be more than a little mutual antagonism. Lieutenant George B. McClellan, for instance, kept a diary in which he several times noted his detestation of the "mustangs," as the volunteer officers were called, because, lacking horses, they rode jackasses. But the military policy pursued by President Polk was far different from the policies pursued in the Revolution and the War of 1812. Instead of summoning an armed mob of militia, Polk called for volunteers who would serve for twelve months or to the end of the war. This gave the officers ample time to drill and train these men until they were on a par with regular soldiers, and solved a problem that had driven earlier American generals to despair.

Even before the volunteers arrived, the West Pointers of the tiny Regular Army demonstrated what professional military training could achieve. Samuel Ringgold of the class of 1818 had led the way in developing field artillery, a weapon that had been all but abandoned by European armies of the 1840's—though Napoleon had used it regularly with devastating effect. Ringgold and three other West Pointers, Captain James Duncan of the class of 1834, Braxton Bragg of the class of 1837, and Randolph Ridgely of the same year, commanded this so-called "flying artillery." In the first clash between the Mexicans and Americans in the tall grass of the plains of Palo Alto, the Mexican army of 6000 drew up in close-packed ranks, expecting the Americans to rush pell-mell upon them as the Texans had done in the past. Eight hundred lancers with gleaming steel-tipped spears were stationed at the head of the army to take the first charge.

Instead, Taylor ordered his 2300 men to halt beyond musket range and sent his West Pointers racing to the front of the army with their horse-drawn guns. In the artillery duel that followed, the eight six-pounders and two eighteen-pounders wreaked unbelievable havoc on the Mexicans. When the enemy sent a column of infantry and cavalry on a flanking movement around the American right wing, Lieutenant Randolph Ridgely of Ringgold's battery hitched up his guns, whipped them into position, and in a matter of minutes a blizzard of canister sent the flankers fleeing into the chaparral. The Mexican army reeled back, decimated, without most of the American infantrymen having fired a single shot. "The infantry stood at order thus as spectators," Sam Grant said later. American casualties were amazingly low: nine killed, forty-five wounded. Unfortunately, one of the dead was Major Ringgold, mangled by a Mexican cannonball in the artillery duel. Carried to the rear, he lived only long enough to know his faith in his new tactics was more than justified.

The next day Zachary Taylor, leaving 600 men behind to guard his wagon train, led 1700 men forward to attack some 5700 Mexicans entrenched along a ravine known as Resaca de la Palma. Once more the artillery, firing canister through dense underbrush, played a major role, but this time Sam Grant and many other West Pointers commanding infantry companies got a chance to show what they had learned about soldiering, too. Much of the fighting was confused small-unit struggles, often hand to hand, and only in the late afternoon, after resisting heroically, did the Mexican soldiers lose heart and flee in wild disorganization across the Rio Grande.

In the next few months "Old Rough-and-Ready" Taylor's ranks were expanded four times by the arrival of thousands of volunteers. Old Rough-and-Ready relieved them of all their duties and drilled them six hours a day from May through September. Though some of the political generals who came with the volunteers were windbags such as Gideon J. Pillow, former law partner of President Polk, regulars and West Pointers were on the whole impressed by the willingness with which these amateurs tackled the task of turning themselves from citizens into soldiers. When Ohio congressman Tom Hamer arrived in camp as a brigadier general, he sought out Ulysses S. Grant, and asked him to help him in his military studies. Hamer wrote home that he found this modest, unassuming young man "a most remarkable and valuable young soldier . . . Today, after being freed from the duty of wrestling with the problem of reducing a train of refractory mules and their drivers to submissive order, we rode into the country several miles and taking our position upon an elevated mound, he explained to me many army evolutions; and, supposing ourselves to be generals commanding opposing armies, and a battle to be in progress, he explained suppositions of the opposing forces in a most instructive way, and when I thought his imaginary force had my army routed, he suddenly suggested a strategic move for my forces which crowned them with triumphant victory, and himself with defeat, and he ended by gracefully offering to surrender his sword! Of course, Lieutenant Grant is too young for command, but his capacity for future military usefulness is undoubted."

A few weeks later, when Taylor with 7000 men attacked some

10,000 Mexicans entrenched in Monterey, Sam Grant had a chance to demonstrate both his horsemanship and his courage. Fighting through streets alive with hissing bullets, the American attack ground to a halt only a block from the center of the city where the Mexicans were massed for a last stand. With almost a third of the 4th Regiment's men killed and wounded, the officers discovered to their horror that almost everyone was out of ammunition. The colonel hesitated to send anyone back through those lead-filled streets alone, to order up more bullets. Sam Grant volunteered, leaped on his horse, and with his body hanging to the sheltered side of the animal Indian-fashion, thundered past intersections where squads of Mexican riflemen were waiting to blaze away at any passing American. As he modestly explained it later, the "flying rate of speed with which he crossed the intersections enabled him and his horse to arrive at headquarters unscratched," with the vital message.

In this desperate, chancy battle of Monterey West Pointers played vital roles in both regular and volunteer units. Chief of staff to volunteer Major General William O. Butler was Albert Sidney Johnston of the class of '26, whom Zackary Taylor called "the best soldier I ever commanded." Johnson had quit the Army in 1834 and become a Texas farmer. He had been a general in that state's war of independence and was first Secretary of War of the temporary republic. In Taylor's army he was serving as a volunteer, heading a regiment of Texans. Cited for his role in a victorious charge on one of the key Mexican fortifications called the Tannery was Colonel Jefferson Davis of the Mississippi Rifles. Like Johnson, he had resigned from the Army and had volunteered at the head of a regiment when war was declared. With casualties distributed almost equally between regulars and volunteers, the battle of Monterey scotched permanently any danger of antagonism between them.

The American artillery, officered almost completely by West Pointers, once again won high praise. Braxton Bragg and his guns went roaring into the suburbs of Monterey side by side with the infantry. Enemy fire wrecked his battery, and Bragg, ignoring shells and bullets filling the air around him, calmly stripped the harnesses from his dead horses. As he withdrew, one of his horse drivers was shot out of his saddle. Bragg halted his battery and ordered another West Pointer, Sam French, to salvage the dead man's sword. When French added the man's pocket knife, Bragg refused it. "It is not public property, Mr. French," said the

Southern puritan, as calmly as if they were discussing a point of military etiquette in a West Point classroom.

Other West Point artillerymen who won high praise from Taylor included scholarly John C. Pemberton of Pennsylvania and buoyant Randolph Ridgely, whose exultant laugh could often be heard floating above his guns as he dueled with a Mexican battery. George Thomas won a brevet captaincy for, among other things, calmly reloading his cannon under fire and blasting a farewell salute practically into the Mexicans' faces before withdrawing from the bloody streets of Monterey.

Taylor's chief of staff was Captain W. S. Bliss of Thayer's '33 class. Called "Perfect Bliss" for his organizational ability, he was famed for the elegance of diction and vigor of expression in his dispatches. He wrote all of Taylor's reports and many observers felt they had not a little to do with winning the Presidency for "Old Rough-and-Ready." Bliss later became Taylor's son-in-law and his private secretary in the White House.

Six months later, the Mexican commander in chief Santa Anna attacked Taylor's approximately 8000 Americans at Buena Vista with a well-trained army of 16,000.

Outnumbered at least two to one, the Americans were on the verge of rout from massive Mexican assaults which had shattered their left flank. As men from Indiana, Arkansas and Kentucky stampeded to the rear, Taylor arrived with some dragoons and Jefferson Davis' red-shirted Mississippi Rifles. Ignoring a painful wound from a musket ball that shattered his heel and embedded splinters of brass from his spur deep in the flesh, Davis led his men in a furious charge that sent the Mexicans reeling back in confusion toward the mountains. But a squadron of Mexican cavalry came pounding in to counterattack. Davis saw that it was up to him and his 300 men to stop this steel-tipped horde from breaking through the American lines and smashing the vital artillery positions behind them. He quickly ordered his men to form a sort of obtuse triangle, which some military historians have called his "V formation." Sternly ordering his men to hold their fire, Davis let the Mexican horsemen ride into the open end of the V and when the Mexicans were only 80 yards away, Davis gave the signal. "Both lines then instantly poured in a volley so destructive," he wrote in his battle report, "that the mass yielded to the blow and the survivors fled." A reporter on the scene declared: "The whole head of the column fell . . . a more deadly crossfire was never delivered."

As he formed his men to deliver another attack on Mexican positions opposite him, Davis was ordered to rush to the opposite flank to stem another emergency. Ignoring his wound, which had already filled his boot with blood, he pushed his gasping men across the rocky terrain to arrive just in time to watch American artillery under Braxton Bragg dueling alone with three lines of charging Mexican infantry. Beside the guns, sidesaddle on his old white horse, sat General Taylor, calmly issuing Bragg a famous order: "Double shot your guns and give 'em hell."

Bragg obeyed, tearing huge gaps in the oncoming Mexican ranks, but the brave peons continued to advance and almost certainly would have captured the battery except for Davis and his Mississippians, who now opened what he called an "eminently destructive" fire on their right flank. Nothing demoralizes soldiers more than an assault from an unexpected direction. The Mexicans broke and fled once more. In seven hours of desperate fighting under the blazing tropic sun, Davis and his men had not once but three times saved the American Army from destruction.

Buena Vista ended the war in northern Mexico. But Taylor's men could not hope to fight their way through the hundreds of miles of mountainous country between them and Mexico City. This job was handed to General Winfield Scott. Much of the artillery and Sam Grant's 4th Regiment of regular troops were shifted to Scott's army, which opened its campaign with an amphibious landing near Vera Cruz and the capture of that city after a brief siege. A shrewd, intelligent general, Scott knew he would need all the military talent he could find if he was to reach Mexico City. On his staff he had Lieutenant Colonel Ethan Allen Hitchcock and Captain Robert E. Lee, the marble model of the class of 1819. Among the engineers serving under Lee was Second Lieutenant George B. McClellan, the second man in the class of 1846, and Lieutenant P. G. T. Beauregard, a top graduate of the class of 1838. Also on hand was Zealous B. Tower, number one in the class of 1841, now an ex-instructor with no more worries about Sam Grants and bonging alarms. Among the generals was William "Haughty Bill" Worth, Thayer's old Commandant of Cadets.

Moving out from Vera Cruz into the unknown interior, Scott soon found his way barred by 13,000 Mexicans under President Santa Anna. The steep mountain ridges, notably Cerro Gordo, which commanded the only pass, were held by strong Mexican batteries. A frontal attack would have been suicidal, and Scott sent out his West Point engineers to find some way to turn the Mexican position with a flanking movement. When an opening exploration by Lieutenant Beauregard revealed there was a good chance of working around the right of the pass, Captain Lee took charge of the reconnaissance. With only a single guide, he prowled through the dense underbrush and found a path that would indeed enable the Americans to get into Santa Anna's rear. He came within a whisker of being captured, spending hours hiding under a log only a few feet from a Mexican patrol.

Returning through the moonlit night with only his amazing memory for terrain to guide him, Lee reported that a flanking movement was possible. Beauregard and Lieutenant Zealous Tower meanwhile had come back with sketches showing the location of all the enemy's batteries, and where Americans could locate cannon high up on the cliffs to enfilade them. Soon engineers, supported by infantry, were dragging cannon up the almost perpendicular slopes. Sam Grant, watching the operation from the American rear, where his regiment was being held in reserve, compared the undertaking as "almost equal to Bonaparte's crossing of the Alps." Lee, meanwhile, went back for another long reconnaissance that convinced him beyond all doubt of the wisdom of a flank march.

So thoroughly did Scott trust Lee's judgment, he assigned to his guidance an entire division of his best troops under Brigadier General David E. Twiggs. Moving out at dawn, they got within 700 yards of the enemy by 11 o'clock that morning, without being discovered. While American batteries blasted the startled defenders, Twiggs' men stormed up the slopes of Cerro Gordo in an irresistible wave. The entire left and center of the Mexican army collapsed and the right wing surrendered. Santa Anna himself escaped with only a handful of troops. The Americans captured 3000 men, 5000 muskets, 43 cannon, with a loss of only 63 killed and 368 wounded. Captain Lee won praise in not one but three separate dispatches.

Advancing to Puebla, 186 miles from Vera Cruz and 93 miles from Mexico City, Scott set up headquarters and awaited reinforcements. Meanwhile, he ordered Lee and Major William Turnbull, of the class of

1819, his chief topographical engineer, to make separate studies of the approaches to Mexico City and prepare a map. Seldom had an army of scarcely 10,000 been confronted by more formidable obstacles. Along the western approaches to the city the road ran on a narrow causeway through marshes between Lake Texcoco on the north and Lakes Xochimilco and Chalco on the south. Commanding the causeway was El Penon, 300 feet high with three plateaus, its base surrounded by a deep trench, its slopes rugged with breastworks from base to crest. It was armed with 30 pieces of cannon and defended by 7000 men under Santa Anna in person. There were other batteries on the causeway itself, and strategically placed for two miles around the fortress, especially at the village of Mexicalcingo.

Reconnaissance by engineers under General Worth soon discovered a road around the lower end of Lake Chalco offering a southern approach to the city. Scott promptly moved his army in this direction, but the Mexicans, operating on interior lines, shifted to meet him, one wing of their army grouping around a hacienda called Padierna near the village of Contreras. Once more Scott called a halt and ordered Robert E. Lee to reconnoiter.

Scouting a seemingly impassable lava field known as the Pedregal, Lee found another lightly guarded road which would enable the Americans to flank the Mexican position. Scott immediately put 500 men to work building a road across the Pedregal for artillery. Though two generals, Gideon J. Pillow and David E. Twiggs, were nominally in charge of the movement, the real leader was Captain Lee.

To maintain communication between the flankers and the main body of the army, Lee trudged back and forth across the three miles of guerrilla-infested, crevasse-gashed Pedregal three times, twice in rain-drenched darkness, setting up a combined attack which in seventeen minutes swept the Mexicans out of their entrenchments. Again Lee gathered citations by the half dozen, General P. F. Smith declaring, "His reconnaissances though pushed far beyond the bounds of prudence were conducted with so much skill that their fruits were of the utmost value—the soundness of judgment and personal bearing being equally conspicuous." Scott, who had sent seven staff officers across the darkened Pedregal in vain, called Lee's night trip "the greatest feat of physical and moral courage performed by any individual in my knowledge pending the campaign."

Only one fortress now barred the Americans' advance to Mexico City—the height of Chapultepec. This guarded two of the five causeways running into the city itself from the southwest. Three other causeways leading up from the south were commanded by batteries at and near the gates, and were in themselves miniature fortresses. If Chapultepec could be captured, the two southwest gates might be taken with comparative ease because the Mexicans had not fortified them as heavily. But reconnaissance by Lee and his subordinates convinced them that taking Chapultepec would be no easy matter. At a council of war, Lee and all the Engineers except Beauregard disagreed with Scott and urged an attack on the southern gates. Scott still preferred Chapultepec, arguing that "he would have more elbow room . . . and that he had reason to believe he would be met by a white flag on taking it." It was one of the few times Scott did not take Lee's advice—but the young Engineer obeyed his commander's order without a murmur of protest. A young naval officer marveled at the way Lee ". . . counselled and advised with a judgment, tact and discretion worthy of all praise."

Artillery fire was all-important in the assault. For two days and nights Lee and other West Pointers toiled on constructing batteries. Lee was everywhere, conferring with the officers in charge of each battery, reporting to Scott, advising other generals on troop movements. At one point Scott, always impatient, decided to attack on the evening of September 12, with little more than two hours' notice. Lee had to summon all his diplomatic skill to talk him out of it. Next came a conference with General Pillow at which Lee sketched the plan of attack that Scott had described to him earlier that day. Lee then spent the rest of the night visiting the batteries to be sure that instructions were understood. By dawn on the thirteenth, he had been 48 consecutive hours without sleep, but he nevertheless took charge of guiding General Pillow's division in its advance. The artillery thundered, driving the Mexican defenders of Chapultepec to shelter, and the infantry rushed forward, West Pointers James Longstreet, George E. Pickett, and Joseph Hooker leading the way across ground known to be thick with Mexican mines.

In another quarter of the front, Sam Grant and his 4th Regiment went charging out to deal with Mexicans attempting to reinforce Chapultepec. There on the road he saw another West Pointer walking up and down in a hurricane of bullets shouting something toward the bushes and rocks nearby. Around him were piled men and horses, dead or kicking. It was Tom Jackson, who had led what might be called a one-gun charge, advancing so far on the north side of the fortress that he had found himself engaging all the batteries on that flank plus fire from a trench in the road ahead. His gunners had all sought the safety of ditches and rocks on the roadside and Jackson was calling them back. "There's no danger! See, I'm not hit!" Haughty Bill Worth himself ordered Jackson to retire, but the young lieutenant gave the general an argument, declaring it would be less dangerous to stay where he was. He then proceeded to guarantee that if Worth gave him fifty soldiers he would take the barricade on the road ahead.

Just then cheers began floating down from the heights of Chapultepec. From the roof of the military college at its very top, the Mexican flag came down and Lieutenant George E. Pickett ran up the Stars and Stripes.

Now there was nothing left but the charge to Mexico City's gates. Robert E. Lee, half paralyzed from sleeplessness, rode to Generals Worth and Whitman with orders not to waste a moment. He reconnoitered the ground and returned to Scott at Chapultepec. Then he toppled from his saddle, unconscious.

The road to the San Cosme and Belim gates was no Sunday promenade. There were well-defended barricades along both routes. Sam Grant, heading for San Cosme, was among the first to go over several of these barriers. Finally the Americans were within musket-shot of San Cosme itself. They found several thousand Mexicans with artillery, grimly determined to make it their last stand. Coolly surveying the formidable defenses, Sam Grant showed that even though he was a mere infantry officer he knew as much about flanking movements as the august Engineers. Stealing past empty houses until he could hear the Mexican guns on his left, he knocked on the door of a locked church, persuaded the priest "with the little Spanish then at my command" to open the door, and together with his men he dismantled a small cannon, carried it up to the church belfry and put it together. "We were not more than two or three hundred yards from San Cosme," he recalled later. "The shots from our little gun dropped in upon the enemy and created great confusion."

General Worth, coming up at this point, sent his aide, Lieutenant John C. Pemberton, to find out who was firing the gun. Pemberton ordered Grant to report to Worth and the general congratulated him, saying that "every shot was effective."

Meanwhile, professional artillerymen were bringing other guns up on roofs not far from Grant's belfry and were soon pouring a stream of fire into the ranks of San Cosme's defenders. By five o'clock Worth decided it was the moment for a frontal assault, and he ordered Lieutenant Henry J. Hunt, '39, forward with a horse gun to blow a hole through the barricade. Thundering through 150 yards of ferocious Mexican fire, Hunt came within fifty yards of the gate before his horses crashed to the pavement in bloody, foaming agony. He and his men leaped off, cut the trace chains and proceeded to duel with the massed batteries behind the barricade. Worth was so stirred he declared in later years, "It has never been my fortune to witness a more brilliant exhibition of courage and conduct."

At the other assault point, the Belen Gate, equally remarkable courage was displayed. Ordered forward to silence the twenty-one cannon defending the gate, artilleryman Fitz-John Porter, '45, soon found himself alone, his captain and senior lieutenant mortally wounded, and most of the gun crews dispersed. Singlehandedly, Lieutenant Porter dragged an eight-inch howitzer to within 100 yards of the gate, and repulsing a sortie with canister, took on the Mexican batteries. William W. Loring, commander of the infantry regiment to which Porter's battery was attached, went on to a distinguished career as a Civil War general, and finally as a soldier of fortune in the service of the Khedive of Egypt. Toward the end of his life he was asked: "Loring, I suppose you have seen as much fighting as anybody. What was the bravest act you ever saw on any battlefield?" Without hesitation Loring replied, "Fitz-John Porter at the assault on the City of Mexico."

Both gates were soon taken by storm, and by 8 P.M. the Americans had heavy cannon inside the city firing warning shells toward the Grand Plaza. With the outer defenses irrevocably breached, Santa Anna fled and the city surrendered.

Except for some haphazard street fighting, the war was over. While the generals argued about who was going to run for President, West Point quietly noted the achievements of its sons. Five hundred and twenty-three graduates fought under Taylor and Scott in Mexico. Forty-nine were killed, 90 were wounded and 452 won promotions—all but five for distinguished services on the field of battle. Forty-three other graduates who had resigned from the service rejoined and held commands in volunteer regiments—nine serving as full colonels. On December 10, 1847, at a victory dinner in Mexico City, Winfield Scott arose and proposed a toast to West Point. "But for its science," he declared, "this army multiplied by four could not have entered the capital of Mexico."

The American achievement had in fact astonished the entire world. When Scott marched into the interior from Vera Cruz, abandoning his base of supply to live off the country, the Duke of Wellington himself had predicted his annihilation. Quartermaster General Thomas S. Jesup pointed out with pride that the Americans had accomplished more in Mexico in six months than France had been able to achieve in Algiers in seventeen years. Landing with 12,000 men, Scott fought a total of 30,000 Mexicans. Although the enemy was always entrenched and on the defensive, the Americans did not lose a single battle. They killed and wounded at least 7000 Mexicans, captured 3730, including thirteen generals and three ex-presidents, 75 field guns, 57 cannon fixed in fortresses and 20,000 small arms.

But the most important point for the professional soldier was the contrast between Mexico and the War of 1812. In Mexico, with less than 6000 men fit for duty, Scott fought his way into the enemy's capital. In 1812, 6000 American militia abandoned the defense of their capital and fled the battlefield with the loss of only nineteen killed and wounded. In the War of 1812, the American government put a total of 521,622 men in the field, only ten percent of them regulars, eighty-eight percent militia and only two percent volunteers. Yet all our attempts to invade Canada were baffled by a professional British army numbering less than 5000 men. In the Mexican War, only 104,284 Americans became soldiers, and only twelve percent of these were militia. Fifty-eight percent were volunteers and thirty percent were regulars. None of the disasters predicted by West Point's Congressional critics had occurred. As for the shrill cries of Alden Partridge that West Point created coddled aristocrats, too scholarly to fight, these also had vanished in the smoke and flame of Palo Alto, Buena Vista, Cerro Gordo and Chapultepec.

V

THE 1850'S HAVE BEEN CALLED West Point's golden years. The Thayer-trained faculty, still built around Mahan, was in full flower. The commanding general of the Army, Winfield Scott, doted on the school. Typical of the Academy's new status in Washington was the announcement by William L. Marcy, President Polk's Secretary of War, that the flags and other trophies captured in Mexico would be deposited in West Point. "Among the considerations which render the U.S. Military Academy . . . an appropriate depository of the trophies . . . of our arms in Mexico is the admitted fact that the graduates of that institution contributed in an eminent degree to our unexampled career of success." New barracks, a riding academy and a new mess hall were added in a handsome improvement program begun by Major Delafield and continued by his successor, Captain Henry Brewerton, 1819.

Off the national stage, that once formidable bugaboo, Alden Partridge, died in frustrated obscurity in 1854, and his wife wrote a pleading letter to Joseph Swift, asking his help in getting one of her sons into West Point. Toward the end of his life, Partridge had met Swift on an Erie Canal boat. Rather than face his ex-friend and protector, Old Pewt had gotten out of the boat and trudged along the towpath with the mules.

But for the men of West Point, these golden years were to be marred by an ugly argument that at the beginning of the 1850's merely loomed on the horizon, a scarcely believable cloud. The vast new territories, fruits of the victorious Mexican War, were, ironically, the source of the turbulence. The South demanded the right to bring slaves into these territories with impunity. In the North the growing group of Abolitionists called on Congress to forbid the spread of slavery a foot beyond the boundary of its present dominion. With the union balanced precariously between fifteen free and fifteen slave states, extremists on both sides began warning of bloody conflict.

As early as 1850, John C. Calhoun was openly stating that secession was the only course left to the South. In Mississippi, Jefferson Davis was equally convinced, and called for a convention at Nashville to plan resistance to Northern "aggression." In New York, William H. Seward spoke for a law higher than the Constitution. Inevitably, this agitation began to infiltrate the Military Academy.

Before the Mexican War the question was considered outside the range of polite discussion. There is a tradition that Ulysses S. Grant and his roommate, Missourian Fred Dent, once got into an argument over slavery, stripped to the waist and were ready to go at each other when both boys simultaneously decided the argument was ridiculous and burst out laughing. Isaac Ingalls Stevens, writing home to his father in 1836, when ex-President John Quincy Adams was attacking slavery in Congress, summed up the prevailing Academy opinion when he said, "Ought the sages of our land like Mr. Adams at this time to agitate a question which, in the opinion of the South infringes upon their rights and which, inflexible as we know them to be in their maintenance, will cause them to look upon a secession from the Union as the only means of preserving them? The South are sensible of the evils of slavery. They deplore the existence of this curse, entailed upon them against their consent by the arbitrary decrees of England and I believe that (if left to themselves) they will adopt some measures to rid themselves of it."

Stevens, as a top student, was a member of the cadet dialectic society, and in another letter he told of having "an animated discussion the other evening on the justice of lynch law. We got very warm; indeed the debate came very near merging into the discussion of abolition. This, you are aware, is a very tender subject and for our Society, a very improper one. For my own part I got very much excited and my free avowal of abolition principles did not tend to allay the feeling which existed among the members."

A high-minded young puritan from Andover, Massachusetts, Ingalls also foreshadowed in another letter what became a major problem within the Academy, as slavery burgeoned into the great national issue of the fifties. "Many of the cadets, chiefly those who come from the slavery states, have a great contempt for our Yankee farmers and even pretend to compare them with their slaves . . . For my own part I shall always respect every man who is honest and industrious and more particularly those who live in the manner that has been ordained by God himself; and whenever any man in conversation with me or in my hearing compares that class of which I am proud to be one with slaves I shall always consider it as an insult offered to myself, and shall act accordingly."

Another incident, underscoring the growing hostility between Northern and Southern cadets, occurred in 1847 when Cadet William L. Crittenden of Kentucky attacked George H. Derby of Massachusetts with his sword. Derby, a humorist who later won national fame under the pseudonym "John Phoenix, Esq., the Veritable Squibob," told his mother how the fight started. "Last Sunday, immediately after the divine service, as I was entering the north barrack door I observed Cadet Crittenden (with whom I was not on very good terms) standing near. Happening to catch my eye as he passed in, he exclaimed, 'What do you mean, sir?'

"Said I to him, 'Mean by what, sir?'

" 'By looking at me, sir,' replied he.

"Said I, 'Do you consider yourself too good to be looked at, sir?'

" 'Yes, sir,' said he, 'I do. And if you give me any more of words, g-d d-n you, I'll run you through.' "

With these words Crittenden placed his hand on his sword. Derby, not giving an inch, said, "You must be a miserable coward to threaten an unarmed man with a sword."

"The words were scarcely out of my mouth," Derby said, "when he drew his sword and chopped me three times over the head, cutting a tremendous gash on my chin bone and wounding my right arm and shoulder—upon recovering from the first effects of the blow I made at him but he was immediately captured and held by a couple of men. Therefore thinking it cowardly to strike him while he was held, I refrained and am consequently sorry to inform you that I didn't get a clip back."

Crittenden had great political influence; he was not expelled. He graduated at the foot of his class, served in the Mexican War, then resigned and ended his life in 1851 facing a Spanish firing squad after leading a nineteenth-century rehearsal for a "Bay of Pigs" fiasco. The expedition, financed by Southern fire-eaters, was supposed to "liberate" Cuba and convert it into the sixteenth and seventeenth slave states. Robert E. Lee was offered the leadership, and wisely turned it down.

There were other reasons for North-South hostility, besides slavery. Southerners generally found it hard to compete with the better-schooled boys from New England. Richard Ewell, writing to his sister in 1836, said, "I have no hopes of getting a good standing at this place. The plebe class consists in all of nearly 150 and is said to be the most intelligent class that has been here for many years. There are several Yankees here who know the whole mathematical course. Of course they will stand at the head of the class. A person who comes here without a knowledge has to contend against those who have been preparing themselves for years under the best teachers and who have used the same class books. The Yankees generally take the lead in almost every class . . ."

Consoling themselves, the Southerners emphasized the military side of the Academy life. They devoutly believed that Southerners were born with the gift of leadership. They substantiated their claims by pointing to the far greater number of resignations among New Englanders to pursue civilian careers. Between the two groups stood the Westerners, a minority in the overall aggregate of Academy graduates, but bulking larger with each passing year as more and more territories organized themselves into states. Both Southerners and Northerners admired the relaxed, easygoing approach of these sons of the border. Plebe John Schofield, in 1849, found himself rooming with "two charming fellows from Virginia." They had hardly learned each others' names when one of them said something about the "blank Yankees." When Schofield flushed, the Virginian said, "You are not a Yankee!"

Schofield replied: "Yes, I'm from Illinois."

"Oh," said the Southern cadet, "we don't call Western men Yankees."

"In that remark," Schofield says, "I found my mission at West Point as in after life to be as far as possible a peacemaker between the hostile sections."

VI

NO MAN TRIED HARDER to be a peacemaker than Robert E. Lee, who became the school's ninth Superintendent on September 1, 1852. After the Mexican War Lee had returned to duty in the Engineering Corps, building forts in Baltimore and elsewhere. On the academic side, he took over from Captain Brewerton a smoothly running Academy. No less an authority than Horace Mann had said, in 1849, when serving on the Board of Visitors, "The committee (on instruction) would express the opinion that when they consider the length of the course and the severity of the studies pursued at the Academy, they have rarely if ever seen anything that equalled the excellence of the teaching or the proficiency of the taught."

Lee brought to his task something new in West Point's history—an ability to combine wide personal appeal among the cadets without endangering the school's discipline. Erasmus D. Keyes of the class of 1832, who came to know the handsome Virginian well during his Superintendency, declared, "Of all the hundreds of southern men with whom I have been intimate, George H. Thomas and Robert E. Lee were the fairest in their judgment of northern men."

From the day he took command, Lee struggled to heal the already mounting sectional bitterness. Again and again he reminded the corps that they were a "band of brothers." As Superintendent, Lee had another advantage, unique in West Point's history thus far. George Washington Custis Lee, his oldest son, was a cadet in the class of 1854. Entering in 1850, Custis had at first shown alarming symptoms of indolence. But some prodding by mail, plus the news that his father was arriving as Superintendent had inspired the young man to an outburst of effort which soon had him rising rapidly in his class. His presence gave Lee an unparalleled opportunity to invite him and his friends for informal visits on Saturday afternoon, or to small dinner parties. On occasion the Lees would use George Washington's silverware, which Mrs. Lee had inherited as Martha Washington's great-granddaughter. This never failed to thrill the cadets.

Lee worried and fretted over each boy's progress. If a prodigal returned to his books, he won praise from the Superintendent. If a cadet did not write home, Lee found out why. When he saw a boy was in danger of failing, he watched his standing week by week, would talk over his case with the faculty and sometimes would call the boy in to discuss his decline during the 7–8 A.M. office hour. Often he wrote parents, urging them to spur an indolent son. If all his efforts proved useless, he frequently chose the only alternative left—he asked the parents to permit the boy to resign to save him the humiliation of dismissal. About one of these failing cadets Lee wrote: "He is a youth of such fine feelings and good character that I should not like to subject him to the mortification of failure to which he might give more value than it deserves. For I consider the character of no man affected by a want of success provided he has made an honest effort to succeed."

When a boy was in danger of dismissal for demerits, Lee sometimes wrote a parent and explained exactly why the young man was in trouble. He made a point of doing this when there was no serious offense involved. "You must not, however," he wrote in one case, "infer that his conduct has been in the least disgraceful or calculated to affect his moral character or standing. His amount of demerit has risen from acts of carelessness, inattention to his duties and to the regulation of police and discipline of the Academy which it is necessary for a good soldier to correct."

One day when Lee was out riding with his youngest son Robert, they came upon three cadets who were far out of bounds. Spotting the Superintendent, the cadets vaulted over the wall by the roadside and disappeared into the woods. "We rode on for a minute in silence," young Lee recalled later. "Then my father said, 'Did you know those young men? But, no; if you did don't say so. I wish boys would do what is right. It would be so much easier for all parties.' "

Lee was always ready to forgive a cadet who repented. Even the few boys who ran away from the Academy and returned days later were given another chance. Once he permitted a cadet who had lied to the officer of the day to remain in the corps when the boy confessed and convinced Lee he had learned a lesson.

Nothing stirred Lee more than a chivalrous gesture. One day a high-spirited joker from New York, Archibald Gracie, Jr., found a way to torment a fellow cadet, Wharton Green, while parading. Gracie again and again stepped on Green's heels, causing him to stumble and receive furious verbal punishment from his cadet sergeant. The moment the march was over, Green proceeded to clobber Gracie right out on the drill field. A tactical officer rushed up and stopped the battle. Green did an instant vanishing act, but Gracie stood his ground, and gave his name and class. When asked who his antagonist was, Gracie answered, "You'll have to ask him, I'm no informer."

Next morning Green appeared before Superintendent Lee during cadet office hours. "Colonel Lee," he said, "Mr. Gracie was yesterday reported for fighting on the parade ground and the other fellow was not."

"Yes, sir," said Lee. "And I presume you are the other fellow."

"I am, sir, and I wish to submit the case in full for your consideration. Don't you think it very hard on him, Colonel, after getting the worst of the fracas to have to take all the penalty?"

"Admitted," said Lee. "What then?"

"Simply this, sir. Whatever punishment is meted out to him, I insist on having the same given to me."

"The offense entails a heavy penalty," Lee warned.

"I am aware of the fact, Colonel, but Mr. Gracie is not entitled to a monopoly of it."

This was too much gallantry for Lee's Virginian nature to resist. "No, sir," he said, "you will get neither report nor penalty for this and neither will Mr. Gracie. I will cancel the report. Don't you think, Mr. Green, that it is better for brothers to dwell together in peace and harmony?"

"Yes, Colonel," said young Green, "and if we were all like you it would be an easy thing to do."

Lee soon found touching, if somewhat unorthodox, proof that his efforts to promote brotherhood in the corps were not in vain. There was another relation in the cadet corps, Fitzhugh, son of his brother Smith Lee. Fitz did nothing to endear himself to his professors, but he had inherited quantities of the Lee charm and he was enormously popular among his classmates. One of the reasons for his popularity was his fondness for breaking the rules. One night Fitz and two other cadets were caught sneaking back on the post after being absent from barracks between 12 and 5 A.M. Thanks to this and other escapades, Fitz piled up 197 demerits by the end of the school year and Colonel Lee decided to deprive him of his summer leave. The jolly young man (someone said he looked and acted like he had been painted by Franz Hals) seemed to take his punishment with good grace, until one night toward the end of July when he slipped out of camp with another cadet about midnight and did not return until 2:30. Caught once more and placed under arrest, Fitz seemed to be a lost cause. Lee could only forward his papers to Washington and recommend a court-martial.

But to the Superintendent's surprise (and secret delight) the entire class came to Fitz's rescue. They made a unanimous pledge not to go out of bounds for the remainder of the school year if Fitz and his companion in crime were forgiven. Though Lee admitted, "that in a military point of view" such an agreement between the school and the corps was irregular, he recommended to the Secretary of War Jefferson Davis that "the pledge be accepted, the charges withdrawn." The Secretary agreed and Fitz survived to graduate, number 45 in a class of 49, in 1856.

Superintendent Lee's favorite cadet was an ebullient young Virginian named James Ewell Brown Stuart. A veritable fountain of charm, "Jeb" never let his decidedly unhandsome face, with its receding chin, trouble him. He always had the best-looking girls on the post swarming around him, and his fellow cadets called him "Beauty" in ironic tribute to his ability to overcome his looks.

Lee's fondness for Stuart can be seen in the way he extricated Jeb from several scrapes. Once, while Stuart was serving as orderly sergeant in the mess room, someone made a derogatory remark, probably about Southerners. Instead of putting him on report, Stuart slugged him, and soon was the center of a battle royal, involving at least four other cadets. Lee could have punished Jeb severely. But he let him off with a simple reprimand, which he turned into a lecture to the corps on "the evil tendency of such offenses."

Less than a month later, Stuart was in trouble again, this time for speaking disrespectfully to one of his instructors. Again, he had responded instinctively to what he considered a slur, and again, the Superintendent could not find it in his heart to do more than issue another reprimand. "It is difficult to understand how one of Cadet Stuart's intelligence should have failed to see the impropriety of this course," Lee said, "as it is to believe that he intentionally committed a fault so utterly at variance with his generally correct deportment . . ."

Why Lee felt this way can be glimpsed from the way Stuart responded to the plight of an earnest young cadet from Maine, Oliver O. Howard.

As devout as he was brilliant, Howard aroused Southern antagonism by his stridently abolitionist views, and his high standing in the class. They began to "cut" him as he walked the Plain—an ostracism that spread until it included almost the entire corps. "For a time," Howard said later, "I confess that my life at West Point was wretched." But when Howard challenged his tormentors and distributed a few black eyes and loosened teeth, Jeb Stuart was among the first to step forward, and by his action make it clear that Howard's ordeal was over. "I can never forget his manliness," Howard said. "He spoke to me, he visited me and we became warm friends." Jeb even introduced the solemn young puritan to his bevy of girl friends, and this, some say, did more to soften Howard's prickly manner than anything else.

Superintendent Lee could also be tough. When he took charge he discovered what was on its way to becoming a pattern at West Point. Toward the end of every Superintendent's reign, discipline began to slide. The Commandant of Cadets, Robert S. Garnett, informed him that a cadet who had reported sick had actually boarded a train and headed for the bright lights of Broadway. His company officer, a cadet lieutenant, refused to testify against him. Lee wrote the War Department angrily declaring that the cadet lieutenant should be court-martialed, but he added that if the Department thought he ought to be dismissed outright—a court-martial board might well have inflicted a lighter penalty—the Superintendent was ready to go along. The rebel wilted after a few days' reflection and decided he was ready to testify against the disappearing cadet.

John Schofield, of the class of 1853, later revealed in his memoirs that he may well have been the originator of these New York expeditions, which Lee discovered were much more common than anyone suspected. Schofield made a bet that he could get to the city and back undetected between the two roll calls he had to attend that particular day. "Old Benny Havens of blessed memory rowed me across the river to Garrison and the Cold Spring ferryman back to the Point a few minutes before evening parade. I walked across the Plain in full view of the crowd of officers and ladies and appeared in ranks at roll call as innocent as anybody. It is true my up train did not stop at Garrison or Cold Spring, but the conductor, upon a hint as to the necessity of the case, kindly slacked the speed of the express so that I could jump off from the rear platform."

With the wholehearted support of Jefferson Davis, now Secretary of War under President Polk, Lee toughened discipline with another new regulation. Previously a cadet could not be dismissed until he had accumulated 200 demerits in twelve months. Lee noted that too many cadets allowed demerits to pile up during the early months, betting on luck and willpower to squeak them through the end of the year. Henceforth a hundred demerits at the end of six months would be fatal.

Another of Lee's problems was a cadet who entered the Academy in July, 1851, as James A. Whistler. In later years he would add McNeill as a middle name and become one of the century's best-known artists. Whistler's long black hair, of which he was extremely proud, won him the nickname "Curly." Army was in his blood and he did his best to cope with the West Point course. But his sarcastic wit and tendency to study only what interested him soon had him in trouble.

Almost from the day he arrived, the boy sat around with a pencil in his hand sketching practically everything he saw. Fortunately, the adjutant of the corps of cadets, William Boggs, took a special interest in the newcomer and noticed this artistic production, which Whistler considered little more than doodling. These discards are part of the collection of Whistler drawings in the West Point library today.

His talent probably saved Cadet Whistler from an early departure. In later years Boggs told how one day during his first summer encampment he noticed a faint column of smoke curling toward the blue sky from a clump of trees. Strolling over to investigate, Boggs found Whistler calmly engaged in roasting corn. As cadet adjutant he could have put him under arrest, but instead Boggs just walked on and never reported him.

Whistler's attitude toward the Academy's course in drawing became evident one day when the professor, William Weir (who had a national reputation), attempted to retouch an India-ink sketch on which the young man was working. When Whistler saw Weir advancing with raised brush, he stepped in front of his drawing and cried out: "Oh, don't, sir, don't, you'll spoil it!"

But it was in the riding hall that Whistler became a legend in his cadet days. Once when a refractory steed pitched him headfirst into the tanbark, the riding instructor dryly remarked, "Mr. Whistler, I am pleased to see you for once at the head of your class!" Another time, Boggs, who was serving as an assistant instructor, heard Whistler arguing with the cadet next to him, trying to persuade him to swap horses. Whistler was riding a huge horse; the other cadet, a big muscular fellow, was sitting on a lightweight pony.

One of the dragoons who was assisting in the instruction overheard the argument and rode up to say, "Oh, don't swap, don't you swap, Mr. Whistler. Yours is a war horse, sir."

"A war horse," exclaimed Whistler. "That settles it, I certainly don't want him."

"Yes, you do," said the dragoon, who obviously knew this man. "He's a war horse, I tell you. He'd rather die than run."

At the end of his first year, young Whistler's health collapsed. The doctors diagnosed a number of diseases, including rheumatism and a possibility of tuberculosis. He missed his final examinations, but a vacation with his mother mended him rapidly, and he returned on August 28, 1853, and passed all his subjects, standing thirty-seventh in mathematics, thirteenth in French and first in drawing. In September he rejoined his class, but the weeks he had spent away from West Point proved fatal. He piled up demerits and ignored almost totally a number of subjects, especially chemistry. In the June, 1853 examinations he was asked to discuss silicon. Whistler rose, the picture of confidence, and said, "I am required to discuss the subject of silicon. Silicon is a gas—"

"That will do, Mr. Whistler," said the examiner.

His failure in chemistry, his low standing in other subjects and his mountain of black marks spelled finis for Cadet Whistler. The young man and his mother objected vigorously to the Superintendent's decision, and a year later Lee was forced to write a long letter to General Totten in the War Office explaining in detail why Whistler could not be reappointed. In later years Whistler came to treat the whole matter as a joke and loved to startle ladies at London dinner parties by remarking, "If silicon was a gas, I would be a major general today."

An Ohio cadet named Philip Sheridan was lucky to have Lee as Superintendent during part of his cadet tour. This future general in chief was not a model student. He was, in the first place, physically déclassé. The long, flowing lines of the West Point uniform looked strange on Sheridan's 5'5" peasant physique, which was long in the arms, short in the legs. At the end of six months he stood fortieth in a class of sixty-five, but he hastened to point out in a letter home that fifteen of the men above him had graduated from college, and thirty of them spoke the

A not very perturbed "spoony" cadet is ambushed on Flirtation Walk in the 1880's and despoiled of his buttons. *Culver Pictures*.

The colored cadet scandal of 1880. J. C. Whittaker of South Carolina was found in his room, seemingly unconscious and bleeding from an apparent assault. An exhaustive investigation concluded that his wounds were self-inflicted. The cadet corps ostracized the thirteen Negro cadets admitted during the first five decades after the Civil War. Nevertheless, five graduated. *Culver Pictures.*

The evolution of a leader. John J. Pershing as the First Captain of the Class of 1886 (above), and as Commander in Chief of the AEF in 1918. "He was the leader in our class, not in his studies, but in everything else," said his roommate. In France Pershing issued an historic order: "The standards for the American Army will be those of West Point." *U.S. Military Academy Archives* (above), *Culver Pictures* (below).

Target Practice at West Point.

The hazing scandal of 1900, as seen by a cartoonist. Ex-cadet Oscar L. Booz died several months after he resigned, and his family blamed the tobasco sauce he was forced to drink as part of his plebe hazing. A Congressional investigation forced the corps to renounce hazing—temporarily. *Culver Pictures.*

French language fluently. The stumpy Irish lad found a friend in his roommate, Henry W. Slocum. After taps the two boys would hang a blanket over the one window of their room and Slocum would tutor Sheridan far into the night. Thanks to this kindness, Sheridan went before the academic board, he later said, "with less uneasiness than would have been the case . . . When it was over, a self-confidence in my capacity was established that had not existed hitherto."

On top of looking more like a private than an officer, Sheridan was an Irish Catholic in a decade when the anti-Catholic feelings of native Americans were running high. The famine of 1848–49 had sent hundreds of thousands of Irish peasants pouring into the United States. An Irish family like the Sheridans, who had come much earlier, felt the sting of the criticism these unlettered primitives drew. In every one of his cadet years Sheridan came close to being expelled for demerits, most of them collected for fighting.

Sheridan's worst fracas was with Cadet Sergeant William R. Terrill. A Virginian with an imperious manner, Terrill gave Sheridan an order on the parade ground one September afternoon in 1851 in what Sheridan later called "an improper tone." The order was to "dress" in a certain direction—to line up more precisely with the cadet to the right and left to maintain precision. Sheridan replied that he was accurately dressed. The cadet sergeant told him in scorching terms that he was wrong. Sheridan lowered his bayonet and charged. Terrill, in one version of the story, danced away from Sheridan's first lunge and ran for his life. By this time Sheridan had regained control of himself, but he had committed an almost unbelievable breach of military etiquette. Terrill placed him on report. Undaunted, the next time Sheridan met his antagonist he swung for his jaw. Terrill was bigger and heavier, and he was in the process of giving his bantam opponent a bad beating when one of the tactical officers interrupted them.

Sheridan was obviously in the wrong both times, but West Point knew a soldier when it saw one. More than once the tactical officers had looked the other way while Sheridan was carried back to the barracks on a shutter after losing another brawl with one of his aristocratic tormentors. Instead of dismissal, the decision was to suspend Sheridan for a year. When he returned to West Point, he went right back to fighting anyone who even hinted at insulting him. At graduation he was within five demerits of expulsion, and there is a tradition, without actual evidence to support it, that Sheridan had actually gone over the limit. But the tactical officers and the Commandant had once more interceded for him, and Lee and the academic board agreed to spare this born warrior for the Army.

No wonder that when Jefferson Davis, at the time Secretary of War in the Cabinet of President Franklin Pierce, visited Lee at the Academy, he was "surprised to see so many grey hairs on his head: he [Lee] confessed that the cadets did exceedingly worry him and that it was perceptible that his sympathy with young people was rather an impediment than a qualification for the superintendency." This was at least one of the reasons why Lee was not averse to a transfer. When Jefferson Davis nominated the Superintendent for lieutenant colonel of the newly formed 2nd Cavalry Regiment, Lee accepted and rode away from West Point to six years of frontier duty in Texas.

Lee's replacement as Superintendent was Captain John G. Barnard. Another top graduate of the class of 1833, he was a distinguished scientist and a prolific writer on engineering subjects. His appointment reflected a mild dissatisfaction with West Point's scholarly achievements. A college education had, by 1850, no longer become the property of a select, often indolent few. The higher education movement was in full swing, and both culture and science were being taught with vigor in dozens of schools. Many of these science programs could trace their ancestry to West Point.

Another strong influence was Rensselaer Institute, which established the first student laboratories for chemistry and physics in 1824 and the first civilian American engineering degrees in 1835. Yale and Harvard began awarding degrees in science around the same time. Because these schools had no military training to worry about, their students were able to go much farther than the average cadet in literature and languages. The ferment produced a drastic change in West Point.

Jefferson Davis, eager to see his old school meet the new competition, approved a recommendation of the 1854 Board of Visitors that the course be made five years instead of four. A growing involvement in Latin America also inspired a suggestion that Spanish be added to the curriculum. Davis agreed and asked the academic board to suggest other subjects that might be added to the expanded course. The board replied that the cadets could profit from the study of constitutional and international law, Spanish, elocution, composition, rhetoric and geography. Of this staggering array, only Spanish was immediately added. As for the cadets themselves, they were considerably more interested in the decision to divide the plebes of 1854–55 into two classes, who would graduate a year apart. There was, as might be expected, not a little grumbling and some loud complaints from the cadets who discovered they were to stay an extra year.

Superintendent Barnard did not have time to do much with the scholastic side of West Point. His tour of duty lasted only eighteen months, and he was replaced by Major Delafield, who thus became the only West Point Superintendent to hold the job twice.

Delafield found himself coping with a new phenomenon—a series of critical reports from the Board of Visitors. The 1856 Board was particularly disturbed by the number of cadets who had been turned back and allowed to continue their studies with the class behind them. They felt the practice was being abused and was lowering discipline and academic standards. The following year the Board went off in another direction, severely censuring the Academy for its dismissal rate. "The class graduating 38 members this year entered the Academy four years ago numbering 98," the chairman lamented. "This disparity occurs in almost every graduating class . . . might not the system be modified without injury . . . ?"

The pressure on the academic side was coupled with another outgrowth of gross favoritism, from another Secretary of War, Simon Cameron, in reappointing cadets who had failed. One year 33 cadets were found deficient by the academic board. Among them was President Buchanan's nephew. Many of the failures waited at West Point, hoping that, as one cadet wrote, "the President could not reinstate his nephew alone without according the same second chance to his classmates." But Buchanan coolly reinstated his nephew and let the rest go down the drain. "The most flagrant piece of injustice that this corrupt administration has been guilty of yet," fumed another cadet.

The growing desperation in the corps led to a serious weakening of cadet honor in regard to examinations. While the corps still despised any man who was caught in a lie, or worse, stealing—which included copying from another cadet's blackboard during an examination—they saw nothing wrong with attempting to acquire examinations in advance. The Academy unwittingly created this temptation by requiring the young instructors who taught the various sections to prepare a list of subjects and questions for each cadet. The purpose, as Ohioan Tully McCrea explained in a letter, was "to facilitate the examinations which are always long and laborious to the old professors who compose the board." Naturally, these lists were kept under lock and key by the instructors. But the intimacy of West Point life made it relatively easy for cadets to figure out the most likely hiding places. Tully McCrea tells of one adventure by twelve of his classmates who were found deficient in French and had five days to prepare themselves for a reexamination. "They knew that they could not learn in five days all that would be required of them at the examination and concluded that if they could not manage some means to get a list of the subjects that they would fail at the examination and be sent off. But how to get the list was the great and difficult question. They first tried to bribe one of the servants of the instructor. She was willing to do all that she could but said that Lieutenant Jenkins kept the list in a desk locked and the key in his pocket . . .

"So this plan failed but they were not inclined to give it up so, for it was almost a matter of life and death to them and they determined to try and enter the house after night. Consequently, three of them disguised themselves and went to the house between two and three o'clock at night when they knew that everyone in the house would be sound asleep. They entered at the window, lit the gas in the room, found the desk that contained the coveted list and unlocked it with a false key. They then sat down and deliberately copied off every subject, placed everything as they had found it, locked the desk, put out the light and came back to the barracks rejoicing. Everyone then knew his subject and it was only necessary to learn it thoroughly to pass the examination."

McCrea then went on to tell how the cadets cleared the next hurdle, which was "not to create a suspicion in the mind of the professors and instructor by appearing to know too much." Although they had the answer to every question memorized, the delinquents would "write down a part of a sentence and examine it as if they were doubtful about it and then they would rub it off the board and put on another, but always ending by putting down the right one." The French professor was dazzled by their performance and could only murmur that he had never seen so much French learned in so short a time in his life.

Another desperate cadet, who was failing in rhetoric, bribed a servant girl to smuggle him into his instructor's house, give him the coveted list and then stand guard while he copied off the questions. He was just finishing when the instructor unexpectedly returned. The servant girl bundled the cadet into a handy wood closet. But the officer, as young McCrea tells it, "took a book and settled down as if he intended to make a stay of some length." The servant girl knew that the cadet was in imminent danger of being missed at the barracks and showed herself more than equal to the emergency.

"Sir," she said, "would you mind reading in another room? I want to clean this and stir up the fire."

The officer meekly submitted, and while the girl made a great clattering with the grate of the fireplace, the cadet escaped out the back door.

Tully McCrea voiced the prevailing sympathy with these tactics in a letter to his sweetheart Belle: "This may appear very strange and bold to you and you may think that is not altogether honest, but you must take into consideration the circumstances under which these cadets were placed. You speak in your letter of your own examination and express fears that you will fail. Now suppose that you did fail, what would be the result? Only a little mortification to yourself and friends which would soon wear off as you progressed in your studies. It is altogether different here; we not only have to experience the most intense mortification but have to sustain the disgrace of a dismissal, disappointment to our friends and forever forego all the advantages that are extended to us here. When you take this into consideration, you will see how desperate a cadet can get when he is in danger of dismissal."

McCrea added: "I hope that I may never have to stoop to such a means to pass an examination." But most of the corps obviously felt that such tactics were in the same daring tradition of making a dash to Benny Havens' or stealing the Superintendent's chickens.

VII

MEANWHILE, BOTH THE NATION and the Academy were showing more dangerous signs of strain. In Kansas, Abolitionists and slave owners murdered and burned. Speech-makers on both sides of the Mason-Dixon Line spewed hatred and defiance. On the floor of Congress itself Northerners and Southerners brawled with words and fists. It was hardly surprising that high-spirited young West Pointers were soon imitating their impassioned elders. Fistfights between Northerners and Southerners became commonplace. When First Captain Edward L. Hartz of Pennsylvania reported a Southern classmate for breaking a regulation in 1855, the Southerner called Hartz an insulting name and the first captain bloodied his nose. The Southerner challenged Hartz to a duel but Hartz contemptuously declined, telling him Pennsylvanians considered dueling stupid and silly. In 1858, three Southerners attacked First Captain William Cushing Paine of Massachusetts with swords, just after breaking ranks one day. The next year came a climactic, symbolic conflict between Wade Hampton Gibbes of South Carolina and Emory Upton of New York. Morris Schaff, who was a plebe that year, called it "the most thrilling event in my life as a cadet; and in my judgment it was the most significant in that of West Point itself."

The real cause of the fight was John Brown's raid on Harper's Ferry, on October 17, 1859. The hideous purpose of Brown's fanatical gesture —nothing less than the massacre of Southern whites by freed Negroes— had appalled and infuriated almost every Southern cadet. An added grievance was Brown's seizure of Colonel Lewis Washington, father of cadet James B. Washington and great grandnephew of the first President. Of less immediate emotional impact, but nonetheless ominous, was the death of George W. Turner of the class of 1831. Turner resigned in 1836 and had been living as a prosperous farmer near Harpers Ferry. He was shot dead while returning the fire of John Brown's riflemen on October 17.

In their furious discussion of Brown's raid, Southern cadets frequently singled out Upton as an example of the extremism that had created Brown. Upton had been a student at Oberlin College, an institution that practically required its graduates to major in abolition, and regularly admitted Negro students. From the day he entered West Point, Upton had been an outspoken Abolitionist. During one heated Southern conclave, Gibbes remarked that Upton had probably had special reasons for enjoying his stay at Oberlin, as many of the Negro coeds would be glad to testify. A Northerner overheard the remark and passed it on to Upton. The next day, just after the battalion had broken ranks after marching back from supper, Upton stopped Gibbes and demanded an explanation. Gibbes declined to give one and Upton demanded the right to a gentleman's satisfaction. Gibbes promptly agreed and a room on the first floor of the 1st Division was selected for the conflict.

A fantastic wave of excitement swept the corps. Eyewitness Morris Schaff tells it best. "A crowd soon gathered on the pavement, on the stoop and packed into the hall. I made my way into the 1st Division . . . and gained a place on the stairway. The sentinel, an inexperienced 'yearling' [sophomore] brushed aside and unheeded, was calling loudly for the corporal of the guard. But no one cared for him or his corporal of the guard or any authority vested in them or in anybody else: the excitement was too great as from time to time during the progress of the battle we could hear angry voices, the scuffling of feet and those other dull sounds which fall so heavily on the ear and mean so much."

Only a miracle prevented the conflict from spreading to the stairs where Northern and Southern cadets were equally mingled. Swarthy Felix H. Robertson of Texas, who was nicknamed "Comanche," howled for his fellow Southerners to use bayonets to defend their rights. Finally the door at the head of the stairs opened and Upton stumbled out, his face bleeding. The bigger, stronger Gibbes had mauled him unmercifully.

Then came an incident that burned its way into the memory of every man there. John Rogers of Pennsylvania, Upton's roommate and second, strode to the head of the stairs and eyed the tangled mob there while many of the Southerners howled insults at him. With eyes that Schaff says were "glaring like a panther's," he called out, "If there are any more of you down there who want anything, come right up."

"I am satisfied," Schaff says, "that the South then and there beheld what iron and steel there was in the Northern blood when once it was up."

Another far more dangerous incident erupted in the middle of a cadet play, later in 1859. One of the scenes called for fierce stage combat between Judson Kilpatrick of New Jersey and Jack Garnett of Virginia. Kilpatrick had become another favorite target for the Southerners because he had reportedly made a Republican speech during his furlough. Both men were good swordsmen and they made the scene come alive with fierce clashes and deadly lunges until it was hard for the audience to separate illusion from reality.

Suddenly Comanche Robertson howled, "Kill him, Jack. Kill him."

Instantly Northern voices roared, "Go it, Kil."

Fortunately the two swordsmen kept their heads and finished the scene without inflicting any real wounds.

Politics seemed involved even in the favorite cadet sport of "deviling" plebes. Morris Schaff tells how he was marched to a room and forced to debate the repeal of the Missouri Compromise with an "animal" from Illinois. The administration had repeatedly tried to stamp out this hazing by encouraging the plebes to resist their tormentors and providing severe penalties, even including dismissal, for serious ill-treatment. Plebes on sentry duty were favorite targets, especially during their first summer encampment. Dozens of stratagems were devised to steal a hapless newcomer's musket. Superintendent Brewerton became so enraged over upper-class tactics during his brief reign that he urged plebe sentinels to use their bayonets on their tormentors.

In 1853, John Schofield was dismissed from the Academy because he allowed "deviling" to go on in a class of boys he was prepping for the entrance examination. Eleven of the thirteen members of the court-martial board were ready to recommend clemency; Schofield had collected clouds of demerits for persistent smoking in his room but was otherwise an above average cadet. Brevet Major Fitz-John Porter was one of two officers who insisted on dismissal. Young Schofield headed for Washington, as many a cadet had done before him, and wrung the heart of his Ohio Senator, Stephen Douglas, who in turn twisted the arm of the Secretary of War and thus he was reappointed. Twenty-five years later, Schofield was to sit in judgment on Porter in one of those ironic reversals that make some West Point lives seem borrowed from Greek tragedy.

Even at this early date, hazing sometimes went too far. One plebe, standing his post for the first time, was tormented by several older cadets. In obedience to orders, he jabbed James Hampden Porter of

Pennsylvania with his bayonet. Porter exploded into a mad rage, rushed into an adjoining tent, seized a musket and drove the bayonet into the plebe's leg, opening an artery. The plebe fainted and almost bled to death before he was rushed to the hospital. Porter was court-martialed and dismissed.

Another respite from politics was the visits of celebrities. Far and away the most famous of this era was that of His Royal Highness, the Prince of Wales, later Edward VII. The royal tour of the former colonies marked a turning point in American-English relations. *Harper's Weekly* declared it "one of the most beneficial measures of Queen Victoria's reign . . . The possibility of war, we think, has been diminished by the prince's visit." Though the prince's call at West Point was, from the international and command point of view, an unqualified success, the cadets were not quite so enthusiastic. The prince debarked from the steamboat *Harriet Lane* at the West Point wharf on October 14, 1860. Thirty-three guns belched from Fort Knox, one for each state. The cadets had been confident that recitations and other academic and military chores would be canceled. Instead, the prince insisted that the Academy routine go on without the slightest interruption while he visited the cadets in their classes. Worse, the corps had to stand under arms for three hours, waiting for the royal party to arrive. "This too," grumbled Tully McCrea, "upon the damp ground . . . without our overcoats." The next day Tully summed up his impressions of the royal personage in rather savage terms. "I suppose you are all curious to hear something of the 'dear fellow,' 'sweet boy' as the ladies call him," he wrote to his fiancée. "Well, the prince has come and gone and we have all been able to live through the mighty event. The conclusion that the cadets have come to is that the prince is a grand humbug in the shape of a well dressed Dutch boy with monstrous big feet. He looked to me like a Dutch Jew and a not very intelligent one at that." The corps was further annoyed when the prince declined their invitation to attend a ball in his honor and eat at their mess. They later found out that the "old fogies"—the Duke of Newcastle and General Bruce, who were in charge of the prince's visit—decided against such democratic mingling for the 18-year-old future king, who was most anxious to attend.

In retrospect, one figure looms above these pre-Civil War Academy years. It is not Morris Schaff, who wrote the most penetrating of West Point's many memoirs; nor Upton and Gibbes, those symbolic battlers;

nor Patrick O'Rorke, who stood first in the class of 1861; nor gifted Alonzo Cushing, fated to be a tragic hero of the North; nor John Pelham, the handsome blond Alabamian who was to become a legend of the South; nor Charles Ball, the enormously popular first sergeant of the corps—but the man who stood at the very bottom of the class of June, 1861—George Armstrong Custer. This ebullient young Ohioan was constantly in trouble. Blizzards of demerits descended on him annually. In 1858–59 he received 98 and 94 respectively for the two six-month periods. The temptation to talk in ranks, play forbidden games of cards, throw snowballs at a passing column, was always more than Custer could resist. He was a noted forager and kept a stew pot up his chimney which was discovered by a sharp-eyed tactical officer. He violently resisted getting his blond hair cut. Then one day, after being repeatedly "hived" (given demerits) for long hair, he had himself shaved bald. In Spanish class he asked the instructor how to say "class dismissed" in Spanish. The instructor told him and Custer led his section in a mad bolt out the door.

Inevitably, such endless defiance of authority made him the idol of the corps. John M. Wright, who entered two years later, flatly declared, "The rarest man I knew at West Point was Custer." In a memoir Wright told of seeing Custer return from furlough. "All of us plebes were standing back unnoticed and uncared for in subdued admiration of the happy fellows receiving such hearty greetings from the gray-coated crowd encircling them, when from a hundred throats went out in various forms of ejaculation the exclamation, "Here comes Custer!" Looking beyond the crowd, I saw a cadet in furlough uniform approaching from the guard tent. I failed to note anything in his appearance that warranted the attention he received. I saw only an underdeveloped looking youth with a poor figure, slightly rounded shoulders and an ungainly walk."

No sooner was Custer back in cadet gray than he went to work on the plebes. "We had been 'yanked' by our tormentors of the class just above us until they had grown tired of the sport," Wright recalled. "For a week past we had enjoyed some degree of repose at night but Custer was to have but one night in camp before the corps went into barracks and that night he devoted to organizing a select band of yearlings who crept out of their tents after taps and under the lead of Custer gave every one of us two or three rides a piece down the several company grounds on our blankets."

Since he rarely looked at a book, Custer was one of those cadets who risked his all to steal an instructor's examination notes. Unfortunately for him, his instructor lived at Cozzens Hotel, which was off limits for cadets. But Custer only regarded this as a double challenge. He stole into the hotel by night, found his way to the instructor's room and discovered the book he wanted. But, alas, in the midst of copying the precious questions he heard someone coming, and in a panic ripped out the page and exited via the window. This, as his roommate Tully Mc-Crea said, spoiled everything. As soon as the instructor discovered that the leaf was missing he knew that some cadet had had it. He therefore changed the questions and the risk and trouble was all for nothing. Custer flunked the exam and was dismissed. But then, in the mysterious way that West Point often manages to spare the obstreperous but born soldier, he was reinstated.

Custer's best friend in the corps was Tom Rosser, a tall, swarthy Texan nicknamed "Tam." Two-thirds of Custer's sectionmates—his best friends—came from slave-holding states. Custer vociferously detested Republicans and Abolitionists. He sent violent denunciations of them home to Ohio. As the political pot came to an ominous boil in 1860, Custer excoriated "black-brown Republicans" who "will either deprive a portion of our fellow citizens of their just rights or produce a dissolution of the union. Southerners," he wrote, "have had insult after insult heaped upon them until they are determined no longer to submit to such aggression."

Even the strongest ties of friendship and family political tradition were strained by the mounting bitterness that seeped into the corps from every direction. The political parties, harried and split by slavery, had named their candidates. Lincoln was the "Black Republican" standard-bearer, and the remnants of the Whig Party out of which the Republicans had grown nominated John Bell of Tennessee. The splintered Democrats nominated Stephen A. Douglas of Illinois, and Southern radicals, seceding from the party, nominated John Breckinridge of Kentucky. In October, 1860, a group of Southern cadets decided to anticipate the November results by holding a straw vote at West Point. "A better scheme to embroil the corps and to precipitate hostilities between individuals," Morris Schaff wrote, "could not have been devised." Schaff, who voted for Douglas, went on to tell of Southern rage and indignation when the tallymen reported 64 votes for Lincoln. "It was always a peculiarity, almost childlike in simplicity, for the Old South to take it for granted that everyone was going its way; it never understood the silence of the puritan," Schaff observed.

Not satisfied with simply voicing their wrath, the Southerners promptly appointed tellers for each division to interrogate cadets personally and discover the names of "the Black Republican Abolitionists" in the corps. They were disappointed. Not a single son of New England, which was solemnly Republican, admitted that he had voted for the Railsplitter. But the interrogations produced violent confrontations between Southerners and Northerners. Fistfights broke out by the dozen. Not even Southern sympathizers such as Custer could stomach the intransigence of the more radical Southerners, which, of course, intensified with the election of Lincoln in November. Morris Schaff recalled an argument that erupted in his room when someone read a statement by Senator Ben Wade of Ohio and a Southerner sneered, "Oh—Ben Wade! Don't read what he says."

Though a Democrat, Schaff came to the defense of his state's Republican Senator. The language soon grew hot, and the Southerner, who towered over the diminutive Schaff, was on the brink of violence when the bugle called everyone for recitation. On the way back from class, Custer and a tall Iowan sidled up to Schaff, who was still expecting a beating, and said, "If he lays a hand on you, Morris, we'll maul the earth with him."

In the South after Lincoln's election, politicians began convening to discuss secession. At West Point on the nineteenth of November, red-haired Henry S. Farley of South Carolina handed in his resignation—the first member of the corps to withdraw. Four days later James Hamilton of South Carolina also resigned. Friends and family had obviously forewarned them that South Carolina would secede on December 20. On December 24, Joseph Coger Dixon of Mississippi sent a telegram to his Governor: "The war has begun. I leave tomorrow." One of Custer's best friends, John "Gimlet" Lea, had taken the solemn step with less fanfare on December 11. But the resignation that reverberated throughout the corps was that of Charles P. Ball of Alabama. He was first sergeant of Company A—the preliminary step to the first captaincy, the most coveted position in the corps. Schaff calls him "one of those rare young men who carry with them the fascinating mystery of promise." Ball almost wept when he said goodbye to his battalion and his classmates in an outburst of pure feeling hoisted him to their shoulders and carried him down to the wharf, where the steamboat waited.

In the first month of 1861, the Gulf states, Mississippi, Florida, Alabama, Georgia, Louisiana and Texas, followed South Carolina into secession. But the number of resigning cadets slowed to a trickle. Though most of these young men were deeply involved with the fate of their native states, they were equally involved with West Point. This was especially true of the first classmen. Five long years they had spent in drill and study. Now they were within three heartbreaking months of examination and graduation. Thus many, such as John Pelham and Tom Rosser, stayed on, hoping against hope. "It would be exceedingly gratifying to me and I know to the whole family . . . receive a diploma from this institution," John Pelham wrote. "But fate seems to have willed it otherwise. I don't see any honorable course other than that of tendering my resignation when Alabama leaves the union and offer my services to her . . ." Pelham's father ordered him to wait. He, like so many others, was desperately hoping the quarrel could be settled short of war.

The cadets were not the only ones who persisted in hoping for the best. On January 23 suave Major Pierre G. T. Beauregard, Louisiana Engineers, became Superintendent of West Point, relieving Major Richard Delafield. Three days after Beauregard arrived to take command, Louisiana seceded. Two days later, under orders from the War Department, Delafield replaced Beauregard as Superintendent.

Only recently has a study of Beauregard's correspondence resolved the mystery of this strange shuffle. Like most Regular Army officers, Beauregard was no politician, and paid little attention to the threats of secession being made throughout the South after Lincoln's nomination. As a loyal member of the Engineering Corps he agreed to take the Superintendent's job, to block a Congressional attempt to open that post to all branches of the officer corps. This was no easy decision for Beauregard. He was in the midst of building a new Customs House for New Orleans, a lucrative job in those days when an engineer was permitted to pocket a small percentage of the overall costs. Nevertheless, as he wrote fellow engineer (and former Superintendent) John Barnard, he had decided to "sacrifice five thousand dollars a year and allow my name to be presented for the position and to do all I can to have you put in charge of the new Customs House here, on the condition that you will resign it

in my favor whenever I return to this city—for I attach much importance to finishing it."

The plan worked beautifully, and on November 20 Beauregard received orders appointing him as Superintendent as of January, 1861. On
his way North he stopped off in Washington and candidly admitted that
if Louisiana seceded, he would have to resign his commission and go
with his state. By the time he arrived at West Point, Louisiana was in
convention, on the brink of voting to secede. Beauregard nevertheless
took command, although he never moved into the Superintendent's
quarters, but spent his brief visit in a room at Cozzens Hotel. His
philosophy can best be glimpsed by his answer to a Louisiana cadet who
went to his room one night and asked him if he should resign. "Watch
me," Beauregard replied, "and when I jump, you jump. What's the use
of jumping too soon?"

When Washington relieved him, Beauregard was shocked. He wrote a
letter insisting that he had no intention of resigning his commission
unless the secession of Louisiana was followed by war . . . "As long as I
remain in the service . . . I shall be most scrupulous in the performance
of all my obligations to the government. So long as I keep my opinions
of the present unfortunate condition of our country to myself, I must
respectfully protest against any act of the War Department that might
cast any improper reflections upon my reputation or position in the
Corps of Engineers." As evidence of his integrity, he declared he had
persuaded several cadets who wanted to resign to stay until hostilities
started. Like so many other West Pointers, Beauregard was desperately
attempting to keep one foot on each side of a steadily widening crevasse.

In this, of course, he was not alone. As late as January 22, 1861,
Thomas Rowland, a Virginia cadet in his second year, was writing
home, "Nothing decisive seems to occur in politics. I hope all will be
settled quietly after these gloomy prospects and we may still look forward to a quiet summer in Old Virginia. Only five months more before
furlough."

The events of the next few weeks made such balancing acts totally
impossible. On January 21, Jefferson Davis had addressed the Senate of
the United States for the last time. He spoke as a soldier who had fought
and bled for his country on the battlefields of the Mexican War, as a
statesman who had "striven unsuccessfully to avert the catastrophe
which now impends." Once more he reiterated the arguments that he

devoutly believed. Not James Kent, but the embittered logic of John Calhoun was his guide as he declared that the equality clause of the Declaration of Independence did not apply to Negro slaves, but to the men of the "political community." Secession of a state had always been a right, and had now become a necessity. Again he voiced the hope that since the sections could not live together peacefully, they could separate peacefully. "In the presence of my God," he said solemnly, in his closing, "I wish you well; and such, I am sure, is the feeling of the people whom I represent."

There was no hatred or bitterness in this farewell. Neither was there hatred or bitterness in the heart of the man who faced Davis across the awful division. As deeply as Jefferson Davis believed in the right of secession, Abraham Lincoln believed in the indivisibility of the Union. He warmly approved of outgoing President Buchanan's order, which required the cadet corps to march to the chapel on Washington's birthday and hear "the friendly counsel and almost prophetic warnings" contained in Washington's farewell address. Solemnly the corps had obeyed. In the small pillared chapel, with the painting of the Republic's eagle flanked by a pleading female Peace and a brooding Roman soldier (symbolizing war) above the altar, they had listened to one of the professors read the first President's urgent advice to "properly estimate the immense value of your national union to your collective and individual happiness."

With classes suspended for the rest of the day, the cadets had nothing to do but discuss politics and impending war. By nightfall emotions on both sides had risen to the point of explosion. The full band that had awakened the cadets that morning with "The Star-Spangled Banner" rather than the trumpet of reveille, turned out for tattoo and boomed its way across the Plain to the stirring strains of "Washington's March" until it reached the sallyport, the arched entrance to the "area"—the inner courtyard formed by the cadet barracks.

As the musicians swung into the sallyport they switched to "The Star-Spangled Banner." On both sides of the area cadets filled every window. Suddenly George Armstrong Custer, outspoken friend of Southerners and the Southern cause, experienced an intense change of heart. Heedless as always of regulations, he roared out a cheer for the flag. At a nearby window his best friend Tom Rosser replied with a cheer for Southern rights. The entire corps instantly took sides and the rival shouts thundered back and forth until every throat was hoarse and aching. After that day there was no longer any doubt that West Point—along with the country—was tragically divided.

Jefferson Davis' election produced another flood of cadet resignations. Yet some Southerners still stayed. John Pelham and Tom Rosser were among them, though they were shaken by a rumor that they might be made prisoners of war after Lincoln's inauguration. Finally, on February 27, Pelham and Rosser wrote virtually identical letters to "His Excellency Jeff Davis."

Being still a member of the Mil'y Academy I don't think it would be exactly proper for me to offer my services to the new government. But I am anxious to serve it to the best of my ability. If you think it would be better for me to resign now than to wait and graduate . . . a single word from you will cause me to resign and as soon as my resignation is accepted, I will consider myself under your orders and repair to Montgomery without delay . . . You know the importance of that portion of the course still to be completed, and also whether my services are needed at present. May I expect a recall if needed?

The agonizingly divided state of mind at West Point can be glimpsed in another letter Pelham wrote to his family.

You need not be afraid of piquing my southern feelings by respecting the stars and stripes. Although I am a most ultra secessionist, I am still proud of the American flag. It does not belong to the North any more than to us and has never had anything to do with our wrongs. I think both sides ought, in justice to the illustrious dead, lay it aside as a memento of our past greatness and our revolutionary renown. I would fight harder and longer to tear the stars and stripes from every northern battlement than for any other cause. They have no right to use it and we should not permit them. It should be stored away with our other household goods, preserved spotless and unstained.

Lincoln's March 4 inaugural appeal to "the better angels of our nature" was ignored by North and South. Massachusetts began raising regiments. Early in March, Georgia papers published a list of the officers of the prospective forces of the state and all the Georgia cadets at the Military Academy were included. On the eleventh of March, the Georgians had a meeting and Morris Schaff tells how his roommate, John Asbury West, came back from it and reported with deep sadness that he had resigned. Schaff was heartbroken. West was his closest friend.

"Until I knew him well—I made friends slowly," he said. "A deep sense of loneliness would come over me at intervals as a cadet, a longing for something, and I suppose that something was a friend." Schaff helped West pack his trunk, then walked with him to the cadet limits near the library. Neither said a word. Finally they threw their arms around each other, and, almost sobbing, said good-bye.

Meanwhile, cadets from the unseceded upper South and border states—Virginia, Arkansas, North Carolina, Tennessee, Kentucky, Maryland—could only watch the mounting tension between the two Presidents over the ownership of Fort Sumter, at the mouth of Charleston Harbor. It was an intensely West Point drama. The man in command at Sumter was Major Robert Anderson, who had been at West Point with Jefferson Davis, and had fought beside him in Mexico. Born in Kentucky, Anderson was married to a Georgia girl, and he had once owned slaves and a plantation in that state. But Anderson saw his responsibility clearly. His duty bound him to defend this fort until his government ordered him to evacuate it.

Again and again, Anderson refused Southern demands to surrender. When Confederate forces in Charleston, commanded by Pierre G. T. Beauregard, cut off Sumter's provisions, Lincoln decided to send a U.S. warship with supplies. Hotheads in the Confederate Congress rammed through a resolution demanding that Davis gain possession of the fort, "either by negotiation or force." Reluctantly Davis told Beauregard to send an ultimatum to Major Anderson. He agreed to surrender in two days—when his provisions were exhausted—if he was not supplied by his government.

Although there was little chance of the supply ship getting close to Sumter—one unarmed ship had tried it and had been driven off by Confederate batteries—the staff officers who presented the final demand rejected this delay and ordered their batteries to open fire. In later life one admitted that they feared Presidents Davis and Lincoln might work out a reconciliation and the chance for war would be lost.

At 4:30 A.M. on April 12, Wade Hampton Gibbes, now a lieutenant in the provisional forces of South Carolina, pulled the lanyard of a huge mortar, and sent the first shell arching high over the bay, to explode above the squat, shrouded Federal fort with an enormous crash. A moment later, his fellow West Pointer, Henry Farley, fired a second shell. The war had begun.

Sometime between 8:00 and 9:30 on the morning of April twelfth the New York newspapers arrived at West Point, their headlines black with the thunderous news. A tremendous wave of excitement swept the nation—and, of course, West Point. All day, as the bombardment continued, the cadets talked of nothing else. That night Custer, his roommate Tully McCrea, and every Northern and Western cadet, held a rally in the Fifth Division. "One could have heard us singing 'The Star Spangled Banner' in Cold Spring," McCrea later recalled. "It was the first time I ever saw the Southern contingent cowed. All of their Northern allies had deserted them and they were stunned."

Throughout the twelfth and the thirteenth newspapers continued to arrive, describing the shells bursting over the fort, the buildings burning, the smoke surging up over the flagstaff. In a letter to his sweetheart on the thirteenth, Tully McCrea wrote, "I do not know whether I can answer your letter properly or not, for my thoughts are with Major Anderson and his little band who are fighting so bravely against such fearful odds at Fort Sumter . . . I suppose this will not interest you, and it is not a proper subject for a letter to a young lady, but I can think of nothing else."

War fever engulfed the Academy as Anderson surrendered the ruins of Sumter after a 34-hour bombardment and Lincoln called for 75,000 volunteers. (In Montgomery, Alabama, Jefferson Davis wired Beauregard that he was grateful that not one Federal soldier in the Fort was killed, and added: "If occasion offers, tender my friendly remembrance to Major Anderson.") Tully McCrea wrote home: "Everything is cast aside. The professors complain bitterly about the deficiency of cadets in their recitations and the superintendent says that something will have to be done about it. I imagine that the only way to prevent it is to stop the war."

Fort Sumter united in fierce indignation every Northern and Western cadet. Union meetings were held in dozens of rooms. Massachusetts and her troops were cheered. Cadets marched out of the barracks to the tune of "Yankee Doodle." They ignored regulations and decorated their rooms with paper American flags. A Virginia-born tactical officer ordered Tully McCrea to take his flags down. McCrea responded by painting his water bucket red, white and blue—the regulations were silent on the color of a cadet's bucket.

The day after the firing on Fort Sumter, the Secretary of War ordered all the officers, professors and cadets at West Point to take a new oath of allegiance. The fifth, or plebe, class was the first group required to take it. Thanks to Tully McCrea we have a vivid description of the ceremony.

The fifth class was assembled to take the oath of allegiance to the United States as we have all willingly done heretofore. As it was supposed that some from the slave states would refuse to take the oath, a great many cadets of the other classes had assembled to witness the ceremony. Everything is done on such occasions to make it as solemn and impressive as possible. The oath is administered in the chapel in the presence of the military and academic staff in full uniform. Ten of the class refused to take the oath and, of course, will be dismissed. When the first one refused, a few southern cadets tried to applaud him by stamping on the floor, but he was immediately greeted with such a unanimous hiss that he could clearly see the sentiments of the great majority present.

The same day that the oaths were taken by some, refused by others, news of Virginia's secession reached West Point. This meant for almost all the cadets from the border states the bitter parting of the ways. By April 22, 32 more cadets had resigned, among them John Pelham and Tom Rosser. Their departure was especially heartbreaking because they had passed their final examinations and were within two weeks of graduation. But they all decided they dared not wait any longer if they hoped to reach their native states and play a part in the war. Unlike Charles Ball, these young men slipped out silently into the night, fearful that a sentry or a secret policeman might arrest them along the way. Patriotic fervor had reached almost hysterical heights in New York, and Southern sympathizers were in danger of being mobbed. Some cadets took a roundabout route home via Albany and the Midwest. Others made red, white and blue rosettes out of ribbons, and thus disguised as union patriots, passed safely through New York.

For some there were still poignant farewell scenes. One of the most touching was the departure of Lieutenant Fitzhugh Lee. He did not believe in secession and frankly told everyone that he "hated to desert the old flag." Tully McCrea told how on Friday evening, April 26, Lee "went to every room and shook hands with every one of us, with tears in his eyes and hoped, he said, that our recollections of him would be as happy as those that he had of us." Later that night, Fitzhugh's fellow officers gathered beneath his window and serenaded him, further proof that, as Tully McCrea said, "he was the most popular officer that I have ever seen at West Point. He was liked by the officers, cadets, ladies and, in fact, by everyone that knew him." The next day, as Lee passed in a horse-drawn omnibus, the cadets gathered in front of the barracks and saluted him by doffing their hats—this was the way officers greeted each other in the Army at the time. It was the corps' way of saying that it regarded Fitz as a true friend.

The first class was graduated ahead of schedule in May and received orders to proceed immediately to Washington. Each cadet was required to take the oath of allegiance to the United States before receiving his diploma. The corps was overjoyed to learn that not a single cadet refused, though several were from the slave states. An emotional scene took place that night in the mess hall when the graduates appeared for dinner. Thunderous applause and cheers greeted the new lieutenants. Mess hall stools were pounded on the floor until they broke to pieces. The excitement reached a climax when Henry W. Kingsbury, adjutant of the corps and considered the best soldier in the graduating class, entered. Deeply affected by the cheers, Kingsbury made a speech on behalf of himself and his class which brought tears to many eyes.

A few days later, the corps' pride and enthusiasm seemed rueful in retrospect. Five of the 45 graduates resigned to take commissions in the Confederate Army and a sixth followed several weeks later. Most were from divided border states, two of which—Tennessee and Arkansas— had not yet seceded when they took their oaths and accepted their diplomas. The shock of this defection produced a new oath which everyone at West Point was required to take on May 13, 1861. The old oath simply stated, "I solemnly swear that I will bear true faith and allegiance to the United States of America and I will serve them honestly and faithfully against all their enemies or opposers whatsoever; and that I will observe and obey the orders of the President of the United States and the orders of the officers appointed over me according to the rules and articles of war." Now cadets were required to add: "That I will maintain and defend the sovereignty of the United States paramount to any and all allegiance, sovereignty or fealty I may owe to any state, county or country whatsoever." Two cadets from Kentucky, John C. Singleton and Myron E. Dunlap, refused to take this oath and were dismissed. Returning home, Singleton changed his mind once more, joined the Union Army, and was killed in action.

There were 278 cadets at West Point on the day Lincoln was elected; of this number 86 were appointees from the Southern states and 65 of these were discharged, dismissed or resigned because their first loyalty was to their native states. From Harvard, Yale, Columbia, Union College, Princeton, all of whom had large contingents from the seceding states, Southerners departed en masse. None of these young men had, of course, taken an oath to support the government of the United States, but the Southern cadets argued that the government of the United States ceased to exist once their native states seceded. Many of the Northern cadets agreed with this reasoning. Henry A. du Pont of Delaware advised one of his Southern friends to take the oath, but the boy quailed before the solemnity of kissing the Bible while his mind remained so divided, and instead resigned.

Not long after the first class left for Washington, the new first class circulated a petition addressed to the Secretary of War asking him to allow them to graduate as soon as possible. Since these young men had been at the Academy for four full years and the Army was desperately in need of men to train the citizen soldiers assembling in Washington, the petition received a warm welcome at the War Department, and the class, led by the brilliant New Yorker Patrick O'Rorke and tailed by its favorite bad boy George Armstrong Custer, departed for Washington on June 24, 1861. Custer, true to his style, was left behind, under arrest and threatened with court-martial. A fight had begun in the summer encampment while he was officer of the day. Instead of breaking it up, he had organized a circle around the combatants and proceeded to act as referee. He wound up in the guardhouse along with the battling cadets.

By now, cadets had no illusions about where they were going. Lieutenant John Grebel, who had been an instructor at West Point in 1858, had been killed in action on June 10, 1861, in the battle of Big Bethel, Virginia. The cadets had read the detailed stories of his death and his burial from Independence Hall in Philadelphia, where he had lain in state for three hours. Along with cheers and chances for glory, these boys knew that war meant death for many of them.

On the last Sunday in the chapel every graduating class from West Point traditionally sang the hymn, "When Shall We Meet Again," which concluded mournfully, "Never, no never." Now the words struck home in a new and momentous way. "In all probability," wrote Tully McCrea, "in another year the half of them may be in their graves, the victims of war or disease." The words, written by an average cadet, declared West Point's readiness to meet a new, more radical test.

VIII

THE DIVISION OF MIND and heart among West Pointers was not, of course, limited to the cadets at the Military Academy. Sam Grant had a father-in-law who owned slaves and considered himself a loyal son of the South. In Louisiana, Cump Sherman presided over that state's military academy. George Thomas was bombarded by letters from his two Virginia sisters who saw him as their contribution to the cause. Braxton Bragg of Mexican War fame was known throughout the Army for his outspoken detestation of secession. But all these men were, at the outbreak of the war, nonentities compared to the man who personified so much of West Point's spiritual and intellectual ideals: Robert E. Lee.

Second in command as a colonel of cavalry in the Department of Texas when the great convulsion seized the union, Lee watched the mounting secessionist fervor with undisguised horror. "I am not pleased with the course of the cotton states as they turn themselves," he wrote to his son Custis in the December after Lincoln's election. "While I wish to do what is right, I am unwilling to do what is wrong either at the bidding of the south or the north. One of their plans seems to be the renewal of the slave trade. That I am opposed to on every ground . . ." When Texas seceded, Lee was on his way North, recalled by General Winfield Scott. As he departed, one of his young officers asked him, "Colonel, do you intend to go south or remain north? I am very anxious to know what you propose doing."

"I shall never bear arms against the union," Lee answered, "but it may be necessary for me to carry a musket in defense of my native state, Virginia."

But before he could leave the state, his commanding officer, Brigadier General David E. Twiggs, the man Lee had counseled so well at Cerro Gordo, surrendered to the Texas government and all the Regular Army officers and men became prisoners of war. When Lee heard the news, tears came into his eyes. "Has it come so soon to this?" he said.

His grief turned to indignation a few days later when the Texas commissioners told him that if he resigned his commission and joined the Confederacy they would guarantee him their full cooperation, but if he refused, they would not allow him to transport his possessions out of the state. Lee bluntly told them that his allegiance was to Virginia and to the Union, not to a revolutionary government in Texas. He went to a friend, asked him to be the guardian of his property and left for Washington with little but the clothes on his back.

In the capital, Lee went almost immediately to Winfield Scott's headquarters where the old general and his favorite lieutenant conferred in private for three full hours. Scott told Lee that he considered a clash between North and South inevitable and he hinted strongly that he himself was too old to take the field as an active commander. He therefore needed someone with Lee's talents for his second in command. Lee went home to his handsome house at Arlington and watched in agony as the peace conference called by Virginia dwindled into collapse. When Twiggs was dismissed from the Army on March first for his surrender of Texas, Colonel E. V. Sumner of the 1st Cavalry was named brigadier general to succeed him. Lee was made a full colonel and given Sumner's regiment. On March 28 the commission signed by Abraham Lincoln was forwarded to him and he accepted it, although he had also been offered, on March 15, a commission as a brigadier general in the Army of the South. Then came the bombardment of Fort Sumter, and war fever sweeping both sections toward the irrepressible conflict.

On April 18, Lee had a final conference with Francis P. Blair, formerly editor of the *Congressional Globe*. The old man was a Lee cousin, as well as a friend of numerous Presidents. Meeting him in his house opposite the State War and Navy building on Pennsylvania Avenue, Blair told the graying colonel that he had been authorized by no less than President Lincoln to ask Lee to assume the command of an army of a hundred thousand men, with the rank of a major general. It was the apotheosis of every soldier's dream. But the mournful Lee could only inform his cousin that he could not accept the offer. He told him that "though opposed to secession and deprecating war, I could take no part in an invasion of the southern states." Desperately Blair talked on, but it was useless. Lee went from his house to Scott's office. The old general was a prime mover in the diplomatic plotting to keep Lee in the Army, and he was crushed by the finality of the Virginian's reply. "Lee," said Scott, "you have made the greatest mistake of your life; but I feared it would be so."

That very afternoon came the news that the convention meeting in

Richmond had voted Virginia's secession, thus sealing Lee's decision for him. The next morning, paying a druggist's bill in Alexandria, he made his only recorded observation on his state's enormous step. "I must say," he remarked sadly, "that I am one of those dull creatures that cannot see the good of secession."

Scott had told Lee he should resign because his position was "equivocal." Yet it took Lee two more days of terrible personal struggle before he could bring himself to write the letter of resignation. In a personal note to Scott, he explained that he would have presented the resignation "at once but for the struggle it has cost me to separate myself from a service to which I have devoted all the best years of my life and all the ability I possessed . . . Save in defense of my native state, I never desire again to draw my sword."

Three days later he discovered how vain this wish was to prove. The defense of his native state involved enormous preparations for war on a scale hitherto unknown. Summoned to Richmond, Lee discovered that he was considered Virginia's finest soldier. When Virginia called, he must respond, and Virginia left no doubt that it was calling him. In an emotional scene, the members of the convention appointed him major general in command of all the military and naval forces of the state.

Other West Pointers who were to play major roles in the unfolding national drama reacted with differing but equally intense emotions. Tom Jackson, professor of engineering at Virginia Military Institute, called the war "the sum of all evils" but he marched his cadets to Richmond to volunteer, and accepted a colonel's commission. His sister, along with most of her fellow West Virginians, denounced him and supported the union.

When Cump Sherman, presiding at his Louisiana Military School, heard that South Carolina had seceded, he burst into tears. Sherman had spent much of his army career in the South. His best friends were Southerners—Braxton Bragg, George Thomas. He poured out his emotions to D. F. Boyd, a Virginia-born professor of ancient languages on the faculty. He called the South's plunge to war "folly, madness, a crime against civilization" that would make him fight "against your people whom I love best."

Then Sherman the professional soldier began to talk. "You people speak so lightly of war. You don't know what you are talking about. War is a terrible thing. You mistake too the people of the north. . . . You

are rushing into war with one of the most powerful, ingeniously mechanical, determined people on earth—right at your doors. You are bound to
fail. Only in your spirit and determination are you prepared for war. In
all else you are totally unprepared, with a bad cause to start with. . . . If
your people would but stop and think, they must see that in the end you
will surely fail . . ."

Braxton Bragg of the scowling eyebrows and fierce discipline, whose
austere, tense soul made him seem almost inhuman to so many, unbur-
dened himself to the friend of his West Point youth. Writing of Sherman's decision to go North, he said, "You are acting on a conviction of
duty to yourself and to your family and friends. A similar duty on my
part may throw us into an apparent hostile attitude, but it is too terrible
to contemplate and I will not discuss it.

"You see the course of events—South Carolina's gone, nothing can
recall her. The union is already dissolved . . . The only question is can
we reconstruct any government without bloodshed? I do not think we
can—a few old political hacks and barroom bullies are leading public
opinion . . . I shall continue to hope, though without reason, that Providence will yet avert the great evil. But should the worst come we shall
still be personal friends."

No wonder Sherman could say years later, "I think I knew Bragg as
well as any living man. His heart was never in the Rebel cause." Appointed commander in chief of Louisiana's military forces, Bragg discovered that Sherman at the military school was in charge of a valuable
arsenal needed to store the state's arms. Realizing that this might make
Sherman look a traitor to Northern friends, Bragg wrote to assure him
that he would hire a man to care for the arms or issue special orders for
Sherman to receive them, so no one could accuse Sherman of cooperation with the rebellion.

This did not satisfy Sherman. A few days later, when Bragg and 500
militiamen seized federal forts in Louisiana and sent the captured muskets to Sherman's arsenal, he spoke his mind and called it an act of war
and a "breach of common decency." He then sat down, and eight days
before Louisiana seceded, resigned as commander of the state's military
academy. He told the governor that he had accepted the position, "when
Louisiana was a state in the union and when the motto of the seminary
was asserted in marble over the main door. 'By the liberality of the
general government of the United States. The union—*esto perpetua* . . .'

I prefer to maintain my allegiance to the Constitution as long as a fragment of it survives."

George Thomas, Sherman's best friend from West Point days, underwent a different kind of agony. On March 12, he refused a call from Governor John Letcher of Virginia to resign from the Army and become the state's chief of ordnance. His sisters redoubled their impassioned pleas to return home. But Thomas, unlike Lee, had no deep ties in Virginia. In twenty-five years since his graduation from West Point, he had spent less than eighteen months with his Southern relatives. His wife was from Troy, New York. For Thomas the memory of his West Point education—the gift of his country—was paramount. Writing to his wife, he said as she later recalled his words, "Turn it every way he would, the one thing was uppermost, his duty to the government of the United States." For making this choice, Thomas's property in Virginia was confiscated and his sisters banished him from the family forever. Until their death they refused to permit the name George Henry Thomas to be mentioned in their presence, stonily declaring that they had no such brother.

One might think that a man who resisted such pressures would be considered doubly loyal. But in the fear-ridden atmosphere of 1861 Washington, Thomas's Virginia birth made him automatically suspect. While dozens of West Pointers who had resigned from the Army years before to enter civilian life were becoming generals in command of volunteers, Thomas replaced Lee as colonel of the 2nd Cavalry, and for a while it looked like he would stay there for the rest of the war.

In this situation Thomas was, of course, not alone. The Lincoln government's approach to organizing the nation for war was little short of chaotic. Essentially, Lincoln reverted to the old state militia system, which had proved so disastrous in the War of 1812. Governors were empowered to raise regiments and distribute all commissions up to the rank of colonel. The Regular Army commander in chief, Winfield Scott, contributed to the confusion by refusing to allow regular units to be broken up and scattered through the volunteer regiments. He feared this would destroy the regular organization, with its carefully developed seniority system.

Thus West Pointers who wanted to serve with the volunteers had to abandon their regular commissions and accept "volunteer" commissions, which would expire at the end of the war. As the conflict lengthened, the old men of Scott's circle faded away, and many West Pointers made this shift. But in the early months of the war, when the volunteer regiments desperately needed their professionalism, hundreds of younger graduates who would have switched gladly were sternly advised against doing so. It was almost insanely ironic that the South, fighting for states' rights, organized their war effort as a nation, while the North, fighting for Federal supremacy, fought as a collection of states.

Fortunately for the Union, George Thomas had an influential friend —William Tecumseh Sherman. Cump, already a volunteer brigadier general, thanks to the influence of his brother John, senator from Ohio, did not forget his old classmate. When Robert Anderson, the hero of Fort Sumter, asked Sherman to join him in a mission to raise a Union army in Kentucky and Tennessee, Sherman eagerly assented. Anderson remarked that he was also considering Thomas and two other officers for the rank of brigadier general but was not sure about Thomas' loyalty. Too many officers of the 2nd Cavalry had resigned and gone South. Sherman excitedly vowed that he would stake his own reputation on Thomas' loyalty. Convinced, Anderson persuaded a hesitant Lincoln to name Thomas as a brigadier general.

Sherman eagerly sought out his old friend to tell him the news. "Tom, you're a brigadier general," he crowed. Thomas, imperturbable as always, did not even smile. For a moment Sherman was overwhelmed with doubts. Was the gossip about Thomas' disloyalty true after all? "Where are you going?" Sherman asked.

"I'm going South," said Thomas.

"My God, Tom," roared Sherman. "You've put me in an awful position. I just made myself responsible for your loyalty."

"Give yourself no trouble, Billy," said Thomas. "I'm going South at the head of my troops."

Sam Grant had less trouble making up his mind about his loyalty. He had been out of the Army for almost a decade. Separated from his family on outpost duty in the far West, he had taken to drink and had resigned as an alternative to being cashiered. Failing as a farmer and businessman, Grant was reduced to clerking in his father's leather goods store, in Galena, Illinois. When a friend who had strong Southern sympathies burst in to shout the news that the delegates of the seceding states had organized the Confederacy and chosen Jefferson Davis as President, Grant, looking down on his secessionist friend from a shelf ladder, growled: "Davis and the whole gang of them ought to be hung."

At Army posts around the nation telegrams reporting the news of

Sumter were received with shock and dismay. Dabney H. Maury, the Virginian who had tried to befriend Tom Jackson, described the reaction at Fort Staunton, deep in Indian territory. "It was some time before we could grasp the details. One after another we took the sheet and started to read aloud its contents and each voice, broken with emotion in the effort, refused to do its owner's bidding . . . It was in no light or unappreciative mood that we sat looking at each other in the silence which followed the reading of the telegram; for we realized the greatness of the sacrifice expected of us, and it was with sad hearts that we turned our backs upon the friends and associations of the happy past and faced the issues of a future which had little to offer us save a consciousness of duty loyally performed."

Perhaps the saddest of these partings occurred in the little adobe town of Los Angeles. Tall, soldierly Captain Winfield Scott Hancock and his wife Almira invited Southerners to a farewell party. Among the guests were George Pickett and Dick Garnett, old friends from West Point and Mexican days, and Lewis Armistead, who had failed to graduate with the class of 1837 but had joined the Army two years later and won three promotions for bravery in Mexico.

Pickett had proved himself a superb soldier in the Mexican War and more recently had won national attention when he stoutly resisted British attempts to bully him into withdrawing his small command from a disputed island in Puget Sound. As for Armistead, soldiering was in his blood. He was a nephew of Walker K. Armistead, 1803, whose defense of Baltimore's Fort McHenry had inspired "The Star-Spangled Banner." Both he and Dick Garnett of the class of 1841 were outspoken in their abhorrence of secession. But they could not refuse when "Old Virginia" summoned them to her defense.

The evening was full of suppressed emotion as everyone strove to conceal his true feelings behind smiles and jokes. But as midnight approached, one of the officers asked his wife to play some of their favorite songs, and she sat down at the piano and struck the notes of "Kathleen Mavourneen," that plaintive melody of parting with the mournful words: "It may be for years, and it may be forever."

Armistead looked across the room at Hancock and tears ran freely down the Virginian's face, thinking of Mexican days, Indian fighting in the Everglades, the long march across the plains and mountains from Kansas to California. He put his hands on Hancock's shoulders and said: "Hancock, good-bye. You can never know what this has cost me, and I hope God will strike me dead if I am ever induced to leave my native soil should worst come to worst." Then he handed Mrs. Hancock a small satchel of mementos and personal items and asked her not to open it unless he was killed. In that case he wanted her to keep his prayer book for herself. "There was," Mrs. Hancock said, "not a dry eye in the party" when they said their final good-byes.

In Philadelphia, another young soldier who had distinguished himself in Mexico, John Pemberton of the class of 1837, wrestled with emotions even deeper than friendship. His wealthy mother—indeed all the other members of his distinguished Pennsylvania family—were wholeheartedly with the Union. But Pemberton's heart was in the South, with his pretty dark-haired wife, Patty, whom he had met and married in Norfolk long before. Even in his cadet days, friends recalled that tall, serious John Pemberton was convinced of the justice of the Southern cause. Yet he had everything to gain by remaining with the North, and his family made it clear that they would consider the decision to side with the South as nothing less than treason.

As Pemberton debated with them, his wife wrote him beseeching letters: "My darling husband, why are you not with us? Why do you stay? Jeff Davis has a post ready for you."

When Pemberton was ordered to duty in Washington, one of his brothers sat up all night with him on the train, making a last desperate effort to dissuade him. In the capital, he was sent by the War Department to seize some Southern-owned steamboats at the wharves. He performed the task with dispatch but he made it clear that he would not participate in any plan to invade Virginia. In a tearful letter to another member of the family, Pemberton's mother summed up her son's travail. "His heart and views are that the South is right and we are wrong . . . We have done all we can—John firmly believes it would be the most honorable and right—'tis only for us he hesitates . . ."

A few weeks later, John Pemberton was an officer in the Confederate Army. Within a few months his two brothers became officers in the Union Army.

Other West Pointers wrestled with the hard choice, which could only be made in the lonely world of the inner conscience. Philip St. George Cooke of Virginia chose the Union, although his own son joined the Confederate Army and a daughter was married to Jeb Stuart. Lee's problem cadet, Archibald Gracie, had resigned from the Army in 1856 to go into business in Mobile, Alabama, and he decided his loyalty lay with his adopted state.

A fiery Virginian, Powell Hill of the class of 1847, debated with his old friend, George McClellan of the class of 1846, before resigning. In earlier days they were competitors for the hand of blonde, blue-eyed Nellie Marcy, daughter of Captain Randolph B. Marcy and one of the capital's reigning belles in the early 1850's. Nellie was inclined to Hill, but her domineering parents had forced her to choose McClellan, who had resigned from the Army and become a prosperous Ohio railroad executive. For a time the rivalry had soured their friendship, but now they thought of West Point days and parted with regret. "Hill, I am truly sorry you are going to leave us," McClellan told him, "but to be frank, I cannot blame you. If I were in your place I would do as you are about to do; but I am an Ohioan and I will stand by my state too."

Altogether, 286 West Pointers opted for the Confederacy. Over 100 other Regular Army officers appointed from civil life resigned to fight under the stars and bars. Although the total was by no means over-whelming—defecting West Pointers and civil appointees together to-talled only one third of the 1108 officers on the active list—Southerners had long dominated the Army, under the benevolent eye of Virginia-born Winfield Scott. The fact that the War Secretariat had been ruled by Jefferson Davis of Mississippi and John B. Floyd of Virginia for eight years prior to 1861 also helped to fill the Army's higher posts with Southerners. The loss of so many prominent officers panicked the politicians in Washington.

In a report issued July 1, 1861, Secretary of War Simon Cameron turned the situation into an attack on West Point. "The large dis-affection at the present crisis of United States Army officers has excited the most profound astonishment and naturally provokes in-quiry as to its cause. But for this startling defection the rebellion never could have assumed formidable proportions . . . The majority of these officers solicited and obtained a military education at the hands of the government—a mark of special favor confined by the laws of Congress to only one in 70,000 inhabitants. At the national Military Academy they were received and treated as the adopted children of the republic. By the peculiar relations thus established they virtually became bound by more than ordinary obligations of honor to remain faithful to their flag. The question may be asked in view of the extraordinary treachery displayed whether its promoting cause may not be traced to a radical defect in the system of education itself."

Cameron was an outspoken opponent of a "cumberous and dangerous standing army." In reality he was voicing the old Partridge-militia hostility to the Military Academy. Unfortunately, in the overheated politics of Washington, he found ready audience. The radical wing of the Republican party hailed the report and called for the abolition of the Academy, even accusing it of causing the rebellion. President Lincoln himself did not help matters when he declared in his message to Congress on July 4, "It is worthy of note that while in this the Government's hour of trial, large numbers of those in the army and navy who have been favored as officers have resigned and proved false to the hand which had pampered them. Not one common soldier or common sailor is known to have deserted his flag . . . This is the patriotic instinct of a plain people."

This attitude filled more than one officer with a sense of impending doom. If the President himself was appealing to the demagogic hatred of West Point to arouse the masses, chaos could be the only possible result. For one thing, Lincoln completely ignored the fact that an officer could resign; an enlisted man could only desert, at the risk of being shot. (Longstreet, enroute to volunteer for the South, was asked by a sergeant if he could join him; he sternly reminded the man he had taken an oath to serve out his hitch.) More important, West Pointers felt that the critics were ignoring the important fact that many Southern-born graduates, such as George Thomas, had remained loyal. They included forty-seven Virginians, seven Tennesseans, eight North Carolinians and six sons of South Carolina, where the secession fever burned hottest.

In the South, with a West Pointer at the helm of the government, there was no hesitation about appointing graduates to important commands. In the North, Lincoln clung at first to the aging residue of the old Regular Army commanders who had won their victories in Mexico and had not seen a battlefield since. Scott, stripped of the Southerners he had favored for positions of trust, was helpless. But in Army camps around Washington and in Illinois, Ohio, and Missouri, a comparative handful of West Pointers, mostly men who had resigned and now returned with volunteer commissions, were vigorously at work, molding an army out of the inchoate civilian mass that had rushed forward in response to the President's call.

The way Sam Grant took charge of an Illinois regiment is a remarkable example of what a professional soldier could accomplish. As always, Grant's beginning could not have been more inauspicious. He wrote a letter to Washington, volunteering his services. The government did not even deign to answer it. A friend wangled him a colonel's commission from the governor of Illinois.

Describing his arrival in the camp, another friend wrote, "He was dressed very clumsily in citizens' clothes—an old coat, worn out at the elbows, and a badly dinged plug hat. His men, though ragged and barefooted themselves, had formed a high estimate of what a colonel ought to be, and when Grant walked in among them they began making fun of him.

" 'What a colonel. Damn such a colonel.'

"A few of them, to show off to the others, got behind his back and commenced sparring at him and while one was doing this another gave him such a push that made him hit Grant a terrible blow between the shoulders, knocking off his hat. Without a word, Grant picked up the hat, dusted it and placed it on his head. Then he turned and looked at the men. For the first time they realized he was a soldier."

Walking around the chaotic camp, Grant noted that there was a guard of 80 men with clubs to keep the men from climbing the fence and going into the city to see girls. Calmly, Grant disbanded the guard and informed the gaping soldiers that from now on each man must be present at roll call—there would be several each day. "The effect of that order," said one of the regiment's junior officers, "was wonderful. There was no more climbing the fence after that."

One of the regiment's privates later recalled, "We could not exactly understand the man. He was very soon called the Quiet Man . . . and in a few days reduced matters in camp to perfect order."

Elsewhere West Pointers were analyzing the strategic situation, and outlining with remarkable accuracy the future progress of the war. Senator John Sherman rode out one day with his brother to have dinner with George Thomas in the Maryland countryside near Williamsport, where Thomas was on cavalry duty. Spreading a map on the floor, the two soldiers placed a dot on Richmond, then marked the cities of Knoxville, Chattanooga, Nashville and Vicksburg. "To me," Senator Sherman wrote in his memoirs, "it has always appeared strange that they were able confidently and correctly to designate the lines of operations and strategic points of a war not yet commenced and more strange still that they should be leading actors in great battles at the places designated by them at this country tavern."

In Braintree, Massachusetts, Sylvanus Thayer, now in semi-retirement, assessed the military alternatives just before the Battle of Bull Run for the benefit of his nephew, Jonathan Moulton. Thayer predicted that whichever side advanced first would almost certainly be defeated "and the greater the number of the advancing forces, the more certain their defeat." It would take, he said, at least three years to make a good army. When Moulton asked him who he thought would make a good commander in chief, he replied, "I don't know. I could name some who might do, but the war must develop that. Our best friends may not make the best generals."

Then Moulton made the mistake of suggesting that the South might produce a military genius who could whip the North. Thayer sprang to his feet. "Are you a traitor with the blood of the Thayers in your veins?" he roared. "If you are not, let me hear no more of that; but if you entertain such an opinion, you are an ignoramus, sir, absolutely an ignoramus." Whereupon he walked out of the room, Moulton said, "as stately as I ever saw him walk out of his office after giving a cadet a sound lecture on his misconduct; nor could I draw him into conversation on the subject for 24 hours after it."

Thayer's prophecy was cruelly fulfilled by the Battle of Bull Run. Unable to resist the political pressure of wild-eyed politicians who visualized a one-battle war, Irvin McDowell, '38, marched 25,000 untrained men against 22,000 equally untrained Confederates commanded by his old classmate Beauregard. Neither general had ever directed an army in battle before, but the Southerner had serving with him the pride of the old Regular Army—thirteen of his fifteen top officers were West Pointers. The result was one of the weirdest battles in history, a Union victory in the morning, a Confederate triumph in the afternoon, which Northern newspapers soon magnified into a disaster.

Bull Run proved little. But the next four years revealed a great deal about the men West Point had trained in the art of war. Unlike the Mexican War when West Pointers fought as company officers in separate Regular Army regiments or served as aides on a general's staff, the Civil War summoned them to prove themselves as military executives at the very apex of the art of war. How well did they succeed?

On the Confederate side, Lee and his immediate lieutenants for a while dazzled the civilized world. Always outnumbered, they repeatedly out-generaled Union armies with daring strategy and tactics. Again and again Lee displayed the virtues of a great captain: audacity, correct evaluation of terrain, ability to gauge his adversary's intentions. More than anyone else, Lee bolstered Dennis Hart Mahan's generalization that "there probably has existed no great engineer who when called upon has not shown himself a superior general; nor a great general who did not fully acknowledge and appreciate the art of fortification . . ." Above all, Lee, in daring to invade the North, was illustrating Mahan's approval of operations "which if carried out to their legitimate ends may change the entire aspect of a war . . . when we abandon the portion of our territory invaded by an enemy to carry the war into his. . . . The entire moveable army strikes at the enemy in the heart of his own country. Such resolutions by great generals are stamped with the mark of true genius."

Even more brilliant, in the opinion of some, were the Shenandoah Valley campaigns of Tom Jackson, better known as Stonewall, thanks to a cry by a fellow West Pointer, Barnard Bee, at the Battle of Bull Run. (Some controversy exists as to whether the epithet was meant to be admiring—or critical of Jackson's refusal to come to his aid.) From April 30 to June 9, 1862, Jackson fought a war of maneuver against four Union commanders who outnumbered him four to one. The grim, praying Virginian whom his second in command, Richard Ewell, believed was certifiably insane, marched his "foot cavalry" over 400 miles, managing on all but one occasion to put into action superior numbers on every battlefield. "Attack the enemy suddenly when he is not prepared to resist . . . Secrecy, good troops and a thorough knowledge of the localities are indispensable," Dennis Hart Mahan had lectured at West Point. "The element of time in war gives . . . the initiative to him who understandingly assumes the initiative. . . . Celerity is the secret of success." Jackson proved that he had paid careful attention to the professor's lectures on the art of war. When he died of wounds after the Battle of Chancellorsville, Lee mourned the loss of the man he called "my right arm."

But we must be careful not to attribute too much to Mahan and West Point. Other Southern generals, who had heard the same lectures, were anything but successful as field leaders. Braxton Bragg, who com-

manded the main Southern army in the West during the most crucial
years of the war, was a failure. Albert Sidney Johnson, considered the
beau ideal of the old Army, after Lee, was anything but a success in the
same theater. Both sides paid Mahan the compliment of reprinting and
widely distributing the weirdly titled book in which he condensed his
military wisdom: *Advanced Guard, Outpost and Detachment Service of
Troops with the Essential Principles of Strategy*. But in this little book
(it was small enough to fit into a man's pocket) there was hardly
enough military lore to sustain a Civil War general. Although Mahan did
his best to deepen it with discussions of Napoleon's campaigns and other
examples from history, the book was essentially a series of strategic and
tactical generalizations, and like all academic statements of what is not a
science but an art, it could be read one way by a cautious man and
another way by an audacious one. In regard to pursuit, for instance,
Mahan recommended it strongly, then proceeded to warn against too
vigorous or "headlong" pursuit which a shrewd general could check and
turn into a counterattack to snatch victory out of defeat. These were the
passages Major General George Meade '35 remembered when Lee fell
back after his shattering repulse at Gettysburg. Meade's tiptoe pursuit
prompted Lincoln to remark a few weeks later, when Lee had successfully reached the safe southern bank of the Potomac, that Meade reminded him of an old woman shooting her geese across the creek.
Mahan himself admitted the weakness of all his strictures when he remarked, in his discussion of the best pursuit: "This is a part of generalship no theory can teach to one to whom nature has not given the
faculties of a general."

The real weakness of the West Pointer in the Civil War was perhaps
best described by Jacob Cox, a citizen soldier from Ohio who rose to the
rank of major general. Cox was not anti-West Point. "It is on the
whole," he wrote in his memoirs, "a salutary popular notion that 'pro-
fessionals' in any department of work are more likely to succeed than
amateurs." The problem, as Cox correctly saw it, was in the experience
of the professional soldier after he left West Point. It was, Cox wrote,
"confined to company duty at frontier posts hundreds of miles from
civilization, except in the case of the engineers, the staff corps and some
of the artillery in seacoast forts. With the same exceptions, the opportunities for enlarging their theoretic knowledge had been small. It was
before the days of post libraries and books of any sort were a rarity at

the garrisons." As for educating men to command armies in the field, Cox concluded it was "absolutely necessary" to note the fact that West Point's curriculum did not pretend to include the military art in that sense. "Its scientific side was in the line of engineering and that only."

Cox recalled a conversation with an unnamed West Pointer in which the soldier mentioned that at the Academy he had read *The Art of War* by Henri Jomini, the French military writer who was the first to attempt to determine the underlying principles that govern warfare. Cox asked him if he had continued his reading into Jomini's history of the Seven Years' War of Frederick the Great which *The Art of War* was only the precis. The officer said no; the latter work had never been translated into English and although he had studied French at the Academy, he had found himself unable to get through even Jomini's brief introductory work and had read that in English translation. The West Pointer, Cox concluded, was admirably equipped to command a battalion or a regiment. He had a thorough knowledge of army regulations, the methods and forms of making returns and conducting business with the adjutant general's office and other army departments. But beyond this routine professional knowledge of army business, Cox felt that "the mental furnishing of the West Point man was not superior to that of any other liberally educated man." But the citizen soldier, he had to admit, needed to acquire "the habit of mind formed in actual service" and familiarity with danger and with the expectation of danger.

There would seem to be some substance to Cox's claim that when it came to commanding the Civil War's huge armies, most West Pointers were, like everyone else, in terra incognita. Sherman in his memoirs confessed that he studied evolutions of the line of battle—essential for anyone leading large masses of men—for the first time in the days before Bull Run.

Irvin McDowell, testifying before a Congressional Committee after the rout, ruefully declared: "I had no opportunity to test my machinery, to move it around and see whether it would work smoothly or not. In fact such was the feeling, that when I had one body of eight regiments of troops reviewed together the general censured me for it, as if I was trying to make some show. I did not think so. For there was not a man there who had ever maneuvered troops in large bodies. There was not one in the army. I did not believe there was one in the whole country. At least I knew there was no one there who had ever handled 30,000 troops. I had seen them handled abroad in reviews and marches, but I had never handled that number and no one here had. I wanted very much a little time, all of us wanted it. We did not have a bit of it."

As in so many other wars after a long period of peace, the battlefield itself was to be the terrible graduate school in which West Pointers learned the ultimate lessons in the art of war.

But competence on the battlefield was by no means the only thing the West Pointer was called upon to demonstrate in the Civil War. The struggle was also our first political war; never before had civilians ordered generals to fight battles or occupy territory so often for purely political considerations. Mexico saw some friction between a Democratic president and Whig generals, but the politicians could do little about the actual conduct of the military operations. Nor could Generals Scott or Taylor, no matter how much they railed against President Polk, turn their armies around and march on Washington, some 2000 miles away. This was anything but the case in 1861. West Pointers found themselves leading huge armies within a day's march of the White House. They fought battles under the often critical eyes of the President, his Cabinet and Congress, all of whom were prone to second-guessing. In such a situation, the Republic's traditional subordination of the man on horseback to the man in office met its severest test.

It was, at the time, a most uneasy topic in men's minds. James Longstreet, as the war broke out, flatly predicted that if it lasted five years the nation would end in a military dictatorship. On the whole, West Pointers resisted this temptation remarkably well, considering the number of times Lincoln was forced to shuffle his high command, in his desperate search for a winning general. Only one graduate showed signs of temporarily forgetting the rules. Almost from the day George McClellan took command as General in Chief he was at loggerheads with Lincoln and his government. McClellan was a prototype of the military intellectual—the sort of man Partridge so savagely criticized. He was also an egotist, quickly dazzled by his position. "By some strange magic," he wrote to his wife, "I seem to have become the power in the land . . . who would have thought, when we were married, that I should so soon be called upon to save my country?"

The men around him, citizen soldiers and West Pointers alike, were, to use Lincoln's phrase, "McClellanized" by his personal charm and imposing military lore. "Little McNapoleon" insisted on fighting the war

as if political considerations did not exist. Worse, he saw no need whatsoever to discuss his strategic plans with his commander in chief. During
the winter of 1861–62, Lincoln repeatedly begged McClellan to undertake even a diversionary operation to sustain civilian morale. McClellan
decided not to move until spring—but did not bother to inform the
President of this decision for months. As a field leader, McClellan was
inept, often failing to reconnoiter before committing his men, and always astronomically overestimating the numbers of the enemy. Never
was his doctrinaire approach to war more evident than when he proposed to Lincoln that the Union assemble 273,000 men and, with this
overwhelming force, land on the Virginia coast and steamroller to Richmond. They would then reembark this host, and repeat the performance
against other Confederate cities. This was Dennis Mahan's maxim of
concentration of force, reduced to absurdity.

But McClellan's political proclivities proved far more dangerous in
the long run. After one of his early interviews with the General in Chief,
Lincoln left muttering: "There is a Presidential candidate." It proved to
be an accurate prediction. But before McClellan ran for President in
1864, he entertained even more alarming thoughts. Major General
Jacob Cox tells in his memoirs of a story that was common in the army
at the time. McClellan, out riding with one of his old Army friends,
remarked: "I understand there is a good deal of talk of making a dictatorship."

"Ah," said the other, "Mr. Lincoln, I suppose."

"Oh no," replied McClellan, "it's me they're talking of."

Cox adds to this story a personal experience. Not long after Antietam
he was invited to dinner in McClellan's tent. The other guests were
Major General Ambrose Burnside, McClellan's best friend, and Major
General John Cochrane, an anti-slavery "War Democrat" from New
York. The conversation turned to the Emancipation Proclamation,
which Lincoln had just issued. Like so many other West Pointers, Mc-
Clellan had no sympathy with Abolitionists, and he regarded the proclamation as a concession by the President to these extremists of the
1860's. McClellan amazed his guests by asking them if they thought he
ought to make a statement against the proclamation, as numerous officers about him were urging him to do.

Everyone present was horrified, and immediately pointed out that any
public statement of his private opinion (which they were perfectly pre-

pared to tolerate) would be little short of insurrection. McClellan, with some hesitation, agreed with this estimate, and immediately claimed that the whole problem was thrust upon him by "others." These men, he said, renewing his tone of careful inquiry, had assured him that the Army was so devoted to him they would "as one man" back up any correction he chose to make of the government's war policy.

Again his exercised guests vehemently disagreed. Cox spoke out strongly, "I said that those who made such assurances were his worst enemies, and in my judgment knew much less of the army than they pretended; that our volunteer soldiers were citizens as well as soldiers and were citizens more than soldiers; and that greatly as I knew them to be attached to him, I believed not a corporal's guard would stand by his side if he were to depart from the strict subordination of the military to the civil authority." McClellan agreed that this was true, and added that "it ought to be so." He then asked their advice on issuing a general order to the Army, to quash this sort of speculation once and for all. After some debate, they finally agreed that this might be a good idea, and McClellan did so, declaring in clear terms the supremacy of civil authority, and advising his men: "The remedy for political errors, if any are committed, is to be found only in the action of the people at the polls."

Since this statement was issued only a few weeks before the 1862 elections, more than a few politicians wondered if McClellan was trying to supply, at least indirectly, ammunition for his own party, the Democrats. Cox believes McClellan was sincere, though he admits that "he must be condemned for the weakness" which made it possible for so-called friends to suggest he take over the government, with no apparent rebuke from him.

McClellan compounded this weakness by actively negotiating with the pro-Southern Democratic politician, Fernando Wood, and others who wanted him to run for the Presidency. In his autobiography, William F. "Baldy" Smith, '45, the irascible genius who served both McClellan and Grant, told how McClellan invited him to his tent one night and showed him a letter he had just written to Wood accepting the candidacy and stating his own ideas on how to conduct the war—largely to conciliate the people of the South and convince them that the Union armies intended no more than the restoration of the pre-war status quo. Smith was appalled by the letter and said to McClellan: "General, do you not see that looks like treason and that it will ruin you and all of us?" After considerable argument, McClellan finally destroyed the letter in Smith's presence and thanked him for his frank and friendly advice.

But a few months later, during the Antietam campaign, McClellan entertained Fernando Wood and his friends at headquarters and this time did write a letter to the North's leading Copperhead agreeing to a campaign platform calling for less war and more conciliation. This almost incredible gesture by a general in the field is also a good explanation for McClellan's failures as a military leader.

Some praised McClellan for resisting the ultimate temptation to dictatorship when he was relieved for the second time from command of the Army of the Potomac. As his special train was about to pull out, several regiments drawn up in formation broke ranks, and, stampeding over their officers, uncoupled McClellan's car from the rest of the train and insisted they would not let him go. They begged him to allow them to march on Washington and "deal" with those who had removed him. McClellan rushed to the platform of the car and gave a short speech urging the men to cease and desist and stand by his successor Ambrose Burnside, "as you have stood by me."

One McClellanized officer wrote home, "What do you think of such a man? He had it in his power to be a dictator—anything he chose to name if he would but say the word, but he preferred retirement rather than ambition. He was not a Caesar." Those inclined to think darker thoughts suspect that McClellan knew that his old friend and classmate Burnside was hopelessly incompetent and foresaw a future in which "Little Mac" would either be recalled to the high command or be speeded on his way to the Presidency by Burnside-led Union catastrophes.

The latter almost proved to be the case. Burnside was about as incompetent as a commanding general could be, without getting shot. The height (or depth) of Burnside's generalship can be glimpsed in a passage from William F. Smith's autobiography; he told of visiting Burnside's headquarters to find him pacing up and down bemoaning the slaughter of his men on the hills of Fredericksburg. Finally he said, "Do you know what I do when you fellows all get away from here at night? I call Robert in here and have a long talk with him, certain that I shall get honest opinions." Robert was a slave whom Burnside had brought with him from New Mexico and had taught to run the engines in his gun factory at Bristol, Rhode Island. When the war broke out he joined the army as Burnside's cook. Smith describes him as "a long, gaunt Negro with a strong face, honest and faithful as human beings can be . . . I did not doubt that Robert's advice was always honestly given," Smith adds, "but I never after that entered into competition with him in the bestowal of it."

McClellan, Burnside, and Fitz-John Porter came close to forming an even more dangerous phenomenon—a military clique. They had been in companion classes at West Point (Porter, 1845; McClellan, 1846; Burnside, 1847). Burnside was McClellan's closest friend. Their letters were addressed to "My dear Burn" and "My dear Mac." Porter was almost as intimate with McClellan. After the failure of the peninsula campaign in 1862, Lincoln removed McClellan and replaced him with John Pope of the class of 1842, who had distinguished himself in the early campaigns in the West. A coarse, rather unpleasant man, Pope issued a proclamation to the Army which said in part: "I have come to you from the west . . . From an army whose business it has been to seek the adversary and beat him . . . It is my purpose to do so and that speedily." He then proceeded to disparage Eastern emphasis on lines of retreat and bases of supply. "Let us study the probable lines of retreat of our opponents and leave our own to take care of themselves."

It was hard to be fond of such an overbearing man, and Porter, who was commanding an Army corps under him, was soon writing all sorts of derogatory comments to Burnside characterizing Pope as an idiot who would lead the Army to disaster. Burnside ran a careless headquarters and allowed many of these personal letters to slip into his public dispatch file, which was forwarded to Washington. A corps commander savagely criticizing the commander in chief was hardly the sort of thing Lincoln and his Cabinet wanted to discover at this crucial juncture of the war. Meanwhile, Pope was maneuvered into a trap by Lee and Jackson. The second battle of Bull Run was another tragedy in the bitter history of the Army of the Potomac. Not a little of Porter's sarcasm was justified after watching Pope flounder wildly around Virginia in search of the elusive Jackson.

When Pope declared that Porter had spent the entire first day of the battle within sound of the guns, yet had not marched to his assistance, and ignored a 4:30 P.M. order to attack without delay, the Secretary of War convened a court-martial composed of two major generals and eight brigadier generals. There was no doubt that Pope's orders were confusing and even militarily unsound. But the Judge Advocate General introduced Porter's messages to Burnside describing the situation in remarks such as "the strategy is magnificent and the tactics in inverse proportion." The court found Porter guilty and sentenced him to be cashiered and to be "forever disqualified from holding any office of trust or profit under the government of the United States." Porter was to spend the rest of his life fighting the verdict.

This "McClellanized" combination of incompetence and hostility to the government's policies intensified Congressional hostility to West Point. Western Republicans complained of the "infernal hold-back, proslavery policy that now rules the army" and declared that Democratic officers were afraid to "adopt a stern and straightforward course" for fear "that they will hurt somebody." A representative charged in the House that there was not "more than one sincere Abolitionist or Emancipationist among the military authorities." Another said that the Academy had produced more open and secret traitors "within the last fifty years than all the institutions of learning and education that have existed since Judas Iscariot's time."

Among the prime attackers was Senator Ben Wade of Ohio who served up the old Partridge chestnuts—West Point was aristocratic, exclusive, a closed corporation and stood in the way of merit being advanced. Even John Sherman, perhaps protecting his political flanks, was forced to join in the general criticism. Pundits outside of Congress added their unfriendly opinions. "The atmosphere, the fume of the bivouac," declared Horace Greeley, editor of the influential *New York Tribune,* "was much more likely to produce military genius than the textbooks of West Point." *Harper's Weekly* declared, "War being an art, not science, a man can no more be made a general than a first-class painter or a great poet by professors and textbooks; he must be born with the genius of war in his breast. Very few such men are born in a century and the chances are rather that they will be found among the millions of the outside people than in the select circle who are educated at West Point."

These slings and arrows continued throughout 1862 and reached a climax in January, 1863, when the annual appropriation for the Military Academy came up for a vote. Senator Lyman Trumbull of Illinois delivered a scathing attack on the Academy curriculum. "Take off your engineering restraints; dismiss . . . from the army every man who knows how to build a fortification and let the men of the north with their strong arms and indomitable spirit, move down upon the rebels and I tell you they will grind them to powder."

"We have advanced to a period when any gentleman without any particular institution can make himself master of any science that he shall see fit to adopt," declared Ben Wade. Abolish West Point and capable state schools of military instruction would spring up "divested of this objection of monopoly of pride, of vanity, of superciliousness that shadows your army and has led almost to the destruction of the activity of your army." James H. Lane topped them all by declaring that if the North were defeated an appropriate epitaph for the fallen nation would be, "Died of West Point pro-slaveryism."

Dennis Mahan, fighting for the school to which he had given his life, flung back devastating rebuttals of these charges in the pages of *The New York Times* and *Army-Navy Journal*. Senator John Sherman and others led a party revolt and the appropriation bill carried 29 to 10.

Understandably, perhaps—they were staring into the cannon's mouth —these congressmen failed to realize that Eastern West Pointers, though they failed to provide gifted leadership to the Army of the Potomac, nevertheless maintained an army in being. At every level and in every arm of the service, especially the artillery, West Pointers helped mould this army into a professional fighting force. More than once, they saved it from total destruction when Lee closed one of his spectacular traps. At Gaines Mill in the 1862 retreat from Richmond, Fitz-John Porter stood alone with his single corps against the assaults of Lee's whole Army, and smashed attack after attack with his massed artillery. The same general, whose career is perhaps the most tragic in West Point annals, repeated the performance, with even more terrible effect, at Malvern Hill a few days later. At Chancellorsville, Federal artillery again did much to blunt the first Confederate rush. It was soon generally acknowledged throughout both Armies that Confederates had the superior infantry, but the Federals had the edge in artillery. More often than not, the Northern guns were commanded by West Pointers.

Typical was the magnificent work of the battery commanded by diminutive twenty-three-year-old Edmund Kirby of the class of 1859 on the second day of the Battle of Antietam. Before the war the battery had been commanded by Confederate Major General John Bankhead Magruder of the class of 1830; at the height of the fierce seesaw struggle, the bloodiest of the war, he peered through his glasses and cried out: "I thought it was. I thought it was. That's my old battery. Take it boys, take it." In three headlong columns, the Confederate infantry responded to the challenge. Coolly, young Kirby's superbly trained gunners met them with a rain of deadly grape and canister. Again and again the infantrymen tried to get forward, only to crumple to the earth. Finally, with the field before him a terrible carpet of slain, Kirby limbered up his guns, and calmly retired to a safer position. Watching the tragic drama, Magruder exclaimed, half in chagrin and half in pride: "Ah, boys, I knew you couldn't take old 'E' Company!"

One of the least recognized but most important individual contributions during the early years of Union disasters in the East was the work of ex-Superintendent John G. Barnard. This gifted engineer was the man who fortified Washington, constructing in the first months of the war no less than 68 enclosed forts and batteries on a perimeter of 14 miles with emplacements for 1123 guns. The entire circuit of the capital's defenses finally included a line of 33 miles, within which Barnard constructed 32 miles of military roads for rapid communications. Three times—after Bull Run, after the disastrous campaigns of 1862 and again in the summer of 1864 when Jubal Early, '37, took over Jackson's role as the Grey Ghost of the Shenandoah Valley, Confederate armies rode to the very outskirts of Washington all but unopposed. But not once did they dare to attack this intricately planned network of fortifications.

In the West meanwhile, a different kind of West Pointer was displaying his talent for a war of rapid movement and fierce concentration of force. Even graduates such as Longstreet, who had known Ulysses S. Grant well, found it hard to see him as a successful general. Writing to Lee on April 2, 1864, Longstreet declared: "If Grant goes to Virginia I hope that you may be able to destroy him. I do not think that he is any better than Pope." Only Richard S. Ewell, who also became a Confederate general, declared in May, 1861, "There is one West Pointer, I think in Missouri, little known and whom I hope the northern people will not find out. I mean Sam Grant. I knew him well at the Academy and in Mexico. I should fear him more than any of their officers I have yet heard of. He is not a man of genius but he is clear-headed, quick and daring."

In the tens of thousands of words that have been written on Ulysses S. Grant, it would be hard to find a better summation of this extraordinary

soldier. Before the war was a year old, Grant electrified the nation with
his capture of Fort Donelson on the Cumberland River, taking between
12 and 15 thousand prisoners by violating one of the prime rules of
military orthodoxy, besieging a fort that held as many or more men than
he commanded. The mortified general who surrendered to him was his
old comrade Simon Bolivar Buckner. Greeting him, Grant could only
think of a day in New York when he had returned from the West
bankrupt and disheartened and his friend had generously loaned him
money. Now without a word, Grant stuffed a roll of greenbacks into
Buckner's hands and walked away.

But it was on Shiloh's bloody battlefield that Grant revealed that
unshakable calm his West Point classmates had seen in him. With half
his army smashed by a surprise Confederate attack, he withdrew the rest
into a fiery semicircle with their backs to the Tennessee River and
fought off repeated Confederate assaults until night fell. Once an hysterical officer rushed up to him and begged him to retreat. Grant looked
surprised. The thought had never even occurred to him. "Retreat?" he
said. "Oh, no, we are all right now. Tomorrow we will drive them."
Which is precisely what he did. It was the Confederate Army that retreated before Grant's counterattacks the next day.

It was after Shiloh, where William Tecumseh Sherman fought brilliantly as one of Grant's subordinate generals, that the great partnership
between these two men emerged. In the first months of the war, Sherman's sharp tongue and mercurial temperament made many people
wonder if he was fit for high command. Now they were puzzled by the
way the loquacious, aristocratic Sherman so quickly conceded the superiority of silent Sam Grant. But this lay at the heart of West Point's
training: results, not personality or background, were what counted, and
Sherman saw early in the war that Grant had an uncanny ability to
produce the result that counted above all others—victory.

Once, in a moment of typical candor, Sherman told a brother officer:
"I'm a damn sight smarter than Grant; I know more about organization,
supply and administration and about everything else than he does; but
I'll tell you where he beats me and where he beats the world. He don't
care a damn for what the enemy does out of his sight, but it scares me
like hell. I'm more nervous than he is. I am much more likely to change
my orders or to countermand my command than he is. He uses such
information as he has according to his best judgment; he issues his

orders and does his level best to carry them out without such reference to what is going on about him."

Seldom has a man forged a friendship more unselfishly than Sherman. After the Battle of Shiloh, Grant was bitterly criticized in the press for his heavy casualties, and intriguers at Army headquarters did their best to discredit him as an incompetent. He was temporarily removed from command and Sherman heard that he was on the brink of resigning from the Army. For a more selfish man, this might have been good news; Sherman stood a fair chance of getting Grant's position. Instead he wrote furious letters to the newspapers defending Grant, then rode to his tent and asked him point-blank if it was true that he was leaving the Army.

"Sherman," said Grant, "you know that I'm in the way here. I have stood it as long as I can and can endure it no longer."

"Where are you going?"

"St. Louis."

"Have you any business there?"

"Not a bit in the world."

Now Sherman unleashed on Grant the full power of his vocabulary. He urged him to stay in the Army no matter what the newspapers or anyone else said about him. Over and over he told the discouraged Grant that the Army and the country needed him. For more than an hour Sherman talked and Grant listened. Then the Quiet Man thanked Sherman and promised he would at least stay in camp and think it over. A week later, while Sherman was on a scouting expedition, he received a note from Grant telling him that he would stay with the Army and ignore his abusers. Sherman assured him that it was the right decision. "You could not be quiet at home for a week when the armies were moving," he said.

It was in their campaign to open the Mississippi that Sherman and Grant discovered their mutual instinct for a new kind of war. But it was the slouchy, silent little man in the dust-covered field uniform who discovered it first. Marching to besiege Vicksburg with Confederate armies threatening on both flanks, Grant received a panicky plea from Sherman to "stop all troops till your army is partially supplied with wagons . . ." Back came Grant's amazing words: "I do not calculate upon the possibility of supplying the army with full rations from Grand Gulf [the Union supply base]. I know it will be impossible without constructing additional roads. What I do expect is to get up what rations of hard bread, coffee and salt we can and make the country furnish the balance."

The baffled Confederate generals, assuming Grant was fighting by the book, committed half their Army to strike at his supply lines. Eighteen thousand soldiers floundered in his rear, and found no supply lines to strike. Meanwhile, in front of Vicksburg, Grant was smashing the divided Confederate forces and hurling them in confusion into the citadel. The commander of the Vicksburg garrison and chief victim of these unorthodox tactics was John Pemberton, whom Grant had known well in Mexico. Watching his beaten army fleeing into the city's fortifications where he knew they faced starvation and eventual surrender, Pemberton said mournfully to a friend, "Just thirty years ago I began my military career by receiving an appointment to a cadetship at the United States Military Academy—and today—the same date, my career is ended in disaster and disgrace."

Pemberton did his utmost to stave off the inevitable. For three months he kept Grant's vastly superior army at bay, while the South frantically tried to scrape together reinforcements to rescue him. Only when his men were reduced to ragged skeletons, too weak to withstand an imminent Union assault, did the Pennsylvanian surrender the great river fortress. Under a small tree on July 4, 1863, he and Sam Grant met to discuss surrender terms. Instead of marching the wasted defenders north to prison camps, where they would have died by the thousands, Grant agreed to parole them all on the promise that they would fight no more.

Many embittered Southerners slandered Pemberton for accepting these generous terms. They thought he should have fought to the death. There were rumors about uncertain loyalty and Northern bribes, cruelly unfair, but inevitable in the superheated emotional atmosphere of war. They were doubly cruel to Pemberton; when he visited his family a few weeks after the surrender, his own children did not recognize him. His hair and beard had turned white.

After the war, Sam Grant came to his defense. He told a story from the days when he and Pemberton were young lieutenants, marching to Mexico City. "An order was issued that none of the junior officers should be allowed horses. Mexico is not an easy country to march in. Young officers not accustomed to it soon got footsore. The order was not revoked, yet a verbal permit was accepted, and nearly all of them remounted. Pemberton alone said, No, he would walk as long as the order was still extant not to ride, and he did walk, though suffering intensely the while." This summed up John Pemberton for Sam Grant. "A more conscientious, honorable man never lived," he said. "All the time he was in Vicksburg and I outside of it, I knew he would hold on to the last."

The ultimate credit for the Vicksburg campaign must, of course, go to Grant himself who made the daring command decisions. But Grant made sure that on his staff were some of the best brains West Point had graduated. At the top of this list of young soldiers who came to be known as "Grant men" was James Harrison Wilson, one of the more brilliant graduates of the class of 1860. Brusque, bold and fearless, Wilson was never hesitant about advising generals. At the Battle of Antietam, when he found Major General Joseph Hooker leaving the field with a foot wound, Wilson told him to his face that he should return to the firing line even if he had to be carried on a stretcher, "with his bugles blowing and his corps flag flying over him."

When McClellan was relieved as commander of the Army of the Potomac, another general advised him to seek a command in the West. McClellan haughtily replied that he did not feel he could take another command even if it were offered to him. Wilson told him that if he were not offered an independent command he should take a corps or a division, failing that, a brigade, and if a brigade were not to be had he should return home to raise a regiment. Failing that, he should shoulder a musket and serve as a private soldier.

Not every general would put up with this kind of subordinate. But Sam Grant saw that Wilson combined brains and gall. He played a key role in the Vicksburg campaign, first proposing the plan of running the city's batteries with the gunboats and transports and marching troops by land to a point south of the city where they could be ferried over the river, to attack from the rear.

When one of the political generals serving under Grant, John McClernand, started a feud with Grant, it was Wilson who ended it with one of his typical confrontations. Bringing McClernand an order from Grant, Wilson was shocked to have it answered by a volley of oaths. "General McClernand," said the twenty-six-year-old Wilson, "I am astonished at what you are saying. You surely do understand the order I have given and I'll repeat it; and now, General, in addition to your highly insubordinate language, it seems to me that you are cursing me as much as you are cursing General Grant. If this is so, although you are a major general and I am only a lieutenant colonel, I will pull you off that horse and beat the boots off you."

McClernand collapsed and apologized. He said he was not cursing, he was "simply expressing his intense feelings on the subject matter." This remark became a standing joke at Grant's headquarters. Whenever Grant heard anyone cursing he would reprimand him, then say he was sure the officer hadn't intended to use profane language, he was just expressing "his intense feelings on the subject."

Another talented Grant man was James Birdseye McPherson, who graduated from West Point in 1853 at the head of his class. William B. Hazen, later a Confederate general, said of him, "He was the best scholar in his class at West Point, the highest moral character of the whole student corps." McPherson served as Chief Engineer on Grant's staff in the campaign against Fort Donelson and was at his side throughout the Battle of Shiloh. Thereafter, on Grant's recommendation, he was made a brigadier general and became military superintendent of railroads in western Tennessee. He knew more about the topography of that vital stretch of country than any other officer in the Union Army. Handsome, courageous, with great personal charm, McPherson rose another grade, thanks to Grant once more, and served as a major general of volunteers during the Vicksburg campaign. He did so well as leader of the 17th Corps he soon had Sherman saying, "If he lives he'll out-distance Grant and myself. A noble, gallant gentleman and the best hope for a great soldier."

William Farrar "Baldy" Smith helped Grant rescue another Union army from a disaster that might have lost the war. Grant was ordered to take command of the Army in the Cumberland in September, 1863, after the Confederates had driven it into the defenses of Chattanooga. By the time Grant and Smith arrived, the army's situation was desperate. They were living on half-rations, with barely enough ammunition for another battle. Supplies reached them only by a wagon haul of 60 miles over the mountains. Secure in the hills above the city, the Confederates controlled every other route.

One day Baldy Smith took a ride along the bank of the Tennessee River, pausing at one point for two hours to study the other shore and the hills above a crossing known as Brown's Ferry. When he returned to headquarters he had in his brain a plan to break the siege. His trained eye saw how the men in blue by a single lunge across the river could seize the south side of the Tennessee and the lightly defended neighboring hills, thus breaking the Confederates' grip on the road to Nashville.

Grant took one look at the plan and immediately authorized it. That very night, Smith threw a pontoon bridge across the river which enabled Grant to pour thousands of men onto the south shore within a matter of hours. The surprised Confederates fell back in disarray, and within five days a flood of supplies was pouring into the Army of the Cumberland by road and by steamer. Sherman said, "I have never beheld any work done so quietly, so well and I doubt if the history of war can show a bridge of that extent, viz. 1350 feet, laid so noiselessly and well in so short a time. I attribute it to the genius and intelligence of General William F. Smith."

Unfortunately, Smith's prickly personality made him so many enemies that in the end not even Grant could protect him. When Grant came East to take full charge of the war, he planned to make Smith his chief of staff and commander of the Army of the Potomac. But other factions in the Army and in Congress disagreed so violently that Grant was forced to abandon the idea. Eventually, after more difficulties, climaxed by a bitter quarrel with his immediate superior, Major General Benjamin Butler, Smith became one of Grant's most vindictive critics. War correspondent Charles A. Dana, who knew Smith well, wrote to him after he had been dismissed by Grant. "If you had neither been able to speak nor write, I have no doubt that you would now have been in command of one of the great armies rendering invaluable service to the cause and making for yourself an imperishable name."

On both sides of the battle line other young West Pointers won high praise and promotion from their seniors. Jeb Stuart led his horsemen on a sensational sweep that completely circled the Union Army, considerably embarrassing his father-in-law, Philip St. George Cooke, who was commanding the Union cavalry, and should have stopped him. Custis Lee, Fitzhugh Lee and later Tom Rosser were not far behind Jeb as daring men on horseback.

But the young West Pointer who seized the imagination of the South was John Pelham. As a captain of the horse artillery in Jeb Stuart's cavalry, he again and again won citations for bravery. At the Battle of Fredericksburg he held up the Union advance for hours, dueling massed

Federal batteries with a single light gun. "Is it not glorious," said Robert E. Lee, watching him, "to see such courage in one so young?" Soon "the Gallant Pelham" became a commonplace phrase. Custer sent a message through the lines: "I rejoice, dear Pelham, in your success." Another graduate, Adelbert Ames of Maine, explained this West Point attitude to a friend. "I'm not disloyal," he wrote, "when I tell you we heard with secret pride of his gallant deeds on the field of battle. It was what we had the right to expect of him—he was our classmate for five years—he was one of the best of us—who should win honors and glory if not he?"

Early on March 17, 1863, Pelham joined Jeb Stuart, Fitz Lee and his old roommate Rosser at Kelly's Ford on the Rappahannock, to repel a reconnaissance in force by Federal cavalry. Normally he stayed in the rear, directing his men to fire their guns with the speed and precision that had won him fame. But today he was returning from a visit to a young lady (a fellow officer said Pelham was "so innocent looking, so childlike and bland in the expression of his sparkling blue eyes, but as grand a flirt as ever lived"), and his regular battery was not on the field. This gave him a chance to join the cavalry in a charge, and, drawing his saber, he rode to the head of a column of the Third Virginia Regiment, and shouted, "Forward!"

A moment later, a shell burst overhead, and Pelham toppled from his horse. His eyes were open, still aglow with battle light, his lips wide in a smile. But from the back of his head blood trickled. A shell fragment had pierced his skull. His comrades rushed him to the nearest doctor, but before the day was over, Pelham was dead. When Jeb Stuart heard the news, he bowed his head on his horse's neck and wept. Three young belles in nearby towns simultaneously went into mourning, in which the whole South joined.

On the Northern side, Custer vaulted from lieutenant to brigadier general, thanks to his reckless daring as a cavalryman. Again and again Custer found himself charging cavalry commanded by Tom Rosser. Rosser once threw back his grey, red-lined cape and boldly reconnoitered the Union lines in full view of Northern sharpshooters. Custer hastily ordered everyone along the front to hold his fire. The next day Custer sent him a message under a flag of truce.

"Tam, do not expose yourself so. Yesterday I could have killed you."

After the Battle of Williamsburg in May, 1862, Custer discovered another classmate, John W. "Gimlet" Lea, lying wounded in a barn.

Custer arranged for Lea to be transported to the home of a Mrs. Durfey in Williamsburg, who had offered to care for him. During the three months of recuperation, Lea fell in love with Mrs. Durfey's daughter and they became engaged.

Not long after, Custer obtained permission from George McClellan to pay Lea a visit before the Union Army withdrew from the Yorktown peninsula. Instead of rejoicing at the news of the Union withdrawal, Lea was downcast. He wanted Custer to be best man at his wedding. Custer promptly took charge; there was no time to lose. In a letter to his sister, he described the ceremony on the borderline between two armies, which took place the following evening.

Lea was dressed in "a bright new Rebel uniform trimmed with gold lace." Custer wore his "full uniform of blue." After the ceremony, the bridesmaid kissed the bride and burst into tears. Teasingly, Gimlet Lea asked: "Why, Cousin Maggie, what are you crying for? Oh, I know— because you are not married; well, here is the minister and here is Captain Custer who I know would be glad to carry off such a pretty bride from the Confederacy." Cousin Maggie apparently hoped she might lure Custer in the opposite direction while he lingered for the next two weeks at the Durfey home. She made eyes at him constantly, meanwhile singing and playing on the piano "My Maryland," "Dixie," "For Southern Rights Hurrah," and other songs of secession. But Custer went no farther than playing cards for the Confederacy, and letting Lea win "every time."

Seldom has any army seen a soldier as flamboyant as Custer. Shortly after he became a brigadier general he vowed he would not cut his blond hair until he entered Richmond. He kept his word until it was hanging a foot long over his shoulders in curls. His old West Point roommate, Tully McCrea, gives a vivid description of him in August, 1863. "He was dressed in a fancy suit of velveteen covered with gold braid, with an immense collar like a sailor's, with his brigadier's star in each corner. Put a fancy cap on his head and a hearty smile on his face and then you have his *tout ensemble*. You may think from this that he is a vain man, but he is not . . . He is a gallant soldier, a whole-souled, generous friend and a mighty good fellow and I like him and wish him every success in his new role of brigadier."

Custer's flamboyance antagonized many strangers, but it never bothered those who knew him from West Point days. For them the color, the vainglory, the strutting, were simply part of being Custer. James Wilson, who became a cavalry general later in the war, was obviously thinking of Custer when he wrote in his memoirs: "The modest man is not always the best soldier . . . Some of the best while shamelessly sounding their own praises, were brave, dashing and enterprising to an unusual degree."

Perhaps the best picture of Custer's strange mixture of ferocity and gaiety was the climax of his rivalry with Tom Rosser, which came in the Shenandoah Valley on October 9, 1864. Beside a stream appropriately known as Tom's Brook, Rosser drew up his men behind stone walls and awaited the Union attack. Custer chose him as his special target, and halting his aides rode forward until he was clearly visible to the watching Confederates. Then he swept his broad-brimmed hat from his head, bowed and led his division in a headlong charge.

Rosser's line broke and Custer chased him for ten miles in what the Union men called the "Woodstock races." The "boy general" (he was twenty-five) captured Rosser's supply train and wagons containing his official papers and trunks of clothes. The next day, Custer came prancing out of his headquarters wearing Rosser's gray uniform, which was six sizes too large for him. Under a flag of truce he sent "Tam" another note, asking him to be sure his tailor made the tails shorter the next time. Custer not only enjoyed the mass madness of war—he added to it.

Throughout the great conflict, other West Pointers had their share of chance encounters with old friends. In the early days more than a few Southerners were still wearing scraps of their Union uniforms. Jeb Stuart retained a battered blue greatcoat which had warmed him during the years he spent as a U.S. cavalryman in Kansas. One day he was reconnoitering the Union lines when he met at a bend in a narrow road a horseman in blue. Stuart recognized him as Delavan Duane Perkins of the class of 1849, who had been assistant professor of mathematics during his cadetship. Cheerfully Stuart called: "Howdy, Perk, glad to see you've come over. What's your command?"

At that very moment, around the bend in the road came a flying battery of Union artillery. With a grin Perkins pointed to it. "Hello, Beauty," he said, "how are you? That's my command right there."

"Oh, the devil," Stuart said. "I didn't know you'd stayed with the Yankees."

Whereupon Jeb beat a hasty retreat, easily outdistancing the encumbered artillerymen.

During the Battle of Bull Run, Stuart used his blue greatcoat to good advantage. Separated from his men after a clash with Union cavalry, he came upon a blue-clad company in a field, behind a rail fence. He rode up to them and roared: "Take down those bars."

The soldiers leaped to obey. Then Stuart drew his sword, gestured to some nearby woods as if he were signaling to a hidden regiment, and shouted: "Throw down your arms. You're all dead men."

An entire company of the 15th Pennsylvania Volunteers promptly dropped their guns, fell upon their faces and surrendered.

Not long after the battle, Stuart led a raid that drove back a Federal force that included artillerymen led by Charles Griffin, another friend from West Point days. Griffin, who was to become a Union general, left behind a note with a local citizen before retreating.

Dear Beauty:

I have called to see you and regret very much that you were not in. Can't you dine with me at Willard's [a famous Washington hotel] tomorrow? Keep your "black horse" off me!

From your old friend,
Griffin

Stuart forwarded the following reply:

Dear Griffin:

I heard that you called, and hastened to see you, but as soon as you saw me coming you were guilty of the discourtesy of turning your back upon me. However, you probably hurried on to Washington to get the dinner ready. I hope to dine at Willard's, if not tomorrow certainly before long.

Yours to count on,
Beauty

Fitzhugh Lee became one of Stuart's division commanders and some months later he decided to emulate his dashing leader. Surprising a Pennsylvania regiment in Leedstown, he killed, wounded or captured about a hundred men. When he learned that the troops belonged to the brigade of his West Point classmate, William W. Averell, he dashed off the following note:

Dear Averell:

I wish you would put up your sword, leave my state and go home. You ride a good horse. I ride a better. Yours can beat mine running. Send me over a bag of coffee.

Fitz

By this time Union cavalrymen were becoming experienced enough to take on the daring Southern horsemen, and Averell decided to pay his classmate a return visit. With five regiments at his back he stormed across the Rappahannock and tore apart one of Fitz's best regiments, the Third Virginia. Only desperate resistance saved the rest of Fitz's smaller command from annihilation. Withdrawing, Averell left behind him a sack of coffee and a note:

Dear Fitz:

Here's your coffee. Here's your call. How do you like it? How's that horse?

Averell

A fever laid George McClellan low not long after he became commander of the Union Army of the Potomac. Hearing of it on the other side of the battle line, Brigadier General George Pickett wrote his fiancée: "I've heard that my dear old friend McClellan is lying ill about ten miles from here. May some loving, soothing hand minister to him. He was, he is, he always will be, even were his pistol pointed at my heart, my dear loved friend . . . You, my darling, may not be in sympathy with this feeling, for I know you see 'no good in Nazareth.' "

Powell Hill had meanwhile become a Confederate major general, and his division was soon famed for the ferocity of its attacks. He seemed to take special pleasure in frustrating the battle plans of his former rival in love, George McClellan. Union soldiers became convinced that more than a little of Hill's pugnacity could be traced to his romantic grievance over Nellie Marcy. Once, after beating off a series of Hill's attacks, the bluecoats were trying to get some well-deserved rest when blaring bugles and rattling musketry announced that Hill had returned for one more assault. "My God, Nellie," groaned a veteran as he pulled on his boots and wearily shouldered his gun, "why didn't you marry him!"

The night before the Battle of Perryville, Kentucky, Philip Sheridan, not yet a top commander, was stalking around the campfires of the Union Army, when he saw a familiar face across the dancing flames. It was his old enemy, William Terrill. After a wrenching debate with his Virginia father, Terrill had chosen to stay with the Union, and was now a brigadier general. Since the day of his near-bayoneting he and Sheridan had not spoken. Now they stared for a silent moment, then Terrill stretched his hand across the fire. Manfully, Sheridan took it in his tough grip, and they sat down together for several hours of reminiscing about cadet days. The next afternoon, trying to rally his men after they had fallen back in confusion before a Confederate assault, General Terrill was mortally wounded, and died that night. His brother, a graduate of VMI, chose the South, and became one of Lee's brigadier generals. A year later, he was killed fighting one of Grant's assaults. The grieving father reportedly raised a tombstone on which he inscribed their names and identical ranks, in the rival armies, and under it, the single line: "God alone knows which was right."

Such pathos was more common than laughter in most of West Point's confrontations. Nowhere was this truer than on the climactic field of Gettysburg. There, after two days of bloody combat, Robert E. Lee chose to make a final desperate assault on the center of the Union lines on Cemetery Ridge. To command the attack he called on Major General George Pickett. Among the brigadier generals under him were Richard Garnett, who dragged himself from a sick-bed, shivering from fever, and Lewis Armistead. Commanding the Union troops of the Second Corps, huddled behind the stone walls atop the ridge, was Major General Winfield Scott Hancock, already nicknamed "Hancock the Superb" for his fighting prowess. Did these old friends think of that farewell party in Los Angeles, two years ago—two years of war, with its fearful compression of time and emotion, that must have seemed like two centuries? Did Armistead in particular remember his solemn words about never leaving his native soil?

Perhaps. We only know that each of them displayed unforgettable courage in the next terrible hours. Through a hail of Confederate artillery, Hancock rode along the entire front of his command, to reassure his jittery men. When one of his aides protested that a corps commander should not expose himself that way, Hancock replied: "There are times when the life of a corps commander does not count." No sooner had the artillery's battering ceased, when out of the woods swept the Southern brigades. Too sick to walk, Dick Garnett rode his horse. Lewis Armistead strode jauntily not far away, putting his black slouch hat on the point of his sword, so that his men could keep track of him.

Fiercely, Hancock's men raked them with artillery fire, but they came steadily on. As they mounted the ridge, Hancock sent Union regiments swarming down their flanks to enfilade them with blasts of musketry. Finally came a tremendous volley from the men on the ridge, sweeping away whole ranks. Dick Garnett fell, riddled by a dozen bullets. But Lewis Armistead strode into the musket smoke, while on the other side of the stone wall, another West Pointer, artilleryman Alonzo Cushing of the class of 1860, ignored mortal wounds to push his one remaining gun forward and fire a final blast of canister in the very faces of the charging Southerners. About the same time, behind the lines, Hancock was toppled from his horse by a minié ball that tore through his saddle and pierced his groin.

Armistead, miraculously untouched, vaulted over the wall, and paused there, his hand on Cushing's cannon. Around him the Union soldiers broke and ran. But on either flank, the blue lines stood firm, and swarms of reinforcements could be seen rushing to fill the gap left by the retreaters. Only then did Armistead realize that he was almost alone. A mere handful of his men had survived the carnage on the hillside. Before he could issue a command, a storm of bullets from the fresh Union troops cut down him and most of his gallant men.

As Union soldiers carried the dying Armistead to the rear, he asked for his old friend. When he heard that Hancock, too, was wounded—fatally, it appeared at the time—Armistead wept, and murmured a message, which some thought expressed his regret at joining the Confederacy—but more likely was his personal sorrow at the news of his friend. A few days later, Almira Hancock opened the suitcase Armistead had given her that last night in Los Angeles. In the prayer book he had wanted her to keep was inscribed a soldier's motto: "Trust in God and fear nothing."

In this hour of terrible defeat, Robert E. Lee showed new greatness. He could have blamed Pickett's failure on his second in command, "Old Pete" Longstreet, who originally had opposed the attack and later supported it with only minimum enthusiasm. Other subordinates had failed him earlier in the three-day holocaust. Instead, Lee told everyone: "It is I who have lost this fight. You must help me out of it the best way you can." Back in Virginia, he told Jefferson Davis he was ready to resign his command. Davis would not even consider the idea.

But the Confederacy had suffered a mortal blow. Never again could Lee take the offensive. Ulysses Grant soon came East, and Lincoln handed over to him full command of the war. With his characteristic simplicity, Grant proceeded to prove himself the first practitioner of total war. "It is my design . . . to work all parts of the army together and somewhat towards a common end," he declared, and proceeded to weave a ring of fire around the dying Confederacy which no amount of military genius or gallantry of spirit could overcome.

When Grant came East, he brought with him Phil Sheridan, whose star had risen steadily in Western battles. Once, early in the war, when intriguers tried to persuade Lincoln to fire Grant, he replied: "I can't do without this man. He fights." For the same reason, Sheridan swiftly became one of the President's favorite generals.

Men would follow this doughty Irishman anywhere. At Lookout Mountain, as his troops prepared to storm the almost perpendicular Tennessee slope, Sheridan whipped out a silver whiskey flask and raised it to a Confederate officer looking down at him from the crest. "Here's to you," shouted Sheridan and took a long swallow. The Confederate answered with a volley from six cannon which narrowly missed decapitating Sheridan. Brushing dirt out of his eyes, Sheridan growled, "That's damned ungenerous; I'll take those guns for that." With a roar, he and his men went surging up the mountain in an irresistible charge.

Sheridan's finest hour imperishably dramatized how leadership can rescue victory from near defeat. Assigned to clear the vital Shenandoah Valley of Confederate troops, he tackled the job with his usual furious energy, smashing the once-potent Southern army under Jubal Early and sending it "whirling through Winchester." But Early was a shrewd, resourceful soldier, and he scratched together his battered regiments and waited until the Union Army lowered its guard, then struck in a dawn attack that caught Sheridan fourteen miles away.

Within minutes Sheridan was on the back of his great black horse, Rienzi, riding to the battlefield. The high pitched "Yi' yi' yi' " of the rebel yell had swept down on the Union camp, sending panicky soldiers fleeing headlong. While a few regiments stood their ground, many more streamed wildly down the pike road—until they met Sheridan. A Vermont private wrote his parents, "The first thing that attracted my attention was the clatter of horses' feet on the pike and the most vociferous cheering I ever heard. When I looked up I saw General Sheridan coming followed by his bodyguard. Sheridan was about 50 yards in advance with his hat in his hand, saying as near as I could understand it, 'Come to the front with me, boys, and we will make this matter all right.' It was an awful moment . . . But everybody and everything followed Sheridan."

An aide described how without "slowing from a gallop, Sheridan pointed to the front; men cheered and shouldered arms and started back . . . As he galloped on his features gradually grew set, as though carved in stone and the same dull red glint I had seen in his piercing black eyes when the battle was going against us was there now."

Onto the chaotic battlefield Sheridan rode, vaulted over a fence manned by Union skirmishers and drove his exhausted horse up a little hill between his men and the Southerners. With magnificent disregard for enemy fire, he rode on to similarly inspire other units. When an infantry colonel hysterically shouted to him, "The army is whipped," Sheridan snarled, "You are, but the army isn't." Up and down the line he rode while behind him rose a mighty roar of men returning by the thousands. Over and over he shouted, "We're going to get a twist on those fellows. We're going to lick them out of their boots."

But Sheridan was also a skilled tactician. Contrary to the poems and stories that immortalized his famous ride, he did not lead his excited men forward in a headlong rush, minutes after he arrived on the battlefield. From 10:30 A.M. until 4:00 P.M., he worked at unscrambling regiments and divisions, bringing up artillery, feeling out the enemy's true strength. It was a totally coordinated army that he sent forward at 4:00 P.M.; yet it was also infused by driving fury. Like unleashed tigers they smashed into the Confederate line "at a double quick with screams of delight and triumph."

The outnumbered Confederates buckled and fled. Now Sheridan seemed to be everywhere at once, lashing his men into pursuit. When he found a group of infantrymen floundering behind the advance, he roared at them to get moving.

"We can't run—we're all tuckered out," gasped a private.

"If you can't run, then shoot and holler," Sheridan said. "We've got the goddamndest twist on them you ever saw."

The Confederate defeat soon became a rout. They lost most of their artillery. Ambulances, ammunition wagons, blocked the road down which they fled, for over three miles. Grant wrote to Secretary of War Stanton. "Turning what bade fair to be a disaster into a glorious victory stamped Sheridan what I always thought him, one of the ablest of generals." Lincoln remarked that he had thought a cavalryman ought to be about 6′4″ but now "5′4″ seems about right."

Around the campfire that night Sheridan told his officers, "I'm going to get much more credit for this than I deserve, for had I been here in the morning, the same thing would have taken place and had I not returned today the same thing would have taken place." Not a man who had spent five minutes on that battlefield agreed with him.

But it was Grant, always Grant, who supplied the relentless determination that fueled the Union armies now. When he was repulsed in his first drive toward Richmond, losing over 15,000 men in the awful chaos of the Wilderness, he drew back his battered divisions, and everyone expected him to retreat north of the Potomac and lick his wounds. Glumly, the blue-clad soldiers trudged along paths made familiar by a dozen earlier retreats. But when they came to a crucial crossroads, they could not believe their eyes. The regiments ahead of them were turning not north, but south! Tremendous cheer burst from the lips of these weary men. For the first time they felt the presence of a leader who fought to win.

Again and again Grant hammered at his gallant adversary, taking fearful casualties, but costing Lee almost as many men. Northern newspapers howled for Grant's head, calling him "the butcher." But Grant never wavered in his conviction that he was shortening the war in the only way a war could be shortened. Grimly ignoring his critics, Grant pondered his maps and moved south, always south. "I propose to fight it out on this line if it takes all summer," he telegraphed the jittery politicians in Washington.

Yet in the worst of this holocaust Grant never forgot he was fighting men who had been classmates and friends. When George Pickett's wife gave birth to a son, the men of his division celebrated the news with bonfires all along their line. Grant saw them and sent scouts to find out why the enemy was illuminating the night. When they reported, Grant turned to one of his generals: "Haven't we some kindling on this side of the lines? Why don't we strike a light for the young Pickett?" Soon answering bonfires were glowing along the Union lines. A few days later, under a flag of truce, blue-clad soldiers delivered a baby's silver service, engraved: "To George Pickett, Jr., from his father's friends, U. S. Grant, Rufus Ingalls, George Suckley."

In the West, meanwhile, Sherman was marching to fame on Grant's simple order, "to get into the interior of the enemy's country as far as you can, inflicting all the damage you can against their war resources . . ." Driving the Confederate Army steadily before him, Sherman demonstrated again and again some of the most brilliant tactics of the war. Always declining to attack the entrenched enemy (commanded by canny Joseph Johnston) Sherman would maneuver three Army corps from flank to flank, swinging the outermost one as much as fifty miles to get in behind the Southern position and force them to retreat once more. An awed Confederate prisoner told one Union soldier: "Sherman ought to get on a high hill and command: 'Attention! Kingdoms by right wheel.'" Another captured rebel declared: "Sherman'll never go to Hell; he will flank the devil and make Heaven in spite of the odds."

Even more than Grant, Sherman used all the military skill West Point had to offer. His was, in fact, the first modern army. Field telegraphers ran their wires right into the front lines so that Sherman could communicate with his rear echelons even under fire. Ahead of the army pressed swarms of topographical engineers charting the terrain and rushing their drawings back in "dark wagons" that multigraphed them so there were copies for Sherman's entire staff. When the retiring Southerners burned bridges, Sherman's engineers, stretching canvas over already constructed frames, then planking the sections with boards, replaced them in a matter of hours. Soon more than one Confederate was convinced that Sherman could do anything. When word arrived that raiders had ruined a railroad tunnel in the Union's rear, a cynic groaned, "Sherman carries a duplicate."

Sherman's own men soon became equally convinced of his omniscience. Once a private wandered past and found the general sleeping against a tree. "A pretty way we are commanded when our generals are lying drunk beside the road," he growled.

"Stop, my man," shouted Sherman, leaping to his feet. "I'm not drunk. While you were sleeping last night I was planning for you, sir; now I was taking a nap."

Through the army went the word: "Uncle Billy sleeps with one eye and one ear open."

Ridding himself of wagon trains as Grant had done before him, Sherman figured to the last decimal point how much each unit could bear on its back. As he crossed into Georgia he had at his fingertips census reports of every county in the state so he would know exactly where his men could forage best. No wonder, as Sherman told a friend, "my men believe I know everything; they are much mistaken but it gives them confidence in me."

Sherman was one of the few generals who used West Pointers to give him an intimate insight into the psychology of his opponent. Evidence of such personal knowledge playing a military role in the war is surprisingly scanty.

Lee, it is true, had the greatest contempt for John Pope. His habit of issuing orders from a so-called "headquarters in the saddle" prompted the great Virginian to one of his few public displays of wit. "Pope has his headquarters where his hindquarters ought to be," Lee remarked. There would seem to be good grounds for arguing that Lee's daring division of his army before the second battle of Bull Run was based on a personal conviction of Pope's incompetence. But this belief had no roots in West Point days.

When Sherman learned that John Bell Hood had replaced Joseph Johnston as commander of the Southern army defending Atlanta, he quickly called a council of war and asked three of his generals who had been at West Point with Hood—McPherson, John Schofield and Oliver O. Howard—what they thought Hood would do. All agreed that the impulsive, impetuous Southerner would attack immediately. Hood had graduated at the foot of the class and was known for his scorn of military scholarship and his fixed belief that courage and spirit were the crucial factors in battle. George H. Thomas, who had taught Hood at West Point and served with him in the 2nd Cavalry in Texas, agreed. The attack came exactly as predicted and was beaten back with terrible casualties.

Capturing Atlanta and thereby rescuing Lincoln's bid for a second term, Sherman now proceeded to make the most daring gamble of the war. Instead of pursuing the Southern army opposing him, he would ignore it and cut a burning swath across the heart of Georgia to the sea. His reasoning, as he described it to Grant, was another basic concept of the West Point soldier: "Instead of being on the defensive, I would be on the offensive . . . The difference in war is a full 25 percent." To this he added the diplomatic argument, "If the North can march an army right through the South, it is proof positive that the North can prevail . . ."

Grant finally gave permission, and with 60,000 men, Sherman proceeded to "march off the map," cutting himself loose from railroad and even telegraph communication with the rest of the world. The British *Army and Navy Gazette* declared: "If Sherman has really left his army in the air and started off without a base to march from Georgia to South Carolina, he has done either one of the most brilliant or one of the most foolish things ever performed by a military soldier . . . The data on which he goes and the plan on which he acts must really place him among the great generals or the very little ones."

So dazzled was the country, reporters began to ask Grant if he wasn't annoyed because "Sherman was absorbing all attention." Grant lit a cigar, then quietly replied: "Jealousy between General Sherman and me is impossible." On December 15, a month to the day after he had disappeared, the commander of Sherman's advance guard wired Washington from Savannah: "We have met with perfect success thus far. Troops in fine spirit and General Sherman nearby." Up and down the land people rushed into country roads, embraced each other with wild exuberance on city streets, shouting: "He's made it. Sherman's at Savannah!"

Another intimate West Point relationship played a key role in Sherman's triumph. When he turned his face to the sea, Sherman left behind him a still potent 40,000-man Confederate Army, led by aggressive John Bell Hood. Sherman knew that Hood might march in the other direction, aiming at a propaganda victory in Tennessee, which could shake Northern confidence badly. But Sherman never so much as looked over his shoulder as he plowed through the South's heartland to the sea. Behind him as commander in Tennessee he had left his classmate George H. Thomas, and he had absolute confidence in "Old Tom."

"We recited together four years in the same section," Sherman said later, "served as lieutenants in the same regiment ten years . . . Never since the world began did such absolute confidence exist between commander and commanded." The only telegram Sherman sent as he shoved off from Atlanta was to Thomas, telling him if Hood attacked he was confident "you will whip him out of his boots."

Thomas was a totally professional soldier, thorough, careful, always insistent on using the latest and best military equipment. Some people accused him of being too cautious, of fighting by the book, but paramount in his book was an idea reiterated again and again at West Point— concentration of force. All Thomas' preparations were aimed at delivering against the enemy, at one chosen point, a massive stroke that would break him apart. Thomas demonstrated this credo early in the Civil War when at Mill Spring, Kentucky, in 1862, he won the North's first clear-cut victory over a Southern field army, utterly smashing the command of Major General George Crittenden and his 4000 Confederates, breaking them up into a fleeing remnant that abandoned even their colors and their wounded.

Thereafter, Thomas and his 14th Army Corps were a bulwark in the long series of battles for control of Tennessee and Kentucky. Somehow he communicated his rocklike character to his men and they became famed for their awesome defensive powers.

Never did Thomas display this genius more brilliantly than on the battlefield named for the little Tennessee creek, Chickamauga. On that terrible day, the Union commander in chief, Major General William Rosecrans, lost both his nerve and his wits, issued a series of contradictory orders that caused the collapse of his right and center and then abandoned the field like a man sleepwalking through a bad dream, leaving Thomas in charge. Grouping shattered regiments around his own still-unbroken lines, Thomas stood off the combined assaults of the entire Confederate Army. As one of his soldiers told it years later, "Disaster is closing in everywhere. Yet under the shadow of a spreading oak near Snodgrass's house is a grizzled soldier, calm, silent, immovable, who resolves to hold the field until night comes—hemmed in by appalling ruin, yet supreme above disaster—the rock of Chickamauga." Thomas' stand on that April afternoon saved the Union Army in the West, the state of Tennessee, and perhaps the war.

Just as Sherman had suspected, Hood decided to take his 40,000 men in the opposite direction and wreck Sherman's success by seizing control of Tennessee and menacing the Midwest. By now the Confederacy was fighting for a stalemate. Grant was hammering Lee in Virginia, and the casualty lists of that awful summer had sent a long shudder through the North. Hood's appearance before Nashville replaced horror with panic.

The politicians in Washington telegraphed frantic orders to attack Hood immediately. Thomas ignored them. Coolly, calmly, he let Hood sit on the hills outside Nashville while he prepared his battle plan. Then he attacked. In two days of sledgehammer blows, Hood's once proud army was broken into shattered fragments. The battle marked the end of the Confederacy between the Appalachians and the Mississippi.

The Southern tide was ebbing faster and faster now. The bravest and the best began to fall. Jeb Stuart rode out with worn horses and thinned ranks to meet a massive Federal cavalry raid, led by Sheridan and Custer, that destroyed tons of vital supplies and equipment, and even threatened to overrun Richmond itself. A fierce fight boiled up around Yellow Tavern, an abandoned inn about six miles from the Confederate capital.

Custer, noting a Confederate battery in an exposed position on Stuart's flank, charged and captured it, rolling up part of the Southern line, and forcing a disordered retreat. In the confused melee that followed, a Union cavalryman fatally wounded Stuart with a hand gun. When Lee heard the news, he wept, undoubtedly remembering that laughing young cadet who visited him on Saturday afternoons at West Point. Weeks later Lee still could "scarcely think of him without weeping."

Only emotion held the battered Army of Northern Virginia together now, a fierce devotion to Robert E. Lee that ran from generals to privates. Twice in the titanic struggle with Grant, Lee reorganized crumbling Confederate defenses and tried to lead a counterattack against the oncoming blue waves. But the men refused to advance. "General Lee to the rear. General Lee to the rear," they roared, until aides had to seize the bridle of Lee's horse, and lead him to safety. Then the ragged men in gray flung themselves forward with a ferocity that blunted one more Union assault.

When Grant was besieging Lee's brilliantly planned field fortifications at Petersburg, Lee had a habit of coming alone into the forward outposts to examine the Union positions. One morning late in November, 1864, he stepped out on the banquette of a work in full view of the numerous Federal sharpshooters and began studying Grant's lines through his field glasses. Immediately Archibald Gracie stepped in front of him. The New York cadet whose gallantry had won Superintendent Lee's admiration was now a Confederate brigadier general. Quietly, Gracie began pointing out various Northern units opposite them.

"General," Lee said, "you should not expose yourself so much."

"If I should not, General Lee, why should you, the commander in chief?" Gracie replied.

Only then did Lee realize that Gracie was covering him with his own body, in case the snipers fired. With a small nod, Lee stepped down from the banquette and continued his walk down the line. A few days later, Gracie was killed by a bursting shell, and Lee bore still another sorrow.

Around the same time came another loss that many in the South felt keenly. Leonidas Polk, the man who had led West Point's religious revival under Thayer, was killed by Union artillery fire while reconnoitering Sherman's front. He had laid aside his Episcopal bishop's robes to don a general's uniform when the war began, and had fought valiantly, if not with any special distinction, in the West. He took advantage of the emotions generated by the South's agony to convert a number of the Confederacy's leading commanders, notably Joseph E. Johnston.

Around the same time, Grant, too, knew the pain of personal loss. Sherman sent a sad telegram from Atlanta, reporting that the most promising of the "Grant men," Major General James McPherson, had been killed instantly by a bullet in the heart while riding to help his men repulse a Confederate assault. "The country has lost one of its best soldiers—and I have lost my best friend," Grant said, and retired to his tent, where for hours he lay alone with his grief.

The immense conflict had its own momentum now. Men began to wonder if the fighting would last for another twenty years. They did not realize that Grant's relentless erosion, his tireless attempts to turn Lee's flank, were forcing Lee to stretch his thinning brigades farther and farther. As 1865 dawned, Lee was holding more than 40 miles of trenches and forts with less than a thousand men to a mile. Finally, in March 1865, a series of concentrated blows tore the Confederate defenses apart, and Lee was forced to abandon Richmond and retreat south.

Grant's pursuit demonstrated the high order of his professional skills. It was, in the words of one military historian, "one of the best operations of its type in the history of warfare." While part of his army smashed at Lee's rear guard, Sheridan raced ahead with another huge force to block the escape routes. The end came when Lee's half-starved, exhausted men stumbled into the little village of Appomattox Courthouse, to find rank after rank of Sheridan's blue-clad troopers commanding the road ahead.

Lee told a courier from Jefferson Davis that the war was ending "just as I have expected it would end from the first." Wearily he summoned his officers and asked their advice. What would the country think if he surrendered? One tear-choked soldier replied: "There is no country. There has been no country, General, for a year or more. You are the country to these men." Lee turned to the huge grim-visaged Longstreet, and asked his opinion.

"Will the sacrifice of the army help the cause in other quarters?" Longstreet asked.

"I think not," Lee replied.

"Then your situation speaks for itself," Longstreet said.

Lee's commander of artillery, Edward Porter Alexander of West Point's class of 1857, then spoke for the younger officers. Why not disband the Army, order the men to "scatter like rabbits and partridges in the bushes?"

Lee recoiled at the thought. He saw that such a decision would create a bitterness between the North and South that might take centuries to heal. "The men would have no rations, be under no discipline. They'd have to rob and plunder," he said. Young Alexander flushed. Later he said that he felt Lee was speaking from a plane so far above him, he was ashamed even to have made the suggestion. But his fervor could not resist one last plea. "A little more blood or less now makes no difference. Spare the men who have fought under you for four years the mortification of having to ask Grant for terms and have him say unconditional surrender . . . General, spare us the mortification of having you get that reply."

Quietly, Lee replied: "General Grant will not demand unconditional surrender; he will give us as honorable terms as we have a right to ask or expect."

Amazing statement! Here was a general on the edge of total disaster, expecting the enemy commander he had frustrated for so many terrible months to give him honorable terms. What else but the spirit of West Point could have given Lee such confidence?

Sheridan was massing his troopers for a final assault, riding along the long blue ranks, growling: "Now smash 'em, I tell you. Smash 'em." Just as his bugles blew the charge, a Southern officer rode through the lines with a letter from Robert E. Lee to Ulysses S. Grant, asking for a meeting to discuss the surrender of the Army of Northern Virginia.

When Grant heard the news, there was, in the words of a newspaperman who had followed him in the field for three years, "no exultation manifested—no sign of joy—and instead of flushing from excitement, he clenched his teeth, compressed his lips and became very pale." Rather than keep Lee waiting, Grant rode to the surrender site in his mud-spattered field uniform. "What General Lee's feelings were, I do not know," he later wrote . . . "but my own feelings . . . were sad and depressed."

Grant was embarrassed to meet Lee resplendent in his best uniform. The Union commander apologized for his tattered appearance, and asked Lee if he remembered a night long ago, when they had met in Mexico. "I have always remembered your appearance," he said, "and I think I should have recognized you anywhere." Lee replied that he did recall the meeting and "often tried to recollect how you looked, but I have never been able to recall a single feature." Obviously trying to ease the tension of the meeting, Grant chatted for some minutes about Mexican days. Finally Lee asked him if he was ready to discuss surrender terms.

Grant stated them promptly and succinctly. "The officers and men surrendered to be paroled and disqualified from taking up arms again until properly exchanged, and all arms, ammunition and supplies to be delivered up as captured property."

Lee nodded. "Those are about the terms I expected to be proposed." At his suggestion, Grant sat down at a small table and wrote them out. Only then did Lee note that the agreement would not permit the Southern cavalrymen and artillerymen to retain their horses, which they owned privately.

Grant pondered for a moment. He finally said. "I will not change the terms as they are written, but I will instruct the officers to let all the men who claim to own a horse or a mule take the animals home with them to work their little farms."

"This will have the best possible effect upon my men," Lee said. "It will be very gratifying and it will do much toward conciliating our people."

The two leaders then discussed the problem of feeding Lee's men. Grant turned to his commissary general. "General Lee has about a thousand or fifteen hundred of our people prisoners and they are faring the same as his men but he tells me his haven't anything. Can you send them some rations?"

Within the hour, three days' rations—fresh beef, salt, hard bread, coffee and sugar—were flowing into the Confederate lines. They were soon followed by Federal troops who, with Grant's permission, shared their food and drink with the half-starved Southerners. When Northern bands began playing and batteries fired victory salutes, Grant sternly ordered a stop to celebrations. "The rebels are our countrymen again," he said. Later that night when someone told Grant that he should have held Lee and his generals for trial instead of paroling them, the stumpy soldier said quietly, "I'll keep the terms no matter who's opposed."

Even before the surrender was signed, George Armstrong Custer called to one of his classmates, "Let's go see if we can find Cowan." They rode to the edge of a stream separating the blue and gray and asked a Southern officer to find Robert V. Cowan of North Carolina who had been two classes behind Custer.

A few minutes later, Cowan rode his horse over the stream and Custer greeted him delightedly, "Hello, you damned red-headed rebel."

While the three young men chatted, Robert E. Lee rode by on his way to see Grant. Sternly Lee ordered Cowan to return to the Confederate side of the stream. Obediently they separated, but then Custer, true to form, signaled that the coast was clear and the three returned to exchange more West Point news. The moment the surrender was formalized, Custer rode to the Confederate camp in search of more friends. He found Gimlet Lea and invited him to dinner. Then he was face to face with another cavalryman, Fitzhugh Lee. With a joyous shout these two birds of a feather embraced each other and rolled on the ground, laughing like schoolboys.

The next day Lieutenant General George Gordon Meade, commander of the Army of the Potomac, rode out to visit Robert E. Lee. Doffing his cap as officers did in the old Army, he said, "Good morning, General."

"What are you doing with all that gray in your beard?" Lee asked.

"You have to answer for most of it," Meade replied.

In Richmond, not long after it was occupied by Federal troops, George Pickett's wife answered a knock on her door, carrying her baby on her arm. There stood "a tall, gaunt, sad-faced man in ill-fitting clothes" who asked if this was George Pickett's home. When the young wife said it was, the stranger introduced himself. "I am Abraham Lincoln."

"The President," gasped Mrs. Pickett.

Lincoln shook his head. "No ma'am, no ma'am; just Abraham Lincoln, George's old friend."

"I am George Pickett's wife, and this is his baby," was all the aston- ished young woman could say.

Lincoln took the baby in his arms, and the little boy gave him a kiss. For a moment the sadness vanished from Lincoln's face. Then he gave the boy back to his mother, and playfully shaking his finger at him, said: "Tell your father, the rascal, that I forgive him for the sake of that kiss and those bright eyes."

At Greensboro, North Carolina, a few weeks later, William Tecumseh Sherman accepted the surrender of the last Southern army in being on terms even more magnanimous than those of Appomattox. To his op- ponent, Joseph Johnston, Sherman even gave the honor of first place in the signers of the surrender document. He issued ten days' rations to all Southern soldiers and loaned them "enough farm animals to insure a crop." Special orders went out to the Union Army to "encourage the inhabitants to renew their peaceful pursuits and to restore the relations of friendship among our fellow citizens and countrymen." Johnston, a man not given to emotional statements, wrote to Sherman, "The en- larged patriotism exhibited in your orders reconciles me to what I have previously regarded as the misfortune of my life, that of having you to encounter in the field."

When Walt Whitman heard the news of Appomattox, he cried: "Affection shall solve the problems of freedom yet!" Certainly not a little of that half-prayer, half-tribute, had been earned by West Pointers, North and South.

Years of Iron

I

THE SPIRIT OF APPOMATTOX vanished when a fanatic blazed a bullet through Abraham Lincoln's brain. The nation reeled down the dreary road to Reconstruction, and decades passed before the bitterness receded. But some West Pointers never ceased striving for reconciliation.

Morris Schaff tells of riding a train from Montgomery to Atlanta late one night some months after the war. It stopped at a lonely station and Charles B. Ball, the handsome ex-first sergeant of Company A, class of June, 1861, entered the car. He had fought through the war, becoming a cavalry colonel. "As soon as he recognized me," Schaff says, "he quickened his step and met me with such unaffected cordiality that the car seemed to glow with new lamps. In view of what had gone before I would not have been hurt had he merely bowed and passed on, for I realized how much there had been to embitter. Yet he sat, and he talked over old times half the night. I could not help wondering as he parted from me whether I could have shown so much magnanimity had the South conquered the North and had I come home in rags, to find the old farm desolate. I doubt it."

General of the Armies Grant greeted his old comrade ex-Lieutenant General "Pete" Longstreet with a smile and a handshake in his War Department office. One version has him locking arms with Longstreet and good-naturedly saying: "Pete, let's go back to the good old times and play a game of brag [a favorite Army card game] as we used to."

That evening Grant entertained Longstreet at his home, and the man who had been second in command of the Army of Northern Virginia recalled in his memoirs how much he enjoyed meeting "old-time personal friends." When he left, Grant walked him to the gate and asked if he cared to have his pardon. Longstreet replied that he did not feel he had committed an offense that required a pardon. Grant said he meant amnesty—which President Andrew Johnson was granting on a selective basis. Old Pete allowed that he would not mind regaining the right to vote and otherwise participate in the Republic. Grant told him to call at his office at noon the next day.

There the victorious commander in chief handed his ex-foe a personal letter to the President urging Longstreet to be included among the forgiven. "I have known him well for more than 26 years," Grant wrote. "First as a cadet at West Point and afterwards as an officer of the army. For five years from my graduation we served together, a portion of the time in the same regiment . . . I shall feel it is a personal favor to myself if this pardon is granted."

President Johnson greeted Longstreet cordially, but the next day informed him with regret: "There are three persons of the South who can never receive amnesty: Mr. Davis, General Lee and yourself. You have given the Union cause too much trouble."

"You know, Mr. President, that those who are forgiven most love the most," Longstreet replied.

"You have a high authority for that," said Johnson, "but you can't have amnesty."

But Grant was persistent, and when a list of names from Georgia came through the War Department with requests for pardons, Grant simply put Longstreet's name on it. For a while Old Pete prospered as a businessman in New Orleans, but he drew the wrath of unrepentant Southerners when he wrote a public letter to the newspaper advising the state to accept Negro suffrage without opposition. Once more Sam Grant came to his rescue. One of his first appointments after he was sworn as President of the United States on March 4, 1869, was Longstreet as surveyor of customs at New Orleans.

The wish to heal wounds, to preserve the spirit of Appomattox, was one of the motives that prompted several West Pointers to meet in the office of Horace Webster (class of 1818), president emeritus of the College of the City of New York, and found an Association of Graduates. The call for the first meeting could not have been sounded by a more symbolic figure—Major General Robert Anderson, defender of Fort Sumter. The idea for the Association was warmly approved by eighty-three-year-old Sylvanus Thayer, still living in retirement in Braintree. Responding to Anderson's urgings to attend the meeting Thayer wrote: "The belief that I am kindly remembered by the graduates still living whose education I had the honor to supervise is the principal source of happiness now remaining to me. To meet them again face to face and to pass a few days or hours in social interview with them would afford me a pleasure I could not deny myself were it possible for me to make the journey to New York. As it is, my spirit can only be there. My old worn out body cannot be."

The Association's first meeting, on May 22, 1869, elected Sylvanus Thayer president, an office that he retained until his death in 1872. Anderson himself had died two years earlier, and the leadership of the Association passed to a pair of sharply different men—George Cullum of the class of 1833 and Charles Davies of the class of 1815. One of Thayer's brighter academic stars, as instructor and later professor of mathematics from 1816 to 1837, Davies was now living in retirement at Fishkill-on-the-Hudson after closing his distinguished career as professor of mathematics at Columbia University. Cullum had come out of the Civil War a major general and served as Superintendent of West Point from 1864 to 1866. Devoted to both the Academy and the Union, Cullum had, with Thayer's help, begun a monumental "biographical register of the officers and graduates of the U.S. Military Academy" and was therefore already deeply involved in the lives and fortunes of West Point alumni. However, he was not inclined to forgive those graduates who had gone South during the war, and his biographical sketches of these men break off with the formula "Joined in the rebellion of 1861–1865 against the U.S.," and resume their individual histories after the war.

Davies played dove to Cullum's hawkish spirit. As the senior living graduate, he gave the address at the first annual reunion, held in the chapel at West Point on June 17, 1870. He was deeply disappointed that no Southerners appeared at this meeting, and forthwith launched a campaign to persuade some to make an appearance. By 1872, several ex-rebels, among them James Longstreet, were listed as paying members of the Association, and that year the first Southerner who had served in the war sat down at the table with his fellow graduates to swap reminiscences and join in toasts. He was Eugene McLean of Maryland, classmate of Longstreet. After serving in the Mexican War and on the frontier, largely in the Quartermaster Corps, he resigned his captaincy in 1861 and became a Confederate major. He was the only Southerner to attend before 1875, and his presence was best explained by his decision to make his home in New York City.

In 1875 Davies launched an all-out effort to recruit Southerners, and that year six appeared. Among them were Longstreet; Joseph R. Anderson (1836) of Virginia, who was a brigadier general in the Confederacy; Sewell Fremont (1841) of New Hampshire, whose marriage to a Carolina girl had persuaded him to become a Confederate colonel; Robert Ransom, Jr., (1850) of North Carolina, Confederate brigadier; and Francis H. Smith (1833) superintendent of VMI. Smith rejected Davies' first invitation, calling himself "an unpardoned rebel, with the rope around my neck." How could he sit down with his old comrades as an equal? Davies in reply begged him not to talk that way. He invited him to stay at his own house, as his guest.

Smith was persuaded, and when he reached Davies' house he found to his amazement "his friends and his neighbors were assembled to meet me—and, with the courtesy of one whose happiness consisted in making others happy, he made this visit the bright hour of my existence. The next day he took me to West Point." Smith never forgot "the emotion which that festive reunion awakened—the warmth of the reception extended me—all the loving work of this dear old friend."

While General Cullum undoubtedly squirmed, Davies rose at this meeting and made a welcoming speech that was both warm and wise. "Having viewed our duties from different standpoints, we have been separated. Viewing them together on this spot and on this anniversary, we are united . . . We turn our eyes to the past only for instruction and our hearts to the future, full of hope and full of joy. In the meeting of today, the country will realize, that if the stream of nationality which flows out from this institution be occasionally interrupted by sandbars or dashed against the rocks, eddies will be formed only temporarily and that the whirling dizzy waters will soon return to their deep and tranquil channel."

II

THIS IS NOT a bad description of what West Point was doing at that time. As early as 1868, young men from Southern states were once more admitted to the plebe class. The value of this swift return to prewar practice was still evident, more than a decade later, when a young Texan named Beaumont Buck marched as a plebe in his first parade. "We were marching back to barracks. . . ." Buck recalled. "The companies were in echelon on that smooth, green drill field, and I was overflowing with pride and enthusiasm at the beautiful sight when suddenly the band switched its tune to 'Dixie'. Think of it! 'Dixie' in that northern state and Yankee region, only 15 years after Lee's surrender! And I, a Texan, marching to it!"

But bringing the Southerner back into the ranks by no means solved all the problems of the Reconstruction era. For West Point it compounded one of the fundamental problems: the status of the Negro. Five years after the war ended, West Point enrolled its first Negro cadet.

Although the North had won the war, Abolitionists, with their doctrine of Negro equality, remained a comparative minority in American society. Perhaps the best index of the prevailing attitude was the state of Connecticut's refusal on October 2, 1865, to grant the vote to some 500 free Negroes within its borders. The Great Emancipator himself had shuddered at the problems of integrating the Negro and strongly favored sending the freed slaves out of the country to colonies in Africa and South America. But the Abolitionists, sitting in Congress as so-called Republican "Radicals," were committed to Negro rights from a political as well as an ethical viewpoint. Ulysses Grant had slipped into the White House with a majority of only 306,000; without 700,000 Negro votes the Republican party would have relapsed into a minority role. It was inevitable, therefore, that West Point should become a public testing-ground for this explosive issue.

With newspapers, politicians and the people watching, it was vital to select the first Negro cadet with care. Benjamin F. Butler of Massachusetts attempted to conduct a search for one, with the aid of President James Fairchild of Oberlin College. But neither man could find a Negro with the proper combination of solid education, rugged physique, and military inclination to survive West Point's ordeal. Butler gave up, and the first two cadets to appear were haphazard appointments of carpetbagger congressmen from Mississippi and South Carolina for the year 1870.

Rufus L. King, who was a tactical officer at West Point at the time, gives the following description of the two cadets, in terms that reflect all too well the prevailing attitude toward the Negro. The young man from Mississippi, whose name was Howard, King described as "a chuckling, bullet-headed little darkie, whose great eyes would wander from object to object as though in search of something to excuse the cachinnation for which his soul was longing." James Webster Smith, the young man from South Carolina, King saw as "a tall, slim, loose-jointed cadaverous party, with arms and legs of extraordinary length, and indescribable complexion, chalky white except in spots where the tan struck through, and occasional deeper splotches of brown; little beady, snakelike eyes, high cheek bones and kinky hair . . . the personification of repulsive gloom."

Smith, in an account published four years later, said that within an hour after he reported on the thirty-first of May, 1870, he was reminded "by several thoughtful cadets that I was nothing but a 'd—d nigger.' " He and Howard were put in the same room to await their preliminary examination. A few nights later, at midnight, a mysterious figure appeared in the doorway of their room and flung the contents of his slop pail over them while they were asleep. Searching through the tobacco quids and other rubbish they found an old envelope addressed to one McCord of Kentucky, another new appointee. He denied having anything to do with the outrage, and the matter was dropped. But a few days later, Smith said, Howard was struck in the face by McCord, when he failed to get out of McCord's way while going into the bootblack's shop. McCord was confined to his room but never punished because a few days later he failed the entrance examination and was sent home.

As might be suspected, Rufus King gives a far different version of the altercation in the bootblack shop. This was a room in the basement of the barracks where the cadets got their shoes shined. According to King, the two Negro cadets came to the tactical officers complaining bitterly of a mass assault. They said that when it came their turn to step upon the shoeblack's bench they had been roughly hustled off with much abusive language. When they insisted on having their shoes blacked in their turn they had been seized by the throat, hurled against the wall and held there by certain young gentlemen whose names they gave, while bowie knives were flourished and dreadful fates were predicted. Smith told the story and Howard corroborated him, going so far as to blurt out, "Yes sah—and pistols too—six shooters."

Within a half hour, King says, three officers were taking testimony in a barrack room. The officer who served as recorder, whom King identifies only as Mr. X, was an ardent Abolitionist, one of the first to recruit colored troops for the Civil War. He was determined to punish the offenders with maximum severity, hoping to head off similar incidents in the future.

Following routine procedure, the two complainants were examined singly. Smith vigorously corroborated his first recital and "unflinchingly" submitted to cross-examination. But Howard did not fare so well. "Every time he told his story," King says, "it differed in important detail from his previous attempt." Sympathetically, Mr. X decided he was "flustered" and dismissed him "to think the matter over for a while." Meanwhile, the six cadets accused by the two Negroes were examined one by one. "Their stories fitted together with exact nicety," King said. "Nor had they had time to concoct one. The instant the affair took place all the implicated parties were placed under surveillance." Six or seven other eyewitnesses were examined and all agreed with the basic story of the defendants. There had been some elbowing and shoving between one cadet and Smith about whose turn it was to step into the bootblack chair. But all the white cadets insisted no violence took place. The moment the shoving began, they said, Smith had called on Howard to follow him from the room shouting, "Now we'll see we get our rights."

The officers recalled Smith, who stuck to his story stolidly, sullenly, but "slipped," King said, on several minor points in cross-examination. "When the discrepancies were pointed out to him, he bit his lip, apparently strove to enlarge a knothole in the floor with the toe of his boot and muttered that that was all he knew about it; he declined to say any more."

Now Howard was recalled. At the second question, King said, he "broke down, hung his head, giggled, stammered, chuckled, experimented with his boot toe on the same knothole and then threw up the sponge with an air of evident relief."

"Do you mean to say that your previous statement was untrue?"

"Yes sah."

"No knives were drawn?"

"No sah."

"Then did the cadets lay hands on you or Mr. Smith or not?"

"No sah; they didn't touch us."

According to King, Howard went on to confess that he and Smith had been put up to the whole performance by letters from Negro friends and carpetbag politicians, who guaranteed to support them the moment they complained. A few days later Howard flunked the entrance examination and was sent home. Smith passed and was duly admitted as the first Negro cadet.

Professor (of French) George L. Andrews, class of 1851, who wrote a long review of the colored cadets at West Point ten years later, said of Smith, "probably a worse selection for the first colored cadet could not have been made. He was malicious, vindictive and untruthful. Instead of contenting himself with manfully meeting trouble when it came, he diligently and successfully sought it." Captain King went even farther, snarling, "Of all the low, tricky, vindictive bipeds that walk the earth, it would have been difficult for the 'friends of the movement' to have selected a specimen better qualified to carry out their plans."

The last word is significant. The radical Republican contempt for West Point—as evidenced by the ferocious attacks they made on the Academy during the Civil War—made soldiers such as King wonder if Smith had not been sent to West Point as part of a conspiracy to destroy the school. At the same time, Professor Andrews pointed out the other side of West Point's dilemma. He told of a gentleman who brought his son as a candidate and seeing Smith and Howard expressed himself with warm approval about the appointment of the two cadets. When one of the tactical officers pointed out that his son might well room with one of them, the man did a 360-degree revolution and spluttered with alarm and indignation.

James Webster Smith's father had been a slave, had been freed by Sherman's army and joined its ranks. His mother was freeborn; he received his first schooling in a "freedmen's school" in Columbia, South Carolina. The teacher was so impressed by his abilities she brought him to the attention of David Clark, a Hartford philanthropist who brought the boy to that city and sent him to the local high school. He then studied for a time at Howard University.

Smith stood tenth in his class during his plebe year, but his personal relations with his fellow cadets grew steadily worse. "Left alone as I was by Howard's failure," he later bitterly recalled, "I had to take every insult that was offered, without saying anything, for I had complained several times to the commandant of cadets and after investigating the matter he invariably came to the conclusion 'from the evidence deduced' that I was in the wrong, and I was cautioned that I had better be very particular about any statements that I might make, as the regulations were very strict on the subject of veracity." Smith told of being ordered to clean quids of tobacco from the company street. When he got a broom and shovel, the upperclassmen supposedly began swearing at and abusing him for not using his fingers, which the corporal of the guard said were "made for that purpose." Whereupon, Smith wrote a complaining letter to his patron, David Clark, who had it published in the newspapers and had copies forwarded to Congress. A board of radical congressmen descended upon West Point for a series of hearings and recommended a number of cadets for court-martial. The Secretary of War declined to cooperate, and issued reprimands instead.

Smith was totally incapable of realizing what he had done in the eyes of the corps. Instead of doing good, he complained, "these reprimands seemed only to increase the enmity of the cadets." Captain Charles King recorded one result of Smith's public complaints. "Reporters were buzzing about the post incessantly . . . next to them in rank as nuisances came the strong-minded women who claimed to represent the Methodist or Baptist faith . . . there was no matter beneath their notice—there was no subject into which they did not pry. The Academy was at their mercy now, for under cover of the interest which all American citizens were supposed to be taking in the colored cadet, these harpies of modern civilization swooped down upon the post and even the personal homes of the officers' families were invaded by them in their hungry curiosity." Professor Andrews concluded, "In a white cadet such conduct would have resulted, not only in complete isolation, but also in treatment (physical punishment) Smith never received."

Before the end of the summer encampment Smith's temper broke under the torment and he attacked a fellow cadet (whom he declared had insulted him) with a dipper, inflicting severe wounds on his head. He was court-martialed with no less a personage than Major General Oliver O. Howard as president of the board. Howard, the Abolitionist cadet who had been rescued from coventry by Jeb Stuart, had lost an arm in the Civil War but stayed in uniform and emerged as one of the most popular Northern soldiers. His presence on the court-martial board guaranteed an impartial verdict. But Smith got more than impartiality. Both he and his opponent in the battle of the dipper were convicted and sentenced to three weeks' confinement and extra duty. To the Academy's astonishment, President Grant "disapproved" Smith's punishment on the highly legalistic ground that it was not severe enough and neither the President nor the War Department had the power to increase it.

In April, 1871, Smith was court-martialed again, this time for the much more serious charge of falsehood. According to Smith, he asked a certain cadet to stop treading on his toes in ranks. He was immediately reported by a cadet corporal for "inattention in ranks." When he detailed the circumstances, both the cadet corporal and the other cadet denied them and the Commandant of Cadets preferred charges against Smith. He was found guilty and sentenced to be dismissed. But once more President Grant intervened and Smith was suspended for a year. Since he had almost completed his first year by the time the final decision returned from Washington, he was "turned back"—forced to repeat his first year.

Smith stood well up in his class the second time around, but when he went into his yearling (sophomore) course, he began to slide steadily downward and eventually found himself treading along the precipice of dismissal in the last section with the "immortals." Meanwhile, he continued his self-defeating policy of encouraging outside publicity. His benefactor, David Clark, wrote a bitter letter to the *New York Daily Tribune* in the summer of 1872, contrasting the treatment Smith received and the supposed favoritism showered on the President's son Fred, who was graduated that year, thirty-seventh in a class of forty-one. In the spring of 1873, Eli Perkins, a friend of the congressman who had appointed Smith, published a long (almost 2000 words) letter in New York's *Daily Graphic* giving his version of the courts-martial and maintaining that Smith's decline in class standing was because "he lived a hermit life, isolated and alone." Smith described himself to Perkins as "rooming all alone with no one to help me and no one to clear up the knotty points. If there is an obscure point in my lesson I must go to the class with it. I cannot go to a brother cadet."

"If you should ask them to help you, what would they say?"

"They would call me a — Nigger and tell me to go back to the plantation."

Even Perkins admitted that the officials of the Academy had made strenuous efforts to guarantee Smith equal treatment. He told how the new Commandant of Cadets, Emory Upton, had sent for him and told him, "You shall not be persecuted into resigning. I am your friend. Come to me and you shall have justice."

But other officers, such as Captain King, were vastly disenchanted with Smith. In his memoir, King tells how the officer who favored Negro rights, Mr. X, one day noted "some stir and disorder, in Company A" as it broke ranks. A moment later the colored cadet rushed into his presence crying, "Mr. X, I claim your protection. I am in fear of my life."

Mr. X calmed Smith and assured him that no harm would come to him. Smith then claimed that on breaking ranks he had been violently assaulted by a cadet from Kentucky. Mr. X sent his orderly for the Kentuckian. "You are accused of having assaulted Cadet Smith on breaking ranks. What have you to say?"

"It is true, sir," said the Kentuckian. "I am sorry but I could not help it. He was kicking me all the way from the mess hall. He had done it time and time again, and at last I lost my temper. He ran as we broke ranks and I was foolish and furious enough to follow and cuff his ears for him. He isn't hurt, sir, half as much as I am."

This was evident, King asserts. The Kentuckian was limping and Smith did not have a mark on him. Nevertheless, Mr. X sent the Kentucky cadet to his quarters, under arrest. Thus, says King, the feeling gained ground among the cadets that the institution was run solely in the interest of the colored man and that Mr. X was a "nigger worshipper."

King tells how the Academy made strenuous efforts to be sure Smith was treated with strict equality in such matters as the location of his room and his seat in the mess hall. When they discovered that the cadet lieutenant of Smith's company refused to sit at the same table and eat with him, he was reported for dereliction of duty, and that night at parade, he was shorn of his sword, plume, sash and gold lace and returned to the ranks.

But the Academy could do little to mitigate the underlying prejudice with which the cadets confronted the Negro. This hostility was obviously immune to preaching, pleas, and disciplinary actions. The only way it could be altered was by the Negro himself. How he coped with this trial by fire was crucial. West Point's faculty watched with great anxiety when the summer of 1873 brought two more Negro appointees. One was Henry Ossian Flipper from Georgia, the second, John Washington Williams from Virginia. Of Williams little is known. He lasted only six months and was dismissed for academic deficiency along with a host of others in his class. But Flipper, well educated at the University of Atlanta, had no problems with his studies. He also, from the beginning, personified a new way of dealing with the corps' prejudice.

He was, first of all, prepared for it. He had given considerable thought to how he was going to handle it. He had the advantage of watching Smith in action, and he drew some sober conclusions from his observations. He was, he later wrote, "particularly careful not to fall into an error which, I think, has been the cause of misfortune to at least one of the cadets of color. If a cadet affront another, if a white cadet insult a colored one, for instance, the latter can complain to the proper authorities, and if there be good reason for it, can always get proper redress. This undoubtedly gives the consolation of knowing that the offense will not be repeated, but beyond that I think it a great mistake to have so sought it." Flipper also disdained any crying out to the governnment for protection. He disapproved of an article in a Negro newspaper that called on Congress to exert its authority on behalf of the Negro cadets. "I disdainfully scout the idea of such protection," he declared. "If my manhood cannot stand without a governmental prop, then let it fall. If I am to stand on any other ground than the one white cadets stand upon, then I don't want the cadetship. If I cannot endure prejudice and persecutions, even if they are offered, then I don't deserve the cadetship, and much less the commission of an army officer."

Flipper then went on to state what he saw as the only answer to rooting out prejudice at West Point. "The remedy lies solely in our case with us. We can make our life at West Point what we will. We shall be treated by the cadets as we treat them. Of course, some of the cadets are low—and good treatment cannot be expected of them at West Point nor away from there. The others, presumably gentlemen, will treat everybody else as becomes gentlemen, or at any rate as they themselves are treated. . . . Prejudice does not necessarily prevent a man's being courteous and gentlemanly in his relations with others."

"The story of the colored cadets might have been quite different if

Flipper had been the first instead of Smith," wrote Professor George Andrews, seven years later.

Another glimpse of the difference between Flipper and Smith can be gleaned from an anecdote Flipper tells about himself, during the few months that Williams was in the school. "It was just after evening call to quarters. I knew Smith and Williams were in our room. I had been out for some purpose and was returning when it occurred to me to have some fun at their expense. I accordingly walked up to the door—our 'house' was at the head of the stairs and on the third floor—and knocked, endeavoring to imitate as much as possible an officer inspecting. They sprang to their feet instantly, assumed the position of the soldier and quietly awaited my entrance. I entered laughing."

Flipper says Smith and Williams promised to repay him, and they did. The next morning Flipper found himself reported for imitating a tactical officer and was required to walk three tours of extra guard duty on three consecutive Saturdays and serve a week's confinement in his quarters. Curiously Flipper does not blame either Smith or Williams for this petty revenge. By the time Flipper wrote his book, *The Colored Cadet at West Point,* Williams and Smith had both been dismissed. Smith's departure (for failure in natural philosophy) triggered angry protests in the radical Republican and Negro press. One writer who signed himself Niger Nigrorum declared that Smith had been "hounded out of the Academy" because when he graduated he would have to be assigned to a white regiment. Citing a half dozen Negro students who had done well at Amherst, Dartmouth, and Yale, the writer asked, "What divinity then hedges West Point and Annapolis? What but the old rebel spirit which seeks again to control them for use in future rebellions as it did in the past." Smith himself published a series of letters in the New National Era and Citizen, a Negro newspaper published in Washington, D.C., severely criticizing West Point and accusing everyone from cadets to the Superintendent of collusion in his dismissal.

Flipper sharply disagreed with these assertions, although he treated Smith with extreme caution. "Of Smith I prefer to say nothing," he wrote. "Of Williams I do express the belief that his treatment was impartial and just. He was regularly and rightly found deficient and duly dismissed." To imply that he should not have been "found" and dismissed simply because he was a Negro, was, in Flipper's opinion "a very shallow reason indeed and one no fair minded man will for an instant entertain." A page later, however, Flipper cannot resist a somewhat masked appraisal of Smith. "I have had an opportunity to become acquainted with Smith's conduct," he wrote, "and that of the cadets toward him. Smith had trouble under my own eyes on more than one occasion . . . But I have not had so much as an angry word to utter. There is a reason for all this and had Niger Nigrorum been better acquainted with it he had never made the blunder he has."

Nevertheless, Flipper makes it clear in his memoir that it required all his strength and self-control to endure the unrelenting pressure of cadet prejudice, not to mention the slanders published against him in Democratic newspapers. One asserted that he had stolen a number of articles from two cadets, had been caught in the act and his guilt established beyond the possibility of doubt. According to the vicious story, the cadets who accused him had been dismissed and Flipper was retained.

Flipper's experience also undercuts considerably Professor Andrews' assertion that the cadets learned their prejudice at home. There would seem to be little doubt that an organized conspiracy existed within the corps to unite every white cadet in a cruel, unrelenting coventry. "It is a remarkable fact that the new cadets, in only a very few instances," Flipper said, "show any unwillingness to speak or fraternize. It is not until they come in contact with the rougher elements of the corps that they manifest any disposition to avoid one . . . When I was a plebe, those of us who lived on the same floor of barracks visited each other, borrowed books, heard each other recite when preparing for examination, and were really on most intimate terms. But alas! in less than a month they learned to call me 'nigger' and ceased altogether to visit me."

He tells an ironic story of a young man who had been a plebe with him and was dismissed at the end of the first six months. Two years later, Flipper met him in New York, while on furlough. By now the entire corps was united in treating Flipper as an outcast, but his exclassmate, knowing nothing of this, hurried across the street, shook Flipper's hand heartily and expressed great delight at seeing him. "He showed me the photograph of a classmate, told me where I could find him, evidently ignorant of my ostracism and wishing me all sorts of success, took his leave," Flipper says.

Flipper's analysis of how prejudice operated within the corps is worth quoting at length, because it is a microcosm of American society yes-terday—and, alas, to some extent today. "There are some, indeed the majority of the corps are such who treat me on all occasions with proper politeness. They are gentlemen themselves and treat others as it becomes a gentleman to do. They do not associate, nor do they speak other than officially, except in a few cases. They are perhaps as much prejudiced as the others, but prejudice must not prevent all from being gentlemen. On the other hand, there are some from the very lowest classes of our population. They are uncouth and rough in appearance, have only a rudimentary education, have little or no idea of courtesy, use the very worst language and in most cases are much inferior to the average Negro . . . What surprises me most is the control this class seems to have over the other. It is in this class I have observed most prejudice and from it, or rather by it, the other becomes tainted. It seems to rule the corps by fear. Indeed, I know there are many who would associate, who would treat me as a brother cadet, were they not held in constant dread of this class." Only the officers were exempt from this contagion. "They," Flipper said, "have treated me with uniform courtesy and impartiality."

Flipper found the conduct of some cadets particularly disheartening. During his yearling (second year) camp, a plebe asked to borrow his first year algebra book so he could do some "boning" during the summer. Flipper "readily consented" and the plebe "went into ecstasies, and made no end of thanks to me for my kindness, etc. All this naturally confirmed my opinion and hope of better recognition ultimately. Indeed I was glad of an opportunity to prove that I was not unkind or ungenerous." Flipper only asked the plebe to take good care of the book. He was planning to save it, as he did all his books, for future use and a souvenir of his cadet life. Flipper's name was on the back, on the cover, and his initial "F" in two other places on the cover. When the plebe returned the book in September, Flipper was appalled to discover the grateful borrower had cut the calfskin from the cover, to remove the telltale name. "Such unmanliness, such cowardice, such baseness even was most disgusting; and I felt very much as if I would like to—well, I don't know that I would. There was no reason at all for mutilating the book. If he was not man enough to use it with my name on it, why did he borrow it and agree not to injure it? Why did he not borrow someone else's and return mine?"

Paradoxically, Flipper could at the same time answer the question,

"What is the general feeling of the corps toward you?" with the words, "A feeling of kindness, restrained kindness, if you please." He goes on to explain, "The majority of the corps have ever treated me as I would desire to be treated. I mean, of course, by this assertion that they have treated me as I expected and really desired them to treat me so long as they were prejudiced." Flipper illustrates the almost superhuman understanding this conclusion required, with several stories.

He once heard a cadet say, when a classmate had been accidentally hurt in light battery drill, "I wish it had been the nigger, and it had killed him." Flipper gave him a cool look. Sometime after this at cavalry drill, he says, "we were side by side and I had a rather vicious horse. One in fact which I could not manage. He gave a sudden jump unexpectedly to me. I almost lost my seat in the saddle. This cadet seized me by the arm and in a tone of voice that was evidently kind and generous said to me, 'For heaven's sake, be careful. You'll be thrown and get hurt if you don't.' "

During Flipper's senior or first class year, he had the good fortune to draw lot number one and therefore had the first choice of all the horses in the stables. "Several classmates hastened to me for the purpose of affecting an exchange of choice. . . . With the avowed intention of proving that I had at least a generous disposition, and also that I was not disposed to consider in my reciprocal relations with the cadets how I had been, and was even then, treated by them, I consented to exchange my first choice for the fourteenth." A few days later, Flipper overheard several other cadets discussing the choice of horses. One of them suggested that Flipper might accept a choice even lower than fourteen. But another cadet cut them off with: "Oh, no, that would be imposing upon Mr. Flipper's good nature."

One night during the winter, when Flipper was on sentry duty during supper, a cadet of the class above him stopped on his post and conversed with him "as long as it was safe to do so." The boy expressed regret that Flipper should be isolated, asked him how he got along in his studies and many other questions. "He assured me that he was wholly unprejudiced," Flipper said, "and would ever be a friend. He even went far enough to say, to my great astonishment, that he cursed me and my race among the cadets to keep up appearances with them, and that I must think none the less well of him for so doing. It was a sort of necessity, he said, for he would not only be cut but would be treated a

great deal worse than I was if he should fraternize with me." As he was
leaving he told Flipper: "I'm damned sorry to see you come here to be
treated so, but I am glad to see you stay."

Other cadets followed this same two-faced policy. One boy repeatedly
called Flipper "nigger" or "damned nigger" in ranks. But once when he
brought to Flipper's room the integration of some differential equation in mechanics (on order of their instructor) he was very friendly,
called him "Mr. Flipper" and said if he desired any further information
to come to his "house."

Flipper never allowed himself to be imposed on in any area that
affected his rights as a cadet. When he became a second classman
he had a right to the front rank in his company. In the spring of
his second class year, when forming a company for a retreat parade,
the sergeant ordered Flipper into the rear rank. The Negro cadet
obeyed, feeling sure that after the company was formed and inspected he
would be placed in the front rank once more. But this did not happen.
He then turned to the sergeant and asked if he could take his place in
the front rank, pointing out several third classmen there. The
sergeant yielded but reported him for challenging the way he was
discharging his duty. Flipper promptly wrote out an explanation for
the Commandant of Cadets who in turn asked for an explanation from
the sergeant. The young man said rather lamely that he had put Flipper
in the rear rank because he saw no third classmen in the front rank.
"This is a little thing," Flipper says, "but it should be borne in mind that
it is nevertheless of the greatest importance . . . any affront to me which
is also an affront to my class and its dignity deserves punishment or
satisfaction. To demand it then gives my class a better opinion of me
and serves to keep that opinion in as good condition as possible."

In the U.S. Military Academy ninety years before Martin Luther
King, Flipper was applying the theory of nonviolence and proving its
power. He quoted with approval the Biblical counsel, "Therefore if thine
enemy hunger, feed him; if he thirsts, give him drink; for in so doing
thou shalt heap coals of fire upon his head." By the time Flipper was a
first classman he was accepted as Smith had never been. The wall of
prejudice remained between him and true social equality in the
corps, but his firm, calm conduct had breached it in a dozen ways. In
June of 1876, when the corps went into camp, Flipper was able to write,
"Nothing is done to make it unpleasant or any way to discourage or

dishearten me." The corps went to Philadelphia to march at the Centennial Exposition. "There not only is the same kindness shown to me," Flipper wrote, "but I find a number of cadets accost me whenever we meet, on the avenues and streets, on the grounds and in the city. They ask questions, converse, answer questions. . . . After the parade on the Fourth of July, every kindness was shown me. Those cadets near me bought lemons, lemonade, etc., and shared with me, and when on another occasion I was the purchaser, they freely partook of my good cheer."

Yet at the same time there appeared in a Philadelphia paper an interview, supposedly with a cadet, describing how the corps treated Flipper. "We don't have anything to do with him off duty," said this unidentified spokesman for the corps. "We don't even speak to him. Outside of duty we don't know him."

Back at West Point as Flipper assumed the duties of a first classman, which included such responsibilities as acting as officer of the guard, he noted that he was no longer referred to as "the nigger," "the moke," or "the thing." Now he regularly heard himself mentioned as "Mr. Flipper." Some cadets expressed shock when they saw Flipper acting as officer of the guard, but his authority was recognized by every cadet, without a moment's hesitation. Even when he reported a recalcitrant cadet and some of the "low ones," as Flipper called the bitterly prejudiced portion of the corps, complained, the Commandant backed Flipper unquestionably. "Your duty was a plain one and you discharged it properly," the Commandant said.

"What is the conduct of this cadet himself afterwards?" Flipper wrote "If different at all from what it was before, it is in my presence at least more cordial, more friendly, more kind. Still there is no ill treatment, assuming, of course, that my own conduct is proper, and not obtrusive and overbearing."

Thus Henry Ossian Flipper became the first Negro cadet to graduate from West Point. He was assigned to an all-Negro regiment, the 9th Cavalry, serving on the Western frontier. But West Point had by no means solved the Negro problem. Flipper left behind him at West Point another member of his race, Johnson Chestnut Whittaker of South Carolina, appointed to fill the vacancy created by Smith's dismissal after several white candidates had been appointed and failed. Whittaker was, temperamentally, another Smith. Flipper had gone through four years without another cadet so much as threatening him with physical harm. Whittaker was in the Academy little more than a month when he was struck in the face by a young man from Alabama, supposedly for sneering at him while passing by. Whittaker reported the affair to the cadet officer of the day, who put the Alabama cadet under arrest. He was court-martialed, found guilty and suspended for six months. Thereafter, perhaps Whittaker learned from Flipper's example. At any rate, he had no more personal difficulties of this sort. But he did poorly in his studies, following Smith's declining course to the foot of the class, and the "immortals."

Meanwhile, Ulysses S. Grant, in the final year of his Presidency, took an unprecedented step, which most observers saw as a grandstand gesture to placate the Negro vote. He persuaded Major General John Schofield, another Civil War notable and former Secretary of War, 1868–69, to accept the Superintendency of West Point. To soothe Schofield's pride, Grant, with the cooperation of General in Chief Sherman, elevated West Point into a department, which made it theoretically equal to such vast realms as the Department of the Pacific, over which major generals normally presided. Schofield accepted the job with great reluctance, feeling, with considerable justification, that he had nothing to gain and everything to lose. But he was a loyal soldier, and when Sherman told him it was for the good of the Army, he yielded.

In 1879 Whittaker hit the bottom of the bottom, and the Academic Board found him deficient. He was now the only Negro cadet in school, and Schofield, perhaps remembering the turmoil caused by Smith's dismissal, decided to turn Whittaker back a year rather than dismiss him. Schofield said Whittaker had "won the sympathy of all by his manly deportment and earnest efforts to succeed."

Unfortunately, Whittaker did no better while repeating his second class course. But the public knew nothing about his problems. Neither his deficiency nor his need to repeat the year had been publicized. Flipper's graduation and Whittaker's otherwise sensible conduct in his relations to the rest of the corps had seemingly defanged the newspaper critics. But on April 6, 1880, came a cataclysm that made all previous tempests seem mild.

A tactical officer, investigating Whittaker's absence from class, found the Negro cadet lying on the floor on his right side, his hands tied in front of him, his feet tied to the side rail of the bedstead, his head bleeding, blood on the floor and on a nearby Indian club. Oddly, there was a pillow under his head. Patches of his hair had been cut off. Broken pieces of a mirror were scattered around him. The Superintendent, the Commandant of Cadets and the surgeon were summoned immediately and reached Whittaker's room within minutes. The surgeon found his skin and pulse were normal, and though he appeared to be unconscious he resisted when the surgeon tried to raise one of his eyelids. A moment later he woke up, and the surgeon noted it was an immediate, not gradual, return to consciousness and he at once appeared to be in full possession of his faculties.

Whittaker told a shocking story. On the previous Sunday afternoon he had found in his room an anonymous note of warning. On the night of the sixth, three masked cadets had entered his room, cut him about the face and head, smashed him in the face with the mirror, struck him on the head with the Indian club, then tied him up and warned him that if he didn't leave the Academy, he would be a dead man. General Schofield was infuriated. He vowed "that every possible effort will be made to detect the perpetrators of this outrage."

Meanwhile, the surgeon and the assistant surgeon were examining Whittaker. His injuries were found to be slight; there were superficial cuts or scratches on his ears, hand and toe, but no other marks or bruises on his head or body. Although he said his nose had bled when they hit him with the mirror, the doctors could find no evidence of it. At the same time, the Commandant of Cadets called before him every cadet in the corps and asked him to state on his word of honor whether he knew anything about either the attack on Whittaker or the note of warning. Knowledge of either was universally denied. At this point the Commandant and the surgeon joined in a report to General Schofield, in which they opined that Whittaker had in some way cooperated with his assailants. Superintendent Schofield showed the report to Whittaker, who at once demanded a Court of Inquiry.

Meanwhile, on the very morning that Whittaker had been discovered, a reporter arrived at West Point and throughout the country sensational stories blossomed. One paper stated that Whittaker's ears had been cut off. All the belaborers of West Point leaped to their type fonts once more, dredging up the by now familiar charge that the Academy had a planned policy of driving out Negro applicants.

The Court of Inquiry met on April 9. Whittaker was the first witness.

Professor Andrews says, "He gave his testimony without nervousness or trepidation, and in a manner to produce a favorable impression." The other cadets also were examined under oath and once more they swore they neither knew nor suspected any member of the corps.

The court found few substantial clues. One story, reported as a rumor, told of three cadets visiting the house of one Ryan, the liquor dealer at Highland Falls, Celtic successor to Benny Havens, on the previous Sunday and declaring in their cups that Whittaker would be "fixed." Ryan was called as a witness and swore that no cadets ever visited his establishment. But his wife and daughter contradicted him to his face and some of the cadets also acknowledged that they had been at Ryan's, but not on that particular Sunday. Finally, the story was traced to three enlisted men stationed at West Point who had taunted Ryan about selling, with the cooperation of his wife and daughter, pleasures more appealing to cadets than liquor. Apparently they said he would sell them even to Whittaker and Ryan in a fury had run them out of his house and later told his milkman about the insult. This was, as far as the Court of Inquiry could determine, the root of the three-cadet story. Other rumors proved equally groundless. The only solid clue was the note of warning.

Zeroing in on this piece of paper, Schofield hired five handwriting experts. On numbered pieces of paper to guarantee anonymity they were given samples of the handwriting of every cadet in the corps. Members of Whittaker's class, who were naturally under stronger suspicion, were forced to surrender from 25 to 57 samples torn from their lecture notebooks. Four of the five men on the first examination declared Whittaker the author of the note.

The experts were then recalled for another round of examinations, the samples being numbered anonymously as before. This time, expert number five, who had declined to accuse Whittaker, discovered that the note of warning was written on a piece of paper torn from a sheet on which Whittaker had written a letter to his mother and that another part of the letter was on paper that Whittaker had originally used to write a requisition for stamps. In the letter to his mother, Whittaker mentioned having received the note of warning, a disastrous faux pas for him, since it showed that the note was written while the sheet of paper was as yet whole. The other experts examined the torn edges of the two pieces of paper and confirmed the conclusion of the fifth expert.

Whittaker was now called before the court once more and questioned closely on certain discrepancies in his testimony. He had given two versions of how he was held when his ears were cut and never did explain satisfactorily why he failed to call for help. Then he was told what the handwriting experts had concluded, with special emphasis on the discovery of the fifth expert. "Only when the discovery was read did he change countenance," says Professor Andrews. Otherwise Whittaker stood his ground and insisted that if the experts said the note was in his handwriting, it only proved that some cadet was a clever forger. This the handwriting experts had already unanimously discarded as an impossibility.

The Court of Inquiry's findings enraged Superintendent Schofield. He was now convinced that Whittaker was "acting under orders from some authority which he believed perfectly competent to protect him from any possible harm." But Whittaker continued to steadfastly deny his guilt and propagandists up and down the country supported him so ably, the President intervened and forbade Schofield to dismiss Whittaker on any grounds but deficiency in his studies. Whittaker stayed on while Schofield fumed and Army Commander in Chief Sherman rushed to his support, denouncing the President and the newspapers for acting "like a pack of hounds barking at they knew not what."

The President and the Secretary of War apologized privately to Schofield, waited a few months and unceremoniously removed him, appointing Oliver O. Howard to replace him. Chief of the Freedman's Bureau, 1865–74 (Howard University is named after him), Howard's reputation with the Negroes was irreproachable, and his presence muffled somewhat the protest over Whittaker's supposed persecution. As for Whittaker, he was found deficient in natural philosophy, the subject he had flunked the year before and had been about to flunk again on the eve of his sensational play for national publicity. In his journal he ascribed his approaching failure to a vindictive hatred of Negroes on the part of the younger instructors. West Point remained convinced of Whittaker's guilt and any fair-minded examination of the case would find the evidence heavily against him. But the definitive truth will probably never be known.

As a final irony, the following year Henry Flipper was arrested and tried by general court-martial at Fort Sill, in Indian territory, for misappropriating and misapplying public funds that were entrusted to him while acting as post commissary, as well as for "conduct unbecoming an officer and a gentleman." He was acquitted of embezzlement but convicted on the second charge. Apparently Flipper had delegated to his civilian domestic employee the authority to mail certain checks to the chief of subsistence in San Antonio. This man was the real embezzler; the checks never reached their destination. But Flipper, meanwhile, was submitting official reports of his subsistence funds, based on the assumption that the checks had arrived. These reports were the basis of the second charge, for which he was dismissed from the service. Flipper spent the rest of his long life as an engineer, working first in Arizona and later in Mexico, where he also doubled as an agent for the Justice Department from 1893 until 1901. He became an authority on Mexican affairs, appeared as a witness before the Senate Foreign Relations Committee several times and ended his career as an engineer with the Pantepec Oil Company in Venezuela, from 1923 to 1930. Retiring, he spent the last ten years of his life in his native Georgia, dying in 1940 at the age of eighty-four.

At West Point, Superintendent Howard found little need for his friendliness toward the Negro. He left before the next colored appointee, John Hanks Alexander, arrived in 1883. Alexander graduated thirty-second in the class of 1887. He was followed by Charles Denton Young, who graduated at the foot of the class of 1889.

One of Young's classmates, Charles D. Rhodes, displayed considerable sympathy for Young in a letter he wrote shortly before graduation: "Our colored classmate, Charles Young, whom we esteem highly for his patient perseverance in the face of discouraging conditions which have attended his cadetship for five years [Young was forced to repeat one year], did poorly in both engineering and ordnance and was given a special written examination in each subject. . . . We are hoping that Young will get through; it would be a terrible disappointment for him to lose the coveted diploma after five years of intensive work." Young was found deficient. But his engineering instructor, Lieutenant George Goethals, made a special plea on his behalf and devoted hours that summer to preparing him for a special reexamination. Young passed by a comfortable margin and received his diploma on August 31, 1899. He retired from the army with the rank of colonel in 1923.

A total of thirteen Negroes were admitted to West Point during the first five decades after the Civil War. Only Flipper, Alexander and Young graduated. During this same period, Annapolis did not even admit a single Negro midshipman.

III

WEST POINT'S FAILURE to cope with the Negro problem was a symptom of a significant shift in the school's inner spirit. As higher education burgeoned throughout America, and more and more first-rate technical schools were founded (including one at Dartmouth, on money left by Sylvanus Thayer), the isolationist trend that had begun in the 1850's became definite, even final. West Point lost its sense of intellectual leadership, and became more and more absorbed solely in producing soldiers. The system became sacred, and it soon developed a rigidity and severity that went far beyond Thayer's regime. It could not be improved by change, only by intensification.

Ironically, the attitude of the man who had created the system was precisely opposite. Although he called himself "a conservative" and did not wish to see "organic changes merely to carry out plausible theories," Thayer also said "nothing should remain static, and all human things are imperfect." As late as 1865, in a letter to George Cullum, he was urging significant changes in the system. He wanted admission through nation-wide competitive examinations, a permanent "Board of Improvement," an "Inspector of Studies" acting as assistant to the Superintendent, and most important, a permanent Superintendent subject only to the orders of the President.

But Thayer was too old to exert any real influence. Hero-worshippers such as Cullum preferred to enshrine him rather than listen to him. More and more, the men in charge confused the rock on which West Point had been founded with the school itself. As the post-Reformation Catholic Church, with its own symbolism of the rock, tended to withdraw into itself and let the modern world go by, so did West Point. The goal became not flexible soldier-scholars, but men of iron.

Hugh Scott entered in 1871 and the following year was caught hazing a plebe, and turned back a year. Later that same year, Scott rescued a fellow cadet from drowning in the Hudson. Many of his classmates thought that his turnback sentence should be reprieved, "But those were not the days of forgiveness at West Point," Scott says. "Stand on your own feet. Behave yourself or take the consequences. Work out your own

The two outstanding West Pointers of the 20th century. Douglas MacArthur, 1903 (above), and Dwight D. Eisenhower, 1915. As cadets they were total opposites. MacArthur graduated first in his class and was First Captain. "He had style," said one contemporary. "There was never another cadet quite like him." Eisenhower drifted desultorily through in the middle of his class, razzing the "file boners" (top students) and frequently threatening to resign from sheer boredom. *U.S. Army Photographs.*

Earl H. ("Red") Blaik as an Army football star in 1920. He returned as head coach in 1941, and restored Army's football eminence. *U.S. Military Academy Archives.*

Michie Stadium at West Point, home of Army football. It is named for Lieutenant Dennis Mahan Michie, Class of 1892, captain of the first Army football team, who was killed in action at San Juan, Cuba, in 1898. *U.S. Army Photograph.*

World War II forced the Academy to abandon its "Napoleonic" summer camp (which Superintendent MacArthur had tried in vain to abolish) and switch to tough, realistic battle training. *U.S. Military Academy Archives.*

On July 1, 1942, the Academy launched a revolutionary new course at nearby Stewart Field. It blended pilot training and traditional West Point curriculum to produce the nation's first "air cadets." *U.S. Military Academy Archives.*

Negro cadets have graduated in growing numbers from the modern Academy. Here Clarence M. Davenport, Jr., Class of 1943, receives his diploma from Undersecretary of War Robert Patterson. Of fifty-four Negro West Pointers, forty-one have graduated since the Army was integrated in 1950. *Culver Pictures*.

New plebe or "beast" carrying his equipment from the supply depot—double-time. Most physical hazing has been abolished, but plebes must still "brace" (stand and sit at super-attention) and endure a year of verbal abuse before being "recognized." *Culver Pictures*.

salvation and root hog or die, were the sentiments which dominated there."

It had been the custom in the classes before Scott's for the yearlings to purchase some rowing shells from the graduating class for their use on the river. But when Scott's class tried to continue this tradition they were met with a firm no, and the shells remained at least four years in the boathouse without being used. "We thought that it was because Fred Grant's class had been too undisciplined," Scott says. "Whenever discipline gets below the standard at West Point, the War Department sends some case-hardened superintendent who pushes the pendulum to the opposite extreme. That is what happened to us . . . We looked back upon the old grey barracks as a jail where we served four years at hard labor."

Colonel T. Bentley Mott of the class of 1886, in his memoirs recalls how in his day the enforcement of discipline had become a kind of automatism. Mott lamented the absence of personal relations in the disciplinary system, especially because it gave to the impressionable young cadet a false notion of how to exercise discipline when he became an officer. He cited a case of a cadet who failed to salute an officer "through carelessness or from a boyish desire to take a chance." At West Point nothing would happen until the next day when the miscreant saw on the bulletin board: "Jones, K. B., failing to salute an officer about 3:50 P.M." Jones now had a chance to submit in writing an explanation of his conduct to the Commandant. The paper would be referred to the officer in question who would state his side of the case. Jones was either given demerits and punishment or his explanation was considered satisfactory. The same routine was followed when an officer inspected Jones's room and found any irregularity. Not a word was spoken; Jones had no idea whether he was "skinned" or whole until he saw the delinquency list.

When he was home on leave, Mott's mother asked him numerous questions about the Academy. Boylike, he bragged about the hardships and proudly described the severity of the punishments. His puzzled mother would ask, "Why do you have to do this?"

"Because it is orders," Mott would roundly declare.

Only then did it occur to Mott that he had no way of finding a better answer to his mother's question. "I had passed two years at a great military school. I stood fairly high in my studies; but I'd never come into contact with an officer except to recite what I had studied in a book, be marked on what I had learned, be inspected to see that I was clean. I was already machine made and the two years that followed removed any lingering protest which nature at first offered to the operation. The only reason for doing anything in life was 'because it was orders' and three years later I heard without surprise an old lieutenant exclaim to a soldier, 'I don't care a damn what you think, I am paid $1600 a year to do your thinking for you.' "

This remark underscored another West Point problem during these years: intellectual stagnation. In the classroom, where Thayer's tradition of small twelve- or thirteen-man sections was continued, few questions were asked. Each morning a slip of paper was handed to each cadet containing the subject he was required to discuss. He went to the blackboard, wrote at the top his name and the subject given him and made such notes or diagrams as he thought he would need. Meanwhile, one man was called to the instructor's desk and asked to recite. The cadet would begin his recitation with "I am required to discuss the subject of so-and-so," or "I am required to solve the following problem." He would then proceed, usually without interruption from the instructor. A perfect recitation required no omissions. The instructor marked the student and called on the next man. The time was carefully measured so that each man recited every day. This was the way mathematics, chemistry, history, English, military science—almost every subject but Spanish and drawing—were taught. "The work of an instructor," says Colonel Mott, "was reduced almost to the sole function of listening to recitations, marking the students, transferring them to higher or lower sections, passing on their examination papers." This instructor could hardly be called a teacher. He was, Mott declared, "a machine for grading cadets upon their knowledge of prescribed texts." He rarely saw his pupils outside the classroom.

Major General George Van Horn Moseley agreed (in his memoirs) with Mott. "In my time the instruction was confined too much to the book," he wrote. "We received too little in a practical way. The applicatory methods were not known or if they were they were not used." As an example, Moseley tells of the way surveying was taught. "We had a certain theoretical course, good as far as it went, I suppose, but the brain, the eye and the hand were never coordinated in this instruction. We seldom saw any surveying instruments and particularly we were never allowed to touch one. I left the Academy believing that a man should be a graduate of the Massachusetts Institute of Technology before he was competent to touch a transit or level."

One day Moseley's instructor gave his class a so-called practical demonstration. He set the transit up on the parade ground, warned the cadets not to touch it, and placed the crosshairs on the center of the ball of the flagpole which could be seen above the trees in the distance, on Trophy Point. He then invited each cadet to step up one by one and observe the crosshairs on the center of the ball. The first half dozen observers came away looking rather confused. Finally, one cadet had the courage to say he did not think the crosshairs were on the center of the ball. The instructor looked again and discovered he was right. Damning the whole class for touching the instrument, he resighted it. Once more confusion reigned until another cadet spoke up and said, "Sir. The crosshairs are a good twenty feet below the ball."

More oaths, another resighting, which once again proved to be wrong. Finally one cadet solved the problem. "Lieutenant," he said, "I think they are raising the top section of the flagpole." Which is exactly what was happening. The quartermaster was raising a new upper section on the pole with a windlass.

"After joining my regiment," Moseley says, "I was told to do a task involving some surveying and running of a line of levels. I borrowed some instruments from a friendly post quartermaster and assisted by a practical surveyor, taught myself how to use them."

West Point's love affair with itself also convinced the academic board that there was no need to seek intellectual inspiration elsewhere. A few of the men who taught engineering and advanced scientific subjects did take short courses at M.I.T. and other civilian schools. But the majority of the instructors learned all their mathematics, history, English, at the Academy. "As a rule," said Colonel Mott, "they know little beyond what they learned as cadets."

Once a man decided to pursue a professorial career at West Point he would ask for another tour of duty there. If he received it he would be on his way to becoming the elite of the instructors, the group from whom associate professors and eventually professors were appointed. "But even these men have not always prepared themselves for their higher functions by taking extended courses at a university or by other contacts with the wider field of learning," Mott complained. "This will explain the changelessness which characterizes the curricula and the methods of instruction."

The languages, history and English (which was dropped completely from 1867–77), fared worst under such a system. "French," General Moseley says, "was taught by men who could not speak it and it was in those days that the French instructors would invariably depart on a few days leave when the arrival of a prominent Frenchman to inspect the Academy was announced." A few years after his graduation, Moseley wrote back to Colonel "Billy" Larned, then head of the drawing department, suggesting some changes in the methods of instruction. "In reply," he says, "I received a letter telling me in very curt terms that I was a mere young upstart in the army and asking me how I could dare criticize the dear old Academy."

Such a system inevitably had deep impact on the cadet corps. Mott tells of an encounter with an upperclassman a few weeks after he entered West Point. "What's your name?" he snapped out, glowering at Mott as if he were about to tear him limb from limb.

"Mott, T. B., sir," he answered.

"Well, Mr. T. B.," said the upperclassman, "are you a candidate for military glory? If you are, take my advice: forget it and bone math."

This, Mott says, was his first encounter with the "God of class standing." But he soon realized, after a few weeks of eating at the mess table, that any enthusiasm about soldiering was looked upon by the corps as rather silly. "The older cadets were quite pitying toward the newcomer who had preserved any youthful illusions on that subject," Mott said. "A junior could show himself as keen as he chose about mathematics or chemistry or engineering and his fellows would applaud. These subjects counted . . . On the contrary, a taste for history, philosophy, art, literature, languages, a sense of tactics and a passion for soldiering were very pretty things but they got you nowhere in the struggle to graduate high."

The dead hand of formalism fell even on the military part of the curriculum. Colonel Cornelius de Witt Willcox of the class of 1885 wrote in his memoirs, "Ordnance and gunnery was well meaning but a holdover from a dead and ought-to-have-been revered past. Our section instructors were up to date but themselves were powerless to change the course. When Mahan went to the artillery and engineering school at Metz he had studied under Noivet, the professor of fortification. He brought back with him plans for a bastion fortification, considered impregnable in the 1820's. Mahan put the plan into his engineering course as a good lesson in the art of fortification.

"A fine and thorough lesson it was," says Colonel Willcox, "so fine and thorough, indeed, that we were still learning it in 1885."

Hugh Scott recalled the almost unbelievable formality of faculty life in this era. "West Point professors were sure enough professors with a lofty dignity all their own and a uniform by which they were distinguished from afar at a single glance—a high hat, a swallow tail coat and a waistcoat with brass buttons. They would take off their high hats to each other 30 feet away in the most ceremonious fashion saying, 'Sir, your most obedient sir,' at the same time bowing and scraping with one foot in a way I have never seen either before or since."

In such an atmosphere, it is easy to see how cadet honor gradually developed a fantastic tinge.

In the early 1870's, when Emory Upton was Commandant, three cadets were suspected of lying to conceal a trip to Highland Falls that one of them had made. They were arrested for making a false report. But before a court-martial could be convened, the first class (seniors) convened a rump court-martial at midnight, found all three guilty and stripped them of their uniforms, thrust them into civilian clothes and escorted them to the post gates where they advised them to put as much distance as possible between the Academy and themselves by morning, if they valued their lives. The next morning a committee informed Upton of their action on behalf of "the reputation of the corps." In an official letter the following day they defended their action. "From the manner in which some members of the fourth class have been conducting themselves of late, and the utter disregard of the truth which they have evinced, we judge that a severe example was necessary to amend this laxity of principle . . ."

The banished boys' parents were outraged. Cries went up from Congress and an investigating committee descended on West Point. They severely criticized Upton and the Superintendent for accepting the cadets' resignation without further investigation. The committee "in extenuation" admitted that "efforts to maintain discipline heretofore seemed not to have been properly sustained by the authorities at Washington and that sentences of courts-martial providing for the dismissal of cadets have almost invariably been remitted . . ." The politicians were still playing their by now familiar game with the Academy. Upton vigorously defended the way he tacitly approved the first class's action, pointing out that two of the three accused cadets freely admitted to the investigating committee that they had lied. Nevertheless, two of the wrong-doers were returned to the Academy the following June, and one graduated.

The first class was probably correct when they pointed out to Upton that they were in a better position to judge a cadet's conduct than the tactical officers, because "little or nothing could be concealed from those who have every opportunity of witnessing and hearing of . . . misdemeanors." But youthful zeal could get out of hand, as is evident from the story of Orsemus B. Boyd.

A New Yorker, Boyd had served with distinction in the Civil War and won an appointment to the Academy in 1863. In the winter of 1865, certain sums of money were stolen from cadets in B Company. The robberies were repeated until the whole corps was in a state of silent fury. Amateur detectives were appointed and their investigation pointed to Boyd as the guilty cadet. One night at evening parade, Boyd was summoned from the ranks, a placard of thief was hung on his back and he was drummed out of the corps. The cadets then broke ranks and began beating him up. Tactical officers quelled the riot and rescued Boyd. Their investigation produced not an iota of proof that he was guilty, but the corps had passed its own decision and Boyd finished his cadetship in coventry.

Only years later, when Boyd, still snubbed by every West Pointer that met him, was serving out a purgatory on the Western frontier did the corps learn that the real villain was Boyd's roommate, John Joseph Casey. A year later, when Casey thought he was dying, he confessed to his roommate Cadet Hamilton that he was the real thief. He lived to graduate, but within a year was accidentally shot at drill by a soldier at Fort Washington in Maryland. Hamilton said nothing until he was on his deathbed several years later.

Casey had done a faultless job of framing Boyd, concealing money that he knew the cadets had marked in Boyd's books. Boyd's friends tried to repair his reputation, but it was a losing battle. As late as 1885, when he died, still a captain of the 8th Cavalry, one classmate, then the secretary of the Association of Graduates, made one last attempt to repair the damage by telling the whole story in his obituary. "If martyrdom wins a crown of glory," he wrote, "then is poor Boyd refulgent in his spirit life . . . the bare recital of the story furnishes the strongest possible argument against a hasty and what can personally be called, snap judgment of the cadets of the two upper classes."

This trend toward harsh moralism was not entirely West Point's fault. It was part of the spiritual atmosphere of the Victorian era. Perhaps the best proof of this judgment was the way the men who succeeded Thayer's faculty intensified the moral emphasis.

The first and best of Thayer's heirs was among the last to go. In the summer of 1871, Mahan suffered a nervous breakdown. Some blamed it on overwork, others on a recommendation of the 1871 Board of Visitors that he be placed on the retired list. Mahan's later years had been marked by repeated depressions. The anguish of the Civil War years, in which he had sided with the Union against his native Virginia, may have been part of the explanation. But he was also undoubtedly suffering from the spiritual weariness that often overtakes intellectual workers at the end of a long career. Advised by the post surgeon to consult a specialist in New York, Mahan boarded the Hudson River steamboat *Mary Powell* on September 16, 1871. As the ship passed Stony Point, the man who had personified Thayer's Academy leaped overboard and vanished into the foam beneath the port paddle wheel.

Six months earlier, Peter Smith Michie had been appointed to the chair of natural and experimental philosophy and for the next 30 years he was to dominate the academic board with even more severity than had Mahan. His testimony, written after 20 years as a professor, was an unqualified endorsement of the status quo. "The writer when he was appointed a cadet was old enough to appreciate the value in mental training and the sound educational advantages derived from the methods of instruction pursued at the Military Academy. Graduating during the war, he found himself in a fortnight in charge of important military duties where he was thrown upon his own resources, and in every case he found that the methods of reasoning in which he had been trained here and the self-reliance which had been inculcated in him by the methods of study were sufficient to solve his problems to the satisfactions of his superior officers."

Michie added to this conviction a Victorian religious fervor which would have appalled Thayer, who died refusing the earnest solicitations of a minister. Michie insisted that his course in physics proved the existence of God and roundly declared that any cadet who declined to be persuaded of this truth did not deserve to graduate from the Academy.

Colonel Willcox in his memoirs describes Michie as a man who had "developed a disposition originally positive and uncompromising into one of masterfulness that brooked no opposition or contradiction. And particularly he had acquired the possibly dangerous conviction that he could from his official contact with any cadet read his character. This led him in some cases to the formation of judgments held by others to be unjust. And yet he was perfectly honest: the Academy was his life and he thought he was protecting it . . . It would be unkind to his memory to conclude that he was heartless: he was severe."

Professor Michie had a son, Dennis Mahan Michie, who was the precise opposite of his solemn father. He apparently sympathized with the cadets, plodding their weary, toilsome rounds. A few days before the January examination, a member of the class of 1885 saw on the cadet bulletin board a unique notice:

"Second classmen,
The course in mechanics has been pretty hard, hasn't it? And tomorrow is the examination. Don't you think you had better look up these. . . .

There followed a list of the hardest subjects in the course, rolling cones, momental ellipsoids—about fifteen in all, written in a boyish hand. The subjects were duly noted and circulated throughout the barracks for intense study that night. "The next day, what was not our delight," Willcox says, "to find the subjects as of the notice, set out in order in both the morning and afternoon sessions." That night the class held a meeting and bound themselves to silence. They knew if any word of the notice got out, they would be examined again. Professor Michie was astonished by how well the class did in the examination. The instructor for another section remarked that if he had not sat on the examination papers ever since they had been printed he would have sworn they had gotten hold of them. Only years after graduation did one of the class nerve himself to tell the professor about the incident. He opined that young Dennis had been the mysterious correspondent. Michie gave him "a queer look" and walked off without a word.

Perhaps the best comment on the West Point of this era is a story told by General Moseley about the fiftieth reunion of the class of 1886. Several soldiers, long retired, had lunch at the Superintendent's house.

One, who was particularly talkative, sat beside Brigadier General Samuel Tillman, for years professor of chemistry. With great glee the 1886 man proceeded to repeat page after page of the chemistry course, not missing a word in long, involved sentences. Finishing, he turned to Professor Tillman and said, "I didn't know what that meant fifty years ago and I don't know what it means today."

IV

THE CADETS FOUGHT the system's rigidities in numerous ways. The professor of Spanish was Patrice d'Janon, native of Venezuela. He had been with the Academy since before the Civil War, serving first as master of the sword and next as professor of Spanish, in itself a comment on one of the perennial problems of government institutions—firing incompetents. Mahan had tried to get rid of d'Janon but got nowhere with his denunciations. The cadets took advantage of his shallow background by giving him a very hard time. In the early 80's, when he was getting on in years, a cadet was translating from Spanish into English: "I have snizzen—" he said.

"No, sir, sneeze," said d'Janon.

"Sir," retorted the cadet, "I willingly acknowledge your superiority to me in Spanish, but I resent your pretense to superiority to me in English. As I respect your Spanish, so I do insist on your respecting my English." A lively discussion now ensued in the section and before the hour was over the cadets had convinced the hapless professor that the principle parts of the verb sneeze were: sneeze, snoze, snizzen.

The following year when the same passage was read out "sneezed," d'Janon corrected it to "snizzen." The section screamed and the cadet, perhaps expecting it, said, "Sir, do you mean to correct my English? As I respect your Spanish," etc., etc. But this time Professor d'Janon stood his ground. He expressed astonishment that he, a Spaniard, should be better acquainted with the intricacies of the English language than native-born gentlemen.

Professor d'Janon used to stroll the campus each morning and pause to see the guard mounted. Once as the outgoing officer of the day was waiting to march off he sidled close to the professor and whispered: "Sir, you would do well to give us our subjects for the examination in Spanish next week and I am asking you to do it."

Outraged, d'Janon spluttered. "That is a very improper thing you have asked me and I shall report you for it."

"Very well, sir," replied the nervy cadet. "I know it is unusual and you may report me if you like, but you know the War Department is anxious to get rid of you and has been trying for several years to find an excuse. If we don't do well in your examination it will have an excuse."

The next day d'Janon collapsed and revealed the subjects.

The professor of drawing, Colonel "Billy" Larned, gave lectures in an amphitheater which George Van Horn Moseley described as "airtight." To complicate matters, the Colonel was in the habit of using a great deal of perfume. Finally one day the corps decided to teach him a lesson and dispatched Cadet Greyson V. "Leper" Heidt to Highland Falls to buy up a dozen or so bottles of five-cent toilet water. Practically everyone in the class doused his handkerchief in the stuff, and Leper, so called because early in his cadet career he was afflicted by a nasty rash, poured some on his head. When Colonel Larned arrived, handkerchiefs were suddenly produced for a universal nose-blowing and the wave of Woolworth scent almost asphyxiated him. "Billy did not use perfume for many a day," said Moseley.

Another weapon was nicknaming the "tacs." One, a diminutive lieutenant named Hoffer, who was rushing a widow, was christened "The Widow's Mite." Another lieutenant, named Allaire, exploded when a plebe inadvertently pointed his rifle at him during target practice. "Don't point that gun at me. Don't you know it will go through 30 inches of wood," he roared, instantly earning himself the nickname "Wooden Willy."

Inevitably, the antics of their classmates also provided some diversion for the cadets. One of the favorite sports was watching a fellow cadet attempting to "bugle it" at the blackboard. After completing an assignment the cadet was supposed to turn around, stand at attention, wooden pointer in hand, and wait for his instructor to call upon him for an explanation. If his mind was a blank, he frequently remained facing the board, praying for the recall bugle to blow. One day Cadet Ike Walton was performing this maneuver. After committing to the board the sum total of his knowledge, which consisted of the number of his subject in the upper left-hand corner, his name in the upper right-hand corner, and diagonally across the otherwise blank board a single straight line, alas, the bugle did not blow, and the instructor said, "I will hear you, Mr. Walton." Cadet Walton executed a beautiful about-face, and pointing to the single straight line said, "Let this be a parallel line."

"Parallel to what, Mr. Walton?" asked the instructor.

"Parallel to nothing—just parallel."

The following day when marks were posted, Walton asked his instructor why he had given him a zero. "Because there was no lower mark I could give you, Mr. Walton," was the steel-tipped reply.

A favorite refuge—in fact the only one—for those who wilted under pressure was the hospital. According to Moseley, "the surgeons were very good in letting a fellow break in for a day or two." Just how well the surgeons understood the game can be seen in the story of Cadet "Sleuth" Newbill.

"Have you pains up and down and across your back?" asked the major in charge of the hospital.

"Yes, sir," replied Cadet Newbill.

"Have you pains in your lower abdomen?"

"Yes, sir," replied Cadet Newbill.

After several similar questions were answered in a prompt affirmative, the surgeon sighed, turned to the hospital steward and said, "Take Mr. Newbill right into the hospital. He is going to give birth to a child."

Another diversion was the "rush." Each year a large portion of the corps met the yearling class as they entered the reservation at the end of their summer furlough. At a signal, both groups would storm toward each other over the Plain and collide in a tremendous crunch that sent them floundering into a mass of shouting, roaring, kicking cadets. Noses were bloodied, eyes blacked, knees wrenched, shoulders dislocated, uniforms wrecked. Each year the melee grew wilder, until finally, in 1886, the Superintendent forbade it. (Stern measures had already limited the custom at other schools.) The first class held a meeting and debated the advisability of disobeying the order. They adjourned without coming to any formal decision. But when the time came for the furlough men to return, most of the first class assembled on the Plain. Hundreds of visitors were on hand—the brawl had obviously become an important annual event.

The state of indecision prevailed only until the first furlough men appeared at the top of the hill. Somebody cheered, "Come on, fellows," and with a frantic Comanche yell the whole first class charged across the sentinel's post while the furlough class bolted from the opposite direction. They met in immense enthusiastic collision and rolled joyfully in the dust while tactical officers danced on the edges of the circle bellowing orders and scribbling names of anyone they could recognize through the haze.

Finally discipline was restored, the rushers were marched to camp, and their names were taken. Five first classmen who happened to be absent from the melee reported themselves to the Commandant as equally guilty, declaring they would have joined the brawl if they had been there. The Commandant considered this insubordination and put them under arrest. The Superintendent telegraphed the War Department for authority to summarily dismiss all the guilty cadets—a move that would have decimated the corps. Cooler heads in Washington refused, and the "Supe" was left with his usual recourse—demerits by the bushel.

Another favorite sport, inherited from earlier decades, was hell-raising. On New Year's Eve, 1879–80, the corps staged a celebration that was remembered for a generation. All the arrangements were undertaken by six men—first class privates. They smuggled fireworks of various kinds onto the reservation and concealed them near Fort Putnam. On the night of December thirtieth, the six conspirators cut supper and lugged the fireworks into the barracks. The corps had a cadet hop on New Year's Eve which ended at eleven o'clock. At this hour the sentries were removed from the barracks and the fireworks were distributed to all those who volunteered to participate. Others were detailed to fire off the reveille gun and as many guns as possible in the siege battery. A gun from Trophy Point was smuggled onto the roof of the barracks. All doors on the ground floor of the barracks were locked from the inside and all cadet officers were locked in their rooms, thereby delaying their appearance.

Everything went precisely as planned. When the cannon roared, tactical officers came rushing toward the barracks, only to be met by an incredible barrage of rockets, cherry bombs and strings of sputtering firecrackers. Only the gun on the roof failed to go off, but this was fired successfully by a daring cadet the following morning, during breakfast. By the time the confused "tacs" reassembled themselves and ordered the long roll beaten, every culprit was on hand to be present and accounted for. The Commandant of Cadets desperately invited one and all to "clear their skirts" by volunteering that they took no part in the affair. Only a handful of the innocent took advantage of this privilege. The entire corps was, therefore, confined to cadet limits for an indefinite period and were prohibited to enter officers' quarters. This meant the loss of what little sociability and extra food and drink a cadet might hope for, but the punishment was accepted with silent glee, because the night of triumph had been so complete.

By far the most popular diversion at West Point, however, was hazing. "Deviling" plebes had been a custom at West Point for a long time. But in the past it consisted largely of practical jokes and had been confined with some exceptions to summer encampment. Now it became a year-long process, beginning with an institution called "Beast Barracks." This system, which became standard in the years after the Civil War, incarcerated incoming plebes for three to six weeks while upperclassmen supposedly taught them the rudiments of drilling, barracks life and other aspects of soldiering. It gradually became an ordeal by torture for every plebe. Day and night he was called "Mr. Dumbjohn, Animal, Thing," and ordered to do exhausting exercises and impossible tasks such as picking all the ants off an anthill one by one.

As the 1870's passed into the 1880's, hazing became more and more sadistic. Superintendent after Superintendent deplored the practice and made vigorous attempts to suppress it. Hazing was announced as abolished at least a dozen times by various authorities, one of them General of the Army Philip Sheridan. Actually it continued with unabated intensity through the turn of the century, when it reached a kind of climax in a tragedy that again put West Point in the nation's headlines.

V

THE SOLDIER WHO WAS the personification of this era at West Point—who in the corps as well as in the history books towers above his fellow soldiers—was John J. Pershing. This rangy Missouri farm boy entered West Point just short of his twenty-second birthday (the legal limit for admittance). Robert Lee Bullard, who was a class ahead of Pershing and was cadet lieutenant when Pershing was first sergeant of Company A, described him: "Regular but not handsome features and . . . a robust, strong body, broad-shouldered and well developed; almost or quite six feet tall, plainly of the estate of man while most about him were still boys; with keen, searching eyes and intent look . . . Pershing inspired confidence but not affection. Personal magnetism seemed lacking. He won followers and admirers, but not personal worshippers."

This was not entirely true. One cadet, a comical fellow named Wylie Bean, within a day of meeting Pershing was telling everyone, "Pershing will be President one day." But Bullard was right about one thing: Pershing's character and personality were perfectly attuned to the West Point of the 1880's. It was, he wrote in his own memoirs years later, "still the West Point of Grant, Sherman, Sheridan, Schofield and Howard. The deep impression these great men made during their visits to West Point in our day went far to inspire us with the soldier's spirit of self-sacrifice, duty and honor." Plain in words, sane and direct in action, Pershing fit perfectly into West Point's impersonal routine. "His exercise of authority was then and always has been since," Bullard wrote, "of a nature peculiarly impersonal, dispassionate, hard and firm." Even in his early days as a cadet when most of his fellows were a trifle reluctant about snapping orders, Pershing effortlessly acquired the habit of command and indicated clearly that he believed he had "an unquestioned right to obedience."

With this intense aptitude for the soldierly side of his profession Pershing combined a lively enthusiasm for the ladies. His tall, erect figure, dark blond hair and gray-blue eyes made him a dazzling companion at West Point dances, and he rarely missed one. "He was a hop goer," Bullard declared, "what cadets called a spoony man." In the company of women, Pershing's icy, commanding manner defrosted, and so, apparently, did the girls.

Another oddity in Pershing's makeup that appeared in his West Point days was tardiness. Most of his demerits were for being late at formations. His classmate, Avery Andrews, said this was because Pershing became "almost oblivious of the passage of time once his mind was absorbed with any particular matter." It was a habit that was later to cause near apoplexy among heads of state and Allied generals who cooled their heels waiting for Pershing to keep appointments.

During his plebe days, on Pershing's own testimony, much of his commanding manner was more surface than substance. He was as appalled by the standard sentry-baiting that all plebes experienced as the rest of his class. Recalling his first guard tour, he said, "I got along all right during the day but at night . . . my troubles began. Of course, I was scared beyond the point of properly applying any of my orders. A few minutes after taps, ghosts of all sorts began to appear from all directions. I selected a particularly bold one and challenged according to orders, 'Halt, who goes there?' At that the ghost stood still in his tracks. I then said, 'Halt, who stands there?' whereupon the ghost who was carrying a chair sat down. Then I said, 'Halt, who sits there?' "

Twenty members of Pershing's class of 1886 graduated with no demerits—perhaps the best testimony to the almost inhuman perfection which the Academy expected, and often got, from the cadets. Pershing's habitual lateness barred him from this elect circle. Scholastically also, Pershing was no leader, graduating thirtieth in a class of 77. French was his nightmare. In his struggles with this language, Pershing came close to reproducing Stonewall Jackson's travails. Avery Andrews tells how cadets were permitted to fall out of ranks at roll call for dinner, as they called their midday meal. Recitations in French were in the early afternoon, and Pershing regularly skipped his dinner to beat the books. "I can truthfully say that I never knew Pershing to show any sign of fear," Andrews says, "but probably his nearest approach thereto was his cadet attitude toward his instructor in French."

The future commander in chief of the A.E.F. also had trouble with the subtleties of the English language. In his plebe year, his roommate Charles C. Walcutt recalls his travails when he was asked in English class to discuss pseudo metaphors. "Pershing . . . made a great struggle to clarify the subject. It was evident he had not made even a beginning in understanding it; however, he struggled on greatly embarrassed, almost hopeless—great beads of perspiration standing out on his forehead. The instructor showed no disposition to throw any light or suggestion that might help. Instead, that dignitary finally said, 'Mr. Pershing, what is a pseudo metaphor?' Pershing could only gasp that he didn't know and sit down."

It was no surprise to anyone that Pershing was named cadet captain in his first class year. In that capacity he led the corps across the Hudson to stand and present arms as the black-draped train bearing Ulysses Grant's body rolled down from Albany to his tomb on the Hudson in New York. Unlike Sherman and Grant, Pershing accepted unquestioningly the Academy's disciplinary ideals. "He was a strict disciplinarian and one who observed very closely his own precepts," said his roommate Walcutt. The plebes of that year took a slightly dimmer view. Charles D. Rhodes noted in his diary on July 5, 1885, "We have an awful mean captain. He turned me out yesterday right in the middle of washing my face, made me bundle on my jacket and hat and go out and pick up two or three matches and minute pieces of paper in front of my tent."

Another reason for the plebes' antipathy to First Captain Pershing was his renown as the inventor of the "jumping Jack" or "string trick." The vigilance of the tactical officers made it difficult to haze plebes safely, until the advent of this brainstorm. Pershing got twenty or thirty plebes out on the company street, and ordered them to count off, so each knew whether he was odd or even in line. When Pershing pulled an imaginary string in one direction, all the odd plebes had to throw their arms out at stiff right angles to their bodies. When the imaginary string was pulled in the opposite direction, the odd men dropped their arms and the even men jumped their legs out, to form a V. The live marionette show was a constant source of upperclass amusement. Best of all, if a tactical officer happened past, Pershing simply dropped his imaginary string and began drilling his victims.

Later in the year, the plebes had their revenge at the hundredth-night entertainment, a post-Civil War custom which was a combination vaudeville show and dance. It permitted the cadets to poke irreverent fun at their officers and even the Superintendent. Pershing was one of the main targets. His part in the program was a carefully kept secret. "He came there with his spoon [girl] and knew nothing of it," Rhodes wrote with glee in his diary. "We plebe ushers were instructed to give Pershing a prominent seat. When his part in the program was reached, the Grand Mogul announced it. Pershing got white around the mouth and in response to cheers and repeated encores had to get up very much embarrassed and make a speech. He is so rarely disconcerted that the audience fully appreciated the joke." A few days later, the rebels struck again. As the corps mustered for evening parade under Pershing's stern eye, along came a shaggy Newfoundland dog belonging to one of the officers, dressed in full uniform. "He had been inveigled into some room," Rhodes said, "and rigged up in an old dress coat with his front legs through the sleeves. The coat was belted to him with a cadet belt and on his head was tied an old forage cap. He passed in review before the battalion standing at ease just as the officer in charge passed and the latter turned very red as he heard shouts of laughter behind him without knowing the cause."

But these were minor ripples in Pershing's outstandingly successful cadet career. His roommate Walcutt summed him up most accurately when he said, "He was the leader of our class, not in his studies, but in everything else." That Pershing achieved this distinction without sacrificing his personal popularity was evidenced by his election as president of the class during their graduation dinner at Delmonico's in New York. His friend Bullard was obviously right when he said that Pershing's habit of command did not give offense. "The man was too impersonal, too given over to pure business and duty." It was also a testimony to how thoroughly the men of the corps accepted the Academy's system and ideals.

VI

WHILE THE ACADEMY pursued its iron goals, graduates of earlier years were acting out other dramas, on the national stage. Ulysses S. Grant added nothing to his own or West Point's reputation by his performance as a two-term President. One might see in Grant's political naïveté the limitations of Thayer's severely scientific-military curriculum. But a more probable explanation is Grant's shy, introverted personality, which was not helped by the isolation from civilian society that America, with its worries about men on horseback, has always imposed on the army officer. Grant's sorry showing tended to obscure from succeeding generations the generally satisfactory performances of some two dozen other West Pointers of this era as congressmen, senators and governors. George McClellan, for instance, was a very competent two-term governor of New Jersey. Totally forgotten is the graduate who almost became President, a far more sophisticated soldier who, some political historians speculate, probably would have erased Grant's aura of careless maladministration: Winfield Scott Hancock. He was nominated by the Democrats in 1880. That year the Republicans came very close to nominating a willing Grant for a third term—which would have made the race for the White House an entirely West Point show. But the G.O.P. chose James Garfield as a compromise candidate, and he edged General Hancock in a very close election, winning with a plurality of only 10,000 out of over 9 million votes.

In the far West, meanwhile, other West Pointers under the leadership of Phil Sheridan, struggled to police the inevitable conflicts that arose between the settlers and the Indians. They fought in vain against the unbelievable stupidity and corruption of the Indian Bureau, which sold repeating rifles to the red men and simultaneously mismanaged the reservations into which the Army was supposed to herd the reluctant tribes. "If I were an Indian," George Armstrong Custer wrote, "I would greatly prefer to cast my lot among those of my people who adhere to the free open plains rather than submit to the confined limits of the reservation, there to be the recipient of the blessed benefits of civilization with its vices thrown in without stint or measure."

Such opinions, and his candid criticism of the Indian Bureau before Congress, got Custer in trouble with politicians and his Army superiors. Relieved of command of the 7th Cavalry as it was about to depart on a crucial expedition to pacify the aroused Sioux, Custer wrote directly to President Grant. "I appeal to you as a soldier to spare me the humiliation of seeing my regiment march to meet the enemy and I to not share its dangers." Even though Custer had accused Grant's brother of being tainted by Indian Bureau corruption, the President was too big a man to resist such a plea. Custer was restored to his regiment and he rode to meet the soldier's death he had risked so often near the Montana stream known as Little Big Horn.

From 1865 to 1898, the United States Army fought no fewer than 943 engagements against the Indians, from skirmishes to pitched battles, in twelve separate campaigns. Yet in 1876, the year of Custer's death, and the climactic year of this long struggle (which Congress did not see fit to call a war until 1890), the politicians in Washington failed to pass an appropriations act for the coming fiscal year. Not until November 21, 1877, when the next Congress cleaned up the mess, could an officer or man of the Army or Navy touch a penny of pay.

This hostility to the Regular Army was a compound of many things— the strong Southern influence in the Democratic party, which resented Army rule in the South during the Reconstruction era, the usual indifference American politicians have traditionally displayed to the professional soldier when the possibility of war seems remote. But not a little of the trouble could be traced to one man—John Logan, senator from Illinois, former major general of volunteers in the Civil War. "Black Jack" Logan, as he was called for his swarthy complexion, was one political general who proved himself a first-class soldier. When James Birdseye McPherson was killed in a surprise Southern attack on the Army of the Tennessee, outside Atlanta, Logan had taken charge of the shaken, wavering regiments. With black hair shining in the sun, swinging his black hat over his huge black horse, he rode among the broken ranks, roaring: "Will you hold this line with me?"

"We will," bellowed the soldiers, and they fell to chanting, "Black Jack, Black Jack, Black Jack," and smashed the Southern attack.

For rescuing Sherman from what could have been a serious reverse, Logan expected to be rewarded with the command of the Army of the Tennessee. Instead Sherman appointed Oliver O. Howard, who had practically no experience commanding Western soldiers and was unpopular with them because of his extreme piety and radical Abolitionist views. Sherman later admitted that he knew Logan deserved the command, but he had yielded to protestations from George Thomas that Logan was unfit for top leadership. The mercurial Logan and the phlegmatic Thomas had clashed several times earlier in the war. Logan was justly enraged and felt he had been victimized by West Point clannishness.

After the war, Sherman personally urged Logan to remain in the Army and went out of his way to assure the Illinoisan of his admiration for his military talents. Logan rebuffed him, and renewed his conviction that "the West Point clique" would forever connive to deprive him of deserved promotion.

Logan returned to politics, and soon emerged as a leader in the postwar Congress. Originally a Democrat, he switched to the Republicans, and went all the way to the rabid radical side, where his animosity toward West Point found congenial company. In 1870 he led a savage attack on the Army budget that slashed appropriations, and even forced a humiliating reduction in Commanding General Sherman's salary and expenses.

Logan also founded the Grand Army of the Republic, and swiftly built it into the most formidable veteran's organization of the nation. He became a specialist at waving what was called "the bloody shirt," and used that technique superbly in 1871 to win his seat as senator from Illinois. His elevation did nothing to abate his wrath. Having reduced the Army to the starvation level, there was little he could do to further humiliate the West Pointers who were commanding it. He therefore shifted his attention to a more personal battle, which was to embroil West Pointers North and South in fierce debate for the better part of two decades—The Fitz-John Porter court-martial.

Porter had refused to accept the verdict that cashiered him for dereliction of duty in the second battle of Bull Run. Tirelessly he sent petitions to Congress, asking the lawmakers to set aside the decision and restore him to his rank. Logan took upon himself the responsibility to uphold the integrity of the court, which had consisted almost entirely of volunteer (non-West Point) officers.

Porter had twice asked President Grant to review his case, and both times had been rebuffed. When Rutherford B. Hayes became President in the election of 1876, Porter tried again, and Hayes appointed a special board, consisting of Major General John M. Schofield, Brigadier General A. H. Terry, and Colonel G. W. Getty to hear testimony. Schofield was then serving as Superintendent of West Point. Thus, by another Greek-like whirl of fate, he found himself sitting in judgment on the man who had almost destroyed his career. Moreover, Schofield knew how Porter had voted years ago in the cadet court-martial involving himself; when he served as Secretary of War for a brief period in 1868, he had taken the trouble to call for the papers and find out.

The board took some two and a half years to interrogate 142 witnesses; Longstreet, Lee's aide-de-camp Charles Marshall, Tom Rosser, Major General Irwin MacDowell, were among them. The Southerners, in particular, contributed invaluable new information about the disposition of their Army, which considerably supported Porter's assertion that the Confederate deployment made it suicidal for him to attack Jackson according to Pope's order. MacDowell, some fifteen years too late, produced dispatches Porter had sent to him, proving that the condemned man could not have received the order at the time claimed by the court-martial board.

On March 19, 1879, the board issued its findings. It completely confirmed Porter's assertion that "the main body of Lee's army . . . must have been on the field at that time." The court-martial's charges, they declared, "bear no discernible resemblance to the facts." Far from being disobedient, Porter's conduct was "obedient, subordinate, faithful and judicious." It had, in fact, "saved the Union army from rout." The board condemned Porter's telegrams to Burnside as "indiscreet." But it wholeheartedly recommended "action . . . to annul and set aside the findings and sentence of the court-martial."

This should have been enough, but with Logan in the Senate, it was only the beginning of another round. Logan's speech, the major opposition statement, took no less than four days to deliver, and filled 891 manuscript pages. In stem-winding prose that would inspire instant slumber today, Logan compared Porter's refusal to march nine miles over terra firma to Washington crossing the Delaware "when the ice was gorging."

James A. Garfield was a power in the House of Representatives, and he had sat on the original court-martial board. Garfield declared that reopening Porter's case "condemns hundreds of leading men from Lincoln down, and leaves a blot on their names." Even Porter's old friend, Burnside, now a senator from Rhode Island, sided with the opposition. He declared on the Senate floor that he would be willing to believe that the Confederate cause was just, before he could be convinced that Porter had not put the interests of one man (McClellan) before the welfare of the Republic. Logan summed up by saying that Porter was no more entitled to be put on the retired list of the Army than was Jefferson Davis.

For two years the debate dragged on, and ended in a stalemate. The Senate passed a bill absolving Porter, but it got nowhere in the House, in spite of the support of West Pointers such as General Joseph Johnston, who was serving as a congressman from Virginia. "I had rather lose an arm than see your enemies succeed in preventing the righting of your grievous wrongs," the ex-Confederate commander in chief told Porter.

Things looked bleak for Porter, until in 1881, Ulysses S. Grant dropped a bombshell. After a moving personal interview with Porter persuaded him to review the case, Grant wrote a letter to President Chester A. Arthur, declaring that he was now thoroughly convinced that "for nineteen years I have been doing a gallant and efficient soldier a very great injustice." Grant said he had been misled by the "totally incorrect" maps introduced at the court-martial. Schofield in his memoirs tells of meeting Grant in 1882, and having a long talk about Porter's case. "He would not permit me to utter a single sentence until he had gone all over the case and showed me that he understood all the essential features as thoroughly as I did, and that his judgment was precisely the same as that which the board had reached."

But as long as the Republicans remained in control of the White House, it was almost useless for Porter's friends and supporters to petition on his behalf. The G.O.P. feared to involve the party in an issue that would arouse Logan and the G.A.R. (Grand Army of the Republic). Not even an article by Grant in the *North American Review*, "An Undeserved Stigma," helped, though it did demonstrate that amazing honesty which so endeared Grant to his contemporaries. It was no small act for him to publicly admit: "As General of the Army when I might have been instrumental in having justice done to General Porter, and later as President, I labored under the firm conviction that he was guilty."

But Logan, in the Senate, remained adamant. Schofield finally approached him directly to see if there was some way to change his mind. The conversation was sad but revealing. In the privacy of his parlor, Logan candidly admitted to Schofield that he now realized he was probably wrong about Porter. He blamed his original stand on Grant, who had assured him that Porter was guilty, when the issue first arose in Congress. Now, although Grant had executed a strategic withdrawal, Logan could not. From a political point of view, he told Schofield it was "too late to change." So the emotion-laden debates continued, until Grover Cleveland was elected President. Then, with dispatch, a bill zoomed through both houses of Congress. Porter was exonerated, and restored to the rank of colonel in the Regular Army.

By now Fitz-John Porter was a white-haired ghost of the daring soldier who had stormed the Belen Gate at Mexico City, and won national attention for his fighting generalship at Gaines Mill and Malvern Hill, where he saved the Army of the Potomac from destruction. Quietly, two days after his vindication, Porter requested his name to be placed on the retired list. His story remains unique in West Point annals, a tangled skein of personal loyalty and personal integrity, which first destroyed, and then resurrected him.

As for Logan, he aimed one more blast at the Academy, a formidable one, which he hoped would bring the entire West Point system tumbling down. It was a book, *The Volunteer Soldier,* a long, turgid tome, published in 1886, a few months after Logan's sudden death. In it he argued that the country needed a completely different approach to obtaining professional Army officers. West Point, he maintained, simply failed to provide the nation with the number of trained soldiers it needed in time of war. The answer as Logan saw it was to dismantle West Point and Annapolis and create military departments at the state colleges throughout the land. Graduates of these schools would take competitive examinations and go on to a revamped West Point and Annapolis, which would function primarily as schools of application. This was, of course, not a new idea, but Logan's criticism of the failure of the Regular Army to adjust to the needs of the volunteers in the Civil War emergency was based on harsh experience. If he had been alive he might have made a formidable issue out of his book. But without his dynamic presence to back it, Black Jack's magnum opus wandered off into obscurity.

VII

MEANWHILE, AT WEST POINT, another kind of emotion was stirring, the kind that would one day be vented in huge stadiums, to the strains of "On, Brave Old Army Team." It seems amazing now, but throughout the first three post-Civil War decades, there was no athletic activity worth mentioning at West Point. Here were some 400 young men between the ages of sixteen and twenty-two grinding away at a monotonous classroom routine day after day with no outlet for their animal energies but a very circumscribed amount of horseback riding, some calisthenics, and fencing instruction from the master of the sword. There was some interclass baseball, and occasionally a football was kicked about the Plain, but the authorities insisted that no matter what the cadet was doing he could not shed his long grey trousers and buttoned coats with their high stiff collars. Then came a happy afternoon in 1888, when Lieutenant Colonel Hamilton S. Hawkins, Commandant of Cadets, happened to see two cadets tossing a rubber ball back and forth. In their buttoned-up condition they looked like a pair of windup toys. After watching for a few seconds, Hamilton asked, "Have you young gentlemen white shirts on?"

"Yes, sir," they said.

"Then," said Colonel Hawkins, "I authorize you to lay aside your jackets."

Soon there were a dozen ballplayers prancing about the Plain in undershirts. When the tactical officers reported them, Hawkins tore up the reports and persuaded the Superintendent, Colonel John G. Parkes, to let the cadets express their native vigor, sans jackets. Within two years a cadet baseball team was playing outsiders, and in 1890 a momentous message arrived from the Naval Academy. Annapolis challenged West Point to a football game.

Nothing happened at first. West Point did not have a football team, and football, while it was soaring to popularity in colleges around the country, had an aura of brutality and questionable ethics. Even the best colleges fielded teams full of professional bruisers who lived and ate at the university but did no studying there. Almost certainly the challenge would have been stillborn, had it not been for Dennis Mahan Michie, the same son of Peter Smith Michie who had leaked his father's exam to the class of 1885. Dennis was now a member of the corps, but he retained the same high spirited fun-loving attitude toward life that made so many wonder how he could be his father's son. He also retained his father's affection. The combination produced the first Army-Navy game.

Dennis had played football at Lawrenceville Prep and had loved the sport. Disregarding West Point's total lack of experience—only three other men in the corps had ever played the game—he decided the Academy could not ignore Navy's challenge. According to one version of the story, he told a good friend, "Old Pete [his father] is dead against it now, but I will bring him around." Which is exactly what he did. When the dour dean of the academic board informed Superintendent John W. Wilson that the honor of the corps required prompt acceptance of Navy's challenge, the Supe instantly issued a stamp of approval.

This by no means solved all the problems. Navy had been playing football since 1882 and their 1889 team had lost only a single game. West Point had neither a coach, practice field or equipment, and the Academy declined to make up for any of these deficiencies. The corps even had to put up half the money for Navy's $275 travel expenses by authorizing a charge of fifty-two cents to be made against each cadet's store account.

The players bought their own uniforms—white-laced canvas jackets and white breeches, black woolen stockings and a black woolen cap with a dash of orange to it. Dennis Michie was both coach and trainer—but the only time he had to drill his volunteers was on a Saturday afternoon when bad weather cancelled the dress parade. Then he had two and a half hours to lead his charges through some elementary gridiron maneuvers on the tanbark in the riding hall. By way of training, the team got up a half hour before reveille and jogged around the Plain. Mighty Yale, hearing of West Point's stirrings, sent their great center "Pa" Corbin down to look things over, and offer some advice and encouragement. "What they don't know about the game," said Corbin, "would fill an encyclopedia, but they have the right type of men for it."

Finally came the great day, November 29, 1890. The Navy team arrived by train that morning. On the way up the hill to the Plain, according to legend, they took a goat from the yard of an Army noncom and made him their mascot. The Army band was on duty, plus most of the cadet corps, faculty officers and their wives, the post's enlisted men, and a group of naval officers from a ship anchored in New York harbor. Altogether the crowd numbered about a thousand, and only the ladies had seats, borrowed from nearby classrooms.

The Navy team trotted onto the field with their white canvas jackets and breeches covered with mud and grime. They were out to remind their untried opponents that this was their seventh game of the year. They even had a cheer which the naval officers promptly delivered:

> Rah, rah, rah!
> Hi ho ha
> U. S. N. A.
> Boom siss bah!
> The Navee!

The Army band struck up a favorite Army song, perhaps "Annie Laurie," as Dennis Michie led his stalwarts onto the field. "On, Brave Old Army Team" was still years in the future. After a pause for "The Star Spangled Banner," Commandant Hawkins gathered the Army team around him and said, "I shall slug (give a punishment tour to) the first Army player who leaves the field in an upright position."

On the very first kick-off Navy demonstrated a clear superiority. Their signals were as salty as their uniforms. "Splice the main brace," shouted "Red" Emrich, their captain and star, and the ball carrier plunged over center. "Tack ship," he roared, and a halfback zoomed around right end. "Wear ship," and he went slicing in the opposite direction. "Anchors in sight," "Veer chains," "Reef topsails," and "Savez the bobstay," were other Navy signals.

The sailors were tricky as well as experienced. Red Emrich went back to punt, faked a kick and ran for a touchdown. Army rooters were outraged, and several officers protested to the referee that such deception was ungentlemanly. Army's players also had trouble with the rules. Truman Murphy grabbed Emrich, spun him around, and suddenly, for no apparent reason, let him go for another touchdown. The shamefaced Murphy explained later, "When I stopped him I heard a lot of yelling from the sidelines. I thought I had done something wrong so I let him go."

The game's basic play was the flying wedge, and the carnage it created was horrendous. Army quarterback Kirby Walker was knocked out four times. One reporter gave history the following description of his fourth and final knockout. "In one grand collision of the sides nearly every man on the field is laid out and four of them cannot arise. One is having his arm jerked into place, another is having his leg pulled, and a third is having his lungs pumped. The fourth, Walker, is unconscious and even the surgeon cannot revive him. He is carried to the hospital and the game goes on."

The final score was Navy 24—Army 0. The sailors scored twelve points in each of the two 45-minute halves. *The New York Times* ran the story on page one in the right-hand column. "West Point was the scene of a mighty battle today," it said. "The flower of the United States Navy invaded the classic precincts of the national Military Academy and captured the flower of the Army. This internecine struggle was not with bayonets nor with cutlasses but only with canvas covered arms and legs and bared heads." Later, shifting into the present tense to give an account of the game, the *Times* reporter wrote perhaps the best summary. "There is not much football in this struggle but the fighting is immense."

The very next day Michie and his cohorts began sounding what has become the perennial cry of the now ancient rivalry: "Wait till next year." But Michie knew that without a coach the chances were good that Navy would only repeat the drubbing. So he persuaded his good friend Lieutenant Daniel Tate, the tactical officer in charge of football, to invite a former Yale star, Harry L. Williams, who was teaching at Siglars Academy in Newburgh, to coach the West Point team. A mountain of a man, Williams promptly accepted the invitation and not only coached the cadets but occasionally scrimmaged with them. This probably did more to toughen the cadets than a decade of training.

"You could tackle him around the thighs," recalled Michie's roommate Harry Pattison, "and your legs would whip out like a shirttail in the wind while he galloped along." To further toughen themselves, the cadets played a five-game pre-Navy schedule in 1891, winning three games, tying one, losing one. But the hidebound Academy was extremely dubious about letting seventeen cadets go to Annapolis for the Navy game. Again Dennis Michie rescued the situation by breaking the news to the Superintendent piecemeal. He first persuaded him to let eleven men go and then only on the eve of the game upped the figure to seventeen.

As usual with every innovation at West Point, the voice of the critic was heard. Grumbled one old grad, "The nation will pay for such idle indulgence on some future battlefield." James McNeill Whistler opined that disputing for a ball kicked around the field was "beneath the dignity of officers of the United States." But the officers of the United States disagreed. Throughout the season, most West Point graduates acted like victims of football fever of the most virulent alumni type. *The Army-Navy Journal* printed scores and play-by-play accounts of each game. Money for uniforms, expenses of visiting teams and the cost of the trip to Annapolis came in a spontaneous stream from Army posts around the world.

In 1891, Michie and his teammates savored the sweet taste of revenge. Minutes after the game started, Elmer Clark, cadet right guard, carrying the ball on a guard's back play battered five yards through the center of the Navy line to score Army's first touchdown against Navy. Captain Michie kicked the extra point and the score was 6–0.

Annapolis clung to its salty east-sou'east signal calling. But Michie, calling plays by the numbers in modern style, repeatedly baffled Navy's stalwarts. The bruising, battering game ended in what *The New York Times* described as "utter rout . . . Michie's black head of hair could have been seen everywhere," the reporter declared, "and every ten yards gained by the Army in the next few minutes was due to his energies." Another reporter said that Michie "played like a lambent flame across the field." On the sidelines an Army officer shouted, "Denny, Denny, Denny," until his face was purple and his voice a feeble whisper. The final score was Army 32, Navy 10.

Army lost the next two Navy games 12–4 and 6–4, but they were close and hard-fought. Then a new Superintendent, Oswald H. Ernst, arrived at West Point and cast a pall over the rivalry. Both he and the Secretary of War were influenced by a near-riot that erupted in the Army-Navy Club in New York, the result of an argument between an admiral and a general over the 1893 game. Ernst favored football ("the surplus animal spirits of the young men finding a vent in football are much less likely to find it in mischievous pranks"), but he saw no good in the Army-Navy game. "The excitement attending exceeds all reasonable limit," he declared. The Secretary of the Army therefore had a conference with the Secretary of the Navy and both declared that neither service team could leave its grounds for a game. This effectively canceled the series, until pressure from the alumni of both schools reopened it in 1899.

But Army football continued to thrive. Yale, Princeton, Harvard,

Dartmouth, Brown, Pennsylvania, Columbia, journeyed to the Plain to slug it out with cadet elevens. In the fall of 1892, the Army Officers' Athletic Association took shape from the haphazard voluntary contributions that had kept football alive at West Point during the first two years. The United States Military Academy Athletic Association was also born to make rules and regulations for this new activity.

Playing in the shadow of Sylvanus Thayer's Academy created some special problems. One fall day in 1893, Butler Ames, Army's right end, was slugging it out with his opposite number, the captain of the Yale team, Frank Hinkey. The spectators loved it, but the new Commandant, Samuel M. Mills, took a far dimmer view. According to legend, Mills had a habit of parading the post with a bugler. If he saw a cadet committing an infraction of the rules, Mills had his bugler blow attention, thereby freezing the victim and making his capture and punishment much simpler. When Ames and Hinkey continued to batter each other in the second half, Commandant Mills lost his temper. As the Army players trotted up to the line of scrimmage, Mills's bugler cut loose and the cadets dropped the ball and snapped to attention. In the hush, Mills's bellow came rolling over the plain. "Mr. Ames. Mr. Ames. If you hit that man again, sir, I'll put you in the guardhouse! And you, man! You, man! If you hit Mr. Ames again, sir, I'll put you off the post!"

All forms of athletics soon leaped into exciting, practically full-grown life at the Academy. Their value was best summed up by the cadet editor of the West Point yearbook, the *Howitzer*. "When a cadet of today graduates, he does not carry with him a feeling of bitterness toward the Academy, as in the pre-athletic period. In his mind he bears memories of recreations and athletic triumphs which soften the asperities of his student life."

"Softened" is the key word here. Athletics did much to make the cadets bear West Point's over-automatized routine during this era. The academic board, still dominated by Peter Smith Michie, steadfastly continued to resist changes in the curriculum. Discipline remained impersonal and severe.

But the nation—and West Point—was about to be drastically transformed by that old familiar catalyst: war. The Cubans were revolting and the Spaniards were doing a reasonably efficient job of suppressing them, with the usual excesses that guerrilla wars make almost inevitable. Prisoners were tortured, civilians shot, and William Randolph Hearst decided to make the independence of Cuba a personal crusade. Things came to a boil when someone—certainly not the Spaniards—sank the battleship *Maine* in Havana harbor. Although Spain did everything short of flagellate herself on the world stage to make amends, Mr. Hearst and his friends had decided the country needed a war. It was, after all, a splendid device for selling newspapers. So the yellow press and a weak President committed the Army to a struggle for which it was almost totally unprepared. The impact on the Army—and eventually on West Point—was vast.

In Search of Progress

I

FOR THE MEN who ran the U.S. Army, the Spanish-American War was a nightmare. The minuscule staffs and the red-tape-clogged routine that administered the scattered 25,000-man Regular Army all but collapsed under the strain of officering and equipping the 200,000 volunteers who swarmed to the colors. Neither Nelson A. Miles, the Army's commander in chief, nor William Shafter, commander of the expedition to Cuba, were West Pointers. But the War Department was the main target of newspaper criticism. Theodore Roosevelt, colonel of the First Volunteer Cavalry Regiment, known popularly as the Rough Riders, complained, "We are not receiving the proper amount of food and what we do get, like most of the clothing issued us, it is more suitable for the Klondike than for Cuba." Men wearing blue woolen uniforms trained at camps hastily thrown up in the South and began dying by the hundreds from epidemics of typhoid and scarlet fever, pneumonia and bronchitis. The rations were atrocious. The men wrote home complaining about "embalmed beef." Dysentery became a major problem.

The nation was astonished to discover that its military hardware was equally deplorable. American soldiers were sent into action carrying Springfield rifles against a Spanish army equipped with Mausers that had twice the range. The field artillery was equally obsolescent. Headquarters for reporting Army snafus was Tampa, the port of embarkation for the Cuban Expedition. Freight cars carrying food, ammunition, tents, clothing, were backed up on miles of siding. "The stench of rotting bacon and spoiled beef tainted the air with the foulest odors," reported a *New York Times* correspondent. "Not in this world or the next shall I see the equal of the mess at Tampa," wrote a *Chicago Herald* reporter. "I have seen sights at dock and railhead I believed unmatched except in some huge insane asylum."

Transports rammed each other at the piers (one actually sank), while hustlers organized tourist groups to "watch the boys go off to war." The men were marched aboard antiquated ships and then left there in the tropic heat for six days while the War Department fussed over sending further orders to General Shafter. Lieutenant Colonel Roosevelt told a newspaper friend, "The soldiers are jammed together like animals on those fetid troop ships. We are in a sewer . . . a festering canal . . . stinking of rot and putrefaction . . ."

The publicity did not improve, even after the war was won. A round-robin letter to the War Department, signed by many officers of the 5th Corps, including Theodore Roosevelt, urged the removal of the Army from Cuba as soon as possible, before "thousands of lives" were lost to epidemic malaria. The War Department yielded to the public clamor and threw up a makeshift camp at Montauk, Long Island, to house convalescent soldiers. Dreadful food and a shortage of tents killed another 250 men there and the *New York World* and the *New York Journal* began a series of "exposés on the scandalous manner in which our heroes are being treated," in which the "armchair soldiers of the War Department" were castigated once more. About the only individual soldiers who emerged from the war with increased reputation were the amateur, Theodore Roosevelt, and the ex-Confederate cavalry leader, "Fighting Joe" Wheeler.

Wheeler, Custer's old classmate Tom Rosser, and Fitzhugh Lee were among the Confederate veterans who donned the Army blue as generals of volunteers. Only 5'5" tall, Wheeler had graduated from West Point in 1859 and won his nickname while wearing blue, defending a wagon train against a horde of raiding Indians. He was the chief commander of Confederate cavalry in the Western theater and served as a congressman from Georgia for seventeen years before returning to active service. By wangling himself a major generalship in Cuba, he became the only man to serve as a corps commander in both the Confederate and United States armies.

At the age of sixty-three, Wheeler more than lived up to his old nickname. A few days after the American Army landed at Siboney, he attacked (without orders) Spaniards holding the village of Las Guasimas. As the Spaniards abandoned their trenches, Fighting Joe reportedly shouted, "Give it to them, lads. We got the damn Yankees on the run." Even if Wheeler confused his wars, this small victory did much to raise the drooping morale of the mismanaged American Army.

During the advance on Santiago, Wheeler ignored a bad case of malaria to mount a horse and lead his men across the San Juan River with bullets and shrapnel whizzing all around him. Undoubtedly John J. Pershing, who was serving as a lieutenant of the 10th Cavalry, an all-

Negro regiment, was thinking of Wheeler when he wrote of the charge up San Juan and Kettle Hills. "White regiments, black regiments, regulars and Rough Riders, representing the young manhood of north and south fought together unmindful of race or color, unmindful of whether commanded by an ex-Confederate or not, and mindful only of their common duty as Americans. . . ."

Wheeler went on to fight with equal courage in the Philippine Insurrection until 1900, and retired as a major general in 1901. When he died in 1906 he was buried in full uniform. Washington fondly told the story of the Confederate veteran who came to pay his last respects and did a double take when he saw Fighting Joe lying there, resplendent in blue. "Jeesus, General," muttered the veteran, "I hate to think of what old Stonewall's gonna say when he sees you arrivin' in that uniform."

But one soldier's exploits could not dim the overwhelming impression of our Army's incompetence. Nor was the situation improved by the undeclared war that broke out in the Philippines, a Vietnam-like conflict that soon escalated into a far bigger war than Cuba. As with Vietnam, many intellectuals violently opposed America's attempt to bring civilization to "our little brown brothers," as William Howard Taft called them. When we paid Spain 20 million dollars for the Philippines, Mark Twain sardonically remarked: "Twenty million dollars! That means a single Filipino costs us around two dollars. Pretty cheap. No wonder we don't care how many we kill." Senator George Hoar denounced the war, telling the administration, "You have sacrificed thousands of American lives, the flower of our youth. You have devastated provinces. You have slain uncounted thousands of people you desire to benefit . . . Your generals are coming home from the harvests, bringing their sheaves with them in the shape of other thousands of sick and wounded. . . ." All this animosity created an anti-Army mood that unfortunately coincided with a major crisis in West Point's history: the Booz hazing scandal.

II

OSCAR L. BOOZ, of Bristol, Pennsylvania, was admitted to West Point on June 20, 1898, at the age of eighteen years, eleven months. He was not a particularly robust young man, and from April 23 to May 14, 1898, he was under the treatment of Doctor William Martin of Philadelphia for acute pharyngitis. According to the later testimony of friends, he was an amiable, easygoing boy and he at first found no difficulty getting along with his fellow cadets. One of his plebe tent-mates called him "a very pleasant sort of fellow . . . He was considered witty. They had a good deal of fun out of him on account of his name." The last remark is significant. Like U. S. Grant and others before him, but with far more tragic results, Booz was singled out by the upperclassmen as a particularly good target for hazing. And hazing had at West Point reached a fine flower of sadistic ingenuity. Among the tasks a plebe might be required to perform were the following:

Bracing—the plebe had to throw his shoulders back until the blades met, draw his chin in until it was depressed against his windpipe, draw his abdomen up and walk so that his toes touched the ground before his heels. Plebes had to brace at all times on the company streets in camp.

Eagling—the plebe was required to stand on his toes with his arms extended, drop to a sitting posture, rise part way waving his arms like wings, again drop to a sitting posture and rise again ad infinitum until the upper-classman was satisfied.

Wooden Willying—the plebe took the regulation gun, drew it up to position fire, dropped it to the position ready and kept this up for anywhere from one to two hundred repetitions.

Footballs—the plebe lay on his back and without bending his knees drew his legs up until they were at right angles with his body and dropped them back to earth. Seventy-five to a hundred times was not considered excessive.

Choo-chooing—a plebe lay on his back and worked both arms and legs in imitation of a locomotive.

Dipping—this is an old-fashioned word for doing push-ups. Sometimes the plebe's hands were placed on a bucket or box to keep his body as straight as possible and to make sure he raised and lowered it by use of his arms alone.

Plebe's rest—a plebe stood on the toe of his left foot and raised his right leg up until he rested the right elbow on his knee and placed his chin in his right hand.

Stretching—a plebe had to hang from the canvas shelf in his tent, legs bent at the knees until he dropped off from exhaustion.

Holding out the gun—the plebe had to hold both arms in front of him at right angles and support upon his hands a regulation rifle.

Swimming to Newburgh—lying face down on a box, a plebe had to kick his feet and work his hands as if he were swimming the Hudson.

Sitting on the bayonet—the plebe assumed a sitting posture with a bayonet under his butt. Loss of equilibrium from weariness or panic was inevitably painful.

Sweating—a plebe was ordered to his tent with the sides and back down and forced to put on his raincoat and wrap himself in bed clothing. Fainting and nausea were frequently the result.

Qualifying—a plebe was forced to eat at one sitting as many as 130 prunes or a soup plate full of molasses. It did not improve his digestion.

Feet inspection—the upperclassmen would inspect a plebe's feet after lights out, intentionally dripping hot grease from the candle on his toes.

Foot in the tent—all an upperclassman had to do was slide his foot into a plebe's tent between tattoo and taps and the plebe had to at once stand on his head, recite and make a left-hand salute with the right foot.

Standing orders—a plebe might be required to stand the entire day, except at mess and sink.

Cold bath—a plebe on orders had to strip himself and dash down the company street while upperclassmen flung buckets of cold water on him.

Obviously, most plebes tried to escape these tortures by being as inconspicuous as possible. Poor Booz had the disadvantage of his name, and he apparently experienced more than his share of them. As a result he tried to protect himself by strictly interpreting his own rights. For instance, during his third week in camp, an upperclassman ordered him to leave the ranks on the way back from supper. Booz ignored him on the grounds that it was against regulations. He thus escaped one or another of the aforementioned ordeals, but the upperclassmen singled him out for a far more serious offense: defiance. A few weeks later someone reported Booz to the "fighting committee."

Every class had one of these committees. Their main purpose was disciplining any plebe who resisted hazing either in words or manner. Under this system, the plebe had to agree to fight an upper-class cadet of his own height and weight or be ostracized by the entire corps. The system was elaborately worked out. Each man was supplied with two seconds from his own class who brought towels, sponges and other equipment. There were a referee, a timekeeper and four sentinels posted at careful intervals to make sure no officers saw anything if they approached.

The cadets fought with bare fists under Marquis of Queensbury rules with two-minute rounds and one-minute rests. But the Marquis never invented the West Point tradition that no matter how badly a man was being beaten, he had to keep on fighting until he was either unconscious or physically incapable of standing up. Between June, 1897, and January, 1901, there were more than forty such fights and in almost every case the defeated party had to go to the hospital; half the time the winner went with him. Of these forty fights, plebes won only four.

Booz knew, therefore, that his chances of victory were practically nil, but he accepted the challenge with apparent confidence and during the first round forced the fight until his opponent landed a solid punch in the face, starting a bloody nose which demoralized him. In his mortification, Booz wept. But he came out for the second round. Almost immediately he took a punch in the stomach which stretched him on the ground. He tried to get up, finally decided it was hopeless and allowed himself to be counted out. He crept back to camp with a bleeding nose, a black eye, a cut under the other eye, several loosened teeth and a bruise on his body near his heart.

No one in the fighting party had any criticism of Booz's performance. But a few hours after he was back in camp the rumor ran through the corps that he was boasting about how he had beaten the system by faking a knockout. Booz was showered with insults. Several first classmen told him bluntly that he would be cut in the corps and in the army if he ever got there. The hapless young man wrote home to his father, telling him of the fight and asking permission to resign. "The fellows here are brutes and they have evil in their minds," he said. His father, naturally irate, refused to let him resign. Meanwhile the bullies in the cadet corps had designed a new punishment for their favorite victim. They began forcing him to drink tabasco sauce with every meal. The doses were fairly small at first, about the size that other cadets were forced to drink as part of the hazing routine. But with Booz the dosage was steadily increased until in a single two-week period he was drinking a full bottle. This ordeal persisted until the end of summer camp, in the last week in August.

When the corps moved back into the barracks, Booz, who had shown considerable scholastic ability while preparing for the Academy, sank almost immediately to the bottom of his class. His roommates reported (later) that he "studied very little . . . he would say he got dizzy and complained of his eyes." Within a month Booz resigned, and on October 19, 1898, he consulted a Philadelphia eye specialist. The doctor decided that his eye trouble was really a by-product of an "exhausted condition —some profound depression of the system."

A year and a half later, Booz died of tubercular laryngitis. In his last delirium he cried out: "Have the tent ready; the inspector is coming" and "they ought to have my throat." Booz's embittered family were convinced that their son's throat condition was directly traceable to the continuous dosage of tabasco sauce. The story, enlarged and distorted by rumor, got into the newspapers, and on December 1, 1900, the day of the Army-Navy football game, newspapers trumpeted that Booz had been beaten, held to the ground and a fiery liquid poured down his throat, followed by a red-hot iron. This brought to the fore still another family—the parents of John Edward Breth, who had entered the Academy in June, 1897, been found deficient in mathematics January 25, 1898, and died in October, 1899, of typhoid pneumonia. Breth's family maintained that his hazing experiences had wrecked his nervous system, leaving him with a permanent twitch. Thus weakened, he was easy prey to the typhoid bacillus. The country boiled with indignation, and on January 4, 1901, a select committee of the House of Representatives, chaired by Charles Dick of Ohio, began hearing testimony on the hazing traditions at West Point, with special emphasis on the fate of Booz and Breth.

The congressmen took testimony in Bristol, Booz's hometown, and then moved to Philadelphia to hear what the surviving members of the Breth family had to say. Although Breth's demise had only a tenuous connection with his ordeal at West Point, in some ways his family's testimony was even more damaging than the Booz witnesses. "When John came home," said his brother, William A. Breth, "he told me he had to do so much 'eagling' that his muscles felt like leather. A cadet named Bender made him sit on the point of a bayonet until he fell off. He was made to sit on it again and during this operation Bender played a violin. On a hot July day, after a hard day's drill, he was compelled to don a raincoat and hold out dumbbells. One night he was dragged out of bed and over rough stones in the company street. On another occasion he was so hardly exercised that the next morning the officer in charge of drill compelled him to drop out because of weakness. My brother considered West Point Military Academy the best in the world but said the upperclassmen ran the place." His sister recalled Breth telling how he collapsed during the third bout of hazing in a single night. On his deathbed, she said, Breth went through choo-chooing motions.

The day after this testimony hit the newspapers, a hazing scandal blossomed at Colby University. A young man described as "a giant in strength" was on his deathbed, suffering daily convulsions as a result of blows on the head and back in the course of inducting him into fraternity. Although in retrospect it makes it clear that West Point was by no means unique in hazing extremism, the news only seemed to redouble Congressional indignation. The following day the committee opened hearings at West Point and Cadet William R. Bettison, president of the first class, took the stand and was grilled mercilessly by the committee. Neither he nor the cadets who followed him were any match for the congressmen, many of whom were lawyers skilled in cross-examination. Though the cadets struggled desperately to avoid it, many were forced to name upperclassmen who had hazed them or their fellows.

By January 20, 1901, it was obvious to everyone at West Point that the Academy was in grave danger. Congress was emotionally prepared to pass a bill that might drastically alter, if not destroy, the school. Fortunately the cadets read the newspapers too, and decided it was time for a change. The presidents of all four classes came forward and presented to the committee the following letter:

Sir: Having become cognizant of the manner in which the system of hazing as practiced at the Military Academy is regarded by the people of the United States, we, the cadets of the United States Military Academy, while maintaining that we have pursued our system from the best motives, yet realizing that the deliberate judgment of the people should, in a country like ours, be above all other considerations, do now reaffirm our former action abolishing the exercising of the fourth class men and do further agree to discontinue hazing—the requiring of fourth class men to eat anything against their desire and the practice of calling out fourth class men by class action—and that we will not devise other similar practices to replace those abandoned.

This gesture won praise from newspaper editors and congressmen. *The New York Times* called it "creditable," and Charles Dick declared he was convinced that "the present cadets will live up to those resolutions." He noted, however, there was "no express promise to cease bracing; and upon some other subjects the resolutions are ambiguous."

One man's testimony suggests that the intransigence displayed by many cadets when testifying before the Congressional committee was by no means rooted out by this graceful letter of surrender. Colonel Clifford Cabel Early of the class of 1905, speaking at a West Point Society Founders' Day dinner at Fort McPherson, Georgia, on March 15, 1957, recalled: "In the winter of 1900–1901 there was, believe it or not, a mutiny at West Point. Although I entered West Point only a few months later, the matter was never discussed or talked about by the upperclassmen and I never knew what it was about. I don't think it was planned or premeditated but developed spontaneously on the spur of the moment. The corps, or a large part of it, on being dismissed in the evening after being marched back from the mess hall, swarmed out on the parade ground. They tore the old saluting gun loose from its moorings and dragged it across the parade ground to in front of the superintendent's quarters where they pointed the gun toward the supe's house . . . As a result of the escapade, five or six first classmen were dismissed from West Point . . . The class of 1902 graduated only 54. Five or six other upperclassmen were suspended a year." Though Colonel Early makes no direct connection between this uprising and hazing, there was no other issue that could have caused such a serious demonstration.

Later in his talk Early briefly referred to the hazing problem and declared as a result of the scandal that hazing had been abolished "for all time." He thus joined a long line of graduates who had made similar declarations.

Neither the Booz scandal nor the most determined efforts on the part of the Academy's administration eliminated hazing. Some of the more violent physical exercises were temporarily dropped; forcing a man to eat obnoxious foods or foreign substances was also largely abandoned. But there persisted in the cadet corps an insistent intuition that hazing made sense at West Point. In their view it tested areas of a man's spirit that might one day become vital factors on a battlefield—the necessity to obey orders that within the limited horizon of a company or a battalion commander may seem stupid and meaningless—the ability to bear disappointment and defeat. Negative capabilities to be sure, but necessary, perhaps even crucial in the personality of the soldier. Hazing was also, of course, a prolonged initiation into the mystique of the corps—a mystique that became more and more intense during the isolation and stagnation of the 80's and 90's. There were also forces outside the Academy that covertly supported the perpetuation of hazing. Congressmen regularly played the old game of helping to reinstate cadets dismissed for hazing. Not merely in the cadet corps itself but probably in a majority of the graduates there was little or no genuine sympathy for critics of the system.

Before the decade was over, another hazing scandal broke out. The situation was much milder—there were no extravagant claims that hazing had killed anyone. Rather, the Senate Committee on Military Affairs, on which sat two Academy graduates, Senator Frank Briggs of Delaware (1872) and Senator Henry A. du Pont, also of Delaware (1861), held a hearing to determine whether Cadet Chauncey C. Devore, a first classman dismissed for hazing a plebe sentinel, ought to be reinstated.

Fortunately for the Academy, one of West Point's best (and least recognized) Superintendents, Hugh L. Scott, was in command at the time. When Scott heard that the cadets dismissed for hazing were seeking reappointments, he rushed to Washington, D.C., to protest to the Secretary of War, Luke Wright, who told him to take the problem to President Theodore Roosevelt.

Scott went back to West Point, thought it over and made a momentous decision that recalled not a little of the Thayer-Jackson crisis. "I'm going to do the most dangerous thing I can possibly do," the Superintendent told his wife. "I'm going to butt right into the President of the United States and the Secretary of War head on. The President is so sure of himself, anyone who differs with him must in consequence be wrong —nobody can possibly be right. . . . The Secretary of War will be sitting right there and all the President will have to do is say to him, 'This bothersome fellow annoys me; he won't let me do what I want to do; send him to the Mexican border, Alaska, or any old place away from West Point,' and all the little reputation I have been all my life building up will be kicked over like a bucket of milk and I will have to go away with a stigma on my record that the President of the United States considers me unfit to command the Military Academy and my career will be over before it is really begun."

Mrs. Scott said: "You know what you ought to do—go ahead and do it. We have lived on the prairie before and I am ready to go back with you and do it again."

Scott journeyed to Oyster Bay with Secretary Wright. After lunch, Roosevelt took the Secretary and the Superintendent to his library and "they began to tell each other what bad boys they had been, the inference being that bad boys like them could come to high places." Scott swiftly realized "that if I did not get in what I had to say I would be steam-rollered by a positive order I could not get changed. The President gave me my chance at last by asking me to tell him again why I had sent those young men away.

"Mr. President," said Scott, "that is the law. The law says if you haze new cadets you shall be dismissed! The culprits do not deny their guilt and there is nothing else to do."

"Oh, yes. Oh, yes. I know, I know," he said. "Congress passed an hysterical law."

"Mr. President, I am not the Supreme Court," said Scott, "to pass on these laws. I have got to take them as they come to me from the War Department. I cannot pick and choose among them. I have taken an oath to obey them and so have you and if you and the Secretary do what you are now contemplating, you will do the greatest damage to the discipline of the Military Academy that anybody has done in this generation."

Scott stood there "waiting for the lightning to strike." But Roosevelt, instead of fulminating, wheeled on the Secretary of War saying: "Luke, we have got to look out here what we are doing."

Scott "came away from Oyster Bay wearing my own hide." But the fight to reinstate the guilty cadets was by no means over. A Senator called Scott to explain that one dismissed boy was the son of an influential constituent. He pointed out the number of favors he had done for Scott and begged him to make an exception. Gritting his teeth, Scott refused. Next came a bill introduced in Congress to reinstate the guilty cadets. The Superintendent was summoned before a Senate committee where he was "subjected like a criminal to a severe grilling not comporting at all with the dignity of the upper House and reminding one of a police court."

Scott's Commandant, Frederick W. Sibley, wavered under the Senatorial crossfire and admitted he thought the mandatory punishment of dismissal was too extreme. He had experienced "much more severe hazing" himself when he was a cadet, he confessed. But Scott was a much tougher witness.

"You have turned out some pretty good officers while hazing has been going on, have you not?" one senator asked.

"In spite of it," Scott replied, icily, and in a pungent sentence summed up what was wrong with hazing. "I believe if a cadet is made to do menial service, if he is browbeaten and humiliated, it is injurious to his character. It is just the same with cadets as with anybody else." At the close of the two-hour session Senator Dick of Ohio, who had sat on the Booz hazing committee, told Scott, "They haven't scored a point on you." The dismissals stood.

Scott had another harrowing experience with Roosevelt. He got up one morning to find a letter on his desk from the President containing the following astonishing statement: "You teach too much mathematics at West Point. I want you to stop it." Roosevelt had obviously succumbed to the wails of congressmen whose appointees had failed in mathematics. As in other days, many congressmen seemed to be convinced "that the Superintendent and faculty lay awake nights searching for some way to send congressmen's appointees away, whereas actually they lie awake pondering how they can possibly keep them there." Scott braced himself for another head-on collision with Teddy, but intervention by friends of West Point in Washington rescued him from this ordeal.

But hazing continued. In 1913, eighteen cadets appealed over the head of the Superintendent to the Secretary of War, protesting severe punishments meted out to them for drilling plebes in "braced" posture. It would take yet another tragedy to drastically alter the hazing system.

III

THE HAZING SCANDALS, the sense of having passed into a new century, the sorry performance in the Spanish-American War (which in truth, if not in public opinion, could not be entirely blamed upon West Pointers) all combined to create a call for changes in West Point and in the Army. The strongest voice belonged to retired Lieutenant General John Schofield, who was president of the Board of Visitors in 1901. Schofield's report severely criticized the narrowness of West Point's education, the overemphasis on science and mathematics, the unsophisticated, overgrammatical approach to languages. "The time has come," he declared, "when those in charge of the Academy should realize there are other requisites to a well-rounded education as applied to the soldier than those that relate to mathematics and their application. There has been too great a tendency to cling to old educational traditions that have influenced, if not entirely shaped the curriculum from the foundation of the Academy." Three years later, Morris Schaff published his graceful memoir, *The Spirit of Old West Point,* which combined invaluable recollections of Civil War days at the Academy with a determined call for a change in attitude toward English, history and other nonscientific subjects.

At least as significant was the death of Peter Smith Michie on February 16, 1901. His passing in the last year of West Point's first century had a finality to it, the solemn guttering of a flame that had been ignited by Sylvanus Thayer, passed triumphantly to Dennis Hart Mahan and finally with dwindling vigor to Michie.

Another influential factor in this mood of change was the centennial of the Academy, which was celebrated on June 9, 10 and 11, 1902. Dr. William R. Harper, president and organizer of the University of Chicago, spoke in praise of West Point's educational achievements. President Theodore Roosevelt declared that during the century "no other educational institution in the land contributed so many names as West Point to the honor roll of the nation's greatest citizens." The Association of Graduates unveiled a commemorative tablet pledging, "The best efforts of our lives shall be to make the record of the second century even more memorable than that of the first."

The Centennial Celebration also laid to rest the last lingering traces of North-South antagonism within West Point. Among the chief speakers on Alumni Day was Edward Porter Alexander of the class of 1857, Lee's chief of artillery. He and James Longstreet headed a phalanx of Southern veterans, and when Alexander mentioned "Old Pete" by name, the room burst into applause and cheering that lasted for several minutes.

Looking back over the years, Alexander declared "that it was best for the South that the cause was lost."

"Whose vision is now so dull that he does not recognize the blessing it is to himself and to his children to live in an undivided country? . . . The right to secede, the state for which we fought so desperately, were it now offered us as a gift, we would reject as we would a proposition of suicide." Then he recalled to his listeners those six wonderful days from April 9, 1865, the surrender at Appomattox, to the fourteenth—the death of Lincoln—when it seemed possible that the nation would be reunited without bitterness. "Time fails me to describe the friendliness, courtesy, generosity with which the whole victorious army seemed filled. The news of the surrender and its liberal terms was received everywhere with similar feelings of generous conciliation."

Now at last, he said, the wounds were healed. "But was all the agony endured for the lost cause but as water spilled upon the sand? Was all our blood shed in vain? No," Alexander declared, "a thousand times no.

"We have given to our children a proud memory and to history new names, to be a theme and an inspiration for unborn generations. The heroes of future wars will emulate our Lees and Jacksons . . . We didn't go into our cause, we were born into it. We fought it out to its remotest end and suffered to the very utmost its dying aches and pains. But they were rich in compensations and have proven to be only the birth pangs of a new nation, in whose career we are proud to own and to bear a part."

Finally, he offered a tribute to West Point "who taught us not the skill to unravel conflicting political creeds . . . but rather to illustrate by our lives manly courage and loyalty to our convictions."

With a mighty roar, the old men who had been young in 1861 sprang to their feet. The band struck up "The Star-Spangled Banner" as it had done on a night long ago at a divided West Point. The gray-headed veterans threw their arms around each other and wept. The next day Secretary of War Elihu Root said: "No army inspired by the spirit of the Military Academy can ever endanger a country's liberty or can ever desert its country's flag."

Root, probably the greatest Secretary of War since Calhoun, expanded and drastically revamped the Army, founded the Army War College and the general staff, and placed West Point in a new educational and military context. He got many of his ideas from a book which had lain in the War Office files for over two decades—Emory Upton's *The Military Policy of the United States*. The first critical analysis of the way America fought its wars and organized its Army, the book was never officially published because some of the most telling points were scored when Upton considered the chaotic way Lincoln and his government had organized the Army for the Civil War. Root exhumed it to support his program of Army reform.

In this new Rootian order, West Point had a cornerstone role. The Secretary saw clearly that the complex nature of modern war and military organization more than justified West Point's role as a basic national school for the preparation of professional soldiers. But the heart of the Academy's education was no longer the tradition of scientific excellence inculcated by Sylvanus Thayer. The new goal was summed up in the official adoption of a motto: Duty, Honor, Country. West Point henceforth would claim to produce, not valuable technicians, but valuable men.

Logically this new concept could—and perhaps should—have created an immediate curriculum revolution at West Point. But most of Root's energies and attention went into reforming the Army beyond West Point. Compared to the rest of the Army, the Academy seemed to be functioning satisfactorily. Although some members of the academic board revealed a lively interest in new ideas, no dominant figure emerged, on the board or among the era's Superintendents, with sufficient force or prestige to lead the drastic overhaul the school needed. Intellectually, West Point drifted in a desultory, vaguely discontented status quo.

This unpleasant truth was effectively smothered by a massive building program, for which Root had extracted $6,500,000 from Congress. A master architectural plan, under the direction of Cram, Goodhue, and

Ferguson of Boston, created the West Point that greets visitors today—massive, gray, machine-made Gothic buildings. The results inspired a flood of magazine articles describing "the new West Point." But behind the more august façade, intellectual stagnation was still the order of the day.

Superintendent Albert Mills, whose tour of duty ran from 1898 to 1906, made a limited breakthrough by persuading Congress to revise the admission standards, which had not changed since 1866, and were woefully elementary compared to what a young man needed to enter Rensselaer Polytechnic, the Columbia School of Mines or even the Naval Academy. On March 2, 1901, Congress passed a new law which made no attempt to specify requirements but simply stated that "all appointees shall be examined under regulations to be framed by the Secretary of War before they shall be admitted to the Academy and shall be required to be well versed in such subjects as he may from time to time prescribe."

But the academic board resisted any extensive changes in the curriculum, although Boards of Visitors repeatedly called for them. Finally, after a notably severe scolding from the 1907 visitors, the board grudgingly created a new Department of English and History and brought in a civilian—Professor John C. Adams of Yale—to head it.

Adams stunned the Academy by dropping Thayer's system of instructors and teaching all the classes himself. His successor, Lucius H. Holt, also of Yale, restored the instructor system and broadened the history curriculum by adding a textbook on political science. But his request for two separate departments for his tandem professorship was flatly rejected. The cadets continued to spend most of their time studying mathematics and engineering.

IV

MEANWHILE, INTO THE corps were marching the men who would lead American armies in the first truly global conflict—World War II. It seems fitting that the cadet who was to prove himself the most brilliant, if not the most beloved, of these generals graduated in 1903, at the very dawn of West Point's second century. As the son of Civil War hero Arthur MacArthur, Douglas MacArthur was a marked man from the day he appeared at West Point. He and two equally prominent classmates, Phil Sheridan, Jr., and U. S. Grant, III, were hazed unmercifully. But MacArthur seemed to attract the toughest treatment. One night he was forced to "eagle" by three separate sets of upperclassmen. During the third session he lost control of his muscles and collapsed in spasms. Summoned before the Congressional committee, MacArthur did his utmost to avoid naming his tormentors. But the congressmen were adamant. Contrary to his memoirs, where MacArthur says he named nobody, he actually compromised and named several upperclassmen who had already been dismissed.

But MacArthur otherwise handled the congressmen with remarkable aplomb. *The New York Times* reported that his self-possession "startled" the politicians. Where other cadets had stumbled and stammered out damaging admissions, MacArthur fielded questions with the cool calm of a professional debater. Patiently explaining plebe traditions ("Sir, I don't think you caught my meaning—" "Again you have not caught the idea"), he did his utmost to mimimize his own suffering. "I have heard it stated, in fact I have seen it in the newspapers," he said, "that I was at one time hazed until I suffered severe convulsions. No such affair took place. I was hazed at the time in question until I was quite tired; I might say more than that. As far as my physical muscles were concerned, I did not have complete control of them but as far as being in convulsions or in any way delirious or anything of that kind or out of my head, I most emphatically deny it . . . I was not obliged to attend hospital for any cause during plebe camp. On the night in question I think I was suffering with a case of exaggerated cramps. That is the only thing I could call it."

[283]

A week later, MacArthur's tentmate Cunningham, who had resigned from the corps, testified before the committee in Chicago and gave a far more graphic description of what his friend had undergone. When asked if he was in violent convulsions, Cunningham replied, "I think if you saw him in the same condition on the street you would call them convulsions." Cunningham said MacArthur's legs were trembling so badly "he asked me to throw a blanket under them in order that the company officers could not hear his feet striking the floor . . . He suggested that if he cried out that we put a blanket in his mouth." MacArthur's courage won him what was then called "a bootlick" from the whole corps. "They were proud of him," Cunningham said.

As for MacArthur himself, he vowed that he would never haze a fellow cadet and if he ever got the chance he would do his utmost to abolish the custom.

Few plebes before or since enjoyed MacArthur's privilege of rooming with a first classman when they moved into the barracks for the first time. Arthur P. S. Hyde of the class of 1900 recalled later he had been "impressed with MacArthur's attention to duty and his manifest determination to make good as a cadet. I therefore invited him to live with me. The invitation naturally came to him as a surprise . . . He asked me for time to run over to the hotel to talk to his mother about my invitation. In a half hour he was back with word that he would be glad to accept."

Hyde was senior lieutenant of A Company and therefore rated the third floor tower room in the first division of the barracks. Aside from a pleasant view of the Plain, the chief advantage of the room was the first classman's right to keep his light on until 11 P.M. Hyde says MacArthur took advantage of this light every night and sometimes was up an hour before reveille the next morning boning with fierce determination to graduate first in his class. Hyde was coasting through in the middle of his class and was amazed by MacArthur's energy. "His only recreation was to spend a half hour after supper each day with his mother."

Both MacArthur's mother and Mrs. Frederic N. Grant, mother of Ulysses Grant III, lived in Craney's Hotel at West Point. They waged a velvet-glove campaign for supremacy through their sons, all the while maintaining an effusive (too effusive, one observer noted wryly) friendship. As Grant and MacArthur boned for the number one position in the corps, the friendship sometimes became a little strained. "They're hair pullin' again," the corps used to say when they saw the two mothers showering compliments on each other. Mrs. Grant had a considerable head start on Mrs. MacArthur: although General MacArthur was campaigning in the Philippines at the time, the MacArthurs were hardly members of the Army's Four Hundred on the Grant level. But Mrs. MacArthur made sure that "Dougie," as she called him, more than made up for this prestige gap. At the end of plebe year MacArthur stood first in his class and Grant was second. But by the end of the course young Grant had dropped to sixth in class standing while MacArthur retained his grip on the number one position. To this triumph MacArthur added the coveted first captaincy in his final year, while Grant had to be satisfied with the post of cadet adjutant.

There is a tradition, denied by some, affirmed by others, that Mrs. MacArthur saved her Dougie from another fate during his West Point years. The handsome young first captain was reportedly engaged to eight girls at the same time. But his mother broke up all the romances before any of them reached the brinkmanship stage. MacArthur's only comment on the story is the highly cryptic, "I have never been so hotly engaged by the enemy."

On the military side, MacArthur was equally outstanding. In his second or "yearling" year, a tactical officer watched Corporal MacArthur drill a squad of plebes, then turned to the cadet captain of 1900 and said, "There's the finest drillmaster I have ever seen." Another man who spent three years in the corps with him summed him up even better. "He had style. There was never another cadet quite like him."

MacArthur showed not only his brains but his individuality early. It was at that time the custom for the cadets to have calling cards engraved, "U.S. Corps Cadets." MacArthur announced to all and sundry that he disagreed with this description and proceeded to lecture his fellows on the fact that the cadet corps was a part of the Army, and Army regulations listed cadets between second lieutenants and sergeant majors. Cadet MacArthur had his cards engraved, "Corps of Cadets United States Army."

Another early flowering of the flamboyant future general could be glimpsed in MacArthur's reaction to finding himself listed with a group of "goats" (men at the bottom of the class) because he had to make up a test in mathematics which he had missed because of illness. MacArthur felt his honor affronted. He went to the professor and declared: "I have not failed my mathematics course and I will not have my name listed with those who failed . . . If my name is not removed from that list by nine o'clock tomorrow morning, I will resign." Mac-Arthur's roommate was appalled and could not sleep all night, certain that his friend's audacity was going to wreck his career before it began. MacArthur went to bed, slept soundly and woke up to find his name had been taken off the list.

In his second and third years MacArthur played left field on the cadet baseball team. "He was a heady ball player," the team captain recalled a half century later. "He was far from brilliant but somehow he could manage to get on first. He'd outfox the pitcher, draw a base on balls and get a single, or outrun a bunt—and there he'd be on first."

MacArthur's interest in baseball allowed two other cadets to pass him in class standing, but in a final burst of fierce energy and determination, MacArthur dropped the sport in the spring of his final year and fought his way back to the top spot. His marks were the highest four-year average anyone had achieved at West Point in more than 25 years.

For all his scholastic and military triumphs, MacArthur knew when to be human. One of his classmates was Hugh S. Johnson, later head of the N.R.A. "Sep," as his friends called him because he had begun his plebe year in September, was the very opposite of MacArthur. He rebelled at the Academy's rules, hated to study and continuously razzed MacArthur. One night during a cadet hop MacArthur strolled into the men's room and found Johnson and some of his pals shooting craps. As first captain he could have put them on report. Instead, he simply said, "I see you fellows prefer boning to dancing," turned his back and walked out.

The cadets went to Washington for William McKinley's inauguration. MacArthur found himself quartered with Johnson on the top floor of old Ebbet House. While MacArthur was out, Sep and his rambunctious friends restaged the battle scene from *Macbeth,* using MacArthur's dress hat for a victim. When he returned he found his beautiful shako, which he was supposed to wear in the parade the next day, pinned to the door with a cadet sword. MacArthur chose to suffer in silence, rather than put Johnson on report.

Neither Johnson nor anyone else could dim MacArthur's enthusiasm for West Point. In 1947, when he was supreme commander in Tokyo, he wrote: "Nearly 48 years have gone since I joined the Long Gray Line . . . The world has turned over many times since that day and the dreams have long vanished with the passing years, but through the grim murk of it all, the pride and thrill of being a West Pointer has never dimmed. And as I near the end of the road, what I felt when I was sworn in on the Plain so long ago I can still say—'That is my greatest honor.' "

As Second Lieutenant Douglas MacArthur sailed off to the Philippines, a far different young man began enduring the terrors of Beast Barracks. Henry Harley Arnold was the son of a surgeon lieutenant with the Pennsylvania Cavalry in Puerto Rico. Deciding one of his sons should go to West Point, the senior Arnold wangled an appointment for his oldest boy Thomas, who promptly turned it down in favor of Penn State and electrical engineering. Arnold *père* therefore designated Harley, as his family called him, although he was supposedly slated for Bucknell and the ministry.

Any fatalist who wishes to bolster his deterministic arguments should study West Point biography, and he might well begin with Cadet Arnold. At West Point he was known as "Pewt" or "Benny" (there is no sign of his later nickname, "Hap"). Summing him up on graduation eve, his yearbook scribe declared: "Pewt's biography might be adequately set forth by filling the required space with sulphurous cuss words and frosting them over with delinquencies." Arnold never even made corporal during his four years. His great interests were football, riding and the "Black Hand," a secret society given to courting trouble of every shape and description. Its greatest success was smuggling an incredible amount of fireworks into the Academy to celebrate New Year's, 1907.

As Arnold himself told it later, "All hell blew loose at the stroke of midnight and in the exploding glare which rose over the Academy, bugles blew, sirens sounded, officers and men tumbled from their beds, the whole reservation was alive! In the center of it all, atop the barracks, I touched off the *pièce de résistance.*" It was an exploding sign that spelled out "1907 Never Again." A sharp-eyed tac spotted Arnold silhouetted against the glare. He was put in solitary confinement and was reposing there when his future wife came up to see him that weekend.

Academically West Point, as Arnold recalled it, was in the doldrums. "After I had once learned how to study in my plebe year, I skated along without too much effort in a spot just below the middle of the class— seldom standing higher than 62nd in a class of 110 nor lower than 66. I had time to play football as a substitute fullback and halfback, to play on the polo squad, place in the shot-put at interclass track meets and with the rest of the cavalry fanatics ride furiously not only at drill but in the Riding Hall and over the reservation on our own." Not once in his four years at West Point did the future commander of the Army Air Force in World War II hear a word about the remarkable feat accomplished by two brothers named Wright in 1903.

Different in still another way was a cadet who entered West Point in 1904. Skinny, high-strung George S. Patton was the grandson of a Confederate general killed at the Battle of Winchester. Patton's father had graduated from the Virginia Military Institute, and the boy had grown up steeped in military tradition, supposedly executing his first battle maneuver by dragging a chicken around the house in imitation of Achilles dragging Hector's body around the walls of Troy. Hypersensitive and ambitious, he made few friends in the corps by flatly declaring he was going to get his major "A" in football and become the first general in his class. He did neither. He made the West Point team four times, but two broken arms in the brutal scrimmages of those days prevented him from ever seeing action in a game. Not until his final year did he win his "A" by starring in an intramural track meet which the corps held each spring. Patton won first place in the 120-yard hurdles, second in the 220-yard dash and first in the 220-yard hurdles. In the last he broke his own Academy record and for this feat received the coveted "A."

In the classroom, Patton was anything but distinguished. Troubles with mathematics forced him to repeat his plebe year, and he finished forty-sixth in a class of 103. But he excelled in the military aspects of cadet life. In fact, he soon became known as a "quilloid," a word the corps used to describe a cadet officer who was prone to put others on report for the tiniest infraction of the regulations. In the 1909 year book, his classmates satirized this tendency in the following vignette:

Confusion reigns supreme. The barracks were being shaken by a violent earthquake and men came tumbling out of their divisions in all stages of dishabille. Suddenly the cadet lieutenant and adjutant appeared in the area, faultlessly attired, as usual. Walking with firm step across the area, he halted, executed a proper about-face and the stentorian tones rang out, "Battalion, attention-n-n! Cadets will refrain from being unduly shaken up. There will be no yelling in the area. The earthquake will cease immediately by order-r-r of Lieutenant Colonel Howze."

West Point cannot claim to have inspired George Patton to be a soldier, but it deepened and broadened that desire. On January 18, 1909, only a few months before graduation, Patton wrote a letter to his bride-to-be's father: "With reference to the profession of a soldier, I think I appreciate most of its drawbacks. As you say, it is very narrowing but don't you think that a man of only very ordinary capacity, in order to succeed against great competition, must be narrow? That is, have only one motive? I have no experience, but from what I have read of successful men, they seem to be of the one-idea sort.

"It is hard to answer intelligibly the question 'why I want to be a soldier.' For my own satisfaction I have tried to give myself reasons but never found any logical ones. I only feel it inside. It is as natural for me to be a soldier as it is to breathe and would be as hard to give up all thought of it as it would be to stop breathing."

George Patton had graduated and gone the way of all second lieutenants when another example of West Point's variety donned cadet gray on June 14, 1911. Dwight David Eisenhower had no military tradition in his family whatsoever. Aged twenty years and eight months, he was older than most of his classmates and at 5'11" was a solid 175 pounds. Although hazing had been "eliminated" thanks to two more Congressional investigations, the upperclassmen drove the plebes so hard "it was double time all the way," Eisenhower later recalled. Ike's first roommate broke down and left after only a few weeks. ("He would put his head down and weep.") Ike himself, on the other hand, "never doubted he would make it" even though 50 of his class left the first Christmas and another 75 fell by the wayside in the three and a half years to come.

One thing that helped Eisenhower survive was his sense of humor. When upperclassmen ordered him and his roommate to appear for inspection after taps in full dress coats, the two plebes arrived wearing the coats, crossbelts and brass, standing in a perfect brace—but without trousers. Furiously, the upperclassmen demanded an explanation. Eisenhower solemnly explained that the order had not said anything about trousers.

Like Grant and Sherman before him, Eisenhower simply refused to take West Point punctilio seriously. "I never could wear my hat straight," he said during a recent reminiscence, "and I couldn't be bothered with dust in the corner of my room." As a result, he accumulated demerits at an accelerating rate throughout his four years (among his slugs for 1912 were: "late at 9:30 gym formation; shoes under bed dirty; failed to execute 'right into line' properly; alcove not in order; in room in improper uniform"), graduating number 125 in conduct. He roomed with a fellow Kansan, Paul Hodgson, and both cadets were soon famous for after-taps talk sessions while a "sentinel" kept an eye peeled for wandering tacs. His classmates remembered Ike's fondness for midnight jawing with the following joke in their yearbook:

Inquisitive civilian—Is Mr. Eisenhower good at athletics?
Caydet—Yes, Mexican athletics.
Inquisitive civilian—What is that?
Caydet—Slinging the bull.

Actually, Ike's athletic skills were considerably more impressive. A natural athlete, he went out for boxing, baseball and track, but his first love was football. Sergeant Marty Maher, the team's trainer, recalled, "Ike was the first cadet on the field for football practice and the very last to leave. I used to curse him because he would practice so late that I would be collecting the footballs he had kicked away in the darkness. He never hit the rubbing table because he would always be out there practicing punts instead of getting a rubdown." As a yearling he quickly won national fame as Army's "plunging halfback." Army had a fine team in 1912, and Ike was close to being its star. In the 19–0 win over Rutgers, *The New York Times* called Ike ". . . one of the most promising backs in eastern football." In the Colgate game, the yearbook recalled, "Eisenhower in the fourth quarter could not be stopped," as Army won 18–7.

But against the Carlisle Indians led by Jim Thorpe, the man many consider the finest football player in the history of the game, they ran into trouble. Neither Eisenhower nor anyone else could stop the rampaging all-time all-American, and Army ended up on the short end of a 27–6 score. Ike limped off the field with a twisted knee, and in the next game against Tufts he reinjured it badly and spent 30 days in the hospital. A few months later he sprang off a horse during riding drill and smashed his unhealed knee so badly there was for a time some doubt about his remaining in the Army. He was allowed to graduate with the injury only by promising never to apply for duty in the cavalry.

Without football Eisenhower found West Point a dull, rather dispiriting place. He served as cheerleader for the Army team, designing colored capes which cadets in the stands could slip over their gray uniforms to spell out ARMY in black and gold. But several times he filled out his resignation papers, only to have classmates talk him out of it. During his third year he also formed a "misogynists' club" with two other classmates who joined in a common vow to remain indifferent to the numerous girls who came to West Point hops. At two recent hops, Ike had been "busted." The charge against him was "Violation of orders with reference to dancing after having been admonished for same," which he later described as "dancing too fast." West Point's dance styles were severely formal.

In his senior year Ike coached the plebe football team, which no doubt was the origin of a quote that appeared under his name in the yearbook, "Now fellers, it's just like this. I've been asked to say a few words this evening about this business. Now, me and Walter Camp we think—" Another hobby, particularly during his final year, was hiking around the hills of West Point studying the remains of the Revolutionary War defenses. But the course simply did not challenge him and he graduated sixty-first in his class, popular but undistinguished.

Far more promising was a friend, Omar Bradley, whose biography Ike wrote in the cadet yearbook. "If he keeps up the clip he started some of us will someday be bragging, 'Sure General Bradley was a classmate of mine.' " This class is in West Point lore "the class the stars fell on." Thirty-six percent of the 164 cadets who won degrees and commissions on June 12, 1915, went on to become general officers. In all they won 111 stars, including two generals of the army (five stars), two generals (four stars), seven lieutenant generals (three stars), twenty-four major generals (two stars), and twenty-four brigadier generals (one star).

Timing is the usual explanation for this extraordinary performance. As Eisenhower and his classmates took their final examinations, a German submarine sank the British liner *Lusitania* at a cost of 1150 lives, including 114 Americans. William Jennings Bryan, President Wilson's pacifist Secretary of State, resigned because he felt Wilson's protest over the sinking was too severe. On the Western front, generals were slaughtering men on a scale hitherto unknown in the history of warfare.

World War I would give these post-1900 graduates an invaluable baptism of fire, and catapult many of them to ranks they would otherwise have taken decades to achieve. But before these young men could stride large into history, the men of the academy's iron era would have a chance to show they had learned something at West Point, too. The first of them, almost forgotten now, unless you happen to live in Staten Island and drive to New Jersey across a bridge named in his honor, was George Goethals, class of 1881. He was to personify what might be described as a last truly great flowering of Thayer's ideal that the men of the corps could not only give America leadership in time of war, but could also make mighty contributions as builders in time of peace.

V

IN 1907, TWENTY-SEVEN YEARS after his graduation, George Goethals was still an obscure major in the Engineering Corps when a distraught Theodore Roosevelt summoned him to the White House and asked him to take charge of the Panama Canal.

Chaos was the order of the day in the Big Ditch that Americans were attempting to dig across the isthmus between North and South America. Two of America's most gifted engineers had resigned in disgust and despair after grappling in vain with the problem of disciplining the army-sized work force of 40,000 workers speaking 45 different languages, and simultaneously organizing the job itself—an unending struggle against rock slides and cave-ins, floods and jungle growth. Chagrined at the resignation of Chief Engineer John F. Stevens, whom he had appointed with vast fanfare, Roosevelt vowed he was going to put the canal in charge of men "who will stay on the job until I get tired of having them there or until I say they may abandon it. I shall turn it over to the Army."

The first thing Goethals did was analyze the unsatisfactory records of his predecessors. Then he asked for a meeting with the President and told him what he thought was wrong. A single phrase summed it up: red tape. The tangle emanated from the seven-man Panama Canal Commission that Congress had forced Roosevelt to create. It was, Goethals said, a Hydra-headed monster that was trying to run a job that was nothing less than a war—a war on the jungle, on nature itself—from swivel chairs 2000 miles away. Bluntly Goethals asked the President to give him absolute authority to make all the decisions.

Roosevelt agreed, and made Goethals both Chief Engineer and chairman of the Commission. He then junked the old Commission and appointed six new members. Inviting them into his office, he introduced them to Goethals in the following no-nonsense fashion. "In appointing you I have only one qualification to make. Colonel Goethals here is to be chairman. He is to have complete authority. If at any time you do not agree with his policies, do not bother to tell me about it—your disagreement with him will constitute your resignation."

[293]

Thus George Washington Goethals, in the best West Point tradition, took full responsibility for the most gigantic construction effort attempted by man. He was greeted in Panama with dismaying hostility by the men on the job. The outgoing engineer, John F. Stevens, was so popular that 4000 workers had signed a petition begging him to remain. Yet within a matter of weeks Goethals had his 400-square-mile domain organized as never before. Up and down the railroad he roamed in a special car, painted a bright yellow, that looked, according to one observer, like "the nightmare offspring of a passenger engine and a taxi." But the "Yellow Peril," as it was dubbed by the workers, was a psychological masterpiece. Its mere appearance galvanized the whole project.

From 6 A.M. in the morning until 10 P.M. at night George Goethals was on the job. On Sundays he took a leaf from his West Point book and held a kind of cadet office hours at which he dispensed justice, soothed quarrels and solved minor personal problems with an almost Solomon-like wisdom.

Soon the whole Canal Zone was singing a song:

> Have they canned you on the run?
> Tell the Colonel.
> Tell the tale of what they've done
> To the Colonel.
> Take your sorrows and your woes
> To the Colonel;
> He will understand, he knows,
> Does the Colonel.

Goethals combined this paternal benevolence with a steely toughness. Once a builder came to him and said: "Now I got that letter of yours, Colonel—"

"I beg your pardon," said Goethals, "but you must be mistaken. I've written you no letter."

"Oh, yes, Colonel, it was about that work at Miraflores."

"Oh, I see. You spoke a little inaccurately. You meant you received my orders, not a letter. You have the orders so that matter is settled. Was there anything else you wished to talk to me about?"

The builder went back to work without another word. When a group of disgruntled troublemakers called a strike, Goethals shipped them out on the next boat. His small police force was equally tough. Arrests averaged 500 a month. Yet by the standards of the early 1900's, when factory owners were sweating women and children twelve to sixteen hours a day, Goethals created the most humane, best paid working conditions in the Western Hemisphere. An Italian newspaperman investigating the lot of thousands of his countrymen working on the job reported, "Very few of the laborers in the service on the Canal Zone have found reason to complain of the too hard or too prolonged work. The great sleeping rooms are in a very excellent condition. The food . . . is good, healthful and abundant."

Simultaneously, Goethals preached and practiced constant economy. Studying a map made by the French company that attempted the first canal on the site, he noticed the name of a construction camp. In a matter of hours he had a gang of men hacking their way through the jungle to the site. The amazed explorers found an entire village—no less than 32 buildings, including mess halls and a completely equipped machine shop. Goethals soon had a thousand men living in it.

Perhaps the best example of his appetite for detail was the story of the empty cement bags. Goethals noted on a report that they weighed more than they should, when baled up in lots of 100 for return to the United States. He soon had a gang of laborers shaking empty bags. Out of them fell enough cement to fill 50 barrels a day.

Robert Wood, of the class of 1900, was one of many young West Pointers who served under Goethals. To them he applied the same basic principle of total responsibility. "I'm making you quartermaster of the Canal Zone," he said to the thirty-two-year-old lieutenant. "The first day we run out of cement, you're fired."

In the humid atmosphere of Panama it was impossible to stockpile cement. Moisture got into it and it solidified. It had to be shipped from the United States in closely coordinated relays. Once, because of hurricanes in the Caribbean, the supply dwindled to a mere four hours' worth. When a ship finally appeared, the frantic Wood met it at the pier with 600 laborers, and they worked 24 consecutive hours to unload the cement and pile it on a special train that raced it to the Gatun locks just in time to replenish the last batch of bags on hand.

Goethals made Wood work at his own exhausting pace. "I'd go home so mad," Wood says. "He worked me like a dog. . . . Every Saturday, every evening. On Sunday I had the morning off but not the afternoon. He never gave me a word of praise."

When Wood told his wife he was convinced Goethals was persecuting him, she demurred: "That old man's very fond of you," she said. Only much later did Wood realize that his "wise wife" was right. "Whenever he had a hard job he'd assign me to it. He knew that was the only way a man grew." Among Wood's jobs was an assignment to unsnarl the clogged Canal Zone pier and rail terminals. He learned so much that in 1917 he was able to clean up an even bigger snafu at French ports, which was threatening the lifeline of the American Army in France. Wood did that job so well he joined Sears Roebuck and soon became its President and the man behind the enormous expansion of that retail giant.

Another favorite Goethals tactic came naturally out of his West Point years. He divided the work up into Pacific and Atlantic divisions. On the Atlantic division he put Army engineers; on the Pacific, civil engineers. "Naturally the competition was intense. Terrific! Which is what he wanted," says Robert Wood.

But above all, Goethals supplied what the Canal had always lacked: the iron determination to see the job through. Slides, explosions, floods —nothing discouraged him. In 1913, when victory seemed almost in sight, a huge collapse at Cucarocha buried men and equipment, destroying months of progress. "What are we going to do?" wailed one of Goethals' lieutenants.

"Hell," snapped Goethals, "dig it out again."

A little more than a year later, on August 15, 1914, the first ship went through Culebra Cut. Though there were thousands of bigwigs and VIP's on hand for the occasion, Goethals permitted only the men who had done the job—the workers and their families—to have the honor of this initial voyage. By then George Goethals, who had not worn a uniform during the seven long years of his monumental achievement, had won the respect and even the veneration of his helpers. Theodore Roosevelt could say without exaggeration, "Colonel Goethals has succeeded in instilling into the men under him a spirit which elsewhere has been found only in a few victorious armies."

Cadet mess hall. Note "braced" plebes in the foreground. The dark-haired waiter is the late Tyrone Power. The photo is a still from the movie, *The Long Gray Line,* filmed at West Point in 1954. *Culver Pictures.*

Sunday parades on the Plain still attract thousands of sightseers each year. The yearly dose of close order drill has been slashed seventy percent to give cadets more time for study and modern battle training. *U.S. Army Photograph.*

The Academy has retained the Thayer tradition of small classes, with emphasis on individual instruction. But cadets no longer "recite" every day. Seminars, lectures, closed circuit television are part of the new curriculum. *U.S. Army Photograph.*

All Fourth Class (freshman) cadets take a course in the use of computers. Later, the computer is used in advanced courses in ordnance, electricity, and military management. Cadets have programmed judge selection procedure and selection and matching of teams for the National Debate Tournament held annually at West Point. *U.S. Army Photograph.*

The modern Academy from the air. This view illustrates with unusual clarity how the twisting Hudson River gave "West Point" its name. Since 1965, the Academy has launched a massive expansion program which will add two new barracks, and raise the corps to 4,280 cadets by 1973. *U.S. Army Photograph.*

VI

GOETHALS' ACHIEVEMENT was quickly forgotten in the shadow of the ghastly slaughter that erupted on the Western front. When a reluctant America finally entered the war, a harassed President turned to that other, truly symbolic man of West Point's iron era—John J. Pershing. Not since Lincoln summoned Grant to command the Union Army in 1864 had an American general been handed anything approaching Pershing's responsibilities. His task, in fact, was unique in our history: to transport and organize on foreign soil the largest American army ever assembled—2,086,000 men—under a single commander. Even before he left his home shores, Pershing confronted what was to become his primary nightmare. The military missions of the French and British proposed that American troops be sent abroad as soon as shipping was available to "join in cooperating with" the Allied armies. Only when Pershing and his small staff reached France did they discover that the Allies were close to military collapse and the British and French generals saw American manpower as their only hope of replenishing their decimated divisions. They wanted not an American army, but American bodies to feed into the Western front's meat grinder. To this demand, which was to grow more insistent as Allied desperation increased, Pershing interposed a blunt and unrelenting no.

Personal tragedy—the death of his wife and three daughters in a fire at the San Francisco Praesidio in 1916—only intensified the aloofness that had marked Pershing as a cadet. In organizing, under such enormous pressure, the massive American Expeditionary Force he relied heavily on men he knew from his cadet days. No less than 14 of the 42 American divisions were commanded by his classmates of 1886. Sixteen others were under the command of officers whom he had known at West Point either in his cadet days or during his tour of duty there as a tactical officer in 1898. Yet for his chief of staff Pershing selected James Guthrie Harbord, a one-time private-corporal-sergeant-and-quartermaster-sergeant of the 4th U.S. Infantry. Pershing had met Harbord when Pershing was serving as a lieutenant in the 10th Cavalry, and had seen him in action later in the Philippines. In 1917 Harbord was an obscure major on duty at the War College, but Pershing sensed in Harbord qualities he himself lacked—an intuitive intelligence and a warm, outgoing personality. Possibly he also wanted a man who would not be awed by memories of the West Point Pershing. A chief of staff must be able to talk as freely to a commanding general as a wife to her husband. This Harbord did to the point of occasionally pounding the table and shouting.

For another key aide Pershing went entirely outside the Army and chose an old friend, businessman Charles G. Dawes, future Vice-President of the United States (under Coolidge). Pershing made Dawes director of purchasing for the A.E.F.

Both these non-West Pointers admired Pershing more and more as they watched him in action, trying to assemble an army and simultaneously preserve it from the French and British devourers. "He decides big things more quickly than he does trivial ones," Harbord noted in his diary. "Two weeks ago, without any authority from Washington, he placed an order one afternoon for 50 million dollars worth of airplanes because he thought Washington was too slow and did not cable the fact until too late for Washington to countermand it, had they been so disposed, which they were not. He did it without winking an eye, as easily as though ordering a postage stamp . . ."

For Harbord, Pershing's major fault was his old West Point flaw, lateness. Harbord found him lacking in time sense "as utterly as a color blind person is without a sense of color or a deaf man is without the sound of music. He is most trying in that respect. An American untried major general may not keep a field marshal waiting or be an hour late to an ambassador's dinner . . ."

For the men he was training Pershing issued an historic order in October, 1917. "The standards for the American army will be those of West Point. The rigid attention, the upright bearing, attention to detail, uncomplaining obedience to instruction required of the cadet will be required of every officer and soldier of our armies in France." No other American General ever attempted to achieve this probably impossible ideal in our era of mass civilian armies. But Pershing never stopped trying. When he inspected a division or a regiment, he insisted on checking out every conceivable detail. He discussed onions with cooks, climbed into hayloft billets, peered down sewage systems, stamped through muddy trenches and emerged without a spot or smudge on his boots and uniform.

Correspondent Heywood Broun, who followed Pershing about France for several weeks, wrote, "His interest in detail is insatiable. He can read a man's soul through his boots or his buttons . . ." Broun quoted a younger officer as saying Pershing's favorite military leader was Joshua "because he made the sun and moon stand at attention." The sight of Pershing's khaki-colored sedan flying his four-star pennant sent chills of alarm through almost every American officer on the Western Front.

Not excepted was Colonel Douglas MacArthur who was serving as chief of staff of the 42nd (Rainbow) Division. War correspondent Frazier Hunt told how Pershing came roaring up to a railhead as the division was returning from 82 days in the line, including a 60-kilometer march. Pershing took one look at the filthy, ragged men and began skinning MacArthur alive before hundreds of grinning soldiers. "MacArthur, I'm going to hold you personally responsible for getting discipline and order into this division. I'm going to hold you personally responsible for correcting measures with the officers at fault. I won't stand for this, it's a disgrace!"

"Yes, sir," was all that Colonel MacArthur could find to say.

Pershing had fought in the Philippines under MacArthur's father, and knew the young colonel personally. Perhaps he was making amends, when, a few months later, he was visiting the Rainbow Division and a message arrived from the British, announcing imminent disaster on their front. Pershing read it without a flicker of expression on his iron visage. But as he left, he said, over his shoulder, "We old first captains, Douglas, must never flinch."

Later he made MacArthur a division commander. Someone noted that the corps commander, Charles Pelot Summerall, had been first captain of the class of 1892. A staff officer jokingly remarked: "This makes it three of a kind, a great poker hand." Perhaps Pershing disliked making light of the first captaincy, or resented the hint of West Point cliquishness; at any rate he all but skinned the hapless joker alive. "I don't want gambling terms used with reference to this army," he growled. "The Expeditionary Force is here not to play cards, but to fight."

There was, of course, a warm, human, personal Pershing behind the soldierly mask, but even those who worked closely with him, such as Frederick Palmer, chief censor of the A.E.F., admitted that his personality appeared "less and less frequently as he became absorbed in the machine he created and drove; and in the lapses, the smile the more quickly faded, the hand drew back more quickly behind the gray stone wall of his West Point training."

Pershing needed every iota of iron in his character to resist the enormous pressure from the French and British in the crisis-filled early months of 1918. By now Russia was out of the war and the Germans were theoretically capable of concentrating some 265 divisions on the Western front against 169 shot-up and dispirited Allied divisions. Ambassadors, generals and self-appointed authorities of all shapes and sizes assaulted Pershing, insisting that the only Allied hope was feeding Americans piecemeal into the trenches where they would fight under British and French command.

Chief among his foes was the scowling French Premier Clemenceau, not without reason called "the Tiger." Clemenceau tried to claw Pershing from the rear, ordering the French ambassador in Washington to tell the American War Department that Marshal Pétain, Pershing's French alter ego, found it impossible to work with the American commander. Pershing, the moment he heard about it, sat down and wrote the French prime minister a sharp letter suggesting, "the inexpediency of communicating such matters to Washington by cable."

When Major General Tasker Bliss, serving on the Allied War Council, allowed British General Sir William Robertson to convince him that 150 battalions of American troops should go immediately into British brigades, Pershing bluntly rejected the scheme. When Bliss suggested that the only solution was to cable Washington to ask for a decision, Pershing replied: "Do you know what would happen if we should do this? We should both be relieved from further duty in France and that is exactly what we should deserve." Finally Bliss conceded, "I shall back you up in the position you have taken."

In admiration of Pershing's stand, Charles Dawes wrote in his diary, "The President of France, the British authorities, Lloyd George, General Bliss, all arrayed against John mean nothing to him except they present reason . . . John Pershing, like Lincoln, recognized no superior on the face of the earth."

For all his intense devotion to "the book" Pershing was capable of taking one of the greatest gambles in history. All through the spring of 1918 he fought off the steadily more violent Allied demands for American units, while the German offensive rolled forward to the Marne, and Paris was in range of the Kaiser's big guns. At Abbeville on May 1,

1918, the Big Three prime ministers, Clemenceau of France, Lloyd George of England and Orlando of Italy, backed by Marshal Foch of France, and Lord Milner of England, confronted Pershing in a climactic clash. Pershing later recalled how "all five of the parties attacked me with all the force and prestige of their high positions." He replied in a bellow that the war could not be saved by feeding untrained American recruits into the Allied armies, and slammed his fist on the table as if he were chewing out a subordinate at his headquarters in Chaumont.

Foch and Lord Milner now took Pershing into another room away from the three prime ministers. "Are you willing to risk our being driven back to the Loire?" Foch cried.

"Yes," Pershing retorted.

When the prime ministers rejoined the group, Lord Milner told Lloyd George, "It's no use, you can't budge him an inch."

When all five renewed the argument, Pershing rose and snapped: "Gentlemen, I've thought this program over very deliberately and will not be coerced."

He stalked out, and the politicians had to eat their own words. Their press secretaries released the following statement: "It is the opinion of the Supreme War Council that in order to carry the war to a successful conclusion an American army should be formed as early as possible under its own commander and its own flag."

A few days later when the German advance shattered the French front, Pershing yielded slightly and permitted two American divisions, the 2nd and 3rd, to go into action under Marshal Pétain's command, but they fought as fully equipped integral units with their own artillery and communications equipment. The 1st Division's 38th Infantry Regiment captured the fortified village of Cantigny on May 28. Commanded by Ulysses Grant Alexander, class of 1887, the 38th proceeded to obey Pershing's orders to hold at all costs, beating off German counterattacks from three sides to win its historic nickname, "Rock of the Marne."

In July the American 1st and 2nd Divisions, still technically under French command, attacked once more at Soissons, and elsewhere along the Marne the 26th, 43rd, 32nd, 42nd and 28th Divisions pushed forward, smashing the German war machine into reverse and proving what Pershing had said all along—that the American doctrine of "fire and movement" was the answer to the stalemate on the Western front. For the first time in four years Germany had lost the initiative and German

Chancellor Von Hertling later wrote: "Even the most optimistic among us understood that all was lost. The history of the world was played out in those three days."

Now Pershing demanded and got his own sector of the front and, marshaling his American divisions, launched the hammer blow of St.-Mihiel. On the very eve of the offensive, Marshal Foch appeared at Pershing's headquarters with the old demand to divide the American Army for service under French commanders in other sectors. Pershing told him, "Marshal Foch, you have no authority as Allied Commander in Chief to call upon me to yield up my command of the American Army."

"I must insist upon the arrangement," Foch cried.

"Marshal Foch, you may insist all you please," Pershing said, sticking out his iron jaw, "but I decline absolutely to consider your plan. While our army will fight wherever you decide, it will not fight except as an independent American army."

St.-Mihiel and the climactic Battle of the Argonne that followed it justified once and for all Pershing's stand. He won his gamble, and the war, not with new tactics (he himself said later, "the principles of warfare as I have learned them at West Point remain unchanged"), but with a personal quality that Prime Minister Clemenceau called "invincible obstinacy" and more friendly Americans called character.

"If he was not a great man," wrote Frank H. Simons, "there have been few stronger." Secretary of War Newton Baker was obviously thinking of Pershing when he said in 1919, "West Point again demonstrated its supreme value to the country in the hour of need. In all walks of life character is the indispensable basis of enduring success. West Point does many things for its men but the highest quality it gives them is character and in the emergency of the World War our success rested on the character of our leaders." More than any soldier of his era, John J. Pershing added form and substance to the words Duty, Honor, Country.

VII

WHEN WORLD WAR I broke out there were 4900 officers of the Regular Army who had had at least one year of commissioned service. About half of them were graduates of West Point. Upon these 4900 fell the task of raising, equipping, organizing, training and commanding the 4-million-man army needed to guarantee victory on the Western front. Some 193,642 emergency officers were commissioned to lead this immense host. West Point graduates dwindled to a mere 1.5 percent of the total. But 74 percent of the 480 generals were West Pointers, and Academy graduates and their fellow regulars were the vital leaven distributed throughout the Army establishment, supplying cohesion and direction. Unfortunately, there were not enough of them, and in their frantic search for more and better officer material, the planners in Washington came close to destroying West Point.

They began by calling out of retirement aged Colonel Samuel E. Tillman, chemistry professor for 31 years, to replace battlefield-bound Colonel John Biddle as Superintendent. The class of 1917, eager to get into the fight, requested and was permitted to graduate in April, two weeks after the declaration of war. As the need for officers escalated, the class of 1918 was graduated in August, 1917, and on June 12, 1918, the class of 1919 marched off to France. No one foresaw the imminent German collapse, and when the Battle of the Argonne began chewing up American divisions, the War Department, in a moment of hysteria, decided to graduate immediately the classes of 1920 and 1921.

Colonel Earl Blaik, future creator of Army's greatest football teams, was a plebe in that momentous October when Cadet Adjutant Beverly St. George Tucker read the order in the mess hall, graduating the second and third classes within a month, on November first. While the mess hall erupted with wild cheers, Adjutant Tucker added another clause—a new plebe class was entering in November, no less than 800 strong. They would be consolidated with the plebes on hand and all of them graduated in June, 1919. General Tillman, who had studied under Mahan and Michie as a cadet and taught with them as a professor, could only look on aghast as the planners in Washington dismantled his beloved Academy before his eyes and turned it into another emergency officers' training camp.

Moreover, the chaos was just beginning. Only 357 of the 800 new plebes showed up, but they were admitted without entrance examinations. Worse, war priorities had consumed the cloth needed for their uniforms and they were issued olive drab A.E.F. gear with leggings and campaign hats circled with orange bands. Called 4th Class A by Superintendent Tillman, they were promptly dubbed Orioles by the cadets. Eight days after the Orioles began enduring a Beast Barracks run by the tactical officers, the Armistice was declared.

Pondering the fact that the class of 1921 had had only seventeen months of West Point training, the War Department reassembled them and marched them back to the Academy on December third. Since they were already commissioned, they were known as the S.O. (Student Officer) class. They arrived wearing regulation second lieutenant uniforms which required salutes from cadets and post enlisted men. They lived separately from the rest of the corps in the south barracks and were treated as cadets by the administration—a status they resented mightily.

Meanwhile, outside West Point's boundaries, the country was going through an emotional hangover. The abrupt ending of the war and the cynical power plays of the victors at the peace table were producing violent reactions against things military. Even before the war was over, some newspapers were muttering against Pershing's attempt to impose West Point standards of discipline on the A.E.F. The *Florida Times Union* of Jacksonville called for the abolition of West Point, declaring, "The road to a commission in the Army or Navy should be through the recruiting offices." A retired major wrote *The New York Times,* declaring every West Pointer should profit from a year in the ranks before he entered the Academy. Soon pacifists were shouting denunciations of West Point's "warmongers and martinets," and with the Academy's traditional four-year course completely disrupted, Congress was in a mood to revamp drastically the whole West Point system. All these critics needed was an excuse to go into action, and they got it from the disorganized semi-disciplined cadet corps, who produced in the winter of 1918–19 still another hazing scandal.

Colonel Earl Blaik recalls the incident in vivid detail. "About nine o'clock on the morning of New Year's Day I was coming down the stairs by the 27th Division of North Barracks when Cadet Harvey Greenlaw, a classmate, called to me from the door of a nearby room. 'Come in here quick! Mr. Bird has passed out.'

"I followed Greenlaw into the room. Cadet Stephen M. Bird was stretched out on the floor, semi-conscious and moaning, 'Water . . . Water . . .' Blood trickled from a corner of his mouth. Two cadets were applying cold towels to his face from the two buckets of water flanking the washstand. On the study table lay a regular 30.06 caliber Springfield rifle."

An Oriole, Bird was a moody, rather artistic young man who wrote poetry in his spare time. An upperclassman, discovering it, had singled him out for special hazing. Bird had tied a string to the trigger of his rifle, placed the muzzle against his chest and fired it. The bullet pierced a lung and Bird died at 6:12 that night.

Congress was, with justification, incensed. In the War Department, Chief of Staff Peyton March, no lover of the old Army (he had feuded furiously with Pershing throughout the war), passed up major generals by the dozen to pluck, from the middle range of the Army's seniority list, Brigadier General Douglas MacArthur to take charge of a chaotic, wavering West Point. An acerbic, thin-lipped intellectual, March had graduated a year after John J. Pershing, but he had imbibed no overwhelming adoration for West Point's traditional ways. "West Point is forty years behind the times," he told MacArthur. Was he ready to undertake a complete overhaul there, aimed at creating a truly modern Academy? March wanted the curriculum revised, the military instruction modernized, and above all an absolute end to physical hazing. MacArthur said he was in complete agreement, and he thus became one of West Point's youngest Superintendents since Sylvanus Thayer.

MacArthur was barely ensconced when, from a highly unexpected source, came one of those teeth-rattling public attacks that have periodically shaken West Point. Dr. Charles W. Eliot, president emeritus of Harvard, in an address to the Harvard Teachers' Association declared: "West Point is an example of just what an educational institution should not be . . . This was shown by the inefficiency and failure of its graduates in the World War." Taking umbrage at these remarks, Major General John W. Ruckman, commander of the North Atlantic Coast Artillery, challenged Dr. Eliot and got for his trouble an even more scorching blast. "In my opinion, no American school or college intended for youth of between 18 and 22 years of age should accept such ill-prepared material as West Point accepts. Secondly, no school or college should have a completely prescribed curriculum. Thirdly, no school or college should have its teaching done almost exclusively by recent graduates of the same school or college who are not teachers and who serve short terms. West Point, so far as its teachers are concerned, breeds in and in, a very bad practice for any educational institution."

This statement brought a full-page reply in Sunday's *New York Times* from Colonel James Gordon Steese, top man in the class of 1907, an engineer on the staff of the War Department. Steese did a good job of refuting Eliot's generalizations about West Point, citing the number of West Pointers who had made their mark in civil life, including seventeen mayors of cities, eight bank presidents, seven presidents of railroads and no less than forty-six presidents of universities and colleges. But he revealed almost too nakedly the prevailing opinion of his era when at the close of his polemic he declared: "We admit that West Point is hard and we admit that it is narrow. We consider that it is well that at least one institution should continue in the United States which holds that the duties of its students are more important than their rights."

Colonel Steese must have been among the more astonished members of the War Department when less than six months later he found newspapers quoting MacArthur's declaration that old rigid Army methods had been swept into history's discard heap by the experience of World War I, necessitating the production of an entirely new type of officer "understanding the mechanics of human feelings."

"When whole nations spring to arms," MacArthur said, "improvisation will be the watchword"; and this required "a liberalization of conception" on the part of the Army officer that "amounts to a change in his psychology of command." The training system at West Point, MacArthur announced, was being rebuilt on this basis and in a burst of premature optimism he added, "The results have transcended my most sanguine expectations; it will be felt throughout the army at large with the graduation of the classes now under instruction." He was achieving this goal, MacArthur said, by a "substitution of subjective for objective discipline, a progressive increase of cadet responsibility tending to develop initiative and force of character rather than automatic performance of stereotype functions."

There was no love lost between MacArthur and graduates who had come up the Army promotion ladder more slowly, and with less flamboyance. Colonel William Addleman Ganoe tells of the reaction to Mac-Arthur's appointment at the West Point Officers' Club. "Fantastic," said one man. "Looks like another effort to wreck the Academy. Who in hell has it in for the place?" MacArthur returned the dislike by deliberately breaking traditions the old grads considered sacred. Post Adjutant Ganoe was astonished when the new Superintendent arrived wearing well-worn infantry puttees bound with straps curled with age, a battered cap and the riding crop which were his trademark in no-man's-land during World War I. "He was just neat enough to pass inspection," Ganoe says. His astonishment trebled when MacArthur brushed aside the standard incoming Superintendent's review of the corps.

"They'll see me soon and often enough," MacArthur told him.

Three months later, after watching the corps in action throughout the usual summer encampment, MacArthur asked Ganoe, "How long are we going on preparing for the War of 1812? Of what possible benefit is cadet summer camp?"

For the first time Ganoe was forced to admit to himself and the new Superintendent that summer camp was a little ridiculous. "The Gilbert and Sullivan sentry with white belts primly walking a prescribed beat and shouting an 'All's well' in the middle of the night; and formal drills in the morning . . . and in the evening reading under electric lights or attending a formal hop in Napoleonic clothing in Cullum Hall; marching to the fife and drum of the Revolution to a palace of a mess hall . . . there rolled over me the ludicrous untimeliness of it all."

The following year, Superintendent MacArthur sent the first and third classes to Camp Dix where they trained with Regular Army troops using modern weapons and tactics developed from World War I experience. But even before he announced this drastic termination of one of the Academy's most hallowed traditions, MacArthur, in obedience to his orders from Chief of Staff March, launched an all-out assault on hazing. Fortunately he had the full support of Adjutant Ganoe and Comman-dant Robert M. Danford.

Danford told how shortly after his graduation he had found himself in command of sixty raw recruits. After watching him in action for a day, his commanding officer called him into his quarters and told him, "Mr. Danford, we do not handle the American soldier the way a yearling handles a plebe at West Point."

Ganoe had had similar experiences. MacArthur added a grim postscript. "There were officers overseas shot in the back by their own men simply because they had been brought up with the mistaken idea that bullying was leadership."

MacArthur first tried to implement his hazing reforms through the tactical officers. He outlined a plan whereby the humiliations of plebedom would be reduced to a minimum. The plebe would still be required to brace, to say sir to upperclassmen and to go through a year without being "recognized" as a social equal, but all other forms of hazing were to be abolished. The tactical officers responded enthusiastically. But when they tried to pass on these orders to the corps, they ran into a wall of stubborn opposition. "Too many felt they were being minimized, not trusted and deprived of using the old harsher ways," Ganoe says. Behind the resisting cadets were legions of old grads who saw the plebe systems as the fountainhead of West Point's greatness. They wrote letters to the recalcitrant cadets, visited them on the post, urging them to maximum resistance. "Graduates came and pounded on my desk," Ganoe says. "My office got letters denouncing the supe as the wrecker of West Point . . . the DOG's [Disgruntled Old Grads] were as set as iron hitching posts."

In desperation, MacArthur decided to make a direct appeal to the cadet corps. With Commandant Danford's help he selected seven cadets to serve as a fourth class customs committee with Cadet Earl Blaik as the chairman. "After two months of conscientious work," Blaik says, "we came up with a pamphlet outlining the new order. We reaffirmed that an upperclassman must not lay hands on a plebe and thenceforth this rule was enforced much more rigidly. An upperclassman must not order a plebe to perform menial tasks. We outlawed such sadism as splits over a bayonet."

Also eliminated was the practice of denying a plebe food for any reason. The committee also reaffirmed the illegality of prearranged fist-fights. But Blaik admits in his memoirs, "It was yet a few years before this order was fully obeyed." Other cadets, scrutinizing the new rules with the fanaticism of guardhouse lawyers, noted that the code did not strike out "qualifying," whereby a plebe could eat unbraced for the rest of the year if he downed an enormous amount of one rather obnoxious food, such as prunes. This custom, too, continued. But Blaik's committee by and large wholeheartedly supported MacArthur's hazing reforms.

An even mightier uproar rose from the DOG's when MacArthur eliminated Beast Barracks, the introduction to West Point which had caused more than one young man to resign on the spot.

MacArthur's conferences with the customs committee suggested still another change in West Point's ways. Too many cadets were totally naïve about the ways of the world beyond West Point. It was time to end the Academy's monastic isolation. Cadets were forthwith ordered to read two newspapers daily and discuss the day's news in the first ten minutes of class. Upperclassmen were granted six-hour leaves on weekends, and during the summer months this was extended to two days, which permitted them to go as far as New York City if they chose. Each cadet was given $5 a month in cash for spending money. Even more revolutionary was the announcement that hereafter first classmen would be treated as junior officers on the post, free to make social calls, visit officers and their families in their homes.

Still another change was produced by Commandant Danford. He came to MacArthur and suggested abolishing the "skin list"—the record of cadet delinquencies. "Every morning I find on my desk a six-inch pack of cadet explanations for delinquencies," Danford told MacArthur. "Written explanations might have been all right back in our day when we were told it was important for us to learn how to write an official letter, when Spencerian penmanship and Victorian form meant more than matter. But now, when an officer has his company clerk perform on the typewriter, explanations take time from more important things."

Danford asked permission to establish a company orderly room on the ground floor of each company's barracks where once a day a tactical officer would handle delinquencies face to face as a company commander did in the Regular Army.

"Do it," MacArthur said.

With MacArthur's approval, Danford also altered the longtime habit of allowing the tactical officers to recommend cadet corps officers. Danford instead devised a rating system based on class standing, military bearing, appearance, leadership, athletics, extracurricular activities and the demerit record. He permitted the cadets to rate each other on military bearing and leadership, a departure that caused more than one DOG to gasp in disbelief.

MacArthur was fortunate in having someone as wholeheartedly behind his disciplinary changes as Danford. But his plans for reform also included the subject matter of West Point's courses, and here he ran into another wall. The academic board sided almost completely with the

DOG's and declined to budge more than a few grudging inches. Although Colonel Ganoe writes glowingly of MacArthur's powers of persuasion in dealing with the tactical officers and the cadets, his charm got him nowhere when he presided over meetings of the academic board.

The conferences in the dim boardroom, with its filigreed mantelpiece carved with figures of great warriors and ponderous medieval table and leather chairs, were frequently acrimonious. At one point when a professor began heckling him, MacArthur brought his fist down on the table and roared: "Sit down, sit. I am the Superintendent. Even if I weren't I should be treated in a gentlemanly manner." Over violent objections, MacArthur decreed that henceforth officers recalled to West Point to serve as instructors would spend the first year of their tour taking refresher courses in their subjects at civilian universities. Each professor was ordered to visit at least three colleges or universities a year.

But the board had the final say on the curriculum. MacArthur and his commandant had only one vote apiece—so reforms in subject matter were minor: the introduction of a slide rule in natural philosophy; the study of the internal combustion engine in chemistry; granting Professor Holt's long frustrated wish to divide his English and history chore into two departments, with him as chairman of the latter; abandoning the study of the Civil War for the history and tactics of World War I. A course in economics was also added, but thereafter progress came to a dull halt. Conferences with individual professors, even unprecedented visits to the section rooms, produced little or no progress.

MacArthur's total changes can be seen at a glance in the following compilation, which sums up how much he added and subtracted from the various subjects:

Mathematics	$-169\frac{1}{2}$ hours
French	$+ 38\frac{1}{2}$ hours
English	$+122\frac{1}{4}$ hours
Drawing	-188 hours
History	$+ 46$ hours
Chemistry	$+ 44$ hours
Spanish	$- 82$ hours
Military Art	$- 84\frac{1}{2}$ hours
Economics and Government	$+ 94$ hours
Engineering	$+ 45$ hours

Since these are figures based on the total number of hours for four years, it is obvious that "minimal" is the only word to describe them. Years later MacArthur was forced to admit: "The success obtained did not even approximate to what I had in mind." MacArthur also got nowhere in his attempt to persuade Congress to double the size of the corps and launch a new building program.

But MacArthur was not the sort of man to let defeat on one front slow him down elsewhere. He now proceeded to throw all his energy into creating a wholly new athletic program for the corps. In this he was ably assisted by one of West Point's more distinguished chaplains, Clayton E. "Buck" Wheat, who had been a three-letter man at the University of the South. Though MacArthur rarely attended chapel, he and Wheat became close friends from the moment the Superintendent watched the chaplain working out with the baseball team. MacArthur was so impressed by his performance at first base he asked him to coach the team. Wheat declined, but soon came to the Superintendent with a suggestion that only the chaplain could have made. Why not abandon the strict Sunday observance rule which had been West Point custom for over a hundred years? It bothered Wheat to see cadets looking wistfully out of their barracks windows or listlessly strolling about the post, forbidden to take part in any athletic activity, or play anything that might be construed as a game.

Not only did Wheat suggest letting the cadets practice baseball, football or tennis on Sunday afternoon, he vowed he was prepared to play with them. MacArthur leaped to his feet, enormously excited. "I approve one hundred percent," he told the chaplain. "Go to it."

With Wheat's enthusiastic support, MacArthur escalated Sunday afternoon exercise into a vigorous intramural athletic program. The cadets had a fairly comprehensive gymnastic program under Master of the Sword Herman Koehler. But MacArthur knew that like most Americans they detested this kind of exercise, and he built his program around competitive sports. Each company was required to field a team in football, baseball, soccer, lacrosse, tennis, basketball, track and field, golf, and polo. And every cadet was required to participate in at least one sport. To make sure nobody had any doubts about his intentions, MacArthur ordered West Point's quartermaster to raze the cadet summer campsite and replace it with a running track. On the stone portals of the gymnasium he had inscribed words which many West Point visitors assume is a quote from some famous educator of another era. Actually, MacArthur, unabashedly espousing the role of an American Wellington, wrote them himself.

> Upon the fields of friendly strife
> Are sown the seeds
> That upon other fields and other days
> Will bear the fruits of victory.

MacArthur's passion for athletics was genuine. He was vastly chagrined when Congress turned down his blueprint for a 50,000-seat stadium by the riverside with elaborate railroad yards to accommodate special trains. "They will never learn to build for the future," he told Ganoe. He hoped that his intramural program would produce better athletes for the Academy's varsity teams, but was mortified to see the Army football team drop three in a row to Navy. Even more agonizing was the baseball team's eleven-to-one loss at Annapolis in 1920. Army made eleven errors, five by the shortstop alone. At varsity practice sessions in baseball, basketball, and football MacArthur was almost always an eager spectator. Once he undertook to show young Earl Blaik, already a football and basketball stalwart, how to hit a curve ball. "Unloosening his blouse, high collar, and Sam Browne belt," Blaik says, "he selected a bat and instructed me on how to cope with that bedeviling number two delivery. When the general had concluded his brief seminar, I couldn't even hit a fast ball. This was the one failure in MacArthur's career."

Among MacArthur's favorite pastimes was talking football in his office with Lieutenant Ollie Oliphant, West Point's great halfback from 1914 through 1917. "If Ollie had a chance to pick up $200 playing a Sunday football game with the Buffalo All-Americans," Blaik says, "MacArthur would give him special weekend leave." When Blaik came down with influenza after playing in a rain-soaked battle with the Tufts football team, MacArthur did his utmost to speed his recovery for the Navy game. "He sent his car and chauffeur to take me for health-restoring rides out to Central Valley and around the Hudson Highlands. The post surgeon ordered me to report three times a day for a glass of sherry." Although Blaik was "weak as a tabby cat" the Monday before the game he showed up at the Polo Grounds with the team and played

58 minutes in a drizzling rain, only to lose a heartbreaker, 6–0 on two Navy field goals.

It is hard to square Blaik's picture of MacArthur with the claim made by another West Pointer that the Superintendent was a remote, largely invisible figure, seen by the corps only from afar. Colonel Ganoe tells of the night in 1921 that the corps celebrated a baseball victory over Navy. The cadets turned out en masse at midnight and paraded past the Superintendent's quarters and around the post, to Fort Clinton, where they built a huge bonfire. A tactical officer, Major C. H. Bonesteel, was so carried away by the excitement he joined the cheering mob and delivered a rousing speech. The next morning, MacArthur gave Commandant Danford an owlish look. "Well, Com, that was quite a party you put on last night."

"Yes it was, sir. Quite a party."

"How many of them did you skin?"

"Not a damn one."

"Good," said MacArthur, banging his desk. "You know, Com, I could hardly resist the impulse to get out and join them."

This was not the only time the corps got out of hand during Mac-Arthur's regime. By far the biggest uproar was on Thanksgiving Day, 1920, during the Runt-Flanker game. This rather mad West Point tradition had emerged sometime between 1900 and 1917. The Flankers were the men of the four tallest companies, A, B, L, and M. The rest of the corps was classified as Runts. A tradition had grown up that if the Runts won on Thanksgiving Day, Army was sure to defeat Navy the following Saturday. The game was therefore rigged to guarantee a Runt victory.

Play began in the usual way, with eleven men to a side, but the Runts had the privilege of unlimited substitution without the need to remove the man whom the substitute was supposedly replacing. After a few plays the field was always swarming with Runts, and although the Flankers often made an initial touchdown or two, they were invariably overwhelmed by the Runts' sheer numbers. Each side had a banner, usually an old bed sheet adorned with designs painted in shoe blacking and red metal polish called "pomade." The banner was jealously guarded, and it was considered a great coup if a patrol from the opposing side sneaked over and wrested it from its owners. Fistfights were common in the course of these forays.

During the World War I chaos, football had been discontinued. In

1919 the Runt-Flanker Game was revived for the first time in three years. Except for an occasional fistfight over the banners there were no unusual incidents. The Runts won as usual and the rival cohorts marched off the field to the strains of improvised bands. Unfortunately, Army lost to Navy the next Saturday.

Thanksgiving Day of 1920 was another matter. As William Jackson Morton of the class of 1923 puts it, "The new plebe class ('24) were given to excess in all things. We called them the militia and they called themselves the Thundering Herd which they certainly were. They decided to drastically alter the traditional Runt-Flanker rivalry."

The game was played on the regular football field in front of Cullum Hall, where the baseball diamond is now laid out. Along both sides of the field were long windrows of straw which had been used to cover the field the night before as a precaution against snow. The moment the Runts made their first touchdown their backers swarmed down on the field and rushed the Flankers' stands. Their objective was not as in the past the Flanker banner, but the Flankers themselves.

"The outnumbered and beleaguered Flankers," says Colonel Morton, "put up a gallant fight but were overwhelmed. All over the field one could see isolated Flankers, each battling like some desperate insect being dismembered by a swarm of ants. Flanker after Flanker had his clothes ripped off him and stood in stark nudity. Then he would spy a windrow of straw and make a dash for it. Before long there were heads of naked Flankers sticking up out of the straw everywhere, beseeching friends and roommates to fetch them clothes. Some of the braver souls who were suffering from the cold rose up and dashed for the barracks, counting on speed to conceal their persons."

Reuniformed in their barracks, the Flankers launched a counterattack, and the morning turned into "a saturnalia." A Runt division would raid a Flanker division and the Flankers would retaliate. The main weapons for repelling the invaders were the cadet water buckets. "Soon all of the halls were awash," says Colonel Morton.

A kind of climax was reached when Major Parker Kalloch, the tactical officer in command of D Company, charged out of his orderly room wearing a resplendent new Brooks Brothers uniform. As he hit the stoop of the 15th Division, two cadets let fly with buckets of steaming hot water, thinking they were scoring on some foes who had just retreated inside the door. Major Kalloch stood there, steaming in more ways than one, his uniform a bedraggled mess, while the culprits ran for their lives.

A few days later Commandant Danford announced that the Runt-Flanker game was herewith and henceforth discontinued. It was too expensive, Colonel Danford said. The cadet store had received requisitions for $7,000 worth of new uniforms to replace those ruined in the riot.

Rather than leave a vacuum, Colonel Danford founded a new and better football tradition—a game between the "Goats," those at the bottom of the class, and the "Engineers"—those at the top. "This was a clever idea because the Goats and Engineers were indiscriminately distributed throughout all companies and divisions of barracks," Colonel Morton says. "There were no longer fixed organizational groups that could be pitted against each other." It also gave the Goats a chance to belabor their hivey superiors once a year, thereby relieving some of the inevitable tensions between them and the intellectual aristocrats.

The class of 1922 also gave Superintendent MacArthur some restless nights. Three of them got hold of a drum of black powder used for the reveille gun and about twenty feet of slow-acting fuse from the engineer warehouse. Thus equipped, they conducted a one-month reign of terror. A handful of powder wrapped in paper and stoutly wound with friction tape made a tremendous bang. Anyone who was fond of catnaps was a prime target. "The demand for lower bunks in the 15th Division took a sudden drop," says H. A. Linn. Other explosions in the central area had tactical officers racing wildly from the "poop decks" to the back windows. Eventually the powder was used up and the devilment boys turned to a new and more ambitious project.

One freezing night in mid-winter, they organized a bucket brigade, and a few minutes of diligent effort produced a small flood in the central area. "Reveille next morning was a thrilling sight," recalls one eyewitness. "You should have seen the first class bucks rushing for the ranks. They passed right through the company, sliding in every conceivable position, gesticulating wildly and then crawling back on all fours. The officer in charge hadn't been warned so he had a lively time too."

More serious was the return of that familiar, often interred ghost, hazing, during the summer tour of duty at Fort Dix in 1921. This time the evil spirit showed up combined with an even more flagrant form of insubordination—the rump court-martial, which had caused the Academy so much grief back in the 1870's. The double whammy began when a plebe who was rather unpopular with his own classmates, had been "braced" and "crawled" by a third classman. (Crawling, still very much in vogue at the Academy today, involves placing an upper classman's jaw about one inch from a plebe's nose and furiously bawling a barrage of questions, orders and insults aimed at reducing the victim to a state of total incoherence.) In this case, the plebe tattled to the commandant, claiming he had been so unnerved by his ordeal that he was failing in his academic courses.

Commandant Danford slugged the upperclassman with a barrel of demerits. Although the plebe flunked several courses, he was permitted to remain at the Academy. This embittered a number of upperclassmen and during the summer of 1921 the first class summoned the rump court in an unused company barracks at Fort Dix. The offending cadet was found guilty of conduct unbecoming a West Pointer and quietly hustled to the nearest railroad station, given money enough to get himself home and warned never again to show his face on the Plain. MacArthur called in Commandant Danford and told him: "Get back to Dix as soon as you can and bust Olmsted."

George Olmsted was the cadet first captain, a superior student, who stood number two in his class. He had nothing whatsoever to do with the impromptu exile. "Sir," one cadet officer told Commandant Danford, "I don't believe the corps will take this order." Danford explained it in terms of World War I experience. When a division failed in combat, its commander was relieved even if he was not directly responsible for the poor performance. Grudgingly, the corps accepted Olmsted's demotion. Olmsted personally never uttered a word of complaint. In the spring of 1921, a few months before his graduation, Danford came to MacArthur and said, "This cadet has been so outstanding, exemplary and loyal and so soldierly and subordinate in his conduct ever since he was reduced to the grade of cadet private, I recommend he be appointed an extra cadet captain so he may graduate with captain's chevrons."

"Do it," MacArthur said, blithely breaking another tradition.

The contretemps at Fort Dix inspired MacArthur to do some thinking about the cadet honor code. Since Thayer's day it had been a basic Academy principle that "a cadet does not lie, cheat or steal." But applying this simple statement to the complexities of everyday life created numerous problems. MacArthur decided it was time to for-

malize the honor code and give it official sanction as a part of West
Point's basic mission. The code belonged to the corps, but it was foolish
to allow the corps to administer it in midnight sessions followed by
surreptitious exiles. MacArthur therefore called together a group of first
classmen and told them to create a committee that would set up ways
and means to build the honor code into the school's system.

A Cadet Honor Committee selected by the corps was made responsible for interpreting the honor system to incoming plebes and sitting as a
jury on violations of the code, under the supervision of the Commandant. The new code made it clear that every man was honor-bound to
report any cadet, even his best friend, whom he knew had violated the
code. At the same time, it specified that the code could not be used
against the corps. For example, if a tactical officer saw a man returning
to his room after taps but could not in the darkness make out who it
was, he had no right to ask every man on that particular floor if he was
out after taps. The Honor Committee made it clear that honor and
regulations were separate and distinct.

This is what the civilian finds especially hard to understand about the
West Point honor system. A man may break the school's regulations by
sneaking off the post for a clandestine dinner or a date and, if he can,
return unscathed; there is not the slightest reflection cast on his honor.
But if the AWOL cadet lied by stating on his absence card that he was
going to the library, he would have violated the code and his roommate
or anyone else who knew about it would be duty-bound to report him.
But neither his roommate nor anyone else is "honor-bound" to report
him for breaking the regulation against going off the post without au-
thorization. Cadet officers or tactical officers, if they catch him, are
under the regulations supposed to report him, but even here there is no
question of honor involved in the decision.

The formalization of the honor code marked another important stage
in the evolution of Thayer's Academy, and it was further proof of
MacArthur's genius as a military educator. From his experience in
World War I, he realized that "in the emergencies of war, success or
failure with all their effects upon the future of a country, may depend
upon an officer's word and upon his undeviating adherence to a principle
or an ideal."

VIII

IN WASHINGTON, D.C., a new President was inaugurated in the spring of 1920, and with him came a new Secretary of War, John W. Weeks. He unceremoniously removed Peyton March before March had finished the customary four-year tour of duty as chief of staff. Into this position of power came John J. Pershing, no friend of Douglas MacArthur or of West Point tradition breaking. Nine months later, Pershing's office issued a terse communiqué.

Brigadier General Fred W. Sladen, commanding Fort Sheridan, Illinois, was today appointed Superintendent of West Point to relieve Brigadier General MacArthur on June 30th. General MacArthur is assigned to the Philippines.

Sladen, a graduate of the class of 1890, was wholeheartedly devoted to his own era. He instantly revoked many MacArthur privileges such as weekend leaves and cadet spending money. Summer camp was restored in all its Napoleonic splendor. The reading of daily newspapers was abandoned and Beast Barracks once more became the province of fog-horned-voiced upperclassmen and shuddering plebes.

But MacArthur's impact on West Point had been too pervasive for any single Superintendent to change. Although Sladen could easily tighten discipline, he could hardly find fault with such programs as the intramural athletic system or the Honor Committee. In fact, Sladen showed that he, like everyone else, was sensitive to the criticism about monastic tendencies by allowing the cadets to launch a magazine, a typical undergraduate publication called *The Pointer*. In the foreword to its first edition, the new Superintendent wrote (in a style that would make a MacArthur wince), "and in that our new publication may well become a factor in guiding our students in the acquiring of experience, it will be one more help in obliterating the charge that our education is too remote from life." In the same first edition, Chief of Staff Pershing too sounded very much as if he were thinking about MacArthur when he wrote: "Heretofore requirements of service have forced the army officer to spend a large portion of his career out of touch with the everyday life of the American citizen. Today, however, the officer finds his principle mission to be the instruction and guidance of those patriotic fellow citizens who volunteer their services for the national defense."

In 1925, MacArthur's insistence on fresh contacts with civilian schools paid off. The Association of American Universities listed the Academy as an approved technological institution, and in 1927 a new Superintendent, Major General Merch B. Stewart, enrolled West Point in the Association of American Colleges. When he took office, Stewart reportedly said: "Everything MacArthur changed is coming back in full force. His principles and practices will be carried on and improved as time goes on."

Actually, Stewart and succeeding Superintendents tended to aim at a compromise between MacArthur and the DOG's of the Sladen wing. They did not abolish summer camp. This Napoleonic anachronism flourished throughout the thirties, while Adolf Hitler and his generals cranked up their Panzer divisions. Discipline remained extremely severe. Listening to the author describe some of the antics of earlier West Pointers, an officer who graduated in the early thirties gasped: "We wouldn't have dared even think of stunts like that."

There were some modest improvements on the liberal arts side of the cadets' education. Beginning in 1931, a cadet lecture committee invited well-known speakers to West Point. Colonel Herman Beukema, successor (in 1930) to Professor Holt as the head of the Department of Economics, Government and History, was a first-class intellect, who labored hard to expand cadet horizons. He added courses in international politics, and in 1940 another course, "The Economics of War." But Beukema and his supporters could only work around the edges of the basic engineering course. Nor was the tactical department much more progressive. The cadets still devoted hours to riding, in preparation for possible careers in the cavalry, and even more hours to intricate close-order drill.

There was no great warmth in the country's attitude toward West Point during these years. The anti-war spirit was still strong, and when the bread lines of the great depression queued up across America, a new generation of social critics, steeped in the pacifist traditions of European socialism, launched another round of attacks on West Point.

In *The New Republic,* Margery Bedinger summed up her opinion in the title of her article, "The Goose-step at West Point." "The instructors at West Point are army officers who know nothing of teaching and have no interest in it," she declared. "At the end of a four-year detail at the Military Academy, all instructors except the heads of certain departments go back to their military duties. Consequently, West Point instructors, except in rare instances, have no more profound knowledge of the subjects they are supposed to teach than they acquired while they were cadets at the Military Academy."

As a result, Miss Bedinger contended, "The cadet is totally ignorant of modern trends in thought, undeveloped emotionally, motivated by set prejudices and burdened with a naïve belief in his own importance." He was, in short, "a man cherishing an attitude toward life that belongs to the dark ages."

Douglas MacArthur as Army Chief of Staff led a desperate rear-guard battle against a hostile Congress that was determined to slash the officer corps and national defense spending to near-suicidal levels. *The World Tomorrow,* a powerful church weekly, asked 53,000 Protestant clergymen, "Do you believe the churches of America should now go on record as refusing to sanction or support any future war?" Sixty-two percent of those who replied said yes. Police carted away anti-war demonstrators when General MacArthur addressed the graduating class at the University of Pittsburgh on June 9, 1932.

Congress, peering across the seas at the Hitler war machine, did not, for once, join in the assault. Instead they voted in 1935 to expand the corps from 1374 to 1960. This inspired another spurt of building, which saw a new North Barracks, laboratory and academic buildings, and the huge Armory-Fieldhouse go up in the same gray Gothic style of the 1906 expansion.

Meanwhile, the Academy tried to answer the newest crop of critics. In 1939, the War Department worked out with the aid of the academic board a statement that claimed to describe and clarify West Point's role in modern America.

The mission of the United States Military Academy is to produce officers of the army having the qualities and attributes essential to their progressive and continuing development throughout their careers as officers and leaders.

The statement went on to spell out in considerable detail what this meant. It declared that the school's goal was "a balanced and liberal education in the arts and sciences" with a "basic military education embracing military history, theory and application of military art, essentials of leadership . . . and the principles of organization, maintenance, training and utilization of military forces in peace and war." Though it took 20 years to accomplish that goal, the push given by Generals March and MacArthur in 1920 had in theory at least brought the Academy up-to-date. But irony seems to be a permanent theme in West Point's history. No sooner had the new West Point's role and mission been clarified when Hitler, Mussolini, and Tojo plunged the nation into the greatest war in history.

West Point's Superintendent, Brigadier General Robert L. Eichelberger, asked for and won a combat assignment on MacArthur's staff in the Southwest Pacific. He left behind him a West Point that was far better prepared to cope with the challenge of total war than the Academy of 1917–18. Almost from the moment he took over as Superintendent, on November 18, 1940, Eichelberger had launched a series of studies for the revision of the curriculum. Horseback riding was almost completely abandoned and additional hours were added to physical training and professional military instruction during the winter months. Eichelberger persuaded Congress to buy available land around the reservation and brought a detachment of Regular Army enlisted men onto the post to assist in infantry training. Probably most important, he enlarged nearby Steward Field from 221.8 acres to 1674.2 acres and made it (on October 20, 1941) an integral part of West Point. Thus, thanks to his foresight, the Academy was ready to launch on July 1, 1942, a revolutionary new course which blended pilot training and traditional West Point curriculum to produce the nation's first "Air Cadets."

Just as this momentous program was getting under way, West Point found itself involved in another fight for survival. Faced as in World War I with the prodigious demand for officers to command an army that was already on its way to 8,000,000 men, War Department planners once more cast covetous eyes on the cadet corps. But this time West Point was prepared to meet the challenge. The new Superintendent, Major General Francis B. Wilby, within a month after he took over on January 13, 1942, had made a rush trip to Washington in search of a Commandant with special skills in training troops. He found one in Colonel Philip E. Gallagher and brought him to West Point with orders to put the corps on a wartime footing. Gallagher went to work immediately, starting with plebe training, which he revamped to include a modified version of the basic infantryman's program. It was called a "fit to fight" course. Armed with rifle and bayonet and wearing the stripped pack and steel helmet of an infantry soldier, the plebes were ordered to move to some distant point on the reservation and solve a tactical problem there—for instance, assaulting a building supposedly occupied by a well-armed enemy. The cadet commander's performance was rated on the speed with which he carried out the mission and the physical condition of his men at the completion of it. Thus the cadets very quickly grasped the importance of achieving a good compromise between speed and available energy in executing battle orders. The hours devoted to these winter exercises, General Gallagher says, were stolen from study time "over dead bodies of academic professors."

Meanwhile, for summer training Gallagher rushed to completion a tactical training area around nearby Lake Popolopen. Starting from zero he built concrete pillboxes, a mock freight train, two moving target ranges, a field firing range for rifles and machine guns, a pontoon and amphibious training area, and a highly realistic town through which platoons of cadets fought hundreds of times in a course called "Combat in Cities." Even more rugged was the 200-yard-long assault course down which a cadet had to charge in no more than four minutes carrying his nine-pound rifle, two hand grenades and his nine-pound combat pack. Crawling down tunnels, bayoneting dummies, grenading his way through an enemy trench, creeping under barbed wire, over shell holes and past booby traps, he was as close to battle realism as human ingenuity could devise it. On top of this intensive training at West Point, the corps was shipped to a regular army training center at Pine Camp, New York, where they were "integrated and maneuvered for about two weeks with the 4th Armored Division."

This program meant the end, once more, of the old formal summer camp which Superintendent MacArthur had tried in vain to abolish. Colonel Gallagher proved himself even more determined than MacArthur. Not only did he raze the camp, he filled in the old latrines which were basements of the Revolutionary Fort Clinton "so that no one could ever bring the corps back to the outdated pre-war type of training." He even put an obstacle course on the parade ground in front of the old campsite, which, he says, "made many ambitious mothers and academic professors very unhappy." Gallagher used third classmen as noncommissioned officers for all training work with plebes. He reorganized the corps into a brigade—necessary because Congress had increased its numbers to 2496. He took first classmen on a tour of the service schools at Forts Benning (infantry), Sill (artillery), and Knox (armor), and adopted a "military aptitude" system (developed by Tactical Officer Captain J. E. Landrum) which rated cadets for their leadership potential. For the first time, a cadet who showed no talent for being a soldier could be dismissed from West Point, no matter how high his academic standing.

In mid-summer, 1942, just as this program was getting into high gear, a board of senior officers and civilians appeared at the Academy. Only much later did one member of the board reveal to Gallagher that they were under War Department orders to consider closing the Academy for the duration and turning West Point into an officers' training school. If the Gallagher training program had not already been in full swing, there was a very strong probability that the board would have voted to close down West Point. Another important factor in the final decision was a plan for a condensed, three-year course, which Superintendent Wilby had had the foresight to prepare, with the help of the academic board. Without the training program and this three-year plan, Gallagher says, it is almost certain that "the Academy would have had its mission radically changed."

IX

MEANWHILE, West Pointers around the world were proving once more that no matter how many problems their old school might have had keeping pace with the modern world, at least some of her graduates were always ready to devise new answers to new kinds of warfare.

Dwight Eisenhower, the "Chairman of the Board," presided over the massive Allied effort in Europe with the deftness of the diplomat and the decision of the general. As commander of ground troops, his classmate Omar Nelson Bradley proved West Point could outthink and out-fight the mighty German war machine. The commander of the Strategic Air Force was Carl Spaatz of the class of 1914. Commanding the armored thrusts of the 3rd Army was George Patton of 1909. In Italy, the man in charge was Mark Clark of 1915. In the Southwest Pacific it was MacArthur and Eichelberger leapfrogging from island to island in a two-year, 2400-mile advance that left 135,000 Japanese troops "rotting on the vine" behind them, to fulfill MacArthur's promise to return to the Philippines.

Less well known, but equally vital, was the work of Lieutenant General Joseph Taggart McNarney of 1915, deputy chief of staff to George Marshall, and the man who reorganized the War Department at the opening of the global conflict. Lieutenant General Leslie James McNair of 1904 worked beside him, in command of training American ground troops in the U.S.A. In the vital job of supply, Lieutenant General Brehon B. Somervell, class of 1914, organized the stupendous logistics of supplying American armies around the world. One in four of the 8,200,000 Americans under arms worked for him, plus over a million civilians. Then there was Lieutenant General Leslie Groves, of the class of November, 1918, who in 1942 was placed in command of "the Manhattan Project." Three years later, the United States had an atomic bomb. The citation of his Distinguished Service Medal reads: "His was the responsibility for procuring material and personnel, marshaling the forces of government and industry, erecting huge plants, blending the scientific efforts of the United States and foreign countries and maintaining completely secret the search for a key to release atomic energy."

X

IN THE SAME ARMY were thousands of West Pointers who led Army corps, divisions, regiments, companies, and who demonstrated again and again what skilled leadership and dedication to West Point's ideals could accomplish. Typical among these men is a moon-faced soldier who joined the long gray line only two years after Dwight Eisenhower graduated in 1915. Anthony C. McAuliffe won his fame with one word which summed up for the whole nation American courage in the grimmest hour of the battle for Germany. Trucked into the key road junction of Bastogne during the Battle of the Bulge, McAuliffe and his eighteen thousand paratroopers of the 101st Airborne Division created a seven-mile perimeter against which 45,000 enraged Germans smashed in vain. Under a flag of truce the German commander sent an emissary to demand the Americans' surrender. They were hopelessly surrounded, declared the Wehrmacht leader, and further fighting could only lead to needless loss of life.

"Nuts," said Tony McAuliffe.

"I thought I understood English, but what does that mean?" said the bewildered German.

"You know what go to hell means?" asked one of McAuliffe's aides.

The German nodded bleakly and retired.

For four more days "the battered bastards of Bastogne," inspired by their laconic commander, held on against almost continuous German attacks. Then the tanks of the 3rd Army broke through and their legendary defense had a happy ending.

McAuliffe's reply overnight made him a symbol of the hard-bitten battle commander. But Tony McAuliffe is far more than that. A first section man at West Point, his Army career presents him as closer to being a symbol of the West Point ideal, a soldier who can think as well as fight, who can make the command decisions on the battlefield or in the Pentagon. In a memoir which he has deposited in the Oral History Collection of Columbia University, McAuliffe, with typical modesty, spends very little time discussing the Bastogne episode. He is far prouder of decisions he made before a shot was fired in the war, when as an obscure major he was brought to Washington to serve under Chief of Staff George Marshall, working on problems of supply and equipment for the wartime Army.

McAuliffe's first assignment was the sort of job that might make a four-star general quail. He was handed a memorandum from Winston Churchill to Franklin D. Roosevelt recommending no less than seven crucial changes in American weapons manufacturing. For instance, Churchill urged the Army to stop making the 37-mm. anti-aircraft gun and switch to the Swedish 40-mm. Bofors. "I didn't sleep the first two nights," McAuliffe says. "I thought I'd go nuts I was so worried. Finally I resolved I just had to take this thing in stride." He spent the next weeks interrogating experts all over the nation, then boiled down a vast mass of data, and, swallowing hard, rejected six out of seven of Churchill's proposals. The only recommendation he approved was the substitution of the Bofors gun for the American 37-mm. weapon.

McAuliffe sent the report in to General Marshall and it was not long before he was summoned before the chief of staff, where he was confronted by an even more formidable figure, the chief of ordnance, Major General Charles M. Wesson, who was nicknamed "Bull" ("not for nothing," McAuliffe adds). Wesson was furious over McAuliffe's recommendation to junk the American anti-aircraft gun, but McAuliffe stood his ground, and for well over an hour the major and the major general slugged it out with facts and figures while Marshall listened. In the end, Marshall ruled in favor of McAuliffe.

Next McAuliffe was assigned the job of finding a radio that would enable American tanks to talk with each other. Police cars in several cities were already using such radios, but the problem was to find a design sturdy enough to take the punishment of tank tactics. McAuliffe collected all available makes and selected the one that looked best to him and the specialists he consulted. But the chief signal officer on the General Staff violently objected to his choice. He wanted to create a board and study the situation for a year and a half or so—which was the prewar Army system. Major McAuliffe went to George Marshall, talked it over with him, and the chief signal officer was abruptly replaced. Within the year American tankers were talking to each other over the airwaves.

But the project that McAuliffe truly pioneered was the DUKW, better known as the Duck. With the Army facing a whole series of amphibious invasions, McAuliffe was told to find a vehicle that could transport supplies from ship to shore in areas where docking and port facilities were nonexistent. He discovered that a man named Putnam had redesigned a two-and-a-half-ton truck into a vehicle that could perform such a task. McAuliffe was impressed by what he saw of the Duck. He invited a United Fruit executive who had considerable experience in "over-the-beach operations" in Central America to check the vehicle out with him, and this expert gave it a very high rating. This convinced McAuliffe, who cornered Major General Brehon B. Summervell, chief of supply, and gave him a report recommending the Duck in highest terms. Somervell took one look and said, "Order 20,000."

Two years later, McAuliffe parachuted into Normandy with the 101st Airborne and fought his way down to Utah Beach. There he saw literally hundreds of Ducks chugging back and forth from the ships off shore, ferrying tons of supplies for the drive into France. "It was one of the most satisfying sights of my life," McAuliffe says.

XI

During World War II, a new kind of Army emerged, by no means as dominated by West Pointers as the A.E.F. of 1918. Of the war's 155 division commanders, only 89, or 57 percent, were West Pointers. The Chief of Staff, George C. Marshall, was a graduate of V.M.I. and many other non-West Pointers such as Lieutenant Generals Lucian Truscott and John R. Hodge were outstandingly successful soldiers. This shift of West Point's influence in the Army's overall command structure is best explained by the growth since World War I of the Army's postgraduate schools.

Here West Pointers and those who enter the Army in other ways compete equally for honors and absorb the really practical knowledge of the art of war. These schools have also made it all but meaningless for the historian to attempt to trace to West Point the military abilities of her graduates. Eisenhower is a good example of a soldier who loafed through West Point; but when he went to the Army Command and General Staff School at Fort Leavenworth, in 1927, he became the student par excellence, finishing first in his class in this graduate course. It was here, and in a self-education program inspired by his friendship with the brilliant Fox Conner (1898), that Ike acquired the generalship he displayed in Europe.

In his memoirs, General Matthew B. Ridgway attributes to the service schools the basic competence of the American Army. West Point, he says, "does not pretend to turn out finished Army officers. Its function in the main is to develop the character of the fledgling officer, to instill in him the ideals and sense of duty, honor and patriotism that will sustain him throughout his career." Here once more we see graphic evidence of the vast shift of West Point's role, from producing skilled technicians to soldiers with character.

At the war's end, James L. Howerton of George Washington University, tried to correlate cadet performance and promotability. Selecting 170 generals who had graduated between 1904 and 1917, he found that only men who had won their stars in the Army Service Forces had significantly higher scholastic records than their classmates. Ground force generals were rarely more than average students. On the other hand, the military managers were under-represented in cadet athletics, while Air Force and ground generals considerably exceeded their classmates in action on the playing fields. Mr. Howerton concluded: "There is only a slight positive relationship between scholastic achievement as Cadets and future success in the Army. There is a high positive relationship between participation in athletics and display of leadership traits as Cadets and future success in the army."

Here, more than anywhere else, may be found the explanation for West Point's hostility to rapid curriculum change. The business of producing soldiers is almost as arcane as running a seminary. Ultimately, in both professions, the nonintellectual components of the personality are the decisive factors in success or failure. This may in turn explain why West Point became during World War II the victim of a virulent American disease: football psychosis.

XII

OVER THE YEARS Army had held its own in Eastern football, placing a fair share of greats on the all-American teams and compiling a respectable won and lost record. But toward the end of the 30's, schools such as Pennsylvania and Cornell began playing big-time football, and Army found it difficult to compete. In 1940 Cornell walloped the cadets 45–0, the worst defeat thus far in West Point's history. Then Pennsylvania handed them an even worse drubbing, 48–0, and they ended the season by losing to Navy 14–0. Brigadier General Robert L. Eichelberger, who had just taken over as Superintendent, called a meeting of the athletic council after the Pennsylvania debacle. "I was impressed Saturday by the way the cadets cheered our team right to the end of that 48–0 beating," he said. "It looks as if we are developing the finest bunch of losers in the world. By the gods, I believe the cadets deserve a football team which will teach them how to be good winners!"

Innovationist Eichelberger put his finger on what he thought was wrong with the West Point game. "Our system of graduate officer coaching is outmoded. We ought to go out and get the best coach in the business. We had him here once and we let him get away. It's high time we got him back. I'm talking about Red Blaik."

Earl Henry (Red) Blaik had resigned from the Army in 1922 after winning the athletic saber as the best all-round athlete in his class. After a stint in business in Dayton, Ohio, Blaik took a part-time job as Army's assistant coach, then decided to make the plunge into full-time coaching and went to Dartmouth, where he created teams that beat Yale in the Yale Bowl for the first time in 52 years.

Another football problem was a decision made almost unilaterally by former Assistant Secretary of the Navy Franklin D. Roosevelt that henceforth West Point must abide by the "three-year rule." This meant that football players who had spent a year on the varsity at another college could play only two years at West Point. In the halcyon days of Army football—it was common practice at many other colleges as well —it was not unusual for a star to play four years on a college varsity, then switch to West Point for another four autumns of gridiron exploits.

Blaik was happy at Dartmouth, but when Eichelberger said, "West

Point needs you, Red," the pull of the corps was strong. Nevertheless, Blaik insisted that Army could not build a winning team unless the Surgeon General abandoned senseless government-imposed weight restrictions. Since 1931 a directive had barred any would-be cadet who exceeded a severely calibrated chart, under which a seventeen-year-old candidate six feet tall could not weigh more than 176 pounds and a 6′4″ man could not weigh more than 198. Football types tend to be big-boned and beefy; Army had spent almost a decade turning away its best prospects. General Eichelberger pulled all the political wires he could find in Washington, while General Edwin ("Pa") Watson, FDR's military aide, twisted arms from his vantage point in the White House. The Surgeon General surrendered, and the War Department issued a ruling that permitted six-footers to weigh as much as 201 and a 6′4″ man 226. With this one essential guaranteed, Blaik agreed to return to West Point as head coach.

In three years, this jut-jawed no-nonsense professional built West Point from a floor mat into the nation's number one football team. World War II helped, of course, draining some of the best players from the nation's colleges and giving the Academy an unparalleled opportunity to scout good football players among the draftees and volunteers of the Army's swelling ranks. Glenn Davis and Doc Blanchard, stars of the Army teams of '44, '45, and '46, became nationally famous as Mr. Outside and Mr. Inside. Blanchard, one of the greatest fullbacks in the history of the game, combined hundred-yard-dash speed with 204-pound hitting power. Halfback Davis was a broken field runner in the Red Grange-Tom Harmon league and a dangerous passer in the bargain.

Blanchard's plebe year exploits inspired one columnist to write a parody of Kipling's poem "Tommy," titled "At Ease, Mister."

If you would go to West Point, lad, and someday earn your stars
You'd better be a man or learn some other trade than Mars
For up there on the Hudson, lad, where Benny set 'em up
The only one a plebe outranks is the superintendent's pup.

Oh, it's Mr. Dumbjohn this and that. Hey, Mister, on your toes.
But it's: "Thank you, Mr. Blanchard," when the football whistle blows.
When the football whistle blows, my lad, when the football whistle blows
Oh, it's: "Thank you, Mr. Blanchard," when the football whistle blows.

The Touchdown Twins sent Army roaring to the very top of big league football. Beginning in 1944, Academy teams racked up five out of six undefeated seasons, two national championships and five Eastern titles. Among their sweetest victories was the 59–0 trouncing of Notre Dame in 1944, erasing twelve previous years of doleful defeat.

That particular victory, according to a well-known West Point historian, Colonel Russell P. ("Red") Reeder, played a part in winning the war in Europe. During the Battle of the Bulge, the Germans infiltrated a number of English-speaking spies wearing American officers' uniforms into rear areas where they caused tremendous confusion by giving false orders to truck convoys, ammunition trains and armored columns. The Germans knew all the American passwords and had up-to-the-minute, beautifully counterfeited identification cards. It was almost impossible to root them out until a military policeman came up with a prize ploy. He strode up to one officer whom he suspected of being a Nazi and said, "Who won the Notre Dame game?"

"The officer did not know what the MP was talking about," Reeder says, "so he was promptly locked up for further questioning and shooting."

Even more marvelous was the excitement when Blaik's Black Knights, as the newspapermen called them, ended a five-year famine by beating Navy in 1944, 23–7, and incidentally completing Army's first unbeaten season since 1916. It was the first time the service rivals fought for the mythical but nonetheless coveted national championship. The game, played at Baltimore's Municipal Stadium, drew a crowd of 70,000 and sold $58,637,000 worth of war bonds. The excitement of graduates on World War II's battlefronts was something to behold. General MacArthur wired: THE GREATEST OF ALL ARMY TEAMS STOP WE HAVE STOPPED THE WAR TO CELEBRATE YOUR MAGNIFICENT SUCCESS. General Eichelberger, the man behind the Blaik breakthrough, piled into a jeep the moment he got the final score and all but swam up muddy mountain trails to tell the good news to Colonel Charles Robert (Monk) Meyer, one of West Point's great 1930 halfbacks, who was commanding a battalion of the 127th Infantry in the hills of Leyte.

Blaik did his best to hold down scores during the booming war years. In 1943, the year before Army really hit its stride, the cadets were running wild against a totally outclassed Temple team. When the score hit 48–0, Blaik gave explicit instructions that Army was not to score again. Minutes later Charlie Sampson, a reserve guard, grabbed a Temple pass and went belting down an open field toward the enemy goal line. Suddenly he remembered Colonel Blaik's order, and when he got to the one-yard line skidded to a halt and grounded the ball. Army now went into a frantic huddle to figure out how not to score. They decided to try a field goal and commissioned Sampson, who had never place-kicked in competition before, to do the job. Sampson astonished himself and everyone else by booting the ball cleanly through the uprights.

In spite of such gestures, the Academy soon discovered that winning too many football games posed almost as many problems as losing too many. The latent hostility to West Point that runs like an ominous thread through the emotions of so many Americans began to focus on the football team. It appeared in its most virulent form immediately after the war, when a still-powerful Army team played a top-ranked Notre Dame team in Yankee Stadium in 1946.

The cadets and Coach Blaik were bombarded by unbelievably scurrilous mail from Notre Dame's subway alumni. There was even a group called SPATNC—"The Society for the Prevention of Army's Third National Championship"—that regularly warned Blaik that "the day of retribution" was fast approaching. The nationwide drumbeating also unbalanced the psychology of the West Point team. Traditionally Academy coaches "built" throughout the season to the Navy game. But the cascade of publicity made the players look on Notre Dame as number one. The coast-to-coast frenzy over their 1946 confrontation completely destroyed any lingering aura of intercollegiate sport. Tickets were scalped for $100 and the great and near-great inundated both schools with demands for choice seats. Biff Jones, Army's athletic director, said, "If Yankee Stadium had a million seats, we would fill it for this game." But the mighty clash turned out to be a dud, both coaches concentrated on not losing, and the score was 0-0.

With Coach Blaik's hearty approval, both schools promptly suspended the series for ten years. A storm of abuse broke over this decision, most of it aimed at Army.

A few years later Blaik's teams were accused of playing dirty football. When Army broke Michigan's three-year, 25-game winning streak on October 7, 1949, a Wolverine professor wrote letters to the Comman-

dant at West Point and to several congressmen, declaring that Michigan's
star halfback Chuck Ordman had been kicked between the eyes and
forced to leave the game with a concussion. Films of the game showed
Ordman had been inadvertently kneed in the back of the head by a
Michigan guard. An unknown and never identified Harvard critic
declared that Army's 1949 team was the dirtiest he had seen in 22
years of playing and officiating. Harvard's coach, Art Valtey, scotched
the canard. West Point's game "was aggressive but not dirty," he said.

But such rumors were a factor in the growing uneasiness about big-
time football at West Point. Fewer and fewer people seemed to appreciate what an amazing achievement it was to have a winning football team
of any dimension at the Military Academy. Nor did anyone realize that
Army had gone to considerable efforts to keep their schedule on a scale
that was suitable for West Point's stature as a national institution, yet
vastly less ambitious than the semiprofessional athletic efforts of the Big
Ten and Notre Dame.

In 1949, when the corps paraded into Philadelphia's Municipal Stadium for the Navy game, the midshipmen saluted them with a scornful
parody of "On, Brave Old Army Team."

> *We don't play Notre Dame*
> *We don't play Tulane*
> *We just play Davidson*
> *For that's the fearless Army way.*

Navy's schedule, which pitted it against a major opponent every week,
was far more difficult and had proved to be disastrous. Coach Blaik
summed up Army's point of view in a statement made shortly before the
1949 Navy game. "We are not making our schedules with a view to the
national championship. Much as we appreciate any honors that come
our way, we are not developing any neurosis about how we may be
ranked. Our type of schedule is sufficiently exacting for the cadets, who
put in a much more rigorous day off the field than any civilian college
student."

Blaik was not exaggerating. Few if any colleges fielded football teams
on which every man was taking a basic engineering course. The cadet
football player lived the same 5:50 A.M.-to-10:30 P.M. day as the rest
of the corps. He was excused from twice-a-week drill with his company
during the football season, and because practice lasted from 4 to 5:30,

he was excused from marching to supper. On Sundays football players were "permitted" to attend 8 A.M. service so they could sit in on scouting reports from 10:30 to 12 o'clock. Even on Saturday mornings of game days at West Point, the football player rose with the rest of the corps at 5:50 and went to his first class. "The general load carried by the cadet, football player or non-football player, far exceeds anything required when I was an undergraduate at the Academy," wrote Coach Blaik in his memoirs.

At the same time, there were some small undercurrents of privilege in the status of the football player. Special tutors, often high-ranking officers on the faculty, volunteered their time to help the stars such as Glenn Davis through the thornier subjects in the curriculum. The players ate together at a training table during football season and inevitably tended to form friendships within the football circle. The hostility to Army's victories outside the Academy were cited by more than a few envious officers and cadets within West Point as proof that football was doing the school positive harm. Some even said that it was a good thing for Navy to beat Army once in a while—a remark that threw the hard-nosed Blaik and his staff into a state of shocked outrage. Snipers called the football players "Blaik boys" and "the chosen cadets." Blaik, of course, with his Army background, was not at all surprised by such a reaction. "Anything obliquely within the Army chain of command that achieves the degree of success and publicity attained by West Point football in those days invites envy from a type of individual present in every community."

Thus the stage was set for West Point's worst scandal. On August 3, 1951, newspapers across the nation blossomed with huge black headlines proclaiming "WEST POINT FIRES 90 BREAKING HONOR CODE." Thirty-seven of the 90 ousted cadets were football players. The scandal had been slumbering at West Point for almost six months. It began when two cadets reported that there was widespread cheating in written examinations. A three-man board of tactical officers was appointed to launch an independent investigation and they began questioning cadets who were under suspicion. Man after man told a dismayingly similar story.

With the expansion of the corps, giving cadets written tests had become an administrative nightmare. Routinely, the Academy began giving the same examinations to different sections of classes on different days. Beginning first with hints and then escalating to more all-out revelations, men who had taken the test began tipping off friends, particularly athletes who were having trouble with a subject. Soon there was what one professor, recalling the scandal, called "a complete intelligence system."

Yet, few if any of the tippers saw themselves as violating the honor code—no more so than George Custer thought he was violating it in 1859 when he squirreled his way into an instructor's room to latch onto the next day's examination paper, or the cadets of Peter Smith Michie's day when they got their unexpected bonus from the professor's sympathetic son.

This is not to deny that the cadets were violating the spirit of the honor code as it might be construed in the eyes of an outsider. It is very difficult to grasp the difference between breaking regulations and violating one's honor in the eyes of the corps. Custom—the general opinion within the corps toward a certain act—has enormous weight in this delicate matter.

The best proof of the offenders' concept of honor was their actions. "Most of the 90 boys condemned themselves by telling the truth," Colonel Blaik said. "Since their acts did not involve cheating in the classroom there was no evidence against most of them. All they had to do was refuse to answer or to plead innocence. To them this would have been dishonorable." Many of the accused had not participated in the system but had merely admitted knowing about it.

For Colonel Blaik, a final agony was the discovery that his son Bob, and his roommate, who was president of the second class, were involved. Blaik pleaded angrily with the Superintendent, Major General Frederick A. Irving, to take the investigation out of the hands of the tactical officers, whom he characterized as young and immature, and place it in the hands of the academic board. Irving, in office only six months, refused, and the board continued its hearings, turning in a report June 8 recommending dismissal for all those who had admitted guilt of any shade or variety.

Two more months of high-level discussion in Washington led to the appointment of a review board consisting of Learned Hand, retired judge of the second United States Court of Appeals; Major General Robert M. Danford, Commandant at West Point under MacArthur; and Lieutenant General Troy H. Middleton, president of Louisiana State

University. This board interviewed none of the violators. They talked only to cadets chosen for them by West Point authorities. In his memoirs, Colonel Blaik makes it clear that he was convinced these cadets were chosen with an eye to blackening the accused and convincing the board that the situation within the corps was so serious that the tactical board's recommendation of dismissal had to be upheld. "They no more represented the majority opinion of the corps," Colonel Blaik insisted, "than the chain of command viewpoint represented a majority opinion of West Point graduates, the Army or the people of America."

Blaik's rhetoric is hard to accept in the face of the elaborate system the miscreants had created for distributing their espionage. The only possible explanation is one that Blaik, of course, labors to rebut throughout his book—that the athletes had become a group apart and were regarded by the corps as somehow special and therefore privileged to break certain rules. This split in the essential loyalty of the cadets to the corps as a whole is one of West Point's recurrent nightmares. Certainly Blaik's athletes were separate from the rest of the corps, not so much through West Point's doing as through the aura conferred on them by a sports-mad American public. But neither this public nor the Army rose up in any notable wrath when the Hand Committee upheld the recommendation for dismissal, and the 90 cadets were ousted by Presidential decree—which gave them no opportunity to ask for a court-martial.

Most of these young men indicated by their silence that they at least regretted what they had done. There were no voices of outraged innocence, although one or two tried to defend themselves with the ultimate cynicism—the claim that the entire corps was involved. Viewing the debacle as history, one can summon sympathy and extenuating explanations for these sad young men. But it is a charitable emotion, perhaps even sentimental. In terms of justice they were plainly and undeniably guilty.

Perhaps the wisest, though unheeded, comment on the situation came from ex-Superintendent Douglas MacArthur. The scandal, he told columnist Bob Considine, "could have been settled quickly, quietly by a reprimand from the Superintendent. That was all that would have been needed except in the case of perhaps two of the boys. And they could have been helped by a kick in the pants."

MacArthur called Earl Blaik down to his suite in the Waldorf Towers to tell him, "Earl, you must stay on. Don't leave under fire." Blaik stayed and rebuilt his wrecked team through seven somewhat bleak years, until in 1958 he produced another unbeaten season, including victories over Notre Dame and Navy, and restored Army's football respectability.

Meanwhile, West Point was grappling with a host of larger problems. The Cold War, the rise of an affluent society, the concept of limited warfare, a new kind of anti-militarism, a younger generation with sharply different demands and expectations—all these things produced a new spirit at West Point—a professed dedication not to permanence but change. The problem was—and is—how to retain the best of the old system in a world steadily more infatuated with newness.

Tradition in Ferment

I

THE GUNS OF WORLD WAR II were silent less than a month when the Army appointed one of its most distinguished soldiers, Major General Maxwell Taylor, Superintendent of West Point. Famed for both his combat leadership with the 82nd and 101st Airborne Divisions in World War II and for his brain power (he stood fourth in the class of 1922), the new Superintendent was a symbol of the Army's determination never again to allow West Point to relapse into the academic or military doldrums. Only nine days after he reached his desk, Taylor received some advice from another even more famous graduate, George Patton:

My dear Max:

I am very appreciative of the opportunity which your letter of 19 August gives me to express my view on the Military Academy. Perhaps since they come from a goat to an engineer, the combined thought may be useful. I collected six West Pointers much younger than myself and talked over various subjects. The results of our conversation, including my own very strong opinions, are expressed here.

Among the changes Patton suggested was a nationwide series of boards of retired generals to advise congressmen on Academy appointments (permitting the politicians to blame rejects on "the evil machinations of Army officers"), and a drastic overhaul of the determination of class standing, giving 50% of the weight to the tactical department. "Nothing I learned in electricity or hydraulics or in higher mathematics or in drawing in any way contributed to my military career. Therefore, I would markedly reduce or wholly jettison the above subjects," Patton declared. He wanted more emphasis on history "studied objectively," and urged that all cadets be required to learn two languages. He also insisted that "gallantry and a desire to attain military prestige can be cultivated." One way to do it, he suggested, might be to require first classmen to memorize and recite each week a citation won by an earlier graduate.

In closing, Patton emphasized that he did not want to turn the Academy into a Benning or a Sill. "I think that the greatest thing you and I got out of it was our profound belief in the greatness of our motto." The honor system, therefore, should not in any way be relaxed.

The Academy blandly ignored Patton's denunciation of the scientific curriculum. Nor did his nationwide boards of generals ever materialize. But his ideas on promoting gallantry, giving more weight to the tactical department, and improving subjects such as history and languages have become part of modern West Point's program, not because George S. Patton, Jr., suggested them, but because they were similar to conclusions reached by numerous other commanding officers during World War II.

Writing from SHAEF on August 31, 1945, Supreme Commander Dwight Eisenhower expressed a similar attitude, with somewhat more sophisticated nuances. "Fundamentally," he said, "I believe West Point is on a sound basis." He went on to recommend "efforts toward improvements . . . more along the human than the technical side. Lessons of cooperation and coordination, in the spirit of friendliness and devotion to a common cause, should be stressed."

When Eisenhower became Army Chief of Staff in 1946, he acted on these convictions, ordering a new course in the psychology of leadership at West Point. World War II's greater duration and complexity had underscored what MacArthur and a few others had grasped from their World War I experience—the American citizen-soldier must be led, not pushed, bullied or prodded into battle. Taylor started the military leadership course, which has since become a basic part of the first classman's curriculum. He also made the Gallagher-Landrum Military Aptitude Rating System a key factor in the cadet's West Point profile.

In a speech delivered to British cadets at Sandhurst, the Royal Military College, Taylor explained how the aptitude system works: "Its procedure is divided into two steps: the first to determine the cadets of doubtful aptitude for the service who should receive special attention; the second to analyze the personality and character of individuals in this small group of doubtful cadets in order to form an idea of their ultimate suitability for the military service."

In step one, each cadet rates every other cadet in his company— about a hundred cadets in all—as a leader. Individually no great accuracy of ranking is expected. But in every company there usually emerges a general consensus as to the best ten percent and the worst ten percent. Once this lower ten are located, the company tactical officer goes to work on them. First he asks certain key cadets in the company to make confidential evaluation reports on each one of these men. From these, the tactical officer himself makes out still another evaluation report and all the data then goes to the Commandant of Cadets, who determines whether or not a particular cadet is so weak in aptitude he ought to be asked to resign. If the Commandant is inclined to issue a thumbs-down judgment, the case is referred to a Brigade Aptitude Board, which consists of experienced officers and at least one psychologist. The Board holds hearings with the cadet and discusses thoroughly all aspects of his problems. It then sends him back to the Commandant with a recommendation for "conditioning" in aptitude or dismissal from the Academy.

The number of cadets thus dismissed has over the years been relatively small. Nor is the decision on an individual cadet made lightly. Rarely is a man dismissed without a previous warning and at least one term on probation during which he can seek help and advice from his tactical officer and from senior cadets.

Perhaps the most important aspect of this innovation has been its impact on the West Point psyche. The confusion between the academic and the military that led earlier cadets to advise plebes to "bone math" and forget about military prowess has to some extent been eliminated. There is, beyond all doubt, a new confidence and a new sophistication in Taylor's words: "An inaptitude for the military service should not be regarded as a stigma on the cadet concerned. In every profession there is some combination of traits and characteristics most favorable for success. The military profession is a highly specialized one, requiring attributes differing in quality and degree from the requirements of most civilian callings."

At the same time, the postwar Academy has insisted on its ability to develop character. "The conduct of war is a business which calls for more than intellectual and physical attainments," Taylor told the Sandhurst cadets. "No great soldier ever rose to eminence as a military commander who was not primarily a man of character. It is for this reason that West Point takes the development of character as a formal objective to be pursued by all available means." When it came to believing in the power of West Point's motto and traditions as character-building influences, the sophisticate Taylor was at one with "Blood and Guts" Patton. "Tradition means much in the life of our cadets. No one can walk across the parade ground without seeing in his mind's eye the

long gray line of men who have passed in review across this Plain. The
fact that Lee, Grant, Pershing, MacArthur and Eisenhower wore the
same gray coat, lived in the same barracks and pursued the same routine
of daily work is a moral influence always at play within the Corps of
Cadets." To these influences he emphatically added the honor system,
which he called "an essential element in the character moulding which
goes on at the Military Academy."

Himself a gifted writer and speaker, Taylor also gave impetus to the
Academy's growing interest in the humanities and the social sciences.
"The cadets should not live in a mental cloister," he declared. "Their
interests must be catholic, avoiding the small horizons sometimes attributed to the military mind." A prime instance of this horizon-widening
during Taylor's regime was the creation of SCUSA (Student Conference
on United States Affairs), which brought to the Military Academy over a
hundred young people from fifty-three civilian colleges as well as six
midshipmen from the U.S. Naval Academy. Guest speakers included
Nelson A. Rockefeller, Dean Rusk, John J. McCloy, Dean Acheson,
Allen Dulles, and W. Averell Harriman.

SCUSA's success has made it an annual event at the Academy.
Most of the visitors have been pleasantly surprised by the level of interest
and learning manifested by the cadets. Claudie Hawley, chief of social
sciences in the Division of Higher Education of the U.S. Office of Education, declared: "It is time for the professional world to realize that
West Point is making a first-rate academic contribution." The faculty
also was interested in the reactions of the student visitors; it was the
first time in 147 years that outsiders of the cadets' own age had a chance
to sit down and get a close look at West Point and its student body. Most
were impressed. "I found that the faculty here is of a quality of which
any civilian college could be proud," commented Charles L. Stewart, a
senior at Amherst. Mary Kohn, a senior at Wellesley, said, "I expected the
cadets to sit on the edge of their seats and just answer 'Yes, sir.' They
don't. They behave just like ordinary students in class—except that they
are a bit more polite." The cadets themselves also profited by coming
face to face with civilians. One upperclassman said that he found "even
the smartest students argue all around a topic, waste a lot of time looking
at a subject from all sides and express themselves vaguely. It's always a
cadet who cuts right through the confusion to the heart of the matter

and offers the concrete proposal that sums the whole thing up. Here at West Point we learn to think in straight lines."

The young man reflected for a moment, then added, "People who have the imagination to think all around a subject are needed just as much as people like us—and the sooner each group learns what it has to gain from the other, the better off we'll all be."

I I

AN ABILITY TO THINK on curves as well as on the straightaway has been the Academy's goal throughout the post-World War II era. As early as 1950, Colonel Herman Beukema was confronting the cadets with lecturers who propounded the philosophy of the opposition. One reporter told of watching an Air Force intelligence officer, recently returned from a tour of duty in Eastern Europe, tell a group of cadets: "Capitalism contains the seeds of its own destruction. Since capitalism is foredoomed, there is no need for Russia to fight. It will not fight unless the odds are so much in its favor that it is merely hastening the inevitable. When the rotten apple is ready to fall, *Russia will shake the tree.*" A lively exchange between cadets and the officer followed the talk. They disputed his points with vigor and authority.

A more recent reporter tells of watching Lieutenant Colonel Wilfred Burton say to one of his English classes: "Army officers are just machines, aren't they? If they are told to go out and massacre the innocent, they go out and massacre the innocent." Politely, but heatedly, one cadet replied: "We just can't accept that, sir."

Breaking out of the cloister has also been a primary concern of the Office of Military Psychology and Leadership which has grown from a single course in 1946 to 130 classroom hours. These include an introduction to psychology and a methods of instruction course to prepare cadets for the vast amount of teaching they will have to do during their Army careers. But the heart of the department is the military leadership course, which is structured around a concept of leadership as a dynamic interaction process, involving the leader himself with his own personality, the group with its particular characteristics and needs, and the situation in which the leader and his group are operating. Sometimes the cadet is asked to play a role. There are also group discussions, training films, tape-recorded skits and numerous case studies.

You have a man in your platoon who is a constant problem throughout training, fighting with other men, once starting a brawl that resulted in three men being hospitalized. Now you are in combat. In the past two weeks the same man has volunteered for three hazardous missions. On one you noticed

[346]

he assumed command of his squad and successfully led members of the squad behind an enemy dug-in position and captured it. Should you recommend him for promotion?

The main focus, however, is not on leading heroic charges or even primarily on solving combat problems. The Academy is more concerned with giving the future lieutenant the ability to deal with day-to-day dilemmas in morale, administration, discipline. As in other areas, the Academy strives to overcome limited horizons by bringing in distinguished guest lecturers. In an average year, most of the lieutenant generals of the Army journey to West Point for a Saturday-morning seminar with first classmen in which they discuss with remarkable frankness problems of their current jobs, plus Army wisdom they have gleaned from earlier assignments.

The most dramatic use of the guest lecturer is in the Department of Tactics, which has made a policy of inviting younger graduates who have distinguished themselves in combat as part of a "military heritage" series.

The talk given by Major David Hughes, Class of 1950, is a good example of how vivid and compelling these narrations can be. Five months after graduation, Hughes and a large part of his class were in combat in Korea (41 were killed, the highest number of deaths in a single class in West Point history). Hughes was a rifle platoon leader and rifle company commander of Company K, 7th Cavalry Regiment, 1st Cavalry Division. He won the Distinguished Service Cross, the Silver Star with Oak Leaf Cluster, Bronze Star for valor, the Purple Heart with Oak Leaf Cluster, and the Greek Cross of War.

Hughes gave the fourth classmen a minute-by-minute, man-by-man account of ten days of combat—September 28 to October 7, 1951. He told how he started out with 7 officers and 200 men to take and hold Hill 339. Two companies of Chinese regulars hit the center of his thinly-spread company, surrounded, infiltrated and cut off his small group from battalion headquarters. He told of jumping into a foxhole as one enemy charge overran a part of the perimeter and finding himself eyeball to eyeball with a Chinese armed with a rifle. By now, with almost a year of combat experience, Hughes had lost confidence in his carbine; he had found the M-1 rifle too heavy to carry along with radio and maps, and a .45 too slow to draw from his holster. Slung low on his hip he carried a

.45 Thompson sub-machine gun lend-leased to the Chinese Nationalists in 1945 and recaptured from Chinese Communists by his unit. The snub-nosed gun saved his life. He shot the Chinese dead before the enemy soldier could bring his rifle to bear in the cramped foxhole. That was the moment, he said, when "I learned what we're asking a private soldier to do."

He went on to detail the chaos and heroism of the succeeding days of combat. He pointed out acts of leadership in his company by West Pointers, enlisted men, a Negro lieutenant and an uncouth, uneducated GI who won a battlefield commission and who carried out the high calling of an officer as well as anyone on the field. "He never would have lasted a day at West Point, or even made it to an OCS," Hughes said. "But what he did on that battlefield made it clear to me that a West Point diploma isn't the only ticket to combat achievement."

A few days later, Hughes was ordered to attack Hill 347. He received 35 replacements at 2 A.M. and they were in battle at 3 A.M. His first sergeant, who had been magnificent in the fight for Hill 339, collapsed. Hughes did not speak a word of censure against him. He made it clear to the cadets that you cannot rescue such a situation by chewing a man out. Soon things were going so badly that one platoon "ceased to exist." Failure was imminent. Then, Hughes said, "I felt what it really means to have responsibility." He told how he simply gathered up the men he had left—there were no more officers—and called forth cooks, drivers, radiomen for additional riflemen. He and a handful of others captured the main enemy bunker on 347, the hill fell and the rest of the unit cleaned out the surrounding bunkers. "It was savage and very ugly."

When it was over, Hughes had 29 animal-like, angry men left, a large hill to hold, and 125 prisoners to guard. "Company K had won for ten days but would never exist again as it was." Meanwhile, there was ominous evidence that the Chinese were marshaling for a counterattack. The men got grenades ready while Hughes debated with himself about the fate of the prisoners in the event of attack. He knew many men would want to kill them so they could defend themselves on the hill. But before the Chinese counterattack, relief came and this agonizing question never had to be faced.

A cadet asked Hughes what he would have done if the relief had not arrived. He said, with total candor, that he didn't know. In such cases a man could only wait until he could postpone his decision no longer.

Summing up, Hughes said, "though officially I was given this ribbon for what is construed to be my part in the capture of Hill 347, I would prefer that you remember that I was only privileged to lead and to be here tonight to represent those unremembered men of Company K that in my memory are still lying down that north slope of Hill 347."

Another cadet raised his hand to ask Hughes if he felt prepared for his job so soon after graduation. "I didn't feel inadequate," Hughes said, but he admitted there were many techniques he didn't know. "I sure as hell knew what Napoleon would do in those cases, but I was a little short in knowing what a second lieutenant would do," he said.

Major Hughes thus returns to one of West Point's basic dilemmas. During a war the Army is inclined to wonder if the Academy should devote more time to training company commanders for combat leadership. In our era of brushfire wars and seemingly permanent hostility between nations, the problem has become even more acute. The Army officer must not only know how to lead in combat, he must also be capable of understanding and utilizing the fantastic technological innovations of twentieth-century warfare. Simultaneously he must possess the kind of diplomatic skills that will enable him not only to win the battles but retain the respect and even friendship of foreign allies. In a word, the Academy is being asked to produce a kind of supersoldier, a combination of George Custer, Leonardo Da Vinci, and St. Francis of Assisi. The achievement is manifestly impossible. Yet the Academy has doggedly tried to satisfy its critics, while retaining its traditional emphasis on mathematics, science and engineering.

III

KOREA PRESENTED WEST POINT'S graduates with the first limited war they had fought in almost a century. The Mexican, Indian and Spanish-American wars were clearly in this category (without the awesome threat of nuclear weapons, held in reserve on either side). The concept proved indigestible to the man who was in many ways the Academy's greatest soldier of this century. Douglas MacArthur's clash with Harry Truman over the President's refusal to allow MacArthur to bomb enemy air bases and lines of supply inside China touched off the most serious crisis in the delicate balance between civilian and military authority since George McClellan toyed with marching on the White House in 1862.

When MacArthur flew home to a national ovation (2850 tons of ticker tape in New York alone) and a Gallup poll reported the public favored the general against the President, 69 to 29, the nation seemed to tremble on the brink. But it is significant that MacArthur, in spite of the ovations, the polls, the tumultuous reception of his emotional speech to Congress, remained entirely alone. West Pointers did not rush to support him, nor, to do MacArthur justice, did he so much as hint that he was trying to overturn the established procedures of the republic. The very most he seemed inclined to do was repeat McClellan's folly, and accept a Presidential nomination from the opposition party.

MacArthur remains a revered name at West Point. But it is the MacArthur who led his patrols into World War I's no-man's-land armed with nothing but a swagger stick; the general who wrecked the Japanese timetable in the Philippines, and saved Australia, and then returned in a campaign that marked him, in the words of one West Point historian, "sui generis, the greatest captain of his age"; the still potent strategist who turned the Korean War from siege to hot pursuit with his brilliant flank thrust at Inchon. The general who clashed with the President finds few admirers in cadet barracks. The majority judgment on him is voiced by the man who succeeded him in Korea, Matthew Ridgway: "It was a boon to the country that the issue did arise and that it was decisively met by the elected head of the government within the ample dimensions of his own high moral courage. . . ."

In 1962, when the passions of Korea had subsided, West Point gave MacArthur its highest tribute, the Sylvanus Thayer Medal. He responded with a speech rich in MacArthur rhetoric, but nonetheless deeply meaningful to every West Pointer:

Others will debate the controversial national and international issues which divide men's minds. But serene, calm, aloof, you stand as the nation's war guardian, as its lifeguard from the raging tides of international conflict, as its gladiator in the arena of battle. For a century and a half you have defended, guarded and protected its hallowed traditions of liberty and freedom, of right and justice. Let civilian voices argue the merits or demerits of our processes of government; whether our strength is being sapped by deficit financing, indulged in too long; by federal paternalism grown too mighty . . . by politics grown too corrupt . . . by morals grown too low; by taxes grown too high, by extremists grown too violent. . . . These great national problems are not for your professional participation or military solution. Your guidepost stands out like a tenfold beacon in the night—Duty, Honor, Country.

IV

THERE IS MORE than a little irony in these words. MacArthur, the man who had fought to involve the cadets in modern society, was here telling them to let it pass them by, to turn back to that moralism with which the West Point of the iron days sought to justify itself. Old men, no longer in touch with the vivid details of the ongoing world, find moralizing an irresistible temptation. The General was human, after all.

Moved though the cadets undoubtedly were by MacArthur's unforget-table closing—"When I cross the river my last conscious thoughts will be of the Corps—and the Corps—and the Corps"—the West Pointers of 1962 were hardly inclined to follow his advice. The Academy was moving, not away, but toward deeper and deeper involvement with the issues and dilemmas that vex our era.

The year 1957 was the great transformation year at West Point. A dynamic new Superintendent, Major General Garrison H. Davidson, decided it was time, not merely to tinker with the curriculum but to revamp it. Davidson's ambitions were MacArthur-size in their scope. Compared to him, Maxwell Taylor had only planted a handful of seeds in a few courses. Davidson appointed five officers, the Ewell Board, to study the personal attributes likely to be essential to the future Army officer. The Board interviewed retired and active Army officers and civilian educators by the score and came up with a group of attributes that would cause most liberal educators to beam. Among the primary necessities of the future officer, they said, was "the ability to think," plus "intellectual curiosity" and "critical original thought." The Board was severely critical of the Academy's ability to encourage these qualities among its graduates. "West Point does not take advantage of natural intelligence or aptitude (or of) . . . prior educational training received." It quoted several prominent educators and military leaders who declared that the Academy's prescribed course system "is designed for the mediocre student and does not challenge the really good student." The Board recommended "some system whereby the cadet is given limited curriculum choice."

Davidson ran into strong faculty resistance. The problem was one that appears at West Point in an almost infinite variety of guises. If too much individuality is allowed, what will happen to the esprit de corps? The conservatives pictured a Hydra-headed group, with history majors having one esprit and economics majors another esprit and physics majors still another peculiar sense of devotion to their own clique.

Ironically, one of West Point's critics, Charles Eliot, anticipated this reply in 1869 when he began electives at Harvard. "It has been alleged," he said, "that the elective system must weaken the bond which unites members of the same class. This is true; but in view of another much more efficient cause of the diminution of class intimacy, the point is not very significant. The increased size of the college classes inevitably works a great change in this respect. One hundred and fifty young men cannot be so intimate with each other as fifty used to be. The increase is progressive."

West Point in 1957 was already ten times larger than Thayer's 250-man Academy. One first classman confessed to the author that only a few weeks before graduation, he met a cadet he did not know, and was startled to discover he was a member of his own class. (The huge numbers have eliminated one old West Point problem. A group of first classmen, asked if they would be influenced by a cadet who was dismissed for disciplinary reasons, and then reinstated, replied candidly: "Most of the class wouldn't have noticed he was gone—or that he'd come back.") It was obviously a new school that Davidson was attempting to vitalize. But for two more years and several tons of curriculum study reports, the Academy hemmed and hawed, and Davidson left, issuing a final cry that electives be made available to "all cadets according to their natural preferences and abilities."

Davidson's frustration underscores the most glaring weakness in West Point's current structure. Superintendents do not stay long enough—the average term in recent decades has been between two and three years—and this only encourages the academic board, all of whose professors have permanent (to age 64) appointments, to resist innovations. Why reach an accommodation with this intruder, who will be gone in a year or two? The twentieth century has made Thayer's 1865 recommendation of a permanent Superintendent look wiser with each passing decade.

In absentia, Davidson finally did get the Academy moving, in its usual glacial fashion. A final curriculum review board, composed of five civil-

ian educators and two general officers, recommended a cautious six
semester hours of electives in the final year, with additional electives
urged for particularly able cadets and more opportunity for these
brighter men to take advanced programs or validate prescribed courses.

This "modified curriculum" was introduced in 1961–62 and has been
steadily expanded. About 60 percent of the cadets take some advanced
studies during their four years, and overall about a third of the corps is
now involved in this program at any one time. Cadets who validate
standard programs may take electives in their third class and second
class years, but most of the school's 110 electives, which range from
nuclear reactor theory to Latin American studies, are taken by first
classmen. They must take a minimum of four and can carry more if they
are qualified. The average cadet takes about five in his four years. Some
top students absorb as many as ten.

Academy spokesmen proudly maintain that about 40 percent of the
core curriculum is now devoted to the social sciences and the humanities,
while 60 percent remains in the general engineering field. They tend to
talk glowingly about the growing elective program and the new freedom
for cadets, but members of the Social Science and English departments
are not so enthusiastic. "In terms of electives," says Colonel George A.
Lincoln, the head of the Department of Social Sciences, "it's really a
90-10 split and that 10 percent hasn't been procured by taking much
away from the basic engineering program. It was achieved primarily by
eliminating anachronisms, such as horseback riding."

This insistence on a science- and mathematics-dominated curriculum
is what disturbs many West Point observers. The obvious solution, foreshadowed in General Davidson's aborted revolution, is a majors program. Already, a good many recent graduates consider their electives a
major. There is no doubt that if a cadet elects English instead of social
sciences, it is likely to have a considerable influence on his career. "I
wish I had gone into social sciences," one young major told this writer
somewhat ruefully. "They really care about their people. Fight for them.
Get them advanced study and so forth."

Inside the Academy pressure is mounting for a majors program, and
not a little of it is coming from current and prospective cadets. Discussing the elective program, one hears very little comment from cadets
about the pleasures of being able to choose courses. Far more frequent
are the complaints about the tiny amount of freedom allowed them, the

number of courses they were prevented from taking by the pressure of the required curriculum. There is a sort of revolution of rising expectations here. Allowing a little freedom has only whetted the cadet's appetite for much more in shaping his course of studies.

Only about 100 cadets, or 3.33 percent, take English electives. The social sciences are more popular. In 1967–68 243 cadets selected the National Security Seminar taught by ex-football star and Rhodes scholar Major "Pete" Dawkins—the largest elective choice. The elite are the cadets who are permitted to elect "computer science fundamentals" and "digital computers." Some have become what one faculty member called "computer bums," devoting 40 and 50 percent of their study time to the computer, and letting their other subjects slide. This may well be a symptom of a larger, all but irresistible movement within the Academy toward permitting a diversification of majors. The academic board has edged a little closer to it by approving for the year 1969–70 something called "Elective Concentration." This will permit cadets to choose six to eight electives in three fields: basic science, engineering science, and national security and public affairs.

In a semiserious look at West Point in the year 2000 (written for *Assembly,* the Association of Graduates Magazine), Colonel Elvin R. Heiberg, professor of mechanics, predicted that the corps would be divided into three major areas of concentration—engineering sciences, public affairs, and physical education. Each brigade would be headed by a deputy dean with the rank of brigadier general. The first brigade would comprise the engineering science majors, the second brigade would be the physical education majors, and the third brigade would be public affairs majors. "Tripled in size," Colonel Heiberg says, "the corps nonetheless would maintain many of its traditions. Rifles and swords would still be carried at parades, thus permitting the Air Force Academy at Colorado Springs to keep alive their old gag, 'Two centuries of tradition unhampered by progress.' "

V

WILLIAM E. SIMONS, an Air Force major who graduated from the Naval Academy, taught at the Air Force Academy and holds a doctorate from Columbia University Teachers College, recently made a searching study published as "Liberal Education in the Service Academies." On the whole he found much to praise at West Point. He noted the Military Academy's class of 1963 was compared with some 2,000 seniors from 175 colleges on an Educational Testing Service examination on knowledge of foreign affairs. The 470 cadets ranked in the eighty-first percentile of the test group. The class of 1962's performance was comparable. Summing up, Simons asked: "Do the potentially liberal studies offered by the service academies in fact provide the students with liberalizing experiences? Allowing for different levels of liberal attainment among different schools and courses, the answer is a definite yes."

At the same time, Simons underscored the need for continuing improvement. He found particular fault with the service academies' tendency to approach education as something that can be divided into standard bite-size units which the students can consume one at a time. "The packaging of courses into finite lesson units is incompatible with the realities of study in depth." He urged the expansion of a method already being tried in the Academy's sophomore history course—a combination of mass lectures to introduce and raise vital issues on major topics with related follow-up discussions in the section rooms throughout the week.

The bite-size critique echoes the late David Boroff, author of *Campus U.S.A.,* who wrote a series of articles on the service academies in 1962–63. Boroff found the cadets' academic load "awesome" and was particularly impressed by the quality of the incoming plebe class. He called them "surprisingly good" and noted that they had higher S.A.T. verbal scores than freshmen in good engineering schools and higher math scores than freshmen in some of the elite liberal arts colleges. In terms of high school achievements, Boroff said, "the plebes remind one of a Harvard freshman class." A study of the class of 1968 more than supports this assertion: 77.8 percent were in the top fifth of their high

[356]

school class; 137 were presidents of their high school student body or senior class; 104 were editors of their school publications; 306 were athletic team captains, 212 of these all-state or all-conference award winners; 112 were members of their high school debating teams; and 327 were president of some school club. Contrary to the rumored equation, only 124, or 12.5 percent, were Eagle Scouts.

When this class entered in 1964, the Superintendent, Major General James B. Lampert, told the Association of Graduates, "You would expect classes such as this to do well at West Point—and they do." By way of proof, Lampert cited the following achievements of that year's graduating class. The cadets achieved a mean score within the top quarter of all seniors taking the standard examination used by colleges to assist in selecting students who should continue in graduate work. In mathematics, the cadets ranked within the top tenth—the ninety-third percentile—of all college seniors. Thirty-two men competed for National Science Foundation Fellowships. Five won and 23 earned honorable mentions. The fellowships were in mechanical, chemical, nuclear and civil engineering, and in economics. Eight other cadets won fellowships sponsored by the Oak Ridge Institute of Nuclear Studies. Seven more were invited to present papers at the Eastern Colleges Science Conference. Overall, the Academy ranks fourth among all U.S. colleges and universities in the number of Rhodes scholars it has produced.

The Academy is still criticized for its insistence on using Army officers for the vast majority of its teaching faculty. But West Point remains convinced that the faculty is, in Maxwell Taylor's words, "well suited to accomplish the objectives of this institution. In developing the motivation and character we desire in our cadets, there is great advantage in placing in the classroom confident, knowledgeable and capable young officers who know their subjects and also can give examples of the practical military applications of the daily subject matter." A former faculty member, essentially agreeing with Taylor, although somewhat sceptical of those "practical military applications," adds: "It is important for the cadet to see older officers of various grades, and they shouldn't all be in the tactical department. It adds to the pride in the uniform to know that there are officers who can discuss Faulkner and Hemingway knowledgeably and if you're so inclined, maybe you can be one too. A civilian faculty teaching the nonmilitary subjects could very easily wind up giving the cadets a giant inferiority complex."

The Academy has steadfastly labored to increase the competence of its faculty. Almost all the instructors now have at least two years of graduate study—the time allotted for a master's degree—and they are usually assigned for a three-year tour of teaching. This is no small chunk of their careers and they know they must do well at it. West Point may fall short if we judge the faculty on purely academic terms. The "union card" is a master's degree, not the Ph.D., which one needs to make his way at Yale and Harvard. But this is still a substantial advance over earlier decades when men were yanked in from the field on a few weeks' notice, given a textbook and told to start teaching. Of the 400 current members, some 300 have master's degrees, and 26 have doctorates. A new program begun in March of 1963 has authorized the Academy to add to the permanent faculty 15 officers to be assigned as associate professors. All of these men will, in the course of things, have had a previous tour with the faculty and will have completed 15 years of commissioned service. If they do not have Ph.D.'s at the time of their appointment, they are expected to enter immediately into doctoral programs.

David Boroff lamented that West Point lacked the "great men" of our best universities who become a kind of legacy from one generation of students to the next. More information on West Point's history would have inclined him to alter this view somewhat. Although there was a hiatus at the end of the Thayer-Mahan-Michie era during the earlier decades of the twentieth century, Herman Beukema certainly passed on a tradition of excellence to Colonel George A. Lincoln, the current chairman of the Department of Social Sciences. Rhodes scholar Lincoln's definition of the soldier's mission is one of the best available proofs of West Point's new sophistication. "The function of the profession of arms is the ordered application of military resources to the resolution of a social problem."

Moreover, Boroff admitted that a "spirited case" can be made for officer teachers. One visiting professor told him, "The students at West Point have a light in their eyes. They haven't been taught by disillusioned professors." Colonel Lincoln argues persuasively that West Point teaching is in some ways superior to that of other universities because the faculty can concentrate on it almost exclusively. "You don't see our people shopping for jobs at scholarly conventions. They don't have to worry about finishing a dissertation or writing scholarly articles that no one reads."

One does not have to be a close listener to detect a certain defensiveness in this statement. Although on one hand the Academy spokesmen will declare that the place cannot be compared to civilian universities (and they are right in the sense of a literal comparison), they are quick to make comparisons whenever they feel the example is to West Point's advantage. Part of this sensitivity, of course, comes from the general assumption among uninformed academics that the Academy turns out glorified Boy Scouts capable of multiplying and subtracting and little else. West Point has been criticized so often over the years and each of its scandals has made the headlines so infallibly, a defensive posture is almost a reflex gesture.

VI

THERE ARE TIMES WHEN the old school, in the best tradition of its most gifted graduates, takes the offensive. In the summer of 1964, the Association of Graduates cranked up a magnificent campaign which placed Sylvanus Thayer in N.Y.U.'s Hall of Fame. For years the Academy had chafed because Thayer was listed in the Dictionary of American Biography as "military engineer, educator." Two previous efforts to place Thayer in the Hall of Fame had fallen short, largely, the Association felt, because the academicians simply refused to accept him as an educator. This time, Thayer made it, along with Jane Addams, Oliver Wendell Holmes, Jr., and Orville Wright. Thayer's citation reads: "Superintendent at West Point from 1817–1833, reorganizing the Academy extensively and effectively. Took a leading role in establishing technological education in the U.S."

Thayer would have been pleased by the way his sons of the twentieth century deployed their forces on his behalf, garnering letters of endorsement from scores of distinguished Americans. The struggle had its interesting sidelights for anyone acquainted with West Point's history. At the very height of the campaign, Thayer had to survive a slashing attack on him by Colonel Lester H. Webb, a retired National Guard officer whose book, *Captain Alden Partridge and the U.S. Military Academy,* attempted to prove that Partridge was a deposed martyr and Thayer a bungling incompetent who stole most of his ideas from Partridge and survived by following a policy of "sordid" repression. In intemperate prose, not unworthy of the man he was defending, Webb asserted that Partridge was an unrecognized superscientist, educator, statesman, and thinker who deserved credit for everything from the cadet motto to the defenses of the Panama Canal.

Today at West Point the spirit of Sylvanus Thayer survives largely by invocation. Thayer himself would never have dreamt of justifying his Academy by claiming it built character. Knowledge was clearly his passion. At the same time, no one at the modern Academy pretends that the school any longer literally imitates Thayer's system. Mathematics class, with its daily "writs" and blackboard performances, is the closest thing to a vestige of Thayer's era. But even here the similarity is more apparent than real. A cadet at the blackboard is not so much reciting as using the board to organize his thoughts and sketch a conceptual model of his problem. He then gives what amounts to a brief lecture to his sectionmates, using what he has written on the blackboard to illustrate and demonstrate his points. His fellow cadets ask him questions and the instructor expands or clarifies various issues whenever he considers it necessary.

One development that is distinctly in the real Thayer tradition (what the man himself stood for, rather than the phony enshrinement which he never wanted) is the spirit of innovation in current classroom techniques. Few universities can match West Point's sophistication in the use of slides, tapes and closed-circuit television. Films are borrowed from the Army, from the U.S. Information Agency, from industry, as well as from commercial and educational TV. They are used selectively. Instead of devoting an entire class to a film, a nine-minute excerpt integrated with the instructor's lecture, will be introduced. A cadet reads a paper on Hitler's conflict with the Catholic Church, and the instructor supplements it by flashing on the blackboard screen blowups of the Apostles' Creed, and the Nazi Creed—a line-by-line imitation the Führer ordered as a replacement. In a typical three-month period in 1966, the Corps watched 1177 closed-circuit telecasts covering such diverse subjects as tactics, ballistics, electricity, and William Faulkner. Cadets also play "candid camera," or as they call it, "candid classroom," watching themselves deliver lectures, to hone their instructional skills. Strolling through the Academy's gleaming TV studios, one can almost see old Sylvanus, that innovator of an earlier century, looking down with a frosty, but nonetheless approving smile.

VII

THE CLASS OF 1965 is a good example of West Point's steady, unsensational transition from old ways to new. They were the first to get weekend passes in sophomore year and the first allowed to drive cars in senior year. They shucked traditional woolen trousers and long-sleeved tunics for short-sleeved, lightweight summer uniforms, and were also allowed to keep their lights on all night if they chose, rather than observe the old 11:30 "lights out" rule.

One of them, commenting on how many of his classmates took all the humanities courses they could get, remarked, "You'd be surprised how many amateur poets there are here. They are all over the place." As these men graduated, the Superintendent was announcing to the Association of Graduates that he had decided to give the incoming plebe class of 1968 Christmas leave for the first time in the Academy's history. First classmen are now permitted to sip cocktails at the officers' club, a privilege that the faculty calls "social training." Morning coffee is served between classes, and some instructors invite cadets to their quarters for evening pizza and beer.

Hazing is still a factor in the West Point picture. "Beast Barracks" is still fondly rolled off the tongue by the faculty to describe the incoming plebes' three-month introduction to cadet life. Recalling his plebe picture, Pete Dawkins ('59) says, "It has the drained, haggard and imploring look of a man who has been picked up by a tornado, blown 20 miles through the air and landed in the top of a tree." Dawkins sounds like a DOG when he calls Beast Barracks a "great evener—everyone—generals' sons, sons of the rich, sons of the poor, sons of all races—faces the same difficulties. Most of them feel the same doubts, anxieties and joys. But when it's all over there is a certain unity, a humility, a sense of consideration for others and a willingness to accept responsibility which makes everything worthwhile."

Today the leveling is done with little or none of the physical brutality that marred earlier hazing. The brace, the stance of superattention, is still very much in vogue while a plebe is being addressed by an upperclassman, and the plebe must be ready to repeat without warning immense quantities of information—the number of kilowatts in the power station, the number of gallons of water in Lake Popolopen. He must be ready to race from the basement to his fourth-floor room, get into his dress uniform and return to the basement in two and a half minutes, an obviously impossible task. For every second he falls behind, or forgets anything on his uniform, he gets unmitigated hell. Idealist Dawkins says that this teaches the plebe that all jobs, no matter how insignificant they may seem, must be done with a precision of which he can be proud. Other graduates see it as a quick way of finding out how well a man reacts to pressure. "It wasn't until I got into combat," says one man, "that I found out how important it was to perform a great many small, detailed actions simultaneously, at maximum speed."

Some of the old hazing habits die hard. As late as 1959 Cadet Dawkins was forced to rebuke one of his fellows for withholding food from a plebe. Dawkins himself, serving as "king of the beasts" in Beast Barracks in his first class year, joined wholeheartedly in yet another effort by Superintendent Garrison M. Davidson to "refine" the approach toward handling the plebes. "They (the faculty) felt that a plebe should be treated in a dignified and gentlemanly manner and still find his experience rigorous and demanding . . . I was thoroughly in accord with the new attitude," Dawkins said. "Such practices as denying plebes food to punish them for making mistakes are methods appropriate to training animals, not men." Dawkins worked closely with other cadet officers to replace brutality with psychological techniques. "Some of the cadet officers were so good with the silent treatment," he says, "that they could send a plebe into a brace that resembled paralysis merely by looking him in the eye."

Today some of the more enlightened upperclassmen have required plebes to replace their traditional gibberish reply to such questions as "How is the cow?" (Answer: "Sir, she walks, she talks, she's full of chalk, the lacteal fluid extracted from the female of the bovine species is highly prolific to the nth degree") with ten-minute lectures on Vietnam. But others still enjoy heaping coals of fire on a plebe's head. On the evening before graduation day, after the final graduation parade, the corps marches back into the area between the barracks and the upperclassmen have about ten minutes left to get in their last licks on the plebes before they are "recognized" as third classmen. They swarm on their favorite targets, send them into braces of unparalleled rigidity and begin roaring questions and demanding answers faster than any human being could possibly supply them. "MISTER, THOSE SHOES WEREN'T SHINED THIS MORNING, THEY WERE SHINED LAST WEEK. WHEN WAS THE LAST TIME YOU SHAVED, MISTER? THAT RIFLE LOOKS LIKE YOU FOUND IT IN A GARBAGE CAN, MISTER. DON'T SAY YES, SIR, NO, SIR, ANSWER ME. THAT'S NO ANSWER." Then the first captain appears on the "poop deck" above the area, issues an order and the roaring tumult ceases. Down the line of plebes the first classmen move, shaking hands with each one, calling him, for the first time in a year, by his proper name. Anyone who watches even this much of the plebe ordeal is convinced that the Academy is still a long way from becoming effete.

Perhaps the biggest change from old to new is the relationship between the tactical officer and his company. In a genuine sense the tactical officer has become a leader, not an ogre devoted to making cadet lives miserable, as he was in Pershing's era. "It just isn't realistic to make an enemy out of a man when he's a cadet," one middle grade officer explained. "After all, in the next two or three years you might find yourself in an awfully tight combat situation with him. Your life can depend on his loyalty and sense of comradeship. That's what we try to elicit these days, not the old-fashioned fear and obedience." Smart salutes are still flung at an officer as he strides around the Academy grounds, but the yearly dose of close-order drill has been slashed by 70 percent. This has led to some DOG grumbling. One member of the class of '35 was heard to mutter as he watched the class of '65 perform in a June parade, "I know they are a hell of a lot smarter than we were, but, damn it, I wish they were doing some of the complex old drills we used to do."

VIII

IN A MAGAZINE ARTICLE written not long after he graduated, football star Pete Dawkins criticized one aspect of cadet life that contributes to a sense, if not the actuality, of isolation—the relatively little opportunity a cadet has to meet the opposite sex. Although there are numerous dances which attract as many as a thousand young women through the Academy gates on a weekend, the affairs are liquorless, kissless, with penalty fraught prohibitions against "Public Displays of Affection." For kissing a girl goodnight in the parking lot a cadet can get 22 demerits, 44 hours of marching with a rifle, and two months' confinement to his room. The Academy is realistic enough not to patrol "Flirtation Walk" (sometimes called "Old Flirty"), a path which winds down the face of the cliff beneath Trophy Point. But this is about the only place where a couple can achieve a modicum of privacy on the reservation. By and large Dawkins is right when he says: "There is little chance for two people really to get to know each other as students at colleges get to know each other, when they study together and have a chance to fight and make up and talk for hours about how each one really feels about life." About fifteen cadets leave each year to marry. They are regarded with sympathy by the rest of the corps, but a more prevailing opinion is stated by one cadet: "It's better to sire an illegitimate child than to marry and violate West Point regulations."

Among the many West Point regulations that exist to be broken, the PDA's prohibition undoubtedly ranks near the top. The Academy itself tacitly admits its unrealism by permitting cadets and their dates to wander the secluded byways of "Flirtation Walk," the path that runs down the face of the cliff near the battle monument.

Cadets maintain that girls are generally curious about "what's behind that little gray suit." There would seem to be some truth in this contention. Mrs. Beatrice E. Holland, who has been a cadet hostess at the Academy since 1953, has a file of 2000 girls who have written asking to attend a West Point weekend. These blind "drags" are essential because so many West Pointers come from remote regions of the country. The more sophisticated girls, such as the Vassar elite, tend to look down on the cadets. "They're nice, but from our point of view limited," one says. But a girl from Briarcliff Junior College commented: "They're healthy, normal boys except that they're neater and stand up straighter."

The battle over the PDA regulation sometimes achieves heroically comic proportions. During the summer of 1961, the new yearlings who were training at Camp Buckner got the habit of meeting their girls at "Flirty" each weekend and strolling along the treelined trail to Lake Popolopen, some pausing to picnic, others to sit on benches and steal a kiss or two as the mood struck them. Several couples went all the way down to the end of the path, spread blankets, and lay watching the water-skiers, the cadets with their ties and hats thrown aside. Suddenly the officer in charge stormed across the lake in his powerboat and as-saulted their positions without a moment's warning. Most of the cadets were caught before they could replace their ties and hats; others retreated into the woods. One of these tacticians returned several minutes later to reconnoiter. Peeping out from under a bush he spied a pair of khaki trousers and whispered, "Hey, did the O.C. catch you?" The khaki trousers stepped around the bush and the sun glinted on the yellow armband that designated the officer in charge. "No," said the iron voice, "but it looks like he did you."

One solution to this problem has been suggested by Colonel Heiberg in his picture of West Point in the year 2000. He envisions a suspension footbridge linking West Point with Constitution Island in the Hudson. A stern sign warns all visitors "OFF LIMITS—UNLESS ACCOM-PANIED BY A WAC OFFICER OR A CODETTE." The puzzled visitor learns from the armed guard at the bridge entrance that the stone buildings on Constitution Island are the barracks and dining hall of the female element of the corps. As he listens to the guard, "two trimly clad, glamorous young ladies in gray skirts, blouses and berets step smartly off the bridge with a crisp 'All right, sir' and head along the road toward the Battle Monument." Discussing the possibility with a member of the West Point faculty, the writer was startled to hear him say he would not be surprised if something very much like this was a reality by the year 2000. "After all," he says, "we have women officers in the Army. Why not send some of them to West Point?"

IX

ONE TRADITION THAT has not changed is cadet hell-raising. In the postwar era beat-Navy stunts have claimed a major share of the corps energy. These have included kidnapping a Navy goat and painting "Beat Navy" on the side of a destroyer anchored in New York harbor and on the roof of the Superintendent's quarters. The climax in this category was probably reached on November 24, 1949, when a B-25 bomber piloted by a West Pointer flew over Newburgh while the cadets fired from fifteen to twenty rounds of blank ack-ack ammunition from anti-aircraft guns at it. Above the Academy the plane dropped a dummy dressed in full Navy regalia who parachuted to the ground while 2000 neighboring civilians rushed to their phones to report another Pearl Harbor.

One day toward the end of his reign, Colonel Red Blaik took his staff out into the hills to hold an impromptu seminar with the plebe class, who were on a practice hike. Blaik was convinced that the current batch of cadets had lost the *joie de vivre* that had characterized the corps in his day. Earnestly, Blaik and his group began telling tales of cadet pranks in the glorious 20's. The plebes listened with amusement and respect, and the Blaikmen, happy that they had contributed a mite to cadet morale, headed back to work. They had not gone 20 steps when they found a mortified plebe sentinel, clothed only in his rifle. Just out of earshot while the Colonel had been talking, this unfortunate had been sand-bagged by first classmen and left walking his post in the altogether.

The class of 1961 was among the more rambunctious of recent years in this department. When the Tacs declined permission for a Saturday afternoon beat-Navy rally, a number of stalwarts climbed to the balcony overlooking the central area and altered the sign hanging there to read, "Go Army—Beat the Tacs." They performed this feat while the Commandant was speaking to a mass of demonstrators, and escaped hot pursuit by the officer in charge. A few nights later they raided the quarters of the officer in charge and "rearranged" his bedding. But the most successful of their escapades was the movement of heavy artillery to positions in front of the mess hall.

This caper was conducted with all the finesse of a military operation

[367]

and the planning and intrigue of a dime-store sabotage novel. While two military policemen sat less than 75 feet away in the darkness, a commando squad from the 1st Regiment used up seven hacksaw blades cutting away the chains that anchored the big guns to the ground. The culprits now waited until one A.M. the following night, when an advanced patrol consisting of members of the track team reported (by radio) that all was clear. "Assault teams" moved out at 2:10 and arrived at Trophy Point at 2:55. All but one of the guns were moved across the Plain to new positions in front of the mess hall without incident. When the assault party returned for the last prize, a contingent of military police dressed in civilian clothes was waiting for them. Final score of the ensuing battle: one cadet escorted to the provost marshal, eight MP's slightly damaged.

X

"DISSS-MISSSSED!" bawled the senior cadet, and the 3000 gray-clad diners in the huge West Point mess hall headed for the doors. The man who gave the order was James Fowler, one of the top men of the class of 1967, and the first Negro son of a Negro graduate to win a West Point diploma. His father is Colonel James D. Fowler, class of 1941. "My father had a rough time getting through here," young Fowler says frankly. "But I haven't had so much as a single prejudiced word." After the handful of Reconstruction graduates, the Negro vanished from West Point for fifty years. The first Negro to break through this wall of de facto segregation was Benjamin O. Davis, now an Air Force lieutenant general. He had to face the same sort of Coventry Henry Flipper and his companions had endured. Davis survived to graduate thirty-fourth in his class. But few Negroes immediately followed him. Of the 54 Negro graduates, 41 have made it since President Harry Truman integrated the Army in 1950.

Currently West Point has the largest number of Negroes in its history—29. There are also two Negro faculty members. "Race is not a personal question here," Cadet Fowler insists, and most of his fellow Negroes seem to agree with him. "I've never had the consciousness of being Negro, just of being me," says Tom Martin, a six-foot-three member of the class of 1968. Negro Major James L. E. Hill, a chemistry instructor, feels many more young Negroes would try for the Academy if they knew how completely prejudice has vanished from the Plain. "Too many kids think about Ben Davis and the hard times he had here, and they think 'well, it's still like that.' It's not. One need not be a genius to get in, nor have political connections. The big thing we need to do is get people to apply."

[369]

XI

IN SPITE OF the Academy's desire to give every boy all the help he can possibly handle (any cadet who wants extra instruction can get it simply by requesting help from his instructor; upperclassmen volunteer for a tutoring squad that does similar work in the barracks in the evening), West Point's attrition rate still remains around 30 percent. This is, of course, an improvement over the 50- to 60-percent rate of earlier eras, but the faculty still regards it as high and would like to see it lowered somewhat.

Among the more interesting things the Academy has discovered from studying this problem is the relationship between physical fitness and academic success. Since 1947, West Point has given all candidates a physical aptitude examination—a battery of six performance tests which usually weeds out about 15 percent of the applicants. Those who pass are rated according to their physical aptitudes in five standard groupings. These have been compared to cadets who failed to graduate. A startling 46.5 percent of the failures come from the lowest 7 percent in physical aptitude. This number is almost twice as great as any of the top three groupings. "We have studied this relationship and others since 1941," says Colonel Frank J. Kobes, Jr., Director of Physical Education. "They remain consistent for each class of cadets. Similarly, the cadets who are among the lowest 7 percent in leadership ratings at the end of the first semester of plebe year tend heavily to be also low in physical aptitude."

There is, of course, an obviously close link between physical aptitude and leadership. As Colonel Kobes, tall and lean himself, says, "If you can't hump up and down hills and through swamps with your men, you're not going to be able to lead them in combat." To guarantee that the West Pointer is not deficient in this vital aspect, the Academy has, under Colonel Kobes's piercing eye, turned MacArthur's intramural program into one of the most comprehensive physical education programs in the world. In plebe year, "basic physical abilities" are taught. Each cadet must pass a test in boxing, wrestling, gymnastics and swimming. The following year they concentrate on orientation in "carryover sports"

—such as squash, handball, tennis, golf—which men can continue to play beyond middle age. In the second and first year classes emphasis is on development of skills in at least two of these carryover sports.

At the same time, cadets in all four years participate twice a week in fall, winter and spring intramural athletics. Each company fields teams in football, golf, soccer, tennis, squash and handball during the fall. In the winter there is water polo, basketball, boxing, handball, skiing, squash, volley ball, wrestling and pentathlon. Spring brings cross-country, softball, tennis, boat racing, lacrosse, squash and handball. Cadets not only play, they act as coaches, managers, and trainers. A cadet can represent his company in a specific sport only twice during his four years of intramural athletic competition (varsity athletes are, of course, excused from intramural play). This rule makes a cadet participate in approximately twelve different sports while he is at the Academy. At the same time the Academy applies its zeal for grading and appraisal to the intramural playing field. All coaches and players rank their team members on ability, team play, sportsmanship and value to the team. Even the coach is rated.

Every member of the squad must play in each contest for a prescribed period of time—approximately 25 percent—and it is up to the coach to juggle his substitutes accordingly. Each sport is assigned a point value based on team size. Thus football, for example, has a higher point value than tennis. The company with the highest ranking is awarded the "Banker's Trophy."

XII

IN MANY WAYS the athletic program and the English program are the two best examples of how the modern Academy has expended intense mental energy in its determination to get the maximum benefit from seemingly peripheral activities. The plebe English course of 89 hours emphasizes formal logic and expository writing. Cadets are required to "take an attitude" toward the subject they write about. "We try to give them a subject on which they are likely to have strong opinions," says Lieutenant Colonel Jack L. Capps, Professor of English, a Ph.D. from the University of Pennsylvania. "Just before they go into Beast Barracks we watch the newspapers closely and select some topic such as LSD or student riots that is likely to have attracted their attention. Those are the sorts of things we ask them to write about. We don't care what attitude they take toward the material—as long as they're not disloyal."

In the spring term the cadet is required to write a library research paper and give two six-minute speeches which are integrated with the work on the research paper. In all the compositions the emphasis is on critical analysis—thought processes, sentence and paragraph structure, are examined for their coherence and logic. The goal is not only to create a reasonably adequate prose style but an ability to present and examine arguments.

For those who validate the standard course by showing "exceptional ability" there is a course in "the evolution of American ideals" that studies the genesis and development of basic issues and motivations in American literature from 1607 to the present. This course is much more strongly oriented toward the seminar approach, and there is less emphasis on the mechanics of writing and more on discussion of ideas. Each cadet does a study in depth on one major author each semester and shares with his classmates the results of this individual exploration. About ten percent of the plebe class takes this advanced course.

The following year comes a survey course in the Western world's great literature. Cadets work their way through selections from the Old Testament, Homer, Aeschylus, Beowulf, Don Quixote, Shakespeare,

Milton, Pope, Swift, Wordsworth, Keats, Tennyson, Browning, into the modern era where they read Eliot's *The Waste Land* and selections from Yeats. Again the emphasis is on the ideational content of the material. The course is divided into three areas; one, Man and Nature; two, Man and his Fellow Man; three, Man and God.

The English department now loses the cadet until he shows up for a half semester in his final year. The emphasis doubles back to the first year and takes up in a more penetrating way the problems of logic, aesthetics, and ethics. The formal logic they learned in plebe year is applied to selected essays by Addison, Darwin, Emerson, Madison, Shaw, Swift, and Thoreau. Discussions in ethics are developed from reading Arthur Koestler's *Darkness at Noon,* Shakespeare's *Hamlet,* and an anthology on the subject. Some attention is also given to aesthetics, using as the basic text *Arts and the Man* by Irwin Edman. But the amount of ground this course contemplates covering in 20 hours is little short of staggering. In discussing the material, the English faculty places primary emphasis on extending the cadet's ability to think and handle a wide range of sometimes conflicting ideas. The course comes as close as anything in the Academy to formally teaching philosophy.

One senses that the modern Academy is bending every effort to prepare West Pointers to defend themselves verbally—or to project the Army's point of view successfully—to a country that they feel has become more and more alienated from military ideals. Listening to Colonel Samuel Hays, head of Military Psychology and Leadership, discuss the problems of shaping contemporary Americans to West Point's ideals is a good way of seeing the larger problem. "More and more in this country the emphasis tends to be placed on individual achievement, individual growth, individual self-realization. We have to change the focus of a man's loyalty from himself to the group. That isn't easy. Especially when we also want to see him grow and develop as an individual. This emphasis on group loyalty runs counter to so much that is taken for granted in American schools and homes today. We must teach him to be intolerant of human weakness, such as equivocation. In the profession these men are entering there is too much at stake to tolerate such things. We have to make them see how important it is to have absolute confidence in the other members of this group. It only takes one barracks thief to demoralize a unit. In war, when you go into combat this group solidarity is absolutely essential. It isn't individual bravery that sends

men up a hill, it's loyalty to the group, the feeling that 'Joe's with me
and I can't let him down.' It isn't easy to convince a young person today
to put himself second and the group first. He has to learn to find ego
supports within the group structure . . ."

Is the problem really so different from Colonel Thayer's troubles with
the high-spirited "gentlemen cadets" of an earlier era of radical American individualism? Yes and no. Earlier American societies were not
nearly so atomized. There were larger kinship and ethnic structures in
which cadets experienced intimations at least of the ultimate loyalty that
West Point was to demand. Today, paradoxically, the gap between West
Point's ways and America's ways seems to have widened—while West
Point has been making strides toward producing students who are intellectually and psychologically more at home with their contemporaries in
every way except this focal point. More than anything else, this explains
the Academy's determination to produce young men who can articulate
and defend its goals. There is not a little similarity between the current
approach and the original goals of the Jesuit universities—to produce
dedicated sophisticates capable of moving easily through all levels of
modern society, without losing the essential sense of devotion to an
ideal.

Other members of the faculty echo Colonel Hays' "It isn't easy." One
colonel says: "We worry about carryover too—whether we can sell
young officers on making the Army a lifetime career." There has been a
slight—estimates vary but it would seem to be about ten percent—rise
in resignations of postwar graduates. The same colonel says: "I just
came back from Washington where I spent several days with younger
graduates who are working in the Pentagon. I was shocked by how
cynical they'd become about a lot of things." The corps was stunned—
and even that is too mild a word—by the court-martial of Lieutenant
Richard R. Steinke, '61, for refusing to accept an assignment to Vietnam. Though thousands of graduates have served there with distinction,
this single failure provoked almost heartsick comments from West
Pointers of all grades—from cadets to General of the Army Omar
Bradley.

breakfast in the cadet mess hall with a different group of first classmen. In class visits he sometimes participated in the seminar discussions. He tried to be present at every varsity athletic contest, "mainly because I got a good chance to talk to individual cadets."

But the already large size of the modern Academy is an inescapable fact that one man's energy cannot possibly overcome. "Every time I went out of my office," Bennett said, "say to a conference at the library, or heading back to my quarters, I fell in step with a cadet and struck up a conversation with him. Of course, I didn't know his name, but it was another way of communicating with the corps."

Above the wainscoting of his big square office are portraits of the 46 previous Superintendents, pitched slightly forward so that they seem to be staring down at the current performer with uniformly formidable eyes. This gallery may explain why General Bennett, discussing his mission at the Academy, harkened back to Sylvanus Thayer. "The Superintendent's role hasn't really changed," he said. "Basically he is an idea man, a planner and an innovator. I've been concerned with the reputation of the school throughout the country, just as Thayer was. I set military standards in the eyes of the cadets. Finally, I tried to evaluate, correlate and criticize what's going on here."

Bennett made it clear that his historical sense was not a stand-pat conservatism. He pointed to a pile of papers on his desk and described them as another step in the continuing curriculum review. "We've got to keep moving. We can't stand still because the world isn't standing still. Above all we've got to teach intellectual curiosity and give our cadets a desire to continue to learn. We have to teach them when to say, 'Why, sir?' and when to say, 'Yes, sir.' "

General Bennett paused to look up at the portraits of his predecessors. "There is a resistance to change here which is only natural in any institution with a 166-year-old tradition. I think there should be resistance. You could lose more than you gain chasing fads. But at the same time I hope you make it clear that this school is committed to growth, not just physically but spiritually and intellectually."

XIV

IT IS 5 P.M. ON A SUNLIT day in May. Squads of cadets trot briskly past in sweatsuits, heading for intramural games. The tennis courts are full and there is a crowd—20 or 30—around one court where a team match is in progress. On the baseball field Army is playing the City College of New York. A few feet away lacrosse players batter each other with their Stone-Age slings. Storm King, Brackanack and Anthony's Nose brood in the fading sunlight, still bare from an exceptionally cold spring.

At Trophy Point where Flirtation Walk wends downward, black old-fashioned cannons squat. Some of them boomed during Sam Grant's years in Mexico, others thundered at Gettysburg and in the Wilderness. The flag floats above the monument to the officers and men of the Regular Army who died for the Union in the Civil War. On the other side of the Plain huge construction cranes tower above the massive additions to the cadet barracks and mess hall. One wing will be named for Douglas MacArthur, the other for Dwight Eisenhower.

How swiftly history converts men into monuments here. Significant monuments, too. MacArthur has been called the last of the cavaliers, the lovers of war in the Jeb Stuart-George Patton tradition. Eisenhower has been compared to the roundhead, who sees war as an unpleasant necessity, and does the job without rhetoric or heroics. Another writer divides our generals into absolutists, who see every war as a crusade, and pragmatists, who are prepared to accept a constabulary role, fighting limited wars wherever necessary, with maximum professionalism.

Ultimately, each West Pointer transcends concepts, as living men must and will. Many types of soldiers, and all the gradations between them, will continue to flourish at the United States Military Academy. If the experience of a century and a half has proven anything, it is the need for richness and variety, not conformity, in our warriors.

One thinks of stolid, steady Walton Walker holding the Pusan perimeter in Korea. Of Matthew Ridgway, using conscious, carefully controlled flamboyance (the hand grenades strapped to his chest, the presence in the front lines) to rally a beaten 8th Army, and turn it north to victory once more. Of Westmoreland, calling on every man in Vietnam to give him a minimum 60-hour week. There is no way to capsulize such men. They represent the old, the eternal mystery of leadership, which West Point has struggled to transmit to each generation of American soldiers.

As the twilight advances, history seems to march with it. It is easy to picture that old Academy band marching at tattoo on February 22, 1861, across this same Plain to the cluster of cadet barracks where George Armstrong Custer and Tom Rosser waited to exchange cheers for the Union and for Dixie. There is young MacArthur drilling a squad of plebes, there is Ike Eisenhower coaching a squad of freshmen football players.

The Superintendent's mansion gleams whitely in the fading light. Thayer's old office has been reconstructed in the basement, as a kind of shrine. Not far away, Thayer's statue stands beneath the budding trees facing the mass of new stone and steel rising before him. A century and a half have passed since the day when the young Major "with a solemn duty to perform" arrived to take charge of a divided, mismanaged, almost forgotten school in an America that was one of the world's have-not nations.

The primal river still flows serenely past the ancient rock on which Thayer founded his school. But today the metaphor loosens. The stability of the rock must be combined with the flexibility of men who see time and change not as enemies, as erosion, but as positive creative dimensions of human experience. Today's West Pointers can still imbibe the meaning of the rock; but it must become more specific in its meaning; they must see clearly its relation to their own characters, the nature of the enormous trust that the nation places in them, in a revolutionary nuclear age. Never again can West Point—or America—afford to confuse moral strength and intellectual growth.

Much depends on how well the corps succeeds. No group of men has participated more fully than West Pointers in the century and a half that saw this raw continent transformed into the most powerful country in the world. Few men will play a more potent role in deciding the uses of that power in the decades to come. For those who wish to be more than spectators of history, West Point, with all its crotchety fondness for the past, remains the school of the future.

A Note on Sources and Methods

RATHER than burden the reader with hundreds of footnotes, I have preferred in my books to discuss my sources in a series of extended notes, which will serve as guideposts to those who wish to explore the subject in greater depth or detail.

SCHOOL OF THE FUTURE

I was fortunate to be the first historian of West Point to make use of the collected and annotated edition of the papers of Sylvanus Thayer, which the West Point Library prepared in 1964–65. Some of Thayer's letters have been available in other USMA Library collections such as the Cullum papers, but the unified collection has enabled me to present a picture of Thayer with more areas of light and shadow. The letters he wrote to Joseph G. Swift in his later years contain valuable new information about the manner and the frame of mind in which he took over West Point. They also shed light on Swift's ambiguous role in the Partridge controversy.

Apropos of recent attempts to rehabilitate the memory of Partridge, these later letters reveal an inflexible detestation for the man on Thayer's part. He protested violently against listing Partridge as a Superintendent of the Academy, calling him "a mere drill master." Anyone who takes the time to plow through Partridge's papers and read the man's helter-skelter prose, particularly his "exposé," as this writer has done, must be puzzled by the pseudoreverence with which some would-be historians, in their desperation for a subject, have treated Partridge. In the overall history of West Point, the debate is of small importance.

I have also drawn on numerous reminiscences of the Thayer era, as well as collections of individual cadet letters. All of these are mentioned in the text where they occur, and are cited in the bibliography. Most of the material concerning the cadets whose extreme behavior brought on Thayer's collision with Andrew Jackson comes from a close study of the records of delinquency in the West Point archives. Previous histories of West Point have treated the subject in a more general way. The rather appalling details make Thayer's decision to leave more understandable. For some perspective on the intellectual and scientific atmosphere of Thayer's era, Frederick

Rudolph's *The American College and University* is helpful. Also valuable, as well as a model of academic history, is Samuel Morison's *Three Centuries of Harvard*.

BAND OF BROTHERS

For the years immediately following Thayer's departure, the most helpful primary sources are *The Life of Isaac Ingalls Stevens* by his son, and *The Making of a Soldier, The Letters of General Richard S. Ewell*. Material on the immortal Benny Havens is somewhere in the twilight zone between legend and objective history, but he cannot be omitted from a West Point narrative. The Porter anecdote about Superintendent Delafield and the rolled overcoats is from Hugh Scott's *Some Memories of a Soldier*, one of the richest and most neglected of West Point memoirs. For the sketches of the individual cadets in this and other sections, I have combined material from cadet letters, the records of delinquency in the West Point archives, minor reminiscences that USMA librarians have industriously collected, and formal biographies. Lloyd Lewis's *Captain Sam Grant* stands out among these, as a particularly vivid recreation of West Point in the late 30's and early 40's. I have drawn on Douglas Southall Freeman's great biography of Robert E. Lee for much of the material on Lee's role in the Mexcian War, and to a lesser extent for Lee's tour as Superintendent.

For West Point during the pre-Civil War years, Schofield's *Forty Years in the Army* is well written and illuminating. I had to cut from my text, with regret, many of his shrewd and rather amusing observations on the severe discipline and the cadets' persistent defiance of it, especially in the matter of smoking. Another extremely valuable book is *Dear Belle, Letters from Tully McCrea to His Sweetheart*, with narrative and editing by Katherine S. Crary. Finally a book more familiar to those who know something of West Point's history, but still worth citing, is Morris Schaff's *The Spirit of Old West Point*. The problem here is separating Schaff's vivid imaginary scenes from his equally rich store of factual memories. The book is also drenched in a sentiment that a contemporary reader may find hard to digest.

For West Pointers in the Civil War, I drew on a wide variety of sources. Douglas Southall Freeman's *Lee's Lieutenants* was especially helpful. Lloyd Lewis's biography, *Sherman, Fighting Prophet,* and Francis F. McKinney's biography of Thomas, *Education in Violence,* were equally enlightening. McKinney especially showed special insight in the rather ambiguous task of connecting generalship to West Point experience. Jacob Cox's memoirs, *Military Reminiscences of the Civil War,* were also illuminating, as well as frustrating. For my portrait of McClellan, which I realize is somewhat controversial, I am primarily indebted to T. Harry Williams' book, *Americans at War*. For my views of Grant and the "Grant men" I have drawn on Clarence Edward McCartney's *Grant and his Generals* and J. F. C. Fuller's consciously iconoclastic *Generalship of U. S. Grant*. Fuller compares Grant and Lee, striking a neutral (British) pose, and gives Grant first prize.

YEARS OF IRON

For my account of the early attempts to reunite Confederate and Federal West Pointers I have drawn on the files of the Association of Graduates and the memoirs of several West Pointers, notably those of Longstreet. The tragic story of the first Negroes at West Point can best be seen through the eyes of the first black man to survive this trial by fire—Henry O. Flipper. His book, *The Colored Cadet at West Point,* reveals almost as much between the lines as it does in the words themselves. Contemporary newspapers, magazines, and the account by George L. Andrews in the *International Review* are the chief sources for the Whittaker debacle. The *Journal of Negro History* has a workmanlike article on Flipper's later career.

For the iron that penetrated West Point's heart and unfortunately also its head during this era I have relied almost entirely on contemporary witnesses. Hugh Scott's *Some Memories of a Soldier* again provides a rich and wise commentary. George Van Horn Moseley's memoir is an historical mine; likewise is the memoir of Cornelius DeWitt Willcox. Both are in manuscript in the USMA Library. Michie's biography of Emery Upton is unintentionally illuminating for this era as well. I depended on him for the account of the rump court-martial that banished the three suspected cadets during Upton's tour as Commandant. The tragic story of Orsemus Boyd is drawn from the files of the Association of Graduates. For my portrait of Pershing I have drawn on Avery Andrews' *My Friend and Classmate* and Richard O'Connor's biography, as well as a number of cadet memoirs in the USMA Library files. The story of how Dennis Mahan Michie brought football to West Point is drawn from a memoir by Brigadier General John M. C. A. Palmer that appeared in *Assembly,* the Association of Graduates magazine. I have supplemented it with newspaper accounts drawn from *The New York Times* and other papers.

IN SEARCH OF PROGRESS

The material on the Booz hazing scandal is drawn from the 1901 House of Representatives hearings. Frazier Hunt's biography of MacArthur adds a few details, as does *The New York Times*. For the sketches of MacArthur, Eisenhower and the other important names of this era I have again drawn on a variety of sources, ranging from unpublished personal reminiscences in the USMA Library, through class yearbooks, to formal biographies. For the sketch of Goethals' achievement in Panama I have relied on several formal histories, but I have supplemented them with material deposited by Robert Wood in the Oral History Collection of Columbia University. Wood's relationship with Goethals is a perfect illustration of the way the men of the iron era practiced leadership. For Pershing's role in World War I, I have drawn on a number of memoirs and biographies. I found Richard O'Connor's book especially illuminating. Also, *The American Army in France* by Major General James G. Harbord.

I only wished space permitted me to devote equal attention to many other West Pointers, such as Charles P. Summerall and Hunter Liggett, who distinguished themselves in France. For those who wish to read more on West Pointers in both world wars, the best book is Colonel R. Ernest Dupuy's *Men of West Point*. For a good picture of the chaos at West Point during World War I, Colonel Earl Blaik's autobiography is dramatic as well as exciting reading. Matthew Ridgway's autobiography, *Soldier,* is also helpful. The best book for the history of the MacArthur era is Colonel Ganoe's *MacArthur Close Up*. It is marred by a tone of extreme hero-worship, but it is a vivid eyewitness account. MacArthur's Superintendent's reports are also illuminating, as are Frazier Hunt's biography and Earl Blaik's book, both of which contribute some anecdotes and insights. I have found other anecdotes in the USMA Library, as well as in *The Pointer* and in *Assembly*.

For the story of how West Point was saved from abolition at the opening of World War II, I have relied on personal communications from several eyewitnesses, notably Major General Philip E. Gallagher. The material on General McAuliffe's Pentagon career I have drawn, with his generous permission, from a memoir deposited in the Oral History Collection at Columbia University. Again it was with regret that I was forced to condense into a few pages the enormous achievements of West Pointers in World War II. On this subject Colonel Dupuy's *Men of West Point* is again a ready and exciting reference. For the material on West Point football, the basic book is Colonel Blaik's autobiography. I have supplemented it with extensive reading in newspapers and magazines. For the tragic cheating scandal I have ultilized a number of personal communications from members of the West Point faculty who were present when this uproar shook the Academy.

TRADITION IN FERMENT

Most of the material in this section is based on unpublished sources—interviews with members of the West Point faculty, letters drawn from

Academy files. Several books were helpful, however, in helping me form judgments and assess trends. William E. Simons' *Liberal Education in the Service Academies* is a perceptive study. With a gesture typical of the hostility that afflicts so much writing about West Point, this book was reviewed in the now defunct *Herald Tribune* as an attack on the service academies. It is neither an attack nor a defense, but a well-reasoned exploration with more pluses than minuses in the final summation. Another illuminating book that ranges far beyond West Point is Morris Janowitz's *The Professional Soldier*. On a smaller scale, the article by the late David Boroff is a useful example of a detached observer's reaction to West Point. The material on the physical education program, the psychological training, and the English program are drawn from personal communications with the heads of these departments, plus personal visits to classrooms, perusal of texts and even of cadet essays which the faculty generously permitted me to examine.

BIBLIOGRAPHY

PRIMARY SOURCES

Adams, John Quincy, *Diary*, Vol. VII, Boston, 1847–77

Alexander, E. P., "The Confederate Veteran," an address on Alumni Day, West Point Centennial, June, 1902, New York, 1902

Andrews, Avery DeLano, *My Friend and Classmate, John J. Pershing*, New York, 1901

Bailey, William Whitman, *My Boyhood at West Point*, Providence, 1891

Blaik, Earl H. (with Cohane, Tim), *You Have to Pay the Price*, New York, 1960

Board of Visitors, 3 vols., 1819–50

Bratt, John, *Diary*, (1842–1918), USMA Library

Chamberlain, John L., "Cadet Reminiscences," manuscript in USMA Library

Chilton, Alexander Wheeler, *Social Life at West Point*, USMA, 1907

Church, Albert E., *Personal Reminiscences of the Military Academy from 1824 to 1831*, USMA, 1879

Congressional Globe, The, Vols. III–XIII, 1836–44

Cox, Jacob Dolson, *Military Reminiscences of the Civil War*, 2 vols., New York, 1900

Cram, Thomas J., "Extracts from Recollections . . . as a Cadet . . . and as an Officer," manuscript in USMA Library

Dawkins, Peter, "My Life at West Point," *The Saturday Evening Post*, May 30, 1959

Early, Clifford C., "West Point—1901 to 1905," typescript in author's possession

Ewell, Richard S., *The Making of a Soldier*, letters, arranged and edited by Captain Percy G. Hamlin, Richmond, Va., 1935

Exposé of Facts Concerning Recent Transactions, Relating to the Corps of Cadets of the United States Military Academy, at West Point, New York, Newburgh, 1819 (Ragland controversy)

Farley, Joseph Pearson, *West Point in the Early '60's*, Troy, New York, 1902

Flipper, Henry Ossian, *The Colored Cadet at West Point*, New York, 1878

French, Samuel G., "Four Letters Written While a Cadet," 1839–40, USMA Library

Gayles and Seaton's Register of Debates in Congress, Vol. VI, Part 1; Vol. XIII, Part 2

Grant, U. S., *Personal Memoirs*, New York, 1885

Hagner, Peter, *Papers*, Southern Historical Collection, University of North Carolina Library

Heintzelman, Samuel P., "Journal . . . while a cadet," USMA Library

Hitchcock, Ethan Allen, *Fifty Years in Camp and Field,* New York, 1909

Hodges, Henry Clay, Jr., *Reminiscences,* USMA Library

Holden, Edward S., *Holden Collection,* Archives, United States Military Academy

Howard, Oliver Otis, *Autobiography,* New York, 1907

Jackson, William Morton, "How the Runt-Flanker Game Became the Goat-Engineer Game," USMA, 1923, typescript in USMA Library

Keyes, E. D., *Fifty Years' Observation of Men and Events,* New York, 1884

King, Charles, "Cadet Life at West Point," *Harper's New Monthly Magazine,* July, 1887

Latrobe, John H. B., *West Point Reminiscences,* West Point, 1887

MacArthur, Douglas, *Reminiscences,* New York, 1964

Mahan, Dennis Hart, *Advanced Guard Outpost and Detachment Service of Troops with the Essential Principles of Strategy and Grand Tactics,* New York, 1947

Mansfield, E. D., *Personal Memories,* Cincinnati, 1879

McCrea, Tully, *Dear Belle, Letters from Tully McCrea to his Sweetheart, 1858–65,* narrative and editing by Katherine S. Crary, Middletown, Conn., 1965

McManus, Bernard T., "Cadet Life at West Point," *Godey's Magazine,* January, 1895

Morgan, George, *Diary,* USMA Library

Moseley, George Van Horn, *One Soldier's Journey,* manuscript in USMA Library

Mott, T. Bentley, "West Point: A Criticism," *Harper's Magazine,* March, 1934

Page, David P., Jr., "Cadet Life," *Infantry Journal,* May, 1924

Partridge, Alden, *The Military Academy at West Point Unmasked,* Washington, 1830

Pickett, George E., *The Heart of a Soldier, As revealed in the intimate letters of,* New York, 1913

Pleasonton, A. J., *Diary,* USMA Library

Proceedings of a General Court-Martial Convened at West Point on 20th October 1817 (Partridge court-martial)

Ramsey, George D., "Recollections of the U.S. Military Academy at West Point, 1814–1820," West Point, manuscript in USMA Library

Register of Delinquencies, Corps of Cadets, 61 vols., 1818–1909

Rhodes, Charles D., "Diary of a Cadet at the United States Military Academy—1885–1889," manuscript in USMA Library

Schaff, Morris, *The Spirit of Old West Point,* New York, 1907

Schofield, John M., *Forty-six Years in the Army,* New York, 1897

Scott, Hugh Lenox, *Some Memories of a Soldier,* New York, London, 1928

Secretary of the Association of Graduates, obituary of Captain Orsemus B. Boyd, USMA Library

Sheridan, Philip Henry, *Personal Memoirs,* New York, 1888

Smith, Francis H., *West Point Fifty Years Ago,* New York, 1879

Swift, Joseph G., *Memoirs,* privately printed, 1890

The Thayer Papers. These include the letters of Sylvanus Thayer, as well as pertinent material from the National Archives, USMA Library

Willcox, Cornelius de Witt, "On the Edge, Personal Recollections of an American Officer," manuscript in USMA Library

SECONDARY SOURCES

"Account of the National Military School of the United States of America," *The Quarterly Journal,* London, April, 1826

Allan, Carlisle V., *Sergeant Major Perry and Cadet Poe,* West Point, 1933

Ambrose, Stephen E., *Duty, Honor, Country,* Baltimore, 1966

——, *Upton and the Army,* Baton Rouge, 1964

Anderson Edward W., "Letters of a West Pointer," *American Historical Review,* Vol. XXXIII, 1928

Anderson, Robert, *An Artillery Officer in Mexico,* New York, 1911

Andrews, George L., "West Point and the Colored Cadets," *The International Review,* November, 1880

Baldwin, Hanson, "Winds of Change Stir the Academy," *Think,* January-February, 1965

Baumer, William H., *Not All Warriors,* New York, 1941

Botkin, Benjamin Albert, *A Civil War Treasury of Tales, Legends and Folklore,* New York, 1960

Boynton, Captain Edward O., *History of West Point,* New York, 1863

Bradford, Ned, ed., *Battles and Leaders of the Civil War,* one-volume edition, New York 1956

Brown, Wesley A., "Eleven Men of West Point," *The Negro History Bulletin,* April, 1956

Brubacher, John S., and Rudy, Willis, *Higher Education in Transition,* New York, 1958

Buck, Beaumont B., *Memories of Peace and War,* San Antonio, Texas, 1935

Bushong, Millard K., *Old Jube, A Biography of General Jubal E. Early,* Boyce, Virginia, 1955

Cajori, Florian, *The Teaching and History of Mathematics in the United States,* Washington, 1890

Catton, Bruce and William, *Two Roads to Sumter,* New York, 1963

Centennial of the United States Military Academy at West Point, New York, 1904

Chambers, Lenoir, *Stonewall Jackson,* New York, 1959

Childs, Marquis, *Eisenhower: Captive Hero,* New York, 1958

Cleaves, Freeman, *Meade of Gettysburg,* Oklahoma City, 1960

Couper, William, *Claudius Crozet,* Charlottesville, Va., 1936

Cullum, George W., *Biographical Register of Officers and Graduates of the U.S. Military Academy,* New York, 1868

Davis, Burke, *Jeb Stuart,* New York, 1957

————, *Our Incredible Civil War,* New York, 1960

————, *They Called Him Stonewall,* New York, 1954

Dawson, George F., *The Life of Logan,* Chicago, 1887

Douglas, Henry Kyd, *I Rode with Stonewall,* Chapel Hill, North Carolina, 1940

Dupuy, Ernest R., *Men of West Point,* New York, 1951

————, *Where They Have Trod,* Washington, 1943

Dyer, John P., *The Gallant Hood,* New York, 1950

Eisenchiml Otto, *The Celebrated Case of Fitz-John Porter,* New York, 1950

Elliot, Ellsworth, Jr., *West Point and the Confederacy*

Fishwick, Marshall W., *Lee After the Civil War,* New York, 1963

Fleming, Walter L., "Jefferson Davis at West Point," *Metropolitan Magazine,* 1908

Flexner, Abraham, *The American College,* New York, 1908

Forman, Sidney, *West Point,* New York, 1950

Freeman, Douglas Southall, *Lee's Lieutenants,* New York, 1942–44

————, *Robert E. Lee,* New York, 1934

Fuller, F. F. C., *Generalship of U. S. Grant,* New York, 1929

Ganoe, William A., *MacArthur Close Up,* New York, 1962

Godson, William F. H., Jr., *The History of West Point, 1852–1902,* Philadelphia, 1934

Halsey, Ashley, Jr., *Who Fired the First Shot?,* New York, 1963

Harbord, James G., *The American Army in France, 1917–1919,* Boston, 1936

Hart, B. H. Liddell, *Sherman,* New York, 1958

Hassler, William Woods, *A. P. Hill, Lee's Forgotten General,* Richmond, Virginia, 1957

Heilberg, Elvin R., "West Point in the Year 2000," *Assembly,* Winter, 1964

Henderson, Colonel G. F. R., *Stonewall Jackson,* London, 1949

Hesseltine, William B., *Ulysses S. Grant, Politician,* New York, 1957

Hofstadter, Richard and Smith, Wilson, eds., *American Higher Education: A Documentary History,* Chicago, 1961

Hollon, W. Eugene, *Beyond the Crossed Timbers, the Travels of Randolph B. Marcy, USMA, 1832,* Norman, Oklahoma, 1955

Howerton, James L., "West Point Generals of the Wartime Army—Their Performance While Cadets at the U.S. Military Academy," master's thesis, George Washington University, April 1945

Hughes, David R., *Ike at West Point,* Poughkeepsie, N.Y., 1958

Hunt, Frazier, *The Untold Story of Douglas MacArthur,* New York, 1954

Hyde, Arthur P. S., "Douglas MacArthur," Rare Book Room, USMA Library (one-page clipping from unidentified magazine)

Investigation of Hazing at the United States Military Academy, Report Number 2768, House of Representatives, 56th Congress, 2nd Session, Washington, D.C., 1901

Janowitz, Morris, *The Professional Soldier,* New York, 1960

Johnston, William P., *The Life of Albert Sidney Johnston,* New York, 1870

Kobes, Frank R., Jr., "Predictive Values of Initial Physical Performance Levels of Freshmen at USMA," USMA Library

Lee, W. Storrs, *The Strength To Move a Mountain,* a biography of George W. Goethals, New York, 1958

Lenney, John J., *Caste System in the American Army,* New York, 1949

Lewis, Lloyd, *Captain Sam Grant,* Boston, 1950

————, "The Holy Spirit at West Point," *The American Mercury,* November, 1930

————, *Sherman, Fighting Prophet,* New York, 1932

Longstreet, James, *From Manassas to Appomattox,* Bloomington, Indiana, 1960

Mahan, A. T., *From Sail to Steam,* New York, 1897

Maher, Marty (with Nardi Reeder Campion), *Bringing Up the Brass,* New York, 1951

Maury, Dabney, H., *Recollections of a Virginian in the Mexican, Indian, and Civil Wars,* New York, 1897

McCartney, Clarence Edward, *Grant and His Generals,* New York, 1953

McKinney, Francis F., *Education in Violence: The Life of George H. Thomas,* Detroit, 1961

Michie, Peter Smith, *General McClellan,* New York, 1901

————, *The Life and Letters of Emery Upton,* New York, 1885

Milham, Charles G., *The Gallant Pelham,* Washington, D.C., 1959

Military Leadership, Office of Military Psychology and Leadership, United States Military Academy, West Point, 1965

Miller, Merle, "The West Point Story," *Argosy Magazine,* January, 1952

Millis, Walter, ed., *American Military Thought,* New York, 1966

Monaghan, Jay, *Custer,* Boston, 1959

Morison, Samuel E., *Three Centuries of Harvard, 1636–1936,* Cambridge, Mass., 1936

Murray, Charles Augustus, *Travels in North America,* London, 1839

Myers, William S., *General George Brinton McClellan,* New York, 1934

Norton, Aloysius A., "A Study of the Customs and Traditions of West Point in the American Novel," manuscript in the USMA Library

O'Connor, Richard, *Black Jack Pershing,* New York, 1961

————, *Hood: Cavalier General,* New York, 1949

————, *Sheridan, the Inevitable,* New York, 1953

INDEX

A Note About the Author

Thomas J. Fleming grew up in Jersey City, N.J., graduated cum laude from Fordham University and from 1958 to 1960 served as executive editor for *Cosmopolitan*. In 1963 he received the Brotherhood Award of the National Conference of Christians and Jews for magazine writing. He is one of the few modern writers who is building a reputation in both the fiction and non-fiction fields as a significant interpreter of the American past and present. *A Cry of Whiteness* (Morrow, 1967), *King of The Hill* (1966), *All Good Men* (1964) and *The God of Love* (1963), are all novels dealing with the inner life of the American city. *The New York Times* has said ". . . Mr. Fleming has as intense an interest in his scrofulous wedge of geography as Faulkner had in his." He has also produced four works of historical non-fiction: *Affectionately Yours, George Washington* (1967), *One Small Candle* (1964), *Beat the Last Drum* (1963), and *Now We Are Enemies* (1960).